PRINCIPLES OF
MARKETING

We work with leading authors to develop the
strongest educational materials in business and marketing,
bringing cutting-edge thinking and best learning
practice to a global market.

Under a range of well-known imprints, including
Financial Times Prentice Hall, we craft high quality
print and electronic publications which help
readers to understand and apply their content,
whether studying or at work.

To find out more about the complete range of our
publishing please visit us on the World Wide Web at:
www.pearsoneduc.com

PRINCIPLES OF
MARKETING

SECOND EDITION

Dr Frances Brassington

Senior Lecturer
Buckinghamshire Chilterns University College

Dr Stephen Pettitt

Pro-vice Chancellor (Corporate Affairs) and Dean, of Luton Business School
University of Luton

FINANCIAL TIMES
Prentice Hall

An imprint of **Pearson Education**

Harlow, England · London · New York · Reading, Massachusetts · San Francisco · Toronto · Don Mills, Ontario · Sydney
Tokyo · Singapore · Hong Kong · Seoul · Taipei · Cape Town · Madrid · Mexico City · Amsterdam · Munich · Paris · Milan

Pearson Education Limited
Edinburgh Gate
Harlow
Essex CM20 2JE
England

and Associated Companies throughout the world

Visit us on the World Wide Web at:
http://www.pearsoneduc.com

First published by Pitman Publishing 1997
Second edition 2000

© Frances Brassington and Stephen Pettitt 1997, 2000

ISBN 0 273 64444 0

Many of the designations used by manufacturers and sellers to distinguish their products are claimed as
trademarks. Pearson Education Limited has made every attempt to supply trademark information about
manufacturers and their products mentioned in this book.

British Library Cataloguing-in-Publication Data
A catalogue record for this book is available from the British Library

Library of Congress Cataloging-in-Publication Data
Brassington, Frances
    Principles of marketing / Frances Brassington, Stephen Pettitt.-- 2nd ed.
        p. cm.
    Includes bibliographical references and index.
    ISBN 0-273-36444-0 (alk. paper)
    1. Marketing. I. Pettitt, Stephen. II. Title.

    HF5415 .B634 1999
    658.8--dc21

                                                          99-056920

10 9 8 7 6 5 4 3 2
04 03 02 01 00

Typeset by 30
Printed and bound by Rotolito Lombarda, Italy

Brief Contents

Contents

Part V
PLACE

Part VI
PROMOTION

23 International Marketing 998

To Adam Stephen Philip,
wishing him a safe journey into this world and a long and happy life.

About the Authors

Stephen Pettitt is Pro Vice Chancellor (Corporate Affairs) and Dean of Luton Business School at the University of Luton. Previously he was the Director of Corporate Affairs at the University of Teesside, and before that, Associate Dean (External Affairs) in the Business School at Teesside. He also worked at the University of Limerick in Ireland for four years as a Lecturer in Marketing and was the Managing Director of The Marketing Centre for Small Business, a campus company specialising in research and consultancy for the small business sector.

He worked initially in various sales and marketing management posts for Olivetti, Plessey and SKF before taking up a career in higher education. He holds a bachelor's degree in geography and an MBA and PhD from Cranfield. In addition to a wide experience in marketing education at all levels, he has undertaken numerous in company training, research and consultancy assignments. He has lectured in marketing and entrepreneurship in France, Poland, Bulgaria, Slovakia, South Africa, Switzerland, the USA and Kenya. He has published over thirty papers and articles along with major studies in tourism innovation strategies, large buyer – small firm seller relationships and small firm development.

Frances Brassington is a Senior Lecturer in Marketing at Buckinghamshire Chilterns University College of Higher Education. She graduated from the University of Bradford Management Centre with a BSc (Hons) in business studies and a PhD. Her first teaching position was at the University of Teesside where she was also MBA dissertation director and marketing section leader. She has taught marketing at all levels and on a wide range of undergraduate marketing modules and programmes and is currently supervising a number of PhD research students. Her own research interests include retail marketing and the use of project based learning in marketing education. She has also designed and delivered marketing programmes for managers and academics in Poland and Bulgaria and has given guest lectures in China and South Africa.

A Companion Web Site accompanies
Principles of Marketing, 2nd Edition
by Brassington and Pettitt

Visit the *Principles of Marketing* Companion Web Site at *www.booksites.net/brassington* to find valuable teaching and learning material including:

For students:
- study material designed to help you improve your results
- 10 MCQs per chapter
- links to articles on the web and a company directory
- extra case studies
- recommended key readings.

For lecturers:
- a secure, password protected site with teaching material
- links to articles, company sites, and marketing resources on the web
- answer guidelines for cases and examination quotes
- downloadable OHPs, an Instructor's Manual, and MCQs.

All web sites mentioned in the text of *Principles of Marketing* will be regularly maintained and updated on the Companion Web Site.

Preface

Introduction

The world within which marketing takes place is a dynamic and potentially very exciting one. By its very nature, marketing reflects social and political change, as well as technological and economic trends. All of these things, as well as their own experiences, influence customers' attitudes to organisations and the product packages on offer. Marketers have to understand this, if they are going to create offerings that will satisfy, or even delight, their customers. There is something of an element of 'magic' to all this, particularly in consumer markets, as the marketer finds the right blend of ingredients to whet the customer's appetite, to stimulate desire, and to generate a sale. Marketing helps consumers to develop emotional bonds with the products they purchase, and to gain psychological as well as functional satisfaction from their use.

Organisational markets too have their own magic. Industrial purchasing might well have a greater element of business-like functionality and cost effectiveness about it, but nevertheless, marketers still have to present the best case to customers, to show them clearly why they should buy from one supplier rather than another. Greater emphasis on long term buyer – supplier relationships means that the marketer not only has to satisfy the organisational buyer's product needs now, but also has to build trust and reassurance so that co-operation can flourish in the future. In essence, this is not that far removed from what the marketer is trying to achieve in a consumer market!

What all this means is that marketing is not a dry, internally focused management function with rigid procedures and sets of rules. It is live, outward looking and interactive. It responds to what is happening both inside and outside the organisation, yet also tries to drive what is happening in order to capitalise on opportunities. This makes marketing fun, but it also makes it dangerous. Marketing creativity and flexibility has to be harnessed within a disciplined and controlled management structure in order to ensure, as far as is possible, that the 'right' things are being done at the 'right' time for the 'right' reasons. Sometimes that means breaking new ground and taking risks.

Marketing is also in the front line of an organisation's attitude to social responsibility and corporate citizenship. Society now expects organisations to ensure that their products are safe and to communicate any risks or problems clearly to the consumer. Organisations are also expected to refrain from selling products in inappropriate ways to vulnerable groups. Marketers have to be able to help the organisation to translate these expectations into practice. Marketers thus have to be creative and flexible, yet disciplined and ethical in everything they do.

In academic terms, the marketing field has reached a sophisticated level of development and is still evolving to incorporate the effects of the changing world. The basic tools of marketing are well established and understood, and theories of consumer and organisational behaviour are becoming increasingly complex. One challenge is to show how all these elements interact with each other in different types of situation, hence the emergence of discrete bodies of literature on international marketing, services marketing, and small business marketing, for example. Another challenge is to explore the impact of emerging issues on both markets and marketers, hence the interest in relationship marketing, 'green' marketing, on-line marketing, and marketing ethics.

The job of a good introductory text book, therefore, is to bring together theory and practice, showing how the two feed from each other. It should cover a wide range of applications, industries and markets, exploring the ways in which marketers are responding to new situations and solving marketing problems creatively. All of this has to be presented within a strong, logical framework that allows the student to develop knowledge and understanding in a structured way. It is also essential, of course, to stimulate the student's interest and curiosity about marketing. Marketing lecturers are privileged in many ways, because their students have already had experience of marketing as consumers. They might be cynical about it, but they have experienced it, and part of the stimulation for the student can be the process of understanding and analysing their own behaviour and responses to marketing activities.

In the light of all this, therefore, this particular textbook aims to be:

- *Comprehensive* in covering a wide range of marketing topics and elements, including the marketing environment, customers and markets, the 4Ps, and specialised applications of marketing. There is particularly comprehensive coverage of the promotional mix to reflect the emerging role of direct and on-line marketing and the sometimes neglected aspects of public relations. Physical distribution and logistics are also given considerably more attention than normal. In a European context, distribution and customer service provision across national boundaries are often critical factors in gaining a competitive edge against nationally based competitors. The wider aspects of international marketing are also well covered. The dedication of a chapter to small business management and franchising reflects the widening application of marketing and the creation of new marketing forms.

- *European* in design and focus. Marketers in most large organisations no longer regard other EU nations as export markets, but as part of one large, single market. This text aims give students this wider European perspective. While there is a bias towards the UK, cases and examples are drawn from across the EU and from further afield to help demonstrate the underlying principles of marketing in practice. It is important that students learn from, and enjoy, examples from across the EU and beyond. 'New' markets are not ignored: examples and cases from China, for instance, are included to show the problems arising from operating in markets in transition.

- *Applied.* Marketing cannot be approached as a purely theoretical course of study. It is essential to show how it works in practice, within the context of market conditions and customer behaviour that can be difficult to predict. To that end, not only does each chapter have a full range of examples and vignettes, but each part of the book also includes an in-depth interview with senior managers who outline their views on the difficulties of putting marketing into practice and some of the problems facing their organisations.

- *Wide ranging* in its coverage of markets and organisations. Marketing is not just about fast moving consumer goods operations which employ dedicated marketing specialists. Marketing happens, formally or informally, consciously or unconsciously, on purpose or by accident, in all organisations. It is important, therefore, to present a wide range of different industries and organisational sizes, in both consumer and organisational markets. Examples have thus been drawn from service industries, non-profit organisations, large and small businesses, (operating domestically and/or internationally. Products considered range from lingerie to condoms, from charities to air travel, from car components to the aerospace industry.

- *A good read.* The text has been written with the needs of the first-time marketing student in mind. The combination of theory, examples and commentary is designed to engage readers' attention and interest, and to lead them painlessly through to a substantial under standing of marketing principles and applications.

Who should use this book

- *Undergraduates* are the prime audience for this text, and the book is intended mainly for use on all purpose introductory marketing modules. The depth and coverage of some topics, however, such as direct marketing, on-line marketing, and marketing communications generally, would make certain chapters useful references for more advanced, specialist modules.

- *Postgraduates* such as MBA or DMS level students will also find in this book a good background text to remind them of basic marketing principles in preparation for more advanced analysis of managerial concepts and case studies. Again, the depth in some of the areas covered would provide useful specialist reading.

Distinctive features of the second edition

The successful features of the first edition of this text have been retained:

- A clearly written and structured text, including chapter objectives and summary.

- A wide selection of vignettes and examples are included in each chapter to illustrate the concepts presented. These are drawn from a range of industries, organisations and countries.

- End of chapter questions give students the opportunity to revise the material presented and to check their understanding of it. Discussion questions, encouraging students to debate issues or to research further into marketing practice can also be used as the basis for seminar work for students working individually or in small groups.

- Each chapter has two short case studies, again drawn from a range of industries, organisations and countries. They have been designed primarily to be discussed within a one hour seminar session and to allow the student to apply the concepts outlined in the text.

■ The complete range of marketing elements is covered, including direct marketing, as well as a selection of specialist applications, such as services marketing, and international marketing.

■ It has been compiled from a European perspective and with a wide European orientation in the examples, vignettes and cases.

■ An instructor's manual that outlines suggested lecture programmes, presents template OHTs, and guidelines on issues arising from the case studies. The manual also suggests how some of the vignettes can be used as seminar material, and offers ideas for further reading and activities.

■ A glossary of key terms is also included, based on the key words highlighted in each chapter.

Some features have been enhanced and some new features introduced:

■ The series of marketing and information technology vignettes is an important innovation in this edition, highlighting the rapidly changing development and application of IT in marketing.

■ Linked with the IT vignettes, we have also paid much more attention throughout this edition to the Internet's contribution to marketing strategies and operations, as a service delivery system, a distribution channel, a research tool and as a communications medium. Drawing all this together, we have added a new section within chapter 18 on on-line marketing. See too, for instance, new Case Studies 13.2 (Amazon's on-line book selling), 15.2 (business to business marketing and IT), and 18.2 (direct selling via the Internet).

■ Throughout the chapters we have given web site addresses (current at the time of going to press) relating to companies, brands and organisations so that students can follow up the stories and seek out their own updates.

■ In terms of case studies, a few 'old favourites' have been retained while others have been updated. A significant number have been replaced to maintain a fresh and topical feel, and regular updates on them will be posted on the website. At the time of writing, issues such as Wal-Mart's entry to the UK market (Case Study 23.1), banana wars (Case Study 3.2), the pricing of soccer club kit (Case Study 10. 1) and even the release of the film *The Mummy* (Case Study 19.1) were still very much in the news and we have thus made as many new cases as possible as up to date as possible.

■ Similarly, we have thoroughly overhauled the examples within the chapters and the marketing in action vignettes, including many items that are of current interest. As with the case studies, we feel that it is important to maintain relevance, freshness and topicality. Additionally, we have also made many of the examples and most of the marketing in action vignettes longer and more comprehensive than in the first edition.

These could easily be used as a basis for classroom discussion as an alternative to a case study.

■ We have reviewed the photographs and retained a few favourite ones. We have taken care to ensure the relevance of the photographs to the text material so that they add value to the student's reading experience.

■ In this edition, we have retained the series of senior mangement perspectives, compiled from lengthy interviews conducted by the authors, although they are now included at the end of each section of the book rather than in a last chapter. By doing this, we feel that they can serve a useful purpose in drawing themes together and providing an applied, integrated summary of the key concepts covered in the part's chapters. These perspectives underline the message that marketing concepts have to be integrated into purposeful strategies that have to be implemented in a real and often difficult world.

Supplements

A wide range of supplements are available to support lectures using *Principles of Marketing*. The unprecedented supplements package has been fully updated to reflect the new edition. Many of these are free to those choosing to adopt the book as their main text.

A comprehensive and easy-to-use manual, designed to help lecturers make full use of the book. Includes:

suggested lecture outlines incorporating the OHPs supplied with the text
outline answers to the end-of-chapter questions for discussion
detailed answers to the case studies within the text, and some supplementary questions and answers
a discussion question and outline answer to each of the Marketing in Action vignettes suggested assignments
10 additional case studies.

100 colour Powerpoint overheads selected from the book are available packaged on CD and included with the Instructor's Manual.

The Financial Times Marketing Casebook has been fully updated with a comprehensive range of interesting and exciting case material, structured to follow the contents of *Principles of Marketing*. Each of the 23 chapters contains 3–4 cases from the *Financial Times* newspaper relating to a specific topic. The chapters are supported by a brief commentary to explain the theory in that section.

Electronic multiple choice question bank contains over 1000 multiple choice questions, arranged in accordance with the structure of the book. Students answer each question and get immediate feedback in terms of which answer is correct. At the end of the test they are given their total score for that session. The software is from Question Mark, the world leader in software for computerising tests, quizzes and surveys.

The *Principles of Marketing* Companion Web Site, is an exciting and involving web site which opens up new possibilities for innovative teaching. The web site includes material specifically targetted at both students and lecturers, additional cases linked to the chapters within the book and the Instructor's Manual and OHPs that lecturers can download and additional multiple choice questions for students to use as self-assessments via the web. The site is located on *www.booksites.net/brassington*, *see* page xiv.

The video contains 6 cases – 4 short (5 minutes appoximately) and 2 long (20 minutes approximately). The cases cover a number of different industries and issues, and is appropriate for use in seminars.

Each case is preceded by a brief summary of the theorectical areas covered in the case and the chapters of the book to which they relate. A number of questions for discussion are included on the web site.

Acknowledgements

It has taken over a year and a half to prepare this second edition of *Principles of Marketing* and there are many people who have helped, directly and indirectly, in its development. Without them it could not have been done.

Particular thanks is due to Neville Hunt of the University of Luton for his hard work and resourcefulness in both sourcing so many new photographs and setting up the senior management interviews. It seems that no challenge was too daunting for him and he gave unstintingly of his time and effort. Our most sincere thanks, Neville. In the latter stages, Neville was ably assisted by Jessica Dos Santos and she too more than earned our gratitude. Other staff of the University of Luton have also been very supportive. Thanks are due to Alison Deacon of the library staff for her help on chapter 6; Brian Mathews for his continued advice on pricing and on services marketing; and Pat Badmin and Gerry Kirkwood for their help in supplying updates and material for some of the cases. All the members of the marketing department within the Business School are thanked for their individual comments and constructive ideas for the book's development.

Colleagues from Buckinghamshire Chilterns University College have been both the sternest critics and the most fervent supporters of this text and have thus made us feel that it was all worthwhile! They have offered constructive insights and feedback on various aspects of the book as well as continuing to supply coffee, comradeship and consolation. Affectionate thanks, therefore, go to Sheena Harland and Kaye 'Fozzie' Foskett in particular, and to George Byars, Mike Clarke, John Cox, and Christine Parsons. Thanks to go to Clive Lewis for explaining the more esoteric aspects of European monetary union and reviewing the relevant material. On the technical side, Ruth Matthews has worked miracles in resurrecting crashed disks and unjamming printers. Heartfelt thanks to them all. Our link with the University of Teesside has also played a role in this project. Thanks to Julie Glover and Alan 'Smiffy' Smith for their friendship and their valuable feedback.

We also thank friends and colleagues from around the world who have contributed to the text and have helped us to deepen our understanding of different markets and cultures. Thanks to: Barra O'Cinneide of the University of Limerick for the provision of case study material. Professor Don Bradley of the University of Central Arkansas for his valuable insights into the impact of the Internet in US marketing applications. Bob Thomas, Managing Director of GEC Marconi in China for his fascinating analysis of the practicalities of marketing in China. We also thank Antònia Pujol from the University of Vic, Spain, Betty Beeler of ESC, St Etienne, and finally, somewhat closer to home, David Pugh, Controller, Retail Sales, Vauxhall Motors for their various contributions to the text.

We are also grateful to Phil Cooper formerly of Chuft Toys and Gifts, Tony and Duncan Lofthouse of Fisherman's Friend, David Moore of Neu Engineering, Joan Capdevila of Grup Colomer, and Graham Hunter of Mars for their courage in allowing us access to their brands and businesses for case study material. We would like to offer general thanks to all those other individuals and organisations who directly and indirectly helped to create the examples, case studies and marketing in action profiles. We are particularly indebted to John O'Connor and Eamon Galvin who contributed the marketing and information technology vignettes.

We are immensely grateful to those people who so willingly gave up their time to give us such interesting insights for the senior management interviews at the end of each section:

Amanda Oswald: Corporate Fundraising Manager, RSPCA.

Ian Aizlewood: Managing Director, Continental Microwave Ltd.

David Burton: Marketing Manager, Eidos Interactive Ltd.

Ian Coomber: Executive Director, Sales and Marketing, Vauxhall UK.

Tony and Duncan Lofthouse: Joint Managing Directors, Lofthouse of Fleetwood Ltd.

Rien van Ruremonde: Managing Director, Nedan Zoetwaren BV.

Tim Pile: Sales and Marketing Director, Alliance and Leicester

Adam Williams: China Country Head, Jardine Fleming China.

During the course of this project, we have come to appreciate the excellent journalistic teams who produce *Marketing, Marketing Week, The Grocer, The Financial Times, The European, The Times, The Sunday Times*, and many other publications that keep us all up-to-date with key developments in marketing across the world.

The Pearson Education team has endured much over the last year, and we would like to thank all those who have helped to bring this second edition to fruition. In particular, we thank Tina Cadle, Nikki Bowen, Stuart Hay, Anna Herbert, Simon Lake, Julianne Mulholland, Jane Powell, and last but certainly not least, Liz Sproat. Their continuous encouragement, support and occasional nagging have been crucial in getting this edition finished. We also thank the unsung heroes behind the scenes, in design, production, marketing, distribution and sales who have made this book the polished, professional package that it is. They've obviously read it!

We were greatly encouraged by the enthusiasm with which the first edition was received and thank all of you who adopted it and used it. We hope you enjoyed the experience and that you will find the second edition even more stimulating. We have appreciated the reviews and feedback (both formal and informal) that we have had from lecturers and students alike and hope that you will stay in contact with us through our website *http://www.booksites.net/brassington*

And finally, yet again we offer our deepest apologies to our friends and family for all the neglect they have had to suffer over the last year. We are sure, however, that they have secretly enjoyed the soap opera that has been the book's progress.

We are grateful to the following for permission to reproduce copyright material:

Figure 1.2 from 'The Marketing Concept: Putting Theory into Practice', *European Journal of Marketing*, 24 (9), pp. 7–23 reprinted with kind permission, MCB University Press Ltd. (Hooley, G. J et al. 1990); Table 5.3 and 5.4 from a survey conducted by Peter Sleight, Target Marketing Consultancy; Tables 7.2 and 7.3 adapted from The UK's Biggest Brands, *Marketing*, copyright A.C. Nielsen (Bainbridge, J. and Curtis, J. 1998); Table 7.5 and 13.2 adapted from *The Retail Pocket Book* 1999, NTC Publications, Henley-on-Thames, p. 60, reprinted with kind permission (Nielsen, 1999); Table 7.6 from EquiTrend, Total Research, London; Table 14.3 VisCap model from Advertising and Promotion Management, p. 293 McGraw-Hill Companies, (Rossiter, J. and Percy, 1987) Table 15.5 from *European Avertising and Media Yearbook* 1997, NTC Publications, Henley-on-Thames, p. 212, reprinted with kind permission; Table 15.10 from *The Marketing Forum* 1999, Richmond Events Ltd.; Table 16.1 and 16.2 from NCH Services Ltd.; Table 19.1 from Mintel Promotional International Group permission from Amanda White; Table 19.2, 19.4 and 19.5 from Exhibition Venues Association; Table 19.3 from European Major Exhibition Centres Association, NEC; Bluewave figure from *http://www. bluewave.com* reprinted with permission; Photograph of Bluewater courtesy of Lend Lease, photographer Adrian Brooks.

Whilst every effort has been made to trace the owners of copyright material, in a few cases this has proved impossible and we take this opportunity to offer our apologies to any copyright holders whose rights we may have unwittingly infringed.

MARKETING AND ITS ENVIRONMENT

Ask anybody what marketing is and it is likely that you will get responses such as 'advertising' or 'making people buy things they don't want'. The first chapters of this book should provide you with fuller, more accurate and more useful definitions than these.

Chapter 1 defines and explores marketing as a philosophy of doing business which puts the customer first, and therefore casts the marketing department in the role of 'communicator' between the organisation and the outside world. Marketers have to tackle a surprisingly wide range of tasks on a daily basis to fulfil that function (hence the thickness of this book), and these too are defined.

Communication is, however, a two-way process. The marketing function does not exist only to deliver the organisation's goods and messages, but also to carry information from a dynamic and changing European environment back into the organisation. Chapter 2, therefore, looks at some of the external influences which affect marketing decisions and thus the way in which organisations choose to do business.

After you have read this section, marketing should mean a lot more to you than 'advertising', and you will appreciate that 'making people buy things they don't want' is the one thing that successful marketers do not do.

1 Marketing Dynamics

LEARNING OBJECTIVES

This chapter will help you to:

1 define what marketing is;

2 trace the development of marketing as a way of doing business;

3 appreciate the importance and contribution of marketing as both a business function and an interface between the organisation and its customers;

4 understand the scope of tasks undertaken in marketing, and the range of different organisational situations in which marketing is applied; and

5 summarise the structure of this book.

INTRODUCTION

You will have some sort of idea of what marketing is, since you are, after all, exposed to marketing in some form every day. Every time you buy or use a product, go window shopping, see an advertising hoarding, watch an advertisement, listen to friends telling you about a wonderful new product they've tried, or even when you go to the library to look at a company's annual report for an assignment, you are reaping the benefits (or being a victim) of marketing activities. When marketing's outputs are so familiar, it is easy to take it for granted and to judge and define it too narrowly by what you see of it close to home. It is a mistake, however, to dismiss marketing as 'just advertising' or 'just selling' or 'making people buy things they don't really want'.

What this book wants to show you is that marketing does, in fact, cover a very wide range of absolutely essential business activities that bring you the products you *do* want, when you want them, where you want them, but at prices you can afford, and with all the information you need to make informed and satisfying consumer choices. And that's only what marketing does for you! Widen your thinking to include what marketing can similarly do for organisations purchasing goods and services from other organisations, and you can begin to see why it is a mistake to be too cynical about professionally practised marketing. None of this is easy. The outputs of marketing, such as the packaging, the advertisements, the glossy brochures, the enticing retail outlets and the incredible bargain value prices, look slick and polished, but a great deal of management planning, analysis and decision making has gone on behind the scenes in order to bring all this to you. By the time you have finished this book, you should appreciate the whole range of marketing activities, and the difficulties of managing them.

Example The UK market for breakfast cereal is worth around £972 million and is the largest in Europe. Constant innovation and good marketing have helped Kellogg (http://www.kelloggs.co.uk) to achieve 43 per cent market share through a wide range of products targeting different consumer tastes and encouraging consumers to snack on cereals throughout the day. The strong brand images of Rice Krispies, Frosties and Choco Krispies, worth about £140 million in sales between them, are clearly targeted at the children's market, while Healthwise, All Bran and Optima meet the growing demand for healthy adult breakfasts. Advertising (particularly through characters such as Tony the Tiger) and promotions (such as in-pack gifts) aimed at children helped to differentiate the products, reinforce brand image and build customer loyalty. Children have a huge influence: 73 per cent of adults surveyed agreed that children influence their purchases of cereals. Premium prices have also reinforced Kellogg's quality image. Thanks to competitors, however, continuing success is not necessarily guaranteed. Supermarket own-brand products, for instance, positioned close to the market leaders and accounting for 26 per cent of the market, have made cereals more of a commodity purchase, undermining premium prices and brand images. To stay ahead, Kellogg will have to continue to plan its product management, communications and pricing strategies carefully (Conley, 1998c; Crosbie, 1997; Gallagher, 1997; Kelly, 1998).

Before launching further into detailed descriptions, explanations and analyses of the operational tasks that make up the marketing function, however, it is important to lay a few foundations about what marketing really is, and to give you a more detailed overview of why it is so essential and precisely what it involves in practice.

This chapter will therefore start by defining what marketing is, by looking at a couple of widely accepted definitions and discussing their implications for organisations. To see how those definitions have emerged, we provide a brief history of marketing and how it has evolved, both as a business function and as a business orientation or philosophy. Building on that, the chapter can then look at the relationship between marketing, the outside world and the rest of the organisation. This will help to establish the role that marketing departments take on, internally and externally, and to define the tools that they use to fulfil those responsibilities. It is important to remember that marketing has a crucial role in helping to set the organisation's overall strategic objectives, and thus we shall discuss the contribution of marketing to defining strategic direction and how the needs of the customer and the needs of the organisation are reconciled.

Finally, to put all of this into context, there will be a practical section discussing the scope of marketing and looking at the variety of marketing applications that exist. To counter the tendency to think of marketing as being relevant only to consumer markets for fast moving physical products, there is a timely reminder of other types of market, such as services and non-profit organisations. This section will also outline the influences that are fundamentally changing the way in which academics and managers think about marketing.

MARKETING DEFINED

This section is going to explore what **marketing** is and its evolution. First, we shall look at currently accepted definitions of marketing, then at the history behind those definitions. Linked with that history are the various business orientations outlined on pp. 11–16. These show how marketing is as much a philosophy of doing business as a business function in its own right. It is important to get this concept well established before moving on to the next section where we discuss philosophy and function in the context of the organisation.

What marketing means

Here are two popular and widely accepted definitions of marketing. The first is the definition preferred by the UK's Chartered Institute of Marketing (CIM; http://www.cim.co.uk), while the second is that offered by the American Marketing Association (AMA; http://www.ama.org):

> **Marketing is the management process which identifies, anticipates, and supplies customer requirements efficiently and profitably.** (CIM)

> **Marketing is the process of planning and executing the conception, pricing, promotion and distribution of ideas, goods and services to create exchange and satisfy individual and organisational objectives.** (AMA, 1985)

Both definitions make a good attempt at capturing concisely what is actually a wide and complex subject. Although they have a lot in common, each says something important that the other does not emphasise.

Both agree on the following points.

Marketing is a management process

Marketing has just as much legitimacy as any other business function, and involves just as much management skill. It requires planning and analysis, resource allocation, control and investment in terms of money, appropriately skilled people and physical resources. It also, of course, requires implementation, monitoring and evaluation. As with any other management activity, it can be carried out efficiently and successfully – or it can be done poorly, resulting in failure.

Marketing is about giving customers what they want

All marketing activities should be geared towards this. It implies a focus towards the customer or end consumer of the product or service. If 'customer requirements' are not satisfactorily fulfilled, or if customers do not obtain what they want and need, then marketing has failed both the customer and the organisation.

The CIM definition adds a couple of extra insights.

MARKETING IN ACTION   **Psion**

The challenge for the marketing manager is to identify what customers want and to deliver it. This is no easy task, as Psion found. Psion dominates the palmtop computer market with a 95 per cent share, despite competing against multinational giants such as Apple, Sharp and Hewlett-Packard. The secret to its success has been careful targeting with different applications, user-friendly technology, innovativeness and updating in a fast moving industry. It is also willing to change its marketing mix to suit emerging circumstances. It has, for instance, been successful in marketing palmtop computing to mobile sales representatives who need to record information during their visits and to download territory information in a user-friendly way.

Competitors' actions can also make marketing plans change. In 1997 Microsoft, one of the world's leaders in computing, entered the same market as Psion with the Windows CE. In response, Psion brought forward the launch of its Series 5 model and shifted the focus of its marketing mix away from advertising, in which it was likely to be outgunned by Microsoft, and into public relations, merchandising and improved communication with existing and potential users. As a result, Psion was able to defend its market share against Microsoft and to improve awareness of the brand among its customers. At times, it was if anything too successful, as demand outstripped production capacity and retailers were left with stocks of only the relatively obsolete Series 3 model. Psion's failure to have adequate stocks contributed towards the growth in sales of the Windows CE in the US market, despite Psion claiming to have a superior product.

Sources: Hamilton (1997); *Marketing Week* (1998a); *Financial Times* (1995); http://www.psion.com.

Innovation at your fingertips.
Source: Psion.

Marketing identifies and anticipates customer requirements

This phrase has a subtle edge to it that does not come through strongly in the AMA definition. It is saying that the marketer creates some sort of offering only after researching the market and pinpointing exactly what the customer will want. The AMA definition is ambiguous because it begins, with the 'planning' process which may or may not be done with reference to the customer.

Marketing fulfils customer requirements efficiently and profitably

This pragmatic phrase warns the marketer against getting too carried away with the altruism of satisfying the customer! In the real world, an organisation cannot please all of the people all of the time, and sometimes even marketers have to make compromises. Efficiency implies working within the resource capabilities of the organisation, and in this case, specifically working within the agreed budgets and performance targets set for the marketing function.

Profitability is a little more questionable. Marketing is now an accepted philosophy within many non-profit making organisations, such as the UK's National Health Service Trust Hospitals, which would certainly accept the need to manage themselves efficiently and cost effectively, but not profitably. That important context aside, most commercial companies exist to make profits, and thus profitability is a legitimate concern. Even so, some organisations would occasionally accept the need to make a loss on a particular product or sector of a market in order to achieve wider strategic objectives. As long as those losses are planned and controlled, and in the longer run provide some other benefit to the organisation, then they are bearable. In general terms, however, if an organisation is consistently failing to make profits, then it will not survive, and thus marketing has a responsibility to sustain and increase profits.

The AMA definition goes further.

Marketing offers and exchanges ideas, goods and services

This statement is close to the CIM's 'profitably', but a little more subtle. The idea of marketing as an **exchange process** is an important one, and was first proposed by

Alderson (1957). The basic idea is that I've got something you want, you've got something I want, so let's do a deal. For the most part, the exchange is a simple one. The organisation offers a product or service, and the customer offers a sum of money in return for it. Pepsi offers you a can of cola and you offer payment; you sign a contract to offer your services as an employee and the organisation pays you a salary; the hospital offers to provide health care and the individual, through taxes or insurance premiums, offers to fund it. A range of further examples is shown diagramatically in Fig. 1.1.

What all these examples have in common is the assumption that both parties value what the other has to offer. If they didn't, then they would not be obliged to enter into the bargain. It is up to the marketer to make sure that customers value what the organisation is offering so highly that they are prepared to give the organisation what it wants in return. Whether the marketer is offering a product, a service, or an idea (such as the environmental causes 'sold' by Greenpeace), the essence of the exchange is mutual value. From mutual value can come satisfaction and possible repeat purchases.

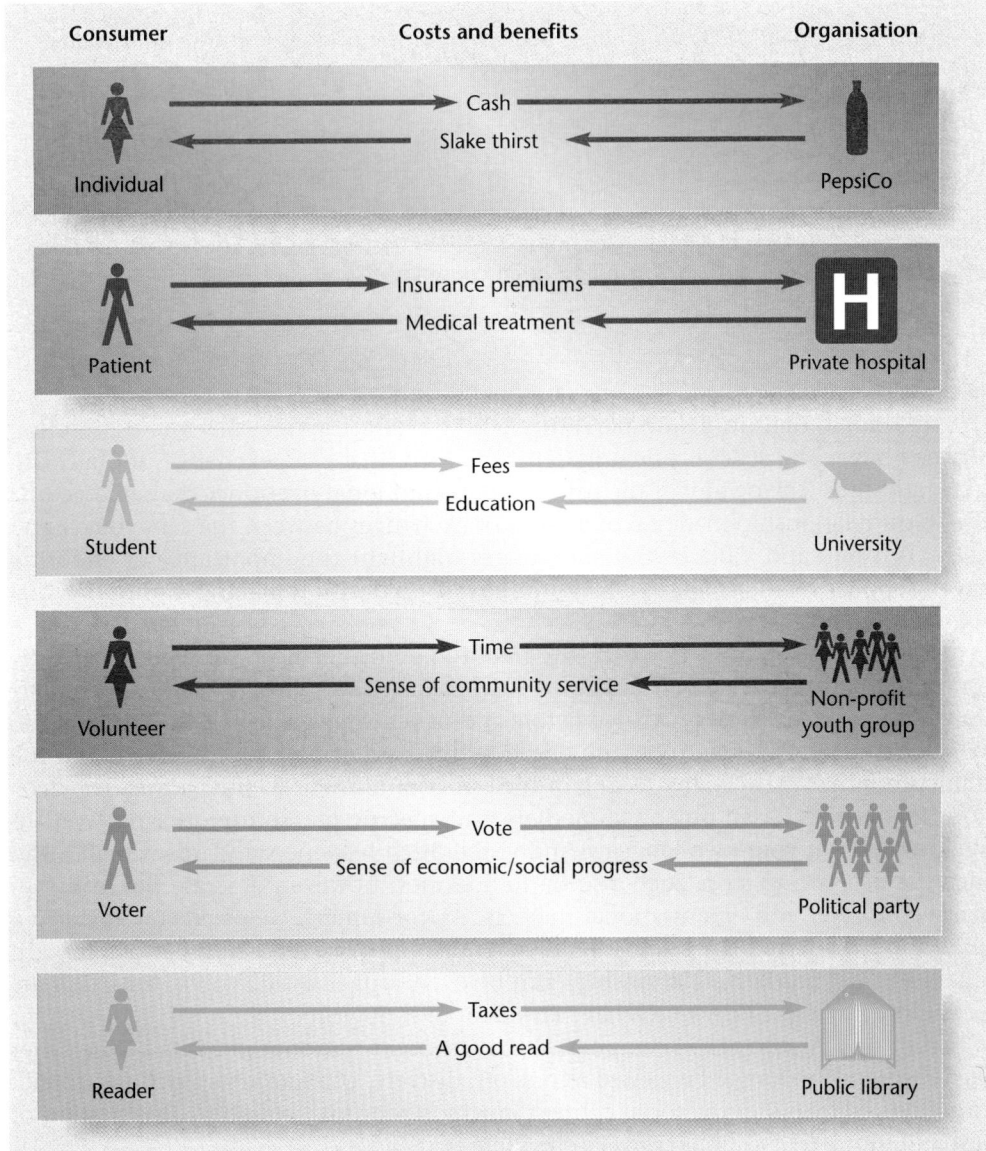

FIGURE 1.1

Exchange transactions

Pricing, promotion and distribution of ideas, goods and services

In saying that marketing involves the conception, pricing, promotion and distribution of ideas, goods and services, the AMA definition is a little more specific in describing the ways in which marketers can stimulate exchanges. It suggests a proactive seller as well as a willing buyer. By designing products, setting sensible, acceptable and justifiable prices, creating awareness and preferences, and ensuring availability and service, the marketer can influence the volume of exchanges. Marketing can be seen, therefore, as a demand management activity on the part of the selling organisation.

Both the CIM and the AMA definitions of marketing, despite their popular usage, are increasingly being criticised as failing to reflect the role and reality of marketing for the 21st century. The two main criticisms centre around the concept of the passive consumer in a discrete exchange, and a failure to address the social context of marketing.

> **Example** Pulling all these marketing activities together is not necessarily easy. P&O (http://www.p-and-o.com) sells sea cruise holidays to consumers. In order to deliver the kind of cruise holiday customers want, P&O has to have the right kind of ships. Fincantieri (http://www.fincantieri.com), an Italian shipbuilding company, constructed *The Grand Princess* for P&O. As Fincantieri's customer, P&O wanted an æsthetically pleasing yet seaworthy 'dreamboat', a floating hotel, built within a set budget and by a set deadline. Fincantieri had to source lighter materials, high tech components and luxury fixtures and fittings to meet the customer's specifications. A soundproof disco and glass lifts for the *outside* of the ship have also had to be designed and built. This was the first cruise ship that Fincantieri had built, and the company clearly believed that if it could meet or even exceed all of P&O's requirements cost effectively, and produce a ship that broke new technical and design ground, then future business would be likely from both P&O and other cruise companies. Since *The Grand Princess*, Fincantieri has also constructed *The Sea Princess* for P&O and has orders worth $4.7 billion, for 12 other cruise liners (Endean, 1998).

Relationship marketing

The traditional definitions of marketing tend to reflect a view that the transaction between buyer and seller is primarily seller oriented, that each exchange is totally discrete, and thus lacking any of the personal and emotional overtones that emerge in a long-term relationship made up of a series of exchanges between the same buyer and seller. Turnbull and Valla (1986) particularly highlight the importance of enduring **buyer–supplier relationships** as a major influence on decision making in international organisational markets.

In some circumstances, however, the traditional non-relationship view is perfectly appropriate. A traveller on an unknown road passing through a foreign country may stop at a wayside café, never visited before and never to be visited again. The decision to purchase is thus going to be influenced by the ease of parking, the decor and the ambience rather than by any feeling of trust or commitment to the patron. The decision, in short, is based on the immediate and specific marketing offering. Well-lit signs, a menu in your own language and visibly high hygiene standards will all influence the decision to stop. Such a scenario does not, however, describe the reality in many consumer and organisational markets. As consumers, we often stay loyal to a small number of familiar brands, retailers and suppliers over a number of years. In organisational markets, relationships can be even longer lived. Volvo, for example, has supplier relationships which have lasted for over 50 years.

Easton and Araujo (1994) emphasise that in organisational markets buyer–seller exchanges can no longer be viewed as one-off, discrete, economic transactions, totally uninfluenced by either the social context in which they take place or consideration of past and future transactions between the same two parties.

> **Example** Marketing is not just relevant to the providers of consumer goods and services that we come into contact with every day. Industrial products often enable those goods and services to be supplied to us. Plasser & Theurer, for example, might not be an instantly recognisable name, yet few railway systems could survive without its products. This Austrian company is a world leader in track-laying and maintenance machines for the railways, with 95 per cent of sales generated outside its domestic market. It has built its reputation by providing machines that improve productivity and efficiency in what was previously the domain of manual labour. It rarely competes on price when chasing business from what are often state-owned or regulated rail authorities. Its focus is on offering better solutions to customers' problems through research and development; offering technical support and user training to help customers get the most out of what is often a £1.25 million investment; and the fast provision of spare parts to avoid costly downtime periods if the equipment is not working. The customers in this market niche appreciate the high-specification, high-quality products that enable them to achieve long-term operational savings compared with costlier alternatives (Frey, 1995; Tulip, 1995).

The rapid rise of **relationship marketing** (see Chapter 18, and p. 166), where organisations develop long-term stable relationships and alliances with other organisations means that:

> Exchange processes are embedded in the dense fabric of social relations and economic exchange is rarely able to rid itself of non-economic exchange baggage such as social exchange, kinship and friendship networks, altruism and gift giving and a host of other psychological and sociological elements not liable to be reduced to the standardised metric of money.
>
> (Easton and Araujo, 1994, p. 75)

Although this statement was made strictly in the context of organisational markets, it is also broadly true in consumer markets. As Chapter 18 on direct marketing shows, direct relationships between individual consumers in mass markets and the organisations that supply them are starting to develop, and this can only increase the importance of the notion of social processes in the definition of marketing. The UK supermarket chain Tesco, for example, through its Clubcard scheme can track the purchases of individual shoppers, creating a database that allows it to communicate directly with consumers in a way that was not possible a few years ago. Thus 30-something males who are not buying their fair share of wine should watch out for the promotional mailshot that will soon be on its way!

Social marketing

'Social marketing' is a fascinating and thought-provoking phrase that is used by a number of writers (Kotler and Zaltman, 1971; Robin and Reidenbach, 1987, for instance). Social marketing is concerned with ensuring that organisations handle marketing responsibly, and in a way that contributes to the well-being of society. It acknowledges that marketing both draws from and contributes to the society within which it operates, in other words it is not about purely unemotional economic transactions. In order to work, it has to interact with people, it has to reflect what they want and what concerns them and, in turn, marketing's images and values become absorbed into popular culture through a synergistic process. At the worst end of the spectrum, for example, it could be argued that marketing, particularly through advertising, encourages people to aspire to things they cannot really afford, and that it encourages materialism and dissatisfaction with what one has. If that is true, then it is certainly a negative social process. At the best end of the spectrum, it could be argued that by developing and opening up mass markets, marketing has brought within the reach of many goods and services that would otherwise only be affordable for a few, and thus marketing is a positive social process. Marketing can also make a positive contribution to the furtherance of altruistic and social causes. The increasing use of marketing techniques by organisations such as Amnesty, Greenpeace and the International Red Cross, for instance, has had a positive impact in bringing 'issues' to a much wider public and precipitating action.

The government's hard-hitting message is 'belt up in the back seat'.

Source: DETR. © Crown copyright (DETR 1998). Reproduced with the permission of the Controller of HMSO.

So definitions of marketing should be moving away from a narrow, organisation-focused perspective, and exchange alone is too narrow a concept for today's approaches and applications of marketing. Further dimensions relating to social contexts and longer-term strategic relationship building are necessary to provide a full understanding of the power of marketing and the influences that shape it.

A definition that includes the important elements of both the AMA and CIM definitions, but perhaps more overtly captures what marketing in today's Europe is all about, is offered by Gronroos (1990):

> **Marketing is to establish, maintain and enhance long term customer relationships at a profit, so that the objectives of the parties involved are met. This is done by mutual exchange and fulfilment of promises.**

This definition still reflects a managerial orientation towards marketing, but emphasises the mutually active role that both partners in the exchange play. It does not list the activities that marketers undertake, but instead is more concerned with the partnership idea, the concept that marketing is about doing something *with* someone, not doing something *to* them. Of course, not all transactions between buyers and sellers can be considered to be part of a relationship, especially where the purchase does not involve much risk or commitment from the purchaser and thus there is little to gain from entering a relationship (Berry, 1983). This was clearly shown in the wayside café example cited earlier. Overall, however, marketing is increasingly about relationships. In many organisational markets, the seller or buyer might even adapt its technology, products or production processes to meet the needs of the other party better, and both parties will gain from the stronger relationship formed (Hallén *et al.*, 1987; Pettitt, 1992).

The idea of fulfilling promises is also an important one, as marketing is all about making promises to potential buyers. If the buyer decides, after the event, that the seller did not live up to those promises, the chances are that they will never buy again from that seller. If, on the other hand, the buyer decides that the seller has fulfilled their promises, then the seeds of trust are sown, and the buyer may be prepared to begin a long-term relationship with the seller.

Between them, therefore, the three definitions offered say just about everything there is to say about the substance and basic philosophy of marketing. Few would argue with any of that now, but marketing has not always been so readily accepted in that form, as the next two subsections show.

The development of marketing

The basic idea of marketing as an exchange process has its roots in very ancient history, when people began to produce crops or goods surplus to their own requirements and then to barter them for other things they wanted. Elements of marketing, particularly selling and advertising, have been around as long as trade itself, but it took the industrial revolution, the development of mass production techniques and the separation of buyers and sellers to sow the seeds of what we recognise as marketing today.

In the early days, the late nineteenth and early twentieth centuries, goods were sufficiently scarce and competition sufficiently underdeveloped that producers did not really need marketing. They could easily sell whatever they produced ('the production era' in which a 'production orientation' was adopted). As markets and technology developed, competition became more serious and companies began to produce more than they could easily sell. This led to 'the sales era', lasting into the 1950s and 1960s, in which organisations developed increasingly large and increasingly pushy sales forces, and more aggressive advertising approaches (the 'selling orientation').

It was not really until the 1960s and 1970s that marketing generally moved away from a heavy emphasis on post-production selling and advertising to become a more comprehensive and integrated field, earning its place as a major influence on corporate strategy ('**marketing orientation**'). This meant that organisations began to move away from a 'sell what we can make' type of thinking, in which 'marketing' was at best a peripheral activity, towards a 'find out what the customer wants and then we'll make it' type of market driven philosophy. Customers took their rightful place at the centre of the organisation's universe. This finally culminated, in the 1980s, in the wide acceptance of marketing as a strategic concept, and yet there is still room for further development of the **marketing concept**, as new applications and contexts emerge.

Historically, marketing has not developed uniformly across all markets or products. Retailers, along with many consumer goods organisations, have been at the forefront of implementing the marketing concept. Benetton, for instance, developed a strong, unique, international product and retail store image, but within the basic formula is prepared to adapt its merchandising and pricing strategies to suit the demands of different geographic markets. The financial services industry, however, has only very recently truly embraced a marketing orientation, some 10 years or more behind most consumer goods. Knights *et al.* (1994), reviewing the development of a marketing orientation within the UK financial services industry, imply that the transition from a selling to a marketing orientation was 'recent and rapid'. They cite research by Clarke *et al.* (1988) showing that the retail banks were exceptionally early, compared with the rest of the sector, in becoming completely marketing driven. The rest have since followed.

MARKETING IN ACTION Marketing myths

The French business magazine *L'Entreprise* gathered together a number of marketing myths to be exploded for the new millennium. One myth relating to consumers and one for each element of the marketing mix have been chosen for discussion.

1 A satisfied consumer is a loyal consumer

Satisfaction helps, but is not necessarily sufficient in itself to guarantee future purchases of a product. After all, satisfaction simply implies that the product has dealt with the problem that the consumer bought it to solve. The next time the consumer is in the market for the same kind of product, other brands offering a better price, a 'new improved' label, more seductive advertising or '20% extra free' might just be more appealing. Marketers have thus to communicate the *unique* benefits of their products very clearly, constantly monitor changes in customer needs, and try to build relationships with their customers. Loyalty schemes, regular mailshots or magazines relating to the company or brand are examples of tools which help the consumer to feel that something over and above the basic satisfaction of the product is being offered.

2 A strong brand is invincible

A strong brand is an attractive target for aspiring competitors. Supermarket own-label products, for example, packaged and branded in a similar way to the mainstream manufacturer brands, have posed a significant threat to them. The perceived unique benefits of the manufacturer brand are unique no longer. Also, if brand manufacturers become complacent, consumers could become bored with the product or their needs might change. A brand name is thus not sufficient protection against a competitor with a similar or 'better' product (in the eyes of the consumer), nor can it guarantee continued consumer loyalty.

3 A big-name brand can sustain a higher price

Price represents what consumers are prepared to give in exchange for a product. If consumers believe that retailer own-label brands are just as good as manufacturer brands, then they will not pay a premium price for the manufacturer brands. Consumers will only pay 37 pence for a can of Heinz baked beans rather than 23 pence for a can of Tesco own-label or 15 pence for Tesco Value Lines beans if they perceive it to have some unique benefit that they value highly (Superior taste? The kids will actually eat them? You get more beans for your money?). The problem for many brand manufacturers is that they do not want to lower prices for fear that the consumer will think that quality has deteriorated. One way of lowering prices without damaging the brand is to offer a discount on bulk purchases. Heinz, for example, offers a four-can pack of baked beans for 99 pence (less than 25 pence per can). The consumer recognises that the lower price is due to bulk buying and does not associate it with brand quality. Single cans are still on sale alongside at the regular price.

4 Members of distribution channels do not influence marketing

For consumer products, retailers, especially the supermarket chains, represent an increasingly important influence on manufacturers' marketing efforts, quite apart from the threat of own-label goods. If, for example, supermarkets will not list (i.e. agree to stock) a new grocery product, then its chances of survival are very slim. Products can also get de-listed if they are not performing to the retailer's expectations or demands and, again, that can be fatal for the product. Manufacturers will also have to plan for incentives to encourage retailers to display the product in the prime areas of the store (the ends of aisles and the eye-level shelves) or to feature it in in-store promotions. The bigger retailers can also drive a hard bargain on the price they are prepared to pay for stock, thus reducing the manufacturer's profit margins. More and more, manufacturers are working in partnership with retailers and wholesalers to minimise the potential problems that retailers can cause and to maximise the benefits gained from the retailer's experience and closeness to the consumer. With more expensive consumer goods too, such as electrical goods, the manufacturer is dependent on the retailer's staff to generate sales and needs to offer partnership, training and incentives to protect market share.

5 Advertising always affects sales

Advertising is often used as a long-term image building tool rather than as a short-term sales booster and thus might not have the direct objective of making sales. It is also difficult to measure the exact impact of advertising on sales, especially as most consumers would not admit to being influenced by advertising. Additionally, strong campaigns can continue to affect the consumer long after they have finished and it can be very hard to pinpoint their role in today's purchases. Nevertheless, a manufacturer who wants to spread information quickly to a lot of people about a new product would still find advertising an effective means of generating early sales. Procter & Gamble's Sunny Delight fruit drink was launched in April 1998 with a £9 million European advertising spend and by August 1998 had generated almost £2 million in sales.

Sources: Agède (1998); Bainbridge and Curtis (1998).

Business orientations

We discuss below the more precise definitions of the alternative approaches to doing business that were outlined above. We then describe the characteristic management thinking behind them, and show how they are used today. Table 1.1 further summarises this information.

TABLE 1.1

Marketing history and business orientations – a summary

Orientation	Focus	Characteristics and aims	Eavesdropping	Main era (generalised)		
				USA	Western Europe	Eastern Europe
Production	Manufacturing	• Increase production • Cost reduction and control • Make profit through volume	'Any colour you want – as long as it's black'	Up to 1940s	Up to 1950s	Late 1980s
Product	Goods	• Quality is all that matters • Improve quality levels • Make profit through volume	'Just look at the quality of the paintwork'	Up to 1940s	Up to 1960s	Largely omitted
Selling	Selling what's produced – seller's needs	• Aggressive sales and promotion • Profit through quick turnover of high volume	'You're not keen on the black? What if I throw in a free sun-roof?'	1940–1950s	1950–1960s	Early 1990s
Marketing	Defining what customers want – buyer's needs	• Integrated marketing • Defining needs in advance of production • Profit through customer satisfaction and loyalty	'Let's find out if they want it in black, and if they would pay a bit more for it'	1960s onwards	1970s onwards	mid-1990s onwards

Production orientation

The emphasis with a **production orientation** is on making products that are affordable and available, and thus the prime task of management is to ensure that the organisation is as efficient as possible in production and distribution techniques. The main assumption is that the market is completely price sensitive, which means that customers are only interested in price as the differentiating factor between competing products and will buy the cheapest. Customers are thus knowledgeable about relative prices, and if the organisation wants to bring prices down, then it must tightly control costs. This is the philosophy of the production era, and was predominant in Central and Eastern Europe in the early stages of the new market economies. Apart from that, it may be a legitimate approach, in the short term, where demand outstrips supply, and companies can put all their effort into improving production and increasing supply and worry about the niceties of marketing later.

A variation on that situation happens when a product is really too expensive for the market, and therefore the means have to be found to bring costs, and thus prices, down. This decision, however, is as likely to be marketing as production driven, and may involve technologically complex, totally new products that neither the producer nor the customer is sure of. Thus CD players, videos, camcorders and home computers were all launched on to unsuspecting markets with limited supply and high prices, but the manufacturers envisaged that with extensive marketing and the benefits gained from progressing along the production and technology learning curve, high-volume markets could be opened up for lower-priced, more reliable products.

Example A modern form of production orientation can occur when an organisation becomes too focused on pursuing a low cost strategy in order to achieve economies of scale, and loses sight of the real customer need. Tetra Pak (http://www.tetrapak.com), the Swedish carton manufacturer, makes 68 billion cartons per year for worldwide customers such as Del Monte and Gerber. The problem was that the cartons were difficult to open, and tended to spill their contents all over the floor. Tetra Pak did not invest in innovation to solve this problem, because it was trying to control costs tightly to maintain its position as a low-cost operator. The result was that its main rival, Norway's Elo Pak, developed a carton with a proper spout and a plastic cap which better met the customers' needs (Slingsby, 1994). This underlines the necessity of talking to customers and being prepared to respond to their problems and needs.

Product orientation

The **product orientation** assumes that consumers are primarily interested in the product itself, and buy on the basis of quality. Since consumers want the highest level of quality for their money, the organisation must work to increase and improve its quality levels. At first glance, this may seem like a reasonable proposition, but the problem is the assumption that consumers *want this product*. Consumers do not want products, they want solutions to problems, and if the organisation's product does not solve a problem, they will not buy it, however high the quality level is. An organisation may well produce the best ever record player, but the majority of consumers would rather buy a cheap CD player. In short, customer needs rather than the product should be the focus.

British farmers have often been accused of adopting a product orientation and neglecting marketing, partly as a result of the protection offered by the EU's Common Agricultural Policy (CAP). There are, however, exceptions. G's Fresh Salads in Cambridgeshire achieved a £1 million increase in overseas sales in one year after employing an export sales manager to find out what European customers wanted, in terms of packaging, quality, delivery and pricing. One of its contracts was to supply the Belgian supermarket chain Delhaize le Lion with lettuces and celery, and this was the UK's first direct delivery of fresh produce to an overseas retail chain (Hargreaves, 1994).

Sales orientation

The basis for the **sales orientation** way of thinking is that consumers are inherently reluctant to purchase, and need every encouragement to purchase sufficient quantities to satisfy the organisation's needs. This leads to a heavy emphasis on personal selling and other sales stimulating devices because products 'are sold, not bought', and thus the organisation puts its effort into building strong sales departments, with the focus very much on the needs of the seller, rather than on those of the buyer. Home improvement organisations, selling for example double glazing and cavity wall insulation, have tended to operate like this, as has the timeshare industry.

Timewell (1994) suggests that banks too have followed this kind of philosophy, developing products that are pushed to customers who do not really want them, and do not use them. The banks have discovered that they do not intuitively know what customers want, and thus they will have to adopt a more customer-centred approach to product development. This should mean less of a 'hard sell' in the future, since the products will at least be in tune with customer needs.

Marketing orientation

The organisation that develops and performs its production and marketing activities with the needs of the buyer driving it all, and with the satisfaction of that buyer as the main aim, is marketing oriented. The motivation is to 'find wants and fill them' rather than 'create products and sell them'. The assumption is that customers are not necessarily price driven, but are looking for the total offering that best fits their needs, and

MARKETING IN ACTION Flower power

Although the market for cut flowers in the UK has traditionally been supplied by small independent florists, in recent years there has been something of a revolution taking place as supermarkets have become increasingly interested in the sector. It has been estimated that the supermarket share of the fresh flowers market has grown to around 30 per cent over the past few years, but more importantly, supermarkets have caused a revolution in what consumers buy, when and how the product reaches the shelves. This affects suppliers and consumers alike.

The supermarket chains have brought their merchandising strategies to the flower market. That means careful shelf planning, display and in-store location to maximise impact. Often, cut flowers are placed in very prominent positions in order to increase sales. The supermarkets have also sought increased shelf life, daily delivery to replenish stocks, and keen prices to stimulate sales. Sales traditionally peak around key public holidays, especially Easter, Christmas and of course St Valentine's Day. In order to spread sales across a wider period, special bouquets are contracted from both domestic and imported packers with the emphasis on flower arranging. Even mail order, the traditional domain of the florists, has been offered by the supermarkets.

Marks & Spencer believes that it is the largest UK fresh florist, offering over 100 varieties of flowers. In one week it sells four million carnations and requires roses all year long from around the world. This type of volume demand has made the UK attractive to both European and international growers. Sierex is one of the Netherlands' top exporters of cut flowers, selling 26 million bouquets a year to European retail chains such as Casino, Promodés and Migros. It is keen to develop the UK market further by providing what supermarket retailers want. Highly attractive bouquets for supermarkets similar to those provided by specialist florists are central to its product offering. Also, through greater efficiency, Sierex believes that it can provide better value for money to supermarket buyers. In order to meet UK supermarket demand, it has introduced daily deliveries and uses North Sea ferries especially equipped with temperature controlled facilities. From further afield, Zimbabwe growers claim that they can now pick, package, label and price so that products can speedily go directly on to UK shelves after a 12-hour flight.

The smaller growers of cut flowers in the UK have found it difficult to respond to increased international competition and changes in the channels of distribution. With limited capacity and volumes they often cannot meet the supermarkets' demand for bulk and year-round supply contracts. One idea being developed by a UK wholesaler and De Montfort University is a virtual marketplace, matching the output of small suppliers with the demands of large wholesalers and supermarkets. If the system is successful, it could result in a just-in-time system that gives smaller suppliers collectively the chance to compete with importers with fresh flowers that have spent less time in transit.

Sources: The Grocer (1998); Matthews (1996); Shapley (1998); Watts (1998).

therefore the organisation has to define those needs and develop appropriate offerings. This is not just about the core product itself, but also about pricing, access to information, availability and peripheral benefits and services that add value to the product. Not all customers, however, necessarily want exactly the same things. They can be grouped according to common needs and wants, and the organisation can produce a specifically targeted marketing package that best suits the needs of one group, thus increasing the chances of satisfying that group and retaining its loyalty.

A marketing orientation is far more, however, than simply matching products and services to customers. It has to emerge from an organisational philosophy, an approach to doing business that naturally places customers and their needs at the heart of what the organisation does. Not all organisations do this to the same extent, although many are trying to move towards it. Hooley *et al.* (1990), as a result of an in-depth study of senior marketing executives, suggested that there are different degrees of marketing orientation, as shown in Fig. 1.2.

The *marketing philosophers*, the biggest cluster of the four in Fig. 1.2, see marketing not only as a function, but as a guiding philosophy of doing business for the whole organisation. In their eyes, marketing is the responsibility of every employee. They also tend to take a more proactive, strategic and planned approach to marketing, and thus have a greater input into corporate strategy.

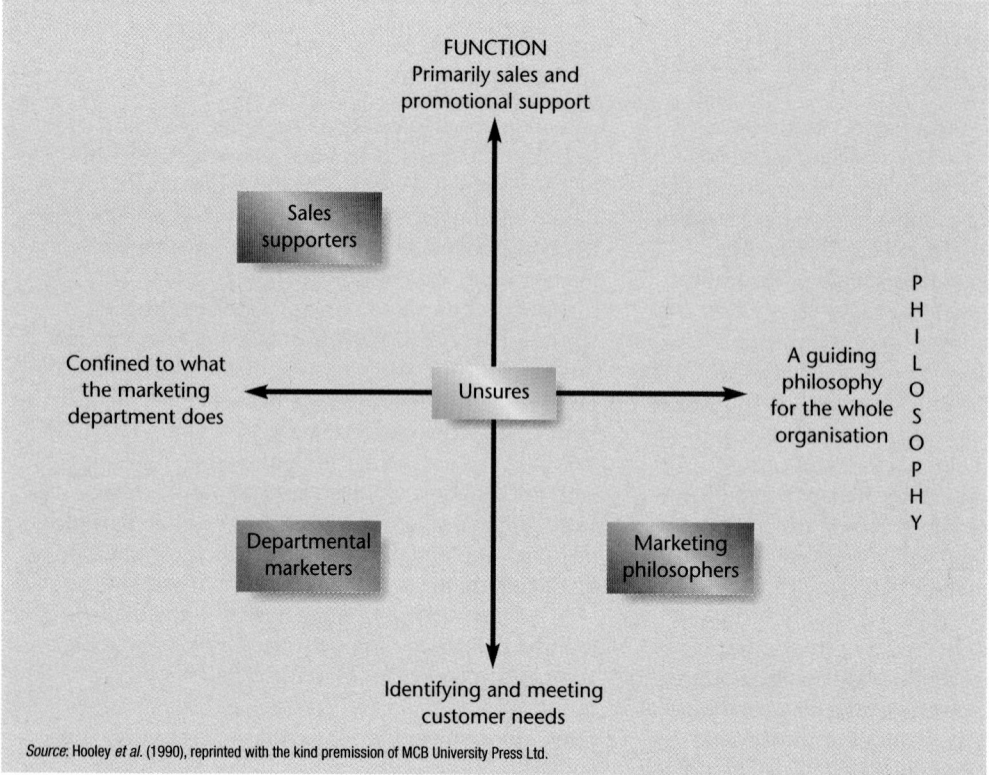

Source: Hooley *et al.* (1990), reprinted with the kind premission of MCB University Press Ltd.

FIGURE 1.2

Marketing approaches

Sales supporters are the smallest cluster, and they see marketing as restricted to the marketing department, with a focus on sales and promotional support.

Departmental marketers see marketing as restricted to the marketing department but, unlike the sales supporters, they also accept the importance of identifying and meeting customer needs.

The 'unsures' cannot decide exactly what marketing is for. Their attitude reflects elements of sales support and customer orientation, but they do not see marketing as confined to the marketing department, nor do they see it as an organisational philosophy. Hooley *et al.* suggest that this implies a laissez-faire attitude to marketing rather than any kind of conscious orientation.

Organisations may evolve from sales support to departmental marketing to the guiding philosophy stage, and organisations that reach the philosophy stage may perform better than those which do not.

The Chief Executive Officer (CEO) of Nestlé fits closely into the marketing philosopher category. His view is that 'Marketing must be a part of general corporate strategy; there is no such thing as isolated marketing' and that 'Marketing is a job for the boss and top management because continuity is important' (Maucher, 1994). He believes strongly in the interaction between marketing function, strategy and philosophy, and longer-term corporate health. He thus feels that the whole organisation can be badly affected when marketing becomes too functional, or 'goes wrong'.

Having thus established the importance of the marketing concept, it is important to look more closely at what its adoption and implementation mean to the organisation.

THE MARKETING CONCEPT IN THE ORGANISATION

What does the philosophy of marketing as a way of doing business mean to a real organisation? In this section we explore the practicalities of implementing the marketing concept, showing just how fundamentally marketing can influence the structure and management of the whole organisation. First, we look at the complexity of the organisational environment, and then think about how marketing can help to manage and make sense of the relationship between the organisation and the outside world. Second, we examine the relationship between marketing and the internal world of the organisation, looking, for example, at the potential conflicts between marketing and other business functions. To bring the external and the internal environments together, this section is summarised by looking at marketing as an interface, i.e. as a linking mechanism between the organisation and various external elements.

The organisational environment

Figure 1.3 summarises the complexity of the external world in which an organisation has to operate. There are many people, groups, elements and forces that have the power to influence, directly or indirectly, the way in which the organisation conducts its business. The organisational environment includes both the immediate operating environment and the broader issues and trends that affect business in the longer term.

Current and potential customers

Customers are obviously vital to the continued health of the organisation. It is essential, therefore, that it is able to locate customers, find out what they want and then communicate its promises to them. Those promises have to be delivered (i.e. the right product at the right time at the right price in the right place) and followed up to ensure that customers are satisfied.

Competitors

Competitors, however, make the organisation's liaison with customer groups a little more difficult, since by definition they are largely pursuing the same set of customers. Customers will make comparisons between different offerings, and will listen to competitors' messages. The organisation, therefore, has not only to monitor what its competitors are actually doing now, but also to try to anticipate what they will do in the future in order to develop counter-measures in advance. European giants Nestlé and Unilever, for example, compete fiercely with each other in several consumer fmcg markets.

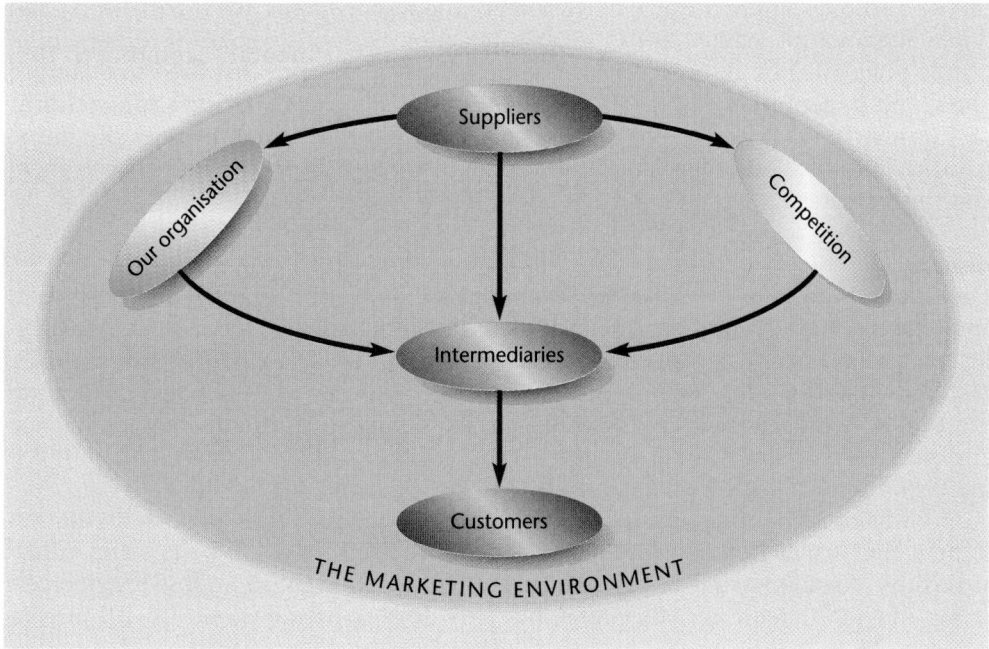

FIGURE 1.3

The organisation's environment

Intermediaries

Intermediaries often provide invaluable services in getting goods from manufacturers to the end buyer. Without the co-operation of a network of wholesalers and/or retailers, many manufacturers would have immense problems in getting their goods to the end customer at the right time in the right place. The organisation must, therefore, think carefully about how best to distribute goods, and build appropriate relationships with intermediaries. Again, this is an area in which competition can interfere, and organisations cannot always obtain access to the channels of distribution that they want, or trade on the terms that they want.

Suppliers

Another crucial link in the chain is the supplier. Losing a key supplier of components or raw materials can mean that production flow is interrupted, or that a lower-quality or more expensive substitution has to be made. This means that there is a danger that the organisation will fail in its promises to the customer, for example by not providing the right product at the right time at the right price. Choice of suppliers, negotiation of terms and relationship building therefore all become important tasks.

The wider **marketing environment**, which will be discussed in further detail in Chapter 2, covers all the other influences that might provide opportunities or threats to the organisation. These include technological development, legal and regulatory constraints, the economic environment, and sociocultural changes. It is essential for the organisation to keep track of all these factors, and to incorporate them into decision making as early as possible if it is to keep ahead of the competition.

This overview of the organisation's world has implied that there are many relationships that matter and that need to be managed if the organisation is to conduct its business successfully. The main responsibility for creating and managing these relationships lies with the marketing function.

Marketing and other business functions

As well as fostering and maintaining relationships with external groups and forces, the marketing function has to interact with other functions within the organisation. Not all organisations have formal marketing departments, and even if they do they can be set up in different ways, but wherever the responsibility for the planning and implementation of marketing lies, close interaction with other areas of the organisation is essential. Not all business functions, however, operate with the same kind of focus, and sometimes there can be potential conflict where perspectives and concerns do not match up. This subsection looks at just a few other functions typically found in all but the smallest organisations and some of the points of conflict between them and the marketers.

Finance

The finance function, for example, sets budgets, perhaps early in the financial year, and expects other functions to stick to them. It wants hard evidence to justify expenditure, and it usually wants pricing to cover costs and to contribute towards profit. Marketing, on the other hand, tends to want the flexibility to act intuitively, according to fast changing needs. Marketing also takes a longer, strategic view of pricing, and may be prepared to make a short-term financial loss in order to develop the market or to further wider strategic objectives.

In terms of accounting and credit, i.e. where finance comes into contact with customers, the finance function would want pricing and procedures to be as standardised as possible, for administrative ease. An accountant would want to impose tough credit terms and short credit periods, preferably only dealing with customers with proven credit records. Marketing, however, would again want some flexibility to allow credit terms to be used as part of a negotiation procedure, and to use pricing discounts as a marketing tool.

Purchasing

The purchasing function can also become somewhat bureaucratic, with too high a priority given to price. A focus on economical purchase quantities, standardisation and the price of materials, along with the desire to purchase as infrequently as possible, can all reduce the flexibility and responsiveness of the organisation. Marketing prefers to think of the quality of the components and raw materials rather than the price, and to go for non-standard parts, to increase its ability to differentiate its product from that of the competition. To be fair to purchasing, this is a somewhat traditional view. The rise of relationship marketing (p. 166 *et seq.*) and the increasing acceptance of just-in-time (JIT) systems (Chapter 12) mean that marketing and purchasing are now working more closely than ever in building long-term, flexible, co-operative relationships with suppliers.

Production

Production has perhaps the greatest potential to clash with marketing. It may be in production's interests to operate long, large production runs with as few variations on the basic product as possible, and with changes to the product as infrequently as possible, at least where mass production is concerned. This also means that production would prefer to deal with standard, rather than customised, orders. If new products are necessary, then the longer the lead time they are given to get production up to speed and running consistently, the better. Marketing has a greater sense of urgency and a greater demand for flexibility. Marketing may look for short production runs of many varied models in order to serve a range of needs in the market. Similarly, changes to the product may be frequent in order to keep the market interested. Marketing, particularly when serving industrial customers, may also be concerned with customisation as a means of better meeting the buyer's needs.

Research and development and engineering

Like production, research and development (R&D) and engineering prefer long lead times. If they are to develop a new product from scratch, then the longer they have to do it, the better. The problem is, however, that marketing will want the new product available as soon as possible, for fear of the competition launching their versions first. Being first into a market can allow the organisation to establish market share and customer loyalty, and to set prices freely, before the effects of competition make customers harder to gain and lead to downward pressure on prices. There is also the danger that R&D and engineering may become focused on the product for the product's sake, and lose sight of what the eventual customer is looking for. Marketing, in contrast, will be concentrating on the benefits and selling points of the product rather than purely on its functionality.

Marketing as a business philosophy

The previous subsection took a pretty negative view, highlighting the potential for conflict and clashes of culture between marketing and other internal functions. It need not necessarily be like that, and this subsection will seek to redress the balance a little, by showing how marketing can work with other functions. Many successful organisations such as Sony, Nestlé and Unilever ensure that all functions within their organisation are focused on their customers. These organisations have embraced a marketing philosophy that permeates the whole enterprise and places the customer firmly at the centre of their universe.

What must be remembered is that organisations do not exist for their own sake. They exist primarily to serve the needs of the purchasers and users of their goods and services. If they cannot successfully sell their goods and services, if they cannot create and hold customers (or clients, or passengers, or patients or whoever), then they undermine their reason for existing. All functions within an organisation, whether they have direct contact with customers or not, contribute in some way towards that fundamental purpose. Finance, for example, helps the organisation to be more cost effective; personnel helps to recruit appropriate staff and make sure they are properly trained and remunerated so that they are more productive or serve the customer better; R&D provides better products; and production obviously churns out the product to the required quality and quantity specifications to meet market needs.

All of these functions and tasks are interdependent, i.e. none of them can exist without the others, and none of them has any purpose without customers and markets to serve. Marketing can help to supply all of those functions with the information they need to fulfil their specific tasks better, within a market-orientated framework. Those interdependencies, and the role of marketing in bringing functions together and emphasising the customer focus, are summarised in a simplified example in Fig. 1.4.

Although the lists of items in the boxes in Fig. 1.4 are far from comprehensive, they do show clearly how marketing can act as a kind of buffer or filter, both collecting information from the outside world then distributing it within the organisation, and presenting the combined efforts of the various internal functions to the external world. The customers box in the figure contains just a few of the issues that concern customers.

FIGURE 1.4

Marketing as an interface

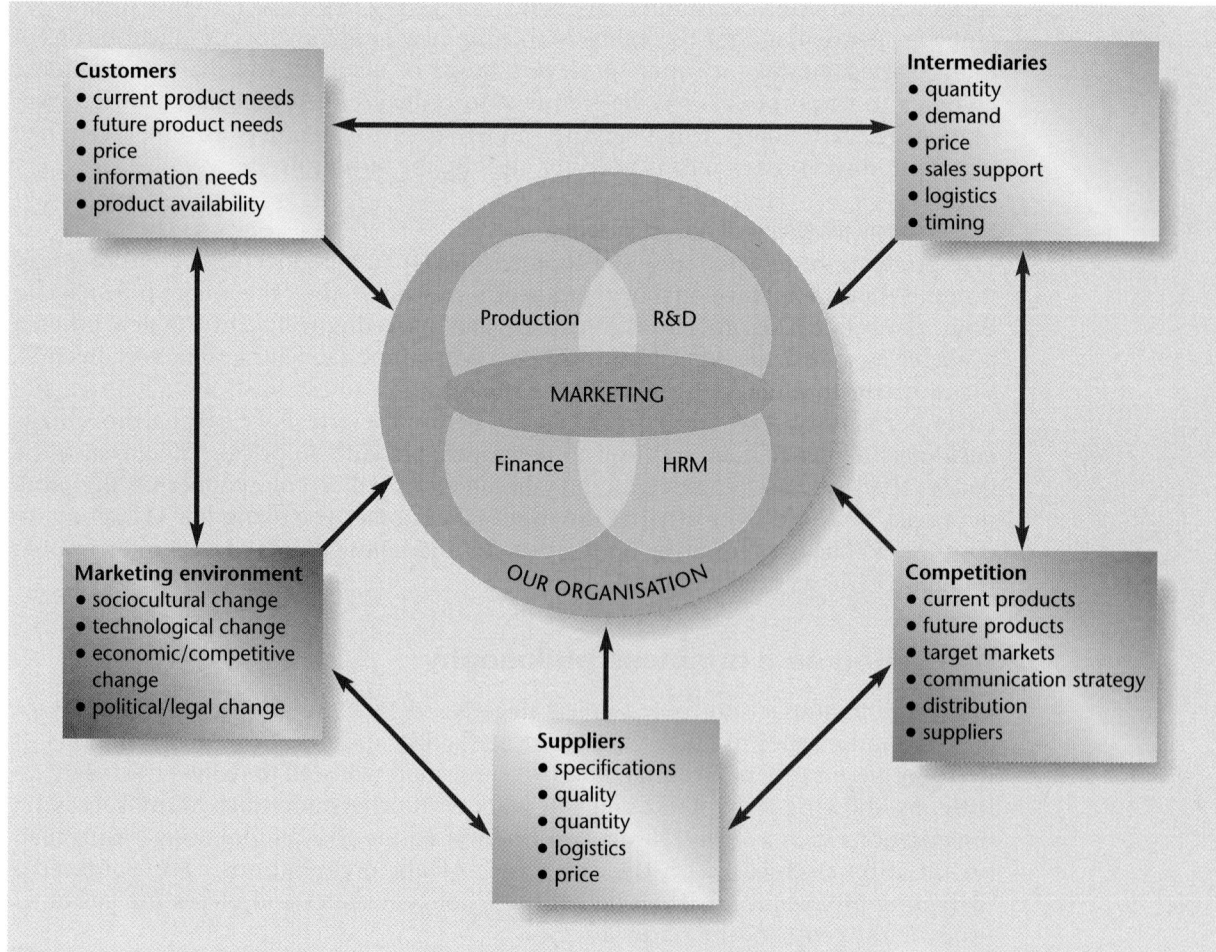

Customer concerns

Current product needs. To satisfy current needs, production has to know how much is required, when and to what quality specification. Production, perhaps with the help of the purchasing function, has to have access to the right raw materials or components at the right price. Keeping current products within an acceptable price band for the customer involves production, purchasing, finance and perhaps even R&D. A sales function might take orders from customers and make sure that the right quantity of goods is dispatched quickly to the right place. Marketing brings in those customers, monitoring their satisfaction levels, and brings any problems to the attention of the relevant functions as soon as possible so that they can be rectified with the minimum of disruption.

Future needs. Marketing, perhaps with the help of R&D, needs to monitor what is happening now and to try to predict what needs to happen in the future. This can be through talking to customers and finding out how their needs are evolving, or working out how new technology can be commercially exploited, or through monitoring competitors' activities and thinking about how they can be imitated, adapted or improved upon. Inevitably, there is a planning lead time, so marketing needs to bring in ideas early, then work with other functions to turn them into reality at the right time. Finance may have to sanction investment in a new product; R&D might have to refine the product or its technology; production may have to invest in new plant, machinery or manufacturing techniques; purchasing may have to start looking for new suppliers; and personnel may have to recruit new staff to help with the development, manufacture or sales of the new product.

When R&D and marketing do share common goals and objectives, it can be a very powerful combination. Marketing can feed ideas from the market that can stimulate innovation, while R&D can work closely with marketing to find and refine commercial applications for its apparently pointless discoveries.

Desired pricing levels. It is rare to find an organisation that can price its products exactly as it wishes without reference to external pressures. Marketing needs to establish what price level the market will bear, and then liaise with production, purchasing and finance to make sure that the organisation can produce the product at that price and still make an adequate profit. If the organisation wants a higher price, then marketing has to make sure that the customers understand and value the benefits they are getting from the product to justify the premium price.

Information needs. If customers do not know about a product or do not understand what benefits it offers them, then they are not going to buy it, and all the internal efforts of the organisation in producing the product will have been wasted. Marketing, therefore, has to liaise with customers to find out what their information needs are and how they fit into the competitive context, and then work with various internal functions to make sure that accurate and timely information is provided.

Product availability. Customers want products to be in the right place at the right time. Marketing, therefore, needs to work closely with those responsible for sales and dispatch to ensure that a distribution network is set up that matches the customer's requirements. This involves both the recruitment of appropriate intermediaries (specific wholesalers and retailers for a consumer product, for example), and the efficient transport of goods from A to B so that they arrive when and where they are wanted, and in good condition. Again, marketing can identify the initial needs, in terms of the required geographic spread of distribution, the preferred intermediaries, and the timing of supply, and then can also help in negotiating the implementation of those needs.

These examples show briefly how marketing can be the eyes and ears of the organisation, and can provide the inputs and support to help each function to do its job more efficiently. Provided that all employees remember that they are ultimately there to serve the customers' needs, then the truly marketing-orientated organisation has no problem in accepting marketing as an interface between the internal and external worlds, and involving marketing in the day-to-day operation of its functions.

MARKETING MANAGEMENT RESPONSIBILITIES

This section outlines specifically what marketing does, and identifies where each of the areas is dealt with in this book.

All of marketing's tasks boil down to one of two things: identifying or satisfying customer needs in such a way as to achieve the organisation's objectives for profitability, survival or growth.

Identifying customer needs

Implicit in this is the idea of identifying the customer. The development of mass markets, more aggressive international competition and the increasing sophistication of the customer have taught marketers that it is unrealistic to expect to be able to satisfy all of the people all of the time. Customers have become more demanding, largely, it must be said, as a result of marketers' efforts, and want products that not only fulfil a basic functional purpose, but also provide positive benefits, sometimes of a psychological nature.

The basic functional purpose of a product, in fact, is often irrelevant as a choice criterion between competing brands – all fridges keep food cold, all brands of cola slake thirst, all cars move people from A to B, regardless of which organisation supplies them. The crucial questions for the customer are how does it fulfil its function, and what extra does it do for me in the process? Thus the choice of a BMW over a Lada may be made because the purchaser feels that the BMW is a better designed and engineered car, gets you from A to B in more comfort and with a lot more style, gives you the power and performance to zip aggressively from A to B if you want, and the BMW name is well respected and its status will reflect on the driver, enhancing self-esteem and standing in other people's eyes. The Lada may be preferred by someone who does not want to invest a lot of money in a car, who is happy to potter from A to B steadily without the blaze of glory, who values economy in terms of insurance, running and servicing costs, and who does not feel the need for a car that is an overt status symbol. These profiles of contrasting car buyers point to a mixture of product and psychological benefits, over and above the basic function of the cars, that are influential in the purchasing decision.

This has two enormous implications for the marketer. The first is that if buyers and their motives are so varied, it is important to identify the criteria and variables that distinguish one group of buyers from another. Once that is done, the marketer can then make sure that a product offering is created that matches the needs of one group as closely as possible. If the marketer's organisation does not do this, then someone else's will, and any 'generic' type of product that tries to please most of the people most of the time will sooner or later be pushed out by something better tailored to a narrower group. The second implication is that by grouping customers according to characteristics and benefits sought, the marketer has a better chance of spotting lucrative gaps in the market than if the market is treated as a homogeneous mass.

Identifying customer needs is not, however, just a question of working out what they want now. The marketer has to try to predict what they will want tomorrow, and identify the influences that are changing customer needs. The environmental factors

MARKETING IN ACTION

Eh-oh, so this is what you want, what you really, really want . . .

Marketers have the job of meeting customers' needs and wants profitably and efficiently. With some goods and services that are linked to fashion and fads, this can mean having to work fast to exploit an opportunity before customers' needs and wants move on to something else. It can also mean working creatively to develop a wide range of goods to encourage and capitalise on demand while it is at a peak. Pop bands and television series are two examples of 'fashion products' that can trigger immensely profitable marketing spin-offs.

Teletubbies, the television series targeted at pre-school children and babies, became the marketing craze of Christmas 1997. Both the BBC and Ragdoll (the programme's production company) earn not only from selling the series to other broadcasters worldwide, but also from licensing the Teletubbies name to manufacturers. The manufacturer pays 10 per cent of the wholesale price of any merchandise, which is then split 60:40 between Ragdoll and the BBC respectively. It is estimated that in 1997, the BBC made £23 million from the Teletubbies and the company which bought the US rights made £15 million in royalties. Products available included soft toys, pyjamas, slippers, puzzles, bubble bath etc. The Teletubbies even released a single, *Teletubbies Say Eh-Oh*, which went straight into the UK charts at number 1. The demand for the soft toys was so great that parents were queueing overnight outside toyshops waiting for deliveries because retailers and manufacturers had failed to predict demand. Part of the problem was that retailers gave orders in January for only 80 000 Teletubbies for the Christmas market. In the autumn, when the real demand picture was becoming clear, Golden Bear, the manufacturer, managed to plan for around one million Teletubbies, but actual demand was nearer three million. Some consumers were becoming entrepreneurial by buying the toys (retail price no more than £13.99 each) and reselling them for £100 or more each.

Teletubbies were not alone in fuelling a Christmas shopping frenzy. Spice Girls dolls also hit the market. Character Group, the dolls' manufacturer, limited pre-Christmas sales to 100 000 dolls, presumably to create excitement as demand was estimated to be nearer two million, and then released a further 400 000 after Christmas to coincide with the Spice Girls' movie. Other Spice Girls merchandise marketed by Character Group included stationery, estimated to have made £10 million. The Spice Girls also had deals in 1997 with Pepsi, Cadbury's, Polaroid, Elida, Fabergé and Asda, among others. The band gets the exposure and the income, while the brand manufacturers benefit from the band's image and character being associated with their products and improving profitability.

Sources: Ayres (1997); Cheary (1997a, 1997b, 1997c); Delves (1997); Hendry (1997); Horsnell (1997); Joseph (1997); Kavanagh (1997); Midgley and Snoddy (1997); Palmer (1998); Wright (1997); http://www.bbc.co.uk.

that affect customer needs and wants, as well as the means by which organisations can fulfil them, are discussed further in Chapter 2. The nature of customers, and the motivations and attitudes that affect their buying behaviour, are covered in Chapters 3 (consumers) and 4 (organisational buyers), while the idea of grouping customers according to common characteristics and/or desired product features and benefits is discussed in Chapter 5. The techniques of market research, as a prime means of discovering what customers are thinking and what they want now and in the future, is the subject of Chapter 6.

Satisfying customer needs

Understanding the nature of customers and their needs and wants is only the first step, however. The organisation needs to act on that information, in order to develop and implement marketing activities that actually deliver something of value to the customer. The means by which such ideas are turned into reality is the **marketing mix**. Figure 1.5 summarises the areas of responsibility within each element of the mix.

First defined by Borden (1964), the marketing mix is the combination of four major tools of marketing, otherwise known as '**the 4Ps**' (product, price, promotion and place). This creates an offering for the customer. The use of the words *mix* and *combination* are important here, because successful marketing relies as much on interaction and synergy between marketing mix elements as it does on good decisions within

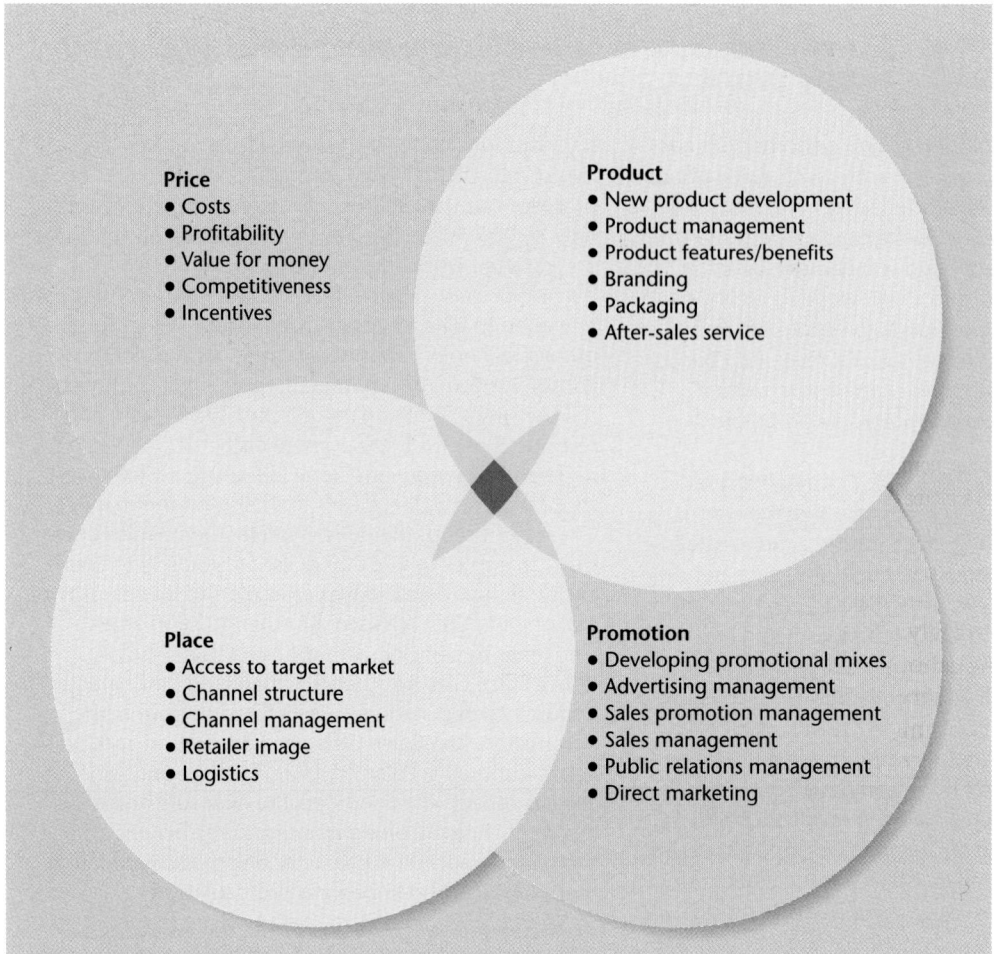

Price
- Costs
- Profitability
- Value for money
- Competitiveness
- Incentives

Product
- New product development
- Product management
- Product features/benefits
- Branding
- Packaging
- After-sales service

Place
- Access to target market
- Channel structure
- Channel management
- Retailer image
- Logistics

Promotion
- Developing promotional mixes
- Advertising management
- Sales promotion management
- Sales management
- Public relations management
- Direct marketing

FIGURE 1.5

The marketing mix

those elements themselves. Häagen Dazs ice cream, for example, is a perfectly good, quality product, but its phenomenal success only came after an innovative and daring advertising campaign that emphasised certain adult orientated product benefits. A good product with bad communication will not work, and similarly a bad product with the glossiest advertising will not work either. This is because the elements of the marketing mix all depend on each other, and if they are not consistent with each other in what they are saying about the product, then the customer, who is not stupid, will reject it all.

We now look more closely at each element of the marketing mix.

Product

This area, discussed in Part III (Chapters 7, 8 and 9), covers everything to do with the creation, development and management of products. It is about not only what to make, but when to make it, how to make it, and how to ensure that it has a long and profitable life. Furthermore, a product is not just a physical thing. In marketing terms, it includes peripheral but important elements, such as after sales service, guarantees, installation and fitting – anything that helps to distinguish the product from its competition and make the customer more likely to buy it.

Particularly with fast moving consumer goods (**fmcg**), part of a product's attractiveness is, of course, its brand imagery and its packaging. Both of these are likely to emphasise the psychological benefits offered by the product. With organisational purchases, however, the emphasis is more likely to be on fitness for functional purpose, quality and peripheral services (technical support, delivery, customisation etc.). As

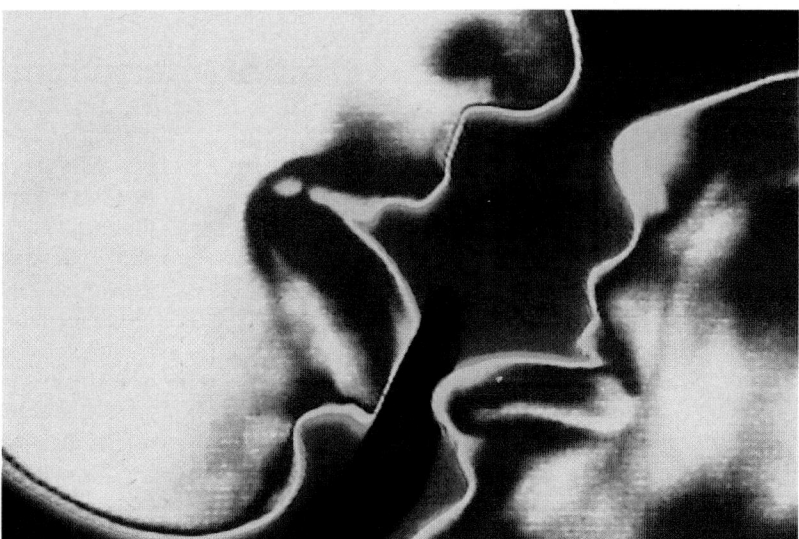

The implied consumer benefit is more than just the taste of Häagen Dazs ice cream.
Source: Euro RSCG.

well as featuring in the product chapters, echoes of these concerns will come through strongly in the chapters on buyer behaviour and segmentation (Chapters 3–5).

Although much of the emphasis is on physical products, it must also be remembered that service markets are an increasingly important growth area of many European economies. The product chapters do cover some aspects of services, but the main discussion of the service product is in Chapter 22, which deals with services marketing.

Price

Price is not perhaps as clear cut as it might seem at first glance, since price is not necessarily a straightforward calculation of costs and profit margins. As Part IV (Chapters 10 and 11) will show, price has to reflect issues of buyer behaviour, because people judge 'value' in terms of their perceptions of what they are getting for their money, what else they could have had for that money and how much that money meant to them in the first place.

Pricing also has a strategic dimension, in that it gives messages to all sorts of people in the market. Customers, for example, may use price as an indicator of quality and desirability for a particular product, and thus price can reinforce or destroy the work of other elements of the marketing mix. Competitors, on the other hand, may see price as a challenge, because if an organisation prices its products very low it may be signalling its intention to start a price war to the death, whereas very high (premium) prices may signal that there are high profits to be made or that there is room for a competitor to undercut and take market share away.

Overall, price is a very flexible element of the marketing mix, being very easy to tinker with. It is also, however, a dangerous element to play around with, because of its very direct link with revenues and profits, unless management think very carefully and clearly about how they are using it. The focus of the pricing chapters, therefore, is on the factors that influence price setting, the short-term tactical uses of pricing in various kinds of market and the strategic implications of a variety of pricing policies.

Place

Place is a very dynamic and fast moving area of marketing. It covers a wide variety of fascinating topics largely concerned with the movement of goods from A to B and what happens at the point of sale. Part V (Chapters 12 and 13) therefore looks at the structure of channels of distribution, from mail order companies that deal direct with the end consumer, to long and complex chains that involve goods passing between several intermediaries before they get to a retailer. The chapters explore the range of

MARKETING AND IT · The impact of information technology

Information technology (IT) is having a profound impact on the way marketing is conducted at the turn of the millennium:

- *Product:* As we will see in Chapter 2, many of today's products have been 'microchipped' – improved and enhanced by adding new chip-enabled facilities to them. Today's cars employ computer chips to manage many of the core systems, from ignition and fuel management systems through to braking control systems. They have also been incorporated into many ancillary components such as digital speedometers, digital clocks, radios and CD players.

- *Price:* The Internet allows companies to market their wares across the globe. This has an impact on international pricing strategies. Internet booksellers like Amazon (http://www.amazon.com) adopted a one price for all when they first opened – typically in US dollars and at up to 40% discount to prices in local stores. When Amazon opened its UK Internet store in 1998 (http://www.amazon.co.uk), it had to adapt its pricing strategy to remain competitive in both jurisdictions as well as being consistent between the UK and the US.

- *Place:* More and more companies are going direct to their customers, often at the expense of their existing relationships with companies and individuals that distribute their products. For example, banks such as Barclays in the UK and Commerzbank in Germany have moved to selling over the telephone and, increasingly, the Internet – a move that has required them to re-evaluate the role of their own branch networks as well as the relationships with independent financial advisers (IFAs) and brokers who promote their life insurance and pensions products.

- *Promotion:* Mass advertising, particularly through the medium of television, has accounted for the majority of advertising expenditure in many companies. The arrival of digital television has increased the choice for viewers, reduced the audiences for individuals television channels but has also allowed companies to target their promotional messages more effectively to specific customer segments.

Source: O'Connor & Galvin (1999).

different intermediaries, and the roles they play in getting goods to the right place at the right time for the end buyer, as well as the physical distribution issues involved in making it all happen.

Do not assume, however, that these channels are merely about the movement and transfer of goods. They are also about power, control, manipulation and competitive advantage, and this is a strong theme throughout these chapters.

For consumer goods, the most visible player in the channel of distribution is the retailer. Manufacturers and consumers alike have to put a lot of trust in the retailer to do justice to the product, to maintain stocks, and to provide a satisfying purchasing experience. Retailers face many of the same marketing decisions as other types of organisation, and use the same marketing mix tools, but with a slightly different perspective. They also face unique marketing problems, for example store location, layout and the creation of store image and atmosphere. Retailing has therefore been given its own chapter which explores its particular concerns.

Promotion

The longest section of this book, Part VI (Chapters 14–19), is basically about communication, which is often seen as the most glamorous and sexy end of marketing. This does not mean, however, that marketing communication is purely an 'artistic' endeavour, or that it can be used to wallpaper over cracks in the rest of the marketing mix. Communication, because it is so pervasive and high profile, can certainly make or break a marketing mix, and thus it needs wise and constant analysis, planning and management.

Chapters 14–19 look at the whole range of marketing communication techniques, not just advertising, but also sales promotions, personal selling, public relations and direct marketing. The activities undertaken within each area, the objectives each can best achieve, their relative strengths and weaknesses, and the kinds of management and planning processes that have to support them are discussed. To put all that into perspective, however, Chapter 14 first looks at the promotional mix as a whole, thinking about the factors that will influence the relative emphasis put on each individual communications area.

That, then, is the traditional 4Ps approach to marketing that has served very well for many years. More recently, however, it has become apparent that the 4Ps as they stand are not always sufficient. In the services sector in particular, they cannot fully describe the marketing activities that are going on, and so an extended marketing mix, the **7Ps**, was proposed by Booms and Bitner (1981), adding people, processes and physical evidence to the traditional 4Ps.

People
Services often depend on people to perform them, creating and delivering the product as the customer waits. A customer's satisfaction with hairdressing and dentistry services, for example, has as much to do with the quality and nature of the interaction between the customer and the service provider as with the end result. If the customer feels comfortable with a particular service provider, trusts them and has a rapport with them, that is a relationship that a competitor would find hard to break into. Even where the service is not quite so personal, sullen assistance in a shop or a fast-food outlet, for example, does not encourage the customer to come back for more. Thus people add value and a dimension to the marketing package way beyond the basic product offering.

Processes
Manufacturing processes, once they are set up, are consistent and predictable and can be left to the production management team, and since they go on out of sight of the customer, any mistakes can be weeded out before distribution. Services, however, are 'manufactured' and consumed live, on the spot, and because they do involve people and the performance of their skills, consistency can be rather more difficult than with normal manufacturing. The marketer, therefore, has to think carefully about how the service is delivered, and what quality controls can be built in so that the customer can be confident that they know what to expect each time they consume the service product. This applies, for example, to banks and other retailers of financial services, fast food outlets, hairdressers and other personal service providers, and even to professionals such as solicitors and management consultants.

Process can also involve queueing mechanisms, preventing waiting customers from getting so impatient that they leave without purchase; processing customer details and payment; as well as ensuring the high professional quality of whatever service they are buying.

Physical evidence
This final area is of particular relevance to retailers (of any type of product), or those who maintain premises from which a service is sold or delivered. It singles out some of the factors already mentioned when talking about retailers within the place element of the traditional 4Ps approach, such as atmosphere, ambience, image and design of premises. In other service situations, physical evidence would relate to the aircraft in which you fly, the hotel in which you stay, the stadium in which you watch the big match, or the lecture theatre in which you learn.

Other than in the services arena, however, the 4Ps are still widely accepted as defining the marketing mix. This book will therefore be structured around them. As you read the subsections on the four elements of the marketing mix, look to see where aspects of people, process and physical evidence are being incorporated or implied within that traditional structure. Relationship marketing, in any type of market for any type of product, is increasingly throwing the emphasis on adding value to products through service. Inevitably, the extra 3Ps are going to impinge on that, and will be reflected in discussing applications of the original 4Ps.

The particular combination of the 4Ps used by any one organisation needs to give it **competitive edge**, or **differential advantage**. This means that the marketer is creating something unique, that the potential customer will recognise and value, that distinguishes one organisation's products from another's. In highly competitive, crowded markets, this is absolutely essential for drawing customers towards your product. The edge or advantage may be created mainly through one element of the mix, or through a combination of them. A product may have a combination of high quality and good value (price and product) that a competitor cannot match; an organisation may have established a 24-hour telephone ordering and home delivery service (place) that cannot easily be imitated; an effective and unique communications campaign combined with an excellent product living up to all its promises (promotion and product) can make an organisation's offering stand out above the crowd.

MARKETING IN ACTION   Virgin Direct

Many organisations claim to be marketing orientated, with their focus on the needs of the buyer. Virgin Direct, for example, decided that personal equity plans (PEPs) were not being properly designed and marketed to the small UK investor. PEPs were sold by financial services companies who then use the money to buy and sell shares on behalf of their PEPs holders. The income from a PEP was tax free. Virgin felt that the financial services companies selling PEPs were charging small investors too much in management fees and that people felt that the purchasing process was complex and daunting. Virgin, therefore, in partnership with Norwich Union, designed a PEP to suit people whose experience of investment went no further than a bank or building society savings account, cut the management fees to a minimum, cut out intermediaries by selling direct over the phone, and then advertised it in comprehensible English rather than in financial jargon. As Virgin said in an advertisement (*Sunday Times* Money Section, 1 October 1995, p. 3):

> *It has none of the things which make most financial products such a drag, such as salesmen, commission and jargon-ridden brochures.*

By 1998 Virgin Direct had become established, selling not just PEPs but also life insurance and pensions. In 1997, the funds under its management exceeded the £1 billion mark from over 200 000 customers. Virgin One, a telephone bank, was launched in 1997 in a venture with the Bank of Scotland, thus bringing together both savings and borrowing.

Success in each of the financial services sectors came from giving customers what they wanted in an easily understood way along with low cost and flexibility.

Each time, the promotional focus was on the difference between traditional financial services providers and the straightforward way in which Virgin dealt with customers. Like the umbrella Virgin brand, Virgin Direct gained increasing public respect and confidence. However, the expansion in the range of services made it difficult to retain the simplicity that was the foundation of its success. Increasingly, different markets for each of the products had to be identified to attract a wider audience and then different messages had to be designed for each one, yet retaining the characteristic forthrightness in advertisements such as 'Beware the charges of the light fingered brigade'.

The new product development manager highlighted the marketing challenge:

> *We need to reach the wider audience that is neglected by the other banks and building societies. These financial institutions have the worst product quality and shoddiest service standards.*

The next stage in the development of Virgin Direct will be interesting, especially now that PEPs have been replaced by ISAs. It is no longer the newest company in the market and now operates in a range of dynamic, competitive sectors. Ultimately it will be the performance of its products that will count rather than the boldness of its advertising.

Sources: Conley (1998a, 1998b); *Marketing Week* (1998a, 1998b); http://www.virgin-direct.co.uk.

Strategic vision

It is clear that individual marketing activities must be looked at within the context of a coherent and consistent marketing mix, but achieving that mix has to be an outcome of a wider framework of strategic marketing planning, implementation and control. Part VII looks at these wider issues, in Chapters 20 and 21.

Strategy is concerned with looking into the future and developing and implementing the plans that will drive the organisation in the desired direction. Implicit in that is the need for strategy to inform (and be informed by) marketing. Strategic marketing thinking also needs a certain amount of unblinkered creativity, and can only be really successful if the marketer thinks not in terms of product, but rather in terms of benefits or solutions delivered to the customer. The organisation that answers the question 'What business are you in?' with the reply 'We are in the business of making gloss paint' is in danger of becoming too inwardly focused on the product itself and improving its manufacture (the production orientation). A more correct reply would have been: 'We are in the business of helping people to create beautiful rooms' (the identification of customer needs). The cosmetics executive who said that in the factory they made cosmetics but in the chemist's shop they sold hope, and the power tool manufacturer who said that they did not make drills, they made quarter-inch holes, were both underlining a more creative, outward-looking, problem-solving way of marketing thinking. Products are bought by customers to solve problems, and if the product does not solve the problem, or if something else solves it better, then the customer will turn away.

The organisation that cannot see this and defines itself in product rather than market terms could be said to be suffering from *marketing myopia*, a term coined by Levitt (1960). Such an organisation may well be missing out on significant marketing opportunities, and thus may leave itself open to new or more innovative competitors which more closely match customer needs. A classic example of this is slide rule manufacturers. Their definition of the business they were in was 'making slide rules'. Perhaps if they had defined their business as 'taking the pain out of calculation' they would still exist today and be manufacturing electronic calculators. Green (1995) discusses how the pharmaceutical companies are thinking about what business they are in. The realisation that patients are buying 'good health' rather than 'drugs' is broadening the horizons of companies such as Sandoz in Switzerland, SmithKline Beecham in the UK and Merck in the USA, all of which have diversified into areas of health care other than research and development of drugs. SmithKline Beecham in particular wants to spread its efforts across what it sees as the four core elements of health care: prevention, diagnosis, treatment and cure.

Therefore the distinction between the product and the problem it solves matters, because marketing strategy is about managing the organisation's activities within the real world in which it has to survive. In that turbulent and dynamically changing world, a marketing mix that works today may not work tomorrow. If your organisation is too product focused to remember to monitor how customer needs and wants are changing, then it will get left behind by competitors who do have their fingers on the customer's pulse. If your organisation forgets why it is making a particular product and why the consumer buys it, how can it develop marketing strategies that strike a chord with the customers and defend against the competition?

Think about a drill manufacturer that is product focused and invests vast amounts of time and money in developing a better version of the traditional electric drill. How do you think it would feel if a competitor then launched a hand-held, cordless, laser gun that could instantly zap quarter-inch holes (controllably) through any material with no physical effort on the part of the operator, and with no mess because it vaporises the residue? The laser company was thinking ahead, looking at the consumer's problem, looking at the weaknesses in the currently available solutions, and developing a marketing package that would deliver a better solution.

What we are saying here is that it is not enough to formulate a cosy marketing mix that suits the product and is entirely consistent with itself. That marketing mix is only working properly if it has been thought through with due respect to the external environment within which it is to be implemented. As well as justifying the existence of that marketing mix in the light of current internal and external influences, the strategic marketer has to go further by justifying how that mix helps to achieve wider corporate objectives; explaining how it is helping to propel the organisation in its longer-term desired direction, and finally, how it contributes to achieving competitive edge.

Ultimately, competitive edge is the name of the game. If marketers can create and sustain competitive edge, by thinking creatively and strategically about the internal and external marketing environments, then they are well on the way to implementing the marketing concept and fulfilling all the promise of the definitions of marketing with which this chapter began.

MARKETING SCOPE

Marketing plays a part in a wide range of organisations and applications. Some of these are discussed specifically in Part VII and elsewhere in this book, while others are implicit throughout the text.

Consumer goods

The **consumer goods** field, because it involves potentially large and lucrative markets of so many individuals, has embraced marketing wholeheartedly, and indeed has been at the root of the development and testing of many marketing theories and concepts. Consumer goods and markets will be a major focus of this text, but certainly not to the exclusion of anything else. Since we are all consumers, it is easy to relate our own experience to the theories and concepts presented here, but it is equally important to try to understand the wider applications.

Industrial goods

Industrial or **organisational goods** ultimately end up serving consumers in some way, directly or indirectly. The cleaned wool that the woolcomber sells to the spinner to make into yarn to sell to the weaver to make into cloth eventually ends up in the shops as clothing; the rubber that Dunlop, Goodyear or Firestone buys to make into tyres to sell to car manufacturers ends up being bought by consumers; the girders sold by British Steel to a civil engineering contractor for a new bridge end up serving the needs of individuals. If these organisations are going to continue to feed the voracious appetite of consumer markets successfully (the right product in the right place at the right time at the right price – remember?), then they also have to manage their relationships with other organisations, in a marketing-oriented way. A study by Avlonitis *et al.* (1997) found that companies in organisational markets that had developed a marketing orientation were a lot more successful than those that had not. The buying of goods, raw materials and components by organisations is a crucial influence on what can be promised and offered, especially in terms of price, place and product, to the next buyer down the line. If these inter-organisational relationships fail, then ultimately the consumer, who props up the whole chain, loses out, which is not in the interests of any organisation, however far removed from the end consumer. As Chapter 4 in particular will show, the concerns and emphases in industrial markets are rather different from those of consumer markets, and thus need to be addressed specifically.

Service goods

Service goods, to be discussed in Chapter 22, include personal services (hairdressing, other beauty treatments or medical services, for example) and professional skills (accountancy, management consultancy or legal advice, for example), and are found in all sorts of markets, whether consumer or organisational. As already mentioned p. 27, services have differentiated themselves somewhat from the traditional approach to marketing because of their particular characteristics. These require an extended marketing mix, and cause different kinds of management headaches from physical products. Many marketing managers concerned with physical products are finding that service elements are becoming increasingly important to augment their products and to differentiate them further from the competition. This means that some of the concepts and concerns of services marketing are spreading far wider than their own relatively narrow field, and this is reflected throughout this book. In between the two extremes of a largely service product (a haircut, for instance) and a largely physical product (a machine tool, for instance), are products that have significant elements of both. A fast food outlet, for example, is selling physical products, burger, fries and a coke, and that is primarily what the customer is there for. Service elements, such as speed and friendliness of service, atmosphere and ambience, are nevertheless inextricably linked with those physical products to create an overall package of satisfaction (or otherwise) in the customer's mind. This mixture of physical and service products is common throughout the retail trade, and thus services marketing not only features in its own chapter, but also permeates those chapters dealing with distribution (Chapters 12 and 13).

Non-profit marketing

Non-profit marketing is an area that has increasingly asserted itself in the economic and political climate of the 1980s and 1990s. Hospitals, schools, universities, the arts and charities are all having to compete within their own sectors to obtain, protect and justify their funding and even their existence. The environment within which such organisations exist is increasingly subject to market forces, and altruism is no longer enough. This means that non-profit organisations need to think not only about efficiency and cost effectiveness, but also about their market orientation – defining what their 'customers' need and want and how they can provide it better than their rivals. Strathclyde Police, for example, broke new ground by advertising on television to highlight the success of its zero-tolerance 'Spotlight' initiative, which it claimed brought about a fall in burglaries, car theft and street robbery, making the city a safer place. The campaign described these achievements to the public to reduce the fear of crime, which is often far greater than the reality. Of course, such a campaign also helps the police force to gain more public support for its methods and operation as well as attracting funding from central government and the local authorities by demonstrating superior performance (Stuart, 1997). Similarly, Oxfam needs public support for its fundraising campaigns. It believes that it is necessary to boost contributions from its retail outlets rather than relying on donations in an increasingly competitive charity market. Despite having over 850 retail outlets in the UK, more than McDonald's, generating over £270 million in sales in 1996, Oxfam had an image of selling junk. Recently, it decided to use advertising to help increase income flow and to dispel negative beliefs about the products on sale. Rather than the traditional approach of focusing on the starving and poor, supermodels were used to demonstrate the quality bargains on sale at an Oxfam store (Cheary, 1997d). Chapter 22 looks in more detail at the particular marketing problems and situations facing non-profit organisations.

Small business marketing

Small business marketing also creates its own perspectives, as discussed in Chapter 21. Many of the marketing theories and concepts laid out in this book have been developed with the larger organisation, relatively rich in management resources, in mind. Similarly, the implementation of these concepts is often discussed under the assumption that the organisation *does* have the expertise, flexibility and resources available to do whatever the market dictates to a high and idealistic marketing standard. Many small businesses, however, simply cannot live up to this. They often have only one or two managers who have to carry out a variety of managerial functions; such businesses often come into existence as a result of the owner/manager's manufacturing skills, and therefore have a production rather than marketing orientation; the manager/s have enough to do managing the day-to-day operation of the business without getting bogged down in strategic planning; they have very limited financial resources for investment in researching new markets and developing new products ahead of the rest. These are a few of the many constraints and barriers to the full implementation of the whole range of marketing possibilities. Throughout this book we therefore takes a closer look at these constraints and considers more pragmatically how marketing theories and practice can be adapted to serve the needs of the small business that wants a long and prosperous future as it develops and grows.

International marketing

International marketing is a well-established field, and with the opening up of Europe as well as the technological improvements that mean it is now easier and cheaper to transfer goods around the world, it has become an increasingly important area of marketing theory and practice. Again, it warrants its own chapter (Chapter 23), not only because of its importance, but also because it creates its own problems. Issues of market entry strategies, whether to adapt marketing mixes for different markets and how, and the logistics of serving geographically dispersed markets all provide an interesting perspective on marketing decision making.

CHAPTER SUMMARY

Marketing is about exchange processes, i.e. identifying what potential customers need and want now, or what they are likely to want in the future, and then offering them something that will fulfil those needs and wants. You thus offer them something that they value and, in return, they offer you something that you value, usually money. Most (but not all) organisations are in business to make profits, and so it is important that customers' needs and wants are fulfilled cost effectively, efficiently and profitably. This implies that the marketing function has to be properly planned, managed and controlled.

Marketing in some shape or form has been around for a very long time, but it was during the course of the twentieth century that it made its most rapid developments and consolidated itself as an important business function and as a philosophy of doing business. By the late 1990s, all types of organisations in the USA and Western Europe had adopted a marketing orientation and were looking for ways to become even more customer focused, for example through relationship marketing.

The marketing orientation has been a necessary response to an increasingly dynamic and difficult world. Externally, the organisation has to take into account the needs, demands and influences of several different groups such as customers, competitors, suppliers and intermediaries, who all exist within a dynamic business environment. Internally, the organisation has to co-ordinate the efforts of different functions, acting as an interface between them and the customer. When the whole organisation accepts that the customer is absolutely paramount and that all functions within the organisation contribute towards customer satisfaction, then a marketing philosophy has been adopted.

Marketing's main tasks, therefore, are centred around identifying and satisfying customers' needs and wants, in order to offer something to the market that has a *competitive edge* or *differential advantage*, making it more attractive than the competing product(s). These tasks are achieved through the use of the *marketing mix*, a combination of elements that actually create the offering. For most physical goods, the marketing mix consists of four elements, product, price, place and promotion. For service based products, the mix can be extended to seven elements with the addition of people, processes and physical evidence.

The marketer has to ensure that the marketing mix meets the customer's needs and wants, and that all its elements are consistent with each other, otherwise customers will turn away and competitors will exploit the weakness. Additionally, the marketer has to ensure that the marketing mix fits in with the strategic vision of the organisation, that it is contributing to the achievement of longer-term objectives, or that it is helping to drive the organisation in the desired future direction.

These marketing principles are generally applicable to any kind of organisation operating in any kind of market. But whatever the application, the basic philosophy remains: if marketers can deliver the right product in the right place at the right time at the right price, then they are making a crucial contribution towards creating satisfied customers and successful, efficient and profitable organisations.

Key words and phrases

Buyer–seller relationships	Marketing	Production orientation
Competitive edge	Marketing concept	Relationship marketing
Consumer goods	Marketing environment	Sales orientation
Differential advantage	Marketing orientation	Service goods
Exchange process	Non-profit marketing	Social marketing
Fmcg products	Organisational goods	4Ps
International marketing	Product orientation	7Ps

QUESTIONS FOR REVIEW

1.1 What essential concepts should a definition of marketing include?

1.2 What is meant by the description of marketing as 'an exchange process'?

1.3 What are the four different types of marketing executive defined by Hooley *et al.* (1990) and how might each manager's approach affect the organisation's atittude to marketing?

1.4 Distinguish between the four main business orientations.

1.5 What are the main groups within the organisational environment that can influence how the organisation operates?

1.6 What factors contribute towards the wider marketing environment?

1.7 How do business functions other than marketing contribute towards satisfying customer needs and wants?

1.8 What is the marketing philosophy?

1.9 What are:

(a) the 4Ps of the marketing mix; and

(b) the 7Ps of the services marketing mix?

1.10 What is competitive edge and why is it so important?

QUESTIONS FOR DISCUSSION

1.1 Which is the most important element of the marketing mix and why?

1.2 Choose a product that you have purchased recently and show how the elements of the marketing mix came together to create the overall offering.

1.3 Choose three different products within the same market and explain how each one is trying to gain a competitive edge over the others.

1.4 Why is the question, 'What business are we in?' so important? How might:

(a) a fast food retailer;
(b) a national airline;
(c) a car manufacturer; and
(d) a hairdresser

answer that question if they were properly marketing orientated?

1.5 How might the application of the marketing concept differ between a small organisation and a very large multinational?

CASE STUDY 1.1

easyJet, easyRide? (A)

In 1997, the deregulation of the European air transport market was completed after 10 years of gradually relaxing the rules to reduce the subsidies given by their governments to state owned airlines, such as Air France and Alitalia, and to abolish monopolies over routes. Open competition on cross-border flights has thus been allowed since 1993 and since 1997 any EU carrier has been able to offer services to and from any EU airport, including domestic flights. These changes have opened up many opportunities for new entrants to the market, such as easyJet, Ryanair and Debonair. All of these airlines operate from secondary airports such as Luton, Stansted and Liverpool and market themselves as low-cost, no-frills carriers or, as Jones (1998) calls them, 'virtually fat-free airlines'.

Founded in 1995 by Stelios Haji-Ioannou, easyJet is typical of the operators in a budget market serving some 10 million passengers per year and growing fast. To keep costs down, as well as operating from secondary airports, easyJet offers a small, carefully selected number of routes and the minimum of service, including no seat allocation or complimentary in-flight meals or drinks. The company really wants to be seen to be saving money and cutting costs. The cabin crew and occasionally the company directors clean the planes after flights; the company handles all its own marketing and advertising in-house; and the marketing director has no secretary and thus has direct contact with customers, even getting an average of 50 calls a month from customers wanting to book flights! Internally, all information (apart from the payroll) is shared to encourage staff

to make suggestions. The chief pilot, for example, suggested that marketing effort should emphasise safety issues more so that the public would not think that cutting prices meant cutting corners.

Low pricing is the main point of the budget airlines' marketing. In 1997, however, the UK government introduced a £10 airport tax on every airline ticket. On a £500 flight with British Airways (BA), for example, an extra £10 makes little difference. When the tax was introduced, however, easyJet had been offering a one-way fare to Scotland of £29. This had to rise to £39 because the ASA (Advertising Standards Authority) had made a general ruling that any advertised flight prices had to include tax. Low pricing from the budget airlines might also have other drawbacks. Some airlines sell less than 20 per cent of the available seats on a flight at the advertised low price, according to Wood and Leathley (1998). They suggest that after the few seats on a flight to Rome advertised for under £100 had gone, other passengers were paying up to £229. Also, there can be little flexibility compared with full-price mainstream airline prices. Passengers might have to book up to three weeks in advance to get low fares; tickets might not be refundable; and a charge might be made for changing tickets (if that is possible at all).

All bookings for easyJet flights are made directly with the company, either by telephone or via its website rather than through travel agents. It is marketing aggressively to boost sales through the website, offering a discount on web bookings. In mid-1998, 3 per cent of bookings worth

£50–60 000 were on-line (the rest were via the telephone), but easyJet was aiming for 30 per cent of bookings and £500 000 of on-line business within one year of that. As a comparison, BA generates 1 per cent of bookings on-line. A joint promotion with *The Times* offering discounted flights to readers was used to promote easyJet's web booking. The website address, www.easyJet.com, was painted on the side of one of the aircraft instead of the usual telephone number.

Because easyJet generates 100 per cent of its business through direct selling, responses and sales generated from different advertising approaches and media can easily be monitored and action quickly taken. As an example, different telephone numbers are occasionally featured in advertisements to monitor response rates from different publications or from advertisements featured in different locations within a publication. Mr Haji-Ioannou has also learned a lot from Richard Branson, not only about running an airline, but also about the art of publicity. When BA launched its budget subsidiary airline, Go, seven easyJet employees, including Tony Anderson (the marketing director) and Mr Haji-Ioannou himself, dressed in orange (the corporate colour) boiler suits and went on the inaugural flight from Stansted to Rome. They also handed out free easyJet tickets to passengers.

Market analysts predict that this sector will grow fourfold between 1998 and 2003 and the budget airlines are confident about their immediate future. Ryanair ordered 45 new aircraft for 1999 and easyJet is aiming for 500 per cent growth by 2003 and spent £500 million on new planes. Nevertheless, competition will also grow and it is likely that the weakest budget carriers will collapse, especially if price is considered the main differentiator. Debonair tried to move away from a price emphasis by adding a few frills. In June 1998, it was the first of the budget airlines to offer complimentary meals and a frequent-flyer loyalty programme. The response from easyJet was typically forthright:

'Being half a budget airline is like being half pregnant.'
(Tony Anderson, quoted by Rogers (1998))

Sources: Beyaztas (1998); Curtis (1998); Hanney (1997); Jones (1998); Mintel (1996); Rogers (1998); Wood and Leathley (1998).

Questions

1 To what extent do you think that easyJet is marketing orientated and practises marketing as defined by Gronroos?

2 Divide easyJet's marketing activities into the 4Ps and explain how they fit together to create a consistent marketing mix. How might the other 3Ps of the services marketing mix fit in?

3 What do you think are the advantages and disadvantages of flying with a budget airline rather than with a mainstream carrier such as BA?

4 Is it possible to be 'half a budget airline' successfully?

CASE STUDY 1.2

Getting to the heart of the dragon

China, with a population of 1.2 billion, represents a huge and largely untapped market for Western companies. Even though it is estimated that only 5 per cent of the population can afford more expensive Western goods, that still yields 60 million potential customers, and up to 10 per cent can afford Western food and drink products. Heinz entered the market with baked beans exported from the UK but labelled in Chinese. Because the price is relatively high for Chinese consumers, Heinz felt that the product would be seen as essentially a middle-class, dinner party type of luxury. Heinz was, however, being initially cautious by shipping out only 1.2 million cans in the first year, which was less than one day's consumption in the UK! Other companies which are committed to the Chinese market, such as Coca-Cola, Pepsi-Cola, Nestlé, Danone and Unilever, already manufacture a number of their brands in China.

Even small and medium sized companies can find good opportunities. William Pitters, a French wine producer, invested FF12 million in a joint-venture winery situated between Shanghai and Beijing. The company is encouraged by the growing westernisation of China's élite. China is not an easy wine market, although it is growing. Average consumption of grape wine is only

0.3 litres per year per person in China, compared with 70 litres per year for a Western European consumer. Traditionally, the Chinese have preferred to drink rice-based wines, but the government is trying to encourage a shift towards grape wines in order to preserve rice stocks for food. William Pitters' immediate objective is to sell Western-style, good quality grape wines in hypermarkets in Shanghai and Beijing for less than £1.50 per bottle.

Any Western companies entering the Chinese market do face a number of problems arising from the fact that China's consumers are only just beginning to come to terms with the marketing orientation that Western companies are offering them. The majority of consumers are not yet very marketing, and especially advertising, literate, although sophisticated urbanites in Beijing, Shanghai or Canton are much more marketing literate than those living in more outlying areas. They are brand conscious, but do not recognise a brand's heritage, nor do they interpret advertising imagery in the same way that Western consumers do. This means that Western companies have to spend a lot on advertising, estimated at £400 million in 1997, and communicate differently. One big difference in their advertising is that advertisers cannot use even mild sexual imagery to sell because it is thought to breach China's 'spiritual civilisation'.

A consumer's age group also affects their attitude to marketing efforts. Ariga et al. (1997), for example, identify a group aged between 18 and 29 who want to look good in the eyes of their peer group by experiencing Western culture through spending a lot of money on the latest, most expensive, big-name Western brands. BMRB International also carried out research into Chinese consumers and found, perhaps not surprisingly, that the under-35s are more positive towards advertising and Western brands ('I like to try new brands') than the over-35s ('I don't pay any attention to the brands I buy'). Pepsi-Cola was particularly interested in targeting children who, as well as having spending power of their own, would also act as 'change agents' with adult groups. Its research indicated that there are 300 million children in China, representing $6 billion in annual spending power.

Retailers are also interested in entering the market. In early 1997, Tesco was considering buying a stake in a Thai retailer with stores in China. The Chinese government is said to be adopting an open-door policy towards top Western retail multiples, and the French hypermarket retailer Carrefour and USA's Wal-Mart are already established in China. Marketers can help the development of the Chinese consumer's marketing awareness. The increase in the number of supermarkets and other food outlets means that consumers are exposed to more brands and are tempted to shop around and to buy. In Shanghai, for example, where consumers spend about 40 per cent of their income on food, there are already 1500 supermarkets and the total is increasing by 200 every year.

Sources: Ariga et al. (1997); Arnaud (1998); Beddall (1998a, 1998b); Bose et al. (1996); Crellin (1998); Crosbie (1998); Graham (1998); Kilburn (1997); http://www.wal-mart.com.

Questions

1 If Heinz wanted to sell baked beans as 'a middle-class, dinner party type of luxury' in Western Europe, how would its marketing mix have to change, and why?

2 What marketing problems do you think that William Pitters, the wine producer, is likely to have faced in the Chinese market?

3 Why are children and young people so important to Western marketers in the Chinese market?

4 Does it matter that China's consumers are less 'marketing orientated' than Western ones?

References to Chapter 1

Alderson, W. (1957), *Marketing Behaviour and Executive Action: A Functionalist Approach to Marketing*, Homewood, Irwin.

Agède, P. (1998), 'Le marketing a aussi ses mythes', *L'Entreprise*, 151 (April), pp. 84–9.

AMA (1985), 'AMA Board Approves New Marketing Definition', *Marketing News*, 1 March 1985, p. 1.

Ariga, M. *et al.* (1997), 'China's Generation III: Viable Target Segment and Implications for Marketing', *Marketing and Research Today*, 25(1), pp. 17–24.

Arnaud, R. (1998), 'Ces Français qui percent en Chine', *L'Entreprise*, 148 (January), pp. 76–80.

Avlonitis, G. *et al.* (1997), 'Marketing Orientation and Company Performance: Industrial vs. Consumer Goods Companies', *Industrial Marketing Management*, 26(5), pp. 385–402.

Ayres, C. (1997), 'Character Toy Firm Hopes to Double Size in Year', *The Times*, 3 December, p. 36.

Bainbridge, J. and Curtis, J. (1998), 'The UK's Biggest Brands, Part 2', *Marketing*, 6 August, pp. 20–1.

Beddall, C. (1998a), 'Tesco Unlocks Door to China', *The Grocer*, 16 May, p. 6.

Beddall, C. (1998b), 'The Walls Come Down', *The Grocer*, 23 May, pp. 32–7.

Berry, L. L. (1983),'Relationship Marketing', in *Emerging Perspectives of Services Marketing*, L. L. Berry *et al.* (eds.), American Marketing Association.

Beyaztas, B. (1998), 'easyJet Pushes Site', *Marketing*, 23 July, p. 10.

Booms, B. H. and Bitner, M. J. (1981), 'Marketing Strategies and Organisation Structures for Service Firms', in *Marketing of Services*, J. Donnelly and W. R. George (eds.), American Marketing Association.

Borden, N. (1964), 'The Concept of the Marketing Mix', *Journal of Advertising Research*, June 1964, pp. 2–7.

Bose, A. *et al.* (1996), 'The Little Emperor: A Case Study of a New Brand Launch', *Marketing and Research Today*, 24(4), pp. 216–21.

Cheary, N. (1997a), 'Asda Signs Spice Girls', *Marketing Week*, 25 September, p. 7.

Cheary, N. (1997b), 'Cadbury Plans Spice Girls Range', *Marketing Week*, 2 October, p. 8.

Cheary, N. (1997c), 'Over Spiced', *Marketing Week*, 2 October, pp. 36–9.

Cheary, N. (1997d), 'Oxfam Retro Retail Breaks the Mould', *Marketing Week*, 6 November, pp. 21–2.

Clarke, P. D. *et al.* (1988), 'The Genesis of Strategic Marketing Control in British Retail Banking', *International Journal of Bank Marketing*, 6(2), pp. 5–19.

Conley, C. (1998a), 'Virgin Direct to Launch Overseas Expansion Drive', *Marketing Week*, 3 September, p. 8.

Conley, C. (1998b), 'Virgin Direct Banks on Serious Approach', *Marketing Week*, 3 September, p. 22.

Conley, C. (1998c), 'Crunch Time for Kellogg', *Marketing Week*, 24 September, pp. 29–31.

Crellin, M. (1998), 'Young China Welcomes West', *Marketing Week*, 16 July, pp. 38–9.

Crosbie, P. (1997), 'Tots Call All the Shots at the Shops', *The Express*, 8 December, pp. 14–15.

Crosbie, P. (1998), 'That's Beanz Meanz Heinz', *The Express*, 23 March, p. 3.

Curtis, J. (1998), 'No-frills Airline, No-frills Culture', *Marketing*, 9 July, pp. 24–5.

Delves, P. (1997), 'Girl Power Tackles Teletubbies', *The Times*, 17 October, p. 6.

Easton, G. and Araujo, L. (1994),'Market Exchange, Social Structures and Time', *European Journal of Marketing*, 28(3), pp. 72–84.

Endean, C. (1998), 'Italy Cruises into Market Leadership', *The European*, 28 September–4 October, pp. 20–1.

Financial Times (1995), 'A Passion for Palmtops', *Financial Times*, 1 November , p. V.

Frey, E. (1995), 'High Tech Solves Low Tech Problem', *Financial Times*, 11 October, p. XVI.

Gallagher, I. (1997), 'We're Cereal Crunchers', *The Express*, 2 December, p. 18.

Graham, M. (1998), 'No Sex, We're Chinese Is the Beijing Slogan', *The Sunday Times*, 27 September, p. 3.12.

Green, D. (1995), 'Healthcare Vies With Research', *Financial Times*, 25 April 1995, p. 34.

The Grocer (1998), 'Dutch Exporter Going Flat out to Grow in Britain', *The Grocer*, 24 January, p. 40.

Gronroos, C. (1990), 'Marketing Redefined', *Management Decision*, 28(8), pp. 5–9.

Hallén, L. *et al.* (1987), 'Relationship Strength and Stability in International and Domestic Industrial Marketing', *Industrial Marketing and Purchasing*, 2(3), pp. 22–37.

Hamilton, K. (1997), 'Profits Slip from Psion's Palms', *The Sunday Times*, 7 September, p. 35.

Hanney, B. (1997), 'BA is Trying to Bring us Down Says easyJet', *The Express*, 12 November, p. 35.

Hargreaves, D. (1994), 'Granting an End to Food Trade Gap: Farmers and Markets are Drawing Closer', *Financial Times*, 11 August 1994, p. 7.

Hendry, A. (1997), 'Parents in the Grip of Tubbymania', *The Express*, 31 October, p. 3.

Hooley, G. J. *et al.* (1990), 'The Marketing Concept: Putting Theory into Practice', *European Journal of Marketing*, 24(9), pp. 7–23.

Horsnell, M. (1997), 'Festive Memo to Parents: Panic Now', *The Times*, 24 October, p. 4.

Jones, L. (1998), 'Airline Boom Stalls', *The European*, 7–13 September, pp. 18–19.

Joseph, C. (1997), 'Tubbies Top the Singles Chart', *The Express*, 8 December, p. 15.

Kavanagh, M. (1997), 'Teletubby Xmas Shortage Looms', *Marketing Week*, 25 September, p. 11.

Kelly, J. (1998), 'It's a Whole New Bowl Game', *The Grocer*, 14 February, pp. 35–8.

Kilburn, D. (1997), 'China Produces Reds – or Whites', *Marketing Week*, 16 October, p. 36.

Knights, D. *et al.* (1994), 'The Consumer Rules? An Examination of the Rhetoric and "Reality" of Marketing in Financial Services', *European Journal of Marketing*, 28(3), pp. 42–54.

Kotler, P. and Zaltman, C. (1971), 'Social Marketing: An Approach to Planned Social Change', *Journal of Marketing*, 35 (July), pp. 3–12.

Levitt, T. (1960), 'Marketing Myopia', *Harvard Business Review*, July/Aug 1960, pp. 45–56.

Marketing Week (1998a), 'The Marketing Society Awards 1998', *Marketing Week*, 26 February, pp. 44–56.

Marketing Week (1998b), 'Virgin Direct Poaches Boss from Australian Insurance Group AMP', *Marketing Week*, 16 July, p. 7.

Matthews, R. (1996), 'Flower Trade with Europe Is Blossoming', *Financial Times*, 24 October, p. 4.

Maucher, H. (1994), 'The Marketing Secrets of a Global Giant', *Director*, 48(4), pp. 54–6.

Midgley, C. and Snoddy, R. (1997), 'Well done. You've Finally Tracked Down a Dipsy. But Does He Talk?', *The Times*, 8 December, p. 3.

Mintel (1996), 'Airlines', *Mintel Marketing Intelligence Reports*, July.

O'Conner, J. and Gavin, E. (1999), Marketing and Information Technology, 2nd edn, Financial Times Pitman Publishing.

Palmer, R. (1998), 'BBC Loses £15m on Teletubbies', *The Express*, 22 October, pp. 1 and 9.

Pettitt, S. J. (1992), *Small Firms and Their Major Customers: An Interaction and Relationship Approach*, unpublished PhD Thesis, Cranfield University.

Robin, D. P. and Reidenbach, R. E. (1987), 'Social Responsibility, Ethics and Marketing Strategy: Closing the Gap Between Concepts and Application', *Journal of Marketing*, 51 (January), pp. 44–58.

Rogers, D. (1998), 'Low-cost Airlines Battle for Skies', *Marketing*, 20 August, pp. 18–19.

Shapley, D. (1998), 'We Can Arrange It', *The Grocer*, 24 January, pp. 37–8.

Slingsby, H. (1994), 'Leader of the Pak', *Marketing Week*, 8 July 1994, pp. 36–7.

Stuart, L. (1997), 'Safe as Houses', *Marketing Week*, 20 November, pp. 32–5.

Timewell, S. (1994), 'Listen to the Customer', *Banker*, 144 (Febuary), pp. 29–30.

Tulip, S. (1995), 'Railtrack Procurement', *Purchasing and Supply Management*, April 1995, pp. 38–40.

Turnbull, P. W. and Valla, J. P. (1986), *Strategies for International Industrial Marketing*, Croom Helm.

Watts, S. (1998), 'Hi-tech Link Gives Flower Growers Way to Bloom', *The Times*, 6 January, p. 18.

Wood, N. and Leathley, A. (1998), 'Get Set, Go: Airline Fares War Takes Off', *The Times*, 23 May, p. 5.

Wright, R. (1997), 'Hamleys Gets Ready for a Spicy Christmas', *Financial Times*, 15 October, p. 22.

2 The European Marketing Environment

LEARNING OBJECTIVES

This chapter will help you to:

1 understand the importance of the external environment to marketing decision making;

2 assess the role and importance of scanning the environment as a means of early identification of opportunities and threats;

3 appreciate the evolving and diverse nature of the European marketing environment;

4 define the broad categories of factors that affect the marketing environment; and

5 understand the influences at work within each of those categories and their implications for marketing.

INTRODUCTION

Marketing, by its very nature, is an outward-looking discipline. As the interface between the organisation and the outside world, it has to balance internal capabilities and resources with the opportunities offered externally. Chapter 1 has already shown, however, that the outside world can be a complex and difficult place to understand. Although the definition and understanding of the customer's needs and wants are at the heart of the marketing philosophy, there are many factors influencing how those customer needs evolve, and affecting or constraining the organisation's ability to meet those needs in a competitive environment. Thus in order to reach an adequate understanding of the customer's future needs and to develop marketing mixes that will satisfy the customer, the marketer has to be able to analyse the external environment and clarify which influences and their implications are most important.

This chapter will dissect the external environment and look closely at the variety of factors and influences that help to shape the direction of marketing thinking. First, the chapter clarifies the nature of the external environment, underlining why it needs to be understood, and what opportunities that understanding offers to the marketer.

Example An alliance between Thyssen (http://www.thyssen.com), Daimler-Benz (htt://www. Daimler–Chrysler.de) and Siemens (http://www.siemens.com), three of Germany's largest companies, is facing a potential threat from the Green Party that could prevent them gaining a worldwide lead in new technology. They have been co-operating to produce the Transrapid train which uses magnetic levitation for propulsion. It has the potential to complete the 180-mile journey between Berlin and Hamburg in one hour, reaching speeds of 300 mph. This technological innovation could become a world beater, creating 18 000 German jobs. So why the problem? The Green Party is concerned with the mental health of the cows which happen to graze under the elevated system and which are thus liable to suffer from the powerful magnetic forces released by the train. The Greens and other environmentalists have already collected 90 000 names on a petition opposing the development and, if the Green party is to occupy an influential position in the government of Gerhard Schröder, it could be even better able to influence plans. This example is seen by many as a watershed in the conflict between the Greens and economic interests. The outcome could help to determine the perceived attractiveness of Germany for foreign investment. The Green agenda does not stop with confused cows, according to *The Sunday Times*, it also proposes a 60 mph speed limit on the autobahns, no further new road building and, perhaps most bizarre, restricting Germans to one foreign holiday every five years (Woodhead, 1998).

Although the environment consists of a wide variety of factors and influences, it is possible to group them under four broad headings: sociocultural, technological, economic and competitive, and political and legal influences. Each will be examined in turn, discussing the various issues they cover and their implications for marketing decision making.

THE NATURE OF THE EUROPEAN MARKETING ENVIRONMENT

This section will first define the broad groupings of environmental influences, and then go on to look at the technique of environmental scanning as a means of identifying the threats and opportunities that will affect marketing planning and implementation within the organisation.

Elements of the marketing environment

Figure 2.1 shows the elements of the external environment in relation to the organisation and its immediate surroundings.

As the figure shows, the elements can be divided into four main groupings, known by the acronym **STEP**:

Sociocultural environment

The sociocultural environment is of particular concern to marketers as it has a direct effect on their understanding of customers and what drives them. Not only does it address the demographic structure of markets, but it also looks at the way in which attitudes and opinions are being formed and how they are evolving. A general increase in health consciousness, for instance, has stimulated the launch of a wide variety of products with low levels of fat and sugar, fewer artificial ingredients and no additives.

Technological environment

Technological innovation and technological improvement have had a profound effect in all areas of marketing. Computer technology, for instance, has revolutionised product design, quality control, materials and inventory management, the production of advertising and other promotional materials, and the management and analysis of customer information. The rise in direct marketing as a communication technique, discussed in Chapter 18, owes a lot to the availability of cheap and powerful com-

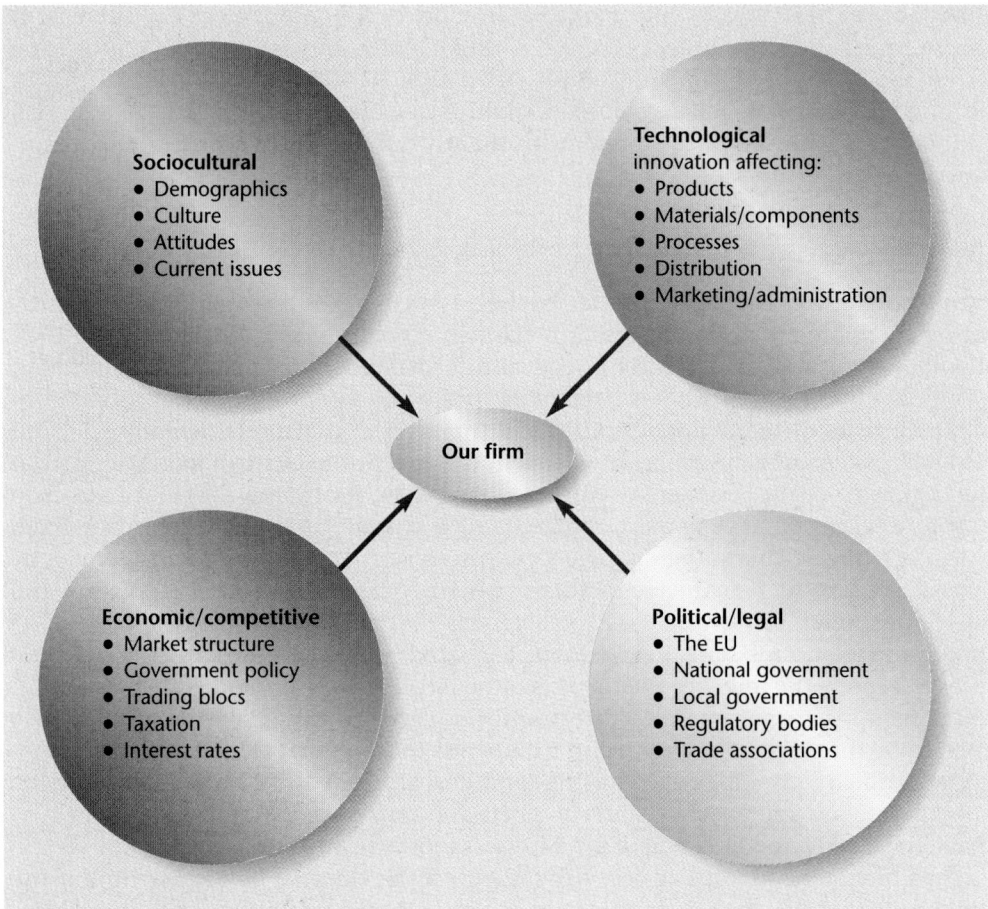

FIGURE 2.1

Elements of the external environment

puterised database management. Technology also affects the development of new processes and materials, as well as the invention of completely new products or applications, such as the multimedia home computer, including a CD-ROM drive, or the development of the low calorie sweeteners that have revolutionised the dieting market.

Economic and competitive environment

The economic and competitive environment covers both macro- and micro-economic conditions which affect the structure of competition in a market, the cost and availability of money for marketing investment in stock and new products, for example, and the economic conditions affecting a customer's propensity to buy. The global recession of the late 1990s, for instance, caused a significant increase in unemployment at all social levels, and thus affected consumers' willingness and ability to buy many kinds of products.

Political and legal environment

The political and legal environment covers the external forces controlled by governments, both national and European, local authorities, or other trade or activity orientated regulatory bodies. Some of the rules and regulations developed and implemented by bodies under this heading have the force of law, while others are voluntary, such as advertising codes of practice. A voluntary agreement covering tobacco advertising in the UK, for example, meant (among other things) that the industry undertook to reduce its expenditure on poster advertising by 40 per cent. Although the code was voluntary, the government made it clear that if the industry failed to comply satisfactorily with the agreement, legislation would be considered. Indeed, in 1999 the government announced that poster and press advertising would be banned from 2001 and 2002 respectively.

Each of the STEP areas will be looked at in more detail on pp. 43 *et seq*. There is, of course, much interdependence between them. Rules and regulations concerning 'green' aspects of products, for example, are a result of sociocultural influences pressurising the legislators and regulators. Certain issues, therefore, such as international, ethical and green issues, will crop up with slightly different perspectives in the discussion of each STEP element.

Environmental scanning

Even a brief discussion of the STEP factors begins to show just how important the marketing environment is. No organisation exists in a vacuum, and since marketing is all about looking outwards and meeting the customer's needs and wants, the organisation has to take into account what is happening in the real world. The marketing environment will present many opportunities and threats that can fundamentally affect all elements of the marketing mix, as we saw in the case of the German manufacturers at the beginning of the chapter. In terms of the product, for example, STEP factors help to define exactly what customers want, what it is possible (and legal) to provide them with, and how it should be packaged and presented. Pricing is also influenced by external factors, such as the competition's pricing policies, government taxation and what consumers can afford. STEP factors also affect promotion, constraining it through regulation, but also inspiring the creativity that develops appropriate messages to capture the mood of the times and the target audience. Finally, the strength of relationships between manufacturers and retailers or other intermediaries is also affected by the external environment. Competitive pressures at all levels of the distribution channel; technology encouraging joint development and commitment in terms of both products and logistics; shifts in where and how people want to buy: all help to shape the quality and direction of inter-organisational relationships.

Thus the marketing mix is very dependent on the external environment, but the problem is that the environment is very dynamic, changing all the time. The organisation therefore has to keep pace with change and even anticipate it. It is not enough to understand what is happening today: by the time the organisation has acted on that information and implemented decisions based on it, it will be too late. The organisation has to either pick up the earliest indicators of change and then act on them very quickly, or try to predict change so that tomorrow's marketing offerings can be appropriately planned.

In order to achieve this successfully, the organisation needs to undertake **environmental scanning**, which is the collection and evaluation of information from the wider marketing environment that might affect the organisation and its strategic marketing activities. Such information may come from a variety of sources, such as experience, personal contacts, published market research studies, government statistics, trade sources or even through specially commissioned market research. Responsibility for collecting and collating the information might lie with individual managers or there could be a committee made up of managers from a range of functions (marketing, R&D, production etc.) which acts as the environmental eyes and ears of the organisation. It is important, however, to limit the amount of incoming information to a manageable quantity, since there is an infinite amount of potentially relevant material out there and a single organisation cannot handle all of it.

The approach to scanning can vary from being extremely organised and purposeful to being random and informal. As Aguilar (1967) pointed out, formal scanning can be very expensive and time consuming as it has to cast its net very wide to catch all the possible influences that might affect the organisation. The key is knowing what is important and should be acted upon, and what can wait.

There is a great deal of skill and perceptiveness involved in assessing the significance of any piece of information and whether it should be acted upon. Volvo, for example, failed to pick up the early signs indicating the emergence of markets for 'people carriers' and four-wheel drive vehicles, and thus missed out on the growth stages of both markets. Organisations that supply components to the motor industry also have to be alert to changing tastes and trends, in order to plan production. According to Daniels (1994), writing in the *Financial Times*, motor industry analysts predicted that airbags would not be accepted by European motorists. What actually happened was that motorists quickly warmed to the idea and began to demand airbags as standard. The motor manufacturers were caught somewhat unprepared, and consequently put a lot of pressure on suppliers to fulfil demand immediately. The motor industry now faces similar decisions on the likely acceptance of and demand for air conditioning, navigation systems and other electronic wizardry. This is overall an issue of monitoring both emerging technology and the way in which consumers' tastes and attitudes towards their cars are changing.

Environmental scanning is therefore an important task, but often a difficult one, particularly in terms of interpretation and implementation of the information gained. The following looks in more detail at each of the STEP factors, and give a further indication of the range and complexity of the influences and information that can affect the marketing activities of the organisation.

THE SOCIOCULTURAL ENVIRONMENT

It is absolutely essential for organisations serving consumer markets, directly or indirectly, to understand the **sociocultural environment**, since these factors fundamentally influence the customer's needs and wants. Despite a 'common market' across Europe, there are still many basic differences in language, culture, cuisine, household size, income levels, spending patterns, women's role in society and perceptions of promotion. These differences must not be overlooked by a marketing manager when planning a European marketing strategy (Jagger, 1998). Many of the factors discussed here will be looked at again in Chapters 3 and 5, and so this is a brief overview of the demographic and sociocultural influences on marketing thinking and activities.

The demographic environment

Demographics is the study of the measurable aspects of population structures and profiles, including factors such as age, size, gender, race, occupation and location. As the birth rate fluctuates and as life expectancy increases, the breakdown of the population changes, creating challenges and opportunities for marketers, particularly if that information is taken in conjunction with data on family structure and income.

If, for example, the birth rate is falling in a particular geographic market, the marketer might interpret it to mean that people are having their childen later in life when they are better established economically. This would mean that the parents have much more money to spend per child, and additionally doting grandparents, aunts and uncles might similarly be inclined to spend more. The marketer might therefore come to the conclusion that there is still a lucrative upmarket niche to be served.

At the other end of the scale is what is known as the 'grey market', consisting of the over-55 age group. As Table 2.1 shows, the over-55s represent around one-quarter of the population of most EU countries. Their numbers are increasing, and because of better health care and financial planning, a significant proportion are able to indulge in high levels of leisure-orientated consumption, especially as they are likely to have paid off any mortgage or similar long-term debt, and are not likely to have dependent children. 'Generational marketing', for organisations seeking to appeal to this target age group, requires a fundamentally different perspective on the part of advertisers, according to Shannon (1998). Attitudes are changing. For example, research into the

The 'grey market' represents a large, distinct and growing opportunity for Saga.

Source: Saga Holidays.

over-50s in Germany revealed that rather than thrift and self-denial, the growing emphasis is on enjoyment through consumption. To communicate effectively to this age group, the focus now has to reflect attitude and lifestyle rather than reinforcing an age-based stereotype. Similarly, Saga, a tour operator for older people, is reviewing its image as it has evolved from being purely a tour operator into travel, publishing and financial services. In 1994, Saga redefined its target market to include the over-50s as well as the over-60s, but it increasingly realised that not only are there differences within this wide age bracket, but also that older buyers can be more discriminating and resistant to being communicated with pejoratively or patronisingly (Shelton, 1998).

Looking at the oldest segment within the over-55 age groups, we see that the growth in the numbers of the over-80s has serious social implications. In the UK, for example, this group represented only 2.3 per cent of the population in 1971, but by the year 2000 that is likely to have risen to 4.6 per cent. This group depends extensively on health and social service provision, and yet is the poorest of the retired groups. At the other end of the age spectrum, it is now common for an individual's educational career to begin at the   age of three and carry on until 23. Again, this has implications not only for the state, but also for educational institutions (public and private) and providers of educational goods and services.

TABLE 2.1

Population by age group, 55 years and over (% analysis)

Latest official estimates at 1 January 1998

	55–59	60–69	70–79	80–89	90+	Total
Austria	5.7	9.1	6.8	3.4	0.4	25.4
Belgium	5.3	10.5	7.1	3.4	0.5	26.8
Denmark	5.3	8.8	7.0	3.4	0.5	25.0
Finland	5.2	9.3	6.5	2.9	0.3	24.2
France	4.8	9.6	6.5	3.4	0.6	24.9
Germany	7.3	10.4	6.6	3.6	0.5	28.4
Greece	6.0	11.7	6.7	3.0	0.5	27.9
Ireland	4.2	7.2	5.4	2.2	0.3	19.3
Italy	6.3	11.1	7.3	3.6	0.5	28.8
Luxembourg	5.4	9.8	5.9	2.9	0.4	24.4
Netherlands	5.0	8.6	6.2	2.7	0.4	22.9
Portugal	5.5	10.4	6.9	2.6	0.3	25.7
Spain	4.9	10.5	7.1	3.0	0.4	25.9
Sweden	5.2	9.0	8.2	4.1	0.6	27.1
UK	5.1	9.2	7.2	3.5	0.5	25.5

Source: European Marketing Data and Statistics 1998, Euromonitor, 33rd edition. Extracted from Table 0221, pp. 124–5.

Clearly, the size of a household combined with its income is going to be a fundamental determinant of its needs and wants, and its ability to fulfil them. Table 2.2 gives some basic data on trends in average household size across Europe.

From Table 2.2, it can be seen that Ireland has a significantly larger household size than elsewhere in the EU. All of this will have a number of implications for marketers selling into Ireland, including the need for larger pack sizes, and more focus on family-orientated products. Across the rest of Europe, differences in average household sizes are less marked, ranging from 2.25 people per household in Denmark to 2.94 people per household in Luxembourg. However, as Table 2.2 shows, some countries are experiencing a pattern of decline in the average household size, for example France, Italy and Portugal. Again, marketers need to be mindful of these changes and to adapt their offerings accordingly. A significant increase in the proportion of single-person households will affect a whole range of marketing offerings, for example solo holidays, smaller apartments, pack sizes and advertising approaches and family stereotypes.

TABLE 2.2

Average number of occupants per household, 1992–96

Country	1992	1993	1994	1995	1996
Austria	2.52	2.51	2.48	2.46	2.47
Belgium	2.71	2.71	2.70	2.70	2.70
Denmark	2.31	2.27	2.26	2.26	2.25
Finland	2.41	2.42	2.40	2.39	2.38
France	2.60	2.58	2.57	2.55	2.55
Germany	2.30	2.34	2.33	2.32	2.32
Greece	2.87	2.88	2.88	2.87	2.88
Ireland	4.09	4.12	4.14	4.16	4.10
Italy	2.80	2.66	2.58	2.57	2.57
Luxembourg	2.87	2.92	2.91	2.97	2.94
Netherlands	2.45	2.45	2.44	2.43	2.43
Portugal	2.85	2.81	2.80	2.78	2.74
Spain	2.63	2.62	2.61	2.60	2.63
Sweden	2.27	2.28	2.28	2.28	2.27
UK	2.72	2.73	2.73	2.73	2.70

Source: European Marketing Data and Statistics 1998, Euromonitor, 33rd edition. Extracted from Table 1607, p. 359.

TABLE 2.3
Consumer expenditure by object 1996 (% analysis)

	Food	Alcoholic	Non-alcoholic drinks	Tobacco drinks	Clothing	Footwear	Housing
Austria	15.8	2.0	0.7	1.6	7.0	1.9	16.4
Belgium	14.0	1.2	0.5	1.4	6.6	1.0	14.8
Denmark	14.4	2.6	0.9	2.9	4.6	0.9	21.2
Finland	14.5	3.9	0.4	2.0	3.5	0.8	21.1
France	13.5	1.9	0.6	1.8	4.3	1.4	18.0
Germany	10.6	2.8	0.8	1.9	5.3	1.0	19.5
Greece	28.9	2.8	1.2	3.7	6.9	0.7	10.2
Ireland	17.8	12.8	1.4	3.8	5.9	1.5	8.5
Italy	18.6	1.0	0.5	1.7	8.2	2.2	15.3
Luxembourg	10.8	1.3	0.7	5.6	5.4	0.6	13.4
Netherlands	11.0	1.5	0.5	1.4	5.5	1.1	17.9
Portugal	30.5	1.3	0.2	1.8	8.5	0.9	7.6
Spain	16.5	1.4	0.5	1.5	6.4	3.1	11.6
Sweden	14.4	2.8	0.6	2.0	4.7	1.0	32.8
UK	9.9	6.2	0.7	2.6	5.1	1.2	17.6

	Household fuels	Household goods and services	Health	Transport	Communications	Leisure	Others
Austria	4.3	8.5	6.5	15.4	2.3	8.0	9.5
Belgium	4.5	9.9	12.8	11.9	1.0	6.7	13.6
Denmark	5.1	5.6	2.2	14.4	2.6	10.3	12.3
Finland	5.2	4.9	5.1	14.9	note (a)	8.7	14.9
France	3.7	7.7	10.2	16.0	2.0	7.5	11.4
Germany	3.7	8.6	6.5	14.4	2.0	11.1	11.8
Greece	1.8	6.3	3.9	12.6	1.4	4.0	15.6
Ireland	3.7	6.9	4.5	11.7	2.3	12.8	6.4
Italy	4.3	9.2	8.0	12.8	1.5	8.9	7.8
Luxembourg	6.0	11.7	7.9	22.2	note (a)	4.6	9.7
Netherlands	2.5	6.5	13.2	11.6	1.4	9.7	15.9
Portugal	note (b)	5.3	2.7	10.4	2.8	5.2	22.8
Spain	3.0	6.9	5.6	16.3	1.0	7.4	18.7
Sweden	5.6	4.7	4.5	13.7	2.1	9.2	1.9
UK	3.2	6.5	1.8	16.7	1.8	10.4	16.3

Notes: (a) Communications included with transport
       (b) Household fuels included with housing

Source: European Marketing Data and Statistics 1998, Euromonitor, 33rd edition. Extracted from Table 1103, pp. 248–9.

What is also important is the level of disposable income available (i.e. what is left after taxes have been paid), and the choices the household makes about saving and/or spending it. Table 2.3 shows how the spending of disposable income varies across Europe.

Clearly, housing is a fundamental cost, but the proportion of income it takes varies widely across Europe, with the Irish and Portuguese spending the lowest percentage on housing. Looking at the food column, however, it is in the less affluent economies, such as those of Greece and Portugal, that people are spending relatively more on food as a percentage of their total expenditure. In some of the other categories, the Dutch spend a higher proportion than anyone else on health care; the Luxembourgeois spend more on tobacco (almost three times more than the Belgians or French); the Irish seem to enjoy their drink (alcoholic and otherwise) and leisure! Of course, patterns of expenditure will be dictated to some extent by national income levels and relative prices.

Such spending patterns are not fixed: they will vary not only because of changes in the demographic and economic structure of the household, but also because of sociocultural influences, discussed in the next subsection. A further factor which cuts across both demographic and sociocultural issues is employment patterns, specifically the number of working women in a community and the rate of unemployment. This influences not only household income, but also shopping and consumption patterns.

MARKETING IN ACTION   A bread and butter market?

In the UK, the bread market is worth around £3 billion a year. Although bread might seem to be a boring, staple product, consumer tastes and demands are quite dynamic, and producers have to remain alert to emerging opportunities and threats. Through the 1980s, the trend was towards brown and wholemeal loaves at the expense of white, because of health concerns. In the 1990s, however, the trend reversed, and it became clear that sales of white bread were growing at the expense of brown and wholemeal. This was partly because children and men actually prefer white bread and partly because of the introduction of premium brands such as Kingsmill and Hovis White, which have moved the product's image away from the low-quality, cheap commodity reputation earned from its use as a weapon in supermarket price wars. Thus while the market for standard and economy bread is declining by 15 per cent a year, the market for premium white increased by 20 per cent in 1997 and is now worth £1 billion per year.

There are also many niches in the market, arising from the consumer's desire for variety and novelty. 'Ethnic' breads have become popular and German (pumpernickel, volkornbrot), French (baguettes, petit pain, brioche, croissants), Italian (ciabatta, focaccia), and Indian (naan, pitta) breads, among others, are now very easy to find on the supermarket shelves, and there are many variants even within these categories. Ciabatta, for example, can be plain, or with olives, or with sun-dried tomatoes, or with pesto. Breads from Spain, Norway, Sweden, the USA and other countries have also appeared. Some of these products are imported, while others are made in the UK. Sainsbury's imports part-baked bread from France and finishes off the cooking process in its in-store bakeries to maximise authenticity and freshness. Alldays, a convenience store, has in-store bakeries called 'L'Art du Pain' which provide fresh baguettes, petit pains, croissants etc. Freshness is especially important, as trends show that the consumer is moving away from mass-produced factory breads, preferring products baked fresh on the premises. The UK market for these 'bake-off' products is estimated to be £540 million and growing.

This trend has made some producers think more creatively about how their products are delivered to the market. Allied Bakeries Group diversified into supplying 90 per cent of the bread needed by sandwich-making companies and establishing in-store bakery operations in supermarkets. Délice de France, for example, offers to delicatessens, convenience stores and garage forecourt shops the 'C'est Magnifique' in-store bakery concept, consisting of an oven, promotional, display and packaging materials, and frozen, part-baked bread products. The retailer gets an 'authentic French product', the smell of fresh baking in store to attract customers and whet their appetites, and complete control over supply, in that they can bake more as it is needed and the supply is always fresh.

Sources: The Grocer (1996, 1998c, 1998e, 1998f); Kelly (1998); Murphy (1997).

As the data presented here have shown, it is dangerous to generalise about demographic trends across Europe. There are wide variations, particularly between the richer northern and western European states and the poorer southern and eastern states. Thus the marketer needs to understand both the differences and the similarities between nations within Europe, as a means of assessing emerging trends and opportunities.

Sociocultural influences

Demographic information only paints a very broad picture of what is happening. If the marketer wants a really three-dimensional feel, then some analysis of sociocultural factors is essential. These factors involve much more qualitative assessment, can be much harder to measure and interpret than the hard facts of demographics and may be subject to unpredictable change, but the effort is worthwhile for a truly marketing orientated organisation.

One thing that does evolve over time is people's lifestyle expectations. Products that at one time were considered upmarket luxuries, such as televisions and fridges, are now considered to be necessities. Turning a luxury into a necessity obviously broadens the potential market, and widens the marketer's scope for creating a variety of products and offerings to suit a spectrum of income levels and usage needs. Televisions, for example, come in a variety of shapes, sizes and prices, from the pocket-sized portable to the cheap, small set that will do for the children's bedroom, to the very large, technically advanced, state-of-the-art status symbol with flat screen and digital connectivity. This variety has the bonus of encouraging households to own more than one set, further fuelling the volume of the market, particularly as improvements in technology and production processes along with economies of scale further reduce prices.

Broadening tastes and demands are another sociocultural influence, partly fuelled by the marketers themselves, and partly emanating from consumers. Marketers, by constant innovation and through their marketing communications, encourage consumers to become bored with the same old standard, familiar products and thus to demand more convenience, variety and variation.

> **Example** The growth of the chilled snacks market reflects the changing lifestyles of many people. The combination of fast refreshment and a treat has become more popular as snackers decide to eat on the move and not to take a long lunch break. People have less time and are demanding more variety, which has created opportunities for manufacturers and retailers to develop new products and offer better displays, more variety and faster check-out service. In response to these demands, the UK sandwich market accounts for 41 per cent of the fast-food business, with an estimated 2.18 billion sandwiches purchased each year. A greater variety of exotic fillings, especially at the premium end of the market, reflects a more discerning customer, although tuna, chicken and ham still predominate. A walk up the aisle of a multiple supermarket will soon demonstrate that attention is being given to offering new tastes and fresher products designed to meet our changing demands (McLoughlin, 1998).

Sandwiches are just one food sector within which consumers are demanding a wider variety of more exotic tastes. This has emerged partly through the influence of ethnic minorities, partly through cheaper, more widespread international travel which reduces hostility to and suspicion of 'foreign food', and partly through the efforts of marketers who have provided the products that have introduced the average supermarket customer to less well-known cuisines. This has all created growing markets in premium-priced chilled ready meals (the UK market for these products is around £578 million per year), and 'cook-in' sauces, which make a wide variety of difficult-sounding dishes such as Chicken Tikka and Lamb Rogan Josh easily accessible.

Consumers want variation and variety not only to stave off boredom, but also as a means of asserting their individuality. Although mass markets are necessary to generate the economies of scale that make products affordable, no consumer wants to think they are identical to their neighbours. They want to feel that their purchasing choices, in everything from their car to the contents of their biscuit tin, create a unique profile that gives them the desired status in others' eyes. Marketers like a certain amount of variety and variation (but not too much or the economies of scale are compromised) because it helps to keep customers loyal (you could use a different variety of one manufacturer's cook-in sauces, if you wanted, every night of the week and still not get bored) and allows scope for the premium-priced niches to emerge.

Fashions and fads are also linked with consumer boredom and a desire for new stimulation. The clothing market in particular has an interest in making consumers sufficiently discontented with the perfectly serviceable clothes already in the wardrobe that they go out to buy new ones every season. For some consumers, it is important for their social integration and their status to be seen to have the latest products and the latest fashions, whether it be in clothing, music or alcoholic drinks. Nevertheless, linking a product with fashion may create marketing problems. Fashions, by definition, are short lived, and as soon as they become widespread, the fashion leaders are moving on to something new and different. Marketers therefore have to reap rewards while they can, or find a means of shifting the product away from its fashionable associations.

More deeply ingrained in society than the fripperies of fashion are underlying attitudes. These change much more slowly than fashion trends and are much more difficult for the marketer to influence. It is more likely, in fact, that the marketer will assess existing or emerging attitudes and then adapt or develop to fit them. As can be seen in Fig. 2.2, there are a number of areas in which changes in societal attitudes have influenced marketing approaches. Each is discussed below.

Environmental issues

Environmental issues have been of major concern in recent years, and this area has caused consumers to think more critically about the origins, content and manufacturing processes of the products they buy. Consumers, for example, want products made with the minimum of pollution and are looking for the reassurance, where applicable, that they come of renewable resources. Many paper products now carry notices stat-

---

MARKETING IN ACTION   ## Chocoholics, stock up!!

The cocoa pod is under threat and that is bad news for chocolate eaters. In a typical year, the British consume 6.83 lb of chocolate per capita, or some 196 300 tons. Germany beats that with 7.10 lbs per capita, a staggering 285 900 tons. Soon all that could change. The Ivory Coast chocolate plantations, the world's largest producers, are suffering from black pod disease. This can drastically reduce a crop by 80 per cent in a wet year. Even worse, the witch's broom fungus is threatening Brazil's crop, and in Malaysia, with large areas deforested for cocoa production, there have also been significant increases in disease and pests.

Environmentalists fear that farming has been too intensive and that the overuse of fungicides and pesticides has resulted in super-resistant bugs. In the past, the cocoa producers moved on to new rain forest clearance to avoid over-farming an area, but now new space is running out and sustainability has become a big issue. This means fewer chemicals and fertilisers and more replanting, rather than abandoning farms at the first sign of lower yields. Cocoa farms are set to become smaller and more diverse. In the natural state, the cocoa tree survives best alongside larger trees which provide shade, but with intensive farming the large trees are cut down and the increase in direct sunlight is believed to have caused many of the problems now being experienced.

As chocolate prices are set to rise and shortages expected, the manufacturers have had to act in order to preserve supplies. Sustainability in farming has become a real issue for the likes of Mars, Cadbury and Nestlé.

Sources: Yoon (1998); Young (1998).

Continental Tyres has found that an active approach to environmental issues is taking it into exciting new areas.
Source: Continental.

Example The car is not really considered to be one of the more environmentally friendly products available, but many component manufacturers are trying to improve the situation. Tyres, for example, are directly and indirectly responsible for a number of environmental problems. They tend to have a short life span, and are difficult to dispose of or to recycle. They can also affect fuel consumption, accounting for up to 16 per cent of a car's average petrol usage, according to industry estimates. Companies such as Pirelli (http://www.pirelli.com) and Continental (http://www.conti.de) are therefore working hard to develop more fuel efficient tyres in parallel with looking at ways of improving their durability. Beyond that, they are also thinking about how they can best use tyres that have come to the end of their life. The manufacturers want to develop tyres that can be retreaded more easily and cheaply, and that can be disposed of in a more environmentally friendly way. If a truck tyre can be retreaded several times, its life span can be increased from 150 000 miles to 375 000 miles. There are also possibilities for turning old tyres into rubber powder that can be incorporated into new ones.

All this development activity is spurred not only by an altruistic desire to become 'greener', but also by pressure from motor manufacturers. The motor manufacturers in turn are reflecting consumer concerns and increasing governmental demands for greener motoring (Simonian, 1995).

ing that they are made of wood from managed forests that are replanted after harvesting. In the same spirit, consumers are also demanding that unnecessary packaging is eliminated and that packaging should be recyclable.

Animal welfare

The issue of animal welfare is linked with environmental concerns, and shows itself in a number of ways. Product testing on animals has become increasingly unacceptable to a large number of vocal consumers, and thus there has been a proliferation of cosmetics and toiletries, for example, which proclaim that they have not been tested on animals. With some products this may only mean that they are made from ingredients that have been separately animal tested and proved safe in the past, but that the current formulation has not itself been tested. Cosmetics retailer The Body Shop has, for example, been at the forefront of positioning itself overtly on this issue, reassuring concerned customers about its own products and publicising the worst excesses of animal testing.

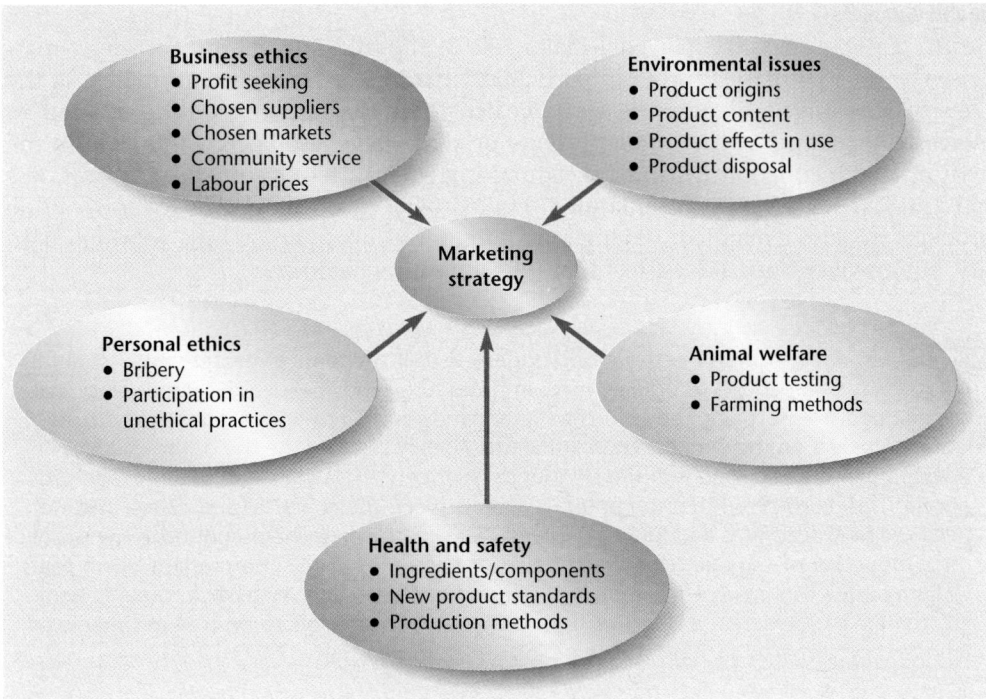

FIGURE 2.2

The impact of
societal attitudes on
marketing strategy

Another area of animal welfare which has captured the public imagination is that of intensive farm production methods. Public outcry against battery egg production, for example, opened new marketing opportunities for free range eggs, since consumers wanted the alternative and were prepared to pay for it. Similarly, outdoor-reared pork and organic beef are starting to appear in supermarkets. Early in 1995, British seaports and airports saw widely publicised, and sometimes violent, demonstrations against the export of live animals, particularly veal calves. The objection was not only that the travelling conditions and times might be less than ideal, but also that the calves were destined to be kept in veal crates on the Continent, a practice which is no longer allowed in the UK. Pressure groups are becoming more adept at using advertising and promotional techniques to activate public opinion. In 1997, the League Against Cruel Sports (LACS) and the International Fund for Animal Welfare (IFAW) co-operated with the Royal Society for the Prevention of Cruelty to Animals (RSPCA) to run a campaign designed to shock. The image of a fox being torn apart by a pack of hounds proved very effective in lobbying support for a parliamentary bill to prevent hunting with dogs. The three non-profit organisations between them spent several millions of pounds on press advertising, mailshots, free phone information lines, and organising mass rallies (Cheary, 1997). As yet, they have not been successful in achieving legislation, despite MORI research which suggest that 71 per cent of the UK population opposes fox hunting and only 1 per cent actually practises it!

While many consumers accept the necessity of farming for meat, there was a much wider backlash against killing and farming for the fur trade. Throughout the 1980s, public revulsion against furs built up and fur products ceased to be regarded as the status symbols they had previously been. Many furriers were driven out of business and many upper-class retailers closed their fur departments. There are small signs, however, that in *haute couture* fur is beginning to make a tentative comeback, presumably as public concern has shifted to other issues.

Health concerns

Health consciousness has played a major role in the thinking behind consumer markets. The tobacco market has been particularly hard hit by increased awareness of the risks of smoking, and pressure from health lobbyists and the public has led to increased regulation of that industry. Food products have also been reappraised in the light of health concerns, with more natural ingredients, fewer artificial additives, less salt and less sugar content demanded. Linked with this, the market for low calorie products has also expanded, serving a market that wants to enjoy tasty food in quantity, but lose weight or at least feel that they are eating healthily.

Example A *Sunday Times* investigation suggested that a chemical preservative, sodium nitrate, was being added to organic meat in order to extend shelf life despite the fact that it is banned from organic foods in the Netherlands and Germany. Allegations of supermarket pressure on the Organic Food Standards Agency to allow the use of the chemical in the curing of organic bacons in the UK raised major concerns with some organic food producers. They considered that the potential link between the chemical and cancer had not been properly dealt with and further believed that supermarkets should not have any say in the production of organic food. Such issues are complex. The supermarkets claim that sodium nitrate can prevent the spread of botulism and, as a further blow to organic farmers, the EU is considering a directive that allows ordinary animals to be sold as organic as long as they have had an 'appropriate period' on an organic farm (Nuki, 1998).

Health concerns also led to a boom in products and services linked with fitness. Health clubs, aerobics classes, exercise videos, sports wear of all kinds and trainers are just some of the things that profited from the fitness boom.

Personal ethics

Apart from concern about the environment, animal welfare and health, all of which might be seen as ethical issues, there has been a subtle shift in people's attitudes to what is acceptable in other areas of their lives. In Western societies, a manageable level of personal debt is now considered normal. Hire purchase agreements, various types of loans and credit cards provide means of achieving a desirable lifestyle now and paying for it later. Previous generations might have been more inclined to take the view that if you want something, you save up for it and buy it outright when you can afford it. Consumers today are also more inclined towards self-indulgence and gratification, without too much guilt, through their consumption. This, it must be said, is openly encouraged by marketers, who want us to believe that we as individuals are special enough to deserve only the best.

The early 1990s saw some conflict between the self-indulgent, self-centred type of conspicuous consumption and external, altruistic concerns about the environment. Although this curbed some of the worst excesses of the late 1980s, the majority of consumers still seemed to be stopping short of radically redefining their attitude to consumption, other than through economic necessity. A study by Dittmar and Pepper (1994) showed that adolescents, regardless of their own social background, generally formed better impressions of people who own rather than lack expensive possessions. In other words, materialism still seems to play a big part in influencing perceptions and attitudes towards others.

Business ethics

Encouraged by various pressure groups and inquisitive media, consumers now want to see greater levels of corporate responsibility, and more transparency in terms of the openness of companies. Bad publicity about employee relations, environmental records, marketing practices or customer care and welfare now has the potential to move consumers to vote with their pockets and shun an organisation and its products. McDonald's, for example, felt sufficiently concerned about stories circulating about its beef and about its record in the South American rain forests to invest in a considerable marketing communications campaign to re-establish its reputation. The Body Shop again features business ethics strongly in its marketing, emphasising, for example, its 'trade not aid' policy with developing countries and native tribes.

Example In 1981 the World Health Organisation introduced a code of practice to end promotional pressures from baby milk suppliers to encourage women to switch from breast feeding to bottle feeding. Breast feeding children up to the age of two could significantly increase infant life expectancy, to the extent of 1.5 million extra babies surviving globally. Unfortunately, only 17 countries adopted the code, which means that in other counties there is immense competitive pressure on suppliers not to comply voluntarily with the code. Promotional activities include free samples. In South Africa, for example, 20 per cent of clinics were provided with free milk samples and in a number of countries gifts to medical staff and bottles and teats to mothers were designed to encourage the mother to bottle feed. Suppliers ignoring these practices are almost certain to lose ground to competition until there is more widespread adoption of the code. This clearly poses an ethical dilemma (*The Times*, 1998).

Consumerism and consumer forces

Many of the influences discussed above might never have taken hold and become significant had it not been for the efforts of organised groups. They themselves often use marketing techniques as well as generating publicity through the media, quickly raising awareness of issues and providing a focal point for public opinion to form around and helping it to gather momentum. Figure 2.3, for example, may remind you of some of the campaigns that have been fought in the interests of raising your awareness of ethical and green issues surrounding the clothing industry.

The UK's Consumers' Association has long campaigned for legislation to protect consumers' rights, such as the right to safe products and the right to full and accurate information about the products we buy. As well as lobbying government and organisations about specific issues, the Consumers' Association also provides independent

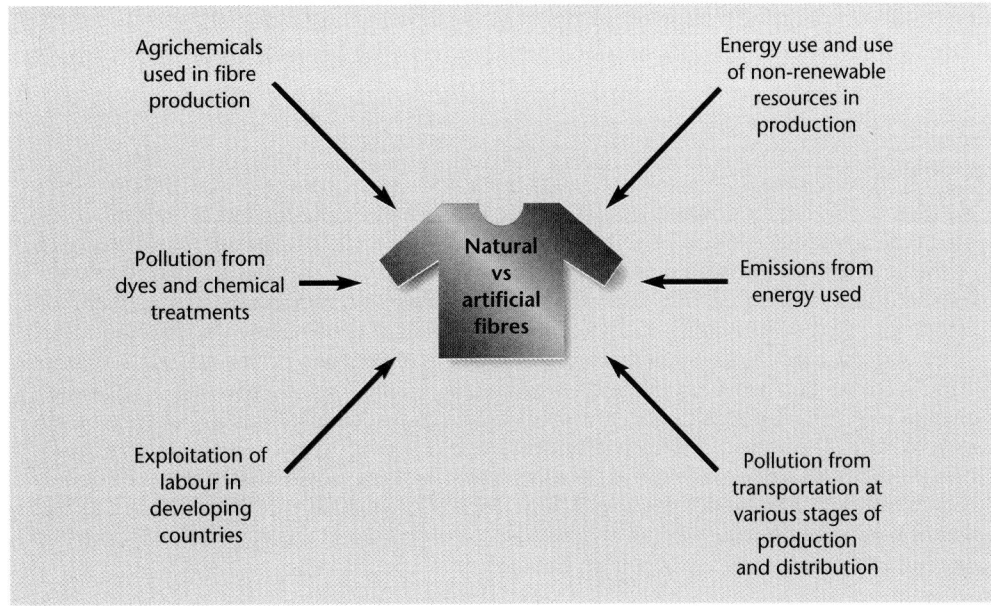

FIGURE 2.3

Green and ethical issues affecting clothing

MARKETING IN ACTION   Watching what we eat

In some cases, individuals can be so powerful in raising public concern that an industry feels that it has to launch a vigorous defence. Lacey (1998), an early advocate of the potential dangers inherent in the link between BSE ('mad cow' disease) and its human variant CJD, considers himself to be a watchdog, telling the public which foods are safe and which are best avoided. Few foods appear to be safe: oranges sprayed with wax to highlight colour, soft cheeses such as Camembert and Brie, yoghurts, bottled water, eggs and frozen foods have all come under scrutiny alongside sausages, burgers and meat pies. With frozen food, for instance, it was claimed that many forms of bacteria can survive the deep freezing process and can be reactivated in well-lit display cabinets. Thankfully, frozen peas, which are often picked and frozen within a few hours, are considered to be of high quality!

The food industry is not impressed. Comments have ranged from 'a personal view that goes against the advice to consumers' to 'nutty professor', 'alarmist propaganda' and a 'man desperate for publicity'. In most cases, the response goes further. The British Soft Drinks Association, for instance, claims that bottled water is not contaminated with animal faeces as it is drawn from deep boreholes and wells. With frozen foods, it is claimed that storage temperatures never reach a sufficiently high level to reactivate any bacteria.

Linked to this debate is the growing controversy over genetically modified (GM) foods. Some believe it is for God alone to engineer food. Prince Charles added to the debate with a report saying that he would not eat food from genetically engineered crops or feed them to his family. At present, there has been no EU directive to ensure that GM food is clearly identified on labelling. Some supermarkets have been criticised for not giving consumers the chance to avoid GM foods through the provision of appropriate information. ASDA, after a survey of its customers, concluded that the issue does not matter. Iceland, however, took the lead by banning all GM food from its own brands and has spoken out against the practice. All of this has posed an interesting challenge to government, the regulators and consumer groups, all of which to date have not been decisive one way or the other.

There is a growing interest in what we eat and individuals, the media and other groups are generating a debate in which both retailers and food producers must participate. Are food standards being maintained or, as Lacey argues, are quality and hygiene being sacrificed for profit?

Sources: Lacey (1998); Rogers (1998).

information to consumers, testing and comparing the features, performance and value for money of competing products in various categories. This information is published in *Which?* magazine, the September 1998 edition issue of which carried reports on hi-fi systems, hairdryers and stylers, personal pensions and Italian wines, for example. In a similar vein, specialist magazines, in fields such as computing and hi-fi, also undertake comparative testing of products of interest to their readership.

High-profile and sometimes militant pressure has been brought to bear on organisations by green groups such as Friends of the Earth and Greenpeace. Although their

Example   Tuna fishing is an activity that has been affected by campaigning leading to the exercise of 'consumer power'. The UK public had been happily buying canned tuna for many years without thinking of anything other than the price, the flavour and the quality of the can's contents. Green pressure groups, with the help of the media, then publicised the fact that the nets that were used to catch tuna also caught dolphins, which could not escape and so died pointlessly. A change in the net design would allow the dolphins to be freed without harm. Public outcry was such that the major tuna producers, such as John West, were encouraged to examine their own sources, and to pressurise their suppliers to change their fishing methods. UK consumers now look for 'dolphin friendly' labels on their cans of tuna. The activities of such pressure groups have not only served to change business practices on specific issues, such as tuna fishing, but also accelerated a general cultural change which has awakened the social conscience of organisations (only partly due to the fear of poor publicity and the loss of customers) and has raised the standards of corporate citizenship that consumers expect from business.

interest is a wider, altruistic concern with ecology rather than consumer rights, they recognise that corporate practices that are harmful to the environment, wildlife and ecology can be partly discouraged by 'bottom-up' pressure. This means raising awareness, changing attitudes and altering purchasing habits among organisations' core customers.

Consumers have also been encouraged to think about their personal health as well as that of the planet. Sometimes sponsored by government (for example through the UK government's Department of Health) and sometimes through independent groups with a specific interest such as Action on Smoking and Health (ASH) or the British Heart Foundation, the public are urged to change their lifestyles and diets. Once it is generally known and accepted that too much of this, that or the other is unhealthy, food manufacturers are anxious to jump on the bandwagon and provide products to suit the emerging demand.

> **Example** Awareness that full fat milk is high in cholesterol has been responsible for a significant shift towards semi-skimmed and skimmed milk which retains most of the vitamin and mineral content but cuts down the fat. Sometimes, a health issue does not even need the support of an organised group to capture the public imagination. A flurry of media coverage about research findings which indicated that eating sugar can actually help weight loss had many of us reaching hopefully for the biscuit tin, purely on medical grounds, of course.

The media have already been mentioned several times as an important channel of communication used by pressure groups to ensure that public awareness is triggered. The media are not, however, passive pawns in all this, simply repeating what they are told. They can magnify a story and give it much more credibility and urgency by the amount and quality of coverage given. Debating issues on current affairs programmes or the publication of editorials and opinion columns in the newspapers stimulates interest and provides the necessary perspectives for the audience to judge how they feel about a particular issue. Some sections of the media behave like pressure groups in their own right. Television consumer programmes, such as the BBC's *Watchdog*, investigate and publicise (usually) bad practice or poor service, highlighting product safety issues, unethical selling methods and fraudulent trading. With audiences in millions, these programmes represent quite a power.

Pressure groups and consumer bodies are not just there to criticise organisations, of course. They also encourage and endorse good practice, and such an endorsement can be very valuable to the organisation that earns it. A consumer who is inexperienced in buying a particular type of product, or for whom that purchase represents a substantial investment, may well look for independent expert advice, and thus the manufacturer whose product is cited as *Which?* magazine's best buy in that category has a head start over the competition. Organisations may also commission product tests from independent bodies such as the Consumers' Association or the Good Housekeeping Institute as a means of verifying their product claims and adding the bonus of 'independent expert opinion' to their marketing.

THE TECHNOLOGICAL ENVIRONMENT

In an increasingly dynamic world, where the creation, launch and maintenance of a new product are more expensive and difficult than ever, no organisation can afford to ignore the **technological environment** and its trends. Even if your organisation does not have the inclination or resources to adopt or adapt new technology, understanding it is important because competitors will exploit it sooner or later, with implications for your product and its marketing. Technological advance can be generated from two main sources, as far as the marketer is concerned. The first source is external to the organisation and perhaps even external to the market. Thus technology developed for other purposes, academic, medical or military, for example, may have spin-off commercial benefits. In this case, the skill for the commercial organisation is spotting the potential application early enough, negotiating the rights to use or develop the technology further, and successfully developing a marketable product from it before the competition. The second source of technological advance is market driven, by organisations searching for specific solutions to specific marketing problems. The R&D work may be undertaken in house, or may be contracted out to specialist agencies or university departments. The range of projects involved may vary from very small to very large, and from the refinement of an existing product to the exploration of completely unknown territory.

The costs and the risks involved can be very high, since there is no guarantee that an R&D project will be successful in delivering a solution that can be commercially implemented. Nevertheless, organisations feel the need to invest in R&D, recognising that they will get left behind if they do not, and are optimistic that they will come up with something with an unbeatable differential advantage that will make it all worthwhile.

Ericsson's commitment to R&D keeps it ahead of the competition.
Source: Ericsson.

Example Ericsson (http://www.ericsson.co.uk), a Swedish telecommunications equipment supplier, has become the dominant force in the international cellular market through a well-planned approach to technological innovation. Its spend on R&D in its radio division amounts to about 16 per cent of sales. It is claimed that this is higher than that of any other mobile phone manufacturer. This effort resulted in applications for over 1000 patents in 1997, and in 1998 Ericsson became the first mobile phone operator to provide access to the Internet using infrared signals through its SH888 model. Ericsson must move quickly with its new products as the typical life span of a new mobile phone product is usually between 12 and 18 months. The total time to bring the SH888 to market was two and half years. The concept was developed in the first year and the rest of the time was spent on product development. If Ericsson lets its commitment to R&D slip, it will fall prey to competition from both Nokia from Finland and Motorola in the USA, which also invest heavily in linking end user needs with new product development (Day, 1998).

To get the best out of the commercial exploitation of technology, R&D and marketers have to work closely together. R&D can provide the technical know-how, problem-solving skills and creativity, while the marketer can help guide and refine that process through research or knowledge of what the market needs and wants, or through finding ways of creating a market position for a completely innovative product. A lot of this comes back to the question 'What business are we in?' Any organisations holding the attitude that they exist to solve customers' problems and that they have to strive constantly to find better solutions through higher-quality, lower-cost or more user-friendly product packages will be active participants in, and observers of, the technological environment. A striking example of this is the Italian firm Olivetti, which began by making manual typewriters, then moved into computers as it saw the likely take-over of the word processor as a means of producing business documentation.

The technological environment is a fast-changing one, with far-reaching effects on organisations and their products. Technological advances can affect the materials, components and products, the processes by which products are made, administration and distribution systems, product marketing and the interface between the organisation and the customer. Each of these areas will now be looked at briefly, to give just a flavour of the immense impact that technology has had on marketing practice.

Example International collaboration in technical development is becoming more common. The European Airbus (http://www.airbus.com) A300 and A310 projects represent technical and commercial successes that could not have been possible at national level, given the strength of American competition from giants such as Boeing and McDonnell Douglas. By collaboration and pooling their expertise and resources, European companies such as Messerschmitt Belkow-Blohm (Germany), Aérospatiale (France), Casa (Spain), Fokker (Netherlands), Sonana (Belgium) and British Aerospace are able to remain players in world markets. International collaboration does not, however, always work as well as the Airbus project. The European fighter aircraft project, instigated and funded by a consortium of European governments, suffered serious setbacks in trying to please all partners on political rather than on purely economic or technical grounds. Government interference, bureaucracy and duplication of effort led to severe cost overruns and delays. Much of this was beyond the control of the various companies involved in the project who were faced with ongoing commitment to developing a product with increasingly questionable commercial viability.

Materials, components and products

Consumers tend to take products, and the materials and components that go into them, for granted as long as they work and live up to the marketers' promises. Technology does, however, improve and increase the benefits that consumers derive from products, and raise expectations about what a product should be. Some technological applications are invisible to the consumer, affecting raw materials and components hidden within an existing product, while others create completely new products.

Low calorie sweeteners

Artificial low calorie sweeteners, for example, are now found in a wide range of food-stuffs. An extremely successful application has been in fizzy drinks, such as colas and lemonades, creating a new segment among diet-conscious adults. Many claim to be able to taste the difference between the regular and diet (or light) versions of the same product, and thus the next stage of the R&D process might be to eliminate this minor discrepancy.

Unleaded petrol

Pressure from those concerned about the environmental and health effects of motor exhaust fumes has led to the development and widespread acceptance of unleaded petrol. The R&D task here was extensive, not only looking at the formulation and quality of the petrol itself, but also requiring adaptation of existing and proposed car engines to be able to take the new fuel with the minimum effect on performance.

Synthetics in clothing

Synthetic fabrics, fibre mixes and dyes have long been research concerns of the clothing industry. Consumers want easy-care clothes that can stand the rigours of machine washing with the minimum of drying and ironing afterwards. They also want their clothes to be hard wearing and for their bright colours to be maintained, despite repeated washing. In this respect, the textile companies can work closely with the detergent manufacturers. More recently, consumer interest has turned back to natural fabrics, such as linen, cotton and silk, and the technological task has been to find ways of treating these fibres to make them easier to care for without compromising their natural characteristics.

Microchips

Microchips are everywhere! Not only are they the heart and soul of our home computers, but they also program our washing machines, CD players and video recorders, among many things. The incorporation of microchips into products has increased their reliability, their efficiency in operation and the range of sophisticated functions that they can perform, all very cost effectively. This in turn has raised consumers' expectations of what products can do, and revised their attitudes towards cost, quality and value for money.

High-tech products

In terms of brand new, innovative high-tech products, the last 15 years or so have opened up a number of new markets, based on invention and the development of commercial processes to allow its exploitation. This is not always an easy or fast process. CD players, videos, camcorders, computers and software have only begun to become common household possessions as technology improves through the man-ufacturers' learning experiences, as a wider range of products tailored towards definable market segments emerge and as costs come down through economies of scale.

Packaging

Technology is not just about the physical product itself. It can also affect its packaging. Lightweight plastics and glass, recycled and recyclable materials and cans that incorporate a device to give canned beer the character and quality of draught are examples of packaging innovations that have helped to make products more appealing, enhance their image or keep their cost down. Additionally, developments in areas such as lamination and printing techniques have increased the attractiveness and quality of packaging, again helping to enhance the product image.

Production processes

The fulfilment of marketing promises can be helped or hindered by what happens in the production process. More efficient production can, for instance, increase the volume of product available, thus potentially meeting a bigger demand, or it can reduce the cost of the product, thus giving more scope to the pricing decision. Production can also contribute to better and more consistent product quality, again increasing customer satisfaction. Here are some examples where technology has influenced production processes and indirectly affected marketing activities.

Computer aided design systems

Computer aided design (CAD) systems have revolutionised product formulation and testing. In terms of design, technology allows ideas to be visualised, tested and accepted/rejected much more quickly than if paper plans and calculations had to be updated. Anything, from the design of a circuit board, through the arrangement of components inside the product, to the external styling and colourways can be fully explored cheaply and quickly. This means that a certain creative impetus can be generated, because the effects of a 'what if?' exercise can be seen almost instantly, and even the wildest ideas can be given space. Sophisticated software can also simulate how the proposed product design might behave in reality under differing conditions, highlighting the probable weak areas and 'bugs'. The outcome for the customer is that products get to the market more quickly, and in a more refined state, and may be cheaper and more reliable.

Computer aided manufacturing systems

Computer aided manufacturing (CAM) systems help to streamline the production process. Computer controlled robotics and other mechanised systems can undertake tasks faster than human operatives, with more consistency and fewer errors. Robots and computers do not get tired or distracted from their tasks! In the long term, this can cut costs, because the labour input is less and there is less wastage through rejects. Again, the customer gets a more reliable, consistent and potentially cheaper product.

Quality assurance and control

Quality assurance (QA) and quality control (QC) are an important part of manufacturing. Technology has improved not only the methods used for testing samples taken from the production line, but also the capacity to detect faults early during the production process. It has also brought the responsibility for QA closer to the shop-floor operative, who can monitor process levels and outputs as they happen and take corrective action or call for help as soon as it is needed. The implications for the customer are again related to costs and reliability. The fewer rejects that occur and the fewer rejects that slip through to the customer, the better for the manufacturer's reputation and relationship with the customer. This is particularly important in organisational markets where just-in-time (JIT) systems operate (*see* Chapter 4 for more on this). This means that a business buying in supplies from another business wants just the right amount to arrive just at the right time to be fed into the production process. There is no scope for error: if a bad batch is delivered, or if there are too many rejects in it, the consequences can be serious as the buyer has no buffer stocks to fall back on. Thus quality has to be right and the buyer has to be able to rely on that quality.

Materials handling

Materials handling and waste minimisation are both concerns of efficient, cost-effective production management, and are again linked with JIT systems. Stocks of materials need to be closely monitored so that further purchases can be triggered when the level gets low; in a large operation, the location of materials needs to be planned so that they can be accessed quickly and spend the minimum amount of time being transported around the site; the packaging and bundling of materials need to be planned to balance out the sometimes conflicting concerns of adequately protecting and identifying the goods, and making sure that they can be unwrapped and put into the production line quickly. Computerised planning models and advances in packaging technology can both help to increase efficiency in these areas. Waste minimisation is clearly desirable if the manufacturer is going to get the most out of the raw materials. Minimisation through quality control was mentioned earlier, but it can also be achieved through good planning of material usage. A clothing factory, for instance, will use computerised layout planning to work out the best arrangement of the garment components on the cloth before cutting, so that the minimum amount of fabric is discarded.

Benefits to service industries

Even what is essentially a service industry can benefit from technology to improve its ability to serve the customer's needs. The telecommunications industry, for example, has used satellite technology, computerised exchanges and fibre-optic cable, for instance, to extend customers' ability to dial direct to virtually any part of the world, relatively cheaply. On the 'hardware' side of the business, telecommunications now encompasses cordless and mobile phones, answering machines, faxes and modems. Technology has also allowed the industry to extend its range of services, such as linking the domestic telephone to burglar alarms, so that the emergency services are automatically alerted to a problem, and the introduction of the chargecard that allows calls made by cardholders from other telephone numbers to be billed to the cardholder's domestic or business number account.

Administration and distribution

There is little point in using technology to streamline the production of goods if the support systems are inefficient or if distribution causes a bottleneck between factory and customer. Distribution has benefited from technology, as has materials handling, through systems for locating and tracking goods in and out. Integrated ordering and dispatch functions mean theoretically that as soon as an order is entered into the computer, goods availability can be checked and the warehouse can get on with the job of fulfilling it, while the computer handles all the paperwork, printing off packing slips and invoices, for example, and updating customer records. All of this speeds up the sending of orders to customers and reduces labour involvement, costs and risks of errors.

Telecommunications linking into computer systems can extend the administration efficiencies even further. Large retail chains, for example, can be linked with their major suppliers, so that as the retailer's stocks reduce, an order can be sent from computer to computer. Similarly, large organisations with sites and depots spread over a wide geographic area can use such technology to link sites, managing and tracking the flow of goods.

Marketing and customers

Much of the technology discussed above has implied benefits for the customer, in producing the right product at the right time in the right place at the right price. Technology also plays a part in the dialogue between buyer and seller, and thus affects the interface between them.

Market research

Market research has benefited from increased and cheaper computer power, which means that large, complex sets of data can be input and analysed quickly and easily.

Databases

Databases are created not only for market research purposes, but also for selling. Relationship marketing, establishing and maintaining a one-to-one dialogue between buyer and seller, is now possible in mass consumer markets. Organisations such as Heinz see this as an exciting development in consumer marketing, and it is only possible because of database technology that permits the storage, retrieval and maintenance of detailed profiles of many thousands, or even hundreds of thousands, of customers. The technology also allows the creation of tailored, personalised marketing offers to be made to subsets of those customers as appropriate.

Advertising media

The advertising media have improved and proliferated through technology. As well as making use of satellite and cable television channels, advertisers can use teletext pages, videotapes and CDs. Improvements in printing technology have led to better reproduction and thus better-quality print advertisements, for example sharply focused, full-colour advertising is now commonplace in newspapers. Technology has also made its contribution to the creative side of advertising, for example with computer animation or computer manipulation of images to create special effects. In addition, the Internet has become an alternative medium for many organisations. It not only allows them to disseminate information about their products, services, news and corporate philosophy, but also to set up interactive dialogue with customers and potential customers. A website can be an exciting communications medium as it can feature sound and video clips and, if the site is well structured, visitors can select the topics that interest them. Also, the information can be updated easily and regularly.

On-line ordering

As briefly mentioned earlier, on-line ordering is a direct link between buyer and seller, allowing for faster reception and processing of orders. Both the Internet and interactive digital television allow potential customers to browse through product information, check availability and place an order, all in the comfort of their own armchairs. However, this technology has yet to make a significant impact on consumer markets. The nearest to on-line ordering that most consumers experience is through telephone shopping, sometimes in direct response to television or print advertising. This is another spin-off from the telecommunications industry, which can now supply sellers with the capacity to handle many hundreds of calls simultaneously.

MARKETING AND IT   ## Searching on the Internet

Information overload has become a problem, and the arrival of the Internet seems, in many ways, to have compounded the problem by making even more information available to consumers. But the Internet comes with a couple of interesting devices designed to help consumers cut through all the data and find the right product or service to meet their needs.

First off, search engines from companies like Lycos (http://www.lycos.com), Yahoo (http://www.yahoo.com) and Infoseek (http://www.infoseek.com) can help you search through cyberspace for information on the most obscure of items. More interesting is the automated robot ('bot') whose job is to search and compare the prices of the same item from different sources. But if all this technology is too much for you, and you are simply looking for the cheapest holiday to Crete, Croatia or the Crimea, why not try an Internet travel agent like Travelocity (http://www.travelocity.com in the US or http://www.travelocity.co.uk if you want to fly from a UK airport). Simply input the details of the destination you want and in seconds you are presented with a choice or routes, airlines and prices to choose from.

Source: O'Connor & Galvin (1999).

Sales force support

Another area that can also be enhanced through computer technology is sales force support. Supplying a sales representative with a laptop computer can give access to current information about products, their availability and prices; it can store customer profiles and relevant information; the representative can update records and write reports while the information is still fresh in the mind; and it can store appropriate graphics to enhance a sales presentation. All of this is easily portable and accessible whether the representative is working in Scotland or Greece.

THE ECONOMIC AND COMPETITIVE ENVIRONMENT

The effects of the **economic and competitive environment** are felt by organisations and consumers alike, and it has a profound effect on their behaviour. In the next few pages we look first at the macroeconomic environment, which provides the overall backdrop against which marketing activities take place. As well as issues of national interest, such as the effects of government economic policy on commerce, we cover the influence of international trading blocs and trade agreements. All of these things may provide opportunities or threats for an individual organisation. We then turn to the microeconomic environment. This is rather closer to home for the organisation, looking at the extent to which different market structures constrain or widen the organisation's freedom of action in its marketing activities and its ability to influence the nature of the market.

The macroeconomic environment

Figure 2.4 shows the basic economic concept of the circular flow of goods and income that makes a market economy go round. Marketing, as an exchange process and indeed as a force that actively encourages more exchanges, is an essential fuel to keep that flow going. The world is not, however, a closed, self-sustaining loop such as that depicted in Fig. 2.4. Its operation is severely affected by the macroeconomic influences generated by government economic policy and by membership of international trading blocs and trade agreements.

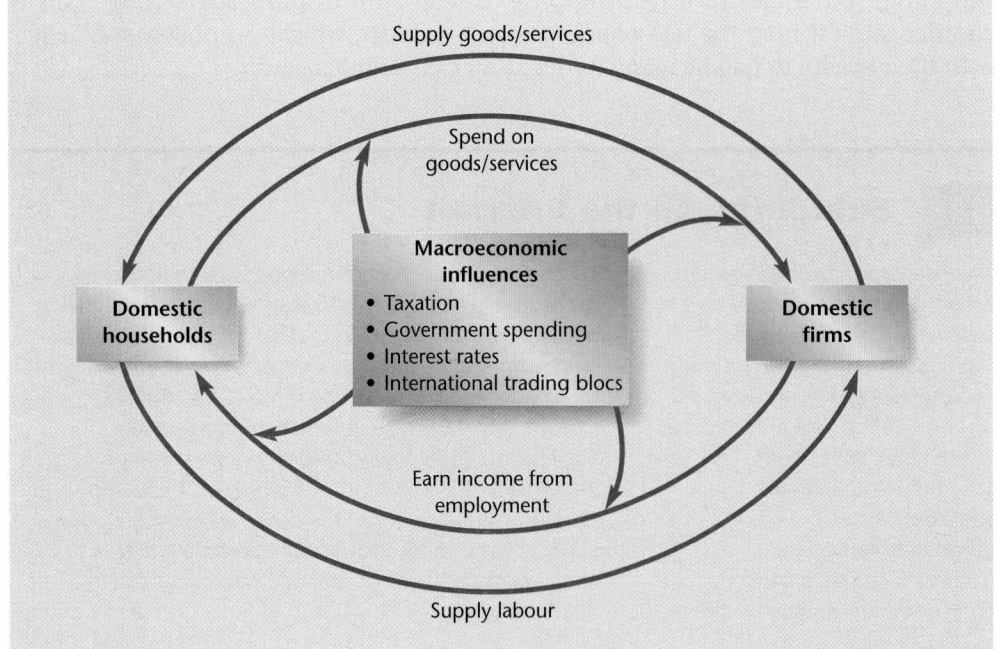

FIGURE 2.4

Macroeconomic influences on the circular flow of goods and income

Governments can develop and implement policies in relation to several macro-economic influences, which in turn affect markets, organisations and customers. Just a few of these are discussed below.

Taxation

Taxes may be direct or indirect. Direct taxation, such as income tax and national insurance contributions, reduces the amount of money, or disposable income, that a household has available to spend on the goods and services that organisations provide. Indirect taxation, such as purchase tax or value added tax (VAT), is collected for the government by the seller, who is obliged to add a percentage to the basic price of the product. Thus a PC sold in the UK may be advertised with two prices: a basic price of £999, then £1174 including VAT.

Some products, such as alcohol, tobacco and petrol, have duty imposed on them, again collected by the seller. Both VAT and duties serve to increase the prices of products for the customer, and marketers need to think about the effect of the tax-inclusive price on the customer's attitude and buying habits. When rates of duty increase, marketers sometimes choose to absorb some of the increase themselves to keep prices competitive, rather than pass on the entire rise to the buyer.

Rates of taxes and duties vary across the EU. The problems faced by brewers because of the higher duty on alcohol imposed in the UK compared with France will be discussed later, on p. 79. The range of goods across which taxes and duties are imposed varies too. In the Netherlands, for example, excise taxes are levied on alcoholic drinks, sugar and mineral oils, regardless of the country of origin. Special consumption taxes are also imposed on cars and motorcycles. A similar list exists in Germany, but also includes tea and coffee. At one end of the spectrum, Italy, Greece and Spain are among those who impose the highest VAT levels, while Luxembourg is at the opposite extreme. The UK has the largest number of goods exempt from VAT (most food, books, newspapers and children's clothing, for example). The EU is working towards narrowing the differences, agreeing for the time being a band of 15 per cent to 19 per cent within which all member countries' VAT rates should fall. Germany, for example, adjusted its VAT rate upwards from 15 per cent to 16 per cent in 1997 to meet the increased burden of its pension system. There were fears that this could fuel inflation without doing much to boost any economic recovery (*Financial Times*, 1997). The Netherlands also sought to increase VAT, but to cut it to 6 per cent on labour-intensive consumer services such as hairdressing (Cramb, 1997). A single European VAT system is still some way off, however.

Government spending

Governments, like any other organisations, are purchasers of goods and services, but on a grand scale. They invest in defence industries, road building and other civil engineering projects, social and health services and many other areas. Such large purchasing power can be used to stimulate or depress economic development, but if a government decides as a matter of policy to cut back on its spending, industry can be very badly hit. Defence, for example, is an area which many governments are reviewing in the aftermath of the ending of the 'cold war'. In the UK, companies such as British Aerospace have had to downsize dramatically as the demand for military aircraft has fallen, both domestically and internationally. At a local government level, the amount of expenditure directed towards local suppliers can be important. Since 1993, Belfast City Council has taken several measures to help local small and medium-sized enterprises (SMEs) to be more successful when bidding for contracts. This was achieved by improving access to buyers, making better information available on calls for tenders, and encouraging more personal contact with SMEs, including feedback on why they were not successful in a bid. Such a policy enables more local spend to stay within the community, thus finding its way into other local products and services. In addition, the successful SME could be better placed to expand its dealings outside the area, further assisting economic development (Barrett, 1998).

Interest rates

Government economic policy affects interest rates, which have an impact on both consumers and business. For many consumers, the most serious effect of a rise in interest rates is on their monthly mortgage repayments. Paying £20 or more per month extra to the mortgage lender means that there is that much less cash available for buying other things, and across the country retail sales can be significantly reduced. Interest rate rises can also affect the attractiveness of credit to the consumer, either when buying large expensive items through instalments, or when using credit cards. A consumer thinking about buying a brand new car, for example, may need a loan, and will look at the repayment levels, determined by interest rates, when deciding how expensive a model can be afforded. To try to reduce this potential barrier to purchasing, many car dealers have entered into arrangements with credit companies to offer 0 per cent financing deals to car buyers.

International trading blocs

Governments also negotiate membership of international trading blocs, and the scope, terms and conditions of international trade agreements. Membership of the EU, for example, and particularly the advent of the single European market (**SEM**),

---

MARKETING IN ACTION   **The Asian crisis**

The causes of the Asian crisis are many and complex, including too much inward investment pushing land prices up; too much borrowing by companies expanding too rapidly; too much lending by the banks to vulnerable companies; and problems with currencies linked closely with the strong US dollar. The subsequent collapse of Asian economies and their descent into recession in 1998 showed clearly just how interdependent different geographic markets are because of inward investment, import and export trade, and the international sourcing of components and raw materials. The impact of the Asian crisis was not only felt by Asian companies, but also by many Western firms. Falling Asian currencies meant that imports became much more expensive, and added to that was rising unemployment which made Asian consumers much more reluctant to spend. Here are a few examples of the practical results of all this:

- Nike blamed the Asian crisis for a drop in profits, as its products had to be discounted in Asia. Future orders too were down 12 per cent (Tomkins, 1997). Nike also had to shed 15 per cent of its Asian workers (August, 1998).
- British pottery companies, such as Portmeirion, Wedgwood and Royal Doulton, were looking to shed 10 000 jobs, 50 per cent of the industry total, partly because of the Asian crisis (Oldfield, 1998).
- Fujitsu closed its UK semiconductor plant with the loss of 570 jobs (Waples and Parsley, 1998).

- Hyundai, in South Korea, planned to lay off over 8000 workers and had to revise its production targets for 1998 down to 900 000 from 1.5 million in the early part of the year (Sivell, 1998).
- Wärtsilä, one of the world's leading suppliers of industrial diesel engines, relied on Asian markets, particularly Indonesia, for 40 per cent of its turnover. After demand collapsed, the company announced several hundred redundancies in its factories in Sweden, the Netherlands, Switzerland and France (Burt, 1998).

Some just about hung on. The French company Inter Parfums depended on Asian markets for 11 per cent of its sales, and was ready for a drop in sales because of the Asian crisis. As a result of the fall in Asian currencies, Inter Parfums had to raise its prices, but could not raise them enough to compensate completely for losses through exchange rates, because that would have priced the product out of the market. The company thus had to tighten up its costs, and both it and its Asian distributors agreed to cut their margins (Gless, 1998).

To some extent, there was some good news for consumers. Falling Asian demand for microchips led to a drop in the prices of computers and falling prices for other imported electrical goods (Smith and Hadfield, 1998). Consumers might well, however, question whether the hidden price of this in terms of job losses and knock-on recession in Western markets was worth paying.

has had a profound effect on the wider commercial dealings of organisations operating within the EU, as well as on the economic and competitive environment. Organisations which exist in countries outside the EU have found it increasingly difficult to sell into the EU, since there are now many more EU-based potential suppliers for purchasers to turn to, and also the logistics of purchasing within the EU are easier.

The EU is not, however, the only major European international trading bloc. The European Free Trade Association (EFTA) was formed originally in 1959 by Austria, Denmark, Norway, Sweden, Switzerland and the UK, and was later expanded to include Finland, Iceland and Liechtenstein. Its philosophy was simply to make trade between the member states easier. Since several EFTA members subsequently became members of the EU, and as the prospect of the single European market (SEM) raised the perceived barriers to entry to EU markets for non-EU organisations, the remaining EFTA countries (except Switzerland) became involved in the idea of the European Economic Area (EEA), formalised by treaty in 1993. Although not full members of the EU, EEA countries now share some of the benefits of the SEM, and certainly face fewer barriers to trade within the EU than they would otherwise have encountered. Participation in the EEA acted as a stepping stone for Austria and Sweden, who subsequently became full EU members. Similar co-operation and association agreements are in progress with the former communist states of central and eastern Europe, with the immediate aim of helping to stimulate their economics and the longer-term aim of including such countries as the Czech Republic, Poland and Hungary some time after 2000. Others, such as Bulgaria and Slovakia, must wait further reform while still benefiting from EU support. The enlargement of Europe will create new opportunities and problems. The population will grow by 28 per cent, but GDP by only 4 per cent when the new nations are allowed to join. GDP in Hungary and Poland, although growing fast, is still one-third of the average EU level. Each nation will have to meet preset criteria and standards for the environment, health and safety and social policy before they will be allowed to enter. All these changes create tremendous opportunities for EU and central European organisations in the run-up to EU enlargement (Barber, 1997).

Beyond the confines of formalised trading blocs, business is often affected by the existence of trade agreements. Some of these are protectionist, in that they are trying to cushion domestic producers from the effects of an influx of imports, while others are trying to liberalise trade between nations. For many years, for example, the UK's textile industry benefited from the multi fibre arrangement (MFA), which protected jobs and businesses by basically restricting the imports of low-priced clothing from various Far Eastern countries. Similarly, Japan agreed to implement voluntary export restraint (VER) with regard to its car industry's sales to Western Europe and the US. This helped to protect domestic car producers and jobs by imposing quotas on Japanese imports. One way of overcoming the restrictions of this VER was international direct investment, i.e. setting up factories within the EU (taking full advantage, by the way, of various EU investment incentives) to produce cars with sufficient local content to be labelled 'European'. Thus those people owning either a Nissan (built in Washington, Tyne & Wear), a Honda (built in Swindon) or a Toyota (built in Derby), for example, are technically driving a British car. From their British manufacturing bases, the companies can legitimately export, without quota constraints, to the rest of the EU under the terms of the SEM. In 1997, 57 per cent of cars manufactured in the UK were exported (Eason, 1998).

The protectionist stance of agreements like the MFA is, however, being overshadowed by wider moves towards trade liberalisation, through the General Agreement on Tariffs and Trade (GATT), for example. The broad aim of GATT is to get rid of export subsidies and import tariffs (effectively taxes on imports that push their prices up to make them less competitive compared with the domestically produced equivalent product) to make international trade a great deal fairer. This means that negotiated VERs, which do not depend on tariffs to control imports, are becoming an increasingly important tool.

Despite liberalisation, governments face the problems of unequal economic performance and opportunity in different regions within their sphere of influence. Governments therefore try to overcome the problems of congestion and rising costs in some areas and underused facilities and infrastructure in others through influencing business decision making with programmes of direct and indirect incentives. In Ireland, for example, the west coast is particularly remote from main European markets, and thus the government offers various tax and capital grant incentives to encourage relocation into the area, indigenous enterprise and business expansion. Similarly, in the Netherlands, a number of assisted areas have been defined to ensure balanced economic growth, including the north-eastern areas of Gronigen, Friesland and Drente, the northern part of Overijssel, and the south-eastern province of Limburg. In these areas, investment premiums are awarded along with cash grants and low-interest loans to encourage R&D investment.

The reunification of Germany posed particular problems for the government in trying to privatise eastern German industry and create an integrated free-market economy across the whole country. The Treuhandanstalt was set up to manage the privatisation of some 8000 previously state-owned industries, and additionally a range of incentives, including grants, subsidies, low-cost loans, accelerated depreciation, low tax, labour retraining support and export credit insurance, were introduced to encourage both domestic and foreign investment.

At EU level, there is a commitment to reducing the disparities between the various regions and developing the less favoured areas. Structural funds awarded from the European Regional Development Fund (ERDF) and the European Social Fund (ESF) particularly help the poorer regions of the EU, such as Greece, Spain, Portugal, Ireland and parts of Italy. The appropriateness and benefits of some of the projects awarded funds have been questioned by some critics, however. As Perry (1994) noted, the Court of Auditors in 1993 reported on projects such as the building of a winter ski resort in Crete, the establishment of a school for waiters on the Costa del Sol in Spain, a fur centre and exhibition hall in Greece, and a Spanish wind farm that switched off when the wind blew too hard! Nevertheless, most projects do achieve their stated objectives and provide a valuable boost to local economies, for example investment in encouraging high technology enterprise in Ireland.

> **Example** Since 1992, the Highlands and Islands region (http://www.hie.co.uk) in Scotland has had Objective 1, most favoured region, status within the EU. This resulted in an additional £242 million to support projects in the region. However, from 2000 onwards, the EU definition is being tightened to include only those areas that generate less than 75 per cent of the average GDP per capita across Europe. The Highlands and Islands generate 80 per cent, but claim that the real problem concerns the sparse population, affecting the range and type of services that can be offered, especially in transport and communication. It is an area larger than Belgium but with one-third of the population of Brussels. Similar low population density regions exist in northern Finland and Sweden. Despite these difficulties, business appears to prosper through a diverse range of small businesses apart from the traditional industries of whisky and oil (Bolger, 1997).

Many of the marketing issues associated with dealing within and with trading blocs, including the SEM, will be considered further in Chapter 23.

EU support keeps communities like this economically viable.

Source: Highlands and Islands Development Council.

The microeconomic environment

The general discussion in Chapter 1 of what marketing is, and its main tools, did not pay particular attention to the structure of markets. It is nevertheless important to think about market structures, because these will influence what sort of competition the organisation is up against, what scope the organisation has to manipulate the 4Ps and how broad an impact the organisation's marketing activities could have on the market as a whole.

Market structures can be defined in four broad categories, based on the number and size of competitors in the market.

Monopoly

Technically, a monopoly exists where one supplier has sole control over a market, and there is no competition. The lack of competition may be because the monopolist is state owned and/or has a statutory right to be the sole supplier to the market. Traditionally in the UK, this applied to public utilities, such as gas, water, electricity, telephone and postal services, and some key industries such as the railways, steel and coal. Government policy during the 1980s, however, was to privatise and open up some of these industries to competition, with the idea that if they were exposed to market forces and were answerable to shareholders, they would operate more efficiently and cost effectively. By 1998 in the UK, the railways and the last part of the electricity and gas industries had all been sold off, while the future of the postal service was still uncertain, being the subject of heated political and public debate. Other EU countries had implemented similar privatisation programmes. The Netherlands, for instance, has privatised its post, telephone and telegraph service (PTT) and Postbank. In Portugal, Electricidade de Portugal, Portugal Telecom and Brisa, the motorway operator, were all heavily over-subscribed on flotation in 1997 (Wise, 1997).

Example The EU has also taken an interest in some state-owned monopolies. In Sweden, as in other Scandinavian countries, there is a state monopoly for retailing alcohol. The EU rejected the Swedish government's claim that it was better able to control retail sales and thus restrict the potential for Swedes to consume too much liquor. The EU considered that Systembolaget's state monopoly to sell wine, spirits and strong beer was a disproportionate measure for preventing alcohol abuse, and that the protected arrangement contravened the EU ruling on the free flow of goods. The grocery trade, for example, was not able to sell in competition with Systembolaget. There were also financial advantages for the Swedish government in maintaining the system, as 6 per cent of the tax revenue in Sweden came from liquor sales and the retail chain's sales were SKr20 billion (£1.6 billion) in 1995 (McIvor and Tucker, 1997).

In practice, although the privatised companies have restructured themselves internally and revised their business philosophies to suit their new status, they still face limited competition as yet. This is mainly because of the barriers to entry faced by potential competitors, such as the massive capital investment required, or the monopolist's domination of essential resources or infrastructure.

The implication of all this is that a true monopoly is hard to find in a modern market economy, although several near-monopolies are operating. In the UK, a monopoly is deemed to exist where an organisation or a group of collaborating organisations control 25 per cent of a market. Where this occurs, or where a proposed or threatened take-over raises the possibility of its happening, the Monopolies and Mergers Commission (MMC) may undertake an inquiry to establish whether the situation is operating in the public interest and whether there is any unfair competition involved.

Example Some travel companies in the UK have been criticised by the MMC for not making clear the connection between airlines, tour operators and high-street travel agents. In a report on travel companies' anti-competitive behaviour, the failure to declare any links could result in consumers not really knowing whether they are receiving impartial advice from a travel agent. This is important because Thomson and Airtours are so dominant in the market. Airtours controls its own airline and the Going Places retail travel agent, while the package tour market leader, Thomson, holds 30 per cent of the market and also owns its own airline and the Lunn Poly travel agency (Curphey, 1997). The major source of complaints was small independent travel agents which, despite claiming to give impartial advice, were losing ground to the big two. Since 1990 the number of independents had dropped by 25 per cent.

Although the MMC did not propose that the travel agencies should be totally independent from the tour operators, it did call for more explicit information about links in all display and promotional materials. It also recommended an end to the 'most favoured customer' clause between travel agent and tour operator which prevented integrated operators from offering bigger discounts on tours from other companies. Despite the problems associated with these integrated systems, there were considered to be benefits from economies of scale, giving rise to wider choice of holidays and more competitive prices (Daneshkhu, 1997).

In theory, monopolists should not need to be particularly bothered about marketing. After all, they have a captive market with no alternative source of supply, so they should be able to price as highly as they want, and not be too concerned about customer service, corporate image, quality, reliability and all the other things that this book covers. In reality, however, monopolies exist with the consent and acquiescence of the government and public opinion, and thus the monopolist is likely to be subject to some kind of control or supervision to make sure that it operates within the public interest. Therefore a strong positive image, good customer service, fair pricing and all the other aspects of marketing soon become essential. Near monopolies, as we have seen, do face competition, at least in sectors of their businesses, and thus have to be more marketing oriented in their thinking.

This discussion so far has been rather parochial in that it has concentrated on national or regional monopolies. In global markets, however, it is even more difficult, if not impossible, to establish and sustain a monopoly.

As a final thought, the concept of monopoly depends on how 'market' is defined. While it is true that currently SNCF, for example, holds a monopoly on passenger rail travel in France, it does not have a monopoly on moving people from Paris to Lyon. To travellers, rail is only one option, and they might also consider travelling to their destinations by air, by coach or by car. In that sense, the traveller's perception of rail, in terms of its cost, reliability and convenience, is developed in a very competitive context. The UK train operators' advertising over the last few years has indeed sought to acknowledge this, by comparing the benefits of long distance rail travel with the disadvantages of road and air journeys. The opening of the Channel Tunnel in particular has brought the comparison of different modes of travel to the forefront, as leisure and business travellers decide whether to take the plane, the train or the ferry to and from the UK.

Oligopoly

Well-developed market economies are far more likely to see the emergence of oligopolies than monopolies. In an oligopoly, a small number of firms account for a very large share of the market, and a number of the privatised ex-monopolies discussed above are moving into this category. The oligopoly creates a certain amount of interdependence between the key players, each of which is large enough for its actions to have a big impact on the market and on the behaviour of its competitors. This certainly occurs in large scale, worldwide industrial markets, such as chemicals, oil and pharmaceuticals, because the amount of capital investment required, the levels of production needed to achieve economies of scale and the geographic dispersion of large customers demanding large quantities make this the most efficient way for these markets to be structured.

Example Oligopolies also occur in consumer markets, however. Petrol retailing in the UK has largely been concentrated in the hands of a few companies, such as Shell, BP and Esso. This has periodically given rise to accusations of collusion, specifically in terms of 'price fixing', which would not be allowed in either UK or EU law. In reality, the organisations within the oligopoly watch each other keenly for signals, and when one makes a price move, the others tend to follow very quickly, because this is a price-sensitive market. It may appear to be orchestrated, but the important thing to emphasise is that each organisation makes its decision independently, on the basis of its analysis of what it sees happening in the market. The petrol oligopoly in the UK became somewhat wider after the entry of the supermarket chains into this market. The supermarket share was thought to have reached around 25 per cent by 1997, with the oil companies closing 5000 petrol stations and losing money on their retail operations (Shingleton, 1998). Shingleton suggests that the main reasons were the supermarkets' better understanding of customers, the oil companies' slowness in responding to the threat by reducing margins, and the supermarkets' ability to differentiate their petrol by associating it with the retail operation while the oil companies suffered from poor brand loyalty. Although the oil companies are fighting back with loyalty schemes and price promotions to match the supermarkets, the damage has been done now that market share has been surrendered.

The entry of supermarkets has changed the face of UK petrol retailing.
Source: DMB&B.

Other consumer oligopolies are less visible to the casual observer. In the super-market, the shopper may see a wide variety of brands of clothes-washing detergents, and thus imagine that there is healthy, widespread competition in that sector. Most brands are, however, owned and managed by either Procter & Gamble (P&G) (Ariel, Daz, Bold etc.) or Lever Brothers (Persil, Radion, Surf etc.), and the proliferation of brands is more to do with fragmented demand and the creation of discrete segments (*see* Chapter 3) than the fragmentation of supply. Again, the supermarkets are the biggest threat to this oligopoly, with their own brands, such as retailer Sainsbury's own brand Novon.

In marketing terms, it is nevertheless still very difficult for a new brand from a new competitor to enter an oligopolistic market, other than in a small niche. This is because the oligopolists have spent many years and vast amounts of marketing money establishing their brands and shares. In the 1998 Marketing/Nielsen Biggest Brand Survey (Bainbridge and Curtis, 1998a), it was reported that P&G had spent nearly £75 million advertising its top six brands, while Lever had spent £30 million on its top two brands, Persil and Comfort, in the previous year. You can begin to see how such levels of marketing expenditure can act as an effective barrier to entry, and how they can meet any threat from a smaller competitor head-on if they wish.

The supermarket's own-brand threat is more serious because of the retailer's inher-ent control over a major channel of distribution which neither of the oligopolists can afford to lose. All of this really leaves only very small gaps in the market for the smaller competitor, such as that filled by products such as Ark and Ecover, two deter-gent brands that positioned themselves as more environmentally friendly than anything else available, appealing to the 'dark green' consumer.

Oligopolists therefore spend their time watching each other, and developing their marketing strategies and tactics on the basis of what the other main players are doing or are likely to do. If, for example, Lever Brothers launches a new brand, or imple-ments a major new marketing communications strategy, P&G would prefer to anticipate it, thus either pre-empting Lever or at least having a calculated response ready when needed. From P&G's point of view this is essential, even if it is only to maintain the delicate status quo of the two companies' relative market shares.

Example Not all oligopolistic markets are made up of organisations from the private sector. In the European airline industry, for example, there is a combination of state-owned and private operators. While British Airways is a privately owned company, Aer Lingus (Ireland), TAP (Portugal), Air France, Iberia (Spain), Sabena (Belgium) and Alitalia (Italy) are primarily state owned. It is claimed that such companies enjoy a higher level of state aid, and that there is a risk of unfair competition. This may arise from direct subsidy, or through government intervention to slow down the pace of unfavourable change. Despite deregulation designed to create more competition on previously monopolistic routes and to encourage price competition, it can still cost more to travel business class return from London to Hamburg than to New York.

Privatisation is still taking place in Europe, although within an increasingly turbulent environment. In Austria, the privatisation plans for Austrian Airlines (http://www.austrianair. com) were delayed due to the turmoil in international financial markets and the prospect of a global economic downturn affecting passenger demand. Shares in airlines privatised earlier, such as Lufthansa and BA, fell in 1998, causing Austrian Airlines to delay its plans and it could also make the two largest state-owned airlines, Air France and Alitalia, reconsider their privatisation timetable (*Flight International*, 1998).

Monopolistic competition

Good marketing practice and the emphasis on differential advantage have created a market structure that might seem a little paradoxical at first sight: monopolistic competition. The idea is that although there are many competitors in the market (with the emphasis on smaller competitors without enough individual influence to create either an oligopoly or a monopoly, as discussed above), each has a product sufficiently differentiated from the rest to create its own monopoly, because to the customer it is unique, or at least any potential substitutes are considered to be inferior. The concept forms the basis of much of the rest of this book.

Perfect competition

Perfect competition is at the opposite end of the spectrum from monopoly, and is about as likely to be found in practice. It involves many small producers, all supplying identical products that can be directly substituted for each other. No producer has the power to influence or determine price, and the market consists of many small buyers, who similarly cannot influence the market individually. There are no barriers to market entry or exit, and all buyers and sellers have complete information about what is happening in the market. All of this is clearly unrealistic. The influence of marketing concepts on even the smallest organisations, along with the development of powerful buyers and sellers in all kinds of markets, consumer and organisational, mean that these conditions cannot hold, and some kind of monopolistic competition or oligopoly soon emerges.

Example Farm produce, such as vegetables, is often cited as an example of near perfect competition. While it is true that the market does consist of many small suppliers, i.e. individual farms, the nature of the buyer is more complex, ranging from a family buying a few kilos of carrots from a farm shop, to the fruit and vegetable wholesalers and supermarket chains that buy such quantities that they can influence price and other supply variables. Even the product itself can be differentiated, for example organic and non-organic, or class I and class II quality. The farmer can also differentiate the offering through grading and packaging the produce to suit the retail customer. Even carrots, therefore, can be seen to be moving towards monopolistic competition.

This section has made implicit reference to concepts of supply, demand and pricing. In Chapter 11, which deals with price setting and modification, we go into more detail on the economics of pricing, supply and demand curves and price elasticity.

THE POLITICAL AND REGULATORY ENVIRONMENT

Quite apart from their effect on the economic and competitive environment, governments have a great influence on the character of the general business environment through their policies and the resultant legislation. Organisations have to exist in and operate according to the laws of the societies within which they do business, and thus in addition to the more general laws of contract and commerce, products have to conform to safety laws; manufacturing processes are subject to pollution controls; copyright and patents protect innovation; and retailers' opening hours are restricted in Germany, for example, by the *Ladenschlussgesetz*, and in the UK by the Sunday trading laws. We look below at the role and influence of national governments and the European Parliament in making rules that have a direct effect on the marketing mix.

Regulation is not only defined through legislation from national governments or the European Parliament, however. Organisations are also subject to rules passed by regulatory bodies, some of which have statutory powers delegated to them from government, while others are voluntary groupings, such as trade associations, with codes of practice to which the organisation chooses to adhere. We examine the nature and influence of such bodies on p. 76–9. Inevitably, governments and other regulatory bodies are influenced in their policy making by other sources, such as lobbyists and pressure groups, and on p. 79–80 we take a wider view of the influences that drive the legislators and rule makers towards their policies.

Overall, therefore, there are three main forces within the **political and regulatory environment**, national and local government, the EU, and various regulatory bodies. The degree of relative influence that each force exerts, and the nature of the tensions between them, will vary from country to country and from industry to industry. These forces are important and necessary because the problem with self-regulation is that it creates tension between what is socially desirable and what those in the industry may consider to restrict commerce unduly. Similarly, there is a risk that the interests of the general public, as represented by pressure groups, may also conflict with the needs and desires of commercial organisations, and that too creates tension that the law makers and regulators have to try to resolve.

National and local government

The obvious responsibility of national governments is to determine and maintain the legislative framework within which organisations do business. This will cover areas such as contract law, consumer protection, financial legislation, competition and trading practices, for example. There are still some variations across Europe, however. In Germany, for example, there are no overall government price controls, yet in the Netherlands, the Price Control Act (*Prijzenwet*) gives the government substantial power to control prices for one year at times of high inflation. Nevertheless, increasingly within Europe national governments are working within EU guidelines, with the longer-term aim of achieving as much consistency as possible between member states.

Within the UK, although Parliament passes legislation and puts it on the statute books, the responsibility for implementing and enforcing it is often delegated to specialist bodies, such as the Office of Fair Trading (OFT), the Monopolies and Mergers Commission (MMC) or the Independent Television Commission (ITC). The role of such bodies is discussed further on p. 76–9.

As well as the legislation they pass that affects the day-to-day business practices of organisations, governments can also have profound effects on the competitive environment. The widespread privatisation of publicly owned utilities and other state-controlled national industries in the 1980s and 1990s, as has already been discussed, presented opportunities for new competitors to enter these markets, as well as profoundly changing the culture and business orientation of the newly privatised companies themselves.

MARKETING IN ACTION Kabo

The Bulgarian company Kabo processes and sells canned fish and vegetables. Although nationalised in 1947, the company prospered because its home market was sheltered and its export business was handled by the state foreign trade organisation. To Kabo, marketing was of little concern and its main priority was production. By the 1980s, the company had 32 products and the overall volume of production was 20 000 tons. Only 5 per cent of sales were generated in the home market, while 70 per cent came from what was then the USSR, and around 20 per cent came from other markets, especially the UK, Italy and the Middle East. The prices between the markets varied considerably, with prices in the EU several times higher than those charged in the USSR. That was not a problem for Kabo, as any losses were made up by state subsidies. By the early 1990s, however, state subsidies had virtually disappeared in the food, tobacco and wine industries. Companies had to become self-sufficient and, because of Kabo's lack of competitiveness, production had fallen to less than

14 000 tons a year and the number of products was down to 12. The free market was now a reality. Kabo faced what were typical problems for many central European organisations as they sought to manage the transition to a free-enterprise, market-based system.

Interest rates soared from around 7 per cent to nearer 45 per cent, making investment problematic. Fuel and energy costs nearly doubled and workers began to look for higher wages. As all this began to affect prices, Kabo's food products became too expensive for the home market and the former Soviet Union had problems paying even the old price levels. Bartering deals, such as petrol in return for canned vegetables, were proposed, at least guaranteeing some form of payment. In other cases, however, no payments were made at all. The state foreign trade organisations disappeared and Kabo had no experience in international marketing and no knowledge of or contacts with international distributors or intermediaries.

Source: Adapted from a case prepared by Ivan Marchevski.

Example Germany currently subsidises the mining industry heavily and this has led to direct conflict with competitors elsewhere in the EU. The subsidies are being used to sustain a high-cost, relatively inefficient industry for fear of a political backlash in the mining areas of the Ruhr and Saarland. The government plans to provide DM1.65 billion for the industry up until 2005 in order to manage a gradual downsizing. This protects nearly 65 000 jobs in the short term, although closures and redundancies are inevitable. Celtic Energy in South Wales believes that it is one of the non-German mining organisations suffering from this policy. In a complaint to the EU commission, Celtic claimed that the true cost of producing high-grade anthracite in Germany is around £100 per tonne, but the Germans are selling it in the UK for £75 per tonne, below prevailing market UK prices. The subsidy, it is claimed, enables the German industry to undercut competition by £5 per tonne (*Financial Times*, 1997; Holberton, 1997; Jowit, 1997; Norman, 1997).

Politically driven deregulation has even made its mark on the public sector, particularly in the UK, where hospitals and police forces now find themselves operating in completely new ways as business units. Hospital pathology laboratories, for example, which traditionally were integrated internal departments, are now being asked to compete against external organisations for their own hospital's business, as well as tendering for contracts from other hospitals and the private sector. These are themes that will be pursued further in Chapter 22.

Local government also carries some responsibility for implementing and enforcing laws made at a national level. In Germany, local government has responsibility for implementing pollution and noise control legislation. In the UK, local trading standards officers may well be the first to investigate claims of shady or illegal business practices. Christmas often heralds a flurry of warnings from trading standards officers about dangerous toys, usually cheap imports from the Far East, that do not conform to EU safety standards. Officers can prosecute the retailer and prevent further sales of the offending goods, but by then, significant numbers of the product may already have been sold.

Example Trading standards officers also look into allegations of short weights and measures. In 1995, for example, they were asked by the angling fraternity in the North-east of England to investigate the practice of selling maggots by the pint. Although officers found that the number and weight of maggots to the pint varied significantly from retailer to retailer, they decided that this was tolerable because of the wriggly nature of the merchandise and, in any case, since this was a long-established method of selling maggots they would not intervene further. It is up to the individual angler to choose a maggot supplier with care!

Local authorities in the UK also have responsibility for granting planning permission. For businesses, this means that if they want to build a factory or supermarket, or change the usage of a commercial building, then the local authority has to vet the plans and grant permission before anything can be done. Sometimes this poses no problem at all, and local authorities go out of their way to encourage new industrial and commercial investment in their regions, as it provides jobs and encourages local economic regeneration. Establishing the Nissan car plant in Washington, Tyne & Wear, for example, not only provided new jobs in the factory itself, but also encouraged companies supplying goods and services to Nissan to locate and flourish close to the factory.

In other cases, however, planning permission can sometimes be a major barrier. Local authorities are under pressure from small retailers who are worried about the major shift towards out of town superstore shopping. The argument is that town centres and small local businesses are dying because people would rather go to the out of town retail park or shopping mall. This means that local authorities are increasingly reluctant to grant planning permission for further out of town developments, seriously affecting the growth plans of many large retailers.

Example Tesco ran into problems when it announced plans to build three superstores on the outskirts of Dublin and Cork, including a £15 million, 86 000 square foot site in North Dublin. Although Tesco had identified Ireland as a major growth area, its plans were set back by the Irish Environment Minister's decision to deny permission for the developments. Tesco now plans 'to contribute to the debate between retailers and the Irish government' through a legal fight. The Irish independent grocers, however, also fiercely oppose the developments, claiming that they would seriously affect any grocery traders within a 30-mile radius of each store. They seriously criticised Tesco for 'exporting a damaging concept' that in the UK has now been seriously restricted (*The Grocer*, 1998a; Tooher, 1998; http://www.tesco.ie).

Problems can also arise with planning permission and land usage at a local level. Safeway is challenging Northumberland Council over its insistence that Safeway should charge customers using its supermarket car park in Morpeth. The local council wants to install pay-and-display machines in the Safeway car park as part of a decision to end free parking in the town. The problem is complex because non-Safeway shoppers used to park there, and although Safeway owns the land, it allowed the local council to manage the car park. Revenue from the car park could be over £100 000 per year (*The Grocer*, 1998g).

Although the EU is making considerable progress towards eliminating national regulations that are contrary to fair and free trade, the scale of the task is great. National environmental laws in Germany and Denmark, for example, have been criticised as favouring local rather than international suppliers. The extent to which regulations affect business, therefore, varies between countries and industries. There is a slow move towards standardisation, which generally means that the advanced industrialised northern European nations are tending to deregulate, whereas the southern nations are tending to tighten up controls. Moves towards deregulation have been accompanied by increased self-regulation within industries.

The European Union

It is unfortunate that the pronouncements from Brussels that make the headlines tend to be the offbeat or trivial ones, such as the proposal to regulate the curve on a cucumber, the redesignation of the carrot as a fruit to allow the Portuguese to carry on their trade in carrot jam, and questions as to whether Cheddar cheese and Swiss rolls can continue to bear those names if they are not made in those places. Despite these delightful eccentricities, the EU works hard towards ensuring free trade and fair competition across member states' boundaries. The development and interpretation of European competition policy has long been an area of debate and controversy. The policy has three main objectives: to create an open and unified European market, to have the 'right' amount of competition in that market and to encourage fair competition unhampered by market abuse and restrictive practices.

The SEM, which officially came into being on 1 January 1993, was the culmination of many years of work in breaking down trade barriers and harmonising legislation across the member states. One area that directly affects marketing is the abolition of frontier controls, so that goods can be transferred from state to state, or carried in transit through states, without lots of paperwork and customs checks. Additionally, road haulage has been freed from restrictions and quotas so that a haulier with a licence to operate in one EU member state can operate in any other. Further European integration is sought through EMU (European Monetary Union) and the introduction of the euro as a replacement for national currencies. This will make cross-border price comparisons a lot easier for customers and create more transparent pan-European competition. The euro will also eliminate problems caused by fluctuating exchange rates, thus reducing the costs of the cross-border movement of goods and encouraging more imports and exports between the countries of the EU. This presents both opportunities and problems to the marketer, which will be discussed further in Chapter 10.

In terms of products themselves, a set of European standards have been implemented through a series of directives, ensuring common criteria for safety, public health and environmental protection. Any product adhering to these directives and to the laws of its own country of origin will be acceptable in any member state. Look for the stylised CE symbol on products as the sign that they do conform to European standards.

Example Defining just what chocolate actually is or is not has caused controversy in Europe among both politicians and chocolate manufacturers. The argument has been going on for nearly 25 years, since the UK and Ireland joined the EU with chocolate that included cheaper vegetable fats rather than a higher proportion of cocoa fats. The chocolate wars have been fought between an alliance of France and Belgium and a number of others against the UK, Ireland and five other states. An EU directive favouring one side over the other would create an unfair competitive advantage and would be a far cry from a single European market in chocolate. In 1997, the European Parliament ruled in favour of the France–Belgium alliance, overturning a previous compromise EU directive. This meant that the term 'milk chocolate' could not be used by the UK and the other states on its side. That vote, if implemented, would mean that products from Ireland, UK, Austria, Denmark, Finland, Portugal and Sweden would have to be renamed 'chocolate with milk and non-cocoa vegetable fats', or at least 'milk chocolate with a high milk content'. Product labels would also have to show clearly that the product contained vegetable fats. The battle looks set to continue. The national governments of the 15 EU states would have supported the compromise directive, but the MEPs appear to have been implacably opposed to it (Bremner, 1997; Tucker, 1997).

In other areas of marketing, harmonisation of regulations and codes of practice across member states has not been so easy, particularly in the marketing communications field, covered by the EU Green Paper on *Commercial Communications in the Internal Market*. This is expected to tackle many of the anomalies in marketing communications practice in different member states but has not yet been published.

Sales promotion, for example, is regulated in very different ways and with very different attitudes across Europe. The UK is very liberal, in that most sales promotion techniques are permitted and are largely regulated through voluntary codes of practice. In Germany, by contrast, many techniques are banned by law or heavily restricted in the way in which they can operate, for instance free gifts are (generally) banned, while there is a restriction on the value of discounts, vouchers or cash refunds. In the Netherlands, free gifts are permitted, but must not exceed 4 per cent of the value of the item to which they are linked. Even these brief examples give an inkling of the nightmares faced by the European marketer trying to trade across borders, and the pressure on the EU to begin to iron out the inconsistencies.

Advertising too is an area of intense debate within the EU. Issues such as the advertising of tobacco and alcohol, advertising aimed at children, comparative advertising and the regulation and control of advertising media are all under consideration. Again, the aim is to find a way of harmonising codes of practice and legislation that differ widely from member state to member state. Direct marketing is a relatively new area which has great potential for the marketing of goods across Europe, and yet here too, a variety of national codes are in operation. In the UK, for example, 'cold calling' telephone selling (i.e. an organisation phoning a consumer for sales purposes without the consumer's prior permission) is permitted, but in Germany it is almost totally banned. Data protection laws (i.e. what information organisations are permitted to hold on databases and what they are allowed to do with it) and regulations on list broking (i.e. the sale of lists of names and addresses to other organisations) also vary widely across the EU. The relevant EU directives include the Data Protection Directive, the Distance Selling Directive and the Integrated Digital Services Network Directive.

Example Another area of marketing where the effects of EU intervention are well publicised is in agribusiness. The Common Agricultural Policy (CAP), designed to regulate the supply of produce, has changed the way in which many farmers run their businesses, with subsidies to help certain sectors and quotas to limit others. Milk quotas mean that dairy farmers can only produce so much liquid milk, and thus some have moved into making and selling cheeses, ice creams and yoghurts to use up their excess.

However, the European Commission hopes to reform the CAP under Agenda 2000 and cut subsidies to farmers to bring European Union prices closer to world market prices. Many significant challenges lie ahead to test the political will. Not only do EU consumers pay more, but food producers are also at a competitive disadvantage in having to buy at EU prices rather than at world prices. Some differences can be substantial, for example for butter and milk powder the price gap is 30 per cent. If, however, the guaranteed prices for agricultural produce across the EU dropped, it could mean more exports to Far Eastern markets which had previously been served by more cost effective producers from New Zealand and Australia (*The Grocer*, 1998b, 1998d; Smith, 1997; Urry, 1997).

Regulatory bodies

Within the UK, there are many regulatory bodies with greater or lesser powers of regulation over marketing practice. Quasi-governmental bodies such as the Office of Fair Trading (OFT) and the Monopolies and Mergers Commission (MMC) have had statutory duties and powers delegated to them directly by government to ensure the maintenance of free and fair commerce.

Slightly more remote from central government, quasi-autonomous non-governmental organisations (QUANGOs) have a specific remit and can act much more quickly than a government department. QUANGOs such as Oftel, Ofgas and Ofwat, for instance, exist to regulate the privatised telephone, gas and water industries respectively in the UK. They advise on pricing policies and competition, and also act as ombudsmen if a consumer has reached deadlock in a dispute with the utility supplier. Following the deregulation of the gas market, Ofgas is trying to bring some order to the slanging matches that developed between rival suppliers. Accusations have been made that companies have been confusing or even misleading consumers with, for example, dubious price comparisons based on very low or very high consumption rates. Ofgas has already acted to stop the worst excesses of doorstep selling, but has also been criticised for not acting quickly enough in some cases. It is, however, difficult for Ofgas to balance its remit to promote competition in a previously strongly regulated sector on the one hand, and its duty to protect the consumer against unfair claims on the other (Benady, 1997b).

Voluntary codes of practice emerge from associations and trade bodies, with which their members agree to comply. The Advertising Standards Authority (ASA), for example, oversees the British Code of Advertising Practice, which covers a variety of advertising media including print, cinema, video, posters, leaflets and teletext. The ASA also supervises the British Code of Sales Promotion Practice, which lays down guidelines for good practice in sales promotions. The philosophy of the ASA is best summed up in its famous slogan, which states that advertising and promotion should be 'legal, decent, honest and truthful'. The ASA is not a statutory body, and can only *request* an advertiser to amend or withdraw an advertisement that is in breach of the code. If the advertiser refuses, the ASA can then *request* the media to refuse to repeat the offending advertisement. Since 1988, however, the Director General of the Office of Fair Trading has had the power under the Control of Misleading Advertisements Regulations to apply for a legal injunction to prevent the re-publication of an advertisement where the ASA's intervention has failed.

Example An example of an adjudication by the ASA involved a poster campaign developed by Saatchi & Saatchi for the holiday firm Club 18–30 in 1994. Copylines such as 'Beaver España', 'Discover Your Erogenous Zones', and 'It's Not Just Sex, Sex, Sex', drew 220 complaints, quite a significant number, which were upheld. The ASA told Club 18–30 to withdraw the advertisements straight away, because they were unacceptable since they had caused widespread offence, and some of them were irresponsible.

Nudity sometimes preoccupies the ASA. Complaints are often upheld if the nudity is not related to the product but included in the advertisement to shock or to gratify. It might be acceptable for Wonderbra to show a woman in her underwear, but this was not acceptable in an advertisement for Denon hi-fi. It showed a naked women on her hands and knees with the speaker between her legs and her mouth open in an expression of terror (Midgley, 1998).

One of the problems that the ASA faces, however, is that it has no authority to vet advertisements before publication, and thus by the time the ASA has enough complaints to act on, the offending campaign has had time to be widely seen and to attract a lot of publicity, because of its sensational nature. Then, when the ASA makes a ruling, further publicity is generated, for instance through opinion articles in newspapers discussing advertising standards which include a picture of an offending advertisement so that the readers know what sort of thing they're talking about. Indirectly, therefore, in some cases, ASA involvement rather defeats its own objectives. Kellogg attracted unwanted controversy over an advertisement suggesting that overweight children are more likely to be bullied but that they can solve their problem by

By the time the ASA forced the withdrawal of a provocative poster campaign by Club 18–30, the company had already benefited from enormous publicity!

Source: Club 18–30.

eating Kellogg's low fat breakfast cereals. The slogan 'sticks and stones may break my bones but names could really hurt me' and the rest of the copy were considered unacceptable by the ASA and Kellogg voluntarily withdrew the advertisement. The case generated widespread publicity in a range of media because of the bullying issue (Sears, 1998).

The Independent Television Commission (ITC) looks after terrestrial television advertising, while the Radio Authority (RA) supervises radio advertising. These two organisations are statutory bodies and carry a great deal of weight, since they have the power to issue and control broadcasting licences, and compliance with the advertising codes of practice is effectively part of the licence. Tobacco advertising on British television is not illegal, it is merely prohibited under the code of practice. Pharmaceuticals, alcohol and diet products are also subject to tight restrictions under the code. All of this means that although the basic philosophy of the ITC and RA is the same as that of the ASA, their concerns are a little wider, covering the timing of advertisements, making sure that the advertisements are suitably differentiated from the programmes, protecting children from unsuitable advertising, prohibiting political advertising and regulating programme sponsorship, among other things.

Example In 1998, the ITC upheld a complaint against a Levi's jeans advertising campaign which showed a hamster execution. The ITC received a record number of complaints, over 200, in the first weekend that the advertisement was screened. Kevin the hamster had nothing to do in life but go round and round on his wheel, until one day it broke and he died of boredom. The sight of Kevin being poked with a pencil to ensure that he was dead was the final straw for many grief-stricken children. Adults simply could not see the relevance to jeans. Levi's did not, of course, mean to shock or offend but just to entertain (*Marketing*, 1998b).

The Institute of Sales Promotion (ISP), the Institute of Practitioners in Advertising (IPA), the Institute of Public Relations (IPR) and the Direct Marketing Association (DMA) are effectively trade associations. All these areas are, of course, subject to prevailing commercial legislation generally, but, in addition, these particular bodies provide detailed voluntary codes of practice setting industry standards for fair dealing with customers. They are not statutory bodies, and only have jurisdiction over their members, with the ultimate sanction of suspending or expelling organisations that breach the code of practice. All of the bodies mentioned here represent organisations with interests in various areas of marketing communications, but trade associations can exist in any industry with similar objectives of regulating the professional practice of their members. There are, for example, the Fencing Contractors Association, the Glass and Glazing Federation, the Association of British Insurers, the British Association of Landscape Industries, and the National House Builders Confederation, to name but a few! As well as regulating business practice, such bodies can also provide other services for members, such as legal indemnities and representation, training and professional development services, and acting as the voice of the industry to government and the media.

Self-regulatory organisations do, of course, exist across Europe, and there are also attempts to introduce internationally accepted codes of practice. In the advertising field, for instance, many national bodies base their codes on the International Code of Advertising Practice issued by ICC in Paris. These guidelines help to harmonise advertising and sales promotion across a range of subscribing countries. The purpose of the code is to ensure that advertising is legal, honest, truthful and socially responsible, and does not hinder fair competition. It also suggests positions on comparative advertising, advertising to children and the avoidance of various types of discrimination. The extent to which the code is adopted varies from country to country. In Germany, for instance, the Deutscher Werberat follows its main provisions, while in Sweden, some legislation goes well beyond the provisions of the international code.

Influences on the political and regulatory environment

The political and regulatory environment is clearly influenced by sociocultural factors, and particularly the pressure of public opinion, the media and pressure groups. Greenpeace and Friends of the Earth, for example, have educated consumers to become more aware of the content, origins and after-effects of the products they buy and use, and this led to the phasing out of chloro-fluorocarbons (CFCs) as an aerosol propellant and as a refrigerant. The green movement has also spurred the drafting of regulations on the acceptable emissions from car exhausts, which has had a major impact on the product development plans of motor manufacturers for the next few years. Similarly, the consumer movement, through organisations such as the Consumers' Association, has also played an important role in promoting the rights of the consumer and thus in driving the regulators and legislators towards laws and codes of practice regarding product safety, selling techniques and marketing communications, for instance.

Not all pressure on legislators and regulators originates from pressure groups or consumer-based organisations, of course. Trade associations or groupings lobby the legislators to try to influence regulation in their members' favour. The freedom created by the SEM to import as much alcohol as you like for your own consumption if it is purchased within other EU member states has created severe problems for the UK brewers. Since duty on alcohol is much lower in France than in the UK, it pays to take a van across the English Channel, stock up on brands of beer and lager that ironically may even have been brewed in the UK, and bring it all back home. The main problem is that some travellers are making a business of it, illegally reselling the goods in the UK at prices that undercut the brewers and their legitimate outlets, yet still making a healthy profit on the trip. According to the Wine and Spirit Association, the UK government is losing £600 million a year on lost excise duty on beer, wine and spirits because of cross-channel shopping. Some £200 million is also thought to be lost from the illegal avoidance of excise duty within a distribution system that makes cut-price, undercover offers to restaurants and wine bars (Willman, 1997). The brewers want UK duty reduced so that it is in line with French rates and makes the 'grey' market unprofitable, but as yet the Chancellor of the Exchequer has not been persuaded.

An area in which the legislators have been pulled in two opposing directions for many years is that of tobacco advertising. On the one hand, ASH (Action on Smoking and Health) has lobbied to get tobacco advertising banned completely and to get the taxes on tobacco raised, as a price disincentive to smokers, while on the other hand, the Tobacco Advisory Council, representing the manufacturers, has waged a counter campaign that has slowed down the pace of restriction and diluted its content. In this case, whatever the legislators do will be unpopular with someone! The UK government's proposed ban on tobacco advertising and sponsorship has pleased the anti-smoking lobby, but means the loss of £57 million per year in advertising revenue. By 2006, when a complete ban on sports sponsorship by tobacco companies is due to come into force, over £50 million of sponsorship will be lost (Higham, 1999).

CHAPTER SUMMARY

This chapter has explored the importance of the external marketing environment as an influence on the way in which organisations do business and make their decisions. The main framework for the chapter is the categorisation of the marketing environment into STEP factors: sociocultural, technological, economic/competitive and political/legal.

Using environmental scanning, a technique for monitoring and evaluating information under each of the STEP headings, organisations can understand their environment more thoroughly, pick up early signs of emerging trends, and thus plan their future activities appropriately. Such information may come from secondary sources, such as trade publications or published research data, or an organisation can commission research to increase their knowledge of the environment. Care must be taken, however, to ensure that all appropriate sources are constantly monitored (but avoiding information overload), and that internal mechanisms exist for disseminating information and acting on it.

The first of the STEP factors is the sociocultural environment. This deals with 'hard' information, such as demographic trends, and with less tangible issues, such as changing tastes, attitudes and cultures. Demographic trends look at how populations are divided in terms of age, sex, income, family size and household structure. Knowledge of these gives the marketer a basic feel for how broad market segments are likely to change in the future, for instance the increase in the number of over-55s, or the increase in one parent families. To gain the fullest picture, however, the marketer needs to combine demographic information with 'softer' data on how attitudes are changing.

The second STEP factor is technology. An organisation's technological advances may arise from the exploitation of breakthroughs from other organisations, or may be the result of long-term investment in R&D in-house to solve a specific problem. Either way, technology can present the opportunity to create a clear differential advantage that cannot be easily copied by the competition. There are four main areas of an organisation that might be influenced by technology: materials, components and products; production processes; administration and distribution; and marketing and customers.

The economic and competitive environment constitutes the third STEP factor, and can be further divided into macro- and microeconomic environments. The macroeconomic environment analyses the effects of the broader economic picture, looking at issues such as taxation, government spending and interest rates. It also takes account of the threats, opportunities and barriers arising from membership of international trading blocs such as the EU and EFTA, and the trading agreements reached within these blocs. The microeconomic environment is a little closer to the individual organisation, and is concerned with the structure of the market(s) in which it operates.

The final STEP factor is the political and legal environment. Laws, regulations and codes of practice emanate from national governments, the EU, local government, statutory bodies and trade associations to affect the way in which organisations do business. Consumer groups and other pressure groups, such as those representing the ecological movement, health issues and animal rights, are active in trying to persuade government to deregulate or legislate, or to influence the scope and content of new legislation.

Key words and phrases

Demographics	Political and regulatory environment	STEP
Economic and competitive environment	SEM	Technological environment
Environmental scanning	Sociocultural environment	

QUESTIONS FOR REVIEW

2.1 What does the acronym STEP stand for?

2.2 What is environmental scanning, why is it important, and what are the potential problems of implementing it?

2.3 What kind of information does the study of demographics cover?

2.4 Why might consumer demands for variation and variety in the products they buy cause problems for marketers?

2.5 To what extent have consumer concerns about environmental issues affected organisations' approaches to marketing?

2.6 Why are consumer groups and other pressure groups a major influence in an organisation's marketing environment?

2.7 Summarise the main implications of the SEM for organisations doing business within the EU.

2.8 In what ways can technology contribute to the marketing environment?

2.9 Differentiate between the macro- and microeconomic environments.

2.10 What are the four main types of market structure?

QUESTIONS FOR DISCUSSION

2.1 What sources of published demographic data are available in your own university or college library?

2.2 Find and discuss examples of products that are particularly vulnerable to changing consumer tastes.

2.3 To what extent, and why, do you think marketers should be seen to lead the way in addressing 'ethical' issues rather than waiting until consumer concern reaches a level where the organisation is prompted to react?

2.4 What are the differences between the ASA and the ITC? Find and discuss recent examples of adjudications by these two bodies (or equivalent regulatory bodies in your own country). Do you agree with their judgement?

2.5 Using Fig. 2.1 as a framework, choose a product and list under each of the STEP factors the relevant influences that have helped to make that product what it is.

CASE STUDY 2.1

Sanpro

Sanpro, otherwise known as female sanitary protection (tampons, towels and panty liners) is a massive market, worth almost £300 million in the UK, but one that is very difficult for marketers to deal with because of the sensitivities involved.

The balance of the market between tampons (for internal use) and towels (for external use) has changed, partly because of technological development, and partly because of consumer health worries. Advances in the field of superabsorbents has meant that towels can be thinner and more discreet, yet still provide reliability and reassurance. This has made them more acceptable to many women. The growth of the towel sector has been stimulated by the Always brand range, owned by Procter & Gamble (P&G). Added to that, publicity over the risks of toxic shock syndrome (TSS) that can arise from tampon use has put users off these products. This means that in 1995 towels had 51 per cent of the market by value, with tampons lagging behind with only 38 per cent. By 1998, sales of Always had overtaken sales of Tampax and were growing much faster.

The competitive structure of this market has also changed over recent years. In 1997, Procter & Gamble (P&G) took over Tambrands, manufacturer of Tampax. Although the market is now dominated by P&G, which claims 58 per cent of the tampon sector with Tampax and 40 per cent of the towel sector with Always, the threat from supermarket own brands has increased. Although the growth in own brands is still slow, the fact that grocery multiples distribute over 60 per cent of all products in this market means that the threat must be taken seriously. One result of all this is to put pressure on the manufacturer brands to maintain a high level of marketing support.

Marketing support in terms of advertising is a very sensitive area. Although press advertising in women's magazines can be quite explicit, many older women in particular are embarrassed about the nature of the product, and do not want to watch television advertisements for tampons, for instance, with other members of the family. Because of this, until 1986 sanpro products could not be advertised on terrestrial television in the UK at all, but gradually the regulatory bodies began to relax the rules. It was only after 1 August 1998, however, that sanpro could be freely advertised around all programmes (except those targeted at children) at any time of day. One of the problems arising from all the restrictions was that the advertisements were often so inoffensive that they did not offer any useful information to women, and clichéd imagery of active young women in tight shorts leading incredibly active and enjoyable lives was felt by many to be patronising.

To try to move away from the clichés, in early 1997, a new $60 million global campaign was launched by Tambrands. The idea was to address women's specific concerns about tampon usage under the umbrella line of 'Tampax. Women Know'. The advertising agency's creative director said,

'We've taken a category that is cloaked in euphemisms and have broken away from the kind of tampon ad that does everything but talk about the product and its use.' (Tylee, 1997)

The 27 countries targeted by the campaign were clustered into three groups:

- Mature markets, such as the USA, Australia and the UK, where tampon usage is widespread and accepted.
- Semi-developed markets, such as Spain and Italy, where women know about tampons, but these are not so commonly used and thus there is still plenty of development potential.
- Emerging markets, such as China and Brazil, where women know very little about tampons at all.

Each cluster requires different messages and even within a cluster, different countries would have different needs and taboos that have to be respected.

Tambrands' development of emerging markets seems to have attracted P&G towards the takeover. P&G felt that it could use its own extensive distribution network across 140 nations to get tampons into countries such as China, India and Vietnam more efficiently and effectively. Tampax had already been launched in China in 1995 and the market was very receptive to the message. These new markets are very important because mature markets, such as the USA and UK in which Tampax has 90 per cent of its sales, are both saturated and highly competitive.

Because of the level of competition and sensitivity about the product, sales promotions play an important role. Teenagers are a prime target for the manufacturers, as a high degree of brand loyalty is established in the early years of usage. Promotions such as free tampon containers, discounts for multiple purchases and joint promotions with skin care brands all help to encourage product trial. Investment in education is also important. Tampax, for example, is committed to providing an education support service to schools.

Sources: Bainbridge and Curtis (1998b); Benady (1997a); Bray (1996); Brower (1997); *The Grocer* (1997); Kelly (1997); *Marketing* (1998a); Murphy (1998); Tylee (1997).

Questions

1 Outline the ways in which the STEP factors affect this market.

2 Why do you think sales promotions are particularly effective for these products?

3 How might the marketing environment differ between the three clusters of countries defined for the Tampax campaign? To what extent can a single, global message be effective?

4 In terms of the marketing environment, how does this product differ from (a) toilet paper and (b)

CASE STUDY 2.2

A friend in need is a friend indeed

Lofthouse of Fleetwood Ltd. is a family owned company based on the coast in the north-west of England. The company began in 1865 when a Fleetwood pharmacist, James Lofthouse, developed a warming lozenge for trawlermen to suck while at sea. That lozenge, branded as Fisherman's Friend, grew from its small beginnings into what is now a global business. Billions of Fisherman's Friend lozenges are sold every year in over 100 different countries. The main ingredients, including menthol, eucalyptus oil and capsicum tincture, make the lozenge a hot prospect and it is endorsed by medical authorities as an excellent means of clearing bronchial congestion. Although purely medicated confectionery, Fisherman's Friend holds FDA certification in the USA and a manufacturer's licence in the UK. This is issued by the Medicines Commission, and its Regional Officer regularly inspects the company's premises. Lofthouse of Fleetwood has also received ISO 9002 accreditation.

Because of its heritage, Fisherman's Friend is perceived in the UK as a 'semi-medicated' product, positioned alongside Tunes and Hall's Mentholyptus cough sweets. In overseas markets, however, where the product has no historical roots, Fisherman's Friend is positioned and accepted as 'adult confectionery'. The UK perceptions are reinforced by the retail trade which, in some cases, still sees Fisherman's Friend as a winter product and so does not give it optimum shelf space in the summer months. It is true to say that in past years, sales have

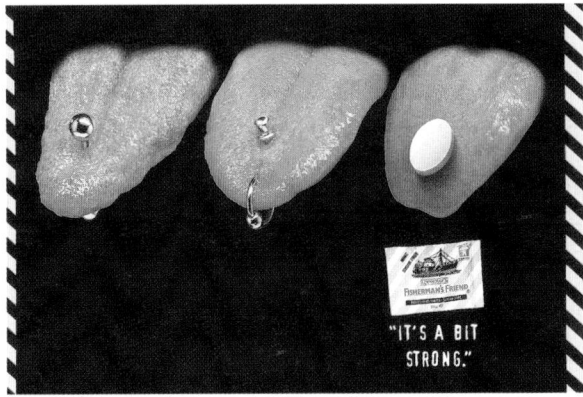

Medicine or sweetie? In any event, brace yourself!
Source: Kelly Weedon Shute Ltd.

experienced peaks and troughs and this is still the case in the UK. In newer markets, where the brand is treated purely as confectionery, there is much less seasonality and the product retains its normal shelf position throughout the year.

Another problem in the UK market for a brand trading on a heritage established over 130 or more years is that many of its loyal buyers are older. The company wants to target a younger market but has found it hard to change the heritage perceptions and create a 'cool' image. The perceptions among the young are still that it is 'the sort of product Granny buys', that 'it'll blow your head off' and that 'I haven't tried it and I know I won't like it'. Despite innovative advertising, those perceptions and the view of Fisherman's Friend being a medicinal product that 'I'll only take as a last resort' still persist. Efforts have been made to get the product sampled by younger consumers. It has been included, for example, in student welcome packs on university and college campuses. Nevertheless, there is still the reaction 'I've tried it once and I didn't like it' to be overcome.

To extend the brand, over fifteen years or so from the mid-1980s, variants on the Original Extra Strong Fisherman's Friend brand were introduced. The first was an aniseed flavoured Fisherman's Friend. This has a milder flavour than the original and is targeted at the younger audience which dislikes the strong flavour of the original. A mint flavour was then developed in order to move the brand further towards the mainstream confectionery sector. Other products have been developed to meet the needs of export markets. The Norwegian market, for example, is very health conscious and wanted a sugar-free version. This caused some manufacturing problems for the company, however. The traditional method of making a hard lozenge did not work well with sugar substitutes as they absorbed too much moisture from the air and turned the lozenges very soggy very quickly. Thus a new method was introduced which compresses dry powders into hard tablets. This is very similar to the way in which the pharmaceutical industry makes aspirin tablets, for instance. The investment in the new method proved to be well worthwhile. Original, mint and lemon sugar-free Fisherman's Friends have all proved successful, not only in Scandinavia but also in the UK and other markets.

The company feels that research is an important basis for the strategic thinking that has driven these developments of the brand. Research has shown, for example, that there are different flavour preferences in different countries and the company exploits this information. Fruit flavours are preferred in southern European markets, such as Greece, Italy, and Spain, where citrus fruits are grown, while northern Europe and Scandinavia prefer the non-fruit flavours. In France and the Far East, consumers have a milder palate, preferring the newer flavours that are less hot than the original Fisherman's Friend. Focus groups are also used as part of the market research effort to test advertising awareness and recall, and price perceptions. Blind tastings have also provided feedback which has allowed the company to identify the potential of new flavour variants.

In all its markets, including the UK, the company uses independent distributors to sell and distribute the product. Lofthouse of Fleetwood has no sales force of its own. 'Our forte is manufacturing quality products. It's what we enjoy and it's what we do best,' said Duncan Lofthouse, a Director of the company. The company does not consider sales, marketing and logistics to be its strengths, and so it contracts out those activities. Nevertheless, the company still involves itself in the major decision making. Its in-house technical and planning department designs the packaging, and the company retains control over its own brand. The company tries to keep a consistent brand image in all its markets, but some adaptation to suit local needs is necessary. For humid markets, such as those in the Far East, the brand's packaging has had to be adapted to include a foil lining to preserve the product and prevent it from going soggy. This gives it the same three-year shelf life as the paper packs have in other markets. Otherwise, the packaging is almost identical in all markets. The Fisherman's Friend brand name is in English on the front of all packs, but the back of the pack varies from market to market. The brand name can be represented in the local script (for example, in China, Thailand and Greece) and the local labelling regulations fulfilled.

Lofthouse of Fleetwood liaises closely with the specialist companies it works with. For example, it has worked for 26 years with an independent sales and marketing company, Impex Management Company Ltd. which represents only Fisherman's Friend. The relationship involves mutual respect and mutual dependency and works well. Impex and Lofthouse of Fleetwood sit down together to discuss the direction of Fisherman's Friend and the business's objectives and five-year plan.

Source: With grateful thanks to Tony and Duncan Lofthouse.

Questions

1 Summarise the STEP factors that might have affected Lofthouse of Fleetwood's marketing decisions.

2 Why is market research so important to this company?

3 Why should Lofthouse of Fleetwood want to reach a younger market? What is it doing and what more could it do to reach this audience?

4 Lofthouse of Fleetwood contracts its marketing activities to an independent company, Impex, so that it can focus on manufacturing. Does this make Lofthouse of Fleetwood a production or product orientated company?

References to Chapter 2

Aguilar, F. J. (1967), *Scanning the Business Environment*, MacMillan.

August, O. (1998), 'Nike Blames Fresh Fall on Turmoil in Asia', *The Times*, 19 September, p. 49.

Bainbridge, J. and Curtis, J. (1998a), 'The UK's Biggest Brands, Part 1', *Marketing*, 30 July, pp. 22–5.

Bainbridge, J. and Curtis, J. (1998b), 'The UK's Biggest Brands, Part 2', *Marketing*, 6 August, pp. 20–1.

Barber, L. (1997), 'Guide to Enlarging the EU Eastwards', *Financial Times*, 8 December, p. 2.

Barrett, P. (1998), 'Local Attraction', *Supply Management*, 12 February, pp. 38–9.

Benady, D. (1997a), 'P&G Gambles on Tambrands', *Marketing Week*, 17 April, pp. 32–3.

Benady, D. (1997b), 'Ofgas Must Dispel Adverting Hot Air', *Marketing Week*, 4 December, pp. 19–20.

Bolger, A. (1997), 'It's Getting Tougher at the Edges', *Financial Times*, 18 December, p. 5.

Bray, L. (1996), 'Privates on Parade', *The Grocer*, 11 May, pp. 35–9.

Bremner, C. (1997), 'All Because the Belgians Do not Like Milk Tray', *The Times*, 24 October, p. 5.

Brower, A. (1997), 'How FCB's Worldwide Tampax Ads Reflect Cultural Diversity', *Campaign*, 9 May, p. 27.

Burt, T. (1998), 'Metra Finnish Group Blames Asian Crisis for Falling Profits', *Financial Times*, September, p. 30.

Cheary, N. (1997), 'Graphic Animal Ads Fox the Watchdogs', *Marketing Week*, 13 November, p. 24.

Cramb, G. (1997), 'Dutch Unveil Plan to Raise VAT', *Financial Times*, 12 December, p. 2.

Curphey, M. (1997), 'MMC to Order Tour Operator Shake-up', *The Times*, 27 October, p. 44.

Daneshkhu, S. (1997), 'Tour Groups May Be Able to Keep Travel Agencies', *Financial Times*, 19 December, p. 1.

Daniels, J. (1994), 'Early Sign of a Change in Attitudes', *Financial Times*, 4 October, XI.

Day, J. (1998), 'The Call of the Wild', *Marketing Week*, 25 June, pp. 41–2.

Dittmar, H. and Pepper, L. (1994), 'To Have is to Be: Materialism and Person Perception in Working Class and Middle Class British Adolescents', *Journal of Economic Psychology*, 15(2), pp. 233–51.

Eason, K. (1998), 'Car Output Highest since 1974', *The Times*, 21 January, p. 24.

Financial Times (1997), 'Germans Go Slow', *Financial Times*, 12 December, p. 13.

Flight International (1998), 'Falling Shares Delay Privatisation Plans', *Flight International*, 154(4640), p. 23.

Gless, E. (1998), 'Comment faire face à la crise Asiatique?', *L'Entreprise*, 151(April), p. 22.

The Grocer (1996), 'Focus on Bread and Morning Goods', *The Grocer*, 6 April, pp. 41–56.

The Grocer (1997), 'Tambrands Taken over by Procter & Gamble', *The Grocer*, 12 April, p. 12.

The Grocer (1998a), 'Irish Vow to Fight Tesco Hypermarket', *The Grocer*, 31 January, p. 5.

The Grocer (1998b), 'Brussels Left to Grasp the CAP Dairy Nettle', *The Grocer*, 7 February, p. 24.

The Grocer (1998c), 'The Upper Crust Prevails', *The Grocer*, 21 February, p. 6.

The Grocer (1998d), 'Brussels Outlines Plans to Cut Milk Rates by 18%', *The Grocer*, 28 February, p. 29.

The Grocer (1998e), 'Magnificence', *The Grocer*, 11 April, p. 42.

The Grocer (1998f), 'White Premium Rises above Bread War', *The Grocer*, 16 May, p. 12.

The Grocer (1998g), 'Safeway Faces Car Park Tussle', *The Grocer*, 16 May, p. 17.

Higham, N. (1999), 'Will Alcohol be the Next Victim of Labour's Ad-bashing Policy?' *Marketing Week*, 24 June, p.19.

Holberton, S. (1997), 'Brussels Check On German Coal Aid', *Financial Times*, 17 June, p. 11.

Jagger, S. (1998), 'State of the European Union', *Marketing Week*, 24 September, pp. 40–1.

Jowit, J. (1997), 'Germany May Face £50mill Coal Claims', *Financial Times*, 21 October, p. 12.

Kelly, J. (1997), 'Personal Services', *The Grocer*, 17 May, pp. 35–7.

Kelly, J. (1998), 'As Good as it Gets', *The Grocer*, 11 April, pp. 37–9.

Lacey, R. (1998), 'Danger Man', *The Grocer*, 12 September, pp. 30–2.

McIvor, G. and Tucker, E. (1997), 'EU Blow to Swedish Liquor Monopoly', *Financial Times*, 5 March, p. 2.

McLoughlin, L. (1998), 'The Need for Speed', *The Grocer*, 18 July, pp. 41–5.

Marketing (1998a), 'ITC Eases Sanpro Ad Curbs', *Marketing*, 25 June, p. 8.

Marketing (1998b), 'Levi's Pulls Hamster Ad after Complaints', *Marketing*, 27 August, p. 5.

Midgley, C. (1998), 'Naked Untruths Earn a Rebuke for Advertisers', *The Times*, 6 May, p. 6.

Murphy, C. (1998), 'Consumer Shift Hits Tampon Sales', *Marketing*, 6 August, pp. 12–13.

Murphy, Y. (1997), 'Let's Make Some Dough', *The Grocer*, 12 April, pp. 37–42.

Norman, P. (1997), 'Germany Reaches Deal to End Mine Closure Protests', *Financial Times*, 14 March, p. 22.

Nuki, P. (1998), 'Big Stores Sell "Organic" Food with Additives', *The Sunday Times*, 4 October, p. 1.5.

O'Connor, J. and Gavin, E. (1999), *Marketing and Information Technology*, 2nd edn, Financial Times Pitman Publishing.

Oldfield, C. (1998), 'Pottery Industry Close to Cracking', *Sunday Times*, 18 January, p. 3.1.

Perry, K. (1994), *Business and the European Community*, Butterworth-Heinemann.

Rogers, D. (1998), 'Stores Dodge GM Food Row', *Marketing*, 18 June, p. 14.

Sears, N. (1998), 'Kellogg's Snub Protests Over Advert "Cruel" to Children', *Daily Mail*, 1 April, p. 35.

Shannon, J. (1998), 'Seniors Convert to Consumerism', *Marketing Week*, 10 September, p. 22.

Shelton, E. (1998), 'Saga Faces Battle to Update', *Marketing*, 18 June, p. 19.

Shingleton, J. (1998), 'The Development of Petrol Retailing in the UK', *Marketing and Research Today*, 26 (1), pp. 32–8.

Simonian, H. (1995), 'Quest for Green Tyre', *Financial Times*, 6 March III.

Sivell, G. (1998), 'Hyundai to Make 8,000 Redundant', *The Times*, 21 May, p. 33.

Smith, D. and Hadfield, P. (1998), 'Can Britain Escape the Asian Vortex', *Sunday Times*, 21 June, p. 1.11.

Smith, M. (1997), 'The Great Survivor: The CAP Is Being Reformed Cautiously', *Financial Times*, 3 November, p. 20.

The Times (1998), 'Companies "Ignore Marketing Codes on Baby Milk"', *The Times*, 10 April, p. 9.

Tomkins, R. (1997), 'Nike Warns of Asia Squeeze as Profits Tumble', *Financial Times*, 19 December, p. 16.

Tooher, P. (1998), 'Tesco Set to Ride out Irish Superstore Ban', *The Express*, 12 June, p. 60.

Tucker, E. (1997), 'MEPs Reject Chocolate Compromise', *Financial Times*, 24 October, p. 20.

Tylee, J. (1997), 'Tambrands Strives for Clear Global Message', *Campaign*, 21 March, p. 7.

Urry, M. (1997), 'Wide Reform of EU Agriculture Policy Urged', *Financial Times*, 28 November, p. 15.

Waples, J. and Parsley, D. (1998), 'Redundant', *Sunday Times*, 20 September, p. 3.5.

Willman, J. (1997), 'Illegal Drinks Trade Costing £600mn', *Financial Times*, 7 November, p. 10.

Wise, P. (1997), 'Brisa Offering: Motorway Operator Draws Strong Retail Demand', *Financial Times*, 25 November, p. 34.

Woodhead, M. (1998), 'Greens Make Germans Fear for Industry', *Sunday Times*, 4 October, p. 3.14.

Yoon, C. K. (1998), 'Bitter Menace: A Shortage of Chocolate', *The Independent*, 5 May, p. 1.

Young, R. (1998), 'Chocolate Lovers Face a Shortage', *The Times*, 6 May, p. 6.

RSPCA

Interview with
Amanda Oswald, Corporate Fundraising Manager

The RSPCA is the UK's best known animal welfare charity. It may be a charity rather than a profit-making business and it may have few tangible products to offer, but marketing still plays a central role in fundraising and furthering its campaigns. We spoke to Amanda Oswald, of the corporate fundraising department to find out what marketing means to the RSPCA and how it is evolving.

Overall, the RSPCA's core operations are:

- *Campaigning*: building awareness of animal welfare issues and lobbying government to take action.
- *The inspectorate*: checking up on animal welfare; following up reports of cruelty and pursuing prosecutions. 'We can deal with anything from a stick insect to an elephant if need be.'
- *Rehoming*: caring for abandoned and neglected companion animals and rehoming them where possible.
- *Education*: a comprehensive programme of contact with schools at all levels and the provision of education materials.

Supporting these operations takes money and effort and thus marketing in the RSPCA has two major roles, fundraising, and furthering the charity's aims. The campaign department, for example, is heavily involved in lobbying both the UK and EU governments to get the law changed on issues such as battery farming (*see* Case Study 19.2). The RSPCA's remit covers England and Wales. Scotland has its own parallel organisation. The RSPCA does link up with similar organisations across the EU, however, to lobby on issues of common concern and that are relevant to the European parliament. The RSPCA is a member of Eurogroup, an affiliation of European animal welfare charities.

Fundraising in the RSPCA is continually evolving. Traditionally, there has been a focus on direct mail and that, along with the direct appeal, has been the major source of fundraising. The pressure on direct mail is increasing, however, because consumers are faced with an increasing amount of very professonial materials from many more charities. So the RSPCA is looking at other areas and sees corporate links as having an important future. The corporate fundraising department was formed in 1998, but in building its work and its contacts is looking five to ten years ahead.

Areas covered include:

- *Corporate relations*: the RSPCA working with a company that wants to associate through sponsorship.
- *Affinity products*: pet insurance; a utilities deal ('Paw Power'); credit cards; and perhaps the next area could be telephone/ Internet access deals. The potential of fundraising from these methods is very high as the charity gains a royalty on sales of these products.
- *Payroll giving*: this has the benefit of generating a steady stream of income and increases the RSPCA profile in companies through the back door because it gives the charity a champion in the company. The problem is that a very low percentage of UK employees are enrolled in payroll giving (only 5%) as yet so its potential is not being fully realised.
- *Trading products*: the sale of merchandise (for example Christmas cards) and licensed products. Although the RSPCA is launching more products via retailers and its own animal centres, for example pet accessories, in general, the charity works through third parties and thus does not get involved in manufacturing and distribution operations. The RSPCA also runs its own company, Freedom Food, which promotes ethical farming practices. Freedom Food is self-financing and accredits farmers adopting ethical farming methods and supports retailers in selling accredited merchandise.

In terms of marketing, it is a three way exchange process in the RSPCA's view:

1 The RSPCA gains money and support both from the public and from corporate donors.
2 The corporate donors get a boost to their 'corporate citizenship' image, benefiting from being seen to be giving something back to the community and caring. Where they use the RSPCA as part of a promotion (for example buy this pack and we'll give the RSPCA 5p – see page 810) they also get a sales and image boost. The RSPCA often finds itself being used as a short-term on-pack promotional tool rather than being in a long-term adopted partnership. Part of the remit of the corporate fundraising department is to change that.
3 The individual donor gets a warm feeling from having given to a worthwhile cause they believe in either directly by giving money or indirectly by buying the promotional packs mentioned above.

Individuals tend to have a portfolio of favoured charities that they are prepared to give to although some can be fickle. If a charity does or says something an individual does not like, there is a strong chance that the charity will be dropped from the portfolio, at least for a while. Awareness of the RSPCA brand is measured compared with other animal welfare charities and causes among both the general public and those with a specific interest in animal welfare causes. Among UK charities, the RSPCA is 7th or 8th in the top ten. The RSPCA also uses external agencies to monitor how demographic profiles are changing. It has found, for example, that younger people are willing to give in other ways. Older people respond better to one-off mail

EXECUTIVE INTERVIEW continued

shots while the younger donors want to give but with minimum effort. Thus they prefer to give by standing order, buying into affinity products, or through buying promotional packs as mentioned earlier. The profile of the general RSPCA supporter is also changing. The classic profile was a female 55+ year-old pet owner, but now more donors are from the 18 to 40 age group, recruited through new schemes such as the affinity card. When the affinity MasterCard was launched, 70% of those who signed up to it were totally new to the RSPCA and many were from that younger age group.

Marketing communication is clearly important in creating and retaining donors. Direct marketing is under strain with response rates dropping. It needs to be better targeted than ever and more creative than ever in thinking of mechanisms for asking for money. The charity has done a lot of work on its databases and their management in tracking the frequency of response, type of appeal responded to, size of donations, spontaneous donation rates, preferred ways of giving etc. to help it plan its marketing better.

The RSPCA makes five appeals per year through direct mail and appeals are tailored to suit different donor groups. High value donors are given much more personal treatment and treated separately from other donors as are legacies. One group, for instance, is payroll givers. Mailings to them are less focused on 'more money please' than on 'do you know about these other ways you can help us?'. The RSPCA is looking to develop the most integrated marketing strategy it can in terms of creating donors and then maximising their value through getting them involved in as many other areas as possible. Thus a donor might sign up for an affinity card, for example, and then be persuaded to buy Christmas cards or set up a standing order for a regular direct donation.

Personal selling is used to make direct face to face appeals:

- *Telemarketing* is used either to follow up a mailing or to act as a pre-mailing flag. The use of this has increased dramatically for anything from a cold approach for a donation to a 'thank you for the donation' call. These activities are contracted out to an agency.
- *Charity street collections* are now less to do with shaking a tin in people's faces, although individual branches do still do this with volunteer collectors, than with getting the public to sign up to a standing order type donation. The RSPCA does not, however, do this in the street?
- *Door to door* selling activities are about getting standing orders or covenants set up. Although this is a relatively new initiative, it has been very successful to date. A consortium of charities including the RSPCA use a field marketing agency specialising in traditional professional door to door selling techniques. This is less popular with older people but most are receptive to it. There is telephone support back up either to verify credentials of door to door callers, or to give reassurance and information.

Advertising supports all the RSPCA's activities. *Campaigning advertising* is hard hitting and emotive e.g. the anti-hunting campaign. These are aimed at the public to raise awareness of an issue and tell a story, for example exactly what fox hunting involves. The objective is ultimately to motivate individuals to start lobbying their MPs/MEPs to get the law changed. The *direct marketers* use smaller, simpler, cuddly advertisements to recruit to their mailing lists. *Corporate advertising* is simply aimed at agencies and businesses and again focuses on the cute animal theme with copy about what a link-up could do for your business.

People do, of course, see more than one type of advertising and more than one type of image but there is no inconsistency really as they are focused on different campaigns, messages, contexts and media and people understand that. Even if they find the tough images a bit disturbing, they understand why they are necessary and the images actually work quite well in getting a sometimes unpalatable message across.

In terms of on-line marketing, a website has been successfully launched although it is not yet possible to make on-line donations. The initial reason for setting the website up was to create a presence and a forum for disseminating information. It generates about 75 000 hits per month. The next stage in development is to improve the security and get it set up for trading and the receipt of donations.

Compared with a mainstream commercial organisation, a charity's organisational drive is different. In commerce it is about profit and revenue, whereas in a charity it is primarily about furthering the cause and only secondarily about raising revenue. It is really something of a product orientation. The RSPCA's main aim, ultimately, is to put itself out of business because there is no more animal cruelty and there are no more campaigns to fight.

Find out why this top dog can be your best friend

The RSPCA is the number one charity for animal welfare, tapping into the interests and concerns of most of the population.

Whatever type of animal your company is, whether you're a blue-chip name like Bank of Scotland or a smaller business like Onyx Cartridge Products, you'd be barking mad not to consider linking up with the RSPCA's corporate programme to raise your profile.

We can work together successfully on all types of cause-related marketing – brand sponsorship, licensing, sales promotions or payroll giving, for example.

For details on forming a pedigree partnership please call Amanda Oswald or Joanna Power today on 01403 223267/269.

Or write to : Amanda Oswald, RSPCA, FREEPOST, Horsham, West Sussex, RH12 1ZH. Fax: 01403 241048 or Email: fundraising@rspca.org.uk.

Source: RSPCA /Target Direct Marketing Ltd.

Part II

CUSTOMERS AND MARKETS

Part I emphasised that the customer is the hub of the marketer's universe, so it is only fitting that Part II should give further consideration to this VIP. The dilemma is, however, that each customer is an individual with unique needs and wants, and no organisation can hope to please all of the people all of the time.

Chapter 3 focuses further on the individual as a customer, examining the influences on buying choices and habits, both psychological and social, while looking at the kinds of decision-making processes through which people might or might not go in making a purchase. This is particularly important given the range of cultures to be found across Europe. Chapter 4 explores similar themes, but this time for organisational customers, highlighting the differences between the personal and the corporate shopper.

Additionally, with improvements in distribution and the relaxation of economic barriers, European market potential for many products is unthinkably huge. Organisations therefore have to find ways of breaking markets down into manageably sized segments for each of which essential needs and wants can be defined. This allows a marketing mix to be designed that can at least please a substantial number of people for most of the time. Chapter 5 looks at ways in which this segmentation process can be designed and implemented. The final chapter in this part, Chapter 6, presents an overview of the role of research in defining, monitoring and assessing buyers, markets and marketing activities.

These four chapters are an important foundation for what follows, because context and meaning can only be given to the organisation's decisions on the marketing mix if there are adequate information flows and clear understanding of customers' needs and wants.

3 Consumer Behaviour

LEARNING OBJECTIVES

This chapter will help you to:

1 understand the decision-making processes that consumers go through as they make a purchase;

2 appreciate how those processes differ between different buying situations;

3 understand the influences that affect decision making, whether environmental, psychological or sociocultural; and

4 appreciate the implications of those processes and influences for marketing strategies.

INTRODUCTION

In contrast to Chapter 2, which looked at the broad backdrop against which marketers have to do business, this chapter focuses closely on the consumer, who is at the centre of many a marketer's universe. While the consumer is part of the marketing environment, and is shaped to some extent by the influences already discussed in Chapter 2, it is also very important to understand the more personal and specific influences affecting consumers and the nature of the decision-making processes through which they go.

Figure 3.1 offers a deceptively simple model of buyer behaviour that summarises the content of this chapter. The decision-making process itself is presented as a logical flow of activities, working through from problem recognition to purchase to post-purchase evaluation. The next section of this chapter deals with this in depth. It is important, however, to recognise that it is difficult to generalise about buying situations, as the nature of the decision-making process is bound to differ according to the kind of product or service that is being considered. Later, therefore (pp. 101 *et seq.*), we discuss how the nature of the product and the situation facing the buyer could change the flow of the decision-making process. Compare, for example, what went into your decision to attend university or college with how you decide whether to visit a Pizza Hut or a nightclub.

Example Although many motorists realise that there is a risk of their car breaking down, it is all too easy for them to think that it will not happen to them, and thus not to bother joining a rescue organisation. The challenges for a breakdown service, such as the UK's Automobile Association (AA), are to get motorists first to appreciate the consequences of a breakdown and the urgent need for a fast rescue, then to understand and value the unique benefits of AA membership, and finally to take action by joining the AA. None of this is easy, especially in a case like this where consumers are expected to buy into a service they hope they will never need and from which the main benefit is psychological 'peace of mind' rather than anything immediately tangible.

A hard-hitting advertising campaign, 'the 4th Emergency Service', was used to cut through motorists' inertia and to communicate both the tangible and intangible benefits from AA membership simply but memorably. The value of the 'real' emergency services is well understood and so the advertisement showed powerful footage of the fire, police and ambulance services at work, as well as the AA. Motorists' respect and perceptions of the professionalism and the essential nature of the emergency services were thus associated with and transferred to the AA (http://www.theaa.co.uk).

The advertisement also brought home to motorists the importance of breakdown cover by inducing a little fear and it did lead to consumer action: AA membership increased by 1.8 million immediately after the campaign's launch. Incredibly, 97 per cent of people who claimed to have seen the advertisement believed that the AA actually is the fourth 'real' emergency service (Clay, 1998). Engendering such a belief, even if it is somewhat mistaken, gives the AA a clear competitive edge in terms of 'professional rescue' over its rivals (who were communicating only in terms of boring issues such as their technical capabilities or how fast they can reach a breakdown) and makes it more likely that the AA will be the first choice of that 97 per cent when they are seeking breakdown cover (Clay, 1998; O'Sullivan, 1997).

The decision-making process is also affected by a number of other more complex influences, as can be seen in Fig. 3.1. Some of these influences relate to the wider marketing environment in which the decision is being made (*see* pp. 104–7). Others, however, relate to the individual purchaser and therefore pp. 107–17 will consider those influences emanating from within the individual such as personality, attitudes and learning. Finally, pp. 117–28 will look at how the individual decisions are affected by their social context, especially family and cultural groupings.

THE DECISION-MAKING PROCESS

Even thinking about your own experiences as a consumer is enough to help you to appreciate the variety of goods that people purchase, the individuality of each purchasing episode and the complexity of the influences affecting the final decision. Nevertheless, there have been many attempts to create models of **consumer decision making** of greater or lesser complexity and detail that try to capture the richness of the experience, such as those proposed by Howard and Sheth (1969) and Engel, Kollat and Blackwell (1978). The Engel, Blackwell and Miniard (1990) model presented here, although more concise and simpler in its outline, provides a framework that still allows us to consider, through discussion, many of the more complex elements. It traces the progress of a purchasing event stage by stage from the buyer's point of view, including the definition of likely information needs and a discussion of the level of rationality and analytical behaviour leading to the eventual decision.

We now look at each stage in turn.

Problem recognition

In trying to rationalise the decision-making process, this is a good place to begin. After all, if you are not aware that you have a 'problem', how can you decide to pur-

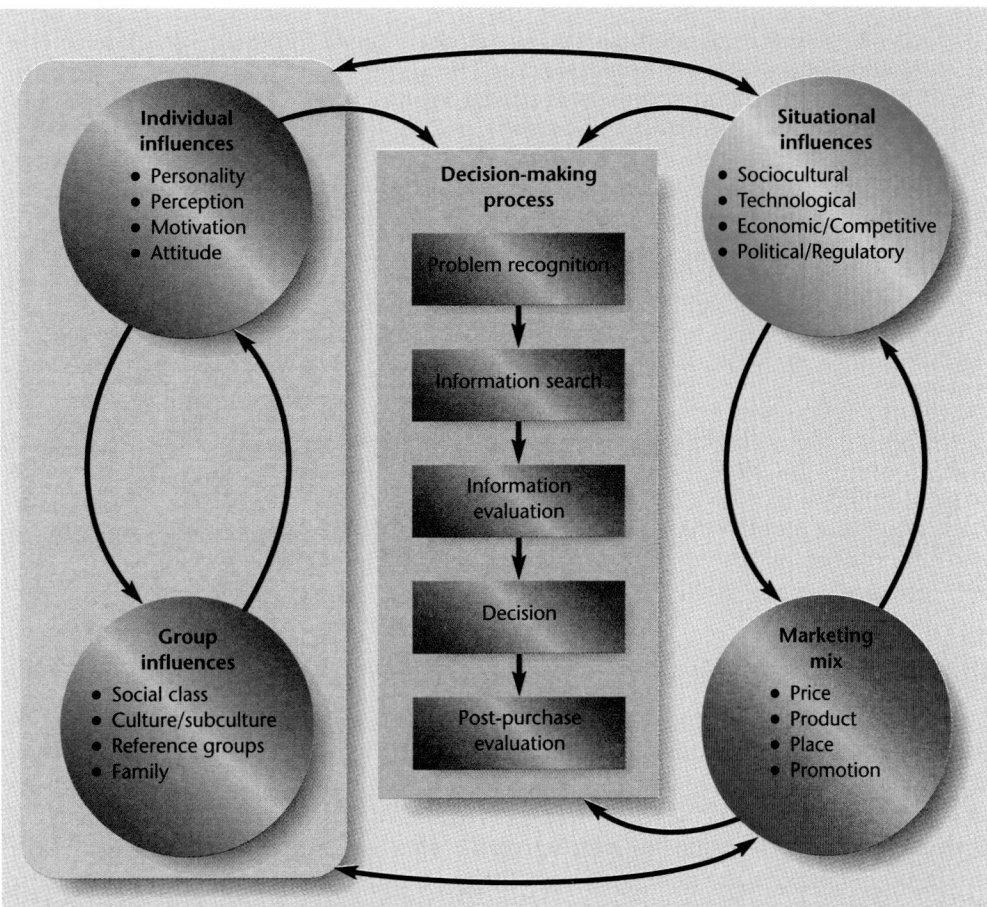

FIGURE 3.1

The consumer buying decision-making process and its influencing factors

chase something to solve it? More functional purchases, such as replenishing stocks of washing powder or petrol, may be initiated by a casual glance at current stock levels. Other purchases may be triggered by a definable event. If, for example, the exhaust falls off your car, you will soon become aware of the nature of the problem and the kind of purchase that will provide the remedy.

Those are very practical and straightforward examples, but not all situations are quite so self-explanatory. Where psychological needs are involved, the **problem recognition** may be a slow dawning or may lead to a sudden impulse, when the consumer, realising that the current position or feeling is not the desired one, decides to do something to change it through a purchase (Bruner and Pomazal, 1988). Imagine, for instance, that you are wandering round the supermarket after a tough day at work. You're tired, listless and a bit depressed. You've filled your trolley with the potatoes, bread and milk you intended to buy, but you also slip a bar of chocolate (or worse!) in there on the basis that it will cheer you up as you drive home. The 'problem' here is less definable, based on a vague psychological feeling, and it follows that the solution is also less definable – it could be chocolate, cream buns, wine or clothing, whatever takes the purchaser's fancy.

What the examples given so far do have in common, however, is that the impetus to go into a purchasing decision-making routine comes from the consumer. The consumer identifies or recognises the problem, independently from the marketer, and looks for a solution. As will be seen in the following sections, marketers can then use the marketing mix elements to influence the choice of solution. It is also possible, however, for marketers to trigger the process by using the marketing mix to bring a problem to the consumer's attention. If one was to be cynical, one could accuse them of deliberately creating problems in order to stimulate purchase.

> **Example** The manufacturers of Radion laundry products ran an advertising campaign in the UK featuring a housewife who suddenly realised that even though the shirt she was ironing had just been washed, there was still a sweaty smell clinging to its armpits. Radion, of course, has the power to eliminate this in the wash. Housewives across the country supposedly became wracked with fear and guilt, asking themselves: 'Do I have this problem? Should I switch to Radion?' A problem had been created in the consumer's mind, and a decision-making process initiated, largely through the marketer's efforts.

There is, of course, a significant difference between being aware of a need or problem and being able to do something about it. Many needs are latent and remain unfulfilled, either because consumers decide not to do anything about it now, or because they are unable to do anything. We might all feel the need for a three-week holiday in some exotic part of the world, but we must be not only willing, but also financially able, to disappear over the horizon. Problem recognition, if it is to lead anywhere, therefore requires both the willingness and the ability to fulfil the emerging need.

Whether the problem recognition is stimulated internally (i.e. originates within the consumer) or externally (i.e. is triggered by marketing or other pressures), there are still several stages left in the decision-making process.

Information search

Defining the problem is one thing, but defining and implementing the solution are something else. The questions to be answered include what kind of purchase will solve the problem, where and how it can be obtained, what information is needed to arrive at a decision and where that information is available. In some cases, consumers will actively search out relevant information with a view to using it in making a decision, but they can also acquire information passively, storing it away until it is needed. Thus Bloch *et al.* (1986) distinguish between ongoing search (browsing and storing for future reference) and purposeful search with a particular objective in mind. Daily, consumers are exposed to a wide range of media all designed to influence awareness and recall of particular products and services. Thus they 'know' that Radion eliminates sweaty smells before they get anywhere near a conscious choice of laundry product in the supermarket. When they do get to the point of purchasing, the manufacturers hope that they will recall that knowledge and use it in making the brand choice.

Similarly, the Cheltenham & Gloucester mortgage advertisement is designed to appeal to someone who is already considering house purchase. It is hardly likely to inspire consumers to move house, but it could be useful if consumers are worried about finding the right mortgage for their circumstances before they start looking seriously. In some cases, a consumer might not be planning to move immediately, but the C&G would hope that they will recall the advertisement when the time does come.

The car exhaust example continues to be reasonably straightforward. You need a new exhaust and a supplier must be found. Since consumers usually fall back on their previous experiences and knowledge before undertaking time-consuming research, you may immediately think of a company that you have used before and have been satisfied with, one whose advertising you have seen, or perhaps you ask a close friend to recommend one. Not all external sources of information are controlled by the marketer – don't forget the power of word of mouth as a marketing tool. Friends, family and colleagues, for example, may all give advice, whether based on experience, knowledge or opinion, to the would-be decision maker in this phase. In choosing a university to study at, for example, many overseas students seek advice from friends who have already studied at various universities to narrow down the number of options to consider. Although the type of product and the importance of the purchase may differ, the basic principle is the same. People are more likely to trust information

The information search is made easy with freefone and on-line access.

Source: C&G.

given through word of mouth, because the source is generally assumed to be unbiased and trustworthy, and the information itself often derives from first-hand experience.

In other situations, the consumer might seek out information from specialist publications, retailers or even from marketing literature. For example, when buying a car, potential buyers will probably visit competing dealerships to talk to sales staff, look closely at the merchandise and collect brochures. Additionally, they might consult what they consider to be unbiased expert sources of advice such as *What Car?* magazine, and begin to take more notice of car advertisements in all media.

In replacing the car exhaust, of course, you might simply turn to the *Yellow Pages* telephone directory and look under 'Exhaust System Dealers'. The impulse buying of chocolate in the supermarket requires even less information searching than that. It is likely to be restricted to seeing what is available within that particular store at that particular time. Think about why this is the case before you get to the later section of this chapter on buying situations (pp. 101–4), where variations in the extent, rationality and formality of the information search in different situations will be discussed.

Hauser *et al.* (1993) emphasise the fact that time pressure can interfere with the information search. They found that consumers spend less time searching for different sources as pressure increases. At the other end of the spectrum, however, **information overload** may cause problems for the potential purchaser. There is evidence to suggest that consumers cannot cope with too much information at product level (Keller and Staelin, 1987). Thus the greater the relevance of the information to consumers, such as the key benefits and applications of the product, the easier it is for them to assimilate and process that information as part of their decision making. In other words, better and more extensive information may actually lead to poorer buying decisions! Similarly, at brand level Jacoby *et al.* (1974) found on the one hand that more on-pack information tends to make it more difficult for the consumer to select the most appropriate brand, but on the other hand that more information positively affected the consumer's level of certainty and satisfaction regarding the selection. There is clearly a fine balance to be achieved between keeping imagery and messages clean, simple and easily understood, and giving consumers enough information to allow them to appreciate the full depth of character of the product and the range of its potential benefits, so that they can develop appropriate expectations and post-purchase evaluative criteria.

MARKETING AND IT   **Surfing the Net**

Information search has been assisted by the growing use of the Internet. Although there is still a long way to go before the Internet is used by a significant proportion of the population, the level of usage rose quickly from around 17 per cent of all UK adults in 1997 (*Marketing Week*, 1998) to around 29 per cent by the end of 1998 (*Marketing Week*, 1999b). An NOP survey revealed that nearly 90 per cent of users source 'general information' through the Internet. According to Shaddick (1998), regular users tend to be more affluent, with an average income of £31 000 compared with the national average of £17 500. This is supported by the NOP findings, which indicate that over 30 per cent of the AB social group has Internet access at home (and some will have access at work instead or as well), twice as many as in any other group (*Marketing Week*, 1999b).

The product areas benefiting from Internet exposure reflect the AB group, including information searching on software, records and CDs, travel, entertainment and books. Information searching on the Internet can be daunting as there are so many websites, but search engines such as Lycos, Yahoo! or Infoseek can guide the consumer to the most obscure information. More interesting is the automated robot, 'bot', which can search and compare prices for the same item from different websites. But if all this technology is too much and you just want to find a relaxing holiday, Internet travel agents such as Travelocity will offer you a selection of holidays to suit your budget, preferred locations, dates, airlines or tour operators.

Source: O'Connor and Galvin, (1999).

Whatever form the information search takes, the data gathered are useless until they are evaluated. However, it is likely that many consumers proceed to evaluation with a minimum of information that furthermore may be too partial, biased or poorly structured for the decision that needs to be made. This is bound to influence the quality of the eventual decision.

Information evaluation

On what criteria do you evaluate the information gathered? A typical *Yellow Pages* may provide up to 10 pages of exhaust system dealerships, featuring over 100 potential outlets within reasonable travelling distance. If you have had no previous experience of any of them, then you have to find a means of differentiating between them. You are unlikely to investigate all of them, since that would take too long, and so you may draw up a shortlist on the basis of those with the biggest feature entries in *Yellow Pages*, or those who also advertise prominently in the local press or on television. Such advertising may emphasise the advantages of using a particular outlet, pointing out to the consumer what the appropriate evaluative criteria are (speed, friendliness or price, for example). Location may also be an important factor; some outlets are closer to home or work than others. You might telephone three or four of them, dismiss any whose telephone manner is either too surly or too patronising, then compare the rest on the basis of price or their ability to do the job immediately.

Meanwhile, back in the supermarket, your information evaluation is likely to be less time consuming and less systematic. Faced with a set of brands of chocolate that are known and liked, the evaluation is cursory: 'What do I feel like eating?' The nearest to systematic thinking might be (in desperation) the evaluation of which one really represents the most chocolate for the price. Of course, if a new brand has appeared on the chocolate shelf, then that might break the habitual, unconscious grabbing at the familiar wrapper, and make a consumer stop and look closely to evaluate what the new product has to offer in comparison with the old ones.

What has been happening to varying degrees in the above examples is that the consumer has started to narrow down from a wide list of potential options to an **evoked set** (Howard and Sheth, 1969), a final shortlist for serious appraisal. Being a part of the consumer's evoked set, and staying there, is clearly important to the marketer, although it is not always easy. Sutton (1987), for instance, found that it was easier for a new product or brand to enter the evoked set than it was for an existing one that had been considered previously, but rejected.

With the car exhaust, constructing the evoked set means narrowing down to the list of outlets that will be telephoned, whereas with the chocolate purchase, the unconscious visual scan across the shelf may lead to a more deliberate choice between a Snickers, a Mars bar and a Twix. To make a choice from within the evoked set, the consumer needs either a formal or an informal means of selecting from the small number of choices available. This, therefore, implies some definition of evaluative or choice criteria.

Again, marketers will be trying to influence this stage. This can be done, for example, through their communications campaigns (more of this in Chapter 14 and subsequent chapters) which may implant images of products in the consumer's mind so that they seem familiar (and therefore less threatening) at the point of sale. They may also stress particular product attributes, both to increase the importance of that attribute in the consumer's mind, i.e. to make sure that the attribute is number one on the list of evaluative criteria, and to ensure that the consumer believes that a particular brand is unsurpassed in terms of that attribute. Radion and residual armpit smells must be inextricably linked in the consumer's mind, and eradication of armpit smells must be important to the consumer. Point-of-sale material can also reinforce these things, for example through displays, leaflets, the wording on packaging (Chapter 7) and on-pack promotions.

Generally, therefore, what is happening is that without necessarily being conscious of it, the potential buyer is constructing a list of performance criteria, then assessing each supplier or available brand against it. This assessment can be based on objective criteria, related to the attributes of the product and its use (price, specification, service etc.), or subjective criteria such as status, fit with self-image or trust of the supplier.

To make the decision easier, abstract attributes, such as 'convenience', 'fun' or 'ease of use', are more likely to be used when direct comparison between choices is not easy (Korfman, 1991), for example chocolate vs biscuits, going to the cinema vs going to a nightclub, or even *Shakespeare in Love* vs *Reservoir Dogs* at the video hire shop! Making any decision can be a demanding exercise in terms of time and mental effort, and thus the consumer often adopts mental 'rules of thumb' that cut corners and lead to a faster decision. The consumer is especially prepared to compromise on the quality and

TABLE 3.1

Consumer market beliefs

Products and brands
- The best brands are the ones that sell best
- National brands (manufacturer or retail) are always better than local ones unless you know better
- Generic brands are well-known brand names sold under a different label
- Keep clear of products new to the market until 'bugs' have been ironed out

Store
- You can tell a store by its window display
- Larger stores offer better prices than smaller ones
- Speciality stores are great for learning about product options, but it is best to buy from a discount store
- A store that offers good value on some of its items probably offers it on all its items
- Small stores give better, more personal service than large ones

Price
- Higher prices within a store often mean higher quality
- Sale items can involve seconds and poorer quality merchandise
- Sales are designed to move poor sellers
- Prices will fall soon after the product is launched

Promotion
- When purchasing heavily advertised products you pay for the label and advertising, not higher quality
- The harder the sell, the poorer the product quality
- Free gifts linked to products mean the product may not be up to much

Packaging
- Big containers are always cheaper per unit than smaller sizes
- Environmentally friendly packaging adds cost to the product
- Quality packaging means a quality product.

Source: Adapted from Duncan (1990).

thoroughness of assessment when the problem-solving situation is less risky and complicated. Table 3.1, based on the work of Duncan (1990), highlights some of the market beliefs widely held by consumers. These beliefs may not relate directly to the specific purchasing situation in hand, but they do act as general decision rules to cut out many of the tedious preliminaries of assessing alternative products. They may focus on brand, store choice, pricing, promotion or packaging, and will serve to limit the size of the evoked set and to eliminate some of the options.

All of this sets the scene for the next stage in the process: the decision.

Decision

The decision may be a natural outcome of the evaluation stage, if one supplier is noticeably more impressive on all the important criteria than the rest. If the choice is not as clear cut as this, the consumer may have to prioritise the criteria further, perhaps deciding that price or convenience is the one overriding factor. In the car exhaust example, the decision making is a conscious act, whereas with the impulse purchase of chocolate, the decision may be made almost unconsciously.

In any case, at this stage the consumer must finalise the proposed deal, and this may take place in a retail store, over the telephone, by mail or in the consumer's own home. In the supermarket, finalising the deal may be as simple as putting the bar of chocolate into the trolley with the rest of the shopping and then paying for it at the checkout. With more complex purchases, however, the consumer may have the discretion to negotiate the fine details of cash or credit, any trade-in, order quantity and delivery dates, for example. This negotiation (*see* Chapter 17 for more on negotiation) may involve further trading of concessions between variables, so that, for instance, you can have your new car within a week as long as you are prepared to accept a red one. If the outcome of the negotiation is not satisfactory, then the consumer may regretfully decide not to go ahead with the purchase after all, or rethink the decision in favour of another supplier – you cannot be certain of your customer until they have either handed over their money or signed the contract!

Suppliers can, of course, make it easy or difficult for potential customers to make their purchases. Lack of sales assistants on the shop floor, long queues or bureaucratic purchasing procedures may all tax the patience of consumers, giving them time either to decide to shop elsewhere or not to bother buying at all. Even if they do persist and make the purchase (eventually), their impression of the supplier's service and efficiency is going to be damaged and this may influence their repeat purchasing behaviour negatively. A traveller who has to queue for 20 minutes to buy a rail ticket from a cashier may well decide to travel by car next time, whereas one who can purchase a ticket quickly through an automated ticketing machine, such as those found in railway stations and more recently in airports around Europe, will have no negative impressions of service provision.

Example The day and night Robo Shop in Tokyo is the ultimate in service provision to make the purchase decision very easy and convenient. The shop has no staff and a wide variety of products from magazines and drinks through to pot plants and watches. Products are behind glass in segregated rows and are ordered, paid for by credit card, and then collected from each display area by a programmed collection bin. This bin empties purchases at the collection point and the customer leaves the store having had no human contact. This could be the next generation of convenience stores, if any lingering doubts about security or hostility to faceless, inhuman service are overcome (*The Grocer*, 1998a).

Even assuming that all these barriers are overcome, the story does not end here. The consumer's involvement with the product does not finish when cash changes hands, nor should the marketer's involvement with the consumer.

Post-purchase evaluation

Whatever the purchase, there is likely to be some level of **post-purchase evaluation** to assess whether the product or its supplier lived up to the expectations raised in the earlier stages of the process. Particularly if the decision process has been difficult, or if the consumer has invested a lot of time, effort and money in it, then there may be doubt as to whether the right decision has actually been made. This is what Festinger (1957) labelled **cognitive dissonance**, meaning that consumers are 'psychologically uncomfortable', trying to balance the choice made against the doubts still held about it. Such dissonance may be aggravated where consumers are exposed to marketing communication that sings the praises of the features and benefits of the rejected alternatives. Generally speaking, the more alternatives that have been rejected, and the more comparatively attractive those alternatives appear to be, the greater the dissonance. Conversely, the more similar to the chosen product the rejected alternatives are, the less the dissonance. It is also likely that dissonance will occur with more significant purchases, such as extended problem-solving items like cars and houses, because the buyer is far more likely to review and assess the decision consciously afterwards.

Clearly, such psychological discomfort is not pleasant and the consumer will work towards reducing it, perhaps by trying to filter out the messages that undermine the choice made (for example advertising for a product that was a rejected alternative) and paying extra attention to supportive messages (for example advertising for the chosen alternative). This all underlines the need for post-purchase reassurance, whether through advertising, after sales follow-up calls and even the tone of an instruction manual ('Congratulations on choosing the Acme Home Nuclear Reactor Kit, we know it will give you many years' faithful service ...'). Consumers like to be reminded and reassured that they have made a wise choice, that they have made the best choice for them. From the marketer's point of view, as well as offering post-purchase reassurance, they can minimise the risk of dissonance by making sure that potential buyers have a realistic picture of the product, its capabilities and its characteristics. Exaggerated advertising simply raises expectations that cannot possibly be fulfilled in reality, and disappointment and dissonance are almost certain. Another way of making sure that the potential buyer's expectations are rooted in reality is to let them sample the product before purchase, where possible. With fmcg (fast moving consumer goods) products, this is relatively simple to do and allows consumers to pass judgement on product benefits based on experience, rather than simply on what an advertiser tells them (*see* Chapter 16 for more on sampling). With a higher priced, less frequently purchased product such as a car, it is more difficult to offer samples, but at least a long test drive can go some way to creating realistic expectations and emphasising potentially negative points before the customer commits to a purchase.

Thus the post-purchase evaluation stage is important for a number of reasons. Primarily, it will affect whether the consumer ever buys this product again. If expectations have not been met, then the product may not even make the shortlist next time. If, on the other hand, expectations have been met or even exceeded, then a strong possibility of lasting loyalty has been created. The next shortlist may be a shortlist of one! It is important to remember that consumers are not passive, inanimate elements in the marketing process. They do not fade away into insignificance if their relationship with a particular product or supplier ends. According to Smith (1993), dissatisfied customers will tell up to 11 other people about their bad experience, which is two to three times more people than a satisfied customer will talk to. Thus it is important for the marketer to consider how the risks of a poor outcome at the post-purchase phase can best be reduced.

> **Example** Consumer post-purchase evaluation is personal and subjective and can sometimes even lead to an exaggerated perception of a product's benefits. Household anti-bacterial sprays and germ killers, for example, appear to get things clean, fresh and sparkling. Their advertising and packaging present a confident, no-nonsense image, they promise protection and the total annihilation of dirt and bugs, and their contents often smell strong and powerful. All of these pre- and post-purchase messages, influences and experiences lead some consumers to think that such cleaning products are an adequate substitute for good general kitchen hygiene. Thus 20 per cent of consumers do not change their dishcloths regularly and over 65 per cent do not wash their hands before preparing food. Some experts have criticised manufacturers for lulling them into a false sense of security. Perhaps, the experts say, consumer education should be a much higher priority so that the limits of such products and their proper role within good hygiene practice are better understood (Norton, 1997).

As has been mentioned already, the marketer can influence the information evaluation that sets up product performance criteria in the consumer's mind. Marketing is about making promises, and the post-purchase evaluation is, to some extent, a measure of how true those promises were. If, therefore, the needs and wants of the consumer have been carefully researched and the marketing mix tailored, balanced and implemented accordingly, then the post-purchase stage should be a happy one for all parties.

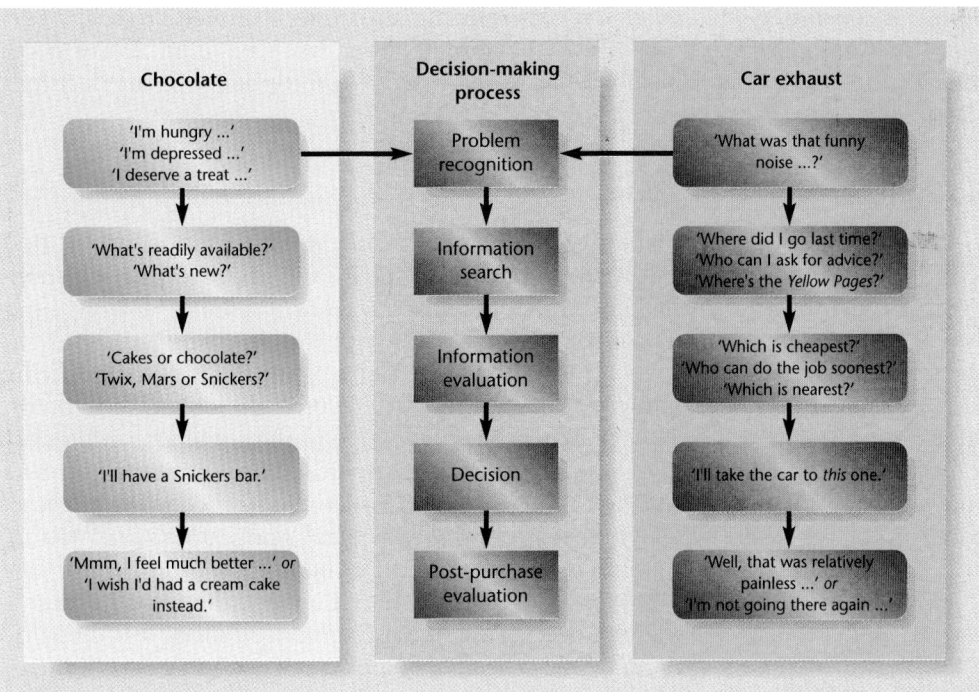

FIGURE 3.2

The decision-making processes for chocolate and car exhausts

Monitoring of post-purchase feelings is an important task of marketing, not only to identify areas in which the product (or its associated marketing mix) falls short of expectations, but also to identify any unexpectedly pleasant surprises the purchaser may have had. The product may, for instance, have strengths that are being under-sold. This is a natural part of the cycle of product and service development, improvement and evolution.

To recap on the stages in the decision-making process, look at Fig. 3.2. This summarises the general process, and then shows its specific application in the context of (a) the impulse purchase of chocolate, and (b) buying and fitting a car exhaust. There are some points to note about the process as presented here. First, the consumer may choose to end the process at any stage. Perhaps the information search reveals that there is no obvious acceptable solution to the problem, or the information evaluation demonstrates that the cost of solving the problem is too high. It is, of course, the marketer's job to sustain the consumer's interest throughout this process and to prevent them from opting out of it. Second, the process does not necessarily have to run from stage 1 to stage 5 in an unbroken flow. The consumer may backtrack at any point to an earlier stage and reiterate the process. Even on the verge of a decision, it may be felt necessary to go back and get more information, just to make sure. Finally, the time taken over the process may vary enormously, depending on the nature of the purchase and the nature of the purchaser. Many months of agonising may go into making an expensive, important purchase, while only a few seconds may be invested in choosing a bar of chocolate. The next section looks more closely at this issue.

BUYING SITUATIONS

In the discussion of the decision-making process, it has been made clear that both the flow and the formality of the process, and the emphasis that is put on each stage, will vary from situation to situation. Some of these variations are to do with the particular environment relevant to the transaction (*see* p. 104 *et seq.*), while others emanate from the consumer (pp. 107 *et seq.*) or from the consumer's immediate social surroundings (pp. 117 *et seq.*). The current section, however, will look more closely at the effect of the type of *purchasing situation* on the extent and formality of the decision-making process.

Routine problem solving

As the heading of this section implies, a **routine problem solving** purchasing situation is one that the consumer is likely to experience on a regular basis. Most grocery shopping falls into this category, where particular brands are purchased habitually without recourse to any lengthy decision-making process. As with the chocolate-buying example above, there is virtually no information search and evaluation, and the buying decision is made simultaneously with (if not in advance of) the problem recognition stage. This explains why many fmcg manufacturers spend so much time and effort trying to generate such loyalty and why it is so difficult for new products to break into an established market. When the consumer thinks 'We've run out of Colgate' rather than 'We've run out of toothpaste', or when beans really does mean Heinz, then the competition has an uphill marketing task on its hands.

As well as building regular shopping habits, i.e. brand loyalty, the manufacturer is also trying to capitalise on impulse purchasing of many products within this category. While toothpaste and beans can be the objective of a planned shopping trip ('When I go to the supermarket, I need to get ...'), some other products may be purchased as the result of a sudden impulse. The impulse may be triggered, as mentioned in the previous section, by a realisation of need ('I'm depressed and this chocolate is just what I need to cheer me up'), or by external stimuli, for example eye-catching packaging attracting the shopper's attention. The trigger need not even be inside the store: the smell of coffee or freshly baked bread wafting into the street may draw a customer into a café on impulse, or an attractive shop window display may attract a potential customer into a clothing store that they otherwise had no intention of visiting (even though clothing is not necessarily a routine problem solving purchase). Whatever the trigger, there is no conscious preplanning or information search, but a sudden surge of desire that can only be fulfilled by a purchase that the shopper may or may not later regret.

Example   In a visual brand audit of the confectionery sector, several types of shoppers were found. The 'blinkered shopper' has mainly rational motives for purchasing, including meeting a functional need such as hunger or oral hygiene. The 'magpie', however, seeks confectionery to fulfil more emotional needs such as giving oneself a treat. Over 70 per cent of consumers purchase something that can be eaten immediately. Packaging is thus crucial for attracting the consumer's attention, leading to purchase. This is particularly true for new products, especially if the brand name is unfamiliar. The behavioural sequence seems to be touch, sense and then select. Manufacturers can support the consumer through this process with attractive design and good on-pack information (*The Grocer*, 1998c).

The items that fall into the routine problem solving category do tend to be low-risk, low priced, frequently purchased products. The consumer is happy that a particular brand satisfies their requirements, and there is not enough benefit to be gained from switching brands to make the effort of information search and evaluation of alternatives worth while. These so-called low involvement purchases simply do not carry enough risk, whether measured in terms of financial loss, personal disappointment or damage to social status, for the consumer to get excited about the importance of 'making the right decision'.

Ehrenberg and Goodhart (1980) proposed a simple three-stage model that covers many routine problem solving purchases. Stage 1 is **awareness** of the brand or product, stage 2 is **trial**, and if the outcome of the trial is satisfactory, stage 3 is **repeat purchase**. Over time, therefore, the repeat purchase becomes habitual, with little or no re-evaluation of the decision. This explains why many manufacturers invest in heavy promotion to generate awareness and trial of new products, as these are necessary foundations for longer-term repeat purchasing behaviour. Later research further supported the relationship between awareness, trial and repeat purchasing, even where consumers indulged in multi-brand and multi-store shopping.

Limited problem solving

Limited problem solving is a little more interesting for the consumer. This is a buying situation that occurs less frequently and probably involves more deliberate decision making than routine problems do. The goods will be moderately expensive (in the eyes of the individual consumer) and perhaps will be expected to last a long time. Thus the risks inherent in a 'wrong' decision are that much higher. There will, therefore, be some element of information search and evaluation, but this is still unlikely to absorb too much time and effort.

An example of this could be a consumer's purchase of a new piece of hi-fi equipment. If it is some years since they last bought one, they might feel that they need to update their knowledge of who makes what, who sells what, and the price brackets in this market. The information search is likely to include talking to any friends with recent hi-fi buying experience, and a trip round locally accessible electrical goods retailers. To this particular consumer, this is an important decision, but not a crucial one. If they make a 'wrong' choice (as defined in the post-purchase evaluation stage), they will be disappointed, but will feel that they have spent too much money to allow them simply to discard the offending product. Having said that, provided that the hi-fi fulfils its primary function of producing music on demand, they can learn to live with it and the damage is limited.

Some healthcare products might fall into this category of purchase, although they are relatively low-value items. The discomfort caused by minor illnesses can be very stressful for sufferers facing another day at work, and thus it is important to take the best remedy to relieve the symptoms and perhaps effect a cure. In addition, such illnesses are so infrequently suffered that consumers might not be aware of medicines available over the counter (OTC). The purchase thus becomes a limited problem-solving exercise. Retailers and manufacturers do not, however, want consumers to wait until they are ill before making a purchase. They are keen to encourage consumers to stock up on remedies such as Hedex or Andrews Seltzer Extra for common ailments while they are well so that when illness strikes, an appropriate treatment is at hand. The trend towards self-medication, in part supported by government initiatives to encourage sales of more OTC medicines, has created a growing market worth £269 million, with SmithKline Beecham capturing over 20 per cent of it (McLoughlin, 1997). Retailers are opening more pharmacies and allocating more shelf space to capitalise on this by reminding consumers of the need to have the right cure for common ailments ready in the home.

Limited problem solving is also likely to occur in the choice of service products. In purchasing a holiday or choosing a dentist (word-of-mouth recommendation?) the consumer has one chance to make the right choice. Once you are on the plane or in the dentist's chair, it is too late and the wrong choice could turn out to be expensive and painful. The necessity to get it right first time is thus likely to lead to a conscious and detailed information search, perhaps even going as far as extended problem solving, to which we now turn.

Extended problem solving

Extended problem solving represents a much more serious investment of money, time and effort from the consumer and, consequently, a much higher risk. Purchases of major capital items such as houses or cars fall into this category. These purchases occur extremely infrequently for most people and, given that they often require some kind of a loan, involve a serious long-term commitment. This means that the purchaser is motivated to gather as much information as possible, and to think quite consciously and systematically about what the decision-making criteria should be. That is not to say that the final decision will necessarily be made on purely functional, conscious or rational grounds. If, for example, two different makes of car have similar technical specifications, price, delivery and after sales service terms, then final differentiation may be in terms of: 'which one will most impress the neighbours?'

The significance of buying situations

So what? Why categorise purchases in this way? After all, one consumer's limited problem-solving situation may be another's extended problem. This matters because it may add another dimension to help marketers develop more efficient and appropriate marketing strategies. If a significant group of potential buyers can be defined who clearly regard the purchase of a hi-fi as a limited problem solving situation, then that has implications for the manufacturers in terms of both how and what to communicate, and where and how to distribute. If consumers are thought to regard a product as a limited problem solving purchase, then perhaps the marketer will prefer to distribute it through specialist outlets, where the potential buyer can get expert advice, and can spend time making detailed product comparisons. Communication may contain a lot of factual information about technical specifications and product features (i.e. what the product can do), as well as selling product benefits (i.e. what all that means to you). In contrast, the same product as a routine problem solving exercise may be distributed as widely as possible, to ensure availability, regardless of retailer specialism or expertise, and the communication might centre on product image and benefits, ignoring the detailed information.

ENVIRONMENTAL INFLUENCES

This section is about the wider context in which the decision making is taking place. All of these environmental influences have already been covered in some depth in Chapter 2, so their treatment here will be brief. What is important is to recognise that decision-making is not completely divorced from the environment in which it is happening, whether the consumer is conscious of it or not.

Sociocultural influences

There are many pressures in this category and pp. 117 *et seq.* looks at them more closely. Individuals are influenced both by current trends in society as a whole and by a need to conform with the norms of the various social groups to which they belong, as well as to enhance their status within those groups.

In wider society, for example, there has been a move in recent years towards demanding more environmentally friendly products, and many consumers who are not necessarily 'deep green' have allowed this to influence their decision making, looking more favourably on CFC-free, recycled or non-animal tested products. Examples of social group pressures can be seen in children's markets. Many parents feel unfairly pressured into buying particular goods or brands because the children's friends all have them. There is a fear of the child being marginalised or bullied because they don't possess the 'right' things, whether those are trainers, mountain bikes or computer games.

MARKETING IN ACTION   Millennium woman

The role of women in society and their participation in business and domestic decision making have changed radically since the 1970s. This is of great interest to marketers as they now find that women have more influence and more spending power. Croft (1998b) reports a survey suggesting that 35 per cent of decision-making business people are women. This is perhaps not surprising, given that it has also been reported that more women than ever in the UK are earning more than £25 000 and that female unemployment is less than half that of men. Building careers also means that women are having babies later in life and thus in the meantime have more confidence and more disposable income to spend on themselves.

Marketers in traditionally male-dominated sectors are now considering how to tap into female spending. Pub chain operators Whitbread (http://www.whitbread.com) estimated that the branded 'female-friendly' pub sector would attract 15 per cent more customers between 1998 and 2003, compared with only 4 per cent for more traditional pub formats (Rushe, 1998). Whitbread is thus spending about £140 million a year on the branded pubs and only £20 million on the others. The company's chief executive told city investors: 'The future is female.' To help women make the decision to go to pubs and to feel good about the experience, brewers are making pubs cleaner (especially the toilets!) and more stylish. They are also offering more food with table service because many women do not like visiting the bar. It is hoped that women will want to go to pubs on their own as well as positively influencing their partners to decide on the pub as a night out.

The DIY industry is also working out how to appeal to women:

> *This industry can grow only if it breaks down the old hairy-chested image and gives women what they want, without expecting them to act like tradesmen.*
> (Phil Duddridge, buyer for B&Q, quoted by Matthews, 1998)

In 1998, 48 per cent of DIY buyers were women, buying either as gifts for partners or for their own use. To encourage this, B&Q is making its DIY stores less intimidating for women, decor colours are increasingly reflecting high street fashion shades, and manufacturers are producing new products specifically targeted at women. Black and Decker (http://www.blackanddecker.com) is developing lighter, easier to use power tools (perhaps it should be called the Girl Power Range?) and Bosch (http:www.bosch.de) runs weekend DIY courses for women (Crosbie, 1998). UniBond (http://www.unibond.co.uk) spent £1 million on a new range of bathroom sealants packaged in aerosol cans to look like hairspray. Much of this is happening because women's attitudes to DIY are changing, partly because there are more single-parent households headed by women, and partly because those women who do have partners get frustrated waiting for men to get round to doing the DIY jobs. The brand manager at UniBond takes this seriously as an influence on buying behaviour:

> *While women traditionally did little more than choose the colour scheme or pick out the wallpaper, a good many have found that rather than asking their husbands to tile the bathroom or paint the ceiling, it is a lot less hassle to do it themselves.* (Jo Wren, brand manager for UniBond, quoted by Matthews, 1998)

This means that women are participating much more in the decision-making process for these kinds of products. They are acting as initiators, deciders, purchasers and users as well as being influencers. Mum is no longer chained to the kitchen sink; she is installing it. Women need more 'female-friendly' information and product design and packaging to help them through the decision-making process. Manufacturers and retailers which provide this are more likely to get the purchase in the first place and then get the positive post-purchase evaluations that lead to repeat business.

Women, however, seem to want some much more fundamental things from retailers as well. A report by agency GfK GB, *Working Women and Retailers*, found that working women in particular hate shopping and feel that retailers do not serve their needs well. Working women are impatient: they do not have much time to shop and hate being delayed in queues. Supermarkets in particular gave cause for complaint, not just because of queues (scanners at checkouts are only effective in saving time if the shopper can pack faster than the cashier can scan – most shoppers just end up getting hot and bothered playing 'beat the scanner'!), but also because of poor lighting, unhelpful staff, crowds and, most of all, changes in store layout. It seems, then, that retailers which want to win female customer loyalty, and particularly that of working women, need to think not only about what they offer and how they offer it, but also about their systems and the extent to which they really understand the shopper (Croft, 1999).

Technological influences

Technology affects many aspects of consumer decision making. Database technology, for example, as discussed in Chapter 18, allows organisations to create (almost) personal relationships with customers. At its extreme, this means that consumers receive better-tailored personalised offerings, and thus that their expectations are raised in terms of the quality of the product, communication and service.

In its wider sense, technology applied to product development and innovation has created whole categories of fast evolving, increasingly cheap consumer 'toys' such as videos, hi-fi formats, camcorders and computer games. Many of these products used to be extended problem solving goods, but they have moved rapidly towards the limited problem solving area, as discussed above (p. 103). Such shifts occur for two main sets of reasons, which are interdependent. First, as the manufacturer learns more through experience about the product, its technology, its manufacture and its marketing, they are able to reduce their costs, make better-quality products and expand the product range to offer a number of different models to suit different kinds of customer. Additionally, over time, competition is likely to increase, again acting as an impetus towards better and cheaper products. Second, as a result of all that, the amount of risk inherent in the purchase reduces for the consumer, who does not, therefore, need to spend quite so much time searching for and evaluating alternative options.

Economic and competitive influences

The early 1990s saw recession and economic hardship across Europe and this inevitably affected consumers' attitudes, as well as their ability and willingness to spend. With uncertainty about employment prospects, many consumers postponed purchasing decisions, adjusted their decision-making criteria or cut out certain types of spending altogether. Price, value for money and a conscious assessment of the need to buy become prevalent influences in such circumstances.

Retailers, in turn, had to respond to the slowdown in trade caused by the economic environment. Money-off sales became prevalent in the high street throughout the year, not just in the traditional post-Christmas period. While this did stimulate sales in the short term, it had one unfortunate effect for retailers. Consumers began to see the lower sale price as 'normal' and resented paying full prices, preferring to wait for the next sale that they were confident would come along soon.

In terms of competition, very few purchases, mainly low-involvement decisions, are made without any consideration of the competition. The definition of what constitutes competition, however, is in the mind of the consumer. The supplier of car exhaust systems can be fairly sure that the competition consists of other exhaust dealers and garages. The supplier of chocolate, however, may be in competition not only with other chocolate suppliers but also with cream buns, biscuits and potato crisps. The consumer's consideration of the competition, however it is defined, may be extensive, formal and time consuming, or it may be a cursory glance across the supermarket shelf, just to check. Competitors are vying for the consumer's attention through their packaging, their promotional mix and their mailshots, as well as trying to influence or interrupt the decision-making process. This proliferation of products and communication can either confuse the consumer, leading to brand switching and even less rational decision making, or provide the consumer with the information and comparators to allow more discerning decision making.

Political and regulatory influences

Political and regulatory influences, emanating either from the EU or from national bodies, can also affect the consumer. Legislation on minimum levels of product safety and performance, for example, means that the consumer does not need to spend time getting technical information, worrying about analysing it and comparing competing products on those criteria. Legislation and regulation, whether they relate to product descriptions, consumer rights or advertising, also reduce the inherent risks of making a decision. This takes some of the pressure off the customer, leading to better-informed and easier decisions and less risk of post-purchase dissonance.

This discussion of the STEP factors is not exhaustive, but simply acts as a reminder that an individual makes decisions within a wider context, created either by society's own dynamics or by the efforts of the market. Having set that context, it is now appropriate to look more closely at the particular influences, internal and external, that affect the individual's buying behaviour and decision making.

PSYCHOLOGICAL INFLUENCES: THE INDIVIDUAL

Although marketers try to define groups of potential customers with common attributes or interests, as a useful unit for the formulation of marketing strategies, it should not be forgotten that such groups or market segments are still made up of individuals who are different from each other. This section, therefore, looks at aspects that will affect an individual's perceptions and handling of the decision-making process, such as personality, perception, learning, motivation and the impact of attitudes.

MARKETING IN ACTION   ## The smell of home baking

By the late 1990s, the home baking market in the UK was worth around £400 million but had been declining. However, manufacturers in this sector began to feel that the market was about to turn. One of the reasons was the rise in the number of cookery programmes on television with 'celebrity chefs' encouraging consumers to get into the kitchen. Consumers began to see that making cakes or pies can be rewarding and fulfilling. In a food culture with a heavy emphasis on time saving and convenience, it is nevertheless unrealistic to expect novice cooks to embrace the concept of baking from scratch wholeheartedly. One way of getting them interested and building confidence is to sell them pre-packaged cake and pastry mixes.

In the 1950s and 1960s, manufacturers of cake mixes learned a valuable lesson: consumers will feel less guilty about using a pre-packaged cake mix and find the experience more rewarding if they can feel involved in the process. The early mixes only required water to be added, but they did not sell well. Then the manufacturers reformulated the mix so that an egg had to be added. This made all the difference, because consumers felt that by choosing an egg, breaking it and beating it into the mixture, they were using expertise and thus really making cakes themselves. In more recent years, there has been little reason to think that consumers are any different in terms of wanting to be involved, but they are ever more demanding in

terms of convenience and variety. Manufacturers have seen that mixes are a real growth area of home baking and have invested in innovation to move away from the more traditional kind of mix that was perceived as being boring and of low quality. Whitworth's and Betty Crocker, for example, developed low fat and fat-free mixes, with an emphasis on premium quality, to meet the needs of the health conscious consumer who wants a guilt-free treat. More seasonal and 'exotic' cakes that consumers would be unwilling to try to bake from scratch have also been successful. Renshaw Viennese Mix and Luxury Stollen Cake Mix both sell well in the run-up to Christmas.

Manufacturers are not just interested in adults. They are also keen to target families and children, as they have identified a trend towards baking as a family leisure activity. To encourage children and sustain their interest and perhaps brand loyalty, Green's launched its Fun to Bake range of children's cake mixes and a Fun to Bake Club maintaining regular contact through a newsletter and recipes. Supercook also launched a range of children's products such as Cookie Treats and Chocolate Factory. Companies such as Spiller's (flour), Tate and Lyle (sugar) and Van den Bergh (margarine) are also keen to draw younger consumers into the baking market to encourage them to develop their baking skills and to take up cooking as a hobby.

Source: Kelly (1998).

Personality

Personality, consisting of all the features, traits, behaviours and experiences that make each of us distinctive and unique, is a very extensive and deep area of study. Our personalities lie at the heart of all our behaviour as consumers, and thus marketers try to define the particular personality traits or characteristics prevalent among a target group of consumers, which can then be reflected in the product itself and the marketing effort around it. This is beginning to trespass on ground that will be covered later in discussion of psychographic or lifestyle segmentation (pp. 187 *et seq.*), which is hardly surprising as personality helps to establish lifestyle as much as lifestyle affects personality.

In the mid- to late 1980s, advertising in particular was full of images reflecting the personality traits associated with successful lifestyle stereotypes such as the 'yuppie'. Independent, level-headed, ruthless, ambitious, self-centred, materialistic traits were seen as positive characteristics, and thus marketers were anxious to have them associated with users of their products. The 1990s saw a softening of this approach, featuring images orientated more towards caring, concern, family and sharing as the route to self-fulfilment.

With high-involvement products, where there is a strong emotional and psychological link between the product and the consumer, it is relatively easy to see how personality might affect choice and decision making. In choosing clothing, for instance, an extrovert self-confident achiever with an extravagant streak might select something deliberately *avant garde*, stylishly daring, vibrantly coloured and expensive, as a personality statement. A quiet, insecure character, with under-developed social skills, might prefer to wear something more sober, more conservative, with less attention-seeking potential.

Overall, however, the link between personality and purchasing, and thus the ability to predict purchasing patterns from personality traits, is at best tenuous. Kassarjian (1971) probably best summed up the situation in a review of previous studies: some showed a strong relationship between personality and purchasing, the majority showed at best a weak relationship, and a few no relationship at all. Chisnall (1985) takes the more cautious line that personality may influence the decision to buy a certain product type, but not the final brand choice.

Getting away from it all means different things to different people.

Source: Hayes & Jarvis.

Perception

Perception represents the way in which individuals analyse, interpret and make sense of incoming information, and is affected by personality, experience and mood. No two people will interpret the same stimulus (whether it is a product's packaging, taste, smell, texture or its promotional messages) in exactly the same way. Even the same individual might perceive the stimulus differently at different times. For example, seeing an advertisement for food when you are hungry is more likely to produce a positive response than seeing the same advertisement just after a heavy meal. Immediate needs are affecting the interpretation of the message. Alternatively, relaxing at home on a Sunday afternoon, an individual is more likely to spend time reading a detailed and lengthy print advertisement than they would if they were flicking through the same magazine during a short coffee break in the working day. Naturally, marketers hope that their messages reach target audiences when they are relaxed, at leisure and at ease with the world, because then the individual is more likely to place a positive interpretation on the message and is less likely to be distracted by other pressures and needs.

Other pressures and needs do create problems for marketers to overcome. All consumers are bombarded with marketing messages every day, and if they tried to pay equal attention and interpret them all objectively, then they would rapidly go mad. There are, therefore, a number of defence mechanisms to protect the consumer from over-stimulation and to make the interpretation process less stressful.

Selective attention

Consumers do not pay attention to everything that is going on at once. Attention filters allow the unconscious selection of what incoming information to concentrate on. In daily life we filter out the irrelevant background noise: the hum of the computer, the birds in the garden, the cars in the street, the footsteps in the corridor. As consumers we filter out the irrelevant marketing messages. In reading the newspaper, for instance, a split-second glance spots an advertisement, decides that it is irrelevant and allows the eye to read around it.

This means that marketers have to overcome these filters, either by creating messages that we will decide are relevant or by building attention-grabbing devices into the message. A print advertisement, for example, might use its position on the page, intense colour or startling images to draw the eye, and more importantly the brain, to it.

Selective perception

The problems do not stop once the marketer has got the consumer's attention, since people are infinitely creative in interpreting information in ways that suit them. It is less threatening to interpret things so that they fit nicely and consistently with whatever you already think and feel than to cope with the discomfort of clashes and inconsistency.

One way of creating this consistency or harmony is to allow perception to be coloured by previous experience and existing attitudes. A particularly bad experience with an organisation's offering creates a prejudice that may never be overcome. Whatever positive messages that organisation transmits, the consumer will always be thinking 'Yes, but...'. Similarly, a negative attitude towards a subject will make the consumer interpret messages differently. For example, someone who is deeply opposed to nuclear power will try to read between the lines of the industry's advertising and PR, looking for cover-ups and counter-arguments. This can distort the intended message and even reinforce the negative feelings. Conversely, a good experience makes it a lot easier to form positive perceptions. The good experience from the past creates a solid foundation from which to look for the best in the new experience.

Selective retention

Not all stimuli that make it through the attention filters and the machinery of perception and understanding are remembered. Many stimuli are only transitory, hence one of the reasons for the repetition of advertising: if you did not notice it or remember it the first time round, you might pick it up on subsequent occasions. Jogging the memory, by repeating messages or by producing familiar stimuli that the consumer can recognise (such as brand names, packaging design, logos or colour schemes), is therefore an important marketing task to reduce the reliance on the consumer's memory.

People have the capacity to remember what they want to remember and to filter out anything else. The reasons for retaining a particular message may be because it touched them emotionally, or it was of immediate relevance, or it was especially entertaining, or it reinforced previously held views. The reasons are many, but the consumer is under no obligation to remember anything.

Learning

Perception and memory are closely linked with **learning**. Marketers want consumers to learn from promotional material, so that they know which product to buy and why, and to learn from experience of the product, so that they will buy it again and pass on the message to others.

Learning has been defined by Hilgard and Marquis (1961) as:

> **the more or less permanent change in behaviour which occurs as a result of practice.**

This implies, from a marketing perspective, that the objective must not only be for the consumer to learn something, but also for them to remember what has been learned and to act on it. Therefore advertising materials, for instance, are carefully designed to maximise the learning opportunity. A 30-second television advertisement selling car insurance over the phone repeats the freephone number four times and has it written across the bottom of the screen so that the viewer is likely to remember it. Demonstrating a product benefit in an advertisement also helps consumers to learn what they are supposed to notice about the product when they use it. The images from Procter & Gamble's advertisement showing the enormous heap of crockery washed by one bottle of Fairy Liquid next to the pathetic heap achieved with a competing product stay in the mind more easily than a simple verbal message would. More generally, showing a product in a particular usage context, or associating it with certain types of people or situations, gives the consumer guidelines about what attitudes to develop towards the product.

Humour, and other methods of provoking an emotional response to an advertisement, can also help a message to stick because the recipient immediately becomes more involved in the process. Similarly, associating a product with something familiar that itself evokes certain emotions can allow those feelings to be transferred to the product. Thus the advertisements for Andrex that feature puppies have helped the British public to learn to think of toilet paper as warm, soft, cuddly and harmless rather than embarrassing.

Motivation

One definition of marketing puts the emphasis on the satisfaction of customers' needs and wants, but what triggers those needs and wants, and what drives consumers towards their fulfilment? Motives for action, the driving forces, are complex and changeable and can be difficult to research, since individuals themselves often cannot define why they act the way they do. An additional problem is that at different times, different **motivations** might take priority and have more influence over the individual's behaviour. Imagine, for example, a traveller driving from Calais to Marseilles. In the early part of the journey, the main priority is to make good time, find somewhere for lunch and provisionally aim to arrive in Lyon in good time to find a reasonable hotel. Long traffic delays on the southbound motorway throw out these plans. It is getting late and the traveller realises that he will not reach Lyon as planned. After seeing a few 'no vacancies' signs, concern starts to mount about the likelihood of finding a room, rather than sleeping in the car. The many hotels passed earlier in the journey were not considered, but now any hotel is likely to be well received. The priority is no longer distance covered but finding the warmth and relaxation of any hotel room. Our traveller's motives, in terms of both content and intensity, have changed during the events of one long-distance car journey. Marketers need to be aware of such influences on patronage motives if they are to market their hotels, restaurants or indeed any business effectively. Think, for example, of the impact on the tired traveller of a well-lit, familiar sign that can be clearly seen from the motorway.

Maslow's (1954) *hierarchy of needs* has long been used as a framework for classifying basic motivations. Five groups of needs, as shown in Fig. 3.3, are stacked one on top of another and form a progression. Having achieved satisfaction on the lowest level, the individual can progress to strive to achieve the goals of the next level up. This model does have a certain logic behind it, and the idea, for instance, that true self-actualisation can only grow from solid foundations of security and social acceptance seems reasonable. However, the model was developed in the context of US capitalist culture, where achievement and self-actualisation are often ends in themselves. It is questionable how far these motives can be extended to other cultural contexts.

Examples of consumer behaviour and marketing activity can be found to fit all five levels.

Physiological needs

Basic feelings such as hunger and thirst can be potent driving forces. After a strenuous game of squash, the immediate craving for liquid overrides normal considerations of brand preference. If the sports centre shop only has one type of soft drink in stock,

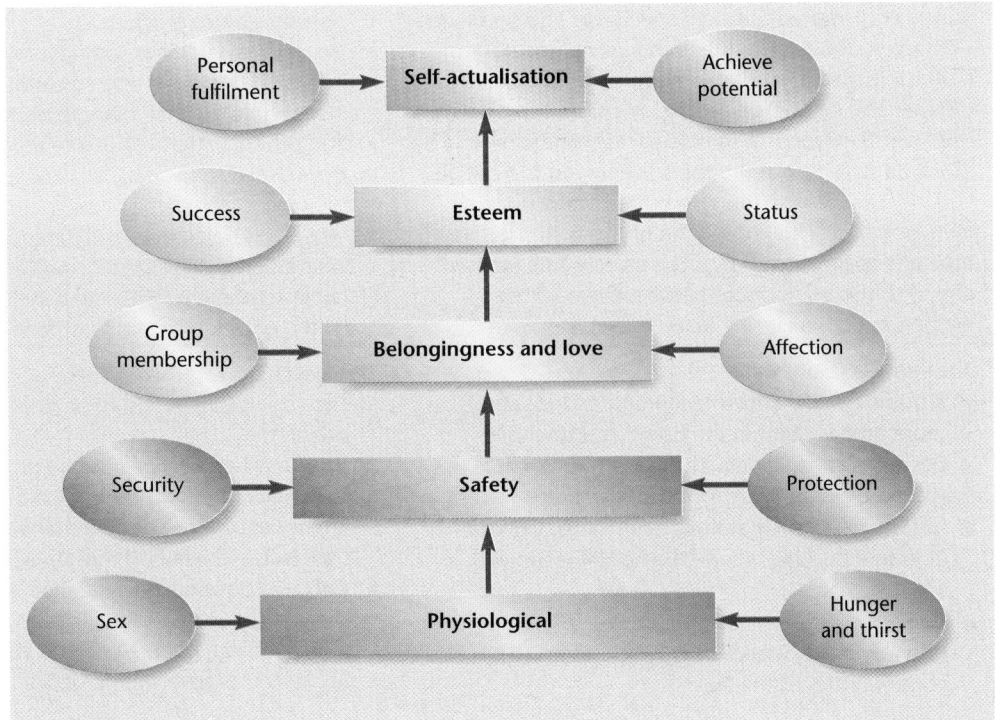

FIGURE 3.3

Maslow's hierarchy of needs

then it will do. Similarly, seasoned shoppers are well aware of the dangers of visiting a supermarket when they are hungry: so much more seems to go into the trolley.

Marketers can capitalise on such feelings. The soft drink manufacturer can ensure that the sports centre stocks that brand and that the product image reflects refreshment and thirst-quenching properties. The food manufacturer can advertise at a time of day when the audience is likely to be feeling hungry so that they are more likely to pay attention to the message and remember it.

Safety needs

Once the individual has taken care of the basic necessities of life, food, drink and warmth, the need for self-protection and long-term survival emerges. In modern Western societies this may be interpreted as the desire for a secure home, protected against intrusion and other dangers (floods and fire, for example). It might also cover the desire for healthcare, insurance services and consumer protection legislation.

The car market in particular has focused on safety needs as a marketing platform. Driving is an inherently dangerous activity, so the manufacturers try to reassure us that their cars are as safe as possible. Various manufacturers have featured side impact bars, airbags and/or anti-lock braking systems in their advertising, showing how these either protect you or help to prevent accidents.

Safety needs in terms of health protection feature strongly in the marketing strategies of products such as bleaches and toilet cleaners. The kind of approach used often appeals to the mother who takes responsibility for safeguarding the health and well-being of the whole family. The threat from bacteria can be eliminated by choosing the right cleanser.

MARKETING IN ACTION   ## A crystal ball would be useful . . . looking ahead to 2010

A Mintel report, *2010: Marketing to Tomorrow's Consumer*, suggests that consumers will retreat into the home, becoming more isolated and changing the nature and emphasis of their spending. This prediction stems from the development and acceptance of interactive media accessible from home, such as the Internet and interactive digital television. It is predicted that over 8 million British households will be on-line by 2003. So why go out shopping when you can get all you want without shifting from the comfort of your own armchair? The implication of this is that leisure time and spending will become more home focused and, if all this turns out to be true, there will be winners and losers in the marketing stakes.

The winners might be:
✔ DIY and home improvement products and services, as more time is spent in the home and the home becomes more valued. The consumer will at least want a pleasant view from the armchair.
✔ 'Brown goods' such as hi-fis, televisions, videos etc., as leisure becomes more of a home-based solo activity.
✔ Computers and computer games, again as a source of home-based leisure activity and as a communications medium.

✔ Time-saving products and services, such as convenience foods and home banking, as work becomes more stressful and demanding and leisure becomes more precious.
✔ Financial services and consultancy, as state welfare provision decreases and consumers become more responsible for their own pensions and seek advice and products that will assure their financial security.
✔ Health foods and drugs, as people become more concerned about their heath and state of mind. Vitamin supplements and functional foods (those with a perceived health benefit such as low-cholesterol margarine) will benefit as people seek to fill the gaps left by their fast food diets.

The losers, however, could be:
✗ Pubs and clubs, as leisure becomes less socially oriented.
✗ Mass-market package holidays, as consumers demand something more exotic or special if they are to venture out of their homes. Mintel predicts that cruise holidays, for instance, could benefit.
✗ Cars, as consumers decide that they prefer a comfy armchair to sitting in traffic jams on congested roads. If more people become able to work from home, if the government decides to impose a car

Continued

park tax or high road tolls, if big gas-guzzling or high-emission cars are taxed further, then fewer cars might be demanded or smaller cars might become more desirable.

✗ *Clothes, shoes and cosmetics*, as those who never go out will be spending less on replacement or fashion items or on personal appearance.

Foresight, the UK government's group of trend spotters, agrees to a certain extent with these views. It predicts that because of the rising divorce rate and the falling birth rate, there will be more single-person households than ever by 2020. Growing self-sufficiency, selfishness and loneliness will accompany this trend. Not all forecasters see this as bleak, however. Some think that on-line shopping will take away the slog of buying basic essentials and leave more time for more enjoyable shopping trips. They see retailers evolving to provide a more entertaining environment, merging retailing and leisure. Borders bookshops already combine book retailing with coffee shops and, in the future, nightclubs and music retailers could merge as could sports shops and fitness clubs,

making an excursion away from the armchair much more appealing and worthwhile.

As well as affecting the mix and the kind of products and services demanded, all these predictions have other implications for marketers. Perhaps more home shopping means more home delivery direct to the consumer and less involvement for retail intermediaries. Perhaps it also means more targeted one-to-one direct communication tailored to the varied needs and interests of all those very individual, self-contained, self-reliant couch potatoes. Perhaps it means more time for more fun. Whatever happens, however, whether these predictions come true or not, marketers do have to try to foresee changing consumer attitudes, habits and demands. They have to try to sort out the contradictions in the different forecasts so that organisations can begin to plan and develop the right products, the right distribution channels, the right communications messages and media, and all the associated marketing strategies so that they are in place at the right time. After all, 2010 is not that far away ...

Sources: Bainbridge (1998); *Marketing Week* (1999a).

Belongingness and love needs

This is about emotional security, wanting to feel accepted and valued by those closest to you. Marketers again play on this need through the portrayal of the family in particular. Over many years, advertising told women that they would be better appreciated and loved as wives and mothers if they did their washing in Persil, cooked with Oxo or fed their husbands cornflakes for breakfast.

Fear of loneliness or personal rejection can be a powerful motivator and features strongly in many marketing campaigns. Toiletries such as deodorants, toothpastes and mouthwashes have all advertised on the basis that you will be more lovable if you use these products, and showing the dire consequences of rejection if you don't. Even anti-smoking campaigns aimed at teenagers have tried this approach, implying that the smell of tobacco on your breath will put off prospective boy/girlfriends.

Esteem needs

This extends outwards from the previous stage to cover the individual's need for success, status and good opinion within wider society. This may include professional status and respect, standing within social groups, such as sports clubs and societies, or 'what the neighbours think'.

These needs are reflected in a wide variety of product and services marketing. Most car advertising, for example, contains some kind of message implying that if you drive this car it will somehow enhance your status and gain the respect of others. This even applies to the smaller, less expensive models, where the esteem arises from notions of 'wise choice' or 'a car that reflects the positive elements of my character'. More overtly, esteem can derive from the individual's sheer ability to afford the most expensive and exclusive items. Perfumes and other luxury products play heavily on the implication that you are a discerning and élite buyer, a cut above the rest, and that using these products makes a statement about who you are and the status you hold. Brand names

This Bentley car makes a statement about the owner's status, satisfying esteem needs.

Source: Rolls-Royce motors.

such as Rolls-Royce, Gucci and Rolex have acquired such a cachet that simply saying 'she owns a genuine Rolex' speaks volumes about a person's social status.

Self-actualisation needs

This is the ultimate goal, the achievement of complete satisfaction through successfully fulfilling one's potential. That may mean anything, depending on who you are and what you want out of life. Some will only achieve self-actualisation through becoming the head of a multinational organisation, while others will find it through the successful raising of a happy and healthy family. This is a difficult stage for the marketer to handle, because it is so individual, and thus the hope is that by fulfilling the other needs discussed above, the marketer can help to propel the individual towards self-actualisation. Only the individual can tell, however, when this stage has been reached.

Interestingly, the traveller from Calais to Marseilles introduced earlier seemed to regress back down from higher order to lower order needs! The initial idea of choosing a nice comfortable hotel that would suitably fulfil his service requirements and match his self-image had to be abandoned. Circumstances brought to the fore the very basic physiological need for sleep and the need for safety, both in terms of stopping driving before tiredness made it dangerous and having a secure roof over his head.

Generally in Western economies the fulfilment of the very basic needs can be taken for granted, however. Real physiological hunger, thirst and lack of safety do not exist for most people. Manufacturers of food products, for instance, cannot therefore assume that just because their product alleviates hunger it will be purchased and accepted. Any one of hundreds of food brands can do that, and thus the consumer is looking to see how a particular product can fulfil a higher order need, such as love or esteem. Consequently, foods are often marketed on the basis that your family will enjoy it and love you more for providing it (Oxo, for example) or because your dinner party guests will be impressed (Viennetta or After Eights, for example). The emphasis, therefore, is largely on the higher order needs (belongingness and love, esteem and self-actualisation).

In contrast, emerging market economies are still in the process of moving away from emphasis on the lower order needs (physiological and safety). When the former Communist states began their difficult transition to market economies, the shortages of basic products meant that people were very concerned simply with survival, acquiring enough bread, tea, milk, meat and other staple items to keep themselves going. Whether a particular product helps you to feel better about yourself is rather irrelevant in those circumstances. Now that the transitions are a few years further on, and because of the impact of the marketing efforts of Western organisations entering these markets, higher order needs are increasingly being considered.

Attitudes

As implied at p. 109 above, an **attitude** is a stance that an individual takes on a subject that predisposes them to react in a certain way to that subject. More formally, an attitude has been defined by Hilgard *et al.* (1975) as:

> **... an orientation towards or away from some object, concept or situation and a readiness to respond in a predetermined manner to these related objects, concepts or situations.**

Thus in marketing terms, consumers can develop attitudes to any kind of product or service, or indeed to any aspect of the marketing mix, and these attitudes will affect behaviour. All of this implies that attitudes play an important part in influencing consumer judgement, whether through perception, evaluation, information processing or decision making. Attitudes play a key role in shaping learning and while they are fluid, evolving over time, they are nevertheless often difficult to change.

Williams (1981), in summarising the literature, describes attitudes as having three different components.

Cognitive
Cognitive attitudes relate to beliefs or disbeliefs, thus: 'I believe that margarine is healthier than butter.' This is a component that the marketer can work on through fairly straightforward advertising. Repeating the message that your product is healthy, or that it represents the best value for money, may well establish an initial belief in those qualities.

Affective
Affective attitudes relate to feelings of a positive or negative nature, involving some emotional content, thus: 'I *like* this product' or 'This product makes me *feel* ...' Again, advertising can help the marketer to signal to the consumer why they should like it, or how they should feel when they use it. For some consumers, of course, affective attitudes can overcome cognitive ones. For example, I may believe that margarine is healthier than butter, but I buy butter because I like the taste better. Similarly, I believe that snacking on chocolate is 'bad', but it cheers me up so I do it anyway.

Conative
Conative attitudes relate to the link with behaviour, thus attitude x is considered likely to lead to behaviour *y*. This is the hardest one for marketers to predict or control, because so many things can prevent behaviour from taking place, even if the cognitive and affective attitudes are positive: 'I believe that BMWs are excellent quality, reliable cars, and I feel that owning one would enhance my status and provide me with many hours of pleasurable driving, but I simply cannot afford it,' or it may even be that 'Audi made me a better offer'.

It is this last link between attitude and behaviour that is of most interest to marketers. Fishbein (1975) developed a model, a further evolution of his earlier 1967 work, based on the proposition that in order to predict a specific behaviour, such as a brand purchase, it is important to measure the individual's attitude towards performing that behaviour, rather than just the attitude towards the product in question. This fits with the BMW example above, where the most important thing is not the attitude to the car itself, but the attitude towards *purchasing* the car. As long as the attitude to purchasing is negative, the marketer still has work to do. While it is usually accepted that other factors, both personal and situational, also influence behaviour, many writers, such as Lutz (1981) and Foxall (1984), still argue that attitude is a key link in the causal chain between perceptions of product attributes at one end and purchasing intentions and behaviour at the other end. Others, such as Joyce (1967), see a two-way relationship between attitudes and purchasing behaviour, so that experience of the product will also influence, through learning, future behaviour.

Attitudes can thus involve feelings (positive or negative), knowledge (complete or partial) and beliefs. A particular female consumer might believe that she is overweight. She knows that cream cakes are fattening, but she likes them. All these things come together to form her attitude towards cream cakes (wicked, but seductive) and her behaviour when confronted by one (five minutes wrestling with her conscience before giving in completely and buying two, knowing that she will regret it later). An advertising campaign for cream cakes, centred around the slogan 'naughty but nice', capitalised brilliantly on what is a common attitude, almost legitimising the guilt and establishing an empathy with the hopeless addict. The really admirable thing about that campaign was that the advertiser did not even attempt to overturn the attitude.

It is possible, but very difficult, to change attitudes, particularly when they are well established and deeply ingrained. Companies like Lada and Aeroflot have been trying for years with varying degrees of success. The nuclear industry has also been trying to overcome hostile and suspicious attitudes with an integrated campaign of advertising, PR and site visits (http://www.bnfl.co.uk). Many people have indeed been responsive to this openness, and have been prepared to revise attitudes to a greater or lesser extent. There will, however, always be a hard core who will remain entrenched and interpret any 'positive' messages in a negative way.

There is a difference between attitudes that relate to an organisation's philosophy, business ethics or market and those that centre around experience of an organisation's specific product or service. An organisation that has a bad reputation for its employment practices, its environmental record or its dealings with suspect foreign regimes will have created negative attitudes that will be extremely difficult to overturn. Similarly, companies operating in certain markets, such as nuclear power, tobacco and alcohol, will never redeem themselves in the eyes of significant groups of the public. People care too much about such things to be easily persuaded to change their outlook. In contrast, negative feelings about a specific product or brand are more amenable to change through skilful marketing. Skoda, for example, launching its new model, the Felicia, tried to overcome the kind of negative attitudes that have led to a plethora of Skoda jokes through an advertising campaign that admitted to the image problem with gentle good humour, but then tried to establish the positive benefits of the brand: 'We've changed the car. Can you change your mind?'

> **Example** Frozen food manufacturers are having a tough time convincing customers that their products are not inferior to chilled products (Hardcastle, 1998). This will not be an easy task, as the image of frozen meals as low cost, low quality and a meal of last resort is deep rooted within many consumers. Old perceptions that typical frozen meals consist of fish fingers, frozen peas and chips die hard. That has not prevented sales growing in recent years, albeit slowly. Taylor Nelson Sofres estimated that the market is worth £2.6 billion. The problem is the growth in chilled products that are perceived to be of higher quality, thus creating downward pressure on the price of frozen meals. Birds Eye Walls

(http:// www.birdseye.com) responded by emphasising quality, improving portion sizes, communicating the benefits of frozen food more strongly, and ensuring that display is first class in new in-store freezers. The company also installed some 'virtual reality microwaves' above the freezers showing a hologram of the various stages in preparing a chicken tikka masala meal (Bray, 1997).

As the cream cake example quoted earlier shows, defining attitudes can provide valuable insights into target groups of customers and give a basis for communication with them. Measuring feelings, beliefs and knowledge about an organisation's products and those of its competitors is an essential part of market research (*see* Chapter 6), leading to a more effective and appealing marketing mix. Identifying changes in wider social or cultural attitudes can also provide the marketer with new opportunities, either for products or marketing approaches. In France, for example, a glossy magazine called *Divorce* was launched focusing on the newly single and the typical problems that they face. The advertising within it was for dating agencies and private detectives! Its existence was due not only to the fact that one in three marriages ends in divorce in France, but also to more liberal attitudes towards divorce and the problems it creates. This new openness and acceptability of divorce are also seen in the UK. VW ran a successful advertisement showing a very happy woman emerging from what the viewer interpreted as a registry office wedding. When she drove away in her VW, however, the slogan painted on the back of the car read 'just divorced'.

In summary, the individual is a complex entity, under pressure to take in, analyse and remember many marketing messages in addition to the other burdens of daily life. Marketers need to understand how individuals think and why they respond in particular ways, if they are going to develop marketing offerings that cut through defence mechanisms and create loyal customers. Individuals' behaviour, however, is not only shaped in accordance with their personalities, abilities, analytical skills etc., as discussed above, but also affected by wider considerations, such as the sociocultural influences that will be discussed next.

SOCIOCULTURAL INFLUENCES: THE GROUP

Individuals are influenced, to a greater or lesser extent, by the social and cultural climate in which they live. Individuals have membership of many social groups, whether these are formally recognised social units such as the family, or informal intangible groupings such as reference groups (*see* pp. 122 *et seq.*). Inevitably, purchasing decisions will be affected by group membership, as these sociocultural influences may help the individual to:

1 differentiate between essential and non-essential purchases;
2 prioritise purchases where resources are limited;
3 define the meaning of the product and its benefits in the context of their own lives; and thus to
4 foresee the post-purchase implications of this decision.

All of these things imply that the individual's decision has as much to do with 'What other people will think' and 'How I will look if I buy this' as with the intrinsic benefits of the product itself. Marketers have, of course, capitalised on this natural wish to express oneself and gain social acceptance through one's consumption habits, both as a basis for psychographic or lifestyle segmentation (which will be discussed later on pp. 187 *et seq.*) and for many years as a basis of fear appeals in advertising (*see* Chapter 14 onwards).

The following subsections look more closely at some of these sociocultural influences.

Social class

Social class is a form of stratification that attempts to structure and divide a society. Some argue that egalitarianism has become far more pronounced in the modern Europe, making any attempts at social distinction ill-founded, if not meaningless. Nevertheless, today social class is established largely according to occupation, and for many years, British marketers have used the grading system outlined in Table 3.2. It has been widely used to group consumers, whether for research or for analysing media readership.

Example The growth of the 'middle class' in the UK will probably mean the end of the official six-class structure adopted since 1921, as shown in Table 3.2. Government statistics suggest that half the UK population are now in the middle class and thus the old groupings are too broad and no longer meaningful. The new 'official' social classification introduced in 1998 has 17 categories, based not only on occupation (as in the old system) but also on the size of an individual's employing organisation and the type of contract, fringe benefits and job security that individual enjoys. It also takes into account how much the employer values that individual. These extra factors make a big difference. Looking only at occupation and income, the top social groups earn twice as much as the bottom ones. Accounting for the extra factors, however, makes the top groups seven times more affluent.

This is perhaps a much more realistic way of defining socioeconomic groups. Under the new scheme, those who acquire 'better' status include large-company managers, teachers, policemen and nurses. Those who slide down the scale, however, include shop assistants, plumbers and traffic wardens. For the marketer, the new system creates smaller, more clearly defined and currently relevant groups for targeting purposes. It still does not, however, get into the mind of consumers or explain their buying behaviour. Does all of this matter? Perhaps it does, as long as the top groups are up to seven times more affluent than the bottom ones (Henderson, 1997; Norton, 1998).

Across the EU, different definitions of social class have been used. In the Netherlands, for example, the population is structured into professional and higher managerial, intermediate managerial, clerical and skilled manual, and finally pensioners and the unskilled. In contrast, Germany defines social groups according to monthly household income while France combines the self-employed with senior management and has classes for professional, white-collar and blue-collar employees. However more fundamental problems can be found in attempting to link consumer behaviour with

TABLE 3.2
UK socioeconomic groupings

% of population	Group	Social status	Occupation of head of household
3	A	Upper middle	Higher managerial, administrative or professional
14	B	Middle	Intermediate managerial, administrative or professional
27	C1	Lower middle	Supervisory or clerical, junior managerial, administrative or professional
25	C2	Skilled working	Skilled manual workers
19	D	Working	Semi-skilled and unskilled manual workers
12	E	Those at lowest level of subsistence	State pensioners or widows, casual or lowest-grade workers

social class. The usefulness of such systems is limited. They rely on the occupation of the head of the household (more correctly called the main income earner), but fail to put that into the context of the rest of the household. Dual income households are becoming increasingly common, with the second income having a profound effect on the buying behaviour of both parties, yet most of these systems fail to recognise this. They tell very little about the consumption patterns or attitudes that are of such great use to the marketer. The disposable income of a C2 class household may be just as high as that of an A or B household, and they may have certain upmarket tastes in common. Furthermore, two households in the A or B categories could easily behave very differently. One household might consider status symbols to be important and indulge in conspicuous consumption, whereas the other might have rejected material-istic values and be seeking a cleaner, less cluttered lifestyle. These contrasting outlooks on life make an enormous difference to buying behaviour and choices, hence the necessity for psychographic segmentation (see pp. 187 et seq.) to provide marketers with more meaningful frameworks for grouping customers.

Nevertheless, as Inskip (1995) argues, a deeply rooted sense of class does affect people's perception of the world and their aspirations. In marketing terms, this may mean that middle-class people generally seek out products that will enhance their self-image, self-belief and sense of success. The working class is more firmly rooted in family values, and although they may still aspire to accumulate possessions, they will not change either those values or themselves fundamentally. Inskip claims that mar-keters do not understand the working class and its needs properly, and thus have either ignored it completely or failed to address it appropriately as they use patronis-ing and stereotypical marketing activities. Since around 46 per cent of the UK population claim to be working class, this is a serious omission. C2 and D consumers do now have money to spend, even if they choose to spend it in areas such as dis-count retailers or mail order catalogues that marketers do not find particularly trendy or exciting. Part of the problem is that most marketers are themselves middle class. They thus find it easier to relate to middle-class customers, and carry their own preju-dices about the working class into their approaches.

Culture and subculture

Culture can be described as the personality of the society within which an individual lives. It manifests itself through the built environment, art, language, literature, music and the products that society consumes, as well as through its prevalent beliefs, value systems and government. As summarised by Chisnall (1985), culture is the total way of life of a society, passed on from generation to generation, deriving from a group of people sharing and transmitting beliefs, values, attitudes and forms of behaviour that are common to that society and considered worthy of retention. Rice (1993, p. 242) similarly defines culture as:

> **The values, attitudes, beliefs, ideas, artefacts and other meaningful symbols represented in the pattern of life adopted by people that help them interpret, evaluate and communicate as members of society.**

Breaking that definition down further, Fig. 3.4 shows diagrammatically the influences that create culture.

Cultural differences show themselves in very different ways. Although eating, for example, is a basic natural instinct, what we eat and when is heavily influenced by the culture in which we are brought up. Thus in Spain it is normal to begin lunch at 4 p.m. and then have dinner after 10 p.m., while in Poland most restaurants would be closing down at those times. Similarly, lunch in Central Europe would almost cert-ainly include sauerkraut, but little fish compared with the wide variety offered on a typical Spanish menu. Even the propensity for eating out may be a cultural factor.

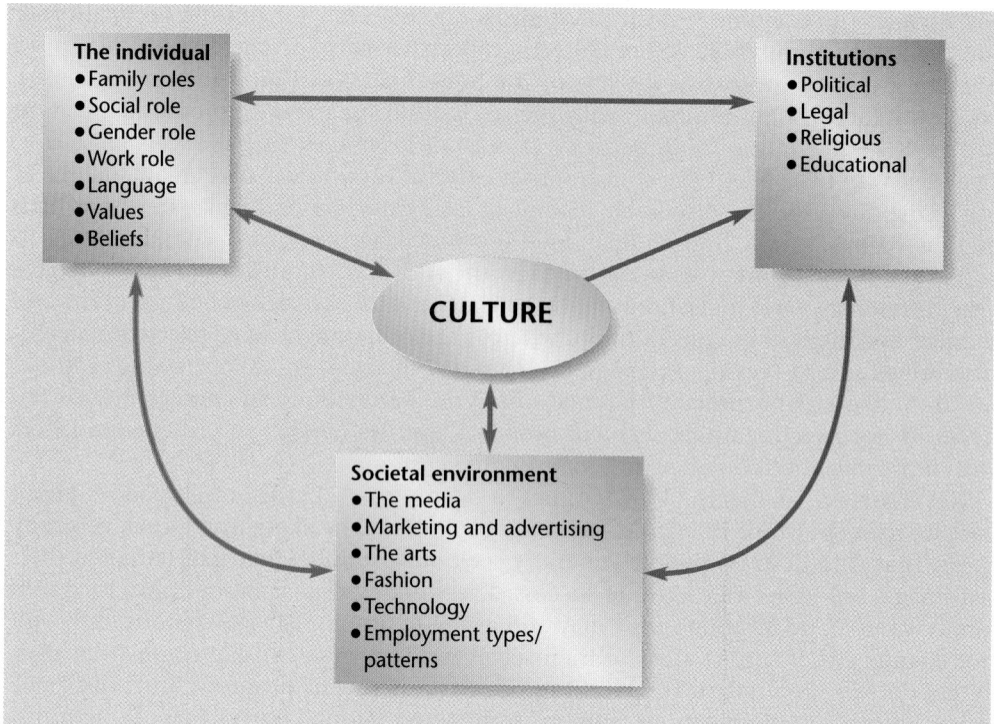

FIGURE 3.4

Influences on culture

Riley (1994), for example, argues that eating out is not a major part of the UK's social culture. Thus the restaurateur has the added marketing task in the UK of overcoming the barrier of the consumer's home orientation and persuading them that eating out is an enjoyable social activity.

Of course, culture goes much further in prescribing and describing the values and beliefs of a society. It influences shopping hours, with many Mediterranean super-markets open for far longer hours in the evening than some of their Northern European counterparts; the beliefs associated with advertising messages and symbols; the lifestyles of the inhabitants; and the products that are more or less acceptable and available in that culture, for example try purchasing an electric kettle in Spain or Italy.

A leisurely meal in pleasant surroundings could be a cultural treat!

Source: Langan's Brasserie.

Culture is thus very important for the marketer to understand, first because marketing can only exist within a culture that is prepared to allow it and support it, and second, it has to act within boundaries set by society and culture. Over the past 10 years or so, for example, it has become more and more socially unacceptable in Europe for organisations to use animals for testing cosmetics. Society has informally rewritten one of the rules and marketers have had to respond. Changing attitudes to tobacco, alcohol and marketing to children are also examples of areas within which cultural change is altering organisations' approaches to business. In the UK, for instance, food marketers have been criticised for aiming too much advertising of products such as sweets, soft drinks, sugary cereals, crisps and fast foods at children. These kinds of product are thought to be of dubious nutritional value, if consumed in excess, and are also thought to be contributing to an increase in dental decay among children.

Any culture can be divided into a number of subcultures, each with its own specific characteristics, yet existing within the whole. It depends on the onlooker's perspective just how detailed a division is required. An American exporter might say that Europe represents a culture (as distinct from the US culture), with British, French, German and other national subcultures existing within it. Dealing with the home market, however, a German marketer would define Germany, or increasingly the German-speaking territories of Europe, as the dominant culture, with significant subcultures held within it. These subcultures could be based on ethnic origin (Turkish, Polish, Asian or whatever), religious beliefs, or more lifestyle-orientated groupings, defined by the values and attitudes held. Language may also be an important determinant of subculture. In Switzerland, for example, the three main languages reflect different customs, architecture and even external orientations. The Ticino region (Italian speaking) probably identifies itself more closely with Milan than Zurich or Basle as a point of cultural reference.

Most European countries, however, have distinct subcultures based on ethnic origin. In the Netherlands there are strong immigrant communities from the Far East, especially Indonesia and Indo-China. In the UK, in cities such as Bradford, Leicester and Birmingham there are strong Asian communities with distinctive lifestyles, retailing and service provision and sense of community. Rafiq (1990) found that Asians have had a significant impact on the structure of UK independent retailing, especially

MARKETING IN ACTION   Marketing to ethnic minorities

It has been argued that companies are ignoring the full potential of ethnic community groups in the UK by not addressing them properly (Gooding, 1998). Ethnic communities account for around 5.5 per cent of the UK population. The challenge for the marketing manager is to recognise whether such groups should be targeted with different products or marketing communications, despite the fact that members of these groups can be, and are, integrated into the same kind of target groups as the rest of the population.

The Asian community, for example, is not in itself homogeneous. There are wide difference in language, religion, country of origin and attitudes. For some, English is their second language. However, people within these groups do not want segregation, tokenism or to be patronised; they want approaches that really address their needs and concerns. The difficulty arises when marketers move beyond targeted media such as

the magazine *Spice* and dedicated cable TV and radio channels. Some advertisers want to use black or Asian actors in their mainstream campaigns, acknowledging that their targeting is inclusive, but they are worried about getting it wrong. They do not want to offend the ethnic audience or alienate the rest of the audience, even though there is no evidence to suggest that this would be the case. Some companies have gone further by developing products specifically for ethnic groups. Revlon and Marks & Spencer are among cosmetics companies that have produced cosmetic ranges for darker skins, for example. Diwali, the Hindu festival of light, is just one of the non-Christian religious festivals to be included in the calendar of the greetings card industry. Nevertheless, even if ethnicity is identified as a legitimate differentiating feature, marketers still have to look deeper than that to understand the consumer more fully.

where there is a high proportion of Asian residents. This is driven by the desire for specialist provision to serve the particular product needs of the subculture, and also to provide services that are more in tune with the needs of that community. In support of subcultures, some local development agencies, as well as universities or colleges, now support specialist units to help new entrepreneurs from minority communities to get started.

In many ways, the tension within ethnic-based subcultures is between cultural assimilation into the main, dominant culture and the preservation of cultural diversity in language, dress, food, family behaviour etc. This tension can be seen even on a European scale, where increased emphasis on travel, rapid communication and pan-European marketing is slowly breaking down barriers at the same time as there is a strong movement towards the preservation of distinct national and regional identities. For example in the West of Ireland, the Gaelic-speaking regions are being heavily supported to prevent relatively small numbers of people from leaving their rural way of life.

As far as the immediate future is concerned, even within a united Europe, people are still celebrating and defending their own cultures and subcultures, and marketers need to recognise and empathise with this. One of the reasons (among many) cited for Disneyland Paris's poor start was that the organisation had underestimated French resistance, in particular, to an undiluted all-American cultural concept in the heart of Europe. Europeans are happy, and indeed eager, to experience Disney on US soil as part of 'the American experience', but cannot accept it, it would appear, within their own culture (http://www.disney.go.com).

Subculture need not only be an ethnic phenomenon, however. The existence of a youth subculture, spanning international boundaries, is widely accepted by marketers, and media such as MTV that reach right across Europe allow marketers to communicate efficiently and cost effectively with that subculture. Brands such as Coca-Cola, Pepsi and Pepe Jeans can create messages that capitalise on the common concerns, interests and attitudes that define this subculture. Pepe Jeans, for example, developed an advertising campaign aimed at the youth market, using MTV, cinema and youth magazines, which featured suicide and alienation from parents as a reflection of youth angst, anxiety and antipathy. Pepe's chief executive was quoted by Steen (1995) as saying:

> **We simply show a world which youth will recognise as being what is around them, one which the older generation may wish wasn't there. It is to be expected that people outside the 12–20 age group may miss the point or be offended.**

The core messages strike at something different from, and perhaps deeper than, national or ethnic culture, and thus may have pan-European currency without necessarily becoming bland in the process. That is not to say that all 16–25 year-olds across Europe should be stereotyped as belonging to a homogeneous 'yoof market'. What it does say is that there are certain attitudes and feelings with which this age group are likely to sympathise, and that these can therefore be used as a foundation for more targeted communication that manages to celebrate both commonalities and differences.

Reference groups

Reference groups are any groups, whether formally or informally constituted, to which an individual either belongs or aspires to belong, for example professional bodies, social or hobby-orientated societies, or informal, vaguely defined lifestyle groups ('I want to be a yuppie'). There are three main types of reference group, each of which affects buying behaviour, and these are discussed in turn below.

Example Controversially, some advertising agencies are trying to appeal to a certain type of youth subculture through advertising that is deliberately violent, offensive and shocking. As Alderson and Olins (1995) report, opinion within the advertising world is divided as to whether such approaches are 'crass, crude or brilliant'. Advertising for Harley-Davidson motorcycles, under the slogan 'Harley-Davidson. A completely irresponsible thing to do' showed, in one advertisement, a woman forced to work as a prostitute because her husband had bought a motorcycle, and in another, an elderly man deprived of an electric wheelchair because his son bought a Harley-Davidson instead. Poster slogans also came in for criticism, such as Great Frog jewellery's 'If you don't like it, fuck off' and Club 18–30's 'Summer of 69'. Those who support such advertising approaches maintain that it simply reflects a mood among the target audience and is therefore acceptable. Those who criticise it, however, maintain that it legitimises unacceptable attitudes and behaviour that marketers should not be endorsing.

Membership groups

These are the groups to which the individual already belongs. These groups provide parameters within which individuals make purchasing decisions, whether they are conscious of it or not. In buying clothing, for example, the purchaser might think about the occasion for which it is going to be worn and consider whether a particular item is 'suitable'. There is great concern here about what other people will think.

Buying clothes for work is severely limited by the norms and expectations imposed by colleagues (a membership group) and bosses (an aspirant group?), as well as by the practicalities of the workplace. Similarly, choosing clothes for a party will be influenced by the predicted impact on the social group who will be present: whether they will be impressed; whether the wearer will fit in; whether the wearer will seem to be overdressed or underdressed; or whether anyone else is likely to turn up in the same outfit.

Thus the influence of membership groups on buying behaviour is to set standards to which individuals can conform, thus consolidating their position as group members. Of course, some individuals with a strong sense of opinion leadership will seek to extend those standards by exceeding them and challenging the norms with the expectation that others will follow.

Aspirant groups

These are the groups to which the individual would like to belong, and some of these aspirations are more realistic than others. An amateur athlete or musician might aspire to professional status in their dreams, even if they have little talent. An independent professional single female might aspire to become a full-time housewife with a husband and three children; the housewife might aspire to the career and independent lifestyle. A young, junior manager might aspire to the middle management ranks.

People's desire for change, development and growth in their lives is natural, and marketers frequently exploit this in the positioning of their products and the subtle promises they make. Bird's Eye frozen meals will not stop you being a bored housewife, but will give you a little more independence to 'be yourself'; buying Nike, Reebok or Adidas sports gear will not make you into Ronaldo, Ryan Giggs or Patrick Kluivert, but you can feel a little closer to them.

Example The growth of designer label suits for men reflects higher disposable incomes and increasing fashion consciousness. The clear fashion statements made in such male magazines as *Loaded* and *FHM* all increase exposure to designer fashion, thus raising the aspirations of male customers and encouraging them to spend a little more on making fashion statements. This has been good news for top designers such as Ralph Lauren, Armani and Versace. Ermenegildo Zegna, the Italian menswear firm selling the Zegna brand and already strong elsewhere in Europe, is now targeting the UK as the next stage in its export development. With a UK market worth over £3 billion in 1996 and off the peg suits fetching over £1000, young men are a lucrative group with which to do business (Oldfield, 1998).

The existence of aspirant groups, therefore, attracts consumers towards products that are strongly associated with those groups and will either make it appear that the buyer actually belongs to the group or signal the individual's aspirations to the wider world.

Dissociative groups

These are groups to which the individual does not want to belong or to be seen to belong. A supporter of the England soccer team would not wish to be associated with its notorious hooligan element, for example. Someone who had a violent aversion to 'yuppies' and their values might avoid buying products that are closely associated with them, through fear of being thought to belong to that group. An upmarket shopper might prefer not to be seen in a discount store such as Aldi or Netto just in case anyone thinks they are penny pinching.

Clearly, these dissociations are closely related to the positive influences of both membership and aspirational groups. They are simply the other side of the coin, an attempt to draw closer to the 'desirable' groups, while differentiating oneself from the 'undesirable'.

Family

The family, whether two parent or single parent, nuclear or extended, with or without dependent children, remains a key influence on the buying behaviour of individuals. The needs of the family affect what can be afforded, where the spending priorities lie and how a purchasing decision is made. All of this evolves as the family matures and moves through the various stages of its life-cycle. Over time, the structure of a family changes, for example as children grow older and eventually leave home, or as events break up families or create new ones. This means that a family's resources and needs also change over time, and that the marketer must understand and respond to these changes.

Traditionally, marketers have looked to the **family life-cycle** as proposed by Wells and Gubar (1966), and shown in Table 3.3. Over the years, however, this has become less and less appropriate, as it reflects a path through life that is becoming less common in the West. It does not, for example, allow for single parent families, created either voluntarily or through divorce, or for remarriage after divorce which may create new families with children coming together from previous marriages, and/or second families. Other trends too undermine the assumptions of the traditional model of the family life-cycle. According to Lightfoot and Wavell (1995), estimates from the Office of Population Censuses and Surveys (OPCS) in the UK forecast that 20 per cent of women born in the 1960s, 1970s and 1980s may never have children. Those who do currently elect to have children are tending to leave childbearing until later in their lives, so that they can establish their careers first. OPCS has noted that

TABLE 3.3
The family life-cycle

Stage	Title	Characteristics
1	Bachelor	Young, single, not living at home
2	Newly married	Young, no children
3	Full nest I	Youngest child under 6
4	Full nest II	Youngest child 6 or over
5	Full nest III	Older, married with dependent children
6	Empty nest I	Older married, no children living at home
7	Empty nest II	Older married, retired, no children living at home
8	Solitary survivor I	In labour force
9	Solitary survivor II	Retired

Source: Wells and Gubar (1966).

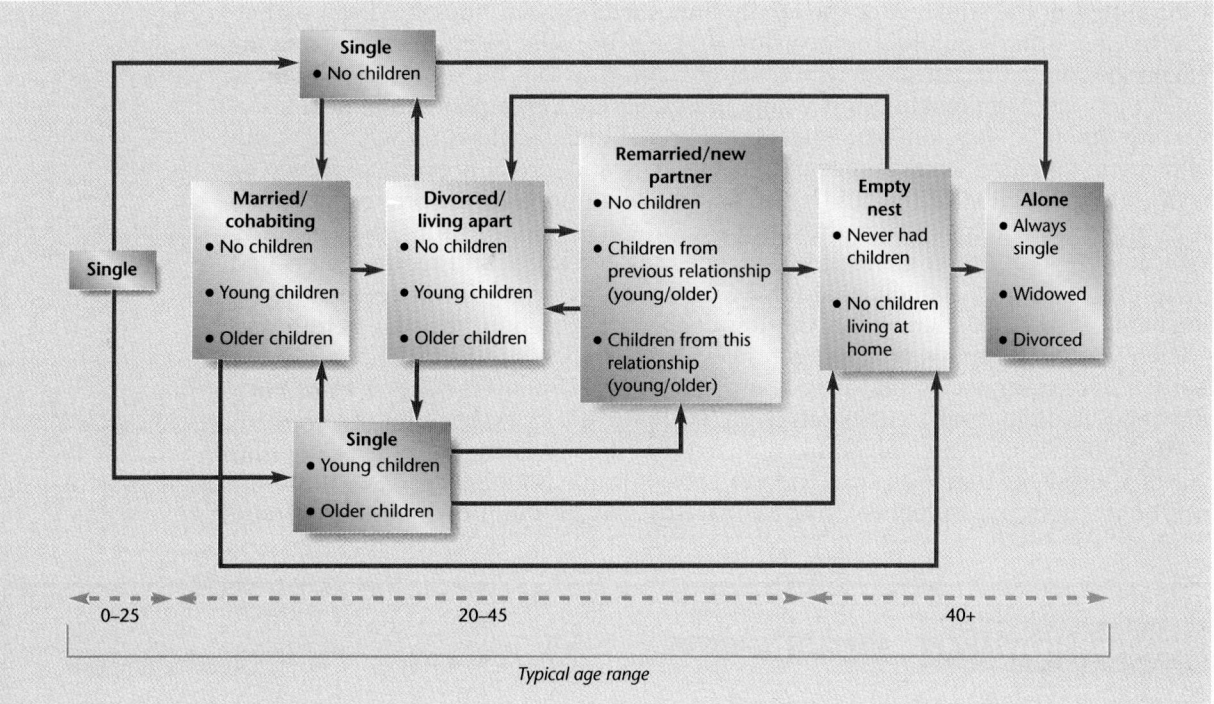

FIGURE 3.5

A modern family life-cycle model

the birth rate among women in their twenties has dropped, while it has increased rapidly for women in their thirties and forties. At the other end of the spectrum, the number of single, teenage mothers has increased alarmingly in the UK to 3 per cent of girls aged 15–19, the highest figure in the EU. Overall, however, European birth rates are falling, leading to 'ageing populations' throughout the EU as the proportion of children in the population falls.

All of these trends have major implications for consumers' needs and wants at various stages in their lives, as well as for their disposable incomes, and this will be explored further in Chapter 5. The marketer cannot make trite assumptions based on traditional stereotypes of the nuclear family, and something more complex than the Wells and Gubar model is needed to reflect properly the various routes that people's lives can now take. Figure 3.5 offers a revised family life-cycle for the way people live today.

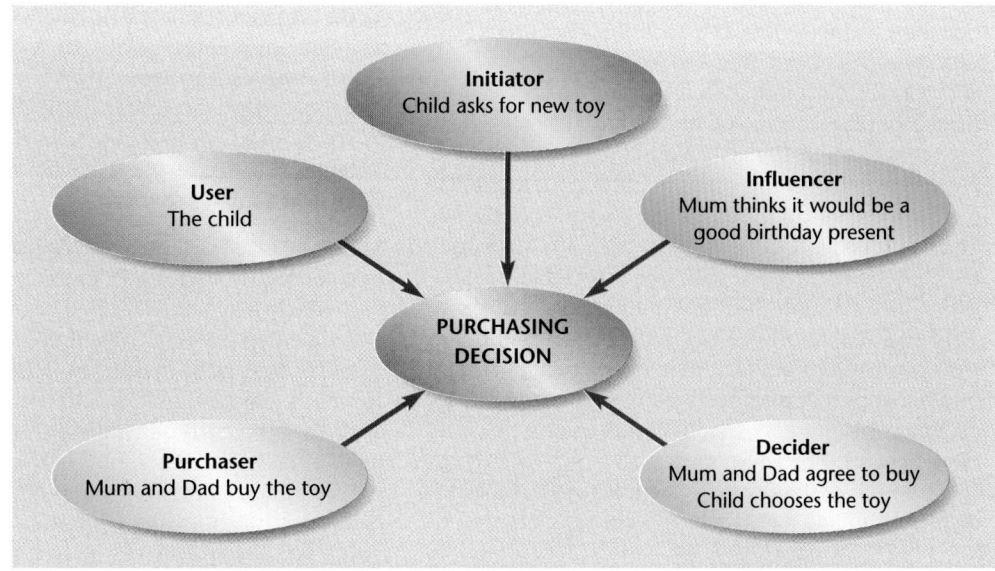

FIGURE 3.6

The family as a decision-making unit

Regardless of the structure of the family unit, members of a household can participate in each other's purchasing decision making. In some cases, members may be making decisions that affect the whole family, and thus Fig. 3.6 shows how a family can act as a decision-making unit where individual members play different roles in reaching the final decision. The roles that any one member takes on will vary from purchase to purchase, as will the length, complexity and formality of the process. The obvious manifestation of the family decision-making unit is in the ordinary week to week grocery shopping. The main shopper is not acting as an individual, pleasing only themselves by their choices, but is reflecting the tastes and requirements of a group of people. In a stereotypical family, Mother may be the ultimate decider and purchaser in the supermarket, but the rest of the family may have acted as initiators ('When you go shopping, will you get me some ...' or 'Do you know that we've run out of ...?' or 'Can we try that new brand of ...?') or influencers ('If you buy THAT, don't expect ME to eat it'), either before the shopping trip or at the point of sale.

The buying roles may be undertaken by different family members for different purchases at different times. Thus in the example of purchasing a bicycle, a child may well be the user and influencer, but the parents may be the principal deciders and

MARKETING IN ACTION   Pester power

Those of us who were brought up in the UK during the 1960s remember with affection a television advertisement that had us all chanting, 'Don't Forget the Fruit Gums, Mum'. That is pester power. Since then, the Advertising Code of Practice has been tightened to prevent advertisers from directly encouraging children to ask for things. Fruit Gums cleaned up their act by changing their advertisement to 'Don't Forget the Fruit Gums, chum'. This does not mean, however, that marketers do not try to reach and influence children.

'Characters' and 'collectables' are all very appealing to children. Heinz, for example, uses Thomas the Tank Engine pasta shapes to appeal to the youngest age group and Barbie and Action Man to target older children. Characters from films (such as Mulan or Hercules) and television and books (Goosebumps, Paddington Bear and Tom and Jerry, for example) are also popular. Collectables, a set of small toys, badges, stickers or other items, one of which is given away with each purchase, can be included in breakfast cereal packs or with children's meals in fast food restaurants. A child wants to collect the whole set and thus pesters Mum to keep buying the relevant brand to build up the collection. The enthusiasm for collectables is also maintained through their 'playground cred', as children swop items with each other or boast about their complete collection. Whatever the gift, character or other appeal, it is all designed to encourage kids to influence their parents' purchasing decisions (Shannon, 1997).

In the UK, pester power influences over £31 billion of adult spending every year, and not just in the obvious areas such as breakfast cereals, soft drinks and toys; 44 per cent of holiday purchasing decisions, 22 per cent of television or hi-fi purchasing decisions and 17 per cent of car purchasing decisions are influenced by children. A survey found that 42 per cent of 14–17-year-olds in Germany similarly influenced major purchases by their parents. Pester power is thus an important influence on adult buyer behaviour and the marketer has the delicate job of ensuring that products, particularly those that are consumed or used by children, have both adult and child appeal (Hardcastle, 1997).

The Family Market Research Panel suggests that the five biggest influences on pester power at the point of sale are (Dwek, 1995):

1 the child's recall of television advertising;
2 a free promotional gift;
3 attractive packaging;
4 a licensed character (e.g. The Lion King, Pocahontas, Power Rangers, Mickey Mouse or Mr Blobby);
5 in-store samples to try.

Market research company ID Magasin found, however, that parents do try to resist pester power by deliberately avoiding areas of the supermarket with child-oriented products. When this is not possible, parents adopt what the company calls a 'cruise missile approach', dashing quickly into the danger area to pick up a planned purchase before the child has too much time to register all the tempting things there. The child still contributes to the purchasing decision, but the parent has much greater control.

buyers. Menasco and Curry (1989) suggest that there are two types of decision-making process within a family. The first is *consensual*, where the family agrees on the purchase but needs to agree how it will be achieved, and thus some problem solving has to be done to enable it to take place. The second type, felt to be more the norm, is *accommodative*, where the family cannot agree and thus bargaining, coercion, power and compromise are used to effect a result.

However, the changing nature of many families, some with two income earners and more participative decision making, others with single parents on limited incomes, is challenging relatively simple generalisations about buying habits and family influences. Many children, for example, now have (limited) independent financial means, and for various purchases, such as clothes and entertainment, they can be considered as decision makers and buyers in their own right.

The 'pester power' of children on family purchases should not be underestimated. A deep impression was made on one of your authors by the sight of a child, about 10 years old, making a very loud fuss in Sainsbury's one afternoon over a packet of bread rolls. Children are not normally interested in bread rolls, but this particular packet had popular cartoon characters all over it and Mother was not being allowed to move her trolley until the rolls were safely in there. More seriously, parents are often prepared to make great sacrifices in other areas of the family budget and their own individual spending in order to prioritise children's needs and wants, as suggested on p. 124.

Children are an important target group for the marketer, partly because of their ability to pester their parents and influence family purchasing, and partly because of the marketer's desire to create brand loyalty as early as possible in consumers' lives. Colgate has sought to promote responsible dental hygiene through a range of educational packages, as shown in the photograph below. Similarly, Kellogg's gave away 800 000 sample packs of Choco Krispies, while McDonald's provides free meal vouchers to be used as prizes by schools. Not surprisingly, many teachers, parents and consumer groups are concerned that the young and vulnerable may be exposed to unreasonable marketing pressures.

Targeting school children, Colgate promotes responsible dental hygiene.

Source: Colgate Palmolive Ltd.

The wider family also affects the individual's purchasing in the same way as other reference groups do, with the same anxieties about conformity, approval, acceptance and opinion leadership.

Clearly, groups of all kinds have the potential to act as both facilitators and inhibitors of consumer behaviour. An aspiration to join a particular group might make a purchasing decision easier, if the marketing package clearly reflects that aspiration, while membership of an economically interdependent household might mean that, regretfully, a purchase cannot be justified. For each purchase, the individual has to decide which group's influence is the strongest or most important and act accordingly.

CHAPTER SUMMARY

This chapter has centred on consumer buying behaviour, in terms of both the processes through which potential buyers pass in deciding whether to make a purchase and which product to choose, and the factors that influence the decision making itself.

The decision-making process was presented as a number of stages: problem recognition, information search, information evaluation, decision and, finally, post-purchase evaluation. The length of time taken over the process as a whole or over individual stages will vary according to the type of product purchased and the particular consumer concerned. An experienced buyer with past knowledge of the market making a low-risk, low-priced routine purchase will pass through the decision-making process very quickly, almost without realising that it has happened. This is a routine problem solving situation. In contrast, a nervous buyer, lacking knowledge but facing the purchase of a one-off, high-risk, expensive purchase, will prolong the process and consciously seek and analyse information to aid the decision. This is extended problem solving. Decision making is influenced by many factors apart from the type of purchase. Some of these factors are external to the consumer, such as social, economic, legal and technological issues existing within the wider environment.

Closer to home, the consumer influences the decision-making process through psychological factors. The type of personality involved; the individual's perceptions of the world and ability to interpret information; the ability to retain and learn from both experience and marketing communication; the driving motivations behind behaviour; and finally the individual's attitudes and beliefs all shape their responses to the marketing offering and ultimately their acceptance or rejection of it. In addition to that, the individual's choices and behaviour are affected by sociocultural influences defined by the groups to which the individual either belongs or wishes to belong. Social class as traditionally defined is of limited help to the marketer, but cultural or subcultural groups provide clearly differentiated groups of potential customers. Other membership groups, formed through work, hobbies and leisure pursuits, provide the individual with norms that act as reference points to aid decision making. Similarly, aspirations fuel people's needs and wants, and thus marketers can attract customers through reflecting those dreams and promising products that can help fulfil them or at least visibly associate the individual with the aspirant group for a while. One of the strongest group influences comes from the family, affecting decisions on what is purchased, how that decision is made and how the individual feels about that purchase.

Consumer buying behaviour is a complex area, covering a wide range of concepts, but nevertheless is an important one for marketers to understand because it lies at the heart of all marketing decisions.

Key words and phrases

Attitude	Information overload	Purchasing situation
Awareness	Learning	Reference groups
Cognitive dissonance	Limited problem solving	Repeat purchase
Consumer decision making	Motivation	Routine problem solving
Culture	Perception	Social class
Evoked set	Personality	Trial
Extended problem solving	Post-purchase evaluation	
Family life-cycle	Problem recognition	

QUESTIONS FOR REVIEW

3.1 What are the main stages of the consumer buying decision-making process?

3.2 Differentiate between the internal and external stimuli that might trigger the buying process.

3.3 What are the potential sources of information that a consumer might use in the buying process?

3.4 Why is post-purchase evaluation important for:
(a) the consumer; and
(b) the marketer?

3.5 Summarise some of the ways in which marketers can 'help' the consumer at each stage in the decision-making process.

3.6 What are the three different types of buying situation and what kinds of products might be included in each of them?

3.7 How and why might the duration of the decision-making process and the extent of information search differ between the three different types of buying situation?

3.8 How do perception and learning affect consumer decision making, and how can the marketer influence these processes?

3.9 What is an attitude and why are attitudes so difficult to change?

3.10 Summarise the stages of Maslow's hierarchy of needs and their marketing implications.

QUESTIONS FOR DISCUSSION

3.1 Outline the main sources of information that might be used in purchasing:
(a) a new car; and
(b) a packet of biscuits.

3.2 Think of a purchase that you have made recently. What products or brands made up your evoked set of alternatives, and what choice criteria did you use to differentiate between them to lead to your eventual purchase?

3.3 To what extent do you think that social class is a helpful concept in improving the marketer's understanding of consumer behaviour?

3.4 Define the three main types of reference group. Within each type, think of examples that relate to you as a consumer, and analyse how this might affect your own buying behaviour.

3.5 How might the roles undertaken by various members of a two parent family vary between the buying decisions for:
(a) a house;
(b) something for tonight's dinner; and
(c) a birthday present for a 10-year-old child?

How would your answer change if it was a one parent family?

CASE STUDY 3.1

Reaching the youth market: Euroteens

The youth market, consisting of teenagers and those in their early twenties, is potentially very lucrative. These consumers have disposable income and are fashion conscious, which means that they are buying often in order to keep up with the latest trends in clothes, music and leisure. Marketers recognise that this group has different needs from older, perhaps more traditional consumers. An increasing number of specialist agencies are now researching young consumers to discover what motivates their purchasing and how they make decisions. Euroquest, for example, a network of market research agencies, produced a survey called *Teenagers Europe*, examining 11–19-year-olds across the UK, France, Germany and Italy. These four countries alone represent a market of 27 million teenagers with £24.8 billion of purchasing power. Their spending priorities are remarkably similar. Clothes are the top priority in Germany, France and Italy, with 'going out' second. In the UK, it is the other way around: 50 per cent of teenagers are fashion conscious and 66 per cent take a lot of care over their appearance; 60 per cent agreed that they could not live without music and thus spending on CDs and related music products is also very high on the list. The average amount of disposable income they have, however, varies from country to country: in the UK it is just over £25 per week, whereas Italy has the lowest figure of around £12. The survey also found that UK teenagers watch television for four or more hours per day, much longer than in any of the other countries, presumably because 75 per cent of UK teenagers have televisions in their bedrooms, again a higher proportion than anywhere else. Perhaps more positively, 90 per cent of UK teenagers use computers, yet again a higher proportion than in any other country. The brand preferences they have in common across all four countries are perhaps as expected: 70 per cent prefer to drink Coke and 60 per cent have visited a McDonald's within last three months.

GfK carried out a similar survey, *Hopes and Fears: Young European Opinion Leaders* across 16 countries in Western, Eastern and Central Europe and in Scandinavia. This survey found that young people are driven by ambition and are afraid of failure. They want to live life to the full. They are very individualistic and do not want to be 'packaged' or classified. As reported by Croft (1998a), they are very suspicious of IT, thinking that it diminishes

human interaction and lacks warmth, and the more intellectual individuals 'show no desire for the Global Village or teleworking'. These young people think that they will work longer and harder than any previous generation because the distinction between home and work is no longer clear cut. Girls are less attracted to interaction through the Internet than are boys and still prefer the telephone. Mobiles are considered to be too expensive, the fax simply is not popular with this generation and most do not have access to e-mail. The survey also concludes that this generation wants to purchase from companies with a strong sense of social responsibility and an ethical culture. Additionally, this generation is not interested in clichés and is very advertising and marketing literate (although Eastern European youth is not quite as cynical . . . yet). Marketers thus need to keep a respectful distance and communicate carefully. As Croft (1998a) puts it, this generation is 'brand aware and brand dismissive . . . nothing is forever'.

These conclusions are echoed by De Parcevaux (1998) in a discussion of French 15–25-year-olds. They are considered to be good at decoding advertising and marketing messages and they have plenty of money to spend on themselves. They conform to the tastes and fashions of their peer group and it is important to them to do so. De Parcevaux suggests that these consumers are:

- *pragmatic and realistic*: they are less receptive to messages of consumption than are older generations and will not be patronised; they like products and messages that do not take themselves too seriously;
- *price sensitive*: 85 per cent of 15–25-year-olds say that a competitive price is an incentive to buy, compared with 60 per cent for environmental issues and 56 per cent for products connected with a humanitarian cause;
- *pleasure seekers*: spending priorities are clothes, going out, hi-fi and video-related products, holidays and leisure; they want anything new, surprising, or aesthetically pleasing, and 75 per cent of them admit to impulse purchasing;
- *keen to assert themselves as individuals*: although they are fashion conscious and peer group influenced, they still want individuality, to differentiate themselves somehow from their friends;

- *flexible in their relationships with brands*: 20–30-year-olds in particular are experienced consumers, have changeable tastes and are prepared to switch brands; for 15–18-year-olds, brands play an important role and they look for 'cult' brands such as cKone;
- *aspiring to universal values*: they want to belong to 'international youth', an identity built from a frontierless culture defined by music and sport;
- *reluctant to do anything that constrains them*: they are not interested in anything hierarchical, organised or too 'packaged' – thus the mobile phone companies' 'pay as you go' schemes are very appealing because there is no contract, no bills and no commitment.

Sources: Croft (1998a); De Parcevaux (1998); Morris (1997); Phillips (1997).

Questions

1 How might the characteristics of French youth, as described by De Parcevaux, affect the marketing mix for (a) clothing, (b) toiletries and (c) soft drinks.

2 How do you think sociocultural influences influence the purchasing decision-making processes of the young people described in these surveys?

3 To what extent is there really a single Euroteen market that is meaningful to marketers?

CASE STUDY 3.2

Premium lagers

The shape of the lager and beer markets has changed as drinkers have become increasingly discerning in the brands that they choose. Although people now generally drink less, they are prepared to spend more and the brewers have realised that quality rather than sheer quantity is what a significant segment of the market wants. The competition is fierce, however, as many brewers, both large and small, try to develop brands with European or even global appeal. In the UK alone, the take-home premium lager market is worth over £620 million and has shown significant growth. The total UK market for beer sold through pubs and clubs (the on-trade) declined by 2.7 per cent in 1997, whereas sales of premium lagers rose by 6.7 per cent. It is a similar story in high street shops, supermarkets and off-licences (the off-trade): the total beer market rose by just over 1 per cent in 1997 while the premium lager sector rose by 15.4 per cent. In addition, 2.6 per cent of women and 5.9 per cent of men are likely to have drunk a premium lager in the last week. Women have become increasingly important customers in this market and by 1998, one in six women were lager drinkers and the numbers were continuing to grow. The top brands are aware of this and are anxious not to alienate women with their marketing communications approaches. Thus the marketing of premium lagers has become more 'sensitive'.

The market leader in both the on- and off-trades is Stella Artois, a Belgian lager, brewed and marketed under licence in the UK by Whitbread (http://www.whitbread.com). It holds about 30 per cent of the market for premium lagers and prides itself on being 'reassuringly expensive'. Its strength in the marketplace, according to Whitbread's marketing manager, has been established by:

> *not going for football and birds in its advertising – it has ads in French and the brand has sponsored tennis. Being different helps.*

Some brands do focus on football, even if they give the birds a miss. Carlsberg not only sponsors the shirts of Liverpool and Hibernian football clubs, but also became the 'official beer of the England team' in the 1998 World Cup tournament. This gave the brand a platform for World Cup sales promotions, special edition cans and a 'Probably the Best Team in the World' advertising campaign.

From Stella's point of view, however, being different and sponsoring tennis are effective ways of appealing to women drinkers and Whitbread does maintain that Stella advertisements are popular among women. Kronenbourg 1664 is number two in the market. It holds a 16.5 per cent market share, with sales growing by 22 per cent per a year. In October 1998, Kronenbourg 1664 launched a £10 million advertising campaign aimed at women aged between 18 and 24. The advertisement emphasised 'Kronenbourg's urban heritage and sophistication' and was designed to be unisex, appealing to both men and women.

▶

The reasons for more women entering this market are many and varied. The huge amounts spent by the brewers on marketing must have a lot to do with it. The big brands have generated a great deal of awareness and desirability for their brands: 'people want to drink a label in the same way they want to wear a label', as Maling (1998) puts it. A buyer for the Iceland retail chain thinks that the rise in the number of female lager drinkers is a result of the Channel Tunnel. More British people are visiting continental Europe, trying and buying lagers at cheaper prices than in the UK and bringing them home. It is also suggested that the trend towards packaging premium lagers in smaller bottles makes them more attractive to women. Market research has found that the impact of women has been felt mainly in the off-trade. This could be a result of the proliferation of lager brands on supermarket shelves, making them just another grocery purchase and easily accessible to women. As part of a £10 million relaunch of Carlsberg Export (number three in the market), Carlsberg-Tetley distributed the product through supermarkets and off-licences for the first time. Perhaps this too is an attempt to reach the growing female market.

The premium lager market faces occasional threats as other drinks, such as white cider and alcoholic lemonades and colas, go in and out of fashion with younger drinkers. The spirits sector has also presented its challenges. Bacardi Breezers (based on rum and fruit juice), Smirnoff Mule (vodka, ginger and lime), Metz (Martini based) and V2 (vodka and Martini) are among the brands launched in the mid- to late 1990s, again targeted at younger drinkers.

Sources: Benady (1998); *The Grocer* (1998b); Maling (1998).

Questions

1 Outline how the buying decision-making process might work for (a) on-trade and (b) off-trade lager purchasing.

2 What individual and group influences are likely to affect someone's choice of lager brand?

3 Why has lager traditionally been targeted at males aged between 20 and 40? How and why is this changing?

4 Given the huge range of premium lagers available, why do you think there is still room in the market for products such as Bacardi Breezers?

References to Chapter 3

Alderson, A. and Olins, R. (1995), 'Yob Commercials Split Ad Agencies', *Sunday Times*, 16 April 1995.

Bainbridge, J. (1998), '2010 Vision', *Marketing*, 4 June, pp. 18–19.

Benady, D. (1998), 'C-T Revamps Export to Draw UK Drinkers', *Marketing Week*, 16 July, pp. 19–20.

Bloch, P. H. *et al.* (1986), 'Consumer Search: An Extended Framework', *Journal of Consumer Research*, 13 (Jun), pp. 119–26.

Bray, L. (1997), 'Focus on Frozen Foods', *The Grocer*, 31 May, pp. 36–8.

Bruner, G. C. and Pomazal, R. J. (1988), 'Problem Recognition: The Crucial First Stage of the Consumer Decision Process', *Journal of Consumer Marketing*, 5(1), pp. 53–63.

Clay, P. (1998), 'Advalue: the Automobile Association', *Marketing Week*, 14 May, pp. 44–5.

Chisnall, P. M. (1985), *Marketing: A Behavioural Analysis*, McGraw-Hill.

Croft, M. (1998a), 'Technology Leaves Teens Cold', *Marketing Week*, 25 June, pp. 38–9.

Croft, M. (1998b), 'Women Who Mean Business', *Marketing Week*, 3 September, pp. 38–9.

Croft, M. (1999), 'Retailers Lose Feminine Touch', *Marketing Week*, 28 January, pp. 38–9.

Crosbie, P. (1998), 'Now Girl Power Plugs in to Joys of DIY', *The Express*, 16 March, p. 3.

De Parcevaux, A.-C. (1998), 'L'art de séduire les 15–25 ans', *L'Entreprise*, Nº 149, February, pp. 84–8.

Duncan, C. P. (1990), 'Consumer Market Beliefs: A Review of the Literature and an Agenda for Further Research', in G. Marrin *et al.* (eds.), *Advances in Consumer Research*, Association for Consumer Research.

Dwek, R. (1995), 'In Front of the Children', *The Grocer*, 2 December, pp. 45–9.

Ehrenberg, A. S. C. and Goodhart, G. J. (1980), *How Advertising Works*, JWT/MRCA.

Engel, J. F., Blackwell, R. D. and Miniard, P. W. (1990), *Consumer Behaviour*, Dryden.

Engel, J. F., Kollat, D. T. and Blackwell, R. D. (1978), *Consumer Behaviour*, Dryden.

Festinger, L. (1957), *A Theory of Cognitive Dissonance*, Stanford University Press.

Fishbein, M. (1967), 'Attitude and Prediction of Behaviour', in M. Fishbein (ed.), *Readings in Attitude Theory and Measurement*, Wiley.

Fishbein, M. (1975), 'Attitude, Attitude Change and Behaviour: A Theoretical Overview', in P. Levine (ed.), *Attitude Research Bridges the Atlantic*, Chicago: American Marketing Association.

Foxall, G. (1984), 'Consumers' Intentions and Behaviour', *Journal of the Market Research Society*, 26, 231–41.

Gooding, H. (1998), 'Racial Integration', *Marketing Week*, 16 July, pp. 41–2.

The Grocer (1998a), 'Automatic Choice', *The Grocer*, 7 February, p. 35.

The Grocer (1998b), 'C-T Goes All the Way', *The Grocer*, 23 May, p. 54.

The Grocer (1998c), 'Bagged Snacks', *The Grocer*, 13 June, p. 36.

Hardcastle, S. (1997), 'Children's Products: Oh Please Mum', *The Grocer*, 6 December, pp. 39–40.

Hardcastle, S. (1998), 'Exploring Frozen Tastes', *The Grocer*, 20 June, pp. 41–6.

Hauser, J. *et al.* (1993), 'How Consumers Allocate Their Time When Searching for Information', *Journal of Marketing Research*, November, pp. 452–66.

Henderson, M. (1997), 'Class Tightens its Grip on Britain', *The Times*, 15 December, p. 7.

Hilgard, E. R. *et al.* (1975), *Introduction to Psychology*, (6th edn.) Harcourt Brace Jovanovich.

Hilgard, E. R. and Marquis, D. G. (1961), *Conditioning and Learning*, Appleton Century Crofts.

Howard, J. A. and Sheth, J. N. (1969), *The Theory of Buyer Behaviour*, Wiley.

Inskip, I. (1995), 'Marketers Develop a Class Consciousness', *Marketing Week*, 13 January, p. 23.

Jacoby, J. *et al.* (1974), 'Brand Choice as a Function of Information Load', *Journal of Marketing Research*, 11 (Feb), pp. 63–9.

Joyce, T. (1967), 'What do We Know About How Advertising Works?', *Advertising Age*, May/June.

Kassarjian, H. H. (1971), 'Personality and Consumer Behaviour: A Review', *Journal of Marketing Research*, 8 (Nov.), pp. 409–18.

Keller, K. L. and Staelin, R. (1987), 'Effects of Quality and Quantity of Information on Decision Effectiveness', *Journal of Consumer Research*, 14 (Sept.), pp. 200–13.

Kelly, J. (1998), 'Hope Lies With our Children', *The Grocer*, 3 October, pp. 39–45.

Korfman, K. (1991), 'Comparability and Comparison Levels Used in Choices among Consumer Products', *Journal of Marketing Research*, August, pp. 368–74.

Lightfoot, L. and Wavell, S. (1995), 'Mum's Not the Word', *Sunday Times*, 16 April.

Lutz, R. J. (1981), 'The Role of Attitude Theory in Marketing', in H. K. Kassarjian and T. S. Robertson (eds.), *Perspectives in Consumer Behaviour*, Scott, Foresman.

Maling, N. (1998), 'Lager Gets in Touch With its Female Side', *Marketing Week*, 24 September, pp. 21–2.

Marketing Week (1998), 'More Connect to Computers', *Marketing Week*, 19 February, pp. 38–9.

Marketing Week (1999a), 'Star Chart', *Marketing Week*, 7 January, pp. 22–6.

Marketing Week (1999b), 'Computers and the Internet', *Marketing Week*, 28 January, pp. 40–1.

Maslow, A. H. (1954), *Motivation and Personality*, Harper and Row.

Matthews, V. (1998), 'Girls Do it for Themselves', *The Times*, 23 January, p. 45.

McLoughlin, L. (1997), 'OTC Healthcare: Grab a 36 Pack Please Dear', *The Grocer*, 28 June, pp. 39–44.

Menasco, M. B. and Curry, D. J. (1989), 'Utility and Choice: An Empirical Study of Wife/Husband Decision Making', *Journal of Consumer Research*, 16 (June), pp. 87–97.

Morris, N. (1997), 'How to Give Youth What They Really, Really Want', *Marketing Week*, 14 August, p. 12.

Norton, C. (1997), '"Dettox Generation" Fails Hygiene Test', *The Sunday Times*, 9 November, p. 10.

Norton, G. (1998), 'Upwardly Mobile Britain Splits into 17 New Classes', *The Sunday Times*, 13 September, p. 1.9.

O'Connor, J. and Galvin, E. (1999), *Marketing and Information Technology*, 2nd edn, Financial Times Pitman Publishing.

O'Sullivan, T. (1997), 'Rescue Mission', *Marketing Week*, 24 April, pp. 38–41.

Oldfield, C. (1998), 'Designer Labels Suit Young Men', *The Sunday Times*, 19 July, p. 3.4.

Phillips, A. (1997), 'The Difficulty of Discovering What Makes Euroteens Tick', *Marketing Week*, 11 December, pp. 28–9.

Rafiq, M. (1990), *Are Asians Taking Over British Retailing?*, Paper 1990:12, Loughborough University Management Research Series.

Rice, C. (1993), *Consumer Behaviour: Behavioural Aspects of Marketing*, Butterworth-Heinemann.

Riley, M. (1994), 'Marketing Eating Out: The Influence of Social Culture and Innovation', *British Food Journal*, 96 (10), pp. 15–18.

Rushe, D. (1998), 'Pubs Cash in on Girl Power', *The Sunday Times*, 21 June, pp. 3–8.

Shaddick, C. (1998), 'Internet Advertising Poised to Change Buyers' Habits', *Marketing Week*, 15 January, pp. 32–3.

Shannon, J. (1997), 'Children Power Comes of Age', *Marketing Week*, 2 October, p. 33.

Smith, P. R. (1993), *Marketing Communications: An Integrated Approach*, Kogan Page.

Steen, J. (1995), 'Now They're Using Suicide to Sell Jeans', *Sunday Express*, 26 March 1995.

Sutton, R. J. (1987), 'Using Empirical Data to Investigate the Likelihood of Brands Being Admitted or Readmitted into an Established Evoked Set', *Journal of the Academy of Marketing Science*, 15 (Fall), p. 82.

Wells, W. D. and Gubar, R. G. (1966), 'Life Cycle Concepts in Marketing Research', *Journal of Marketing Research*, 3 (Nov.), pp. 355–63.

Williams, K. C. (1981), *Behavioural Aspects of Marketing*, Heinemann Professional Publishing.

4 Organisational Buying Behaviour

LEARNING OBJECTIVES

This chapter will help you to:

1 understand the nature and structure of organisational buying;

2 appreciate the differences between organisational and consumer buying;

3 analyse the reasons that purchasing varies across different buying situations; and

4 link organisational buying with the development of marketing strategy.

INTRODUCTION

The essence of the marketing philosophy was described at the beginning of this book as the satisfaction of customers' needs and wants through the provision of the right products and services, at the right time, in the right place at the right price. This remains true whether that customer is an individual or an organisation. All organisations, whether making products or delivering services, purchase goods and services from a range of suppliers so that they can run their own operations. Consider, for example, a small local garage. It may purchase not only petrol, but also spare parts, tools, supplies, some capital machinery, confectionery, and accountancy services, for instance. Compare that with a large steel producer or car assembly plant and the thousands of suppliers that are dealt with regularly.

Example ICI (http://www.ici.com) targeted savings of over £500 million from its Symphony supply chain project. The aim of the project was to rationalise the supplier base and to create better value for ICI from the remaining suppliers. Of the company's £7 billion annual spend, just 9000 suppliers accounted for £5.5 billion and 44 000 for the remaining £1.5 billion. By establishing more group-wide deals, improving information technology for ordering and tracking, and developing a clear preferred supplier framework, Symphony brought significant savings. Previously, for example, there were nearly 60 suppliers across Europe for steel drums. After Symphony, Van Leer in the Netherlands gained the group contract, resulting in significant savings to ICI from purchasing in larger quantities at better terms from just one supplier (*Supply Management*, 1998).

There are, therefore, sufficient differences between individuals and organisations in what they purchase and the ways in which they go about their purchasing to make separate consideration worthwhile.

This chapter looks at the special characteristics and problems of organisational markets, beginning with a definition of organisational marketing and a classification of organisational customers. The characteristics of organisational markets are then discussed, and attention is given to the ways in which they differ from consumer markets. The buying decision-making process is analysed, laying the foundations for looking at the roles that individuals and groups play within it. The last two sections examine the criteria, both economic and non-economic, that affect organisational purchasing and the importance of long-lasting buyer–seller relationships.

In your wider reading you may come across the terms *business-to-business marketing* and *industrial marketing*. Generally speaking, these terms are often used interchangeably with 'organisational marketing'. This text, however, uses the term organisational marketing as a constant reminder that not all organisations that make substantial purchases, for example government departments, universities and hospitals, are in business in the profit-making sense of the word, nor are they in industry in the narrow manufacturing sense. Thus, as pp. 137 *et seq.* will show, the term organisational marketing covers a wide range of purchasing relationships between a wide range of organisations without excluding or indeed offending any one of them. First, however, it is important to define more precisely what organisational marketing is.

DEFINING ORGANISATIONAL MARKETING

Organisational marketing is the management process responsible for the facilitation of exchange between producers of goods and services and their organisational customers. This might involve, for example, a clothing manufacturer selling uniforms to the army, a component manufacturer selling microchips to IBM, an advertising agency selling its expertise to Kellogg, Kellogg selling its breakfast cereals to a large supermarket chain, or a university selling short management training courses to local firms. Whatever the type of product or organisation, the focus is the same, centred on the exchange, the flow of goods and services that enable other organisations to operate, produce, add value and/or re-sell. Figure 4.1, even though it only offers a simplified view of this flow, gives an idea of the number and complexity of exchanges involved in getting products to the end user or consumer.

The steel producer, for example, takes raw materials (and we will not even begin to consider the mining, refining and transport processes that go into the production of the iron ore and coke that the steel producer buys) and turns them into steel that is then pressed into panels or cast into components to sell on. The car producer can then assemble these components, along with others from different sources (glass, plastics, paints, fabrics, tyres, electrics etc.), with the finished car as the output to be sold on.

Both the steel producer and the car manufacturer use more than just the components and raw materials that make the physical product, however. Both of them also buy in various services and supplies that support the main production without directly providing a physical part of it. For example, proper planned maintenance of plant and machinery is essential for safe and consistent production. The steel producer will perhaps use contract engineering service companies to do this work and would consider it as contributing indirectly to the end product. Similarly, the supplies and services used by the quality control function or the managers and administrators that keep a smooth flow of goods and orders in and out of the organisation support the end product indirectly. Thus an organisation may have to purchase not only raw materials and semi-finished goods, but also financial, technical and management consultancy services.

Once the cars or the spares leave the car manufacturer, the retail showroom, i.e. the car dealership, as a *re-seller*, takes the products and sells them to the general public with little change other than perhaps the addition of number plates and fine tuning of the engine. Most of the *value added* comes from intangible elements of customer service.

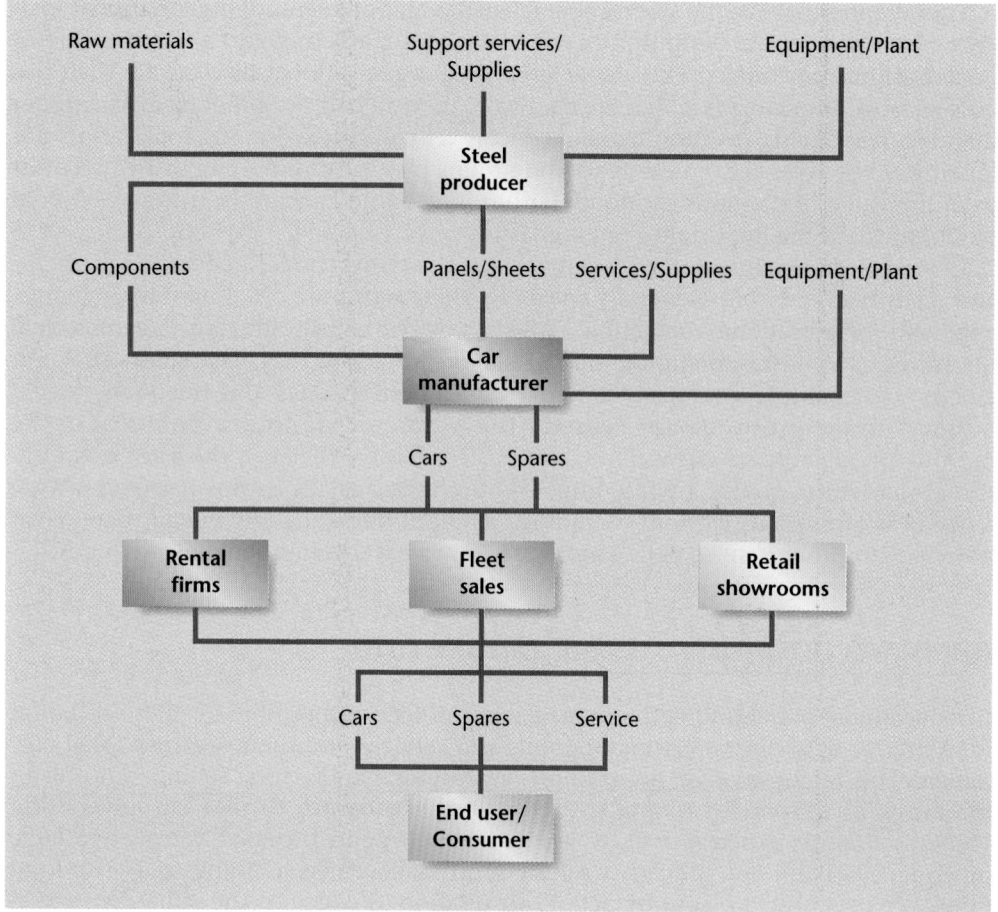

FIGURE 4.1

Flows within an organisational market

Even at the re-seller level, there are also other support services to consider. A car dealership selling to the general public, for instance, would put a lot of thought into the design and ambience of the showroom, the training of its sales and service staff and its advertising and other promotional activities. All these services can be bought in and add to the successful sale of the physical product.

All of this goes to show that organisational marketing and purchasing is a complex and risky business. An organisation may buy many thousands of products and services, costing anything from a few pennies to many millions of pounds per item. The risks are high in these markets where a bad decision, even on a minor component, can bring manufacturing to a halt or cause entire production runs to be scrapped as sub-standard.

Example The building of Oslo's new airport for Kr11.4 billion represents a complex task in ensuring that the 150 separate contractors all meet the required service and performance standards over the five-year building period. All contracts were placed in accordance with GATT rules and EC directives on public procurement and advertised in a special publication to invite any interested company to bid. Non-Scandinavian companies were free to bid, but very few bothered to tender and those that did, other than in very specialised areas, tended to be unsuccessful due to uncompetitive prices.

A two stage bidding process was introduced. First, a pre-qualification stage established which bidders actually had the capability to do the job; the second stage was a closed bidding system (i.e. no bidder knows what anybody else has bid) between a small number of potential suppliers. At least three bids were sought for each contract, and project management and control skills were important criteria for the final decision. This was because an essential requirement was the ability to work alongside other contractors, often against tough deadlines. In cases where a particular supplier was preferred, but the final bid price was considered too high, post-tender negotiations were held to see if further reductions were possible (Nordby, 1996).

There are several differences between organisational and consumer marketing, as Table 4.1 shows. If a consumer goes to the supermarket and finds that their preferred brand of baked beans is not there, then it is disappointing, but not a disaster. The consumer can easily substitute an alternative brand, or go to another supermarket, or the family can have something else for lunch. If, however, a supplier fails to deliver as promised on a component, then the purchasing organisation has a big problem, especially if there are no easily accessible alternative sources of supply, and runs the risk of letting its own customers down with all the commercial damage that implies. Any failure by any link in this chain has a severe impact on the others.

Thus the links have to be forged carefully, and relationships *managed* over time to minimise the potential problems or to diagnose them early enough for action to be taken. Policy decisions have to be made about purchasing, for example whether to source from one supplier only (**single sourcing**) or from several suppliers (**multiple sourcing**), and how the purchasing process should operate (who is authorised to do what and with what safeguards). All these issues will be addressed later in this chapter.

TABLE 4.1

Differences between organisational and consumer marketing

Organisational customers often/usually ...	Customer customers often/usually ...
■ purchase goods and services that meet specific business needs ■ need emphasis on economic benefits ■ use formalised, lengthy purchasing policies and processes ■ involve large groups in purchasing decisions ■ buy large quantities and buy infrequently ■ want a customised product package ■ experience major problems if supply fails ■ find switching to another supplier difficult ■ negotiate on price ■ purchase direct from suppliers ■ justify an emphasis on personal selling	■ purchase goods and services to meet individual or family needs ■ need emphasis on psychological benefits ■ buy on impulse or with minimal processes ■ purchase as individuals or as a family unit ■ buy small quantities and buy frequently ■ are content with a standardised product package targeted at a specific market segment ■ experience minor irritation if supply fails ■ find switching to another supplier easy ■ accept the stated price ■ purchase from intermediaries ■ justify an emphasis on mass media communication

A final reminder of the volume and variety of organisational buyer–seller relationships is provided in Fig. 4.2, which shows in detail the wide range of goods and services essential to a clothing manufacturer. All these goods and services represent relationships that have to be established, maintained and sustained.

ORGANISATIONAL CUSTOMERS

So far, only one kind of organisational buying situation has been considered in detail, that of a profit-making organisation involved in transactions with other similarly oriented concerns. There are, however, other kinds of organisation that have different

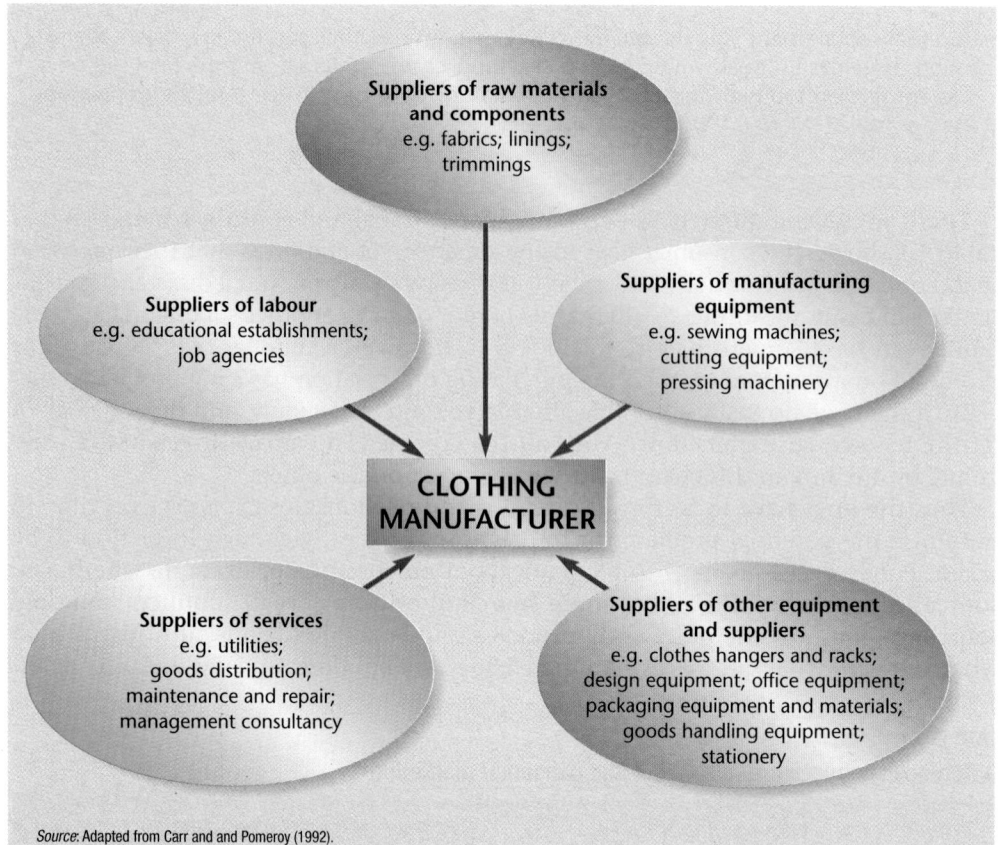

FIGURE 4.2

A clothing manufacturer and its suppliers

philosophies and approaches to purchasing. Overall, there are three main classes: commercial enterprises, government bodies and institutions, each of which represents a lot of buying power.

Commercial enterprises

Commercial enterprises consist of profit-making organisations that produce and/or re-sell goods and services for a profit. All the members of the flow shown in Fig. 4.1 fall into this category, which can be further divided into a number of subgroups.

Users

Users purchase goods and services to facilitate their own production, although the item purchased does not enter directly into the finished product. Examples of this are CAD/CAM systems, office equipment and management consultancy services. Large chemical and steel process manufacturing plants may source a wide range of services from a myriad of local, and often small, suppliers. Plumbers, cleaners, caterers and travel agents thus supply services that are an indirect means to an end rather than a direct influence on production. Although some vetting and inspection may take place before these suppliers are allowed on to the list of approved suppliers, these procedures are far less rigorous than those imposed on companies wishing to supply goods and materials that do directly enter or support the production process.

Original Equipment Manufacturers

Original Equipment Manufacturers (OEMs) incorporate their purchases into their own product, as the car manufacturer does with the electrics, fabrics, plastics, paint, tyres etc. Some of these components will be recognisable even after the OEM has finished with them, for instance a tyre is a recognisable element of a car and is usually strongly branded by the original supplier, whereas others, such as the paint, are incorporated anonymously. Recognisability is important for the tyre manufacturer as a means of developing links with the end consumer and encouraging brand loyalty when it is time to buy new tyres. OEMs' purchasing is very closely linked with forecast demand for their end products, and needs good buyer–seller co-ordination as it has to be tied in with production schedules.

Re-sellers

Re-sellers purchase goods for re-sale, usually making no physical changes to them. As mentioned above when discussing the car dealership, the value added stems largely from service elements. A full outline of the role and function of re-sellers can be found in Part V of this book. This group is the closest to the end consumer of the product and should, therefore, be able to feed valuable information back up the chain on what the end market really wants.

Government bodies

Government bodies are very large, important purchasers of goods and services. In the UK, the National Health Service has a £5.5 billion supplies budget per year, while the Ministry of Defence has an annual spend of over £9 billion on equipment and supplies. Purchasing power of this magnitude makes them both highly attractive targets for suppliers.

This group of organisational buyers includes both local and national government, as well as European Commission purchasing. The range of purchasing is wide, from office supplies to public buildings, from army bootlaces to battleships, from airline tickets to motorways, from refuse collection to management consultancy. Although some purchases may be very large, expensive and high profile, involving international suppliers, as is often seen in defence procurement, others are much more mundane and routine, and involve very little public concern.

Because of the traditional bureaucracy and public accountability surrounding government sector purchasing, there are specialised purchasing procedures that are often more explicit and formal than those found in many commercial organisations. Such a procedure might be:

The development of precise specifications for the good or service
For more innovative and large-scale projects, the development of specifications may be done in conjunction with specialist consultants and the potential suppliers' development personnel.

Tendering for the right to supply
Organisations are requested to bid or tender for the right to supply. Some jobs are only open to tender from organisations already on an approved list, while others are open to anyone.

Assessment of tenders
The submitted tenders are assessed and the winning one is chosen.

Tendering is a very competitive process that demands that the suppliers are well tuned into the procedures and are able to find out early what tenders are on offer. Much of this is down to having the right contacts within the purchasing organisation and maintaining good relationships and communication links with them (within ethical boundaries, of course). These issues of buyer–seller relationships are expanded further at p. 150 and pp. 166 *et seq*. It is often too late to establish contact once formal bidding has begun. The contact and reputation building necessary for next year's bids needs to be done this year.

The EU, as part of the single European market (SEM) initiative, issued a Public Services Directive stating that for any of its purchasing needs of 200 000 ECU (five million ECU for construction bids) or more, the contract must be advertised openly for tender across all community boundaries. In 1987 some 12 000 tender notices were published in the *EC Official Journal* and this had risen to 90 000 by 1995, although this was estimated to be still a long way from the total number that should have been published. The Public Services Directive aimed to encourage more cross-border trading, especially for smaller companies, but it has been criticised for creating more bureaucracy and actually doing little to help smaller companies to compete across Europe (Nolan, 1997a). It was suggested in a *Eurostrategy* survey of 1600 suppliers that only 41 per cent of them had obtained information from the *Official Journal* and just 4 per cent had actually won business in another member state. The final selection must be made on objective, non-discriminatory criteria within defined European standards.

> **Example** Europe's largest multinational aerospace project, the Eurofighter aircraft, is a good example of the complexity of purchasing management when national governments are involved. After many years in the design and development stage that began in 1982, the first production orders for 620 aircraft were agreed only after much wrangling. The allocation of the work involved had to satisfy the needs of all the governments involved, Italy, the UK, Spain and Germany, and their air forces.
>
> The prime subcontractors for the production orders are also the shareholders of the consortium company Eurofighter GmBh (http://www.eurofighter-typhoon.com). This is an alliance between Alenia, British Aerospace, Construcciones Aeronautics SA (CASA) and Daimler-Benz Aerospace (DASA). They in turn deal with 400 suppliers worldwide that supply aircraft components and systems. The governments of each nation are keen to ensure that their prime contractors and supply industries achieve a good share of production, not only for the long-term trade benefit in sales and employment, but also to facilitate technology transfer to their national suppliers. It is claimed that the Eurofighter is the most advanced multi-combat aircraft and that the order book is the largest for military jets in the world. The long-term order potential is extremely attractive to the nations concerned. In the UK alone it has been estimated that 40 000 jobs have been secured by the project (Kahn, 1997). As a compromise, therefore, the share of work allocated to each of the prime subcontractors was linked with the number of aircraft ordered by that nation's airforce: the greater the number of aircraft purchased, the greater the production allocation to the prime subcontractor. Germany, therefore, received 30 per cent of production with 180 Eurofighters ordered, the UK 37 per cent for 232 aircraft ordered, Spain had just 14 per cent for an order of 87 aircraft, and Italy got the rest (Varley, 1998a, 1998b).

Institutions

This group includes (largely) non-profit making organisations such as universities, churches and independent schools. These institutions may have an element of government funding, but in purchasing terms they are autonomous. They are likely to follow some of the same procedures as government bodies, but with a greater degree of flexibility of choice. A university, for example, has to purchase a wide range of products and services in order to teach and undertake research and consultancy. Large capital projects, such as a new lecture theatre, perhaps part financed by government, may be subject to tendering and closed bidding (i.e. a potential supplier makes a bid without knowing what price anyone else has quoted). Many other supplies are purchased with varying degrees of efficiency and formality from a range of different suppliers. A typical university may deal with over 5000 suppliers, although the bulk of purchases may come from just a few of them.

CHARACTERISTICS OF ORGANISATIONAL MARKETS

The differences between consumer and organisational markets do not lie so much in the products themselves as in the context in which those products are exchanged, that is, the use of the marketing mix and the interaction between buyer and seller. The same model of personal computer, for example, can be bought as a one-off by an individual for private use, or in bulk to equip an entire office. The basic product is identical in specification but the ways in which it is bought and sold will differ.

The following subsections look at some of the characteristics of organisational markets that generate these different approaches.

Nature of demand

Derived demand

All demand in organisational markets is derived from some kind of consumer demand. So, for example, washing machine manufacturers demand electric motors from an engineering factory, and that is an organisational market. The numbers of electric motors demanded, however, depend on predictions of future consumer demand for washing machines. If, as has happened, there is a recession and consumers stop buying the end product, then demand for the component parts of it will also dry up.

Figure 4.3 represents the links in the chain stretching from forestry to reading material. At each stage in the process, there are different influences on the activities and behaviour of the organisations, yet these have implications both up and down the chain. In northern Europe, for example, between 30 and 40 per cent of the population read newspapers, whereas in southern Europe it is closer to 10 per cent. An increase in that reading rate to bring it closer to the northern level would have a great impact on those supplying paper to the newspaper industry in that region. Similarly, the increase in demand for high-quality, full colour special interest publications (for instance CD review magazines) affects the type, quality and quantity of paper and printing processes demanded.

Neu Engineering's systems are vital for the safe storage of dry ingredients such as sugar.

Source: Neu Engineering.

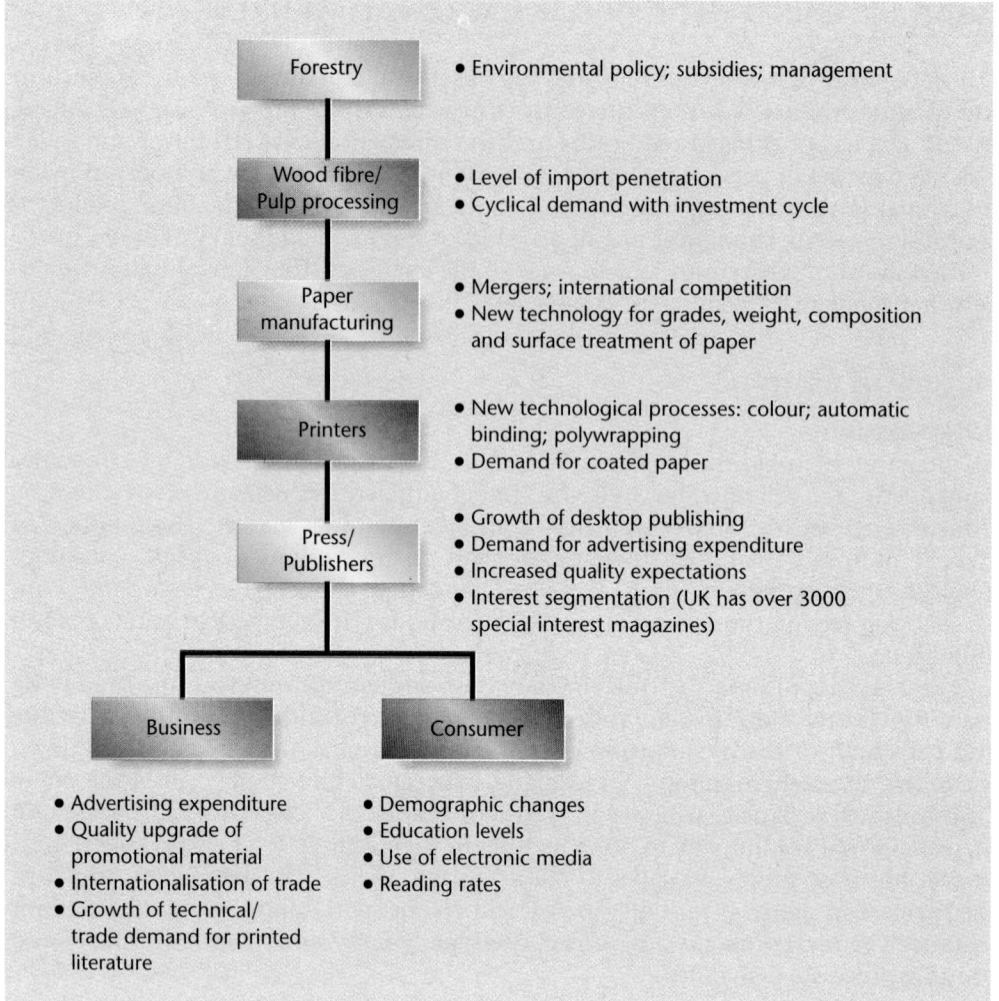

Forestry
- Environmental policy; subsidies; management

Wood fibre/ Pulp processing
- Level of import penetration
- Cyclical demand with investment cycle

Paper manufacturing
- Mergers; international competition
- New technology for grades, weight, composition and surface treatment of paper

Printers
- New technological processes: colour; automatic binding; polywrapping
- Demand for coated paper

Press/ Publishers
- Growth of desktop publishing
- Demand for advertising expenditure
- Increased quality expectations
- Interest segmentation (UK has over 3000 special interest magazines)

Business
- Advertising expenditure
- Quality upgrade of promotional material
- Internationalisation of trade
- Growth of technical/ trade demand for printed literature

Consumer
- Demographic changes
- Education levels
- Use of electronic media
- Reading rates

FIGURE 4.3

Influences on an organisational purchasing chain

Example Transport accounted for 26 per cent of aluminium use in Western countries in 1997, and the second biggest sector was construction, using 20 per cent. It is important, therefore, that aluminium producers such as Alcan should follow usage trends very closely in those markets. In the motor industry, for example, the trend is towards greater aluminium content in passenger cars. Aluminium content was 85kg per car in 1997 and it is expected to rise to 130kg by 2005. By substituting aluminium for steel, the overall weight of a car can be reduced, leading to better fuel consumption, reduced exhaust omissions, improved safety with reduced braking distances, and overall allowing more scope for new, sometimes weighty features such as air conditioning (Batchelor, 1998). The manufacturers of substitutes, such as steel, must also follow trends very carefully if they are to plan capacity over the next 10 years.

Another problem with derived demand is that the further up the supply chain an organisation is, the more remote it is from the end consumer and the further ahead it has to look in order to predict demand. In the fashion industry, for example, organisations such as ICI and DuPont that produce dyes and fibres have to be two years ahead of the market. This means that in spring 2000 they will be deciding what colours and fabrics will be fashionable in spring 2002! Figure 4.4 shows how those two years are used up in the product development process.

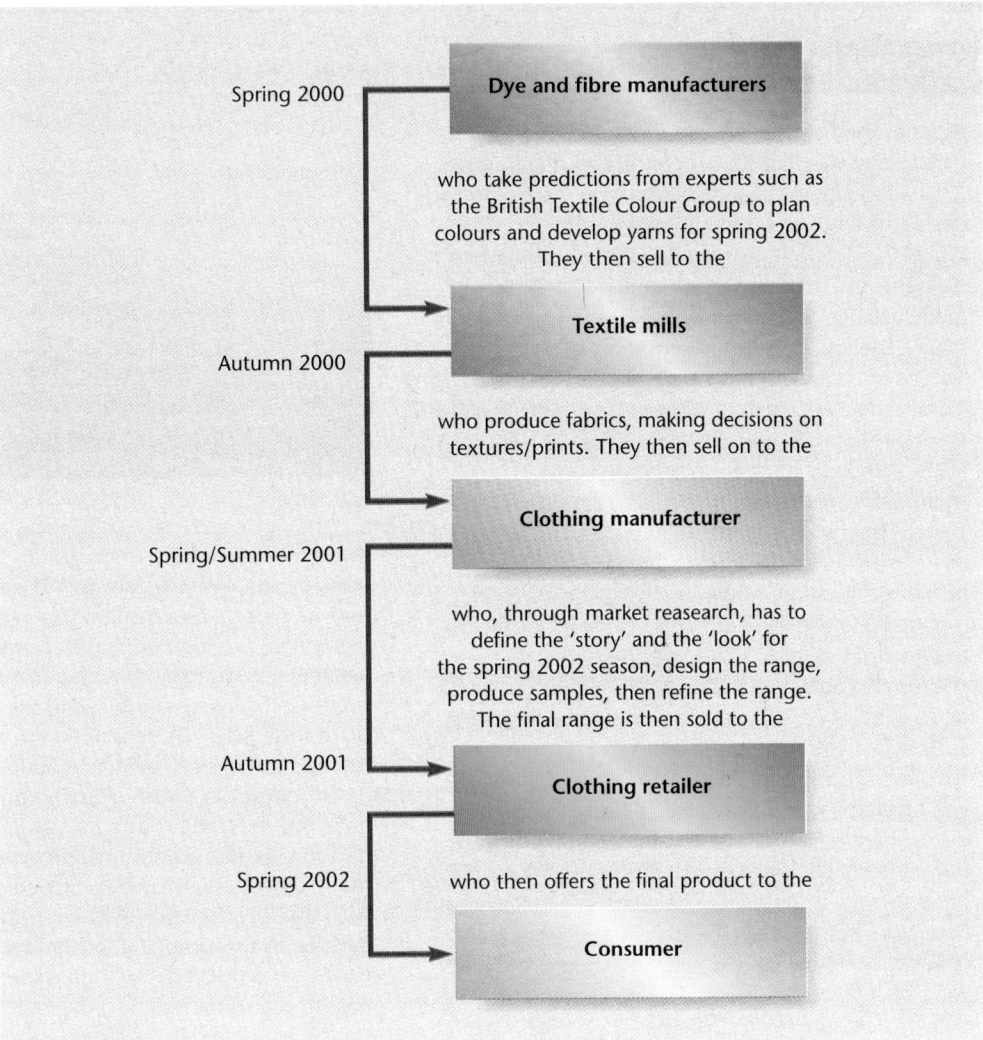

Spring 2000

Dye and fibre manufacturers

who take predictions from experts such as the British Textile Colour Group to plan colours and develop yarns for spring 2002. They then sell to the

Autumn 2000

Textile mills

who produce fabrics, making decisions on textures/prints. They then sell on to the

Spring/Summer 2001

Clothing manufacturer

who, through market reasearch, has to define the 'story' and the 'look' for the spring 2002 season, design the range, produce samples, then refine the range. The final range is then sold to the

Autumn 2001

Clothing retailer

Spring 2002

who then offers the final product to the

Consumer

FIGURE 4.4

Derived demand in the fashion industry

Joint demand

It is also important to note that organisational demand is often closely linked with demand for other organisational products. For example, demand for casings for computers is linked with the availability of disk drives. If there are problems or delays with the supply of disk drives, then the firm assembling the computer might have to stop buying casings temporarily. This emphasises that there is often a need to plan and co-ordinate production schedules between the buyer and a number of suppliers, not just one.

Such tight and crucial links are not common in consumer markets. A close example, however, is that demand for carpets can be linked with the level of buying and selling activity in the housing market, but the two things are not as inextricably tied as in the organisational situation above.

Inelastic demand

Elasticity of demand refers to the extent to which the quantity of a product demanded changes when its price changes. Elastic demand, therefore, means that there is a great deal of price sensitivity in the market. A small increase in price will lead to a relatively large decrease in demand. Conversely, inelastic demand means that an increase in price will make no difference to the quantity demanded.

A car battery, for instance, is just one component of a car. A fall in the price of batteries is not going to have an impact on the quantity of cars demanded, and the car

MARKETING IN ACTION   Pendolino – on time, on track

As far as the negotiation and delivery of high technology specifications is concerned, the Italians succeeded where the British failed, by managing to develop a high-speed train based on tilt technology. Called Pendolino, it was the result of considerable dialogue and trials between Fiat Ferroviaria, the manufacturer, and Italian Railways, the customer. Its main benefit was its ability to run on existing track. Speeds of up to 155 mph were realised on the Rome to Florence line and trials in the Alps, notorious for severe curves, resulted in journey times up to 20 per cent faster. Although track signalling and some installations had to be upgraded to cater for high speeds, the benefit of faster travel often attracted more passengers. The technical requirements were only part of the specification, however. The first-class format also required a fine level of attention to detail in the interior design and provision of on-board services.

From humble beginnings in the 1970s, the latest generation of Pendolinos are now sweeping across Europe in an industry traditionally dominated by local suppliers. The approach adopted by Fiat Ferroviaria was often the same: Pendolino was built under licence by local manufacturers with some equipment from Fiat. In Portugal, for example, five of the 10 Pendolinos ordered were to be built in Italy and five in Portugal by Sorefame. In the Czech Republic, Pendolinos were needed for the Berlin–Prague–Vienna service. These were built by a consortium of Fiat, Siemens and Czech railway stock builder CKD Praha.

When the Finns were interested in purchasing Pendolino, however, a whole new range of customer specifications had to be considered. Finnish track gauge is wider, for instance, the train had to be wider and taller, underfloor air intakes had to be moved to

Source: Fiat Ferroviaria

avoid blockages from driving snow and new electrical transmission gear was needed to suit the Finnish railway system. As a result of the prototypes, eight Pendolinos were ordered in December 1997 to the value of FM616 million, with a further option on 15 more, and all were produced in the Fiat Ferroviaria plant near Turin. These trains were introduced on the Helsinki to Tampere service in 2000.

Although the British, French and German markets have proved to be tough for the Pendolino, because of home-produced designs, progress continued to be made elsewhere in Europe. Slovenia is experimenting with three Pendolinos, with an option on 30 more, initially on the Ljubljana to Maribor line, but with a view to eventual links with Budapest and Munich. Poland is also considering the Pendolino, but it will not be easy for Fiat Ferroviaria as it will be competing with bids from other manufacturers, including Adtranz, Siemens and Alstom (Gough, 1998a, 1988b).

Sources: Freeman Allen (1994; 1995a; 1995b; 1996); Gough (1998a; 1998b); http://www.railway-technology.com.

---

manufacturer will demand neither more nor fewer batteries than before the price change. In this context, and indeed in any manufacturing situation where a large number of components are used, demand is inelastic. Any price changes will be passed on in higher prices charged to the manufacturer's customers or be absorbed into the total costing of the product, or will cause the manufacturer to look for alternative components or cheaper sources of supply (but that takes time and effort and may have implications for production processes, quality and specifications). Whatever happens, demand will not change and in the short term cannot change, since the manufacturer has obligations and orders to fulfil.

Structure of demand

One of the characteristics of consumer markets is that for the most part they comprise many potential buyers spread over a wide geographic area, that is, they are diffuse, mass markets. Think of the market for fast food, for example, which McDonald's has shown to have worldwide appeal to many millions of customers. Organisational markets, in contrast, differ in both respects.

Industrial concentration

Organisational markets tend to have a small number of easily identifiable customers, so that it is relatively easy to define who is or is not a potential customer. McDonald's can persuade non-customers to try its product and become customers; in that sense, the boundaries of the market are fuzzy and malleable, whereas a manufacturer of kilns to the brick and roofing tile industry would have problems in trying to extend its customer base beyond very specific types of customer.

This kind of concentration opens up all sorts of marketing possibilities in terms of relationship building and personal contact that just would not be feasible in consumer mass markets. It allows more focused targeting and, in some cases, the dedication of specific members of staff to service that relationship, or the establishment of regional offices and/or distribution facilities.

Considerable knowledge, experience and trust can build up between buyers and suppliers. Where there is a finite number of known customers, most organisations in the trade know what the others are doing, and although negotiations may be private, the outcomes are very public. An example could be an airline's decision to buy an Airbus or a Boeing, and whether to purchase or lease the aircraft.

Geographic concentration

Some industries have a strong geographic bias. Such geographic concentration might develop because of resource availability (both raw materials and labour), available infrastructure or national and EU government incentives. Traditionally, heavy industry and large mass producers, such as shipbuilders, the coal and steel industries and the motor industry, have acted as catalysts for the development of a range of allied suppliers. More recently, airports and seaports have given impetus to organisations concerned with freight storage, movement, insurance and other related services. In Baden-Württemberg in Germany, it is claimed that the regional investment in 36 science parks and high technology research has created the highest number of scientists per capita in Europe. Similarly, with 75 patent applications per 100 000 inhabitants, it has produced more innovation than anywhere else in Germany (Genillard, 1993). This new form of geographic concentration provides obvious opportunities for a range of service providers, whether software specialists or marketing consultants!

Concentration can, however, lead to a high degree of mutual dependency. A small, highly specific customer base can leave a supplier very vulnerable if something goes wrong. The closure of a coach works in Shannon, Ireland, resulted in a number of small suppliers also going out of business because they could not find new markets for their skills quickly enough.

SKF sells bearings direct to larger OEMs across Europe, especially in the automotive, electrical and mechanical engineering sectors.

Source: SKF.

Buying process complexity

Consumers purchase primarily for themselves and their families. For the most part, these are relatively low-risk, low-involvement decisions that are made quickly, although there may be some economic and psychological influences affecting or constraining them, as Chapter 3 has shown. In contrast, organisational purchasers are always buying on behalf of other people (i.e. the organisation), which implies certain differences from the consumer situation. These differences give rise to much more complexity in the buying process, and the marketer must appreciate them when designing strategies for encouraging trial and reordering. The various dimensions of complexity are as follows.

Organisational purchasing policy

Certain systems and procedures for purchasing are likely to be imposed on the organisational buyer. There may be guidelines on favoured suppliers, or rules on single/multiple sourcing or on the number of quotes required for comparison before a decision can be sanctioned. Often, a purchasing manual is provided for all staff who may be involved in dealing with suppliers. This manual would outline organisational rules and approaches to purchasing, and might list approved suppliers and the procedures to be undertaken for approving a new supplier.

> **Example** Purchasing business travel can be a big headache for organisations. Drinks company Seagram (http://www.seagram.com) has 7000 business travellers and spends around $200 million a year on airfares, hotels, car hire etc. By outsourcing operational matters and analysing expenditure carefully, the company was able to make $15 million of savings with a new travel policy. A preferred carrier scheme was introduced, for example, encouraging airlines to offer better prices. Similarly, a UK company spending £7 million on airline tickets made £450 000 of savings by not using 'The World's Favourite Airline' (Bartram, 1999).

An organisation's decision whether to source from a single supplier or from multiple suppliers is another important aspect of **purchasing policy**. With a single source, the purchaser needs to be assured of the continuity and consistency of supply, as well as value for money. Table 4.2 outlines the advantages and disadvantages of alternative sourcing strategies.

Ramsay and Wilson (1990), in a study of sourcing strategy, challenged the growing belief in Japanese models of long-term single sourcing. They proposed that large, powerful, high spending organisations might gain more by using competitive pressure to keep a number of suppliers on their toes. This would also reduce the buyer's vulnerability to supply interruption from strikes or breakdowns. Segal (1989) found that the decision whether to adopt single or multiple sourcing was often the result of an overriding organisational attitude to suppliers, arising from whether the buyer wanted close, long-term relationships with suppliers, or an arm's-length, competitive type of atmosphere. Segal does concede, however, that other factors, such as product type, market structure and location, might also influence the decision.

Further restraints might also be imposed relating to how much an individual is allowed to spend under particular budget headings on behalf of the organisation before a second or more senior signature is required. Linking individual spending limits with the most appropriate quotation procedure could give rise to a matrix such as that shown in the hypothetical example in Table 4.3.

This matrix provides clear guidelines on who should be involved, for what amount, and the types and methods of quotation required. However, even in this matrix, much would depend on the nature of the organisation. Clearly, for a car manufacturer placing high volume, repetitive orders, the order value categories would be completely inappropriate.

TABLE 4.2

The advantages and disadvantages of alternative sourcing strategies

(a) Single sourcing

Advantages	*Disadvantages*
■ Improved communications and understanding between buyer and supplier	■ Increased costs through lack of competitive pressure
■ Increased responsiveness to buyer's needs	■ Increased supply vulnerability
■ Shared design of quality control systems	■ Reduced market intelligence and thus flexibility
■ Elimination of supplier switching costs	■ Improved supplier appraisal capacity
■ Improvement in product cost effectiveness	
■ Reduced prices through larger volumes	
■ Reduced prices through reduced supplier costs	
■ Enhanced ability to implement JIT systems	

Source: Adapted from Treleven (1987).

(b) Multiple sourcing

Advantages	*Disadvantages*
■ Increased competitive pressure	■ Perceived lack of commitment
■ Improved supply continuity	■ Increased costs
■ Improved market intelligence	■ Less supplier investment
■ Improved supplier appraisal effectiveness	■ Reduced willingness to adapt
	■ Higher operating costs

Source: Adapted from Hahn (1986) and Ramsey and Wilson (1990).

TABLE 4.3

Purchasing guidelines

Estimated value of order	*Method of enquiry*	*Type of quote*	*Authorisation*
Below £500	Phone/In person	Oral	Junior manager
£500 – £2000	Written/Catalogues	Non-competitive	Middle manager
£2000 – £20 000	Written	Competitive quotes	Senior manager
Above £20 000	Written	Tenders	Board

In addition to the formal requirements associated with purchasing, guidelines are often produced on ethical codes of practice. These do not just cover the obvious concerns of remaining within the law and not abusing authority for personal gain, but also address issues such as confidentiality, business gifts and hospitality, fair competition and the declaration of vested interests.

Professional purchasing

The risk and accountability aspects of organisational purchasing mean that it needs to be done professionally. Much negotiation is required where complex customised technical products are concerned and, even for small components used in manufacturing, defining the terms of supply so that they are consistent and compatible with production requirements (for example performance specification, delivery schedules and quality standards) is a significant job. Most consumer purchasing does not involve so great a degree of flexibility: the product is standard and on the shop shelf, with clearly defined price, usage and function; take it or leave it.

Different types of production and operating systems will help to shape an organisation's purchasing task. An inflexible or technology-driven manufacturing organisation, such as a continuous production plant, allows little scope for varying the types of purchases made and needs suppliers who will conform to the standards required for maintaining the system (Sheth, 1977). Furthermore, according to Hallén (1980), if there is no guaranteed economic and stable flow of materials at a consistent quality level, the system will be severely impaired. It is thus critical for the suppliers in such a system to be able to meet the demands of the customer's technology.

Mass production systems are often rigid in the short term, although with careful planning they can be reorganised and modified to accommodate new products. At times of model changes and reorganisation, there may be an opportunity for the supplier to adopt new technical solutions, but often it is the buyer who will determine requirements and dominate the supply situation. This contrasts with unit production, where close discussion and joint development may take place to develop designs and specifications that meet the requirements of the application.

MARKETING IN ACTION   **B&Q goes green**

B&Q, the UK DIY retail chain, has taken a firm position on environmental and ethical issues related to the products it sources and sells. The company has appointed an Environmental Controller to review its suppliers and their production methods and the environmental impact of their products. A number of initiatives have already been introduced, including:

■ The Rugmark scheme in India, and more recently in the Philippines, which put pressure on suppliers not to use child labour. Local social pressure groups have been employed to undertake supplier audits and to report back to B&Q if the standards agreed are violated.

■ A campaign against the use of solvents in paint. Because of the harmful effects of these, B&Q sought to develop a labelling scheme to measure solvent content as a forerunner to reducing it. The scheme simplified the way in which solvent content is described and aims to reduce solvent content in paint by 30 per cent across the B&Q range.

■ Special effort has been made with the timber supply chain. By establishing certification through the Forest Stewardship Council, suppliers are expected to meet certain standards of forest management and conservation. As part of this programme, B&Q started to source hardwood garden furniture from Bolivia (where standards have been met) rather than from Indonesia and Vietnam.

Although the threat of the withdrawal of business is most significant to any supplier which does not conform to an environmental audit initiated by B&Q, it is hoped that suppliers will become more proactive and drive the agenda for change, rather than waiting for the buying organisation to create pressure. B&Q would like more partnerships in which it can work with suppliers to create a greener, more ethical environment. Such an approach could be especially beneficial in developing countries where suppliers could learn new methods through co-operation with customers from developed nations.

Devising a green and ethical purchasing policy is not without difficulty. Established environmental standards such as ISO14000 do not always distinguish between the production process and the source of materials. There is a problem of potential conflict between the environment and profit, and between negotiating a good deal with suppliers and the cost impact of the demands made on suppliers. Retail chains such as B&Q operate in highly competitive markets and cannot always pass on the higher cost of environmentally friendly products to the customer. The benefits are often less tangible and must be measured in image and public relations terms. Even that can be difficult as, for example, forest fires in Indonesia caused by land clearance for the timber trade are hardly likely to attract the headline 'B&Q: not involved in causing forest fires'.

Source: Edwards (1997).

In supplying components for these British built fighter aircraft, suppliers have to be as innovative and as technologically advanced as British Aerospace itself.

Source: British Aerospace.

Group decision making

The need for full information, adherence to procedures and accountability tends to lead towards groups rather than individuals being responsible for purchasing decisions (Johnson and Bonoma, 1981). A full discussion of the role and structure of groups (*buying centres* or *decision-making units*) can be found at pp. 161 *et seq*. While there are group influences in consumer buying, for example the family unit, they are likely to be less formally constituted than in the organisational purchasing situation. It is rare, other than in the smallest organisations or for the most minor purchases, to find individuals given absolute autonomy in organisational spending. Mattson (1988) found that product related aspects of the purchase strongly influenced the area of the organisation involved in the purchase, while the size of expenditure influenced the managerial level of those involved.

Purchase significance

The complexity of the process is also dictated by the importance of the purchase and the level of experience the organisation has of that buying situation (Robinson *et al.*, 1967).

For instance, in the case of a **routine rebuy**, the organisation has bought this product before and has already established suppliers. These products may be relatively low-risk, frequently purchased, inexpensive supplies such as office stationery or utilities (water, electricity, gas etc.). The decision-making process here is likely to involve very few people and be more a matter of paperwork than anything else. Increasingly, these types of purchase form part of computer-based automatic re-ordering systems from approved suppliers. A blanket contract may cover a specific period and a schedule of deliveries over that time is agreed. Bearings for the car and electrical motor industries are sold in this way. The schedule may be regarded as definite and binding for one month ahead, for example, but as provisional for the following three months. Precise dates and quantities can then be adjusted and agreed month by month nearer the time. Increasingly, with JIT systems, schedules may even be day or hour specific!

A **modified rebuy** implies that there is some experience of buying this product, but there is also a need to review current practice. Perhaps there have been significant technological developments since the organisation last purchased this item, or a feeling that the current supplier is not the best, or a desire to renegotiate the parameters of the purchase. An example of this is the purchase of a fleet of cars, where new models and price changes make review necessary, as does the fierce competition between suppliers who will therefore be prepared to negotiate hard for the business.

The decision making here will be a longer, more formal and involved process, but with the benefit of drawing on past experience.

A technical modified rebuy, therefore, is related to changing design and performance specifications, while a commercial modified rebuy involves issues such as price and delivery. The former type may be decided by technical personnel, whereas the latter is more likely to concern the purchasing department.

New task purchasing is the most complex category. The organisation has no previous experience of this kind of purchase, and therefore needs a great deal of information and wide participation in the process, especially where it involves a high-risk or high-cost product. One example of this might be the sourcing of raw materials for a completely new product. This represents a big opportunity for a supplier, as it could lead to regular future business (i.e. routine or modified re-buys). It is a big decision for the purchaser who will want to take the time and effort to make sure it is the right one. Another situation, which happens less frequently in an organisation's life, is the commissioning of new plant or buildings. This too involves a detailed, many-faceted decision-making process with wide involvement from both internal members of staff and external consultants, and high levels of negotiation.

Laws and regulations

As we saw in Chapter 2, regulations affect all areas of business, but in organisational markets, some regulations specifically influence the sourcing of products and services. An obvious example would be the sourcing of goods from nations under various international trade embargoes, such as Iraq in the 1990s. More specifically, governments may seek to regulate sourcing within certain industrial sectors, such as utilities.

Example In Germany in 1994 there was some debate over allowing third parties access to distribution grids to supply electricity and gas. As things stood, the large German utility companies, such as RWE, Bayernwerk and PreussenElektra, had exclusive rights to supply municipalities. This guarantees supply, but restricts choice and price competition. One small town wanted to break its agreement with RWE and seek bids from cheaper alternative suppliers, perhaps even from the Netherlands. The German government, however, was reluctant to deregulate and open its borders unless there was reciprocal access for German utilities into other countries (Dempsey, 1994).

Buyer–seller relationships

Apart from the tangible characteristics of buyer–seller relationships, as formalised in a negotiated, legally drawn-up contract that lays out both parties' responsibilities, obligations and penalty schemes (for late delivery, for instance), there are also less concrete factors shaping the way in which two organisations do business.

Where there is a small number of identifiable customers, then it is possible for the buyer and the seller to build experience, knowledge and trust in each other to an intimate level that consumer marketers can only dream of. Suppliers can tailor their offerings to suit particular buyers, leading to long-term relationships with joint development potential.

One of the problems of such close relationships, however, is dependency. In the short term, the purchaser comes to rely on regular supplies conforming to quality standards, while over a longer period, either party may come to regard the other as essential. For example, a small injection moulding firm found itself selling 80 per cent of its output to a large multinational manufacturer of domestic vacuum cleaners. Since the purchasing organisation also had two alternative suppliers on the sidelines,

EDI: the carrot and the stick

EDI (electronic data interchange) allows companies to enter into dialogue with each other to exchange information or to place and rack orders, for example, and it plays an important role in the buyer–seller relationship. It is used by large organisations, such as Glaxo-Wellcome, ICI, Marks & Spencer, Courtaulds and the major car manufacturers, who can use EDI to dictate prices and business terms to their smaller suppliers. In return, the supplier can receive a substantial amount of business through electronic trading, but does tend to get locked into the relationship with the buyer. Nevertheless, it can help the supplier to reduce costs as well as being more responsive to the needs of the buyer. Kingcup mushrooms, a small UK company with fewer than 30 employees, trades with supermarket chain Tesco using EDI. Tesco submits its orders through EDI, then Kingcup picks up the orders and can submit its invoices in return. The cost to Kingcup is around £1 per invoice, significantly cheaper and quicker than more traditional methods of doing business (O'Connor and Galvin, 1999).

Supermarkets hold a lot of information that is of great interest to suppliers and can be used as a way of improving collaboration and relationships with suppliers. Data sharing is not new, but in 1998 supermarket chain Sainsbury's was looking at new ways of providing data to suppliers and using it collaboratively. An Internet-based EDI system, JSNet, was developed, allowing 4000 suppliers to access data on sales, stock levels and availability of their products. General information for suppliers is also available on JSNet, as is the means for all parties to share ideas. In addition, Sainsbury's invited its 20 leading suppliers to participate in trialling software, also implemented via the Internet, that allows buyer and supplier to negotiate and plan joint promotions or other marketing activities using standardised forms and procedures. The data thus generated can then be distributed directly to all departments involved, for instance the supplier's logistics and marketing departments, to ensure accurate, smooth and timely implementation of the plans (Whitworth, 1998).

it was able to exert considerable influence over the small supplier who could not afford to lose the business. These issues are covered more fully at pp. 166 *et seq.*

The result of all the above complex factors working together is to make organisational purchasing a much longer, more formalised process than in consumer markets. Organisational buying decisions have to be justified to managers, accountants and shareholders, and are, therefore, likely to be more rationally made, to be based on more solid information and to reflect more collective responsibility than a consumer decision. They are also more likely to lead to long-term, mutually valuable, interdependent relationships between specific buyers and sellers.

BUYING DECISION-MAKING PROCESS

It is just as important for marketers to understand the processes that make up the buying decision in organisational markets as it is in consumer markets. The formulation of marketing strategies that will succeed in implementation depends on this understanding. The processes involved are similar to those presented in the model of consumer decision making described in Chapter 3, in that information search, analysis, choice and post-purchase evaluation also exist here, but the interaction of human and organisational elements makes the organisational model more complex.

There are many models of organisational decision-making behaviour, with different levels of detail, for example Sheth (1973), Webster and Wind (1972) and Robinson *et al.* (1967). How the model is formulated depends on the type of organisations and products involved; the level of their experience in purchasing; organisational purchasing policies; the individuals involved; and the formal and informal influences on marketing. Figure 4.5 shows two models of organisational decision making and, on the basis of these, the following subsections discuss the constituent stages.

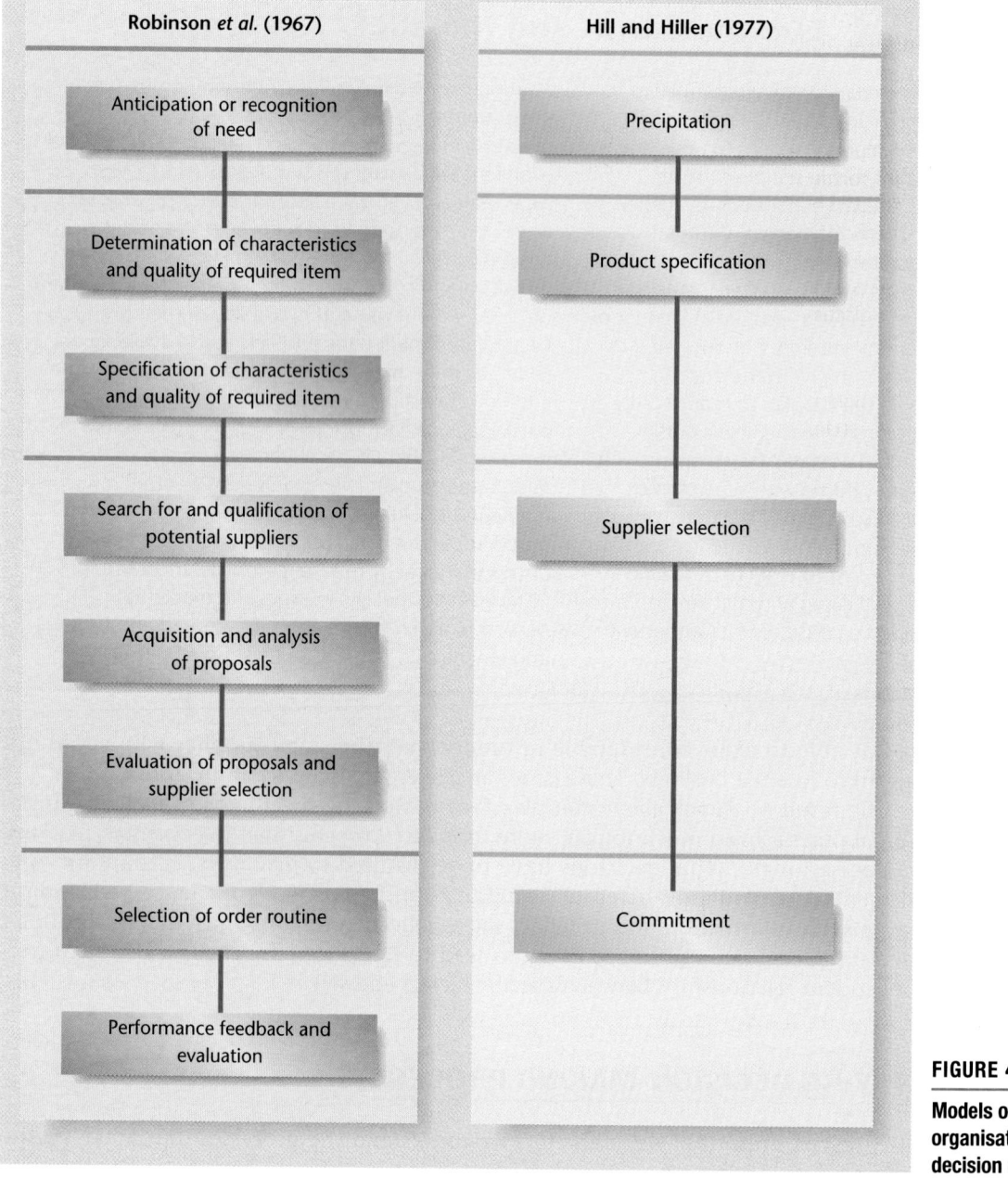

Robinson et al. (1967)

- Anticipation or recognition of need
- Determination of characteristics and quality of required item
- Specification of characteristics and quality of required item
- Search for and qualification of potential suppliers
- Acquisition and analysis of proposals
- Evaluation of proposals and supplier selection
- Selection of order routine
- Performance feedback and evaluation

Hill and Hiller (1977)

- Precipitation
- Product specification
- Supplier selection
- Commitment

FIGURE 4.5

Models of organisational buying decision making

Precipitation

Clearly, the start of the process has to be the realisation that there is a need, a problem that a purchase can solve. The stimulation could be internal and entirely routine: it is the time of year to renew the photocopier maintenance contract. It could be a planned new buy precipitated, for example, by the implementation of expansion plans or the imminent production of a new product. It could also be something more sudden and dramatic than that, such as the failure of a piece of plant or machinery, or a lack of stock.

External influences can also stimulate a need. If the competition has invested in new technology, then other organisations will have to consider their response. Attending trade exhibitions, talking to visiting sales representatives or reading the trade press might also generate awareness of opportunities, whether based on new technology, cost reduction or quality improvements, which would stimulate the buying process.

> **Example** Potential suppliers may have to help the customer to realise that they have a need. Security Backup Systems, for instance, has to stimulate potential clients to be aware of the importance of storing essential data away from their normal premises, in case of fire or theft. This means exposing potential clients to a problem that they may not have even thought about, and offering a solution that they may not have realised was available. In offering an automatic off-site backup service for PCs and networks, the company uses tele-marketing to raise the awareness of risk, outline the cost and arrange a follow-up meeting to discuss the client's needs in detail.

Changes in the wider business environment can also trigger a need. The privatisation of electricity supply in the UK created a competitive market for supplying large industrial users. Organisations such as Ford, Tesco and Abbey National have appointed energy buyers with responsibility for undertaking a modified rebuy review of the electricity supply market. The energy buyers ensure that what was always considered a routine repurchase in the past can now be bought with the most advantageous long-term supply contracts from the most appropriate supplier. Thus changes in the energy environment have precipitated changes in purchasing decisions and processes.

Not all needs can or will be fulfilled and it is possible for the decision-making process to stop here, or be postponed until the organisational or environmental conditions are better. Nevertheless, some opportunities will be followed through and these move on to the next stage, **product specification**.

Product specification

Unlike a consumer, for whom half the fun of shopping is often not quite knowing exactly what is wanted, an organisation must determine in some detail precisely what is required, and the greater the strategic significance of the purchase, the more true this is. Think about buying a component to be incorporated into another end product. The physical characteristics of that component must be specified, in terms of its function, its design, expected quality and performance levels, its relationship and compatibility with other components, but there are also the less tangible but no less important considerations of quantity required, delivery schedules and service back-up, among others.

These specifications will need the combined expertise of engineers, production managers, purchasing specialists and marketers (representing the interests of the end customer), balancing ideals against cost and practicality. A key decision early on will be whether to develop a specification based on known particular needs and then locate a suitable supplier, or to locate the supplier first and then adapt the specifications to suit what they can offer. Even external consultants and suppliers could be involved in particularly complex situations. In the first instance, a general specification will be issued to potential suppliers, but a more detailed one would follow later, perhaps after a shortlist of two or three suppliers has been drawn up.

Where specifications are largely set by the seller rather than the buyer, reports and publications can be used to compare the different features and performance of competing products. The publication *What to Buy for Business*, for example, reviews in detail a wide range of business equipment and services, from franking machines to company health insurance. A typical edition reviews such issues as supplier lists, technical data, guidelines on running costs, discounts and after-sales service for various product categories. All of this helps the organisational buyer to make a more informed choice.

A level of fine detail in specifications is understandable in an engineering context, but is not appropriate in all circumstances. An organisation wanting to develop a corporate brochure, for example, might have a certain amount of in-house expertise within its marketing department, but will issue a general brief to a number of external agencies in order to get a fresh perspective in the light of current practice. The brief may specify the number of pages for the brochure, the scope of the content, the target audience and an indication of the price that the organisation is prepared to pay, but the fine detail will be deliberately vague to allow the agency plenty of creative scope. The agency 'interprets' the brief, then makes proposals to the client who can reject or negotiate from there.

It is also worth while at this stage to define the criteria or priorities for choice. It may not necessarily be cost. If a machine has suddenly broken down, then speed of delivery and installation may be of the essence. In the case of new technology, the choice may hinge on compatibility with existing facilities, the future prospects for upgrading it or the service support offered.

MARKETING IN ACTION **Buying machine tools**

MBM Technology, based near Brighton in the UK, operates an Aerospace Equipment Division to provide design and manufacturing services to the aerospace, defence and commercial sectors. In order to produce the high-quality and high-specification products required by their customers, MBM has to select very carefully the machine tools used to manufacture its specialist assemblies. A detailed assessment of the machine purchase is made before the final selection decision.

At the outset, a detailed assessment is made of the objectives of the purchase. This covers such areas as capacity needed, replacement priority, and the new tool's potential to help MBM serve its own customers better. This could cover reduced lead times, lower manufacturing costs, higher product quality tolerances, or the flexibility to cope with changes in customer needs. After that stage a team is called together, briefed on the project and asked to translate business needs into a technical specification. The team members come from different backgrounds so that they can pool their expertise. The selection criteria cover technical and commercial considerations.

After the specification has been finalised, suppliers are asked to provide quotations. Trade magazines, buyers' directories and guides and exhibitions are used to build a list of reliable sources from which to seek quotes. Some flexibility is offered in the specification to allow for any new ideas or developments of which the buying team are unaware. Typically, an initial list of around 30 suppliers will be drawn up and then a general screening process will reduce that to three. These three will then be invited to detailed negotiations.

At this stage, what is desired is matched with what can be achieved. A distinction is sometimes drawn between 'needs', 'wants' and 'likes'. This enables a guide to be given on those factors in the specification and criteria that are or are not open to negotiation. Firm requirements might involve little discretion, whereas 'likes' can be more flexible. In selecting a supplier, MBM pays particular attention to running costs, spares and maintenance, warranty, health and safety factors, proven track record and long-term stability. MBM also places particular importance on teamwork and the rapport between buyer and seller during the negotiations. The company values the opportunity to develop a relationship based on trust, commitment and understanding, as even after the supplier selection, after sales service, installation and maintenance all call for ongoing contact with the supplier.

In the final stages a purpose-built test piece may be used to assess the actual performance of competing machines in technically advanced applications. All these technical factors, along with commercial considerations such as delivery and price, are used to guide the final decision. Such a comprehensive buying process is typical of more complex industrial purchases where a range of factors need to be considered in the supplier selection process to find the best match.

Source: Northam (1994).

Supplier selection

The next stage involves the search for a suitable supplier which can best meet all the specified criteria. Sometimes, the inclination to search for potential suppliers can be quite low, and the purchasing department will keep files on who can do what. If existing suppliers can do the job, then they are likely to be favoured. On other occasions, it may be necessary for buyers to be proactive by openly seeking new suppliers and encouraging quotations from those who could meet their requirements. Nevertheless, there is often a bias towards existing suppliers who are known and trusted.

There are some advantages in this approach. Existing suppliers are at least a known quantity, and the purchasing organisation will have experience and a realistic view of their capacity to perform. The existing relationship means that there should be better mutual understanding, good working relationships between members of staff within the two organisations and an appreciation of the constraints under which each of them works. Automatically pushing business towards the existing supplier does, however, have its risks. Is the purchasing organisation becoming too dependent on the one supplier? Will this extra business strain the production capacity of the supplier? Is the purchasing organisation missing out on other suppliers with better technology which are anxious to prove themselves? Some exploration of who and what exists beyond the 'usual' supplier makes sense.

Much depends, of course, on the nature of the purchasing task. A low-risk, frequent purchase might not warrant that kind of search effort, and the existing supplier might simply be asked to tender a price for resupply. One or two other known suppliers might also be requested to quote for the job, just as a checking procedure to make sure that the existing supplier is not taking advantage of the established relationship.

In a high-risk, infrequent purchase (i.e. the new task situation), a more serious, lengthy selection procedure is likely to be implemented. There will be complex discussion, negotiation, revision and reiteration at a high level with a number of potential suppliers before a final decision is made. Additional problems may be caused where different suppliers will be expected to work closely together, such as on the building of a new manufacturing plant, for instance. Their compatibility with each other, their reliability and their ability to complete their part within strict time limits dictated by the overall project schedule may all affect the decision making.

> **Example** Fiat, the Italian car manufacturer, decided to move towards 'lean production' methods, looking at ways of lowering total costs within relatively small production batches. The construction of new facilities at Melfi for producing the Punto and at Pratola Serra for engine manufacture meant finding suppliers which, from a capital investment perspective, were willing to install highly standardised automated equipment designed for ease of operation and maintenance. Close co-operation with potential suppliers was necessary from an early stage to ensure that suppliers could improve plant capability and meet cost and delivery requirements.
>
> Fiat's supplier selection criteria for production equipment evolved from the price and service focus of 1980s to include quality, reliability and standardisation. The level of know-how and technological expertise, the supplier's problem solving capability and its willingness to innovate through its own R&D efforts were all important considerations. Previous experience of working with Fiat, adherence to quality standards and not lease the supplier's workload also featured in the final selection stage. Fiat would have been unhappy about dealing with a supplier which was already at the capacity, as this could have led to delays. The final decision, therefore, was not just about price, but also involved detailed technical and performance factors so the Fiat could get what it considered to be 'the best performance at the best price' (Bombaci, 1996).

Commitment

The decision has been made, the contract signed, the order and delivery schedules set. The process does not, however, end here. The situation has to be monitored as it unfolds, in case there are problems with the supplier. Is the supplier fulfilling promises? Is the purchased item living up to expectations? Are deliveries turning up on time? The earlier such problems are diagnosed, the more likely it is that remedial action can be taken with the least disruption to production schedules. Commitment, therefore, comes in two parts, the contractual commitment and the review and evaluation process.

The purchasing manager of a large computer assembly plant in Ireland was clear cut in his requirements. He claimed: 'In my experience, 85 per cent of the business is lost or gained on quality and delivery, not on prices. We want what we order when we want it' (Pettitt, 1992, p. 208).

With the introduction of new purchasing strategies, such as JIT, the pressure on suppliers increases. Suppliers have to earn customer commitment through consistency, quality and delivery. Failure to live up to these promises can be very costly for production schedules.

Some buyers adopt formal appraisal procedures for their suppliers, covering key elements of performance. The results of this appraisal will be discussed with the supplier concerned in the interests of improving their performance and allowing the existing buyer–seller relationship to be maintained. New suppliers are sometimes eased into critical supply situations so that their performance can be carefully assessed. Small trial orders can grow into larger batches. This approach is especially used where larger firms are dealing with smaller suppliers.

Other buyers are less tolerant and keep their suppliers under constant threat. A buyer of injection moulded plastic parts, for example, has a policy of withdrawing business from a supplier which fails to meet delivery schedules. Two alternative suppliers are kept in reserve in case this happens. In another company, the buyer of automotive components places the emphasis on quality consistency. If a supplier falls short of quality standards, then again, alternative sources will be activated. Both these examples demonstrate the need for a true marketing orientation among suppliers of fulfilling the customer's needs and wants exactly. These customers are too important to lose, and any complaints have to be handled quickly, efficiently and effectively in order to maintain levels of customer satisfaction.

In a study of the European aircraft industry, Paliwoda and Bonaccorsi (1994) found a trend towards reducing the supplier base to allow closer co-operation and relationships to develop. Airframe manufacturers increasingly expect suppliers to fund development costs from their own resources, and in the avionics and power systems areas, a shift to single (or much reduced) sourcing forms the basis for a preferred supplier system.

In concluding this discussion of the buying process as a whole, we can say that the Hill and Hillier (1977) model has provided a useful framework for discussing the complexities and influences on organisational buying. It is difficult, however, to generalise about such a process, especially where technical and commercial complexity exists. Stages may be compressed or merge into each other, depending on circumstances; the process may end at any stage; there may have to be reiteration: for example if negotiations with a chosen supplier break down at a late stage the search process may have to begin again.

At each stage, a number of decisions have to be made that may well affect the character of the next stage. These various decision factors are summarised in Table 4.4.

Thus if a decision is taken in the specification stage to adopt a certain type of technology, that may then narrow down the choice of potential suppliers. The process will also vary according to whether the purchase is a new task or a re-buy. Remember too that although organisational buying is assumed to be more rational than consumer buying, it still involves the less than predictable human element, and where groups of people are concerned in the buying process there is plenty of scope for its smooth flow to be interrupted. The next section looks in more detail at these human elements.

TABLE 4.4

Decision problems in the organisational purchasing decision-making process

Stage	Decision problems
Precipitation	Do we need to make a purchasing decision or not? What benefits (e.g. cost savings) are we looking for?
Product specification	What quantity are we likely to need? How often? What are the 'must have' attributes? What are the 'would like' attributes? What is our required quantity level? What level of service/support do we want from supplier? What price band are we thinking of?
Supplier selection	Do we want to use existing and/or new suppliers? How do we construct a shortlist of potential suppliers? On what criteria do we select the supplier: price, ability to meet specifications exactly, past experience, solvency, culture? To what extent, and on what features, are we prepared to negotiate?
Commitment	Does the product actually meet our needs? Is the chosen supplier living up to its promises? How do we continue to motivate/evaluate this supplier? How often do we review their status?

ROLES IN THE BUYING PROCESS

A potential supplier attempting to gain an order from a purchasing firm needs to know just who is involved in the decision-making process. As has already been established, organisational purchasing is unlikely to be the result of one person's deliberation and decision. Thus the aspiring supplier wants to know not only who is involved, but at what point in the process each person is most influential and how they all interact with each other. Then, the supplier's marketers can deal most effectively with the situation, utilising both the group and individual dynamics to the best of their advantage, for example tailoring specific communication packages to appeal at the right time to the right people, and getting a range of feedback from within the purchasing organisation to allow a comprehensive product offering to be designed.

Clearly, the amount of time and effort the supplier is prepared to devote to this will vary with the importance and complexity of the order. A routine re-buy may consist of a telephone conversation between two individuals to confirm the availability of the product and the fine detail of the transaction in terms of exact price and delivery. A new task situation, however, with the promise of either a large contract or substantial future business, provides much more scope and incentive for the supplier to research and influence the buying decision.

The rest of this section takes a more focused look at some of the functional areas involved in the decision-making process, detailing their interests and concerns. This lays the foundations for the next (p. 161) which then examines how these functional areas operate within a group setting.

Purchasing

The role of the purchasing department is to handle relationships with suppliers by, for instance, sourcing suppliers, soliciting tenders, evaluating offers and negotiating or reviewing performance. Purchasing acts as the interface between other internal functions, such as production and finance and external suppliers, and thus has to reflect and represent those internal needs. This means that the function cannot act in isolation, except in the case of very well-established routines.

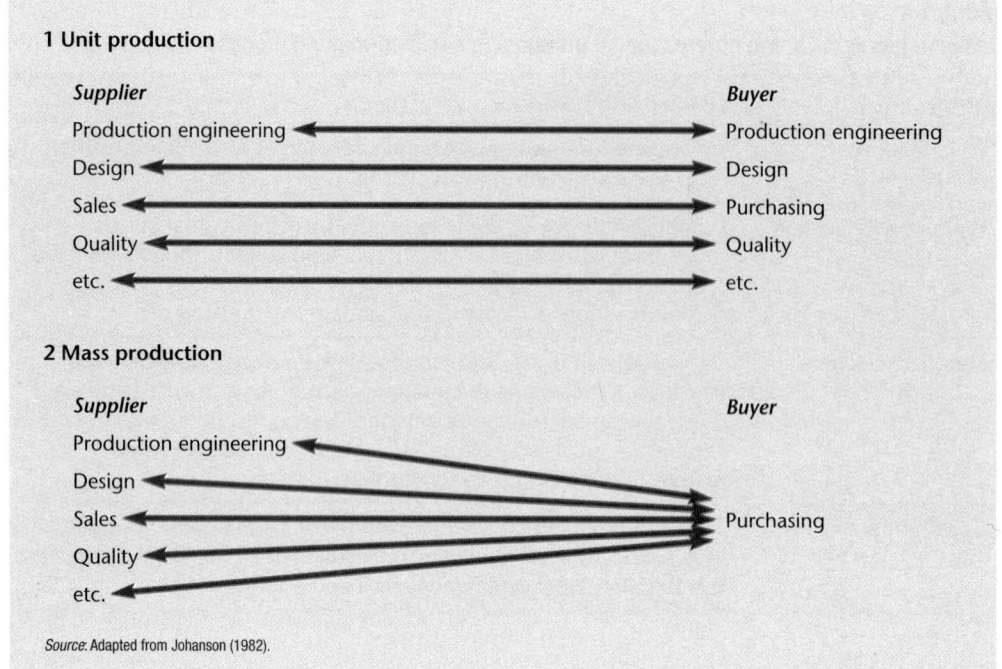

1 Unit production

FIGURE 4.6

Models of buyer–seller contact in organisational markets

Source: Adapted from Johanson (1982).

The role of purchasing will often vary according to the technology being used and the kind of contact needed with suppliers. In Fig. 4.6, where unit or small-batch production takes place, such as in building a large gas turbine or specialist vehicles, there may be considerable contact between different departments within the selling and buying organisations. This is because a whole range of specification, quality, design and production issues may have to be discussed before, or even during, the transactions. The role of purchasing in such a situation tends to be less central to the whole process, and is more focused towards offering support in such matters as contracts and supplier suitability etc. In mass production, however, given the need for consistency, reliability and possibly frequent and critical exchanges, the role of purchasing may be enhanced to ensure the free flow of goods into the organisation. The other internal departments may channel their efforts and be co-ordinated through the purchasing department.

Example The purchasing manager at Avis UK (http://www.avis-europe.com), the car rental company, has to buy and re-sell cars for the fleet. There are around 22 000 vehicles in the fleet, each of which has a profitable life expectancy of just six months in the hire business, so Avis represents an attractive target for car manufacturers. The role of the purchasing manager is to plan the fleet by size and model over the year to supply the rental side of the operation. The purchasing manager negotiates with the manufacturers, ensures pre-delivery inspection and allocates vehicles to the various rental outlets. Because of its size, Avis tends to deal with a range of manufacturers, often more than 10, but cannot rationalise down to just a few because it wants to offer more choice to its customers. Although pan-European purchasing is growing, it is still a small part of Avis's total spend (McInerney, 1996).

Purchasing rarely initiates the decision-making process, except for routine re-buys or where it acquires information to suggest that a change of policy or supplier could lead to better efficiency. Thus its key role is in the supplier selection and commitment stages, that is, in locating 'good' suppliers, establishing terms and liaising with them.

The main concerns of purchasing are security and consistency of supply, especially where large-scale production schedules are concerned. Lowest cost is, therefore, unlikely to be its prime criterion. The whole area of purchasing is growing in importance as organisations seek cost savings, raised quality levels and better integration with suppliers to strengthen their overall competitiveness in the supply chain. This means developing a clear understanding of the relative significance of individual purchases and of different types of purchases. Figure 4.7 details the various products and services purchased by a university, classified by the security/risk required and the value of the purchases. Strategic cells SS and SC suggest long-term supply contracts and careful selection of suppliers. The more tactical areas are divided into *acquisition* (TA), where the priority is minimising effort, and *profit* (TP) where the concern is with savings and improving margins through tendering. With business travel in the TP cell, for example, travel agencies would be required to bid on a regular basis, indicating the service level offered and their discount structures. Such a matrix is a valuable guide to an organisation in selecting those product areas that require special attention.

Production/operations

With prime responsibility for meeting targets for the end product in both quantity and quality terms, the production function also has a great interest in the security and consistency of supply. If a critical component is concerned, then it will be anxious to ensure that the component meets quality and design specifications in order to be entirely compatible with the production flow.

Production staff may, therefore, be mainly involved in the precipitation and specification stages, although if they have an interest as users of the purchased product, they are not going to be entirely absent from the other stages.

In some cases, the production process may have to be adapted to accommodate a particular supplier's technology. This is widespread practice in organisational markets (Johanson and Wootz, 1986; Valla, 1986). While some of these adaptations are driven by logistical concerns alone, issues relating to ease of handling, fit with other organisations' production systems and cost effectiveness may also be considered.

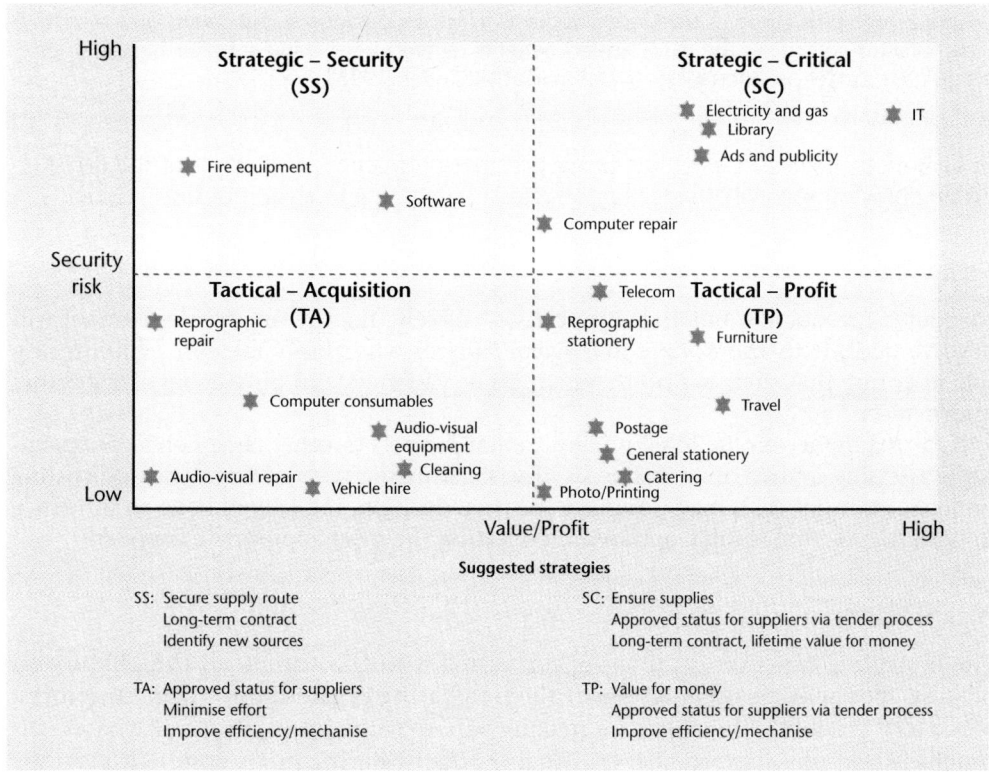

FIGURE 4.7

Commodity positioning matrix

Engineering

Engineering is usually concerned with specification and design, for example when sourcing a component or designing new production facilities, advising production on more efficient methods. Applications engineers may work closely with suppliers to develop solutions to problems, for example pooling their expertise to use CAD systems to design components that both perform to the purchaser's specifications and are feasible, given the supplier's technical capacity and talents. They can also feed specific information back to the supplier to solve a specific end-customer's problem.

R&D

Where R&D has been given a free-ranging brief to look for new, radical solutions to problems, then it is likely, as in the case of engineering, to have close contact with suppliers in the interests of joint development.

Johnson & Johnson, for example, are researching new approaches to wound dressings that involved close liaison with textile suppliers to develop fabrics of the right density, texture and quality for medical use and that could withstand sterilisation. At the same time, it also worked with another supplier to develop an adhesive that not only fulfilled its prime functions of being non-allergenic and sufficiently adhesive (although not too much so), but could also be supplied in a form that would allow it to be easily and efficiently incorporated into a production run. This proved to be a somewhat sticky problem.

In addition, development has to be done within given cost parameters. If the proposed solution to an R&D problem looks likely to push the price of the end product up beyond what the market will bear (taking into account the unique selling points offered by the new development), then further development work has to be done to reduce the costs or find alternatives.

> **Example** Ericsson, the Swedish telecommunications company, invests heavily in R&D to retain a competitive edge. To achieve this, it seeks R&D co-operation with some suppliers from a very early stage in the design process. This co-operation is not based on low-cost manufacturing but on the value added benefits derived from good supplier partnerships that bring better products faster to the market (Ahlinder, 1996).

In such cases, R&D staff are going to have a strong influence at all stages of the decision-making process, somewhat reducing the role of purchasing to an administrative one.

Finance

For routine production-orientated purchases, is likely that the finance department will devolve budgets to appropriate managers. Finance will simply take on a monitoring role to ensure that there are no irregularities or variances and provide regular internal information.

It takes a higher-profile role in major capital projects or other large items of expenditure, assessing returns on investments, investigating methods of financing and costing projects, for instance. It may not make the final decision, but it does have an influence in both shaping the feasible options and selecting the most appropriate supplier.

Marketing

The marketing function is primarily concerned with the outputs of the production process, representing the interests of the purchasing organisation's own customers. Marketers' concerns, therefore, are making sure that the implications of whatever is purchased do not compromise the final product offering or its competitive edge.

Marketers are likely to approve of options that enhance the offering, perhaps in terms of better quality or improved reliability, thus favouring innovative, reliable suppliers.

Overall, in relation to functional roles in the decision-making process, just who is involved and in what capacity is an amalgam of many factors. The further removed the situation is from routine re-buys, the more people are involved and the more formal and time consuming the process is likely to be. Organisational size, structure and culture will also play a role in defining the process, for instance through the degree of delegation of responsibility and devolved decision making.

THE BUYING CENTRE

The previous section implied that individuals within the purchasing organisation, as well as having functional roles and concerns, can also play different roles within the decision-making process that cross functional boundaries. This section, therefore, looks at these non-functional roles, and how they interact to form a **buying centre** or **decision-making unit** (DMU).

Table 4.5 compares buying centres in consumer and organisational markets, indicating the membership, the roles they play and the functional areas that may be involved.

Users

Users are the people who will use the end product, for example an operator who will use production machinery, or a secretary who will use a word processor. These people may trigger the purchasing process through reporting a need, and may also be consulted in setting the specifications for whatever is to be bought.

TABLE 4.5

Comparison of DMUs in consumer and organisational markets

Consumer	Example	Organisation	Example
Initiator	Child pesters parents for a new bike.	**User**	Machine breaks down; the operator reports it, thus initiating the process. May also be asked to help with specs for replacement.
Influencer	Mother thinks about it and says, 'Well, perhaps he has grown out of the old one.'	**Influencer**	User may influence; may also involve R&D staff, accountants, suppliers, sales reps, external consultants.
Decider	Father agrees and they all go to Toys 'Я' Us where the final decision is the child's, but under restraints imposed by parents' credit card limit.	**Decider**	May be a senior manager with either an active or a passive role in the whole process. May also be the buyer and/or influencer.
Purchaser	Parents pay the bill.	**Buyer**	Handles the search for and negotiations with suppliers.
User	The child.	**Gatekeeper**	Secretarial staff preventing influencers reaching the decision maker; R&D staff withholding information.

Influencers

Influencers can affect the outcome of the decision-making process through their influence on others. Influence could stem formally from expertise, for example the advice of an accountant on the return on investment from a piece of capital machinery or that of an engineer on a supplier's technical capability, or it could be an informal, personal influence. Their prime role is in specification, information gathering and assessment.

Deciders

Deciders have the formal or informal authority to make the decision. For routine re-buys, this may be the purchasing officer or someone in a functional role, but organisational structures may dictate that the final decision rests with top management, who are fed information and recommendations from below. The decider's role and level of involvement, therefore, will vary widely, depending on individual circumstances.

Buyers

Buyers have the authority to select and negotiate with suppliers. Buyers with different levels of seniority may exist to handle different types of transaction, for example a routine re-buy could be handled by a relatively junior clerical worker, whereas the high-cost, high-risk new buy might require a senior purchasing manager of many years' experience. Where devolved budgeting exists, the buyer may not belong to a formal purchasing department at all, but be someone who also has a functional role such as R&D or marketing.

Gatekeepers

Gatekeepers have some control over the decision-making process, in that they can control the flow of information by denying access to key members of the buying centre. For example, a secretary or purchasing manager may prevent a sales representative from talking directly to an executive, or intercept brochures and mailshots and throw them in the wastepaper basket before they reach the decision maker. Technical staff can also act as gatekeepers in the way in which they choose to gather, present and interpret information to other members of the buying centre.

Bear in mind that the buying centre is not necessarily a fixed entity from transaction to transaction or even within a single transaction. It can be fluid and dynamic, evolving to meet the changing demands of the unfolding situation; it can be either formally constituted (for a major capital project, for instance) or loosely informal (a chance chat over coffee in the canteen between the purchasing manager and an R&D scientist); it can consist of two or three or many people. In other words, it is what it needs to be to do the job in hand.

When analysing the make-up of the buying centre, we should look not only at the allocation of roles between the different functional areas of the organisation, but also at the seniority of the members. Higher expenditure levels or purchases that have a critical impact on the organisation may involve much more senior management. Of course, input from the lower levels of the hierarchy will help to shape the decision, but the eventual authority may rest at board level. Thus, for example, a bank's decision to introduce a new account control system may be taken at a very senior level.

Also, an individual's contribution to it may not be limited to one role. In a small business, the owner/manager may be influencer and buyer as well as decider. Similarly, in a larger organisation, where routine re-buys are concerned, the buyer may also be the decider, with very little call for influencers. Whatever the structure, however fluid the buying centre is, it is still important for the aspiring supplier to attempt to identify the pattern within the target organisation in order to create effective communication links.

Having thus established decision-making structures, the next step is to examine the criteria applied during the process.

BUYING CRITERIA

In the previous sections, the emphasis in terms of decision making has largely been on rational, functionally oriented criteria. These task-related or economic criteria are certainly important and reinforce the view of the organisation as a rational thinking entity. It is dangerous, however, to fall into the trap of forgetting that behind every job title lurks an individual whose motives and goals are not necessarily geared towards the greater good of the organisation. Such motives and goals may not form a direct, formally recognised part of the decision-making process, but nevertheless, they can certainly cause friction and influence the outcomes of it.

Economic influences

As has been stressed throughout this chapter so far, it is not always a matter of finding the lowest priced supplier. If the purchasing organisation can make the best use of increased reliability, superior performance, better customer service and other technical or logistical supports from its suppliers, then it can offer a better package to its own customers, with the rewards that brings. This route can also result in lower total costs, since it reduces production delays due to substandard components or delivery failures, and also improves the quality consistency of the purchaser's own end product, thus reducing the costs of handling complaints and replacing goods.

The main criteria have already been discussed in the previous sections of this chapter, so here is a summary of them:

Appropriate prices
The appropriate price is not necessarily the lowest, but one representing good value for money taking into account the whole service package on offer.

> **Example** Building a Formula One racing car from scratch is not an easy business. Stewart Grand Prix's three racing cars are each made from 1400 components sourced from over 1000 suppliers. The costs per car can be staggering. To design and develop a car can cost £1 million, a similar amount is spent on tyres, and then some £5 million of spares are needed every season. The buying criteria are led completely by design and performance technology and the high specification of such cars often means locating special suppliers. Lead times can, however, be short, especially if a re-work is necessary on a component that needs to be upgraded. Because of the high specification, price is nearly always of secondary importance in the buying decision. Instead, good relationships leading to component improvement, reliability, safety and quality are dominant (Nolan, 1997b). After all, who wants to be the buyer who saved a few pence on the component that caused a breakdown during the big race? (http://www.saunalahti-fi)

Product specification
Product specification involves finding the right product to meet the purchaser's specified needs, neither more nor less. There are, of course, various trade-offs between specification and price. The main point is the closeness of the match and

the certainty that it will be maintained throughout the order cycle, or that the supplier will be able to meet increasing and changing demands as technology progresses. This is particularly important in areas such as electronics where product life-cycles are getting shorter and shorter.

Quality consistency

It is important to find a supplier with adequate quality controls to minimise defects so that the purchaser can use the product with confidence. This is especially true for JIT systems, where there is little room for failure.

> **Example** Velden Engineering (UK) manufactures a wide range of component parts and assemblies for various industries and applications, such as medical and aeronautical. In such sensitive areas, it needs to ensure that everything supplied is right first time, as failure can be very expensive indeed. Its customers not only expect compliance with standards such as BS5750 and ISO9002 but also to be supplied with finished components or tested assemblies that can go straight into the production process on a JIT basis. This is a crucial factor in supplier selection.

Supply reliability and continuity

The purchaser needs to be sure that adequate supplies of the product will be available as and when needed, especially where JIT systems are involved. This may mean sacrificing the economies of scale achieved through sourcing from one supplier for the risk-spreading advantages to be had from sourcing smaller amounts from a number of suppliers.

> **Example** Sogea/Satom, a French civil engineering firm, builds large projects such as roads and bridges in sub-Saharan Africa. An early decision in any project is whether to source supplies locally or to ship them in from Europe. In Africa, the three main elements of the company's purchasing criteria, price, quality and delivery, are often beyond local suppliers. Despite being local, they cannot offer the consistency and reliability needed to achieve tough deadlines in construction projects. A significant proportion of materials and equipment is, therefore, imported from Europe, despite the risks of transport delays. One exception is plant hire, but even in that case, the company is often dealing with branch offices of international suppliers which are used to meeting exacting standards (Bouchard, 1996).

Customer service

Buyers require reassurance that the supplier is prepared to take responsibility for its product by providing fast and flexible back-up service in case of problems. This aspect might also include an appraisal of the supplier's longer-term capacity and willingness to become involved in joint development activities. Some customer service is delivered even before the sale is made.

> **Example** Nedalo (UK) (http://www.energy.rochester.edn) is a joint venture between Nedalo BV from the Netherlands and Eastern Electricity from the UK, selling small scale combined heat and power equipment. Nedalo (UK) undertakes free feasibility studies and site assessment to establish for the customer the scale of the savings and the most appropriate usage. The company also offers discounted electricity schemes and the free installation and maintenance of its units. This last area, maintenance, is a good example of the importance of post-sales service. All of these additional services matter to buyers of plant and equipment, but the cost savings also matter. The Edwardian International Hotel near Heathrow airport estimated that the successful installation of a Nedalo unit has saved about £40 000 per year (Gutteridge, 1995).

Non-economic influences

Powers (1991) summarises non-economic influences under four main headings: prestige, career security, friendship and social needs, and other personal needs. We look at each of these in turn.

Prestige

Organisations, or more specifically the individuals who make up organisations, hanker after 'status'. They want to be seen to be doing better than their competitors or other divisions within the same organisation. So, for example, they may be prepared to spend a little more when the office accommodation is refurbished on better-quality furnishings, decor and facilities to impress, instil confidence or even intimidate visitors to the site.

The robot supplier must collaborate with the car manufacturers to develop the right production system.

Source: Vauxhall Motors Ltd.

Career security

Few people involved in the decision-making process are truly objective about it. They may well be chiefly and genuinely concerned with finding the best solution to the problem, but at the back of the mind there is always the question, 'What does this mean for my job?'

First, there is the risk element. A problem may have two alternative solutions, one which is safe, predictable and unspectacular, and one which is high risk, but promises a high return. If the high-risk decision is made and it all goes wrong, what are the consequences? The individual may not want to be associated with such an outcome and thus will push for the safe route.

Second, there is the awareness of how others are judging the individual's behaviour in the decision-making process: 'Am I prepared to go against the main body of opinion on a particular issue that I feel strongly about or will that brand me as a trouble-maker and jeopardise my promotion prospects?'

Friendship and social needs

Needs such as friendship can be dangerous and can sometimes stray very close to ethical boundaries. It is necessary, however, to value trust, confidence and respect built on a personal level between individuals in the buying and selling organisations. It does help to reduce the perceived risk of the buyer–seller relationship.

Other personal factors

The three categories discussed above all provide useful insights into the human elements of organisational behaviour, but their emphasis is still on the relationship between the individual, the job and the organisation. Remember too the individual's personal profile, issues such as demographic characteristics, attitudes and beliefs, discussed in Chapter 3 in the context of consumer behaviour. These, coupled with factors like self-confidence and communication skills, can all shape the extent to which that individual is allowed to participate in and influence the outcome of the decision-making process. A young, recent business graduate with forthright views, for example, may provoke negative reactions in older managers who have progressed through more traditional routes and feel that they have accumulated a wealth of experience, even if the graduate's views are valid.

A further dimension of non-economic forces is trust. Trust is the belief that another organisation will act in such a way that the outcomes will be beneficial to both parties and that it will not act in such a way as to bring about negative effects (Anderson and Narus, 1986). Trust can be built at an organisational level, but can also stem from a series of personal relationships between employees. Lorenz (1988), for example, found from a study of subcontracting in France that personal contacts were a major cause of organisational trust. From that trust can come a whole series of activities that can enhance the relationship, as considered in the following section.

RELATIONSHIP MARKETING

One matter that has been emphasised repeatedly in this chapter is the potential risks inherent in poor purchasing decisions. The quality of the relationship between the buying organisation and an existing supplier could prove to be a major factor in reducing those risks, and is inevitably going to influence decision-making processes. The history of previous transactions between two organisations leads to understanding, expectations and perhaps an active desire to continue to trade, even at the cost of short-term sacrifice.

There has, therefore, been an increased focus in recent years on the place of buyer–seller relationships in explanations of marketing and decision making in organisational markets. Porter (1990) goes further in suggesting that an organisation with advantageous relationships with supplier networks has a competitive edge, because of the synergy between them in terms of joint problem solving and information exchange.

MARKETING IN ACTION   Nokia's global sourcing

The mobile phone market is growing at a very rapid rate as usage spreads from business to domestic use. Nokia (http://www.nokia.com) is one of the market leaders and in 1995 produced over 5.5 million handsets. The purchasing challenge for the company is to ensure that supplies can be regularly adjusted to meet growing demand from its five factories across three continents. It must also be sure that suppliers are capable of producing components that are in line with expected technological advances in a market in which innovation is used to gain competitive advantage.

Given the world-wide scale of production and the need sometimes to adjust product specifications to meet local requirements, purchasing has been divided into two different organisations. First, *local procurement* deals with day-to-day purchasing for the factories. Its primary role is not to source components, but to ensure that adequate supplies of components are available for production. *Global sourcing* is the other organisation. This actually sources materials, negotiates prices and terms, makes delivery arrangements, establishes quality procedures and sets supplier performance standards for appraisal. There is a close link between global sourcing and the R&D and manufacturing experts to ensure that the right technology is available and that it will continue into the future.

Nokia operates on formal contracts with suppliers, specifying prices, quality, quantities etc. Suppliers are expected to meet these standards and are monitored at a local level to ensure that they comply. By aggregating demand from each of the production units, Nokia is able to get better terms from suppliers because of the scale of the contracts. It insists, however, that a supplier should offer only one collection point in the world from which components can be collected, regardless of where they were produced. Nokia is the supplier's problem to handle its own logistics to ensure that the various products arrive in time at that collection point. It then arranges for carriers to handle the transport, customs etc. to ensure that components arrive on time at Nokia's own plants. This arrangement simplifies the ordering procedures for Nokia's local procurement teams.

Quality monitoring of components is critical so that Nokia can ensure that its own products meet standards. Targets are set for failure rates and robustness, for example, and the company asks each supplier to present its plan for meeting those targets over the lifespan of the contract. Nokia has to be convinced, as it does not inspect goods on arrival. It expects suppliers to take care of testing and to guarantee that they are meeting standards on a consistent basis. When problems do occur, they are normally identified at the local buying points, but it is global sourcing that takes the necessary action with suppliers.

Nokia insists on each supplier nominating an account manager who they regard as being responsible for the relationship between the companies on a global basis. The account manager is expected to be senior enough to be credible within Nokia and to carry influence within the supplier's top management if urgent action is required. By establishing clear lines of communication, issues such as annual purchasing agreements to cover forecasting, capacity planning and allocation can be fed through one point. It is then the responsibility of the account manager to link with the rest of the supplier's organisation to ensure that it all happens. It is the supplier's responsibility to adjust its own internal organisation to meet Nokia's requirements.

Although most of the collaboration is on commercial matters, in some areas closer technical co-operation is required. With 'application-specific integrated circuits' (purpose-designed complex microchips), for example, it is necessary for Nokia's engineers to work closely with the supplier's technical staff to create the most appropriate specification. The purchasing function's fear about such arrangements, however, is that it could become locked into a single supplier and this in turn could, it believes, jeopardise supply continuity, especially when the demand for a component is suddenly increased.

Nokia has refined its relationship approach to component suppliers over a number of years. It believes in partnership, openness and trust to ensure that it can plan its capacity and production schedules with a high degree of certainty that suppliers will not let it down. Although Nokia takes a tough stance on suppliers which do not meet their promises, there are benefits in the highly prescribed, efficient procedures imposed.

Source: Taimi (1996).

This final section of the chapter looks at some of the characteristics of buyer–seller relationships that add a further dimension to the understanding of the decision-making processes already covered.

Durability

Durability refers to the longevity of relationships in organisational markets that might even outlast individuals and managerial generations. Not all exchanges evolve into long-term durable relationships. In low-cost, low-risk purchasing situations there will be minimal concern about long-term relationships. For example, paperclips for the office are a standard product and there is plenty of choice in the market, and thus convenience and possibly low price will be the main concerns.

However, as complexity increases and as it becomes apparent that value can be created by developing a stable, well-tuned relationship, then there may be mutual advantage in continuity. This may emerge for two types of reason. The first relates to the economic dimension, the second to the social dimension.

Economic dimension

Joint development has already been mentioned a few times in this chapter. If a supplier has invested time, effort and money in improving quality or products, or in developing special operating processes or services to suit a particular customer, then the supplier will want the relationship to be sustained so that returns on that investment can be realised. Similarly, the purchaser will not want to start the process from scratch with a new supplier. If the relationship has led to a specialist complex package, then either party may become dependent on the other. In other words, the purchaser cannot easily get the same thing from an alternative supplier and the supplier cannot easily find an alternative customer.

Social dimension

There is a certain security and comfort in dealing with someone you know. There is an existing level of trust, knowledge and friendship to build on. Strengths and weaknesses are known quantities, thereby reducing the risks of taking on a new supplier or customer.

Some relationships can be very long lasting and resistant to change, despite the temptations of competitors' marketing wiles. It is difficult for an outsider to break into such well-developed and managed relationships. A number of studies have been undertaken into the duration of buyer–seller relationships. Valla (1986) found that 40 per cent of French buyer–seller relationships studied had lasted for over 20 years; Johanson and Wootz (1986) found that 30 per cent of German relationships studied had lasted for more than 16 years, and in the UK, 40 per cent of relationships studied had been in existence for over 11 years (Cunningham, 1986). These results certainly give food for thought. Whether involvement in such relationships has offered protection against the worst ravages of economic recession is a study yet to be undertaken.

Approaches to supplier handling

The way in which the purchasing organisation decides to deal with its suppliers can have a fundamental effect on the future of the buyer–seller relationship. According to Spekman (1988), there are two polarised approaches that lead to very different relationships.

Adversarial approach

The purchasing organisation pressurises the supplier to minimise prices and, by insisting on short-term contracts and using multiple sourcing, keeps the supplier alert and sweating. The purchaser is unlikely to be interested in helping the supplier unless there is a direct cost saving to be had. This purchaser will rarely need special products and

TABLE 4.6

Collaborative vs adversarial approaches to supplier handling

Adversarial	Collaborative
■ Multiple suppliers	■ Few suppliers
■ Regular price quotes	■ Long-term relationship; mutual investment
■ Adversarial negotiations	■ Partnerships
■ Sporadic communication	■ Frequent, planned communication
■ Little co-operation	■ Integrated operations
■ Quality and time scales to meet lowest threshold	■ Quality and time scales 'designed in'
■ Emphasis on lowest unit price	■ Emphasis on lowest overall cost

Source: Adapted from Spekman (1988).

services and certainly will rarely be prepared to pay for such things. This is a legitimate approach in appropriate circumstances, where there are plenty of alternative sources of supply, the product is fairly standard and price really is the driving criterion.

Collaborative approach

In a collaborative approach, close ties are forged between buyer and seller and there are much interest and value in close co-operation and integration. Such an approach can support valuable work in product design, specification and quality; advanced production processes; flexible scheduling and delivery; and special inventory. There are, however, the risks of becoming too 'cosy', complacent and blinkered, as well as the inherent dangers of mutual dependency.

Collaborative approaches are particularly crucial in JIT environments, as Table 4.6 shows, neatly summarising the reasons that collaboration rather than confrontation should be considered in critical supply situations.

Supplier relationship portfolio

The focus so far has been on the relationship between one purchaser and one supplier. In reality, a purchaser is likely to maintain a portfolio of suppliers and to develop different levels and intensity of relationship with each, based on need and value.

Some suppliers have the potential to be long-term important partners in joint innovative development, and therefore the purchaser may encourage co-operation in improving both technical capability and quality, while others will be developed as guaranteed, secure, reliable sources of supply. Both of these will deserve a collaborative approach to handling. Others, however, will merit no special consideration, for example where there are plenty of alternative sources readily available, and will be retained at arm's length somewhere nearer the adversarial end of the handling spectrum. It is the job of purchasing to advise on an appropriate portfolio.

Relationship life-cycle

Much emphasis has been put on the potential durability of a buyer–seller relationship, but as with any kind of relationship, it is dynamic, changes its nature over time and is unlikely to last indefinitely. This evolution can be broken down into five stages of the **relationship life-cycle**, as proposed by Dwyer *et al.* (1987).

Awareness

Awareness occurs as each party learns of each other's existence and potential. This could come about as a result of a sales visit, a trade exhibition or any other means of making an initial contact.

Exploration

Exploration is about discovery and has all the insecurities of adolescent relationships. It is about gaining experience, testing each other out with no real commitment and with high uncertainty over the outcomes. This could mean small trial orders and perhaps even some pre-order assessment.

Expansion

Expansion has the characteristics of romance and the early days of marriage. Partners are working together, valuing the benefits, building orders and mutual trust. There is a rising level of commitment and the partners may even be making special adaptations to suit each other better. The uncertainty is much reduced, and members of staff from the two organisations may be starting to build sound working and social relationships.

Commitment

In the commitment stage, the novelty has worn off, but the partners are comfortable with each other and have built a predictable, stable nest round themselves. There is high mutual trust and respect, well-developed personal networks, and the seller has become a major supplier of special products and services, perhaps to the point where there is a high level of mutual dependency. Most relationships remain in this stage, but a few move on to the next stage.

> **Example** A good example of the benefits of collaboration is seen in the relationship between the Lawson Mardon Group (LMG), a plastic blow moulder, and Jeyes, a consumer cleaning goods manufacturer. Jeyes needed 200 different types of plastic bottle in a variety of sizes from 250 ml to 5 litre. Seventeen machines were needed to produce the required volume of containers. Jeyes switched from in-house production to buying in from LMG. The risks of thus extending the supply chain were reduced when LMG located its factory next door to Jeyes', with a conveyor belt running between the two for continuous production and supply. Both parties benefited from this arrangement. LMG had a long-term seven-year supply contract with flexibility to allow for changing raw material prices, giving it a secure foundation for building a wider customer base. Jeyes was able to focus on its core business, freed of the responsibility of churning out plastic bottles, yet retaining security and flexibility of supply, delivery reliability, and maintaining quality standards.

Dissolution

This stage is possibly the equivalent to disillusionment and divorce. If stability and satisfaction have been reached in the maturity stage, then the most likely source of danger is complacency. Lack of innovation or service responsiveness on the seller's part, for example, could encourage the purchaser to turn to a younger, more versatile supplier with a good marketing-orientated approach ('I can tell your current supplier doesn't understand you any more. Let me show you my blueprints ...').

> **Example** Sometimes the dissolution can be carried out with respect and dignity. A small supplier of engineering components, for example, found that its major customer was going to phase out its purchases from that supplier over the next two years. The customer had decided to make the components itself, but acted responsibly by phasing the supplier out over time rather than all at once. Instant termination of the contract would have had a devastating effect on the supplier, which depended on this customer for 60 per cent of its business. At least it now had two years to find alternative customers or to re-organise the business.

Much remains to be explored in the evolution of buyer–seller relationships. Little is really known about the stages, their underlying determinants and the specific factors that trigger change. However, it is clear that when the relationship between two parties is examined in depth, patterns of evolution do emerge and the key decision points that shape the relationship become apparent.

CHAPTER SUMMARY

The focus of this chapter has been organisational buying behaviour and buyer–seller relationships. Organisational marketing is about exchanges between organisations, whether they are commercial enterprises, government bodies or institutions.

Organisational markets have a number of distinct characteristics, including the nature of demand (derived, joint and inelastic), the structure of demand (concentrated in size and in geography), the complexity of the buying process and the risks inherent in it. The decision-making process that organisational purchasers go through has elements in common with consumer decision making, but is likely to be formalised, to take longer and to involve more people. Stages in the decision-making process include:

- *Precipitation*: beginning the process through recognising a need.
- *Product specification*: defining what is required and the priorities or criteria on which a supplier will be selected.
- *Supplier selection*: searching out potential suppliers, soliciting bids and assessing them in order to make a final choice.
- *Commitment*: drawing up contracts and developing and maintaining a long-term, mutually valuable relationship.

Staff with various functional backgrounds, such as purchasing, marketing, accounting, engineering, production and R&D, will be involved in the process and form a buying centre. The membership of the buying centre, the roles played and who takes the lead may vary from transaction to transaction or even from stage to stage within a single process.

The decision-making process is affected not only by rational, measurable economic criteria (price, specification, quality, service etc.), but also by non-economic influences (prestige, security, social needs, personality) emanating from the individuals involved.

The on-going buyer–seller relationship is increasingly being recognised as a major influencer of organisational marketing strategies. Relationships can be durable and resistant to change, leading to mutual co-operation and the full exploitation of synergy between the two organisations. Other less significant relationships can, however, be kept deliberately superficial. The purchasing organisation has to develop a portfolio of different relationships of varying closeness and depth to suit the whole spectrum of its needs.

Relationships do develop over time and pass through a number of developmental stages, from the initial *awareness* stage, through *exploration* and *expansion* phases, establishing trust, to *commitment*. Some relationships then pass on to *dissolution*, perhaps through complacency, or one party's neglect of the other.

Key words and phrases

Buying centre	Multiple sourcing	Relationship life-cycle
Decision-making unit (DMU)	New task purchasing	Routine re-buy
Derived demand	Organisational marketing	Single sourcing
Joint demand	Product specification	
Modified re-buy	Purchasing policy	

QUESTIONS FOR REVIEW

4.1 What are the different categories of organisational customer and how do they differ from each other?

4.2 What is derived demand and how might it affect organisational purchasing?

4.3 Why does organisational buying vary across different types of organisation, sometimes even within the same industry?

4.4 What are the main differences between organisational and consumer buying behaviour?

4.5 Outline the main stages in the organisational buying decision-making process.

4.6 What factors influence the complexity and the amount of time spent on the decision-making process?

4.7 What is a buying centre?

4.8 How might people in different functional roles (for example R&D or marketing) participate in organisational buying?

4.9 Define the main economic and non-economic influences on organisational decision making.

4.10 Why is it that in some buyer–seller relationships strong bonds and co-operation develop?

QUESTIONS FOR DISCUSSION

4.1 From the supplier's point of view, how might the marketing approaches aimed at a customer making a new task purchase differ from those aimed at a routine re-buy customer?

4.2 How are supplier handling strategies changing as organisations seek to improve their competitiveness?

4.3 What are the stages in the buyer–seller relationship life-cycle, and how is each characterised? What difference might the stages make to the seller's marketing approaches?

4.4 You are the purchasing manager of a large organisation with an enormous annual spend. Most of

your contracts are awarded by tender. What would your attitude be to the following offers from potential suppliers, and to what extent would they influence your decision making:

(a) A bottle of whisky at Christmas?

(b) An invitation to lunch to discuss your requirements?

(c) An offer of the free use of the supplier's managing director's Spanish villa for two weeks?

(d) £1500?

4.5 What do you think are the advantages and disadvantages of long-term, close buyer–seller relationships?

CASE STUDY 4.1

Keeping the wheels turning in the motor industry

The motor industry has developed new strategies over the past decade to build stronger relationships with some suppliers in order to achieve greater efficiencies.

Fiat realised at the end of the 1980s that it had weaknesses in its operation that suppliers could help to solve. For many years, it had purchased largely on price, a policy that had encouraged short-term thinking and little innovation in quality from suppliers. Fiat now needed to encourage suppliers to become involved in the design process and then to invest in their own quality improvements to benefit Fiat. It began to offer a long-term relationship based on trust and, in return for the supplier's investment and commitment, offered it an exclusive contract. Thus 92 per cent of the parts in the Punto were single sourced. This was part of a programme of cutting back the number of main suppliers from 500 to 130, providing 90 per cent of Fiat's parts needs.

Volvo (http://www.volvo.com) similarly must achieve maximum product cost savings and be able to build good, efficient and effective relationships with suppliers to assure quality and remain competitive. About 35 per cent of the value of Volvo cars is produced by Volvo and the balance, worth some SKr23 635 million, is purchased externally. Swedish suppliers contribute 25 per cent of the external balance, German suppliers 33 per cent, the Japanese 12 per cent, Belgians 10 per cent and the British only 3.8 per cent.

In building a supplier base, Volvo sets tough prerequisites for supplier selection and has moved to single sourcing so that any one component can be supplied by one supplier for all models. The initial criteria for selection are that the supplier must:

- be known as a world-class supplier;
- have a recognised and appropriate R&D facility;
- operate proven and appropriate production processes;
- maintain high quality standards;
- implement aggressive cost and productivity development;
- operate a policy of openness;
- be prepared to establish resident engineers close to Volvo's plant at Gothenburg.

Following the initial selection, the final selection has meant some painful decisions as Volvo has had to terminate some relationships despite a long period of successful trading. In addition to meeting the general prerequisites, suppliers are increasingly expected to co-operate with a modularisation programme initiated by Volvo. This means that a supplier takes responsibility for a complete part of the car and thus deals with other component suppliers in the assembly of that part. Areas covered include dashboards, carpets and sound-absorbing materials. The modularisation programme has enabled Volvo to reduce the number of suppliers with direct contracts. With the Volvo 850, for example, the number of suppliers with direct contracts was 270 and this was expected to fall to around 150 after modularisation for the new model.

All these developments have created a climate for closer partnerships between supplier and manufacturer. Volvo takes a cautious approach in the early years to establish whether it can trust the supplier and be confident of its promises. It believes that it can only build between 15 and 20 really close partnerships over the next few years, but as a result it will become more competitive and have access to the technology and engineering skill residing within its supplier partners.

Source: Palm (1996).

Questions

1 Both Fiat and Volvo have adopted a policy of moving towards single sourcing. Why do you think they have done this? What are the disadvantages of such a policy?

2 Some 35 per cent of the value of a Volvo car is produced in-house. If Volvo was looking to increase this percentage, what kinds of suppliers are least likely to lose business to Volvo's in-house operation?

3 How might the composition of the buying centre and the implementation of the purchasing decision-making process differ if a company like Volvo is buying (a) a car component or (b) stationery supplies for its offices?

4 You are the sales director of a small company that produces car components. What information are you going to need, and what factors will you have to take into account, before approaching Volvo with a view to becoming one of its suppliers?

CASE STUDY 4.2

Philips cultivates suppliers

Philips is a global operator in the electronics market with factories all over the world. In order to compete and to ensure customer satisfaction, Philips has to manage its quality and purchasing strategy very carefully. The company recognises that customer satisfaction depends on the quality of what happens on the production line, which in turn depends on the performance of suppliers. If any of the links in the chain breaks down or fails to meet the required standard, then all the glossy advertising in the world is not going to make up for the customer's disappointment in a product that is unavailable, or does not work properly, or fails to meet its technical expectations.

Total quality, therefore, is an ingrained philosophy throughout Philips' operations, resulting in better products and better processes. 'Philips Quality' has five simple but important principles:

(a) Strive for excellence.
(b) Customer first.
(c) Demonstrate leadership.
(d) Value people.
(e) Supplier partnership.

Directly or indirectly, many of these principles could not be properly implemented without good relationships with the right suppliers. Philips cultivates supplier relationships based on trust and co-operation, sharing experience and expertise to benefit not only the buyer and the supplier, but also the end customer. Together, Philips and its suppliers develop technology, solve problems, learn from experience and try to avoid errors and misunderstandings.

Clearly, Philips cannot develop and maintain deep relationships with every one of its suppliers. Instead, it assesses its suppliers to discover which are the most important in terms of their strategic significance to Philips' business. These receive the most attention and investment in relationship building. Philips has three categories of supplier:

1 *Supplier–partners*: this might be the smallest group, but these are the most important suppliers and Philips builds intense, involved relationships with them. An important focus of

the co-operation is innovation, the development of new expertise and new opportunities. These suppliers might well have essential knowledge and/or expertise that Philips could not otherwise access or develop for itself. This makes these suppliers extremely significant strategically, as their loss could seriously undermine Philips' current business and future direction.

2 *Preferred suppliers*: these suppliers are less important, but there is still good reason for Philips to work closely with them on issues such as quality, logistics and price to gain mutual benefit. The supplier does adapt itself to suit Philips' requirements, to some extent, but there is not the same mutual dependence as in the first category.

3 *Commercial suppliers*: these are the least important suppliers and although Philips will encourage better performance in terms of quality etc., it is unlikely to get involved in helping the supplier to achieve it.

Philips also emphasises the importance of supplier revaluation as a basis for improving future performance. A supplier's actual performance is measured against mutually agreed targets in terms of quality, logistics, costs and responsiveness.

Source: European Purchasing and Materials Management (1993/94).

Questions

1 Why should Philips go to all this trouble to develop relationships with suppliers? Why doesn't it just choose suppliers on the basis of the lowest price?

2 What do you think each of the five principles of 'Philips Quality' actually means in practice? How are they consistent with the marketing concept and what impact might they have on the marketing mix?

3 Suggest what criteria Philips might use to decide what category a particular supplier falls into.

4 What is the purpose of supplier evaluation? What do you think Philips might do if it found that a particular supplier had under-performed in terms of costs and quality?

References to Chapter 4

Ahlinder, H. (1996), 'Staying in Touch', *European Purchasing and Materials Management*, No. 7, pp. 51–5.

Anderson, J. C. and Narus, J. A. (1984), 'A Model of the Distributor's Perspective of Distributor–Manufacturer Working Relationships', *Journal of Marketing*, 48 (Fall), pp. 62–74.

Anderson, J. C. and Narus, J. A. (1986), 'Towards a Better Understanding of Distribution Channel Working Relationships', in K. Backhaus and D. Wilson (eds.), *Industrial Marketing: A German–American Perspective*, Springer-Verlag.

Bartram, P. (1999), 'Trim those Wings', *The Grocer*, 6 February, pp. 38–9.

Batchelor, C. (1998), 'Market Has Grown Faster than any Other Sector', *Financial Times*, 28 October , p. II Aluminium.

Bombaci, F. (1996), 'Lean Machine', *European Purchasing and Materials Management*, No. 7, pp. 205–11.

Bouchard, A. (1996), 'Into Africa', *European Purchasing and Materials Management*, No. 7, pp. 317–21.

Carr, H. and Pomeroy, J. (1992), *Fashion Design and Product Development*, Blackwell.

Central Office Of Information (1993), *Britain 1993: An Official Handbook*, HMSO.

Commission of the European Communities (1990), *Public Procurement: Opening Public Service Contracts*, Background Report ISEC/B30/90, 9 November.

Cunningham, M. T. (1986), 'The British Approach to Europe', in P. W. Turnbull and J-P. Valla (eds.), *Strategies for International Industrial Marketing*, Croom Helm.

Dempsey, J. (1994), 'Big is No Longer Beautiful', *Financial Times*, 21 November, VIII.

Dwyer, F. R. *et al.* (1987), 'Developing Buyer–Seller Relationships', *Journal of Marketing*, 51(2), pp. 11–27.

Edwards, N. (1997), 'Here Today, Green Tomorrow', *Supply Management*, 11 December, pp. 24–6.

European Purchasing and Materials Management (1993/94), 'Philips Quality', *European Purchasing and Materials Management*, 1993/94(2), pp. 51–5.

Freeland, J. R. (1991), 'A Survey of JIT Purchasing in the United States', *Production and Inventory Management*, 32(2), pp. 43–50.

Freeman Allen, G. (1994), 'Italy's Pendolino: The Second Generation', *Modern Railways*, April, pp. 227–8.

Freeman Allen, G. (1995a), 'Europeview', *Modern Railways*, Nov., p. 707.

Freeman Allen, G. (1995b), 'Europeview', *Modern Railways*, March, p. 165.

Freeman Allen, G. (1996), 'Europeview', *Modern Railways*, June, p. 395.

Genillard, A. (1993), 'Plenty of Scientists But No Monkeys', *Financial Times*, 29 April, p. 39.

Gough, J. (1998a), 'Pendolino Order Confirmed', *Modern Railways*, February, p. 109.

Gough, J. (1998b), 'Pendolinos Ordered', *Modern Railways*, February, p. 111.

Gutteridge, S. (1995), 'Financing Small Scale CHP Schemes', *Purchasing and Supply Management*, Feb., pp. 41–2.

Hallén, L. (1980), 'Stability and Change in Supplier Relationships', in L. Engall and J. Johanson (eds.), *Some Aspects of Control in International Business*, Uppsala.

Hill, R. W. and Hiller, T. J. (1977), *Organisational Buying Behaviour*, MacMillan.

Johanson, J. (1982), 'Production Technology and the User–Supplier Interaction', in H. Håkansson (ed.), *International Marketing and Purchasing of Industrial Goods: An Interaction Approach*, John Wiley and Sons.

Johanson, J. and Wootz, B. (1986), 'The German Approach to Europe', in P. W. Turnbull and J-P. Valla (eds.), *Strategies for International Industrial Marketing*, Croom Helm.

Johnson, W. J. and Bonoma, T. V. (1981), 'The Buying Centre: Structure and Interaction Patterns', *Journal of Marketing*, 45 (Summer), pp. 143–56.

Kahn, S. (1997), '£40 bn Eurofighter Gets Final All-clear', *The Express*, 22 December, p. 38.

Lorenz, E. H. (1988), 'Neither Friends Nor Strangers: Informal Networks of Subcontracting in French Industry', in D. Gambetta (ed.), *Trust: Making and Breaking Cooperative Relations*, Basil Blackwell.

McInerney, M. (1996), 'Planning a Fleet', *European Purchasing and Materials Management*, No. 7, pp. 223–34.

Mattson, M. R. (1988), 'How to Determine the Composition and Influence of A Buying Centre', *Industrial Marketing Management*, 17(3), pp. 205–14.

Nolan, A. (1997a), 'Watching the Directives', *Supply Management*, 27 February, pp. 14–15.

Nolan, A. (1997b), 'Finding the Right Formula', *Supply Management*, 13 March, pp. 14–15.

Nordby, K. (1996), 'Moving with the Times', *European Purchasing and Materials Management*, No. 7, pp. 307–14.

Northam, S. (1994), 'Look Before You Leap', *European Purchasing and Materials Management*, 1994(3), pp. 251–7.

O'Connor, J. and Galvin, E. (1999), *Marketing and Information Technology*, 2nd edn, Financial Times Pitman Publishing.

Paliwoda, S. and Bonaccorsi, A. J. (1994), 'Trends in Procurement Strategies Within the European Aircraft Industry', *Industrial Marketing Management*, 23(3), pp. 235–44.

Palm, C. (1996), 'Purchasing the Volvo Way', *European Purchasing and Materials Management*, No. 7, pp. 193–6.

Pettitt, S. J. (1992), *Small Firms and Their Major Customers: An Interaction and Relationship Approach*, unpublished PhD Thesis, Cranfield University.

Porter, M. E. (1990), *The Competitive Advantage of Nations*, The Free Press.

Powers, T. L. (1991), *Modern Business Marketing: A Strategic Planning Approach to Business and Industrial Markets*, St Paul MN: West.

Ramsay, J. and Wilson, I. (1990), 'Sourcing/ Contracting Strategy Selection', *International Journal of Operations and Production Management*, 10(8), pp. 19–28.

Robinson, P. J. *et al.* (1967), *Industrial Buying and Creative Marketing*, Allyn and Bacon.

Segal, M. (1989), 'Implications of Single vs Multiple Buying Sources', *Industrial Marketing Management*, 18(3), pp. 163–78.

Sheth, J. (1973), 'A Model of Industrial Buying Behaviour', *Journal of Marketing*, 37(Oct), 50–6.

Sheth, J. (1977), 'Recent Developments in Organisational Buying Behaviour', in A. G. Woodside *et al.* (eds.), *Consumer and Industrial Buying Behaviour*, Elsevier.

Spekman, R. E. (1988), 'Strategic Supplier Selection: Understanding Long Term Buyer Relationships', *Business Horizons*, 31(4), pp. 75–81.

Supply Management (1998), 'ICI Symphony Delivers Big Savings', *Supply Management*, 9 April, p. 9.

Taimi, K. (1996), 'The Face in the Supermarket Window', *European Purchasing and Materials Management*, No. 7, pp. 159–69.

Trevelen, M. (1987), 'Single Sourcing: A Management Tool for the Quality Supplier', *Journal of Purchasing and Materials Management*, 23(1), pp. 19–24.

Valla, J-P. (1986), 'The French Approach to Europe', in P. W. Turnbull and J-P. Valla (eds.), *Strategies for International Industrial Marketing*, Croom Helm.

Varley, P. (1998a), 'Preparing for the 18 Month Aircraft', *Supply Management*, 26 March, p. 17.

Varley, P. (1998b), 'Smooth Operator', *Supply Management*, 10 September, pp. 37–8.

Webster, F. E. and Wind, Y. (1972), *Organisational Buyer Behaviour*, Prentice Hall.

Whitworth, M. (1998), 'JS' Revolution in Data Supply', *The Grocer*, 30 May, p. 4.

5 Segmenting Markets

LEARNING OBJECTIVES

This chapter will help you to:

1 understand the potential benefits of breaking markets down into smaller, more manageable parts or segments;

2 explain the ways in which market segments are defined in both organisational and consumer markets;

3 understand the effects on the marketing mix of pursuing specific segments; and

4 appreciate the role of segmentation in strategic marketing thinking.

INTRODUCTION

Building on the understanding of buyer behaviour and decision-making processes outlined in Chapters 3 and 4, this chapter concerns a question that should be very close to any true marketer's heart: 'How do we define and profile our customer?' Until an answer is found, no meaningful marketing decisions of any kind can be made. It is not usually enough to define your customer as 'anyone who wants to buy our product' because this implies a product-orientated approach: the product comes first, the customer second. If marketing is everything we have claimed it to be, then the product is only a small part of a total integrated package offered to a customer. Potential customers must, therefore, be defined in terms of what they want, or will accept, in terms of price, what kind of distribution will be most convenient for them and through what communication channels they can best be reached, as well as what they want from the product itself.

Example The business-class flyer is an important source of revenue for the airline industry. This group of customers differs significantly from leisure- and economy-class customers. Business travellers sometimes need to book at short notice, travel to tight schedules, travel frequently and could need to change arrangements at the last minute. Airlines have adapted their service provision to meet the needs of this group. Fast check-in facilities, first- or business-class travel options and lounges, special boarding arrangements and loyalty schemes are all important for attracting these customers. Airlines also advertise specifically to the business traveller and keep their pricing competitive within the business flyer segment on competitive routes such as London–Brussels. The business traveller group is not, however, homogeneous. There are subsegments such as frequent flyers whose characteristics and needs are slightly different. In the UK it is estimated that there are 3 million business-class flyers, but only 300 000 of them make more than 10 flights per year. Interestingly, *The Sun* and *The Daily Mail* are the most popular media with all business flyers, whereas *The Times* and *The Daily Telegraph* are very popular with frequent flyers (Clemens, 1997).

Remember too that in a consumer-based society, possession of 'things' can take on a symbolic meaning. A person's possessions and consumption habits make a statement about the kind of person they are, or the kind of person they want you to think they are. The organisation that takes the trouble to understand this and produces a product that not only serves its functional purpose well, but also appears to reflect those less tangible properties of a product in the purchaser's eyes, will gain that purchaser's custom. Thus sport shoe manufacturers such as Reebok and Nike not only developed shoes for a wide range of specific sports (tennis, soccer, athletics etc.), but also realised that a significant group of customers would never go near a sports facility and just wanted trainers as fashion statements. This meant that they served three distinctly different groups of customers: the professional/serious sports player, the amateur/casual sports player and the fashion victim. The R&D invested in state-of-the-art quality products, combined with the status connected with the first group and endorsement from leading sports icons, helped these companies to build an upmarket image that allowed them to exploit the fashion market to the full with premium-priced products. This in turn led to the expansion of product ranges to include branded sports and leisure clothing.

All this forms the basis of the concept of segmentation, first developed by Smith (1957). Segmentation can be viewed as the art of discerning and defining meaningful differences between groups of customers to form the foundations of a more focused marketing effort. The following section looks at this concept in a little more depth, while the rest of the chapter will examine how the concept can be implemented and its implications for the organisation.

THE CONCEPT OF SEGMENTATION

The introductory section of this chapter has presented the customer-oriented argument for the adoption of the segmentation concept. There is, however, also a practical rationale for adopting it. Mass production, mass communication, increasingly sophisticated technology and increasingly efficient global transportation have all helped in the creation of larger, more temptingly lucrative potential markets. Few organisations, however, have either the resources or the inclination to be a significant force within a loosely defined market. The sensible option, therefore, is to look more closely at the market and find ways of breaking it down into manageable parts, or groups of customers with similar characteristics, and then to concentrate effort on serving the needs of one or two groups really well, rather than trying to be all things to all people.

It may help you to understand this concept better if you think of an orange. It appears to be a single entity, yet when you peel off the skin you find that it is made up of a number of discrete segments, each of which happily exists within the whole. Eating an orange is much easier (and much less wasteful and messy) if you eat it systematically, segment by segment, rather than by attacking the whole fruit at once. Marketers, being creative folk, have adopted this analogy and thus refer to the separate groups of customers that make up a market as **market segments**.

The analogy is misleading, however, in that each segment of an orange is more or less identical in size, shape and taste, whereas in a market, segments may be very different from each other in terms of size and character. To determine these things, each segment has its own distinct profile, defined in terms of a number of criteria, referred to as *bases* or *variables*, set by the marketer. The choice of appropriate criteria is very important and thus a significant proportion of this chapter is devoted to thinking about the bases by which segments might be defined in both consumer and organisational markets. Leading on from this, there is also the question of influences that might affect an organisation's choice of segmentation variables. Then, once an organisation has defined its market segments, what is it supposed to do with the information? This too is addressed in this chapter.

Organisational and consumer markets, in general, tend to be segmented differently and will, therefore, be discussed separately, beginning with organisational markets. If you are unsure of the difference between these two types of market, then revise the content of Chapters 3 and 4 before you go any further.

SEGMENTING ORGANISATIONAL MARKETS

The overall concept of segmentation applies equally to both consumer and organisational markets, but the variables by which they are segmented do differ. One major feature of organisational segmentation is that it can focus on both the organisation and the individual buyers within it. Additionally, there is the need to reflect group buying, that is, the involvement of more than one person in the purchasing decision. All of this can be compared with a family buying situation in a consumer market, but operating on a much larger scale, usually within a more formalised process.

Wind and Cardozo (1974) suggest that segmenting an organisational market can involve two stages:

1 *Identify subgroups* within the whole market that share common general characteristics. These are called **macro segments** and will be discussed further below.

2 *Select target segments* from within the macro segments based on differences in specific buying characteristics. These are called **micro segments** and are discussed at p. 180.

Macro segmentation bases

Macro segments are based on the characteristics of organisations and the broader purchasing context within which they operate. Defining a macro segment assumes that the organisations within it will exhibit similar patterns and needs, which will be reflected in similar buying behaviour and responses to marketing stimuli.

The bases used for macro segmentation tend to be observable or readily obtained from secondary information (i.e. published or existing sources) and can be grouped into two main categories, each of which will now be discussed.

Organisational characteristics
There are three organisational charactistics: size, location and usage rate.

1 *Size.* The size of an organisation will make a difference to the way in which it views its suppliers and goes about its purchasing. A large organisation, for instance, may well have many people involved in decision making; its decision making may be very complex and formalised (because of the risks and level of investment involved), and it may require special treatment in terms of service or technical co-operation. In contrast, a small organisation may operate on a more centralised decision-making structure, involving one or two people and with simpler buying routines. The UK clearing banks, for example, tend to segment their business customers by size. Small businesses need sympathetic local support, and the banks target the new start-up segment of the small business market with advice packs and promises of cheap financing along with the support of their own banking adviser.

2 *Location.* Organisations may focus their selling effort according to the geographic concentration of the industries they serve. Such specialisation is, however, slowly breaking down as the old, heavy, geographically based industries, such as shipbuilding, mining and chemical production, become less predominant. Additionally,

there is the emergence of smaller more flexible manufacturers, geographically dispersed in new technology parks, industrial estates and enterprise zones. Nevertheless, there are still examples of geographic segmentation, such as that of computer hardware and software sales, or in the financial sector, which is concentrated in London, Frankfurt, Zurich and the major capitals of the world. Organisations providing certain kinds of services might also look to geographic segments. A haulage company might specialise in certain routes and thus look for customers at specific points to make collection, delivery and capacity utilisation as efficient as possible.

3 *Usage rate.* The quantity of product purchased may be a legitimate means of categorising potential customers. A purchasing organisation defined as a 'heavy user' will have different needs from a 'light user', perhaps demanding (and deserving) different treatment in terms of special delivery or prices, for example. A supplier may define a threshold point, so that when a customer's usage rate rises above it, their status changes. The customer's account may be handed over to a more senior manager and the supplier may become more flexible in terms of co-operation, pricing and relationship building. It is generally a better investment to make concessions in order to cultivate a relationship with a single heavy user than to try to attract a number of light users, as implied in Chapter 4.

Product or service application

This second group of segmentation bases acknowledges that the same good can be used in many different ways. This approach looks for customer groupings, either within specific industries as defined by standard industrial classification (SIC) codes, each with its own requirements, or by defining a specific application and grouping customers around that.

The SIC code may help to identify sectors with a greater propensity to use particular products for particular applications. Glass, for example, has many industrial uses, ranging from packaging to architecture to the motor industry. Each of these application sectors behaves differently in terms of price sensitivity, ease of substitution, quality and performance requirements, for instance. Similarly, cash-and-carry wholesalers serve three broad segments: independent grocers, caterers and pubs. Each segment will purchase different types of goods, in different quantities and for different purposes.

The macro level is a useful starting point for defining some broad boundaries to markets and segments, but it is not sufficient in itself, even if such segmentation does happen too often in practice. Further customer-orientated analysis on the micro level is necessary.

Micro-segmentation bases

Within a macro segment, a number of smaller micro segments may exist. To focus on these, the organisation needs to have a detailed understanding of individual members of the macro segment, in terms of their management philosophy, decision-making structures, purchasing policies and strategies, as well as their needs and wants. Such information can come from published sources, past experience of the potential buyer, sales force knowledge and experience, word of mouth within the industry, or at first hand from the potential buyer.

Micro segmentation reflects, to some extent, the nested approach to organisational market segmentation suggested by Bonoma and Shapiro (1984). This means starting with broad characteristics, that is, the demographic profile of the customer (understanding the industry, organisational size etc.) and then developing increasingly fine detail by working through their operating variables (product, technology, quality etc.), purchasing approach (DMUs, power, buyer–seller relationships etc.), situational factors (delivery lead times, order size etc.) and, finally, personal characteristics (the individuals concerned).

An overview of common bases for micro segmentation is given in Table 5.1. If some of the terms given within the table seem a little vague, revise Chapter 4 that goes into them all in much more detail.

Gathering, collating and analysing such depth of information is, of course, a time-consuming and sometimes difficult task, and there is always the question of whether it is either feasible or worth while. However, there are benefits in defining such small segments (even segments of one!) if it enables fine tuning of the marketing offering to suit specific needs. Given the volumes of goods and levels of financial investment involved in some organisational markets, the effort is not wasted. An organisation that has a small number of very important customers would almost certainly treat each as a segment of one, particularly in a market such as the supply of organisation-wide computer systems where individual customer needs vary so much. In contrast, in a market such as office stationery, where standard products are sold to perhaps thousands of organisational customers, any segmentation is likely to centre around groups aggregating many tens of customers on the macro level.

Overall, this section has shown that it is useful to be able to segment organisational markets, and that it can be done in a number of ways relating to the nature of both the product sold and the buying organisation. The emphasis here has essentially been a practical one, treating the buying organisation as a rational entity. Chapter 4 (particularly pp. 165 *et seq.*), in looking more deeply at the organisation as the sum of its human parts, demonstrated some of the potential irrationalities that make micro segmentation so fascinating. In consumer markets, rapid progress has also been made towards expanding concepts of segmentation to include what might be termed the less rational influences on purchasing, as the following section shows.

TABLE 5.1
Basis for micro segmentation in organisational markets

- Product
- Applications
- Technology
- Purchasing policies
- DMU structure
- Decision-making process
- Buyer–seller relationships

SEGMENTING CONSUMER MARKETS

Segmenting consumer markets does have some similarities with organisational segmentation, as this section indicates. The main difference is that consumer segments are usually very much larger in terms of the number of potential buyers, and it is much more difficult, therefore, to get close to the individual buyer. Consumer segmentation bases also put more emphasis on the buyer's lifestyle and context, because most consumer purchases fulfil higher-order needs (*see*, for example, Maslow's hierarchy of needs, discussed at pp. 111 *et seq.*) rather than simply functional ones.

Geographic segmentation

Geographic segmentation defines customers according to their location. This can often be a useful starting point. A small business, for example, particularly in the retail or service sector, operating on limited resources, may look initially for custom within its immediate locale. Even multinationals, such as Heinz, often tend to segment geographically by dividing their global organisation into operating units built around specific geographic markets.

In neither case, however, is this the end of the story. For the small business, simply being there on the high street is not enough. It has to offer something further that a significant group of customers want, whether it is attractively low prices or a high level of customer service. The multinational organisation segments geographically, partly for the sake of creating a manageable organisational structure, and partly in recognition that on a global scale, geographic boundaries herald other, more significant differences in taste, culture, lifestyle and demand. The Single European Market (SEM) may have created a market of some 400 million potential customers, yet the first thing that most organisations are likely to do is to segment the SEM into its constituent nations.

> **Example** Take the marketing of an instant hot chocolate drink, made with boiling water. In the UK, virtually every household owns a kettle, and hot chocolate is viewed either as a bedtime drink or as a substitute through the day for tea or coffee. In France, however, kettles are not common, and hot chocolate is most often made with milk as a nourishing children's breakfast. Thus the benefits of speed, convenience and versatility that would impress the UK market would be less applicable in the French market. France would require a very different marketing strategy at best or, at worst, a completely different product.

Geographic segments are at least easy to define and measure, and information is often freely available from public sources. This kind of segmentation also has an operational advantage, particularly in developing efficient systems for distribution and customer contact, for example. However, in a marketing-oriented organisation, this is not sufficient. Douglas and Craig (1983), for example, emphasise the dangers of being too geographically focused and making assumptions about what customers in a region might have in common. Even within a small geographic area, there is a wide variety of needs and wants, and this method on its own tells you nothing about them. Heinz divides its global operation into geographically based subdivisions because it does recognise the effects of cultural diversity and believes in 'local marketing' as the best means of fully understanding and serving its various markets. It is also important to note that any organisation segmenting purely on geographic grounds would be vulnerable to competition coming in with a more customer-focused segmentation strategy.

In summary, therefore, there is limited scope for the application of geographic segmentation on its own. It may be useful for service-based products that require the customer to come to you. For example, hairdressers attract business from a geographic catchment area centred on their salon, but even so, they still segment further on other criteria (for instance sex, age and trendiness). In manufacturing, geographic segmentation may also be useful for organisations operating with very limited resources. By confining its operations to a small geographic area, the organisation can develop a focus that will allow it to expand gradually as business builds up. In the main, however, it is used as a foundation for other, more customer-focused segmentation methods, such as those described below.

Demographic segmentation

Demographic segmentation tells you a little more about the customer and the customer's household on measurable criteria that are largely descriptive, such as age, sex, race, income, occupation, socioeconomic status and family structure.

Demographics might even extend into classifications of body size and shape! In the UK, for example, the proportion of overweight men has risen to almost 50 per cent of the male population, while 40 per cent of the female population are overweight. The overweight thus represent a significant marketing opportunity. The clothing retailers High and Mighty and Evans primarily target larger men and women respectively. Furniture manufacturers are redesigning their products to cope with bigger and heavier people, while cars, trains and airline seats are also having to be adapted (Palmer and Cohen, 1993).

MARKETING IN ACTION   Go for bust

The British bra and lingerie company Gossard (http://www.gossard.co.uk) has found that a geographic approach to market segmentation can have some validity. The types of product that sell best in various countries are different, partly for the practical reason that women vary in average size across Europe, and partly because of cultural and lifestyle factors. While the British female figure averages around sizes 12–14, German women tend towards sizes 14–16 and the French towards 10–12. Italian women want to be seductive and thus buy a lot of basques; the Germans are practical and look for support and quality; the French want to be fashionable and impress other women; and the Scandinavians want natural fibres. This is, of course, a grossly generalised survey, but the basic trends are there and give Gossard a basis for developing appropriate new products and strategies for different markets.

Not all bra brands are constrained by geographic markets, however. Playtex (http://www.playtex.com) sells 1.5 million Wonderbras across Europe every year

and sales are still growing at around 5 per cent. The Wonderbra was designed to target younger women, aged between 18 and 35, wanting a fashionable, fun, sexy bra that allows them to make the most of their assets. This appeal was reinforced by advertising slogans such as 'Hello, Boys', 'Mind If I Bring a Couple of Friends?' and 'In Your Dreams' alongside scantily clad, beautiful models. Playtex realised, however, that such an approach is inappropriate for younger girls and was reported to be in the process of developing an extension of the Wonderbra with a more relevant marketing campaign for the under-18s. A further usage segment for Playtex is active women who play sport or take strenuous exercise and a sports Wonderbra would offer the right kind of support and comfort during exercise. It is possible for an individual woman to be a member of two segments: she might buy the 'fashion' Wonderbra (and perhaps even a number of them in different colours) for normal day or evening wear and the sports version for her leisure pursuits.

Source: Broadhead (1995); Sage (1997a; 1997b).

Gossard designs different products for different European markets as both taste and average sizes differ across regional boundaries.

Source: Gossard.

As with the geographic variable, demographics are relatively easy to define and measure, and the necessary information is often freely available from public sources. The main advantage, however, is that demographics offer a clear profile of the customer on criteria that can be worked into marketing strategies. For example, an age profile can provide a foundation for choice of advertising media and creative approach. Magazines, for instance, tend to have readerships that are clearly defined in terms of gender, age bands and socioeconomic groups. The under-35 female reader, for example, is more likely to go for magazines such as *Marie Claire*, *Bella* and *Cosmopolitan* than the over-35s who are more likely to read *Prima*, *Good Housekeeping* and *Family Circle*.

One of the problems facing organisations looking to European markets in particular is that socioeconomic definitions vary widely across different countries, as already shown at p. 118. Efforts are, however, being made to develop a uniform scale, applicable across national boundaries and relevant to the needs of marketers. The outcomes of one such project, reported in Marbeau (1992) and Quatresooz and Vancraeynest (1992) suggest a definition of social grade based on the terminal education age of the main income earner in a household, his or her further education and professional training, and his or her occupation. Additionally, an economic status scale is proposed, based on a household's ownership of 10 carefully chosen consumer durables.

MARKETING IN ACTION | A weighty segment

Obesity is big business for some companies. The Russians lead the world with over half the population classified as being at least 20 per cent fatter than they should be. They are followed by Americans (33 per cent), Belgians (23 per cent), the British at 22 per cent, and finally the Italians at 20 per cent. It is an expanding segment in more ways than one. Fast food, more eating out and less exercise have all combined to increase obesity over the last 10 years in the United States and Europe.

Lands End, a catalogue group based in the US but also selling in Europe, decided to expand the sizes available for the woman with the fuller figure. Its research indicated that this segment had considerable trouble finding stylish clothes, especially casual wear, so the catalogue offered larger sizes of items such as jeans, sweaters, T-shirts, blouses, shorts and sleepwear. The company was astounded at the success of the new sizes.

Pinault-Printemps-Redoute, the large French catalogue and retail group, purchased a 40 per cent stake in the US catalogue firm Brylane, which had established a good share of the outsize men and women segment. About 40 per cent of its business is in the bigger sizes and it caters for men up to a 28 inch neck and 72 inch waist. Catalogue shopping is especially attractive to this segment, as the consumer is sometimes too embarrassed to visit a retail store.

Some really large people argue that being fat is not a character flaw, but largely genetic. Others take fat-reduction programmes very seriously, creating opportunities for weight watchers' clubs, special diet foods, slimming pills and a myriad of publications designed to provide practical 'how to lose weight' advice and diets. In 1997, for instance, a pill was launched called Beer Blok that claimed to reduce beer bellies if taken before a pint was drunk. Men have also been turning to electronic slimming devices, traditionally the preserve of women. Men are now the largest group buying machines that electrically massage the stomach, a convenient way of sipping a beer while undergoing some light exercise! Although such machines cannot reverse years of neglect, they can assist in the removal of the extra flab generated by over-indulging in the pub for too long.

Understanding the obese and overweight target segment is critical to successful marketing. Such consumers do not want to be patronised, embarrassed or called 'fat'. There is often denial, blaming metabolism and genes rather than lifestyle. The Department of Health also found that people from advantaged groups in the UK tend to be thin and those from the lower social class tended to be fat. Just 11 per cent of social class one suffers obesity, but this rises to 25 per cent in social class five. This has been explained variously as being due to less exercise combined with poor diet, with the emphasis on processed, cheap and fatty foods. The difficulty for the marketer when communicating with this segment is whether to go with the 'fat' image, using shock tactics emphasising the beer belly to sell the 'cure', or whether to use more subtle approaches showing what you could be like if you were a little lighter.

Sources: Austin (1998); Brodie (1998); Wavell (1997).

This provides a way of comparing different countries without the problems of varying exchange rates, varying purchasing power or income measurement. The extent to which such a system becomes common European currency remains to be seen.

On the negative side, demographics are purely descriptive and, used alone, assume that all people in the same demographic group have similar needs and wants. This is not necessarily true (just think about the variety of people you know within your own age group). Additionally, as with the geographic method, it is still vulnerable to competition coming in with an even more customer-focused segmentation strategy. It is best used, then, for products that have a clear bias towards a particular demographic group. For instance, cosmetics are initially segmented into male/female; baby products are primarily aimed at females aged between 20 and 35; school fee endowment policies appeal to households within a higher income bracket at a particular stage of the family life-cycle. In most of these cases, however, again as with the geographic method, the main use of demographic segmentation is as a foundation for other more customer-focused segmentation methods.

Geodemographic segmentation

TABLE 5.2
ACORN Group D

- Older terraced housing – pre-1914
- Tenement flats
- Low income
- Inadequate ventilation/heating/cooking facilities
- Government grants have led to some modernisation
- Lack of suitable play areas for children
- In larger towns: young families
- In smaller towns: elderly population
- Few modern retail facilities

Source: CACI Information Services.

Geodemographics can be defined as 'the analysis of people by where they live' (Sleight, 1997, p. 16) as it combines geographic information with demographic and sometimes even lifestyle data (see below) about neighbourhoods. This helps organisations to understand where their customers are, to develop more detailed profiles of how those customers live, and to locate and target similar potential customers elsewhere. A geodemographic system, therefore, will define types of neighbourhood according to their characteristics. Table 5.2 gives an example of how CACI's ACORN (A Classification Of Residential Neighbourhoods) profiles one of its 54 neighbourhood types.

A number of specialist companies, including CACI, offer geodemographic databases and some of these are shown in Table 5.3. Most of them are generally applicable to a range of consumer markets, although Residata, for instance, is specifically designed for the insurance industry, and some, like ACORN, have developed variations on the main database to suit different industries or geographic regions.

The databases vary considerably in the sources of data they use and the number of variables they employ to define and describe the clusters (neighbourhood types). CAMEO, for example, uses 48 variables to define up to 44 clusters, whereas MicroVision uses 185 variables to define up to 200 clusters. The more recent systems, such as PeopleUK and Pixel, are different from their predecessors in that they classify individuals and households rather than just neighbourhoods (anything up to 115 households). Pixel, for example, defines 1250 types of individual in terms of gender, age group, length of residency, household composition, property type, shareholdings and directorships, and Experian claims that 92 per cent of the UK population fits into those types (Sleight, 1999a).

Geodemographic systems are increasingly becoming available as multimedia packages. MOSAIC is available on CD-ROM, giving the manager access to colour maps, spoken commentary on how to use the system, photographs and text. Experian and other providers are also working on customised geodemographic packages, tailored to suit a particular client's needs.

TABLE 5.3

Examples of geodemographic classifications

Organisation	Classification system	Examples of data sources used
ABC Ltd	Residata	Housing types and structure; risk indices; insurance data; PAF; unemployment statistics; census
CACI	ACORN	Census data
	Lifestyles UK	Lifestyle data; ER; Census; share ownership
	People UK	LIfestyle data; ER; Census; share ownership
Claritas UK	SuperProfiles	Credit data; CCJs; ER; TGI
	PRIZM	Lifestyle data; share ownership; company directors; PAF; unemployment statistics; births and deaths
	Lifestyle Universe	Lifestyle data; ER; CCJs; PAF; share ownership
Equifax	MicroVision	Lifestyle data; share ownership; company directors; CCJs; ER; risk indices; unemployment statistics; census
EuroDirect	CAMEO	Census data
Experian	MOSAIC	Census data; credit data; CCJs; PAF; ER; company directors; access to retail centres Pixel Company directors; share ownership; ER

Key: CCJs: County Court Judgments: Consumers who have been taken to court for debt recovery

ER: Electoral Register: gives names, addresses and number of adults of 95 per cent of UK households

PAF: Postcode Address File: Royal Mail's database of all addresses in the UK by postcode

TGI: Target Group Index: detailed market research on consumer media usage and on some 3500 brands, 25 000 adults per year

Source: Adapted from Sleight (1997, 1998, 1999a, 1999b).

Such systems are invaluable to the marketer across all aspects of consumer marketing, for example in planning sampling areas for major market research studies, or assessing locations for new retail outlets, or finding appropriate areas for a direct mail campaign or door-to-door leaflet drop. O'Malley *et al.* (1995) point out that retailers

CCN's MOSAIC geodemographic system is availabe on CD-ROM, thus enhancing its user-friendliness and flexibility.

Source: Experian.

Scottish blood

It is not just consumer goods manufacturers or retailers which use geodemographic databases for targeting. The Scottish National Blood Transfusion Service wanted to increase the number of blood donors. Using CACI's software and data, groups of people living in Scotland judged to have 'the greatest propensity to give blood' were identified. These groups mainly consisted of affluent people in managerial or professional jobs and less well-off people with a strong public-spirited attitude who are likely to live alone near the centres of towns (O'Connor and Galvin, 1999).

TABLE 5.4

Applications of geodemographic and lifestyle data

Application	Percentage of respondents
Targeting direct mail	55.6
Market segmentation	47.0
Customer database building	41.1
Media analysis	34.4
Retail location analysis	29.8
Sales force organisation	13.2
Other applications	12.6

Source: Survey conducted by Peter Sleight, Target Market Consultancy. Reprinted with kind permission.

find geodemographics invaluable. This is because setting up a new retail store location is very capital intensive and represents a long-term commitment. Retailers thus need to monitor a trade area in terms of its catchment, shopper profiles and competitive effects. Geodemographics can help to achieve this.

A survey carried out by Target Market Consultancy (Sleight, 1997) found that 75 per cent of respondents use geodemographic or lifestyle data within their businesses. Table 5.4 lists the most popular applications for the data.

Psychographic segmentation

Psychographics, or **lifestyle segmentation**, is an altogether more difficult area to define, as it involves intangible variables such as the beliefs, attitudes and opinions of the potential customer. It has evolved in answer to some of the shortcomings of the methods described above as a means of getting further under the skin of the customer as a thinking being. The idea is that defining the lifestyle of the consumer allows the marketer to sell the product not on superficial, functional features, but on benefits that can be seen to enhance that lifestyle on a much more emotional level. The term *lifestyle* is used in its widest sense to cover not only demographic characteristics, but also attitudes to life, beliefs and aspirations.

Plummer (1974) was an early exponent of lifestyle segmentation, breaking it down into four main categories: activities, interests, opinions and demographics.

Activities

The activities category includes all the things people do in the course of their lives. It therefore covers work, shopping, holidays and social life. Within that, the marketer will be interested in people's hobbies and their preferred forms of entertainment, as well as sports interests, club memberships and their activities within the community (voluntary work, for instance).

Interests

Interests refers to what is important to the consumer and where their priorities lie. It may include the things very close to them, such as family, home and work, or their interest and involvement in the wider community. It may also include elements of leisure and recreation, and Plummer particularly mentions areas such as fashion, food and media.

Opinions

The category of opinions comes very close to the individual's innermost thoughts, by probing attitudes and feelings about such things as themselves, social and cultural issues and politics. Opinion may also be sought about other influences on society, such as education, economics and business. Closer to home for the marketer, this category will also investigate opinions about products and the individual's view of the future, indicating how their needs and wants are likely to change.

Demographics

Demographic descriptors have already been extensively covered, and this category includes the kinds of demographic elements you would expect, such as age, education, income and occupation, as well as family size, life-cycle stage and geographic location.

By researching each of these categories thoroughly and carefully, the marketer can build up a very detailed and three-dimensional picture of the consumer. Building such profiles over very large groups of individuals can then allow the marketer to aggregate people with significant similarities in their profiles into named lifestyle segments. As you might expect, because lifestyles are so complex and the number of contributory variables so large, there is no single universally applicable typology of psychographic segments. Indeed, many different typologies have emerged over the years, emphasising different aspects of lifestyle, striving to provide a set of lifestyle segments that are either generally useful or designed for a specific commercial application.

In the USA, for example, advertising agencies have found the Values And Life Style (VALS-2) typology, based on Mitchell (1983), particularly useful. The typology is based on the individual's *resources*, mainly income and education, and *self-orientation*, i.e. attitude towards one self, one's aspirations and the things one does to communicate and achieve them. The segments that emerge include, for example, *Achievers*, who fall within the category of 'status oriented'. They have abundant resources and are career minded with a social life that revolves around work and family. They mind very much what other people think of them, and particularly crave the good opinion of those who they themselves admire. The implication is that Achievers have largely 'made it' in terms of material success, in contrast to *Strivers* (who are likely to be Achievers in the future) and *Strugglers* (who aspire to be Achievers, but may never make it). Both these segments are also status oriented, but are less well endowed with resources and still have some way to go.

Example Participation in an ever-increasing range of sports and outdoor activities is a feature of modern lifestyles. This can be a great leveller, as performance is related to ability rather than a participant's financial means or social standing. Marketers have, however, created another form of status hierarchy through the increasing emphasis on the labels and brands of sports clothing and equipment. Whether the sport is golf, cycling, sailing, tennis or even hill walking, the choice of equipment seems to be based just as much on fashion and image statements as on functional benefit. This phenomenon is not only seen in clothing and equipment. Elida Fabergé launched a new range of bodycare products, Physio Sport, which aimed to attract worldwide sales of £300 million within two years. The target is 'serious' sports people of either sex and the range covers personal freshness, washing, hair washing and chafed skin (Barnard, 1998; *The Grocer*, 1998a).

With the advent of the SEM, many organisations have been trying to produce lifestyle-based psychographic segment profiles that categorise the whole of Europe. One such study, carried out by Euro Panel and marketed in the UK by AGB Dialogue, was based on an exhaustive 150-page questionnaire administered across the EU, Switzerland and Scandinavia. The main research areas covered included demographic and economic factors, as well as attitudes, activities and feelings. Analysis of the questionnaire data allowed researchers to identify 16 lifestyle segments based on two main axes, innovation/conservatism and idealism/materialism. The results also identified 20 or so key questions that were crucial to matching a respondent with an appropriate segment. These key questions were then put to a further 20 000 respondents, which then allowed the definition of 16 segments, including for example Euro-Citizen, Euro-Gentry, Euro-Moralist, Euro-Vigilante, Euro-Romantic and Euro-Business.

Paitra (1993) similarly defines three Euro-segments:

The Moderns

Representing some 30 per cent of Europeans, the Moderns have flexible purchasing power and are open to change, with cosmopolitan tastes and a liking for the exotic and foreign. They have no problem thinking about themselves as European and as nationals of their own country at the same time. They are more likely to be Italian or French than British or German.

MARKETING IN ACTION   **Retail therapy**

Although the clothing market in the UK is worth around £14 billion per year, it is still important for a fashion retailer to define its target customer very clearly so that it can create a strong image and store atmosphere that will appeal directly to such a customer. Marketers have defined four female segments in the clothing market, each with different needs and different expectations:

- *The fashion enthusiast* is the youngest shopper and is likely to be a teenager. She spends a lot, three times more on average than an adult shopper, and often buys on impulse. She loves shopping and sees it as a social event, a fun day out. Because of this, she tends to shop with a group of her friends and it is important to her to gain their help in making choices and to gain their approval of what she does buy. Group shopping generates an air of excitement and adventurousness, and this store image and atmosphere matter a lot as a means of enhancing the buzz. This shopper is not, however, too concerned about quality in the clothes she buys, looking rather for their ability to make a fashion statement. She accepts that fashions come and go and thus her clothes can be 'disposable' rather than durable. Preferred retailers include New Look, Miss Selfridge and Top Shop.
- *The price-led replacer* is a bargain seeker, likely to shop at stores such as BhS and anxious to get good value for money. She is likely to be between 25 and 44 years old with limited income. She is a pragmatic shopper who will take time to search out the best bargains and is thus very demanding. She responds to the kind of store that provides comfortable surroundings (because she is going to spend quite a bit of time in there assessing the merchandise), yet creates bargain-hunting excitement with lots of bright colours and 'money-off', 'prices slashed'

messages. She does not spend a lot, however, nor does she spend often.

- *The 30-somethings* are the biggest demographic group of all and the second highest spending. In her thirties with a career, she is into 'aspirational dressing', that is, reflecting her career ambitions and lifestyle aspirations through the way she dresses. She likes shopping and buys frequently, often on impulse. She is also likely to shop with her long-suffering partner in tow: to endorse choices? To pass compliments? To blame when she decides after the purchase that she does not like the garment after all? She likes stores that are user friendly with a reasonable level of service and that allow lots of interaction with the merchandise on offer, thus she wants pleasant changing rooms and plenty of mirrors. The kind of retailers she likes include French Connection, Next and Oasis.
- *The interested label seeker* is something of a clothes snob and has a lot of money to spend. She looks for exclusivity and high quality and is extremely label conscious. She patronises small independent retailers and does not shop in the big chain stores because they are neither expensive enough nor exclusive enough for her: she would not want anyone to see her in Marks & Spencer's or to identify what she was wearing as coming from there. She is prepared to spend a lot of time browsing to get the right 'look', but demands a great deal of personal service. She thinks that she is independently minded and can not be 'sold to', but in reality will probably be influenced by the flattery and attention of suitably professional sales staff. If she is satisfied with what she buys, she is prepared to be loyal to a store and spend a significant amount of money in it on a regular basis.

Source: Channel 4 series *Shop 'Til You Drop*, broadcast 1998.

The Go-betweens

Representing 40 per cent of Europeans, this group have experienced a change in their attitudes, but not enough to change their buying habits, and thus they are torn between habit and the thrill of the unexpected. They could become Moderns, but are still too tied to their home culture, education and the society within which they live. Marketing approaches that are obviously pan-European are less likely to influence or affect them than approaches that appear to be rooted in their own culture etc. This group are more likely to be British or Spanish than French, Italian or German.

The Traditionals

Accounting for the remaining 30 per cent of Europeans, this group holds on tight to local, regional and national traditions. They are very conformist, in that they have a great respect for authority, prefer an ordered existence and resist change, as a bringer of chaos. They are largely unattracted to international or pan-European brands, preferring the very familiar, habitually purchased products that they have always bought. This group is most likely to be German, with some representation in the UK and Italy, and is less likely to be found in France or Spain.

Paitra is convinced, as the above typology shows, that there is no such thing as the generic Euro-consumer. He strongly feels, however, that the Euro-segment that transcends national boundaries does exist, and that international, qualitative studies are going to become increasingly important to marketers in defining and locating such segments.

Despite the extent and depth of research that has gone into defining typologies such as these, they are still of somewhat limited use. When it comes to applying this material in a commercial marketing context, the marketer still needs to understand the underlying national factors that affect the buying decisions for a particular product. These Euro-segments give only a very general flavour of trends and changing attitudes, as part of the sociocultural marketing environment, and are still too simplistic, given the cultural diversity within the EU.

Nevertheless, there are compelling reasons for such methods of segmentation being worth considering and persevering with, despite their difficulties. Primarily, they can open the door to a better-tailored, more subtle offering to the customer on all aspects of the marketing mix. This in turn can create a strong emotional bond between customer and product, making it more difficult for competitors to steal customers. Euro-segmentation adds a further dimension, in that it has the potential to create much larger and more profitable segments, assuming that the logistics of distribution allow geographically dispersed members of the segment to be reached cost effectively, and may thus create pan-European marketing opportunities.

The main problem, however, as we have seen, is that psychographic segments are very difficult and expensive to define and measure. Relevant information is much less likely to exist already in the public domain. It is also very easy to get the implementation wrong. For example, the organisation that tries to portray lifestyle elements within advertisements is depending on the audience's ability to interpret the symbols used in the desired way and to reach the desired conclusions from them. There are no guarantees of this, especially if the message is a complex one (more of this in Chapter 14). Additionally, the user of Euro-segments has to be very clear about allowing for national and cultural differences when trying to communicate on lifestyle elements.

In summary, psychographic segmentation works well in conjunction with demographic variables to refine further the offering to the customer, increasing its relevance and defendability against competition. It is also valuable for products that lean towards psychological rather than functional benefits for the customer, for instance perfumes, cars, clothing retailers etc. For such a product to succeed, the marketer needs to create an image that convinces consumers that the product can either enhance their current lifestyle or help them to achieve their aspirations. Solomon (1994) summarises the uses of psychographic segmentation as:

1 to define a target market;

2 to create a new view of the market: breaking away from stereotypes;

3 to position the product: making sure product attributes fit with the deeper needs of the customer;

4 to better communicate product attributes: influencing advertising themes and content;

5 to develop overall strategy: identifying opportunities and trends, for instance;

6 to market social and political issues: to home in on groups with basically sympathetic attitudes and beliefs, or to identify those who need more persuasion.

Behaviour segmentation

All the categories of segmentation talked about so far are centred on the customer, leading to as detailed a profile of the individual as possible. Little mention has been made, however, of the individual's relationship with the product. This needs to be addressed, as it is quite possible that people with similar demographic and/or psychographic profiles may yet interact differently with the same product. Segmenting a market in these terms, therefore, is known as **behaviour segmentation**.

End use

What is the product to be used for? The answer to this question has great implications for the whole marketing approach. Think about soup, for instance. This is a very versatile product with a range of potential uses, and a wide variety of brands and product lines have been developed, each of which appeals to a different usage segment. A shopper may well buy two or three different brands of soup, simply because their needs change according to intended use, for example a dinner party or a snack meal. At this point, demographic and psychographic variables may become irrelevant (or at least secondary) if the practicalities of usage are so important to the customer. Table 5.5 defines some of the possible end uses of soup and gives examples of products available on the UK market to serve them.

TABLE 5.5
Usage segmentation in the soup market

Use	Brand examples
Dinner party starter	Baxter's soups; Covent Garden soups
Warming snack	Crosse & Blackwell's soups
Meal replacement	Heinz Wholesoups
Recipe ingredient	Campbell's Condensed soups
Easy office lunch	Batchelor's Cuppa Soups

Example Even the humble potato has become a victim of usage segmentation. The pre-bagged potatoes sold by some supermarkets are now labelled to indicate suitability for various uses, and thus the shopper can see precisely what is best for baking, roasting, chipping or boiling. Although it is still possible to buy a bag of 'general-purpose' potatoes, the shopper is left with a vague feeling that these are somehow second best for everything!

Benefits sought

This variable can have more of a psychological slant than end usage and can link in very closely with both demographic and psychographic segments. In the case of a car, for example, the benefits sought may range from the practical ('reliable'; 'economic to run'; 'able to accommodate mum, dad, four kids, a granny, a wet dog and the remains of a picnic') to the more psychographically orientated ('environmentally friendly'; 'fast and mean'; 'overt status symbol'). Similarly, the benefits sought from a chilled ready meal might be 'ease of preparation', 'time saving', 'access to dishes I could not make myself', 'a reassuring standby in case I get home late one evening', and for the low-calorie and low-fat versions, 'a tasty and interesting variation on my diet!' It is not difficult to see how defining some of these *benefit segments* can also indicate the kinds of demographic or lifestyle descriptors that apply to people wanting those benefits.

McCain decided to re-brand its oven-ready chips range to fit with the 'surprisingly good for you' slogan. Rather than emphasising speed and convenience, the plan was to educate consumers and make them aware of the 'health benefits' of oven-ready chips. The 'only 5% fat' claim and other facts such as 'the high-fibre option' were designed to exploit growing consumer interest in health matters (*The Grocer*, 1998b).

Usage rate

Not everyone who buys a particular product consumes it at the same rate. There will be heavy users, medium users and light users. Figure 5.1 shows the hypothetical categorisation of an organisation's customer base according to usage. In this case, 20 per cent of customers account for 60 per cent of the organisation's sales. This clearly raises questions for marketing strategies, for example should we put all our resources into defending our share of heavy users? Alternatives might be to make light users heavier; to target competitors' heavy users aggressively; or even to develop differentiated products for different usage rates (such as frequent-wash shampoo).

Again, this segmentation variable can best be used in conjunction with others to paint a much more three-dimensional picture of the target customer.

Loyalty

As with usage rate, loyalty could be a useful mechanism, not only for developing detail in the segment profile, but also for developing a better understanding of which segmentation variables are significant. For instance a carefully thought-out market research exercise might help an organisation to profile 'loyal to us', 'loyal to them' and '**switchers**', and then discover what other factors seem to differentiate between each of these groups. More specifically, Wind (1982) identified six loyalty segments as:

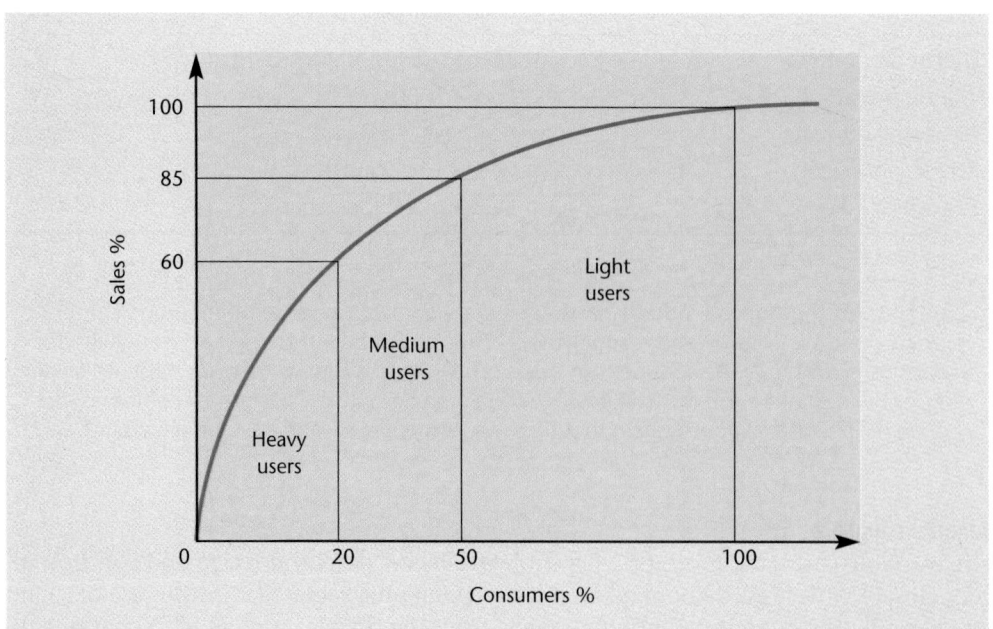

FIGURE 5.1

Consumer product usage categories

1 current loyal users who will continue to purchase the brand;

2 current customers who might switch brands or reduce consumption;

3 occasional users who might be persuaded to increase consumption with the right incentives;

4 occasional users who might decrease consumption because of competitors' offerings;

5 non-users who might buy the brand if it was modified;

6 non-users with strong negative attitudes that are unlikely to change.

To many loyal customers, beanz really does mean Heinz!

Source: H.J. Heinz.

What is certain is that brand loyalty can be a fragile thing, and is under increasing threat. This is partly as a result of the greater number of alternative brands available and incentives or promotions designed by competitors to undermine customer loyalty. The most serious threat in the UK, however, has come from supermarket own brands, many of which look uncannily like the equivalent manufacturer brands but undercut them on price. Consumers thus believe that the own brands are just as good, if not identical, and are thus prepared to switch to them and to be more price sensitive. There is more on this issue in Chapter 13.

Assuming that loyalty does exist, even a simple combination of usage rate and loyalty begins to make a difference to the organisation's marketing strategy. If, for example, a large group of heavy users who are also brand switchers was identified, then there is much to be gained from investing resources in a tightly focused marketing mix designed to turn them into heavy users who are loyal to a particular company. Repeat business is important to Burger King. The company has estimated that a single customer can be worth over 100 burgers and fries over a lifetime, amounting to over £3000. This means that losing a customer through dissatisfaction is an important loss of revenue (Denny, 1998).

Attitude

Again, trespassing on the psychographic area, attitude looks at how the potential customer feels about the product (or the organisation). A set of customers who are already enthusiastic about a product, for example, require very different handling from a group who are downright hostile. A hostile group might need an opportunity to sample the product, along with an advertising campaign that addresses and answers the roots of their hostility. Attitude-based segments may be important in marketing charities or causes, or even in health education. Smokers who are hostile to the 'stop smoking' message will need different approaches from those who are amenable to the message and just need reassurance and practical support to put it into practice. Approaches aimed at the 'hostile' smoker have included fear ('look at these diseased lungs'), altruism ('what about your children?') and vanity (warning young women about the effect on their skin), but with little noticeable effect.

Buyer readiness stage

Buyer readiness can be a very valuable variable, particularly when one is thinking about the promotional mix. How close to purchasing is the potential customer? For example, at a very early stage the customer may not even be aware that the product exists, and therefore to get that customer moving closer to purchase, the organisation needs to generate *awareness* of the product. Then there is a need for information to stimulate *interest* in the product. The customer's ability to understand and interpret that information may lead to *desire* for the product, which in turn stimulates *action*: the purchase itself.

Have your cake and eat it

Research has discovered four basic usage segments in the cake market (Davenport-Firth, 1998). First, there is the 'everyday, everyone' segment. These buyers are likely to be women buying for the family and so they want the kind of cakes that can go into packed lunches or that can just be there in the kitchen if anyone in the family fancies a snack. Examples of the kinds of products these shoppers buy are jam tarts and fruit cake. The second segment, 'every day for me', consists of consumers who are looking for a self-indulgent treat, some comfort or a reward. This is perhaps the impulse purchase of a chocolate éclair

'because I deserve it', which the family will never find out about. Shoppers in the 'special everyone' segment are buying a treat for the whole family. It could be the case, for instance, that Sunday lunch is the only meal that the family eats together and thus mum wants to buy something a little more special for dessert, such as a Viennetta or a chocolate gâteau. The final segment, 'special treat for an occasion', is concerned with impressing people outside the immediate family. If friends are coming round for a meal then the shopper might be looking for a luxury gâteau or an Entenmann's cake.

Figure 5.2 summarises this progression, and Chapter 14 will consider further its influence on the promotional mix.

Behavioural segmentation, therefore, examines closely the relationship between the potential customer and the product, and there are a number of dimensions on which this can be done. Its main achievement is to bring the relationship between customer and product into sharper focus, thus providing greater understanding of the customer's specific needs and wants, leading to a better defined marketing mix. Another advantage of this kind of segmentation approach is that it provides opportunities for tailored marketing strategies to target brand switchers or to increase usage rates. All these benefits do justify the use of behavioural segmentation, as long as it does not lead to the organisation becoming product centred to the neglect of the customer's needs. The customer must still come first.

Multivariable segmentation

As has been hinted throughout the previous sections, it is unlikely that any one segmentation variable will be used absolutely on its own. It is more common for marketers to use a **multivariable segmentation** approach, defining a 'portfolio' of relevant segmentation variables, some of which will be prosaic and descriptive while others will tend towards the psychographic, depending on the product and market in question. The market for adult soft drinks, includes age segmentation along with some usage considerations (for example as a substitute for wine as a meal accompaniment), some benefit segmentation (healthy, refreshing, relaxing), and lifestyle elements of health consciousness, sophisticated imagery and a desire for exotic ingredients.

The emergence of geodemographics in recent years, as discussed at pp. 185 *et seq.* above, is an indicator of the way in which segmentation is moving, that is, towards multi-variable systems incorporating psychographics, demographics and geographics. These things are now possible and affordable, as Chapter 6 will show, because of increasingly sophisticated data collection mechanisms, developments in database creation and maintenance (*see* Chapter 18) and cheaper, more accessible computing facilities. A properly managed database allows the marketer to go even further and to incorporate behavioural variables as the purchaser develops a trading history with a supplier. Thus the marketers are creeping ever closer to the individual consumer. The UK supermarkets that have developed and launched store loyalty cards that are swiped through the checkout so that the customer can accumulate points towards

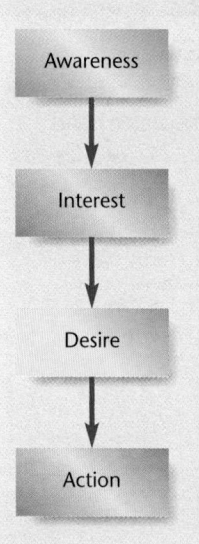

FIGURE 5.2

The AIDA response hierarchy model

discounts, for example, are collecting incredibly detailed information about each individual shopper's profile. It tells them when we shop, how often, which branches of the store we tend to use, how much we spend per visit, the range of goods we buy, and the choices we make between own brands and manufacturer brands. The supermarkets can use this information to help them define meaningful segments for their own customer base, to further develop and improve their overall marketing mix or to make individually tailored offers to specific customers.

IMPLEMENTATION OF SEGMENTATION

This chapter so far has very freely used the phrase 'segmenting the market', but before segmentation can take place, there has to be some definition of the boundaries of that market. Any such definition really has to look at the world through the consumer's eyes, because the consumer makes decisions based on the evaluation of alternatives and substitutes. Thus a margarine manufacturer cannot restrict itself to thinking in terms of 'the margarine market', but has to take a wider view of 'the spreading-fats market' which will include butter and vegetable oil based products alongside margarine. This is because, generally speaking, all three of these product groups are contending for the same place on the nation's bread, and the consumer will develop attitudes and feelings towards a selection of brands across all three groups, perhaps through comparing price and product attributes (for example taste, spreadability, cooking versatility and health claims). This opens up a much wider competitive scene, as well as making the margarine manufacturer think more seriously about product positioning and about how and why consumers buy it. Similarly, the adult soft drinks market cannot be too restrictive in its market definition. It is still competing to a certain extent with the more traditional soft drinks (both the fizzy ones such as colas and lemonades and the still fruit juices) and alcoholic drinks, as a substitute. The key to its continued growth and success lies in pulling it away further from the wider, mainstream beverages markets (alcoholic and non-alcoholic), through clear differentiation in terms of all elements of the marketing mix, to reduce the 'substitute' effect. The various manufacturers involved can then concentrate more on competition and further segmentation within the adult market.

This whole issue of market definition and its implications for segmentation comes back, yet again, to what should now be the familiar question of 'What business are we in?' It is a timely reminder that consumers basically buy solutions to problems, not products, and thus in defining market segments, the marketer should take into account any type of product that will provide a solution. Hence we are not in 'the margarine market', but in the 'lubricating bread' market, which brings us back full circle to the inclusion of butter and vegetable oil based spreads as direct competitors.

It is still not enough to have gone through the interesting exercise of segmenting a market, however it is defined. How is that information going to be used by the organisation to develop marketing strategies? One decision that must be made is how many segments within the market the organisation intends to target. We look first at **targeting**.

Targeting

There are three broad approaches available, summarised in Fig. 5.3, and discussed in detail below.

Concentrated

The concentrated approach is the most focused approach of the three, and involves specialising in serving one specific segment. This can lead to very detailed knowledge

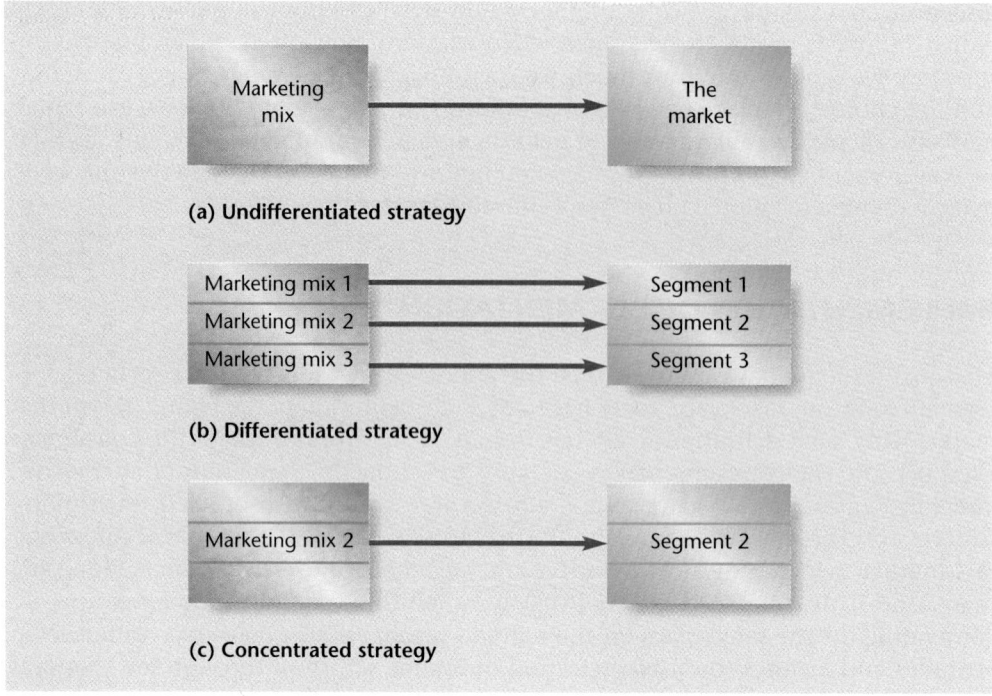

(a) **Undifferentiated strategy**

(b) **Differentiated strategy**

(c) **Concentrated strategy**

FIGURE 5.3

Segmentation
targeting strategies

of the target segment's needs and wants, with the added benefit that the organisation is seen as a specialist, giving it an advantage over its more mass-market competitors. This, however, carries a risk of complacency, leaving the organisation vulnerable to competitive entry into the segment.

Example From its origins in 1884, the Italian company Bulgari (http://www.bulgari.com) has built an outstanding reputation for fine jewellery to compete alongside Cartier (France) and Tiffany (USA). Whenever such companies innovate, they concentrate on the luxury segment of the market, fearing a major loss of reputation if they become associated with a downmarket new product.

Up until the early 1990s, Bulgari concentrated on opening new stores to sell jewellery rather than undertaking any significant product innovation. There are now over 60 Bulgari stores worldwide, especially in Europe and Asia. There are risks, however, in concentrating on just one product area and so the company has plans to diversify into perfumes, silk scarves, ties and a range of leather goods, china and crystal ware. Despite the innovation, the company is still following a concentrated targeting approach aimed at the high disposable income, luxury end of the market (Rawsthorn, 1997).

In terms of management, concentration is attractive because costs are kept down, as there is only one marketing mix to manage, and there is still the potential for economies of scale. Strategically, the concentration of resources into one segment may lead to a stronger, more defendable position than that achievable by competitors which are spreading their effort more thinly. However, being a niche specialist may make it more difficult for an organisation to diversify into other segments, whether through lack of experience and knowledge, or through problems of acceptance arising from being identified with the original niche.

The benefits also need to be weighed against the other potential risks. First, all the organisation's eggs are in one basket, and if that segment fails, then there is no fallback position. The second risk is that if competitors see a rival establishing and clearly succeeding in a segment like this, then they may try to take some of it.

Differentiated

As Fig. 5.3 implies, a differentiated strategy involves the development of a number of individual marketing mixes, each of which serves a different segment. For example, Ford manufactures a range of cars, covering a number of different segments, from the Focus at the bottom end of the price range, generally intended for the younger female driver, to the Scorpio in the higher price bracket, intended for the status seeking executive.

As with the concentrated strategy, this approach does allow the organisation to tailor its offerings to suit the individual segments, thus maintaining satisfaction. It also overcomes one of the problems of concentration by spreading risk across the market, so that if one segment declines, the organisation still has revenue from others.

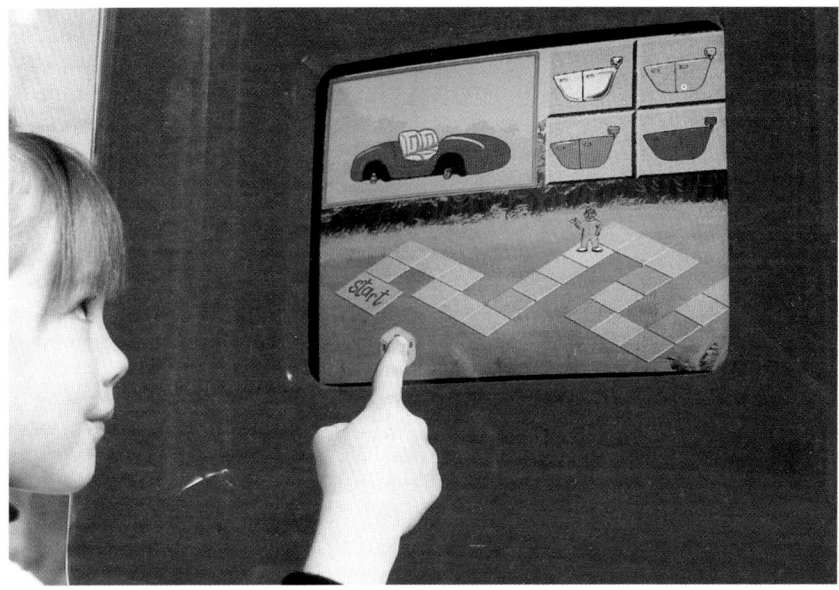

When she grows up, she'll be designing her own car through Daewoo's interactive screens.

Source: Daewoo.

To be implemented properly, this approach requires a detailed overview of the market and how it is developing, perhaps leading to the early detection of new opportunities or emerging segments. This knowledge is valuable for an organisation with a healthy curiosity about its environment, but is acquired at a cost (in terms of both finance and managerial time). It also leads to increased costs in trying to manage the marketing mixes for a number of products, with possible diseconomies of scale.

Overall, a differentiated strategy dilutes the organisation's efforts through the thin spreading of resources. The organisation must, therefore, be very careful not to overreach itself in the number of segments it attempts to cover. Nevertheless, it can help an organisation to survive in highly competitive markets.

Example H J Hall Sock Group manufactures branded socks, but found the UK market of the early 1990s very difficult. Quite apart from the fact that the average British male acquires only five new pairs of socks a year, there is fierce competition from cheap imports, market traders and stores' own brands (Marks & Spencer, for example, cornered 20 per cent of the sock market in 1990). H J Hall Sock Group has survived by targeting a number of specialised segments that the bulk manufacturers would not consider worth while. Thus the firm has supplied soccer teams (including the English, Irish and Scottish national sides), Middle Eastern armies and the top end of the fashion market (Darwent, 1993).

197

Undifferentiated

The undifferentiated approach is the least demanding of the three approaches, in that it assumes that the market is one great homogeneous unit, with no significant differences between individuals within that market. Thus a single marketing mix is required that serves the needs of the entire market. The emphasis is likely to be, therefore, on developing mass communication, mass distribution and as wide an appeal as possible.

An undifferentiated approach does have some apparent advantages. It involves relatively low costs, as there is only one marketing mix that does not require the depth of research, fine tuning and updating that a concentrated or differentiated strategy would entail. It could also lead to the possible maximisation of economies of scale, because of having a single product in a potentially large market.

It is naive to hope that you can please everyone. What is likely to happen in reality is that some people will like your product offering more than others, and thus a segment (not of your own definition) will emerge by default. Because your product has not been tailored to that segment, it is unlikely to be exactly what that segment wants, and therefore any competitor who does target the segment more closely will attract those customers. This is similar to what is happening in the potato example cited at p. 191 above, where the 'general-purpose' product is becoming overshadowed and pushed into a perceived 'second-best' position by usage specific varieties.

> **Example** Through processes taking place beyond the farm gate, many food manufacturers can introduce more differentiation in what could easily be a homogeneous market. Olive oil producers are a good example. The olive picked from the tree can be processed and packaged in many different ways and thus differentiation is created through the processing, cleaning, pressing and filtering of the olives and the suggested end use of the oil. The problem in the UK is that many consumers are not particularly familiar with olive oil use and do not always understand the differences between, for instance, virgin oil and refined grades. Instead, they tend to regard olive oil in terms of its country of origin. The challenge is thus to educate consumers so that they can select the right olive oil for different uses (Crosskey, 1997).

If an undifferentiated approach is possible at all, then it might best be suited for products with little psychological appeal. For example, petrol is essentially a very ordinary product that many of us purchase regularly but never even see (unless we are not very adept with a self-service pump). It makes the car go, regardless of whether it is a Rolls-Royce or a Lada and, traditionally, the only discriminating factor between brands has been price. Petrol retailers have now begun to create market segments, through the petrol itself (as with unleaded and petrols with extra additives); through the extended product (providing car washes, mini-supermarkets etc.); and also through strong corporate images that create brands and engender loyalty. All of this is moving the petrol retailers away from undifferentiated strategies.

Quite apart from the advantages and disadvantages connected with each of the alternative approaches above, there are a number of factors influencing the choice of targeting strategy.

Marketing theory may well point to a particular strategy as being ideal, but if an organisation's resources cannot support and sustain that strategy, then an alternative must be found. A smaller organisation may, for example, need to adopt a concentrated strategy (perhaps based on a geographic segment in a consumer market, or on a specialist niche in an organisational market) to generate the growth required to allow a wider coverage of the market.

It is also important to make the choice of strategy in the context of the product itself. As has already been indicated, certain types of product lend themselves more readily to

MARKETING IN ACTION   Blue Circle's standardised boiler

The market for gas-fired domestic central heating boilers is fragmented across Europe, largely on a geographic basis. This is not only because the climate and the nature of housing vary so widely in different places, but also because plumbing standards and techniques are different. Consequently, there are thousands of different types of boiler available but each one is mainly focused on its home country. Those companies that do try to achieve a pan-European approach tend to take an existing product and make significant adaptations to make it suitable for other countries.

Blue Circle, a UK company, has boiler interests in France, Germany and the Netherlands, as well as in the UK, but each national division largely pursues its own home market. The parent company, however, spotted an opportunity to create a truly pan-European boiler for a niche segment and put together a team of 40 engineers and marketers from across Europe to develop the product. Condensing boilers save energy and cut carbon dioxide emissions, but only account for about 5 per cent of the European market. Other companies make them, but on a country by country basis. Blue Circle thought that if it could develop a product that was 90 per cent standardised for any country, it could achieve economies of scale in manufacture as well as saving on the development costs normally associated in the industry with redesigning the product for each

market. It also felt that the product would have a cross-border appeal to a market segment looking for 'greener' approaches to heating and that this segment would have considerable future potential.

The design process, with its target of 90 per cent standardisation, was not easy. The design had to be flexible enough to be easily adapted with the minimum of fuss to suit different national preferences and conventions on, for example, the type of boiler, the type of gas used, design and safety regulations, location within the house (apparently in the UK, gas boilers tend to be in the kitchen; in the Netherlands they are in the attic; in Germany, in the cellar) and electronic controls. Nevertheless, the target was achieved through a kind of modular design, with the added benefit that the interaction between engineers from different countries led to many improvements and simplifications in boiler design generally.

The product was launched in 1995, first in the UK and the Netherlands, then later in Germany and France. Although the product itself was standardised, other elements of the marketing mix were tailored for different countries. Even the product name varied, from Envoy in the UK to Runner in the Netherlands and Ecotherm in Germany.

Source: Marsh (1995); http://www.bluecircle.co.uk.

certain approaches, for example a product with many potential variations that involve a high level of psychological relationship with the customer (such as clothing or cosmetics) is better suited to a differentiated or concentrated approach. Other products with a more functional bias can be treated in a more undifferentiated way.

It must be reiterated, though, that undifferentiated approaches are becoming increasingly rare. Salt used to be held up to marketing students as the prime example of a commodity product sold in an undifferentiated way. Table 5.6 demonstrates how all that has changed.

The product's life-cycle stage (*see* Chapter 8 for a full definition of this concept) might also affect the choice of strategy. For example, an innovative new product, of which neither the industry nor the consumer has past experience, may first be marketed with an undifferentiated strategy in order to gain practical knowledge of the market's behaviour and reactions. It is very difficult to undertake meaningful market research in advance of launching such a new product, because the market may have problems conceptualising the product or putting it into context. It will be in the growth and maturity stages of the life-cycle that differentiated strategies will emerge as competitors enter the market and organisations learn from experience.

That last comment is a reminder that strategic decisions cannot be taken in isolation from the activities of the competition. If competitors are clearly implementing differentiated strategies, then it is dangerous for you to adopt a more dilute, undifferentiated approach. It may make

TABLE 5.6

Differentiation in the salt market

- Table salt
- Cooking salt
- Sea salt
- Rock salt
- Alpine rock salt
- Iodised salt
- Low-sodium salt
- Garlic salt
- Celery salt

  et cetera!

more sense to identify the segments within which the competition is strong and then to assess whether it would be possible to attack them head-on in those segments or to find a different niche and make that your own. Thus competition is affecting not only the choice of approach, but the actual choice of segment(s) to target.

BENEFITS OF SEGMENTATION

The previous sections of this chapter should at least have served to show that market segmentation is a complex and dangerous activity, in the sense that the process of choosing variables, their measurement and their implementation leaves plenty of scope for poor management and disappointment. Nevertheless, there are few, if any, markets in which segmentation has no role to play, and it is important to remember the potential benefits to be gained, whether looking at the customer, the marketing mix or the competition.

The customer

The obvious gain to customers is that they can find products that seem to fit more closely with what they want. These needs and wants, remember, are not only related to product function, but also to psychological fulfilment. Customers may feel that a particular supplier is more sympathetic towards them, or is speaking more directly to them, and therefore they will be more responsive and eventually more loyal to that supplier. The organisation that fails to segment deeply enough on significant criteria will lose custom to competitors that do.

The marketing mix

This is a timely reminder that the marketing mix should itself be a product of understanding the customer. Market segmentation helps the organisation to target its marketing mix more closely on the potential customer, and thus to meet the customer's needs and wants more exactly. Segmentation helps to define shopping habits (in terms of place, frequency and volume), price sensitivity, required product benefits and features, as well as laying the foundations for advertising and promotional decisions. The customer is at the core of all decisions relating to the 4Ps, and those decisions will be both easier to make and more consistent with each other if a clear and detailed definition of the target segments exists.

In the same vein, segmentation can also help the organisation to allocate its resources more efficiently. If a segment is well defined, then the organisation will have sufficient understanding to develop very precise marketing objectives and an accompanying strategy to achieve them, with a minimum of wastage. The organisation is doing neither more nor less than it needs to do in order to satisfy the customer's needs and wants.

This level of understanding of segments that exist in the market also forms a very sound foundation for strategic decisions. The organisation can prioritise across segments in line with its resources, objectives and desired position within the market.

The competition

Finally, the use of segmentation will help the organisation to achieve a better understanding of itself and the environment within which it exists. By looking outwards, to the customer, the organisation has to ask itself some very difficult questions about its capacity to serve that customer better than the competition. Also, by analysing the competitors' offerings in the context of the customer, the organisation should begin to appreciate the competition's real strengths and weaknesses, as well as identifying gaps in the market.

DANGERS OF SEGMENTATION

The benefits of segmentation need to be balanced against the dangers inherent in it. Some of these, such as the risks of poor definition and implementation of psychographic segmentation, have already been mentioned.

Other dangers are connected with the essence of segmentation: breaking markets down into ever smaller segments. Where should it stop? Catering for the differing needs of a large number of segments can lead to fragmentation of the market, with additional problems arising from the loss of economies of scale (through shorter production runs or loss of bulk purchasing discounts on raw materials, for instance), as mentioned at p. 197 above. Detail needs to be balanced against viability.

Within the market as a whole, if there are a number of organisations in direct competition for a number of segments, then the potential proliferation of brands may simply serve to confuse the customer. Imagine five competitors each trying to compete in five market segments. That gives the customer 25 brands to sort out. Even if customers can find their way through the maze of brands, the administration and marketing difficulties involved in getting those brands on to the supermarket shelves can be very costly.

As Chapter 4 showed, such problems are less likely to occur in organisational markets. Where an organisation has a very small number of high spending customers, each one can legitimately be treated as a separate segment with its own marketing mix tailored to it.

CRITERIA FOR SUCCESSFUL SEGMENTATION

Cutting through the detail of how to segment, and regardless of the complexities of segmentation in different types of market, are four absolute requirements for any successful segmentation exercise. Unless these four conditions prevail, the exercise will either look good on paper but be impossible to implement, or fail to deliver any marked strategic advantage.

Distinctiveness

Any segment defined has to be *distinctive*, that is, significantly different from any other segment. The basis of that difference depends on the type of product or the circumstances prevailing in the market at the time. It may be rooted in any of the segmentation variables discussed above, whether geographic, demographic or psychographic. Note too the use of the word *significant*. The choice of segmentation variables has to be relevant to the product in question.

Without a significant difference, segment boundaries become too blurred, and there is a risk that an organisation's offerings will not be sufficiently well tailored to attract the required customers.

Tangibility

It must be remembered that distinctiveness can be taken too far. Too much detail in segmentation, without sound commercial reasoning behind it, leads to fragmentation of effort and inefficiency. A defined segment must, therefore, be of a sufficient *size* to make its pursuit worthwhile. Again, the notion of size here is somewhat vague. For fmcg goods, viable size may entail many thousands of customers purchasing many tens of thousands of units, but in an organisational market, it may entail a handful of customers purchasing a handful of units.

Proving that a segment actually exists is also important. Analysis of a market may indicate that there is a gap that existing products do not appear to fill, whether defined in terms of the product itself or the customer profile. The next stage is to ask why that gap is there. Is it because no organisation has yet got round to filling it, or because the segment in that gap is too small to be commercially viable? Does that segment even exist, or are you segmenting in too much detail and creating opportunities on paper that will not work in practice?

Accessibility

As well as existing, a defined segment has to be *accessible*. The first aspect of this is connected with distribution. An organisation has to be able to find the means of delivering its goods and services to the customer, but this may not be so easy, for example, for a small organisation targeting a geographically spread segment with a low-priced infrequently purchased product. Issues of access may then become an extension of the segment profile, perhaps limiting the segment to those customers within a defined catchment area, or those who are prepared to order direct through particular media. Whatever the solution to problems of access, it does mean that the potential size of the segment has to be re-assessed.

The second aspect of access is communication. Certain customers may be very difficult to make contact with, and if the promotional message cannot be communicated, then the chances of capturing those customers are much slimmer. Again, the segment profile may have to be extended to cover the media most likely to access those customers, and again, this will lead to a smaller segment.

Defendability

In talking about targeting strategies at pp. 195 *et seq.* above, one of the recurrent themes was that of the competition. Even with a concentrated strategy, targeting only one segment, there is a risk of competitors poaching customers. In defining and choosing segments, therefore, it is important to consider whether the organisation can develop a sufficiently strong differential advantage to defend its presence in that segment against competitive incursions.

Example Sock Shop in the UK, a niche retailer selling a vast variety of both 'fun' and serious products for feet could not, in the end, defend its position against high street retailers such as Marks & Spencer copying the basic idea and selling similar products more cheaply and more conveniently.

Organisational markets

Most of the above discussion has centred on consumer markets. With specific reference to organisational markets, Hlavacek and Ames (1986) propose a similar set of criteria for good segmentation practice. They suggest, for example, that each segment should be characterised by a common set of customer requirements, and that customer requirements and characteristics should be measurable. Segments should have identifiable competition, but be small enough to allow the supplier to reduce the competitive threat, or to build a defendable position against competition. In strategic terms, Hlavacek and Ames also propose that the members of a segment should have some logistical characteristic in common, for example that they are served by the same kind of distribution channel, or the same kind of sales effort. Finally, the critical success factors for each segment should be defined, and the supplier should ensure that it has the skills, assets and capabilities to meet the segment's needs, and to sustain that in the future.

CHAPTER SUMMARY

This chapter has focused on the complexities and methods involved in dividing markets into relevant, manageable and targetable segments in order to allow better-tailored offerings to be developed.

In organisational markets, segmentation techniques are divided into macro and micro variables or bases. Macro variables include both organisational characteristics, such as size, location and purchasing patterns, and product or service applications, defining the ways in which the product or service is used by the buyer. Micro segmentation variables lead to the definition, in some cases, of segments of one customer, and focus on the buyer's management philosophy, decision-making structures, purchasing policies and strategies, as well as needs and wants.

In consumer markets, five main categories of segmentation are defined: geographic, demographic, geodemographic, psychographic and behaviour based. Between them, they cover a full range of characteristics, whether descriptive, measurable, tangible or intangible, relating to the buyer, the buyer's lifestyle and the buyer's relationship with the product. In practice, a multivariable approach to segmentation is likely to be implemented, defining a portfolio of relevant characteristics from all categories to suit the market under consideration.

The implications of segmentation are wide reaching. It forms the basis for strategic thinking, in terms of the choice of segment(s) to target in order to achieve internal and competitive objectives. The possibilities range from a niche strategy, specialising in only one segment, to a differentiated strategy, targeting two or more segments with different marketing mixes. The undifferentiated strategy, hoping to cover the whole market with only one marketing mix, is becoming increasingly less appropriate as consumers become more demanding, and although it does appear to ease the managerial burden, it is very vulnerable to focused competition.

Segmentation offers a number of benefits to both the consumer and the organisation. Consumers get an offering that is better tailored to their specific needs, as well as the satisfaction of feeling that the market is offering them a wider range of products to choose from. The organisation is more likely to engender customer loyalty because of the tailored offering, as well as the benefits of more efficient resource allocation and improved knowledge of the market. The organisation can also use its segmentation as a basis for building a strong competitive edge, by understanding its customers on a deeper psychological level and reflecting that in its marketing mix(es). This forms bonds between organisation/product and customer that are very difficult for competition to break.

There are, however, dangers in segmentation, if it is not done well. Poor definition of segments, inappropriate choice of key variables or poor analysis and implementation of the outcomes of a segmentation exercise can all be disastrous. There is also the danger that if competing marketers become too enthusiastic in trying to 'out-segment' each other, the market will fragment to an unviable extent and consumers will become confused by the variety of choice open to them.

On balance, segmentation is a good and necessary activity in any market, whether it is a mass fmcg market of international proportions, or a select organisational market involving two or three well-known customers. In either case, any segment defined has to be distinctive (i.e. features at least one characteristic pulling it away from the rest that can be used to create a focused marketing mix); tangible (i.e. commercially viable); accessible (i.e. both the product and the promotional mix can reach it) and finally, defendable (i.e. against competition).

Key words and phrases

Behaviour segmentation	Geographic segmentation	Multivariable segmentation
Brand loyalty	Lifestyle segmentation	Psychographics
Buyer readiness stages	Macro segments	Switchers
Demographic segmentation	Market segments	Targeting
Geodemographics	Micro segments	

QUESTIONS FOR REVIEW

5.1 What is the difference between macro and micro segmentation in organisational markets?

5.2 What variables might be included in micro segmentation?

5.3 What is geographic segmentation and how is it used in consumer and organisational markets?

5.4 What are the main demographic variables used in consumer markets?

5.5 What is geodemographic segmentation and how can it help the marketer?

5.6 What, according to Plummer, are the four main components of psychographic, or lifestyle, segmentation?

5.7 Why is psychographic segmentation so difficult and so risky to do?

5.8 In what major way does behavioural segmentation differ from the other methods? Outline the variables that can be used in behavioural segmentation.

5.9 What are the three approaches to targeting available to marketers?

5.10 What factors might affect the marketer's choice of targeting strategy?

QUESTIONS FOR DISCUSSION

5.1 How might the market for personal computers, sold to organisational markets, be segmented?

5.2 Find examples of products that depend strongly on demographic segmentation, making sure that you find at least one example for each of the main demographic variables.

5.3 Choose a consumer market and discuss how it might be segmented in terms of benefits sought.

5.4 For each targeting strategy, find examples of organisations that use it. Discuss why you think they have chosen this strategy and how they implement it.

5.5 How can market segmentation influence decisions about the marketing mix?

CASE STUDY 5.1

Neu Engineering

Neu Engineering is a project management company which designs, builds (with the help of subcontractors), installs and maintains industrial plant for a wide variety of customers. It specialises in pneumatic conveying, that is, moving powders, granules and other dry products around a factory or other industrial site. The conveying systems usually move the materials by either blowing them or sucking them through pipelines. There is more to the system than just pipelines, however, as the company also incorporates silo storage, mixing, weighing, drying or cooling equipment into the system. The industrial buyer is offered a complete, customised package. Thus a food processing company might need to store sugar under suitably cool and dry conditions, then move it from the silo in weighed batches to a mixing vat along with other ingredients, such as flour or milk powder that have travelled through their own section of the conveying system. Neu Engineering also takes a serious and innovative approach to safety and environmental issues. Many powders are potentially explosive; sugar and milk powder, for example, and an explosion in a custard powder factory (which did not have a Neu Engineering system installed) demolished the side of the building. Systems have to be able to prevent or contain any such incident safely. It is also important to protect workers from any dust emissions or leakages by ensuring that the system has appropriate exhaust and/or ventilation built in.

The majority of Neu Engineering's business comes from clients in three main industries.

1 *Pharmaceuticals*: customers in this market include Johnson & Johnson, Glaxo-Wellcome, Nycomed and Zeneca. Customers such as these value the fact that Neu Engineering has the expertise to build a system to standards demanded by the FDA (the Food and Drug Administration, the US regulatory and licencing body). They are also concerned with protecting their materials from contamination, preventing any leakage into the working environment, appropriate controlled storage, and absolute accuracy in weighing and mixing. Thus Neu designs and installs 'automatic dispensaries' for tablet production on Zeneca's factories in Macclesfield and Reims which deliver all those

benefits, as well as giving the computerised recordability, traceability and repeatability required by FDA regulations. Neu Engineering is a leader in this market because it entered the market early and is recognised as a specialist.

2 *The food industry*: customers such as Cadbury, Tate and Lyle, Birds Eye, Heinz, Kellogg and Nestlé also require fully contained, temperature-controlled and hygienic systems in storing and conveying a wide variety of solid ingredients for their food products. Flour, sugar, chocolate granules, coffee beans, peas, and barley are among the materials that travel successfully around factories in Neu Engineering systems. The company built a system to intake, convey, batch, weigh and mix the spices for Birds Eye's 'Steakhouse' production line, for example. This replaced manual materials handling, improving efficiency and accuracy. Neu Engineering also won a contract to build ten cereal plants in Russia. There is even something of a second-hand market. Sweden's leading confectionery manufacturer, Marabou, sold a storage, conveying and weighing system to another company, Kungsornen, which dismantled it then moved it 100 miles and rebuilt it!

3 *Plastics*: customers in this industry include ICI, BP, Amoco, Kellogg and Samsung. This industry is a large user of pneumatic conveying systems and, compared with pharmaceuticals, requires heavy-duty systems that can move anything up to 60 tonnes per hour over 500m. This is one of the most competitive of the three main markets that Neu Engineering is in and, although the jobs tend to be big, profit margins are almost half those that can be gained in the other markets. It is also a more cyclical industry than the others. Every five years or so, when the industry is in a boom phase, all the plastics manufacturers expand fast and there are plenty of opportunities for companies such as Neu Engineering. When it is in a slump, however, the manufacturers have too much capacity and there is no expansion and thus no new contracts. It is therefore dangerous to be too dependent on such an industry. Nevertheless, as in other industries, innovation wins business. Neu Engineering spent over £100 000 developing an innovative high-pressure, low-

velocity conveying system which has been installed at plants in Spain, the Netherlands, Malaysia and Argentina.

Sometimes it is not easy to win customers; it took Neu Engineering five years to 'get into' Kellogg, but once successful, the inherent quality of the product ensures that up to 80 per cent of its business is repeat business. Neu Engineering would ideally like to focus in the future on key regular customers. It firmly believes that only by being a market driven company will it be able to tackle the challenges of the new millennium. A strategy for the future is a strategy for success.

Questions

1 What macro and micro segmentation bases are in evidence in this case?

2 What, if anything, do those segmentation bases have in common with those used in consumer markets?

3 Why do you think Neu Engineering gains such a high proportion of repeat business?

4 What kind of targeting strategy is Neu Engineering using now, and what strategy is it moving towards? To what extent do you think this move is a good idea?

CASE STUDY 5.2

The pink pound

The value of the gay market in the UK has been estimated at something between £6 billion and £8 billion per year. According to the magazine *Gay Times*, average income in the gay community is £17 000 and the income of the average gay household is £36 000. This is higher than for the population as a whole, which is reflected in the fact that 77 per cent of *Gay Times* readers are in the ABC1 socioeconomic groups, compared with only 43 per cent for the general population. This affluence was also emphasised in a report *In the Pink?*, by marketing consultants Grey Matter. This report suggested that the gay consumer is trend setting and likely to spend significant amounts of disposable income on fashion, travel and entertainment. It is relatively easy to reach the gay market through magazines such as *Gay Times*, *Attitude* and *Diva*.

There are some companies producing goods and services specifically targeted at gay consumers. These include legal and financial services, housing developments, travel agencies and funeral services. Some gay consumers feel that they have encountered prejudice and been given bad advice by mainstream companies and so it is important that such services are offered by companies specialising in the gay consumer's needs. The holiday market is particularly attractive, as it has been estimated that 79 per cent of the UK's gay community takes two or more overseas holidays per year. Alternative Holidays, a company offering exclusively gay holidays, began with European Gay Ski Week, which attracted 400 gay holidaymakers. The company then expanded into other destinations. RSVP is a company that charters cruise ships for exclusively gay cruises. Many other companies, such as In Touch Holidays and Sensations, offer gay holidays.

The housing market also offers opportunities to target the gay market. Gay consumers' affluence means that they are willing and able to pay for a quality development with good security. In Manchester, for instance, Bellway built 93 apartments for the gay market selling for £100 000 each. London estate agents have also seen a big rise in demand for gay-only properties and are urging developers to build many more. Some past developments sold out before they were even completed. Inner-city areas are popular with gay property buyers as they want to be near the nightlife and are not bothered about issues such as the quality of local schools or access to family-orientated amenities. City developments are also appropriate because these buyers want spacious apartments, but do not need lots of bedrooms. A survey carried out by the mortgage industry found that gay borrowers are less likely to default on loans than the rest of the population, not only because there is a higher proportion of well-paid professionals among gays, but also because there is no risk of children or high-cost divorces draining a household's income.

It is, of course, possible for mainstream companies to make a specific appeal to the gay segment. Companies such as Bass and Virgin have shown their commitment to the gay market in different ways. Bass runs 28 gay bars with a turnover of over £8.7 million and spent £2 million refurbishing just one of them. Virgin sells gay merchandise in its Megastores, organises gay shopping nights, sponsors the gay pressure group Stonewall and also backs Gay Pride events. Both companies have worked hard to ensure that their corporate culture and policies are 'gay friendly'. *In the Pink?* does suggest that companies should emphasise their trustworthiness in the gay consumer's eyes by, for example, ensuring that they offer equal opportunities and treat their gay staff fairly, that they are visible at gay trade fairs and exhibitions, that they join the Gay Business Association and that they demonstrate on-going commitment in their relationships with gay consumers and staff. According to *Gay Times*, companies that patronise the gay community by making token gestures or using sensationalist gay imagery simply alienate the audience. Gay

consumers will boycott any company that they regard as exploitative, hypocritical or insensitive.

Although there are growing acceptance and tolerance of homosexuality, there is still a lot of prejudice and some companies are nervous about associating themselves with this segment. *Gay Times* has been rebuffed by some companies as an advertising medium and the Henley Centre had to abandon plans for a market research report on the gay market because it could not find enough big name clients who were prepared to buy it.

Sources: Fry (1998); Leake (1997); Thompson-Noel (1997).

Questions

1 To what extent does the gay segment conform to the criteria for successful segmentation?

2 What segmentation bases are relevant to the gay housing and holiday markets?

3 What are the risks and rewards for a mainstream company targeting the gay segment?

References to Chapter 5

Abratt, R. (1993), 'Market Segmentation Practices of Industrial Marketers', *Industrial Marketing Management*, 22, pp. 79–84.

Austin, M. (1998), 'Slimming Craze Has Men All of a Quiver', *The Sunday Times*, 8 March, p. 1.14.

Barnard, P. (1998), 'Class Wars in the Great Outdoors', *The Times*, 24 January, p. 49.

Bonoma, T. V. and Shapiro, B. P. (1984), 'How to Segment Industrial Markets', *Harvard Business Review*, May/June, pp. 104–10.

Broadhead, S. (1995), 'European Cup Winners', *Sunday Express*, 7 May, p. 31.

Brodie, I. (1998), 'Bigger Waistlines Mean Healthier Bottom Lines', *The Times*, 9 March, p. 50.

CACI Information Services (1992), *The Acorn User Guide*, CACI Ltd.

Clemens, J. (1997), 'Business Flyers Make Profits Soar', *Marketing Week*, 7 August, pp. 26–7.

Crosskey, P. (1997), 'Sales Press Forward', *The Grocer*, 3 May, pp. 41–2.

Darwent, C. (1993), 'A Socking Success', *Management Today*, February, pp. 44–6.

Davenport-Firth, D. (1998), 'Smile, You're on Candid Camera', *The Grocer*, 14 November, p. 45.

Denny, N. (1998), 'Listening to Your Customers is Vital', *Marketing*, 19 November, p. 18.

Douglas, S. P. and Craig, C. S. (1983), *International Marketing Research*, Prentice-Hall.

Fry, A. (1998), 'Reaching the Pink Pound', *Marketing*, 4 September, pp. 23–6.

The Grocer (1998a) 'Getting Serious with Physio Sport', *The Grocer*, 6 June, p. 37.

The Grocer (1998b), 'Taking the Guilt out of Eating Chips', *The Grocer*, 24 October, p. 73.

Hlavacek, J. D. and Ames, B. C. (1986), 'Segmenting Industrial and High Tech Markets', *Journal of Business Strategy*, 7(2), pp. 39–50.

Leake, J. (1997), 'Pink Pound Powers Gay House Boom', *The Sunday Times*, 10 August, p. 19.

Marbeau, Y. (1992), 'Harmonisation of Demographics in Europe 1991: The State of the Art. Part 1: Eurodemographics? Nearly There!' *Marketing and Research Today*, 20(1), pp. 33–40.

Marsh, P. (1995), 'Down in the Boiler Room', *Financial Times*, 21 August, p. 8.

Mitchell, A. (1983), *The Nine American Lifestyles: Who Are We and Where Are We Going?*, MacMillan.

O'Connor, J. and Galvin, E. (1999), *Marketing and Information Technology*, 2nd edn, Financial Times Pitman Publishing.

O'Malley, L. *et al.* (1995), 'Retailing Applications of Geodemographics: A Preliminary Investigation', *Marketing Intelligence and Planning*, 13(2), pp. 29–35.

Paitra, J. (1993), 'The Euro-consumer: Myth or Reality?', in C. Halliburton and R. Hunerberg (eds.), *European Marketing: Readings and Cases*, Addison-Wesley.

Palmer, R. and Cohen, J. (1993), 'Bunter's Back as Model Shape for the Future', *Sunday Times*, 25 April.

Plummer, J. T. (1974), 'The Concept and Application of Lifestyle Segmentation', *Journal of Marketing*, 38 (Jan.), pp. 33–7.

Quatresooz, J. and Vancraeynest, D. (1992), 'Harmonisation of Demographics in Europe 1991: The State of the Art. Part 2: Using the ESOMAR Harmonised Demographics: External and Internal Validation of the EUROBAROMETER Test', *Marketing and Research Today*, 20(1), pp. 41–50.

Rawsthorn, A. (1997), 'Bulgari Jewellers: the Luxury to Diversify', *Financial Times*, 10 December, p. 4.

Sage, H. (1997a), 'Playtex Aims Wonderbra at Teenagers', *Marketing Week*, 21 March, p. 7.

Sage, H. (1997b), 'Wonderbra Needs New Ideas to Push up Sales', *Marketing Week*, 5 June, p. 20.

Sleight, P. (1997), *Targeting Customers: How to use Geodemographic and Lifestyle Data in Your Business*, 2nd edn, NTC Publications.

Sleight, P. (1998), 'The Ultimate System?', *Database Marketing*, November.

Sleight, P. (1999a), 'Reacting Fast', *Database Marketing*, February, p. 8.

Sleight, P. (1999b), 'Measuring the Risk', *Database Marketing*, February, pp. 15–17.

Smith, W. R. (1957), 'Product Differentiation and Market Segmentation as Alternative Marketing Strategies', *Journal of Marketing*, 21 (July).

Solomon, M. R. (1994), *Consumer Behaviour*, (2nd edn.) Allyn and Bacon.

Thompson-Noel, M. (1997), 'Potent Power of Pink Purchasing', *Financial Times*, 26 April, p. 14.

Wavell, S. (1997), 'Fat of the Land', *The Sunday Times*, 2 November, p. 5.6.

Wind, Y. J. (1982), *Product Policy and Concepts, Methods and Strategy*, Addison-Wesley.

Wind, Y. J. and Cardozo, R. (1974), 'Industrial Marketing Segmentation', 3 (March), pp. 153–66.

Marketing Information and Research

LEARNING OBJECTIVES

This chapter will help you to:

1 recognise the importance of information to an organisation and the role information plays in effective marketing decision making;

2 understand the role of a marketing information system and a decision support system, and develop an awareness of the various types of information available;

3 become familiar with the various steps involved in the marketing research process;

4 outline the sources of secondary and primary data, understand their role and the issues involved in their collection and analysis; and

5 appreciate some of the ethical concerns surrounding marketing research.

INTRODUCTION

The nature and role of market research in Europe have seen significant changes in recent years, as organisations increasingly look to do business in a wider range of EU markets. To be effective in penetrating these markets requires specialised and sophisticated approaches to identifying, assessing and satisfying market demands in a competitive environment. In a community with 15 member states, each with subtly different needs and market characteristics, effective information on the markets that are of interest is essential to help the organisation to make a better decision on the most appropriate market entry and competitive strategies. To support all this, the organisation also needs a properly designed and managed information system to enable timely and appropriate information to be available for the marketing decision maker.

Every aspect of marketing considered in this book, including the definition of markets and market segments, the formulation of an integrated strategy based on the 4Ps and planning and control mechanisms, requires the collection and analysis of information. The better the planning, data collection, information management and analysis, the more reliable and useful the outputs become, and thus marketers are able to make decisions that are more likely to satisfy the needs and wants of selected market segments. The organisation that is prepared to contemplate making a significant change to its marketing effort, without first assessing likely market reaction, is running a very high risk of failure.

In general, gathering information on the actual or potential market-place not only allows the organisation to monitor trends and issues concerning its current customers, but also helps it to identify and profile potential customers and new markets, and to keep track of its competition, their strategies, tactics and future plans. In this context, market research and information handling offer the organisation a foundation from which it can adjust to the changing environment in which it operates.

Example At the heart of the marketing concept is the need for organisations to strive constantly to satisfy their customers' needs and wants. This means that it is important for those who develop the organisation's strategies and policies to understand how the customer is thinking and feeling. At a conference held by The Marketing Society, the President of the Burger King (http://www.burgerking.com) fast-food chain explained what happened when his company stopped listening to its customers in the UK (Denny, 1998). Burger sales were falling and so the company raised its prices to compensate for lost revenue, which in turn led to even fewer customers. Market research revealed that customers did not want to have to wait for more than three minutes for a meal and yet 60 per cent of them were having to do just that. As a result of these findings, the company began to focus much more on customer service and on ensuring that the concerns of both customers and staff were heard. All of this, accompanied by a new product launch, the Big King, and an advertising campaign centred on quality and taste solved the problem, leading to a 1.5 per cent increase in Burger King's market share.

Decision makers in even the biggest companies, therefore, cannot afford to be complacent or assume that they know what the customer wants. Good, up-to-date, relevant research, with its implications understood at the highest levels, can ensure that an organisation keeps up with its customers.

Marketing information and research principles and practice are often similar across a wide range of situations in consumer and organisational market contexts, although they may, of course, become market specific in terms of their focus. Thus assessing the market for machine tools in Germany and Spain, for example, may differ in terms of the sources of data and information used, but the need for the careful selection of key information sources and the design of a user survey of key potential buyers may well follow similar lines.

This chapter first considers the role of marketing research and discusses the structure of the marketing information system (MIS) as a means of collecting, analysing and disseminating timely, accurate and relevant data and information throughout the organisation. It then looks at the marketing research planning framework. The stages in designing and implementing a marketing research project are considered, from defining the problem to writing a brief and then executing the project and disseminating the findings. The chapter also looks in detail at sourcing and collecting secondary (or desk) research, from existing or published sources, and primary (or field research) derived from scratch through surveys, observation or experimentation for a specific purpose. The important aspects of designing samples and data collection instruments are explored in some depth, since however well managed the rest of the research process is, asking the wrong questions in the wrong way to the wrong people is a recipe for poor quality marketing information.

Finally, because marketing research is potentially such a complex process, with so much riding on its findings, and because organisations often delegate it to agencies, it is important that it is carried out professionally and ethically. There is, therefore, a section on ethical issues involved in marketing research at pp. 249 *et seq.*

Throughout this chapter, the terms *client* and *researchers* have been used. Client means the organisation that has commissioned the marketing research, whether from an external agency or from an in-house department. Researchers mean the individual or the team responsible for actually undertaking the research task, regardless of whether they are internal or external to the client organisation.

MARKETING RESEARCH: DEFINITION AND ROLE

Marketing research is at the heart of marketing decision making and it is important to understand what it involves and its place within the organisation. This section thus discusses the meaning of marketing research and the role that it plays in helping managers to understand new or changing markets, competition, customers' and potential customers' needs and wants.

Defining marketing research

Marketing research is a critical input into marketing decisions and can be defined as:

> **Marketing research is the function which links the consumer, customer, and public to the marketer through information – information used to identify and define marketing opportunities and problems; generate, refine, and evaluate marketing actions; monitor marketing performance; and improve understanding of marketing as a process. Marketing research specifies the information required to address those issues; designs the method for collecting information; manages and implements the data collection process; analyses the results; and communicates the findings and their implications.**
> (AMA definition as quoted by McDaniel and Gates, 1996)

Marketing research links the organisation with the environment in which it is operating and involves specifying the problem, gathering data then analysing and interpreting those data to facilitate the decision-making process. Marketing research is an essential link between the outside world and the marketer through the information used to identify and define marketing opportunities and problems, generate, refine and evaluate marketing actions, monitor marketing performance and improve understanding of marketing as a process. Marketing research thus specifies the information required to address these issues and designs the methods for collecting the necessary data. It implements the research plan and then analyses and interprets the collected data. After that, the findings and their implications can be communicated.

The role of marketing research

The role of marketing research in consumer markets has become well established across the EU. It is particularly important for manufacturers, because of the way in which retailers and other intermediaries act as a buffer between manufacturers and their end consumers. If the manufacturer is not to become isolated from market trends and changing preferences, it is important that an accurate, reliable flow of information reaches the marketing decision maker. It might be very limiting if only feedback from the trade were used in making new product and marketing-mix decisions.

Another factor facing the consumer goods marketer is the size of the customer base. With such a potentially large number of users and potential users, the onus is on the organisation to make sure that it generates a backward flow of communication from those customers. The potential size of consumer markets also opens up the prospect of adapting products and the general marketing offering to suit different target groups. Decisions on product range, packaging, pricing and promotion will all arise from a well-understood profile of the different types of need in the market. Think back to Chapter 5, where the links between market segments and marketing mixes were

Example   Marketing research is not just about consumers. Whitbread (http://www.whitbread.com), which markets Stella Artois, the best-selling lager brand in the UK, carried out a distribution survey among stores operating under the Spar name (*The Grocer*, 1998a). These are independent retailers which have joined a kind of co-operative to give them the benefits of a nationally known trading name (Spar) and centralised bulk buying. The good news for Whitbread was that 79 per cent of these Spar stores stocked Stella cans, but the bad news was that 21 per cent, more than 400 retailers, did not. Furthermore, fewer than 50 per cent of stores stocked bottled Stella. This represents much more detail than Whitbread would possess from its own sales records alone and opens up a number of opportunities for it, for example undertaking further research to discover the reasons for not stocking the brand, targeting the non-Stella stores with incentives to encourage them, or working more closely with Spar's central purchasing operation to improve the take-up of the brand among stores.

discussed in more detail. Marketing research is essential for ensuring that segments exist and that they are viable, and for establishing what they want and how to reach them. As markets become increasingly European and global in their scope, marketing research plays an even more crucial role in helping the organisation to Europeanise its marketing effort, and to decide when to standardise and when to vary its approaches as new markets are opened up.

In organisational markets, the role of marketing research is still very similar to that in consumer markets, in that it helps the organisation to understand the marketing environment better and to make better informed decisions about marketing strategies. Where the two types of market may differ is in the actual design and implementation of marketing research, because of some of the underlying factors peculiar to organisational markets, such as the smaller number of customers and the closer buyer–seller relationships, as introduced in Chapter 4. Despite any differences, the role of marketing research is still to provide an essential insight into opportunities, markets and customers.

An organisation can collect its data in different ways. Data can come from secondary sources (published data, discussed at pp. 225 *et seq.*) or primary sources (data collected for a particular research project, discussed at pp. 228 *et seq.*). Primary data

Whitbread is working to ensure that this bloke's glass need never be empty again.

Source: Whitbread.

might be collected by commercial market research agencies, which will undertake specific, commissioned projects for clients. These agencies can vary considerably in size and specialisation, depending on whether they are large multinationals or small operations. Some will offer the full range of services, but others will choose to specialise in particular areas of marketing research, such as large-scale field surveys.

However, marketing research can also be undertaken by the organisation's own marketing research department, if it has one, and secondary data can be obtained from a range of commercial and government-sponsored bodies. If it is decided to undertake the research internally, the organisation has to be sure that the range of expertise exists to cope with the problem in hand. The problem is that the greater the in-house expertise available, the more expensive and difficult it is to keep it employed throughout the year.

A larger organisation, such as KLM, tends to be better equipped for formal marketing research, as it recognises that it can become remote from customers, whereas a smaller organisation has more day-to-day contact with its customers, although that can lead to a narrow view, being oblivious to new ideas and opportunities. Whatever its situation, an organisation must be confident that it is sufficiently well informed to be able to make marketing decisions with the support of timely and accurate information.

Example KLM, the Dutch airline (http://www.klm.com), carries out two different annual research surveys among business travellers. The first survey focuses on the 50 000 Dutch business people who are members of its frequent flyer programme, and looks at issues such as check-in procedures, in-flight service and value for money. The second survey is much wider. It is undertaken in conjunction with two magazines, *Time* and *Newsweek*, which have 175 000 readers between them who are also business travellers. This survey looks at attitudes towards KLM as a business airline compared with other carriers (Rijkens, 1992). Between the two surveys, KLM can begin to build a picture of how well it is meeting the needs of existing customers and how it can improve its service to them, and can also monitor perceptions of its perceived position in the market as a basis for developing strategies for attracting new customers.

Marketing research can take many forms, from being a highly specialised project requiring expert knowledge and considerable expense, to being quite informal and inexpensive. The amount of time and cost to allow for each project will, of course, vary considerably. An organisation with a proper respect for marketing research and the support it offers to decision makers will allow a project to take as long as it needs, and to cost as much as it needs, to solve the defined problem, without getting lost in irrelevant fine detail.

The need for marketing research sometimes arises because the organisation needs specific details about a target market, which is a well-defined, straightforward descriptive research task. Sometimes, though, the research need arises from a much broader question, such as why a new product is not achieving expected market share. The organisation may have a theory about the nature of the problem, but it is up to marketing research to establish whether any assumptions are correct and to check out other possibilities. In practice, most marketing researchers spend a fair proportion of their time on informal projects, undertaken in reaction to specific requests for marketing information. Often these projects lack the scientific rigour associated with the more formal definition of market research. However, problems of a more innovative and complex nature have to be solved through major, formal pieces of market research, simply because of the risks involved in going ahead without the fullest possible insights. International market research is becoming increasingly important as organisations expand into new, unfamiliar markets. A survey among 557 buyers of market research in 12 different countries showed that half the respondents regularly buy international market research. The Finns came out on top, with 47 of their 50 respondents buying international data, while the Greeks came bottom. The British and French were about average, just ahead of the Dutch and Italians (Gofton, 1994).

MARKETING IN ACTION   ## Spicing up the UK market

Planning to expand into a foreign market poses a number of market research problems. Gathering information such as population size and breakdown, ethnic and religious background and legal and regulatory issues could be a straightforward task of consulting secondary sources, but at some point the company needs to look more closely at the market for its own product, probably with primary research. Is there indeed an established market in the target country? What brands already exist there? What are their marketing mixes and strategies? Who buys the product? How often? How do they use it? How acceptable would our brand be?

Sharwood's, for instance, a UK ethnic foods manufacturer, undertook extensive research, asking those kinds of questions, before it entered the US market. As a result of this research, it developed 40 new products catering specifically for the needs and tastes of the US consumer, including products that are sweeter than those in the UK and with less fat and sodium.

Sources: The Grocer (1998b); Mackenzie (1998).

TYPES OF RESEARCH

So far, the discussion of marketing research has been very general and has not distinguished between different types of research. There are, however, three main types of research, each suitable as an approach to different kinds of problem.

Exploratory research

Exploratory research is often undertaken in order to collect preliminary data to help clarify or identify a problem, rather than for generating problem solutions. Before preparing a major proposal, some exploratory work may be undertaken to establish the critical areas to be highlighted in the main body of the research.

Example   An American manufacturer of high-pressure fire-fighting hose nozzles wanted to enter the European market with its most recent innovative design. Before it made a serious commitment to detailed market research across Europe to establish customer reaction and the market entry strategy, some exploratory research was undertaken. This made use of secondary data to establish who the competition would be, what the safety and product standards across Europe were and, not least, what the trends and profile of purchasing by the different fire-fighting authorities were. In addition, a small number of key interviews were held with purchasing bodies in Germany, France and the UK to establish the procedures for trial and adoption in those markets.

This provided a valuable insight into the characteristics of European markets and revealed that significant differences existed in what had been believed to be a relatively homogeneous market. In this case, exploratory research helped to identify the areas that the main survey would consider in more depth and ensured that the company's original assessments and expectations were tested before detailed surveys were designed.

Exploratory research can be conducted through a number of different techniques. Secondary sources of information may be enough (*see* pp. 225 *et seq.*), or the organisation may wish to undertake small-scale qualitative research such as surveys of knowledgeable persons or small group discussions (*see* p. 231). In some circumstances, the organisation may even choose to use observational research (*see* pp. 233 *et seq.*)

for its exploratory data. However, whatever the method chosen, in each case the purpose is to make an initial assessment of the nature of a marketing problem, so that more detailed research work can be planned appropriately.

Descriptive research

Descriptive research aims to provide the marketer with a better understanding of a particular issue or problem. Descriptive research can range from quite specific briefs, for example profiling the consumers of a particular brand, assessing the actual purchase and repurchase behaviour associated with that brand and the reasons behind the behaviour exhibited. Most research in this category tends to be of a large-scale survey type, designed to provide a means of better understanding of marketing problems through the presentation of both quantitative and qualitative data (*see* below).

Causal or predictive research

This type of research is undertaken to test a cause-and-effect relationship so that reasonably accurate predictions about the probable outcome of particular actions can be made. The difficulty with this kind of research for the marketing manager is that to be confident that more of x does cause more of y, all the other variables that influence y must be held constant. The real-world laboratory is rarely so obliging, with competitors, retailers and other middlemen, and the marketing environment generally, all acting independently, doing things that will change the background conditions. Thus researchers trying to establish, for instance, whether or not a promotional 10 per cent price reduction would increase sales volume by 15 per cent during a specified period are faced with the problem of ensuring that all the other variables that might influence sales volume are held constant during the research. Random sampling may help in this process, so that the 10 per cent offer would only be made in a random selection of stores, with the other stores offering normal terms. Any difference in the performance of the product in the two groups of stores is likely to have been caused by the special promotion, since both the 'normal' and the 'promotional' product have been subjected to identical environmental factors, impacting on all the stores, during the same period.

The origins of research data

There are two main types of data, which are generated by fundamentally different research approaches.

Qualitative research

Qualitative research involves the collection of data that are open to interpretation, for example people's opinions, where there is no intention of establishing statistical validity. This type of research is especially useful for investigating motivation, attitudes, beliefs and intentions, rather than utilising probability-based samples. With this approach, many of the methods used to generate data are grounded in the behavioural sciences. They are often based on very small-scale samples and, as a result, cannot be generalised in numerical terms. Although the results are often subjective, tentative and impressionistic, they can reflect the complexity that underlies consumer decision making, capturing the richness and depth of how and why consumers act in the way they do. According to Chisnall (1986, p. 147)

> **for all its limitations, qualitative research is able to provide unique insights to inspire and guide the development of marketing strategy and tactics.**

Quantitative techniques, despite their statistical rigour, are rarely able to capture the full complexity and the wealth of interrelationships associated with marketing activity.

A range of methods can be adopted within the qualitative framework. These include:

- survey research/questionnaires
- focus groups
- in-depth interviews
- observational techniques
- experimentation.

All of these are discussed further at pp. 229 *et seq.*

Quantitative research

Quantitative research involves the collection of information that is quantifiable and is not open to the same level of interpretation as qualitative research. It includes data such as sales figures, market share, market size, consumer product returns or complaints, and demographic information (*see* pp. 182 *et seq.*) and can be collected through primary research, such as questionnaire-based surveys and interviews, and through secondary sources, including published data.

Quantitative research usually involves larger-scale surveys or research that enable a factual base to be developed with sufficient strength to allow statistically rigorous analysis. Most of us have been on the receiving end of quantitative research at some time or another, having been collared by an interviewer armed with a clipboard interviewing respondents in the street. The success of quantitative research depends in part on establishing a representative sample that is large enough to allow researchers to be confident that the results can be generalised to apply to the wider population. It is then possible to specify that 'Forty-five per cent of the market think that ... whereas 29 per cent believe ...' The research can be undertaken through telephone interviews, face-to-face interviews, or mail questionnaires (*see* pp. 232 *et seq.*), and can also utilise secondary data sources (*see* pp. 226 *et seq.*).

Continuous research

A large number of research projects are developed specifically to better understand and to overcome marketing problems as they are identified. At pp. 222 *et seq.* we trace the development of such projects from inception through to final evaluation. Some research, however, is conducted on a continuous basis. **Continuous research** is available on an ongoing basis for a subscription or agreement to purchase the updated findings. Usually offered by market research agencies, syndicated research provides much useful data on an ongoing basis. In the UK, retail purchases by consumers are tracked by A C Nielsen, while Target Group Index (TGI), produced by MRB, plots the fortunes of some 5000 brands. Similar services are available in all the main European markets. The quality of such research is very high, but the important advantage is shared cost, since Nielsen data, for example, are essential to any large multiple retailer or brand manufacturer and they will all buy the data. The price for each organisation is still far, far less than the cost of doing or commissioning the research individually. The big disadvantage, of course, is that competitors also have access to exactly the same information.

There are a number of different approaches to generating continuous data.

Consumer panels

Market research companies recruit large numbers of households which are prepared to provide information on their actual buying and consumption patterns on a regular basis. The panel may be constituted to provide as wide a coverage of the population as possible, or it may be defined to home in on a particular segment. The make-up of a consumer panel can be quite specific. The Pre- and Post-Natal Survey (PNS), operated in the UK, runs a regular survey of 700 pregnant women and 600 mothers with babies up to six months old. For manufacturers of baby foods, nappies, toiletries and infant medicines, such inside information can be invaluable. At the other extreme, Taylor Nelson AGB offers Superpanel, claimed to be the largest in Europe with 8500 households and 28 000 individuals providing purchasing information weekly.

Data can be extracted from consumer panels in two main ways: home audits and omnibus surveys.

Home audits. The consumer is expected to throw nothing away, and that includes cans, wrappers and all other forms of packaging. Refuse is placed in a special container that is checked at regular intervals by an independent auditor, who also checks the food cupboard and fridge/freezer. Sometimes additional questions are asked to supplement the survey. Increasingly, electronic terminals are installed in homes to allow regular tracking of brand usage. Nielsen Homescan has around 9000 homes linked to in-home scanners that record grocery purchases as well as collecting answers to survey questions. Information is simply downloaded to the research company on a regular basis using a modem. This method is increasingly replacing the old-style consumer diary, which recorded the same kind of information but using pen and paper technology!

Television viewership panels are very similar, in that they involve the recruitment of households and the installation of in-home monitoring equipment. This time, the objective is to use the equipment to enable minute-by-minute recording of audience viewing by channel. From these data, organisations such as AGB and RSMB are able to provide detailed ratings for programmes and viewing patterns during commercial breaks, a critical factor in the sale of advertising time.

Consumer panels enable buying profiles to be built up over time and provide much useful information for brand managers. Panel data are particularly useful for assessing consumer loyalty, brand switching and the frequency and quantities purchased.

Omnibus surveys. An omnibus survey, as the term suggests, enables an organisation to participate in an existing research programme whenever it is felt appropriate. When an organisation wants to take part, it can add a few extra questions to the next round of questionnaires sent to the large number of respondents who are regularly contacted. The big advantage is cost, although normally the number of questions that can be asked on behalf of a specific organisation is very small. The speed with which answers are received is also an important factor.

To speed up the collection and input of data, many research companies, such as Access Omnibus Surveys, use CATI (computer-aided telephone interviewing), or CAPI (computer-aided personal interviewing), as used by RSGB Omnibus. Such techniques allow Access to offer its Face to Face omnibus survey, which interviews 2000 adults aged 15 or over every week. IPSOS-RSI's Capibus GB also offers 2000 adults weekly and its Autobus GB offers 500 motorists every week. Some omnibus providers also offer European surveys. Capibus Europe covers France, Germany, Italy, Spain and the Netherlands and interviews 1000 adults weekly in each of those countries. Autobus Europe similarly interviews 500 motorists on a monthly basis in each of four countries: France, Germany, Italy and Spain. If the sample definition across Europe is similar, and if the fieldwork is designed and delivered in a similar manner, then the findings from different markets become far more comparable. This could be especially important during a launch of a new brand or a pan-European advertising campaign.

Retail audits

The retail audit concept is perhaps the easiest to implement, as it relies on trained auditors visiting selected retail stores and undertaking regular stock checks. Increasingly, the use of barcode scanning is providing even more up-to-date information on what is sold where and when. Changes in stock, both on the shelf and in the warehouse, indicate an accurate figure for actual sales to consumers by pack size. This information is especially useful for assessing brand shares, response to sales promotions and the amount of stock being held within the retail trade. Along with information on price levels, the brand manager has much useful information with which to make revised marketing mix decisions.

MARKETING INFORMATION SYSTEMS

In order to serve the information needs of the organisation and to support decision making, marketers need to focus not only on collecting data and information, but also on how to handle and manage issues of storage, access and dissemination. A research report is no use to anyone if nobody knows where it is or that it exists, or if the people who need it do not have the authority or means to access it. Thus it is vital to develop a system of organising and structuring information into a meaningful form to provide timely flows to managers, whether on an *ad hoc* or a continuous basis. The complexity of managing a continuous flow of information into the organisation demands a well thought-out information gathering, storage and retrieval system. There is little point in having a highly complex information system that cannot readily deliver what managers want, when they want it and how they want it. Any system must be responsive to the needs of the users.

A marketing information system (**MIS**) has been defined as:

> **an organised set of procedures and methods by which pertinent, timely and accurate information is continually gathered, sorted, analysed, evaluated, stored and distributed for use by marketing decision makers** (Zikmund and d'Amico, 1993, p. 108).

Nowadays, most of these systems are data based and use high-powered computers. System requirements need to co-ordinate data collection and decision support, as shown in Fig. 6.1. The MIS should be tailored to the specific requirements of the organisation. These will be influenced by the size of the organisation and the resources available as well as the specific needs of decision makers. While these needs are likely to be broadly similar between organisations, they will not be exactly the same and therefore the design of the systems and their sophistication will vary. What is important is that the information is managed in a way that facilitates the decision-making process, rather than just being a collection of data gathering dust.

> **Example** Market research information as part of the MIS has a direct impact on marketing decisions and strategies. When Procter & Gamble (P&G) was about to relaunch its Pampers nappy brand in the Netherlands, its competitor, Peaudouce, made an active effort to recruit women in the maternity hospitals for a database. The feedback from information collected from these women helped R&D to develop a new nappy, samples of which were sent out to the women and more feedback requested. This helped to increase Peaudouce's market share by more than 35 per cent, despite P&G's spend on Pampers' relaunch (Miles, 1998).

It can be seen from Fig. 6.1 that an MIS provides a comprehensive framework for managing information. Information comes in a variety of forms and from a range of sources, any of which can be of critical importance to any organisation, whether large or small, profit or non-profit orientated, government or private, local, national or multinational. In the current fast changing, information-rich, technological environment, organisations tend to be overwhelmed with information. Along with generating huge amounts of data about their day-to-day activities (sales, customer details, incoming and

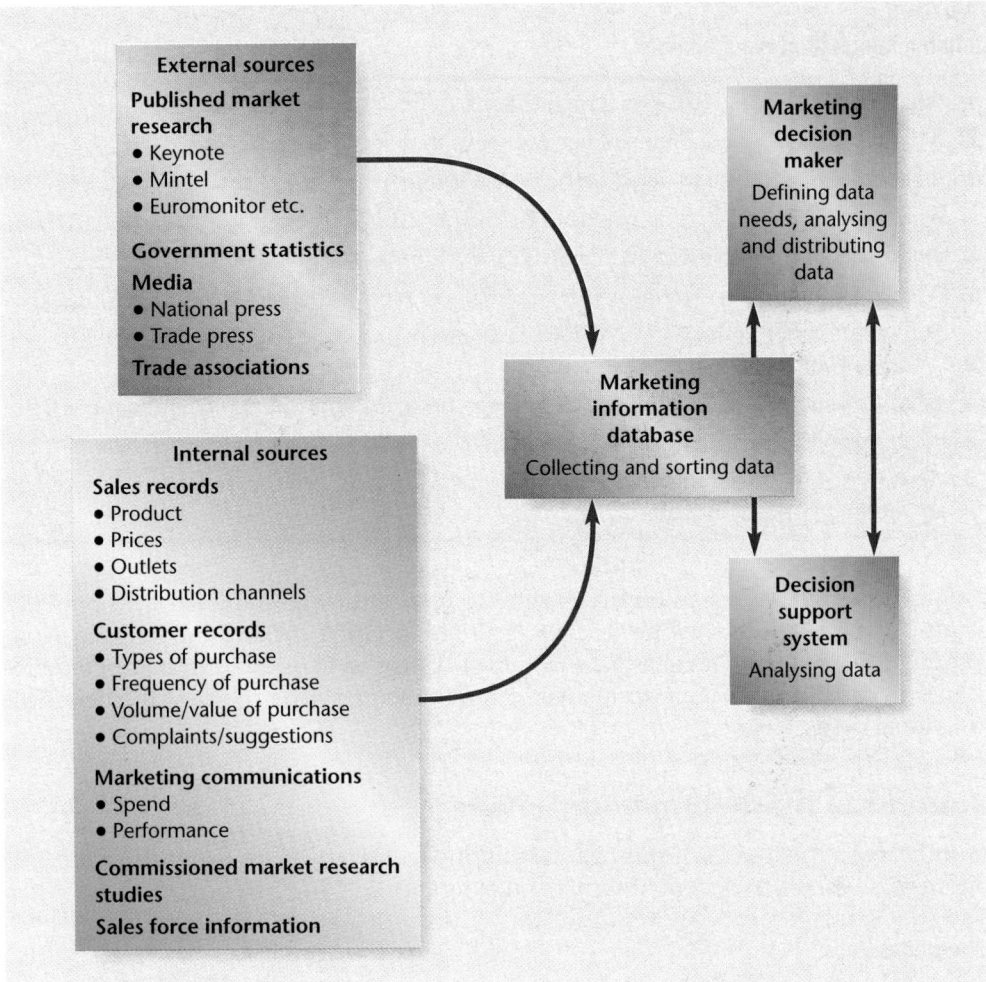

FIGURE 6.1

The marketing information system

outgoing orders, transactions, service requirements etc.), organisations are usually in various stages of gathering other data about competitors, new product tests, improved service requirements and changing regulations, for example. The problem often becomes not how to get the data but what to do with them, and how they should be managed to turn them into useful information. This is where the MIS comes in, to provide a means of managing information, even for small or medium-sized organisations. Unless the organisation has a system that can collect, evaluate, analyse and distribute this information, providing it in a form that is useful, the organisation is not getting the maximum benefit from what it has. Timeliness of information, whether it be for short- or long-term decision making, is also of importance, as the provision of immediate feedback or projected trend details to decision makers can provide a competitive advantage in the market-place.

The other requirement of information is that it should be appropriate to the needs of those using it. Just as you may have difficulty identifying the information you need to make decisions about a range of options facing you, such as whether to update your computer, buy the new software version of your word processing package, go on an overseas holiday, or even look for a new job, organisations encounter the same problems, but usually on a much larger scale. They have to manage the information they have, identify what information they need, and present it in the form that the various decision makers require. Not all information that the organisation has is necessarily appropriate for all marketing decision makers. It is therefore important to identify the

TABLE 6.1

Defining information requirements

- What decisions do you make on a regular basis?
- What types of information do you need to make these decisions?
- What types of information do you regularly receive?
- What types of information do you need but do not currently get?
- What types of specific information are you likely to request?
- What is the time frame in which you would like to receive the information (daily, weekly, fortnightly, monthly, half-yearly etc.)?
- What are your areas of specific interest?
- What are your likely sources of that information (internal reports, trade magazines etc.)?
- What are your data analysis requirements?
- What formats for the information (summary, table, graphs, print, computer disk/file etc.) are most appropriate for you?

various needs of those decision makers and to ensure they are supplied with only the information that meets their needs. This facilitates decision making and helps to avoid information overload. The questions in Table 6.1 help to identify information requirements by getting managers to answer a range of questions relating to their own individual needs.

Sources of marketing information

As indicated at the outset of this chapter and in Fig. 6.1, there are two main sources of information for a MIS system, internal and external:

External sources

External sources are either *ad hoc* studies using secondary and primary research, or continuous data provided by the various syndicated and omnibus studies mentioned earlier. Information comes from sources external to the organisation, such as customers, suppliers, channels of distribution, strategic alliance partners, independent third parties, commercial agencies, industry associations, CSO, Eurostat etc., and external sources like the Internet. These are increasingly being recognised by the business community as a potential means of keeping up with developments in research and a range of other business-related areas, as well as providing a computer link with many millions of computer users, both individual and organisational. The challenge for the marketing manager is to integrate these findings into the organisation to effect change. Much will depend on the purpose of the research. Some may be specifically designed to support decisions of a tactical nature that need to be addressed as a matter of some urgency, others are part of a longer-term strategic development process indicating trends and opportunities.

Internal sources

Information also comes from internal sources within the organisation. These include the internal record keeping system (production, accounting, sales records, purchase details etc.), marketing research, sales representatives' field reports, call details, customer enquiries and complaints, product returns etc. All of this information, again, must be managed appropriately and distributed in a timely fashion if it is going to be used effectively to assist decision making.

The development of Electronic Point of Sale (EPOS) technology has revolutionised the flow of information within retail operations, providing a base for fast and reliable information on emerging trends. Either by using a laser barcode scanner or by keying in a six-figure code, retailers can be right up to date in what is moving, where and what the immediate impact will be on stock levels. Retail managers can monitor movement on different product lines on a daily basis and adjust stock, orders and even in-store promotions, based on information either from individual stores or across all the branches. Tesco, with its Clubcard loyalty scheme, can track and record the purchasing and shopping habits of millions of individual customers, and tailor its marketing offerings, both locally and nationally, based on solid, internally generated information. Direct response marketing, as will be discussed further in Chapter 18, similarly allows a wide range of organisations to build databases of information about individual customers.

The flow of sales force information into a MIS provides access to up-to-date profiles on customers' expectations, account problems and competitive activity. The key is to structure the data entry at sales representative level so that there is as little delay as possible in the flow. Gathered as part of the sales representative's daily reporting routine, information on calls made, orders, new accounts plus other interesting snippets all enable a closer link between sales and marketing decision making.

Organisations thus get everyday information, often as a matter of course, from a variety of sources that can influence their decision making, but *intelligence* means developing a perspective on the information that provides a competitive edge, perhaps in new product opportunities or the opening up of a new market segment.

Sometimes environmental scanning can provide useful insights. By deliberately looking at the various influences on product markets, an organisation may spot early warning signs before the competitors are aware of them. This will help in the forward planning process and will be especially useful as an input to strategic development decisions.

DECISION SUPPORT SYSTEMS

The availability and use of a range of computer-based decision support systems (**DSS**) are changing the way information is used and presented to decision makers, and the way in which they interpret it. While a MIS organises and presents information, the DSS actually aids decision making by allowing the marketer to manipulate information and explore 'What if ...' type questions. A DSS usually comprises a software package designed for a personal computer, including statistical analysis tools, spreadsheets, databases and other programs that assist in gathering, analysing and interpreting information to facilitate marketing decision making. By having the DSS connected to the MIS, marketers further enhance their ability to use the information available. Effectively, this brings the MIS to the desktop, and even to the personal laptop, with the appropriate connections, servers and modems. This can encourage wide use of information, although there may be some problems about restricting access to more sensitive areas and ensuring that the complexity can be handled from a systems perspective.

The use of simple spreadsheets and databases, for example, allows an organisation to keep track of customers' ordering details, payments, returns and product complaints on an individual basis. From this information, marketers can project future sales, keep track of complaints, identify who their regular customers are, what quantities they are buying, as well as patterns of purchase etc. One of your authors failed to visit her local supermarket as frequently as the retailer would have liked, despite having a store loyalty card. This resulted in a very polite letter reminding her of the benefits of buying at that store rather than elsewhere and telling her about a few promotional offers that might be of interest. Thus overall the DSS can be used with statistical analysis to try to identify significant patterns and trends, in both sales and customer behaviour, as well as for predicting the future course of those trends and the impact of marketing decisions on them.

The MIS or DSS will never replace decision makers, only help them. Marketing decisions still need the imagination and flair that can interpret 'hard' information and turn it into implementable tactics and strategies that will maintain competitive edge.

MARKETING AND IT   **DSS and data mining**

In the 1980s, software companies such as Holos and Comshare were at the forefront of computerised DSS which provided up-to-date information to senior executives in a clear, understandable format. Since then, many other companies have moved into the DSS market, including the manufacturers of data-mining software tools. Data mining is the computerised analysis of large databases of company data to find new correlations that give an insight into customer behaviour and help to develop competitive advantage. In the insurance industry, for example, it has long been recognised that female drivers are a lower risk than their male counterparts and thus can be offered cheaper car insurance premiums. Data mining is used to find further subsegments of female drivers with different risk and price profiles.

American Express was one of the first companies to use data mining to show how credit card holders shop and spend, and which stores, hotels and restaurants they prefer. The Royal and Sun Alliance insurance company also used data mining to increase the response rate to its direct marketing campaigns. The company found that by mailing just 20 per cent of its database, it still achieved a high number of responses. The trick was to find the right 20 per cent, using data-mining technology.

Source: O'Connor and Galvin (1999).

THE MARKETING RESEARCH PROCESS

When an organisation has decided to undertake a research project, it is important to make sure that it is planned and executed systematically and logically, so that the 'right' objectives are defined and achieved as quickly, efficiently and cost effectively as possible. A general model of the marketing research process is presented here, which can be applied to a wide range of real situations with minor adaptations. The broad stages, and the decisions and problems associated with them, from the initiation of the research through to the final review of the outcomes, should be common to most research exercises. The model is shown in Fig. 6.2, and although it may suggest a logic and neatness that is rarely found in practice, it does at the very least offer a framework that can be tailored to meet different clients, situations and resources. Each stage in the process will now be discussed in turn.

Problem definition

Problem definition is the first and one of the most important stages in the research process, because it defines exactly what the project is about and as such influences how the subsequent stages are conducted, and ultimately the success of the project itself. The organisation sponsoring the research, whether it intends to use in-house researchers or an agency, needs to define precisely what the problem is and how that translates into research objectives. This may also lead to the identification of other concerns or problems that need to be included in the project. For example, if the fundamental problem has been defined as 'People are not buying our product', the organisation may feel that it should not only explore people's attitudes to the product itself, but also look at how they rate the product on other aspects of the marketing mix in comparison with the competition.

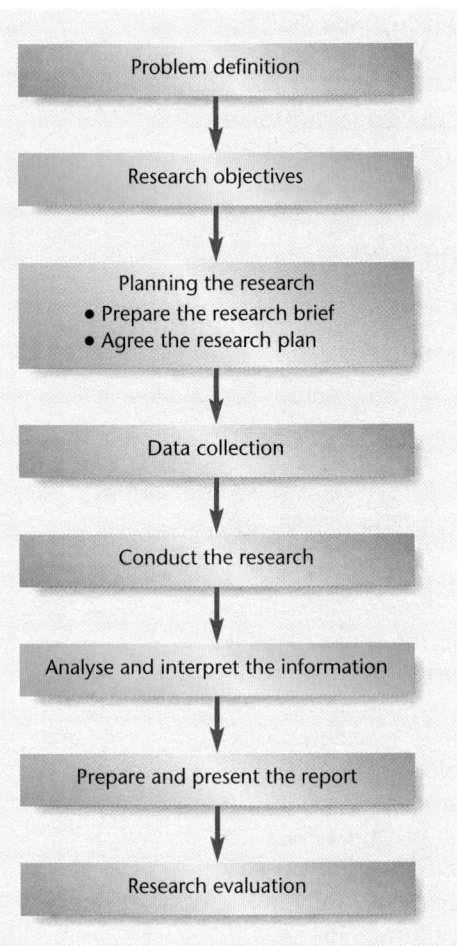

FIGURE 6.2

The market research process

Once the broad nature of the problem has been established, the next stage involves more precise definition of objectives.

Research objectives

The tight specification of research objectives is important to ensure that the project is developed along the right lines. Usually, primary objectives need to be distinguished from secondary objectives. The primary objective for an electric components manufacturer seeking to enter the French market, for example, might be to establish the market potential for the products specified and to indicate appropriate market entry strategies. The secondary objectives tend to be more specific and comprehensive. For the components manufacturer they might include:

- defining market trends and competitive structure over the past five years
- profiling the existing main suppliers in terms of strengths and weaknesses (products, prices, distribution, branding, service etc.)
- identifying the main buyers of electrical components
- identifying the main buying criteria when purchasing
- surveying potential trade and end users for willingness to switch supply source.

The list above is not exhaustive, but the main point is that objectives clearly drive the whole research process, and should provide the necessary foundations for whatever management decisions will have to be taken at the end. In all cases, the research objectives need to be clearly and concisely stated in writing to ensure that the research brief can be adequately prepared.

The skill at this stage lies in being sufficiently broad minded and flexible to avoid being misled by assumptions and prejudices that may not be valid, yet being focused enough to allow the project a strong sense of direction and a chance of being achieved within time and cost constraints. To be successful at this stage, the project team needs good communication and a solid understanding of the issues involved. This is where exploratory research may be useful, in eliminating some of the possibilities or filling some basic gaps in knowledge and understanding. This could involve some preliminary discussions with distributors, experts or customers. The information collected, including any secondary data, can then be used to prepare the research brief for the formal commissioning of work.

Planning the research

The planning stage falls into two main parts: first, the preparation of the research brief, and second, agreeing the research plan. This applies equally whether the research is conducted in-house or not.

Prepare the research brief

The research brief originates from the client. Its quality and precision can vary widely. In some cases, the client has a vague idea of what the problem is, but is not sure what the underlying causes or dynamics are. They thus rely heavily on researchers to specify the problem and then decide on the best research design, effectively asking them to undertake the first two stages of the research process. In many ways, the development of this kind of brief is rather like consultancy and may be part of that kind of overall process.

In other cases, however, the brief may be highly specified for researchers. The organisation has already undertaken the first two stages of the research process and thus has made a detailed analysis of the current situation, identified the problem that needs to be addressed and formulated its exact requirements. The brief can then be handed over complete to either a marketing research agency or the in-house department.

The main points of the research brief (adapted from Hague, 1992) will be:

- a definition of the problem, including its history
- a description of the product to be researched
- a description of the market to be researched
- specific research objectives
- time and financial budget
- reporting requirements.

This brief may be the subject of modification and negotiation during the meetings.

Agree the research plan

On the basis of the brief, a research plan needs to be agreed before the project begins. Not only is this important for cost and timing considerations, but it also ensures that the data generated will enable management decisions to be resolved without the need for further analysis. There is nothing worse than completing a major research project only to find that the results are at best of only partial use to managers!

The details of the research plan will vary according to the project. Many of the points that will be covered in the subsequent stages of the research process need to be outlined in the plan. This will help the clients to appreciate the specification they are contracting for, and indeed open any debate about the time and cost constraints early enough to negotiate changes. The research plan ideally should contain:

- background information for the research
- research objectives (based on decisions that need to be made and the criteria to be used)
- research methods (secondary and/or primary)
- type of analysis to be employed
- degree of client involvement
- data ownership
- details of subcontractors (if any)
- level and timing of ongoing reporting
- format of final report
- timing and cost of research.

An organisation with a major research project may well ask a number of research agencies to tender for the business. Each agency will obviously propose different research plans. These need to be evaluated alongside the organisation's more usual buying criteria. The final decision by the clients should be based on confidence that the chosen agency can best meet its information needs through the research plan proposed, but within any constraints imposed.

Data collection

The first requirement in preparing the research plan is to identify clearly what additional data are needed and then to establish how they are to be collected. This may involve collecting both primary and secondary data, or just primary data.

Secondary research

Sometimes also referred to as *desk research*, secondary research consists of data and information that already exist and can be accessed by an organisation. Thus, for example, it would include published government statistics and published market research reports. All of the data included in the tables in Chapter 2, for example, come from secondary sources. The advantage of secondary research is that it can be much cheaper and quicker to access, and may provide information that the organisation would not otherwise have the time, resources or inclination to gather. The organisation does, however, need to be careful that secondary data are current and that they are appropriate and applicable to the problem in hand. We will look in detail at secondary research below.

Clearly, if secondary research is available that answers the question or solves the problem, then that is the quickest and most efficient way of gathering the necessary data. In many cases, however, secondary data may not be directly applicable, or may only give half the picture. This means that a market research project will often incorporate both primary and secondary research, each complementing the other.

Primary research

Sometimes also called *field* research, primary research is undertaken by, or commissioned by, an organisation for a specific purpose. The required information does not already exist in any available form and so the research has to be undertaken from scratch. If an fmcg manufacturer, for example, wants to find out in detail about what motivated consumers to try their brand specifically, then it is likely that they will have to undertake primary research. The advantage of primary research is that it is exactly tailored to the problem in hand, but it can be expensive and time consuming to undertake. We will look in detail at methods of primary research at pp. 228 *et seq*.

Once the researchers have recognised that information is needed that is not currently available, they must decide from what source they can most effectively get that information. It is well worth checking secondary data sources first to see what has already been done. The pursuit of secondary data should be exhaustive, as secondary data are usually far more cost effective and quicker to collect than primary data. However, because secondary data were collected for another purpose they are not always in a form that is useful or appropriate, and thus they often have to be re-analysed to convert them into a form that can be used for a particular project. Even if secondary data are available, or can be converted, they may still not be sufficient to meet all the researchers' needs, and thus a primary research study may still have to be developed to fill the gaps or further explore the issues. If there are no appropriate secondary data commercially available, then a primary research study will have to be developed from scratch.

SECONDARY RESEARCH

There is little point in commissioning expensive primary research if the data needed have already been obtained by other organisations, either on a commercial basis or as part of their normal information-gathering and dissemination activity. Secondary data can be either internal or external to the organisation. The former is considered to be part of the normal MIS (marketing information system), as outlined at pp. 218 *et seq*. External secondary data offer valuable information to researchers, once sourced. There is a wide variety of sources to consider, such as government departments and agencies, university libraries, higher education research organisations, other libraries, industry associations, trade and professional bodies, commercial information sold to industry or published in magazines or newspapers or on-line, to name but a few. Of course, as already mentioned, the major drawback with secondary data is that the

MARKETING IN ACTION   Retailing information

With shoppers making anything between 100 million and 110 million food shopping trips per week, retailers are inevitably interested in how many of those trips come their way. This is not just a big-name retailer's 'market share by number of visits' ego trip, however. Adding in the detail about who makes those trips, why and how often helps retailers to understand their customers better, and detail about traffic density (number of trips per ft^2) and average spend per trip can help retailers to assess individual store performance. Research by Harris International in late 1997 shows that on average a shopper visits a grocery store 2.8 times per week, part of a trend towards more frequent, but quicker and less bulky shopping trips. The 25–34-year-old age group accounts for more than 25 per cent of spending, yet on average only represents something between 21 and 23 per cent of the number of shoppers. Only 18 per cent of this age group takes a shopping list with them, compared with 38 per cent of the 65+ group and an average of 25 per cent of all shoppers. Information like this, which looks at both the industry averages and data for specific retailers, helps the retailer not only to identify opportunities (attracting more 25–34-year-olds or trying to encourage them to do more list-less impulse buying) but also to compare its performance with its main competitors (Harris, 1998).

information has been collected for purposes other than this particular research project, and may not be in a suitable or usable form.

Secondary data can nevertheless play a variety of roles in the research process. Its main role is probably in providing background information on industries and markets, in terms of trends, dynamics and structure. Some of this information may be useful in its own right in informing management decision making, although it is more likely to provide pointers for further primary research. It can also provide useful information that may assist in sample selection for surveys by indicating the main competitor and customer groups.

Sources of secondary data

It would be impossible to list all potential sources of data, as the number of sources is vast and much will depend on the type of research project in question. A discussion with a business librarian will soon reveal how extensive such a list can be! However, a number of the more commonly used sources are listed in Table 6.2.

Using secondary data

Secondary data vary widely in terms of relevance and quality. Boyd *et al.* (1977) suggest four criteria for evaluating secondary data sources:

1 pertinency of the data;
2 who collects the data and why;
3 method of collecting data;
4 evidence of careful work.

Although secondary sources of data are widely used, as they tend to be low cost and usually easily obtainable once a source has been identified, the criteria above do suggest some potential problem areas. Often the data fail to get down to the micro level necessary to support management decisions. The focus is often at industry level rather than the sector or segment of particular interest, perhaps within a defined geographical area. Some data may have been collected to promote the well-being of the industry, rather than to provide wholly accurate figures, and sometimes they are not always accurate because of their source, their age or the way they were collected. However, for most surveys the sorting, sifting and analysis of secondary data are useful for purposes ranging from developing sample frames (*see* pp. 236 *et seq.*) to providing comprehensive insights into market size, structure and trends.

TABLE 6.2

Sources of secondary data

EU sources from Eurostat, the EU's statistical office These and other publications are available from Euro-info centres and European Documentation Centres	*European Economy* *Panorama of EC Industry* *CRONOS* *REGIO* *COMEXT*	Economic trends in member states Trends in 100+ product groups Economic and social trends in member countries Demographic database Intra-EU trade and extra-EU trade data
UK government sources from the Central Statistical Office Other European Government Statistics Offices: INSEE (France) Instituto National Estadistica (Spain) Central Bureau voor de Statistiek (Netherlands)	*Annual Abstract of Statistics* *Regional Trends* *Social Trends* *Monthly Digest of Statistics* *Census of Production* *Census of Distribution* *Business Monitor* *Digest of Tourist Statistics* *Guide to Official Statistics*	 Manufacturing industry statistics Retail and wholesale statistics Product market information Statistics on the tourism industry A list of all available UK government publications
Chambers of Commerce		Local information and business contacts
Trade associations		Specialist reports and/or libraries for members
Commercial publications Published by Dun & Bradstreet Published by Euromonitor Published by Mintel Published by NTC Publications Published by Keynote Reports Published by Newman Books Published by Graham and Trotmans Published by Pricewaterhouse Coopers Published by ELC International Published by CBB Research Published by Manor House Press From other publishers Other useful organisations	*Dun's Europa* *Who Owns Whom* *Key British Enterprises* *Datastar* *Retail Monitor International* *European Directory of Retailers and Wholesalers* *European Marketing Data and Statistics* *International Marketing Data and Statistics* *World Marketing Data and Statistics* *Retail Trade International* *Consumer Europe* *The Book of European Forecasts* *Market Research Europe* *Market Research International* *Mintel Market Intelligence* *European Lifestyles* *European Marketing Pocket Book* *Retail Pocket Book* *British Shopper* *Market Sector Overviews* *Industry Trends and Forecasts* *Directory of European Retailers* *The Major Companies of Europe* *Guide to European Companies* *Europe's 15,000 Largest Companies* *Directory of European Industrial and Trade Associations* *Store Buyer International* *Kompass* *Yellow Pages* Economist Intelligence Unit Financial Times Management	Information on top European enterprises Information on which companies own other companies and brand names Top British enterprises; similar publications available country by country On-line database of international companies Monthly report on retail trends and statistics Information on 3000 distribution companies across Europe Statistics on 250 consumer products across Europe Data on lifestyles and trends across Europe Monthly Journal Monthly Journal Monthly market research reports on various consumer goods Data about consumers in EU countries Data and statistics about European consumer markets Data and statistics on UK retail industry Data and statistics on UK consumer shopping habits Research reports on consumer goods Research reports on industries 4000 retailers 8000 companies 9000 retail buyers Information on who manufactures what; various European editions
On-line sources	http://www.dis.strath.ac.uk http://www.europages.com http://www.eiv.com http://www.dti.gov.uk	Summary of sites with business information European business directory Country reports and news Overseas trade and market information

FT Profile

FT Profile is a good example of an on-line market research service as it offers a wide range of information. Its coverage includes:

- *News*: access to publications such as the *Financial Times, International Herald Tribune, Les Echoes, Frankfurter Allgemeine Zeitung* and *The South China Morning Post*, as well as to global news databases such as *World Reporter, Asia Intelligence Wire* and *Textline*.
- *Countries*: profiles and analyses of every country and region in the world, with information ranging from political issues and country risk intelligence to foreign trade data, and details of economic policy, transport, visa regulations and hotel listings.
- *Companies*: an extensive collection of detailed information about companies and their activities. This includes company news, credit ratings, corporate issues, products, company rankings and

turnover, as well as access to millions of company reports and over 10 000 stockbroker reports on thousands of companies worldwide.

- *Industries*: company and industry news, statistics and trends, research and development information, newsletters and tendering information. Access to trade press and business publications such as *Lloyd's List, Cable Satellite and TV News* and *Japan Textile Week* is also possible.
- *Markets*: comprehensive market coverage, including trends, advertising spend, brand activity and information on emerging markets, as well as full market research reports on consumer products, services and industries all over the world. Over 200 trade titles covering the marketing industry are included, ranging from *Campaign, Marketing Week* and *Brand Strategy* to *Predicast MARS* and *Asian Advertising and Marketing*.

Source: O'Connor and Galvin (1999).

PRIMARY RESEARCH

Once the decision to use primary research has been made, researchers have to define what data need to be collected and how. This section looks specifically at 'how'. First, there is an overview of primary research methods. For example, the data needed may be drawn from personal interviews, telephone or mail surveys, involving customers, non-customers, suppliers, retailers or any other group of interest. These are not, however, the only methods of data collection and thus the section also looks at observational and experimental research methods.

Whatever method is chosen as most appropriate to the client's information needs, researchers then have to think about defining a sample of individuals or organisations from the total population of interest (defined as a market segment or an industry, for instance). This topic is covered in some depth at pp. 236 *et seq*. Finally, of particular interest to those conducting surveys, pp. 239 *et seq*. look specifically at questionnaires.

Research methods

The three most commonly used methods for collecting primary data are interviews and surveys, observation and experiments.

Category management

Category management (CM) is a partnership between a supplier or a small number of suppliers and a retailer. A category is a group of brands that have something in common that makes them complement each other, compete directly or act as substitutes for each other. Examples of categories might include breakfast cereals,

dairy products, bagged snacks or hot beverages. The objective of CM is to streamline the number of brands offered in the store in a category and to manage logistics, space allocation on the shelf, pricing and promotions for the category as a whole to enhance sales and profits for both the retailer and the supplier.

Continued

Research has a big role to play in developing and implementing CM, but according to Reed (1998) it is a very different, more complex kind of research. Before CM, retailers and major manufacturers tended to stick to their own areas and confine their research problem to those areas. Retailers thus mainly worried about how customers shop and manufacturers mainly worried about consumer behaviour connected with brands and brand image. Under CM, both sets of concerns come together and add a further dimension relating to how brands fit together and interact with each other within a category. Certainly, market research objectives that are to influence CM decisions have an impact on what kind of research is done. More research, for example, is likely to be carried out in the retail environment itself and researchers will be looking for representative samples of category users rather than representative households (Reed, 1998). For market research companies, all this means bigger, more complex research studies, and the need to ensure that objectives are well defined and that findings are clearly communicated.

The Harris Research Centre undertook research for brand manufacturer Van den Bergh Foods to discover in detail how shoppers in store buy 'yellow fats' as part of a category management exercise. To answer the client's questions, this complex research involved (Qureshi and Baker, 1998):

- *36 hours of shopper observation using remote control video equipment.* This allowed researchers to see how shoppers naturally behaved at the fixture: how long they spent, how they reacted to point of sale material, what products they picked up, what they selected etc.
- *1200 entrance/exit interviews.* Entrance interviews establish what intentions shoppers have when

starting the shopping trip, including whether they intend to buy a specific brand of yellow fat or just any brand, or whether they have no intention of buying at all. Exit interviews of the same consumers then record what actually happened, whether they bought what they planned or switched brands, or impulse purchased something that they had not intended to buy on entering the store.

- *1300 shopper interviews at the fixture.* This allows researchers to probe the reasons that shoppers think they are behaving as they are, as it is happening. Thus the researcher can ask about price awareness, influences on selection, reasons for final selection etc.
- *200 in-store, in-depth interviews.* This helps researchers to check out shopping routes around the store and to gain deeper insights into how shoppers behave in the store as a whole.
- *72 accompanied shopping interviews.* A researcher visits the shopper at home before a shopping trip and investigates pre-shopping behaviour and decisions. Then the researcher accompanies the shopper around the store and gathers information about issues connected with the retailer (e.g. branding of the store, colour schemes, layout, queueing, parking, fixtures, service etc.), but putting the emphasis on their relationship with the category and how the shopper buys that category.

The results of all these primary research methods give Van den Bergh a detailed and three-dimensional view of not only how its brands fit into the consumer's life at home, but also their role and impact on the shopping trip, how its brands and the competitors' brands affect the consumer's decisions and behaviour at the fixture, and how those brands fit into the retailer's store.

Interviews and surveys

Interviews and surveys involve the collection of data directly from individuals. This may be by direct face-to-face personal interview, either individually or in a group, by telephone or by a mail questionnaire. Each of these techniques, considered in turn below, has its own set of advantages and disadvantages, which are summarised in Table 6.3.

Personal interviews. A personal interview is a face-to-face meeting between an interviewer and a respondent. It may take place in the home, the office, the street, a shopping mall, or at any prearranged venue. In one extreme case, a holiday company decided to interview respondents who were at leisure on the beach. One can imagine the varied responses!

TABLE 6.3

Comparative performance of interview and survey techniques

	Personal interviews	Group interviews	Telephone survey	Mail survey
Cost per response	High	Fairly high	Low	Very low
Speed of data collection	Fast	Fast	Very fast	Slow
Quantity of data collectable	Large	Large	Moderate	Moderate
Ability to reach dispersed population	Low	Low	High	High
Likely response rate	High	Very high	Fairly high	Low
Potential for interviewer bias	High	Very high	Fairly high	None
Ability to probe	High	High	Fairly high	None
Ability to use visual aids	High	High	None	Fairly high
Flexibility of questioning	High	Very high	Fairly high	None
Ability to ask complex questions	High	High	Fairly high	Low
Ability to get truth on sensitive questions	Fairly low	Fairly high	Fairly high	High
Respondent anonymity	Possible	Fairly possible	None	None
Likely respondent co-operation	Good	Very good	Good	Poor
Potential for respondent misunderstanding	Low	Low	Fairly low	High

There are three broad types of personal interview:

(a) the in-depth, largely **unstructured interview**, taking almost a conversational form;

(b) the **structured interview**, which allows the interviewer far less flexibility to explore responses further and results in a more programmed, almost superficial interview;

(c) a combination of these, the **semi-structured interview**, which is based around a programmed script, but the inclusion of some open-ended questions gives the interviewer scope to pursue certain issues more flexibly.

The unstructured interview can be used for collecting quantitative data, but is rather more useful for exploring attitudinal and motivational issues. Although a standard set of questions may be used as a guide, there is often considerable scope for the interviewer to explore some topics in more depth if additional unforeseen themes emerge in the interview. Generally, the questions are more of a checklist than a rigid format to follow. Given that an unstructured interview may provide one or two hours of intense exploration, it is important that the interviewer is properly briefed, can judge whether the respondent is starting to go off at a tangent or raising new issues of real relevance, and can adjust to the changing pattern of the interview. Often high level interviewing skills are needed, along with a sound knowledge of the product-market concept being examined. These interviewing skills must also include the ability to record the interview accurately if a tape recorder or video recorder is not being used. Further problems that can emerge in the data analysis stage will be considered below.

The main advantage of the unstructured interview is the depth that can be explored and the ability to push the respondent on meaning and accuracy. However, the time taken to complete an interview, and the cost of each interview, make large-scale surveys of this nature prohibitively expensive. In organisational markets, they are often used on a small-scale basis to fill gaps left by other approaches such as mail or telephone surveys.

The structured personal interview adopts a standard questionnaire in wording, layout and order that the interviewer must follow strictly. Little use is made of open-ended questions and the questionnaire is carefully designed for ease of recording information and progress through the interview. This may be especially important if the questionnaire is being administered in the street, thus interrupting a respondent's planned shopping trip. The use of a standardised questionnaire means that the responses from a large number of individuals can be handled with considerable ease, as there is no need for further interpretation and analysis. Furthermore, the inter-

Primary data collection is a familiar sight in the majority of high streets and shopping centres. The interviewer relies on interviewees being amenable and giving up some time.

viewer retains control over the completion of the questionnaire. This approach is used by opinion pollsters and organisations seeking to quantify responses to predetermined questions. As less skilled interviewers are needed, the whole process can be completed more quickly than the unstructured interview, in terms of both field work and data processing. The limitations stem mainly from the need to design and pilot the questionnaire very carefully to ensure that it meets the specification expected of it. We look more closely at some of these questionnaire issues at pp. 239 *et seq.*

Group interviews and focus groups. Group interviews are used to produce qualitative data that are not capable of generalisation to the wider population, but do provide useful insights into underlying attitudes and behaviours relevant to the marketer. A group interview normally involves between six and eight respondents considered to be representative of the target group being examined. The role of the interviewer is to introduce topics, encourage and clarify responses and generally guide proceedings in a manner that is effective without being intrusive.

In this kind of group situation, individuals can express their views either in response to directed questions or, preferably, in response to general discussion on the themes that have been introduced. Often, the interaction and dialogue between respondents are more revealing of opinions. So that participants will relax enough to open out like this, it is often helpful to select the group concerned to include people of a similar status. For example, a manufacturer of an innovative protective gum shield for sports persons organised different group interviews for sports players (users) and dentists (specifiers). Further subdivision could have been possible by type of sport, or to distinguish the casual player from the professional.

Group interviews are especially useful where budgets are limited or if the research topic is not yet fully understood. If secondary data have clearly indicated in quantitative terms that there is a gap in the market, group interviews may be useful in providing some initial insights into why that gap exists, whether customers are willing to see it filled and with what. This could then provide the basis for more detailed and structured investigation. There are of course dangers in generalisation, but if between four and six different discussion groups have been held, some patterns may begin to emerge. For the smaller business with limited funds, group interviews may provide a useful alternative to more costly field techniques.

Telephone interviews. Telephone interviews are primarily used in industrial markets in Europe as a means of reaching a large number of respondents relatively quickly and directly. Whereas there is variation across Europe in home telephone ownership, virtually every business is connected and so a readymade network exists to reach targeted respondent groups. It is far more difficult to ignore a telephone call than a mail survey, although the amount and complexity of information that can be gathered are often limited. In the absence of any visual prompts and with a maximum attention span of probably no more than 10 minutes, the design of the questionnaire needs to be given great care and piloting is essential to ensure that the information required is obtainable.

The range of applications is wide but the telephone is especially useful for usage and purchase surveys where market size, trends and competitive share are to be assessed. Other applications include assessing advertising and promotional impact, customer satisfaction studies and establishing a response to a very specific phenomenon, such as the launch of a new export assistance scheme. Kwik Fit Exhausts telephones its recent customers to establish the degree of satisfaction with their recent purchase.

The interviewing process itself is highly demanding. Being able to generate interest and keep the attention of the respondent is critical, yet at the same time the information required must be collected in an effective and unbiased manner. The use of software packages can enable the interviewer to record the findings more effectively and formally and to steer through the questionnaire, using loops and routing through, depending on the nature of the response. With the demand for such surveys, a number of agencies specialise in telephone research techniques.

Example In October 1998, Teletext Research, a joint venture between Channel 4 and research company Vivid Interface, was launched in the UK (Campbell, 1998). Teletext Research allows displays of questionnaires on domestic television sets and consumers can respond using the buttons on their remote controls. The information is processed through a database and sent to client companies via the Internet. Clients who commission this kind of research can access 28 million adults (potentially) on a nationwide basis or they can focus on a specific region. They have to offer some kind of incentive, however, to encourage consumers who have to make a freefone call to register for the survey and to get an identity number to allow them to access the relevant Teletext pages.

The system has many potential uses for marketers, for example supermarkets could use it to do further research into loyalty card holders or brand manufacturers could use it to get immediate feedback on advertising campaigns. The obvious advantages of the system are that it is cheaper and much faster than more traditional methods and it opens up easy access to an enormous number of potential respondents. There could, however, be some problems. The response rate for any single survey conducted this way might be somewhat unpredictable and researchers will have to think about sampling issues (for example sample size or self-selecting samples – see pp. 236 *et seq.*). In particular, they might have to watch out for 'professional' respondents who have nothing better to do than fill in every survey that is offered to them and rake in the freebies!

Mail questionnaires. This popular form of research involves sending a questionnaire through the post to the respondent for self-completion and return to the researchers. Questionnaires can, of course, also be handed out at the point of sale, or included in product packaging, for buyers to fill in at their own convenience and then post back to the researchers. Hotels and airlines assess their service provision through this special kind of mail survey, and many electrical goods manufacturers use them to investigate purchasing decisions.

While the mail survey has the advantage of wide coverage, the lack of control over response poses a major problem. Researchers cannot control who responds and when and the level of non-response can create difficulties. Response rates can drop to less than 10 per cent in some surveys, although the more pertinent the research topic to the respondent, and the more 'user friendly' the questionnaire, the higher the response rate. Offering a special incentive can also work (Brennan *et al.*, 1991). In a survey of Irish hotel and guest house owners, the offer of free tickets to a local entertainment facility proved an attractive incentive. Other larger-scale consumer surveys promise to enter all respondents into a draw for a substantial prize.

There are other obvious things that can be done to ensure higher response rates. A clear, spacious and user-friendly layout, gentle reminders and follow-up approaches to non-respondents and a supportive, persuasive covering letter all assist in increasing the responses. However, the non-respondents in themselves may pose a problem. It is important to assess whether the respondents, as a group, may be different from the late and non-respondents. Those who think more strongly about a topic, for example, are more likely to respond than those with a more marginal interest, perhaps representing casual or light users.

Mail surveys are especially prevalent in organisational markets, where target respondents can be more easily identified from contacts or mailing lists. The process of mailing can also be readily implemented and controlled using the organisation's normal administrative and mailing infrastructure already set up for response logging, address label generation, folding and franking etc. One way of trying to improve response rates for organisational mail surveys is to warn or notify the desired respondent in advance that the survey is on its way. Haggett and Mitchell (1994), reviewing the literature on pre-notification, found that overall it increases response rates by around 6 per cent and on average reduces by one the number of days taken to respond. The telephone shows the best results, increasing responses by 16 per cent, while postcards only manage a 2.5 per cent improvement. There is, however, no evidence to suggest that the quality of the response is also improved.

There is no one best method to select from the group discussed above. Much will depend on the nature of the research brief, especially in the light of the resources available and the quality and quantity of information required for decision making. A direct face-to-face interview, for example, allows for deeper exploration by the interviewer, an evaluation of body language and generally higher response rates, but it has the disadvantages of possible misinterpretation, distortion or bias in the interviewer's report, especially if the interviewer is inexperienced, poorly trained or poorly supervised. There is also a chance that the interviewee will give what they feel to be more acceptable responses, rather than their genuine belief about a particular question. All of these factors, including the type of questions asked and the structure of the interview, have the potential to influence and distort the results of the survey.

The other factor that has become of significant concern is the cost of the research survey. Face-to-face interviews, especially if conducted on an in-depth basis, tend to be the most costly and time consuming, thus making this form of survey less attractive. Other survey techniques, such as group interviews, telephone surveys and mail questionnaires, all provide alternative, cheaper ways of gathering data. Each of them, however, also has its own set of limitations. Ultimately, the decision on choice of technique has to put aside absolute cost considerations and think in terms of finding the most cost effective way of collecting those vital data.

Observational research

This method involves, as its name implies, the observation by trained observers of particular individuals or groups, whether they are staff, consumers, potential consumers, members of the general public, children or whoever. The intention is to understand some aspect of their behaviour that will provide an insight into the problem that has been identified by the marketing research plan. For example, trials are often conducted with new products in which consumers are asked to use a particular product and are observed while they do so, thus giving information about design, utility, durability and other aspects, such as ease of use by different age groups, and whether people naturally use it in the intended way. This provides an opportunity to test the product and observe how it is used first hand.

Another form of observational research that deliberately seeks feedback on employee performance is *mystery shopping*. This allows a researcher to go through the same experience as a normal customer, whether in a store, restaurant, plane or showroom. As far as the employees are concerned, they are just dealing with another customer and they are not aware that they are being closely observed. The 'shopper' is trained to ask certain questions and to measure performance on such things as service time, customer handling and question answering. The more objective the measures, the more valuable they are to marketing managers in ensuring that certain benchmark standards are being achieved. In a survey of 80 of the UK's largest retailers, almost all claimed to use mystery shopping with the aim of identifying training needs, boosting company standards and improving staff performance (Cramp, 1994).

MARKETING IN ACTION   In bed with the consumer?

Culture Lab, a behavioural research company, has taken the art of observational research to its limits with Project Keyhole, in which researchers live with a family for a number of days (but not the nights!) and record everything. The big advantage is that the researcher can see not only what is bought, but also how it is used in the home environment. The researcher can also observe the quirkier aspects of behaviour, for example how it changes according to time of day or mood etc. Culture Lab's clients get a customised piece of very detailed qualitative research; each client is allocated its own group of households and can research whatever it wants within them.

The main difference between this technique and more traditional forms of observational research is the way the research gets so close to the consumer. Because researchers stay with consumers for several days in their own homes, the presence of the researchers is eventually ignored and the behaviour observed is natural as well as taking place in the right context. It is also true to say, however, that this can be expensive and time-consuming research. It does produce a mass of data that can be very difficult to interpret, especially as those data have to be interpreted to suit the needs of a single client. There is a risk that researchers get involved in too much detailed observation that ends up giving the client no more than a less intensive exercise would have done. It is also important to remember that all this detailed information is related to a very limited number of households and individuals. Can the conclusions be generalised over an entire mass-market customer base?

Source: Curtis (1998).

The potential problems that can be experienced with interviews are also likely with observation where human observers are used. That is, the training and supervision of observers are of great importance and, since it is more subjective, the likelihood of misinterpretation is higher. On the other hand, mechanical observation tools may be used to overcome bias problems, such as supermarket scanners monitoring the purchases of particular consumers or groups of consumers, and the Nielsen people meters, used to monitor the viewing and listening habits of television watchers and radio listeners.

Other devices can be used to observe or monitor closely the physiological responses of individuals, such as their pupil dilation (using a tachistoscope) when watching advertisements, to indicate degree of interest. A galvanometer, which measures minute changes in perspiration, can also help to gauge a subject's interest in advertisements.

In some ways, observation is a more reliable predictor of behaviour than verbal assertions or intentions. Where interaction is not needed with the respondent, or

Hidden cameras discreetly observe this shopper as she browses, selects and rejects brands.

Source: J Walter Thompson Ltd.

where the respondent may be unable to recall the minutiae of their own behaviour, direct observation may be a valuable additional tool in the researcher's armoury. It is particularly informative when people are not aware that they are being observed and are thus acting totally naturally, rather than changing their behaviour or framing responses to suit what they think researchers want to see or hear. Observation can be relevant in both consumer and industrial markets. In the latter, observation at exhibitions and shows can provide useful insights into behaviour. Also, the actual tracking of buyer decisions and experiences as they work through the system (i.e. order processing, packaging, delivery, invoicing, after sales service etc.) can reveal much about operating procedures for usage, buying and logistics in a way that would be difficult to discover and fully understand through post-purchase questioning.

Experimentation

The third method through which primary data can be collected is by conducting an experiment. This may involve the use of a laboratory (or other artificial environment), or the experiment may be set in its real-world situation, for example test marketing a product (more on that in Chapter 9). In the experimental situation, researchers manipulate the independent variable(s), for example price, promotions or product position on a store shelf, and monitor the impact on the dependent variable, for example sales, to try to determine if any change in the dependent variable occurs. The important aspect of an experiment is to hold most of the independent variables constant (as well as other potentially confounding factors) while manipulating one independent variable and monitoring its impact on the dependent variable. This is usually possible in a laboratory, where control of the environment is within the power of researchers, but far less possible in a real-world situation where a myriad of external complications can occur that can confuse the results.

For example, a manufacturer may want to find out whether new packaging will increase sales of an existing product, before going to the expense of changing over to the new packaging. The manufacturer could conduct an experiment in a laboratory, perhaps by setting up a mock supermarket aisle, inviting consumers in and then observing whether their eyes were drawn to the new packaging, whether they picked it up, how long they looked at it and whether they eventually chose it in preference to the competition. The problem with this, however, is that it is still a very artificial situation, with no guarantees that it can replicate what would have happened in real life. Alternatively, therefore, the manufacturer could set up a field experiment, tri-alling the new packaging in real stores in one or more geographic regions and/or specific market segments and then monitoring the results.

Not all experimental research designs need to be highly structured, formal or set up for statistical validation purposes. For example, side by side experiments where shop A offers a different range or mix from shop B, which in all other respects is identical to shop A, can still reveal interesting insights into marketing problems, even though the rigour of more formal experimental designs is not present.

Sampling

Particularly in mass consumer markets, time and cost constraints mean that it is impractical to include every single target customer in whatever data gathering method has been chosen. It is not neces-sary even to begin to try to do this, because a carefully chosen representative sample of the whole population (usually a target market) will be enough to give the researchers confidence that they are getting a true picture that can be generalised. In most cases, researchers are able to draw conclusions about the whole population (i.e. the group or target market) based on the study of a sample. The skill, therefore, lies in making sure that the selected sample is indeed representative. If it is not, then the results of the research may not give an accurate picture of the relevant population and decisions made are likely to be wrong. While it is true that a sample is never absolutely identical to the population that it is supposed to repre-sent, if selected correctly it will tend to have the same characteristics as that population and conclusions drawn about the sample should reflect those of the population. In other words, the reliability of the results from the sample is high and decisions can be based on those results with confidence.

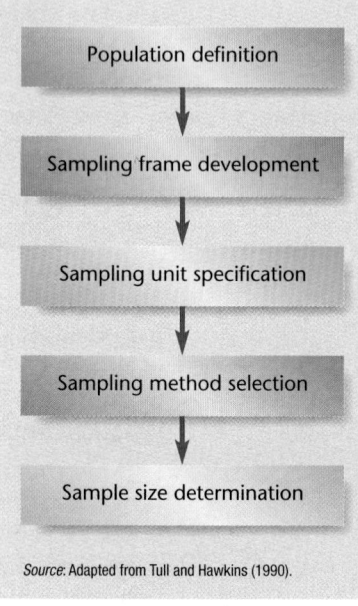

Source: Adapted from Tull and Hawkins (1990).

FIGURE 6.3

Stages in the sampling process

Figure 6.3, based on Tull and Hawkins (1990), shows the main stages in the **sampling process**. Each will be considered briefly in turn:

Population definition

The population to be surveyed will derive from the overall research objectives. Often this will be based on a target market or segment, but even then further definition based on markets, products or behaviours is unlikely to be necessary to create a tightly defined population. In consumer markets, the population may be defined by any of the variables considered in Chapter 5, provided that researchers can use them opera-tionally. In organisational markets the population is usually defined in terms of organisational characteristics and industries.

Sampling frame

The sampling frame is the means of access to the population to be surveyed. It is basi-cally a list from which individual names can be drawn. Registers of electors or lists of organisations compiled from directories such as *Kompass* and *Dun and Bradstreet* are examples of possible sampling frames. Internal customer records may also provide a sam-pling frame, although researchers need to be very sure that such records give a complete picture, and that there is no doubt that this is the required population for the study, rather than just a cheap, quick and easy way of generating an extensive list of names.

Sampling unit

The sampling unit is the actual individual from whom researchers want a response. In consumer markets, the sampling unit is usually the name attached to the address in the sampling frame. In organisational markets, however, this stage can be complex because, as we saw in Chapter 4, organisations have a number of individuals concerned with decision making. So if an organisation wanted to survey builders' merchants across Germany, a two-stage process might have to be used. First, the sample unit might be represented by the individual firm selected, and then a secondary stage might focus the individual within that organisation who should be the subject of attention (the sampling element). It is very important to identify the right individual, as the responses of the purchasing manager in this case may be different from those of the managing director.

Sampling method selection

The next step in the process is to select the sample method, which is the means by which individual sample units and elements are selected from the larger sampling frame. The main and early decision is whether to use probability or non-probability sampling methods.

Probability sampling. Random, or *probability sampling*, where each member of the population has an equal or known chance of being selected for the sample, offers specified levels of confidence about the limits of accuracy of the results. So if a retailer wanted to do a survey to establish satisfaction levels with checkout services, it might decide to interview every thirtieth customer coming through the checkouts during research sessions held at different times of the week. At the end of the process, the retailer might be able to conclude that the findings were correct to the 95 per cent level of confidence – in other words there was only a one in 20 chance that the sample was biased or unrepresentative.

Stratified sampling is an important method of probability sampling, which involves the division of the sampling frame into defined strata or groups that are mutually exclusive. Random probability samples are then drawn independently from each group. This method is widely used in organisational markets, as they naturally divide into discrete layers or bands, reflecting for example company size, geographic location, market shares or purchase volumes. Researchers could decide, therefore, to take a 100 per cent sample (census) of all the larger firms (defined perhaps by turnover or number of employees) and then use random sampling with the rest. By effectively restructuring the sample frame in a manner best suited to the project, greater confidence can be enjoyed that the sample closely reflects the population in question.

An alternative form of stratified sampling is *area sampling*. Returning to our survey of German builders' merchants, the first stage would be to divide Germany into regions and then randomly select a small number of those regions as the basis for the sample. Within each chosen region, researchers randomly select the organisations for the sample. They may end up studying merchants in the Leipzig, Karlsruhe and Hannover areas, rather than a sample from across Germany that would involve considerable time and expense to follow up.

With a random sampling method, it is important for researchers to ensure that the sampling frame used does enable each member to have an equal chance of being selected. Furthermore, actually obtaining responses from the selected sample can be quite difficult. What if the thirtieth customer through the checkout doesn't want to stop? What if there's nobody at home when the interviewer calls round or phones? What if the sampling frame is out of date and the selected consumer has moved house or died? Any of these circumstances violates the ideal of the random sample.

Non-random sampling. *Non-random samples* are much easier to identify than random samples because they are not based on the same strict selection requirements and allow researchers a little more flexibility. The results from these samples are not representative of the population being studied and may lack the statistical rigour generated by random sampling, but they are still often of considerable use to researchers. Two main non-random sampling methods may be used:

1 *Judgemental sampling*. This method is widely used in organisational market research. Sample units are selected deliberately by researchers, because they are felt to represent better sources of the required information. Given the concentrated nature of many industries, if a contracting company for pipework cleaning wanted to enter a new geographical market, for example, it would probably make sense to survey the larger users if that was the target segment of interest, rather than draw at random from all users, large and small. Of course, no inference could be drawn about the wider population from such a sample method.

2 *Quota sampling*. Quota samples are formed when researchers decide that a certain proportion of the total sample should be made up of respondents conforming to certain characteristics. It may be decided, for example, that for a particular study, the sample should consist of 400 non-working women aged between 25 and 35, 250 full-time working and 350 part-time working women in the same age group. This breakdown may reflect the actual structure of the market under consideration. Each interviewer is then told how many completed questionnaires to bring back within each quota category. The choice of respondents is not random, since the interviewer is actively looking for people who fulfil the quota definitions and, once the quota is full, will reject any further respondents in that category. The criteria for defining quotas often use geographic or demographic factors, for example age bands, employment, the structure of the family unit, location, car owners etc., whatever is felt to reflect the structure of the market.

The advantage of quota sampling is that it is quicker and cheaper to do than a full random sample would be, as no sample frame has to be devised and researchers do not have to worry whether the sampling frame is up to date or not. Furthermore, interviewers are not committed to following up specific respondents. Under a quota sample, if a particular respondent does not want to co-operate, then that's fine – the interviewer will look for another one.

Sample size

A final yet very important consideration in the sampling process is sample size. While it may be true that the larger the sample, the greater the confidence that it truly represents the population of interest, there is no point in spending more time and money pursuing any bigger sample than you have to. With random sampling based on statistical analysis, researchers can have confidence within prescribed limits that the sample elements are representative of the population being studied. It is not so much the size of the sample selected that matters, as the tolerated risk of sampling error that researchers are prepared to accept and the cost that is incurred in adding to the number of sampling elements.

Example The Chartered Institute of Marketing (CIM) carried out a survey among UK companies, of all sizes and in all sectors, to see what they thought the impact of the Euro would be and how prepared they were for it (Mazur, 1998). The survey received 200 responses, broken down by size of company as follows:

<50 employees	38	per cent
50–100 employees	12	per cent
101–500 employees	22	per cent
501–1000 employees	8	per cent
1001–5000 employees	9.5	per cent
5001–10 000 employees	2.5	per cent
>10 000 employees	8	per cent

To what extent and why do you think that this is a representative sample?

As one would expect, the higher the levels of confidence required, the greater the size of the sample needed. In Europe, surveys of consumer buying habits are often around 2000 units, which would typically yield a 95 per cent confidence level that the sample reflects the characteristics of the population. In organisational markets, sample sizes of between 300 and 1000 can be used to produce high levels of confidence. With stratified samples, provided that the strata have been carefully defined according to relevant characteristics, even smaller sample sizes may be permissible, especially if they are supported by a full census of some of the more critical groups.

Questionnaire design

The questionnaire is a commonly used research instrument for gathering and recording information from interviews, whether face-to-face, mail or telephone surveys, as described earlier. Researchers soon learn that the best planned surveys soon fall apart if the questionnaire is poorly designed and fails to gather the data originally anticipated. Even the most professional researchers can still make mistakes that only come to light when the responses come back, i.e. when it is too late. To minimise the risk of disappointment, however, there are several dimensions to consider in questionnaire design.

Objectives

The aim of a questionnaire is closely linked with the overall purpose of the research. It is tailormade to meet the information requirements of the study and therefore lies at the heart of the research process. If the questionnaire is to fulfil its role properly as a means of data collection, then there are several areas that need to be analysed, as outlined in Table 6.4.

TABLE 6.4
The objectives of a questionnaire

Objective	Suggestions
To suit the nature of the target population	Pitch the questions in a way they can understand; ask questions they can be expected to be able to answer given their knowledge and experience.
To suit the research methods	For example, a telephone survey cannot use the kind of visual aids that a face-to-face interview can; a postal survey is less likely to get responses if it is lengthy or if it is probing feelings/attitudes.
To suit the research objectives	It must be designed appropriately to gather the right information for answering the research questions – no more, no less.
To collect the right kind of data	The quality and completeness of responses are important for a successful survey. There must also be the right depth of data, whether it is factual or probing attitudes, beliefs, opinions, motivations or feelings.
To aid data analysis	Ensure that it is as easy as possible to take the raw data from the questionnaires and input them accurately into any analytical framework/software package being used.
To minimise error and bias	Ensure that the questionnaire is 'tight' enough to allow it to be administered by any interviewer, to any respondent, at any time, in any location with consistency. Also ensure that questions cannot be misinterpreted or misunderstood.
To encourage accurate and full responses	Avoid leading or judgemental questions; ensure clarity in the way questions are asked; ensure that respondents feel at ease rather than threatened or intimidated by the questions.

Some thought also needs to be given to ensuring that the questionnaire will retain the interest of the respondent, so that full completion takes place. It is easy with self-administered questionnaires for the respondent to give up if the questionnaire becomes tedious, seems to be poorly explained, or is too long or complex. When an interviewer is involved, the motivation can still be lost, despite the best efforts of the interviewer, although it takes more courage for a respondent to terminate a face-to-face interview in mid flow than simply to put a pen down.

It is thus important to make sure that the questionnaire takes as little time as possible to complete. Research in the US found that 20 per cent of consumers thought that questionnaires in general, including 30-minute telephone surveys, were too long (McDaniel *et al.*, 1985). According to Gander (1998), the 30-minute survey is still common, making the interviewer's job much more difficult.

Types of questions

There are two main types of question that can be asked in a questionnaire: **open-ended questions** and **closed questions**. The category of open-ended questions has many significant style variations within it, but they all allow considerable scope for the respondent to express views on the selected theme (and in some cases, on other themes!). Closed questions force the respondent to choose one or more responses from a number of possible replies provided in the questionnaire.

MARKETING IN ACTION **Scoring with sponsorship**

Match, a football magazine targeted at under-16 year olds, distributed 20 000 questionnaires in one of its issues. In one of the questions, it wanted to know whether respondents could associate brands with footballers. Respondents were faced with the question: 'Can you tell us the make of football boot the following players wear?' and a list of 27 footballers' names. There was also space left for the respondent to write in a brand name. No brand names were suggested in the survey and so the respondent had to come up with them unprompted as well as associating them with the right footballer.

Asking the question in this way means that it is more likely that respondents really know the answer, rather than making the kind of guesses that might have arisen if a list of brands has been offered as a prompt or if

multiple-choice questions had been used. Perhaps not surprisingly, given the readership profile, over 70 per cent linked Ryan Giggs with Reebok, 67 per cent linked David Beckham with Adidas and 66 per cent linked Alan Shearer with Umbro and Paul Ince with Adidas. In fact, the top 15 footballers in the list all scored at least 30 per cent correct responses (McDonald, 1998).

Findings like this will please companies that spend a great deal of time and money finding out which personalities are 'hot' among the target market. It is not just football players, such as David Beckham with a deal worth around £2.5mn, who benefit from sponsorship. Adidas signed up boxer Prince Naseem, reportedly for £10mn, because its monthly research showed that he was extremely popular with the 16–24-year-old market (Wilkinson, 1998b).

Open-ended questions. Questions such as 'In the buying of garden furniture, what factors do you find important?' or 'What do you think of the trend towards out-of-town shopping centres?' are open ended because they do not give a range of potential answers for the respondent to choose from. In both cases, interviewers could be faced with as many different answers as there are respondents. Using such questions can, therefore, be rewarding, because of the rich insights given in a relatively unrestrained manner. The difficulties, however, emerge in recording and analysing the responses, given their potential length and wide variations. Nevertheless, it has been argued that using open-ended questions can help to build the goodwill of the respondent through allowing an unrestricted response (Chisnall, 1986).

Closed questions. Closed questions fall into two broad groups, dichotomous and multiple-choice questions. *Dichotomous questions* allow only two choices, such as 'yes or no' or 'good or bad'. These questions are easy to ask and easy to answer.

With careful pre-coding, it is also relatively easy to analyse responses and to use them for cross-tabulation with another variable, for example to find out whether those who say that they do use a product pay more attention to product-specific advertising than those who say that they do not use it. The problem with dichotomous questions is that it can take very many questions to obtain a relatively small amount of information. This can be critical where the length of the questionnaire needs to be constrained.

Multiple-choice questions are a more sophisticated form of closed question, because they can present a list of possible answers for the respondent to choose from. This could be, for example, a list of alternative factors that might influence a purchasing decision (price, quality, availability etc.), or it could reflect alternative levels of strength of feeling, degree of importance or other shades of variation in response to the variable under consideration. Figure 6.4 gives examples of different types of multiple-choice question.

These questions need to be designed carefully, to incorporate and group as wide a range of answers as possible, since restraining the amount of choice available creates a potential source of bias. The alternative responses need to reflect the likely range, without overlap or duplication, since this too may create bias. By offering an 'other, please specify' category, these questions provide some opportunity to collect responses that were not originally conceived (but that should have been identified in the pilot stage) or responses that do not fit neatly into the imposed structure. However, the advantage of multiple-choice questions is that again they are relatively straightforward to analyse, if pre-coding has been used.

Multiple choices can also be used to overcome some respondent sensitivities. If asked 'How old are you?' or 'What do you earn?' as open questions, many people may refuse to answer because the questions are too specific and personal. Phrasing the question as 'To which of these age groups do you belong, 17 or under, 18–24, 25–34, 35–44, 45 or over?' allows respondents to feel that they have not given quite so much away. It is unlikely in any case that knowing a respondent's exact age would be of any greater use to researchers. The bands need to be defined to reflect the likely scope of responses from the target respondents, and to be easy for them to relate to. Professionals, for example, will be more likely to relate to bands based on annual salary than manual workers, who are more likely to know what their weekly wage is. The scope of responses will also vary between these two groups. The bottom band in a survey aimed at ABC1 socioeconomic groups may be 'less than £15 000', whereas the equivalent of this figure in weekly wage terms may provide the top band for a C2DE-oriented survey.

To which of the following age groups do you belong?		Which of these daily newspapers do you regularly read?	
(a) 17 or under		(a) *The Times*	
(b) 18 – 24		(b) The *Daily Telegraph*	
(c) 25 – 34		(c) The *Daily Mail*	
(d) 35 – 44		(d) The *Sun*	
(e) 45 or over		(e) Other (please specify)	

How do you travel to work?		On average, how often do you go to the supermarket?	
(a) Private car		(a) More than 4 times a week	
(b) Taxi		(b) 2 or 3 times a week	
(c) Bus		(c) Once a week	
(d) Train		(d) Once a month	
(e) Other (please specify)		(e) Less than once a month	

FIGURE 6.4

Examples of multiple-choice questions

Rating scales are a form of multiple-choice question, widely used in attitude measurement, motivational research and in situations where a number of complex, interacting factors are likely to influence a situation. There are a number of scaling methods, including:

1 *Likert summated ratings.* A large number of statements, relevant to the research study, are built up from preliminary research and piloting. These statements are then given to respondents who are asked to respond on a five- or seven-point scale, for example 'strongly agree', 'agree', 'neither agree nor disagree', 'disagree' and 'strongly disagree'. The responses are scored from 5 (strongly agree) down to 1 (strongly disagree). The average score across all respondents can then be used to establish the general strength of attitude towards the variable under consideration. An examination of the pattern of individual responses may also reveal issues of interest to the marketer.

   Likert scales are very popular with researchers because of their relative ease of implementation. The statements must, however, be carefully derived and relevant to the phenomena being studied. The scale itself must accurately reflect the range of respondents' views.

2 *Semantic differential scales.* These scales were developed to measure differences in the meaning of words or concepts. This method involves a bipolar five- or seven-point rating scale, with each extreme defined by carefully selected adjectives representing opposite extremes of feeling. A study of retail store atmosphere might offer a series of scales including 'warm – cold', 'friendly – unfriendly', or 'fashionable – unfashionable', for example. Once the scales have been defined, the product (or whatever) is rated on each of them to reveal a profile of the respondent's opinion. Such scales can also be used for measuring corporate image or advertising image and for comparing different brands. In the latter case, if two products are plotted at the same time on the same scales, significant differences may emerge, and help the marketer to understand better the relative positioning of products in consumers' minds.

Examples of both types of rating scale can be found in Fig. 6.5.

The wording of questions. The success or failure of a questionnaire lies as much in the detail as in the grand scheme and design. This includes the detailed wording of questions so that the respondent fully understands what is required and accurate responses are encouraged. The next few paragraphs raise a number of pertinent issues.

It is always important to ensure that the *meaning of words and phrases* is fully understood by the respondent. Particular effort should be made to avoid the use of jargon and technical language that may be unfamiliar to the respondent. Additional complications arise from surveys that are intended for pan-European implementation, as commonly used phrases may not translate well into different cultures.

Ambiguity can lead to misunderstandings and thus poor or inaccurate responses. A question such as 'Do you buy this product frequently, sometimes, seldom or never?' seems to be clear and unambiguous, but think about it for a minute. What does 'frequently' mean? To one respondent it might mean weekly, to another it might mean monthly. Researchers should therefore be as specific as possible.

A further source of ambiguity or confusion occurs when the respondent is asked to cope with too many concepts at once. Two questions should therefore never be *piggy backed*, i.e. asked in one question, such as: 'How important is price to you, and how do you think we could improve on value for money?'

Leading questions may tempt the respondent to favour a particular answer. This is not, of course, the essence of good research. Thus asking 'Are you, or are you not, in favour of capital punishment?' is more balanced than 'Are you in favour of capital punishment?', which is edging the respondent towards 'Yes' as an answer. Even the

Likert scale

	Strongly agree	Agree	Neither agree nor disagree	Disagree	Strongly disagree
Safeway's prices are generally lower than those of other supermarkets					
Safeway's offers the widest range of groceries					
Safeway's staff are always friendly and helpful					
I never have to queue too long at the checkout					
Supermarket own brands are just as good as manufacturers' brands					
Low prices are important to me in choosing a supermarket					
Supermarkets should provide more personal services					

Semantic differential scale

	1	2	3	4	5	6	7	
Modern								Old-fashioned
Friendly								Unfriendly
Attractive								Unattractive
Spacious								Crowded
High quality goods								Low quality goods
Wide choice of goods								Limited choice of goods
Convenient opening hours								Inconvenient opening hours
Tidy								Untidy
Short queues								Long queues
Low prices								High prices

FIGURE 6.5

Examples of rating scales

choice of one word in a question may be seen as leading. 'Should the UK stay in the EU or not?' is a very different question from 'Should the UK leave the EU or not', because each question triggers different associations and emotions.

Questions that are *too closed* are a kind of leading question that may also frustrate researchers. 'Is price an important factor in your purchase?' begs the answer 'Yes', but even if it was a balanced question, the responses tell very little. It does not indicate how important price is to the respondent or what other factors influence the purchase. An open-ended or multiple-choice question might tell much more.

Researchers need to be sympathetic to people's *sensitivity*. Some areas are highly personal, so building up slowly may be important and 'soft' rather than 'hard' words should be used, for example 'financial difficulties' rather than 'debt'. Of course, the more sensitive the information, the more likely the respondent is to refuse to answer, lie or even terminate the interview.

Coding and rules. It is more important to obtain accurate and pertinent information than to design a questionnaire that embraces everything but rarely gets completed. Hague (1992) proposes an *ideal length* for three different types of questionnaire:

- telephone interviews: 5 to 30 minutes
- visit interviews: 30 minutes to two hours
- self-completion: four sides of A4, 20–30 questions.

A street interview would need to be very much shorter than 30 minutes to retain interest and prevent irritation.

The *layout* of the questionnaire is especially important for self-administered questionnaires. A cramped page looks unappealing, as well as making it difficult to respond. Where an interviewer is in control of the questionnaire, the layout should assist the recording and coding of responses and ease of flow through the interview to maintain momentum. Most questionnaires are now designed with *data coding* and ease of analysis in mind. This means that all responses to closed questions and multiple choices need to be categorised before the questionnaire is released, and that the layout must also be user friendly for whoever has to transfer the data from the completed questionnaire into a database.

The *order of the questions* is important for respondents, as the more confusing the flow and the more jumping around they have to do, the less likely they are to see it through to completion. Similarly, to assist the interviewer, the more routing and skipping that are built into the questionnaire, the easier it is to administer.

Support materials and explanation can be very important. For a mail survey a covering letter can be reassuring and persuasive while, at an interview, the interviewer needs to gain the respondent's attention and interest in participation. Visual aids, such as packaging or stills from advertising, can also get respondents more involved, as well as prompting their memories.

Piloting

Whatever care has been taken in the design of the questionnaire, problems usually emerge as soon as the questionnaire is tried on innocent respondents. Piloting a questionnaire on a small-scale sample can help to iron out any 'bugs', so that it can be refined before the full survey goes ahead. Initially, a fresh eye from colleagues can eliminate the worst howlers, but for most projects, it is best to set aside time for a full field pilot. This would mean testing the questionnaire on a small sub-sample (who will usually not then participate in the main survey) to check its meaning, layout and structure and, furthermore, to check whether it yields the required data and whether it can be analysed in the intended manner.

Conduct the research

Once the research plan has been developed and the methods of collection and proposed analysis identified, it is necessary to go about conducting the research itself.

Careful market research is an important ingredient in launching new fmcg products.

Source: St Ivel Chilled Products.

This stage will vary according to the type of research. The demands of a consumer survey involving perhaps thousands of respondents over a wide geographic area are very different from those of a select number of interviews in depth.

Particularly in primary research, it is this part of the process that often presents the biggest problem, because the collection of the data should not be left to poorly trained or badly briefed field researchers. Using people who do not recognise the importance of their role may cause them to take less care, allow bias to be introduced into the process or, at the extreme, to cheat in some way so that they can ostensibly fulfil their obligations, but with the minimum effort and with no regard for truth or accuracy.

During the development of the research plan those involved, who are usually well qualified and trained, are at pains to ensure the accuracy of data collection, realising that important decisions may be made on the results. They are therefore very careful in what they do and how they go about structuring the research. On the other hand, those who will be responsible for actually collecting the data, field workers, interviewers and even their supervisors are more removed from the design and development process and less aware of the implications of data quality (or lack of it). Furthermore, they may not be adequately prepared in terms of training (poor interviewing skills or data-recording techniques), they may not be motivated (often being poorly paid and employed on a part-time basis) or they may not be appropriately or adequately supervised (such as when conducting research over a wide geographic area). Each of these shortfalls has the potential to distort the results of the research itself. It must be said, however, that the research industry is well aware of these problems and has developed quality control standards, especially with regard to interviews and contact with the general public, with which reputable suppliers of marketing research comply.

Example Recruiting market research interviewers is not an easy job. Staff have to be prepared to work afternoons and evenings to make sure that they get representative samples of all kinds of workers. They also have to be well organised and good at managing themselves and their time, especially if they are working out in the field rather than in a telephone interview call centre, for example. All researchers need a strong sense of responsibility and have to be prepared to take an ethical approach to what they do. Field researchers have to be tough, to cope with less co-operative interviewees or to deal with the stranger kinds of people one meets when spending a lot of time hanging around city streets with a clipboard.

Research companies take a great deal of care in recruiting and training researchers. Some companies undertake lengthy initial telephone screening, partly to give applicants a better idea of what the job entails and partly to help develop a profile of the candidate. Many companies then insist on a face-to-face interview to check a candidate's appearance (especially for field researchers), their interaction skills and their ability to deal with situations. This is important because staff are effectively representing the research company and its clients and they have to be able to develop a rapport with interviewees quickly, reassure them and hold their attention, often through a fairly long and detailed survey.

Research company Gallup maintains that only 1 out of 16 candidates makes it through its selection procedures, a clear indication that the company sees the quality of its staff as an important asset. Those recruiting interviewers for telephone research call centres are less concerned about the appearance of their staff but more concerned about their telephone voice and ability to establish rapport without the face-to-face contact. Some companies even recruit people with certain regional accents to help this process (Gander, 1998).

There are a number of areas, in any kind of face-to-face research, where careful attention to detail can pay dividends. The prime purpose of the interviewer is to deliver the questions in an orderly, structured and accurate manner, where appropriate asking secondary questions, and finally accurately recording the responses of the respondent in line with the measurement instruments selected. The greater the need for the interviewer to depart from a carefully prepared script and *modus operandi*, the greater the skill involved and the higher the cost of the interview. This is particularly emphasised in the implementation role of the interviewer who conducts a group discussion or an in-depth interview. The dangers of interview bias are always present where the interviewer records what they think has been said or meant, not what has actually been said in response to a question. This sort of bias can be particularly pronounced where open-ended questions are being used.

The whole area of data collection can be particularly difficult for a new business that does not have the resources to employ field researchers. It is bad enough that the entrepreneur has to design the research, perhaps as part of a feasibility study, without having to find the time and develop the expertise to carry it out accurately.

New technology is making a big impact in the implementation of field research by assisting in the questioning and recording process. Computer-aided telephone interviewing (**CATI**) and computer-aided personal interviewing (**CAPI**) mean that interviewers using laptop computers and modems can download questions from the central system and then quickly return completed data by the same route. By entering data as the interview is being conducted and using the screen to move between questions, the interviewer can achieve marked improvements in efficiency, recording accuracy and control of the process.

MARKETING AND IT ## CATI: computer-aided telephone interviewing

Two days before the Swedish general election in September 1998, the Prime Minister, Göran Persson, remained narrowly ahead of the opposition leader, Carl Bildt, in the popularity stakes. A telephone survey undertaken by research company SIFO found that 37 per cent of Swedes preferred Persson's ruling Social Democrats, while only 25 per cent opted for Bildt's conservative Moderate Party. This was in sharp contrast to the previous year, when Bildt was riding high as he returned to Swedish politics after two years as an independent peace mediator in Bosnia. In 1998, however, neither the Social Democrats nor the Moderate Party was predicted to win a majority in the election and they would have to scramble for the support of five smaller parties, according to SIFO.

SIFO's telephone poll was conducted using CATI, a technique originating in the US in the 1960s that has become technologically advanced and commonplace in survey companies. CATI is, however, capital intensive and some market research companies have set up subsidiaries specialising in the technique. MORI's On-Line Telephone Surveys, for example, was established in 1988 and is one of the largest CATI specialists in the UK with 80 interviewer stations. In Sweden, which boasts the highest proportion of telephone-based surveying in Europe, SIFO's 700 part-time interviewers and 200 CATI stations make it the largest and most sophisticated CATI specialist in the country.

Source: O'Connor and Galvin (1999).

Analyse and interpret the information

While the quality of the research data is essential, it is the analysis of the data, i.e. turning raw data into useful information, that provides the most value to the organisation. It is on the basis of the reports prepared from the data analysis that significant managerial decisions are likely to be made. Few surveys are undertaken without a detailed consideration of how to code, enter and classify the data generated. The use of sophisticated computer hardware and software packages provides a powerful means of processing large quantities of data relatively easily. CAPI, CATI, scanners that can read completed questionnaires, complex statistical analysis and data manipulation have improved the speed, accuracy and depth of the analysis itself. However, it is still the human element, the researcher's expertise in identifying a trend or relationship or some other nugget hidden within the results, that provides the key component for decision makers and transforms the data and techniques used into valuable information.

Researchers need to be conversant with such statistical techniques as correlation analysis, regression analysis, multivariate analysis, factor analysis, cluster analysis and the repertoire of significance tests. These techniques fall into either the descriptive category or relational, ranging from simple cross-tabulations through to highly sophisticated multivariate analysis.

Some care needs to be exercised in the interpretation of quantitative data. Outputs of calculations should never overrule sound common sense in assessing the significance and relevance of the data generated. There is sometimes the danger of analysis paralysis, where the use of highly sophisticated techniques almost becomes an end in itself, rather than simply a means of identifying new relationships and providing significant new insights for management. While the old saying that trends, differences or relationships are only meaningful if they are obvious to even the untrained statistical eye may be going too far, it does highlight the danger of misinterpreting cause and effect and the differences between groups of consumers, arising from over-reliance on finely balanced statistics pursued by researchers.

Not all data are quantitative, of course. Qualitative data arising from in-depth interviews or group discussions pose a different kind of challenge to researchers. Whereas quantitative data have to prove their reliability when compared with the wider population, qualitative data can never be claimed to be representative of what a wider sample of respondents might indicate. The main task of qualitative data, therefore, is to present attitudes, feelings and motivations in some depth, whether or not they are representative of the wider population.

To handle qualitative data analysis, great care must be taken in the recording of information. Video or taped interviews are thus helpful in enabling classification and categorisation of the main points to be checked and explored in depth. Similarly, issue or content analysis enables particular themes to be explored across a range of interviews. For example, if researchers wanted to identify the barriers to exporting in small firms, they might define such themes as market entry, market knowledge, finance or using agents as indicative of the main barriers to be assessed. The data

---

MARKETING IN ACTION   **Statistics: as simple as ABC**

Marketers who want to buy advertising space in newspapers and magazines are clearly going to be interested in how many people buy or have access to any particular publication and who they are. Counting readers is not, however, a simple task. The Audit Bureau of Circulation (ABC) is responsible for collating and publishing circulation data from publishers and also sets the rules for how circulation should be measured and over what period. Its complex rules for reporting circulation have had to take into account anything that might distort the underlying circulation figures, such as subscriptions, vouchers for free issues, a strike at the printer's or money-off promotions. Bulk sales are also difficult to account for. If a publisher sells 100 copies of a magazine to an airline that then leaves a copy in each of its aircraft for a month, how many people read it?

In January 1999, ABC tightened the way in which it reports circulation figures for newspapers and magazines so that the statistics show what percentage of the circulation is not paid for, i.e. given away free. The impact of the promotional tactics used by supermarkets on the figures is, however, causing concern to ABC. If, for example, a supermarket offers three magazines for the price of two as a special offer, then the consumer is not paying for one of them. If the supermarket pays the full price of that 'free' magazine to the publisher, however, then neither the publisher nor ABC will know that it was free to the consumer and it will show as 'paid for' in the ABC statistics. The distinction between 'paid for' and 'not paid for' publications could be important data to an advertiser. In the past, a publisher might have given away free copies of a magazine to boost circulation and to make it look more attractive to advertisers, thereby increasing the value of the advertising space. Advertisers might also be more interested in the regular purchaser who pays for the magazine and who is likely to spend time reading it. The one-off customer who buys it because it is on special offer might be less likely to read it in detail, and the customer who gets it free might not read it at all!

Sources: Day (1998); Wilkinson (1998a).

analysis might be supported by a range of quotations from the interviews. Because of the richness and complexity of this kind of data, skilled psychologists are often used to explore and explain much of what is said and, indeed, not said.

So although the risks of bias are great in qualitative analysis, both in data selection and analysis, and although the results can, in untrained hands, be rather subjective and conjectural, the advantage arises from the fresh insights and perspectives that more rigorous statistical techniques would simply not generate.

Prepare and present report

The information provided by researchers must be in a form that is useful to decision makers. Too often, research reports are written in highly technical language or research jargon that, to a layperson, is confusing or meaningless. Marketers who want to use these reports to make decisions need them to be easily understandable. A report that is too complex is all but useless. The language and the use of visual aids, such as graphs and charts, become critical elements in the presentation and interpretation of research reports. Various software packages, such as Microsoft's Powerpoint, greatly assist presentation through incorporating graphs, pie charts, histograms and other illustrations, in full colour. All of this helps the marketing decision maker to under-stand the main points of the research findings. That is why the formal presentation of the report, whether written or verbal (which allows the client to ask questions and seek clarification of points made), should be given as much thought, care and atten-tion as any previous stage in the research process.

Although a verbal presentation can play an important part in sharing understand-ing, it is the report itself that has the power to influence thinking significantly. Arguments can be carefully presented, with data used appropriately in their support, and the detail surrounding the main findings can be displayed to increase the client's confidence that the research was well executed to plan. There are no standard report formats, as much will depend on the nature of the research task undertaken.

The main areas covered, which closely follow the issues discussed in this section, are summarised in Table 6.5.

TABLE 6.5
The report

Title page	Contains, for example, report title; client; research company; date
Contents	Shows clearly the structure and content of the report and where in the report to find it
Preface	Sets the background to the report defining the marketing problem; summarises the researchers' interpretation of the original brief
Executive summary	Summarises the main points of the report, including conclusions and recommendations
Research methods	Explains how the research was done and why, with respect to the objectives of the research
Findings	Presents and collates the data collected
Conclusions	Interprets the data; draws out the key points
Recommendations	Identifies action and priorities arising from the conclusions and examines their implications
Appendices	Contain the fine detail that is not needed for the main body of the report or that would clutter up the report too much, e.g. a copy of a questionnaire, raw data or peripheral background information

Research evaluation

Research projects rarely go completely to plan. Although greater care in conducting pilot studies and exploratory research will make it more likely that the actual outcomes will match those planned, problems may still emerge that will require careful consideration in weighing up the value of the project. Thoughtful analysis of the planning, conduct and outcomes of the project will also teach valuable lessons for the future to both clients and researchers.

This stage can involve a review of all aspects of the research plan described above. Any deviations need to be understood, both in terms of the current results and for designing future research. With regard to the research project undertaken, the most important point is whether the research actually provided a sufficient quality and quantity of information to assist management decision making. Sometimes, the research objectives may have been ambiguous or poorly framed in the context of the marketing problem being addressed. Ultimately, it is the marketing manager who must take responsibility for ensuring that the objectives and research plan were compatible and reflected the requirements, although researchers can help in this task.

> **Example** Perhaps the ultimate test for the value of the research is what action or decisions were made as a result of it. A small manufacturer of made-to-order fabricated metal cabinets had seen sales and profitability decline over several years. Market research identified changes in customer buying preferences away from the specifications offered by the firm, and profiled a more competitive climate, caused by new entrants. This study led to a fundamental rethink of the quality of the products being offered and the need to open up new markets.

Far too often, research is undertaken but the findings are only partially accepted, or at worst ignored, as not conforming to preconceived notions and prejudices. Although poorly designed and executed research is best ignored, and researchers have the responsibility for presenting the findings of the research accurately and persuasively, the true value of the project lies in the extent to which it offers added power to the manager for making better decisions. This kind of evaluation helps the client to understand better when research was a 'good buy' or a 'bad buy' and how to improve things next time around.

ETHICS IN MARKETING RESEARCH

The ethical concerns surrounding market research have been the subject of an ongoing debate in the industry for a long time. Because much consumer research involves specific groups of consumers, including children and other groups that might be considered vulnerable, it is essential that the researchers' credibility is maintained and that the highest standards of professional practice are demonstrated. This is vital if researchers are to maintain the confidence of their clients, as well as that of the general public and the government, and so the industry has established a set of professional ethical guidelines. Members are expected to comply with these guidelines, although there is still some debate about their interpretation. The market research guidelines include such matters as protecting the confidentiality of respondents or clients, not distorting or misrepresenting research findings (for example, two major newspapers could both claim to be the market leader by using readership figures gathered over different time spans and failing to mention the time period), using tricks to gain information from respondents, conducting an experiment and not telling those being studied, and using research as a guise for selling and sales lead building.

The European Society for Opinion and Marketing Research (ESOMAR), a leading marketing research association, is actively trying to encourage members to stamp out the practice of 'sugging' (selling under the guise of market research) through an agreed code of practice.

There is a conflict of interest between selling and research. Selling requires clear, persuasive communication outwards from the organisation, while research needs to preserve neutrality if the respondent is to open up fully. Research can certainly inform the selling process, helping the marketer to make better, more effective decisions, but if the two become confused or merged with each other then neither functions particularly well. For example, a new small business entrepreneur organised interviews with potential customers for 'market research purposes'. However, although the session began with a face-to-face in-depth interview based around a questionnaire, the respondent started to 'freeze' half way through, as the 'researcher' started to enthuse about the benefits of the new manufacturing service planned. That respondent would not take kindly to being manipulated into listening to a sales pitch when he thought that he was doing a new business a favour by participating in research. Any goodwill (or potential sales) will almost certainly have been destroyed.

Codes of conduct are therefore especially useful in influencing the behaviour of the more responsible organisations within the industry. Within the UK, the Market Research Society has an extensive code of conduct covering such areas as professional ethics, sampling conditions and practice and the presentation of findings. ESOMAR has developed a similar, internationally based code of practice to augment local specifications.

BMRA, the British Market Research Association, is a trade association representing the interests of market research companies and helping to regulate them. It requries its members to subscribe to a code of conduct and insists that its larger members are accredited by the Market Research Quality Standards Association (BMRA, 1998). Of course, not all providers of market research are committed to compliance and not all bad practice can be eliminated, but considerable progress is being made across Europe.

CHAPTER SUMMARY

Marketing managers find it impossible to make decisions effectively without a constant flow of information on every aspect of marketing. Everything, from defining target markets to developing marketing mixes to making long-term strategic plans, has to be supported with appropriate information. The key question, however, is whether the organisation recognises the worth of the information it has, and whether it is prepared to use information intelligently to make decisions, rather than putting more value on its own prejudices about how the market works.

The organisation needs to co-ordinate its information, collected from a variety of sources, including primary research, into an MIS. A formal MIS brings everything together under one umbrella and provides timely and comprehensive information to aid managers in decision making. DSS build on the MIS, also to help decision making. The DSS uses a variety of computer tools and packages to allow a manager to manipulate information, to explore possible outcomes of courses of action and to experiment in a risk-free environment.

There are three different types of market research, exploratory, descriptive and causal, each one serving different purposes. Depending on the nature of the problem under investigation, any of the three types of market research may use qualitative or quantitative data. Rather than individually pursuing a series of marketing research studies, an organisation can participate in *continuous research*, undertaken by a market research agency on an ongoing basis and usually syndicated.

There is a general framework for the conduct of a marketing research project that can be applied to almost any kind of market or situation. It consists of eight stages: problem definition, research objectives, planning the research, data collection, research implementation, data analysis, reporting findings and research evaluation.

Secondary research provides a means of sourcing marketing information that already exists in some form, whether internal or external to the organisation. Secondary data can be used to paint an overall background picture to a more specific marketing problem or to help to focus primary research objectives. Secondary data can be very wide ranging and can provide much depth, but the organisation needs to be sure of how and why the data were originally collected and that the data are relevant and up to date before relying on them totally. The data may thus need to be re-analysed or worked over before they can be used with confidence.

Gaps in secondary data can be filled through *primary research*. The main methods of primary research are interviews and surveys, observation and experiments. Surveys may take place through face-to-face interviews, by telephone or by mail. Group interviews or focus groups allow interviewers to explore issues with several people at once. The group interaction often adds another interesting dimension to the research, with members debating with each other and generating ideas from each other. Observational research can be used to collect information about how people react to products and how they use them. Experimentation can also be used, although it is orientated more towards causal research allowing, for example, researchers to test whether manipulating one marketing mix variable will have a significant effect on sales. Experiments may take place under artificial laboratory conditions or they may take place in the field.

Sampling is a crucial area for successful market research. There is no need to survey an entire population in order to find answers to questions. As long as a representative sample is drawn, answers can be generalised to apply to the whole population. There are five important areas connected with sampling: population definition, drawing up the sampling frame, defining the sampling unit, the sampling method and the sample size.

Questionnaires are often used as a means of collecting data from the sample selected, but they need to be carefully designed with a number of issues in mind. They must reflect the purpose of the research, collect the appropriate data, whether those are factual classification data or opinion-based data, accurately and efficiently, and facilitate the analysis of data. Inherent in all that are the needs to minimise errors and bias and to encourage full and accurate responses.

Key words and phrases

CAPI (computer-aided personal interviewing)	Focus groups	Quantitative research
	Marketing research	Rating scales
CATI (computer-aided telephone interviewing)	MIS (marketing information system)	Sampling process
		Secondary research
Closed questions	Open-ended questions	Semi-structured interview
Continuous research	Primary research	Structured interview
DSS (decision support system)	Qualitative research	Unstructured interview

QUESTIONS FOR REVIEW

6.1 Why is *market research* an essential tool for the marketing manager?

6.2 What is the difference between *primary* and *secondary* research?

6.3 What kinds of marketing problems might be addressed through:
(a) *exploratory*;
(b) *descriptive*; and
(c) *causal* research projects?

6.4 Differentiate between *qualitative* and *quantitative* research, highlighting their relative advantages and disadvantages.

6.5 What are the *criteria for evaluating secondary sources* and why are they important?

6.6 What is *observational research* and in what circumstances might it be more appropriate than interviews or surveys?

6.7 What are the main stages in the *sampling process* and what does each involve?

6.8 How does *quota sampling* work and what are its advantages?

6.9 Define the stages of the *market research process* and outline what each one involves.

6.10 Discuss the role and content of an *MIS* and how it might relate to a *DSS*.

QUESTIONS FOR DISCUSSION

6.1 Without looking back at pp. 226–8, how many *sources of secondary data* can you list? Check your list against pp. 226–8 and then investigate what your library has to offer.

6.2 Evaluate the appropriateness of each of the different *interview and survey-based primary research methods* for:

(a) investigating the buying criteria used by organisational purchasers;
(b) defining the attitudes of a target market towards a brand of breakfast cereal;
(c) profiling purchasers of small electrical goods; and
(d) measuring levels of post-purchase satisfaction among customers.

Clearly define any assumptions you make about each of the situations.

6.3 Design a questionnaire. It should contain about 20 questions and you should use as many of the different types of question as possible. Pay particular attention to the concerns discussed at pp. 239–44 of the chapter. The objective is to investigate respondents' attitudes to music CDs and their purchasing habits. Pilot your questionnaire on 12 to 15 people (but preferably not people on the same course as you), analyse the results and then make any adjustments. Within your seminar group, be prepared to discuss the rationale behind your questionnaire, the outcome of the pilot and any data-analysis problems.

6.4 Why is an ethical approach to marketing research important and what are the main areas of concern?

6.5 Why is a sound *research brief* important, what should it contain and how does it influence each of the subsequent stages in the process?

CASE STUDY 6.1

Kings Hotel

As a rough guide, assume that £1 = 25 Polish zloty (zl) approximately.

The Kings Hotel is situated on the inner ring-road, some ten minutes walk from the historic centre of the Polish city of Kraków. It is near the Wavel castle, the ancient Polish Royal Palace which is a major tourist attraction. The Kings Hotel is the second oldest hotel in Kraków and up to now little has been spent on improvement. The hotel is split into four operating units.

1 A three-star hotel (the front part), with 72 beds. The price of a double room is 1200 zl per night, and that price remains the same all year.
2 A two-star hotel (the rear part), with a mix of bedrooms sleeping up to four per room, and a total capacity of 78. The price is 600 zl per night for a double room, and again the price is constant all year round.

As a comparison, prices at the nearby Hotel Majestic, one of the best in Kraków, are 1455 zl in low season and 2190 zl in high season.

3 A disco bar with a street entrance. This is rented out privately, but infrequently.

4 A restaurant at the front of the hotel at ground floor level, primarily serving hotel guests.

The hotel management has avoided tour bookings wherever possible. It did deal with the Polish airline LOT a few years ago for block bookings, but found that more profitable business from independent travellers had reached a sufficient level to reduce the need for such trade. Prices are already comparatively low, and no discounts are offered to private individuals or groups. Most of the customers in the summer season are tourists and outside that period they tend to be business travellers, especially visiting university staff and local government officers.

Little promotion is undertaken, but a multi-language brochure has been designed. Good relations are maintained with the Kraków tourist office, which finds accommodation for travellers, and the hotel advertises in tourist board publications. The hotel also advertises on a poster site at the local airport. The real concern is that most other hotels have already been modernised to achieve Western European standards. An independent traveller had found the Kings Hotel room plain and a little shabby, but spacious and clean. It did have a television and an en-suite bathroom with a shower, but no drinking water. The hotel itself looked somewhat 'tired' and lacked extra facilities, such as room service, porters and direct dial international telephone facilities. To receive breakfast, the guest had to get a voucher from reception and then walk out of the hotel, round the corner into the hotel's restaurant.

The manager thus decided that some development would be necessary if the hotel was going to meet the needs of the independent traveller better. He hoped that a questionnaire for independent guests would provide a valuable insight into the type of customers visiting the hotel and the sort of facilities they would like to see.

The manager asked his two children, who were students on a tourism management course, to prepare a questionnaire that could be given to guests as they arrived at the hotel. The questionnaire would be given to them as they checked in, along with a letter explaining the purpose of the exercise. A box would be provided at reception for completed questionnaires. He briefed his children on the type of information required and suggested that they should have a summary report of the data analysis and information ready in two months' time. This would give him some ideas before the start of the summer season in four months' time.

The questionnaire was as follows:

QUESTIONNAIRE

1 Are you male or female?

2 How old are you ___ years ___ months

3 How did you travel to the Hotel?

Car   ____

Airline   ____

Train   ____

Coach/bus   ____

Other   ____

4 How long do you normally stay in a hotel?

1 week   ____

2 week   ____

More than 2 weeks   ____

5 Have you been to this Hotel before?

6 If you had to choose between the following, which do you think are the most important for the hotel to provide?

A larger car park ___, bath in every room ___, computerised booking ___, shop ___, bar ___, an automatic telephone system ___, don't know ___

Thank you for helping with this questionnaire, which when completed should be put in the box at the reception desk.

Source: Adapted from a case prepared by Pat Badmin.

Questions

1 To what extent and why do you feel that the research method employed is appropriate for gathering the information needed?

2 Criticise the questionnaire outlined in the case in terms of the choice of questions, their wording and their response mechanism.

3 What marketing problem is this research trying to help solve? What information do you think the hotel manager would actually need in order to investigate this problem?

4 Design your own questionnaire of up to 20 questions to address the manager's problem. Explain your choice of questions and the response mechanism, and discuss when and how you would undertake the survey.

CASE STUDY 6.2

Gathering information on an up and coming market

The condom market can be viewed as a bit of a laugh, as a bit of an embarrassment, as a moral outrage, or as deadly serious, given the risks of sexually transmitted diseases or unwanted pregnancy. To condom manufacturers, however, it is a commercial business just like any other which must be based, as with any company, on sound marketing information about consumers and their buying behaviour.

Condom purchases vary between planned and impulse buys. An NOP Health Monitor survey found that travelling abroad either for business or pleasure often led to planned purchases before the trip. The report found that 81 per cent of people thought a holiday to be the most likely occasion for casual sex, while in the 48–55 age group, 18 per cent thought a business trip more likely. Although men were the larger group of pre-holiday purchasers, 58 per cent of women expecting a sexual experience on holiday travelled with condoms purchased at home. Such planned purchases are actively encouraged by condom manufacturers, as the customer can be assured of a quality product and a familiar brand by buying at home.

Impulse or reminder purchases represent the second group, where availability is essential for continued sales. The policy of Durex is to suggest to retailers that condoms should be easy to find, self-selected, preferably from special displays, and clearly priced to avoid any interaction with sales staff or at the checkout. This reflects the changes taking place in distribution patterns. Condoms are no longer sold exclusively in pharmacies or barbers' shops, but also in supermarkets as a toiletry alongside razors and shampoos. This exposes the product to both men and women, and encourages customers to treat condoms as a normal part of the regular shopping routine. ASDA believes that women represent the largest purchase group in its stores. A variety of different types of outlet have been targeted to accommodate the change in purchase patterns, such as late night grocery stores and vending machines in 'strategic places' such as discos, pubs and student social facilities. New outlets such as off-licences and record shops began putting condoms on self-service display, while 24-hour stores cater for the distress and impulse segment.

Pack sizes tend to be larger in the grocery store, reflecting planned purchases. Despite all these changes, it has been estimated that 30 per cent of consumers still have some reservations about purchasing condoms.

In parallel with changes in distribution patterns, condoms have experienced considerable expansion in the range of products available. In recent years, they have become stronger, more sensitive and more reliable. Variations in strength, size, colour, texture and flavour have all been offered to the market. Products such as Ultra Strong, Extra Safe, Arouser, Safe Play and Fetherlite are all offered by the clear market leader, London International Group (LIG) as variants within the Durex brand family. Durex has 21 per cent of the world market for condoms, and 40 per cent of the European market and over 80 per cent of the UK market by volume. Jiffi represents the other main player in the market with such names as Rainbow (nine colours), Cocktail (four flavours) and Flavours (eight fragrances). Mates, launched in 1987 and now owned by Ansell International, is another key player in the UK market.

Government health campaign advertising has worked well for the manufacturers in creating generic demand for the product. In 1984, only 31 per cent of males and 35 per cent of females said that they would use a condom the first time they had sex with someone, but by the early 1990s, this had increased to 69 per cent of men and 78 per cent of women. It has also made it easier for manufacturers to advertise directly and more explicitly, although they still have to be careful not to offend people too much or else they will not listen to the message.

Nevertheless, developing new products in this market and getting the approach right is not always easy. Durex claims that it bases its product development on in-depth research into people's sexual habits and attitudes, developing brands to meet different consumer needs and preferences. Durex failed, however, with a new brand called Assure, targeted at young women. It was packaged in a pastel coloured unbranded box, to keep in a handbag. The target market turned out to be confident enough to buy the brand that suited them best, regardless of the discretion, or lack of it, in the packaging design. One brand that is well targeted is Jiffi, targeted at the 16 to 24 year-old group. Jiffi treats condoms as a necessity that can be fun, fashionable, flavoured, and brightly coloured. This is reflected in its branded T-shirts and boxer shorts flaunting slogans such as 'Real Men Come in a Jiffi' and 'Where All the Big Knobs Hang Out'. In contrast to this, Mates focuses on size, supporting its range of different sized condoms with a 'size does matter' advertising campaign. The company claims that a pilot study indicated that men can tell the difference between shapes and sizes and that choosing the right condom makes a difference.

Sources: Bray (1997); Cheary (1997); Kelly (1996); Lane Fox (1995).

Questions

1 Briefly outline the types of market research information that might be useful to a condom manufacturer.

2 What are the problems of undertaking primary consumer research for a product like this? How can these problems be overcome?

3 Thirty per cent of buyers still have some reservations about purchasing condoms. Suggest a programme of primary research that might tell the manufacturers why this is.

4 To what extent do you think it would be ethical for condom manufacturers to undertake a survey of 14–16 year olds?

References to Chapter 6

Boyd, H. W. *et al.* (1977), *Marketing Research*, 4th edn., Irwin.

BMRA (1998), 'BMRA – What Does BMRA Stand For?', advertisement in *Marketing Week*, 25 June, p. 50.

Bray, L. (1997), 'Focus on Condoms', *The Grocer*, 15 February, pp. 49–50.

Brennan, M. *et al.* (1991), 'The Effects of Monetary Incentives on the Response Rate and Cost Effectiveness of a Mail Survey', *Journal of the Market Research Society*, 33(3), pp. 229–41.

Campbell, L. (1998), 'Teletext Tool to Boost Research', *Marketing*, 29 October, p. 14.

Cheary, N. (1997), 'The Long and Short of It', *Marketing Week*, 16 October, pp. 39–43.

Chisnall, P. M. (1986), *Marketing Research*, 3rd edn., McGraw-Hill.

Cramp, B. (1994), 'Industrious Espionage', *Marketing*, 18 August, pp. 17–18.

Curtis, J. (1998), 'Keeping Up with the Jones's', *Marketing*, 19 November, pp. 28–9.

Day, J. (1998), 'Asda Takes on the News Trade Giants', *Marketing Week*, 25 June, pp. 14–15.

Denny, N. (1998), 'Listening to Your Customer is Vital', *Marketing*, 19 November, p. 18.

Gander, P. (1998), 'Just the Job', *Marketing Week*, 25 June, pp. 51–4.

Gofton, K. (1994), 'Moving in on More Markets', *Marketing*, 10 March, pp. 26–9.

The Grocer (1998a), 'Spar Missing Out on Stella', *The Grocer*, 3 October, p. 59.

The Grocer (1998b), 'Sharwood's Praised for Tailored Approach to US', *The Grocer*, 19 December, p. 8.

Haggett, S. and Mitchell, V. W. (1994), 'Effect of Industrial Prenotification on Response Rate, Speed, Quality, Bias and Cost', *Industrial Marketing Management*, 23(2), pp. 101–10.

Hague, P. (1992), *The Industrial Market Research Handbook*, 3rd edn., Kogan Page.

Harris, J. (1998), 'Footfall Focus', *The Grocer*, 28 February, pp. 39–40.

Kelly, J. (1996), 'Something for the Weekend', *The Grocer*, 27 January, pp. 43–5.

Lane Fox, H. (1995), 'Durex Stretches its Brief', *Marketing*, 10 August , p. 14.

MacDonald, R. (1998), 'Football Scores in Youth Sector', letter published in *Marketing Week*, 29 January, p. 39.

Mackenzie, S. (1998), 'Boundary Commission', *Marketing Week*, 29 January, pp. 57–60.

Mazur, L. (1998), 'Failing the Euro Test', *Marketing*, 3 December, pp. 26–7.

McDaniel, C. and Gates, R. (1996), *Contemporary Marketing Research*, 3rd edn, West.

McDaniel, S. *et al.* (1985), 'The Threats to Marketing Research: an Empirical Reappraisal', *Journal of Marketing Research*, 22 (February), pp. 74–80.

Miles, L. (1998), 'Combined Strengths', *Marketing*, 3 December, p. 33.

O'Connor, J. and Galvin, E. (1999), *Marketing and Information Technology*, 2nd edn, Financial Times Pitman Publishing.

Qureshi, B. and Baker, J. (1998), 'Category Management and Efficient Consumer Response: the Role of Market Research', *Marketing and Research Today*, 26 (1), pp. 23–31.

Reed, D. (1998), 'Categorical Truths', *Marketing Week*, 25 June, pp. 45–9.

Rijkens, R. (1992), *European Advertising Strategies: The Profiles and Policies of Multinational Companies Operating in Europe*, Cassell.

Tull, D. S. and Hawkins, D. T. (1990), *Marketing Research: Measurement and Method*, MacMillan.

Wilkinson, A. (1998a), 'ABC Rules to Curb Paper Price Wars', *Marketing Week*, 29 January, pp. 16–17.

Wilkinson, A. (1998b), 'In the Name of Sport', *Marketing Week*, 25 June, pp. 34–7.

Zikmund, W. G. and D'Amico, M. (1993), *Marketing*, West.

Continental Microwave Ltd.

Interview with
Ian Aizlewood, Managing Director

Continental Microwave Ltd. (CML) is a medium sized manufacturer of communications equipment, for both fixed and mobile links, for broadcasting, telecommunications, PTT and other communications applications world-wide. Its customers range from the BBC, CNN and other national broadcasters, to UK and US defence departments. We last spoke to Ian Aizlewood, CML's Managing Director, three years ago when he emphasised the importance of lasting buyer-seller relationships and the difficulties of selling what is effectively capital equipment in a technologically dynamic global market with relatively few potential customers. Since 1996, sales have grown and CML now has more digital television transmitters in operation in the world than any other company. It is still an overall growth market that is not yet mature. Digital television, for instance, means more channels, more choices and more broadcasting especially in sport which requires outside broadcasting equipment, of course. In our most recent meeting, therefore, we first asked Ian how CML's markets and marketing strategies had developed since then.

In 1996, Ian had commented that there was a lot of nationalism in purchasing decisions, for instance German customers tended to prefer to buy from German suppliers and French customers from French suppliers. This is still true with France and Germany the best European examples of nationalistic purchasing. CML has moved on in ways of addressing the issue, having decided that it would be a very long-term slog to use standard selling methods using sales representative in those markets. In France, for instance, CML developed an alliance with French electronics giant Thomson. Thomson purchases exclusive CML satellite systems, puts its own branding on them and then resells them in France or beyond if it wishes. Thomson has thus taken a high tech subsystem to build into its projects and CML equipment has effectively become a component. From the customer point of view, CML has persuaded Thomson to resell on its value added competence: projects. If Thomson and CML both offer a mobile system in a van, even if it is the same system, the vehicle will be different and thus the two companies are actually offering two different packages, pleasing more customers between them that way. Through Thomson's patronage, CML is actually achieving significant additional sales. 'We do not deal direct into France any more, yet sales thanks to Thomson, have gone from zero to millions in France, and through into the rest of the world.'

One of the observations that Ian made in 1996 was that German customers often demand local type approvals to discourage non-German suppliers. Germany is slowly changing, but is still using specifications and testing requirements against external suppliers. One technique is to ask for extra tests which are very expensive to do. CML has to consider its priorities – is spending £10 000 on this test

better than spending it on something else? The fundamental mandate is to meet financial targets per trading period from limited resources. So if a better return is expected from, say, the Far East than from Germany, money will not be spent on extra German testing. German specifications should be identical to those in any other EU country but it is hard to complain for fear of being branded a troublemaker. It is important to remember, though, that Germany is not 'Germany': it is a federal state made up of culturally different länder, and local agents are needed. There is competition between the länder and it cannot be treated as 'a nation'. So the options are either a strategic alliance with a major indigenous company or appointing multiple agents, one for each of the strategically important länder.

The question for CML is whether it is enough to stay with an agency solution, or whether an alliance would be better. The company does not feel, however, that it needs Germany at the moment. Germany's political and, more specifically, its slow privatisation evolution inhibits early adoption of new technology such as digital television, for instance. The UK has already adopted it but it may be another 5 to 8 years in Germany because its development needs:

- commercial drive: in the UK there has been OnDigital and BSkyB pioneering the market
- an advanced government that is into privatisation which Germany does not have
- a national body which gets kudos from high tech prestige, e.g. the BBC research.

The overall feeling is that Germany is a more traditional, less price sensitive marketplace in which open tender principles do not apply to the same extent.

As in 1996, non-aligned and Commonwealth countries still provide the major export focus for CML. The EU is significant but business is hard to get. The cost per result is high but CML has cracked most of the EU and gets what it regards as its fair share of business.

CML has also looked at eastern Europe as a whole, but it is a fragmented market and with the collapse of the state infrastructure, there is a new business philosophy. CML has taken on a front line salesman (the others are product or highly technically competent regional managers) who knows the markets and can open doors, generate leads and gather information. CML is also doing something similar in Germany, building market research information. The company had never had to do it before because it always knew its customers, but the market research is helping CML to make a higher than ever market impact.

One market that is orthodox and traditional and thus suits an orthodox and traditional supplier is China, and CML broke into this market with a £1mn order. If the Chinese managers buy the wrong thing, it stays with them because they do not have the job mobility and are held responsible. In buying, they thus probe a supplier's commitment as well as its

EXECUTIVE INTERVIEW continued

product. CML was the third contender for supplying a satellite news system. The first two were not making the right commitments. CML's commitment was demonstrated with a competent first line agent who knows the product and visits customers regularly whether they have problems or not to do some 'positive stroking'. China operates a little like the old USSR – if Moscow bought, they all bought. In China, the regional operators are looking at what systems have been bought in Beijing and tend to buy the same. They are risk averse. The buying decision is not just about specification but also longer term relationships and this is in the manager's own self-interest in a long-term job. Since this first order, regional orders have come in.

In other markets, the buying imperative is somewhat different and the world as a whole is becoming tougher. The things that generate loyalty, i.e. customers treating communications systems as a capital purchase, are different. The telecoms industry, for example, now has a high management staff turnover so purchasers do not really care about the long-term implications of their decisions because they will be long gone by the time it is realised that they made bad choices. It is a similar situation in the broadcasting industry. Professional broadcasters used to operate their own technical teams, testing potential products and insisting on high specifications. They do much less of it now because a lot of major television companies' work is contracted out to freelancers. Many commercial broadcasters too have lost their engineers who now operate as contracted 'facilities' houses competing for business. While long term loyalties do still exist, they are the exception rather than the rule. Thus the market is now more price-driven and customers cannot justify paying a premium for what they see as 'over specification'. It used to be that conservatism was king and customer service important, but the new companies do not think like that. A customer, especially one in the third world, now has to justify not buying the cheapest, although over time when problems begin to arise with cheap systems, this could reverse.

CML cannot compromise on quality because that is the foundation for its reputation but what the company has done is create simplified products that retain the quality integrity. These 'simple yet elegant' products have been value engineered to get their costs down and simplified in non-tech areas (e.g. extraneous functions removed but can be added back if the customer wants them for an extra price). There is a conflict between higher specifications and decreasing prices. Development effort goes into reducing the size and weight and bringing the cost down. One example is CML's new portable microwave link. It's flexible. It does four jobs and although it does not perform any single function better than the old models, it is much more practical in usage. It is two-thirds of the manufacturing cost of the old model and is highly versatile for the customer.

Another area of change is tendering processes. In more organised international tenders, it is a two stage process which is now predominant in major institutions such as ministries, post/telegraph companies and national broadcasters:

1 In the first stage, the tender with its commercial pages removed is submitted to a panel of engineers who are looking at its technical aspects. Does it meet the specifications? Is the system fit for the required purpose? This panel passes equipment 'fit for purpose' and can

only look at the specifications. All tenders are supposedly treated equally and the same questions asked of each tenderer. If one tenderer has a bright idea, the others will be asked if they can do it too. This panel passes through the tenders that meet the specification, say 5 out of 8, to the next stage:

2 a commercial panel which looks at the commercial data and makes a decision based on best price.

Thus the decision-making has been divided between the technical people and the commercial people. In traditional broadcasting organisations, for example, the decision-making used to be down to one or two key people with both technical and commercial knowledge.

CML is effectively selling development projects and works closely with its customers to make sure everything goes as it should. The company uses customer training as a carrot, although it is really a form of relationship building. It gets customers' staff onto CML's premises and allows interaction. The managing director's role in this is largely social in that he endorses what others have said to customers and reassures. The managing director has a major role in the early stages of a relationship, providing a senior presence and getting involved in introductions. For instance in developing business in Nigeria or Algeria, he would visit ministers and other influencers as well as customer companies. Once the contract is won, regional managers take over. The company is conservative in advertising but trade fairs and exhibitions are important. There are two big European shows: Montreux and the International Broadcast Convention in Amsterdam and one major US show, The National Association of Broadcasters. The company maintains a presence at three or four smaller shows for example China, Australia and eastern Europe.

With grateful thanks to Ian Aizlewood, Managing Director of Continental Microwave Ltd.

The ultimate in mobile communications equipment.

Source: Continental Microwave Ltd.

PRODUCT

Chapter 7 poses a very simple question, 'What is a product?', and finds that the answer is somewhat less simple. It is related to what the buyer really wants from the product, whether that consists of practical performance, psychological benefits or both, and the ways in which marketers choose to communicate that through the product via branding, packaging, design and quality.

Following an analysis of this complex anatomy of the product, Chapter 8 can then look critically at more detailed product management issues, such as the product life cycle and its influence on marketing decision making, the importance of developing a balanced portfolio of products and brand management. It also opens the debate about the advantages or otherwise of pan-European branding.

One of the lessons to be learned from the product life-cycle theory is that most products have a finite life span. As a product matures, therefore, decisions have to be made about what to do next. Chapter 8 examines some possibilities, such as relaunching an improved version of the product, while Chapter 9 takes the route of new product development, that is, allowing the product to die and replacing it with something new. The processes and problems of new product development are fully explored.

7 Anatomy of a Product

LEARNING OBJECTIVES

This chapter will help you to:

1 define and classify products and the key terms associated with them;

2 understand the nature, benefits and implementation of branding;

3 appreciate the functional and psychological roles of packaging;

4 understand the broad issues relating to product design and quality and their contribution to marketing.

INTRODUCTION

The product is at the heart of the marketing exchange. If the product does not deliver the benefits the customer wanted or if it does not live up to the expectations created by the other elements of the marketing mix, then the whole exercise has been in vain. Remember that customers buy products to solve problems or to enhance their lives and thus the marketer has to ensure that the product can fully satisfy the customer, not just in functional terms, but also in psychological terms. The product is important, therefore, because it is the ultimate test of whether the organisation has understood its customer's needs.

Example In 1994, German motor manufacturer BMW (http://www.bmw.com) bought the UK's Rover group. By early 1999, however, BMW was having to make some tough decisions about the future of the Rover brand name within its product range, fundamentally re-examining the relationship between Rover and the BMW brand, which is well known for excellence. BMW was happy to keep Rover's world beaters, Land Rover and Mini, as niche brand names, but the problem was with the other loss-making Rover cars. Although the Rover 200 and 400 were the principal models, they failed to make a big impact in the main markets and the Rover 75, the first model introduced with BMW influence, was not launched until 1998. In that year, Rover's sales slumped and they were not helped by delays in launching the new Mini. The long-term hope was that the Rover 75 would become a parallel premium brand for those consumers who did not want a BMW.

The main dilemma was whether BMW should ditch the Rover brand name (http://www.rovercars.com) or persist with its emphasising a tradition of refinement and relaxing motoring in contrast to BMW's 'ultimate driving machine'. Rover's range extended below the cheapest BMWs, so there was a danger that a unified brand name might threaten the prestige and image of BMW that had been developed over many years. However, some managers in BMW wanted to see a Series 2 introduced below the

▶

3 Series anyway, while others feared that this would stretch the core brand values too far and destroy the carefully nurtured marque. Retaining separate brands such as the Rover 75 can, however, be expensive, because it has only a few components or parts in common with the BMW range, thus reducing the opportunities for economies of scale (Lorenz and Woodhead, 1999; Hutton, 1999).

The above example raises a number of interesting questions about what makes a product, the importance of brand image and customer perceptions of it, and the interaction between the product and other elements of the marketing mix. Clearly, marketers have to understand the nature of these questions and base strategic decisions about the development and management of product offerings on the answers. To start the process of thinking about these issues, therefore, this chapter examines some fundamental concepts. The definition of product and ways of classifying products lead to some basic definitions of product ranges. Then, the underlying concepts that give the product its character and essential appeal to the buyer will be examined. These include branding, packaging and labelling, design, style and quality, and the role of peripheral areas such as guarantees in enhancing the product offering. The wider issues of product management and new product development will then be discussed in the following two chapters. The first task for this chapter, meanwhile, is to define the meaning of the term *product*.

MEANING OF A PRODUCT

The product is one half of the exchange that interests marketers (price is the other half; *see* Chapters 10 and 11). A formal definition of product may be that:

> **a product is a physical good, service, idea, person or place that is capable of offering tangible and intangible attributes that individuals or organisations regard as so necessary, worthwhile or satisfying that they are prepared to exchange money, patronage or some other unit of value in order to acquire it.**

A product is, therefore, a powerful and varied thing. The definition includes tangible products (tins of baked beans, aircraft engines), intangible products (services such as hairdressing or management consultancy) and ideas (public health messages, for instance). It even includes trade in people. For example, the creation and hard selling of pop groups and idols are less about music than about the promotion of a personality to which the target audience can relate. Does a Spice Girls fan buy their latest album for its intrinsic musical qualities or because of the Spice Girls name on the sleeve? Politicians too try to sell themselves as people with caring personalities in exchange for your vote at election time. Places are also saleable products. Holiday resorts and capital cities, for example, have long exploited their natural geographic or cultural advantages, building service industries that in some cases become essential to the local economy.

Whatever the product is, whether tangible, intangible or the Spice Girls, it can always be broken down into bundles of benefits that mean different things to different buyers. Figure 7.1 shows the basic anatomy of a product as a series of four concentric rings representing the **core product**, the **tangible product**, the **augmented product** and finally the **potential product.**

The *core product* represents the heart of the product, the main reason for its existence and purchase. The core benefit of any product may be functional or psychological and its definition must provide something for the marketer to work on to develop a differential advantage. Any make of car will get the purchaser from A to B, but add on to that the required benefits of spaciousness, or fuel economy or status

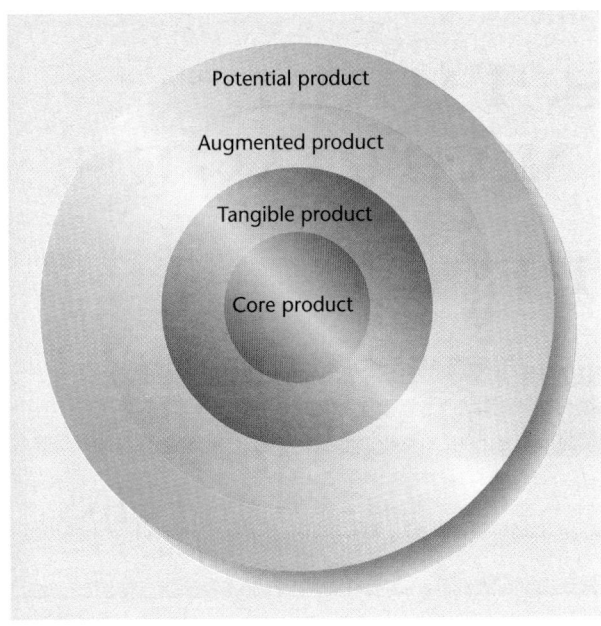

Potential product

Augmented product

Tangible product

Core product

FIGURE 7.1

The anatomy of a product

enhancement, and a definition of a core product to which a market segment will relate begins to emerge. The core benefit of a holiday could be to lie in the sun doing absolutely nothing, being pampered for two weeks, at one end of the spectrum or, at the other end, to escape from the world by seeking adventure and danger in unknown terrain. Although it might be argued that an Club 18–30 holiday could satisfy both those core benefit requirements, generally speaking very different packages will emerge to meet those needs.

The definition of the core benefit is important because it influences the next layer, the *tangible product*. The tangible product is essentially the means by which the marketer puts flesh on the core product, making it a real product that clearly represents and communicates the offer of the core benefit. The tools used to create the product include design specification, product features, quality level, branding and packaging. A car that embodies the core benefit of 'fast and mean status symbol', for example, is likely to have a larger engine, sexy design, leather upholstery, lots of electric gadgets, built-in CD player, definitely be available in black or red metallic paint (among other choices) and certainly carry a marque such as BMW rather than Lada.

The *augmented product* represents add-on extras that do not themselves form an intrinsic element of the product, but may be used by producers or retailers to increase the product's benefits or attractiveness. A computer manufacturer may offer installation, user training and after sales service, for instance, to enhance the attractiveness of the product package. None of this affects the actual computer system itself, but will affect the satisfaction and benefits that the buyer gets from the exchange. Retailers also offer augmented products. An electrical retailer selling national and widely available brands such as Hoover, Zanussi, Indesit or Hotpoint needs to make its own mark on each transaction so that the buyer will want to shop there again in the future. Augmenting the product through extra guarantees, cheap financing, delivery and breakdown insurance is more likely to provide memorable, competitively defendable and relatively inexpensive mechanisms for creating a relationship with the consumer than is price competition.

Finally, the *potential product* layer acknowledges the dynamic and strategic nature of the product. The first three layers have described the product as it is now, but the

Example A long haul flight in cramped economy-class accommodation next to the 'passenger from hell' is everybody's nightmare. Airlines are now working hard to make life a little easier. Current or planned improvements include beds on long haul journeys, more comfortable seat designs, noise cancellation technology and, as a last resort, a 'sleep-enhancer spray' to help passengers nod off. This is because airlines have come to realise that the more experienced traveller is not always prepared to put up with 'cattle-class' travel conditions. Research has shown that it is physical discomfort that puts people off long haul travel rather than lost luggage, jet lag or other negative effects.

Airbus Industrie (http://www.airbus.com) is already offering to fit beds below the passenger cabin, which is increasingly necessary, given that the new generation of aircraft is capable of flying for 15 hours non-stop. Some airlines do not want to wait, however. Singapore Airlines has fitted retractable partitions between the seats at head level for business-class travellers. Swiss Airlines has introduced ergonomically designed seats that adjust themselves automatically to support the passenger's back when reclined. It is the economy-class passengers, however, who will have to wait a little longer to be pampered (Bray, 1998).

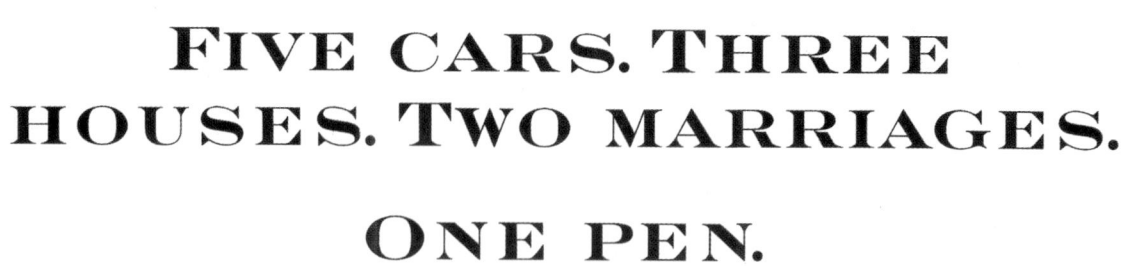

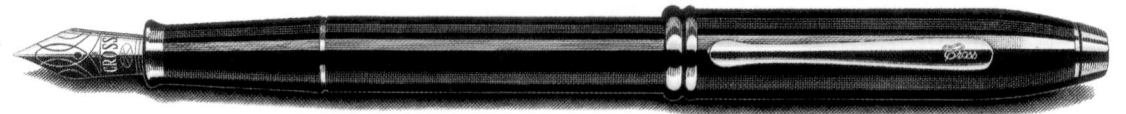

FIVE CARS. THREE HOUSES. TWO MARRIAGES.

ONE PEN.

Guaranteed for a lifetime. Available from jewellers, stationers, pen specialists and leading department stores.

CROSS
SINCE 1846.

marketer also needs to think about what the product could be and should be in the future. The potential product can be defined in terms of its possible evolution, for example new ways of differentiating itself from the competition.

Doyle (1998), however, takes a slightly different view. He considers that the potential product reflects such high levels of added value and differentiation that the product is better protected against competitors and substitutes. Achieving this kind of potential has been one of the foundations of success for such organisations as Marks & Spencer, Kellogg and Levi over many years. Thus Kotler is saying that potential simply reflects what might be done with the product in the future, whereas Doyle is saying that it provides a strategic focus in itself.

In summary, all four layers of product contribute to the buyer's satisfaction, but the outer two depend on the definition of core product to determine how they are realised. The core itself may be functionally based, in terms of what the product is supposed to do, or it may be benefit or promise based, in terms of how this product will make you feel. It is, however, in the outer layers, the tangible and augmented product, that most of the overt marketing competition takes place.

> Durability is a key element in Cross Pens' tangible product
> *Source*: Travis Sully Harari.

PRODUCT CLASSIFICATION

To bring order to a wide and complex area of marketing, it is useful to be able to define groups of products that either have similar characteristics or generate similar buying behaviour within a market. Such classification schemes allow some generalisations to be made about appropriate marketing strategies for each group.

Product-based classification

A product-based classification groups together products that have similar characteristics, although they may serve very different purposes and markets. There are three main categories: **durable products**, **non-durable products** and **service products**.

Durable products
Durable products last for many uses and over a long period before having to be replaced. Products such as domestic electrical goods, cars and capital machinery fall into this group.

Non-durable products

Non-durable products can only be used once or a few times before they have to be replaced. Food and other fmcg goods fall into this category, as do office consumables such as stationery and computer printer cartridges.

Service products

Services represent intangible products comprising activities, benefits or satisfactions that are not embodied in physical products. Items such as financial services, holidays, travel and personal services create problems for marketers, because of their intangibility and inherent perishability. Services are so different that they warrant their own chapter in this book (Chapter 22).

The nature and implementation of the marketing mix are likely to be very different for each of these categories of product. A durable is likely to be an infrequently purchased, relatively expensive good. It may require selective distribution through specialist channels and a communications approach that is primarily centred on information and function rather than psychological benefits. In contrast, a non-durable is likely to be a frequently purchased, relatively low-priced item requiring mass distribution through as wide a variety of outlets as possible and mass communication centred on psychological benefits. Services have to find ways of either bringing the service to the consumer or persuading the consumer to come to the service delivery point. Communication has to develop both functional and psychological benefit themes as well as reassuring the potential customer of the quality and consistency of the service offered.

These outlines are, of course, broad generalisations of limited use and it is not difficult to think of exceptions within each category (compare cars and washing machines in the durable group, for instance). Although these classifications are ostensibly based

---

MARKETING AND IT   ## Using IT to turn products into services

Products that are viewed as commodities by consumers cannot command a premium price in the marketplace. Marketing managers, therefore, sometimes augment the product to differentiate it from its competitors and to enhance its value or make it more difficult to replicate. IT can be used in this way to add service features to a product. Remote monitoring services, for example, can be added to consumer or organisational products:

■ *Industrial equipment*: remote monitoring sensors are routinely incorporated into machine tools, chemical processing plant and other industrial equipment to monitor operation. If there is a problem or malfunction, the machinery can either be reset remotely or the remote monitoring system can alert and dispatch an engineer before the equipment fails completely and causes further damage.
■ *White goods*: remote monitoring can also be applied to consumer goods. In 1998 Merloni, a company that sells over seven million kitchen appliances every year under the Ariston and Indesit brand names, launched a new service linking domestic appliances

with remote 'diagnostic centres' via the telecommunications network. For a fee of perhaps £30 per year, an appliance can be hooked up to Merloni's network of service centres across Europe, which means that the consumer does not have to worry about anything going wrong.

■ *Security services*: house alarms no longer simply let the entire neighbourhood know that an intruder is on the premises. Many now automatically alert the police and/or a security company. In many ways, this is no more than another form of remote monitoring service for which a price premium can be charged.
■ *Cars*: many taxi firms now advertise the fact that their cars are fitted with global positioning system (GPS) technology. This allows the company to schedule taxi movements more efficiently as it has more accurate information on precisely where any taxi is located at any time. Sometimes referred to as an in-car navigation system, this form of remote monitoring is also available to private motorists in the UK through the Automobile Association.

Source: O'Connor and Galvin (1999).

on product characteristics, it has proved to be impossible to talk about them without some reference to buyer behaviour, so perhaps it is time to make this dimension more explicit and instead to think about user-based classifications of products.

The following subsections deal in turn with consumer markets (goods purchased for personal or family consumption – *see* Chapter 3) and organisational markets (goods purchased for business or institutional use – *see* Chapter 4). Although both groups look for satisfaction from their purchases, the kinds of products they buy and the buying influences and behaviour that predominate are very different, thus meriting separate treatment. It is important to note that even the same product can be marketed very differently, depending on whether it is aimed at a consumer or an organisational purchaser, as will be shown, for example, at p. 269 *et seq.*

User–based classifications: consumer goods and services

The contents of this section are very closely linked with the content of pp. 101 *et seq.*, where differences in buyer behaviour were based on whether the purchase was a routine response situation (i.e. a familiar, low-risk and frequently encountered situation), a limited problem-solving situation (some unfamiliarity, medium risk, less frequently encountered) or an extended problem solving situation (no experience, very infrequent, high-risk purchase). If we begin with these behavioural categories, it is possible to identify parallel groups of goods and services that fit into those situations, giving a very powerful combination of buyer and product characteristics for outlining the basic shape of the marketing mix.

Convenience goods

Convenience goods correspond to the routine response buying situation. They are relatively inexpensive, frequent purchases. The buyer puts little effort into the purchasing decision and convenience often takes priority over brand loyalty. This is especially true of supermarket-based shopping. If the desired brand of breakfast cereal is inexplicably unavailable within the store that the shopper is visiting, they will probably buy an alternative brand or do without rather than take the trouble to go to another shop.

The marketing implications of such a product definition are similar to those outlined for the non-durable in p. 265 above. Wide distribution needs to be assured to make it as likely as possible that the product will be under the consumer's nose. Communication needs to be aimed directly at consumers to get them as involved as possible with the product through the creation of brand image to offset brand-switching indifference. Packaging and brand imagery need to be as attention grabbing and as memorable as possible to facilitate recognition and positive brand choice at the point of sale. The market may well be price sensitive and thus the producer and retailer should be prepared to accept low margins and to seek profit through volume.

Example The growth in petrol station forecourt retailing was very high during the 1990s. No longer content with just selling petrol, a number of oil companies either run their own forecourt shops selling convenience foods or have entered into arrangements with specialist retailers. By 1999 Esso, for example, had 1980 branded shops, while BP/Mobil had 1858. The latter had also been experimenting with joint shop development with supermarket chains Safeway and Budgen's. Texaco was even more adventurous, with tie-ins to Dunkin' Donuts, Pizza Hut, Burger King, Upper Crust and McDonald's in order to offer a range of fast foods. All of these forecourt food and grocery shops trade on the convenient locations and long opening hours associated with petrol retailing, as well as looking for impulse purchases (Linnell, 1998).

The types of goods involved may be staple items, such as groceries, but could also include impulse or emergency purchases. For example, a consumer browsing through a bookshop with no particular intention to buy may be caught suddenly by a particular title, jacket design or author's name and make an immediate decision to buy. In an emergency, such as dealing with a burst water pipe in the home, convenience takes on a less lazy definition. The need for a solution to the consumer's problem develops an urgency that precludes extensive shopping around. In both the impulse and the emergency situations, the key to making a sale is essentially the same: be in the right place at the right time with the right product and be ready to ambush the unsuspecting customer.

Shopping goods

Linked with limited problem solving behaviour, **shopping goods** represent something more of a risk and an adventure to consumers, who are thus more willing to shop around and plan their purchases and even to enjoy the shopping process. Comparison through advertisements and visits to retail outlets may be supplemented by information from easily accessible sources, such as consumer organisations' published reports, word of mouth from family and friends and brochures, as well as advice from sales assistants in the retail setting. A moderately rational assessment of the alternative products based on function, features, service promises and guarantees will lead to a decision.

The effort required by this process is worth it if the purchase is significant or if the consumer will have to live for a long time with the consequences of the decision (*see* the hi-fi example at p. 103). Whether a purchase falls into this category depends on the individual consumer's perceptions of the importance and complexity of the purchase, as well as their previous experience within the market concerned. One consumer's shopping good is another's convenience or speciality good. Within the shopping goods classification, there may be brand and/or store loyalty involved, or no loyalty at all. There may also be a pre-existing short list of preferred brands within which the detailed comparison and final choice will be made.

The implications of all this for the marketer affect all aspects of the marketing mix, not just product. The mass distribution strategies of the convenience good may no longer be appropriate. The consumer is more likely to seek out certain specialist retailers and see what they have available than to purchase impulsively from a supermarket shelf, because of the nature of the product and the buying behaviour it invokes. This makes the careful targeting of key retailers essential. A hair-dryer manufacturer needs a presence in Curry's, Comet and Argos, because those are the places the consumer will go to seek market information. Hair-dryers are a grey area, in the sense that for a significant number of consumers they are closer to convenience items than shopping goods. In that case, a major manufacturer with a recognisable, reassuring name such as Braun or Philips can display and sell products very successfully through a supermarket type of outlet.

Example Travel Inn, the Whitbread-owned budget accommodation chain, has mainly used service standardisation, careful price positioning, good location planning and ease of accessing information and reservation as the main ways of competing with similar offerings from Granada Travel Lodge and Novotel's Formula One. The central reservation service covering all 400 sites, for instance, means that it is very easy for potential guests to make price comparisons, check availability and to book. Some £2mn is spent on advertising, although, unlike many of the motel chains in the USA, a freefone number is not used and the service is not open 24 hours. Perhaps in time more travellers will use the website, http://www.travelinn.co.uk, to make a reservation (*Marketing*, 1998).

The volume of goods sold will be lower than for a convenience item, but the margin on each unit will be much higher. Price sensitivity could go either way with these products. A consumer who is confused by the amount of information to be analysed and is having difficulty comparing competing products on the basis of performance and features may resort to price as the deciding factor. A more expensive one may be purchased on the basis that it must be a better quality product, or a cheaper one may be bought on the basis that it will do the job and there's no point spending more on fancy frills.

Communication might also take two directions. Establishing a strong corporate name is important, so that when the consumer enters the market the name either springs to mind as an obvious choice or at least seems very familiar, and therefore comforting, when it is encountered. Organisations such as Ariston, Zanussi and Hotpoint have used mass advertising in this way, so that even consumers who are not currently interested in buying kitchen appliances are aware that they exist and have some perception of what the company name stands for. The hope is that these perceptions will be transferred to the actual products at the appropriate time.

The other direction for communication is that of working closely with the retail trade. If a consumer seeks information at the point of sale to guide product choice, then obviously any manufacturer wants its product to be the one with the strongest retailer backing. Providing training or incentives (*see* Chapter 16 on trade sales promotion) to retailers or individual sales assistants, as well as help with point-of-sale displays and provision for joint promotion (*see* Chapter 16), all help to forge stronger links between producer and retailer with a view to developing a competitive edge.

Speciality goods

Speciality goods equate with the consumer's extensive problem-solving situation. The high-risk, expensive, very infrequently purchased products in this category evoke the most rational consumer response that a manufacturer could hope to find. It is not entirely rational, however. The psychological and emotive pull of a brand name like Porsche could still override objective assessment of information, leading to a biased, but happy, decision for the consumer. If you allow the inclusion in this category of products like designer perfumes, those that cost several hundred pounds for 50 ml and would be a once (or never) in a lifetime purchase for most consumers, then rationality goes right out of the window and the purchase is made entirely on the basis of the dream and the imagery woven around the product.

The products in this category need very specialist retailing that will provide a high level of augmented product services, both before and after the sale. Limiting distribution to a small number of exclusive and well-monitored outlets not only protects the product from abuse (for example inappropriate display or sales advice), but also helps to enhance the product's special image and the status of the buyer.

Example   Choosing where to go on an annual holiday is a high-risk decision for many households. The television consumer 'watchdog' programmes are full of holidays that went wrong! In its 1999 campaign, Thomson Holidays decided to focus on the dangers of selecting a holiday on price-based criteria rather than on the basis of quality and peace of mind. The campaign featured a 50-second television advertisement incorporating the line: 'Would you risk the love of this fine woman for the price of a *curry*?', as Roland Rivron berated a fellow passenger for seeking a cut price deal. Although as number one in the industry Thomson could easily emphasise price deals and reduce its profit margins, it believes that the best long-term interests of its brand name are served by focusing on quality, not just value for money. According to the advertising and branding manager:

> 'We see our task as trying to stop the downward price spiral. A holiday is one of the most important purchases you make during the year; if you were buying a car you wouldn't make an instant decision if one were cheaper by £20'.

(McLuhan, 1999)

Thomson's campaign seeks to differentiate its holidays.

Source: Thomson Holidays Ltd.

The (relatively) very low volumes sold of these products are compensated for through their high profit margins. Prices are high not only to reward the producer and retailer for their care for the product and its buyer, but also because the buyer is likely to perceive a high price as a positive benefit (*see* Chapter 11 on the pricing of luxury goods and on psychological pricing), enhancing the status of the purchase.

Communication will be a more extreme version of the shopping goods scenario, with much emphasis on name and image building. This is likely to focus more on the psychological benefits of choosing that manufacturer or that product rather than on the functional benefits as such. At these price levels, function and quality can almost be taken for granted: it is the extra intangible psychological 'something' that differentiates between competing products. There is also going to be even closer co-operation between manufacturer and retailer, who will take care that any joint promotional efforts do not compromise the product's quality or status level.

Unsought goods

Within the **unsought goods** category, there are two types of situation. The first is the sudden emergency, such as the burst water pipe or the flat tyre. The organisation's job here is to ensure that the consumer either thinks of its name first or that it is the most accessible provider of the solution to the problem.

The second unsought situation arises with the kinds of products that people would not normally buy without aggressive hard-selling techniques, such as timeshare properties and some home improvements.

User-based classifications: organisational goods and services

This type of classification of organisational goods and services is linked closely with the discussion at p. 149 *et seq.*, where the spectrum of buying situations from routine rebuy to new task purchasing was discussed. The novelty of the purchase influences the time, effort and human resources put into the purchasing decision. If that is then combined with the role and importance of the purchase within the production environment, it is possible to develop a classification system that is both widely applicable and indicative of particular marketing approaches.

Capital goods

Capital equipment consists of all the buildings and fixed equipment that have to be in place for production to happen. Such items tend to be infrequently purchased and, given that they are expected to support production over a long lifetime and that they can represent a substantial investment, they are usually regarded as a high-risk decision in the new task category. This category might also include government-funded capital projects such as the building of motorways, bridges, housing and public buildings like hospitals and theatres.

The purchasing organisation will therefore use extensive decision making, involving a wide range of personnel from all levels of the organisation and perhaps independent external consultants as well. The seller will also have to be prepared to spend a great deal of time and effort researching the buying organisation and cultivating a relationship with its key personnel during the decision-making process. In some cases, the seller might have to become involved in developing a tailormade product for the buyer. Such purchasing is likely to centre on rational criteria, so the seller will have to bid for the contract, communicating the quantifiable benefits of the product, in competition with a number of alternative suppliers.

Example Despite the dynamic developments in the power of PCs, some applications still require more powerful, top of the range computers. Unlike PCs, the price of these computers has not dropped significantly. A new concept, the 'distributed supercomputer', is challenging the position of these supercomputers, however. In scientific, medical and industrial applications, the clustering of PC computer technology can provide a powerful platform. NASA required high-performance, 1 gigaflop (one thousand million operations per second) for a project but only had $50 000 to spend, well short of the cost of high-performance, top of the range computers. By using PCs linked together with a Linux operating system, however, it was able to meet its computing requirements. The potential for clustered PCs is enormous and will make high-powered facilities available to a much wider range of users (Talacko, 1999).

Accessory goods

Accessory goods are items that give peripheral support to the production process without direct involvement. Included in this group, therefore, will be items such as hand tools, fork-lift trucks, storage bins and any other portable or light equipment. Office equipment is also included here, such as wordprocessors, desks, chairs and filing cabinets.

Generally speaking, these items are not quite as expensive or as infrequently purchased as the capital goods. The risk factor is also lower. Buying the 'wrong' desk will not jeopardise the organisation in the same way as would buying the 'wrong' production machinery. An unreliable fork-lift truck can disrupt production, but even so, it is relatively quick and simple to replace. All of this indicates that the length of and the degree of involvement in the purchasing process will be scaled down accordingly into something closer to the modified rebuy situation.

The seller's main task, therefore, would appear to be to ensure that the prospective purchaser has all the relevant up-to-date information to hand. The purchase of office equipment, for example, might be delegated to the office manager without reference to more senior management, within an overall budget. The office equipment supplier then needs to maintain regular contact, making sure that the latest catalogue is in the office manager's hands, so that when a purchasing decision is due, that is the catalogue that is used. Regular visits from a sales representative can help to communicate or negotiate special offers and deals, as well as providing a human point of contact for the office manager.

Raw materials

Raw materials arrive more or less in their natural state, having been processed only sufficiently to ensure their safe and economical transport to the factory. Thus iron ore is delivered to British Steel; fish arrives at the Findus fish-finger factory; beans and tomatoes are delivered to Heinz; and fleeces arrive at the textile mill. The raw materials then go on to further processing within the purchaser's own production line. The challenge for the supplier of raw materials is how to distinguish its product from the competition's, given that there may be few specification differences between them. Often, the differentiating factors in the purchaser's mind relate to non-product features, such as service, handling convenience, trust and terms of payment, for example.

Semi-finished goods

Unlike raw materials, semi-finished goods have already been subject to a significant level of processing before arriving at the purchaser's factory. They still, however, need further processing before incorporation into the ultimate product. A clothing manufacturer, therefore, will purchase cloth (i.e. the product of spinning, weaving and dyeing processes), which still needs to be cut and sewn to create the ultimate product.

Components and parts

Components and parts are finished goods in their own right, which simply have to be incorporated into the assembly of the final product with no further processing. Car manufacturers, for example, buy in headlamp units, alarm systems and microchips as complete components or parts and then fit them to the cars on the assembly line.

There is an important distinction to be drawn here between products specified by the supplier and those specified by the buyer. If the components are buyer specified, then the sales representative's main responsibility is to make sure that the right people are talking to each other. This might mean, for instance, co-ordinating the efforts of applications engineering personnel within the selling organisation with the engineering and specifying staff within the buying organisation. Even when the product has been agreed, there is still a need to maintain the relationship. This would be particularly critical if specific capital investments have been made by either party. Buyer specified products will be discussed further at p. 327 *et seq*.

In contrast, supplier specified products demand clear appreciation of customer needs, carefully designed and priced products and effective selling and promotion to exploit the opportunities identified by market research. Often, the competitive edge comes from designing unique parts for targeted applications, which can be delivered to a standard and consistent quality level to meet customer requirements.

Supplies and services

Finally, there are several categories of minor consumable items (as distinct from the accessory goods discussed above) and services that facilitate production and the smooth running of the organisation without any direct input.

Operating supplies. Operating supplies are frequently purchased consumable items that do not end up in the finished product. On the factory floor, these will include things like the lubrication oils for the production machinery. In the office, this group mainly includes stationery items such as pens, paper and envelopes, as well as computer consumables such as printer toner or ink cartridges and floppy disks.

Maintenance and repair. Maintenance and repair services ensure that all the capital and accessory goods continue to operate smoothly and efficiently. Maintenance and repair may take place on a planned basis, regularly servicing and checking equipment. They may also be called in on a trouble-shooter basis, when an actual problem develops. Remember, though, that maintenance and repair are not just about looking after equipment, but also about looking after the working environment, from mending the roof to emptying the office wastepaper baskets. This category can also include minor consumable items, such as cleaning materials, which assist in providing this service.

Business services. Business services may well be a major category of purchases for an organisation, involving a great deal of expenditure and decision-making effort, since they involve the purchase of services like management consultancy, accounting and legal advice and advertising agency expertise. This takes the discussion back to new task purchasing and its associated problems of involvement and risk.

UNDERSTANDING THE PRODUCT RANGE

Very few organisations are single-product companies. Most offer a variety of different products and perhaps a number of variations of each individual product, designed to meet the needs of different market segments. Car companies clearly do this, producing different models of car to suit different price expectations, different power and performance requirements and different usage conditions, from the long distance sales representative to the family wanting a car largely for short journeys in a busy suburban area. The same happens in organisational markets. Ingersoll-Rand, for example, has developed a whole range of portable compressors for use on construction sites. These range from small units that will run a single tool to high-capacity, high-pressure specialist units. A construction or engineering contractor can choose the appropriate unit to do the job in hand most cost effectively and most efficiently. Service companies also vary their products to suit different customer groups. A business school will offer undergraduate and postgraduate courses; post-experience courses for practising managers; full-time and part-time courses; tailored training packages for industry; and consultancy.

To understand any product fully, it is essential to appreciate its position in the wider family of the organisation's products. The marketing literature uses a number of terms when talking about the product family that are easy to confuse because of their similarity. Here are some definitions that sort out the confusion and offer some insight into the complexity of the product family. Figure 7.2 shows how all of these terms apply to the products produced within the Consumer Healthcare division of SmithKline Beecham.

FIGURE 7.2

SmithKline Beecham consumer healthcare product mix

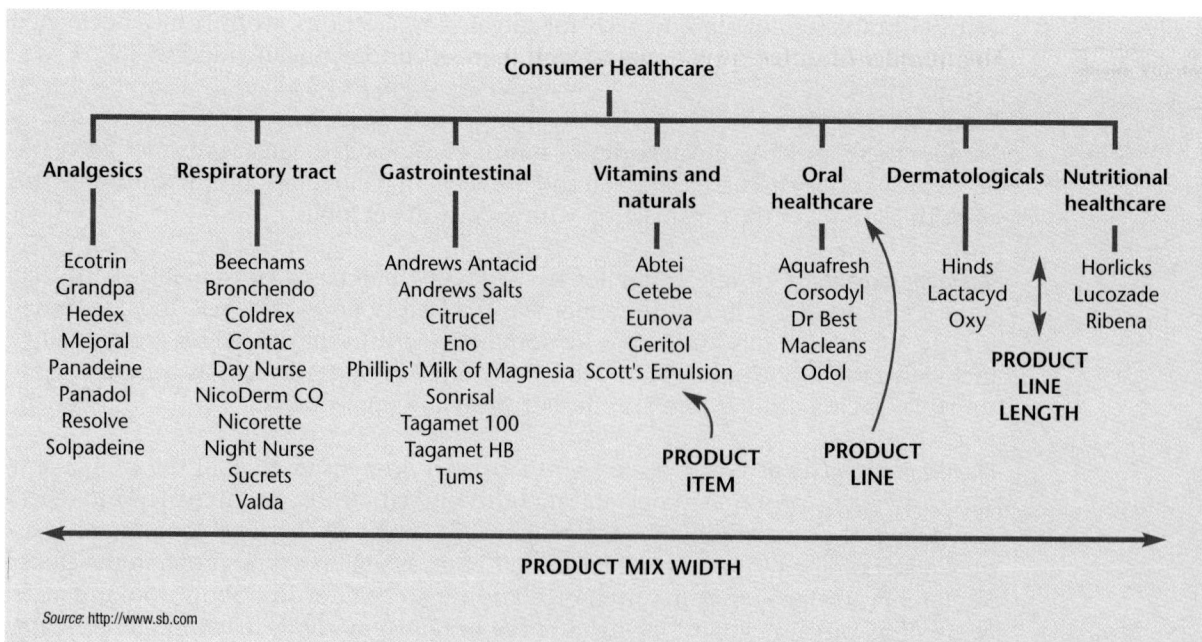

Source: http://www.sb.com

Product mix

The **product mix** is the total sum of all the products and variants offered by an organisation. A small company serving a specialist need in an organisational market may have a very small, tightly focused product mix.

Specialist companies also exist in consumer markets, of course. Van Dyck Belgian Chocolates, for example, offers boxed chocolates, chocolate bars, liqueur chocolates, fruit-flavoured chocolate, nut chocolates etc. A large multinational supplier of fmcg goods, such as Nestlé, has a very large and varied product mix, from confectionery to coffee to canned goods.

Product line

To impose some order on to the product mix, it can be divided into a number of **product lines.** A product line is a group of products that are closely related to each other. This relationship may be production orientated, in that the products have similar production requirements or problems. Alternatively, the relationship may be market orientated, in that the products fulfil similar needs, or are sold to the same customer group or have similar product management requirements. A company such as Minolta may define three of its product lines as still cameras, video cameras and photocopiers. These labels make sense because those three groups involve different technologies, and also because they sell to very different customers and markets.

Product item

A product line consists of a number of **product items**. These are the individual products or brands, each with its own features, benefits, price etc. In the fmcg area, therefore, if Heinz had a product line called table sauces, the product items within it might be tomato ketchup, salad cream, mayonnaise, reduced calorie mayonnaise etc.

Product line length

The total number of items within the product line is the **product line length**. Bosch, for example, might have a product line of DIY power tools, as shown in Fig. 7.3. Its equivalent industrial range of power tools would probably be even longer.

Product line depth

FIGURE 7.3

Bosch DIY power tools product line

The number of different variants of each item within a product line define its *depth*. A deep product line has many item variants. A deep line may be indicative of a

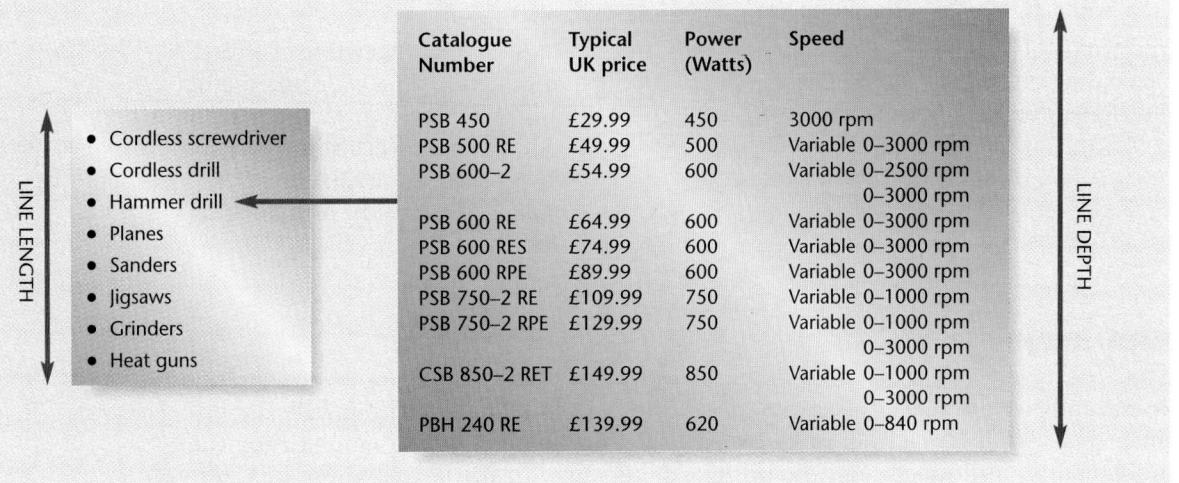

	Catalogue Number	Typical UK price	Power (Watts)	Speed
• Cordless screwdriver	PSB 450	£29.99	450	3000 rpm
• Cordless drill	PSB 500 RE	£49.99	500	Variable 0–3000 rpm
• Hammer drill	PSB 600–2	£54.99	600	Variable 0–2500 rpm 0–3000 rpm
• Planes	PSB 600 RE	£64.99	600	Variable 0–3000 rpm
• Sanders	PSB 600 RES	£74.99	600	Variable 0–3000 rpm
• Jigsaws	PSB 600 RPE	£89.99	600	Variable 0–3000 rpm
• Grinders	PSB 750–2 RE	£109.99	750	Variable 0–1000 rpm
• Heat guns	PSB 750–2 RPE	£129.99	750	Variable 0–1000 rpm 0–3000 rpm
	CSB 850–2 RET	£149.99	850	Variable 0–1000 rpm 0–3000 rpm
	PBH 240 RE	£139.99	620	Variable 0–840 rpm

LINE LENGTH

LINE DEPTH

TABLE 7.1
The Lynx brand

Product type	Fragrance					
	Africa	Mirage	Java	Tempest	Oriental	Nevada
Body spray	O	O	O	O	O	O
Shower gel	O	O	O	O	O	O
Aftershave	O	O	O	O		
Roll-on deodorant	O	O	O	O		
Deodorant stick	O	O	O			
Aftershave gel	O	O				

Source: Elida Gibbs, *Male Toiletries Retailing*, Spring/Summer 1995, p. 1.

differentiated market coverage strategy where a number of different segments are being served with tailored products. If we look again at the Bosch example in Fig. 7.3, we can break hammer drills down into a number of variants, giving a depth of ten, each of which has different performance and application capabilities, as well as fitting into different price segments.

Similarly, in an fmcg market, Table 7.1 shows the Lynx brand produced by Elida Gibbs. Taking into account the various combinations of product type and fragrance, Lynx has a depth of 25. This depth does not aim to cover different market segments, but does offer sufficient variation and choice to keep the target segment interested and loyal. The line includes all the basic male toiletry products so that the customer does not need to purchase anything from outside the line, and the variety of fragrances allows the customer to experiment and have a change from time to time!

Voodoo injects a touch of magic into the Lynx range.

Source: Elide Fabergé Ltd.

Product mix width

The *width* of the product mix is defined by the number of product lines offered. Depending on how broadly or narrowly defined the product lines are, a wide mix might indicate an organisation with a diverse interest in a number of different markets, such as Nestlé. A wide mix in an organisational market might indicate a specialist technology being supplied for very different applications to customers in different industries.

These definitions will be important for the next chapter's discussion of managing the product mix.

BRANDING

Branding is an important element of the tangible product and, particularly in consumer markets, is a means of linking items within a product line or emphasising the individuality of product items. Branding can also help in the development of a new product by facilitating the extension of a product line or mix, through building on the consumer's perceptions of the values and character represented by the brand name. This points to the most important function of branding: the creation and communication of a three-dimensional character for a product that is not easily copied or damaged by competitors' efforts. The prosaic definition of brand, accepted by most marketers, is that it consists of any name, design, style, words or symbols, singly or in any combination that distinguish one product from another in the eyes of the customer.

Branding is a very important activity in consumer markets. *Marketing*'s annual survey of Britain's biggest brands shows how much business a brand can bring to its owner and the level of advertising support that brands can command. Table 7.2 gives details of the top 10 brands from the 1998 survey, while Table 7.3 shows the top 10 fastest-growing brands in the UK in 1998.

An organisation's approach to branding depends on its overall product mix and individual line strategy, as will be shown at pp. 284 *et seq*. First, however, it is necessary to look a little more closely at the meaning of branding, beyond the raw definition already presented.

TABLE 7.2
The UK's top 10 brands, 1998

Brand	Owner	Sales (£mn)	Ad. spend (£mn)
Coca-Cola	Coca-Cola	580+	31.41
Walker's crisps	PepsiCo	400–405	6.88
Nescafé coffee	Nestlé	285–290	6.24
Andrex toilet tissue	Kimberly-Clark	205–300	9.25
Ariel laundry products	Procter & Gamble	200–205	21.91
Persil laundry products	Lever Bros	195–200	20.59
Pampers nappies	Procter & Gamble	190–195	11.62
Pepsi	PepsiCo	190–195	10.91
Stella Artois lager	Whitbread	165–170	3.92
Müller yoghurt	Müller	160–165	2.46

Source: adapted from Bainbridge and Curtis (1998a).

TABLE 7.3
The UK's 10 fastest-growing brands, 1998

Brand	Owner	Sales (£mn)	Change (% year on year)	Ad. spend (£mn)
KittenSoft kitchen towels	Fort James	10–15	113.3	1.68
Nouvelle toilet tissue	Fort James	20–25	52.0	2.34
Onken yoghurt	Onken	10–15	43.1	0.59
Pampers baby wipes	Procter & Gamble	20–25	36.5	1.31
Cadbury's chocolate fingers	Premier Brands	15–20	35.6	0.00
Dolmio pasta sauce	Master Foods	50–55	31.5	6.69
Stella Artois lager	Whitbread	165–170	31.1	3.92
Vanish stain remover	Benckiser	15–20	29.5	7.47
Nicorette smoking cessation	Parmacia & Upjohn	20–25	28.9	3.90
Budweiser beer	Anheuser-Busch	75–80	27.8	10.05

Source: adapted from Bainbridge and Curtis (1998b).

The meaning of branding

The definition of brand provided above offered a variety of mechanisms through which branding could be developed, the most obvious of which are the name and the logo. As with the product mix jargon discussed in the previous section, you are likely to meet a number of terms in the course of your reading and it is important to differentiate between them.

MARKETING IN ACTION   ## Life begins at 40, Barbie

At the age of 40, when many women start to worry about spreading waistlines or a few wrinkles, Barbie keeps her figure and youthful looks and continues to entertain generations of children. Mattel (http://www.mattel.com) launched the Barbie doll in 1959 and then allowed her to evolve as product technology developed and consumer tastes changed. By 1997, Barbie's sales had reached over £100mn in the UK and nearly £1bn worldwide.

Millennium Barbie showed the results of the third major facelift since her birth. The 1959 Barbie had heavy makeup, which was replaced by a more natural look in 1967 and a happier-looking Barbie in 1977. The millennium look required a more intelligent and sophisticated appearance to reflect the changing role of women in society. In addition, the open lips have closed and the nose has been made a little thinner. The bimbo image might well have gone (except for her bust!), but the fictional world in which Barbie undertakes every kind of career going, keeps Ken hanging on and owns an improbably extensive wardrobe still enthrals.

Source: Hussey (1998).

Brand name

A brand name is any word or illustration that clearly distinguishes one seller's goods from another. It can take the form of words, such as Weetabix and Ferrero Rocher, or initials, such as AA. Numbers can be used to create an effective brand name, such as 7-Up. A browse through the telephone directory of any British town is likely to reveal a small company called A1 Taxis. The A1 name is popular with small operators partly because it has connotations of quality, but mainly because the quirks of alphabetical order mean that it comes very early in the telephone book listing and is thus more likely to attract a potential customer's attention. Brand names can also be enhanced by the use of an associated logo, such as the one used by Apple computers, to reinforce the name, or through the particular style in which the name is presented. The classic example of this is the Coca-Cola brand name, where the visual impact of the written name is so strong that the onlooker recognises the design rather than reads the words. Thus Coca-Cola is instantly identifiable whether the name is written in English, Russian, Chinese or Arabic because it always somehow *looks* the same.

The strategic issues surrounding the choice and use of brand name are examined further at p. 283.

Trade name

The trade name is the legal name of an organisation, which may or may not relate directly to the branding of its products.

Example   Cadbury's, (http://www.cadbury.ac.uk) as an organisation, has deliberately developed a strong image for the Cadbury corporate name to act as an umbrella for all its product brands. Hence its products benefit both from the affection that consumers hold for the corporate name and from the individual character developed for Cadbury's Flake, Cadbury's Dairy Milk, Cadbury's Drinking Chocolate and all its other products.

Some companies prefer to let the brands speak for themselves and do not give any prominence to the product's parentage. Washing powder brands produced by either Lever Brothers or Procter & Gamble do not prominently display the company name, although it is shown on the back or side of the pack. Few consumers would realise that Persil, Surf and Radion come from the same stable. Similarly, RHM produces brands such as Paxo that have no obvious corporate identity.

There is more on the strategic implications of the degree of corporate branding used at pp. 284 *et seq.*

Trade mark

A trade mark is a brand name, symbol or logo, which is registered and protected for the owner's sole use. To bring the UK into line with EU legislation, the Trades Marks Act, 1994 allowed organisations to register smells, sounds, product shapes and packaging, as well as brand names and logos. This means, as discussed by Slingsby (1994), that the Coca-Cola bottle, the Toblerone bar and Heinz's tomato ketchup bottle are as protectable as their respective brand names. Advertising slogans, jingles and even movements or gestures associated with a brand can also be registered as trade marks. The Act prevents competitors from legally using any of these things in a way that may confuse or mislead buyers, and also makes the registration process and action over infringement much easier. By 1996 it was also possible to register trade marks for the whole of Europe by filing a single application to the Community Trade Mark Office in Alicante, Spain, rather than having to apply for registration country by country.

Trade marks are valuable properties, as organisations invest much time and money in creating them and educating consumers about what they stand for. This means that there is also value in trade that capitalises on the illegal use of brand names. Companies such as Nike and Reebok have put a great deal of effort into trying to stem the flow on to the market of counterfeit, low-cost copies of their brands. These counterfeits, allegedly sourced from the Far East, are poor-quality goods that damage the company name and image if purchased as 'originals'. Even organisational markets are not immune to this trend, which has been seen in the markets for motor spare parts and aircraft parts, among others.

Example Duracell (http://www.duracell.com) became worried about counterfeiting in 1998 and warned all stockists to be on the look-out for copycat Duracell products. The fake products were thought to be of poor quality and even potentially dangerous if the mercury leaked. Duracell was especially concerned with the impact on customers who experienced poor performance and became dissatisfied with the brand because they could not tell that the product was counterfeit. Even dealers had to be eagle-eyed to spot the fakes. The packs were shorter and wider, the words on the pack were different and the tester was displayed

Brand mark

The brand mark is specifically the element of the visual brand identity that does not consist of words, but of design and symbols. This would include things like McDonald's golden arches, Apple's computer symbol, or Audi's interlocking circles. These things are also protectable, as discussed under trade marks above.

The benefits of branding

Branding carries benefits for all parties involved in the exchange process and in theory at least makes it easier to buy or sell products. This section, summarised in Fig. 7.4, looks at the benefits of branding from different perspectives, beginning with that of the buyer.

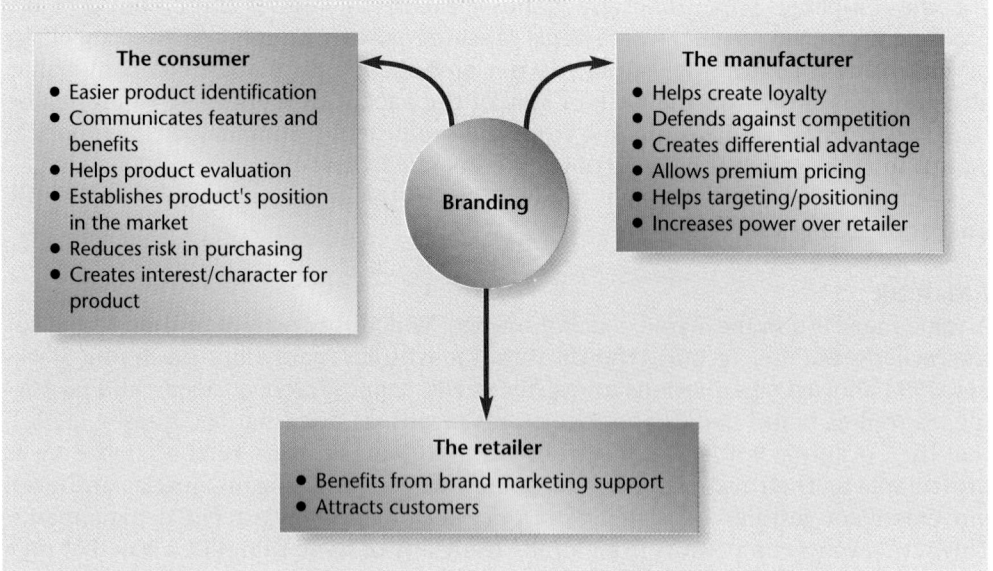

FIGURE 7.4

The benefits of branding

Consumer perspective

Branding is of particular value to the buyer in a complex and crowded market-place. In a supermarket, for example, brand names and visual images make it easier to locate and identify required products. This is expecially important as it has been estimated that the average consumer inspects just 1.2 brands per purchase on average (Kahn, 1998). Strong branding can speak volumes about the function and character of the product and help consumers to judge whether it is their sort of product, delivering the functional and psychological benefits sought. This is especially true for a new, untried product. The branding can at least help the evaluation of product suitability, and if there is an element of corporate branding (as discussed with Cadbury's above) it can also offer reassurance about the product's quality pedigree.

This all aids in the shopping process and reduces some of its risks, but it goes further. Giving a product what amounts to a three-dimensional personality makes it easier for consumers to form attitudes and feelings about the product. It gets them sufficiently interested to want to be bothered to do that. This has the double effect of creating brand loyalty (the product as a trusted friend) and of creating something special in the consumer's mind that the competition would find difficult to touch.

It is especially important for companies to build trust when they are asking consumers to become involved with them in life-transforming tasks, such as taking out a pension or other significant personal finance package. It is then necessary to establish a real relationship rather than an arm's length, 'take the money and run' transaction. This relationship manifests itself not only through the product or service consumption, but also through the brand's values, which are essential for building trust and winning affection (Mitchell, 1999).

A final slant on this issue of relationship between buyer and brand is that the brand's name and image are as individual and evocative as a person's name and facial features. If you mention the name of a mutual friend to someone, the name triggers the recall of the friend's face and personality as well as the listener's attitude towards that person. The name acts as a shorthand label for a large bundle of complicated descriptors and emotions. The brand's name serves the same purpose. This means that for an established brand, relatively short, sharp communication can achieve a wealth of response from the target audience.

'Passion brands' such as football club Manchester United (*see also* case study 10.1), religions, pressure groups, political parties etc., reflect the 'buyer's' inner belief in values and create very strong emotions. They do not have 'consumers' and 'targeted products'; they have followers, who buy into what the brand stands for and who feel part of a community. This generates enormous potential for additional revenue from such things as merchandise, media products (for instance, Manchester United has its own television channel), alliances with other service providers for events and affinity cards (Mitchell, 1998).

Manufacturer perspective

The manufacturer benefits, of course, from the relationship of the buyer with branding. The ease of identification of the product at the point of sale, the connotations of quality and familiarity and the creation of a three-dimensional product personality all help the manufacturer. The manufacturer's key interest is in the building of defendable brand loyalty to the point where the trust, liking and preference for the brand overcome any lingering price sensitivity, thus allowing a reasonable measure of premium pricing and the prevention of brand switching.

> **Example** Asia's economic difficulties made a big impact on luxury brands. It was estimated that some luxury goods companies had between 30 and 50 per cent of their sales in Asia, so any downturn was almost inevitably going to have a significant effect. LVMH, owner of French luxury brands such as Louis Vuitton, Moet & Chandon champagne and Christian Dior, reported a 7 per cent drop in profits in the first half of 1998. Watch company Tag Heuer reported its sales down by 22 per cent in Asia. Luxury brand manufacturers were thus forced to increase their marketing efforts in Europe and the US to try to compensate. Gucci, for example, managed to increase overall sales through offsetting serious decline in Asia against increased effort in Europe.
>
> It was not only export sales to Asia that were hit by the recession. Declining numbers of tourists from Japan, Korea and Indonesia also made an impact on sales in European high streets, shopping malls, hotels and other leisure and tourism service providers (Cunningham, 1998).

Other more subtle advantages of branding for the manufacturer are linked with segmentation and competitive positioning strategies. Different brands can be used by one organisation to target different segments. Because the different brands have clearly defined individual characteristics, the consumer does not necessarily link them and thus does not become confused about what the organisation stands for. Even where there is a strong corporate element to the branding, as with Ford cars, the individual models within the range are clearly seen as separate products, serving different market needs, with price differences justified in terms of design and technical specification. Consumers view this wide range of brands positively, as a way of offering as tailored a choice as possible within the confines of a mass market.

Strong branding is also important for providing competitive advantage, not just in terms of generating consumer loyalty, but also as a means of competing head-on, competing generally across the whole market in an almost undifferentiated way or finding a niche in which to dominate. Research published by the European Brands Association supports the 'virtuous circle' of brand investment: heavy *advertising* creates *brands* which *grow market share* to enjoy greater *economies of scale* in advertising and promotion, which enables *higher R&D* and *advertising spend* to *introduce more innovation* and branded products (Lightfoot, 1998). Brand imagery can help to define the extent of competition or exaggerate the differentiating features that pull it away from the competition. Table 7.4 examines the toilet soap market, identifying the different levels of competitive activity in different market segments, as represented by available brands.

Retailer perspective

The retailer benefits from branding to a certain extent. Branded products are well supported by advertising and other marketing activities, and so the retailer has some assurance that they will sell. Branded products do draw customers into the store, but

TABLE 7.4
The UK's toilet soap market, 1998 (selected brands)

Manufacturer	Family segment	Luxury/beauty	Skincare	Cosmetic	Deodorant
Lever Brothers	Knight's Castile	Lux		Dove	Shield
Cusson's	Imperial Leather	Pearl		Cusson's Mild Cream	Lifebuoy
Procter & Gamble	Fairy	Camay		Ulay Conditioning Bar	
Colgate Palmolive	Palmolive				Fresh
Smith & Nephew			Simple		
Own label			The Body Shop		
			Boots Natural		

Source: Based on information from Mintel Market Intelligence (Novermber 1998), 'Soap, Bath and Shower Additives'.

MARKETING IN ACTION   **Brand assets**

Brand valuation emerged through the 1990s as an important measure for brand owners assessing the effectiveness of their brand marketing strategies, their long-term advertising and even the overall worth of the company. Brands represent a financial value to a company reflected through the goodwill component of a balance sheet. The attractiveness of the Rolls-Royce brand to BMW or the Volvo brand to Ford reflects the strong brand values that make them worthwhile names to own.

Interbrand Newell & Sorrell, in research for trade magazine *Marketing Week*, plotted the growth in brand values for top US and UK companies between 1988 and 1998. Brand value was calculated by comparing market capitalisation with net tangible or physical assets. The difference between these two figures shows the goodwill gap, i.e. the extent to which potential investors value a company over and above its tangible assets such as plant and machinery. Although these differences can be accounted for by a range of factors, such as management ability, patents and distribution strength, research has found that a significant part of the difference can be accounted for by the worth of the brands. In the case of Coca-Cola the figure is 4000 per cent of the tangible assets, Cadbury Schweppes is 33 per cent or £1.5bn and Scottish & Newcastle Breweries is 158 per cent.

A similar study by Interbrand and Citibank examining stock market performance found that those companies that were heavily branded tended to outperform the rest of companies in the FTSE 350 index by between 15 and 20 per cent over a 15-year period. Brand value clearly makes a difference to companies.

The history of brand valuation can be traced back to 1988 when Rank Hovis McDougall (RHM) successfully defended against a hostile takeover by including the value of its brands in its balance sheet. Since then, organisations such as Burmah Castrol, Cadbury Schweppes, ICI and Disney have all used brand-valuation techniques for management and acquisition purposes. The value of brands to many companies has now become so important that it has been argued that the chief executive should ultimately be the brand manager and that all staff need to realise that they are in the front line of brand delivery. Such an approach is clearly demonstrated by Richard Branson at Virgin, where the strength of the Virgin brand name has successfully carried it into many sectors.

The recognition of brands as assets is likely to become more emphasised in future as finance directors and accountants increasingly use brand-valuation techniques in balance sheets. In December 1998, the UK Accounting Standards Board recommended through Standards 10 and 11 that the value of acquired brands should be included in company accounts. Shareholders will be asking more often what the 'real' value of the brand portfolio is for enhancing their own yield value.

Sources: Baird (1998); Butterfield (1998); Butterfield and Haigh (1998).

---

the disadvantage is that if a brand is unavailable in one store, then the shopper is likely to patronise another instead. The retailer may prefer the shopper to be less brand loyal and more store loyal! Supermarkets have always recognised the value and necessity of manufacturer-branded goods, but they have also looked for ways of reducing the power that this gives the brand owner. This issue will be looked at in detail in the next subsection.

Lest this discussion should seem too enthusiastic about branding, we now turn to some of the disadvantages. Echoing one of the risks of segmentation (discussed in Chapter 5, p. 201), there is the danger of proliferation if brands are created to serve every possible market niche. Retailers are under pressure to stock increasing numbers of lines within a product area, which means in turn that either less shelf space is devoted to each brand or retailers refuse to stock some brands. Both options are unpleasant for the manufacturer. The consumer may also begin to see too much choice and, at some point, there is a risk that the differences between brands become imperceptible to the consumer and confusion sets in.

Types of brands

The discussion so far has centred on the brands created and marketed by manufacturers and sold through retail outlets. An area of growing importance, however, is the brand created by a wholesaler or retailer for that organisation's sole use. This development has taken place partly because of conflicts and power struggles between manufacturers and retailers (*see* Chapter 12), and partly because the retailers also need to generate store loyalty (*see* Chapter 13) in a highly competitive retail sector.

This section, therefore, distinguishes between the brands emanating from different types of organisation.

Manufacturer brands

Most manufacturers, particularly in the fmcg sector, are at arm's length from the end buyer and consumer of their product. The retail sector is in between and can make the difference between a product's success and failure through the way the product is displayed or made available to the public. The manufacturer can attempt to impose some control over this through trade promotions, but the manufacturer's best weapon is direct communication with the end buyer. Planting brand names and recognition of brand imagery in the consumer's mind through advertising or sales promotion gives the manufacturer a fighting chance of recognition and selection at the point of sale. Furthermore, the creation of a strong brand that has hard-core loyalty can tip the balance of power back in favour of the manufacturer, because any retailer not stocking that brand runs the risk of losing custom to its competitors.

The creation and management of a manufacturer brand generate many responsibilities and costs in terms of promotion, distribution, quality control and product development, but if the process is managed effectively, then it does represent a valuable asset, both financially and strategically.

Retailer and wholesaler brands

The growth of **own-label brands** (i.e. those bearing the retailer's name) has become a major factor in retailing. Supermarkets and clothing stores, in particular, have been very active in creating physical products exclusive to the store, reflecting the retailer's name. The responsibility for the development and maintenance of the brand falls on the retailer. The retailer may or may not manufacture the products directly, but either way, the product will not admit its provenance. 'Manufactured in the UK for J Sainsbury PLC' is the nearest you are likely to get.

Why do it? One possible problem a retailer has is that if a consumer is buying a recognised manufacturer's brand, then the source of that purchase is less relevant. A can of Heinz baked beans represents the same values whether it is purchased from a corner shop or from Harrod's. Retailers can differentiate from each other on the basis of price or service, but they are looking for more than that. The existence of a range of exclusive retailer brands that the consumer comes to value creates a physical reason for visiting that retailer and no other. These brands also serve the purpose of giving the consumer 'the retailer in a tin', where the product in the kitchen cupboard is a constant reminder of the retailer and embodies the retailer's values in a more tangible form, reinforcing loyalty and positive attitudes.

Other reasons include the fact that the retailer can earn a better margin on an own brand and still sell it more cheaply than a manufacturer's brand. This is because it does not face the product development, brand creation and marketing costs that the manufacturers incur. The retailer's own brand is sold on the back of the retailer's normal marketing activity and not with the massive advertising, promotion and selling costs that each manufacturer's brand has to bear. Even the comparatively small production runs involved with retailers' brands need not increase costs too much, if the own brand is either the manufacturer's brand with a different label or a slight variation.

The use of own label varies across different retailers. Some retailers, such as Kwik Save, use their own label to create a no-nonsense, no-frills, value-for-money, generic range. Others, such as Marks & Spencer, Sainsbury's and the Albert Heijn chain in the Netherlands, have created own brands that are actually perceived as superior in quality to the manufacturer's offerings. The penetration of own labels also differs. Table 7.5 shows the percentage of own-label business across different products.

It is apparent that some supermarkets are using own-brand products increasingly as a central pivot around which to cluster a select but small number of manufacturer brands. Given that own-label products seem to put so much power into the hands of the retailers, why do manufacturers co-operate in their production? For a manufacturer of second string brands (i.e. not the biggest names in the market), it might be a good way of developing closer links with a retailer and earning some sort of protection for the manufacturer's brands. In return for the supply, at attractive prices, of own-brand products, the retailer might undertake to display the manufacturer's brands more favourably, or promise not to delist them, for example. The extra volume provides some predictability for the manufacturer and it also could help to achieve economies of scale of benefit to both parties.

The danger, of course, is that of the manufacturer becoming too dependent on the retailer's own-brand business. The supplier–buyer relationship needs to be carefully monitored and handled (*see* pp. 150 *et seq.*). Some retailers, such as Marks & Spencer and the Irish retailer Dunne's, demand a high level of influence over the operations of their own-label suppliers, to the point of expecting to take a significant proportion of

TABLE 7.5

UK grocery own-label trends 1997-98

	1997	1998	% change
Cooking salt	89.8	91.1	+1.5
Canned apricots	77.1	82.8	+7.4
Milk	80.1	80.2	+0.1
Honey	72.8	75.1	+3.1
Demerara sugar	64.2	69.8	+8.8
Canned peas	54.6	60.4	+10.7
Canned beans	45.4	43.6	−3.9
Cotton wool	95.2	97.0	+1.9
Aluminium foil	84.5	84.4	−0.2
Cat litter	68.4	66.5	−2.8
Toilet tissue	49.7	48.8	−1.9
Sunburn products	16.5	25.5	+54.2

Source: adapted from *The Retail Pocket Book 1999*, NTC Publications, Henley-on-Thames, p. 60. Reprinted with kind permission.

the supplier's output, yet retaining the right to drop a supplier which fails to live up to expectations. The smaller, more vulnerable organisation in particular needs to develop an active policy of diversification to offset the strategic risks of over-dependency.

A final twist in the evolution of the own-brand scene over the past few years has been an increasing consumer cynicism, giving credence to the view that retailers' own brands are only the manufacturers' brands with different labels, but much cheaper. To counter this, some big manufacturers have made it explicit that they do not operate in the own-brand market. Nescafé and Procter & Gamble have advertised on this basis and Kellogg's packaging actually states, 'We don't make cereals for anyone else'. Their fear is understandable. Why continue to spend more on manufacturer brands when you can get the same goods cheaper with an ASDA label on them?

The battle between own-label and manufacturer brands is expected to intensify in the coming years, especially as own labels confront the manufacturers' claims of better quality head on by also positioning themselves on quality as much as on price (Kahn, 1998).

Branding strategy

This chapter has already hinted at a number of important dimensions to be considered in developing and maintaining a branding strategy. Each one will now be treated separately.

Selecting a brand name

If all the benefits to the buyer mentioned at p. 277 *et seq.* are going to be achieved through branding, then the name becomes a crucial choice. It must be memorable, easy to pronounce and meaningful (whether in real or emotional terms). As manufacturers look increasingly towards wider European and international markets, there is a much greater need to check that a proposed name does not lead to unintended ridicule in a foreign language. Neither the French breakfast cereal Plopsies (chocolate-flavoured puffed rice) nor the gloriously evocative Slovakian pasta brand Kuk & Fuk are serious contenders for launch into an English-speaking market. From a linguistic point of view, care must be taken to avoid certain combinations of letters that are difficult to pronounce in some languages. The combination 'th' is fine in English but not in French, while the combination 'cz' poses no problem to a Polish speaker but challenges most of western Europe. The danger is, of course, that by trying to avoid challenging anyone linguistically, imagination is lost and the Eurobrand becomes the Eurobland. Some brand names such as Adidas, Findus, Mars and Lego have nevertheless managed to avoid the pitfalls. Birds Eye, while retaining the bearded sea captain and pack design for its fish products, becomes Iglo in Germany and Captain in France (Ensor, 1997).

Language problems apart, the ability of a brand name to communicate something about the product's character or functional benefits could be important. Blackett (1985) suggests that approaches to this can vary, falling within a spectrum ranging from freestanding names, through associative names, to names that are baldly descriptive. This spectrum is shown with examples of actual brand names in Fig. 7.5. Names that are totally freestanding are completely abstract and bear no relation to

FIGURE 7.5

The brand name spectrum

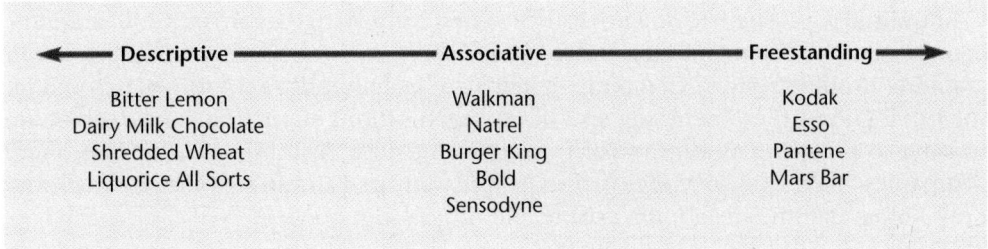

← Descriptive	Associative	Freestanding →
Bitter Lemon	Walkman	Kodak
Dairy Milk Chocolate	Natrel	Esso
Shredded Wheat	Burger King	Pantene
Liquorice All Sorts	Bold	Mars Bar
	Sensodyne	

the product or its character. Kodak is a classic example of such a name. *Associative* names suggest some characteristic, image or benefit of the product, but often in an indirect way. Pledge (furniture polish), Elvive (shampoo) and Impulse (body spray) are all names that make some kind of statement about the product's positioning through the consumer's understanding of the word(s) used in the name. The extremely prosaic end of the spectrum is represented by descriptive names. Names such as Chocolate Orange, Shredded Wheat and Cling Film certainly tell you about what the product is, but they are neither imaginative nor easy to protect. Bitter Lemon, for example, began as a brand name and was so apt that it soon became a generic title for any old bottle of lemon-flavoured mixer. Somewhere between associative and descriptive names come a group with names that are descriptive, but with a distinctive twist. Ex-Lax (laxative), Lucozade (fizzy glucose drink) and Bacofoil (aluminium cooking foil) are names that manage to describe without losing the individuality of the brand.

In summary, there are four 'rules' for good brand naming. As far as possible, they need to be:

1 *distinctive*, standing out from the competition while being appealing to the target market and appropriate to the character of the product;
2 *supportive* of the product's positioning with respect to its competitors (pp. 318 *et seq.* will discuss positioning in further detail), while remaining consistent with the organisation's overall branding policy;
3 *acceptable*, recognisable, pronounceable and memorisable, in other words user-friendly to the consumer; and finally,
4 *available*, registerable, protectable (i.e. yours and only yours).

With respect to this last point, it is important to ensure that the suggested brand name is not infringing the rights of existing brands. This is particularly difficult with international brands.

As mentioned earlier, the establishment of the Community Trade Mark Office means that a single registration can protect all aspects of a brand's identity across Europe. A trade mark search carried out by an agent, costing anything from £200 (for checking out a proposed name) to £2000 (for a detailed search), can help to reassure an organisation that it is not likely to infringe the rights of others. This all suggests that great care needs to be taken when developing brand identities. In order to minimise the risk of either choosing an inappropriate name or the inadvertent breach of another organisation's registered trade marks, many organisations do use professional consultants who specialise in brand concept development and testing and trade mark searches.

Product range brand policy

For most fmcg organisations, the decision on whether to brand the product range or not is an easy one. Branding is essential for most products in these markets. Difficulty arises with some homogeneous products because in theory the customer does not perceive sufficient difference between competing products to make branding feasible. As suggested at p. 198 in the discussion on undifferentiated products, however, there are fewer and fewer truly homogeneous products to be found. Petrol brands, for example, have now been created that differentiate on the basis of service factors and the use of sales promotions as an integral part of the offering.

Branding is of even less significance when supplying organisational markets, because of the differences in buyer behaviour. There is, however, increasing interest in branding in some sectors. Computer systems are heavily branded for instance and, at the other end of the purchasing spectrum, organisations supplying consumables are turning to branding as a means of trying to engender customer loyalty. Stationery companies, such as Arjo Wiggins fine papers with its Conqueror, Connoisseur and Keay Kolour brands, are branding paper and other office goods.

Once the decision to brand has been made, there are still a number of choices, one of which is the degree of independence that the brand is to be given in terms of its relationship with both other brands and the originating organisation.

Generic brands represent one extreme, where a single brand image covers a wide range of different products. This is mainly found in supermarkets, where a range of very low-priced, basic staple products are packaged with the minimum of frills and often the minimum permissible information on the packaging, such as Tesco's Value Lines. This is still a form of branding, in the sense that it is creating a distinctive character for a set of products.

At the opposite extreme, individual products are given entirely separate individual brand identities. There is thus no obvious relationship between different products produced by the same organisation. This is known as *discreet branding*. It is a useful policy to adopt if the intention is to compete in a number of different segments because it reduces the risk of one product's positioning affecting the consumer's perception of another product. It also means that if one product gets into trouble, perhaps through a product tampering scare or through production problems causing variable quality, the other products are better insulated against the bad reputation rubbing off on to them too. The big disadvantage of the discreet approach to branding, however, is that each brand has to be set up from scratch, with all the expense and marketing problems associated with it. The new brand cannot benefit from the established reputation of any other brand.

One way of allowing brands to support each other is by using a *monolithic* approach to branding, which uses a family name (usually linked with the corporate name) with a single brand identity for the whole product range.

Example Heinz (http://www.heinz.com) is a prime example of the monolithic approach. The Heinz brand is well respected and very strong, but individual Heinz products have little identity of their own. Brand names are descriptive and always include the word Heinz to link them, such as Heinz Cream of Tomato Soup, Heinz Baked Beans, Heinz Low Calorie Mayonnaise etc. Even the label design of each product shows that it clearly belongs to the Heinz family, further drawing the products together. Such family unity creates a strong overall image and allows new products easy entry into the existing product lines (although it might take consumers a while to notice a new flavour of soup in among the rest). It is also possible to achieve economies of scale in communication, if desired, and distribution, through treating the family as a unit rather than as a number of independent products. The danger is, however, that if one product fails or gains a bad reputation, the rest may suffer with it.

A compromise between monolithic and discreet branding is an approach that allows individual brand images, but uses a corporate or family name as a prominent umbrella to endorse the product. Some organisations, such as Ford and Kellogg, use a *fixed endorsed* approach. Here, there is a rigid relationship between the company name and the brand, with a high degree of consistency between the presentation of different brands (but not as extreme as the Heinz approach). A *flexible endorsed* approach, such as that practised by Cadbury's, gives the brand more latitude to express its individuality. The company name may be more or less prominent, depending on how much independence the organisation wants the brand to have. These products seem to enjoy the best of both worlds. The family name gives the products and any new products a measure of credibility, yet the individuality of the products allows variety, imagination and creativity without being too stifled by the 'house style'. Marketing costs are, however, going to be higher because of the need to develop and launch individual identities for products and then to communicate both the family image and the individual brand images.

Developing a brand extension policy

A kind of flexible endorsement that does not involve the corporate name is where a brand name is developed to cover a limited number of products within a product line.

Example Reckitt and Colman established the Dettol brand name in 1933. This name has now been expanded to include a whole range of clearly related products, such as Dettox, Dettol antibacterial soap, foam bath, antiseptic cream, pain relief spray and handwash in a mini-family, again capitalising on the established reputation of the 'parent' product.

Reckitt and Colman brands have gained worldwide sales so that few kitchen and bathroom cabinets are without some. Most of its brands, such as Lemsip, Lysol or Dettol, are strong and thus 70 per cent of sales come from products that are either number one or two in their markets. With that kind of strength, it makes sense to extend the brand names to gain maximum impact (Urry, 1999).

This example raises the issue of *brand extension*. Dettol has been very successful in launching variants or new products. Such a policy is cost efficient in that it saves the cost of developing totally new images and promoting and building them up from nothing: for example, easyJet is actively extending its brand name into 'easyEverything'. The launch of cyber cafés is the first such move using a formula similar to the one that made easyJet so successful. The cafés offer low-cost Internet access to the public with easyJet's trademark no-frills service. Consideration of brand extension also begins to highlight some of the marketing issues involved in branding that will be discussed further in the next chapter on product management.

In summary, any individual organisation is faced with a range of decisions including whether or not to brand, the character of its brands and the degree of independence each brand is given. A smaller organisation with limited resources and a limited number of products may take a monolithic approach, whereas a larger organisation may be better able to create discreet brands if it chooses. Whatever the situation, however, the branding and brand management decisions have to be made in the context of market segments, positioning and the competitive environment. Branding can be a strain on resources if the brand identity is not well established or if it is under threat.

The strength of the Dettol brand has allowed numerous extensions.

Source: Reckitt and Colman Products Ltd.

An organisation that uses branding effectively, whether creating a monolithic brand family, a fixed or flexible endorsed set of brands or taking a discreet branding approach, is in a powerful position with the retail trade in gaining shelf space and co-operation. It can also be in a better position to engender consumer loyalty, whether to an individual product or to a range (which would allow product switching within the variety offered in the range, without the loss of overall sales). All of this helps to make branding a very active and strategically important area in marketing.

PACKAGING

Packaging is an important part of the product that not only serves a functional purpose, but also acts as a means of communicating product information and brand character. The packaging is often the consumer's first point of contact with the actual product and so it is essential to make it attractive and appropriate for both the product's and the customer's needs.

> **Example**   McVitie's (http://www.unitedbiscuits.co.uk) has managed to differentiate its Jaffa Cakes (http://www.jaffacakes.co.uk) brand from supermarket 'look-alike' own brands by producing innovative packaging for mini-Jaffa Cakes. The pack consists of six individually sealed plastic segments, joined by perforations, which can be easily separated. The pack is bright orange, with the texture of orange peel to emphasise the nature of the product. Each segment provides a portion of Jaffa Cakes and can be packed into a lunch box or just used as a convenient snack. Meanwhile, the other five segments remain sealed and therefore stay fresh until required.

Packaging is any container or wrapping in which the product is offered for sale and can consist of a variety of materials such as glass, paper, metal or plastic, depending on what is to be contained. The choice of materials and the design of the packaging may have to take account of the texture, appearance and viscosity of the product, as well as its perishability. Dangerous products such as medicines or corrosive household cleaners need special attention. Other design issues might include the role of the packaging in keeping the product ready for use, the means of dispensing the product and the graphic design, presenting the brand imagery and the statutory and desired on-pack information.

Naturally, there is a cost involved in all of this and thus the organisation needs to be reassured that a particular solution to its packaging needs and problems will either serve a functional purpose or enhance the product's image and competitive standing in the market. Equally, trying to save money by skimping on packaging could be a false economy. If the packaging does not work (literally or metaphorically), then the customer is likely to reject the whole product. Although it can cost £100 000 to create a packaging design for an fmcg product, it seems a very reasonable sum compared

> **Example**   Heinz (http://www.heinz.com) undertook a re-packaging exercise to bring greater coherence to the appearance of its soups, pasta meals and beans. For convenience foods, packaging design has to be clear and distinctive to attract busy shoppers moving through supermarkets. Research had indicated to Heinz that shoppers were moving more quickly through aisles and spending less time on shopping. Although the traditional packaging colours for tomato soups and beans were retained, colour was used to emphasise the distinctiveness of other ranges. 'Big Soup' labels were, therefore, presented with a dark green background rather than red. Similarly, 'Chef's Specials' pasta meals, such as ravioli and macaroni cheese, appeared with a yellow background including the traditional Heinz keystone design, rather than in their original orange and bright green respectively (Smith, 1998).

with the £3 million or more that will be spent on the advertising to launch that same product. McKenzie (1997) found that the packaging design was becoming a vital element in developing a brand proposition to the consumer both in advertising and point-of-sale promotion. This could be the case both for a new product launch and for relaunching existing products that might be starting to look tired.

With the rise of the self-service ethos in consumer markets, packaging has indeed grown in importance. It has to communicate product information to help the consumer make a choice, to communicate brand image and positioning and, mostly, to attract attention at the point of sale and invite the consumer to explore the product further. Even in organisational markets, packaging is important. To serve organisational customers' needs, suppliers have to think about how best to bundle quantities of product together for ease of handling for fast-moving products, how best to protect products that will be held for a time in storage or how to make it as easy as possible for a customer to unpack and introduce a component or product into a production line.

Thus packaging is an important part of the overall product offering and has a number of marketing and technical dimensions, some of which are discussed below.

Functions of packaging

Functional

First among the functions of packaging are the practicalities. Packaging must be *functional*: it must protect the product in storage, in shipment and often in use. Packaging may consist of a number of layers, each serving a different purpose. A packet of frozen beefburgers, for example, may have an outer cardboard box. This protects the product in transit and handling, creating units of a standard size that can easily be packaged together for delivery to the retailer. The outer box also allows the retail display to be attractive and tidy, presenting necessary product information, cooking instructions and selling points to the consumer. Within the box, the burgers may be sealed in groups of six inside clear plastic wrapping. This prevents them from suffering 'freezer burn', a natural process of deterioration in unprotected frozen food. The individual burgers are finally separated from each other with a single sheet of film to prevent them from sticking together.

Frozen food is not the only area in which it is necessary to preserve freshness. Jars of coffee and cans of dried milk, such as Marvel, have an inner seal that serves the double purpose of keeping the product fresh until it is opened and reassuring the customer that the product has not been tampered with before purchase.

Other packaging functions centre on convenience for the consumer, both in terms of ease of access and ease of use. The ring-pull tins now used for canned sardines, for example, have made the sweat and (usually) bloodshed associated with the old-style key-operated tins a thing of the past (corned beef canners take note!). An example of packaging that also helps the usage of the product is shower gel. The lid of the pack, incorporating a hook, is removed and clipped to the bottom of the pack to allow it to be hung in the shower. A self-sealing mechanism in some packs means that the contents do not drip out unless the pack is purposefully squeezed. In the convenience food sector, ease of use has come with the development of packaging that can be placed straight inside a microwave oven and thus serves as a cooking utensil. These last examples also underline the necessity for packaging materials, design and technology to develop in parallel with markets and emerging market needs. Consumer pressure for fewer preservatives and additives in food products has also encouraged the development of packaging that better preserves pack content. Conversely, advances in packaging technology can themselves lead to the opening up of new opportunities. The development of the 'widget', a device incorporated into beer cans, has opened up the market for canned beer that behaves and tastes like draught.

A less positive driving force behind packaging development was the sad spate of attempts at corporate blackmail through product-tampering scares. Manufacturers and retailers alike became very concerned to hasten the development of packaging that was difficult to interfere with without leaving an obvious trace. Many jars or packages now have at least a visually prominent seal on the outer pack with the verbal warning that the product should not be used if the seal is damaged.

Promotional

In addition to offering functional information about product identity and use, packaging also serves a *promotional* purpose. It needs to grab and hold the consumer's attention and involve them with the product. This means that the packaging is actually adding value to the brand; this can be achieved through the combination of materials, shape, graphics and colour.

Finally, packaging can literally be used for promotional purposes. It gives the manufacturer a powerful medium of communication. It can be used, for example, as a means of distributing coupons, for advertising other related products, announcing new products, presenting on-pack offers or distributing samples and gifts. A special can was developed for Lucozade Sport, for example, that allowed 'instant win' vouchers to be sealed into the packaging, separate from the liquid. There is more on all of this in Chapter 16 on sales promotion.

> **Example** The added psychological value of the packaging is an absolutely essential part of some products. Perfumes, for example, rely heavily on their packaging to endorse the qualities of luxury, expense, exclusivity, mystery and self-indulgence that they try to represent. Champagne, a perfume by Yves St Laurent, comes in a crimson-lined gold box, which opens out like a kind of casket to reveal an elegant bottle representing a champagne cork, complete with gold wire. It is estimated that the packaging for such a product actually costs about three times as much as the content of the bottle itself. Closer to the mass market, Easter eggs are also an example of the packaging outshining the content. Novelty carton shapes, bright graphics, ribbons and bows are central to the purchasing decision and dull any natural inclination to compare the price with the actual chocolate content.

Packaging in the marketing mix

Packaging plays an important part in the marketing mix. This chapter has already outlined its functional importance, its communication possibilities and its crucial role as a first point of physical contact between the buyer and the product. Effective and thoughtful packaging is recognised as means of increasing sales.

Even the choice of the range of pack sizes to offer the market can reinforce the objectives of the marketing mix. Trial-size packs, clearly labelled as such, help with new product launch (*see also* Chapter 16) by encouraging low-risk product trial. Small-sized packs of an established product may reinforce a commitment to a market segment comprising single-person households or infrequent users. Larger packs target family usage, heavy users generally or the cost-conscious segment who see the large pack as better value for money. The increase in out-of-town shopping by car means that consumers are far better able than ever before to buy large, bulky items. This trend has developed further into the demand for multiple packs. When the US warehouse club Costco first opened in the UK, it only sold in bulk quantities such as gallon jars of HP Sauce, 10-kilo packs of dishwashing powder and 4-kilo packs of minced beef. These sizes were, however, later found to be somewhat larger than the customer really wanted, even when buying in bulk. Pack sizes may also be closely linked with end-use segmentation (*see* p. 191). Ice-cream can be packaged as either an individual treat, a family block or a party-sized tub. The consumer selects the appropriate size depending on the end use, but the choice must be there or else the consumer will turn to another brand.

Any organisation needs to appreciate the different packaging demands of different markets. Ensor (1997) examined differences in packaging preferences across Europe. Cans are more popular in France and Spain than card or foil because of the small size and lower prevalence of refrigerators and microwaves, yet soup is traditionally sold in packets. Germans prefer their cake wrapped in foil as they believe it means a fresher product, while the French like a cellophane window so that they can inspect the cake. In France and Spain, packaging has to work hard in the hypermarkets because of the wide range of products stocked in each category and thus colour, shape, type and size of pack all have an impact on the shelf. Retailer Albert Heijn, with over 650 stores in the Netherlands, some of them small, prefers smaller pack sizes. All of this means careful research in European countries so that the most appropriate package can be developed.

Another demand relates to waste packaging. The framework of the European Packaging and Packaging Waste Directive 1994 requires schemes for the recovery of at least half of all waste packaging and for the recycling of at least one quarter to be set up. This has led to some criticism from the trade (Bickerstaffe, 1999). It is argued that the escalating costs of implementing regulations are out of all proportion to the environmental benefits. The focus is on the environmental impact of packaging, not on the material and energy used throughout the distribution chain or on the goods wasted because of inappropriate packaging. Food has a value often 10 times that of packaging and better packaging could reduce food waste. The regulations are, however, getting tougher. In the UK, the 1999 Packaging (Essential Requirements) Regulations enable Trading Standards Officers to enforce a ruling that all packaging must be minimal by volume and weight in line with safety, hygiene and consumer acceptance. The regulations also require that the packaging should be recyclable and, if not, that the environmental impact should be minimised.

In contrast, the European Commission is in dispute with the Danish government over its adoption of a very tough stance that bans aluminium cans for beer and soft drinks and also bans non-refillable glass and plastic bottles. In the view of the energy and environment minister Svend Auken:

> **The Commission wants us to allow any form of disposable packaging ... Denmark does not want to find itself submerged in packing and does not want to deal with problems caused by extra waste.**
>
> (as quoted in *European Policy Analyst*, 1998b)

The Commission maintains that the ban acts 25 a barrier to the free movement of goods within a single market and as a form of protection against competition from non-Danish companies.

In developing a new product or planning a product relaunch, an organisation thus needs to think carefully about all aspects of packaging and its integration into the overall marketing mix of the product. The technical and design considerations, along with the likely trade and consumer reactions, need to be assessed. Consumers in particular can become very attached to packaging. It can be as recognisable and as cherished as a friend's face and consumers may not, therefore, take kindly to plastic surgery! Sudden packaging changes may lead to a suspicion that other things about the product have also changed for the worse. All of this goes to show that, as with any aspect of marketing, packaging design and concepts need careful research and testing, using where possible one of the growing number of professional consultancies in the field.

Labelling

Labelling is a particular area within the packaging field that represents the outermost layer of the product. Labels have a strong functional dimension, in that they include warnings and instructions, as well as information required by law or best industry practice. Labels state, at the very least, the weight or volume of the product (often including a stylised letter 'e', which means that the variation in weight or volume between packs is within certain tolerances laid down by the EU), a barcode and the name and contact address of the producer. Consumer demand has also led to the inclusion of far more product information, such as ingredients, nutritional information and the environmental friendliness of the product. Information about the extent to which the packaging is made of recycled materials or can be recycled is also much more common now.

The European Commission is struggling to develop common standards for product labelling across Europe based on successful schemes such as Germany's Blue Angel and the Scandinavian Nordic Swan. The Ecolabel, based on the well-established Blue Angel scheme, gives a consumer reassurance that the products displaying it conform to EU environmental standards. A number of washing machines carry the Ecolabel, reflecting standards in energy, water and detergent consumption. Food labelling about additives and nutritional values has also received attention and this is likely to evolve further with public concern about the identification of genetically modified foods. There has, however, been some concern expressed that the information is too complex and confusing to the consumer and there may be a need to show information in a more graphical way. Despite the potential problems, the EU Parliament has proposed an elaboration of the Ecolabel logo, with additional information, and its extension to retail and service providers (*European Policy Analyst*, 1998a).

The prominence and detail of health and safety instructions are also becoming increasingly important, as organisations seek to protect themselves against prosecution or civil liability should the product be misused. These instructions range from general warnings to keep a product out of the reach of children, to prohibitions on inhaling solvent-based products, through to detailed instructions about the use of protective clothing.

Clear labelling in terms of the matters discussed in this section is important and necessary. The information may be incorporated into the outer packaging as a whole or there may be a distinctive and separate label. Many organisational products, for example, may be plainly wrapped and bear a very functional label, serving to identify only the product and its use.

PRODUCT DESIGN, QUALITY AND GUARANTEES

Design

The preceding discussion of packaging has already mentioned one aspect of design. But there is far more to design than just pretty logos, graphics and attractive packaging. Design is an integral part of the product itself, affecting not only its overall aesthetic qualities but also its ergonomic properties (i.e. the ease and comfort with which it can be used) and even its components and materials. All of this together can enhance the product's visual appeal, its ability to fulfil its function and its reliability and life span.

Industrial designers have to tread a fine line between innovativeness and customer expectations. Microsoft, for example, has designed an ergonomic computer keyboard that allows the wrists and hands to maintain a much more natural position while typing, reducing the risk of strain and making the typist more relaxed. The new keyboard looks good too, with gentle curves replacing the familiar boxy shape of traditional keyboards. The benefits are unquestionable, yet people are so used to the old design that despite the discomforts, they are slow to make the change. Innovative design can, nevertheless, be the making of a product.

Example Dyson vacuum cleaners (http://www.dyson.com) are designed to operate without a dust bag, giving the technical benefits of better suction and no risk of blockages or burst bags. The design innovation goes further, however, affecting the aesthetics of the product too. The upright model, the Dyson Dual Cyclone, is generally the same kind of shape as the traditional uprights of companies such as Hoover, yet there are subtle details of styling, colouring and design (for instance the see-through dust collection chamber) that clearly differentiate it from the competition and give the message that here is something more advanced, more futuristic, more exciting than you are used to. All these design advantages allowed Dyson to price its initial product at double the price of the best-selling units and 25 per cent higher than even the highest-priced competitor. Despite the price premium, it achieved a 60 per cent share of the upright cleaner segment, including strong sales to the C and D socioeconomic groups (Miles, 1995).

MARKETING IN ACTION **You can have any colour you like as long as it's grey**

What colour would you like your computer, madam, grey or beige? That used to be the way to sell PCs until Apple's launch of the iMac in September 1998. Apple had been somewhat pushed into a specialised niche, mainly in the education and graphic design markets, but wanted a better presence in the mainstream home PC market. In creating a product for this market, it still wanted to be distinctive and so decided to introduce colour and high styling into its new iMac home PC. The iMac still emphasised Apple's strengths as being easy to use and ideal for first-time buyers, but also emphasised its 'look' rather than its speed or more technical aspects of performance. The conical outer casing of translucent plastic was markedly different from any PC that had gone before. Apple selected a strap line to reflect the design differences with 'Think Different', supported by 'Chic. Not Geek' and 'Sorry, No Beige'. The early signs were that the change in approach had been successful. Apple reversed the trend in its declining market share and appeared to be attracting more fashion-conscious new users.

Other manufacturers are now considering introducing stronger style elements. Hewlett-Packard plans to launch coloured PCs, although market leaders Compaq and Packard Bell NEC are waiting a while, preferring to emphasise applications, value and reliability rather than 'slinky design'.

Sources: Rosier (1999); Wilkinson (1998), http://www.apple.com.

Despite the success stories, it must nevertheless be said that design is often not given the recognition or priority that it deserves. Lorenz (1994) gives two broad reasons for this. First, design does not have a clear place in strategic planning, or indeed in the set of strategic concepts that many managers use. Design and its potential contribution is simply not well enough understood by most managers. Second, because design has traditionally been a lowly function, smothered by marketing or engineering departments, it is not given a proper weighting in decision-making processes. Governments have, however, recognised the importance of design in helping industry to gain a sustainable competitive edge in global markets. Bodies such as the UK's Design Council, the Netherlands Design Institute and the French Agence pour la Promotion de la Création Industrielle promote and support good design practice. The EU also encourages design with initiatives such as the biannual European Community Design Prize aimed at small and medium-sized businesses.

Quality

Unlike design, quality is a very well-understood concept among managers. Many organisations now recognise the importance of quality and have adopted the philosophy of total quality management (TQM), which means that all employees take responsibility for building quality into whatever they do. TQM affects all aspects of the organisation's work, from materials handling to the production process, from the product itself to the administrative procedures that provide customer service. Marketers, of course, have a vested interest in all these manifestations of quality, because creating and holding on to customers means not only providing the quality of product that they want (and providing it consistently), but also supporting the product with quality administrative, technical and after-sales service.

In judging the quality of the product itself, a number of dimensions may be considered, as shown in Fig. 7.6.

Performance

Performance is about what the product can actually *do*. Thus with the Bosch hammer drills mentioned earlier (*see* Fig. 7.3), a customer might perceive the more expensive model with a variable speed of 3000 rpm as being of 'better quality' than the more basic two-speed drill. The customer might have more difficulty judging between competing products, however. Black & Decker, for example, produces a range of hammer drills that are very similar to the Bosch ones, with minor variations in specification and price levels. If both the Bosch model and the equivalent Black & Decker model offer the same functions, features, benefits and pricing levels, the customer might have problems differentiating between them in terms of performance and will have to judge on other characteristics.

Durability

Some products are expected to have a longer life span than others and some customers are prepared to pay more for what they perceive to be a better-quality, more *durable* product. Thus the quality level built into the product needs to be suited to its expected life and projected usage. Thus a child's digital watch fitted into a plastic strap featuring a licensed character such as Barbie or Batman, retailing at around £5, is not expected to have the same durability or quality level as a Swiss Tissot retailing at £125. Disposable products in particular, such as razors, biros and cigarette lighters, need to be manufactured to a quality level that is high enough to allow them to perform the required function for the required number of uses or for the required time span, yet low enough to keep the price down to a level where the customer accepts the concept of frequent replacement.

Reliability and maintenance

Many customers are concerned about the probability of a product breaking down or otherwise failing, and about the ease and economy of repairs. As with durability, some customers will pay a price premium for what are perceived to be more *reliable*

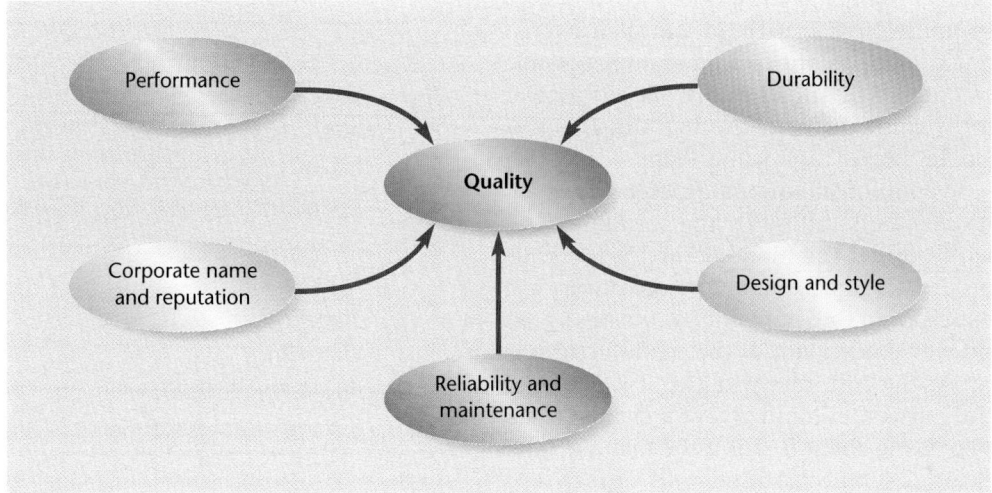

FIGURE 7.6

Product quality dimensions

products or for the peace of mind offered by comprehensive after-sales support. These days most makes of car, for example, are pretty reliable if they are properly maintained and so car buyers may differentiate on the basis of the cost and ease of servicing and the cost and availability of spare parts. For example, among the appealing features of the Trabant are its durability, its reliability and a mechanical simplicity that allows many repairs to be done by the owner.

Design and style

As mentioned earlier, the visual and ergonomic appeal of a product may influence perceptions of its quality. The sleek, stylish, aerodynamic lines of the Lambourghini contrast sharply with the functional boxiness of the Lada. Packaging design can also enhance quality perceptions. In the 1998 Design Effectiveness Awards, the winner was the Psion Series 5 palmtop, as discussed at p. 5 in Chapter 1.

England's Fly Fishers also used innovation in design and style to carve out a new market niche. The company designed an inflatable fishing jacket that not only matched those already on the market for style, but also had the added advantage of a life-saving device that gives automatic self-inflation and is self-righting. This means that the jacket will inflate even if the wearer is unconscious or unable to inflate an orthodox lifejacket and that the head will be kept above water. Just the thing for the unfortunate fisherman taking a premature dip, and not bad for sales either, as the company exports its goods throughout Europe and the Americas (Warman, 1997).

Corporate name and reputation

If, after all that, customers are still uncertain about the relative quality offerings of the alternative products under consideration, they may fall back on their *perceptions of the organisation*. Some may feel that Black & Decker is a well-established, familiar name, and if they have had other Black & Decker products that have served well in the past, then that might swing the quality decision in Black & Decker's favour. Others may decide in favour of Bosch because of its associations with high-quality German engineering.

Marketers recognise that quality in the market-place is a matter of perception rather than technical specification. This is particularly true in consumer markets, where the potential customer may not have the expertise to judge quality objectively and will use all sorts of cues, such as price, packaging or comparison with competitors, to form an opinion about quality level. A survey by Total Research called EquiTrend, measured brand quality perception among consumers of over 170 brands in some 30 product and service categories. Table 7.6 shows the top 10 brands from the 1998 EquiTrend and their overall quality ratings out of a maximum possible score of 10. Incidentally, Bosch power tools came 12th in the list and Black & Decker power tools came 19th.

Even in organisational markets, the quality agenda is still set by the customer, who will soon let the manufacturer know if its product is unacceptably inconsistent or if its response to complaints or queries is too slow or inadequate. If the manufacturer is lucky, the customer will give it warning of their discontent and give it a chance to do something about it, but if the manufacturer is unlucky, the customer will simply stop

TABLE 7.6

Brand quality ratings, 1998

Rank	Brand	Perceived quality
1	Mercedes-Benz Cars	8.46
2	BMW Cars	8.31
3	Disney World, Florida	8.01
4	Cadbury's Dairy Milk Chocolate Bars	7.96
5	Lego Toys	7.95
6	Duracell Batteries	7.95
7	Sony Televisions	7.89
8	Fisher-Price Toys	7.80
9	Kodak Photographic Film	7.78
10	Kellogg's Corn Flakes Cereal	7.68

Source: EquiTrend, Total Research, London. Reprinted with kind permission.

The high quality German engineering heritage enhances a quality reputation.

Source: Robert Bosch Ltd.

buying from it. This further underlines the need for some kind of constant dialogue with customers to ensure that the warning signs are picked up early. In general, investment in quality is good for business, creating satisfied and loyal customers.

Guarantees

One way in which an organisation can emphasise its commitment to quality and its confidence in its own products and procedures is through the *guarantees* it offers. Although customers are protected under national and EU laws against misleading product claims and goods that are not fit for their intended purpose, many organisations choose to extend their responsibility beyond the legal minimum. Some will offer extended warranties. Double-glazing companies, for example, routinely offer 10- or 15-year guarantees on their windows, which is fine as long as the company is still in existence in 10 or 15 years' time! Others are less ambitious and simply offer 'no questions asked' refunds or replacements if the customer is unhappy with a product for any reason at all. Retailer Marks & Spencer has operated such a policy for many years and, although this can be abused, it is generally highly valued by customers. In a completely different market, Rover cars offered a similar scheme in which the customer was entitled to a full refund within a month of purchase, regardless of their reasons for returning the car. Such schemes not only reflect the organisation's confidence in its product and its commitment to customer service, but also reduce the risk to the customer in trying the product.

The EU has agreed to draft a law that will entitle consumers across 15 member states to a two-year guarantee on goods purchased, quadrupling the mandatory warranty period in some countries such as Germany, Greece and Spain. Under this legislation, the buyers of defective goods will be able to demand repair, replacement or a price reduction or money back (Smith, 1999).

It may also be possible for the organisation to use its guarantees to create a differential advantage over its competitors. The danger is, however, that promises can be copied. The largest UK supermarket chains, for example, trying to shift the emphasis away from price competition to quality of service, are all now offering very similar packages, including refund and replacement schemes on any product that fails to satisfy. Perhaps the real differentiator will be the speed, efficiency and courtesy with which those promises are fulfilled. In strategic terms, the biggest potential problem is that once similar guarantees have become widespread within a particular market or industry, they start to be seen as a normal part of the product package and their impact may be lost as customers look for other differentiating factors.

CHAPTER SUMMARY

This chapter has provided a broad introduction to the product element of the marketing mix. Product is *defined* as covering a wide variety of goods, services and ideas that can be the subject of a marketing exchange. The product itself is layered, consisting of the core product, the tangible product and, finally, the augmented product. Using the tangible and augmented product, manufacturers, service providers and retailers can create differential advantage.

Products can be *classified* according to either their own characteristics (durable, non-durable or service) or buyer-orientated characteristics. In consumer markets, these are linked with the frequency of purchase and the length and depth of the inform-ation search. In organisational markets, they are more likely to relate to the final use of the product. An organisation's product mix, made up of individual product items, can be divided into product lines. These are groups of items that have some common link, either operational or marketing based. Product mix width is established by the number of product lines, while product line depth is defined according to the number of individual items within a line.

Branding is an important way of creating differentiated tangible products. It helps the manufacturer to establish loyalty through the three-dimensional character imposed on the product, as well as deflecting consumer attention away from price. Branding is carried out not only by manufacturers, but also by retailers who want to create a more tangible character for themselves, as well as wanting consumers consciously to prefer to shop at their outlets.

Branding issues concerning manufacturers include the choice of *brand name* and the choice of product range *brand policy. Packaging* is another important element of the tangible product. *Labelling*, as a specific area of packaging, covers the legally necessary information to be included on the pack as well as the additional information the consumer demands.

Product *design* is an important but often under-estimated function, as it can help to create differential advantage, by building in new useful features or benefits and emphasising the way in which the product differs. In many organisations, however, design is not given the priority, resources or consideration that it deserves, partly because of its traditionally lowly status and partly because it does not feature strongly in the kinds of strategic planning frameworks that managers commonly use. *Quality* is also an important concept, but its contribution, unlike that of design, has been fully recognised and through TQM programmes it has been integrated into all aspects of organisational performance.

Guarantees reflect the organisation's confidence in its products and its procedures and reduce the perceived risk to the potential customer in trying a product. These guarantees or manufacturers' warranties are over and above any legal protection to which the customer is entitled. Guarantees can create a differential advantage, provided that the competition cannot copy them, or they might be necessary simply to keep pace with competitors who implemented them first.

Key words and phrases

Augmented product	Non-durable products	Shopping goods
Branding	Own-label brands	Speciality goods
Convenience goods	Potential product	Tangible product
Core product	Product items	Unsought goods
Durable products	Product lines	
Manufacturer brands	Product mix	

QUESTIONS FOR REVIEW

7.1 What, other than physical goods, might be classed as products?

7.2 What is the *augmented product* and why might it be important?

7.3 Define *durable* and *non-durable* products and summarise the likely marketing differences between them.

7.4 What is a *speciality product* and how might its marketing mix and the kind of buying behaviour associated with it differ from those found with other products?

7.5 What are the six different categories within the *user-based product classification system* for organisational products?

7.6 Why do you think the EU felt it necessary to extend the range of things that can be registered as trade marks?

7.7 What benefits does branding offer the consumer?

7.8 Why do retailers develop *own-brand products*?

7.9 What are the advantages and disadvantages of *monolithic* branding compared with *discreet* branding?

7.10 How can design contribute to the success of a new product?

QUESTIONS FOR DISCUSSION

7.1 Choose three different brands of shampoo that you think incorporate different *core products*.

(a) Define the *core product* for each brand.
(b) How does the *tangible product* for each brand reflect the *core product*?

7.2 Adapt Fig. 7.1 to suit the specific example of a personal computer:

(a) for family use; and
(b) for the use of a small business.

How do your two diagrams differ from each other, and why?

7.3 Choose a manufacturer of consumer products and list all the brands it sells. How might these brands be grouped into product lines and why? (You might find Fig. 7.2 helpful.)

7.4 List as many functions of packaging as you can.

7.5 Develop a weighted set of five or six criteria for 'good' labelling. Collect a number of competing brands of the same product and rate each of them against your criteria. Which brand comes out best? As a result of this exercise, would you adjust your weightings or change the criteria included?

CASE STUDY 7.1

Celebrating the success of the brand

In 1995, the UK market for confectionery was worth around £3.27bn. The UK has a very sweet tooth. The British munch their way through 9.08 kilos of chocolate each every year in a market dominated by Cadbury's (29 per cent share), Nestlé-Rowntree (25 per cent) and Mars (21 per cent).

Mars (http://www.mars.com) is a long-established player in the worldwide chocolate market and some of its brands have been around since the 1930s. The company has done a lot of

▶

innovation by extending and developing products under its existing brand names rather than creating completely new brands. It has six core brands: Mars, Milky Way, Galaxy, Bounty, M&Ms and Snickers. Thus Milky Way Magic Stars, Mars Bar Light, Galaxy Caramel, Galaxy Hazelnut, Galaxy Ripple and Galaxy Swirls, among others, have all been introduced.

Mars had no presence, however, in the £624mn boxed chocolate sector in which rivals Cadbury's and Nestlé-Rowntree were dominant, but as it is a very valuable sector, representing around 19 per cent of the total market in 1995, Mars really wanted to change this. Boxed chocolates can be further divided into four distinct segments:

- *luxury gift*: for example premium-priced Belgian chocolates;
- *traditional gift*: assortments such as Black Magic and Milk Tray;
- *family sharing*: boxed assortments of loose, individually wrapped sweets such as Roses (15 per cent share of the boxed chocolate sector) and Quality Street (13 per cent); and
- *mints*: boxed after-dinner mints such as After Eights.

The main growth in the early 1990s was within the family sharing segment, which grew by 12 per cent between 1990 and 1995. Mars felt that there was a gap there. As it had already invested in creating miniature versions of its known and loved brands, there was an obvious choice to bring the various miniatures together as a boxed chocolate selection. Mars hoped to exploit the synergy between the core brands to create a new product with a strong image offering variety to the consumer. A new brand identity, Celebrations, was developed to create a distinctive identity for the selection that was clearly separate from all of the core Mars brands and that would not compromise their positioning.

Celebrations, developed specifically for the UK market, consists of twist-wrapped miniatures of Mars brands Topic, Snickers, Mars Bar, Maltesers, Bounty, Galaxy, Galaxy Caramel and Galaxy Truffles. They come in 300g and 500g boxes, similar in shape to those used by Roses and Quality Street. Roses and Quality Street are both formidable and well-established brands, but within the box, their main offer is variety. The individual sweets have no brand value in themselves. Mars felt that with Celebrations, it was offering a much more attractive proposition based on variety and strong individual brand characters within the box.

Celebrations was test marketed in the Tyne-Tees television area in 1996 before a national roll-out. The test market began in late October 1996 and was designed to assess the product's performance in the crucial run-up to Christmas. A 30-second television advertisement, 'poking fun at all things mini', was commissioned and screened as a vital part of generating awareness and establishing product image within the test-market area.

As a result of the test market, Mars made minor alterations to Celebrations, finalised sales forecasts and went ahead with a national launch. The launch took place in September 1997 so that the product would be sufficiently well established to exploit the Christmas market. Initially, Mars spent £500 000 on a 'Celebrations Express' celebrity-laden train to travel around the country and then a £2mn advertising campaign began in October. Trial packs (65g retailing at 49p) and an instant win promotion with £1 million in cash prizes completed the £3.5mn launch package. A strong relationship with retailers such as Tesco allowed Mars to negotiate prime shelf space and a wide frontage for the brand, as well as offering extra loyalty card points as a promotion with each purchase.

Mars was also keen to ensure that the new product was not discounted by retailers, as that might damage its image. To avoid this, it produced the small trial packs to act as an incentive to consumers to try the brand and stimulate re-purchase of the bigger packs. While there could be cause for conflict between retailer own brands (for example Tesco's Occasions) and Celebrations, Mars was careful to demonstrate how Celebrations could contribute positively to extending the retailer's range within a growing sector. The retail trade was thus very receptive to the product.

Table 7.7 compares the pack sizes and retail prices of Celebrations and other brands with which it was directly competing at the time of its launch.

TABLE 7.7 Celebrations and competing brands

Brand	Size (g)	Price (Tesco, 19.9.97)
Roses	227	£1.85
Quality Street	227	£1.85
Occasions (Tesco own brand)	227	£1.50
Celebrations	300	£2.59

Mars hoped that all its launch activities, as well as product exposure on shop shelves, would mean that every adult in Britain would have seen the brand's logo at least 50 times by Christmas 1997. Such an impact was probably essential if it wanted to achieve its targets for the brand:

- £30mn sales in the four months after the national launch;
- £75mn sales per year within three years; and
- to be in the top 10 of confectionery brands within two years.

By 1998, in *Marketing*'s 'Ten Hot Brands to Watch', Celebrations was number 3 (Bainbridge and Curtis, 1998a). Its first Easter egg had been a success and, by October 1998, the shops were prominently displaying a range of special Christmas packs. By early 1999, the brand was established as third in the family sharing segment and was estimated to be worth about £50mn, with an 8.1 per cent share of the boxed chocolate sector.

Sources: Authers (1996); Bainbridge and Curtis (1998a, 1998b); Bentley (1996); Gilchrist (1995); *The Grocer* (1997); *Marketing* (1999); Mintel (1996a, 1996b); Rees (1995); Tylee (1996); Waples (1997); and with grateful thanks to Graham Hunter, Celebrations Brand Manager, Mars Confectionery.

Questions

1 What is the core product that Celebrations offers?

2 What is the role of packaging for a product like Celebrations?

3 What are the advantages and disadvantages of using existing brand names for this new product launch?

4 How does Celebrations differentiate itself from its competitors?

CASE STUDY 7.2

The market with no stiff competition

Viagra was something of an accidental discovery. Scientists testing an angina drug found that as a side effect, it seemed to cure impotence in many patients. It did not take long for its manufacturer, Pfizer (http://www.pfizer.com), to decide to focus on its unexpected benefit and to develop the product further as an anti-impotence drug. The drug was licensed by the US FDA (Food and Drugs Administration) and launched in the US in April 1998, amidst a huge fanfare of serious and not so serious media hype. In the first month, 570 000 new prescriptions for Viagra were issued, generating $100mn in revenue. The number of prescriptions peaked in May at over 1.2mn, but then started to fall.

In June, Pfizer started a campaign estimated to be costing tens of millions of dollars on consumer-oriented advertising in popular magazines such as *Time*, *Life* and *Newsweek*. The start of the campaign alone was estimated to have cost around $30mn. The main reason for this seems to have been a desire to regain control over the brand image, ensuring that it was positioned as Pfizer wanted it to be and that accurate information was given to the public. The enormous level of publicity that Viagra had generated was not necessarily a good thing. The publicity was out of Pfizer's control, meaning that it could be inaccurate and/or damaging to the brand image. The thousands of jokes made about the brand could well have had a negative effect, making patients embarrassed about owning up to an impotence problem and asking for the drug. Pfizer waited until the worst of the publicity had died down before launching its campaign to make sure that its message was heard properly and that the drug was taken more seriously. It also waited until the number of prescriptions started to droop in order to inject new life into the product. This fall was not a surprise, as market analysts had been expecting an early peak due to pent-up demand before the drug's launch, because it was the first relatively simple solution to a common problem. This, along with all the media hype, had led to a rapid take-up after its introduction.

Despite the campaign, by October revenue had fallen to just $40mn per month. Some felt that this was more than a simple levelling off in demand and that it had more to do with reports of a number of deaths from cardiac problems, possibly exacerbated by the drug. In January 1999, after around 130 deaths, *Medical Marketing and Media* reported that the FDA was requiring Pfizer to change the label on Viagra to draw the user's attention to the risk of death, heart attacks and hypertension, among other effects noticed after the drug had been launched.

Pfizer also faced other problems with Viagra. The hype about the drug was such that a lot of people wanted it and a lot of people wanted to supply it. There was a proliferation of websites offering it, such as http://www.xtra-med.com offering Viagra for anything from $6 per dose, posted to you in a plain package. Because the Internet is a global network with no central regulatory control, however, it is difficult for Pfizer to do much about this. Both Pfizer and the American Medical Association are adamant that prospective Viagra patients should undergo a full physical examination before a prescription is given. Websites, however, only take prospective patients through a series of questions about their medical history that are evaluated by a doctor, who then approves or fails to approve the prescription. If a buyer really wants the drug, it can be relatively easy to work out the 'right' questionnaire answers to ensure that the doctor approves the prescription. Anyone who is prepared to lie like that is hardly likely to be put off by website disclaimers and warnings about the folly of supplying false information.

All the US publicity was heard in Europe and made the European market a little more difficult to enter. When Viagra was eventually licensed in Europe late in 1998, the UK health minister pronounced that Viagra would not be made available on the National Health Service (NHS). This had a lot to do with NHS priorities: impotence is not high on the list, apparently, and there were fears about the cost to the NHS if all the hype produced the same sort of level of demand as in the US. Other European governments, such as Germany, Austria and France, took a similar view. Some observers, however, feared that this would push Viagra into the black market and that it would deny valuable treatment to those who were genuinely suffering because of impotence. Pfizer

believes that Japan will be the last country to license the drug, because its regulations require more trials and then a two-year wait after the results of these for government screening to be completed. Meanwhile, Japanese men are taking trips to Hawaii to pay $600 to get a medical examination and a three-month supply of Viagra.

Viagra's fame has also meant that Pfizer picked up a number of uses of the brand name in other companies' advertising and was threatening legal action against such infringement of its trade mark. *FHM* magazine, for instance, advertised an increase in its circulation figures by featuring a bottle of Viagra and the line 'Getting Bigger Has Never Been Our Problem'. A strongly worded warning from Pfizer's legal department is usually enough to stop particular cases of the brand name's abuse. Companies that have asked if they can use the brand name in advertising or for other marketing purposes have been refused permission.

Sources: Amaha (1998); *Business and Health* (1998); Gopal (1998); Greenhalgh (1999); *Marketing Week* (1998); *Medical Marketing and Media* (1999); Petersen (1998); *Time* (1998–99); West (1998a, 1998b); Wirth Fellman (1998).

Questions

1 What issues do you think a pharmaceutical company like Pfizer has to take into account when deciding on a brand name for a new drug?

2 How would you classify Viagra as a consumer product?

3 'There's no such thing as bad publicity.' So why is Pfizer worried about media coverage, the website prescription of Viagra and the use of the name in other companies' advertising?

4 To what extent do you think the packaging considerations are the same for Viagra and a mainstream fmcg product?

References to Chapter 7

Amaha, E. (1998), 'Potent Potion', *Far Eastern Economic Review*, 18 June, p. 56.

Authers, J. (1996), 'Sales Success Less Sweet as Chewers Avoid Sugar', *Financial Times*, 2 January, p. 6.

Bainbridge, J. and Curtis, J. (1998a), 'The UK's Biggest Brands, Part 1', *Marketing*, 30 July, pp. 22–5.

Bainbridge, J. and Curtis, J. (1998b), 'The UK's Biggest Brands, Part 2', *Marketing*, 6 August, pp. 20–3.

Baird, R. (1998), 'Asset Tests', *Marketing Week*, 1 October, pp. 28–31.

Bentley, S. (1996), 'Mars Launches Attack on Boxed Chocolate Sector', *Marketing Week*, 7 June, p. 8.

Bickerstaffe, J. (1999), 'We're Really Snowed Under', *The Grocer*, 27 March, p. 46.

Blackett, T. (1985), 'Brand Name Research – Getting it Right', *Marketing and Research Today*, May, pp. 89–93.

Bray, R. (1998), 'Soon You May Be Sleeping in Comfort', *Financial Times*, 19 November , p. V.

Business and Health (1998), 'Virtual Viagra', *Business and Health*, December, p. 11.

Butterfield, L. (1998), 'Brands Become the Biggest Assets of All', *Sunday Times*, 20 September, p. 3.8.

Butterfield, L. and Haigh, D. (1998), *Understanding the Financial Value of Brands*, The Institute of Practitioners in Advertising.

Cunningham, S. (1998), 'Top Brands Feel the Heat', *Times*, 3 October, pp. 26–7.

Doyle, P. (1998), *Marketing Management and Strategy*, 2nd edn, Prentice-Hall Europe.

Ensor, J. (1997), 'Interpreting the European Market', *The Grocer*, 15 March, p. 67.

European Policy Analyst (1998a), 'Environment Report', *European Policy Analyst*, 3rd quarter, p. 67.

European Policy Analyst (1998b), 'Environment Report', *European Policy Analyst*, 4th quarter, p. 60.

Gilchrist, S. (1995), 'Victory is Sweet in Egg War', *The Times*, 15 April, p. 21.

Gilmour, F. (1989), 'Brand Blueprint', *Marketing*, 28 September, pp. 34–5.

Gopal, K. (1998), 'Please Pass the Viagra', *Pharmaceutical Executive*, October, pp. 28–30.

Greenhalgh, T. (1999), 'On the Pill', *Accountancy*, January, p. 58.

The Grocer (1997), 'Mars Set to Celebrate Nationally', *The Grocer*, 2 August, p. 52.

Hussey, M. (1998), 'Seriously, It's Barbie', *The Express*, 26 January, p. 19.

Hutton, R. (1999), 'Rover 75: the Last in Line That Goes Back to 1904?', *Sunday Times*, 7 February, p. 3.5.

Kahn, B. (1998), 'Mastering Marketing: Part Four Brand Strategy', *Financial Times Supplement*, pp. 4–6.

Lightfoot, W. (1998), 'Never Mind the Low Prices, Feel the Quality', *The European*, 5–11 October, p. 22.

Linnell, M. (1998), 'Prime Time at the Pumps', *The Grocer*, 6 February, pp. 34–6.

Lorenz, A. and Woodhead, M. (1999), 'Scrapped', *Sunday Times*, 7 February, p. 3.5.

Lorenz, C. (1994), 'Skin-deep Styling is Not Enough', *Financial Times*, 13 June, p. 17.

McKenzie, S. (1997), 'Package Deal', *Marketing Week*, 11 September, pp. 67–9.

McLuhan, R. (1999), 'Thomson Ads Go For Service', *Marketing*, 28 January, p. 21.

Marketing (1998), 'Travel Inn Seeks Agency for Push', *Marketing*, 17 December, p. 2.

Marketing (1999), 'Celebrations Boosts Mars' Sales by £50mn', *Marketing*, 11 February, p. 9.

Marketing Week (1998), 'Pfizer Acts to Stem the Rising Tide of Ads Using Viagra Branding', *Marketing Week*, 3 September, p. 11.

Medical Marketing and Media (1999), 'New Viagra Labelling Warns of Deaths', *Medical Marketing and Media*, 34 (1), p. 32.

Miles, L. (1995), 'Mothers and Fathers of Invention', *Marketing*, 1 June, pp. 26–7.

Mintel (1996a), 'Boxed Chocolates', *Market Intelligence*, June.

Mintel (1996b), 'Chocolate Confectionery', *Market Intelligence*, July.

Mitchell, A. (1998), 'Sky's the Limit for New Breed of Passion Brands', *Marketing Week*, 17 September, pp. 44–5.

Mitchell, A. (1999), 'How Brands Touch the Parts Others Can't Reach', *Marketing Week*, 18 March, pp. 22–3.

O'Connor, J. and Galvin, E. (1999), *Marketing and Information Technology*, 2nd edn, Financial Times Pitman Publishing.

Petersen, C. (1998), 'Viagra Fall Out Continues Abroad', *Pharmaceutical Executive*, September, p. D21.

Rees, J. (1995), 'Mars Launch Attacks Cadbury's Milk Tray', *Marketing Week*, 13 October, p. 5.

Rosier, B. (1999), 'Putting Colour into PC Sales', *Marketing*, 11 March, p. 18.

Slingsby, H. (1994), 'Distinguishing Marks', *Marketing Week*, 11 November, pp. 40–1.

Smith, A. (1998), 'Heinz Soups up its Old Image', *Financial Times*, 2 October, p. 13.

Smith, A. (1999), 'Accord Reached on Product Guarantees', *Financial Times*, 23 March, p. 2.

Talacko, P. (1999), 'Clustered PCs Do a "Super" Job', *Financial Times*, 1 February, p. 12.

Time (1998–99), 'What Goes Up', *Time*, 28 December–4 January, p. 154.

Tylee, J. (1996), 'AMV Ad Puts Mars in Boxed Chocolate Arena', *Campaign*, 18 October, p. 8.

Urry, M. (1999), 'Reckitt & Colman Awaits Invitation to the Takeover Ball', *Financial Times*, 4 February, p. 29.

Waples, J. (1997), 'Mars to Wage War on Roses', *Sunday Times*, 14 September, p. 3.1.

Warman, C. (1997), 'Happy Landings for Anglers Who Cast off', *The Times*, 20 October, p. 40.

West, D. (1998a), 'Honeymoon over for Viagra?', *Pharmaceutical Executive*, November, pp. DTC22–4.

West, D. (1998b), 'On-line Prescriptions Have Adverse Reactions', *Pharmaceutical Executive*, November, p. DTC28.

Wilkinson, A. (1998), 'Cutting Edge Apple iMac Takes on PCs', *Marketing Week*, 14 May, pp. 19–20.

Wirth Fellman, M. (1998), 'Preventing Viagra's Fall', *Marketing News*, 31 August, p. 1.

8 Product Management

LEARNING OBJECTIVES

This chapter will help you to:

1 understand the product life-cycle concept, its influence on marketing strategies and its limitations;

2 appreciate the importance of product positioning and how it both affects and is affected by marketing strategies;

3 understand the scope and implications of the various decisions that management can take with regard to product ranges, including deletion;

4 define the role and responsibilities of the product or brand manager; and

5 outline the issues surrounding pan-European branding.

INTRODUCTION

The previous chapter defined what a product is and some of the terms that are used in talking about products within organisations and markets. Even that general overview raised a number of strategic issues relating to how an organisation is supposed to manage such an important resource as its product range. This chapter addresses those issues.

Products need managing throughout their working lives. Someone has to decide what products should be created and when is the best time to launch them. Someone has to help the product to capitalise on its strengths and iron out its weaknesses. Someone has to decide whether an older product, past its prime, should have its life extended through modification or marketing strategy or whether it should be allowed to die peacefully. Such decisions are critical to an organisation's strategy, since after all the product range is at the heart of the supplier–buyer relationship. Product management, therefore, requires clear lines of authority and effective and efficient organisation. In consumer markets, many product management decisions are made by the marketing manager, but in organisational markets, responsibility is shared across a range of functional areas, including research and development (R&D), engineering and after-sales service personnel.

This chapter is concerned with the strategic concepts and tools that help those managers, whether marketers or engineers, to make the best decisions about their products. The first concept presented is that of the product life-cycle. This traces the life story of the product, helping managers to understand the pressures and opportunities affecting products as they mature. The important area of new product development is considered in the next chapter, but the difficulties of supporting a product in its early stages are addressed here as being crucial to the future well-being of the product. Within a product range, some products can live very long and profitable lives, such as Smarties, Dettol, Bovril, Mars Bar and, of course, Coca-Cola.

To create and sustain long-lived brands such as those listed above, the product range needs to be managed in sympathy with changes in the customer and competitive environment through the concept of product positioning and repositioning. This may involve changes in marketing strategies, including promotion, packaging, design or even in the target market profile. In the 1960s, for example, Coca-Cola introduced the can of coke for the first time in addition to the traditional bottle. This changed the way in which the product was purchased and consumed and thus its image. Every product has to be assessed and managed according to how the consumer perceives it in relation to the competition. This is a natural extension of the targeting decision discussed at p. 195 *et seq.*

> **Example** In 1998, chocolate manufacturer Cadbury's (http://www.cadbury.co.uk) introduced a 'Managing For Value' (MFV) programme designed to identify and support only those products that actually made profit or had long-term potential. This was bad news for some brands, such as Wiggley Worms, which were dropped, but good news for others, which gained more attention and resources. Turkish Delight, for example, despite having had no UK advertising since 1994, generates high profit margins from low chocolate content and so plans were made to support the brand with advertising. Other brands, such as Dairy Milk, Creme Eggs, Fuse, Caramel, Wispa and Time Out, continued to be supported with campaigns of over £1mn per brand. Nevertheless, Cadbury's can never afford to be complacent. The introduction of Celebrations by Mars, for instance, took significant market share from Cadbury's Roses as we saw in Case Study 7.1. This emphasises the need for Cadbury's not only to support existing profitable brands, but also to give new product development a high priority, either for introducing innovative new brands or for responding to competitors' moves (Murphy, 1999).

The natural processes of product maturity and decline lead to the discussion of product deletion issues. No product has an infinite life span and deciding the best time either to refresh and relaunch a product or to withdraw it altogether is difficult. It requires a critical review of the product's market performance, an analysis of its past (and potential future) contribution to overall profitability and a sound grasp of what is happening in the market.

Finally, this chapter returns to the practical problems of managing these processes, presenting a brief overview of product management structures as a foretaste of the more detailed review in Chapter 21.

THE PRODUCT LIFE-CYCLE

The **product life-cycle** (PLC) concept reflects the theory that products, like people, live a life. They are born, they grow up, they mature and, eventually, they die. During its life, a product goes through many different experiences, achieving varying levels of success in the market. This naturally means that the product's marketing support needs also vary, depending on what is necessary both to secure the present and to work towards the future. Figure 8.1 shows the theoretical progress of a PLC, indicating the pattern of sales and profits earned. The diagram may be applied either to an individual product or brand (for example Kellogg's Cornflakes) or to a product class (breakfast cereals).

The PLC concept offers no hard and fast rules for product management, but it can act as a useful guide for thinking about what a product has achieved and where it is heading in the future. There are, however, some reservations about the usefulness of

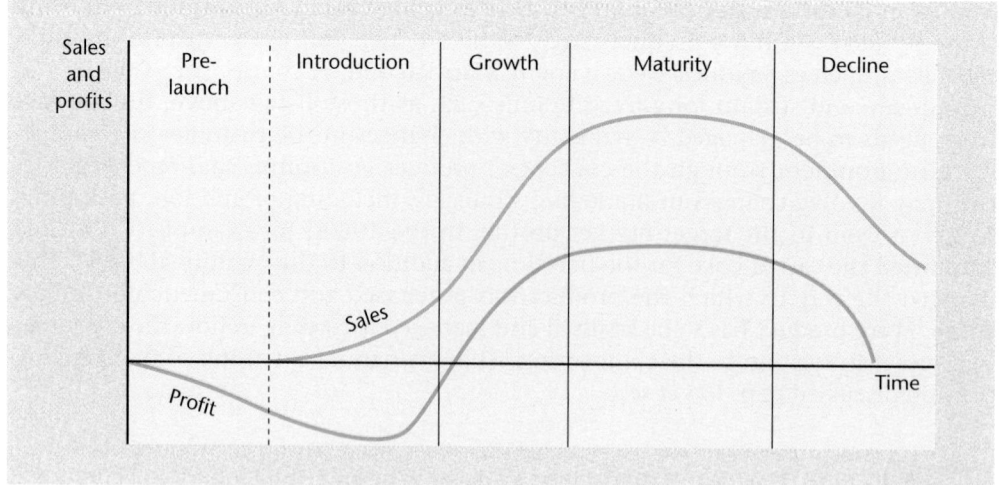

FIGURE 8.1

The product life-cycle

this concept (Dhalla and Yuspeh, 1976). As you read the rest of this section, think about what those reservations might be, then compare your thoughts with the critical appraisal of the concept at pp. 308 *et seq*. First, it is important to describe in some detail the stages of the PLC. Figure 8.1 indicates that there are four main stages, introduction, growth, maturity and decline, and these are now discussed in turn along with their implications for marketing strategy.

Stage 1: Introduction

At the very start of the product's life as it enters the market, sales will begin build slowly and profit may be small (even negative). A slow build-up of sales reflects the lead time required for marketing efforts to take effect and for people to hear about the product and try it. Low profits are partly an effect of the low initial sales and partly a reflection of the possible need to recoup development and launch costs.

The marketer's main priority at this stage is to generate widespread awareness of the product among the target segment and to stimulate trial. If the product is truly innovative, there may be no competitors yet and so there is the added problem of building primary demand (i.e. demand for the class of product rather than simply demand for a specific brand) as a background to the actual brand choice.

In most cases, the new product is an addition to an existing market and will either be targeted at a different segment or be offering additional features and benefits. There are a number of problems facing the marketer. First, there is a need to gain distribution. With new fmcg goods, the retail trade may be hard to convince unless the product has a real USP (unique selling point), because of the pressure on shelf space and the proliferation of available brands. In parallel with that, there is still the task of generating awareness among consumers and moving them through towards a purchase. The decision on the product's price, whether to price high or low or whether to offer an introductory trial price, could be an important element in achieving that first purchase.

Given the failure rate of new products and the importance of giving a product the best possible start in life, the introduction stage is likely to make heavy demands on marketing resources. This can be especially draining for a smaller organisation, but nevertheless is necessary if the product is to survive into the next stage: growth.

Stage 2: growth

In the growth stage, there is rapid increase in sales. One reason for this might be that word is getting around about the product and the rate of recruitment of new triers accelerates. Another reason is that the effects of repeat purchases are starting to be seen. There is some urgency at this stage to build as much brand preference and loyalty as possible. Competitors will now have had time to assess the product, its potential and its effect on the overall market, and will thus have decided their response. They may be modifying or improving their existing products or entering a new product of their own to the market. Whatever they do, they will deflect interest and attention away from the product and there is a risk that this will flatten the growth curve prematurely unless the company takes defensive steps.

Example The retail chain Electronics Boutique (http://www.ebworld.com) is in a fast-moving growing sector, driven by new games software and associated equipment. In some cases, 50 per cent of sales for a new game can be generated in the first weekend after its release and so getting the timing and stock levels right is critical. The launch of a new generation games console by Sega in 1999 was expected to help double the market for consoles within one to two years (Swann, 1998).

Figure 8.1 shows that profits start to rise rapidly in this stage. This too might be affected by competitive pressure, if other organisations choose to compete on price, forcing margins down. Again, repeat purchases that build brand loyalty are the best defence in these circumstances.

Even though the product might seem to be still very young and only just starting to deliver its potential, towards the close of the growth stage might be a good time to think about product modifications or improvements, either to reinforce existing segments or to open up new ones. This is about keeping one step ahead of the competition. If the initial novelty of your product has worn off, buyers might be vulnerable to competitors' new products. This might also threaten the security of your distribution channels, as heavy competition for shelf space squeezes out weaker products perceived as heading nowhere. This all reinforces, yet again, the need for constant attention to brand building and the generation of consumer loyalty, as well as the necessity for the cultivation of good relationships with distributors.

Another good reason for considering modifying the product is that by now you have real experience of producing and marketing it. The more innovative the product (whether innovative for your organisation or innovative within the market), the more likely it is that experience will have highlighted unforeseen strengths and weaknesses in the product and its marketing. This is the time to learn from that experience and fine tune the whole offering or extend the product range to attract new segments.

Example Themed restaurants such as Planet Hollywood (http://www.planethollywood.com) were part of a major growth sector during the 1990s. The number of themed restaurants doubled between 1993 and 1998 and accounted for 7 per cent of all restaurant sales in the UK. They were the 'cool' places to be seen, linked with celebrities and supermodels. Factors such as increased affluence, a greater number of tourists and more working women all helped to fuel growth, leading to higher prices as the supply of new restaurants was not able to keep up with demand. By the end of 1998, however, it appeared that the growth stage was ending, as sales levelled off and fashion moved on. For some, paying higher prices for what was essentially mass-market food became unacceptable and the value-for-money offering was increasingly perceived as poor. The Fashion Café in London, launched in 1997, went into receivership and a number of other companies also had a difficult year (Daneshkhu, 1998).

This is not to imply that an organisation should advocate change for the sake of change. Any changes must be the result of detailed analysis of what is happening in the market and projections of what is likely to happen in the event of various developments taking place. It is strategic change, it is planned change, it is purposeful change in the best interests of the organisation, the product and the customer.

At some point, the growth period comes to an end as the product begins to reach its peak and enters the next stage: maturity.

Stage 3: Maturity

During the maturity stage, the product achieves as much as it is going to. The accelerated growth levels off, as everyone who is likely to be interested in the product should have tried it by now and a stable set of loyal repeat buyers should have emerged. This is not a cause for complacency, however. There are few new customers available and even the laggards have purchased by now. This means that there is a high degree of customer understanding of the product and possibly of the market. They know what they want, and if your product starts to look dated or becomes unexciting compared with newer offerings from the competition, then they might well switch brands. Certainly, the smaller or more poorly positioned brands are going to be squeezed out. In these circumstances, the best hope is to consolidate the hard-core loyal buyers, encouraging heavier consumption from them. It may also be possible to convert some brand switchers into loyal customers through the use of sales promotions and advertising.

At this stage, there is likely to be heavy price competition and increased marketing expenditure from all competitors in order to retain brand loyalty. Much of this expenditure will be focused on marketing communication, but some may be channelled into minor product improvements to refresh the brand. Distribution channels may also need careful handling at this stage. Unless the product remains a steady seller, the retailer may be looking to delist it to make room on the shelves for younger products.

The sales curve has reached a plateau, as the market is saturated and largely stable. Any short-term gains will be offset by similar losses and profits may start to decline because of price competition pressure. It is thus very important to try, at least, to retain existing buyers. Sooner or later, however, the stability of the maturity phase will break, either through competitive pressure (they are better at poaching your customers than you are at poaching theirs) or through new developments in the market that make your product increasingly inappropriate, pushing the product into the decline stage.

Example It is possible for the marketer to take action to extend the maturity stage or even to stimulate new growth in the market. Scotch whisky is a mature product (in all senses of the phrase) in its biggest markets, the UK and France. This is partly because of the high level of competition in the market, over 2000 brands, and partly because of the image of whisky as 'something your parents drink'. The potential to inject new life into the market has come from the trend in countries such as Portugal, Spain and Greece, where whisky is commonly drunk with water, ice or cola by the under-30 age group. If whisky manufacturers can successfully give their brands a more youthful emphasis and a more consistent European image, then they may be able to extend the life-cycle still further.

Berenson and Mohr-Jackson (1994) suggest that organisations often turn to new products rather than rejuvenating existing ones to extend their life-cycles. They consider that rejuvenation can be a better option, provided that the organisation thinks about five issues:

1 Why the product is going into decline.
2 Whether the marketing environment is right for a rejuvenation strategy.
3 What the product name communicates to the market.
4 Whether there is still a potential segment worth reaching.
5 Whether there is any possibility of creating value for customers.

These questions can help the organisation to assess the relative advantages of rejuvenation over a full new product launch.

Stage 4: Decline

Once a product goes into decline for market-based reasons, it is almost impossible to stop it. The rate of decline can be controlled to some extent, but inevitably sales and profits will fall regardless of marketing effort.

> **Example** Butlin's holiday camps (http://www.butlins.co.uk) grew rapidly in the 1950s as the C2, D and E socioeconomic groups in particular had more leisure time and more disposable income for family holidays. However, by the 1970s, trends in the marketing environment were working against the established Butlin's concept. Holiday-makers found cheaper and sunnier alternatives in Spain, rejected the highly regimented and enclosed atmosphere of the holiday camp and came to expect much higher standards of facilities and entertainment.
>
> During the 1990s, Butlins slowly changed the nature of the holiday experience on offer. Gone are 'holiday camps' in favour of 'holiday centres' and 'chalets' have given way to 'holiday villages'. Knobbly knees competitions and beauty contests are strictly yesterday's entertainment. Now it is indoor whirlpools, wave pools and multi-sports centres. The year round entertainment centre for all the family has replaced the groups of lads looking for a good time. All of this required a major investment programme. At the Skegness camp alone since 1972 the company has used 200 000 litres of paint in refurbishment and recently completed a £40mn facelift. All these efforts are designed to stop long-term decline through careful product repositioning (Young, 1998).

Decline can often be environment related rather than a result of poor management decisions. Technological developments or changes in consumer tastes, for example, can lead to the demise of the best-managed product.

Some products are deliberately sacrificed on the altar of consumer demand. Fashion products with a naturally short life-cycle capitalise on shifting consumer tastes and the rise and fall of popular icons, and are managed with the expectation of a short maturity and a quick decline.

> **Example** Whatever the fashion in new cars, in India there are some models that still sell well despite having been around since the 1950s. The Ambassador, based on the Morris Oxford, and the Contessa, based on an old Vauxhall design, are still purchased by loyal customers. Nearly 40 per cent of Ambassadors are sold to taxi operators, because of their rugged and reliable reputation on what are sometimes poor roads. The local manufacturer, Hindustan Motors, even plans to give the Contessa an upgrade to keep customers happy (Bose, 1998).

Faced with a product in decline, the marketer has a difficult decision of whether to try slowing down the decline with some marketing expenditure, or to milk the product by withdrawing support and making as much profit out of it as possible as it heads towards a natural death. In the latter case, the withdrawing of marketing support aimed at distributors in particular is quite likely to speed up the delisting process.

The problem with a declining product is that it can absorb a great deal of management time for relatively little reward. Decisive action is called for so that management effort can go into the newer products that need it. There are a number of possible options for dealing with declining products. The option of complete deletion is considered separately at p. 325 *et seq.*

Milking or harvesting

The strategy of milking or harvesting centres around the idea of allowing nature to run its course with little or no marketing support. The product is allowed to fade away naturally while the profits are reaped. After all, if a product has had a long and useful life and has built up a good solid core of loyal users, it is not going to die overnight and the organisation might as well extract the last little bit of return on the investment it has made in the product over the years. Let the buyers drift away gradually and let the product die when it is no longer economic to produce it or when the retailers drop it.

This strategy has the advantage of maximising the useful life of the product, as well as generating the cash and the time to help establish new products. The slow decline of the product gives the organisation adjustment time to get used to the declining cash flow and to find other means of generating revenue. It is also less of a shock to the consumer (and other interested parties in the market) than the sudden disappearance of what might still be a popular product, with all the resentment that would cause.

Phased withdrawal

The milking strategy has a certain amount of drift attached to it. The product can continue indefinitely, as long as there is a purchaser out there. With a phased withdrawal, however, the ultimate cut-off date for the product is set, along with a number of interim staging posts. The interim stages might involve pulling the product gradually from different channels of distribution, or might focus on withdrawal from geographic areas.

The planned withdrawal does have some certainty about it. The organisation knows in advance what is going to happen to the product and can take that into account when planning its marketing strategies. It also allows time to plan replacement products (with the possibility of phasing them in as the old product is phased out) and does not prematurely cut off the income from the declining product. For the customer, however, there is an element of unpleasant surprise if the product disappears suddenly from their favourite retailer or from their area.

Car manufacturers normally operate on a phased withdrawal basis, so that both dealers and the public are well aware of when new models will be launched.

Contracting out or selling

A way of keeping loyal users of the product happy is to sell the brand to a niche operator or to subcontract its marketing and/or production. To a smaller, perhaps more flexible firm, the remains of the product's market might represent a manageable challenge that could earn what seems to it to be a satisfactory return. This way, the originating organisation is rid of a product it no longer wants, consumers do not lose a product that they do want, and the subcontractor or buyer gains access to, and experience with, a brand that it could probably never have built for themselves. Quaker, for example, bought the US soft drink brand Snapple for $1.7bn. Although the brand was declining at the time of its purchase, Quaker felt that it had the management and marketing skills to make it successful.

Once the decision is made and the implementation plans drawn up, the process can be allowed to run its course with the minimum of managerial interference.

Facets of the PLC

The PLC is more of a guide to what could happen rather than a prescription of what will happen. At its best, it does provide some useful indications at each stage of some of the marketing problems and issues that could arise. It is, after all, a form of collective wisdom based on the history of many brands.

In reality, however, it is too general and superficial a concept to stand alone. Before applying the concept in practice, it is necessary to dig deeper and think about a number of issues before the PLC becomes a really useful tool.

Length of PLC

How long is a piece of string? It is very difficult to predict how long it will take a product to move through its life. The length of the PLC varies not only from market to market, but also from brand to brand within a market. Some board games, for example, such as Monopoly, Scrabble and more recently Trivial Pursuit, are well-established, long-term sellers, whereas other games, particularly those linked with television shows (remember Countdown, Blockbusters and Neighbours board games?) have much shorter spans.

It is even more difficult to predict when the key transition periods from one stage to the next will happen, yet this is critical information for planning strategy changes. The problem is that the length of the PLC is affected by so many things. It is not only the pace of change in the external environment, but also the organisation's handling of the product throughout its life. The organisation's willingness and ability to communicate effectively and efficiently with both the trade and the consumer, its policy of supporting the product in the critical early period and its approach to defending and refreshing its products will all affect how the PLC develops.

Self-fulfilling prophecy

Linked with the previous point, there is a real danger that the PLC can become a self-fulfilling prophecy. A marketing manager might, for example, imagine that a product is about to move from growth into maturity. Theory may suggest appropriate marketing strategies for this transition and, if these are implemented, the product will start to behave as though it is mature, whether it was really ready for it or not. This demonstrates a basic marketing dilemma: should the PLC drive marketing strategies, or should the PLC be defined as an outcome of strategies derived through other means?

The shape of the PLC

The shape of the PLC offered in Fig. 8.1 is necessarily a generalisation. Products that get into marketing problems at any PLC stage will certainly not follow this pattern. Products that spend relatively longer in one stage than another will also have distorted PLC curves. A product that has a long and stable maturity, for instance, will show a long flat plateau in maturity rather than Fig. 8.1's gentle hillock. Different market circumstances could also distort this hypothetical curve. Five different scenarios, the innovative product, the imitative product, the fashion product, the product failure and the revitalisation, each with its own PLC shape, are shown in Fig. 8.2.

Innovative product. The innovative product is breaking totally new ground and cannot really utilise consumers' previous experience as a short cut to acceptance. The marketer will have to overcome ignorance, suspicion and scepticism, thus extending the introduction stage. People feel that they have managed perfectly well without this product in the past, so why do they need it now? This is a question that both microwave oven producers and 3M, the manufacturer of Post-It Notes, have managed to answer to the customer's satisfaction. Having to educate the market from scratch is neither easy nor cheap. Sony, in introducing the Walkman, had to undertake this task and, of course, it not only laid the foundations for its own product, but also broke the ground for 'me too' subsequent imitative entrants.

As said at p. 304, the introductory stage does hinge on creating awareness, encouraging trial of the product and winning over the retail trade. In the case of innovative products, this is an even more crucial, but much longer process.

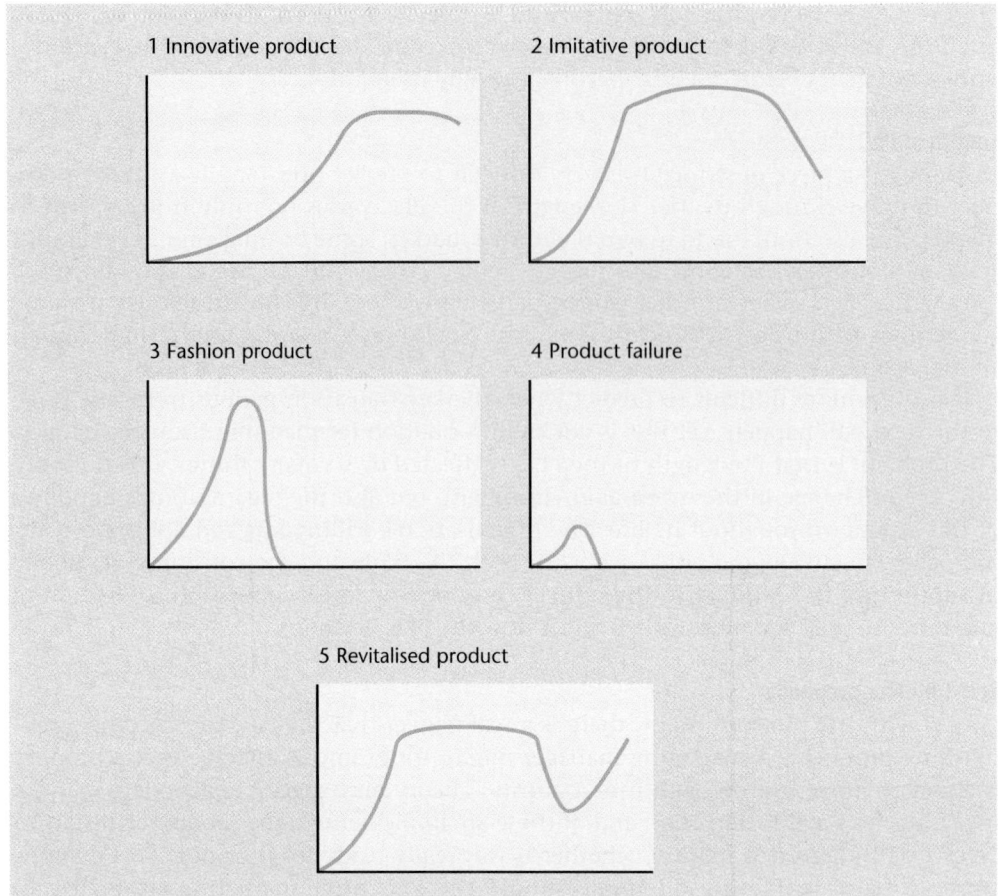

FIGURE 8.2

PLC Variations of a theme

Imitative product. Imitative products, such as new confectionery brands or the first non-Sony personal stereo, do not require as much spadework as the innovative product. They take advantage of the established market and the buyer's existing knowledge and past experience, and thus will move into the growth stage very quickly. The main considerations for the imitative marketer are establishing clear, differentiated positioning of the product against existing brands, encouraging trial and making repeat purchase as easy as possible.

Fashion product. Fashion products have a naturally short PLC. Fads are an extreme form of fashion product, accentuating the rapid sales increase followed by the rapid decline. The timing of entry into the market is critical and those who succeed in making a quick return in these markets are those who spot the trend early. There is little opportunity for late entrants. It is interesting to note that some fads retain a hard core of enthusiasts, for example skateboarding.

Example The party dresses designed for the Christmas market appear in high-street shops in late autumn and disappear again after the January sales. This implies a Matterhorn-shaped PLC curve as shown in Fig. 8.2(3), with a very rapid rise to a short maturity and an equally rapid decline. Such an ephemeral existence requires a lot of forward planning, as there is no time to adjust the marketing mix once the product is launched. Note, however, that not all clothing products conform to this model. Women's tights, for example, are a staple product enjoying a long and fairly stable maturity, with minor adjustments to packaging and colour ranges.

Product failure. Some products never even achieve a growth stage: they fail. This may be because the product itself is badly thought through or because it never gained awareness or distribution. New food products from small manufacturers without the resources to create strong brands may fail because they simply cannot gain mass distribution from retailers unwilling to take risks with unknown producers or brands.

Revitalisation product. The revitalisation phase of the PLC shows that marketing effort can indeed influence the course of a life-cycle. By updating a product, either through design or through a fresh marketing approach, new life can be injected to regenerate customer and retailer interest and loyalty. Tango, for example, was a standard, uninteresting fizzy orange drink until some surreal, controversial and imaginative advertising repositioned it as a trendy teenage drink.

Product level, class, form and brand

As said at the beginning of this section, the PLC can operate on a number of different levels. It is important to distinguish between the PLCs of total industries (such as the motor industry), product classes (such as petrol-driven private vehicles), product forms (such as hatchback cars) and individual brands (such as the Fiat Uno). Rink and Swan (1979) argue that there is a need for a clear definition of the distinction between these four categories of PLC so that the manager can fully understand the context within which the brand is evolving.

Industries and product classes tend to have the longest PLCs, because they are an aggregate of the efforts of many organisations and many individual products over time. An industry, such as the motor industry, can be in an overall state of fairly steady maturity for many years even as individual product forms and brands come and go. In the motor industry, for example, the hatchback is probably a mature product form, while the people carrier is still in its growth stage. Although a number of hatchback 'brands' have come and gone, the number of people carrier 'brands' is still growing. At the same time, the earliest entrants in the European market are starting to reach maturity.

Focusing down further to the individual brand level, it can be even more difficult to judge the nature of the PLC because there are so many competitive factors to take into consideration. Each factor, for example a competitor's pricing or promotional approach, has an influence on the strategies formulated for the brand and a direct effect on its success or failure. A brand's growth phase may not be as rapid as hoped or may not achieve as high a level of share as planned if a major competitor can find a way of distracting the market's attention during the critical launch period. To some extent, a predictable range of likely competitor actions and their outcomes can be foreseen and contingencies can be built into product planning to account for them. Nevertheless, it is still very difficult to forecast sales, to define the best strategies for each stage, the duration of each stage and the overall curve dynamic. The PLC concept provides no guarantees, despite its neatness. There are too many unpredictable factors influencing a product's life and too much depends on the quality of the care, commitment and imagination with which the product is managed.

Despite these weaknesses, the PLC is a well-used concept. Product marketing strategies should, however, take into account other considerations as well as the PLC, as the next section shows.

MARKETING IN ACTION   The yo-yo craze: it just keeps coming back

Fads and crazes are especially challenging to marketers as it is very hard to predict whether they will take off, how fast and for how long they will last. If the predictions and timing are wrong, then the marketer risks either being too slow to benefit before the craze passes or being left with unsold stock. The trouble with fad products, however, is that traditional marketing rules do not apply. There is no point in building for the long term if there is not going to be one and thus being flexible enough to capitalise quickly on a craze is critical.

Fad products often crop up in the toy market which, in the UK alone, is worth around £800mn per year. The yo-yo is a craze toy with a different kind of product life-cycle because it keeps coming back! Popular for short periods in the 1960s, 1970s and 1980s, sales suddenly burst into life yet again in 1998. In 1997, the UK's largest independent toy retail chain, The Entertainer Group, hardly sold a yo-yo. In the first quarter of 1998, however, sales went up to between 3000 and 4000 yo-yos per week. By the end of the year the sales level had reached between 15 000 and 18 000 per week. The British Association of Toy Retailers estimated that sales nationally were approaching 150 000 per week and the yo-yo become the top-selling toy for pre-teen children. In an era of sophisticated computer games and in a market faced with an ever-increasing array of tempting toys, it was not a bad performance for a simple wheely thing on a piece of string.

So why did the yo-yo make a comeback? Some argue that the craze was fuelled by parents who saw it as a wholesome and nostalgic alternative to letting their kids gaze at a computer screen all day. A more likely explanation, however, is that marketers made the yo-yo a more acceptable play alternative by careful product development and a marketing campaign selling the yo-yo's benefits as an outdoor toy, emphasising its street credibility. Product improvements encouraged ease of use, for example the 'centrifugal clutch system' makes it easier to perform tricks, even for beginners. To encourage children to practise their skills and to reinforce brand awareness, yo-yo company Yomega started a reward

The Rolls-Royce of yo-yos!

Source: Yomega Corporation Inc.

programme called 'Tricknology'. If children buy the yo-yos from accredited stores they can be tested to earn certificates at bronze, silver, gold and platinum levels.

Skills development was not the only attraction. Through design and colour, the yo-yos became fashion accessories rather than just toys and some kids even began collecting them! Although yo-yos can be purchased for as little as £1, the average sale value was between £8 and £15, with premium products costing up to £100. Children became brand conscious, looking for the 'coolest' names such as Yomega X-Brain and Pro Yo III, and perhaps the fact that some schools banned yo-yos from playgrounds only served to enhance the 'cool' factor. The critical question for marketers, however, was always going to be how long the yo-yo renaissance could last: a craze, by definition, cannot last for ever. The product is mature, yet appears to reinvent itself on a cyclical basis before it slips into decline. As yo-yo means 'come back' in the Tagalog dialect of the Philippines, even though the current craze will end, the yo-yo is almost guaranteed to make another reappearance – eventually!

Sources: Gray (1998); Rigby (1998); Wright (1998), http://www.yomega.com.

MARKET EVOLUTION

The marketing manager needs to understand how markets develop over time, in order better to plan and manage products, their life-cycles and their marketing strategies. Three components are involved in market evolution: the way in which customers adopt new products, the evolution and acceptance of technology and, finally, the impact of competition.

The diffusion of innovation

The product life-cycle is clearly driven by changes in consumer behaviour as the new product becomes established. The rate at which the growth stage develops is linked in particular to the speed with which customers can be led through from awareness of the product to trial and eventual adoption of the product, in other words how fast the AIDA model (*see* Fig. 5.2 on p. 194) works. The problem is, however, that not all customers move through it with equal speed and eagerness and some will adopt innovation more quickly than others. This has led to the concept of the **diffusion of innovation** (Rogers, 1962), which looks at the rate at which innovation spreads across a market as a whole. Effectively, it allows the grouping or classification of customers depending on their speed of adoption into one of five adopter categories, as shown in Fig. 8.3.

Innovators

Innovators are important in the early stages of a product's life-cycle to help get the product off the ground and start the process of gaining acceptance. They form only a small group, but they buy early and are prepared to take a risk. In consumer markets, innovators tend to be younger, better educated, more affluent and confident. In organisational markets, innovators are likely to be profitable and, again, willing to take risks in return for the potential benefits to be gained from being first.

Innovators may be category specific. A consumer who is an innovator in the hi-fi market, for example, may be a laggard when it comes to small kitchen appliances or photographic equipment. It depends on the individual's interests and inclinations and to some extent on what kinds of product they think are important in establishing their status in other people's eyes. Within a particular product category, the innovator may continue to show innovative tendencies over time, wanting to be the first with a series of new products. Thus those who were the first to adopt car phones may also be the first to adopt in-car computerised navigation systems.

Early adopters

Early adopters enter the market early, but are content to let the innovators take the real pioneering risks with a new product. They do, however, soon follow the lead of the innovators and are always alert to new developments in markets of interest to them. Once the early adopters begin to enter the market, the growth stage of a PLC can then develop.

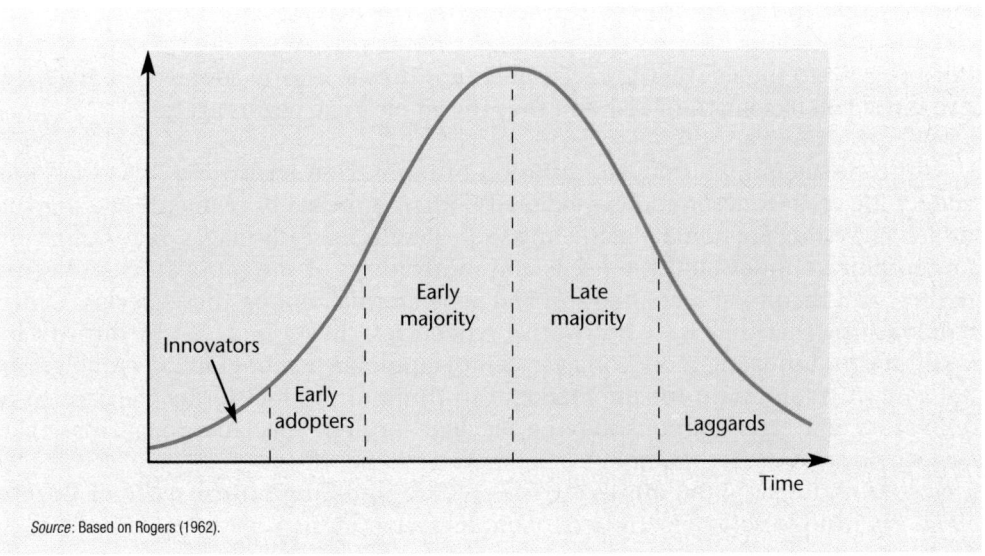

FIGURE 8.3

Diffusion of innovation: adopter categories

Source: Based on Rogers (1962).

313

Both innovators and early adopters tend to be opinion leaders and thus it is important for the promoter of a new product to target them and win them over. The mass market, however, looks particularly to the early adopters for a lead, as they are more of a mainstream group than the innovators. The early adopters are thus critical for making a product generally acceptable and for spreading word-of-mouth recommendations about the product's value and benefits.

Early majority

With the *early majority* the mass market starts to build up, as more and more people enter it. The early majority are more risk averse than previous groups and want some reassurance that the product is tried and tested before they will commit themselves to it. This group may be relatively well educated, with above-average incomes, but that may depend on the nature of the product concerned. DVD players, for example, have entered this stage, but many consumers may be holding back until the price comes down. When a product does reach the early majority, social pressure may begin to build: 'You really must get yourself an ice-cream maker – you can't possibly manage without one.' This begins to move the product towards the late majority.

Late majority

The *late majority* customers are perhaps less interested or bothered about the product category, or are content to wait until they see how the market develops. They are a little behind the early majority and want even more reassurance about the product's benefits and worth. The late majority may have more choice of alternative products in the market, as competition builds, and will certainly have the benefit of the accumulated knowledge and experience of the previous groups. Once the late majority has been converted, the product is likely to be reaching its mature stage, a steady plateau of repeat purchases, with very few new customers left to enter the market.

Late adopters or laggards

The last remaining converts are the *late adopters* or *laggards*. They may be very averse to change and have therefore resisted adopting a new product, or they may have had attitudinal or even economic problems coming to terms with it. Alternatively, they may just have been very slow in hearing about the product or in relating its benefits to their own lifestyles. They may be in the lower socioeconomic groups or they may be older consumers.

The benefits of being among the late adopters are that others have taken all the risks; the ephemeral brands or manufacturers are likely to have disappeared; it may thus be easier to identify the best products on the market; and the price may be falling as competitors fight for share among a shrinking market. By the time the late adopters get into the market, however, the innovators and early adopters are likely to have moved on to something else and thus the whole cycle begins again!

As this discussion has implied, diffusion of innovation has strong links with the product life-cycle concept and can be used both as a means of segmenting a market and for suggesting appropriate marketing strategies. In the early stages, for example, it is important to understand the needs and motivations of the innovators and early adopters and then to attract attention and generate trial among these groups. Other than knowing that they have innovative tendencies, however, it can be difficult to profile the groups using more concrete demographic or psychographic variables. In that case, it is important for the marketer to think in product terms. Perhaps hi-fi innovators and early adopters may be reached through specialist magazines that review new products, for example.

According to Gatignon and Robertson (1985), building on the work of Rogers (1962), six main factors affect the rate of product adoption:

1 *Relative advantage*: additional benefits and value added compared with alternatives.
2 *Compatibility*: fit with consumer tastes, needs, attitudes etc.
3 *Complexity*: the less complex the product or the more user friendly it is, the quicker the rate of adoption.
4 *Divisibility*: whether it can be tried on a limited basis to reduce the risk of trial, e.g. computer software demonstration disks.
5 *Communicability*: ease of communicating benefits.
6 *Perceived risk*: what it will cost the buyer in terms of both money and pride if the purchase turns out to be a 'wrong' decision.

The marketer can consider these factors when developing products and their marketing mixes. Market research can help to define compatibility and to determine the most attractive relative advantage. Risk can be reduced through warranties, free samples, trial prices and pack sizes or 'satisfaction or your money back' promotions. Communication can be helped through product demonstrations or samples.

Technological impact

Technology also evolves over time. Sometimes this evolution is gradual, allowing the product to develop incrementally through new models and upgrades, but with no major shocks to the customer. Sometimes, however, technical breakthroughs occur that radically alter the expectations of the market and its competitive structure. Such technological discontinuities tend to create a period of intense change and disturbance to the *status quo* as new products emerge that capitalise on the breakthrough. Whole industries can be wiped out by these changes if adaptation does not take place (Tushman and Anderson, 1986). The demand for black and white televisions, steam locomotives and mechanical cash registers changed dramatically as a result of technological discontinuity. Fortunately for many organisations, such radical changes are rare and take some time to work through to the market.

Technological innovation can thus be used to extend the product life-cycle, by helping to refresh and update the product, but it can also shorten a life-cycle by rendering a product obsolete.

Competitor entry timing

In the same way that consumers can be classified according to their willingness and ability to adopt innovation, competitors can be classified according to their timing in entering a market. In any specific product market, competitors can be categorised in five main groups:

Pioneers

Pioneers are the innovative organisations that create new markets or are the first to get to the market. They may invest heavily in R&D and marketing to keep the new ideas flowing and to commercialise them. This group might include organisations such as Sony, 3M and Philips.

Early imitators

Organisations that are *early imitators* see what the pioneers have done, recognise the market's potential and then copy them. An early imitator's product is likely to be a 'me too' product, with very little to differentiate it from the pioneer. Any differentiation is likely to arise from elements of the marketing mix other than product. The entry of early imitators may coincide with the growth stage of the life-cycle when there is enough demand and enthusiasm to support a number of very similar competing products.

315

Early differentiators

An organisation that takes the basic product and improves it or adds new features is an *early differentiator*. The early differentiator's product does, therefore, offer distinct features and benefits, but builds on the pioneer's original product concept. The entry of such competitors is likely to happen during the growth stage.

Early nichers

As a market moves towards saturation and maturity, the level of general competition becomes intense and any new entrant is likely to look for a specific *niche* segment. This segmentation could be based on any of the variables examined in Chapter 5, such as product benefits, price sensitivity or psychographics.

Late entrants

In an established mature market, it will be difficult for a new entrant to compete unless it has some means of clear differential advantage. This could be in terms of price, distribution or promotional weight. A *late imitator* is unlikely to be able to achieve these things without the strong financial backing provided by its other products in other markets, or by acquiring an established product in the market, as with Quaker's acquisition of Snapple mentioned earlier. For a small organisation without such backing, entering a market at this stage could be a high-risk, unfeasible strategy. Clearly, these categorisations are somewhat generalised, but they do add another dimension to the PLC. They help in understanding how a market's PLC might evolve and what kinds of marketing strategies are appropriate at each stage given the competitive environment. Many of these issues will be further explored in Chapter 20.

Managerial responses

By using the PLC together with analysis of customers, technology and competitors, as outlined above, the marketing manager can begin to paint a detailed picture of the factors that are likely to influence the shape of the PLC, its duration and the strategies that might be appropriate at each stage. Table 8.1 summarises this approach from the point of view of a pioneer organisation, looking at the projected PLC of a radically new consumer product. As the PLC's externally generated characteristics unfold, the organisation's strategies also develop, as a means of either minimising threats or maximising opportunities. However, the manager needs to exercise caution in assuming that the future will unfold neatly according to plan. In a marketing environment that is witnessing reduced new product development cycle times, customer-driven product development and increasing global competition, there is less certainty than ever. Models that appear to be conceptually very simple and predictive then become very dangerous managerial tools.

MANAGING THE PRODUCT MIX

In a dynamic marketing environment, the product mix is not static. The effects of changing technology, evolving competition and changes in customer needs mean that it is most important for an organisation to find ways of keeping its product ranges fresh and interesting. This opens up a number of management problems, requiring planned procedures and strategies in order to:

1 retain and maintain existing products so that they continue to meet their objectives;
2 modify and adapt existing products to take advantage of new technology, emerging opportunities or changing market conditions;
3 delete old products that are close to the end of their working lives and no longer serve their purpose; and finally,

TABLE 8.1
PLC Stages: Characteristics and strategies

	Introduction	Growth	Maturity	Decline
Market characteristics				
Type of customer entering market	Innovators	Early adopters	Early majority Late majority	Late adopters
Type of competitor entering market	Pioneer	Early imitators Early differentiators Early nichers	Late entrants	
Number of products on the market	One	Few	Many	Declining
Technological development	Discontinuity – radically new concept	Incremental – fine tuning – differentiation	Incremental – possibility of interruption by discontinuity?	None or minor
Financial characteristics				
Sales	Low	Growing rapidly	Growing slowly	Declining
Costs per customer	High	Average	Low	Low
Cash flow	Negative	Acceptable	High	Acceptable
Profit	Negative	Rising rapidly	High	Declining
Main marketing objectives				
Re consumer	Gain awareness Generate trial	Widen acceptance Generate trial/repeat sales	Remind/reinforce Encourage loyalty	Milk last sales
Re competition	Establish premier position	Defend	Compete	
Re distribution	Gain acceptance	Widen distribution Increase shelf space	Maintain shelf space	Keep product available
Re product	Establish	Fine tune	Refresh/relaunch/vary Maintain	Drop/sell
Marketing mix				
Product range	Basic Brand building	Enhanced	Extension/variety Brand image reinforcement	Rationalisation
Price	Skimming – capitalise on early entry	Lower Penetration	Low Match/beat competition	Steady
Channels of distribution	Limited	Increasing	Maximum	Declining
Consumer promotion focus				
• Advertising	High: Awareness	High: Image building	M">Moderate: Remind/reinforce	Minimal: Remind
• Sales promotion	High: Trial	High: Repeat purchase	Moderate: Short-term share gain	Low: Reward loyalty
Trade promotion				
• Ads/promotions	High: Awareness/acceptance	Minimal: Reinforce/defend	Moderate: Defend/relaunch	Minimal: Remind
• Personal selling	High: Awareness/acceptance	Lower: Repeat orders	Moderate: Reinforce/relaunch	Minimal: Repeat orders

4 introduce a flow of new products to maintain or improve sales and profit levels and to form a firm foundation for tomorrow's markets. This latter point will be dealt with separately in Chapter 9.

An organisation, therefore, needs a balanced **product portfolio**, capable of sustaining it satisfactorily over its planning horizons. Note that the portfolio ideally must be *balanced*, containing neither too many new nor too many declining products. Too many new products could put an organisation at risk, as product launch is resource intensive with no guarantee of success. At the other extreme, too many declining products could threaten the future of the business, as sales and profits start to fall. Even if replacement or diversification plans are in place, unless they are implemented over a longer period, the organisation could find itself coping with too much change and new product risk. In an ideal world, mature but still strong products can provide the stable cash flow against which a planned programme of new product establishment and declining product deletion can take place.

Positioning products

A crucial decision, which could affect the length of a product's life and its resilience in a market over time, concerns the product's positioning. **Product positioning** means thinking about a product in the context of the competitive space it occupies in its market, defined in terms of attributes that matter to the target market. The important criterion is how close to the ideal on each of those attributes, compared with competing products, your product is judged to be by the target market. Harrod's, for example, is positioned as a high-quality, exclusive departmental store. In order to reinforce this positioning with its target market, Harrod's (http://www.harrods.com) makes sure that its product ranges, its staff expertise, its displays and overall store ambience are of equally high quality.

It is the target customer's definition of important attributes and their perception of how your product compares on them that matter. Marketing managers have to stand back from their own feelings and must ensure that the attributes selected are those that are critical to the customer, not those that marketing managers would like to be critical. The range of attributes judged to be important will vary according to the particular market segments under consideration. Chapter 5 offered further insights into the relationship between segmentation and product characteristics.

Further need for managerial objectivity arises when a positioning exercise is carried out. While managers may take steps to create a product and marketing package that they think will fill a previously defined position, they still need to ensure that they closely monitor the target market's opinions to make certain that the required image and message are being conveyed.

The concept of product positioning is clearly focused on a customer-based perspective, but it still has serious implications for product design and development. The decision about positioning is made during the product's development and will be reflected in a whole range of the product's characteristics, including brand image, packaging and quality, as well as in the pricing and communication elements of the marketing mix.

Defining and selecting an appropriate position for a product involves three stages.

Stage 1
Detailed market research needs to be carried out during the first stage in order to establish what attributes are important to any given market segment and their order of preference. This background research will centre on a class of products rather than on individual brands within the class. Thus a particular segment, for example, might regard softness, absorbency and a high number of sheets on the roll as the three most important attributes of toilet tissue, in that order of preference.

Stage 2
Having identified the important attributes, in the second stage further research now shortlists the existing products that offer those attributes. Brands such as Kleenex Velvet and Andrex might be seen as fulfilling the needs of the toilet tissue segment mentioned above.

Stage 3

In the third stage, it is necessary to find out:

(a) what the target market considers to be the ideal level for each of the defined attributes; and

(b) how they rate each brand's attributes in relation to the ideal and to each other.

The conclusions from this hypothetical research may be, for instance, that while Andrex has more sheets per roll than Kleenex (thus apparently achieving a better rating for Andrex on an important attribute), in relation to the ideal Andrex is perceived to have too many (too bulky for the roll holder), whereas Kleenex might be perceived to have too few (runs out too quickly). Both products could thus improve their offering.

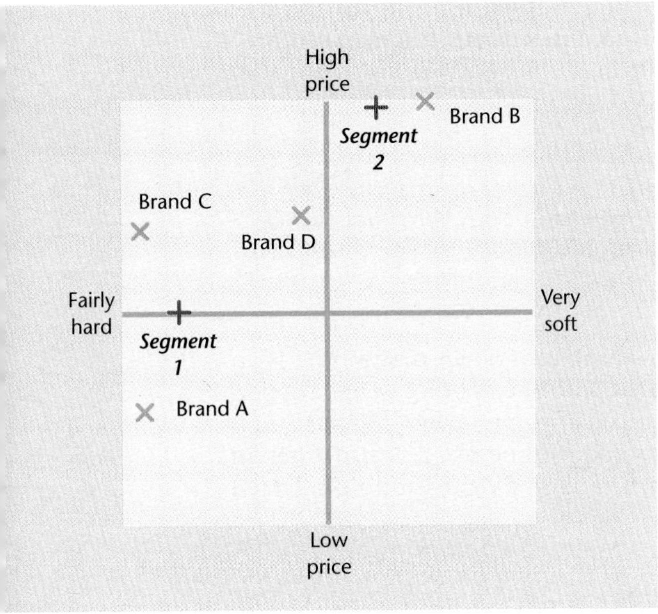

Once the positioning process has been completed for all the relevant attributes, it is useful to be able to visualise the complete picture graphically, by creating a *perceptual map* of the market. Figure 8.4 shows such a hypothetical map of the toilet tissue market, using price and softness as two dimensions that might represent important attributes. This shows that Brand A is serving the bottom end of the market in Segment 1, offering a cheap, purely functional product, whereas Brand B is aimed at the discerning customer in Segment 2 who is prepared to pay a little more for a gentler experience. Brand C seems to be closer to Segment 1 than Segment 2, but is overpriced compared with Brand A for a similar quality of product. Brand D is floating between the two segments, with nothing to offer that is particularly appealing to either.

In some cases, of course, two dimensions are insufficient to represent the complexities of target market opinion. Although this creates a far more difficult mapping task, any number of further dimensions can be included using multidimensional scaling techniques (Green and Carmone, 1970). Figure 8.5 expands the mapping of the toilet tissue example to include additional dimensions. In such a case, the map is an invaluable aid to understanding complex product relationships, almost at a glance, saving many pages of confusing verbal description.

As can be seen from Fig. 8.5, Segment 1 wants high performance and Brand E is well positioned to serve its needs. Segment 2 is fairly concerned about performance characteristics, but also thinks that the aesthetics of the tissue are important, so that it co-ordinates with bathroom decor and fittings. Brand E might be able to serve this segment better by expanding its colour range, without alienating Segment 1. Segment 3

FIGURE 8.4

Perceptual map of the toilet tissue market

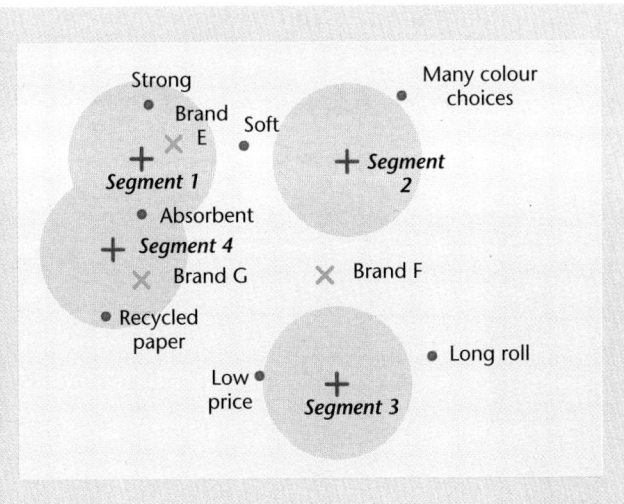

FIGURE 8.5

Multidimensional perceptual map of the toilet tissue market

is the value-conscious economy segment that wants the largest number of sheets per roll for the least amount of money. Segment 4 has more of an environmental conscience than the others and Brand G is well positioned for them. Brand F, however, is poorly positioned to serve any of the existing segments and its managers need to think carefully about which direction to take with it.

Perceptual mapping helps to provide insights into appropriate competitive actions. For instance, a fundamental decision could be whether to try to meet the competition head-on or to differentiate your product away from them. The map can show just how far away from the competition your product is perceived to be and where its weaknesses lie, leading to an understanding of the marketing tasks involved in improving the product offering. If the intention is to differentiate, the map can indicate whether your product is sufficiently different in terms of attributes that matter and whether market niches exist that your product could be adapted to fill.

> **Example** Volvo focused on safety as an important attribute of a family car at a time when its competitors were communicating performance and value for money. Volvo was not perceived as providing outstanding performance or value, so it decided to differentiate and create a niche for itself in a segment for which safety was a very high priority.

All of this implies that assessing and defining meaningful product positioning is an important early step in marketing management. This process can bring to light opportunities, it can highlight potential dangers of cannibalising one's own products and it can help to define competitive pressures, strengths and weaknesses. It is also a step in making the decision to modify a current product range by repositioning selected products.

Repositioning and modifying products

Positioning might have to be adjusted for many reasons as both the product and its market mature. Developing technology, evolving competition, changing customer needs and wants all mean that products have to be constantly appraised and reviewed. Nevertheless, a major **product-repositioning** exercise can be very costly and risky (alienating or confusing existing buyers and failing to attract new ones, for instance). This means that the marketing manager needs to be sure that the changes

Lucozade was very successfully repositioned as a fitness drink.

Source: SmithKline Beecham.

will be perceptible and relevant to the target market, that the market is willing to accept change and that the repositioning will produce measurable benefits.

It is important to distinguish here between a fundamental repositioning exercise and minor product refreshment. The latter is a natural part of the PLC, when small changes that suggest progress and improvement are implemented to prevent the product image from becoming stale. Car manufacturers, for instance, will change their colour ranges and redesign various accessories each year, but the market does not interpret these as anywhere nearly as radical as a repositioning would be. Fine tuning the product itself can be done without seeking to reposition and, conversely, repositioning can take place through pricing, promotion or distribution without any change to the product. Kellogg, for example, used advertising to reposition its Cornflakes brand as an adult snack that can be eaten at any time of day rather than as a basic and rather boring children's breakfast. The slogan 'Have you forgotten how good they taste?' implies a long-established brand heritage, with connotations of familiarity, reassurance and quality.

Repositioning has a number of serious implications. It might involve redefining or enlarging segments and it may well involve redesigning an entire marketing strategy. Such a fundamental revamp of a product is most likely to take place in the maturity stage of the PLC, when the product is beginning to fade a little.

There are three main areas for repositioning and product improvement.

Quality

As discussed at pp. 292 *et seq.*, quality has a number of dimensions. With physical products, quality can be defined in terms of reliability, durability and dependability, which are generally applicable across most products. There are, however, product-specific quality dimensions that the target market could use as indicators of a quality product, such as speed, taste, colour, materials, ingredients and even price and packaging (*see* Chapter 11 and pp. 289 *et seq.*).

MARKETING IN ACTION **Repositioning for good health**

Lucozade (http://www.lucozade.com) used to be positioned as an invalid's drink, with the slogan 'Lucozade aids recovery'. Its advertising in the 1960s used to show a poorly child being tended by a caring mother who gave him Lucozade. As general health and living conditions have improved, however, this became too much of a niche position. If people only bought Lucozade when there was sickness in the household, the purchase frequency and volume would be very low, especially when compared with other more mainstream fizzy drinks. In the 1980s, therefore, Lucozade was repositioned to capitalise on the growing health boom. Instead of being a semi-medicinal 'illness' drink, with all the negative connotations that implies, it became a specially formulated, glucose-rich, energy drink for active and busy people, and this positioning was endorsed by sports celebrities, e.g. Daley Thompson. It still retained its premium price and quality image, but created much more positive connotations and a rationale for more frequent purchase and consumption. The repositioning was achieved partly through packaging, for instance in a 'one-shot' bottle (no longer just the large size bottle), selling alongside other soft drinks (colas etc.), and partly through powerful celebrity advertising featuring current sports heroes.

The popularity of energy drinks has, however, led some to question their real value. A study of many energy 'sports drinks' has resulted in concerns about the validity of some of the claims being made. Despite being positioned as 'healthy', many drinks had high sugar content, with one brand dishing up 19 level teaspoons of sugar in one serving, and some had caffeine levels three times higher than those of traditional colas. Sue Dibb from the Food Commission summed up the concerns:

Sports dieticians do not recommend high energy drinks as a regular part of the diet of someone training or doing sport recreationally. For extra energy, a banana is healthier. (Hawkes, 1997)

As the public becomes more informed, discerning and wary of marketing claims, brand personalities and values will have to evolve too. But then again, if it tastes good and you enjoy it, perhaps that is enough!

> **Example** The Jaguar brand name (http://www.jaguarcars.com) has such strong associations with quality in the luxury car market that the company decided to extend the brand into aircraft. Jaguar linked up with Raytheon in the US to produce the Beech King Air Jaguar special edition. Jaguar quality manifests itself through the interior fittings and furnishings, leather seats, Jaguar green carpeting, special colours and liveries and even walnut cabins. All the aircraft registrations will end with XJ to emphasise the Jaguar link. The Jaguar XJ8 car costs over $50 000 in the USA and the Jaguar special edition plane over $2.6mn, some $66 000 more than the same aircraft without the special edition interior (Brennan, 1997).

Quality for service products tends to arise from the customer's perceptions of the physical support mechanisms and the infrastructure that help to create an appropriate interactive environment. An efficient appointments system, friendly reception and provision of coffee and magazines in a pleasant waiting area, for example, all add to the perceived quality of a service operation in the minds of customers. Naturally, this must be reinforced by consistent, reliable and satisfactory delivery of the service itself.

In changing the quality of a product, the movement can be towards either relatively higher quality or relatively lower quality. Lowering the quality is likely to lose existing customers, but at the same time could open up an expanded market if it brings the product into a more affordable price range. Lowering the quality does not necessarily mean making actual changes to the product; it can be an act of omission. An organisation could make a conscious decision to withhold any further development and modification resources from a product, despite seeing competing products improve. This means that the organisation's product quality is declining relative to the rest and may indicate that the product is being phased out and that resources are being saved for investment in future products.

Raising the quality of a physical product could be achieved perhaps through better components or refined manufacturing. For a service product, it could mean major refurbishment for the premises or developing the way in which the experience is packaged. Whatever the product or the means employed, raising the quality offers the prospect of charging higher prices and increasing profit margins. It might, however, lead to increased competition from other organisations greedy for a share of that prosperity. The other point to consider carefully is whether the target market will either recognise or value the newly raised quality.

> **Example** Seat (http://www.seat.com), the Spanish subsidiary of Germany's Volkswagen group, is seeking to reposition itself away from a cheap and basic image as a motor manufacturer. The long-term aim is to rival the likes of the Alfa Romeo as a sporty and stylish brand. Although this may be a lengthy project, the launch of the Toledo in 1998 represented an important step in that direction. Using style and design along with more powerful engines, Seat hoped to make an impact on the medium to large vehicle class. The Ibiza, a completely new car launched in 2000 in the small hatchback class, is the next model built with the new requirements (Simonian, 1998).

Design

Thinking in an aesthetic rather than an engineering context, design affects the impact of the product on the senses. This concept can be difficult to handle, as it covers areas such as the appearance, texture, taste, smell, feel or sound of the product, all of which involve the customer in some very subjective assessments. These areas do, however, provide many combinations of variables that could offer the opportunity for change. If the objective is to reposition a product, just changing its visual appearance or its packaging (probably with 'new improved...' splashed across it) could give customers sufficient cues and justification for revising their opinions of it.

> **Example** Design is clearly an important factor in fashion clothing markets. Brand names become closely associated with certain characteristics or a certain 'look' that helps to position them in the 1990s. Jaeger, for example, was closely associated with traditional, classic looks, but the organisation felt that it needed to be more fashionable and stylish as the brand's growth had slowed compared with its competitors. The solution was to retain a core classic range, so as not to alienate loyal customers, but to supplement it with capsule collections of more fashionable merchandise. This signalled a subtle rather than radical shift in Jaeger's positioning to widen and refresh its appeal.

It must be stressed that any design changes are a waste of time and resources unless they matter to the market, can be communicated to that market and are implemented to achieve defined objectives.

Performance

Like design, performance relies on the customer's initial, rather impressionistic assessment. A more concrete appreciation of performance may only come after product use. The kind of factors under consideration here include convenience, safety, ease of handling, efficiency, effectiveness and adaptability to different situations. A car's performance, for instance, can be measured in terms of its acceleration, braking ability or fuel economy, depending on what is important to the buyer. Improving the fuel economy at the expense of acceleration might change the character of the car, making it less appealing to a 'boy racer' type of segment, but positioning it more firmly and more positively in the 'heavy urban usage' segment. Even the fuel itself has been repositioned in terms of its performance-enhancing capabilities, with some brands promising to be more engine friendly or to improve engine performance.

Quality, design and performance are often inextricably interlinked. Proposed changes under one heading have implications for the others. Improving a car's fuel economy may involve better-quality components under the bonnet as well as a more aerodynamic body design.

It does not really matter whether a proposed change is classified as relating to quality, design or performance, or all three. What does matter is that as part of the product management process, all the relevant options are assessed to make sure that the product continues to achieve its maximum potential, either within its existing segment(s) or through repositioning into a new one. Quality, design and performance all provide possibilities for the major or minor changes that will ensure this.

Product range management

The discussion above concentrated on the adjustment and adaptation of existing products and their marketing mixes to reposition the offering in the customer's mind. Taking this concept a step further, the organisation may wish to leave existing products as they are and use the assessment of positioning to identify opportunities for new products to fill or extend the current range. This approach to new product development may use existing products as a basis, rather than the more radical departures envisaged in the next chapter. These decisions are all part of the ongoing product audit, constantly checking to make sure that product offerings continue to serve the market's needs and wants. A major advantage is that all the positive attitudes and perceptions of the original brand's customers can be transferred to the new product that evolves (Aaker and Keller, 1990).

Two broad options are available: extending the product line and filling the product range.

Extending the product line length and depth

Extending the product line involves looking at the current range and deciding whether to extend it upwards, downwards or in both directions. An upwards extension might involve introducing a higher priced, higher-quality, more exclusive product, while a downwards extension might require a basic, no-frills product at a rock-bottom, mass-market price.

In thinking about such an extension, the marketer needs to be sure that the gaps thus filled are worth filling. Will sufficient customers emerge to take up the new product? Will the trade accept it? Is it a significant profit opportunity? Will it simply cannibalise existing products? This last issue is particularly important; there is no point in extending a product range downwards if the main effect is to pull customers away from an existing mid-range product.

Extending upwards. Extending upwards has a number of attractions, assuming that the organisation has the ability to produce a suitably attractive and consistently high-quality product offering. An upwards extension could create a product with higher margins (*see* Chapter 11) as well as enhancing the organisation's image. It also helps to build a kind of staircase for the customer to climb. As the customer becomes more affluent or as their needs and wants become more sophisticated, they can trade up to the next product in the range and still maintain their loyalty to one organisation. A business school, for example, with established post-experience management programmes at certificate and diploma levels, might extend its product range upwards to include an MBA. The intention would be that students should work their way through all three qualifications in the course of their management careers. Similarly, a bank might create a new savings scheme offering higher rates of interest for balances over £10 000 to prevent a customer with such funds from taking their money elsewhere.

> **Example** Pringle, a Scottish knitwear firm best known for its sweaters and golf sponsorship, tried to extend upwards into luxury goods, such as high-quality luggage and accessories. At the same time, it was also expanding sideways into non-knitwear clothing and its own retail outlets. This combination of upwards and sideways expansion did not work well. The Pringle brand name was appearing on too many items that were too far removed from its core image. This diluted the impact and exclusivity of the name and meant that customers did not perceive the luxury goods as being suitably classy or élite.

Extending downwards. The downwards extension can be used to attack competitors operating at the volume end of the market. It can build a larger base of sales if a lower-priced product broadens the number of potential customers. Then, by introducing people to the bottom of the range product and forming some kind of relationship with them, it may be possible to get them to trade up, thus assisting sales of the mid-range product. This would be the ideal situation, but do remember the risks of cannibalisation if the bottom of the range product acts as a magnet to existing mid-range customers. There can be a risk of undermining brand equity by extensions at the bottom of the range. This can cause an overall loss of equity to the whole range that is greater than the incremental sales of the new products (Reibstein *et al.*, 1998).

Careful thought also needs to be given to the logistic implications of extending downwards if it opens up bigger markets. This might mean shifting higher volumes of goods to more outlets, as well as increased commitment to mass communication in order to reach the greater number of potential buyers. Hi-fi manufacturers, for instance, make sure that they extend their ranges downwards, partly to catch the mass market with cheap and cheerful, value for money music systems, and partly to try to encourage brand loyalty in the younger buyers who will eventually trade up the range. Similarly, Heinz has managed to extend downwards in the beans market by undertaking own-label manufacture for retailers. This has allowed it to gain a position at the price sensitive, discount end of the market without damaging the overall brand image.

Both kinds of range extension clearly have benefits and risks that need to be assessed before a decision can be made. The biggest danger, perhaps, is that of stretching scarce management and cash resources so thinly that current products suffer from neglect and new extensions to the range never have a real chance of becoming established on a firm foundation.

Filling the product range

The option of **filling the product range** involves a very close examination of the current range, then creating new products to fill in any gaps between existing products. This could be a relatively low-cost option, as it would be likely that existing distribution and promotional activity could be applied to the new products. As implied in the previous section, the range extension option is opening new ground, thus requiring a possible review of distribution and promotional activity.

One way of filling out the range could be to increase the number of variants available. The product remains the same, but it has a range of different presentations. Thus a food product might be available in single-serving packs, family-sized packs or catering-sized freezer packs. Tomato ketchup is available in squeezy bottles as well as in glass ones.

Manufacturers of laundry detergents have long used range filling as a means of keeping consumer interest and persuading them to buy different products for different uses. This means that when the UK supermarket Safeway launched its own brand of laundry products, Cyclon, it had to provide a wide range of variants in order to compete with the established brands in the market. Thus the range included biological, biological with fabric conditioner, non-biological and coloureds washing products. All of these are available as powder or liquid, standard or concentrated, in boxes and bottles or in refill bags and pouches, and in different sizes. Excluding different pack sizes, this provided the shopper with over 30 different choices!

Filling the range can be a useful strategy for keeping the competition out, by offering the consumer some novelty and a more detailed range of products closer to their needs, and to add incrementally to profits at relatively low risk. The danger, however, is the risk of adding to costs, but with no overall increase in sales. This is the risk of cannibalisation, of fragmenting existing market share across too many similar products. There is the added irony that the consumer might well be indifferent to these variants, being perfectly satisfied with the original range.

Deleting products

The final stages of a product's life are often the hardest for management to contemplate. The decision to eliminate a poor seller that may be generating low or even negative profits is a tough one to make. The economic rationale for being ruthless is clear. A product making poor returns absorbs management time and can quickly drain resources if it is being kept alive by aggressive selling and promotion. Such a product may also have a marginal competitive position and be unlikely to recover any significant share in the market. As the product's sales volumes inevitably decline, its unit costs start to increase (*see* Chapter 11) and the product becomes a burden.

There is, however, often a reluctance to take action. There are various reasons for this, some of which are purely personal or political. Managers often form emotional attachments to the products they have looked after: 'I introduced this product, I backed it and built my career on it.' If the offending product was launched more recently, then its deletion might be seen as an admission of failure on the part of its managers. They would, therefore, prefer to try just once more to turn the product round and to retain their reputations intact.

> **Example** The Metro is dead. It was introduced in the early 1980s as the replacement for the Mini and the saviour of motor manufacturer British Leyland (BL, subsequently Rover). It was neither. BL is no more and the Mini is still in production as a niche, cult car. The Metro never gained as much popular affection as the Mini and will probably best be remembered as the car in which so many learned to drive after the British School of Motoring built its fleet around the economical brand. The real problem for the Metro was that it was left behind in terms of quality, design and performance, as the small car segment became more attractive to other manufacturers such as the Japanese companies, Ford and General Motors. Selling on price requires high-volume sales and the Metro did not achieve enough nor did it have sufficiently unique benefits to offer. Even the British School of Motoring eventually switched to the Vauxhall Corsa. By the late 1990s, once BMW had taken over the Rover group, the termination decision was easy to make (Eason, 1998).

Other reasons for being reluctant to delete a product are based on a desire to offer as wide a range as possible, regardless of the additional costs incurred. While there is still some demand (however small) for a particular product, the organisation feels obliged to continue to provide it, as a service to its customers. Suddenly deleting that product might result in negative feelings for some customers. Car owners in particular become attached to certain models and react badly when a manufacturer decides to withdraw them from the available range.

Managers may also find it difficult to calculate the full product cost. Where costs are shared between several different products, for example, there may be a number of justifiable ways of splitting those costs, depending on what you want to prove. Coming to an agreement that a product is covering its variable costs and making at least a contribution to fixed costs and overheads is useful, but it is only a beginning. Opportunity costs also have to be considered, which means defining what else could be done with the resources (manufacturing, financial, labour and management) that are being invested in this product. If those resources could be employed more profitably on something else within the strategic context of the business, then the product in question may be less secure.

All of this means that there is a need for a regular systematic review to identify the more marginal products, to assess their current contribution and to decide how they fit with future plans.

If new life can be injected into a product, then all well and good, but if not, then there are three broad options.

Phase out

Phasing out means allowing a gradual decline of the product with little change during the year, as long as it is making some contribution. There will then be a review at the end of the year to decide whether to continue with the product any longer or not.

Run out

Running out entails a deliberate effort to sell more in the product's main markets, but without heavy marketing expenditure. Self-financing promotions may be the most that the organisation will allow. In this situation, the organisation expects to lose sales, but will make a greater return on each sale because of the lack of investment in marketing support.

Drop or sell

In the worst case, the organisation finds that it can no longer sustain a product that is making little or no contribution. Major customers may be notified in advance to allow them adjustment, stocking or re-sourcing time. With fair warning of the product's demise, customers are less likely to be caught by surprise and thus less likely to feel angry that they have not been informed. They may not like the decision, but at least they have time to discuss it and get used to it.

As a general rule, many companies have not introduced regular deletion procedures (Avlonitis, 1985; Greenley and Bayus, 1994). The price of this failure is long and sometimes unprofitable product ranges, which serve the needs of neither the customer nor the manufacturer.

CUSTOMER SPECIFIED PRODUCTS

So far, the assumption has been made that the manufacturer or the service provider specifies the product. Particularly in organisational markets, this is not always the case, as a specific customer might have such unique requirements that standard product offerings will not suffice. The supplier's skill lies in designing and developing a standard specification that can be used as a basis for fine tuning and compromise in accordance with individual customer needs.

To provide customised products, the supplier needs to develop technical capabilities. This might mean investment in capital goods, machinery and plant to allow customer specifications to be met. A heavy haulage company, for example, will have to be able to load large items on to trailers but may only have the ability to handle items up to 500 tonnes. Any heavier object that a customer may want to have transported is beyond the haulier's technical capability. As well as technical capability, a supplier might have to be able and willing to be responsive in the design, production and delivery of the product or service. In the case of the haulier, extensive negotiation

---

MARKETING IN ACTION   **Making records**

The music industry is in trouble because of changes in consumer demand and tastes. In 1998, sales outside the US tended to be stagnant or declining. Sales dropped in Germany by 6 per cent in the first half of 1998. There are particular problems with increasingly short product life-cycles and thus products that become obsolete very quickly. Singles enter the charts at a higher point, but stay there for a much shorter time than previously. Another problem is that traditionally, singles were used almost as a marketing device to sell albums, which generated the real profits. In the 1990s, however, the singles charts were dominated by dance acts that generally do not sell albums. There is concern within the industry that these acts are too ephemeral and that the record companies are not able to do enough to nurture and develop talent over time, because they are under too much pressure to churn out immediate, short-term hits. Parallels are drawn with bands such as Pink Floyd, the Rolling Stones and other big names from the 1960s and 1970s. Recording companies took risks and these artists were given the space and time to develop. As a result, they still sell and their record companies have rich back catalogues of their material that earn a steady profit.

Even the super acts of the 1980s are no longer guaranteed to drive sales upwards. U2, Michael Jackson, Madonna, George Michael and Prince, while maintaining a loyal following, do not generate the kinds of sales volumes to maintain growth. Only the Spice Girls and Alanis Morissette can claim outstanding success in terms of over 40 million albums sold, but there are few others. The lack of really big sellers makes it less likely that casual listeners will buy.

There have also been other shifts in consumer demand. The tendency is for diversity in musical tastes and thus a typical album sells around 200 000 copies rather than one big hit selling two million. This adds to marketing and distribution costs. There is also a growing belief that music is losing its glamour and becoming a commodity rather than having the special appeal or 'star quality'. The growth of the MP3 player, which allows consumers to download music from the Internet, could be another blow to the industry. CD prices have been exceptionally high in parts of Europe compared with the Far East and in the UK there have been allegations of overcharging. The *Titanic* soundtrack, for example, retailed at £14.49 in the UK when it could have been picked up in Hong Kong for around £8. Despite all these difficulties, there are still opportunities for really big acts rather than compilations, old tunes, remakes and fading stars. Watch this space!

Sources: Baird (1998); Townsend (1998); Wroe (1995).

will be necessary on the collection, movement and installation of any load, although what is possible is restricted by the haulier's available technology. If suppliers claim to be prepared to be responsive to special requirements, they must be sure that their own suppliers can be equally responsive if necessary.

In some organisational markets, a supplier might have to adapt facilities or even invest in new facilities, just to serve the needs of one or two customers. Small manufacturing subcontractors often invest in new machinery to service one or two major customers in the hope that further business may then be found, given their expanded capabilities and capacity. In this case, the supplier's investment in its ability to meet customised needs can give it a means of generating customer loyalty. However, if those customers can still easily source the same goods from elsewhere, then such specific investment might be dangerous (Blois, 1980). Nevertheless, preparedness to adapt and invest for a specific customer is widespread in organisational markets. Sometimes it is instigated by the customer and sometimes by the supplier as a means of winning orders (Cunningham, 1986; Turnbull and Valla, 1986). Often, however, a smaller supplier does not have the luxury of choice and is expected to adapt itself as a sign of commitment to a larger customer. In return, the supplier perhaps gets slightly longer-term contracts and other forms of co-operation from the customer.

> **Example** Anglo-French engineering group Alstom (http://www.alstom.com) recently won a contract to maintain the fleet used by Great North Eastern Railway (GNER). Alsthom had to respond to GNER's demand for greater reliability of electronic equipment on high-speed trains. Reliability matters to GNER, as the company's operating performance is closely monitored in such areas as punctuality and cancellations. Alstom is required as part of the contract to investigate parts with unsatisfactory reliability and to propose improvements to methods of manufacture or overhaul. The overall aim is to ensure that the parts made or supplied by Alstom closely meet GNER's standards for achieving lower failure rates and improved reliability (Batchelor, 1998).

This example highlights the amount of time and effort that a buyer might have to put into sourcing a customised product successfully. It also explains why some buyers may be prepared to sacrifice precision of specification and make do with a standardised product instead, where possible. To develop a specification, and then find and assess suppliers who are willing and able to meet it may be too time consuming and expensive to be justified. In some cases, however, it cannot be avoided. A crucial component of a larger system, such as a unique printed circuit board (PCB) for a machine-tool operating system, will have to be customised. Interestingly, there are suppliers of PCBs who specialise in the low-volume, prototype, customised end of the market. They provide fast service and technical responsiveness and then as soon as the PCB moves out of the development stage and into full-scale mass production, the contract is handed over to other high-volume, low-unit-cost manufacturers.

Even if a supplier has the capability to produce to customer specifications, the job still has to be done efficiently and within a cost structure that leads to an acceptable price from both parties' perspectives. The trade-off between price and specification will depend on many factors, such as how critical the product is to the buyer, whether high prices can be passed on to the buyer's ultimate customer and the nature of the market niche occupied by the buyer. In some situations, the product is not completely customer specified, but is a compromise between customer needs and suppliers' technical capabilities. This means that there has to be 'give and take' in the advice and design stage to produce a valued and cost effective package. This is especially true where physical products are purchased that do not actually enter into the buyer's own product, but help the buyer to enhance its service or production capability offering to its own customers.

Even consumer markets may be able to offer customer specified products, within limits. Fitted furniture has to be supplied to fit room dimensions, although the customer is likely to choose from a range of pre-fabricated types of unit which will then undergo minor adjustments to make them fit. Clothes can be tailormade to fit an individual, although again, the range of styles and fabrics within which that can be done may be predetermined and limited. In Pizza Hut, customers have plenty of flexibility to design their own pizzas, but within a range of toppings specified by the organisation. This strikes a successful yet delicate balance between cost effective production and the personal touch so valued and so difficult to achieve in mass markets.

MARKETING AND IT   Customer specified products

In consumer markets, customer specified products are not just confined to pizzas. Most products in the 'design your own' category are, however, just a little more expensive, allowing producers to find a balance between cost effective production and achieving an adequate return for the added service. Here are three examples of how consumers are invited to design their own products:

■ *Dell Computers*: Dell is the world's leading direct seller of personal computers and increasingly sells over the Internet. Prospective customers can visit Dell's website (http://www.dell.com) to design and assemble a PC to their own specification. Once the order has been accepted over the Internet, the PC is assembled to order and shipped within days.

■ *Andersen Windows*: in the US, Andersen Windows uses multimedia applications in retail outlets to integrate customers into its supply chain and effectively sell to a market of one. The systems allows customers to input a 3-D representation of their home, choose where the new windows are to go and then experiment with different window frames.

■ *Rover Group*: multimedia point-of-sale systems are also used by the UK based Rover Group to allow potential customers to 'configure' their own car. The kiosks have been rolled out to Rover dealers in the UK and elsewhere across Europe.

Source: O'Connor and Galvin (1999).

PRODUCT MANAGEMENT AND ORGANISATION

There is a range of management structures for marketing, depending on the tasks required and the environmental opportunities and threats. A traditional functional organisation that emphasises sales and distribution lacks the holistic approach to marketing so necessary for successful brand development. Also, in some organisations, the number of products to be managed may be large. This means that some kind of focus is needed to ensure that each product gets appropriate management support and attention, as well as to exploit the synergies between products and between their marketing strategies.

Products are extremely important as revenue earners and so they need careful management. Product-centred management structures can help to ensure that they do get the care they deserve. A product or brand manager handles part of a range or even an individual brand if it is very critical. **Product managers** operate across all functional areas, especially marketing, but also liaise with R&D, production and logistics to ensure the best opportunities and treatment for their product(s). Their job is to manage the product throughout its life-cycle, from launch, through any modifications, to its eventual demise. It can often be a total commitment and may include commissioning research, liaising with distribution and even handling sales with major account negotiations. The product manager will also be involved in planning advertising approaches, media selection and packaging.

Product managers clearly cannot undertake all this alone. They play a key role in a project team, taking the product through from idea to commercialisation. These teams are always multifunctional, because of the need to consider project viability from all angles. If the launch is successful, then the day-to-day management of the product will be turned over to the product manager, with less input from the initial team.

In terms of planning, controlling and monitoring product performance, the product manager is likely to have to produce an annual product plan, specifying actions, resources and strategies for the coming trading period. This helps the manager to justify the investment of resources in the product and also allows early recognition of problems with the product and proposed corrective action.

This kind of product management structure is used in larger fmcg organisations in particular, where there is significant emphasis on new product development and major mass-market brands. It may also be applicable in some organisational markets, but as Davis (1984) suggests, the structure and complexity of some organisational markets mean that other options may also have to be considered. If, for example, the same product or component is sold to a range of different end users, then it may be better to divide management responsibility by end user (or segment) rather than by product. A car component, for example, may be sold to car manufacturers, servicing and repair workshops or specialist retailers. Each of these customer groups needs different handling and the component manufacturer may prefer to have specialist marketing managers for each one. A different approach is to divide marketing management responsibility on a geographic basis, particularly where international marketing is the norm. The logic is the same as for the end-user focus: each territory has a unique profile and very different demands and handling needs, requiring a specialist manager. Both of these alternatives, allocating responsibility by end user or geographic area take account of the day-to-day marketing needs of the organisation's products, but potentially leave an unfilled gap for a 'product champion'. The last thing the organisation wants is for managers to develop the attitude that they only sell the product and that its wider strategic development is 'somebody else's problem'.

EUROPEAN PRODUCT STRATEGY

Creating a brand that can be established across Europe, a **Eurobrand**, is neither easy nor cheap, as the motor industry has found in striving to create a 'world car' that can suit all tastes internationally. Many smaller companies feel that they have a sufficiently difficult job on their hands creating and maintaining a presence in their own local national market without worrying about the rest of Europe. Even some of the bigger household name organisations, such as Nestlé, have consolidated their European presence as much through the acquisition of companies in each local market as through establishing pan-European brands.

Lynch (1994) is uncompromisingly blunt in defining the criteria essential for Eurobrand building:

1 *Resources*: Lynch estimates that a marketing communications budget of no less than $60 million is needed for three years to establish the brand, unless, of course, a much longer-term phased introduction is planned.
2 *Quality*: The need for consistent quality in both the product itself and the production, logistical and administrative procedures that support it should not be under-estimated. Operating on a pan-European basis is more difficult than operating within a national market.
3 *Timing*: According to Lynch, it will take at least five years to establish a Eurobrand and short-term returns on investment should not be expected.

These three criteria alone put Eurobranding out of the reach of most organisations. There are also practical considerations, for example culture and language. These can affect everything from the brand name (remember Plopsies and Kuk & Fuk; not to mention other gems from non-English speaking markets, such as Fanny, Spunk, Bum and Crap?), to the imagery associated with the brand, to the advertising. The marketer has to decide whether to use an identical approach in all corners of the European market, or whether to make adaptations, perhaps to the advertising or the packaging, for particular local or cultural conditions. (More detailed discussion on these issues will be found in Chapter 23 on international marketing.) As Wolfe (1991) points out, only around 40 per cent of European adults understand English, the most widespread language, which means that packaging will have to be multilingual, or as non-verbal as possible, or produced in a number of different language versions.

Example Scott Worldwide, manufacturers of the Baby Fresh brand of baby wipes, found a compromise solution (Cramp, 1995). Because it had expanded into various international markets over a number of years, there was no consistent brand image. Pack sizes, colours and graphics varied greatly from country to country. After much research, the pack size, colour and basic graphic imagery were standardised and a series of animal icons designed to signify product variants. Within that framework, there were designated areas on the pack where local flexibility was allowed, for colour or message variation.

Halliburton and Hunerberg (1987) found that strategic variables such as positioning and product range transferred more readily across borders than pricing, which needs to reflect local conditions. Advertising and distribution tended to vary between stand-ardised and differentiated approaches. It is, however, difficult to generalise. Nescafé, while giving the impression of being a standardised international brand, actually varies in blend, flavour and product description to suit local taste (Rijkens, 1992). This highlights the difference between the concept and the brand in terms of standardisation. For Nescafé, there is often considerable conformity across Europe on packaging, labelling and basic communications mix strategies, whereas specific message design and pricing are subject to more local control. Bolz (1992) also found more of a standardised, pan-European approach in the areas of product specification, brand name, design and packaging than in pricing and promotion. The decision to standardise is also influenced by external factors, such as the homogenisation of demand, the exist-ence of global segments, economies of scale and global competition in the sector. Factors such as retail structure and the legal and technological environments, however, tend to create barriers to standardisation.

All of this assumes that there is a pan-European market for the product, demanding volumes that justify the investment. Despite the potential problems, however, there are many pan-European brands (some of which are also global brands). The car manufacturers successfully sell the same model across Europe, while Procter & Gamble, Johnson & Johnson, Colgate Palmolive, Heinz and Nestlé all maintain pan-European fmcg brands. Although many of those brands have been around for many years, it is still possible to launch a new brand on a pan-European basis. Gillette's Natrel deodorant was launched with heavy marketing support across the EU, using not only identical product and brand imagery in all countries, but also identical packaging and advertising.

Example Outside the fmcg area, many organisations with well established products have restructured themselves to make the most of the opportunities offered by the SEM. Whirlpool Europe, for example, which makes domestic appliances such as dishwashers and washing machines, spent several years restructuring itself on a pan-European basis. This has meant centralising and streamlining production and administrative support as well as reorganising the sales effort. Rather than maintaining a sales force for each European country, it developed two pan-European sales organisations, each concentrating on different types of distribution channel because, as the company itself said:

'Channels across borders have a lot more in common than different channels within a country.'

All of this not only increases production and administrative efficiency, and provides a sales force better tailored to the market's needs, but also allows the organisation to use its European size to compete effectively against national competitors in each country. In organisational markets, as Chapters 4 and 7 have already indicated, there is a far higher propensity to adapt product offerings to suit individual customers, regardless of geographic boundaries. The nature and significance of these product adaptations will vary according to market structure, technological forces and the importance of the buyer–seller relationship. However, Europroducts have been developed in some organisational markets such as software, computers, trucks and machine tools, where any adaptations tend to be minor, for example trucks for the UK market need to be right-hand drive!

In summary, the advantages of pan-European branding are:

■ defining segments across borders, increasing the size of the potential market
■ achieving economies of scale in production, administration, marketing and sales effort
■ gaining competitive advantage over nationally orientated competition.

Colgate toothpaste: recognisable anywhere in Europe.

Source: Colgate Palmolive Colgate UK Ltd.

The potential dangers of pan-European branding are:

■ a segment too geographically spread to be served efficiently
■ presenting a bland product through trying to be all things to all people and trying to avoid cultural or linguistic problems
■ high investment and long lead times, stretching resources and patience to breaking point
■ making so many concessions to local differences that you end up with a series of loosely related products rather than a single pan-European brand.

As more Eurobrands evolve, it has been argued, there will be fewer new brands introduced at a national level and more that are targeted across wider European markets to appeal to Eurosegments, using common brand names, packaging and positioning (Guido, 1991). In support of this view, Doyle (1998) considers that the focus should be on appealing to a particular segment rather than focusing on standardisation or adaptation issues. Thus there may be a wide diversity of products, appealing to segments that are free of geographic boundaries.

CHAPTER SUMMARY

This chapter has tackled some of the more detailed issues connected with managing products from their conception to their eventual decline. The product life-cycle (PLC) concept is the foundation for the idea that products do move through stages in their lives and that they may, therefore, have different marketing needs over time. The PLC suggests four stages: introduction, growth, maturity and decline. Inevitably, the PLC is a very general concept, perhaps too general to be of real use, and there are many practical problems in using it.

For an organisation, product management is important not only for making sure that existing products live profitable and efficient lives, and that they are deleted at the most appropriate time, but also to enable it to plan for the future and the flow of new products, taking advantage of new technologies and other opportunities. This implies the need for a balanced portfolio of products: some still in development, some in the early stages of their lives, some more mature and some heading for decline.

One way of ensuring that products get the most out of their life-cycles is to think about how they are positioned. This means defining what attributes or benefits are important to the market, then researching how your product, its competitors and a hypothetical ideal product are rated against those criteria, then analysing each brand's position in relation to the others and to the ideal. Perceptual mapping, using two or more dimensions, can help to visualise the state of the market. All of this can stimulate debate as to whether a product needs to be further differentiated from its competitors or brought closer to the market segment's ideal.

Rather than repositioning existing products, an organisation may choose to introduce new products, based on existing ones, to fill perceived gaps. Current ranges may be extended up market, down market or in both directions. The organisation needs to make sure, however, that any such extensions are acceptable to the trade and to customers, do not stretch resources too thinly and will not compromise or cannibalise existing products. A further option is to fill out an existing product range, without moving up or down market, perhaps by increasing the number of variants available, for example in terms of pack sizes or packaging formats.

The decision to delete a product can be a difficult one. Emotional attachment to products, a reluctance to admit defeat or difficulty in proving that a product is making a loss may all delay deletion. When a product is to be deleted, there are several options. Phasing out allows gradual decline; running out means a deliberate selling effort in main markets but without heavy support; drop or sell means deleting the product completely.

Customer specified products cause their own marketing difficulties for manufacturers, as the product has to be produced efficiently, to specification and within cost constraints. The manufacturer may have to adapt facilities in order to make what the customer wants. Sometimes products are not totally customer specified, but involve a compromise between manufacturer and buyer.

In fmcg companies in particular, product or brand managers may be given the responsibility of looking after a particular product or group of products. Although a similar product management structure may be found in organisational markets, alternative options may be considered. Management responsibility may be divided by end user or on a geographic basis, again because the needs of different regions may differ. In either case, the organisation can develop managers with depth of expertise relating to a specific group of end users or a particular geographic market.

The creation of the SEM opened up opportunities for pan-European branding. For many smaller organisations, however, this is not a serious issue and they do not have the resources or the real desire to move beyond their own national boundaries. Organisations interested in pan-European branding need abundant resources, to be sure that they can deliver consistent quality in all aspects of the operations and marketing and that they are prepared to support the brand through a long lead time before the product begins to make a return on its investment.

Key words and phrases

Diffusion of innovation	**Filling the product range**	**Product portfolio**
Eurobrand	**Product life-cycle (PLC)**	**Product positioning**
Extending the product line	**Product manager**	**Product repositioning**

QUESTIONS FOR REVIEW

8.1 Define the four stages of the *product life-cycle*.

8.2 What might be the main concerns for a marketing manager dealing with a *mature* product?

8.3 To what extent is the *PLC* limited in its applicability as a management tool?

8.4 What are the alternative ways of allocating *product management* responsibility in organisational markets?

8.5 Discuss the relationship between *product adopter categories* and the *stages of the PLC*. What are the implications for the marketer?

8.6 Define *product positioning* and summarise the reasons why it is important.

8.7 Why might *product repositioning* be necessary, and in what ways can the organisation achieve it?

8.8 Differentiate between *product line extension* and *filling out the product range*. In what circumstances might each be appropriate?

8.9 Find examples of *product line extension*, both up market and down market. Try to analyse the marketing thinking behind the extensions.

8.10 Outline the alternative *product deletion methods* available and the advantages and disadvantages of each.

QUESTIONS FOR DISCUSSION

8.1 In what ways might *customer specified products* complicate the product management task?

8.2 Why is *product management* essential?

8.3 Choose a consumer product area (be very specific – for example, choose shampoo rather than haircare products) and list as many brands available within it as you can.
(a) What stage in the *PLC* has each product reached?
(b) What stage has the *product class* or *form* reached?

(c) Does any one organisation own several of the brands and, if so, how are these brands distributed across the different *PLC stages*?

8.4 What circumstances might lead an organisation towards *pan-European branding*?

8.5 Find an example of:
(a) a successful *pan-European brand*; and
(b) an unsuccessful *pan-European brand*.
What do you think has contributed to the success/failure?

CASE STUDY 8.1

Alcopops

Alcopops (alcoholic soft drinks or alcoholic carbonates) are ready-to-drink products containing a mix of alcohol and a soft drink such as cola, lemonade or other fruit flavours and a strength of between 4.7 and 5.5 per cent ABV (alcohol by volume). This compares with lager's alcoholic content of between 4 and 4.5 per cent. The alcopops category does not include mixed drinks based on spirits (e.g. vodka, whisky or gin) or ciders.

The first product launched in the UK market was Hooper's Hooch, an alcoholic lemonade, in the hot summer of 1995. Two Dogs and Lemonhead soon followed. Alcopops were an instant success, mainly because their branding was perceived as 'cool' and dynamic by drinkers who like to 'discover' new products. Added to that was a great deal of controversy over their ethical position and targeting, helping to create a cult atmosphere around the market. Particular concern was expressed about the use of cartoon characters on the labels (although many of these were later dropped).

Controversy dampened neither the consumers' nor the producers' enthusiasm and within little more than a year there were over 100 brands in the UK market. Despite negative publicity, the alcopops sector continued to show substantial growth, estimated at 20 per cent a year through 1996, and new alcopop products continued to enter the market. However, in summer 1997, reports suggested that even the leading brands, Hooper's Hooch and Two Dogs, were experiencing problems and that growth in the £350 million market was levelling off, perhaps even heading towards decline. All brands had suffered from the fact that major retailers such as the Co-op and Iceland had stopped selling alcopops altogether and shelf space in the major multiples was becoming increasingly scarce. The Co-op had explained its decision to ban alcopops from its shelves:

> We feel we should not sell products that in our opinion are likely to appeal to, and be consumed by, people who are not old enough to buy them from us.
> (Shannon, 1997)

The retailer felt that it was respecting the concerns of customers and pressure groups, and that alcopops were different from ciders and lagers because their imagery was clearly targeted at the under-18s.

Two Dogs had always been a poor second behind Hooper's Hooch and had also been delisted by Sainsbury's in 1996 because it was not selling well. In December 1996, Hooper's Hooch had 68 per cent of the market, while Two Dogs had only 5 per cent. In an attempt to regain a significant position in the market, therefore, Two Dogs announced a £1mn advertising campaign in August 1997 to communicate its new look (a more adult design with more emphasis on the label on the word 'alcoholic') and taste (more lemony). Considering that the launch advertising spend on Two Dogs had only been £500 000, this represented a significant investment. Hooper's Hooch was not standing still, however. In October 1997, it too announced a £1mn redesign and £7mn advertising campaign to reposition the brand as a more adult and less sugary drink. The words 'alcoholic lemon' on the label were replaced with 'alcoholic drink' and the overall look was made 'unambiguously adult'. The blackcurrant version was axed and replaced with grapefruit.

These relaunches were not just driven by the need to defend or build market positioning and share. Research showed that 59 per cent of people felt that alcopops encouraged under-age drinking. The media and pressure groups such as Alcohol Concern were vociferous in their criticism. The new Labour government made it clear that if the industry could not regulate itself properly, then legislation and even a complete ban would be seriously considered. All of this encouraged the Portman Group, the alcohol industry's watchdog, to investigate complaints about the targeting of alcopops towards under-age drinkers and to tighten up the code of practice in the market. Although no complaints against Hooch were upheld by the Portman Group, Hooch's owner, Bass, wanted to be seen to be taking a responsible lead in overtly repositioning its brand away from the teenage market. Other brands did not escape criticism. Seventeen brands were examined and thirteen had a case to answer. Five brands were axed as a result of the investigation and a further eight brands were required to rename or repackage themselves. Even without the Portman Group's intervention, some kind of shakeout was inevitable in such a crowded market with over 100 brands competing for space and custom. As a management consultant dramatically said:

> The shelves had started to groan with ill-thought-out me-too products which lacked taste or marketing support. (Willman, 1997)

By May 1998, a lot of the 'me too' brands had gone and the value of the market had dropped to £174mn, with Hooch still the biggest seller at 2 million bottles per week, down from its peak of 2.5 million.

Sources: *The Grocer* (1997a, 1997b); *Marketing* (1997); *Marketing Week* (1997a, 1997b); Marsh (1997a, 1997b); *Mintel* (1997); Murphy (1998); Shannon (1997); Teather (1997); Willman (1997).

Questions

1 Draw the product life-cycle for (a) the alcopops market and (b) Hooch, explaining your reasoning. What types of life-cycle have you drawn (*see* Fig. 8.2)?

2 To what extent and why do you think that the product life-cycle concept could be a useful tool for a market like this?

3 What do you think are the main factors from the marketing environment that have influenced product management decisions in this market and what impact have they had?

4 Can the repositioning of Hooch as an older, more sophisticated drink succeed? Why? How might this affect the shape of its life-cycle?

CASE STUDY 8.2

Diamonds are for ever . . . and so are the payments

In 1998, the diamond industry was in trouble. Demand from South East Asia and Japan had declined dramatically because of the turmoil in financial markets and although the US still remained a lucrative market, there was so much over-supply that producers could not maintain profitable prices. The world trade in rough or uncut diamonds is dominated by De Beers from South Africa, with around 70 per cent market share. In 1998, however, De Beers' sales of rough diamonds fell by 28 per cent to $3.3bn. Although De Beers only mines around half of world production, through its Central Selling Organisation (CSO) it manages the distribution of 80 per cent of all diamonds, either by entering into distribution contracts with other mining companies or by buying diamonds on the open market.

De Beers considers its current arrangements as a 'benevolent monopoly', concerned with protecting consumers' investments in diamonds and maintaining suppliers' price levels. Thus in the past, De Beers could influence world prices for diamonds by adjusting supply to meet fluctuations in demand. If prices started to fall because of weak demand, it could cut supply and sustain prices by producing diamonds to keep in reserve as 'buffer stocks' rather than for the open market. This is an expensive option as it means carrying stock worth up to $5bn. This does little to stimulate demand for the benefit of all producers. De Beers can direct its production into buffer stocks and so is more immune to short-term market fluctuations than smaller producers that cannot afford to carry increased buffer stock levels.

The company was thus in a strong monopoly position and could dictate to the market – as long as consumers valued diamonds. De Beers has spent over 100 years building a glittering image for diamonds. Slogans such as 'diamonds are for ever' and 'diamonds are a girl's best friend' helped consumers to attribute 'luxury', 'special', 'mystique' and 'romantic' characteristics to diamonds and also made De Beers a very wealthy organisation. De Beers also invented 'occasions' products, such as the 10th wedding anniversary diamond eternity ring ('show her you would marry her all over again'), the 25th anniversary necklace and the 'sweet 16' pendant. De Beers' $200mn annual promotional spend has tended to go on generic advertisements for diamonds, which benefits the whole market, rather than on specifically promoting its own name. It is possible for De Beers to establish its diamond brand, as it has developed the technology to etch minutely and invisibly the De Beers logo and a serial number on its top-quality diamonds. This could become a guarantee of quality and differentiate its products from the competition.

This might have to happen. In 1998, the slump in demand was so severe that prices for rough diamonds continued to fall, despite cutbacks in production and supply. In addition, some producers left the De Beers controlled CSO, preferring to supply to the open market at lower prices that will stimulate extra demand and weaken the CSO's dominance.

In the longer term, of course, demand might recover. Sales could increase with the expected 1.5 billion individual parties expected for the year 2000 celebrations. It has been estimated that if just 1 per cent of people involved in these celebrations bought diamonds it would add between 20 and 25 per cent to the 70 million pieces normally sold annually. This would help strengthen the position of the CSO. Alternatively, it seems likely that De Beers' dominance could be eroded as, for example, new Canadian mines come on stream and take an estimated 10 per cent market share. In this event, *The Economist* (1998–99) sees De Beers as the Coca-Cola of luxury goods, facing competition but with the marketing and distribution skills to be successful. A director of De Beers understands the task ahead:

> *We must now compete for the consumer's discretionary dollar – not just against other jewellery, but against weekends in Paris, Dior dresses and luxury cars. (The Economist, 1998–99)*

But will diamonds continue to be a girl's best friend?

Sources: The Economist (1997–98, 1998–99); Gooding (1998); Morrison (1998); Newland (1998), http://ww.edata.co.za; http://www.adiamondisforever.com).

Questions

1 To what extent is it in a marketing manager's interests to restrict supply of a product and maintain high prices?

2 If diamonds are in the same market as weekends in Paris, Dior dresses and luxury cars, what are the implications for the way they might be marketed?

3 Should De Beers commit itself to developing its own brand? What are the potential risks of doing this?

4 How do you think that the market for diamonds is likely to change in the future as new producers come on stream?

References to Chapter 8

Aaker, D. A. and Keller, K. L. (1990), 'Consumer Evaluation of Brand Extensions', *Journal of Marketing*, 54 (June), pp. 27–41.

Avlonitis, G. J. (1985), 'Product Elimination Decision Making: Does Formality Matter?', *Journal of Marketing*, 49, pp. 41–52.

Baird, R. (1998), 'Rock's Road to Ruin', *Marketing Week*, 12 November, pp. 26–9.

Batchelor, C. (1998), 'Novel £25m Rail Contract Will Reward Reliability', *Financial Times*, 7 October, p. 9.

Berenson, C. and Mohr-Jackson, I. (1994), 'Product Rejuvenation: A Less Risky Alternative to Product Innovation', *Business Horizons*, 37(6), pp. 51–7.

Blois, K. J. (1980), 'Quasi-integration as a Mechanism for Controlling External Dependencies', *Management Decision*, 18(1), pp. 55–63.

Bolz, J. (1992), *Wettbewerbsorientierte Standardisierung der Internationalen Marktbearbeitung*, Darmstadt.

Bose, K. (1998), 'Ageing Contessa Gets a Facelift as HM Seeks Admirers', *Financial Times*, 14 October, p. 32.

Brennan, S. (1997), 'Jaguar Gets its Claws into a Luxury Plane', *Times*, 28 February, p. 47.

Cramp, B. (1995), 'Refreshing Change', *Marketing*, 19 January, pp. 21–3.

Cunningham, M. T. (1986), 'The British Approach to Europe', in P. W. Turnbull and J.P. Valla (eds.), *Strategies for International Industrial Marketing*, Croom Helm.

Daneshkhu, S. (1998), 'Themed Restaurants Lose Their Flavour as Fashion Changes', *Financial Times*, 26 October, p. 8.

Davis, E. J. (1984), 'Managing Marketing', in N. A. Hart (ed.), *The Marketing of Industrial Products*, McGraw-Hill.

Dhalla, N. K. and Yuspeh, S. (1976), 'Forget the Product Life Cycle Concept', *Harvard Business Review*, Jan–Feb, pp. 102–12.

Doyle, P. (1998), *Marketing Management and Strategy*, 2nd edn, Prentice-Hall Europe.

Eason, K. (1998), 'Any Rush to Buy the Very Last Metro?', *The Times*, 24 January, p. 49.

The Economist (1997–98), 'Glass with Attitude', *The Economist*, 20 December–2 January, pp. 89–90.

The Economist (1998–99), 'De Beers is It', *The Economist*, 19 December–1 January, pp. 89–90.

Gatignon, H. and Robertson, T. S. (1985), 'A Propositional Inventory for New Diffusion Research', *Journal of Consumer Research*, 11 (March), pp. 849–67.

Gooding, K. (1998), 'Diamond Industry between a Rock and a Hard Place', *Financial Times*, 29 October, p. 36.

Gray, R. (1998), 'How the Yo-yo Bounced Back', *Marketing Week*, 22 October, p. 21.

Green, P. E. and Carmone, F. J. (1970), *Multidimensional Scaling and Related Techniques in Marketing Analysis*, Allyn and Bacon.

Greenley, G. E. and Bayus, B. L. (1994), 'A Comparative Study of Product Launch and Elimination Decisions in UK and US Companies', *European Journal of Marketing*, 28(2), pp. 5–29.

The Grocer (1997a), 'Many Alcopops Axed', *The Grocer*, 9 August, p. 7.

The Grocer (1997b), 'Hooch Revamp "Nothing to do with Furore"', *The Grocer*, 6 September, p. 6.

Guido, G. (1991), 'Implementing a Pan-European Marketing Strategy', *Long Range Planning*, 24(5), pp. 23–33.

Halliburton, C. and Hunerberg, R. (1987), 'The Globalisation Dispute in Marketing', *European Management Journal*, 4 (Winter), pp. 243–9.

Hawkes, N. (1997), 'The "Sporting" Drink with 19 Spoons of Sugar', *The Times*, 21 October, p. 5.

Lynch, R. (1994), *European Business Strategies: The European and Global Strategies of Europe's Top Companies*, Kogan Page.

Marketing (1997), 'New-look Two Dogs in £1m Push', *Marketing*, 7 August, p. 4.

Marketing Week (1997a), 'Drinks Companies Rapped for Marketing of Alcopops', *Marketing Week*, 28 August, p. 9.

Marketing Week (1997b), 'Tougher Code May Force New Alcopops Ban', *Marketing Week*, 11 September, p. 10.

Marsh, H. (1997a), 'Will Codes Squash Alcopops?', *Marketing*, 22 May, p. 16.

Marsh, H. (1997b), 'Two Dogs Bites at Alcopop Rival', *Marketing*, 21 August, p. 3.

Mintel (1997), 'Alcoholic Soft Drinks', *Market Intelligence*, March.

Morrison, S. (1998), 'Ekati Mine Opens in Canada', *Financial Times*, 14 October, p. 36.

Murphy, C. (1999), 'Cadbury's Quiet Revolution', *Marketing*, 11 February, pp. 24–5.

Murphy, C. (1998), 'Alcopops Review their Strategies', *Marketing*, 30 July, pp. 14–15.

Newland, F. (1998), 'On the Rocks', *Marketing Week*, 16 July, pp. 34–7.

O'Connor, J. and Galvin, E. (1999), *Marketing & Information Technology*, 2nd edn, Financial Times Pitman Publishing.

Reibstein et al. (1998), 'Mastering Marketing Part Four: Brand Strategy', *Financial Times Supplement*, pp. 7–8.

Rigby, R. (1998), 'Craze Management', *Management Today*, June, pp. 58–62.

Rijkens, R. (1992), *European Advertising Strategies: The Profiles and Policies of Multinational Companies Operating in Europe*, Cassell.

Rink, D. R. and Swan, J.E. (1979), 'Product Life Cycle Research: A Literature Review', *Journal of Business Research*, 78 (Sept.), pp. 219–42.

Rogers, E. M. (1962), *Diffusion of Innovation*, The Free Press.

Shannon, W. (1997), 'Why We Banned These Alcopops', *Marketing*, 19 June, p. 7.

Simonian, H. (1998), 'Seat Completes Transformation with New Model', *Financial Times*, 29 September, p. 35.

Swann, C. (1998), 'Electronics Boutique Trebles', *Financial Times*, 1 October, p. 28.

Teather, D. (1997), 'Bass Ages Alcopop', *Express*, 4 September.

Townsend, M. (1998), 'Music Fans Fleeced in Great CD Rip-off', *Express*, 2 July, p. 28.

Turnbull, P. and Valla, J.P. (1986), 'The Strategic Role of Industrial Marketing Management' in P. W. Turnbull and J.P. Valla (eds.), *Strategies for International Industrial Marketing*, Croom Helm.

Tushman, M. L. and Anderson, P. (1986), 'Technological Discontinuities and Organisational Environments', *Administrative Science Quarterly*, Winter, pp. 439–65.

Willman, J. (1997), 'Keeping Fizz in Alcopops', *Financial Times*, 11 September, p. 8.

Wolfe, A. (1991), 'The Single European Market: National or Euro-Brands?', *International Journal of Advertising*, 10, pp. 49–58.

Wright, R. (1998), 'Craze for Yo-yos Comes Full Circle to Boost Sales', *Financial Times*, 7 October, p. 1.

Wroe, M. (1995). 'Slipped Discs', *Marketing Business*, February, pp. 18–22.

Young, R. (1998), 'Butlin's Braces Itself for Winds of Change', *Times*, 30 April, p. 13.

9

New Product Development

LEARNING OBJECTIVES

This chapter will help you to:

1 define the various types of product 'newness' and the marketing implications of each;

2 understand the reasons for new product development;

3 analyse the eight stages in the new product development process;

4 appreciate the reasons for new product failure; and

5 outline some current trends in R&D management.

INTRODUCTION

Chapter 8 considered issues of product development, modification and deletion within the context of an existing product portfolio. Sometimes, however, to satisfy strategic objectives it is not enough just to manipulate existing products. Organisations need a flow of new products to keep their portfolios fresh, their customers interested and their sales growing. This chapter, therefore, is devoted entirely to **new product development** (NPD).

Obviously, the pace of NPD will vary depending on the pressures to change and the scale of change required. Complex, technology-based products, such as new drugs, may be launched and then continue as stable products for a number of years, with any further development effort focusing on minor changes and improvements. In fmcg markets, however, there is more likely to be a rapid rate of NPD. Despite the promising hopes held for some of these new products, it is a stark fact that most, up to 90 per cent, will fail to achieve their potential and will not survive. This is a sobering thought, given the time, resources and money that often go into developing a new product.

> **Example** Gillette was optimistic about the addition of a third blade to its men's razor. The Mach 3 was the most significant new product for the company since the launch of the Sensor in 1990 and the Mach 3 launch went well in the US and in Europe. Nevertheless, the launch was not without difficulty and around $1bn was spent in manufacturing upgrades and marketing to ensure a successful launch. Significant improvement is important to Gillette in order to maintain its world dominance in the shaving equipment market (Griffith, 1998).

The fact is that nobody can give any guarantees that any new product will succeed and the more radical the new product idea, the more true this becomes. NPD is not just about *invention*, it is also about *innovation*. Invention is about the creation of ideas and physical products, but innovation is about finding appropriate applications and commercialising those ideas and products. It is something of a cliché, but the British are generally thought to be good at invention but very poor at innovation, whereas the Japanese are astute when it comes to defining and exploiting the commercial possibilities of an idea or product.

It is, however, possible to assess or minimise the risks of NPD through effective and efficient planning and management of the NPD process. This chapter will later outline a framework, identifying the stages of NPD and the relevant questions that should be asked of any NPD project. First, however, it is necessary to discuss in more detail the definition of 'new products', as it is always important to clarify the context within which NPD is being undertaken. We consider also the rationale for pursuing an active programme of planned new product launches and point out that in some circumstances, organisations could be failing strategically through their inaction and reluctance to commit themselves to NPD.

The particular emphasis of this chapter is on the introduction of the framework to guide NPD from initiation through to commercialisation. It can be argued that such a procedure can reduce but not eliminate the risks associated with new product launch. An examination of the causes of new product failure reveals that many failures could be avoided with better analysis and research in the development stage. In reality, not all new products are manufacturer initiated and driven. In some organisational markets, the NPD approach may be customer led or a joint effort between buyer and supplier. The final section in this chapter, therefore, examines the underlying approach and rationale for various types of co-operative new product development.

THE MEANING OF A NEW PRODUCT

This section looks at precisely what a new product is, exploring definitions of 'new' from the organisation's point of view and then discussing the problem from the buyer's perspective.

Types of newness

The term 'new product' appears to be pretty clear cut. There are, however, differing degrees of newness that can make a significant difference to the way in which an organisation handles that product. The risks, opportunities and strategies associated with that product will partly depend on the type of newness in question. At one extreme, newness could simply involve a new pack size or colour, while at the other extreme, the product could represent a radical, mould-breaking innovation. There are, of course, many options between these two extremes.

A number of these options are of particular interest and will now be discussed in turn.

New to the company, new to the market

The most exciting option is the product that is new to the company and new to the market; it represents a completely new idea that has never been offered before. Technological breakthroughs often provide the basis for such radical new products. It is not so long since the invention and commercialisation of the home video recorder, the CD player and the personal computer (to name but three) created vast new markets and made a huge impact on the lifestyles of many individuals.

One problem with this category of new product is that potential buyers might be suspicious of a totally new concept – will it be reliable, will it be superseded, will I look a fool in two years' time for having bought it? The second problem is in persuading potential buyers that they actually need this product. After all, if one had lived one's life without a video recorder, why get excited about its invention? Marketers

Example As we saw in case study 8.1, Alcopops were radically new products that quickly gained acceptance among young, fashion-conscious consumers. It took a little longer, however, for the market (and the publicity) to settle down and for marketers to understand the longer-term potential of the product. After the competitive shakeout in 1998, Bass decided to position Hooch more firmly as a more masculine and adult drink for the 20-to-24-year-old group, through a sharper taste and redesigned packaging. The repositioning was also emphasised by a new advertising campaign launched in 1998. One television advertisement featured the special powers of Hooch, as a man answering the call of nature split a urinal and another featured a mosquito drunk on Hooch cutting through glass. It was hoped that all these actions would establish Hooch as a more sophisticated drink with a longer-term future than a passing fad (Maling, 1998). This shows that even after a new concept has been launched, it needs to be refined as both consumers and marketers learn from experience.

How long have you been drinking Yakult?

20 YEARS
Miguel de Souza, BRAZIL

5 *years*
Dick Borst, HOLLAND

5 years
Jodi Phillips, AUSTRALIA

7 months
Mrs P.I. Godd, UK

years
Toki Uchara, JAPAN

These are just a handful out of millions worldwide who have put their trust in Yakult since its introduction in 1935. Yakult is a delicious, refreshing drink for everyone – it's rich with the active ingredient, *Lactobacillus casei Shirota* – a natural, friendly bacterium.

Yakult's discoverer, Dr Minoru Shirota, was an eminent scientist and humanitarian.

People of all ages from 16 countries around the world drink Yakult daily. In this, our founder's centenary year, we invite you to try Yakult. You'll find it in the chilled dairy section of supermarkets throughout the UK. **Yakult**

To support our customers throughout the UK, Yakult has produced a jargon free 'Guide to the Gut'. For your free copy just ring the Yakult Consumer Information Centre on: 0345 697 069 (local rate call).

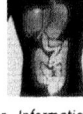

his novel product started its UK
'e among trend setters in London

urce: Travis Sully Harari.

have to address both these problems. The key to them both, perhaps, lies in targeting a segment of innovators and opinion leaders (*see* pp. 313 *et seq.*). If they accept the product, then maybe the suspicion of the rest of the market will be reduced because they can see that other people have bought it. Furthermore, when the rest of the market sees that people they look up to (opinion leaders) have embraced the new product, desire for the product becomes a social need for its intangible status benefits rather than a real need for its core function. Generally, the whole marketing mix needs to be handled with care. If the market has no experience of anything quite like this, there is no clear reference point against which to develop a market-orientated marketing mix.

If the risks and marketing problems are so great, then why engage in this kind of innovation? If it works, then there is the respect and reputation gained from being first, not only with the market, but also with shareholders, potential investors and even potential employees (visibly successful organisations attract the brightest candidates). In marketing terms, there is the opportunity to establish a strong, prime position in the market before the real competition starts. Against this, the innovative organisation is bearing the costs and risks of development and market creation and has to face the prospect of competitors coming in later with cheaper imitative products (*see* pp. 315 *et seq.*), unless it pursues proactive further development to stay ahead.

MARKETING IN ACTION   **Launch it before it melts!**

The ice-cream industry experienced a significant level of new product development in 1999 as the top three brand manufacturers sought to retain their market positions. Innovation was seen as the key for recovering lost sales volume caused by dismal summers since a sales peak of £1bn in 1995. There is still plenty of scope in the UK market, as consumption per head is one of the lowest in Europe. Take-home ice creams have 57 per cent of the market, dominated by convenient multipacks for the freezer, premium and luxury brands. Impulse purchases, especially on hot summer days, account for 32 per cent of the market, but sales can fluctuate more because of the effects of cold summers.

Premium products, multipacks and luxury products are outperforming more traditional blocks and cones and so it is these areas that attracted the attention of some manufacturers, although others were seeking to revitalise the more stagnant areas. In 1999, over 40 new products were planned by the big three manufacturers, Birds Eye Walls, Nestlé and Mars. But just what does new product development mean in the ice-cream market?

For Birds Eye Walls (http://www.birdseye.com), it is a combination of targeting particular market segments with 'new' products. In the impulse sector, for example, Magnum Double, a chocolate-coated ice cream with a thick caramel fudge, is an extension of the Magnum family that has accumulated sales of £50.5mn. Solero has been reformulated with sorbet in the ice cream and new flavour variants are planned. The children's market is catered for by such new products as Star Wars,

building on the renewed interest in the films, and Mr Spot, containing strawberry jelly sweets. Meanwhile, the take-home sector saw new flavours of Viennetta, including apricot, and a brand repositioning for Carte D'Or with new transparent packaging and new blueberry and other exotic flavours.

The other manufacturers have also planned their form of new product innovation. Nestlé introduced Extreme Duo into the UK following on from success elsewhere in Europe. Häagen Dazs is especially concentrating on putting most of its popular tub flavours on to sticks. Pillsbury plans to spend £7mn launching 10 new products covering range and flavour extensions and again shifting from stick to tub or vice versa depending on the original launch version. Belgian manufacturer Ijsboerke concentrates on high-juice water ices and its new Funky Dunky, a sorbet stick shaped like a papaya, and Popito, shaped like a clown's face, are two designs that could catch the imagination of the more adventurous. At the very top end of the ice-cream market is Hill Station, using double cream milk and tropical spices to create unusual flavours such as cinnamon, spiced coffee, stem ginger and nutmeg ice creams. New product launches for that company are usually associated with offering new flavours in the standard 500ml tubs that retail at £3.95. But the most interesting new product launch in this market has to be the neon-blue Viagra Man and the pink Viagra Lady ice-cream flavours launched in the Zio Ciro ice-cream shop in Rome!

Sources: Hardcastle (1999); Kelly (1998); Oleck (1998).

New to the company, a significant innovation for the market

Where a product represents a significant innovation for the market, the core product concept itself is familiar, but there is a new twist to it that makes it innovative and exciting. Examples of this might be the first combined washer-dryer, the first fax machine to operate with ordinary paper or the first car fitted with a catalytic converter.

The marketing task is perhaps a little easier here, because the basic product concept is a familiar one. The main job is one of communicating the nature of the innovation and the added benefits it confers on the product. The consumer can compare the new product with the old from their own experience and thus reach an opinion as to the value of the innovation. A family that has had to live with the inconvenience of the space taken up by a washing machine and a tumble dryer in a small house would not need much persuading about the benefits of a combined machine.

> **Example** Robot vacuum cleaners could be the answer to the household arguments about whose turn it is to do the cleaning. Electrolux (http://www.electrolux.com) has developed a domestic robot, Noo-Noo, that can be left indoors to clean carpets without supervision. Not only will it traverse the room, it will also steer around the wine glass or book left over from the previous night's entertainment. It takes about 20 minutes to clean a typical room and if the doors are left open it will work its way around the ground floor. Using advanced electronics for navigating and understanding cleaning tasks, the product is one of the pioneers of a new generation of household robots currently under development that are designed to make our lives a little easier. They will radically transform the product ranges of domestic appliance manufacturers. Mass production may soon start for Noo-Noo and after that we could see two-legged robotic waiters, gutter cleaners, bedmakers, decorators and mechanical guard dogs. For many people they can't come quick enough (Nuki and Connor, 1997; Young, 1997).

New to the company, a minor innovation for the market

A product that represents only a minor innovation for the market is less exciting than the previous option from the market's point of view, as the product offered is not particularly different from what already exists. The challenge and the burden of newness rest much more heavily on the organisation than on the market. An organisation might, for example, enter the existing video recorder market for the first time with a machine that is easier to program than any competitor's product. While this is a worthwhile feature that will attract interest, it is not sufficiently innovative to turn the market upside down.

In this situation, there should not be too much risk involved in the product concept itself, as that is largely established, tried and tested. The risks and problems arise from trying to gain distribution and break into an established market that may consist of a number of powerful competitors who will use marketing counter-measures to prevent the successful entry of a new product.

New to the company, no innovation for the market

An organisation offering a product that represents no innovation is offering a completely imitative product, based on a competitor's approach and technology, and the market perceives little difference between them. Many organisations consciously decide to take this 'me too' approach to NPD (*see* pp. 346 *et seq.*). For a smaller organisation with limited resources, it makes sense to let the bigger competitor spend the time, effort and money developing the radical new concepts (as with products that are either new to the market or significant innovations), then when the market is established and known, it can launch a slightly cheaper imitation and get a foothold in the lower end of the market. The imitator may be able to achieve a cost advantage, if it has learned from the experience of the innovator. Sony suffered from this with the Walkman. It invented the concept, developed it into a viable commercial proposition, created the market and launched the first product, yet within a couple of years, it was facing stiff competition from a whole range of cheaper 'me too' imitations offering no significant new features. *See also* pp. 315 *et seq.* for further discussion about imitative products.

Customer-orientated perspectives

As implied in the previous section, it is the customers' view of newness and their reaction to that newness that count. This section looks more specifically at the buyer's degree of learning and adjustment to the new product as reflected in their buying behaviour and their use of the product or service, linking all of this with the supplier's perspective discussed above.

The buyer's approach to dealing with new products has to be put into the context of the level of innovation within a market, which can be categorised in three ways, **continuous innovation**, **dynamically continuous innovation** and **discontinuous innovation**, as shown in Fig. 9.1.

Continuous innovation

In a market characterised by continuous innovation, new product introductions are regular occurrences. No new behaviour is really required of the consumer, who is used to sizing up new products regularly and includes that activity as a matter of course in the decision-making process. It imposes a small amount of low-risk, limited decision making on what would normally be a routine response situation (*see* pp. 102 and 266 *et seq.*).

Fmcg markets, such as that for laundry detergents, often see new product launches, usually with minor or no innovation incorporated in them. 'Now washes even whiter', 'Washes cleaner at even lower temperatures', 'More concentrated cleaning power than ever', 'With added stain digesters' are the types of phrase that appear on laundry products to signify some level of continuous innovation. Consumers may see them in the supermarket, look at them, then make a decision as to whether to try them or remain loyal to their existing brand. This emphasises that the key task for the marketer with such new products is to generate awareness and gain distribution.

Dynamically continuous innovation

A market characterised by dynamically continuous innovation tends to involve new products with a degree of significant innovation. Because the innovation represents a big change in a familiar product, it is likely to require some change in buying

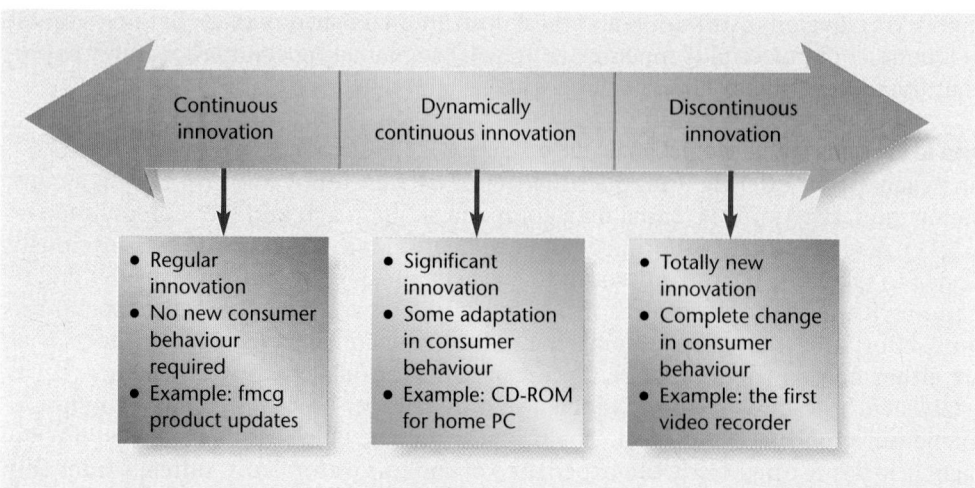

FIGURE 9.1

The innovation continuum

MARKETING IN ACTION   ## Nutraceuticals

Continuous innovation can capitalise on changing consumer tastes and concerns. Food manufacturers, for example, have produced lower fat, lower sugar or lower calorie versions of familiar products over the years. In some cases, they are now moving towards adding more ingredients to their foods. There is a growing market for 'nutraceutical' foods with added health-giving ingredients. Thus SmithKline Beecham (http://www.sb.com) introduced Ribena Juice and Fibre, which the company claims can help to reduce cholesterol levels; MD Foods, a Danish company, has introduced Gaio, a yoghurt containing a particular cholesterol-reducing culture; and a French company has launched Carres Memoire, a brand of chocolate that is supposed to improve memory.

Johnson & Johnson (J&J) (http://www.johnsonand johnson.com), recognising the growing interest of health-orientated customers, entered the market through the acquisition of the margarine brand Benecol, from the original brand owner, Raisio in

Finland. It is claimed that the margarine can cut blood cholesterol by between 10 and 14 per cent. The gamble for J&J is whether Benecol will be as popular in the UK as in Scandinavia. Despite a considerable price premium, Raisio gained 4 per cent of the Finnish margarine market and J&J expects that its reputation in the healthcare sector will assist in the promotion of Benecol in the UK and that similar market shares can be gained. The price differential is designed to reflect the value of the product benefits, £3.50 for a 250g pack compared with a normal margarine price of around 60p.

Independent experts were less sure of the potential for J&J. Leatherhead Food Research Association believed that consumers would not see a beneficial relationship between the medical expertise in the main J&J product lines and the nutraceuticals. Consumers might want natural, healthy food, not prescription food, and this could reduce the potential for the brand.

Sources: Beenstock (1998); *The Grocer* (1996).

behaviour. While the buyer has a familiar frame of reference for the product, the new features and benefits have to be understood and integrated into that familiar picture. The introduction of the electric toothbrush, for instance, might have caused problems for some consumers. The function would be well understood, but what are the advantages of an electric one over a manual brush? How do I know that it's safe? This is related to limited problem solving situations (*see* p. 103) and thus emphasises the need for the marketer to provide information and to explain the new benefits to the prospective purchaser. In selling a fax machine that does not require special paper in order to receive incoming messages, marketers do not need to explain the function and benefits of the fax itself, which are very well established, but they do need to show how the plain paper feature differentiates the machine from the competition and how it saves money and time etc.

Discontinuous innovation

Discontinuous innovation represents the biggest upheaval for the potential customer and relates most closely to extended problem solving (*see* p. 104). It requires a whole new learning experience for the customer, with new patterns of consumption behaviour. The consumer has to understand the underlying concept of the product and then relate it to their own life, visualising how it will fit in. This process is linked to the issues of suspicion and acceptance raised in the discussion of the marketing problems of products new to both the market and the organisation. Customers need hard information about what the product is and what it does, but they also need guidance on its benefits and what that means to them. There is also a role here for product demonstrations. The microwave oven, for example, was greeted with incredulity when it was launched, because it was difficult to believe that it could do all the things promised without compromising the quality of the food. The advertisements could achieve a certain amount, but 'seeing is believing', and seeing the machine in action and tasting the results were essential for proving that it did live up to its promises.

THE IMPORTANCE OF NEW PRODUCT DEVELOPMENT

Having looked at the outcomes of NPD, in terms of degrees of innovation and their impact on the potential customer, it is now time to think more clearly about why NPD is so important. Organisations do not operate in a static environment, but are constantly facing the consequences of changing technology, changing customer tastes and preferences and changing competitor product ranges. Any organisation that is positively managing its product portfolio will recognise that its existing products are in different stages of their life-cycles and can be modified to maximise their potential, but, inevitably, new products will be needed to replace the mature and declining ones.

Although it is an important part of a product strategy, NPD can be a very risky business. The commercial and financial risks can be very high, with many new products failing. As reported in a newspaper article by Mitchell (1994), of 12 000 new grocery and toiletry products launched in the UK during 1995, 90 per cent will have been dropped within months of their launch. The failure rates can thus be very high, yet organisations are increasingly driven to NPD as a means of gaining competitive edge. The investment in NPD can be very substantial in some industries. According to Elliott and Beavis (1994), for example, the UK pharmaceutical industry invests 12 per cent of its sales revenue in R&D, compared with the UK average of 1.6 per cent. Furthermore, analysis undertaken by the Department of Trade and Industry of the R&D investment of the UK's listed companies showed that the pharmaceutical companies accounted between them for nearly one-third of all UK R&D spending in 1993 (Caulkin, 1994). The added ingredients for the 'nutraceutical' products mentioned earlier can take up to 15 years to develop and cost anything from $10mn to $100mn.

The organisation, therefore, needs a new product strategy that is linked with the overall strategic plan of the business. It is essential to look ahead and assess how much sales or profit will have to be generated from today's or tomorrow's new products in three or five years' time. Our discussion of the product life-cycle (*see* pp. 303 *et seq.*), pointed out that it takes time to get a new product established, and the one that is intended to be the big revenue earner in five years' time might have to be launched now and therefore should already have spent some time in development.

The approach to NPD can be either reactive or proactive.

Reactive approach

The *reactive* approach is taken by the organisation that is happy to respond to what others do, rather than seeking to outmanoeuvre its competitors. This organisation is happy to let others take risks and face the problems of breaking new ground, then it will enter the market when it is clear that further opportunities exist. The organisation may be late into the market, but may have the production or marketing muscle to capitalise on the situation. This organisation avoids costly launch errors and can even eventually use that experience to extend the technology.

The reactive organisation is most likely to have its emphasis on application and design engineering. As said earlier, however, the imitative market entrant does have the problems of breaking into an established market in which others may already have built reputation and market share. With the Walkman market, Sony had the established lead and the quality reputation, so the imitators concentrated on getting manufacturing costs down to allow them to produce cheaper, lower-quality products to create a new segment at the bottom end of the market.

Proactive approach

The *proactive* organisation deliberately sets out to find new ideas and seeks to commercialise them early before the competition step in. This approach requires a strong commitment to R&D, consumer research and market awareness. It also needs willingness to take risks and the kind of organisational culture that encourages enterprise. Such an organisation may deliberately scan the environment for opportunities and then develop products to fit the perceived gap in the market. If the organisation, however, has insufficient resources to develop an idea from scratch, it may then seek or initiate joint ventures or licences.

Proactive NPD is far from easy and there are a number of considerations to be taken into account when thinking about this approach. First, such an investment in NPD is expensive and time consuming, with no guarantees of success. This commitment, therefore, really needs to take place against a backdrop of an existing portfolio comprising steady profit-earning products, in order to keep the organisation and the NPD process ticking over. Furthermore, a new product in the early days after its launch may continue to consume more resources than it generates, so the organisation needs to be sure of its short-term cash flow. Finally, fast-moving changes in the marketing environment mean that there is an increasing tendency for life-cycles to shorten, with the result that organisations are under pressure to produce successful new products more often, yet with shorter payback periods (*see* Chapter 11).

Example Lego (http://www.lego.com) is being proactive in its approach to innovation with toy bricks. It is helping to fund a project at the Massachusetts Institute of Technology in the US to produce intelligent toys. The project aims to develop bricks, balls and badges that can be programmed to interact with an infra-red beam. This will allow far higher levels of interaction between the child and the toys than is available through pulling strings or manipulating buttons. The Lego bricks, called Crickets, will produce light, sound and motion so that the bricks can interact with each other as well as with the child. Further development will allow the crickets to be programmed using a PC. All of this will create a new experience for children and, of course, keep Lego sales very healthy in the electronic age (Prigg, 1997).

Either way, perhaps one of the main motivating forces for NPD is a justifiable paranoia: if our organisation does not invest in NPD, the competition certainly will and that will place us at a longer-term disadvantage. It is important, however, to manage the NPD process appropriately within the organisational context and structure.

Cooper and Kleinschmidt (1987) compared product successes and failures against various factors that might affect the likelihood of success. The most important factor was having a good-quality, well-managed NPD process. This was closely followed by a need for the new product to offer a clear competitive advantage. Other important factors included synergy between the new product and the organisation's technological and marketing strengths; the quality and thoroughness of the early stages of the NPD process; the effectiveness of the technological and marketing inputs into the NPD process; and, of course, having top management support. This, then, emphasises the importance of the NPD framework, the subject of the next section.

THE NEW PRODUCT DEVELOPMENT PROCESS

This section develops an eight-stage framework that can guide the NPD process. Shown in Fig. 9.2, it is presented as a logical sequence, narrowing down from a broad spread of potential general ideas in the first stage to the commercialisation of a single, highly developed concept in the final stage. Clearly, the implementation of the process will vary according to the particular organisation involved and the market context within which it is operating. Some stages may be truncated, others may be extended, according to circumstance. In a complex, high-technology market, the process may be extremely formal and take many years to complete, while in a fast-moving fashion market, the process may be reiterated three or four times a year, for

each new season. Nevertheless, despite the variations, it is still important to recognise that such a framework or process brings a degree of
rigour to NPD that can help to reduce the risks and problems of failure
(Booz-Allen, Hamilton Inc., 1982).

Each stage in the NPD process will now be discussed in turn.

Idea generation

Any new product has to start somewhere as the germ of an idea. In view
of the investment and commitment that will be given to this process, it
is important in the early stages to let the corporate imagination range as
freely as possible, just to make sure that all the options have been
thought of. There is a need for an ongoing flow of new ideas. It does
not matter how ridiculous some of them might sound; at this stage anything goes and you never know what potential an idea might have.
Ideas can always be abandoned at the next stage if serious appraisal
shows them to be inappropriate. Rarely do these ideas emerge out of
nowhere, however. Some ideas develop from a combination of recognising emerging market needs and exploring technical feasibility. Thus
ideas may be either problem or opportunity driven. Whatever the
source of ideas, however, some kind of formal mechanism is usually
needed to generate and collect them. There are, however, dangers in
becoming formulaic in idea generation. The director of the design consultancy Elmwood suggested that many UK organisations stifle
creativity rather than create a culture for the free flow of creative ideas
from staff within the organisation (Croft, 1998). Many ideas are simply
ignored rather than being welcomed.

There are a number of main sources of new product ideas:

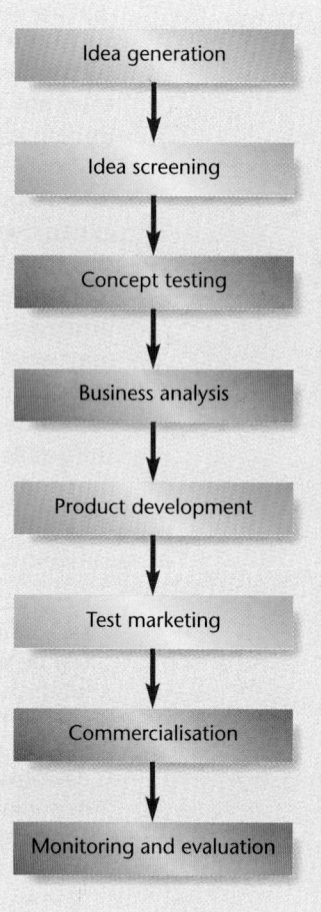

Research and development

R&D is the obvious source of new product ideas. After all, that is what an organisation's R&D staff are paid to do. In some organisations, the R&D department can be
given a very tight brief ('Develop something that conforms to these specifications'); in
others, they can be given freedom to range widely ('Do what you want, as long as you
deliver something we consider commercially viable'). The first approach has the
advantage of making sure that R&D activity and expenditure are controlled, since it is
problem or project driven and has defined aims and objectives. The second approach,
however, allows R&D scientists full creative scope to do what they are good at, and it
does throw up products that otherwise would never have been conceived.

R&D work can also vary from being completely self-sufficient, working only
within the company environment, to collaborative research with other organisations, external institutes or universities. This latter approach allows the organisation
to draw on a much wider pool of expertise on a particular project than they could
ever reasonably hope to employ for themselves, but has the drawback of placing the
work in a more public arena where the competition might detect it. There is more on
this at pp. 365 *et seq.*

Generating and developing ideas through R&D can involve fairly long time-scales,
with far from certain reward. Maintaining an R&D department is thus expensive, yet
essential for a proactive organisation. Sometimes, external inventors approach an
organisation with their own ideas. They might wish to sell the idea to the organisation or to enter into a collaborative development deal, splitting the profits. The Black
& Decker Workmate began life as such an idea.

FIGURE 9.2

**The new product
development process**

Competitors

There are two categories of competitor to consider here: actual and potential. Actual competitors are those who operate in your existing market and have products there already. Looking in detail at the products themselves and assessing the marketing strategies around them can lead to an understanding of the concept's strengths and weaknesses and thus how it can be improved. This analysis can form the basis of a new improved version, albeit a potential 'me too' product, with a more focused marketing strategy.

Potential competitors operate in areas from which others are currently absent. If the organisation's strategic plan suggests a need to redefine the market, then potential competitors may become actual competitors. This could, for example, apply to export markets. An organisation thinking of entering a foreign market would need to assess existing coverage of that market and develop its own product and marketing offering accordingly.

In some situations, there may be no intention of entering into direct competition with the potential competitors studied, but every intention of lifting ideas from them. A study of tourism innovation in Ireland (Pettitt, 1989) found that a common source of new products was visits by entrepreneurs to other countries, where they picked up new ideas. Also in Ireland, efforts have been made by the Irish Development Authority and the Irish Goods Council to build up an ideas bank from looking at import substitution possibilities. This involved identifying product sectors such as foodstuffs and electronics where home producers could be given help to develop products and thus enter the market.

> **Example** Entrepreneurs may also identify a specific gap in a market and use that as the basis for establishing a business. A couple designed a carrying case for their daughter's ballet tutu, because there was nothing on the market other than bin liners that could hold a tutu without damaging it! In its first year of trading by direct selling to consumers, that small company expected a turnover of £300 000 and was beginning to receive enquiries from dancewear shops wanting to stock the product, and even football clubs wanting bags made up in their team colours.

Employees

Employees can be encouraged to suggest new product ideas through suggestion boxes and competitions. Organisations such as Toyota, Kodak and General Motors operate such schemes. Employees may be able to think of improved ways of producing the product or new features to incorporate. It is very easy to underestimate the vested interest of the work-force in the organisation's products and their knowledge. After all, they work with the organisation's products on a daily basis and their jobs depend on continued progress and development within the market. A number of methods of generating new ideas from employees have been proposed (Croft, 1998). These include awards, allowing time and space for new ideas, forming cross-functional teams, training staff in creative thinking and always adopting a positive attitude to new ideas, however wild they may be. Often, appointing a 'director of change, creativity and growth' can act as a focal point for the fostering of ideas.

Employees who have regular contact with customers and the trade should be given special attention. Service engineers and sales representatives, for example, come into contact with customer problems as a normal part of their working day and may thus generate potential ideas that can offer product opportunities. It is important, therefore, to make sure that such employees are encouraged to have discussions with customers and that the reporting mechanisms are in place to capture and collate the information arising from them.

Customers

The organisation is in business to serve the customer's needs and wants and so it is crucial to be in touch with customers, not only on the informal basis discussed above, but also through formal research techniques. Monitoring changing customer attitudes and feelings about products and markets and their usage patterns provides fertile ground for new ideas. Whether this research is regularly purchased secondary data or opportunity-driven commissioned research, it may reveal important gaps early enough to allow the organisation to gain competitive advantage in its NPD programme.

> **Example** In the development of its 9000 Communicator all-in-one voice, data and personal organiser, Nokia extensively used market research in the NPD process. Qualitative research and consumer feedback on design were undertaken at the pre-concept stage, before any formal product development began. This enabled Nokia fully to understand potential users' needs and how they were likely to use any new product once it was launched (Day, 1998).

In organisational markets, customers are a particularly important source of product improvement and innovation ideas. Von Hippel (1978), looking at scientific instrument markets, found that 82 per cent of major improvements and 70 per cent of minor improvements in four different instruments arose from customer suggestions. Some organisations go as far as to identify lead users, those customers whose needs are evolving ahead of the market in general. Working with lead users, organisations can develop their innovative ideas and products early and then adapt them for the wider market (Von Hippel, 1986). Similarly, Bonaccorsi and Lipparini (1994) found that a leading Italian firm derived significant improvements in NPD through close, co-operative partnerships with innovative suppliers.

Licensing

Licensing can be a useful way of getting access to new products without the time and expense of full-scale NPD. Licensing is a contractual relationship in which a manufacturer (licensor) who owns trade mark or patent rights over a product or technology allows another organisation (licensee) to manufacture and market that product in return for royalties or other payments. Licences are often used as a means of entering international markets without direct investment, and are further considered in that context in Chapter 23. A small US manufacturer of orthopaedic aids and specialist hospital equipment, for example, had neither the resources nor the know-how to get into the European market. It thus searched for an English-speaking organisation based in Europe that would act as a licensee for the products. Grolsch, a Dutch brewer, decided to expand the number of licensing agreements for its premium brands as part of its efforts to reduce costs and to better penetrate western markets. In the UK, the beer is brewed by Bass and an expansion to Australia was expected. In the US, no licensing agreements were to be sought as only imported beers attract premium prices there (Cramb, 1999).

A licensing agreement may cover the use of patents, manufacturing expertise or technical services, but a major issue is often whether or not the licensor's trade mark will be used. Nevertheless, a co-operative agreement between licensor and licensee can generate benefits in terms of new technology and ideas for both parties. The licensing route is attractive for smaller organisations with limited resources, either as an exporting strategy (as a licensor) or as a means of product range development (as a licensee).

Organised creativity

A number of techniques for encouraging staff to develop new ideas exist. Majaro (1991) suggests brainstorming, synectics, attribute listing, forced relationships and morphological analysis.

Brainstorming. Brainstorming involves a group of 6 to 10 people in an intensive session focusing on a specific problem. The purpose is to generate as many ideas as possible, however wild they are. The benefit of the group session is that one person's idea may spark off other ideas from the rest of the group. In discussing brainstorming, Osborn (1963) suggests that there should be no negative comments about any idea during the sessions; that outlandish ideas should be accepted; that the more ideas generated, the better; and that ideas can be combined to create better ones.

Synectics. Synectics is a group technique similar to brainstorming, but less problem specific. This frees the group from any mental strait-jacket and allows it to enter into more exploratory thinking.

Attribute listing. Attribute listing means listing all the attributes of a product and then changing each one in search of a new combination. Osborn (1963) suggests thinking in terms of other uses, adaptation, rearrangement, reversal, magnifying or minimising attributes, combination or substitution.

Forced relationships. Forced relationships as a technique considers products in relation to each other. Manufacturers of telephones, computers and hi-fi equipment, for example, may generate new product ideas by thinking of their products in relation to, say, a car and considering the technology involved, the design and styling and how the product would fit into the car's cockpit fascia.

Morphological analysis. Morphological analysis means looking at a problem and its components and then finding connections and solutions. Thus thinking about a golf buggy might lead to consideration of options relating to fuel source, power transmission, body shape and surface contact.

Agencies and consultants

Many agencies and consultancies specialise in providing information to organisations to assist in the generation of new product ideas. In the fashion industry, for example, agencies exist to predict colour and fabric trends so that designers and manufacturers can develop appropriate ranges for future seasons.

General Intelligence

Apart from the specific sources already mentioned, there is also a range of external sources, most of which are not specific to the organisation. These sources provide very general information that can be interpreted by the organisation to reveal possible new ideas. Such sources include trade magazines, exhibitions, distributor comments, government agencies, libraries and general research publications.

Despite the range of sources of new ideas, only a few ideas are likely to amount to anything. A large and regular supply is therefore needed. If an organisation really wants a successful NPD programme, it must ensure a systematic and ongoing effort.

Once the pool of ideas has been collected, it is time to move on to the next stage, idea screening.

Screening ideas

This second stage of NPD is where a preliminary scan of the ideas is conducted, in order to eliminate those that are unlikely to prove appropriate or successful. This means undertaking an assessment of an idea's potential, using information that is already available within the organisation. If the idea does not seem to fit within what is already known, or if nobody seems prepared to make out a case for following it through, there is little point in investing in more serious and costly external research and testing. It is best to drop bad ideas (after a fair hearing) as soon as possible, partly to allow concentration on the better ideas and partly to prevent a bad idea gaining unjustified management momentum as time goes on.

The objective of this stage is thus to assess whether the idea fits with the broad strategic plans and development directions of the organisation. It is also important to establish whether the idea's implementation is technically feasible. Usually, the idea and its preliminary screening analysis are presented to management as a proposal. This will describe the product arising from the idea, outline how it complements existing products, analyse its market segments, define and analyse the competition, and forecast its likely margin and its sales profile over time so that recommendations can be made whether or not to proceed.

Many organisations use a semi-formal weighting procedure to establish the relative importance of various screening criteria. This produces a score for each idea, allowing them to be compared with each other. Table 9.1 shows an example, suggesting the main criteria that might be applied for screening assessment purposes. In this case, Idea 1 scores significantly better than the other two.

It can be seen that each specific factor assumes a different weighting, according to its overall importance in a successful launch. In some cases, management has a maximum of 100 points to divide between all the relevant criteria. Having such a limited number of points to distribute means that there is likely to be an overt, critical discussion on why particular criteria have been included and why certain criteria deserve more points than others. This in itself is a useful process, forcing managers to think hard about how their market ticks.

Some care clearly needs to be taken in assessing ideas on such criteria. Ideas at the extreme ends of the spectrum (the excellent or the complete non-starters) pass through this process very easily, but the ones in the middle, on the borderline between 'accept' and 'reject', could be more difficult to assess. The numerical score itself has a spurious certainty about it and, in reality, for a borderline idea, it should be possible to override the score and argue about its strengths and weaknesses on a more qualitative level. Remember that the assessment criteria and their weightings are in themselves management judgements, based on perceptions of previous experience, and thus there is always room for doubt or argument.

TABLE 9.1
Idea screening criteria

Criterion	Weighting	Idea 1		Idea 2		Idea 3	
		Raw score	Weighted score	Raw score	Weighted score	Raw score	Weighted score
Fit with corporate strategic goals	15	8	1.20	3	0.45	5	0.75
Fit with marketing strategic goals	15	7	1.05	3	0.45	5	0.75
Market growth	5	9	0.45	9	0.45	3	0.15
Size of target market	10	6	0.60	8	0.80	9	0.9
Access to market	10	4	0.40	9	0.90	7	0.7
Differential advantage offered	10	9	0.90	5	0.50	7	0.7
Profitability potential	10	7	0.70	7	0.70	4	0.4
Timing	5	8	0.40	7	0.35	9	0.45
Synergy with existing products	5	7	0.35	3	0.15	6	0.3
Synergy with existing technology	5	7	0.35	3	0.15	2	0.1
Synergy with existing distribution channels	5	3	0.15	8	0.40	8	0.4
Synergy with existing skills and assets	5	6	0.30	4	0.20	5	0.25
Total	100	81	6.85	69	5.50	70	5.85

Note: Raw score = marks out of 10; Weighted score = (raw score × weighting)/100

Concept testing

Once an idea has been accepted in principle at the internal screening stage, it needs to have some external endorsement. This, then, is the third stage of NPD: **concept testing**, which can be defined as:

> '**A printed or filmed representation of a product or service. It is simply a device to communicate the subject's benefits, strengths and reasons for being.**'
>
> (Schwartz, 1987)

Concept testing starts to describe, profile and visualise the product in a way that potential customers would understand. What is presented to potential buyers at this stage may still only be sketchy concepts, in the form of working statements, drawings or storyboards, or it may go as far as models and mock-up packaging. There are two main types of concept statement: core ideas and positioning statements. Core ideas consist of short, general statements of what the product can do. There is no attempt to sell, as such, and all this type of statement is doing is testing whether the basic idea is acceptable or attractive. Positioning statements may comprise several paragraphs, focusing on main and secondary benefits, as well as outlining aspects of the product's marketing mix. Here, the researcher is trying to get as close as possible to assessing a realistic package that the potential customer might encounter in the market-place.

The overall objective, then, is to assess the relative attractiveness of each idea to the people whom the organisation hopes will eventually buy the product. The kinds of questions asked are included in Table 9.2. Such an assessment provides management with further information about the strengths and weaknesses of each idea and a rating on a scale from 'definitely would buy' to 'definitely would not buy'.

This stage of the process sometimes produces surprises (there would be no point doing it if it did not). Management's favourite ideas can be rejected by the consumer, while apparently weak or borderline ideas emerge with hidden appeal. Whatever the outcomes, management should now have a fuller picture of each idea and may, therefore, reject a few more and carry a small number through to the next stage, a thorough business analysis.

TABLE 9.2
Concept testing

Hypothetical concept statement for a self-chilling beer can
'A can of beer that cools itself, whatever the outside temperature. When the sealed can is opened by pulling a tab, the pressure releases a special capsule that can chill a can from a room temperature of 23°C down to 5°C in thirty seconds. The taste of the beer is unaltered and it will feel as if it has come straight from the fridge. The can will still be fully recyclable and requires no special storage. The price of the drink may rise by around 5%.'
A group of consumers may then be asked the following questions to establish such factors as need, perceived value, the impact on trial, how to communicate benefits and likely usage rates:
■ 'What problems do you find with the temperature of beer served from a can?'
■ 'Do you understand the benefits of the new can?'
■ 'Do you believe in the benefits offered?'
■ 'Will these benefits be important to you?'
■ 'Would you require any more evidence to support the claims made?'
■ 'Do you think that the new price of the beer is fair for the value offered?'
■ 'Would you certainly/probably/not sure/probably not/certainly not buy beer in these cans?'
■ 'Would the new can increase your total purchases of beer or would they remain the same?'

Business analysis

The fourth stage of NPD requires the product concept to be specified in greater detail so that production, marketing and financial projections can be made. It may involve, for example, forecasting new product sales and the rate of repeat purchase. Some of the issues addressed at this stage may well be the same as those included in the preliminary screening earlier, but here, the organisation is looking for more depth, more rigour and more evidence. Beyond this stage, it can become very expensive to drop an idea because of the capital investment and management time involved in developing and creating prototypes of both the product and its marketing strategy. It is important, therefore, that this stage should be thorough and that management is fully convinced and committed to any idea carried beyond it.

There are three main dimensions to consider: marketing, finance and production.

Marketing strategy

It is particularly important to show evidence of the nature of the *market*, its shape, size, dynamics, competitors and likely competitor reaction, along with any customer feedback gained so far. Further research may be undertaken at this point to clarify or further explore specific areas of concern. All of that activity looks at the external picture. It is also essential to demonstrate the internal strategic benefits to be gained and the demands that will be made on marketing resources by continuing with a particular product idea. Thus the product's relationship with the existing product portfolio, its distribution, sales and promotional needs all have to be addressed in some detail. None of those considerations, however, can make sense without some kind of outline of the marketing programme envisaged for launching and sustaining the product, considering all elements of the marketing mix.

All of these elements have to be fully costed and linked with a range of alternative sales and profit projections that are realistic and both optimistic and pessimistic.

Production

Satisfactory marketing of the product is not enough. The organisation has to be able to *produce* it as well. Detailed analysis, therefore, is needed on all aspects of manufacturing, such as material and component sourcing and storage, factory space, labour and machinery requirements. Thought also needs to be given to whether introducing this product will affect other production lines and schedules. Again, all this needs to be costed in the context of various possible levels of production. Only then can the sales and profit projections be appreciated. The sales figures projected may look healthy in themselves, but may actually be below the threshold for economies of scale to operate on the production side. This might mean that the product can only just break even at best, unless its production costs can be brought down, or its marketing strategy is revised radically to open up a bigger market at a higher price.

If the costs of production are thought to be too high, or if the disruption to current activities is too great, then it might be decided that it would be better to sub-contract manufacture to another organisation, in which case an extremely careful and detailed analysis of the risks and benefits would have to be undertaken, along with a detailed search for potential suppliers.

Financial analysis

Both of the areas discussed so far, marketing and production, have *cost* implications. These need to be fed into detailed calculations of the costs associated with different volumes and a breakeven analysis. Decisions also need to be made on the level of fixed costs and overheads that would need to be apportioned to the product. The financial analysis would also have to decide how to treat the R&D and development costs associated with the product, in terms of the amount to be charged to the product and over how many years it should be recovered.

The objective of the financial analysis is to provide information about the return on the investment in development, the likely payback period and the product's profit sensitivity should its market share develop in various ways, both good and bad. Chapter 11, on pricing, will develop these concepts further and look at how they might have an impact on the pricing decision.

Competitive response

One of the most difficult things to gauge in all of this is competitive reaction. That is why all of these analyses have to include an element of 'what if?' about them and take account of good, average and poor sales performance. Patent protection or heavy branding may help to protect against the competition launching a 'me too' product too quickly, but if a product launch threatens the competition's existing market shares, then the organisation concerned will have to be prepared for swift and damaging competitive response. That will reflect not only on its sales, but also on its marketing costs if, for example, an advertising or price war results.

Product development

The business analysis has brought through one or two ideas with real potential. Now, it is time to commit significant investment to produce the actual product. Everything that can be done theoretically has been done. Any further analysis requires a *real* product in order to allow demonstration, product trials, performance assessment and usage testing.

Just how problematic this fifth stage of NPD is depends on how innovative the new product is. The process may be more straightforward if the product utilises known technology. With a new shape of potato crisp, for example, more of the risk will lie in the organisation's ability to create a market presence than in its ability to produce a consistent quality product. With new engineering products (such as components), capital investment items (such as production machinery) or even new food types (such as microwavable frozen chips), extensive development work will be required before production reaches an acceptable level of efficiency, quality and consistency.

> **Example** Paxman is a supplier of high-powered diesel engines for locomotives, yachts and electrical generators. In 1993 it launched a new engine, the VP185, which performed 15–20 per cent better than the company's previous model that had been used in Intercity 125 locomotives. Before launch, however, the VP185 had to undergo extensive testing. In 1991 it underwent a British Rail type test, where its performance and ratings under different power demands were examined. Once it had passed these tests and gained British Rail Type Approval, it was fitted into a locomotive for further testing in the field for some 8000 hours under realistic operating conditions (Ford, 1994). Similarly, Siemens spent five years and between DM100 mn and 200 mn developing a new series of gas turbines. These too underwent extensive testing trials, the results of which, in terms of thermal efficiency and electrical output, were used by Siemens as part of its marketing approach (Baxter, 1995).

The staff involved at this stage will depend on the nature of the technology concerned. Design engineers, development engineers, R&D scientists, manufacturing and tooling experts may all play a part with an engineering or capital product. With foodstuffs, extensive laboratory testing, along with initial taste trials, may be required. The organisation will call on any type of expertise, whether available internally or consulted externally, in order to get it right. In any case, a sound appreciation of product specification and legal requirements (touching on safety, health or performance, for example) is necessary.

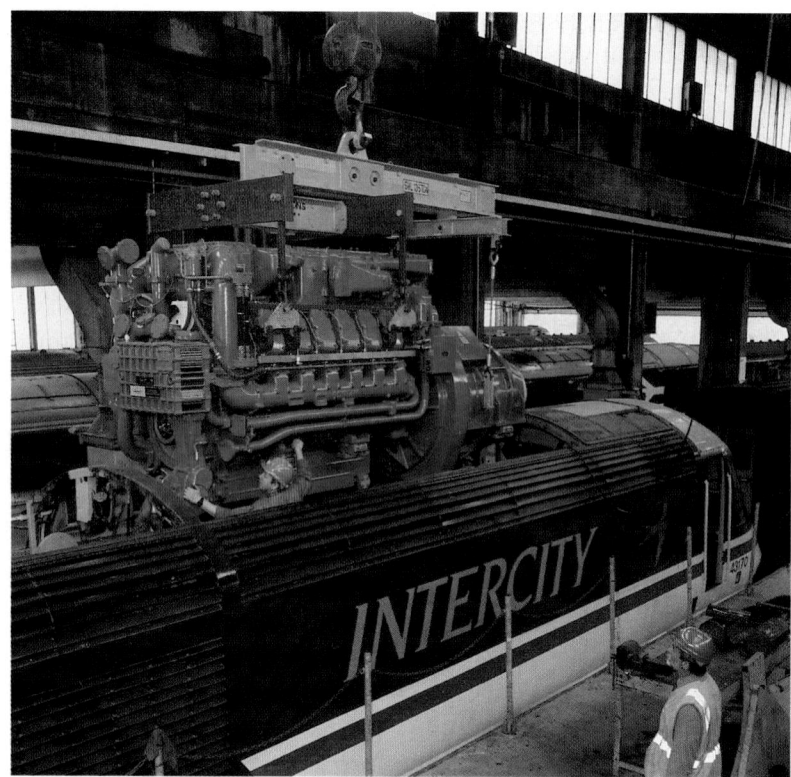

In the product development stage, this Paxman VP186 diesel engine underwent extensive testing.

Source: GEC Alstom Diesels.

Example British Biotech received a major blow to its product development plans when the trials of its pancreatitis treatment Zacutex revealed no significant difference in the mortality rates of those taking the drug compared with those taking other treatments. After extensive phase III trials, £30mn in development costs and several years of effort, these results meant that the future prosperity of the company rested on the success of its anti-cancer drug, Marimastat. That too is under extensive field trials (Smy, 1999).

It is impossible to specify a length of time for this development process. An aircraft takes many years to develop and involves many different areas of expertise, from interior design to micro-electronics. A fashion product may take a matter of weeks, by necessity. However long it takes, the objective is to answer questions on whether the product can be made cost effectively, within business plan guidelines, and whether it is capable of performing consistently under realistic conditions.

Towards the end of the development phase, if the product is looking good, plans can be made for market and customer testing. In fmcg markets, this means developing brand identity, packaging, labelling, promotion, pricing and launch strategy etc. When Churnton, a new cheese, was launched in the UK it was subjected to trial tasting sessions in Safeway supermarkets. This allowed the manufacturer to gauge the likely repeat purchase rates (80 per cent) and to refine its promotional pitch. In organisational markets, this stage is more likely to involve the development of appropriate support manuals and associated training or installation guides so that a realistic test can go ahead.

Test marketing

Particularly in consumer markets, before the decision is made to proceed with a full launch, the potential product can be offered on a limited basis in a defined geographic area, under conditions that are as realistic as possible. Within the UK, this geographic area is likely to correspond with a regional TV area to allow advertising to run only within the boundaries of the test market. This enables an assessment to be made of the likely outcomes of a full national launch.

Test marketing, the sixth NPD stage, answers a number of critical questions about the product. It gives an indication of whether the target market will actually buy the product and whether they will repeat the purchase or not. It shows the trade response to the product and how it performs in reality against the competition. Conducting market research to monitor the progress and outcomes of the test market can assess trade and consumer response to elements of the marketing mix, identifying which aspects are successful and which might need revision, and it can also offer valuable information on how the market rates the various product attributes and benefits. Again, this can identify where product improvements need to be made before the full launch.

Example The pressure to bring products to market more quickly has meant that alternative ways of test marketing that ensure speed and absolute secrecy offer powerful benefits to fmcg manufacturers. Virtual reality (VR) can be used to create a retail environment by placing a headset on the consumer and simulating a real store. A new package called Concept VR (http://www.vrweb.com) allows the environment to be easily modified and merchandise to become even more life-like. Once in the virtual store, the shopper can browse, pick up products, examine packaging, check prices and even change their mind and swop a product that has already been placed in the virtual trolley with a new find. Although still in its infancy, and often used alongside more conventional methods to assess consumer reaction to the product offering, the potential of VR could be enormous in allowing a number of alternatives, for example a selection of different packaging designs, to be tested quickly and cheaply (Hart, 1998).

Test marketing is not an extension of the development stage. Much of the product testing should already have been undertaken and the obvious bugs ironed out. This stage may be seen as a trial run for the major launch, in which all the elements of the planned marketing offering are assessed.

In summary, test marketing offers a number of benefits:

1 it is a real test in a real environment;
2 it offers a last chance for fine tuning;
3 it gives the opportunity to vary some of the mix variables. For example, a test market might take place in two geographically different (but demographically similar) regions, each of which has a different advertising approach, with all other elements of the marketing mix held constant. This might help to decide which advertising approach is the more effective in terms of generating sales or creating the right product image;
4 it allows the assessment of things that are difficult to predict on paper, such as awareness generated, propensity for repeat buying etc.

All of this allows the adjustment of the overall business plan and the launch strategy. It is especially important as a guide for the fine detail, such as how much to produce initially, where to supply, whether to run more or less advertising etc.

Test marketing seems like a good idea, but there are a number of areas that need careful consideration before a decision is made on whether to test market or go straight into a national launch.

Test area selection

If the results of the test market are going to be scaled up to give a picture of the total market, then the organisation needs to be absolutely sure that the test market is indeed representative of the overall target market. The criteria for selection will vary from product to product, taking into account factors such as distribution structure, media availability, competitor activity and the detailed breakdown of the target market profile.

Competitive response

Even within an area selected as being as typical as possible, there are risks that the test marketing may go wrong. Competitors will not sit back passively and let another organisation proceed with test marketing. If they find out that test marketing is to be conducted in a particular region, they may at least try to distort the results. They could do this quite simply by running sales promotions, either aimed at the trade, so that the retailers stock up with competitors' products and will be less willing to take on large quantities of the test-marketed product, or aimed at consumers to divert their attention from the test product.

A potentially more serious problem of test marketing is that it gives the competition a great deal of warning and much detail about what is planned. This might just give them enough lead time to bring forward their own plans and launch their own version of the product with full knowledge of the test marketers' position. This is especially easy if the basis for the new product lies in relatively superficial aspects such as packaging or branding rather than in fundamental product attributes or technicalities.

Timing and duration

Other problems relate to the timing and the duration of the test market. The organisation needs to ensure that any seasonal factors affecting sales are taken into account when planning and evaluating the test market. Also, the duration of the test market needs to be carefully considered. If it goes on for too long, then all that happens is that the organisation stops learning anything useful or new and this unduly delays the big launch. A prolonged test market means that the competition is being given a longer lead time to think of a response to the national launch. Too short a test market period, however, might mean that important effects are missed. Enough time must be allowed to enable the target market to become aware of the product, try it, then settle down into a regular purchasing pattern. It may also take some time for advertising and other promotional efforts to reach their full potential.

All three of the areas discussed above must be taken into account when planning and evaluating the effects of a test marketing exercise. In particular, the typicality of the test area and the possible effects of untypical behaviour or spoiling tactics from the competition need to temper the way in which the results are scaled up to reflect the national picture.

If the risks of test marketing are too great, especially with the delay and the danger of competitors' alternatives coming on to the market, then there are a number of alternatives.

1 *Simulated test market.* This is a much reduced version of the full test market discussed above and involves the introduction of a brand to a number of selected stores. Free samples might be distributed and consumers questioned about their buying habits and brand preferences. These consumers are then tracked through their product usage, questioned on their assessment of the product's attributes and repurchasing behaviour.
2 *Controlled distribution minimarkets.* Again, this technique is often store specific. Purchase of the new product is monitored electronically and, if possible, repurchases are also tracked.

Both of these methods lower the costs of test marketing, as well as being quicker to produce results. Most importantly, however, they make a less public impact, allowing the organisation to keep elements of its product launch plans away from the competition's direct scrutiny.

Overall, provided it is carried through with thought and sufficient time is available to do it properly, test marketing can be a very valuable step in the launch process, especially for products that eventually pass through mass distribution channels.

Its role is less clear cut, however, with services and organisational products.

Test marketing for services

Cowell (1984) points out that test marketing for services is not always possible. Large service providers, such as airlines or banks, who produce mass-market services can test a new service package on an individual route or in an individual region. This will help them to answer the question of whether they have developed a product that is really attractive to the people it was designed for and whether they are selling it effectively. There will then be an opportunity for refining the service itself and its delivery, and perhaps its marketing strategy, before offering the product from all the organisation's service outlets.

Many small service providers, however, are geographically centred anyway and thus the test market is the entire real market! In this case it may be less a matter of test marketing and more a matter of pacing the development of the business. Thus the market may be tested initially with a compact range of core services and then the organisation can open out to a greater range of services when viability has been established.

Test marketing for organisational products

According to Moore and Pessemier (1993), there are several reasons for test marketing not being appropriate for organisational products:

1 *Market structure*. The market may consist of a small number of potential customers in total, or a very small number of customers may account for a large proportion of sales in this market. Either way, a test market would become tantamount to a full launch.

2 *Buyer–seller relationships and customisation*. In many organisational markets, close and durable working relationships develop, which in turn lead to joint product development. This means that the potential buyer is involved in NPD from the start, with an implied commitment to purchase what is effectively a customised product at the end of it. Since the buyer is involved in prototype testing as part of the joint development process, and since issues such as price and availability are also negotiated as part of the development, test marketing as such is a rather redundant concept.

3 *The product's life span and purchase frequency*. Some organisational products, such as capital equipment for example, have very long life spans and are thus purchased very infrequently. This means that although there may be many potential customers in total, at the time that an organisation with a new product is ready to test market it, there may actually be very few potential customers ready to consider the product *now*. Again, this effectively means, therefore, that the test market would consist of all potential customers who are able and willing to buy.

Clearly, much depends on the type of product. Low-cost, low-risk, relatively frequently purchased goods that are applicable across a range of business customers lend themselves to consumer-type test marketing. On the other hand, test marketing is less applicable to customer specified or high-cost, high-risk capital items (which tend to be developed with the co-operation of the customer anyway) with a very limited number of customers in the whole market. Where test marketing is appropriate, Hart (1993) suggests that it can be done geographically, in a particular region or in a small foreign market, or that it can be tested in a particular industry or market segment. Moore and Pessemier (1993) advocate the use of trade shows and exhibitions (of which more in Chapter 19) as a means of exposing new products or prototypes to a range of 'expert' scrutiny to get feedback on what amendments might have to be made before full commercialisation. The problem with this, of course, is that the ideas are exposed to competitors as well as to potential customers.

Commercialisation

By the seventh stage, commercialisation, everything that can be done to ensure the successful launch of the new product has been done. The surviving product is now ready for its full launch.

> **Example** Nintendo (http://www.nintendo.com) has little option but to launch new games as soon as possible, usually on an international scale. The life-cycle for new software titles is normally very short and the company generates a significant proportion of its sales in the run-up to Christmas. This pressure to launch can have serious consequences when things go wrong, as with *Yoshi's Story* in 1997. After receiving excellent reviews, Nintendo believed that the title could be an outstanding success. Unfortunately, the game was delivered late because the software designers would not let the product go until it was just right, manufacturing volumes were too small to meet demand and the stocks that did become available often went to the wrong markets and channels. As a result, sales performance was disappointing and by the time the problems were solved, the market had moved on. In 1998, *Yoshi's Story* was available at a 50 per cent discount (Abrahams, 1998).

Any significant changes to the product after the test marketing stage can be very expensive, not just in terms of direct costs, but also in opportunity cost terms if a competitor gets in sooner. This is especially true with products that have a short life-cycle, such as high technology consumer products. It is also true that significant changes after the test market effectively take the whole NPD process back a stage or two, if the changes fundamentally change the concept so that further business analysis, product development and test marketing have to take place.

Assuming, however, that no significant changes happen, the product is now ready to launch. Many of the topics covered in this book as a whole apply to the details of the marketing programme for the product launch. Areas such as positioning (pp. 318 *et seq.*), strategies for the introduction stage of the product life-cycle (p. 304), price setting (Chapter 11) and the initial promotional programme (all the chapters in Part VI) are of particular relevance to new product launch.

In terms of how to go about launching the product, there are two main alternatives at this stage:

Immediate national or international launch (the sprinkler strategy)

Making the product available in all target markets at the same time achieves two things. First, it makes a big impact, providing a single focus for a large PR, advertising and promotional blitz. Second, it allows little scope for the competition to sneak in, either with a launch of its own to eclipse yours or with a loud promotional voice to distract the market from your new product. If you are investing considerable promotional resources in making a big issue out of the national launch, it will be difficult and expensive for the competition to shout louder than you.

The risk of a national launch, however, is that it leaves the organisation open to teething troubles. A test market can reduce those risks, but it cannot guarantee against them. Working in a carefully managed test market is different from day-to-day operation on a national scale. Production routines that work well on the sort of quantities required for a test region may not scale up as well or as efficiently as planned, for example. Both consumers and the trade have long memories, and early problems with supply or quality will taint an organisation's and a brand's reputations.

Rolling launch (the waterfall strategy)

A **rolling launch** or waterfall strategy is an alternative to the high impact approach (Kalish *et al,* 1995). It involves building towards full national coverage by starting with one or two recognised distribution areas, then gradually adding new regions to those already served as experience and success accumulate. This means that the organisation can concentrate on getting the logistics of distribution and production right and can also fine tune marketing strategies in the light of experience.

Whether to use this approach depends a great deal on the resources available. A smaller or less well-established company could have difficulty in financing and managing a full national launch, yet could make an effective impact within a limited region. Success within that limited region would then finance the addition of further areas to the new product's distribution. The decision might also depend on the organisation's experience in NPD and any similarity between the new product and existing ones. If the new product is part of a family of related brands, then it might make sense to go for the national launch through the same distribution channels and with similar marketing strategies as are used for the other brands. Even if the brand is free standing, i.e. unrelated to existing products, if it makes use of the same sales or distribution channels, then again, a national launch might be feasible.

In some cases, rolling out can have an international dimension. In Ireland, with a small domestic market, organisations can start with that home base as almost a test market, but to achieve significant volume sales, they then have to roll out to attack the UK and other European markets as they gain experience.

Kalish *et al.* (1995) argued that the expected life-cycle of the product, the difficulty or familiarity of foreign markets and the state of competition in those markets are all important determinants of whether a 'sprinkler' or 'waterfall' approach is appropriate.

Monitoring and evaluation

As with any marketing activity, the story does not end just because all the practical tasks within a particular framework have been completed. There always has to be time given over to reflection on how well the process itself has been implemented and how successful or otherwise the outcomes have been. NPD, as a particularly difficult activity to manage and get right, deserves that kind of review more than most.

Part of this final NPD stage will relate to the *process* and part to the *performance* of the product itself after launch. The process may be reviewed in terms of whether each stage was given due consideration, whether the right kinds of people were involved in it, whether it needed more time or resources, whether it took more time and resources than it need have done or whether the quality of the information, analysis and decision making was as high as the organisation would wish. Taking time to address such issues might at least lead to a better and more efficient NPD exercise on the next occasion.

No matter how good the management and implementation of the NPD process, the real measure of its success is the product to which it gave rise. Before the product is launched, performance criteria will be set for it. These criteria might include volume or value sales targets, market share relative to competition, trade take-up of the product or promotion objectives linked with awareness generation, product trial or attitude formation. Setting such criteria allows forecast performance to be compared with actual performance. Any mismatch between the two needs to be carefully analysed to find out whether it arose from poor management decision making, lack of information, poor forecasting or unforeseen market conditions. In any event, lessons need to be learned for the future. Some further insights into the problems of evaluating new product failure are given at p. 363 *et seq.*

The entire NPD process presented here follows a logical pattern of stages, from initial idea generation through to commercialisation and evaluation. As each stage progresses, the number of ideas being followed through reduces and the investment of money and time becomes greater and more serious. At any stage, it is possible for the organisation to terminate the process or to backtrack to an earlier stage. If, for example, business analysis shows that the favoured idea is not feasible for whatever reason, then the idea generation stage may be run again to find something on a slightly different track. Although the longer the process goes on, the more expensive it gets, it is still cheaper to drop a new product just before it is launched than to face the public embarrassment and the massive costs of a market failure. The aim of the whole NPD process is to reduce the considerable risks of failure, but each stage is sufficiently complex to leave plenty of scope for an organisation to get it wrong.

Mistakes in managing the NPD process can lead to two types of wrong outcome, broadly speaking. The first is a decision to launch when the product should not have been allowed out (a *go error*) and this is discussed in the following section. The second is a decision not to launch a new product that eventually could be successful (a *drop error*).

All the time, the organisation is having to balance the risk of rushing the NPD process and making either of those two types of error against the costs of prolonging it. The organisation also has to decide how much commercial risk it is prepared to take. If it is too risk averse, then there is a greater danger of a drop error, while if it is too daring, there is a greater risk of a go error.

MARKETING AND IT   ## Getting to market more quickly

The increasing use of IT in the design and manufacture of products is shortening the time it takes to get products through the NPD process and into the market-place. A senior executive at the American drugs company Eli Lilly (http://www.elililly.com), for example, describes its business as '50% IT, 50% pharmaceuticals'. This comment highlights the increasingly crucial role played by computer and telecommunications technologies in the fast-moving, high-pressure world of global pharmaceuticals, in which a day's delay in bringing a product to market can cost over $1mn in lost revenue. Some companies believe that they can cut the clinical trial process by half, from 30 months to 15 months, simply by managing the process better. Traditionally, a clinical trial depended on a lengthy and largely paper-based system that began with the general practitioner filling in a form after seeing a patient and sending it back to the company conducting the trial, which then input the data for analysis. More recently, doctors have been given computers with which to input the data directly and clinical research assistants, who normally visit the doctors every six weeks, have been provided with mobile computers and digital telephones so that they can access the latest clinical trial information remotely.

Source: O'Connor and Galvin (1999).

NEW PRODUCT FAILURE

New product failure is a very real and very common phenomenon. The introduction to this chapter stated that something like 90 per cent of new products fail. Failure can also be very expensive. While a larger organisation can carry a certain level of loss from a failure (although that does not mean that it either encourages or enjoys it), a small, newly formed organisation may go out of business completely if its one and only project fails.

Failure is sometimes a difficult thing for managers to cope with, especially if they think that it will reflect badly on either their status or their career prospects. Failure is, therefore, sometimes rationalised or hidden. It might be justified, by saying that the failed product was not really not part of the organisation's objectives or that it did not really fit with the organisation's capabilities. Poor top management support or lack of development resources are commonly cited as reasons for failure. Deeper analysis often reveals many other reasons.

Failure defined

Even the term 'failure' needs to be more precisely defined, as it can carry shades of meaning.

Outright failure – lost money

A product may be a failure because it is not covering its variable costs and it is not making any contribution to fixed costs and profit (*see* Chapter 11). Such failures could arise either because the sales volumes are too low (*see* below) or because there was a major miscalculation of unit production or distribution costs.

Outright failure – major negative market response

Another type of outright failure occurs when the market has rejected the product outright. It has not come anywhere near its sales targets and therefore is likely to be either losing money or not earning as much as the organisation forecast.

Partial failure – failure to make contribution to fixed costs and profit

A partial failure occurs when the product has been accepted by the market, but for some reason is not living up to financial expectation. Again, this may be a result of the miscalculation of costs. This is only a partial failure, because the product's standing in the market seems to be satisfactory and while that is the case, and while the product is managing to cover its variable costs at least, it might be redeemable with a certain amount of effort.

Partial failure – failure to achieve its set objectives

When a product fails to achieve its set objectives, the issues involved are similar to those discussed above in relation to monitoring and evaluation. Failure is a relative term and thus a product can superficially seem to be performing well in the market and making a comfortable contribution to fixed costs and profit, yet still be labelled a failure because it is performing below expectations. The question is, of course, whether those expectations were realistic in the first place.

Partial failure – no longer fits organisational strategy

A product cannot be blamed for failing to fit in with organisational strategy. Particularly if the NPD process has been long and difficult, by the time the product is launched the organisation might have moved on strategically. This may mean that the product no longer fits easily into the desired product portfolio, or that the management views it as out of keeping with the kind of image it now wishes to project. At this point, the organisation faces a number of options such as repositioning (*see* pp. 318 *et seq.*) or deletion (*see* pp. 325 *et seq.*).

There are many reasons for products failing, and some of the more frequently quoted include:

1 Too small a target market, which is too specialised for the volumes originally planned or those needed for breakeven.
2 Insufficient differentiation from existing offerings, leading to another 'me too' imitative product.
3 Poor or inconsistent product quality.
4 No access to the market, because the organisation is unable to get trade distribution and does not have sufficient resources to sell direct.

5 Poor timing in terms of the industry life-cycle. Launching too early (before the market is fully formed and ready) or too late (after the peak has passed) has an impact both on the resources needed for a successful launch and on the investment pay-back period.

6 Poor marketing, through either an insufficient spend or a badly allocated spend. It may be that not enough attention was paid to the main competitive alternatives, leading to a marketing strategy that was unable to cut through competitors' activities.

In an ideal world, every one of these reasons for failure is avoidable. Within the NPD framework presented, all these issues of competitive activity, state of the market, market size and production capability should be addressed and the organisation should not be caught out by such failures after launch. In the real world, however, time is short, managers are under pressure to make decisions within very tight deadlines, information is expensive and incomplete, corners are cut, assumptions are made, risks are taken and, sometimes, a product launch simply does not work out.

> **Example** Sometimes, test marketing might not reveal all the likely difficulties that will be experienced at launch. MD Foods (http://www.mdfoods.com) had to withdraw the cultured dairy product Gaio as consumer groups disputed its claim to lower cholesterol levels. In 1999, the same company withdrew the Pact range of functional foods, including yoghurt with folic acid launched in 1998. Again, advertising restrictions on the health claims meant that the product could not move beyond a niche position (Pring, 1999).

A study of 2250 product launches concluded that only one in seven met the 'success criteria' of £1mn sales or a 2 per cent market share in the first year after launch. For grocery and health and beauty products, the success rate of existing names tended to be greater than that of new names. The survey findings suggested that the majority of successful new products were promoted for the first 12 weeks, but unsuccessful products were not promoted at all. The failed products also appeared to suffer from unsufficient market research data and an over-reliance on exaggerated claims to create consumer interest and sales. Interestingly, successful products tended to be priced above average for the sector and were launched with the retailers' objectives in mind (Morley, 1999).

It also needs to be emphasized that although the process presented in this chapter is a cool, rational approach to the NPD problem, it has to be implemented by people who often have their own agendas. (Refer back to pp. 165 *et seq.* to remind yourself of the issues involved.) Managers become emotionally attached to their own pet projects and will sometimes take the risk of seeing a product through to launch come what may, rationalising away any warning signs. Some may see the new product as their big career break or as a means of differentiating themselves from their colleagues in the eyes of senior management. Some may take a gamble on a borderline project for the personal rewards and status that success would bring. Such human interest might well drive a difficult launch to success but, equally, it might drive it to an inevitable failure.

TRENDS IN NPD PROCESS MANAGEMENT

The main message from this chapter should be that NPD is a necessary, costly and risky process. It requires adequate levels of investment and management commitment if it is going to succeed in ensuring that tomorrow's products are ready when needed (Brown and Eisenhart, 1995). It also requires time, however, which perhaps is the scarcest commodity of all. As competitive pressures increase and as the life-cycles of products become shorter, the temptation is to push a new product out on to the market as quickly as possible. This sense of urgency is further heightened by financial pressure, particularly in periods of recession, where the emphasis is on keeping development costs as low as possible and putting a new product out to begin to recoup its development costs as soon as possible. In fmcg markets, for example, the NPD time has been reduced from around two years to between three and six months in some cases (Matthews, 1995). Clearly, there is a great risk here of launching an under-developed, under-researched, second rate product, which may well fail before the marketers can fine tune the offering after launch.

Research and development

Reducing the NPD time does not necessarily mean compromising the effectiveness of the process. Renault has managed to cut both the costs and time taken in NPD through changes in its management structure. By opening a Technocentre in 1995, the whole process of NPD from conception through prototyping and final development was cut from just over eight years to just over three. Previously the stages had been sequential and geographically dispersed, but the new centre enabled better co-ordination and project management. It also cut the cost of developing and launching a new car model by anything from 10 to 25 per cent.

Not all organisations have the funds to invest in that kind of long-term commitment to R&D. There has been a tendency in some organisations to cut back on R&D during recession. In the recession of 1989/90 in the UK, for example, R&D expenditure fell by 8 per cent. Others have invested heavily as a key part of their strategic development.

> **Example** The pharmaceutical industry invests heavily in R&D to ensure a regular flow of new products. Most companies spend more than 15 per cent of their sales revenue on R&D and, in the period from 1981 to 1999, the industry as a whole increased its spend from $5bn to $40bn per year. Despite these increases, there has been a downward trend in new drug launches from the 50 to 60 molecular entities per year in the 1980s to just 35 worldwide in 1998. With the intensity of R&D effort going on, however, many of these new drugs are genuinely innovative. Lead times can be very long between finding a new molecule to product launch, typically 10 to 12 years, largely due to extensive clinical trials and the need to meet tough regulations. Considerable attention is being given to bringing lead times down through better project management and through the use of new laboratory technologies.
>
> The industry as a whole had 11 307 projects in progress in 1998, with Novartis (http://www.novartis.com) in Switzerland having 208 and Hoechst Marion Roussel of Germany 122. Having too large a development portfolio can be a sign of poor screening that does not eliminate weaker projects. With development costs for a drug reaching as much as $600mn, R&D has a major role to play in finding ways in reducing overall project costs (Cookson, 1999).

Looking to reduce costs, yet to tap into as wide a range of innovative technology as possible, organisations are increasingly turning to **outsourcing R&D**, i.e. contracting out R&D to other organisations such as commercial or government laboratories, consultants and universities. There is indeed little point in an organisation's trying to re-invent or develop a technology for itself if there is another organisation that can do that work better and whose expertise can be bought. A survey reported by Houlder (1995a) indicated that by 1996, European businesses would be 24 per cent reliant on external technology.

There are, however, a number of potential problems arising from outsourcing. The contracting organisation may not ultimately have total control of what might become a critical technology for its business and, furthermore, may run a higher risk of details of that technology being leaked to competitors than if the R&D were totally in-house. Time lags might also be a problem, since it takes time for an organisation to realise it has a problem that is worth outsourcing; to locate a suitable contractor; to brief them on the background to the organisation and its R&D needs; then to discuss and refine the terms and conditions of the required work. The internal implications of outsourcing also need to be carefully thought through. The organisation may lose its internal R&D impetus altogether, becoming rather too dependent on external bodies for its innovation. Where internal R&D and outsourcing do exist in parallel, the organisation will also have to be careful to avoid attitude problems towards the external ideas (for example, internally sourced ideas might be given priority in terms of implementation, time and resources).

Half-way between outsourcing and the Renault approach is the idea of partnership, or **collaborative R&D** (Houlder, 1995b). This means that two or more organisations pool their resources and their expertise to undertake a specific project that will benefit both/all of them.

As with outsourcing, collaboration is a way of sharing costs and tapping into a wider field of expertise, but unlike outsourcing, both the risks and the potential commercial benefits are also shared. Before matters reach this stage, however, a big problem with collaboration can be finding an appropriate partner in the first place. In industries where there is close buyer–supplier co-operation, collaborative R&D partnerships can emerge naturally within the supply chain. Microprocessor manufacturer Intel, for example, entered into a joint development venture with Hewlett Packard.

With the exception of companies whose circumstances are similar to those described above, most smaller, low profile companies do not find collaborators easily,

Rapid analysis of new chemical entities using the very latest advances in chromatography and mass spectrometry to reveal their structure and likely properties.

Source: Glaxo Wellcome plc R&D

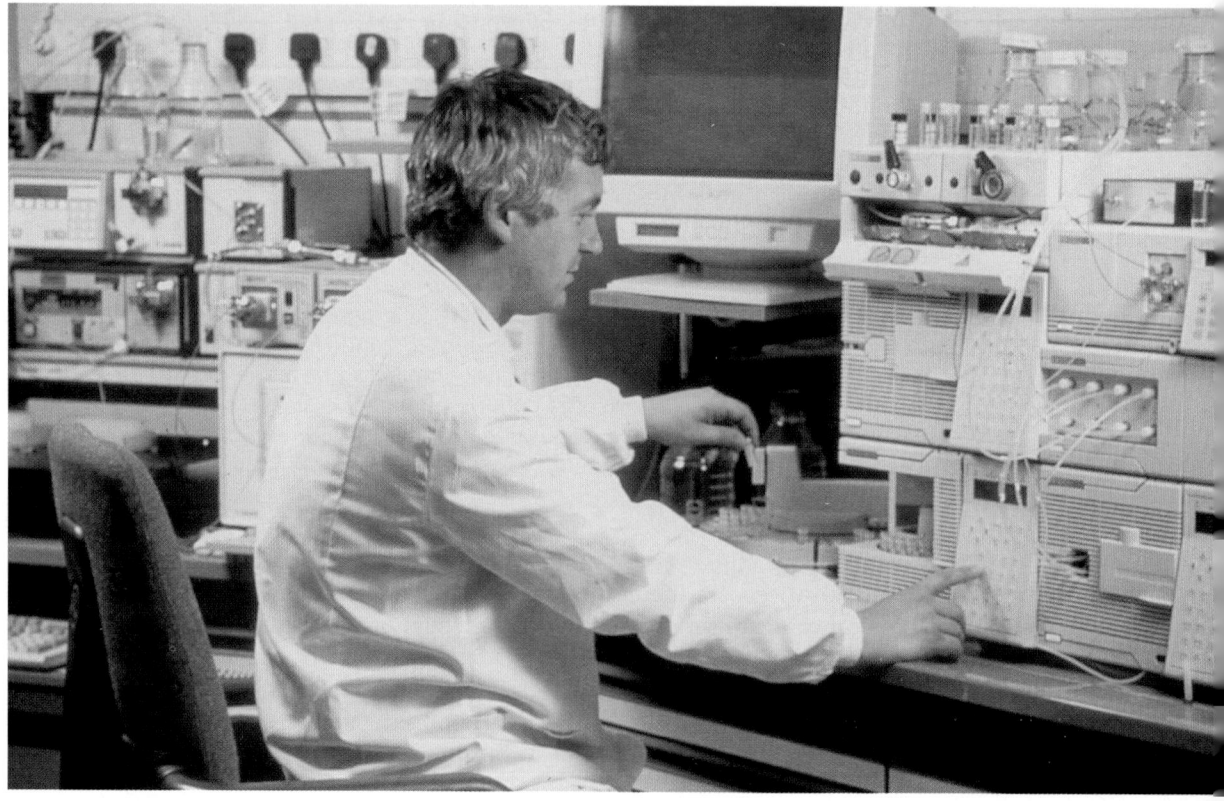

particularly where the nature of the R&D concerned may cut across industries or scientific disciplines. This all, however, further assumes that organisations know precisely what kind of partner they are looking for and for what purpose or objective. Some ideas for collaboration only emerge after organisations have come together and talked to each other about their respective problems and areas of expertise. With this in mind, national governments, the EU, universities and other bodies with an interest in promoting innovation have promoted conferences, forums and clubs (e.g. the European Industrial Research Managers' Association) to allow dialogue between organisations that otherwise might never even think of talking to each other. It was at such a forum organised by the government-backed Centre for the Exploitation of Science and Technology that Yorkshire Water and Siemens came together to develop a sensor for monitoring toxic waste.

MARKETING IN ACTION   ## The Merc and the moose

The launch of the Mercedes A Class has been described as 'one of the costliest and most embarrassing errors of modern motoring industry'. Few could have expected problems as the car was paraded at the Frankfurt show in September 1997. It was described as Mercedes' 'wackiest offering' that was sure to be a winner. Many innovative design features were incorporated into this major departure for the company. It was given a vote of confidence by many of the motoring journalists – that is, until Robert Collins, a Swedish journalist, decided to put the car through its paces.

The problem was simple: he found that it was very difficult to keep all four wheels on the road! Despite spending five years, 3000 test miles and £870mn on its development, Mercedes' process did not include putting the car through its paces on a slalom course at ordinary driving speeds. Just days after the car was launched, Robert Collins did just that and managed to flip the car over. Three people incurred minor injuries and the journalist thought that the car's instability on certain manoeuvres was obvious. His report first appeared in a Swedish magazine and soon made big headlines around Europe.

Just why did Mercedes (http://www.mercedes.com) miss such an obvious point? The 'elk-avoidance test' was invented in Sweden because of the number of accidents caused by elk crossing the road without looking! Such testing is hardly necessary on typical French or German roads, but in Sweden the ability to brake and swerve on ice to avoid an elk can actually save the driver's life, never mind the elk's. Despite

conducting extensive tests before the launch, Mercedes' engineers overlooked the elk avoidance test and this proved to be an extremely costly oversight. Mercedes originally thought that such a test was not representative of normal driving conditions, but the trouble was that most other rival cars passed the elk test at higher speeds than the A Class could.

Production had to be stopped for 12 weeks at a cost of £100mn while the car went through a redesign to improve stability. Three thousand cars were recalled from all around Europe. Stabilisers were fitted to both axles, the body lowered, the tyres widened and an advanced electronic stability programme, normally reserved as an option for top-of-the-range Mercedes cars, was fitted as standard to a car selling at around £15 000.

The damage was not just limited to the delayed launch and 40 000 frustrated enquirers in the UK alone. The negative publicity had the potential to harm Mercedes' high-quality brand name and the company certainly did not want to be associated with an 'unsafe' car. Even some of the German motoring press were slated for not spotting the weakness and for being too sympathetic to home producers. It cost £100mn for a relaunch to convince a now sceptical public that the problem had been solved and that they could buy with confidence. The campaign seems to have worked. Despite the early difficulties, the redesign did help restore public confidence and sales started to build according to plan after the three-month stoppage.

Sources: Eason (1998); Eason and Boyes (1997); Hutton (1998); Simonian (1997).

Finally, as a form of summary of this section, Table 9.3 brings together the advantages and disadvantages of using the three types of R&D approach discussed: in-house, outsourcing and collaboration.

TABLE 9.3

Advantages and disadvantages of various ways of organising R&D

	Advantages	Disadvantages
Outsourcing	Reduced costs Access to wider technology Access to a wide pool of R&D talent Use only when needed Solves specifically defined problems Access to facilities	Information leaks Requires trust Lose in-house R&D impetus Time lags Lack of control/motivation Lack of control over critical technologies Good communication needed
Collaboration	Shared costs Access to wider technology Access to wider facilities Access to a wide pool of R&D talent Shared risks Multi-industry/cross-disciplinary synergy possible Involvement/development of in-house R&D function	Shared benefits Needs trust Danger of domination by one partner Danger of unequal benefits Locating a suitable partner
In-house	Secrecy Total control over process Total control over critical technology Industry/company/product knowledge among researchers Quick response/always available Reap all the rewards	Cost Limited expertise Limited facilities May be too close to the problem Permanent resource to be funded and maintained

Organisation for NPD

As this chapter has made clear throughout, NPD is a serious and necessary business and accordingly needs the right kind of management support and organisational structures if it is to flourish and produce results. This section looks in further detail at the kinds of teams and individuals who might be involved in NPD.

Product or brand manager

A product or brand manager has responsibility for a single product or brand family, and thus has developed extensive knowledge of a specific market. The brand manager may be able to spot new opportunities in that market or ways of stretching or filling product lines. The risk, of course, is that the brand manager is too involved in managing the current product, or is too emotionally attached to it to threaten its future with a new product. Quite apart from that, an individual who is a good brand manager may not necessarily be equally good at developing and appraising new product opportunities. Thus although the brand manager has a valuable role to play, the NPD process is likely to involve others.

Market manager

A market manager has responsibility for a particular market, which may be defined in terms of customer type or product type. An organisation manufacturing and selling motor spares may define its markets as independent garages, franchised car dealerships, multiple chains such as Kwik Fit and mass retailers such as Halfords. Market managers develop deep knowledge of the customer needs and wants within their own markets, but as with the brand managers, their expertise is best deployed as part of a wider team.

'Oreal aims to lauch 2000 new products every year – because we're worth it.

* source*: L'Oréal.

New product manager

A new product manager is employed specifically to seek out new product opportunities and is likely to be found in a consumer market where the emphasis is on marketing rather than technical innovation. The existence of such a post formalises commitment to new products and ensures that the NPD process is in the hands of someone who understands how it works and will take responsibility for implementing it. Nevertheless, the new product manager may need to draw on the expertise of others within the organisation.

Venture team

The Renault approach discussed above is an example of the venture team. This is a group of selected individuals from various functional areas who are given the freedom to work solely on NPD, unhindered by other responsibilities and relatively independent of the rest of the organisation. In the Renault case, this went as far as providing a separate, purpose-built site for the team to work in. Such an approach clearly signals a long-term, serious investment and commitment to NPD.

New product committee

A new product committee may take responsibility for defining the organisation's new product policies, aims and objectives and may also make the ultimate decision about which new products to launch. Such a committee is likely to consist of senior managers from a range of functional areas, thus not only co-ordinating NPD strategy and effort throughout the organisation, but also visibly endorsing commitment to NPD at the top level.

Task force

A task force is a temporary team, brought together from the various functional areas of the organisation to tackle a specifically defined NPD project. Unlike members of a venture team, however, the task force members may have to cope with their involvement in NPD in addition to their normal duties, although in some cases they may be temporarily seconded to the task force full time. Once the NPD problem is solved, the task force disbands.

Clearly, the number of individuals concerned and the range of functional areas involved in an NPD exercise will vary according to the size of organisation and the nature of the NPD task in hand. Thus within a single organisation, a variety of flexible NPD approaches may be employed to suit different conditions.

CHAPTER SUMMARY

This chapter has been concerned with new product development (NPD) as a means of enabling organisations to maintain the pace of innovation in their industries and to keep themselves ahead of the competition. There are, however, different degrees of newness. A product might be completely *new to the market*. Such products are totally innovative and can emerge from technological advances. Alternatively, a product might be a *significant innovation for the market*, where the basic product concept is familiar, but there is a new twist to it. The other two options represent *minor* or *no* innovation to the market. These are products that either offer little change (of minor but not fundamental interest to the market) or are purely imitative.

The buyer's attitude to new products may also be influenced by the rate at which new products are introduced into the market. In fmcg markets, for instance, there is *continuous innovation*, where new product launches are fairly common and it is difficult (and expensive) to get the consumer deeply excited about any single launch.

New product development is important to organisations for many reasons, including the need to maintain competitive advantage through innovation and better serving the customer's changing needs and wants. There are two types of approach to NPD. The first is to be *reactive*, to wait and see what others do and then follow or imitate, and the second is to be *proactive*, to set the pace and standard and be the one whom others follow or imitate. Whatever the approach, NPD is not an easy activity and there are many potential problems that can arise. In order to minimise the risks, therefore, the NPD process needs careful and skilful management. An eight-stage framework, building from the initial idea generation through to actual product development, test marketing and launch, helps to define the necessary NPD activities and shows how they fit together in a logical sequence.

Even with a well-planned, resourced and managed NPD framework, things can go wrong. An organisation may decide to launch a product that should have been rejected (a *go error*) or to dump a product that could have succeeded (a *drop error*). Such errors reflect the delicate balancing act that NPD represents: risk vs safety, investment vs uncertain rewards, speed to market vs taking enough time to make a considered and well-researched decision, proactiveness vs reactiveness.

Many new products do fail, for a variety of reasons. It should be emphasised, however, that many common reasons for failure, such as too small a target market, insufficient differentiation, poor quality, poor distribution, poor timing or poor marketing, are entirely avoidable if the NPD process is researched and handled correctly. The reality is, however, that many organisations are under pressure and do not feel that they have the time and resources to do things as thoroughly as they should.

It is possible to cut the time spent on the NPD process by more effective and efficient management, although this requires long-term commitment and investment. Other organisations have attempted to reduce the costs of NPD by outsourcing their R&D, that is, by using external bodies to undertake work on their behalf. While this allows the organisation to tap into wider technology and expertise, it may compromise commercial secrecy, increase the time taken for the NPD process and remove much control from the organisation. Another trend is that of collaborative R&D, where organisations enter into complementary partnerships to achieve specific R&D goals. Both partners benefit from shared risks and from synergy between their respective skills and industrial experience.

Key words and phrases

Collaborative R&D	Discontinuous innovation	Outsourcing R&D
Continuous innovation	Dynamically continuous innovation	Rolling launch
Concept testing	New product development (NPD)	Test marketing

QUESTIONS FOR REVIEW

9.1 What is the difference between *dynamically continuous innovation* and *discontinuous innovation*?

9.2 What is the difference between *reactive* and *proactive* NPD?

9.3 What are the eight stages of the NPD process?

9.4 List as many potential general sources of new product ideas as you can.

9.5 What kind of criteria are likely to be taken into account during the *idea screening* stage?

9.6 What is *concept testing* and why is it a crucial stage in the NPD process?

9.7 How are marketing, production and financial concerns brought together at the *business analysis* stage?

9.8 What might be the main causes of uncertainty at the *business analysis* stage?

9.9 What is the role of the *product development* stage for an fmcg product?

9.10 What is the difference between *outsourced* and *collaborative* R&D?

QUESTIONS FOR DISCUSSION

9.1 Find an example of a new product for each of the *types of newness* categories discussed at pp. 340 *et seq.* What particular marketing problems do you think the organisations launching each of those products might have had?

9.2 What are the potential benefits and pitfalls of using a screening approach based on rating ideas against weighted criteria?

9.3 How might the *product development* stage differ for:

(a) an fmcg product; and
(b) an organisational product?

9.4 To what extent do you think that *test marketing* is a good idea?

9.5 Find examples of two recently launched fmcg products, one of which was given a *full national launch* and the other of which was *rolled out* gradually. Why do you think the particular approach chosen was appropriate for each product?

CASE STUDY 9.1

Media revolution: the big one?

The launch of digital television in the UK in the autumn of 1998 marked the start of another potential revolution that could radically change many aspects of marketing. At the heart of digital television is increasing viewer choice and catering for an increasing number of minority interests through targeted channels. There is little doubt that viewing habits will change and with it advertisers' media selection and spend, and the use of associated technology such as interactive services. There are also implications for the consumer electronics manufacturers who supply televisions, sound systems and video products. Digital transmission is in wide screen format and flat screen technology is also compatible. The issue is not so much whether digital television will succeed as a concept, as just how fast the pace of change is going to be.

Sky Digital (BSkyB) http://www.skydigital.co.uk, launched its digital service first with the promise of 200 audio and visual channels. It was soon followed by ONdigital (http://www.ondigital.co.uk), jointly owned by established broadcasters Granada and Carlton. Whereas Sky relies on satellite dishes, ONdigital concentrated on aerial reception, as aerials still dominate UK viewing, making it the first terrestrial digital service in the world. Both systems require associated equipment as part of the subscription package. Older satellite dishes are not compatible with digital transmission, while ONdigital requires the purchase of a on-set receiver box and thus there is little price differential between the two systems. This could change as the new generation of television sets with built-in receiver boxes is launched. ONdigital wanted to give Sky a run for its money, spending £90mn to promote its launch. It planned to offer only 30 channels, with just 15 available at launch. These included popular favourites such as Sky Sports, UK Gold and The Cartoon Network, as well as news channels from the BBC, ITV and Channel 4.

The key to digital's success will be the rate of its uptake by the consumer. BSkyB predicted that around 50 per cent of homes would have digital television within three to five years and that Sky itself would control a 50 per cent share. In the first month, Sky Digital attracted 100000 subscribers and was predicting a further 200000 within the following two months. To try to achieve this, BSkyB spent £60mn to get subscriptions for Sky Digital, targeting the 75 per cent of homes that did not already subscribe to multi-channel television. The campaign included a 90-second television advertisement, 3500 posters, press advertising, a 32-page supplement to the *Times*, the *Sunday Times* and the *Daily Mail* and £50000 on a website.

Despite all this spending, however, a survey in September 1998 revealed that although 84 per cent of people had heard of digital television, there was still considerable ignorance of the technology needed and the availability of the service. The government has not yet announced when analogue signals will be switched off, but the pundits expect it to happen sometime between 2010 and 2015. As television sets are replaced on average every eight years, over 50 per cent of people should have integrated sets within five years, long before the expected end of analogue transmission.

ONdigital had the potential to reach 60 per cent of homes at launch, but could not produce enough receiver boxes. Only between 10 000 and 20 000 boxes were available at launch and from this stock over 4000 were taken by retailers for display models. The problem was attributed to a shortage of key components and, until it was solved, the number of possible subscribers was very limited. A further 70 000 receivers, however, were expected to be made available in the two months following launch. The rate of take-up might also be affected by the cost of changing televisions. Widescreen televisions are more expensive than conventional sets and integrated sets will attract premium prices for a time. Some people prefer to rent until the market settles down and prices start to fall. Few people want to purchase a television set that could be obsolete in a few years.

The proponents of digital television claim that the main attractions for the viewer will be choice and picture/sound quality. The availability of choice is not disputed, but there are problems in finding the most appropriate channel from the myriad on offer. The biggest aid to the viewer will be electronic programme guides (EPGs), which will generally be the first thing seen when the television is switched on. In time, these EPGs will develop from being mere listings to intelligent systems that can sort by topics such as sport or news and perhaps even guide you to your favourite programme based on previous viewing behaviour. Some, however, think that some of the claims made for digital are exaggerated, especially for pin-sharp pictures and CD-quality sound. Unless the current picture suffers from ghosting or light snowing there could be little discernible improvement and some areas will benefit from digital reception, while others may receive no reception at all.

Sources: Ap Gwilym (1998); Crawford (1998); Crawford and Murphy (1998); Fry (1998); Richards (1998a,1998b); Snoddy (1998).

Questions

1 What factors are likely to influence the rate of acceptance and subscription to digital television?

2 After the events described in this case, both Sky Digital and ONdigital started to give away their dishes/set-top boxes free. What are the advantages and disadvantages of this?

3 To what extent is the introduction of digital television a response to consumer demand?

4 How is digital television likely to affect the market segmentation and targeting strategies of consumer goods manufacturers generally?

CASE STUDY 9.2

Because I'm worth it

French company L'Oréal generates a turnover of over £6bn from its worldwide interests in cosmetics, skincare and haircare markets. Two of its operating divisions within consumer markets are L'Oréal Paris (which owns brands including Elnett, Elvive, Recital, Plénitude and various cosmetics lines) and Laboratoires Garnier (Ambre Solaire, Fructis, Maybelline New York, Belle Color, Nutralia and Synergie, among others). To achieve and maintain its number one position in markets that are moving fast in terms of both technology and fashion, L'Oréal has had to invest heavily in innovation. The company employs more than 2000 chemists, biologists and pharmacists and spends about 3 per cent of turnover on R&D. Unilever and Procter & Gamble, L'Oréal's main competitors, spend only 1.5 per cent and 1.7 per cent respectively of their cosmetics turnover (which is 20 per cent lower than that of L'Oréal in any case). The aim of L'Oréal's R&D is to deliver 2000 new formulae to the marketers, who can then launch 2000 new products every year. Nicolas Rosselli, assistant head of haircare products, said:

> Innovation is our driving force. In the salons of our customers who are professional hairdressers, one sees that there is a marked demand for differentiation. Each customer wants to be able to offer consumers something that the others do not have.

This means that L'Oréal always has to be at the forefront of fashion and has to have new products and services ready to offer when the market wants them.

Some new product ideas are initiated by marketing and R&D then has to be responsive in coming up with a formula. Marketers had noticed, for instance, that young Japanese people were fed up of having black hair but had found that hair colourings used in the West gave very poor results on their hair. R&D took the problem and developed a product that began by bleaching the hair to prepare it to take the desired colour. The resulting Féria range was an instant success. There is not always a quick response, however. Marketers wanted a fruit-based shampoo range and it took R&D 10 years to come up with the formulae for the Fructis range! As well as working on ideas initiated by marketing, it is important for the scientists to have some freedom to work on their own long-term ideas and projects, even if there is no immediately obvious commercial application, which can then be patented to protect them from the competition. L'Oréal owns the patents for around 110 molecules.

There is a delicate balance to be struck between 'creative' R&D, promising long-term solutions, and 'marketing led' R&D, maintaining the impetus to keep launching new commercially viable products, which L'Oréal has tried to find through a three-level structure:

1 *Advanced research*: this is the 'creative' level taking the longer-term view. It is critical for advancing knowledge in the skin, hair and nails areas relevant to L'Oréal; for developing new ingredients; for better understanding and improving the effectiveness of new ingredients and products; and for better understanding their toxicological effects.

2 *Applied research*: this level takes over ideas from both L'Oréal's own advanced research and from what has been done outside the company to refine new raw materials and to put new technology into practice. The manager of applied research said that although it does not take very long to develop and synthesise a molecule, it takes a lot longer to evaluate its effectiveness, mix it with other ingredients to create a useable product, find the means of making it on a commercial scale and get it accepted by the regulatory bodies. It is important that every new L'Oréal product is exciting, offers a new and clear benefit and proves itself acceptable in use. This makes globalisation very complicated, because of diverse regulations, consumers and cultures. Another job for applied research is to watch the competition, examining in detail the world's press, surfing the web and getting hold of other companies' new products. About 1000 arrive every year, and between 700 and 800 of them are examined in minute detail by about 20 people who do nothing else.

3 *Product development*: at this level, formulae are further refined and the products, including the packaging, actually created. Development is especially important as the interface with marketing, and development staff and marketers work closely together. The international

marketing director for Lancôme care products, Marie-Hélène Ahrweiler, is as interested in the science as the marketing: 'I see research every day and our researchers live every day with marketers.' She even takes scientists with her to Japan or to the US, for example, to see what is going on at the point of sale and to look at what sort of competition is there in the store.

Underlying the development work is a clear focus on the product, thanks to continual exchanges between R&D and marketing. It is important that researchers do not lose sight of industrial reality, especially at the applied research and product development levels. Informal contacts are encouraged and it is not unusual to see scientists participating in product launch activities. But there are also more formal contacts. At Lancôme, for example, formal meetings include:

- one day per month to discuss the progress of current projects;
- monthly themed meetings to discuss specific topics, for example wrinkles or greasy skin;
- two or three meetings per year for the scientists to reveal their new goodies to the marketers;
- product launch meetings to agree the scientific and marketing platform for each product;

- an annual strategy meeting with board-level managers to look at plans for the next three to five years.

The reward for all this effort can be very high. The Fructis range, for example, took 10 years to develop and when the tests showed spectacular results on the quality of hair, it was launched in France in July 1996. Within six months, it had sold nearly 5mn units and had captured nearly 8 per cent of the French shampoo market and 14 per cent of the conditioner market. Similar success followed as it was rolled out into international markets, not only in western Europe but also in Scandinavia, Russia and Chile.

Sources: Alexandre (1998); L'Oréal (1998), http://www.loreal.com.

Questions

1 Why is new product development so important for a company like L'Oréal?

2 What are the potential risks of launching up to 2000 products a year into global markets?

3 What do you think are the problems of managing the R&D–marketing interface? Do you think that L'Oréal has solved those problems?

4 To what extent does L'Oréal follow the new product development process outlined in Fig. 9.2?

References to Chapter 9

Abrahams, P. (1998), 'Nintendo's Errors Could Well End up Costing It the Game', *Financial Times*, 17–18 October, p. 21.

Alexandre, R. (1998), 'L'Arme Secrète de L'Oréal', *L'Essentiel du Management*, May, pp. 15–22.

Ap Gwilym, A. (1998), 'Digital TV is upon Us . . . with 140 Channels', *Express*, 27 September, p. 61.

Baxter, R. A. (1995), 'Birthday in Berlin', *Financial Times*, 16 May, p. VII.

Beenstock, S. (1998), 'Spreading the Health Benefit', *Marketing*, 3 December, pp. 18–19.

Bonaccorsi, A. and Lipparini, A. (1994), 'Strategic Partnerships in New Product Development', *Journal of Product Innovation Management*, 11(2), pp. 134–45.

Booz-Allen, Hamilton Inc. (1982), *New Product Management for the 1980s*, Booz-Allen, Hamilton Inc.

Brown, S. and Eisenhart, K. (1995), 'Product Development: Past Research, Present Findings, and Future Directions', *Academy of Management Review*, 20 (2), pp. 343–78.

Caulkin, S. (1994), 'Research into R&D Spending Pays Off', *The Observer*, 19 June, p. 8.

Cookson, C. (1999), 'Development Times Static', *Financial Times*, 15 March, p. III.

Cooper, R. G. and Kleinschmidt, E. J. (1987), 'New Products: What Separates Winners From Losers?', *Journal of Product Innovation Management*, 5 (Sept.), pp. 169–84.

Cowell, D. (1984), *The Marketing of Services*, Butterworth-Heinemann.

Cramb, C. (1999), 'Grolsch Targets Mature Markets', *Financial Times*, 10 February, p. 35.

Crawford, A-M. (1998), 'Sky Digital Aims to Go Upmarket', *Marketing*, 1 October, p. 5.

Crawford, A-M. and Murphy, C. (1998), 'How Marketers Will Tackle Digital', *Marketing*, 1 October, pp. 18–19.

Croft, M. (1998), 'Time to Nurture Creativity', *Marketing Week*, 12 November, pp. 40–1.

Day, J. (1998), 'The Call of the Wild', *Marketing Week*, 25 June, pp. 41–2.

Eason, K. (1998), 'Mercedes Gets Baby out of a Tight Corner', *The Times*, 23 January, p. 7.

Eason, K. and Boyes, R. (1997), 'Costly Mercedes "Baby" Grows into a PR Disaster', *The Times*, 13 November, p. 13.

Elliott, L. and Beavis, S. (1994), 'Feeling Frail After 15 Year Slimdown', *The Guardian*, 8 November, p. 14.

Ford, R. (1994), 'VP185 – Paxman's Powerful New Diesel Engine', *Modern Railways*, March, pp. 141–2.

Fry, A. (1998), 'Channelling Digital Choice', *Marketing*, 24 September, pp. 27–8.

Griffith, V. (1998), 'Turmoil Blunts Gillette's Product Launch', *Financial Times*, 30 September, p. 29.

The Grocer (1996), 'Wonder Spread From Finland', *The Grocer*, 18 May, p. 9.

Hardcastle, S. (1999), 'Giving It a Lot of Stick', *The Grocer*, 20 March, pp. 49–51.

Hart, D. (1998), 'The Virtues of Virtual Reality', *The Grocer*, 11 July, pp. 50–1.

Hart, N. A. (1993), *Industrial Marketing Communications*, Kogan Page.

Houlder, V. (1995a), 'Revolution in Outsourcing', *Financial Times*, 6 January, p. 7.

Houlder, V. (1995b), 'Partners in Innovation', *Financial Times*, 24 March, p. 16.

Hutton, R. (1998), 'Born-again Baby Benz', *Sunday Times*, 1 February, p. 2.24.

Kalish, S. *et al.* (1995), 'Waterfall and Sprinkler New Product Strategies in Competitive Global Markets', *International Journal of Research in Marketing*, 12, pp. 105–19.

Kelly, J. (1998), 'Digging for Scoops', *The Grocer*, 16 May, pp. 42-4.

L'Oréal (1998), advertising supplement to *The Grocer*, 10 October.

Majaro, S. (1991), *The Creative Process*, Allen & Unwin.

Maling, N. (1998), 'Hooch Tries £6m TV Comeback', *Marketing Week*, 26 November, p. 8.

Matthews, V. (1995), 'Innovators Out to Beat the Odds', *Financial Times*, 9 February, p. 19.

Moore, W. L. and Pessmier, E. A. (1993), *Product Planning and Management: Designing and Delivering Value*, McGraw-Hill.

Morley, C. (1999), 'Set For a Splash', *The Grocer*, 3 April, pp. 28–9.

Nuki, P. and Connor, S. (1997), 'Robot Vacuum Cleaner Clears the Decks for Domestic Bliss', *Sunday Times*, 30 November, p. 1.3.

O'Connor, J. and Galvin, E. (1999), *Marketing and Information Technology*, 2nd edn, Financial Times Pitman Publishing.

Oleck, M. (1998), 'Double Viagra with Nuts, Please', *Business Week*, 26 October, p. 4.

Osborn, A. F. (1963), *Applied Imagination*, 3rd edn, Schreiber.

Pettitt, S. J. (1989), *Innovation in Tourism*, Unpublished report for Shannon Development Co., Ireland.

Prigg, M. (1997), 'Lego Toys with Talking Bricks', *Sunday Times*, 30 November, p. 13.

Pring, A. (1999), 'MD Foods Takes Pact out of UK', *The Grocer*, 16 January, p. 5.

Richards, A. (1998a), 'The Digital Deception', *The Express*, 27 September, p. 9.

Richards, A. (1998b), 'OnDigital Seeks Revolution in Middle England', *The Express*, 8 November, p. 61.

Schwartz, D. (1987), *Concept Testing: How to Test New Product Ideas Before You Go to Market*, American Marketing Association.

Simonian, H. (1997), 'Mercedes-Benz "A Class" of its Own', *Financial Times*, 9 September, p. 5.

Smy, L. (1999), 'British Biotec Abandons Development of Key Drug', *Financial Times*, 26 March, p. 21.

Snoddy, R. (1998), 'First Digital TV Service Walks on Air', *Times*, 16 November, p. 4.

Von Hippel, E. (1978), 'Successful Industrial Products from Customers' Ideas', *Journal of Marketing*, 42 (Jan.), pp. 39–49.

Von Hippel, E. (1986), 'Lead users: A Source of Novel New Product Concepts', *Management Science*, 32 (July), pp. 791–805.

Young, R. (1997), 'Robot Vacuum Bites the Dust', *Times*, 1 December, p. 3.

Eidos Interactive Ltd.

Interview with
David Burton, Marketing Manager

Eidos, a global publisher and developer of 'entertainment software', is perhaps best known for its *Tomb Raider* game featuring heroine Lara Croft. In the fast moving games market, Eidos is committed to constant new product development. It indirectly employs over 500 development staff and launches 20 or more games every year. Eidos' marketing manager, David Burton, explained to us how the new product development and launch process takes place, but first told us about the company's perception of its core customers and their relationship with games.

Eidos is targeting different kinds of consumer in different countries. The US consumer, for example, prefers easier games and has more of a taste for action than for problem solving. This is reflected in the marketing approaches and product content which is tailored to suit each market. The UK and German consumers are similar and sophisticated in their tastes, taking a more cerebral approach to a game. The French want games that 'look nice' thus more graphically impressive games tend to have higher profit expectations in that territory. Thus the packaging and the message are also different from market to market. In the USA for instance, the imagery, is more obvious and straightforward on the packaging, and character based rather than setting the scene and the mood. In terms of segmentation, Games Publishers also get information from Sony Computer Entertainment which conducts market research on a quarterly basis across Europe using focus groups, telephone interviewing etc. They have identified types of customer (e.g. 'casual gamers', 'bedroom PlayStations' etc.), their buying and playing patterns and how they are evolving which helps Eidos target its products and devise its marketing strategies.

Having said all that, in general, the product itself is pretty consistent across the world. Compromises are made in the development stages to make a game more or less appropriate for most places, typically voices are dubbed or subtitles added. Difficulty levels can be tweaked but there can be no hard editing because that would have too many knock on effects on continuity within the game.

It takes two very expensive years to develop a game. The normal sequence of events is that the game development team gets a game idea and then Eidos works out how to sell it. It is thus a product-led process and mainly internally orientated. First, the game development team get an idea. This team consists of guys who know the market and are into the comics/games scene themselves. The team is primarily developing games for the hard core gamer who buys 12 or more games per year.

One year into development, the game then goes to 'product testing'. A team of 20 or 30 employees, mainly men aged between 16 and 20, play the game exhaustively, noting any bugs or problems with it and making suggestions as to how the game-play, user interface and general entertainment experience can be improved. 'Real customers' do not get involved until late in the process when Eidos is committed to the development of the game. It is not unknown for games to be shelved late in their development if it is felt they will not be a 'winner', though this is rare.

'Producers' monitor the whole process and look at costs, quality, and timescales etc. Are the developers working to the original brief? What feedback have we had? Is any updating or adaptation necessary? A game can be delayed for a year, for example, because new technology comes in and the whole thing has to be upgraded. Early adopters buy the new upgraded hardware and so games have to be upgraded too sometimes even before launch. There is thus a strong relationship between the software and the hardware. The hardware companies need big games or else their consoles will not sell. They are looking at the price and quality of the games. Sony and other hardware companies do not contribute to game development costs although they will supply the hardware for the development process. Eidos is always looking at new hardware and technology to take advantage of, but waits until it is sure that it has achieved penetration into a critical mass of homes before adopting it.

The marketing run-in starts ahead of the launch. Game Development teams may be keen to add to their creation right up to the last minute before its scheduled completion date, and getting them to call it a day and wrap up the game can be a challenge. Thus the teams are incentivised positively and negatively to achieve complete on time. The marriage of high tech and creativity is an uneasy one, and it is hard to bring all the elements together on schedule.

EXECUTIVE INTERVIEW continued

To try to get away from the product-led approach, a game called *Saboteur* was designed in reverse to a 'recipe' developed from popular, proven action/adventure titles. Eidos concluded that such a product needed:

- *passion*: Saboteur is based on a Bruce Lee type of film. The hero's father has been killed and his sister kidnapped and so he is out for revenge.
- *hand to hand combat*
- *a unique feature*: in this case, the unique feature is the hero's dog which is part of the action and can be made to perform.

Whichever way round the development process works, 95% of the marketing effort is put into the launch. Once a game is out, the media interest wains and using chart-track reports Eidos knows within 2 weeks whether a game is a retail winner or not. Launch costs vary running as high as £1mn for a UK campaign. The two main communications spending areas are on co-operative advertising with the trade and then specialist print and television media. PR, both internal and external is also very important. Within broad parameters, the launch budget is determined on a percentage of predicted sales or forecast revenue. It is difficult to forecast because lots of games are being launched all the time. Much depends on what else is being launched at the same time as a product, particularly rival games of the same genre. The success of a game also depends on what is happening in the wider entertainment field. Games are competing for a mind share of the consumer's leisure time. Thus if a good film has just been released, that can have a negative effect on time spent gaming, whereas if the weather is bad during the summer, that can have a positive effect.

The retail shelf life of a PC or console game can be as short as 90 days and most profit is made within this period. Given the potential brevity of the product life-cycle, lead times between ordering and production are very short, a matter of days. Stock outs are rare but short-lived, and are most likely to occur around the Christmas rush. The life-cycle can be extended by re-releasing re-packaged games, for instance under the Eidos 'Premier' brand name at a budget value for money price level. This catches the new users or laggards. Compilations, i.e. packaging a couple of previously released titles together also works. Games are sold at a standard trade price and it is up to the retailer to set a retail price from there. There are standard benchmarks for pricing in different markets, though there are no huge pricing differences between them, particulary as Eidos does not want to encourage 'grey imports' and upset its retail customers!

In terms of distribution channels, once upon a time specialist independent retailers were the largest buying group, but the entry of retailers like Virgin, Game and HMV in recent years means that most sales now come from high street multiples. Internationally, exclusive distributorships are sometimes awarded in a particular country. The biggest Europen markets are Germany, France, Italy, Spain and Scandinavia. Eidos has been one of the last companies to get into direct sales over the Internet. The UK does, however, supply mail order and on-line sales companies.

Every new product is a gamble and success cannot be guaranteed. One of Eidos' biggest successes, however, has been *Tomb Raider*. Eidos wanted a different action-character and so went for a sexy female, Lara Croft. The games enormous popularity took the company by surprise. Eidos believe that while many factors contributed, a major factor may be that male fans have developed an emotional bond with Lara; an element of protectiveness, 'caring for her', in the player's mind. Interestingly, Lara also appeals to female players, 20% of *Tomb Raider* sales are made to women, the largest segment for any game.

As well as the product benefits of entertainment, excitement and testing problem solving skills, there were several other factors in the success of *Tomb Raider*:

- its superior technology which it has managed to retain through from *Tomb Raider 1* to *Tomb Raider 4*, thus keeping ahead of the competition
- the Lara appeal: this has led to an urban myth that there are secret codes built into the program relating to sex. It's not true!
- its launch coinciding with the emergence of the 'girl power' zeitgeist.
- *Tomb Raider* appeals to a wider family market that might, for instance, only be buying a game or two at Christmas and its income facilitates other new product developments. Paramount is making the *Tomb Raider* film and it is hoped that this will have a positive impact on the brand.

For the future, downloading games from the Internet is a possibility, but Eidos believes that there will always be a market for boxed games because it represents a tangible product and is more 'real' (cf. real books vs. on screen text). The interactive Entertainment industry is still in its infancy, a maximum of 15 years old, with a lot of young people working in it who have not experienced any other types of business. Eidos itself is a young firm which has experienced tremendous growth in its four years of existence and feels that the industry does have a bright future: 'the interactive experience has very few limits, its appeal will never go away'.

With grateful thanks to David Burton, Marketing Manager of Eidos Interactive Ltd.

Part IV

PRICE

It is natural to assume that the price of a product is very closely related to the cost of producing it. Since the purpose of marketing is to create and hold a customer at a profit, pricing policies have to reflect a reward to the organisation for its efforts. Manufacturing costs, however, are only the beginning of the story. Chapter 10 looks into a number of influences on pricing decisions, such as distribution channels, long-term marketing and corporate objectives, competitor pricing and customer expectations, and finds that it is far from being a simple arithmetic 'cost plus' calculation.

Price is an important indicator of the positioning of the product for potential customers who sometimes have too little experience of the product or the market to judge it by other factors. Price is often equated with quality or used as a means of comparing competing products. For some products, such as motor insurance, price can even be the primary criterion for choice with wide implications for the organisation. A price-sensitive market means that the organisation might have to find ways of cutting costs or increasing volume to maintain profits or it might be able to use creative marketing to reposition into less sensitive segments.

Linking with this, Chapter 11 examines the rationale behind a number of pricing strategies open to organisations, from deliberately setting high prices through to aggressive low-price strategies. Pricing can also be used as a short-term tactical tool, as a means of diverting customers' attention away from competitive products, for example, and trying to influence their behaviour. Whatever is done, however, pricing must be consistent with the message generated by the other elements of the marketing mix or else the buyer may become confused or suspicious.

10 Pricing: Context and Concepts

LEARNING OBJECTIVES

This chapter will help you to:

1 define the meaning of price;

2 understand the different roles price can play for buyers and sellers and in different kinds of market;

3 appreciate the nature of the external factors that influence pricing decisions;

4 explore the internal organisational forces that influence pricing decisions;

5 understand the impact of the single European market and the euro on pricing.

INTRODUCTION

At first glance, **price** might seem to be the least complicated and perhaps the least interesting element of the marketing mix, not having the tangibility of the product, the glamour of advertising or the atmosphere of retailing. It does, however, play a very important role in the lives of both marketers and customers, and deserves as much strategic consideration as any other marketing tool. Price not only directly generates the revenues that allow organisations to create and retain customers at a profit (in accordance with one of the definitions of marketing in Chapter 1), but can also be used as a communicator, as a bargaining tool and as a competitive weapon. The customer can use price as a means of comparing products, judging relative value for money or judging product quality.

Ultimately, the customer is being asked to accept the product offering and (usually) to hand money over in exchange for it. If the product has been carefully thought out with the customer's needs in mind, if the distribution channels chosen are convenient and appropriate to that customer, if the promotional mix has been sufficiently seductive, then there is a good chance that the customer will be willing to hand over some amount of money for the pleasure of owning that product. But even then, the price that is placed on the product is crucial: set too high a price, and the customer will reject the offering and all the good work done with the rest of the marketing mix is wasted; too low, and the customer is suspicious ('too good to be true'). What constitutes 'a high price' or 'a low price' depends on the buyer, and has to be put into the context of their perceptions of themselves, of the entire marketing package and of the competitors' offerings. Pricing has a spurious certainty about it because it involves numbers, but do not be misled by this; it is as emotive and as open to misinterpretation as any other marketing activity.

It is thus important for the marketer to understand the meaning of price from the customer's point of view, and to price products in accordance with the 'value' that the customer places on the benefits offered.

> **Example** An ordinary Barbie doll sells through the toys section of a mail order catalogue for between £3.99 and £9.99, depending on her outfit. A Barbie doll dressed as Scarlett O'Hara from the film *Gone With the Wind* was sold through an advertisement in a Sunday newspaper colour supplement for £69.95. The higher price was justified because the Scarlett doll was a limited edition collector's item, with her own certificate of authenticity, and her dress had been copied exactly from the film. The advertisement sold Scarlett as an heirloom or as an investment, suggesting that it was possible that her value might increase over time. It was not a toy, and thus the features and benefits offered were very different from those offered by the £3.99 doll and valued much more highly by the adult target market.

This chapter expands on these initial concepts of price. It will look further at what price is, and what it means to marketers and customers in various contexts. It will also examine more closely the role of price in the marketing mix, and how it interacts with other marketing activities. This sets the scene for a focus on some of the internal factors and external pressures that influence pricing thinking within an organisation. The final section of the chapter tackles some of the issues affecting pricing on a Europe-wide basis.

THE ROLE AND PERCEPTION OF PRICE

Price is the *value* that is placed on something. What is someone prepared to give in order to gain something else? Usually, price is measured in money, as a convenient medium of exchange that allows prices to be set quite precisely. This is not necessarily always the case, however. Goods and services may be bartered ('I will help you with the marketing plan for your car repair business if you service my car for me'), or there may be circumstances where monetary exchange is not appropriate, for example at election time when politicians make promises in return for your vote. Any such transactions, even if they do not directly involve money, are exchange processes and thus can use marketing principles (go back to Chapter 1 for the discussion of marketing as an exchange process). Price is any common currency of value to both buyer and seller.

Even money-based pricing comes under many names, depending on the circumstances of its use: solicitors charge fees; landlords charge rent; bankers charge interest; railways charge fares; hotels charge a room rate; consultants charge retainers; agents charge commission; insurance companies charge premiums; and over bridges or through tunnels tolls may be charged. Whatever the label, it is still a price for a good or a service, and the same principles apply.

Price does not necessarily mean the same things to different people, just because it is usually expressed as a number. You have to look beyond the price, at what it represents to both the buyer and the seller if you want to grasp its significance in any transaction. Buyer and seller may well have different perspectives on what price means. We now turn to that of the buyer.

The customer's perspective

From the buyer's perspective, price represents the value they attach to whatever is being exchanged. Up to the point of purchase, the marketer has been making promises to the potential buyer about what this product is and what it can do for that customer. The customer is going to weigh up those promises against the price and decide whether it is worth paying (Zeithaml, 1988).

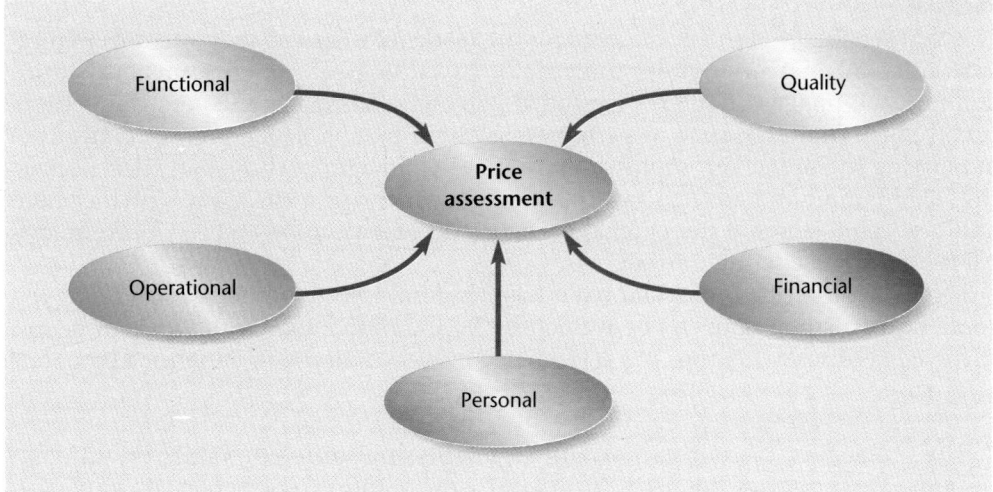

FIGURE 10.1

Factors influencing customers' price assessments

In assessing price, the customer is looking specifically at the expected benefits of the product, as shown in Fig. 10.1.

Functional

Functional benefits relate to the design of the product and its ability to fulfil its desired function. For example, a washing machine's price might be judged on whether or not it can handle different washing temperatures, operate economically and dry as well as wash.

Quality

The customer may expect price to reflect the quality level of the product (Erickson and Johansson, 1985). Thus a customer may be prepared to pay more for leather upholstery in a car, or for solid wood furniture rather than veneer, or for hand-made Belgian chocolates rather than mass produced. Quality perceptions may be to do with the materials or components used in the product, as in these examples, or with the labour involved in making it. Quality may also, however, be a less tangible judgement made on the basis of corporate image. BMW, Heinz and Cadbury's are perceived as quality companies, and therefore they are perceived as producing quality products. The consumer can thus accept that those organisations might charge higher prices.

Operational

In organisational markets, price may be judged in relation to the product's ability to influence the production process. For example, a new piece of machinery might be assessed on its ability to increase productivity, make the production line more efficient or reduce the labour content of the finished goods. Even in a consumer market, operational issues might be considered. For instance, the purchase of a microwave oven increases the operational efficiency of the kitchen, both making it easier to cater for the staggered mealtimes resulting from the modern family's fragmented lifestyle, and giving the chief cook more time to pursue other interests.

Financial

Particularly in organisational markets, many purchases are seen as investments, and therefore the expected return on that investment is important in judging whether the price is worthwhile or not. New machinery, for example, is expected to pay for itself over time in terms of increased efficiency, output, labour saving etc. Note that this judgement is made not only in terms of production outputs, but also in terms of long-term cost savings, efficiency gains and productivity improvements.

Personal

Personal benefit is a difficult category for the marketer to gauge, as it attempts to measure price against intangible, individual, psychological benefits such as status, comfort, self-image (Chapter 3 reminded you about these benefits) etc. Some high-involvement products, such as perfumes, use high pricing deliberately as a means of amplifying the upmarket, sophisticated, exclusive images portrayed in their packaging, distribution and advertising strategies, thus increasing the status enhancement and 'feel good' factor of the purchase. Chapter 11 will examine aspects of psychological factors in price setting further.

Remember too that organisational markets are not immune from the effects of personal factors. Purchasing can be influenced by the individual motivations of people involved (as discussed at pp. 165 *et seq.*), and even by a desire to enhance a corporate self-image.

The problem is, of course, that different buyers put different values on different benefits. This endorses the need for market segmentation (*see* Chapter 5), which can begin to sort out groupings of like-minded customers so that appropriately tailored marketing mixes (including price) can be developed.

So far, it has been assumed that **price perceptions** and judgements of value are constant in the mind of the potential buyer. They are, however, variable according to circumstances. For example, a householder thinking of replacing water pipes would probably be very price sensitive and get quotes from a number of plumbers before making a decision. A burst pipe in the winter, however, would have that same householder paying almost any price to get a plumber round immediately. In any such distress purchase, the value placed on immediate problem solution justifies paying a **premium price**.

Another factor influencing price perception is scarcity. Where supply is severely limited and demand is high, prices can take on a life of their own and begin to spiral.

The seller's perspective

Price is a distinctive element of the marketing mix for the *seller*, because it is the only one that generates revenue. All the other elements represent outgoing costs. Price is also important, therefore, because it provides the basis of both recovering those costs and creating profit.

MARKETING IN ACTION Putting you in the picture

Camera manufacturers produce wide ranges of products, priced differently, to cater for different segments' needs. At the bottom end of the market is the customer who sees a camera simply as a means to an end. This customer wants to capture a moment and does not want to get too involved in how that is done. The camera should be unobtrusive but do all the work. This provides the basis for the compact cameras with 35 mm lens, built-in flash, auto focus, motorised advance and rewind, which retail for between £25 and £200. The serious amateur, on the other hand, may be interested in the process of taking the picture, and thus wish to have some involvement and control over the composition and technical specifications of the photo. SLR cameras catering for this market allow lenses with different focal lengths to be attached, allowing the photographer control over shutter speed and light metering and allow the choice of automatic or manual focusing. These customers want 'photographs' rather than 'snapshots' and because they appreciate the role of the camera in creating a good photo, they want more quality, durability, features and benefits. This means that they will be prepared to pay more for their cameras than the 'snapshotter' will, and thus SLR cameras retail at various levels from £200 up to £2000 or more. The snapshotter would find such a camera too complicated, bulky, time consuming and irritating to use and would thus not value its features and benefits so highly.

Example Tickets for the 64 soccer matches in the 1998 World Cup in France were scarce. It was alleged that over half of the 2.5 million tickets available for the 64 matches had gone to French fans one way or another, and then after foreign soccer federations and tour operators had received their share, only 110 000 tickets were left for sale to individual fans all over the world. It was estimated that on the first day that these tickets went on sale, 20 million callers tried to get through to a telephone hotline with only 90 operators! Not surprisingly, tickets for the big games became hot property. A couple of days before the England vs Argentina match, tickets were changing hands on the black market for £700 each. Some Argentinean supporters simply could not afford that, having already paid up to £1000 for a ticket for Argentina's first-round match against Japan (Gwin, 1998; Lee, 1998).

$$\text{Profit} = \text{Total Revenue} - \text{Total Cost,}$$

where total revenue is the quantity sold multiplied by the unit price, and total cost represents the costs of producing, marketing and selling the product. Quantity sold is itself dependent on price as well as on the other marketing mix elements. The motor industry has suggested that although a car dealership selling a large number of cars every year could well generate 80 per cent of its turnover from car sales, it is generating only just over one-third of its total profits from those sales. In comparison, the workshop might only generate 5 per cent of turnover, but 25 per cent of profit. This reflects the fact that for some products, competitive pressures may keep margins tight. To increase profit in such areas, therefore, the organisation may have to find a way of either reducing the costs involved, or justifying higher prices.

The seller, however, must always take care to think about price from the perspective of the customer. In pure economic terms, it would be assumed that reducing a price would lead to higher sales because more people could then afford and want the product. As the introduction to this chapter suggested, however, a low price may be interpreted as making a negative statement about the product's quality, and a sudden reduction in price of an established product may be taken to mean that the product's quality has been compromised in some way. Even petrol, the stereotypical homogeneous product, has been a victim of this.

Similarly, a high price may not always be a bad thing for a seller. If buyers equate price with quality (and in the absence of information or knowledge of the market, it may be the only indicator they pick up), then a higher price might actually attract customers. Part of the psychological benefit of the purchase for the customer might well be derived from its expense, for example in purchasing gifts where one feels obliged to spend a certain amount on the recipient either to fulfil social expectations or to signal affection. The higher the price, the more exclusive the market segment able to afford the product or service. Many more rail travellers, for example, choose to travel second class than in the higher-priced first-class accommodation.

Photographs, and not 'snapshots', are what this camera's buyers are paying for.

Source: Olympus Optical Company (UK) Ltd.

The seller also needs to remember that sometimes the cost to the customer of purchasing a product can be much greater than its price. These broader considerations might have an inhibiting effect on purchase. A consumer buying a DVD player for the first time, for example, will not only look at the ticket price of the machine, but also weigh up the costs of replacing favourite video cassettes with discs. A business buying a new computer system has to consider the costs of transferring records, staff training and the initial decrease in productivity as they learn to find their way around the new system and the costs of installation (and of removing the

old equipment). The whole marketing strategy for a product has to recognise the real cost to the customer of accepting the offering and work to overcome such objections, whether through pricing, a better-tailored product offering or effective communication and persuasion.

Example The roller towel had been replaced by hot-air dryers and paper towels in many organisations' washrooms on the basis that these were cheaper, easier to service and more hygienic. The cotton towel industry has fought back, however, demonstrating that when consumables, transport, labour, dispenser costs and disposal are taken into account, the roller towel system can be up to 58 per cent cheaper to operate per month (Smith, 1994). Added to that, the industry has improved the design of roller dispenser cabinets and the laundering standards to overcome the poor hygiene image, and has proved that cotton is much more efficient and consistent at drying. In industries such as food processing, catering and pharmaceuticals where hygiene standards are becoming increasingly stringent, and in a world where environmental friendliness is a serious concern, it is not surprising that the combination of cost advantage and performance benefits found in cotton roller towels is irresistible!

Whatever type of market an organisation is in, whatever market segments it seeks to serve, it must always be aware that price can never stand apart from the other elements of the marketing mix. It interacts with those elements and must, therefore, give out signals consistent with those given by the product itself, place and promotion. Price is often quoted as a reason for not purchasing a product, but this reflects a tendency to use price as a scapegoat for other failings in the marketing mix. Price is a highly visible factor and at the point of purchase it hits the buyer where it hurts – in the pocket. As has been said before in this chapter, if the rest of the marketing mix has worked well up to the point of sale, then the price should not be too great an issue, because the buyer will have been convinced that the benefits supplied are commensurate with the price asked. Price is seen here as a natural, integrated element in harmony with the rest of the offering. It could be argued that a buyer who is wavering and uses price as the ultimate determinant of whether to purchase is either shopping in the wrong market segment or being ill served by sloppy marketing.

PRICING CONTEXTS

This section summarises the impact on pricing of the issues and characteristics prevailing in various kinds of market. It highlights the fact that pricing is not just a cost-driven exercise, but a skill that requires knowledge and understanding of both the customer and the external environment.

Consumer markets

There is much competition for *consumers'* disposable income. This is reflected in both the range of different product markets available for them to spend in and the variety of products competing in any one market. Consumers also have a great deal of discretion over whether they spend or not. There are very few real necessities and, on many occasions, consumers buy because they want to, rather than because they need to.

Also, as a result of the fact that consumers are largely buying to please themselves, their assessment of competing products in most markets is often informal, irrational or even non-existent. As discussed in Chapter 3, psychological factors can play a much greater role than analytical skills. Even where hard product information is provided, the consumer does not necessarily make the effort to digest it properly or retain it. It may simply be used selectively as support for a decision that has already been made. Price too, as has already been pointed out, may be interpreted variously, depending on the individual customer. If you want the product badly enough, then you will justify the expense somehow.

All of this makes it very difficult to identify scope for *price negotiation* and, indeed, in most consumer markets, the unit price of the goods is so low that there is no need for such a tool. The price is on the product; take it or leave it. There are some exceptions, however. Consumers expect to negotiate the price of a new car with the dealer, and the dealer recognises this and sets the opening price at a level where he can afford to be beaten down 10 or 15 per cent. This has almost taken on the aura of a ritual and, in many cases, it actually adds to the psychological benefits of car buying because consumers feel that they have been astute enough to drive a hard bargain, which enhances their self-image.

Nevertheless, price is still an important element of the consumer product's marketing mix. **Price banding** can be a useful addition to a market segmentation exercise, as a segment that is prepared to spend £10 to £20 on a product needs to be served differently from a segment prepared to pay £30 to £40. In making planned purchases of clothes, for example, consumers will sometimes decide to buy a certain item and set the price band within which they are prepared to shop. They then seek out the item within the band that offers the best value in terms of colour, fabric, style etc. If they cannot find anything satisfactory within that band, only then will they consider shifting to another price band.

A consumer for whom price is the primary consideration in comparing competing offerings is said to be **price sensitive**. In dealing with such consumers, marketers have to be particularly careful to get the price right because customers are less likely to be seduced by non-price factors into moving outside their preconceived price band.

Example In the tyre market, the budget segment represented something like 25 per cent of the European market in 1995, largely thanks to the increasing number of own brands and the influx of cheaper non-European products. In response to this, the manufacturers of the top brands expanded their product ranges to cater for the price-sensitive segment, either by manufacturing own brands for tyre retailers, or by creating new budget brands. In 1995, for example, Michelin and Continental agreed to produce and distribute jointly a low-cost brand. Many tyre manufacturers also have own brand supply agreements. Goodyear manufactures the Suburbanite brand for the UK wholesaler Tyreco Trading, Rainbow for the French Arc-en-Ciel retailing group, and also manufactures for the Swiss ESA buying group. This last agreement has the potential to open up a wide own brand market for Goodyear because ESA is a member of the Tecar buying co-operative with 5500 partners across France, Germany, Switzerland, Austria, Italy and Denmark. It would thus be very lucrative for Goodyear if the ESA deal could be expanded to the other Tecar members. The own brand market thus allows the manufacturers to participate in the budget end of the market without compromising their premium brand images. As the marketing and sales director of Pirelli Reifenwerk in Germany was quoted as saying:

'A top of the line brand will never or only seldom be an option for the price conscious consumer. However, we don't want to overlook this price sensitive market segment, leaving it to bargain suppliers'

Source: Davis (1995).

Price sensitivity can, therefore, be a meaningful way of differentiating between groups of customers.

Retail and wholesale markets

Retail and wholesale markets take a far more rational approach to price interpretation than do consumer groups. As intermediaries, they have to look in two directions, at both the manufacturer and the consumer. They have to be realistic about what price they themselves can charge for a product to their customers, and this in turn establishes what kind of price they are looking to pay to the manufacturer, if they are to maintain a reasonable profit margin. This price also needs to reflect the services in respect of selling the product that the intermediary has to perform.

Looking in the opposite direction at the consumer, retailers and wholesalers will also expect pricing structures to reflect demand. For example, if a product is going to have mass-market appeal and will sell in high volumes, then the intermediaries will need to be able to sell it at a competitive price, especially if it is a new brand entering an established market.

Price discipline is also expected, in the sense that manufacturers should not be seen to be selling direct to the public at lower prices than the retailers could set. Price discipline sometimes goes further than this, and retailers become upset if they think that manufacturers are selling to other retailers at lower prices. The major UK supermarket chains, for example, were incensed when they thought that manufacturers were selling branded lines to warehouse clubs such as Costco more cheaply than to themselves. The manufacturers justified any lower prices on the basis of the quantities ordered. Manufacturers also expect price discipline from retailers, however. Kellogg's decision to stop supplying a discount chain because it was selling Kellogg's products at below cost was upheld in the courts.

Intermediaries are also knowledgeable about alternative product offerings and will therefore use price as a bargaining weapon where they can. Manufacturers in turn may well be willing to make price concessions in order to gain distribution through a powerful retail chain. Another means by which the retailer can keep prices lower is by offering own-brand goods. These compete directly with the manufacturers' brands, but tend to be sold at lower prices. Where a market is under severe price pressure, manufacturers may have to rethink their product policies. Chapters 12 and 13 explore many of these points in more detail, looking closely at the often complex relationships between manufacturers, intermediaries and consumers.

Service markets

Services, as Chapter 22 will show, are different from tangible goods. Because a service is intangible, it is very difficult to assess its quality before purchasing it. Often, **price comparison** is the nearest a potential buyer can get to working out the relative quality of similar competing offerings. A hungry traveller stopping in a strange town may be faced with two restaurants on opposite sides of the road. Both have similar menus, both look to be equally clean, attractive and well patronised. The traveller may then look at their relative prices and decide that the more expensive of the two might give bigger portions, use better ingredients or offer better service.

Another peculiar feature of services is that they are perishable, in that they happen at a particular time and place and, if there is no customer there, the 'product' is lost. A service is not like a packet of cornflakes that can sit on a supermarket shelf until it is sold. If, for example, there are empty seats on a flight from Amsterdam to Berlin, then those unsold tickets represent wasted product and therefore lost revenue because that same flight can never take place again. Pricing, however, can help to ensure that these losses are minimised. Reducing the cost of a ticket as the flight time gets closer may encourage someone to purchase it. The airline may not make as much profit on that ticket as it would like, but as long as it is covering its variable costs and making a contribution to fixed costs and profit, then that is better than no sale at all.

MARKETING IN ACTION   The sweet smell of success?

Demand for honey appears to have been quite sticky, despite changes in prices. Total worldwide demand has varied little over recent years, but fluctuations in price can be very high. In 1995, for example, prices rose by 50 per cent because of poor harvests from the main producers as hurricanes, droughts and disease all took their toll on production.

European honey production is small compared with China's (140 000 tonnes) and Russia's (about 231 000 tonnes). The UK's 1500 main apiarists (including 10 big producers), for example, produce only about 3000 tonnes per year, worth about £12mn. European production has been hit hard by disease. The Varroa mite, which wipes out bee colonies, made its first European appearance in Germany in the 1970s. Since then, about 40 per cent of German beekeepers have gone out of business. Varroa arrived in the UK in 1992 and within five years had spread to 51 counties in England and Wales. In Hampshire, 70 per cent of colonies were lost because of it in 1995/96. Only Ireland and Scotland are free of the mite in Europe.

Manmade problems arise too. In early 1998, the French government launched an investigation into 'mad bee disease', which had wiped out over one-third of France's 30 000 tonne honey output. It is thought to be caused by an insecticide which affects the bee's sense of direction, so the bee cannot find its way back to the hive and dies. Problems do not just exist in Europe, however. There are between 3000 and 3500 apiarists producing between 2000 and 3000 tonnes of honey per year in South Africa. South African production has been hit not only by the Varroa mite, but also by African killer bees that interbreed with the honey bees and make them more aggressive,

more likely to migrate away from the hive and likely to produce less honey. An estimated 500-tonne honey shortage in South Africa in 1998, therefore, prompted the government to issue permits to import natural honey.

When production falls but demand does not, prices are likely to rise partly through domestic producers having to raise prices to cover their costs and partly through the cost of imports to fill the gap. Germany, for example, is the leading nation in per capita consumption of honey for spreading and in cooking, demanding 90 000 tonnes every year, and yet only 20 000 tonnes of that comes from home producers. The rest is imported mainly from Mexico and Argentina. Honey packers and importers are in the front line in adapting to changes in prices. The price of Chinese honey in the mid-1990s was around $1200 per tonne, although it had earlier dropped as low as $700 per tonne. Since China is the market leader, producers from Argentina, Mexico and Australia tend to follow Chinese prices. The Chinese government imposed a system of export licences to seek to stabilise prices, since the price of honey has a direct effect on the level of interest shown in beekeeping by Chinese farmers.

Another factor influencing European prices for honey has been the success of Chinese producers in meeting the product range requirements and quality levels demanded by the US market. The increase in Chinese exports to the USA means that there is less available for export to Europe, increasing prices. Supply-side considerations thus tend to be the main influences on honey prices, as well as the lead taken by the major producing nations.

Sources: Guild (1996); Heath (1998); MacIntyre (1998); Mead (1997); van Zyl (1998).

An airline represents service marketing on a very large scale, with many skilled employees able to deliver consistent quality service to many customers simultaneously. Many service businesses, particularly in the field of personal services such as hairdressing or dentistry, are reliant on the skills of one or two individual service providers. In such cases, price may be used as a means of restricting demand, by excluding those who cannot afford the price (or those who do not place sufficient value on that service).

Non-profit markets

Non-profit organisations, discussed further in Chapter 22, differ in that they see themselves as existing and operating for the benefit of the public rather than for the creation of profits. Their objectives, therefore, are to encourage people to use their services or products, or to participate in their activities. Pricing can have a major role in achieving that, if goods and services are sold at cost or subsidised to a point where they are visibly below market rates. Some activities, such as minority interest arts events, could not be produced on a commercial basis unless ticket prices were astronomically high, and therefore public subsidy or sponsorship is essential to keep prices down to an affordable and accessible level.

Public benefit need not always be about increasing and encouraging demand. Environmental awareness means that many pressure groups are concerned about the impact of visitor numbers on popular beauty spots. The provision of access, facilities and amenities, along with the erosion of footpaths, has a devastating effect on the place. This has led to consideration of using entry fees or high car-parking fees as a means of discouraging visitors. Similarly, in the years before it pedestrianised the city centre, the city of Oxford implemented very high car parking charges to deter shoppers from bringing their cars into a congested city centre and to encourage the use of 'park and ride' public transport. Zermatt has gone one step further and has banned all vehicles unless they have a special permit. This is to protect the local environment and the ambience of the town, in view of the large number of tourists who visit the area every year.

Unlike the practice in most ordinary consumer markets, where the price is directly exchanged between buyer and seller, in the non-profit sector price sometimes passes through a third party. When this happens it can blunt the consumer's price sensitivity. Where medical services are paid for through an insurance policy, for example, the consumer can begin to think that the visit to the doctor is 'free' and the connection between the service and its price is lost. Such disconnection can lead to overuse of a 'free' service, causing pricing problems for the service provider. Next year's insurance premiums rise to compensate and consumers grumble about it, becoming even more determined to get their money's worth.

In public services, paid for through taxation, moves have been made to reduce the disconnection between price and service by imposing direct charges that contribute towards the cost of maintaining and improving service provision. Prescription charges made under the UK's National Health Service do not in most cases cover the full cost of the drugs supplied, but contribute towards it and remind the user that the service is not 'free'. In some cases, the charges levied do not even recoup the costs of collecting them, such as the tolls on the Humber Bridge. Raising these charges to a more economic level would potentially cause both political difficulties and public outcry, as happened when the tolls were set on the newly opened Skye bridge. In France, however, the tolls on the Loire bridge between St Nazaire and St Brevin have been abolished to encourage economic regeneration in the region. The private consortium that built the bridge still had 16 years left of its rights to collect tolls, but the two local authorities concerned bought up those rights, thus giving them the freedom to drop the toll.

Organisational markets

In organisational markets, the difference between price and real cost is particularly marked. As mentioned above at p. 385–6, the costs of installation, training, scrap, financing etc. are all used to put the price of major purchases into perspective. Add to this the costs and risks incurred if it turns out that a bad purchasing decision has been made, and you can begin to appreciate why organisational buyers spend so much time and effort analysing potential purchases from all angles. It is rarely the case that the lowest price on paper wins the order. Deeper analysis may reveal that the lowest price actually incurs the highest cost. Mehta (1995), for example, in discussing capital investments, suggests 12 points that affect the total cost and that should form part of the buying centre's evaluation criteria. These points refer to technological and commercial factors, and are listed in Table 10.1.

An organisation's sensitivity to price may well vary according to the type of item being purchased. More time will be spent considering the price of a component (such as an aircraft engine) that represents a high percentage of the cost of the finished product than on one that represents a fraction of 1 per cent (such as the rivets that hold the engine on the aircraft).

Many organisations try to eliminate unnecessary cost and waste by using **value management**. Value management involves teams who look very closely at processes and products to analyse where the greatest costs are being incurred, and where the greatest value is added. This focuses attention on the critical areas of the production process where cost savings in terms of bought-in components, production methods or systems will yield the greatest benefits. Value management teams are likely to include members from all the different organisational functions, as well as possibly representatives of suppliers' companies. Once priority areas for cost saving have been identified, the supplier can be instrumental in helping to find solutions, perhaps by looking critically at its own cost profile or by working co-operatively with the buyer to develop new, more efficient components. It has been claimed that value management can achieve savings of between 20 per cent and 30 per cent of the cost of bought-in parts (*Purchasing and Supply Management*, 1995).

It is also characteristic of organisational markets that many prices are negotiated, particularly with critical components, custom-made goods, or high-volume bulk purchases. It is common to find that purchases are put out to tender, putting the onus on the seller to design an acceptable offering at a good value price. Both of these areas are considered in Chapters 11 and 14.

TABLE 10.1

Technological and commercial factors affecting the total cost of a capital investment

1	Cost of necessary accessories to achieve full capacity	Transport; installation; commissioning costs; manuals
2	Cost and need for spares	Cost of spares including sourcing; importing; delivery time/cost
3	Actual performance of same equipment in other companies	Assess reliability; running costs; operator problems; maintenance
4	Demonstration and guarantees	Supplier's ability to 'prove' what the equipment can do; promises on spares availability; servicing
5	Eco-friendliness	Dust, noise, smoke, fumes and other pollutant outputs; cost of safe effluent disposal
6	Safety	Safety of operators and others; long- and short-term effects on health
7	Cost of providing special operating conditions	Provision of new facilities, e.g. air conditioning or pressurised chamber
8	Any supplier's costs associated with installation/trials	Travel and accommodation costs incurred while supplier sets up equipment and runs tests. Is the buyer responsible for this?
9	Training costs	Training operators; costs incurred until they become efficient and achieve output/quality level required
10	Other service costs	Other service needed during installation
11	After-sales service costs	Repairs; maintenance; downtime while awaiting repair
12	Cost of preventive maintenance	Frequency of servicing required; complexity and time needed for scheduled maintenance; cost of downtime and staffing

Source: adapted from Mehta (1995).

All of this highlights one of the distinctions between consumer and organisational markets: consumer markets tend towards fixed prices set and controlled by the seller, whereas organisational markets tend to operate more flexibly, with the buyer having a lot more bargaining power.

EXTERNAL INFLUENCES ON THE PRICING DECISION

The previous sections of this chapter have shown that there is more to pricing than meets the eye. It is not a precise science because of the complexities of the marketing environment and the human perceptions of the parties involved in the marketing exchange. There will always be some uncertainty over the effect of a pricing decision, whether on distribution channels, competitors or the customer. Nevertheless, to reduce that uncertainty, it is important to analyse the range of issues affecting pricing decisions. Some of these are internal to the selling organisation, and are thus perhaps more predictable, but others arise from external pressures, and are therefore more difficult to define precisely. There is also some variation in the extent to which the organisation can control or influence these issues. Figure 10.2 summarises the main areas of *external influence*, while this section of the chapter defines them and gives an overview of their impact on the pricing decision, in preparation for the more detailed scrutiny of price setting and strategies in Chapter 11.

Customers and consumers

As pp. 382 *et seq.* and 386 *et seq.* showed, pricing cannot be considered without taking into account the feelings and sensitivities of the *end buyer*. Different market segments react to price levels and price changes differently depending on the nature of the product, its desirability and the level of product loyalty established.

> **Example** The discerning coffee drinker who likes the taste of Nescafé and always buys that brand may not notice when the price rises, but even if they do spot the price rise, they might still continue to purchase Nescafé because they value the brand's benefits so highly. A segment that perceives coffee as a commodity and does not mind what it tastes like as long as it is hot and wet might be more inclined to be price sensitive. They might have been buying the same brand on a regular basis, but if its price rises then they certainly will notice and switch to something cheaper.

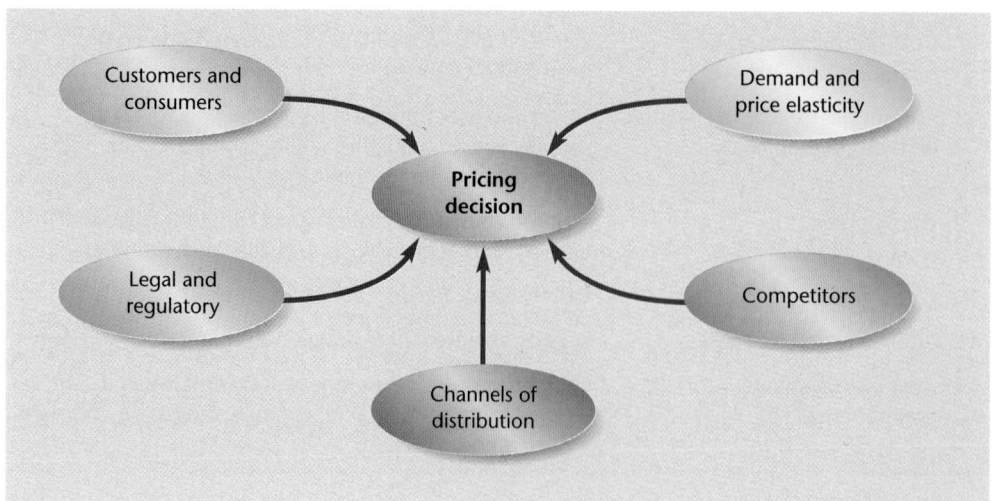

FIGURE 10.2

External influences on the pricing decision

The marketer has to be careful to set prices within an area bounded at the bottom end by costs and at the top end by what the market will tolerate. The bigger that area, the more discretion the marketer has in setting price. The organisation can increase its pricing discretion either by reducing costs (thereby lowering the bottom boundary) or by raising the consumers' threshold (by better-targeted communication or by improving the product offering).

The consumers' upper threshold is difficult to define as it is linked closely with perceptions of the product and its competitive standing. A product perceived as better than the competition will have a higher upper threshold than one perceived as poor value. In the latter case, the upper limit on price may be very close to cost. Similarly, a product with strong brand loyalty attached to it can push its upper limit higher because the product's desirability blunts any price sensitivity, enabling a price premium to be achieved.

Demand and price elasticity

Customers' attitudes towards price and their responsiveness to it are reflected to some extent in economic theories of *demand*.

Marketers' pricing objectives and the estimation of demand are thus very closely linked (Montgomery, 1988). As pricing objectives change, for example if there is a decision to move upmarket into a premium-priced segment, the nature and size of potential demand will also change. Similarly, it is important for the marketer to be able to estimate demand for new product. The definition of demand is flexible here; it may mean demand across an entire product market, or demand within a specific market segment, or be organisation specific.

Chapter 21 will look at some of the techniques used to establish sales and market potential in terms of usage or product sales with different market conditions. Using this information, it is possible to address an issue that has long been of concern to economists: the relationship between price and demand.

Demand determinants

For most products, it seems logical that if the price goes up, then demand falls and, conversely, if the price falls, then demand rises. This is the basic premise behind the standard demand curve shown in Fig. 10.3, which shows the number of units sold (Q1) at a given price (P1). As price increases from P1 to P2, demand is expected to fall from Q1 to Q2. This classic demand curve may relate either to a market or to an individual product. As an example, if the dollar is weak against other currencies, Americans generally find foreign holidays more expensive and thus do not travel. Similarly, the Asian financial crisis reduced the number of Japanese tourists.

The shape of the demand curve, however, will be influenced by a range of factors other than price. Changing consumer tastes and needs, for example, might make a product more or less desirable regardless of the price. The economic ability to pay is still there, but the willingness to buy is not. Fluctuations in real disposable income could similarly affect

Brand values justify a premium price.

Source: Nestlé UK Ltd/McCann Erickson Advertising Ltd.

FIGURE 10.3

The classic demand curve

demand, particularly for what could be considered luxury items. In a recession, for instance, consumers may cut back on demand for foreign holidays or new cars. In this case, the willingness exists, but the means to pay do not. The availability and pricing of close substitute products will also change the responsiveness of demand. For example, the introduction of the CD player into the mass market had a disastrous effect on demand for record players.

All of these factors are demand determinants that the marketer must understand in order to inject meaning into the demand curve. As Diamantopoulos and Mathews (1995) emphasise, however, demand curves are very subjective in nature. They depend very much on managerial judgements of the likely impact of price changes on demand, since most organisations do not have the kind of sophisticated information systems that would allow a more objective calculation. In reality, then, it is a *perceived* demand curve that drives managerial decisions rather than a 'real' one.

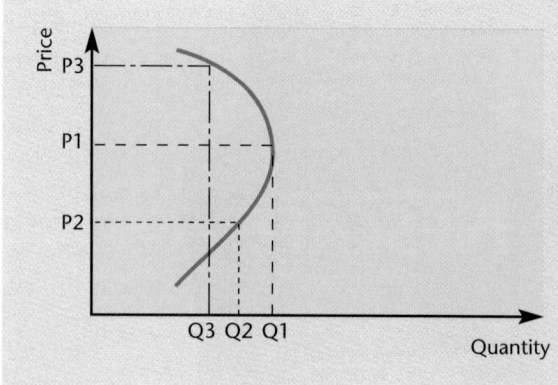

FIGURE 10.4

The boomerang demand curve

Not all products conform to the classic demand curve shown in Fig. 10.3. Some products with a deep psychological relationship with the consumer, perhaps with a high status dimension, can show a reverse price–demand curve in which the higher the price the higher the demand. As Fig. 10.4 shows, as the price goes down from P1 to P2 and demand falls from Q1 to Q2, the product loses its mystique and demand falls. There is, however, still an upper threshold beyond which the good becomes too expensive for even a status-conscious market. Then as the price rises higher, beyond P3, a more normal relationship holds true in which higher price leads to lower demand. This creates a boomerang-shaped demand curve. Knowing at what point the curve begins to turn back on itself could be useful for a marketer wishing to skim the market. Price too high and you could have turned the corner, becoming too exclusive.

Example Fine fragrances, especially those with designer names, might fall into this category of demand curve. The fragrance houses have been careful to price them sufficiently highly to position them well away from ordinary toiletries. This means that fine fragrances appeal not only to a well-to-do segment who can easily afford this sort of product on a regular basis, but also to those who aspire to be part of this élite and are prepared to splash out what seems to them to be a large sum of money occasionally to bring themselves closer to a world of luxury and sophistication. In either case, the high price is part of the appeal and the excitement of the product. The higher the price, the bigger the thrill. If the price became too high, however, the aspiring segment would probably fall away and live out their fantasies with something more affordable. They might find £30 to £80 acceptable, but £70 to £120 might be perceived as too extravagant. Even the élite segment might have its upper threshold. If the price of designer-label fine fragrances becomes too high, then they might as well buy the designer's clothes instead if they want to flaunt their wealth and status!

Another dimension of the demand curve is that marketers can themselves seek to influence its shape. Figure 10.5 shows how the demand curve can be shifted upwards through marketing efforts. If the marketer can offer better value to the customer or change the customer's perceptions of the product, then a higher quantity will be demanded without any reduction in the price. It is valuable for the marketer to be able to find ways of using non-price-based mechanisms of responding to a competitor's price cut or seeking to improve demand, to avoid the kind of mutually damaging price wars that erode margins and profits. This may create a new demand curve, parallel to the old one, so that demand can be increased from Q1 to Q2 while retaining the price at P1.

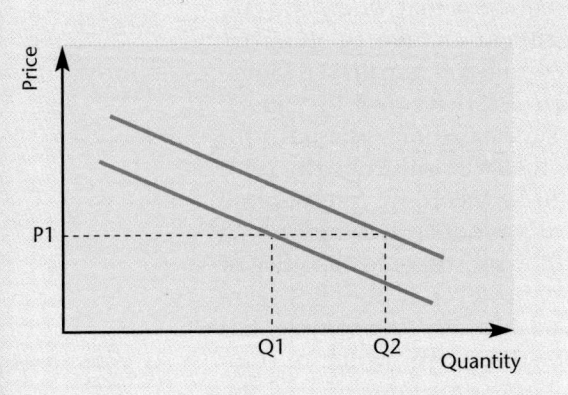

FIGURE 10.5

The parallel demand curve

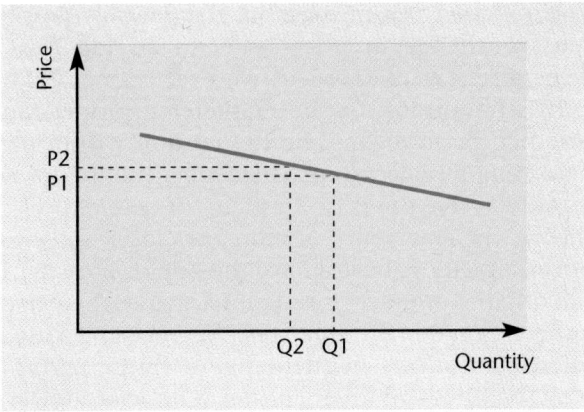

FIGURE 10.6

The elastic demand curve

Price elasticity of demand

It is also important for the marketer to have some understanding of the sensitivity of demand to price changes. This is shown by the steepness of the demand curve. A very steep demand curve shows a great deal of price sensitivity, in that a small change in price, all other things remaining equal, leads to a big change in demand. For some essential products, such as electricity, the demand curve is much more shallow; changes in price do not lead to big changes in demand. In this case, demand is said to be *inelastic* because it does not stretch a lot if pulled either way by price. The term *price elasticity of demand* thus refers to the ratio of percentage change in quantity over percentage change in price:

$$\text{Price elasticity} = \frac{\%\ \text{change in quantity demanded}}{\%\ \text{change in price}}$$

Thus the higher the price elasticity of demand, the more sensitive the market. Goods like electricity will have a price elasticity much closer to zero than do goods like convenience foods. For most goods, as the quantity demanded usually falls if the price rises, price elasticity is often negative, but by convention, the minus sign is usually ignored. To summarise, there are three possible forms of elasticity:

Elastic demand. Where demand is elastic, a small percentage increase in price (from P1 to P2) produces a large percentage decrease in quantity demanded (from Q1 to Q2), as shown in Fig. 10.6. The price elasticity is greater than one (ignoring the minus sign). The effect on total revenue is that a rise in price leads to a reduction in revenue, because the extra income from the price rise does not fully compensate for the fall in demand. Conversely, a fall in price increases demand to the point where total revenue rises, because the income from the new customers more than compensates for the decrease in revenue from existing ones.

Inelastic demand. Where demand is inelastic, a small percentage increase in price (from P1 to P2) produces a very small percentage change in quantity demanded (from Q1 to Q2), as shown in Fig. 10.7. The price elasticity will be between zero and one. In total revenue terms, income increases as the price increases, and falls as the price falls. The change in demand is not sufficient to compensate, as it is with elastic situations.

FIGURE 10.7

The inelastic demand curve

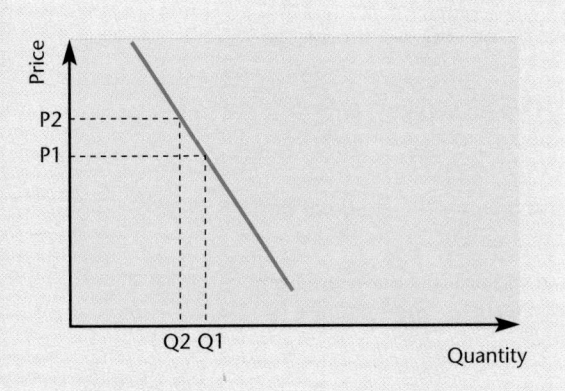

Unitary demand. An unlikely, but theoretically possible, situation is that where the percentage change in price leads to an identical percentage change in quantity demanded. The price elasticity is exactly one, and total revenue will remain the same.

It is important for the marketer to understand price elasticity and its causes, whether for an organisation's brand or within the market as a whole, as a basis for marketing mix decisions. There are a number of factors that will influence the price sensitivity (i.e. the price elasticity of demand) of customers. According to economic theory, the emergence of more, or closer, substitutes for a product will increase its price elasticity as buyers have the option of switching to the substitute as the price of the original product rises. From a marketing perspective, however, it does not seem quite so simple. The emergence of vegetable-based spreadable fats, for example, has offered consumers an alternative to butter and thus something with which to compare the price of butter. Further than that, however, it has completely changed the character of butter's demand curve from that of a necessity (a fairly flat straight line) to that of a luxury (more of a boomerang shape). Those who now choose to buy butter because of its superior taste or because of the status it bestows on the contents of the buyer's fridge will be no more price sensitive now than they ever were and, indeed, may even be less so.

As well as looking at the influence of substitutes on the shape and steepness of demand curves, it is also interesting to consider the relative importance of the purchase to the buyer. A purchase involving a relatively large cash outlay compared with the buyer's income will make that buyer more price sensitive. As discussed in Chapter 3, the more risky and infrequent the purchase, the more rational the buyer becomes, and more important the value for money aspects of the offering become. A rise in the price of cars, for example, might deter a potential buyer from replacing an old car. Table 10.2, based on the work of Nagle (1987), lists nine factors that affect

TABLE 10.2

Factors influencing price sensitivity

1 The unique value effect	The better differentiated the product, the lower the price sensitivity
2 The substitute awareness effect	The greater the number of substitutes available, the greater the price sensitivity
3 The difficult comparison effect	The more difficult it is to make a direct comparison between different products, the lower the price sensitivity
4 The total expenditure effect	The smaller the proportion of total spend this product represents, the lower the price sensitivity
5 The end benefit effect	The greater and more valued the end benefit of the product, the lower the price sensitivity
6 The shared cost effect	A buyer bearing only part of the cost of a product will be less price sensitive
7 The sunk investment effect	Buyers who have already bought complementary products or who are 'locked in' to a system will be price sensitive
8 The price–quality effect	The higher the quality and the prestige image of the product, the lower the price sensitivity
9 The inventory effect	Buyers who hold stocks of the product are more likely to be price sensitive than are those who purchase for immediate consumption

Source: Based on Nagle (1987).

TABLE 10.3

Factors influencing price sensitivity in organisational markets

1 The total expenditure effect	The smaller the proportion of the total spend this product represents, the lower the price sensitivity
2 The penalty for failure effect	The greater the cost of failure if the wrong choice is made, the lower the price sensitivity
3 The overall saving effect	The greater the overall savings or improvement in performance the product makes, the lower the price sensitivity
4 The contribution to quality effect	The higher the quality of the buyer's own product, the lower their price sensitivity
5 The degree of customisation effect	The more customised or differentiated the product, the lower the price sensitivity
6 The end customer sensitivity	The more price sensitive the buyer's own customer, the more price sensitive the buyer becomes
7 The buyer's ability to absorb costs	The more profitable the buyer and the better able to absorb costs, the lower the price sensitivity
8 The buyer's ignorance effect	The less the buyer knows and the looser their purchasing specifications, the lower their price sensitivity
9 The decision maker's motivation effect	The less motivated the decision maker in terms of cost minimisation, the lower the price sensitivity

Source: Based on Porter (1980).

price sensitivity generally, while Table 10.3, based on Porter (1980), looks at sensitivity specifically in the context of organisational markets.

Elasticity of demand will vary greatly between different types of product. Within the food sector, Bolton (1989) found that whereas coffee brands and convenience foods are very price elastic, certain types of fresh fruit and vegetables are price inelastic. As a final thought on price elasticity, it is interesting to consider how it has been deliberately manipulated in the case of tobacco products. The UK government has pursued a consistent policy over the years of imposing increasingly punitive taxes on tobacco as a social welfare issue. Basically, the aim has been to push tobacco prices up to the point where price elasticity comes into operation and smokers give up the habit because it is too expensive. This point has not yet been reached, as addicts are proving to be remarkably resilient in absorbing the price rises and maintaining their inelasticity.

Channels of distribution

An organisation's approach to pricing has also to take into account the needs and expectations of the other members of the *distribution chain*. Each of them will have a desired level of profit margin and a requirement to cover the costs associated with handling and reselling the product, such as transport, warehousing, insurance and retail display, for example. Even with a service product, such as insurance or a holiday, distributing through agents who claim commission on sales to cover premises, staffing, administration and profit has an impact on the price of the service.

All of this tends to erode the manufacturer's pricing discretion, because effectively it adds to the producer's costs and takes the total much nearer to the consumer's upper limit. How much erosion there is will depend on the balance of power between manufacturer and intermediaries.

Competitors

The point has been made several times during the course of this chapter that pricing decisions have to be made in a *competitive* context. The level and intensity of competition and the pricing decisions that other organisations make in the market will influence any producer's own pricing. It is not just about relative positioning ('If the budget version is £10 and the premium quality version is £70, then if we want to signal a mid-range product we have to charge £45'). It also concerns strategic decisions about the extent to which the organisation wishes to use price as an aggressive competitive weapon. Price and non-price competition will be discussed further in Chapter 11.

The influence of competition on price will depend on the nature of the product and the number and size of competitors within the market.

Monopoly

Few monopoly situations, where there is only one supplier serving the whole market, exist. Traditionally, monopolies have been large state-owned enterprises providing public services such as utilities, telecommunications and mail, or operating economically crucial industries such as steel and coal. Legislation protected the monopoly from competition. In theory, monopolists have no competitive framework for pricing and can, therefore, set whatever prices they like as the customer has no choice but to source from them. In practice, however, governments and independent watchdog bodies have imposed regulations and pressurised monopolists into keeping prices within socially acceptable limits. Even if that was not enough, the growth of international competition and the availability of alternatives also have an impact. The price and availability of fuel, oil, gas or nuclear power, for instance, all affect the price and demand for coal.

The last 15 years or so have seen UK government policy moving towards privatising state-owned organisations and creating conditions that will allow free-market competition to emerge. This is already evident in the telecommunications market, where the emergence of new competition changed the way in which British Telecommunications develops its service and pricing policies.

Oligopoly

The UK's deregulated telecommunications market is an oligopoly, where a small number of powerful providers dominate the market between them. Each player in the market is very conscious of the rest and makes no move without due consideration of the likely competitive response. Pricing is a particularly sensitive issue in such markets and, where oligopolists choose to price very closely with each other, accusations of collusion are bound to arise. Sudden changes in price by one organisation might be construed as a threat by the rest, but prior and public notification of price rises, as will be discussed at Chapter 11, can be used to defuse suspicion.

These developments are not surprising, as a price war between oligopolists is something that all parties involved would prefer to avoid. Since oligopolists are likely to be fairly evenly matched, it is difficult for any one of them to be sure that it can win. While the war goes on, the consumer may be happy, but the oligopolists are simply eroding their profit margins to dangerously thin levels, not gaining any competitive ground, and causing themselves much stress about the eventual outcome.

Monopolistic competition

Most markets fall into the category of monopolistic competition where there are many competitors, but each has a product differentiated from the rest. Price is not necessarily a key factor in these markets, as product features and benefits serve to differentiate a product and diffuse the competitive effect. The emphasis in these markets is on branding or adding value so that the customer is prepared to accept a different

Discount pricing

In the early 1990s, the media accused the biggest UK supermarket chains of keeping their basic prices artificially high to maintain their profits. The entry of discounters and warehouse clubs was thus seen as disturbing the established oligopoly, with the media hopeful (and the supermarkets fearful) that this would trigger a price war. In the short term, price did indeed become a prominent feature of the supermarkets' marketing mixes, with Sainsbury's (http://www.sainsbury.co.uk) advertising that 'Good Food Costs Less at Sainsbury's' and Tesco (http://www.tesco.co.uk) introducing its *Value Lines*, generic products selling at bottom of the range prices, for example. Over time, however, the supermarkets managed to reassert themselves as an oligopoly by managing to focus the customer's attention on quality, consistency and service rather than price, thus differentiating themselves as a group further from the discounters. The price issue did not entirely go away, but was subtly reformulated as a 'value for money' message, largely communicated through selected own-brand items and specific short-term price-oriented promotions rather than price wars across the whole range.

Thus by 1998, the discounters had carved out a market share of no more than 2.4 per cent. The lack of significant progress by the hard discounters such as Aldi and Lidl in the UK market has not been repeated in their home country, Germany, where discounters have captured around 25 per cent of the market. German shoppers often use more than one shop and seek out low-priced commodity items from the discounters. In the UK, however, longer working hours, more working women and an emphasis on convenience have favoured the large, out of town supermarkets that offer easy parking, a wide range of products, good service, heavy merchandising and the facility for shoppers to pay by credit card (Robinson, 1999).

price from its competitors. Miele, a German manufacturer of kitchen and laundry appliances, for example, has developed a reputation for selling very high-quality goods at a price premium. It can thus price its products substantially higher than those of its competitors, because Miele's customers believe that they are getting good value for money in terms of quality, durability and service.

Perfect competition

As with its direct opposite, the monopoly, perfect competition is hard to find. It implies that there are very many sellers in the market with products that are indistinguishable from each other in the eyes of the buyer. There is, therefore, little flexibility on price, because no one seller has either enough power to lead the rest or the ability to differentiate the product sufficiently to justify a different price. If one seller increases the price, either the rest will follow suit or customers will change suppliers, bringing the aberrant supplier back into line. One supplier's reduction in price will attract custom until such time as other suppliers follow suit.

To avoid this kind of powerless stalemate, most markets have evolved into offering differentiated products, even with the most uninteresting commodities (*see* the example at p. 199 on salt, for instance). Nor does the equality of suppliers last for long in most markets. One or two more astute or powerful suppliers usually emerge to lead the market into monopolistic competition.

> **Example** A visit to the local fruit and vegetable market demonstrates a near perfect market at work. Products are clearly priced, the merchandise is usually visible for comparison and competing suppliers are contained within a defined area. Depending on the season, many prices are set at similar levels. If any differentiation does take place, it could be with a smile, the free provision of a carrying box, or a discount for buying particular goods in quantity (if carrots, for instance, are priced on every stall at 18p per kg, one might differentiate by offering 2 kg for 30p).

Legal and regulatory framework

European marketers increasingly need to understand the national and European *legal and regulatory framework* when setting and adjusting prices. Aspects of this were discussed at pp. 72 *et seq.* Some organisations, such as public utilities, tend to have their pricing policies carefully scrutinised by the government to make sure that they are in the public interest, especially where a near monopoly is operating. Even after privatisation, such organisations are not entirely free to price as they wish. As mentioned in Chapter 2, for example, the privatised water, gas, telephone and electricity companies in the UK are answerable to quasi non-governmental organisations (QUANGOs), watchdog bodies set up by the government. Even the National Lottery has its pricing, distribution of funds and profits overseen by a QUANGO, Oflot.

These are high-profile cases involving large and important organisations whose activities fundamentally affect the whole population and the economy. For the most part, however, Europe subscribes to the idea that a free market should determine prices without governmental interference. Authorities, whether national or EU based, will nevertheless become involved in pricing issues where they feel that unfair competition or price fixing is taking place. In the UK, for example, the Office of Fair Trading (OFT) is the first port of call for complaints about pricing and if the OFT cannot resolve the problem, it may refer the case to the Monopolies and Mergers Commission (MMC). It in turn may refer a case to the EC.

> **Example** The Office of Fair Trading (OFT) undertook an eight-month investigation to check out the profit levels of the four leading UK supermarkets, ASDA, Safeway, Tesco and Sainsbury's. This reflected, it was claimed, growing concern over the difference between prices in the UK and in mainland Europe and the USA. Although the supermarkets argued that price differences are influenced by higher land costs, higher fuel costs and higher taxes and duties on some items, the matter was still referred to the MMC for adjudication.
>
> The OFT noted that even when high-profile price-cutting campaigns are launched, the cuts often only match a competitor's price move. It is also claimed that the cost of cuts are sometimes borne by suppliers who are put under pressure to cut their supply prices to cover promotional price cuts, thus preserving retailers' margins. The MMC inquiry is unlikely to rule before 2000 and will cover all retailers operating 10 or more stores with 600m^2 of grocery sales area. The MMC ruling should decide whether current arrangements inhibit or promote competition and whether they are in the consumer's interest (Cunningham, 1999; Gannaway, 1999; *The Grocer*, 1999).

In 1998, for instance, the UK government's Department of Trade and Industry acted on the MMC's 1997 report on pricing in the electrical goods market and banned manufacturers from imposing a 'recommended retail price' or refusing to supply retailers who discount. It also became illegal for retailers to pressurise suppliers not to supply goods to their discounter rivals. Suppliers now have to set down their criteria for selecting retailers (price is not a legitimate criterion) and retailers can demand written explanations of any refusal to supply (Caine, 1997; Young, 1998). This all happened because in 1995, the OFT referred to the MMC complaints from discounters that they had been refused supplies without adequate reason.

In the UK, resale price maintenance, that is, the power of manufacturers to determine what the retail price of their products should be, was abolished in the early 1960s, although it was retained in a few selected product areas. One area in which resale price maintenance is still practised is vitamins, minerals and dietary supplements. The idea behind this price maintenance is to protect small, neighbourhood pharmacies by ensuring that the bigger high-street chains have no price advantage over them. Some bigger retailers resent this, however. The supermarket chain ASDA cut up to 20 per cent off the prices of brands in those categories, forcing the manufacturers to take ASDA to court to uphold their right to dictate the price. The case went against

VISION DIRECT

Contact lens replacement at a fraction of the cost

Example Sometimes, in order to maintain higher prices and margins, retailers can put pressure on manufacturers to refuse to supply other retailers who might be prepared to discount. A survey undertaken by the *Sunday Times* suggested that consumers were paying over £100 a year for contact lenses as a result of pricing agreements between high-street opticians and lens manufacturers. The survey revealed that for a six-month supply of disposable, ultra violet filter lenses the prices varied from over £140 at Dolland & Aitcheson and Vision Express down to £79 at Vision Direct (http://www.visiondirect.co.uk).

The opticians lost their monopoly position in 1984 for supplying contact lenses and new competitors such as Vision Direct grew through mail order. Vision Direct complained to the OFT that contact lens manufacturers were being put under pressure by the high street opticians to withdraw supplies from it. The opticians argued that under the 1989 Opticians Act, contact lenses can only be supplied if the sale is effected by a registered doctor or optician. The mail order companies had, however, found legitimate ways around the Act. It could be argued that the high street opticians objected because they knew that they could not compete on price because they need more expensive high street locations and testing and diagnostic services. Despite its lower prices, Vision Direct claims to make a 20 per cent margin on its contact lens price levels (Nuki, 1997).

ASDA, which then had to increase prices again and await the outcome of an OFT review of the situation. In the meantime, all the major supermarkets pointedly and heavily discounted their own-label vitamins, minerals and supplements, as they are perfectly entitled to do.

Within the EU, some industries have negotiated selective distribution agreements that effectively allow them to control prices by having the right to decide who should or should not be allowed to sell their products.

Finally, at a more mundane level, manufacturers and retailers may be obliged by law to include duty or tax as part of their pricing. Alcohol and tobacco in particular are targeted by many governments for high rates of duty, partly as a public health measure (keep the prices high to discourage over-consumption), and partly as an excellent revenue earner. In the UK, petrol is also subject to high rates of duty (with a higher rate on leaded petrol than on unleaded or diesel). Excise duties and VAT account for 80 per cent of the cost of a litre of unleaded petrol and the actual cost of the fuel is only around 8p per litre. As shown in Table 10.4, petrol prices vary widely across the world, and this is often explained by differences in tax rates rather than by competitive pressures.

BLE 10.4
leaded petrol price per litre, July 1998

JSA	17.7
Poland	37.3
pain	46.8
witzerland	49.2
Germany	58.0
rance	64.0
JK	65.5
taly	65.6
Sweden	68.0
Norway	72.2

rce: Nuttall (1998).

As mentioned at p. 63, varying rates of VAT are charged on various categories of products across the EU. When the UK government decided to impose VAT on domestic fuel, the gas and electric companies had no choice but to add it to their customers' bills, thus increasing the overall price of these utilities.

INTERNAL INFLUENCES ON THE PRICING DECISION

Pricing is, of course, also influenced by various *internal factors*. Pricing needs to reflect both corporate and marketing objectives, for example, as well as being consistent with the rest of the marketing mix. It is also important to remember, however, that pricing may also be related to costs, if the organisation is looking to generate an acceptable margin of profit. Figure 10.8 summarises the internal influences on price, and the rest of this section discusses each of them in further detail.

Organisational objectives

The area of *organisational objectives* is an internal influence, linked with corporate strategy. Marketing plans and objectives have to be set not only best to satisfy the customer's needs and wants, but also to reflect the aspirations of the organisation. These two aims should not be incompatible! Organisational objectives such as target volume sales, target value sales, target growth in various market segments and target profit figures can all be made more or less attainable through the deployment of the marketing mix and particularly through price.

Corporate strategy is not simply concerned with quantifiable target setting. It is also concerned with the organisation's relative position in the market compared with the competition. Pricing may be used to help either to signal a desire for leadership (whether in terms of lowest cost or price, or superior quality) or to establish a clearly differentiated niche, which can then be emphasised and consolidated through the other elements of the marketing mix. In launching the *Midnight Sun* brand of butter on to the UK market, the Finnish company Valio used high-quality silver packaging as well as pricing the product to match the market leader, Lurpak, to communicate an upmarket image to the customer.

At the other end of the pricing spectrum, discount supermarket chains, such as Netto, Aldi, Lidl and Kwik Save, are trying to achieve objectives relating to price leadership in the market. Obviously, low pricing within their stores is their primary tool, but this can only be achieved through cost reduction (hence the minimalist retail environment and low levels of customer service) and accepting lower profit margins (1 per cent, compared with the industry average of between 5 per cent and 8 per cent). Achieving all of this is also dependent on attracting many more customers

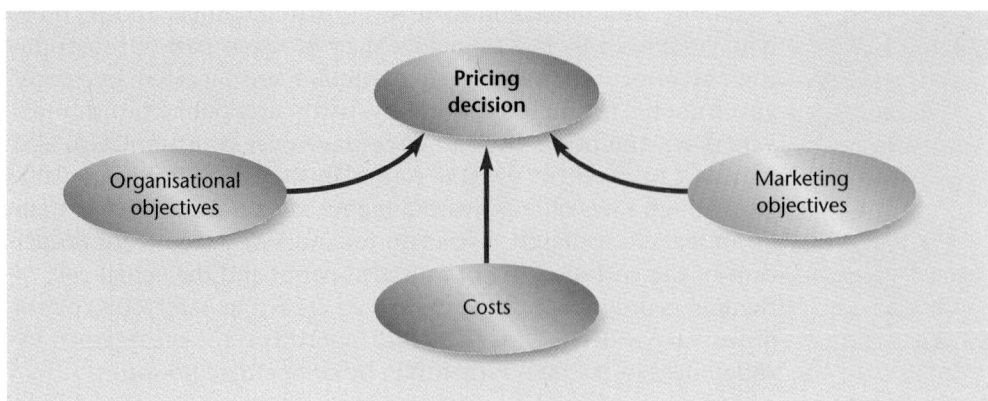

FIGURE 10.8

Internal influences o
the pricing decision

through the doors to generate the higher volume of sales needed to make a reasonable profit. The higher volumes also give the discount retailer scope for negotiating more favourable terms with the manufacturers for bulk buying.

Organisational objectives can change over time as the organisation and its markets evolve. A new business, or a new entrant into a market, faces initial problems of survival. There is a need to generate orders to use excess capacity and to establish a foothold in the market. Relatively low pricing (at the sacrifice of profit margins rather than quality) is just one possible way of doing that. Once established, the organisation can begin to think in terms of target profits and building a competitive position, which may involve a revised approach to pricing. Using price as part of an integrated marketing mix, the organisation can aim to achieve market leadership in terms of whatever criteria are important. Once leadership is achieved, objectives have to be redefined to maintain and defend that leadership, thus keeping competition at arm's length.

Corporate objectives can also have both short- and long-term dimensions to them. In the short term, for example, a small business on the verge of collapse might use low price as a survival tactic to keep it afloat, even if its longer-term ambitions include quality leadership at a higher price.

Marketing objectives

As the previous subsection has implied, marketing and organisational objectives are very closely interrelated and influence each other to a great extent. The distinction, though, is that while organisational objectives relate primarily to the operation, the well-being and the personality of the organisation as a whole, *marketing objectives* are more closely focused on specific target markets and the position desired within them.

Marketing objectives are achieved through the use of the whole marketing mix, not just the price element, emphasising again the need for an integrated and harmonious marketing mix. An organisation may have a portfolio of products (*see* pp. 317 *et seq.*) serving different segments, each of which requires a different approach to pricing. Such a differentiated strategy can be seen in telecommunications, with British Telecommunications developing a range of tariffs for both domestic and business users to suit different needs and priorities.

> **Example** In 1999, the manufacturer of KEF loudspeakers (http://www.kef.com) had 13 models in its range, priced from £129 for the KEF Coda 7 (a value for money, functional introduction to the range) to £3299 for the KEF Reference Model Four (a premium product in terms of sound quality and performance). As long as the market recognises the functional and quality differences between the models in such a range, the wide spread of prices need not cause confusion or conflict as to what the organisation stands for.

In that sense, it is no different from a car manufacturer making a cheap and cheerful £8000 run-about model at one end of the range and a sleek, executive £40 000 status machine at the other. The key is to use the other elements of the marketing mix to support the price or to provide a rationale for it. The concept of the product portfolio and the management issues surrounding it are fully covered in Chapter 20.

Another product concept that might influence the pricing of a particular product over a period of time is the product life-cycle (*see* pp. 303 *et seq.*). In the introductory stage, a lower price might be necessary as part of a marketing strategy to encourage trial. Advertising this as 'an introductory trial price' would be one way of preventing 'low price = low quality' judgements. As the product becomes established through the growth and early maturity stages, and gains loyal buyers, the organisation may feel confident enough to raise the price. As indicated earlier, this has to be done with due reference to the competitive situation and the desired positioning for both product

Premium pricing for a premium product.
Source: KEF Systems Ltd.

and organisation. In late maturity and decline, it is possible that price reductions could be used to squeeze the last breath out of the dying product.

Costs

From a marketing perspective, price is primarily related to what the customer will be prepared to pay for a particular product offering. The actual *cost* of providing that offering cannot, however, be completely ignored. Marketing is about creating and holding a customer at a profit, and if an organisation cannot produce the product for less than it can sell it for, then its presence in that market is questionable.

The cost of producing the product, therefore, represents a floor below which the product cannot be sold profitably. However, defining cost may not be so straight-forward. In a hotel, for example, the majority of its costs are fixed in the short term (staffing, facilities provision, maintenance, etc.) and are incurred regardless of the room occupancy. The variable costs associated with an actual guest (such as laundry and consumables) are relatively low. In setting the price of a room, therefore, the organisation has to reflect both the estimated variable costs and an element of contri-bution towards fixed costs and profit based on predicted levels of business, so that in the long run all costs are met and an acceptable level of profit made.

In the short term, however, it may not be possible to adhere strictly to a cost-recovery formula. The price has to stand in a competitive and unpredictable environment, and may have to be flexible enough to be used as a competitive weapon or as a promotional tool to maintain volume of sales. Thus a hotel may be prepared to let a room at a discount of anything up to 40 per cent of the normal rate at a quiet time of the year when the supply of hotel rooms far exceeds the demand. This is acceptable as long as the price covers the variable costs of letting that room and makes some contribution towards fixed costs and profit. Similarly, at busy times when rooms are hard to find, the hotels can afford to stand by their published rates.

Another important dimension of cost is the concept of joint or shared costs that are divided between a number of products produced by one organisation. Central provi-sion of, for example, R&D facilities, maintenance, quality assurance and administrative costs has to be paid for through revenue generated and therefore has to be reflected in prices. Often the rules for allocating these costs across product lines are arbitrary, and not necessarily closely linked with predicted sales and the market's price sensitivity.

It is therefore clear that costs do play an important role in price setting. They will be further discussed in Chapter 11.

THE EUROPEAN INFLUENCE ON PRICING

Much of the general discussion on pricing in this chapter and the next is applicable to any organisation, whether it is trading solely within its own national boundary or on a Europe-wide basis. The impact of increasing European integration, however, culminating so far with EMU (European Monetary Union) and the launch of the euro on 1 January 1999, creates fresh challenges for pricing decision makers. Although only non-cash transactions are now possible, in 2002 the euro will become a hard currency, replacing the domestic currencies of individual member states that entered the eurozone in the first wave.

The impact of the SEM

The creation of the SEM meant the removal of fiscal, physical and technical barriers to trade, and an increase in the number of organisations operating in more than one country. In marketing terms, as discussed in earlier chapters, the SEM opened up the possibility of pan-European products, or at least of products that are largely standardised across Europe but with adaptations to suit local tastes, preferences or marketing environments. Price may be the element of the marketing mix that is most likely to be adapted for local conditions, as incomes, spending patterns and price sensitivities vary widely across the EU. Price is also a very flexible tool, far easier to adapt than a product!

The implications of the SEM on pricing were predicted by Quelch and Buzzell (1989), who suggested at that time that prices would be forced downwards because of:

1 *decreased costs* through higher-volume sales with more common packaging (and other marketing elements) across the EU and cheaper logistics (since technically there are no import/export regulations and paperwork to fulfil) that also tend towards uniformity;
2 *the opening up of public procurement contracts* to broader competition from across the EU, hence leading to keener prices;
3 *foreign investment*, raising production capacity;
4 *the rigorous enforcement of competition policy*, fewer trade restrictions, less opportunity for building monopolies;
5 *a general increase in competitive activity*, forcing prices down.

Smith (1998) questioned whether the SEM had really achieved all the benefits originally expected, especially when a single currency was not available to support a single market. An Institute of Directors survey found that 38 per cent of UK firms actually found that costs increased as a result of the SEM. Another survey by the European Commission found that just 12 per cent of Portuguese, 17 per cent of Dutch and 20 per cent of French firms surveyed believed that the SEM had worked for them. The two areas of particular concern were state aid that made fair foreign competition more difficult (*see* the example of German coal in Chapter 2) and in public procurement, where 90 per cent of contracts are awarded within the domestic market. Both of these barriers prevented the realisation of the full benefits of price competition.

The launch of the euro and the creation of Euroland, comprising the 11 member states currently participating in the single currency, is a logical extension of the SEM and some of the expected benefits from the SEM are also being claimed for the euro. These are:

1 *Greater price transparency across member states*

Price variations across Europe can be very large. A report by Lehman Bros on 53 products across Europe found that prices varied on average by 24 per cent after the effects of VAT and other taxes were removed (Smith, 1999). These price differences reflect pricing strategies that exploit differing price sensitivities and the amount of local competition in member state markets. The introduction of the euro makes price comparisons much easier and allows consumers to buy products across borders more easily. It is unlikely that German shoppers are going to make many journeys just to buy products from Greece, but if they start hopping over the border to the Netherlands on a regular basis, it could cause problems for local traders. The advent of the euro does not necessarily mean that prices will become identical across Europe, but it does mean that prices will be open to more detailed comparison. This will be especially true in organisational markets, where buyers can more readily access information on suppliers from other member states.

2 *More opportunity for Eurobrand building with a common positioning*

The euro could lead to increased Europe-wide branding activity (Philips, 1998). As the prices for a particular brand become similar across Europe, there is more reason for positioning that product in the same way across all countries. If manufacturers do want to vary the positioning of a Eurobrand, however, then it will have to be done through brand image rather than pricing. Iced tea, for example, is very popular in mainland Europe, but not in the UK. If the product was priced in euros, it would be difficult to sell it more cheaply in the UK to try to stimulate demand, because consumers in other European markets might notice and resent it. The manufacturers would thus have to try more subtle approaches to the UK market.

3 *No exchange rate fluctuations and currency hedging*

EMU aims to eliminate exchange-rate uncertainty and to create more stable economic environments across member states through a convergence of interest rates. It is too early to state whether these benefits are being realised, although the ability to quote prices in euros and to deliver at that price is a significant improvement for suppliers. They do not have to make allowances for any unforeseen exchange rate fluctuations or exchange costs. Without the need to create a contingency for fluctuations, there is the possibility that transaction costs could be reduced and some of the benefit passed on to customers.

But there are also potential problems:

1 *The risk of brand positioning confusion during changes*

There are fears that the euro could disturb established price perceptions and consumer brand values in member state markets (Shannon, 1998). If consumers do become confused about prices, it could disturb markets, especially for the brand leaders. For example, differences in prices, when converted from local currencies into euros, will have varying psychological significance in different markets. If a brand is 12 francs cheaper than the brand leader in France, 12 francs sounds like a big price difference. However, the difference is only 2 euros, which sounds like a much smaller saving. In contrast, in the UK, a £1 price difference between brands seems substantial and at 1.5 euros, it seems even better. In both cases, the real price gap is the same in both local currency and in euros, but the consumer is interpreting the gap differently. Retailers are aware of this and some, like the French supermarket chain Leclerc, are using 'reference brands' as a starting point for euro pricing and setting the prices of other brands from that to take account of the way in which consumers interpret price gaps.

2 *Lack of harmonisation of VAT and other sales taxes across Europe will still create differences*
This problem is considered in more detail in the following section. Sometimes it is difficult for the consumer, as in the case of price differentials in euro car pricing, to differentiate between the tax effects and deliberate attempts to create different pricing levels.

3 *Difficulties for those European countries not in the first wave of EMU*
The 11 countries in the first wave – Austria, Belgium, Finland, France, Germany, Ireland, Italy, Luxembourg, the Netherlands, Portugal and Spain – are on track for the use of a hard euro in 2002. In the meantime, they can transact in the euro and in consumer situations indicate dual pricing, listing both euro and domestic hard currency prices. In those countries not in the first wave, such as Sweden and the UK, suppliers have to respond to a new situation when dealing with the other 11 member countries. Should they continue to quote only in their domestic currency or should they work on euro pricing, even though they are not part of the zone?

Marsh (1998) identified two types of British companies that should be concerned with the euro. First, those with direct exports to the eurozone will need to trade very early in the euro, as they will be given little choice by their customers. The second group are the suppliers to those domestic customers who in turn are further down the supply chain involved in the eurozone. This group might also have to price in the euro to minimise the fluctuation risks in the overall supply chain. The complex and extensive Europe-wide supply chains will drive euro usage for all EU members. Most larger companies are already operating with the euro, although most are currently adopting a non-confrontational approach in encouraging suppliers to price in both euros and local currencies.

In Sweden, larger companies such as Volvo, Ericsson and SKF were planning for a euro transition long before the changeover date, but Burt (1998) found that those companies with fewer than 30 employees had not concerned themselves with euro effects and were vulnerable to unplanned changes in their pricing strategies. There appears to be little doubt that most organisations in non-participating states will have to respond to the euro, a situation confirmed by Volvo when it stated that 'we will be changing over to the single currency for all our purchasing within the euro area next year' (Lars Persson, Volvo). Regardless of outstanding political decisions, in organisational markets the euro is a reality as a trading currency.

4 *Prices could rise if non-EU competition is stifled*
The effect of creating the eurozone could be to create a much more closed economy than previously experienced by the individual countries comprising the EU. Euroland will become comparable with the USA, which generates 11.5 per cent of its GDP from international trade, compared with 8 per cent in Japan. The average in Europe is 13 per cent, although it is 20.9 per cent in Germany and 23.6 per cent in Britain (Lightfoot, 1998). If the closer integration of Europe has the effect of making it more difficult for outsiders to compete, there is a danger that in some areas, especially where industries experience some protection, prices may not fall but rise.

It is too early to understand fully the effects of the creation of a eurozone. The hard currency is still a few years away and many consumers are not fully familiar with the possibilities. Some retailers such as Tesco are listing dual prices in Ireland and can accept non-cash euro payments. Similar dual pricing is becoming a feature in supermarkets elsewhere in Europe, especially where the number of credit card transactions is high, as in Portugal. The Dutch retailer Albert Heijn is preferring to wait, however, until just before the launch of the hard currency before creating dual pricing (McClintock, 1999).

Consumer goods manufacturers might not have to move to euro pricing that is the same across all countries if there are sound distribution or marketing reasons for differences. Pricing is, after all, only one component of the full value and cost of a product to the consumer. The growth of European travel and Europe-wide media, however, will both act as a force for consistent pricing. The impact will be far greater in organisational markets and it is probably this factor that will eventually persuade the non-EMU nations to join, in order to retain national competitiveness in key employment sectors despite the political fallout and economic uncertainty associated with the perceived loss of sovereignty.

Price differentials

As the euro grows in popularity and becomes an accepted hard currency, **price differentials** across Europe are more likely to follow differing tax rates rather than marketing strategy considerations (Kelly, 1998). As mentioned in Chapter 2, VAT and excise rates do vary considerably across the EU, and moves towards harmonisation still have some way to go, with the result that countries such as Denmark with its 25 per cent VAT rate are still well above the average of 15 per cent. Until such time as EMU is fully implemented and tax rates are harmonised, however, the capacity for price differentials remains and the reasons for those differentials are not always clear.

The *Sunday Times*, for instance, commissioned a study of mobile phone charges across Europe. The results showed that the British consumer had an average monthly bill in excess of £25, 20 per cent higher than in France, Germany or Norway, and twice as expensive as in Italy. The newspaper concluded that not only were rental charges higher in the UK but there were also many hidden costs that created a complex web of tariffs that consumers found difficult to understand. The higher prices have been partially attributed to the slower growth in mobile use in the UK compared with other European countries. Published articles such as this mobile phone study all help to raise public perception of the differences and create pressure for more uniformity in pan-European pricing (Nuki and Hamzic, 1998).

MARKETING AND IT   Cross-border pricing and the Internet

Another factor to consider in cross-border pricing is the Internet. In Europe, many companies will probably have to adopt a 'one price fits all' policy for goods and services, regardless of national boundaries, as the euro comes into force and Internet sales become more commonplace.

One specific aspect of Internet selling that deserves a special mention because of its likely impact on price harmonisation is the Internet auction. There electronic auctions are ideal for selling off 'perishable' services as their 'sell by' date approaches. Examples of perishable services include flights and holidays. As their departure dates approach, the value of unsold seats and hotel rooms plummets almost to zero. Most major airlines have begun to auction unsold seats, following the lead of American Airlines and the Hong Kong-based Cathay Pacific in 1996. For airlines and travel agents, the economics of Internet auctions are inescapable. Selling off unsold capacity by auctioning it at a discount one or two days before its 'sell by' date can improve profitability dramatically. Achieving 100 per cent passenger loadings on aircraft will, in theory, quadruple net profits, even if ticket prices have to be discounted by 25 per cent. On a more practical level, there is still the question of passenger acceptance. While low fares might be popular, crowded aircraft are not. Some passengers might shy away from full flights. As one commentator puts it, 'I mean, I hate when those middle seats are full, don't you?'

Source: O'Connor and Galvin (1999).

Price differentials might also arise according to consumers' willingness and ability to pay. The price of tea and coffee in Swiss cafés is something of a shock to the foreign traveller, but is widely accepted by the Swiss themselves who are willing and able to pay such prices. Implicit in all this is the necessity for the marketer to understand the pricing context of the local market, and to see it through the consumer's eyes.

Example In a comparison of typical French and British shopping baskets, Pring and Eggleston (1998) found that some foods and toiletries also represented excellent value in France. The French are well prepared for the British invasion. At Carrefour in Cité Europe, English is widely spoken, the signs are bilingual and in-store tasting sessions are widely used to extend the British palate. Real price comparisons are, of course, difficult to make if exchange rate fluctuations and the effects of bulk buying are taken into account, but the pleasures of the day out and a full shopping basket are proving to be extremely attractive to Brits from all over the country.

It is necessary to understand the consumer's living standards, life-style, aspirations and purchasing patterns, as well as the alternatives open to that consumer in terms of competitors and substitutes. The organisation might also have a brand-building job to do to establish credibility in the European consumer's eyes. A brand that has been carefully nurtured over the years in its home market to achieve a position where it can command a handsome price premium may mean nothing to the consumer in another European country. The organisation might even have to price low to get into that market against strong local competition, and then begin to build reputation.

There are still wide differentials between car prices in different parts of Europe. The reality is that it costs far more to buy an identical model in some European countries than in others. As shown in Table 10.5, for example, in 1998 it cost 58.5 per cent more to buy a Ford Mondeo in the most expensive country than in the cheapest. The introduction of the euro will remove one of the main reasons provided by manufacturers for price differentials, currency fluctuations, so that comparisons will be easier to make.

The price differential between the UK and the rest of Europe has become so marked that the OFT may be close to referring carmakers and their franchised dealers to the MMC. A VW Golf, for example, can be purchased for more than 28 per cent less in the Netherlands than in the UK. Although the differences can in part be explained by the strength of the pound, it has also been suggested that the use of recommended resale prices, strong encouragement not to discount beyond a certain level and bonus payments to dealers all lead to higher prices. In addition, a premium is often charged in the UK for supplying right hand drive vehicles.

It is not just in the UK that large price differentials can be found. VW lost a test case in 1998 and was fined ECU 102mn for competitive abuses that breached single-market rules. The Commission found that VW's Italian dealers were told not to sell cars to German, Italian and Austrian citizens, despite car prices being 30 per cent cheaper in Italy. The growth of the Internet is likely to cause more cross-border shoppers to think about where they purchase their car. This, along with the euro, should create greater price transparency, which could cause a shift of buyers from northern Europe, where prices tend to be higher, to southern Europe where they are lower. VW predicts that by 2000, VW prices will not vary by more than 5 per cent to 10 per cent across Europe, unless there are special tax factors such as in Denmark and Ireland (Bowley, 1998; Griffiths, 1998a; Townsend, 1998).

TABLE 10.5

EU Car Price Differentials (as at 1 May 1998)

Small cars %		Medium cars %		Large cars %	
Opel Corsa	24.0	VW Golf	43.5	BMW 318i	12.0
Ford Fiesta	44.7	Opel Astra	26.0	Audi A4	13.0
Renault Clio	33.8	Ford Escort/Orion	33.8	Ford Mondeo	58.5
Peugeot 106	21.1	Renault Mégane	27.9	Opel Vectra	18.2
VW Polo	36.7	Peugeot 306	46.2	VW Passat	36.4

Source: European Commission, as reported by Bowley (1998).

Parallel trading

Parallel trading takes place when products sold in one country find their way into another country, where they are resold at higher prices. Such trading can even apply to services. Some passengers have found it cheaper to phone Calais to buy a UK–France ticket for Le Shuttle than to buy it in the UK.

Parallel trading is increasingly difficult to avoid, especially as retailers source more widely, looking for price bargains across Europe and beyond. Consumers too may be tempted by parallel trading, for example as they notice the car price differentials already outlined, or if they value the differences in alcohol and tobacco prices. Pressure is building for some national governments to set up legislative barriers to make parallel trading less attractive, despite the fact that this might go against the spirit of the SEM. Such barriers might include the payment of local VAT rates when bringing back into the country goods that command high prices at home but that are available more cheaply in neighbouring countries. Denmark, for instance, is concerned about cross-border parallel imports from Germany.

> **Example** Honda (http://www.honda.co.uk), the UK motorcycle market leader, became very concerned about parallel imported motor cycles and threatened to take legal action against those unofficial dealers that persisted with the practice. It estimated that parallel imports accounted for 25 per cent of bikes sold each year and were undermining UK price levels and causing safety risks for customers. Examples quoted were of customers themselves assembling high-powered machines delivered from elsewhere in the EU in crates. In some cases, customers did not know the difference between authorised and parallel importers. The Honda action follows recent EU rulings favouring the trademark owners of Levi jeans and Silhouette sunglasses (*see also* Case Study 11.1) (Griffiths, 1998b).

CHAPTER SUMMARY

This chapter has discussed the basic principles behind an element of the marketing mix that is often neglected or given insufficient strategic consideration. Pricing is a broad area, defined as covering anything of value that is given in exchange for something else. 'Price' is a blanket term to cover a variety of labels and is a key element in the marketing exchange. Price is usually measured in money, but can also involve the bartering of goods and services.

Price serves a number of purposes. It is a measure against which buyers can assess the product's promised features and benefits and then decide whether the functional, operational, financial or personal advantages of purchase are worthwhile or not. This assessment opens up the difficult area of price perception. Price may well be communicated as a fixed amount of money, but what that sum really represents is something very individual that can change as the buyer's needs and circumstances change.

The seller faces the difficult job of setting the price in the context of the buyers' price perceptions and sensitivities. In a price-sensitive market, finding exactly the right price is essential if customers are to be attracted and retained. The seller also needs to remember that price may involve the buyer in more than the handing over of a sum of money. Associated costs of installation, training and disposal of old equipment, for example, are taken into account in assessing the price of an organisational purchase.

The relationship between buyer and price differs according to the type of customer and the type of market. Consumers are likely to be more influenced by non-price factors in making their personal purchasing decisions within preconceived price bands. Nevertheless, there are some price-sensitive segments who will use price as a primary purchasing criterion. Wholesalers and retailers are more pragmatic about price. They know what the consumer is willing to pay and thus seek prices from manufacturers that allow them to sell competitively to the public, yet still cover their costs and an acceptable profit margin. In service markets, price may be used as a means of regulating the demand pattern, either dropping the price to ensure the fullest take-up of the service, or increasing the price to limit the number of customers to a level that the service provider can cope with. Non-profit organisations may also use this latter strategy, for example to protect conservation areas from 'human pollution'. Organisational markets represent the situation where both buyer and seller are likely to take as rational a view of price as possible.

The pricing decision is influenced by a number of factors, some of which are external to the organisation and some of which are internal. The external influences include customers, channels of distribution, competition and legal and regulatory constraints. Corporate and marketing objectives set the internal agenda in terms of what pricing is expected to achieve, both for the organisation as a whole and for the specific product. The organisation's costs relating to the development, manufacture and marketing of the product will also affect price.

The creation of the SEM opened up new opportunities for pan-European marketing, with lower costs, but also with more price competition. Currently, price differentials can be quite wide in some product sectors across Europe. This might be because of differing local market conditions or because of differing tax rates. Tax harmonisation has not yet been achieved in the EU. Price differentials might also arise from different consumer profiles, knowledge and attitudes to brands and products. Wide differentials in prices across Europe might create a discerning shopper who crosses borders in search of bargains, particularly for high-priced infrequent purchases such as cars. The introduction of the euro, however, should mean more price transparency and consistency.

Key words and phrases

Premium price	Price differentials	Price perception
Price	Price discipline	Price sensitivity
Price banding	Price elasticity of demand	Value
Price comparison	Price negotiation	Value management

QUESTIONS FOR REVIEW

10.1 What factors affect the customer's interpretation of price?

10.2 In what kind of circumstances might a high price actually be better for a seller than a low one?

10.3 How can a seller distract the customer's attention from a high price?

10.4 Define price discipline and explain what it means to both manufacturers and retailers.

10.5 What are the particular problems of pricing service products?

10.6 List the internal and external influences on pricing decisions.

10.7 Define price elasticity. Why is this an important concept for the marketer?

10.8 In what ways can competition influence pricing decisions?

10.9 To what extent and why do you think that costs should influence pricing?

10.10 What factors influencing European prices are likely to increase or reduce price differentials over the next five years?

QUESTIONS FOR DISCUSSION

10.1 Choose a manufacturer that produces a range of products serving different price segments in a consumer market. How does the manufacturer 'justify' the different prices?

10.2 Find an example of a price-sensitive consumer market. Why do you think this market is price sensitive and is there anything that the manufacturers or retailers could do to make it less so?

10.3 Compare consumer and organisational attitudes to price, explaining how and why they differ.

10.4 To what extent do you think the classic demand curve as shown in Fig 10.3 is a useful guide for the marketing manager in practice?

10.5 Choose a consumer product and explain the role that pricing plays in its marketing mix and market positioning.

CASE STUDY 10.1

Home win for soccer clubs

Love it or hate it, Manchester United is big business. It is a worldwide brand name that generates a loyalty and affinity that enables the soccer club, like many others, to develop merchandise, media products and alliances with service providers on a scale not thought possible in the era before the English Premier League was established. In 1997, United earned £27mn profits from merchandising. Sales have been helped as soccer has repositioned itself from a working-class game, sometimes dominated by violent youth, to a family entertainment dominated by middle and higher earners. In the UK, it has been estimated that United's share of the fan market is 20 per cent, so it is a major force in marketing terms.

Manchester United can be considered a typical 'passion brand', characterised by a sometimes fanatical following and a strong sense of belonging that is far removed from the discerning and rational consumer. Its following spreads far wider than its Old Trafford ground and many supporters have never seen a live game. To some, such a following brings special ethical issues for clubs as:

fans have an insatiable appetite for anything related to their favourite team, so clubs have a huge responsibility not to exploit them. (M. Pearce, TSM UK)

There is a risk of over-commercialisation, which can undermine the special relationship between the club and the consumer. Manchester United, along with other leading clubs, ran into this problem among accusations that it was putting pressure on suppliers of replica kits to keep prices artificially high in a sector worth £200mn. The Office of Fair Trading (OFT) was called in to investigate these claims. The OFT is not interested in premium prices generally, but it does take an interest if suppliers seek to keep prices artificially high by insisting that sports shops sell goods at prices comparable to those in the club shops. This reduces the opportunity for price competition.

The problem does not just relate to club shirts. Tesco claimed that it was refused supply of World Cup shirts and so had to resort to unofficial middlemen to get England and Scotland kit, which it then sold at 25 per cent less than sports shop prices. A selection of 1998 club kit prices for children and adults is listed in Table 10.6 to show the differences between prices at club shops. High-street prices closely follow these club shop prices.

TABLE 10.6
Club kit prices

Club	Child shirt	Child full kit	Adult shirt	Adult full kit
Arsenal	£30	£51	£38	£64
Chelsea	£30	£55	£40	£72
Derby County	£21	£38	£25	£48
Leeds United	£28	£50	£37	£64
Manchester United	£30	£53	£40	£71
Newcastle	£30	£51	£40	£67
West Ham United	£30	£54	£40	£70

Source: Farrell (1998).

Manchester United had already run into some criticism in the 1997 season when it issued a fourth strip to wear during the season, each one costing £80 for an adult and £63 for children. This followed on from a survey by the Consumers' Association in 1995, which found that United charged the highest price for first team shirts and had issued six new kits in three seasons. The guidelines laid down for clubs specify that they should not change their kit more than once every two years, although the need to have several 'away' kits can circumvent this guideline.

It has been estimated that clubs earn around £10 per shirt in addition to any retainers paid by the suppliers. In 1997, United sold 500 000 strips, compared with typical gates of around 50 000 for matches. The absence of a new strip in the 1997–98 season, however, meant a drop in merchandise sales of 16 per cent on the previous year's level. Thus the incentive for clubs to change kits is clear and does not necessarily relate to fashion or sponsorship. United, with its aim to dominate European football, recognises the value of expanding merchandising sales to the full. There are plans to open 150 stores selling team merchandise across Europe, Scandinavia and Asia and a web page, http://www.ManUtd.com, has been launched. For many clubs, what happens on the pitch or terrace is just a small part of a powerful marketing organisation.

Sources: Crosbie (1998); Farrell (1998); Gee and Twomey (1998); Hemsley (1999); Mitchell (1998); Nissé (1998).

Questions

1 Why is merchandise so important to a Premier League soccer club? Why has Manchester United gone into retailing when its core business is football?

2 What do you think are the internal factors influencing a club like Manchester United's pricing decision for replica kit?

3 What kind of factors are consumers taking into account when assessing the retail price of replica kit? Do you think they are sensitive to price or to the number of new kits that come out?

4 Why do you think the kit prices listed in the table above are so similar from club to club (with the notable exception of Derby County)?

CASE STUDY 10.2

Pricing a pinta

Most consumers in the UK have two main choices when it comes to buying milk. They can either have it delivered daily to their doorsteps, in traditional one pint bottles, priced at about 48p per pint, or they can buy in cartons or plastic bottles from the supermarket, priced between 21p and 28p per pint, depending on the size of the container. The average price differential between doorstep and supermarket milk is 14p. The price of the doorstep pint partly reflects the cost and value of the service provided, and partly the higher operating costs of a relatively inefficient distribution system. Doorstep delivery companies, such as Unigate and Dale Farm Express, have to run and maintain fleets of milk floats and between them employ around 20 000 people to make the deliveries, pick up the empty bottles, and collect the money from individual households. In contrast, supermarkets are buying in bulk and having deliveries made in bulk to regional depots, which is much more cost effective. In order to improve economies of scale and cost effectiveness, in 1998 the major supermarkets all cut the number of milk suppliers used, for example Tesco cut the number of its suppliers from eight to four.

The basic price of milk used to be controlled by the Milk Marketing Board, which had a monopoly over supply. In 1994, however, the milk market was deregulated, opening the market up to free competition. The immediate effect was an increase of between 8 per cent and 11 per cent in milk prices. Most dairy farmers in England and Wales joined a cooperative called Milk Marque (http://www.milk-marque.co.uk) which, with control over 65 per cent of supplies, could easily push for higher prices in the interests of its members. Upward pressure on prices has also arisen from EU agricultural policy, with the introduction of milk quotas. Because of this, it was estimated that in the mid-1990s, supply in the UK only met 85 per cent of demand.

Against this general background, supermarkets have seen milk as a valuable loss leader, bringing customers into the store and reinforcing 'value for money' images. In 1999, a six pint bottle cost £1.27, just over 21p per pint. The supermarkets still watch each other's milk prices carefully, and try to match them. If one breaks ranks, the others soon follow. A result of this is that the supermarkets are barely breaking even on milk. They are often making as little as 2p gross margin per pint, which is not sufficient even to cover the cost of the chilled storage.

One other major reason for milk still being so cheap, despite the best efforts of Milk Marque and the companies supplying milk to the supermarkets, is to do with changing consumer habits and lifestyles. There has been a decline in milk consumption generally, and it is perceived as having a boring, commodity image, particularly among young people. In addition, the more milk consumers buy from supermarkets, the greater the supermarkets' economies of scale and price negotiation power. Partly because of the convenience of 'one stop' shopping and partly because of the price, the supermarkets' share of the milk market has risen rapidly (*see* Table 10.7).

TABLE 10.7
Shares of the milk market

	Supermarket % market share	Doorstep delivery % market share
1980	10	90
1990	38	62
1995	55	45
1997	62	38

Mintel also suggests that smaller households have more erratic milk consumption patterns, and thus buying from the supermarket makes more sense. Some industry pessimists estimated that eventually the supermarkets would capture 85 per cent of the market, but by 1999, the decline in doorstep deliveries had slowed and the supermarkets did not seem to be taking any more market share. To slow the decline, doorstep delivery companies have tried to make the milkman special. Milk Marque launched a magazine targeted at women called *Home and Life* available only from the milkman for £1. The first issue sold 350000 copies. In late 1997, Dale Farm Express entered into an agreement with Lever Brothers and Kellogg to deliver bulky fmcg products to homes on the milk round. This idea failed, however, because of retailer opposition (although they still deliver peat and household cleaning products). They have also experimented with running promotions and competitions through milkmen to try to generate loyalty.

Nevertheless, many consumers find that purchasing milk from the supermarket is actually more convenient than a doorstep delivery. Improvements in milk quality and its processing means that its shelf life has increased, so that consumers can buy enough milk in bulk to last up to 10 days. The four and six pint bottles take up less room in the fridge than the equivalent number of glass bottles would, and consumers can buy as much as they want whenever they want rather than being tied to a certain number of pints per day. The customer does not have to worry about being at home either to take the milk in every day, or to pay the delivery person weekly (and check the bill, of course).

If consumers do not want or appreciate the service offered by the doorstep delivery, they will not be prepared to pay a premium for it. Also, as the gap between doorstep and supermarket prices widens, the bigger that premium becomes and the smaller the number of consumers who will pay it.

Sources: Gilchrist and Hornsby (1995); Maitland (1996a, 1996b); Mintel (1998); Murphy (1997); Smith and Urry (1998); Stuart (1997).

Questions

1 Summarise (a) the internal and (b) the external factors influencing the price of milk from the farmer's point of view.

2 What kind of pricing strategy do you think the supermarkets are using for milk and why?

3 Assess the threat to the doorstep delivery companies and the steps they are taking to counteract the threat. Is there anything else they could do?

4 What role does Milk Marque play in all this? What might happen if Milk Marque did not exist?

References to Chapter 10

Bolton, R. N. (1989), 'The Robustness of Retail Level Price Elasticity Estimates', *Journal of Retailing,* Summer, pp. 193–219.

Bowley, G. (1998), 'On the Road to Price Convergence', *Financial Times,* 12 November, p. 45.

Burt, T. (1998), 'Who is Prepared for the Single Currency', *Financial Times,* 3 December, p. 39.

Caine, N. (1997), 'Fridges, Hi-fis to be 10% Cheaper', *Sunday Times,* 3 August.

Crosbie, P. (1998), 'Clubs Face Probe into Price of Young Fans Kit', *Express,* 24 February, p. 13.

Cunningham, S. (1999), 'MMC to Check Out Supermarket Prices', *The Times,* 26 March, p. 29.

Davis, B. (1995), 'An Upheaval in the Retail Market', *Financial Times,* 6 March, p. II.

Diamantopoulos, A. and Mathews, B. (1995), *Making Pricing Decisions: A Study of Managerial Practice,* Chapman & Hall.

Erickson, G. M. and Johansson, J. K. (1985), 'The Role of Price in Multi-attribute Product Evaluations', *Journal of Consumer Research,* 12, pp. 195–9.

Farrell, S. (1998), 'Clubs Accused of Fixing Replica Soccer Kit Prices', *The Times,* 24 February, p. 6.

Gannaway, B. (1999), 'It's Crunch Time', *The Grocer,* 27 March, p. 16.

Gee, J. and Twomey, J. (1998), 'The Cup Kit Rip Off', *Express,* 27 May, p. 9.

Gilchrist, S. and Hornsby, M. (1995), 'The Vanishing Milkman Means Loss of 2200 Jobs', *The Times,* 24 March, p. 1.

Griffiths, J. (1998a), 'Time for a Better Deal', *Financial Times,* 29 October, p. 18.

Griffiths, J. (1998b), 'Honda Threatens Dealers Over Parallel Imports', *Financial Times,* 27 November, p. 10.

The Grocer (1999), 'Price Wars are Phoney', *The Grocer,* 10 April, p. 4.

Guild, A. (1996), 'Honey Market Hits A Sticky Patch', *Financial Times,* 19 March, p. 29.

Gwin, P. (1998), 'World Class Ticket Quandary', *Europe,* May, p. 31.

Heath, V. (1998), 'Honey makes Money for Big-scale Bee-keeper', *The Times,* 12 May, p. 25.

Hemsley, S. (1999), 'Match of the Day', *Marketing Week*, 18 March, pp. 43–7.

Kelly, J. (1998), 'Disharmony Ahead on Value Added Tax', *Financial Times*, 3 December, p. 39.

Kortge, G. D. and Okonkwo, P. A. (1993), 'Perceived Value Approach to Pricing', *Industrial Marketing Management*, 22, pp. 133–40.

Lee, A. (1998), 'FA Appeal Wins 30 Extra Tickets for England Fans', *The Times*, 29 June, p. 3.

Lightfoot, W. (1998), 'Will the Euro be Strong and Stable?', *The European*, 14–20 December, p. 36.

MacIntyre, B. (1998), '"Mad Bee" Disease Hits French Honey Supply', *The Times*, 9 April, p. 20.

Maitland, A. (1996a), 'Price Rise Prompts Fresh Outcry Over Milk Marque', *Financial Times*, 16 January, p. 7.

Maitland, A. (1996b), 'Surge in Supermarket Milk Price Eases Squeeze on Processors', *Financial Times*, 28 February, p. 9.

Marsh, P. (1998), 'Acceptance of the Inevitable Gains Currency', *Financial Times*, 15 October, p. 21.

McClintock, L. (1999), 'Euro Dawns but Shoppers Shrug', *The Grocer*, 9 January, p. 17.

Mead, G. (1997), 'Virus Endangers UK Honey Bees', *Financial Times*, 5 August, p. 23.

Mehta, S. (1995), 'Investing in Capital Assets', *Purchasing and Supply Management*, March, pp. 16–19.

Mintel (1998), 'Milk', *Market Intelligence*, March.

Mitchell, A. (1998), 'Sky's the Limit for New Breed of Passion Brands', *Marketing Week*, 17 September, pp. 44–5.

Montgomery, S. L. (1988), *Profitable Pricing Strategies*, McGraw-Hill.

Murphy, C. (1997), 'Is Delivery Coming Home?', *Marketing*, 9 January, p. 13.

Nagle, T. T. (1987), *The Strategy and Tactics of Pricing*, Prentice Hall.

Nissé, J. (1998), 'Manchester United Plans to Open 150 Club Stores', *The Times*, 29 September, p. 30.

Nuki, P. (1997), 'Contact Lens "Cartel" Can Cost Customers £100', *Sunday Times*, 26 October, p. 1.10.

Nuki, P. and Hamzic, E. (1998), 'British Mobile Phone Users Pay Double Foreign Rates', *Sunday Times*, 4 December, p. 1.7.

Nuttall, R. (1998), 'Why Does Petrol Cost So Much?', *Express*, 19 July, pp. 76–7.

O'Connor, J. and Galvin, E. (1999), *Marketing and Information Technology* (2nd edn.), Financial Times Pitman Publishing.

Philips, G. (1998), 'Staking a Claim on the Future', *The Times*, 21 October, p. 33.

Porter, M. E. (1980), *Competitive Strategy*, Free Press.

Pring, A. and Eggleston, S. (1998), 'Calais Run for Your Money', *The Grocer*, 3 October, pp. 32–4.

Purchasing and Supply Management (1995), 'Value In, Cost Out', *Purchasing and Supply Management*, June, p. 29.

Quelch, J. A. and Buzzell, R. D. (1989), 'Marketing Moves Through EC Crossroads', *Sloan Management Review*, 31(1), pp. 63–74.

Robinson, P. (1999), 'Economical with the Facts', *The Grocer*, 16 January, pp. 32–4.

Shannon, J. (1998), 'Euro Puts a Tax on Brand Values', *Marketing Week*, 26 February, p. 27.

Smith, A. and Urry, M. (1998), 'Supermarkets Skim Some Excess Fat from Dairy Suppliers', *Financial Times*, 17 November, p. 28.

Smith, R. (1994), 'Hand Drying for the Future', *European Purchasing and Materials Management*, No. 3, pp. 119–25.

Smith, D. (1998), 'How Single Is the Single Market?', *Management Today*, January, pp. 55–8.

Smith, D. (1999), 'Life with the Euro', *Sunday Times*, 3 January, p. 3.5.

Stuart, L. (1997), 'Dairy Tale', *Marketing Week*, 26 June, pp. 36–7.

Townsend, M. (1998), 'Action at Last on Great Car Price Scandal', *Express*, 7 July, p. 13.

van Zyl, (1998), 'Beekeeping Can Be Sweet as Honey', *Finance Week*, 11 December, p. 25.

Young, R. (1998), 'Shops Freed to Set Own Price on TVs and Fridges', *The Times*, 21 May, p. 10.

Zeithaml, V. A. (1988), 'Consumer Perceptions of Price, Quality and Value', *Journal of Marketing*, 52 (July), pp. 2–22.

11 | Pricing Strategies

LEARNING OBJECTIVES

This chapter will help you to:

1 understand the managerial process that leads to price setting and the influences that affect its outcomes;

2 appreciate the multiple and sometimes conflicting objectives impacting on pricing decisions;

3 define a range of available pricing strategies and their application in different market and competitive situations;

4 understand the available pricing methods and tactics, and their most appropriate use; and

5 appreciate some of the special issues affecting pricing in organisational markets.

INTRODUCTION

Economists' models of pricing tend to be based on costs and simplified models of demand structures without taking into account the reality of the marketing situation. It is rare to find that pricing can be achieved through the simple application of a formula, since the actions of marketers and competitors, as well as the perceptions and behaviour of consumers all have an influence on the pricing decision. Chapter 10 outlined many of these internal and external influences. The reality of pricing is that organisations do not have perfect information, as the economists assume, nor are consumers and competitors passive players in the process. Thus a certain amount of skill is required to assess how both consumers and competitors will respond to a particular pricing decision in the context of a particular marketing mix. The pricing decision is only simple for an organisation that consciously follows the rest of the market rather than tries to lead it.

Example Research by the Henley Centre suggested that different groups of consumers value time differently. 'Cash rich' but 'time poor' customers might be prepared to pay more for their products and services if they can access the service more quickly and conveniently than if they waste time queuing. This has led to some supermarkets considering the introduction of a fast-moving checkout line in which customers pay more for the benefit of moving through the line more quickly. One problem is avoiding offence to the majority of customers who want good service but are not prepared to pay a premium. There could also be problems if the majority of customers elect to take the fast lane. Research has suggested that one in four full time workers would be interested in using such a system.

Another way of using price to manage retail store traffic is 'off-peak discounts'. B&Q, for example, offered a 10 per cent discount to pensioners if they used the store on a Wednesday. The technology also exists to allow retailers to change prices throughout a store for all customers for a brief period during the day. Thus if the first hour's trading on a Monday morning is particularly quiet, for instance, the store can have a 'happy hour' to bring shoppers in earlier (Bird, 1998a, 1998b; Nuki, 1998; Rufford and Nuki, 1997).

Building on the foundations of price influences laid down in Chapter 10, this chapter examines the stages that organisations go through to establish the price range and to set the final prices for their products. Figure 11.1 gives an overview of the process. Setting price objectives, stage 1, ensures that the corporate and marketing objectives of the organisation are taken into consideration in the pricing decision. Stage 2, estimating demand, assesses likely market potential and consumer reaction to different price levels, and was covered in at pp. 392 *et seq*. Within this structure, marketing managers can then begin to define pricing policy in stage 3. This is the guiding philosophical framework within which pricing strategies and decisions are determined. Pricing strategies deal with the long-term issues of positioning within the market and the achievement of corporate and marketing objectives. Establishing cost–volume–profit relationships at stage 4 checks that the estimated sales of the product can generate acceptable levels of income at any given price in order to cover costs and make an adequate profit. Implicit in all of this is the fact that pricing has to take place in a competitive environment, and thus the marketing manager must assess how competitors will react to various possible prices, and the extent to which the proposed price reflects the desired competitive positioning of the organisation and its products.

These first four stages culminate in stage 5, pricing tactics and final adjustments that focus on the practical application of pricing in the marketing mix and in the context of the market segments to be served. Pricing procedures set the method by which prices are calculated in the light of strategies to arrive at the final figure. Tactics, however, allow those prices to be varied on a planned, structured basis or in the shorter term on a one-off or irregular basis, perhaps to take advantage of sudden market opportunities or to overcome unforeseen difficulties.

Although Fig. 11.1 presents a neat, logical flow, in reality the pricing decision is likely to involve many reiterations and merging of stages. Some stages may be omitted, others may be extended to take into account special conditions within a market. There may also be conflict, for example between corporate level pressure to maximise profit and competitive assessment that indicates a market that is already well served at the higher-priced end. Such conflicts need to be resolved to avoid the risks of inconsistent pricing within a poorly defined marketing mix. It is also difficult to generalise about the price-setting process, not only because it operates uniquely in every organisation, but also because it will vary greatly between different types of product and market depending on the dynamics and maturity of the specific situation.

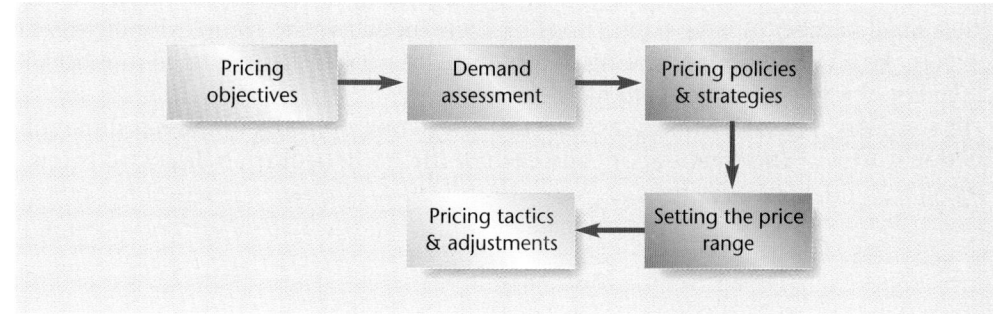

FIGURE 11.1

Determining a price range – overview

Finally, this chapter reviews some of the special considerations connected with price setting in organisational markets, such as negotiation, tendering and the setting of internally derived transfer prices between different departments or divisions of an organisation.

First, however, we discuss the general stages of the pricing process outlined in Fig. 11.1, beginning with pricing objectives.

PRICING OBJECTIVES

Any planned approach needs to be founded on what has to be achieved, and that applies as much to pricing as to anything else. Its role in the marketing mix as well as its role as the generator of revenue and profit has to be defined. In that sense, price is a delicate balance between serving the customer's needs and wants and serving the need of the organisation to recoup its costs of manufacturing and marketing and to make a profit.

Price objectives, therefore, should be closely linked with organisational and marketing objectives (Baumol, 1965). Some of these may be financially based, whereas others may be related to volume of sales. Pricing objectives thus have implications for many functional areas of the business, such as finance, production and distribution, as well as for marketing. Those other functional areas may also influence pricing. If in the short term, for example, finance detects a cash flow problem, marketers may be pressurised into dropping prices to convert products into cash quickly. In the longer term, the corporate strategists may see the organisation's only means of survival to be the defeat of a major competitor, and price may be a key weapon in that. This also underlines the fact that objectives need not be absolutely fixed; they can vary in the short- or long-term to meet changing needs and pressures.

> **Example** One-2-One (http:www.one2one.co.uk), the smallest of the UK's big four mobile phone companies, wanted to secure a larger market share in the run-up to Christmas 1998. The three months leading up to Christmas are especially busy, with new subscribers signing up and so One-2-One decided to use price as a weapon to beat its rivals. In order to increase the number of subscribers, it offered free calls on workdays between noon and 2pm from signing up until June 1999. It was hoped that this would attract customers wanting to make personal calls during the lunchtime period (Cane, 1998).

Inevitably, where there are so many objectives relating to so many functional areas, conflicts will arise. In that case, management must work to ensure that compromises and decisions are made, and priorities set in the best interests of the organisation and its customers.

As with objectives in any area of management, pricing objectives must be clearly defined, detailed, time specific and never inconsistent with each other (Diamantopoulos and Mathews, 1995). Clearly, these ideals are easier to achieve in an organisation dealing with a small number of large transactions or a few products. The complexity increases, however, for an organisation dealing in a number of markets, with a large number of customers, or with a number of products.

In summary, Fig. 11.2 shows the basis of conflicting objectives between different functional areas of the organisation, and each of these will be further discussed below, starting with financial objectives.

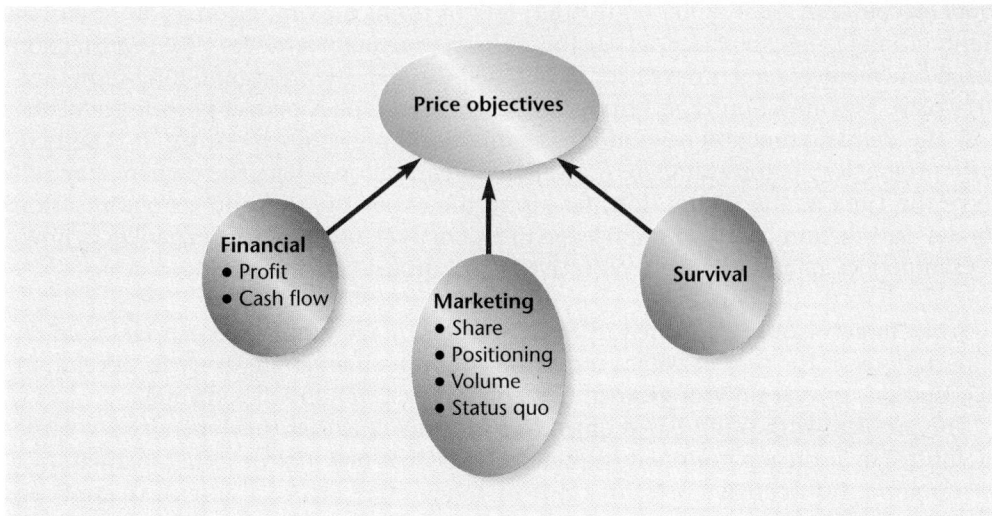

FIGURE 11.2

Conflicting price objectives

Financial objectives

Financial objectives can have both short- and long-term dimensions. For instance, the necessity to generate sufficient cash flow to fund the day-to-day operation of the organisation is a short-term objective, whereas the need to generate funds to allow reinvestment in research and development is a longer-term goal. Long-term objectives ultimately provide the means of satisfying shareholder expectations and generating the means of investing in sound foundations for the future.

Most financial objectives centre on either profit or cash flow. We look at profit-based objectives first.

Profit

Return on investment. Pricing is used in the context of return on investment as the means of achieving a specified rate of return on the investment made in the product. One of the interesting questions relating to return on investment (ROI) is the length of time it should take to recoup that investment and begin generating clear profit. If a long-term ROI is acceptable, that gives the marketer the opportunity to build the product strategically, creating and protecting market share through planned market penetration with strong marketing support. It means that the product can be allowed to develop at its own pace with less risk of its existence or position being threatened by management looking for a quick, clear profit.

Short-term ROI implies more of a performance orientation. The product is under pressure to generate large amounts of cash to pay for itself and make a clear profit quickly. The danger is that these pressures can lead to inappropriate marketing strategies, for example setting too high a price or attempting to make a niche product into a mass-market item to generate volume sales in order to bring in revenue. This lack of patience can, therefore, jeopardise the product's success and thus severely reduce the eventual return on the organisation's investment.

There is a skill involved in setting target ROI, not only because it assumes a degree of knowledge of revenue and cost behaviour that may not be possessed, but also because it has to balance the short-term pressure to bring money in against the possible longer-term strategic desire to build market position slowly but thoroughly. The more volatile and the less predictable the market environment into which the product is being launched, the more problematic becomes the ROI decision.

Profit maximisation. Economics texts often talk of profit maximisation as an organisation's ultimate goal. In reality, an organisation may actually settle for profit satisfaction based on whatever targets have been negotiated through the short- and long-term business plan. Maximisation is an impossible ideal, as it implies perfect knowledge of the cost and demand function beyond the organisation's previous experience. It is particularly impracticable, for example, in a smaller organisation where the owners may not have the time or the inclination, let alone the expertise, to build a maximisation model. Satisfaction based on knowledge of the market and previous experience, however imperfect, may be the main objective to be fulfilled through pricing.

Profit targets can be measured in actual or percentage terms, and can be based on expectations of the way in which the product and its market are likely to develop or expectations of year-on-year growth, namely that past trends will continue.

The problem with profit-based objectives for pricing is that they encourage a sense of control over the environment or predictability that may not be either justifiable or sustainable. Competitive pressures, for instance, may create a downward pull on prices during the course of the accounting period, which will compromise target profits. Alternatively, an organisation that sets its profit targets too high may create a pricing structure within the market that attracts new entrants who are prepared to undercut and accept lower profit expectations in order to develop market share.

Cash flow

The pressure to generate cash quickly from a product may be especially great if the product has a short life-cycle, such as goods utilising the merchandising rights associated with a film (e.g., *Titanic* or *Godzilla*). There may also be pressure if a producer feels that there is only a short lead time available to capitalise on a new product before heavy competition enters the market.

Cash flow considerations are also strong where an organisation has high operating costs and/or fluctuating or seasonal demand. A retailer who stocks lawnmowers, for example, may be prepared to sell the machines at a lower price at the end of the summer in order to turn the stock into hard cash, to avoid the costs of keeping the stock over the winter and to clear the warehouse in preparation for the latest models to be introduced next spring. All of this is worth the reduced margins on the mowers sold cheaply.

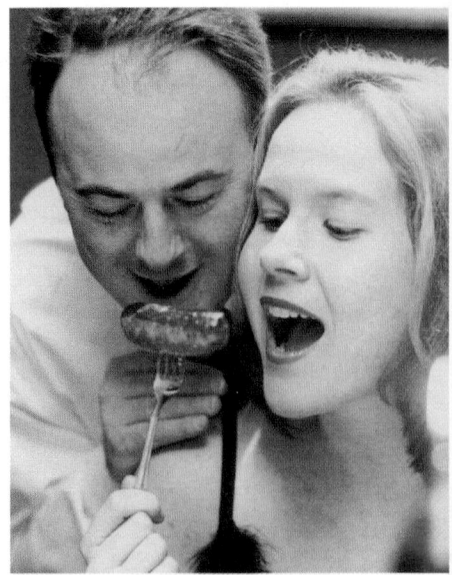

Love is ...

Source: Mr Lazenby's/Northern Profile

Sales and marketing objectives

Clearly, sales and marketing objectives are important influencers of the pricing decision. Target market share, relative position within the market and target volume sales can all be affected through pricing choices.

Market share and positioning

An organisation's marketing objectives may relate to either maintaining or increasing market share. The implications of this for pricing need to be carefully considered. Maintenance of market share in a highly competitive market may mean that prices cannot be increased for the next trading period, or even that they have to be reduced to face competitors who undercut. Increasing market share may mean aggressively low pricing to attract switchers from competing products. Alternatively, high prices might help to establish a high-quality position that appeals to more discerning customers.

The interaction between price and quality, and the need for consistency between them, are shown in Fig. 11.3. Where price and quality are equal, or where quality level exceeds price, the

MARKETING IN ACTION Premium sausages

Lazenby's (http:www.lazenbys.co.uk) has helped to create a premium-priced, upmarket niche within a sausage market that was dominated by mass-produced products sold on low price. The company has become the market leader in the premium sausage niche market, a move that has proved highly profitable for a relatively small firm in the market. The business started in 1983 with just one Dicker-filler, a hand-operated sausage machine. At that time, UK supermarket sausage prices were between 49p and 69p per pack. Lazenby's positioned itself at around the £1 mark, a price that meant that it took five years before the first supermarket contract was won. Meanwhile, the brand image developed, centred on a traditional image of a smiling butcher, Mr Lazenby, suitably attired in a clean, white butcher's apron.

By 1997, sales of premium sausages had really taken off, and the sector was worth over £100mn within the whole £520mn UK sausage market. Many manufacturers had developed premium brands and in the constant search for differentiation had introduced products made from more and more exotic meats (venison, wild boar, ostrich and kangaroo, for example), herbs, spices and added ingredients (such as beer, cranberry and mushroom). Mr Lazenby has had to be as innovative as the rest. In 1998, the Mr Lazenby brand was extended to include a crispy coated sausage in 'hot and spicy' and 'Chinese' flavours to appeal to the youth market. Special occasions also provide sausage opportunities. The exotic Mr Lazenby sausage containing oysters, pork and ginger was a one-off concoction targeted, perhaps not surprisingly, at all those lovers on Valentine's Day 1999.

The quality theme extends throughout the raw material and production process. The combination is simple: 100 per cent pork, natural skins and real flavourings. Price tends to be used by consumers as a quality indicator in the sausage market, although in reality, higher-priced products do not always use higher-quality ingredients.

Despite occupying a premium position, Lazenby's still had some tough negotiating to do with the larger supermarket chains as it expanded its distribution. Richard Lazenby, the owner, claimed:

'I know for a fact that one major UK supermarket chain is making margins of 45 per cent on our products and 90 per cent of that is profit – but it's always the supplier who ends up having to carry the can.'

Pressures on margins and the need to reinvest in new equipment to retain the leadership position in a growth market means that premium prices are an essential part of the overall strategy.

Sources: Darwent (1996); Mintel (1997); *Supermarketing* (1998, 1999).

consumer certainly benefits and thus the seller may have established a useful position. If the price exceeds the quality, however, to the bottom left of the matrix, the offering represents bad value for money and the seller is likely to lose customers unless something is done to remedy the inconsistency.

Obviously, price is not the only factor affecting performance. Astute use of advertising, for example, may help to achieve market share objectives without giving way so much on price. Using price this way as a competitive weapon may be less effective than hoped, since price moves are too easily copied by other organisations.

		Product quality		
		Low	Medium	High
Price	Low	Economy position	Value position	Excellent value strategy Underpriced?
	Medium	Poor value position Overpriced?	Medium value position	Value position Underpriced?
	High	Poor value strategy Overpriced?	Poor value position Unsupported price premium	Premium positioning

FIGURE 11.3

Price–quality matrix

Volume sales

Seeking volume sales may well be related to market share objectives, but arises more from an operational focus on capacity. In different kinds of production activity, pricing may be used as a means of maintaining the operational smooth running of the organisation. With continuous production, involving the mass production of identical products, there is the ability to pile up stocks of the finished product until it is sold. At some point, however, the stockpiles may become unacceptably large, leading to pressure to sell at a discount to clear them. In a recession, for instance, many car manufacturers face this problem if they keep their production lines running at more or less normal capacity in the hope that the market will pick up soon.

Batch or unit production, involving the production of small numbers (even down to one-off jobs) of different goods at a time, is more concerned with keeping the business afloat than with the running of a particular line. Shipbuilding operates in this way; while one job is being carried out, management are looking to fill the order book for the future, whether with large multimillion-pound projects or with small maintenance jobs just to keep the work-force occupied and make a contribution to overheads. Pricing is used very aggressively in such markets to win the contract that will secure the short- or long-term future of the organisation.

In a service industry, because of the inherent perishability of the product, price becomes more important as the deadline for service delivery approaches. In a hotel, for example, if it means the difference between letting a room tonight and not letting it, then price may become negotiable for an eleventh-hour potential guest. Pricing is also used extensively in service situations as a means of evening out fluctuating demand. Again, in the hotel industry, weekend or midweek special deals help to direct demand to the quieter parts of the week, allowing the hotelier to maintain occupancy rates while still recouping the variable costs of so doing.

Status quo

Linked closely with maintaining market share, the objective of preserving the *status quo* implies an organisation that is happy for things to continue as they are and does not want the market's boat to be rocked. Even a market leader may be happy simply to retain share rather than seek even more, and may prefer not to challenge a smaller, lower-priced competitor for fear of damaging its own position in the process.

Example Icelandair's (http://www.icelandair.is) average fare to the USA is 35 per cent lower than that of bigger airlines such as SAS, and it carries more Norwegians and Swedes to Florida than any other airline. The other airlines are happy for Icelandair to do this, however, since the airline is not perceived as a serious threat because of the small scale of its operations, and because a significant proportion of transatlantic travellers would prefer to pay a little more not to visit Reykjavik!

One of the problems of using pricing as a means of gaining share is indeed the risk of a price war. One organisation reduces its prices and then all the others start a downward spiral of undercutting. The ultimate outcome of this is that margins become increasingly small, the weakest organisations fall by the wayside, relative market shares are unlikely to change, and nobody wins other than the consumer. This is a very expensive way of maintaining the *status quo*. Even a smaller supplier may elect to maintain the *status quo* by matching rather than challenging competitors' prices. According to Perks (1993), to win a price war, an organisation should only target weaker competitors, fight from a position of strength and extend the war over a long period to wear down the competition.

An organisation may, of course, choose to match prices in some product areas, but not in others. Even the upmarket UK supermarkets, for example, are seen to compete aggressively on price on a select number of basic product lines, yet quietly make up for this by charging price premiums on others.

Price as a stabiliser can, therefore, be a very powerful force. It also strengthens the arguments for a philosophy of profit satisfaction rather than maximisation, as discussed at p. 420 above, through the trade-off between the perceived gains and losses of failing to follow on price.

Price matching rather than undercutting may well maintain the *status quo*, but it also opens the door for non-price competition, where the focus is on the other elements of the marketing mix. An organisation that can demonstrate that it offers a better product (by whatever criteria matter to the target market) can neutralise, to some extent, the market's sensitivity to price. This is difficult to do, but it does mean that it is easier to build and retain loyalty, thus defending against competitive erosion of both market share and margins. The more price sensitive the customers, the less loyal they are.

Survival

In difficult economic circumstances, survival can become the only motivating objective for an organisation. Long-term strategic objectives have no currency if you are likely to be out of business tomorrow. Imagine a small company that has found that its market does not have the potential it originally predicted. Price is a very obvious and flexible marketing mix element to change in order to keep goods flowing out and cash flowing in. As discussed at p. 422 above, even a larger firm, such as a shipbuilder, may be prepared to suffer short-term losses to keep the operation intact, even though this cannot be sustained indefinitely without reducing the size of the operation in some way.

Example The American airline PanAm, in its last few years before bankruptcy, attempted heavy price discounting and frequent-flyer bonus mileage points as a means of staving off collapse. The consumer gained from the lower fares and incentives, but even at those prices, the company did not generate sufficient traffic to pull it out of its financial problems.

PRICING POLICIES AND STRATEGIES

Pricing policies and strategies guide and inform the pricing decision, providing a framework within which decisions can be made with consistency and with the approval of the organisation as a whole. Policies and strategies help to specify the role of pricing and its use in context of the marketing mix (Nagle, 1987). Such frameworks are especially important in larger organisations where pricing decisions may be delegated with some discretion to line managers or sales representatives. They need sufficient rules to maintain a consistent corporate image in front of the market without being unduly restricted.

There are many situations in which a sales representative, for instance, may need policy guidance. Imagine a sales representative visiting a customer who tells him that a competitor is offering a similar product more cheaply. Company policy will help the representative to decide whether or not to get involved in undercutting or whether to sell the product benefits harder.

Other situations where policy and strategy guidelines may be of use include responding to a competitive price threat in a mass market, setting prices for new or relaunched products, modifying price in accordance with prevailing environmental conditions, using price with other marketing mix elements and, finally, using price across the product range to achieve overall revenue and profit targets. Some of these situations are discussed in more detail below. In any situation, guidelines can provide the basis for more detailed pricing strategies designed to achieve price objectives.

New product pricing strategies

In addition to all the other pressures and risks inherent in new product development, as discussed in Chapter 9, it is important to get the launch price right as it can be difficult to change it later. It can be easy and tempting to set a low price to attract customers to a new launch, but this can establish attitudes and perceptions of the quality and positioning of the brand that would be difficult to overturn. A subsequent price rise might be viewed with some hostility by the customer. The safest route to low price entry with an option of raising it later is to make the price a promotional issue. Clearly signalling the low price as an introductory offer, a short-term trial price both attracts attention and encourages trial of the new product, and when the price does rise to its 'normal' level, there is no confusion or suspicion in the customer's mind.

> **Example**   In April 1999, to coincide with the release of the Rugrats movie (http://www.nick.com/rugrats_movie), the Rugrats Snack Box was launched containing a vitamin C-enriched drink, a packet of raisins, a packet of crisps and a 'harvest bar'. The trial price of the box was 99p compared with a normal retail price of £1.19. This would encourage retailers to stock the product, as consumers would be more likely to give it a try for less than £1 (*The Grocer*, 1999).

Another aspect of the high or low price setting decision is the likely impact on the competition. A high price might encourage them to enter the market too, as they see potentially high profit margins. The organisation launching the new product may not, however, have too much choice. Internal pressure to recoup development costs quickly, as discussed at p. 419, may force a high price, or alternatively a price-sensitive market might simply reject a high price and force prices lower.

According to Monroe and Della Bitta (1978), much depends on how innovative the new product is. A new brand in a crowded market can be precise with its price positioning as there are many competitors to compare with, and both the price setter and the consumer can 'read' the price signals clearly. A completely unknown product, such as the very first domestic video recorder, has no such frame of reference. The price setter can work on three things. First, the prices of other domestic electrical goods might give clues as to the sort of prices consumers expect to pay. This is a tenuous link because this new product is so obviously different it may not be comparable, especially in the mind of an opinion-leading consumer. Second, market research may have been carried out to discover how enthusiastic consumers are about the new idea, and hypothetically what they would pay to possess it. Again, this may be misleading because the consumers have no experience of this product and may not themselves be able to foresee in theory how they would respond in practice. Third, the price setter can work on internal factors such as costs, breakeven analysis and return on investment. This serves as a starting point and experience and emerging competition will allow a more realistic price structure to evolve. It is a dangerous route, however. If that cost-based price turns out to be inappropriate, rescuing the product could be almost impossible, particularly if astute competitors are learning from your mistakes and launching realistically priced products themselves.

With all this in mind, the high or low entry price decision boils down to two alternative strategies, **skimming** or **penetration**, first proposed by Dean (1950).

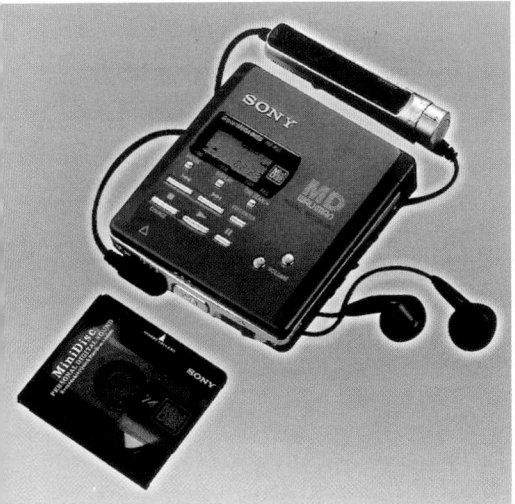

Price skimming was short but sweet.
Source: Sony UK Ltd.

Price skimming

In order to skim, prices are set high to attract the least price-sensitive market segments. Such pricing might appeal, for instance, to opinion leaders who want to be seen to be first with any new product regardless of the price, or to those who seek status and see high price as the mark of an exclusive product.

Skimming has a number of advantages. It allows the organisation to establish a quality brand image that could serve as a stepping stone to future development of lower-priced, more mass-market versions. If the product in question is a difficult one to produce, then pricing to keep the market small and exclusive can also give breathing space to gain learning experience on lower volumes while still marketing the product in a real market. The risk here, of course, is that high price raises high expectations, and if that learning experience does not go well, then the market will think that the product quality is too poor or inconsistent to justify the price, a bad reputation will stick and the future of the product becomes questionable. Finally, it is easier to reduce price than to raise it. If an initial high price does not generate the required response, it can be slowly lowered until an appropriate level is found.

Example Organisations with new products may not have long to enjoy the fruits of skimming. The Sony Walkman, for example, had a honeymoon period as the only product of its type, and could thus price itself high. As competitors began to infiltrate the market with imitations, the market's price profile began to develop and although Sony remained a premium-priced brand, it would never again have the freedom to skim as it chose.

Penetration pricing

In an attempt to gain as big a market share as possible in the shortest possible time, an organisation may price aggressively below existing competition, deliberately paring its margins for the sake of volume. This is *penetration pricing*. It may be a necessary strategy if cost structures are such that a very large volume of sales is required to break even or to achieve economies of scale in production or marketing terms. It is a risky strategy because it could establish a poor-quality brand image and also, if it does not work, it would be very difficult to raise the price.

It is, nevertheless, a legitimate strategy to seek to deny the competition volume share within the market. Penetration pricing of a new product, particularly in a market where product differentiation is difficult, reduces the attractiveness of market entry to competitors unless they can be sure that they can produce and market much more efficiently and on a tighter cost base. Penetration pricing is also useful in elastic demand situations where price is a critical factor for the buyer.

As emphasised above, the choice of launch price should take into account future plans for the pricing and positioning of the product. Some products can enter a market with a skimming price and retain it, particularly luxury goods that are well differentiated from each other and have an element of uniqueness about them. The Swiss company Bueche Girod, for example, advertised a 9 carat gold and diamond ladies' watch for £1675 with a matching necklace for a further £2975. In markets where a new product has a high level of technological innovation and customers have no benchmark against which to compare prices, the introductory price may skim, but this will give way to something more competitive as rival products enter the market, economies of scale are achieved and costs reduce with the learning curve. In contrast, penetration pricing at launch sets an aggressive, value for money stance that the manufacturer would find hard to break away from, regardless of what the competition do. This product will always have to be priced competitively.

Product mix pricing strategies

A product that is part of a product range cannot be priced in isolation from the rest of the range. The range has to be viewed as an entity, and different products serve different purposes that come together to benefit the whole. In seeking to serve the needs of a number of market segments and build a strong competitive defence across the market, one product may be allowed to earn a relatively low return while another is skimming.

Within an individual product line (*see* pp. 272 *et seq.* for the distinction between range and line), such as SLR cameras, each product within the line offers additional features and their pricing needs to be spaced out accordingly. Customers see the set of products within the line and relate the price steps with additional features, benefits or quality. This may also encourage consumers to trade up to a more expensive model in the line as they begin to indulge in a type of marginal analysis: 'For an extra £20 I can have a zoom facility as well. Seems like a better deal ...'. The process may not be so rational. As discussed at p. 385, price may be used as an indicator of quality in the absence of other knowledge or indicators. Thus a buyer may find a model within the product line at (or slightly beyond) the preconceived spending limit and feel that the best possible quality purchase has been made, regardless of whether the product benefits and features are useful or appropriate.

Rather than presenting a predetermined collection of standard products with standard prices, some organisations prefer to offer a basic-priced product to which the consumer can then add extras, each of which adds to the overall price. The beauty of this is that the basic price seems very reasonable and affordable, and thus the consumer can easily get to the stage of wanting the product. Once that stage is reached, the odd few pounds here and there for extra features seems insignificant, even though the final total price may be somewhat higher than the consumer would have been comfortable with in the first place. At least the customer is getting a personally tailored purchase.

Example Holiday packages prominently feature low prices on their brochures to attract attention and make themselves seem eminently affordable. Two weeks in the sun for only £99 per person soon increases to something closer to £300 when airport transfers and taxes are added, along with the supplements for a local departure, insurance, better-quality accommodation with a sea view, full board, and an August rather than May holiday. Buying a car is also a minefield of extras. Delivery charges, taxes, registration plates, metallic paint, sunroof, alarm system, central locking are among the items that may not necessarily be quoted in the advertised price.

The problem with any such approach is knowing what to leave out and what to include in the basic price. A basic price that does not include non-optional items such as tax is likely to lead to an unimpressed customer. There is also the danger that a competitor who comes in with an all-inclusive price may be seen as attractive by customers who feel that they have been deceived by overpriced extras that are actually essentials. In the USA, both General Motors and Ford led the car market in offering *one-price selling* or *value pricing*, where they offered vehicles with a fixed set of options at a fixed, non-negotiable price. Such moves take away the uncertainty about what the real price will be and what is or is not included in the price, as well as relieving the buyer of the ordeal of having to haggle over price (Moskal, 1994).

This discussion has raised issues of the psychology of pricing, which will be further discussed at p. 438 *et seq.*

Managing price changes

Prices are rarely static for long periods. Competitive pressures may force prices down, either temporarily or permanently, or new market opportunities might increase the price premium on a product. The pressure of cost inflation means that the marketing manager has to decide whether to pass these cost increases on to customers through prices charged, and when. However, changing prices can have a serious effect on profit margins and on market stability. If the changes are too significant, whether on transatlantic air fares or the price of vegetables in the local market, it is almost inevitable that competitors will respond in some way. Price changes not only cause ripples through the market, but also have an impact on sales volume. Normally, it is likely that a price cut will increase volume, and it is sometimes a very fine calculation to predict whether the profit margin earned on the extra volume gained more than compensates for the lost margin caused by the price cut. At various times, an organisation might be faced with the prospect of initiating price changes, or of responding to competitors' price changes.

Initiating price cuts

Initiating price cuts can be a very dangerous activity. Any organisation considering such a move needs to think through carefully the likely impact of any changes on both customers and competitors. Table 11.1 shows how much extra volume needs to be sold to make up for the lost margin on any given price cut. It can be seen that if the initial gross profit margin was 30 per cent and a price cut of 10 per cent was introduced, unit sales would need to increase by 50 per cent just to maintain the original profit level. For even the best of organisations, assessing the likely impact of such a price cut on the market is a tough challenge.

Nevertheless, organisations still do cut prices from time to time. They may do so for short-term tactical reasons, such as clearing excess stock, or as part of a more fundamental strategic 'value for money' repositioning. Much depends on whether the organisation sees itself as a price leader or follower in the market. A leader may wish to make the first move, leaving competitors with the problem of whether to respond, and how. There are a number of reasons for cutting price, including the following.

Capacity utilisation. Where excess production capacity is found in a market, there is a temptation to lower prices to levels that do not cover full costs, but at least cover the variable cost and make some contribution towards fixed overheads, just to keep the production lines busy. Such price cutting cannot carry on indefinitely, but might serve a useful purpose in the short term until either recovery or shakeout.

> **Example** Airlines use price variations in order to maximise the revenue from a flight and to ensure that a minimum number of seats remain unsold. There could well be 20 or 30 different fares on a typical transatlantic jet, with some tickets purchased six months in advance and others purchased on a stand-by basis. Airline capacity planning and fare setting might differ from flight to flight even within one airline on the same route. As a general rule, as soon as the first-class and business-class seats have been sold with full-fare-paying passengers, the cost of the flight has been covered. The sale of seats in economy class is therefore translated into direct profit and for this reason the challenge is to maximise the return in economy class by selling all the seats at prices appropriate to the season and market conditions on that route (Walters, 1998). So it may be £6000 for a Concorde ticket to New York, or if you prefer something a little cheaper, with many restrictions, it could be less than £200 (but not on Concorde, of course!).

TABLE 11.1

The impact of price reductions on sales volume

If you cut your price by: %	If your gross profit margin is (%)						
	5	10	15	20	25	30	40
	you need an increase in unit sales of (%):						
1	25.0	11.1	7.1	5.3	4.2	3.4	2.6
2	66.7	25.0	15.4	11.1	8.7	7.1	5.3
3	150.0	42.9	25.0	17.6	13.6	11.1	8.1
4		66.7	36.4	25.0	19.0	15.4	11.1
5		100.0	50.0	33.3	25.0	20.0	14.3
6		150.0	66.7	42.9	31.6	25.0	17.6
7		233.3	87.5	53.8	38.9	30.4	21.2
8			114.3	66.7	47.1	36.4	25.0
9			150.0	81.8	56.3	42.9	29.0
10			200.0	100.0	66.7	50.0	33.3
11			275.5	122.2	78.6	57.9	37.9
12			400.0	150.0	92.3	66.7	42.9
13				185.7	108.3	76.5	48.1
14				233.3	127.3	87.5	53.8
15				300.0	150.0	100.0	60.0
16				400.0	177.8	114.3	66.7
17				566.7	212.5	130.8	73.9
18					275.1	150.0	81.8
19					316.7	172.7	90.5
20					400.0	200.0	100.0
21					525.0	233.3	110.5
22					733.3	275.0	122.2
23						328.6	135.3
24						400.0	150.0
25						500.0	166.7

Market dominance. If an organisation enjoys a strong price and cost leadership position and is not likely to fall foul of competition legislation, it may pay to seek an even more dominant position through selective or across the board price cuts. Such action could help to eliminate or at least squeeze some competitors, but an organisation following this strategy also runs the risk of making customers more price sensitive.

Market defence. If a market segment is under attack or if demand is weak compared with other alternatives, it may pay an organisation to defend its position by lowering prices to minimise the impact of the threat. This could be a dangerous strategy in the long term, but by creating short-term difficulties for the attacker, it may help the organisation to retain share.

A sudden unsignalled price cut might be seen by competitors as the first move in a price war. An organisation needs to be sure that it can win and be sure of what it is going to achieve by such an aggressive act. An advance warning of a price increase is less likely to be viewed with hostility. It gives the competition time to reflect on its implications and to make a considered response, which does not necessarily mean a panic descent into further undercutting. It also allows good customers to stock up at the old prices or enables further negotiation time in organisational markets. Many annual subscriptions to magazines are offered to readers at the existing rate, with a clear indication that the subscription rate will rise in the near future. This is an incentive to 'act now'. An early notification of price increases, often associated with the introduction of new and revised products, gives a short-term flurry of excitement to the market as customers aim to beat the deadline.

Responding to competitors' price cuts

When a competitor initiates price cuts, whether selective or across the board, a very careful response needs to be planned. Much again will depend on how and why the change has taken place. Is it overt and threatening, covert and threatening or clearly signalled with some attempt at justification, for example spare capacity?

The response to a competitor's price cut can take three broad forms: ignoring the decrease, responding head-on by matching or undercutting the competitor or deflecting the decrease, as the supermarkets did (*see* p. 399), by emphasising added value rather than price.

Ignoring the decrease. This can be a high-risk strategy if the price cut is significant and clearly related to an aggressive campaign to gain market share. Once share is lost it is very difficult to win it back.

> **Example** Many years ago, Bic (http://www.bicworld.com) created turmoil in the pen industry with low pricing, disposability and heavy promotion through mass distribution. Many traditional suppliers failed to spot the threat emerging across Europe quickly enough and lost substantial market share by not responding. The desirability of matching a price cut may depend on whether it is perceived to be a short-term or long-term measure. If it is longer term, there may be a case for introducing an economy brand and repositioning the threatened product slightly more upmarket. This is effectively what happened in the pen industry, as suppliers introduced higher-quality, well-differentiated pens, while seeking to match the lower Bic prices through new cheap alternatives based on a similar competitive formula.

Undercutting. Responding by *undercutting the competitor* might easily lead to a flurry of price cuts, stimulating a price war in which the consumer may well be the only winner. Sectors such as petrol, transatlantic air fares, supermarkets and cross-channel travel have all experienced price wars in recent years. Price war threats are especially prevalent in oligopolistic markets, but many organisations seek to avoid them for the kind of reasons discussed on p. 422 (Lambin, 1993).

Deflecting the cut. *Deflecting the price cut* may be an appropriate option if the cut is not very severe and sufficient brand loyalty and differentiation have reduced customers' price sensitivities. Various options can be used to add value to the product at existing prices. This could include larger pack sizes, more features, more services, better packaging or promoting the product quality and benefits more aggressively. In extreme circumstances, of course, the only commercially sensible option may be to concede defeat and move on.

> **Example** Intel (http://www.intel.com), the silicon chip manufacturer, has come under increased pressure from price-cutting competitors such as AMD (http://www.amd.com) and Cyrix (http://www.cyfix.com). For many years, Intel had the PC processor market to itself and although making just one component in the PC, through branding and end-user advertising it established a high level of awareness for a product that is not seen by the majority of consumers. Although it did lower prices when new competitors entered the market in the mid-1990s, it did not regard this as a sustainable long-term approach and has therefore also sought to compete on non-price factors. First, it launched the Pentium II processor that offered speed advantages, and second, it undertook an advertising campaign to reinforce the Intel brand for all its chips. The television campaign aimed to show the importance of speed in real-life situations. The visual imagery was of a sky diver waiting for his parachute to open when a Windows alert box appears, telling him that he needs a faster processor. The purpose of the campaign was to encourage end users to specify Intel when they purchased their new PC. Although costs were increased, this was considered to be preferable to becoming involved in a protracted price-cutting exercise (McLuhan, 1998).

The main difficulty with responding to price increases is that decisions often have to be made quickly in order to protect short-term volumes and there might be too little time for detailed 'what if ...?' planning. Thus the surprise of a sudden price cut from a competitor and the speed of response needed can lead to poor decisions in the long run. The nature of the response will, in part, reflect the organisation's strategic plans and the importance of the product under threat. If it is central to future development, then careful but decisive action may be needed. If it is a marginal product, perhaps in the later stages of its life-cycle, there may be less sense of urgency.

Initiating price increases

Not all price changes involve cuts. Price increases may also be initiated, whether because of cost pressures or for legitimate strategic reasons. As with initiating price cuts, however, any move to raise prices needs to be considered very carefully, to assess customer and competitor response. The likelihood of customer acceptance of the price increase can be estimated from previous experience and from known sensitivity within price ranges. Much, however, will ultimately depend on whether competitors choose to ignore the increase or to follow suit. This assessment need not be based entirely on guesswork. Previous experience, actual and anticipated market conditions, demand stability or volatility and not least an estimation of production capacity within the industry might all influence the likely reaction. Sometimes cost pressures, perhaps arising from increases in wage rates or in raw material prices, affect all competitors in the market, making a general price increase more likely.

Cost pressures. Manufacturers can no longer assume that higher raw material prices can be passed on automatically to customers through higher prices. However, depending in part on the relative bargaining positions, reduced costs might not necessarily be reflected in lower prices to the customer. In the 12 months to June 1998, for instance, food manufacturing prices fell by 1.4 per cent and raw material costs by 7.9 per cent, whereas food retail prices rose by 0.5 per cent.

Curbing demand. Not all price increases are cost driven. In situations where demand is buoyant and shortages are starting to emerge, the supplier can use price to curb demand or to capitalise on the profit opportunity. This can be achieved in several ways other than through a straight price rise. One method is to withdraw concessions or discounts. Thus, for example, the number of cheap seats available on a particular flight often reflects the likely level of overall demand. This emphasises the flexibility and responsiveness of pricing as a marketing tool, since thanks to on-line booking systems, the airline can adjust its discounts in accordance with sales levels. An indirect way of raising prices is to 'unbundle' the product or service so that elements that were originally included in the price are now charged as extras. What used to be an all-inclusive price for a restaurant meal, for instance, may suddenly no longer include drinks or a service charge. Similarly, installation and training might begin to be charged to the purchaser as an additional cost on a new office word-processing network.

Responding to competitors' price increases

When an organisation is faced with a competitor's price rise, it has to decide whether and how to respond. There are three possible responses: respond in kind by matching the competitor's move; maintain price levels, but differentiate the product by emphasising how much better value it now represents; or refuse to respond at all. Responding in kind is perhaps the safest option from a market stability perspective. Many organisations prefer to follow others in implementing price rises, rather than taking the leadership risks. Smaller firms may use the leader's price as a reference point, follow the price and continue to compete on non-price factors such as location, service and adaptability. Promoting further differentiation may be the best option for defending a niche.

Even if the price increase is replicated, the higher margins can be ploughed back into adding value. This could mean offering more product per sale, or including services that were originally charged for or increasing promotional activity to develop stronger product loyalty. Not responding at all is perhaps the highest-risk option, if it is perceived as an aggressive response designed to gain market share. Smaller firms may have more flexibility in their response, as their actions are likely to have only a marginal impact. For example, larger airlines are unlikely to care whether or not Icelandair follows their price increases.

The specific response selected will primarily depend on how much the other organisations in the market want market stability and to shelter under the price umbrella created by the price leader.

SETTING THE PRICE RANGE

Once the strategic direction of the pricing decision has been specified, a price range needs to be set within which the final detail of price can be established. A pricing method is needed that can generate purposeful and sound prices throughout the year. The method and its rigidity will obviously vary depending on whether the organisation is setting one-off prices for a few products or many prices for a large product range or is in a fast-moving retailing environment.

There are three main pricing methods, which take into account some of the key pricing issues already discussed. They are cost based, demand based and competition based. The organisation may adopt one main method of operation or use a flexible combination depending on circumstance. Each method will be discussed in turn, once the general principles of cost–volume–profit relationships have been established.

The cost–volume–profit relationship

The demand patterns discussed at pp. 393 *et seq.*, although established and understood in their own right, also need to be understood in the context of their relationship with costs, volume of production and profit. The marketer needs to understand how the organisation's costs behave under different conditions, internally and externally generated, in order to appreciate fully the implications of marketing decisions on the operation of the organisation. The marketer should understand the different types of costs and their contribution to the pricing decision. The four most important cost concepts are fixed costs, variable costs, marginal cost and total cost. These are now defined.

Definitions of costs

Fixed costs. Fixed costs are those that do not vary with output in the short term. This category thus includes management salaries, insurance, rent, buildings and machine maintenance etc. Once output passes a certain threshold, however, extra production facilities might have to be brought on stream and so fixed costs will then show a step-like increase.

Variable costs. Variable costs are those that vary according to the quantity produced. These costs are incurred through raw materials, components, and direct labour used for assembly or manufacture. Variable costs can be expressed as a total or on a per unit basis.

Marginal cost. The change that occurs to total cost if one more unit is added to the production total is the marginal cost.

Total cost. Total cost is all the cost incurred by an organisation in manufacturing, marketing, administering and delivering the product to the customer. Total cost thus adds the fixed costs and the variable costs together.

To reiterate what was said in Chapter 10, costs may not be the only factor involved in setting prices, but they are an important one. No organisation would wish to operate for very long at a level where its selling price was not completely recovering its costs and making some contribution towards profit.

There are two main approaches to examining the cost–volume–profit relationship: marginal analysis and breakeven analysis.

Marginal analysis

Marginal analysis is concerned with what happens to a business when production or sales changes by just one unit. The focus is, therefore, on what is happening to costs and revenues at the very edge or margin of operations. Thus the marginal cost is the additional cost incurred by the production of one more unit and, similarly, the marginal revenue is the extra income derived from selling one extra unit.

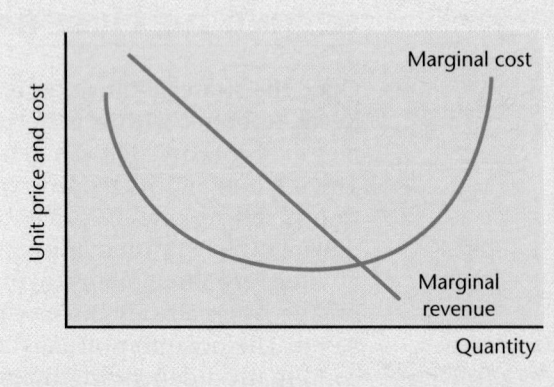

Figure 11.4 shows a situation where the marginal cost is high at low-quantity production levels. As production levels increase, marginal cost then decreases because of both production and marketing economies. Then, however, a point is reached where the organisation is overstretching its production capacity, and inefficiencies arising from overworked labour and machinery send the marginal cost upwards again.

FIGURE 11.4

Marginal cost and revenue

Meanwhile, the marginal revenue curve in the same figure shows how each additional unit sale affects total revenue. The pressure to expand sales, thus broadening the market, leads to lower prices, to make the product more affordable and therefore to lower revenue. Thus marginal revenue usually shows a downward slope. The message is simple: each additional unit sale, at least theoretically, generates less revenue than the previous unit sold because the price is falling.

At the heart of marginal analysis lies the search for the point where marginal revenue is equal to marginal cost. Up to that point, each additional unit sale generates more revenue than it incurs costs, and therefore it is worth producing and selling that unit. Beyond that point, however, the situation is different. Each additional unit begins to incur more cost than it can earn in revenue.

FIGURE 11.5

Profit maximisation

Thus it becomes increasingly uneconomic to carry on producing extra units. This is all summarised in Fig. 11.5, which shows the relationship between profit and price, total revenue, and total cost.

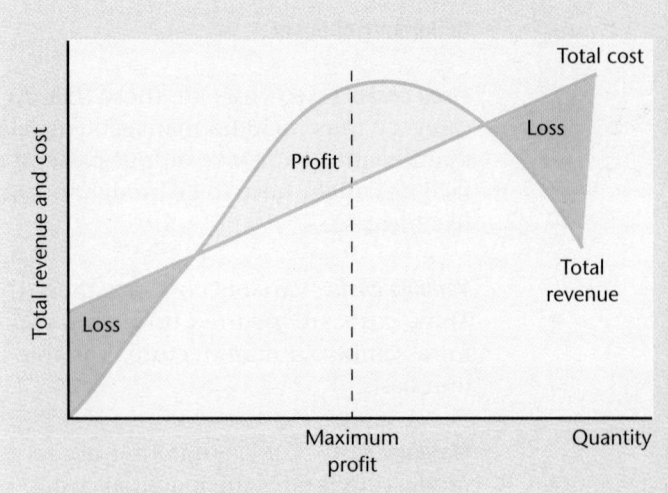

All of this may seem to be somewhat theoretical and far removed from the realities of pricing in real markets. Emerging strategic opportunities or changing competitive situations may be more urgent motivators of pricing decisions than whether producing one more unit is economic or not. No organisation can operate without due consideration of competitors' actions and price threats, which can soon change the best-laid revenue analysis.

The model can have some bearing in more stable, less dynamic markets, where there is reasonable and predictable knowledge of cost schedules and demand sensitivity. Marginal analysis can at least demonstrate the folly of chasing sales for the sake of sales. In most new product situations where information is scarce or incomplete, or where a competitive market is very volatile, however, such analysis becomes rather more academic.

Breakeven analysis

Breakeven analysis offers a simpler, more convenient approach to examining the cost–volume–profit relationship. It is a technique that shows the relationship between total revenue and total cost in order to determine the profitability of different levels of output. The breakeven point is the point at which total revenue and total cost are equal (i.e. no profit is made, nor are any losses incurred). Producing beyond this point generates increasing levels of profit.

Knowing how many units at any given price would have to be made and sold in order to break even is important, especially in new product and small business situations where an organisation has limited resources to fall back on if losses are incurred. Combining the breakeven analysis with known market and competitive conditions may make an organisation realise that it cannot compete unless it either reduces costs or develops a marketing strategy to increase volume sales.

Take, for example, a small engineering company wishing to produce a component to be priced at £200. The average variable cost per unit is £100, while the total fixed costs to be recovered are £200 000 per year.

$$\text{The breakeven point} = \frac{\text{total fixed costs}}{\text{unit price} - \text{variable costs}}$$

$$= \frac{£200\ 000}{£200 - £100}$$

$$= 2000 \text{ units per year.}$$

Figure 11.6 shows this information in a breakeven chart.

Breakeven analysis helps to show the impact on contribution to fixed costs and profit of alternative price levels. It is mechanically very simple to calculate, provided that costs are known, and any spreadsheet package can be used to set up a model to test the impact of different prices or cost structures. Breakeven is particularly useful in situations where fixed costs represent a high proportion of total costs. Once the

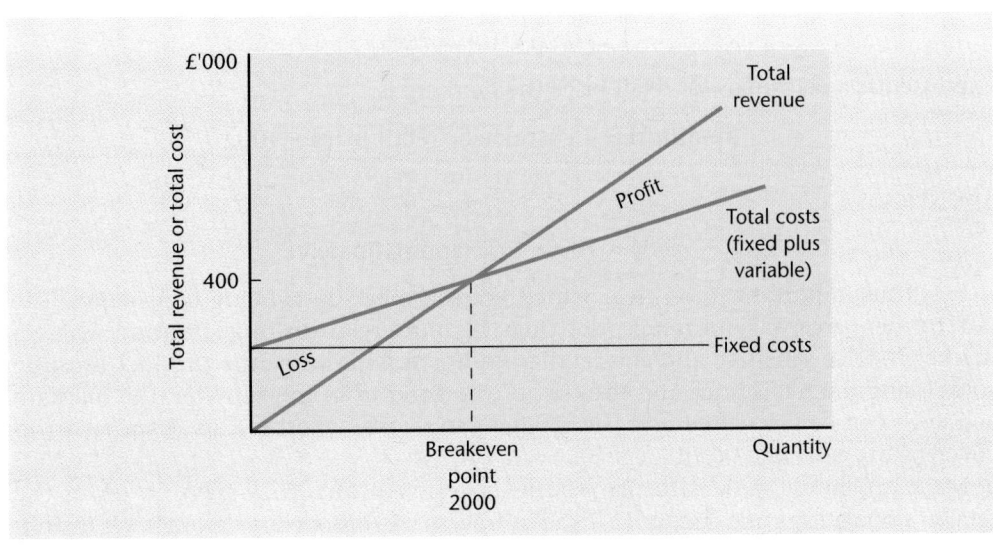

FIGURE 11.6

Breakeven chart

breakeven point is reached, the fixed costs are all covered and any sales beyond that are mostly profit (because the variable cost component is so low). If this is a price-competitive market, therefore, it is useful to know where the breakeven point is so that prices can be set as low as possible, but without crossing the breakeven point into loss.

The problem with the approach is that it focuses internally on cost structures and externally on a potentially simplistic relationship between price and sales. It must always be tempered by an appreciation of realistic market and competitive conditions, and put into the context of how the organisation can use other marketing techniques to bolster or develop demand to achieve sales more effectively.

Cost-based methods

The emphasis in *cost-based* pricing methods is on the organisation's production and marketing costs. Analysis of these costs leads to an attempt to set a price that generates a sufficient profit. The obvious disadvantage is the lack of focus on the external situation. An organisation implementing such a method would need to be very sure of the market's response. It is, however, a simple method to use, drawing the sort of direct parallels between cost and price that make accountants very happy. There are some variations in cost-based pricing.

Mark-up

Especially in the retail sector, where it can be difficult to estimate demand patterns for each product line, percentage mark-up is used as a means of price setting. This means that the retailer starts with the price paid to the supplier for the goods and then adds a percentage to reach the retail price to the customer. In fmcg high-volume markets this can be as low as 8 per cent, whereas in low-volume fashion clothing markets it can be 200 per cent or more. Mark-ups may be standard across all retailers in a particular sector, although the smaller business may have to accept a lower mark-up to compete with the retail prices of bigger operators who can negotiate better cost prices from suppliers. A retailer such as Costco that deliberately violates the mark-up traditions of its sector can be seen as initiating an all-out price war.

Mark-up can be expressed as a percentage of cost or as a percentage of the retail selling price. If a French wine merchant, for instance, buys a bottle of wine from a vineyard for 20F and adds 15F as the mark-up, thus achieving a retail price of 35F, then the mark-up as a percentage of the cost is:

$$\textbf{mark-up/cost price} \times 100.$$

That is:

$$15/20 \times 100 = 75\%.$$

Expressed as a percentage of retail price the mark-up is:

$$\textbf{(retail price – cost price)/retail price} \times 100.$$

This gives:

$$15/35 \times 100 = 43\% \text{ (approximately)}.$$

It is thus important to be clear which kind of mark-up is being considered. The latter type, percentage of retail price, may be more relevant in a situation where a market is price sensitive and the retailer knows at what price the product must be sold. Using the retail price and the cost of the good from the supplier, the mark-up achieved can be calculated and the retailer can decide whether this is sufficient to cover selling costs and profit.

Mark-ups must work hard. As well as covering profit, they have to cover the retailer's operating costs. Figure 11.7 shows how mark-ups operate through the distrib-

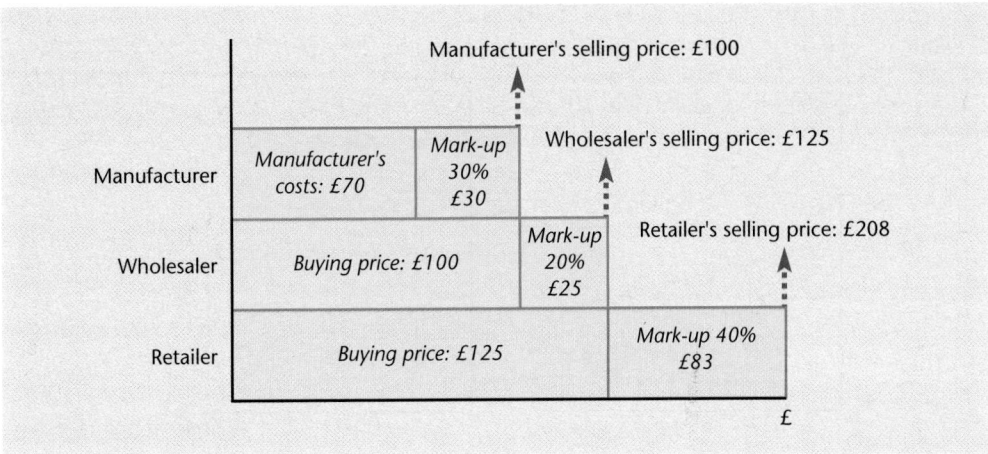

IGURE 11.7

Mark-up in the
distribution chain

ution chain. Sometimes the mark-ups become bigger the closer one is to the end consumer because of all the services the retailer is expected to supply, such as personal selling and attractive product displays. Each mark-up down the chain may be considered a reward for services rendered. The wholesaler's mark-up for instance, recognises the efficiency brought to the market by the wholesaler, in providing a central meeting point for manufacturers and retailers (there is more on the role of the wholesaler in Chapter 12). The wholesaler's mark-up poses an added difficulty for the small retailer. In paying for the services rendered by the wholesaler, the small retailer sacrifices some of its own mark-up if it still wishes to sell at a price close to that of the big operator who buys direct from the manufacturer.

Although this is basically a cost-based pricing method, it does not operate in isolation from external events. Retailers will be wary of implementing a mark-up that leads to a retail price way out of line with the competition, or that violates the consumer's expectations. This is particularly evident in the comments on the small retailer in the preceding paragraphs.

Cost-plus pricing

Cost-plus pricing involves adding a fixed percentage to production or construction costs. It is mainly used on large projects or for custom-built items where it is difficult to estimate costs in advance. The percentage will be agreed between buyer and seller in advance, and then just before, or after, the project's completion, buyer and seller agree the admissible costs and calculate the final price. It sounds straightforward enough, but in large, complex construction projects, it is not so easy to pin down precise costs. Problems arise where the seller is inflating prices, perhaps through the use of transfer pricing (*see* p. 448), and it can take some time for buyer and seller to negotiate a final settlement.

An industry operating on this kind of pricing method, using a standard percentage, is orientated less towards price competition, and more towards achieving competitiveness through cost efficiency.

Experience curve pricing

Over time, and as an organisation produces more units, its experience and learning lead to more efficiency. Cost savings of between 10 per cent and 30 per cent per unit can be achieved each time the organisation doubles its experience, as shown in Fig. 11.8. In Fig. 11.8 (a), an aggressive pricing strategy is being adopted, as prices are being set in anticipation of future cost savings to be derived from increased experience. In Fig. 11.8 (b), however, a more moderate approach is being adopted, in which prices fall with cost savings as they are achieved.

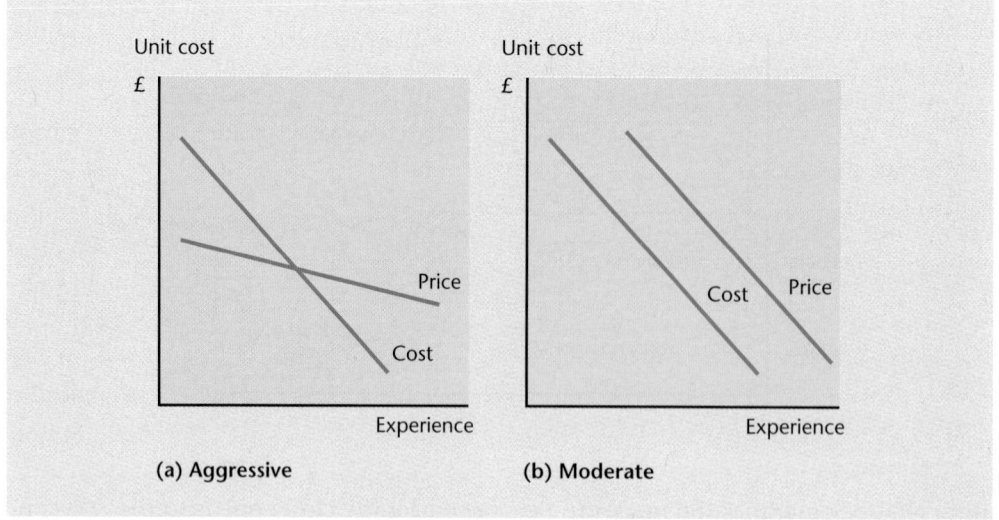

FIGURE 11.8

Experience curve
pricing strategies

Some organisations use this learning curve, essentially predicting how costs are going to change over time, as part of the price-planning process. Such planning means not only that the organisation is under pressure to build the volume in order to gain the experience benefits, but also that if it can gain a high market share early on in the product's life, it can achieve a strong competitive position because it gains the cost savings from learning sooner. It can thus withstand price competition.

Although the savings are made mainly in production, there is still a close link with the volume share and price-dominating strategies discussed earlier. Fax machines and mobile phones are examples of products that are reducing their relative prices, partly because of the experience curve effect.

The problem with cost-based methods is that they are too internally focused. The price determined has to survive in a market-place where customers and competitors have their own views of what pricing should be. An organisation's price may thus make perfect sense in cost terms and generate a respectable profit contribution, but be perceived as far too high or far too low by customers in comparison with the features and benefits offered. The price may also be way out of line compared with a competitor with a different kind of cost base.

Demand-based pricing

Demand-based pricing looks outwards from the production line and focuses on customers and their responsiveness to different price levels. Even this approach may not be enough on its own, but when it is linked with an appreciation of competition-based pricing, it provides a powerful market-orientated perspective that cost-based methods just do not provide.

At its simplest, demand-based pricing indicates that when demand is strong, the price goes up, and when it is weak, the price goes down. This can be seen in some service industries, for example, where demand fluctuates depending on time. Package holidays taken during school holidays at Christmas, Easter or in the summer when demand is high are more expensive than those taken at other times of the year when it is more difficult for families to get away. Similarly, holidays taken when weather conditions at the destination are less predictable or less pleasant are cheaper because there is less demand. Even within the course of a single day, travel prices can vary according to demand. Tickets on shuttle flights between Heathrow and UK regional airports vary in price depending on when the peak times for business travellers occur.

Tea producers work hard to add
value to the tea drinking
experience.

Source: Advertising Archives.

Time for a cup of tea

Tea producers are often very dependent on the fortunes of their competitor nations' harvests and the impact this has on the big buyers at auction, especially in Russia and the UK. The UK supermarkets tend to buy mainly from Kenya, often at one-tenth of typical supermarket retail prices, so there is some protection for consumers from price rises due to poor crops. The Russians are no longer prepared to buy low-quality Georgian tea and are therefore creating more demand for other countries' produce. Demand for tea in western Europe is more static, however, because of the popularity of soft drinks. All of this sets the scene for tea producers to develop their pricing strategies.

Tata Tea (http://www.tatatea.com), India's largest tea group, benefited in 1997 from large increases in international prices for tea. These were brought about by setbacks to the harvest in Kenya because of droughts and floods, and in Indonesia because of the currency crisis and domestic troubles. Kenya and Indonesia, along with China, are India's main competitors in world markets. By 1998, however, the global supply had recovered in those countries and the price for tea

started to fall back to more normal levels.

Tata Tea has sought to minimise the effects of fluctuations in world supply and demand patterns. It sells nearly 70 per cent of its production pre-packed rather than as a bulk commodity. The pack format may not interest supermarket buyers, but does offer Tata some protection from price fluctuations, as it can create larger margins between the cost price and selling price and, like the UK supermarkets, can absorb a certain amount of fluctuation. In order to maintain a stronger price position, Tata has also had to invest in quality. It has established R&D facilities looking at all aspects of tea operations and has invested $37.8mn on new gardens and processing factories. It has also prioritised building a brand name as a high-quality tea producer to assist it in maintaining better prices. As well as being a major exporter, Tata has built a domestic market share of 35 per cent. Through its successful marketing strategy, it has grown at well above the industry average and has not been so badly affected by fluctuations in world market prices.

Sources: Bose (1998); Cole (1998).

There is an underlying assumption that an organisation operating such a flexible pricing policy has a good understanding of the nature and elasticity of demand in its market, as already outlined at pp. 393 *et seq*.

There are a number of interesting and more subtle forms of demand-based pricing.

Psychological pricing

Psychological pricing is very much a customer-based pricing method, relying as it does on the consumer's emotive responses, subjective assessments and feelings towards specific purchases. Clearly, this is particularly applicable to products with a higher involvement focus, i.e. those that appeal more to psychological than to practical motives for purchase. All the following are examples of psychological pricing.

Prestige pricing. Prestige pricing is used by the consumer as a means of assessing quality, as discussed at p. 382 *et seq*. The high price attracts the status-conscious consumer, the discerning customer for whom price is no object. Luxury goods such as fine jewellery, designer clothing and porcelain all need to be priced at high-prestige levels. A lower price would deter that group of customers from buying.

Odd-even pricing. Odd-even pricing is the technique of ending a price with certain numbers, usually odd ones, for example £4.99 or 199 pesetas. It is a widely practised method, which seems to have an effect on the buying public. The research on the subject is far from conclusive, but Blattberg and Neslin (1990), among others, found that an increase in sales could be achieved simply by ending the price of the goods with a 9 rather than any other digit. It would appear that consumers view prices ending in 9 as lower prices and think that retailers offering such prices are better value. Further, when consumers were asked to recall the prices later, the prices ending with 9 were recalled as lower than they really were. In some situations, retailers can strive for the opposite effect. If £4.99 is a bargain, then £5.00 emanates quality. This is all far from being proved conclusively, however.

> **Example**   A study by Gendall *et al.* (1997) found that odd pricing produces greater demand than a slightly higher price, and thus a kink in the downward-sloping demand curve. With products such as low-priced grocery items, however, there is no difference between .99 and .95 price endings in terms of demand.

Price lining. Price lining is a technique that is favoured in a product mix strategy in which a number of products are sold at specific price points. Sometimes an organisation will work back from these price points regardless of the cost differences between the products in the line. For example, a clothing retailer might sell ladies' skirts at £25, £40 and £55, capitalising on customers' ideas of price banding (*see* p. 387). At one extreme, the skirts at each of these prices might all be purchased from the supplier at the same price, but they are marked up to price points on the basis of style, colour and the expected response of the typical customer.

Too many price points may confuse customers and may prevent differentiation. Three or four price points is better than trying to operate eight or nine. Figure 11.9 shows a stepped demand curve where demand is inelastic within particular price bands represented by different price points. Price lining works because it makes it easier for the customer to

FIGURE 11.9

The stepped demand curve

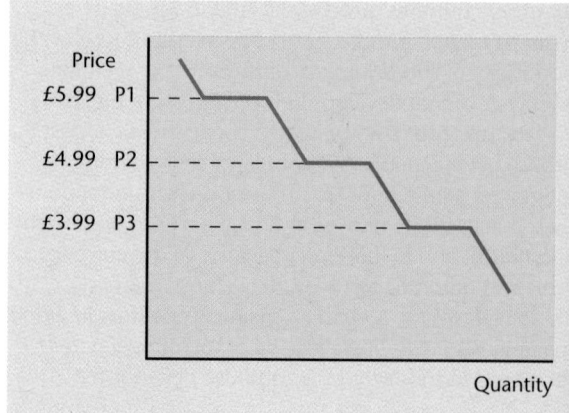

choose. As the price is held constant within the band, choice can be made on other, perhaps aesthetic, grounds such as fabric, style or colour.

Bundle pricing. Bundle pricing involves assembling a number of products in a single package to save the consumer the trouble of searching out and buying each one separately. It makes it easier to buy, attracting the shopper who is short of time or is risk averse. Personal computers are often sold in this way, with all the hardware, software and peripherals bundled as a package that will enable the user to start some serious computing within minutes. Bundling has a psychological benefit, but it also has an economic rationale, perhaps leading to a lower overall price to the consumer or lower marketing costs for the supplier.

Promotional pricing. Promotional pricing is closely linked with the discussion in Chapter 16 on sales promotion. It can be used to stimulate a market or to reinforce perceptions of value in the short term. Selecting a limited number of lines for a price promotion, as practised in the retail sector for example, attracts consumers' attention, draws them into the store and makes them feel as though they are benefiting from a bargain. The retailer hopes that the costs of providing a number of such price leaders are recouped by the sales of full-priced items, either to new customers or to existing customers spending the money they saved on the bargains (sales that would not otherwise have been made).

Time-specific markdowns. End of season sales, one-day sales, sales of the type 'sale ends Saturday' are common in the retail sector. A greater level of psychological excitement can be created among customers by providing a limited number of cut-price goods on a first-come first-served basis. Those who do not get the bargain of their choice still spend in the store and enjoy the thrill of the chase. More sedately, retailers and manufacturers use price promotions based on rewards for spending over a certain amount, or coupons rewarding repeat purchase as a means of offering the customer that little something extra.

Whether intended to stimulate demand, to encourage product trial, to take the risk out of purchase or to reward consistent and loyal behaviour, all these price promotion techniques show the flexible use of price as a tactical weapon in the marketing mix, supporting and supported by the other mix elements.

Price differentiation. Price differentiation involves the use of different prices for different segments. The same basic product is offered, but the associated services differ. A drink from a vending machine, for example, is more expensive than one from a supermarket because of the convenience, the machinery and its maintenance and the refrigeration. First-class travel on an aircraft costs much more than economy class not because it gets travellers to their destination any more quickly, but because of the extra comfort and easier check-in procedure. In both cases, the same core product is being offered, a can of Coke or a journey from A to B, but price variations are justified by both peripheral services and psychological benefits.

When geographical segmentation is being used to support price differences there are special risks, as suggested in Chapter 10's discussion of the euro. Wildner (1998) proposed that the risks of international price differences increase with:

■ the price of the product;
■ the ease with which individuals can transport the goods;
■ the frequency with which the goods are bought by people with higher incomes;
■ the frequency with which the goods are purchased through the Internet;
■ the frequency with which goods are offered by mail order.

Overall, demand-orientated pricing, regardless of how it is implemented, can be very powerful in achieving a strong, defendable market position. It can also lead to higher profit levels. The problem, however, lies in the difficulty of estimating demand response.

Competition-based pricing

This chapter has frequently warned of the danger of setting prices without knowing what is happening in the market, particularly with respect to one's competitors. According to Lambin (1993), there are two aspects of competition that influence an organisation's pricing. The first is the *structure of the market*. Generally speaking, the greater the number of competitors, i.e. the closer to perfect competition the market comes, the less autonomy the organisation has in price setting. The second competitive factor is the product's *perceived value* in the market. In other words, the more differentiated an organisation's product is from the competition, the more autonomy the organisation has in pricing it, because buyers come to value its unique benefits.

> **Example** The *Express* newspaper ran an article questioning the wisdom of consumers' perceived value of bottled water. The chief executive of the UK Water Companies Association, representing 17 small operators in England and Wales, was quoted as saying that bottled water was 'one of the great cons of the 20th century'. Compared with tap water, the claims that bottled water added to health and vitality were fanciful, especially as regulation has now improved tap supplies. Furthermore, tap water costs about 0.07p per litre and bottled water around 50p, a price differential of 700 per cent for essentially the same product (Crosbie, 1997b).

Most markets are becoming increasingly competitive, and a focus on competitive strategy in business planning emphasises the importance of understanding the role of price as a means of competing. An organisation that decides to become a cost leader in its market and to take a price-orientated approach to maintaining its position needs an especially efficient intelligence system to monitor its competitors. Levy (1994) looks at organisations that offer price guarantees in organisational markets. Any supplier promising to match the lowest price offered by any of its rivals needs to know as much as possible about those rivals and their cost and pricing structures in order to assess the likely cost of such a promise.

In consumer markets, market research can certainly help to provide intelligence, whether this means shopping audits to monitor the comparative retail prices of goods, or consumer surveys or focus groups to monitor price perceptions and evolving sensitivity relative to the rest of the marketing mix. Data gathering and analysis can be more difficult in organisational markets, because of the flexibility of pricing and the degree of customisation of marketing packages to an individual customer's needs in these markets. There is a heavy reliance on sales representatives' reports, information gained through informal networks within the industry and qualitative assessment of all those data.

Competitive analysis can focus on a number of levels, at one end of the spectrum involving a general overview of the market, and at the other end focusing on individual product lines or items. Whatever the market, whatever the focus of competitive analysis, the same decision has to be made: whether to price at the same level as the competition, or above or below them.

An organisation that has decided to be a price follower must, by definition, look to the market for guidance. The decision to position at the same level as the competition, or above or below them, requires information about what is happening in the market. This is pricing based on the 'going rate' for the product. Conventional pricing behaviour in the market is used as a reference point for comparing what is offered, and the price is varied from that. Each supplier to the market is thus acting as a marker for the others, taking into account relative positioning and relative offering. Effectively, pricing is based on collective wisdom, and certainly for the smaller business it is easier to do what everyone else does rather than pay for market research to prove what the price ought to be, and run the risk of getting it wrong. In a seaside resort, for example, a small bed and breakfast hotel is unlikely to price itself differently from the one next door, unless it can justify doing so by offering significantly better services. Within an accepted price range, however, any one organisation's move may not be seen as either significant or threatening by the rest.

The dangers of excessive price competition, both in terms of the cost to the competitors and the risk to a product's reputation, thus attracting the 'wrong' kind of customer, have already been indicated. But if neither the organisation nor the product has a particularly high reputation, or if the product has few differentiating features, then price competition may be the only avenue open unless there is a commitment to working on the product and the marketing mix as a whole. An extreme form of competitive pricing is practised through tendering, which is discussed at p. 446.

PRICING TACTICS AND ADJUSTMENTS

Pricing tactics and adjustments are concerned with the last steps towards arriving at the final price. There is no such thing as a fixed price; price can be varied to reflect specific customer needs, the market position within the channel of distribution or the economic aspects of the deal.

Price structures

Particularly in organisational markets, *price structures* give guidelines to the sales representative to help in negotiating a final price with the customer. The concern is not only to avoid overcharging or inconsistent charging, but to set up a framework for pricing discretion that is linked with the significance of the customer or the purchase situation.

> **Example** At one extreme, price structure may involve a take it or leave it, single price policy such as IKEA operates. It offers no trade discount for organisational purchasers, seeing itself largely as a consumer-orientated retailer. Compare this with some industrial distributorships, which offer different levels of discount to different customers. Most try to find a middle ground, between consistent pricing and flexibility for certain key customers.

FIGURE 11.10

From list price to actual price

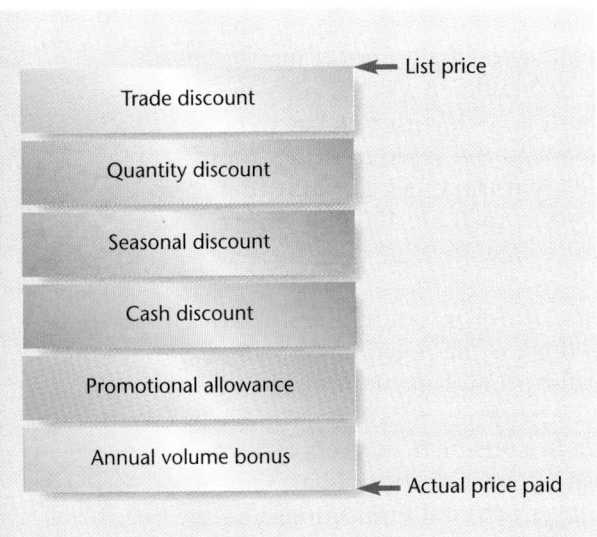

Special adjustments

A variation on price structures, *special adjustments* to list or quoted prices can be made either for short-term promotional purposes or as part of a regular deal to reward a trade customer for services rendered. Figure 11.10 shows the range of discounts and other incentives that can mean that the price paid for an item (for example home appliances) is significantly less than the list price.

As the channel of distribution becomes deeper or wider, there is a need for more structure and careful planning of special adjustments to price structures. There are three main types of special adjustment, which are not mutually exclusive.

Discounts

Discounts consist of reductions from the normal or list price as a reward for bulk purchases or the range of distribution services offered. The level and frequency of discounts will vary according to individual circumstances. Blois (1994) points out that most organisations offer discounts from list prices and that these discounts form an important part of pricing strategies. There are also different types of discount.

Trade discounts. Trade discounts, sometimes called functional discounts, are based on the services that the buyer (a retailer or wholesaler) is expected to perform in the future in reselling the goods. They are normally well understood between buyer and seller, and may be agreed as part of an annual negotiation. The value of the discounts depends on the services to be performed and the location of the buyer in the distribution channel. The closer the buyer is to the end consumer, the higher the service charges and the greater the discount. Different markets have their own traditional discount structures established, but of course any member may seek to violate tradition for competitive reasons.

Quantity discounts. Quantity discounts encourage bulk purchases. Bulk discounts come into force if a single order exceeds a certain volume or value level. Cumulative discounts build up over time. At the end of a trading period, the quantity purchased is totalled and a percentage rebate given back to the buyer. Both types of discount encourage larger purchase quantities, and the cumulative discount also encourages loyalty over time.

There are examples of both types of discount in consumer and organisational markets. The promotional technique of 'buy two and get the third free' is effectively a bulk discount and is found on many products in many supermarkets. Similarly, a promotion that requires a consumer to collect tokens then send them off for a cash rebate is a form of cumulative discount. In organisational markets, a retailer may be offered a twelfth case of a product free if 11 are initially purchased (quantity discount), or a rebate on the number of cases of a product sold by the end of the trading period (cumulative discount).

Seasonal discounts. Seasonal discounts are usually offered to offset cash flow difficulties, as discussed earlier at p. 420, or to overcome the problems of utilising capacity in quieter periods. Examples are discounts for buying heating fuel in the summer, retailers being offered discounts for stocking up on seasonal merchandise earlier, or car hire tariff reductions over weekends. Such discounts could be seen as a form of reward to the purchaser for taking on the risks of an early purchase.

Cash discounts. Cash discounts encourage prompt payment in a form that is easiest and cheapest for the seller to handle. They can operate at all levels of all types of market. A small retailer, buying supplies from a wholesaler, may be offered a better price per case of a product if immediate payment is made than if a 30-day invoice has to be sent. A small retailer, for example, might purchase goods to the value of £1000 and the bill might specify: '£1000, 2/10 net 30'. This means that if the bill is paid within 10 days, the customer can have a 2 per cent discount on the total of £1000; otherwise the £1000 is payable in full within 30 days of the invoice date. In some cases interest may be charged if the bill is not settled after 30 days.

It can sometimes be difficult to make the rules stick. If, for instance, a customer takes the discount but pays after the 10-day deadline, there is the potential for a dispute. From the customer's perspective, the discount for prompt payment may not always be particularly attractive when compared with the short-term cash flow implications of losing the use of that money. Sometimes in consumer markets a cash discount will even be given to consumers who use cash or cheques rather than credit cards, reflecting the extra cost to the retailer of processing credit card transactions.

Allowances

Allowances are similar to discounts, but usually require the buyer to perform some additional service. Trade-in, for example, makes a transaction more complicated because it involves the exchange of a good as well as money for whatever is being purchased. It is a common practice in the car market, where consumers trade in their old cars as part exchange for a new one. The qualitative judgement of the value of the trade-in disguises the discount offered, and it is further complicated by the attitudes of the respective parties. A car that is an unreliable liability to the owner may have potential to a dealer with a particular customer in mind or a good eye for scrap. The owner thinks they are getting a good deal on the old car, while the dealer thinks they can actually recoup the trade-in value and make a bit more besides.

Promotional allowances, often used as trade incentives, mean that a retailer can be rewarded for participating in point-of-sale promotions, or joint advertising, through cheaper or free goods. The retailer also reaps the added benefit of the synergy gained from being associated with the promotional activities of leading brands.

Geographic adjustments

Geographic adjustments are those made, especially in organisational markets, to reflect the costs of transport and insurance involved in getting the goods from buyer to seller. In consumer markets, they can be seen in the case of mail-order goods, which carry an extra charge for postage and packing.

In organisational markets, the terms of delivery and what is or is not included in the price need to be established in advance as part of the negotiated contract. An ex-works price does not include any delivery costs; effectively, the buyer collects. A price quoted as FOB (free on board) means that the seller is obliged to deliver the goods to some agreed point, be that an airport, a railhead, a goods depot or whatever, and then the buyer bears the charges from there. A price quoted as CIF (cargo, insurance, freight) generally means that the seller incurs all costs to the buyer's door.

Zoned pricing relates price to the geographic distance between buyer and seller. A DIY warehouse, for example, might add a £5 delivery charge to any destination within five miles, £7.50 for up to 10 miles, £10 for up to 15 miles and so on, reflecting the extra time and petrol involved in delivering to more distant locations. Operating a single zone means that the delivery price is the same regardless of distance, as is the case with the domestic postal service, which charges on the weight of letters rather than the destination. The international mail service does, however, operate on a multiple-zone basis, dividing the world up into areas and pricing to reflect different transport costs.

From a marketing perspective, the key decision is the extent to which freight costs can be absorbed, and how far they can be used as a negotiating tool with customers. This is an especially critical question for a smaller organisation as it begins to develop business outside its home market.

ISSUES IN PRICING

There are several issues connected with pricing that should be considered in the setting and managing of prices in organisational markets.

Negotiating prices

In organisational markets and even in some consumer situations where high-value purchases such as cars are involved, *negotiation* usually takes place. This determines the final price agreed between the parties and the nature of the offer package that will be provided for that price. Negotiation is therefore concerned with the communication

---

MARKETING IN ACTION **A baa-gain offer ewe can't refuse**

Caledonian MacBrayne (http://www.calmac.co.uk), a ferry owner operating the Hebrides to Scottish mainland service, ran into trouble when trying to segment the market for travel by price. The company was anxious to encourage more island farmers to use the ferries to take their sheep to the market on the mainland. The farmers on the remote island communities of Uist, Barra, Mull and Colonsay need to take their sheep to the markets in Oban in the western Highlands. The normal prices for the five-hour sailing between Barra and Oban were £104 return for a car and £29 per passenger, but under the sheep discount scheme, the price was just £2.35 per sheep, with no charges for car or passenger.

It did not take long for the canny farmers to work out how to use the system. Some cars were packed with sheep, but others just had one woolly passenger along with suitcases and passports. The farmers were using the scheme to take a holiday on the mainland and beyond. It was even more perplexing when a few weeks later the cars returned with tanned drivers and sheep still on board. This did not mean a flood of sheep sunning themselves on the Costa Del Sol; they were being left with friendly farmers on the mainland, so even the sheep had a holiday. They certainly rarely made it to the market!

Caledonian MacBrayne sheepishly admitted that it had got into a mess with an initiative designed to help the local economy and its own profits without fleecing customers. A councillor for the Western Isles Council was quoted as saying that: 'We do know that there has been some serious evasion of fares and certain people's sheep seem to have become quite well travelled recently.' Was this woolly scheme one baa-gain offer too many?

Sources: Coles (1998); Harris (1998).

---

processes that take place between the two parties to arrive at a mutually acceptable bargain. Lysons (1993, p. 215) defined negotiation as:

> 'any form of verbal communication in which the participants seek to exploit the relative strengths of their bargaining positions to achieve explicit or implicit objectives within the overall purpose of seeking to resolve the identified areas of disagreement.'

Many negotiations revolve around price and/or cost trade-offs with the rest of the commercial package offered. Thus a buyer may agree to pay a slightly higher price than it had intended if the seller agrees to deliver more quickly than originally suggested.

Baily (1987) identified four main situations where negotiation may be used:

1 an established supplier wants to increase the price or to change the offer package;
2 the buyer wants an established supplier to reduce the price or to change the offer package;
3 a potential supplier wants to oust the existing supplier;
4 there is no regular supplier and it is a new task purchase.

On a slightly smaller scale, hotel managers regularly have to negotiate deals with organisations for conference and banqueting contracts. Issues such as accommodation, menus, local transport, facilities and the overall price all have to be agreed and offer considerable scope for discussion.

Increasingly, negotiation is part of the continual exchange process that characterises a long-term business relationship. In these situations both parties may seek co-operative negotiation. This is where a win–win deal, with both parties getting something that they want, is the best outcome, as it is in the interests of both parties for the relationship to continue. There is little point in one party obtaining a short-term advantage that might lead to longer-term mistrust and poor supply from the other. If, for example, a buyer who purchases a large proportion of the total output of a small firm drives prices down to a level that is uneconomic for the small supplier, supply problems and even discontinuities might start to occur. Such problems might arise because the small supplier compromises on quality or processes in order to meet the new, tighter cost targets.

> **Example** Considerable negotiation was necessary to create the 'supplier parks' feeding many of Europe's car assembly plants. This involved suppliers dedicating facilities to the production of complete modules for the car plants and delivering them in sequence into the car manufacturers' own assembly lines. The supplier parks enable centralised logistics and planning services, which reduce costs for the component manufacturers while the manufacturers are able to lower their stockholding costs as more is being held by the supplier. This method enabled Ford to cut costs by 20 per cent on its Ka, which is produced in Valencia. Ford was also able to lower the number of parts it handled by nearly one-third compared with earlier models. To achieve these win–win benefits from contract negotiation requires a high level of trust and confidence about the durability of the relationship between the component supplier and the car manufacturer (Chew, 1997).

In other situations, there may be competitive negotiation, where neither party has any real intention of creating a long-term relationship. These deals can easily become win–lose deals, where one or other party gains at the expense of the other. For example, an organisation purchasing a second-hand piece of capital machinery cannot expect the seller to be concerned with the long-term reliability of that equipment. It is up to the buyer to check out and assess the state of that machinery. Sometimes, competitive negotiations break down completely and neither party gains anything. The seller fails to sell and the buyer fails to buy, and effectively this is a lose–lose arrangement!

There are many potential areas of the offer that might have to be negotiated, and Fig. 11.11 highlights typical areas of concern. Of course, these will vary from situation to situation. The key skill in effective negotiation is the ability to negotiate elements of the package in terms of a trade-off. Thus the trade-in allowance may be increased if payment is made in total up front, or a discount may be increased if the customer collects the item at its own expense. Not all elements of negotiation will involve price, but virtually all of them will involve cost. A good negotiator will concede on areas that cost little, but are highly valued by the other party. An organisation selling a photocopier might agree to send out an engineer within two hours of any repair call, in order to secure a higher price for the machine. The buyer gets the peace of mind of knowing that it will not be left with a broken-down photocopier for too long and will feel that the slightly higher purchase price is thus justified, while the seller will be confident that the machine is so reliable that the agreement will never, or rarely, be put to the test!

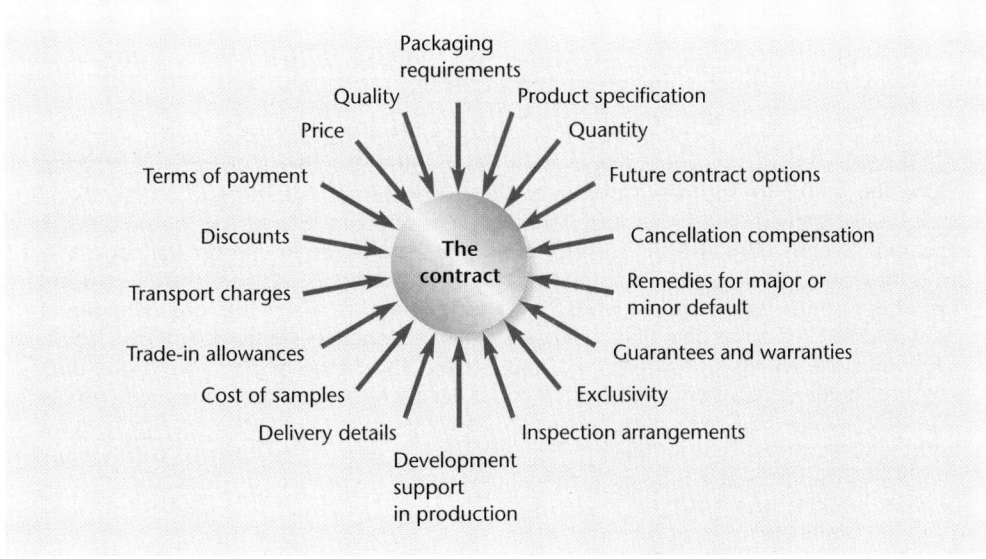

FIGURE 11.11

Negotiation variables

Generally, the more the buyer is locked in to the supplier's specification, the more limited the alternative sources and the greater the urgency of demand. This tends to enhance the negotiating position of the supplier. There is more on negotiation, and the relative power balance between the negotiating parties, in Chapter 17.

Tendering and bidding

Tendering is another feature of pricing in organisational markets. Tenders are offers made by suppliers concerning the price, terms and conditions of supply. The successful supplier's tender may then form the basis of detailed negotiation to finalise the terms of the deal, but with the clear understanding that it will be awarded the contract. Tendering is widely used in capital goods purchasing where large sums are involved. Many services ranging from training contracts and management consultancy to cleaning and plumbing can also be purchased through tenders. Some invitations to tender are restricted to approved or selected suppliers, while others are open to any organisation that wants to bid. A large organisation, for example, may encourage a wide range of smaller businesses to bid for its catering or cleaning services, although fairly strict criteria may be applied to eliminate the weaker bids. Tenders are often advertised in the relevant trade press. *Construction News*, for example, contains details of private and public tenders called for, in the UK, EU and worldwide. Thus invitations to tender can range from applications for pre-qualification for the design and construction of the Bhairab Bridge in Bangladesh to the dredging of Scalloway harbour for the Shetland Islands Council.

> **Example** When BA had up to £2bn to spend on new aircraft, it decided to put the order out to tender even though it knew that it would be a two-horse race between Boeing and Airbus. The reason for this approach was to encourage the aircraft manufacturers to come up with more imaginative financing deals. BA was seeking an arrangement beyond conventional leasing whereby the manufacturers also took on some of the capital risk of buying aircraft, leaving BA free to concentrate on running a competitive airline (Jones, 1998).

The first phase of the tendering process is normally an initial expression of interest. The buyer will let it be known, perhaps through advertisements in relevant trade publications, that they are about to begin a particular purchasing process, and will invite potential suppliers to express an interest in submitting a tender. This is effectively a pre-qualification stage, as the buyer can weed out potential suppliers with a dubious reputation or those who are unlikely to be able to meet the technical or commercial requirements. The remaining potential suppliers who have expressed an interest in the contract can then be invited to prepare and submit a formal tender, a process that in itself can involve much time, effort and expense.

> **Example** When Railtrack called for expressions of interest in the development and supply of a signalling system for the West Coast main line, 17 expressions of interest from across the world were received. Only nine organisations were selected to prepare formal tenders, including Siemens, ABB and GEC Alsthom. All nine were based in Europe. Railtrack, after the eight-week bidding period, intended to offer contracts to at least three of the bidders. This is because the work required was so wide ranging and complex that no one organisation would be likely to be able to do it all better than anyone else (*Modern Railways*, 1995).
>
> However, the winning of the contract was not the end of the negotiation for the three successful bidders. In an effort to reduce costs, Railtrack then sought to reduce costs by 30 per cent on the £2.1bn project. This was to be achieved not just by hard bargaining but also by greater attempts at partnering. Thus contractors were to be involved earlier in any project and to participate fully in specification development in order to maximise cost-saving measures (Hope, 1998).

It is not always the lowest tender that wins, however. A buyer might consider a certain bid too low, and might doubt the bidder's ability to deliver what they promised at an acceptable quality level. Sometimes, therefore, a buyer might feel that a higher price is worth paying to be more certain of the outcome and to cut down the risk of potential problems as the project unfolds.

> **Example** As China's economic system has adopted more 'free-market' characteristics, the government has moved to more open bidding procedures rather than awarding contracts to 'preferred suppliers' without tendering being opened up to others. The Yantai municipal government in Shandong province claims to have saved 675 000 Yuan ($81 000) when it purchased 180 computers. Forty bids were received and five passed through to the final decision phase. This method of procurement is new in China and has already been used for such items as vehicles, photocopiers, air conditioners and medical appliances (Chuanjiang Ju, 1999).

The tendering might end, as in many of the examples quoted above, with further negotiation to finalise the fine detail of the contract. However, it is also possible, usually where smaller jobs are involved, for the buyer to ask for sealed bids. This means that the winning supplier is selected with a minimum of contact, and thus there is no further negotiation of terms. The buyer either takes or leaves the supplier's original offer. In these cases, potential suppliers seek to influence the tendering process well before the formal invitations to tender are issued. By building contacts, influencing specifications and raising its reputation, a supplier may feel that its total offering, not just its price, might receive a more sympathetic hearing from the buyer when it comes to analysing the formal tenders. This, of course, raises issues of what constitutes fair and ethical practice, as discussed in Chapter 4.

Aircraft purchasing involves complex negotiation with manufacturers.

Source: British Aerospace Photo Library 1999.

Transfer pricing

In larger organisations, there is often a considerable amount of internal trading between different divisions of the company and across national boundaries. A typical car manufacturer may concentrate production of engines, body parts and transmission systems in different divisions and in different locations. Fiat and SKF both have transfer price arrangements for 'selling' parts and finished products respectively to other parts of their own organisations. Transfer prices are thus used to cover the movement of goods or services across organisational boundaries. These prices may be set at commercial rates, based on full overhead recovery and profit criteria, or at a reduced rate agreed within the group. Where transfer prices cover the movement of goods across national or trading bloc boundaries, there is clearly scope to use them creatively as a means of shifting funds around the world with the maximum tax advantages. With different rates of corporation tax in different countries, prices can be manipulated to minimise the organisation's total tax liability.

According to Livesey (1976), there are three different types of transfer prices:

Negotiated prices

With *negotiated prices*, business units or divisions are encouraged to act in a semi-commercial manner in determining transfer prices to other business units. This means negotiation between the two parties, but there are dangers in this approach. If one buying unit decides that it can get a better deal elsewhere, another part of its own organisation may be left with idle capacity, with the result that overall profits suffer. The organisation may avoid this problem by making it compulsory to source internally. This, however, distorts the negotiating position by creating a captive buyer and a captive seller, both of whom know that they will have to reach some kind of agreement.

Market prices

External (*market*) prices are used as a guide to what the buying unit should be prepared to pay. They are commonly used in organisations where business units act as profit centres and therefore cannot afford to give away their outputs too cheaply to other business units. Unfortunately, as this and the last chapter have shown, there may be some debate as to what exactly constitutes a representative price, given the various trade-offs that are possible. List prices or average prices rarely reflect market reality.

> **Example** Nokia Data, the Finnish computer company that is part of the Nokia group (http://www.nokia.com), built its European growth strategy around an approach that gives considerable pricing discretion to local managers in each country. However, the organisation still needed to develop a fair transfer price arrangement that took into account the various local pricing conditions across Europe. It was thus agreed that each local business unit would pay a transfer price set at its local market price less the appropriate local margin of 30 per cent to 40 per cent.

Cost-based systems

The previous methods of transfer pricing have taken the line that the transfer price should reflect what the component concerned is worth either to the buying unit of the organisation or to the end customer. In contrast, the *cost-based systems* approach looks simply at what it cost to produce the component. There are many options within this approach, based on marginal cost, full cost or marginal cost plus a percentage for overhead recovery. The problem with this approach is that it does not reflect market changes or lower cost structures elsewhere. It also does not reflect the opportunity cost of the production capacity used, especially where limits are being reached. In other words, the business unit supplying the component might have external customers clamouring to buy more at much higher commercial prices than the internal cost-based market pays. If the supplying unit cannot expand its capacity or divert sales from the internal to the external market, then it might be losing out severely on a profit opportunity. With a cost-based pricing method, it cannot make up for any of that lost external business through higher internal prices. Despite these weaknesses, this approach is the most popular of all those on offer.

Given all these complications and the lack of any ideal method of transfer pricing, some organisations are happy to allow business units to purchase from the best source, whether internal or external to the organisation. Across Europe, different nations have different policies towards intra-organisational transactions. In the Netherlands, for example, special provisions for determining taxable profit can eliminate distortions caused by transfer pricing so that, for tax purposes, the terms and conditions are comparable to those imposed on transactions between unrelated parties. If there is a doubt, therefore, market prices can be used to ascertain appropriate prices for tax purposes. Similar principles apply in Germany and controls can be stringent. If a German subsidiary company is burdened with costs and expenses that do not reflect the market situation or conditions that could reasonably be imposed on third parties, then the tax authorities can become involved.

CHAPTER SUMMARY

This chapter focuses on the process of setting prices and managing the pricing process. The first step in price setting is the consideration of the organisation's pricing objectives, whether they relate to *financial targets* or *sales targets*. Financial targets can centre on either profit or cash flow. Sales objectives can relate to desired market share and the organisation's position within the market, or to volume sales targets. Pricing, along with the other elements of the marketing mix, can be used to influence both sales and consumers' perceptions of products.

Other influences on pricing objectives involve strategic assessment of the market and the organisation's position within it, and analysis of competitors' likely response to price decisions. Organisations have to weigh up the risks, however, of triggering a price war where price competition leads to a downward spiral of price cutting, risking the health of all parties. For organisations in trouble, the possibility of dropping prices as a temporary survival mechanism might be a means of keeping the business intact.

Any estimates of demand in the market have to be put into the context of what the individual organisation can be expected to achieve. *Marginal analysis* is one method of finding an optimum level of production that covers costs and makes a profit. A simpler, more realistic approach to looking at the relationship between costs, profit and production volume is *breakeven analysis*. This calculates the volume of sales required, at a given price, to cover costs and begin to make a profit. It is then up to the organisation to work out whether it can produce (at least) that volume and whether it has the marketing skills to sell so much.

This information, along with an evaluation of competitors' activities, can guide the organisation towards appropriate pricing strategies, methods and tactics. *Skimming* (high, premium pricing signalling a quality good) and *penetration* (pricing low to gain large market share quickly) are examples of possible strategies for launching new products on to the market. Pricing an individual product also has to take the context of the rest of the *product mix* into account, as well as the pricing moves made by *competitors* within the market.

Methods of arriving at prices can either be cost based (operationally centred), demand based (customer centred), or competition based (copying or differentiating from the rest). In practice, some consideration is given to all three methods as all these elements are central to successful marketing strategy. Pricing tactics allow the organisation to take advantage of short-term or unique opportunities by manipulating price to offer discounts, allowances or geographic adjustments to individual customers or groups of customers.

In most organisational markets and in some consumer purchasing situations, *negotiation* may be necessary to arrive at a final price. Negotiation tends to trade off price against other elements of the total offering, in that the seller is trying to obtain the highest price possible in return for features, benefits or services that are valuable to the buyer, but cost little to the seller. In an ideal situation, therefore, both parties come away from the negotiation feeling reasonably happy that they have achieved a bargain that gives them most of what they want. This is particularly important if the buyer and seller are part of an ongoing business relationship, and will have to trade with each other again in the future.

In organisational markets, potential suppliers are sometimes asked to *tender* or bid for a contract. This means that the supplier offers a price along with details of what the buyer can expect for that price, and the buyer decides which supplier should get the contract. Sometimes invitations to tender are open to any bidder, sometimes they are restricted to a chosen few, selected on the basis of past history, areas of expertise or reputation. Contracts are not always awarded to the lowest bidder, as issues of risk reduction, quality of service and reliability may enter the decision. Very large companies with a number of different operating divisions or with multinational subsidiaries might also become involved in *transfer pricing*. Transfer prices may be used as a means of moving money from one country to another, or from one profit centre to another, and thus do not necessarily relate closely to open market prices.

Key words and phrases

Breakeven	Price objectives	Psychological pricing
Discount	Pricing method	Skimming
Mark-up	Pricing policies and strategies	Tendering
Penetration	Pricing tactics	Transfer pricing

QUESTIONS FOR REVIEW

11.1 Define the various stages involved in *setting prices*.

11.2 List the *financial objectives* that might be achieved through pricing decisions and outline the ways in which pricing might help to achieve them.

11.3 How can pricing help to achieve *marketing* and *sales objectives*?

11.4 In what circumstances might a high price be justified for a *new product launch*?

11.5 What factors might prompt an organisation to initiate either a *price cut* or a *price rise*?

11.6 What are the possible responses for an organisation facing a *competitor's price cut*?

11.7 What contribution can:
(a) marginal analysis; and
(b) breakeven analysis
make to the pricing decision?

11.8 What are the advantages and disadvantages of *cost-based pricing methods*?

11.9 Why are *discounts* an important feature of organisational product pricing for both the seller and the buyer?

11.10 Define *transfer pricing* and summarise the various available methods of calculating a transfer price.

QUESTIONS FOR DISCUSSION

11.1 Define *penetration pricing* and find an example of an organisation that has used it for one of its products.

11.2 How can organisations justify charging *different prices* for different products within their product ranges?

11.3 Define three methods of *psychological pricing*, then find and discuss examples of each one in practice.

11.4 To what extent and why do you think that a marketing manager's pricing decision should be influenced by the competition's pricing?

11.5 Develop a checklist of five important points that you would like a sales representative to bear in mind when trying to achieve a favourable outcome from price negotiation with a potential customer.

CASE STUDY 11.1

Rip-off clothing?

For many years, the owners of high-quality brands have maintained tight control over where and how their goods are sold through selective distribution strategies. In 1997, however, the UK supermarkets started to take an interest in brand names such as Sony, Nike, Adidas and Levi Strauss and wanted to stock them and sell them at a discount. Surprisingly, the supermarkets did not find this to be a straightforward task. Tesco, for example, had approached companies directly, but had been refused supplies on 'image criteria'. Levi Strauss said that it would supply Tesco if it met its distribution criteria relating to location, affinity with the target consumer, other brands stocked, presentation and staff training. The problem is that a supermarket is unlikely to deliver the 'young consumers that are interested and involved in clothing' that Levi's wants, nor indeed is it likely to meet the high standards demanded on the other criteria.

Tesco turned to other sources of supply from the grey market, which consists of importers, wholesalers and distributors with surplus stock that they are prepared to sell. This is not necessarily a satisfactory source as it cannot guarantee regular supplies, it might not have the latest designs or models, and it might not have the full product range. The margins on grey-market products are not necessarily attractive. It has been estimated that Tesco bought Levi jeans from Mexico for £26 per pair and was selling them at £30 (compared with a high-street price of £55). The main objectives are publicity and attracting customers into the stores rather than making profits. Nevertheless, the grey market is better than nothing, and Tesco successfully sourced and sold millions of pounds worth of Calvin Klein, Levi, Nike and Adidas clothing at half the normal high-street price.

It is not just clothing brands that are subject to selective distribution. Tesco got hold of Sony PlayStations, Walkmans, camcorders and hi-fi systems from the grey market in Germany to sell at up to 50 per cent discount in the UK. It had approached Sony to get 'first-hand' supplies, but Sony refused on the grounds that Tesco could not provide advice to prospective buyers or after sales service. Once Tesco had accessed goods from Germany, Sony then refused to supply instruction books in English to go with the products or to honour guarantees on them. Tesco got the instruction manuals from elsewhere and arranged its own guarantees.

Meanwhile, Tesco complained to the OFT that Calvin Klein and Levi Strauss had deliberately withheld supplies from it because it wanted to discount them. A Tesco spokesman said:

'We believe that it is unfair that Tesco shoppers cannot get access to branded products that are openly on offer elsewhere in the world . . . At present it is perfectly legal for a manufacturer to refuse us supplies simply by saying they don't want their products sold next to food. This is plainly ridiculous and amounts to a restrictive practice.' (as quoted by Crosbie, 1997a)

The OFT refused to support Tesco in its complaint against Levi Strauss and cleared Levi of price fixing. A further blow fell in July 1998 when the European Court ruled that it was illegal to import designer goods from the grey market outside the EU and re-sell them in the EU without the manufacturer's permission. This ruling was the result of an action brought by an Austrian spectacles company, Silhouette, against a discount retailer that had been sourcing Silhouette frames from Bulgaria and selling them cheaply in the EU.

▶

The European Commission defended its Silhouette ruling on the basis that it would guarantee the consistent quality of products circulating within the EU. This ruling could threaten what is a £100mn market in the UK and means that companies such as Tesco need to be careful about the source of their grey-market goods.

It is difficult to judge whether the manufacturers are indulging in price fixing or not. The *Sunday Times* set up a fictitious company to see if it could get supplies of top American brands directly from the manufacturers. The manufacturers were keen to supply what they thought was a new chain of 20 stores, until it was made clear to them that the intention was to discount the goods. Virtually all of them refused to deal with the company unless it maintained the recommended retail prices.

The manufacturers have always argued that they have spent a great deal of time and money building exclusive, quality brands and that supermarkets do not provide the right kind of selling ambience because they give the impression of a commodity type of routine purchase. The manufacturers also claim that supermarkets cannot give the kind of personal service and expertise that their customers expect and demand. Nevertheless, a MORI poll showed that 79 per cent of UK consumers think that companies like Tesco ought to be free to sell whatever brands they want, including Levi's. The Consumers' Association also feels that supply restrictions exist to allow the manufacturers to maintain power in the marketplace and sustain high profit margins. If retailers do not comply with manufacturer demands, they do not get supplies. The argument is far from being over.

Sources: Alderson and Nuki (1998); Ap Gwilym and Justice (1998); Bremner and Farrell (1998); Crosbie (1997a, 1997c, 1998a, 1998b); Lee (1998); Linton and Townsend (1998); Mitchell (1998).

Questions

1 Why do the manufacturers seems to want to maintain high prices for their goods? What sort of pricing strategy are they implementing?

2 How are external factors affecting Tesco's pricing strategy for products like Levi's?

3 Discuss the advantages and disadvantages of allowing supermarket retailers unrestricted access to 'first-hand' supplies of branded products like these and the freedom to set whatever retail price levels they want, from (a) the manufacturer's (b) the retailer's and (c) the consumer's points of view.

CASE STUDY 11.2

Pricing in a volatile market

Pulp is the main raw material for paper production, whatever the quality or grade, and demand is derived ultimately from the magazines, newspapers, packaging and blank paper that we consume. Pulp is mainly offered on the open market by paper mills that cannot consume all they produce in their own continuous paper production. This is a worldwide business, but many of the mills are concentrated in Scandinavia, North America and Brazil. It is a very fragmented industry and no single producer has more than a 6 per cent share of the overall market. The 10 largest producers hold less than 50 per cent of the market between them.

Many of the products in the paper market are treated as commodities, traded mainly on price. It is thus a cyclical market that experiences considerable price volatility. This was particularly marked during the mid to late 1990s when pulp prices halved, resulting in considerable problems for producers. Prices fell sharply because companies expanded too fast and added too much extra capacity. Supply thus began to outstrip demand and prices fell as producers tried to get rid of excess stock. When prices are high, producers want to invest in more capacity to take advantage of it. But it takes two years to get a plant up and running, by which time demand has passed the peak and prices are lower. The producers then dump all that extra new capacity on to the market and contribute to a further, steeper decline in prices.

Additional price uncertainty destabilised the market to some extent because of the entry of lower-cost South American and Asian producers into markets traditionally served by Scandinavian, European and North American suppliers. This, coupled with the over-capacity in the market, also put downward pressure on prices. The Asian economic crisis made its own contribution to price volatility. An Indonesian pulp producer estimated that currency devaluation decreased its operating costs by up to 15 per cent, thus making it very price competitive. Asia produces between 5 and 10 per cent of pulp in the global market, which is enough to have an effect on prices.

If the industry as a whole could cut back on production, then this might help to increase prices. Reducing capacity is not easy, however. Some companies were reluctant to do it because they had invested so much capital in building capacity in the first place. Unions and governments also had a voice in what happened. Strong Canadian unions lobbied hard to prevent jobs being cut, thus pressurising companies to maintain capacity, and the provincial government in British Colombia even bought a 53 per cent stake in a producer to prevent it from closing down, thus preserving jobs and capacity. Other companies did cut back hard. International Paper, for instance, cut 9000 jobs and sold off $1bn of assets.

For the bigger companies, consolidation through takeovers and alliances has meant that they can develop bigger global market share and perhaps have a greater influence over market prices. UPM-Kymmene, for instance, a Finnish company which is the largest in Europe, took over a North American producer in order to increase its coverage of the global market. It also entered into an agreement with Asia Pacific Resources International to take advantage of growing, emerging markets. Although in the short term after the economic crisis, Asian demand for pulp imports dropped by about 50 per cent, in the longer term the market is thought to have great growth potential. Swedish company Stora entered into a joint venture with a Brazilian partner with a view to building a $1.5bn production plant in Brazil where operating costs are much lower.

Focusing on niche markets was also a viable way out, particularly for smaller companies. Becoming a specialist would allow a company to develop a significant share of the niche market and give it more opportunity to influence prices for particular products. For example, Sappi, a South African company, is the world's largest producer of coated wood-free paper. It achieved this dominance of a niche market through acquisition. The aim was to get into a position to influence prices and reduce volatility.

It was estimated that despite the consolidations and capacity cutting, in early 1998 there was still around 13 per cent over-capacity in the market depressing prices. Add to that the fact that stock levels were at their highest for three years and that a further 500 000 tonnes of capacity were due to come on stream in 1998, and it seemed unlikely that prices would recover in the short term.

Sources: Ashurst (1997); Burt (1997); Burt and McIvor (1997); Hargreaves (1997); McIvor (1997); Morrison (1997); Thoenes (1997).

Questions

1 What are the main causes of price volatility in a market? To what extent and how have these general causes applied in the pulp and paper market?

2 What effect do you think consolidation in the industry will have on (a) the biggest producers and (b) their customers?

3 Assess Sappi's strategy. Do you think that it can succeed?

4 Is price volatility in a customer's interests?

References to Chapter 11

Alderson, A. and Nuki, P. (1998), 'Exposed: How US Designer Labels Rip off British Consumers', *Sunday Times*, 5 July, p. 1.1.

Ap Gwilym, A. and Justice, E. (1998), 'Spectacular Deals', *Express*, 29 April, pp. 28–9.

Ashurst, M. (1997), 'Rich Parents Cushion Volatility', *Financial Times*, 8 December, p. 4.

Baily, P. J. H. (1987), *Purchasing and Supply Management* (5th edn.), Chapman & Hall.

Baumol, W. J. (1965), *Economic Theory and Operations Analysis*, Prentice Hall.

Bird, S. (1998a), 'Pay Up to Check Out', *The Express*, 15 June, p. 22.

Bird, S. (1998b), 'It's Cut-price Happy Hour for Shoppers', *The Express*, 6 July, p. 16.

Blatterg, R. C. and Neslin, S. A. (1990), *Sales Promotion: Concepts, Methods and Strategies*, Prentice Hall.

Blois, K. (1994), 'Discounts in Business Marketing Management', *Industrial Marketing Management*, 23(2), pp. 93–100.

Bose, K. (1998), 'High Quality Crop Keeps Tata Tea Cosy', *Financial Times*, 16 October, p. 27.

Bremner, C. and Farrell, S. (1998), 'European Court Outlaws Designer–label Discounts', *The Times*, 17 July, p. 13.

Burt, T. (1997), 'Strategies Are Redefined', *Financial Times*, 8 December, p. 4.

Burt, T. and McIvor, G. (1997), 'Consolidation on a Roll', *Financial Times*, 1 October, p. 21.

Cane, A. (1998), 'One-2-One Offers Free Calls in Autumn Strategy', *Financial Times*, 19 October, p. 25.

Chew, E. (1997), 'Supplier Parks Cut Parts Bills', *Automotive News Europe*, 2 (7), p. 18.

Chuanjiang Ju (1999), 'Government Benefits from Open Bidding System', *China Daily*, 7 April, p. 3.

Cole, R. (1998), 'Storm in a Teacup Brewing as Price Trend Unsettles Market', *The Times*, 2 June, p. 31.

Coles, J. (1998), 'Sheep Day Return', *The Express*, 13 October, p. 16.

Crosbie, P. (1997a), 'The Big Brand Price Scandal', *The Express on Sunday*, 14 September, pp. 22–3.

Crosbie, P. (1997b), 'Bottled Water Supplies Century's Biggest Con', *The Express*, 18 September, p. 9.

Crosbie, P. (1997c), 'Fashion Price War in Store', *The Express*, 23 October, pp. 1–2.

Crosbie, P. (1998a), 'Store's War on High Cost of Top Name Sportswear', *The Express*, 28 January, p. 4.

Crosbie, P. (1998b), 'Tesco Hit Squad in £5mn War on Sony', *The Express*, 16 February, p. 9.

Darwent, C. (1996), 'Bangers and Cash', *Management Today*, June, pp. 72–4.

Dean, J. (1950), 'Pricing Policies for New Products', *Harvard Business Review*, 28 (Nov.), pp. 45–53.

Diamantopoulos, A. and Mathews, B. (1995), *Making Pricing Decisions: A Study of Managerial Practice*, Chapman & Hall.

Gendall, P. *et al.* (1997), 'The Effect of Odd Pricing on Demand', *European Journal of Marketing*, 31 (11/12), pp. 790–813.

The Grocer (1999), 'Rat Snack', *The Grocer*, 10 April, p. 52.

Hargreaves, D. (1997), 'A Bad Time to Swamp the Market', *Financial Times*, 8 December, p. 2.

Harris, G. (1998), 'Islanders Discover Sheep-day Return', *The Times*, 13 October, p. 3.

Hope, C. (1998), 'Railtrack Signals Intent', *Construction News*, 22 October, p. 6.

Jones, A. (1998), 'BA Puts Aircraft Order out to Tender', *The Times*, 24 February, p. 27.

Lambin, J. J. (1993) *Strategic Marketing: A European Approach*, McGraw-Hill.

Lee, J. (1998), 'Tesco Looks to Europe in Fight Over Levi Jeans', *The Times*, 21 March, p. 27.

Levy, D. T. (1994), 'Guaranteed Pricing in Industrial Purchases: Making Use of Markets in Contractual Relations', *Industrial Marketing Management*, 23(4), pp. 307–13.

Linton, L. and Townsend, M. (1998), 'End of the Line for our Designer Bargains', *The Express*, 17 July, p. 7.

Livesey, F. (1976), *Pricing*, MacMillan.

Lysons, C. K. (1993), Purchasing, *M&E Handbooks* (3rd edn.), Pitman Publishing.

McIvor, G. (1997), 'Smoothing out the Peaks and Troughs', *Financial Times*, 8 December.

McLuhan, R. (1998), 'Speed is the Issue for Intel', *Marketing*, 3 December, p. 23.

Mintel (1997), 'Sausages and Meat Pies', *Market Intelligence*, December.

Mitchell, A. (1998), 'Levi's Must Give Choice Back to its Consumers', *Marketing Week*, 29 October, pp. 30–1.

Modern Railways (1995), 'Railtrack Shortlists West Coast Main Line Signalling Bidders', *Modern Railways*, August, p. 506.

Monroe, K. B. and Della Bitta, A. J. (1978), 'Models for Pricing Decisions', *Journal of Marketing Research*, 15 (Aug.), pp. 413–28.

Morrison, S. (1997), 'New Calls for Sector Consolidation', *Financial Times*, 8 December, p. 6.

Moskal, B. (1994), 'Consumer Age Begets Value Pricing', *Industry Week*, 21 February, pp. 36–40.

Nagle, T. T. (1987), *The Strategies and Tactics of Pricing*, Prentice Hall.

Nuki, P. (1998), 'Shoppers Will Pay to Jump Queues', *Sunday Times*, 14 June, p. 10.

Perks, R. (1993), 'How to Win a Price War', *Investor's Chronicle*, 22 October, pp. 14–15.

Rufford, N. and Nuki, P. (1997), 'Rush-hour' Shoppers Face Higher Prices as Stores Test Dual Charging', *Sunday Times*, 7 December, p. 1.11.

Supermarketing (1998), 'Mr Lazenby's Launches Crispy Coated Sausage', *Supermarketing*, 5 June, p. 16.

Supermarketing (1999), 'Valentine's Day Sausage', *Supermarketing*, 15 January, p. 13.

Thoenes, S. (1997), 'Survival of the Cheapest', *Financial Times*, 8 December, p. 5.

Walters, J. (1998), 'Can Airlines Win the Price Wars?', *Marketing*, 29 October, pp. 18–19.

Wildner, R. (1998), 'The Importance of Understanding Consumer Reactions', *Marketing and Research Today*, 27 (4), pp. 141–7.

Vauxhall Motors UK

Interview with
Ian Coomber, Executive Director

Vauxhall Motors UK is owned by General Motors and is a sister company of Opel. It sells cars in the UK that have been manufactured either in the UK or Europe and holds some 15% UK market share. We visited Ian Coomber, Vauxhall UK's Executive Director, Sales and Marketing to find out about the complexities of pricing a car and how the pricing decision evolves with the new product development process. Ian described a six stage process and each stage will now be discussed in turn:

1 Product Positioning

The pricing decision for a new model is broadly based on the planned product positioning of the car and on the prices of directly competing models as specified in the business plan. This is agreed by senior management before any serious production and design development even begins.

Rarely is a new model in the motor industry completely unique and so it is usually possible to identify direct competition and use their prices as a reference point. This in itself is not enough, of course. The business plan is a crucial document that indicates how price will vary over the life of the model and how returns on investment will vary with different price assumptions within the context of the business environment. The plan has to consider, for example, what manufacturer allowances and discounts will be offered during the model's life cycle and whether any changes in list price are planned from the outset. All of this is covered at this stage with alternative cost-volume production options presented to guide decision making.

Setting a broad price level early also helps to guide the designers so that they can develop sensible specifications within reasonable cost levels. Without these guidelines, when designing in additional benefits they could get carried away.

The decision to go ahead with a new model is not just a pricing issue. The numbers might well add up to an attractive opportunity but management judgement is needed to assess whether the market will buy the proposed model in sufficient volume at the price point agreed and whether the initial concept stacks up against the competition, both in terms of what is currently offered and any forthcoming new models. Market analysis and research can provide a broad indication of general acceptability, but will not necessarily guarantee customer reaction to the detailed concept. Further research is necessary.

The outcome of this stage is the decision whether to go ahead with the development of the proposed model or not. If a commitment is made, then even now it is considered too late to change or reposition the concept.

2 Determining the specification options

This very important stage helps establish the exact specification profile to offer for the model and determines how it will compare with competitor offerings. The objective of this stage is, therefore, to determine the various accessory/ specification packages throughout the planned model's range compared with the competitor set, and then to determine how much the customer is willing to pay. The competitor set derives from the market leader and other main models targeting the same segment and the various specification options are listed. Then, to find out how much a customer will be prepared to pay, there is heavy emphasis on pricing research. This is undertaken using pricing research clinics in which small groups of customers are confronted with a fibreglass model and a mock up interior of the vehicle. Different specification options relating to styling, space, safety or comfort features for example can be added or taken away from the model. The research then plots the responses of the groups to the various option changes to test their willingness to trade off between price and purchase preference. This can be tracked by computer, using conjoint analysis.

The method can be summarised as:

- Car A (Vauxhall) offers the first price and specification set to be tested
- Car B (another vehicle from the competitor set) has a different price and specification.

The customer selects their preferred one and then the price or the specification of the other is varied to find the point at which the customer will switch. This enables Vauxhall to assess the value of the specification to the potential customer. After this has been repeated enough times, a profile emerges as to which specification combination and price level is most competitive for the new model.

'We don't use cost plus pricing at all at this stage; it really is market based. It concerns the perception of value according to different specification bundles. The analysis of the trade offs really is useful as, for example, we can find out what air conditioning or heated seats are worth to real potential customers.'

These group research activities are not just concerned with the UK. Increasingly, Vauxhall views Europe as one market, but sometimes evidence is collected to suggest that different specification options are preferred in some markets. Normally, these research groups take place in the major markets only, though sometimes they can be extended to the smaller markets also. It has been found that the specifications do have to be tailored, for example in central Europe customers tend to look for an emphasis on safety, high specifications and functionality, whereas in the Mediterranean zone, the emphasis is on style, flair and air conditioning. In Scandinavia, heating systems and chain fitments can be high priorities.

3 Price Modelling

After the group research, and the resultant price – specification trade offs, the company is in a position to determine the impact of different specification options on sales and market share. By establishing the specification options we can better predict the profitability impact beyond the cruder cost – volume – profit measures used in the initial assessment. Vauxhall is not looking to be the cheapest in the segment, but to select a list price based upon comparative specification options. For example when pitching against the Renault Mégane with the Zafira, a higher price was chosen because the Zafira has a unique feature in its 7 seat capacity.

The impact of special promotions and allowances can also be introduced in more detail at this stage, before a final decision on the list price. A report is then made to a special committee comprising senior management from Vauxhall Europe and General Motors Europe. Typically, this group includes representatives from both marketing and finance and purchasing along with the Managing Director. They can make recommendations on the list price position based on the general market data and the findings of the group research analysis and the wider pan-European marketing positioning, though the final decision is always made locally. Judgement is also necessary as sometimes new entrants and their impact on the planned sales development have to be considered.

Thus competitive benchmarking is crucial in arriving at the list price of a model, but then the focus has to shift to encouraging potential customers to 'walk up the range' from basic to high specification models.

4 List Price Structure

This is an important area for marketing as often the perceived value to the customer of the extra specifications gained from walking up the range is far greater than the cost of providing them. The further the customer can be moved from the basic model, the greater the opportunity for higher margins and profitability. All of this is planned from the outset using the results from the pricing research in order to establish the detailed price points within the range and the size of the price gaps. There are standard industry statistics on the perceived value of additional specification items, but the trouble is that this information is available to all manufacturers. They all use a similar methodology, with clinics and conjoint analysis techniques to the fore.

Sometimes, the manufacturer's pricing objective is actually to limit demand to match the available supply, however. During the first year or so of a model's life, when teething problems in production in the ramp-up phase are likely to occur, demand can be deliberately restricted by charging a premium or by not offering any special allowances or discounts. Where there is an opportunity to charge a premium, Vauxhall does consider doing so. Because diesel engines, for example, are more expensive to produce, Vauxhall always seeks a higher price to reflect increased costs. Nevertheless, normally cost is just one determinant of the price and at the time the final list price is determined, cost plays only a minor role compared with perceived value relationships.

5 Price variations

Even though Vauxhall goes to great lengths to get the list prices right, allowances also have to be built into the pricing structure to allow flexibility for sales promotions. List prices for cars tend to be fairly stable as the trade does not like frequent changes which can lead to uncertainty or confusion for customers. Extra support through increased allowances is the typical way of gaining short term sales with the benefit that they add value in the consumer's mind rather than focusing on the model's price. Free car insurance, extended warranties, low cost credit, free servicing etc are all powerful ways of adding value and their introduction and withdrawal are forms of price re-alignment. In addition, Vauxhall's buying power means it can often obtain these kind of benefits more cheaply than the cost and thereby offering the customer a better deal.

In the old days dealers were given a 17% discount and through hard bargaining a consumer could knock the dealer's retail price down. The emphasis was on price negotiation and the margin lay with the dealer, thus the manufacturer had less scope to add value through sales promotion. Now, the dealer discount is down to 10% which means that dealers have less scope for reducing prices and manufacturers can now introduce allowances for anything between 3% and 7% depending upon market circumstances. Early on, few allowances are offered in order to restrict demand, but later, once all the production problems have been resolved, allowances are used more heavily. These allowances are usually built into the business plan and are especially useful for extending the life of the product or for boosting sales of an old model before the introduction of a new one. Some models are so successful and unique that Vauxhall does not seek to introduce any significant allowances.

All these allowances are heavily researched to establish their perceived value to the customer the impact of changes on sales. The difficulty with allowances is that they can be difficult to take away and customers may come to expect them as a norm. The British in particular are becoming far more prepared to complain if quality or service is found wanting.

6 Dealer pricing

As indicated earlier, the standard approach in the motor trade is to offer the dealer a discount on list prices, usually around 10%. They then take possession of the stock and take responsibility for storage, financing and service. They are, after all, tying up a lot of capital in a dealership. There is often not much margin left these days for serious price discounting, but that is welcomed in the industry. It has been found that the greater the scope for discounts, the greater the price competition and channel instability.

Additional allowances are given, based on dealer performance, usually on a quantity of sales basis or customer satisfaction basis. Vauxhall has a firm policy that any dealer can benefit from these additional allowances as it is regarded as unfair to treat dealers differently. Sometimes extra bonuses are given to promote a particular model or features, if Vauxhall is trying to move stock or combat a potential competitor threat.

Overall, this system has evolved over many years and Vauxhall has developed considerable experience in examining pricing options and integrating market, value based and cost based data to make list price and allowance decisions. There is still scope for management judgement, but research plays a major role in informing decision-making. Vauxhall is watching Internet car buying trends as this could change the current approach, although we are many years away from that. Car buying is still an emotional rather than a commodity purchase and this favours a visit to the dealer, direct personal contact and even a test drive. However, if having decided what model to buy, the consumer then uses the Internet to shop around for the best price, almost on a commodity basis, then the dealer distribution system could be undermined. It all depends upon whether customers are prepared to trade service and security for price. No doubt Vauxhall will research that through its clinics if it thinks that such a shift is likely to happen.

With grateful thanks to Ian Coomber, Executive Director, Sales and Marketing of Vauxhall UK.

Part V

PLACE

Place, or distribution, can become the element of the marketing mix that causes the biggest headache to a manufacturer. The other three mix elements remain under the manufacturer's control, but once the product is out of the factory gate, it is at the mercy of the middlemen within the distribution channel. Chapter 12 defines the main types of distribution channel available to manufacturers and discusses the advantages or otherwise of each. It also focuses on both the importance of cultivating good relationships within distribution channels and, where possible, ways of gaining and maintaining control over channel members. The final part of Chapter 12 looks at the logistics function, and how goods are moved cost effectively from the manufacturer through the distribution channel to the end customer.

Chapter 13, in contrast, centres on the retailer as the main interface between manufacturer and end consumer. Retailers face particular problems, such as choice of location, merchandising and image development, which are all discussed in this chapter. Many of these problems are, at heart, centred on making decisions on elements of the marketing mix, but the application in retailing gives them a different and interesting angle. This chapter also looks at the rapidly emerging field of Internet retailing.

Marketing Channels and Logistics

This chapter will help you to:

1 define what a channel of distribution is and understand its contribution to efficient and effective marketing effort;

2 differentiate between types of intermediary and their roles;

3 appreciate the factors influencing channel design, structure and strategy and the effect of conflict and co-operation within channels;

4 define logistics, appreciating the importance of customer service and its implementation within logistics;

5 identify the functions involved in logistics and the decisions contributing to their management.

INTRODUCTION

Part of the responsibility of a marketing orientated organisation is to get the product to the customer in the right place at the right time. This has led to the development of extremely efficient and sophisticated distribution systems. Imagine what life would be like for a consumer without those familiar distribution systems. The onus would be on us as consumers to find out what is being supplied, when and where. Without the back-up of a customer orientation, issues of supply, location, timing, quantity and assortment would all be resolved to suit the supplier's, not the customer's, abilities and preferences. This is fine, as long as demand outstrips supply and consumers are prepared to invest considerable time and even money in sourcing goods. Such a scenario is not impossible. Before the changes in eastern Europe, a consumer's first activity after finishing work was often to join the queues for essential items of food such as bread.

This indicates the importance of a sound distribution infrastructure, both in the structure of a modern economy and as a tool in the marketing mix, and provides the main theme of this chapter. This topic is often referred to as 'place' to cover the decisions and strategies that enable the product to flow to the consumer, whether from the market, direct to the home, via a wholesaler or from a retail outlet.

The chapter begins with a definition of channels of distribution, highlighting the role played by different types of intermediaries, and looks at the relative merits of using intermediaries compared with direct selling. Attention then turns to the strategic decision making necessary to design and implement a channel strategy. While the

The motor industry in Europe is a good example of the complexity surrounding the design, building and maintenance of distribution channels. Europe has over 470 million people and 155 million cars. It also has over 30 manufacturers supplying national sales organisations in each of 24 countries, who in turn supply more than 100 000 retail outlets. In Germany alone, there are 17 000 dealers and 9000 sub-dealers, while in France there are 4000 main dealers and 19 000 sub-dealers. In the UK, the figures stand at 6700 and 600, respectively. Assuming that around 13 million cars are sold each year in Europe, that means an average of around 130 cars per outlet, although this will vary widely between different countries and car manufacturers. The car manufacturers, are concerned with a whole range of decisions in order to remain competitive, yet provide good customer service and achieve marketing objectives through their distribution channels.

main emphasis will be on the manufacturer selecting a channel structure and strategy to achieve market coverage and marketing objectives, the power of the intermediary should not be forgotten. In many countries, the power of negotiation rests with the intermediary, who may select or deselect manufacturers' products. Such action has a major impact on the manufacturer, but little impact on the intermediary.

Although channels of distribution are important economic structures, they are also social systems involving individuals and organisations. This chapter, therefore, also considers issues associated with the general conduct of the relationship. Such relationships may be characterised by conflict, co-operation, trust or a climate of mutual hostility and discontent, despite the economic pragmatism that binds both parties together.

This chapter also examines the processes of physical distribution that enable products to flow from manufacturer to consumer. After an initial review of some of the key concepts, the difficulty of balancing customer service against distribution costs is considered in terms of the total logistics system, which highlights the need for adopting a 'total' approach to distribution management. The various functions and management decisions are then examined in the context of the main choices that lead to different distribution cost and service profiles. These include transportation modes, storage and materials handling.

Of course, in service situations there is no product movement or storage because production and consumption are normally simultaneous. In that case, the channel of distribution is primarily concerned with providing access to the booking and reservation system and in handling the sales and negotiating process associated with such access (*see* Chapter 22). The emphasis in this chapter, therefore, will be the movements of physical goods.

DEFINITION OF MARKETING CHANNELS

A **marketing channel** can be defined as the structure linking a group of individuals or organisations through which a product or service is made available to the consumer or industrial user. The degree of formality in the relationships between the channel members can vary significantly, from the highly organised arrangements in the distribution of fmcg products through supermarkets, to the more speculative and transient position of roadside sellers of fruit and vegetables.

It is interesting to compare the highly developed food distribution systems of western Europe with those struggling to emerge in Poland. In the UK, although there are over 74 000 food and drink retail outlets, owned by over 58 000 businesses, the top seven multiples account for around 70 per cent of retail sales in the sector (A.C. Nielsen, 1999). The dominant multiples have had a significant impact on branding and product range, service and distribution, innovation and in raising general quality standards in the grocery trade. In

Poland, by contrast, there are around 100 000 retail outlets concerned with food and groceries and over 90 per cent of them are owned by small independent retailers. The large number of outlets reflects low car ownership patterns and frequent shopping trips. Supermarkets, as opposed to small shops and kiosks, account for less than 10 per cent of overall food business. This retail sector could well see dramatic change as the current system means difficult and expensive physical distribution, limited shelf life, limited product ranges, variable displays and greater difficulties for branded-goods manufacturers in creating a uniform and consistent presence (Keller, 1996).

There are several different types of **intermediary**, each with a slightly different role. These will now be defined, and then we shall look at the ways in which these intermediaries come together to create different kinds of distribution channels between manufacturer and consumer. As a means of summarising all of this, this section will finally consider the rationale for using intermediaries at all.

Types of intermediary

Many marketing channels involve the physical movement of goods and the transfer of legal title to the goods, although the physical movement may be separate from the change of title, especially if external transport carriers are used. As the goods pass from hand to hand, each intermediary adds a *margin* to the price of the goods, which may or may not reflect the value added. Various functions are performed by the various types of intermediaries in return for their margins. Some purchase an assortment of products from various suppliers and then add value by storing, breaking bulk, and then adding services (e.g. credit, delivery) during the resale process. In some situations product transformation may take place, especially in packaging and in the image of the product, which may be enhanced by in-store promotion.

However, not all intermediaries between the manufacturer and consumer necessarily take legal title to the goods, or even physical possession of them, as the following descriptions show.

Wholesalers

Wholesalers do not normally deal with the end consumer but with other intermediaries, usually retailers. However, in some situations sales are made directly to the end user, especially in organisational markets, with no further resale taking place. An organisation may purchase its catering or cleaning supplies from a local cash and carry business that serves the retail trade. A wholesaler does take legal title to the goods as well as taking physical possession of them.

Retailers

Retailers sell direct to the consumer and may either purchase direct from the manufacturer or deal with a wholesaler, depending on purchasing power and volume. Retailers come in many different formats, sizes and locations as we shall see in Chapter 13.

Distributors and dealers

Distributors and dealers are intermediaries who add value through special services associated with stocking or selling inventory, credit and after-sales service. Although these intermediaries are often used in organisational markets, they can also be found in direct dealing with consumers, for example computer or motor dealers. The term usually signifies a more structured and closer tie between the manufacturer and intermediary in order that the product may be delivered efficiently and with the appropriate level of expertise. Clearly, some retail outlets are also closely associated with dealerships and the distinction between them may be somewhat blurred.

Franchisees

A franchisee holds a contract to supply and market a product or service to the design or blueprint of the franchisor (the owner or originator of the product or service). The franchise agreement covers not only the precise specification of the product or service, but also the selling and marketing aspects of the business. The uniformity of different branches of McDonald's is an indication of the level of detail covered by a franchise agreement. There are many products and services currently offered through franchise arrangements, especially in the retail and home services sector, considered in Chapter 22.

Agents and brokers

Agents and brokers are intermediaries who have the legal authority to act on behalf of the manufacturer, although they do not take legal title to the goods or indeed handle the product directly in any way. They do, however, make the product more accessible to the customer and in some cases provide appropriate add-on benefits. Their prime function is to bring buyer and seller together. Universities often use agents to recruit students in overseas markets.

Euro Food Brands acts as a food broker for a small number of continental European brand manufacturers that want to develop in the UK market. By representing such brands as Ducros (peppercorns) and illycaffé (coffee), it selects products that are original and well established in their home market. Then it supplies the major multiples, cash and carries, department stores and 1000 restaurants directly (*The Grocer*, 1999c).

The specific role of each channel member will vary depending on a range of market and strategy issues. The next subsection looks at how these intermediaries relate to each other, and discusses further the specific roles that each plays in getting goods to end users.

Channel structure

The route selected to move a product to market through different intermediaries is known as the *channel structure*. The chosen route varies according to whether the organisation is dealing with consumer or organisational goods. Even within these broad sectors, different products might require different distribution channels.

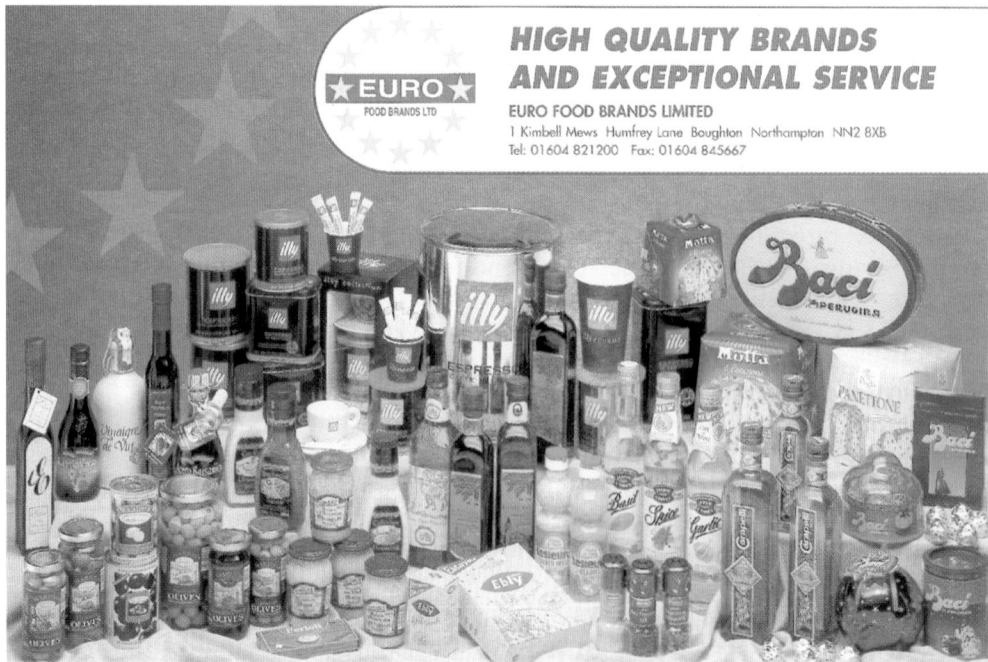

This company distributes specialist European brands throughout the UK market.

Source: Euro Food Brands Ltd.

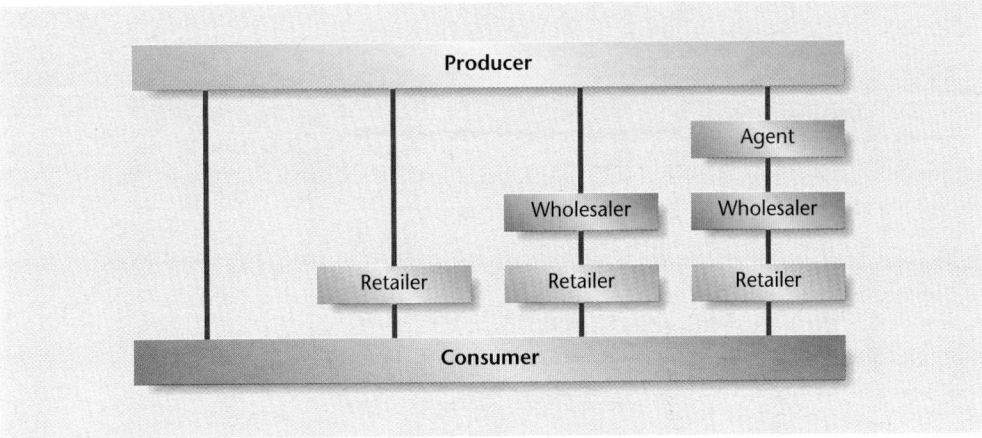

Consumer goods

The four most common channel structures in consumer markets are shown in Fig 12.1. As can be seen, each alternative involves a different number of inter- mediaries, and each is appropriate to different kinds of markets or selling situations. Each will now be discussed in turn.

Producer–consumer (direct supply). In the producer–consumer channel, the manufacturer and consumer deal directly with each other. There are many variants on this theme. It could be a factory shop or a pick-your-own fruit farm. Some manufacturers sell direct to the public through mail order. The increasing cheapness and ease of setting up cus- tomer databases (to be discussed in detail in Chapter 18) mean that direct selling by telephone or mail order is becoming a more attractive distribution option. Alternatively, goods may be sold through a network of sales offices. Door-to-door sell- ing, such as that practised by double-glazing companies, and party plan selling, such as Tupperware and Ann Summers parties, are all attempts by producers to eliminate intermediaries. Clearly, this route has the advantage of control and simplicity, but this must be weighed against the cost and resource efficiency of directly building a company-owned sales and distribution force.

Producer–retailer–consumer (short channel). The producer–retailer–consumer route is the most popular with the larger retailers, since they can buy in large quantities, obtaining special prices and often with tailormade stock-handling and delivery arrangements. This route is typically used by large supermarket chains and is most appropriate for large manufacturers and large retailers who deal in such huge quantities that a direct relationship is efficient.

Figure 12.2 shows a highly simplified form of the goods and information flow between a manufacturer and a retailer. The fast capture and processing of information are critical for the efficient and effective functioning of such systems. Tesco, for exam- ple, has automated its business chain to such a degree that orders, invoicing and payments are all triggered by shoppers passing through the checkouts.

In the car trade, a local dealer usually deals directly with the manufacturer, because, unlike fmcg products, there is a need for significant support in the supply infrastructure and expertise in the sales and service process. This is an example of the grey area between retailing and distributorships, discussed at p. 461.

Producer–wholesaler–retailer–consumer (long channel). The advantage of adding a wholesaler level can be significant where small manufacturers and/or small retailers are involved. A small manufacturing organisation does not necessarily have the skills or resources to reach a wide range of retail customers and, similarly, the small corner shop does not have the resources to source relatively small quantities direct from many manufactures.

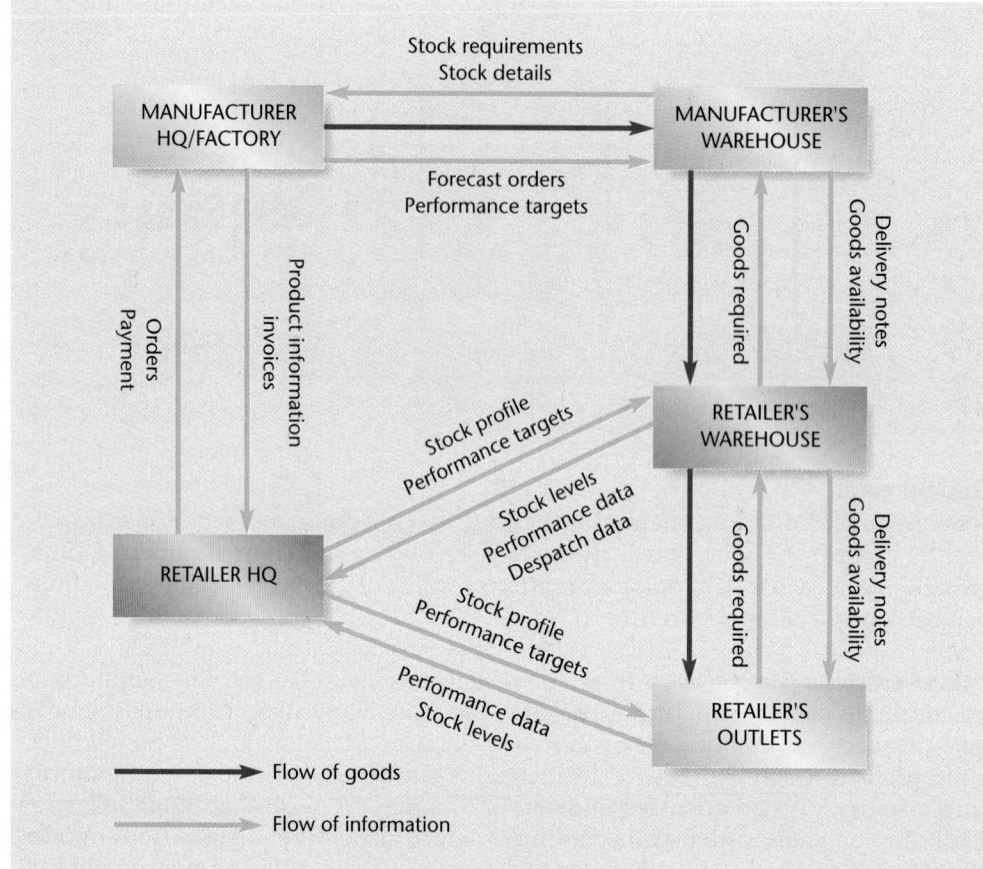

Stock requirements
Stock details

MANUFACTURER
HQ/FACTORY

MANUFACTURER'S
WAREHOUSE

Forecast orders
Performance targets

Orders
Payment

Product information
invoices

Goods required

Delivery notes
Goods availability

RETAILER HQ

Stock profile
Performance targets

RETAILER'S
WAREHOUSE

Stock levels
Performance data
Despatch data

Goods required

Delivery notes
Goods availability

Stock profile
Performance targets

Performance data
Stock levels

RETAILER'S
OUTLETS

→ Flow of goods

→ Flow of information

FIGURE 12.2

The flow of products and information between a large manufacturer and a large retailer

The wholesaler can provide a focal point for both sides, by buying in bulk from manufacturers, then splitting that bulk into manageable quantities for small retailers; bringing a wider assortment of goods together for the retailer under one roof; providing access to a wider range of retail customers for the small manufacturer; and similarly providing access to a wider range of manufacturers' goods for the small retailer. Effectively, the wholesaler is marketing on behalf of the manufacturer.

Example The independent grocery sector is serviced by a number of wholesalers and cash and carry providers. Nearly two-thirds of the trade is through cash and carries in which the retailer can be offered greater choice or more items than the delivered wholesaler handles (*The Grocer*, 1999a). The delivered sector is growing, however, and the major multiple depot wholesalers are taking business from the smaller cash and carries and the unaffiliated groups.

Sugro UK, a Nantwich-based wholesale group that is part of a German-based parent company, is an amalgam of 84 wholesalers and cash and carry operators specialising mainly in confectionery, snacks and soft drinks. It services 43 000 outlets including 16 000 CTNs (confectionery, tobacco, news establishments), 6500 convenience stores, 2400 petrol forecourts and around 5000 pubs. The advantages for small independent retailers sourcing from the group are mainly linked with the group's centralised bulk buying from major manufacturers, the availability of Sugro own brands on some lines, as well as an efficient and comprehensive stocking and delivery service (Gilbert, 1995).

The wholesaler can also act on behalf of relatively large manufacturers trying to sell large volumes of frequently reordered products to a wide retail network. Daily national newspapers, for example, are delivered from the presses to the wholesalers, which can then break bulk and assemble tailormade orders involving many different titles for their own retail customers. This is far more efficient than each newspaper producer trying to deal direct with each small corner shop newsagent.

Producer–agent–wholesaler–retailer–consumer. This is the longest and most indirect channel. It might be used, for example, where a manufacturer is trying to enter a relatively unknown export market. The agent will be chosen because of local knowledge, contacts and expertise in selling into that country, and will earn commission on sales made. The problem is, however, that the manufacturer is totally dependent and has to trust the quality of the agent's knowledge, commitment and selling ability. Nevertheless, this method is widely used by smaller organisations trying to develop in remote markets, where their ability to establish a strong presence is constrained by lack of time, resources or knowledge.

Organisational goods

As highlighted in Chapter 4, organisational products often involve close technical and commercial dialogue between buyer and seller, during which the product and its attributes are matched to the customer's specific requirements. The type and frequency of purchase, the quantity purchased and the importance of the product to the buyer all affect the type of channel structure commonly found in organisational markets. Office stationery, for example, is not a crucial purchase from the point of view of keeping production lines going and, as a routine repurchase, it is more likely to be distributed through specialist distributors or retailers such as Staples, Office World or Rymans. In contrast, crucial components that have to be integrated into a production line are likely to be delivered direct from supplier to buyer to specific deadlines. The variety of organisational distribution channels can be seen in Fig. 12.3. Each type will now be discussed in turn.

Manufacturer–user. The direct channel is most appropriate where the goods being sold have a high unit cost and perhaps a high technical content. There is likely to be a small number of buyers who are perhaps confined to clearly defined geographical areas. To operate such a channel, the manufacturer must be prepared to build and manage a sales and distribution force that can negotiate sales, provide service and administer customer needs. In some cases, the sales representative will both sell and install the product, as happens with computer software applications.

Manufacturers may also operate their own sales branches or offices. These organisations are owned and operated by the manufacturer, but fulfil many of the functions and roles of a wholesale operation. They allow the manufacturer to retain more control over the way in which the distribution channel works, and can increase the effectiveness and efficiency of the links between manufacturers and their customers, but they may also be a necessity if the manufacturer needs wholesale services that are not available on the open market.

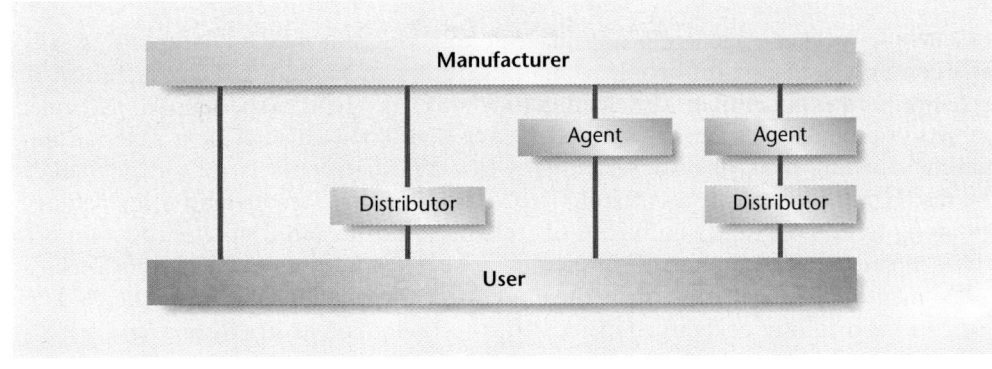

FIGURE 12.3

Channels structure organisational markets

AB Konstruktions-Bakelit, one of Sweden's largest manufacturers of industrial plastic components, deals directly with customers such as Volvo, Saab and Alfa Laval. This is because of the need for considerable dialogue during the design and development stage to ensure a close fit between the customer's specification and components that are made to order. There would be a very high risk of misunderstanding if a third party were introduced.

Sales branches tend to be situated away from the manufacturer's head office in areas where demand is particularly high. They are a conveniently situated focal point for the area's sales force, providing them with products and support services so that they in turn can better meet their customers' needs more quickly. Sales branches may also sell products themselves directly to small retailers or wholesalers.

Sales offices do not carry stock, so, although they might take orders from local customers, they are only acting as agents and will pass the order on to head office. Again, they provide a locally convenient focus in busy areas.

Manufacturer–distributor–user. Less direct channels tend to be adopted as the number of customers grows, the size of customers reduces, and the number of intermediary functions also increases. Building materials, for example, are often sold to builders' merchants, who then sell to the building trade based on lower order quantities, and consequently with a greater range of stock availability but greater proximity to local need. The philosophy is similar to that of the short channel of distribution discussed in the consumer context on page 463.

This less direct type of structure can also apply to software products. Moser GmbH is one of the leading software houses in Germany and specialises in selling to trade and handicraft organisations. Although it had over 10 000 software installations in Germany and the Netherlands, it decided to seek expansion elsewhere in Europe. This was done by selling through other software and system houses which already had the sales and technical appreciation to generate sales for Moser.

Manufacturer–agent–user. Sometimes an agent is introduced to act on behalf of a group of manufacturers in dealing with users in situations where it would not be economically viable to create a direct selling effort, but where there is a need for selling expertise to generate and complete transactions.

Teijo Pesukoneet from Nakkila in Finland specialises in technically advanced cleaning machines for metal components in enclosed cabinets. Although it has its own sales offices in Sweden and Norway, it operates through agents in other main European markets such as the UK and Germany. Agents are trained to handle technical queries and sales enquiries but relay orders to Finland for direct delivery.

Generally speaking, agents do not take title to goods, but may buy and sell, usually on a commission basis, on behalf of manufacturers and retailers. They facilitate an exchange process rather than participating fully in it. They tend to specialise in particular markets or product lines and are used because of their knowledge, or their superior purchasing or selling skills, or because of their well-established contacts within the market. The distinction between an agent and a broker is a fine one. Agents tend to be retained on a long-term basis to act on behalf of a client, and thus build up working rapport. A broker tends to be used on a one-off, temporary basis to fulfil a specific need or deal.

The main problem with agents is the amount of commission that has to be paid, as this can push selling costs up. This cost has to be looked at in context and with a

MARKETING IN ACTION South African oranges

The next time you tuck into a South African orange, stop to think of the many stages in the distribution channel through which the product has moved, from the South African orange growers to the local supermarket. Each year South Africa exports some 50 million cartons of oranges, with western Europe consuming over 50 per cent of them. The industry is made up of 200 private farmers and 1200 growers in co-operatives. Many growers and co-operatives pool their output for marketing and distribution purposes under the Capespan International selling operation. The challenge for Capespan has been to align its distribution strategy with increased international competition, greater customer sophistication and the demands of ever-powerful supermarket chains. Product freshness, variety, quality and supply must all meet customer demand and the product must move smoothly through the supply chain from grower to buyer.

The oranges move from the growers to the fruit-handling facilities run by Capespan near the major ports such as Durban, Cape Town and Port Elizabeth. Capespan purchases the oranges and then adds handling and transportation costs and a profit margin. The services provided include some initial de-greening, environmental control, labelling and packing, all before shipment. It also arranges shipment, increasingly in large bulk bins for ease of handling, from the ports. At this stage, data is collected on the fruit, size, type, quality grade, treatment and origin. Another service that Capespan undertakes is to move the oranges to cold storage before they depart for Europe.

European ports such as Sheerness and Tilbury have been selected as destinations. A partnership approach between Capespan and the port authorities has resulted in a specialist infrastructure for handling and storing palletised or binned oranges. In order to ensure that the right oranges arrive at the right EU port, data is sent to

Capespan planners in Europe, who then decide which fruit should be unloaded at which port to meet local demand. On arrival, Capespan re-inspects the produce. Where necessary, the cartons are labelled and quality control checks undertaken to ensure that the fruit is consistent with specific buyers' expectations. This all helps to preserve the reputation of the Capespan brand name, Outspan. There are plans to add more valuable services such as pre-packing, size grading and fruit preparation for fresh fruit salad. After processing, the oranges are ready either to enter the UK domestic distribution chain or to go for further storage. Because an electronic data system has been used, fruit that has ripened during transit is ready to leave port quickly in 'table-fresh' condition.

Shipment can be to external pre-packers contracted by the supermarkets or straight to the wholesale and supermarket distribution systems at regional or central warehouse collection points. These shipments fulfil orders placed either direct by the supermarkets or through selling agents dealing with Capespan in the UK. Some oranges go into the fruit and vegetable distribution chain and end up being sold in markets and through wholesalers dealing with specialist fruit and vegetable stores.

With the deregulation of the South African industry, other importers have started to deal directly with the South African industry. Eurodix in Peterborough markets oranges under its own brand name, Sovereign, and ships them directly to customers after import. It has employed its own staff in the packhouses in South Africa, who inspect the fruit purchased and also grade and pack it. In the UK, Eurodix checks quality for appearance and taste, and then pre-packs and delivers to meet customer demand. It is the first distributor in the UK to be appointed outside the complex, but single-channel, system used for South African citrus fruit.

Sources: Shapley (1998b); http://www.networking.ibm.com, 'The Sweet Taste of Success'.

sense of proportion. That commission is buying sales performance, market knowledge and a degree of flexibility that would take a lot of time and money to build for yourself, even if you wanted to do it. The alternative to using agents, therefore, may not be so effective or cost efficient.

Manufacturer–agent–distributor–user. A model comprising manufacturer–agent–distributor–user links is particularly useful in fast-moving export markets. The sales agent co-ordinates sales in a specified market, while the distributors provide inventory and fast restocking facilities close to the point of customer need. The comments on the longest channel of distribution in the consumer context (*see* p. 465) are also applicable here.

The type of structure adopted in a particular sector, whether industrial or consumer, will ultimately depend on the product and market characteristics that produce differing cost and servicing profiles. These issues will be further explored in the context of the main justification for using marketing intermediaries, described next.

Rationale for using intermediaries

Every transaction between a buyer and a seller costs money. There are delivery costs, order picking and packing costs, marketing costs, and almost certainly administrative costs associated with processing an order and receiving or making payment. The role of the intermediary is to increase the efficiency and reduce the costs of individual transactions. This can be clearly seen in Fig. 12.4.

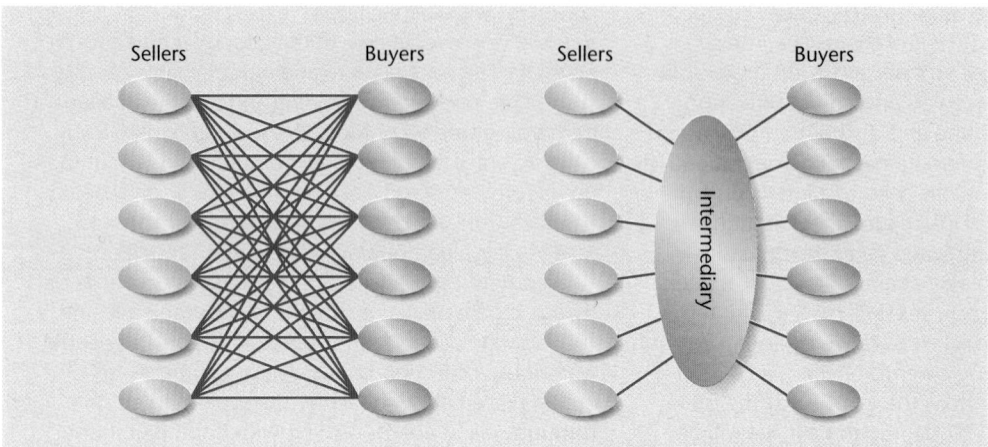

FIGURE 12.4

The role of intermediaries

If six manufacturers wished to deal with six buyers, a total of 36 links would be necessary. All of these transaction links cost time and money to service, and require a certain level of administrative and marketing expertise. If volumes and profit margins are sufficient, then this may be a viable proposition. However, in many situations this would add considerably to the cost of the product. By using an intermediary, the number of links falls to just 12, and each buyer and each seller only needs to maintain and service one link. If this makes sense when considering only six potential buyers, just imagine how much more sensible it is with fmcg goods where there are millions of potential buyers! On economic grounds alone, the rationale for intermediaries in creating transaction efficiency is demonstrated.

However, there are other reasons for using intermediaries, because they add value for the manufacturer and customer alike. These value added services fall into three main groups (Webster, 1979), as shown in Fig. 12.5.

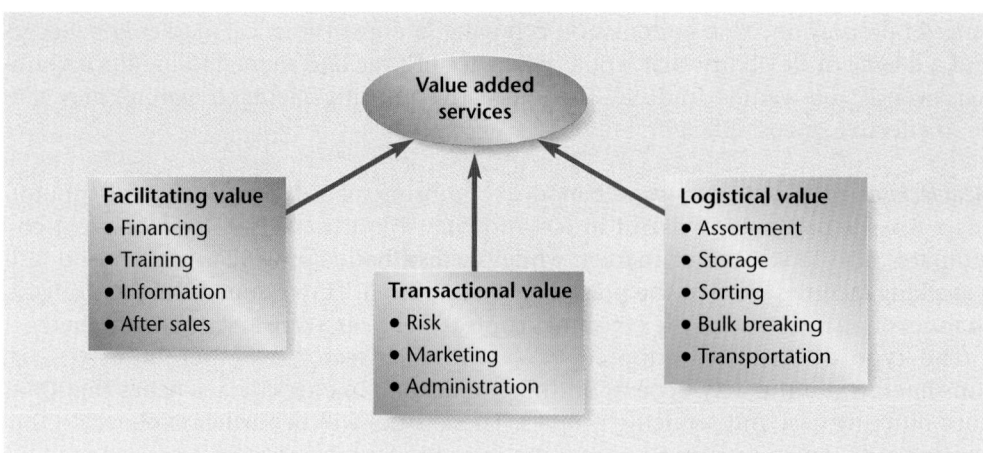

FIGURE 12.5

Value added services provided by intermediaries

Transactional value

The role of intermediaries in assisting transaction efficiency has already been high-lighted. To perform this role adequately, the intermediary, as an interconnected but separate entity, must decide on its own strategic position in the market-place, and therefore assemble products that it believes its own desired customers need and then market them effectively. The selection is extremely important, and requires careful purchasing in terms of type, quantity and cost to fit the intermediary's own product strategy.

The *risks* move to the intermediary, who takes *title* to the goods and, as legal owner, is responsible for their resale. Of course, it is in the manufacturer's interest to see the product moving through the distribution system in order to achieve sales and profit objectives. However, the risk of being lumbered with obsolete, damaged or slow-moving stock rests with the intermediary, not the manufacturer. This is a valuable service to that manufacturer.

With the transfer of title and risk, the need to *market effectively* increases. Intermediaries may recruit and train their own sales forces to resell the products that they have assembled. This is another valuable service to the manufacturer, as it means that the product may have a greater chance of being brought to the attention of the prospective customer, especially in organisational markets. An intermediary can use the full range of promotional weapons available, including advertising, point-of-sale promotion and direct mail (*see* Chapters 15, 16 and 18). An industrial distributor may have a sales counter or a telephone sales operation, or it may have an external field sales force to sell the product in question (Anderson and Narus, 1986). The intermediary may take sole responsibility for this function, or carry it out in co-operation with the manufacturer, sharing the decisions and the expenses.

> **Example** Dexion is a leading storage equipment manufacturer, handling everything from small orders from independent retailers through to fitting out large automated warehouses. For these larger contracts Dexion has its own sales force to deal with the complexity of agreeing the design and installation, the price and building a long-term relationship. One system installed with British Central Electrical, part of the OTRA NV electrical wholesaling group, had to be specially designed to handle 25 000 items with 24-hour turnaround. The small user market, however, is served by 50 UK Dexion distributors. This mixed channel system has enabled Dexion to expand to over 100 countries and become a market leader (http://www.dexion.com). The emphasis is on fast ex-stock supply and local sales and marketing based on sound knowledge.

Logistical value

A critical role for the intermediary is the assembly of an *assortment of products* from different sources that is compatible with the needs of the intermediary's own customers. This assortment can operate at product or brand level. A drinks wholesaler, for example, may offer a full range of merchandise from beer to cognac, but within each category considerable brand choice may also be offered. The benefit to the customer is the wide choice available from one source, supported perhaps by a competitive and comprehensive pre- and post-sales service. However, for other intermediaries the choice may be more limited. If one manufacturer occupies a dominant position, the choice of competing brands may be severely restricted to just complementary products. In many car dealerships, for example, only one manufacturer's new cars can be sold, although there might be more flexibility over second-hand cars.

Assortment strategy is a critical variable in a retailer's marketing strategy. The key is to build an assortment to reflect the needs of the target market.

> **Example** Assortment strategy can be clearly seen in the music business. Some stores specialise only in classical or rock and associated sheet music. Others aim to provide a little of everything, but primarily concentrate on the bestsellers in CD and tape. A further group aim to provide depth of range by covering many older, slower moving titles.

In any of these strategies there are risks in misjudging changes in customer fads or tastes. This is particularly noticeable in high fashion areas where even the sale rails do not move assortments that have been left behind. The trend, however, in a society where disposable incomes are increasing, is for deeper choice within more specialised assortments, whether the all-Japanese store in North London or cuckoo-clock shops in Berne.

A further dimension of logistical value is the *accumulation and storing of products* at locations that are appropriate and convenient to the customer. The small manufacturer can make one large delivery of output to the wholesaler's warehouse, where it can be stored until a retailer wants it, and broken down into smaller lots as necessary. The hassles of transporting small quantities to many different locations, finding storage space and insuring the goods are taken away from the manufacturer.

> **Example** A walk around a market in a developing country reveals row upon row of sellers with small tables offering piles of undifferentiated home-grown carrots or turnips and little else, a far cry from town centre markets in the UK or France. By using intermediaries, farmers or market gardeners do not need to find their own markets. A fruit and vegetable wholesaler can accumulate small quantities of different products from specialist growers, sort them, and then make larger deliveries of assorted goods to the next point in the chain, thus gaining economies in transport costs.
>
> Soleco is France's largest producer of pre-packed salads and fresh stir-fry and snack vegetables. Trading under the Florette and Manon brands, it enjoys a 42 per cent share of the French pre-packed salad market. To make the business a success, it had to invest in high levels of quality control, strict temperature control and specialist preparation machinery. It also needed regular supply. Not only has it contracted with 450 French growers, but about 15 per cent of its supply needs comes from Italy, Spain and Portugal. All crops are allocated batch numbers as part of an ISO 9001 system. All of this enables the consumer to enjoy top quality, fresh produce and provides Soleco with sales of over £75mn (Shapley, 1998a).

Sorting is a very basic step in the logistical process, and means grouping many diverse products into more uniform, homogeneous groups. These groups may be based on product class and further subdivided by such factors as size, shape, weight and colour. This process may also add value by *grading*, which means inspecting, testing or judging products so that they can be placed into more homogeneous quality grades. These standards may be based on intermediary or industry predetermined standards. Large supermarket chains, for example, are particularly demanding about the standardisation of the fruit and vegetables that they retail. If you look at a carton of apples in a supermarket, you will see that they are all of a standard size, colour and quality. Mother Nature hasn't quite worked out how to ensure such uniformity, so the producers and wholesalers have to put effort into sorting out and grading the top quality produce for the High Street. The second-class produce ends up in less choosy retail outlets, while the most irregular specimens end up in soup, fruit juices and ready meals.

A further important role for the intermediary, as already implied, is **bulk breaking**, the division of large units into the smaller, more manageable quantities required by the next step in the chain. Whereas a builder's merchant may purchase sand by the lorry load, the small builder may purchase by the bagged pallet load, and the individual consumer by the individual bag. The value of bulk breaking is clear to the DIY enthusiast, who certainly would not wish to purchase by the pallet load. There is, of course, a price to pay for this convenience, and the consumer would expect to pay a higher price per bag purchased individually than the builder would pay per bag purchased by the pallet load.

A final role is in actually *transporting the product* to the next point in the chain. Lorry loads may be made up of deliveries to several customers in the same area, thus maximising the payload, and with careful siting of warehouse facilities, minimising the distances the products have to travel. Again, this is more efficient that having each manufacturer sending out delivery vans to every customer throughout the country.

Facilitating value

The intermediary also offers a range of other value added services either to the manufacturer or to the customer. Not only do intermediaries share the risks, as outlined above, they also provide a valuable *financing* benefit. The manufacturer only has to manage a small number of accounts (for example with two or three wholesalers rather than with 200 or more individual retailers) and can keep tighter control over credit periods, thus improving cash flow. As part of the service to the consumer, retailers may offer credit or other financial services such as credit card acceptance, easy payment terms and insurance. Manufacturers selling direct would not necessarily be interested in such financial services.

Other activities also add value. Local demonstrations and consumer *training* provided by intermediaries enable the manufacturer to avoid costly labour inputs. Market *information* and *feedback* are precious commodities, as we saw in Chapter 6. The intermediary is much closer to the market-place, and therefore alert to changes in consumer needs and competitive conditions. Passing on this information up the channel of distribution can enable manufacturers to modify their marketing strategies for the benefit of all parties. While there is no replacement for systematic, organised market research, information derived from sales contacts and meetings with intermediaries provides specific, often relevant intelligence. For the small manufacturer, with very limited market research resources, this can be particularly invaluable.

All the above functions need to be performed at some point within the marketing channel. The key decision concerns which member undertakes what role. This decision may be reached by *negotiation*, where the power in the channel is reasonably balanced, or by *imposition*, when either manufacturer or retailer dominates. Whatever the outcome, the compensation system in terms of margins needs to be designed to reflect the added value role performed.

An appreciation of added value dispels the commonly held belief that involving intermediaries simply increases the price of goods to the consumer. It also dispels the view of some small business marketers that they cannot afford to pay a margin to the intermediary, and so must deal direct. Clearly if intermediaries, especially wholesalers, were eliminated, the services provided would still need to be performed and, in many cases, this would be done somewhat less efficiently. The result could be a rise in prices or a severe limitation on the availability of less popular products, or perhaps even to put smaller manufacturers out of business. If, for example, wine distributors were eliminated, retailers then would have to create trading relationships with individual wineries worldwide, and might never find out about new, specialist wines. At the same time, immense problems would be created for wine producers in finding retail outlets, organising delivery and absorbing distribution costs.

Ultimately, the existence of intermediaries gives everyone a fighting chance of concentrating on what they are best at doing, whether that is producing, selling or consuming.

CHANNEL STRATEGY

With the various added-value roles implicit in the marketing channel, decisions need to be taken about the allocation and performance of these roles, the basis of remuneration within the system and the effectiveness of alternative configurations in enabling market penetration to be achieved competitively and efficiently. This is **channel strategy**. As indicated earlier, these decisions do not necessarily revolve around the manufacturer, despite the origins of the product.

Channel structures

The basic forms of channel design were outlined in Figs 12.1 and 12.3. These are known as conventional channels, in which the various channel activities are agreed by negotiation and compromise, recognising that both sides need each other. The particular structure adopted should reflect the market and product characteristics, taking into consideration such factors as **market coverage**, value, quantity sold, margin available etc. (Sharma and Dominguez, 1992). The structure can be described by the number of levels utilised, ranging from the simplest (two layers) through to the most complex (five or more layers).

Where a manufacturer needs to reach distinct target markets, a dual or multiple distribution approach may be adopted, which means that each target market may be reached by two or more different routes. For example, IBM will sell direct to large users and organisations, but will go through the retail trade to reach the consumer segment. This pattern works well, provided that discreteness is maintained and as long as the arrangement reflects the various buyers' differing pre- and post-purchase servicing needs. However, problems can emerge if the same product is sold to the same target market through different channels. A book publisher, for example, may create some friction with the book trade if it actively encourages direct ordering and other subscription services at lower prices than the retail trade can manage. This potential for conflict may well increase as direct marketing and home shopping gain in popularity.

Market coverage

One way of thinking about which types of channel are appropriate is to start at the end and work backwards. The sort of questions to ask relate not only to the identity of the end customer, but also to their expectations, demand patterns, frequency of ordering, degree of comparison shopping, degree of convenience and the associated services required. All of these elements influence the added value created by place, and the density and type of intermediaries to be used, whether at wholesaler or distributor or retail level. Market coverage, therefore, is about reaching the end customer as cost effectively and as efficiently as possible, while maximising customer satisfaction. To achieve this, three alternative models of distribution intensity can be adopted, as shown in Table 12.1, each of which reflects different product and customer requirements from place. They are discussed below, in turn.

Intensive distribution

Intensive distribution occurs where the product or service is placed in as many outlets as possible, and no interested intermediary is barred from stocking the product. Typical products include bread, newspapers and confectionery, but more generally, most convenience goods (*see* p. 266) fall into this category. The advantage to the consumer is that convenience and availability may be just around the corner, and they can invest a minimum of time and effort in the purchasing process. Using this kind of market coverage also assumes that availability is more important than the type of store selling the product, hence the growth of non-petrol products on sale in garages.

TABLE 12.1

Alternative distribution intensities: general characteristics

	Intensive	*Selective*	*Exclusive*
Total number of outlets covered	Maximum	Possibly many	Relatively few
Number of outlets per region	As many as possible	A small number	One or very few
Distribution focus	Maximum availability	Some specialist retailer knowledge	Close retailer/consumer relationship
Type of consumer product	Convenience	Shopping	Speciality
Number of potential purchasers	High	Medium	Low
Purchase frequency	Often	Occasionally	Seldom
Level of planned purchasing by consumers	Low	Medium	High
Typical price	Low	Medium	High

However, if a product is on sale in every corner shop, it can be difficult for the manufacturer to ensure that the product is being maintained to the desired standard. This may not be a problem with canned or packaged goods, but with more perishable refrigerated or frozen foods, for example, the manufacturer's quality standards may be seriously compromised by poor handling. Even minor irritations can affect the consumer's attitude and satisfaction. In many less well-development retail markets, for example, many small shops do not have the refrigeration facilities to allow them to sell ice-cold cans of Coke.

Intensive distribution usually involves a long chain of distribution (manufacturer–wholesaler–retailer–consumer). It is an efficient means of getting the product as widely available as possible, but total distribution costs may be high, especially where small retailers are concerned and unit orders are low.

Selective distribution

As the term suggests, a more selective approach is designed to use a small number of carefully chosen outlets within a defined geographic area. These are often found with shopping products (again, *see* p. 267) where the consumer may be more willing to search for the most appropriate product and then to undertake a detailed comparison of alternatives. Unlike intensively distributed goods, which can virtually be put on a shop shelf to sell themselves, selectively distributed products might need a little more help from the intermediary, perhaps because they have a higher technical content that needs to be demonstrated, for instance. Manufacturers may also need to invest more in the distribution infrastructure, point-of-sale materials and after sales service. It may thus pay to select a smaller number of intermediaries, where support such as training and joint promotions can be offered and controlled.

Example   The major fine fragrance manufacturers have long adopted a selective distribution strategy. Their rationale for this is that they are selling a luxury, upmarket product that needs to have an appropriate level of personal selling support and the right kind of retail ambience to reinforce and enhance the product's expensive image. In the early 1990s, they repeatedly refused to supply discount chemist chains such as Superdrug in the UK, who wanted to undercut the prices charged by upmarket department stores and other existing fragrance retailers. Pressure from Superdrug and other discount retailers which obtained unofficial but perfectly legal supplies from third parties has thus led to wider availability of fragrances and a significant focus on price competition from all but the most upmarket retailers.

The selective distribution approach is not unique to consumer goods. An Irish distributor of tractor seats for a UK organisation was required to carry local stocks and to fit the replacement seats to conform with European safety standards. Such regulation and control are only possible if a manageable number of outlets are allowed to handle the product. The Irish distributor, therefore, had major territorial rights across the west and south-west of Ireland. It was meant to handle all replacement sales by building up relationships with farmers, farm equipment repair shops and service agents.

Exclusive distribution

Exclusive distribution is the opposite of intensive distribution, and means that only one outlet covers a relatively large geographic area. This type of distribution may reflect very large infrastructure investments, a scattered low density of demand or infrequently purchased products. In organisational markets, the impact on the customer may not be particularly significant if a sales force and customer service network are in place. However, in consumer markets there may be some inconvenience to the customer, who may have to travel some distance to source the product and may effectively have no choice about who to purchase from.

Example In consumer markets, the obvious example of exclusive distribution is new cars. A particular dealership will have the right to sell brand new Ford cars, for example, within a defined geographic area. Ford goes even further, in that it will not consider any multi-franchise proposal. This means that the dealer cannot sell Ford cars and Fiat cars, for example, from the same premises. Similarly, Ford will not give permission for any of its dealers to operate any motor related business within 50 km of the Ford franchise. If consumers do not like that dealership for some reason, then they will have to travel some distance to find the next Ford dealer, or else buy a Renault locally instead.

Such an exclusive approach may even fit in with the product's own exclusivity. It would also be appropriate where high degrees of co-operation in inventory management, service standards and selling effort are required between manufacturer and intermediary.

Example When Mustang, an American-based manufacturer of small four-wheeled construction vehicles, wanted to build a presence in the UK market, it appointed a sole distributor offering a sales force experienced in selling small equipment into the building trade.

Influences on channel strategy

There are several alternative channel design decisions facing the manufacturer who has a choice, but there are also several factors that may constrain these choices. These factors are outlined below, and are shown in Fig. 12.6. While it may be desirable to adopt an optimal design in terms of marketing effectiveness and efficiency, rarely do organisations have the luxury of a clean sheet of paper. More often, they inherit the consequences of previous decisions, and the risks of changing design midstream need to be carefully considered before any planned improvement.

Organisational objectives, capabilities and resources
The channel strategy selected needs to fit in with the organisation's objectives, capabilities and resources. If the objective is to generate mass appeal and rapid market penetration, then an intensive distribution approach would be necessary. This would have to be supported, however, with an equally intense investment in other market-

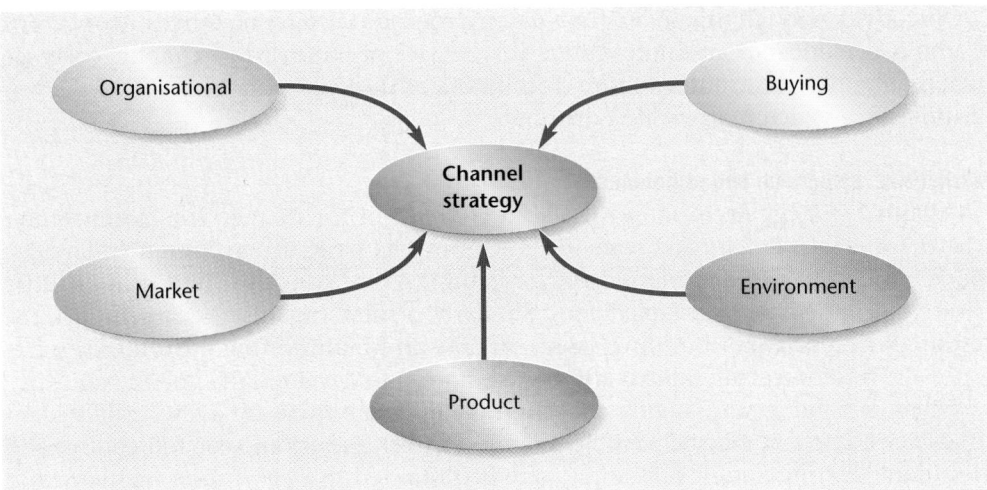

FIGURE 12.6

Factors influencing channel strategy

ing activities such as promotion. If the focus was on repositioning upmarket into a more exclusive niche, then a selective or even an exclusive distribution approach would be called for.

An organisation that wishes to control marketing activities, and is well endowed with resources, may assume many of the channel functions directly. A small organisation with a small market share may have little choice but to concentrate on manufacture and direct dealing with an intermediary. A lack of resources and a lack of expertise and contacts may leave no option.

MARKETING IN ACTION   Borsalino

The trouble with being a hat producer is that the market is in long-term decline. Over the last 50 years, the wearing of hats has become a rarity in social situations and hats are now often worn only on special occasions. Borsalino, an Italian hat producer based in Alessandria, produced two million hats in 1913, but only 200 000 in 1995. Despite having been in the business since 1857 and developing a roaring export trade in the first half of the century, there was no guarantee that success would continue. Borsalino has an international brand reputation and is regarded as being at the forefront of hat fashion. It has managed to retain its 'small multinational' status throughout. In 1900, it exported 60 per cent of its production and by the 1990s the figure was 65 per cent. All this has been achieved by careful product positioning and a distribution strategy that enables a specialist, premium, worldwide niche to be exploited. Over 65 per cent of the company's production is exported to far-off destinations such as Seoul, Osaka and New York, as well as around Europe. When Guiseppe Petrone joined Borsalino in 1993 as managing director, he decided to try to relaunch the company, building on its premium image. He was quoted as saying, 'Other manufacturers produce hats – we make a Borsalino'. As its own

literature proclaims, 'who speaks of Borsalino, talks about a symbol of an utterly Italian style and elegance'. Borsalino is positioned alongside Ferrari, Campari and Gucci as a status product. Prices can go up to L500 000 for a man's hat.

The renewed marketing effort gave rise to a review of the marketing channel strategy. Previously, Borsalino had sold through 300 designated retailers outside Italy and through 400 retailers in Italy. In order to give itself more control and marketing push at the point of sale, Borsalino decided to open its own outlets at key centres in locations such as Moscow, Tokyo, Berlin and Hamburg, along with 'shops within shops' in department stores in Paris, Seoul and New York. It refurbished its own shops in Milan and opened new stores in Florence and Asti. The opening of these outlets enabled closer contract with customers and an opportunity to launch new lines in the women's and youth markets, where the company had a weaker presence. It also enabled a co-ordinated store identity to be developed, from which new accessories and lines such as Ecuadorian straw hats and Montecristi Panamas could be launched, drawing on the established reputation.

Source: Simkins (1996); http://www.borsalino.com.

Objectives may change over time as environmental circumstances evolve. For example, demands for an improved delivery service or increased geographic coverage may require new distributors, more distributors or incorporating better service levels in the service structure of existing distributors.

Market size, dispersion and remoteness

No channel strategy decision can ignore the impact of the market. If a manufacturer wishes to penetrate a market some distance from its base, it may lack the contacts, market knowledge or distribution infrastructure to deal directly. There may be little choice but to deal with intermediaries. Similarly, a small organisation might lack the resources necessary for building sales contacts and maintaining customer service, especially if resources are limited and there is a need to develop sales volume quickly.

When demand is more highly concentrated, or where there are a few, readily identifiable customers, it may be possible to build a direct operation, keep full control and eliminate intermediaries. Efficiency may be obtained in negotiation, delivery and support services. By way of contrast, a large, dispersed market, such as that for magazines, may require a well-structured, efficient chain of intermediaries.

Buying complexity and behaviour

Understanding customer needs and buying criteria goes to the heart of effective marketing and has a major influence on channel selection (Butaney and Wortzel, 1988). Questions such as who buys, where they buy and how frequently they buy all indicate the kind of intermediary best suited to reach target customers. Matching the inter-mediary with customer needs, buyer expectations and product position is a challenging task. The move to out of town shopping, with its advantages of easy parking, convenience and large assortments under one roof, has meant a refocusing of effort by some manufacturers to ensure that they are well represented. Similarly, if a product occupies a specialist position, there is little point in dealing with a wholesaler that is primarily concerned with mass distribution.

Understanding the product classifications presented in Chapter 7 is also likely to influence design. Convenience, routine decisions may require much more widespread distribution than shopping goods where a more systematic evaluation of the selection criteria may suggest the type of intermediary required in terms of service, range, display and demonstration, etc.

Product characteristics

Products that are complex to purchase, install or operate, products that are of high unit value and products that are customer specific tend to be distributed directly to the customer or through highly specialised intermediaries. This reflects the need for close dialogue during the pre- and post-sale situations that may be lost if additional parties are involved. By way of contrast, fairly standard, routinely purchased, low-unit-value products tend to be distributed intensively through intermediaries.

Example McQuillan Engineering Industries (MEI) is a supplier of a wide assortment of components for aircraft interiors, such as overhead bins, galleys, sink units and even nuts and bolts. However, although considerable stocks are held, everything is manufactured to customer designs and specifications, and when demanded they can be assembled on site. Customers include Boeing, Saab and Airbus. With a specialism in batch or prototype production, the distribution and sales method is direct because of the complexity of individual customer orders. This contrasts with replacement parts for domestic electrical equipment, which are standardised by model and are widely stocked either in manufacturers' warehouses or though intermediaries such as repairers.

Other product factors may also have an impact. Highly perishable products need short distribution channels to maintain product quality or to assist in rapid turnover. Items that are non-standard or difficult to handle or items that have the potential to create transport problems may be less attractive to intermediaries (Rosenbloom, 1987).

Changing environment

The changing business environment, discussed in Chapter 2, creates new problems and opportunities for channel design. Three issues demonstrate the effect.

Technology. Technology offers the potential for closer integration between the manufacturer and the intermediary. On-line systems may enable direct access to stock availability, electronic ordering and automated dispatch with the minimum of negotiation, if any. Electronic point-of-sale (EPOS) data can facilitate very rapid responses within the distribution system. Smaller organisations still relying on older technology such as the telephone and manual checking may soon become marginalised.

Working patterns. The growth in the number of women working has had a profound effect on some distribution channels, making some channels more difficult to operate, such as door-to-door selling during the daytime, while home shopping and convenience shopping outside usual trading hours have become much more widely accepted.

European Union regulations. Generally speaking, manufacturers have the right to decide which intermediaries should or should not distribute their products. Both national and European regulatory bodies start to become interested, however, where exclusion of certain intermediaries might be seen as a deliberate attempt to distort competition or to achieve price fixing. Chapter 10 (at p. 400) referred to the MMC's investigation of the refusal of major manufacturers to supply electrical goods to discount retailers. The outcome hinged on whether the refusal to supply was based on a legitimate concern over the quality of the retail premises and staff, or whether it was an illegal attempt to prevent retail prices falling.

Manufacturers also need to be careful over the restrictions that they try to impose on intermediaries as part of a contract. They might, for example, insist that an intermediary does not carry competing products. This is usually permissible, depending on the market structure, the definition of what constitutes competition and whether there is any direct alternative available to an intermediary who does not wish to accept such a clause.

Selecting a channel member

The final phase of the channel design strategy is the selection of specific intermediaries. There may be a number of reasons that a selection decision needs to be made, some of which are not part of a new strategic formulation or realignment. Typical examples would be:

■ to add more intermediaries to increase market penetration
■ to replace existing intermediaries because of poor performance or contract termination
■ to add new intermediaries to service a new product range
■ to create a network of intermediaries for market entry.

Whatever the reason, the selection decision should be compatible with the overall channel strategy. The selection decision tends to become more critical as the intensity of distribution itself becomes more selective or exclusive. In mass-distribution decisions, such as those concerning products like confectionery, any willing outlet will be considered. However, where a selective distribution approach is adopted, great care must be taken over the final selection of intermediary, as a poor decision may lead to strategic failure. For example, the selection of a wholesaler to allow entry into a new European market may be critical to the degree and speed of penetration achieved.

> **Example** Klemm is part of the Ingersoll-Rand group and specialises in a range of German-built piling and drilling rigs for construction sites. Its channel approach is often to appoint sole distributors in target countries. Thus in the UK, Skelair handles all sales, while in the Netherlands, Drilcon has exclusive rights. Klemm seeks to develop a close and effective relationship with its distributors. Although individual domestic markets may be relatively small, the selling task is complex in defining machines for applications and good after-sales service is also crucial. This demands close technical support and a level of trust and confidence between manufacturer and distributor (http://www.klemm-bt.com).

In situations where organisations need to select intermediaries on a fairly frequent basis, it would be useful to select on the basis of predetermined criteria. Table 12.2 highlights a range of issues that should be examined as part of an appraisal process.

The relative importance of the various criteria will vary from sector to sector and indeed over time. Inevitably, there is still a need for management judgement and a trading off of pros and cons, as the 'ideal' distributor that is both willing and able to proceed will rarely be found.

Reverse selection

Not all manufacturers have the power or ability to design their channel strategy and to select the ideal members. Effectively, the intermediaries have the choice of whether or not they will sell the products offered. This luxury of choice is not just restricted to supermarkets and large multiple retailers. Travel agents can only stock a limited number of holidays, and are very careful about offering new packages from smaller tour operators. In some industrial distribution channels, the intermediary can decide whether or not to stock ancillary products around the main products that it sells on a dealership basis.

Reverse selection also suggests that intermediaries are proactive in looking for new manufacturers to complement their supply sources, or at a minimum that they are considering whether to extend the assortment being offered. In many organisational situations it is the buyer that initiates the contact process with suppliers.

TABLE 12.2
Selection criteria for intermediaries

Strategic	Operational
■ Expansion plans	■ Local market knowledge
■ Resource building	■ Adequate premises/equipment
■ Management quality/competence	■ Stockholding policy
■ Market coverage	■ Customer convenience
■ Partnership willingness	■ Product knowledge
■ Loyalty/co-operation	■ Realistic credit/payment terms
	■ Sales force capability
	■ Efficient customer service

Klemm used the drilling rig expertise of its UK distributor, Skelair International, to develop sales in the UK.

Source: Skelair International.

EMERGING FORMS OF CHANNEL STRUCTURE

The traditional view of channels of distribution suggests a group of independent manufacturers and intermediaries working together within negotiated guidelines and operating functions to exploit a market opportunity. This does reflect the situation in many cases, where mutual benefit forces consensus rather than competitive behaviour between channel members.

However, a growing number of channels are being effectively led and managed by one channel member who can control the policies, strategies, actions and returns of the other members. These are called **vertical marketing systems** (VMS), and represent an advanced form of channel integration. Such integration may improve supply consistency, lower costs and lead to more effective marketing. Before we examine in more detail the various forms of channel integration, we now provide a brief review of the types of competition that may be experienced in channels. This review forms the basis for an appraisal of the benefits of integration.

Competition in channels

Not all competition in channels comes from traditionally expected direct sources, as we see from Fig. 12.7. Sometimes, internal channel competition can reduce the efficiency of the whole channel system. Each of the four types of competition identified by Palamountain (1955) is considered in turn below.

Horizontal competition
Horizontal competition, as can be seen in Fig. 12.7, is competition between intermediaries of the same type. This type of competition, for example between supermarkets, is readily visible. Each one develops marketing and product range strategies to gain competitive advantage over the others.

479

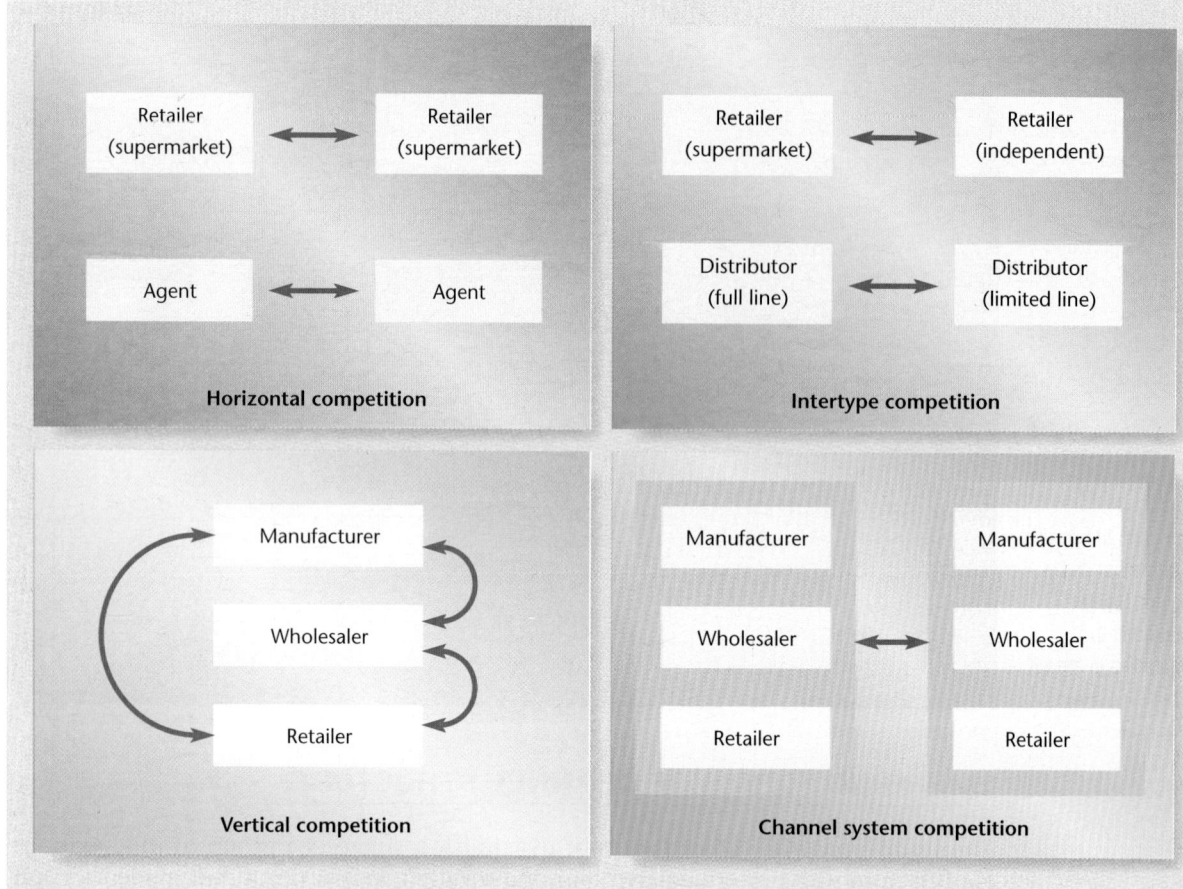

FIGURE 12.7

Competition in channels

Internet distribution

The Internet has the capacity either to enhance a distribution channel or to destroy it. It provides the opportunity for one channel member to bypass another and enter into direct sales with its customers. It is important that channel members examine the impact of the Internet on their business and identify how it will change power and profitability relationships (Clemons, 1999). Three examples from the travel, retail and organisational markets highlight the potential of Internet distribution.

Some in the travel industry already suggest that the Internet will replace many existing travel agents and create a new direct channel between the provider of a service, hotel, airline or car rental company and the consumer (Kumar, 1999). A prime role for the travel agent is to source information for customers and to provide an informed interface to the service provider's reservation system. The Internet can provide both

these benefits, especially as users become more familiar with the powerful search engines available. KLM has made on-line ordering easy. The user selects the place of departure, destination, date and time of travel and enters credit card details. Tickets can be made available through the new e-ticketing machines installed at airports (http://www.klmuk.com). easyJet even offers a small fare reduction for an Internet booking (http://www.easyJet.com). Perhaps it is not surprising, therefore, that the travel agents' share of domestic airline reservations in the USA declined from 82 to 50 per cent in the late 1990s. Europe could be on the verge of a similar revolution.

Similarly, there will be less need for travel agent involvement in hotel bookings. Not only do some hotel chains already have direct freephone and e-reservation systems, but new intermediaries are also emerging to perform many of the tasks of the travel agent on the

continued

Internet. Pegasus Systems Inc. provides e-commerce and transaction processing for the worldwide hotel industry. The system allows travel agents, corporate travel departments and individuals to access hotel room availability and to make reservations electronically. TravelWeb (http://www.travelweb.com) is connected to 26 000 hotels in 170 countries. In addition to the hotel photos, maps, weather information and special deals available, an airline reservation can also be made with over 300 carriers. The average number of visitors per day is 55 000.

In situations where there is no product to be physically delivered, the impact of Internet distribution is likely to grow considerably over the next 10 years. Even in the grocery trade, there is expected to be large growth despite the additional logistical problems of home delivery. It has been suggested that sales in the UK could grow to £1bn by 2004 from the current level of just £8mn. This could represent a serious challenge to retailers and branded-goods manufacturers alike, as there will be little opportunity for in-store sensory cues and merchandising. The promotional effort will have to switch to the ease with which the site can be browsed and products compared, along with subsequent ordering and service delivery reliability (*The Grocer*, 1999b). Typical grocery retail sites can be found at http://www.tesco.co.uk and http://www.jsainsbury.co.uk.

On-line procurement within business-to-business markets is still in its infancy in Europe, but is expected to grow dramatically. The USA is more advanced in developing the necessary applications than is Europe. The County of Los Angeles uses an e-procurement system to source maintenance, repair and small parts needs. This has meant that it is to eliminate the need for warehouses and deal directly with suppliers, considerably reducing paperwork and materials-handling costs (Nairn, 1999).

MarketSite (http://www.commerceone.com) allows a 'virtual trading community' to be created in which suppliers and buyers can meet in a web-based marketplace. The site in the USA has 5100 suppliers and five million items can be accessed on-line. In the UK, BT has signed a licensing deal to develop the European market. Both BT and Boots are using the system to purchase goods and services such as travel, computer hardware and software, stationery and maintenance service on-line. The expected benefits include better order tracking, streamlined buying processes and reduced purchase-cycle times.

Despite the potential of the Internet in allowing manufacturers to deal directly, rather than through intermediaries, care has to be taken not to destroy the existing network unless it is recognised that it has become outdated. Mixed channel approaches, with direct and indirect sales, can cause channel conflict, thus reducing the effectiveness of the whole distribution operation. The principles of good channel-management design still apply to Internet distribution, but entirely new ways of working are now becoming possible. These possibilities will force all those in a channel to examine carefully the real value added that is being offered and whether there are more cost-effective alternatives.

Sources: Clemons (1999); *The Grocer* (1999b); Kumar (1999); Nairn (1999); http://www.commerceone.com, 'BT and Boots Kick off Business'.

Intertype competition

Intertype competition, refers to competition at the same level in the channel but between different types of outlet. Thus, for example, the battle between the department stores, the high-street electrical retailers and large out of town warehouse operations to sell hi-fi equipment to the same customer base is a form of intertype competition. The manufacturer that has a choice may need to develop different approaches to handle each retailer type. Of course, there are dangers if a manufacturer is seen to give unwarranted preference to one type over another, given the intense rivalries that can develop. This may start to lead to dysfunctional channel behaviour.

The supermarket chains, for instance, were dismayed by the fact that the big brand manufacturers agreed to supply Costco, the warehouse club open to the general public, when it first set up in the UK. The argument was that the manufacturers were supplying Costco at lower prices than those offered to the supermarkets, and thus Costco could further undercut them. The supermarkets threatened to delist brands if the manufacturer did not even out the price differentials, but in the end did not carry out the threat. Even the strongest supermarket chain cannot risk being without certain key brands.

Vertical competition

Vertical competition can soon become a serious threat to the integrity and effectiveness of a channel. Here, the competition is between different levels in the channel, such as wholesaler and retailer, or even retailer and manufacturer. This type of competition can soon lead to internal rivalry, where the focus shifts from co-operative market penetration, focused outwards, to mutual cannibalism, focused inwards.

Example Mars became concerned with the premium pricing of its chocolate products in smaller convenience stores. As prices were set higher than those of the multiples, consumers were switching to larger packs from the supermarkets. Mars was also concerned that consumers would not pay a premium for convenience and thus sales would be lost. Mars had a similar experience in France during the 1990s when the price premium increased but the convenience stores' share compared with that of the multiples slumped to 7 per cent of confectionery sales. One response from Mars could be to extend price-marked packs to encourage all retailers to maintain similar prices (*The Grocer*, 1998b, 1998c).

Channel system competition

The last form of channel competition is where a particular channel is in competition with different, parallel channels. The focus for the operator, therefore, is on ensuring that its system is more efficient and competitive than the others. The emphasis is on total channel efficiency, which may, however, involve some suboptimisation in the interests of a more effective chain.

Example The car manufacturers operate through competing channel systems, especially where there are exclusive arrangements with dealers. Ford, therefore, wants to make sure that its channel system is functioning better than Renault's or Honda's to create extra value for existing and potential customers. This has implications for all aspects of marketing, including promotion, distribution, customer service, technical support and product development.

Vertical marketing systems

To minimise the risks of internal competition within the channel and the risks of conflict, channel members, who wish to co-operate and gain the maximum possible benefits from channel membership, may form closely knit vertical marketing systems (VMS). These systems can become highly organised and dominated, to a point where the independence of some of the members disappears into a vertically integrated channel, with one member owning all or some of the other levels. There are three types of VMS.

Corporate vertical marketing systems

A corporate VMS exists where an organisation owns and operates other levels in the channel. This may be at any level, and the dominant organisation may be manufact- urer, wholesaler or retailer. *Forward integration* means that the manufacturer owns and operates at the retail or wholesale level. A number of oil companies, for example, own their own petrol stations, while Firestone, the tyre manufacturer, owns its own tyre retailers. *Backward integration* occurs when the retailer owns and operates at a wholesale or manufacturing level. Retailers such as C&A operate in backwardly integrated markets.

> **Example** The corporate VMS has the advantage of creating a channel that is tailormade for the owner's product and marketing objectives. Furthermore, those objectives are shared throughout the channel. The owner also has ultimate control over the activities of the channel and its members. In the UK, the top three tour operators, Thomson, Airtours and First Choice, each have equity stakes in other holiday service companies. Thomson, for example, owns Thomson Holidays, the Britannia charter airline and the Lunn Poly travel agency. In these situations, care must be taken to allay public fears that such close arrangements could restrict customer choice and result in biased advice from travel agents supporting one tour operator at the expense of others.

Contractual vertical marketing systems

The most prevalent form of VMS is the contractual VMS. Members of the channel retain their independence, but negotiate contractual agreements that specify their rights, duties and obligations, covering issues such as stock levels and pricing policies, for example. This prevents unnecessary internal conflict and suboptimal behaviour. Three types of contractual system are commonly found.

Retail co-operatives. A retail co-operative exits where groups of retailers agree to work together and to combine and increase their purchasing power by supporting their own wholesaling operation. This sort of agreement helps the small independent retailers who are members of the co-operative with greater range, access to promotion and more competitive pricing.

Wholesaler voluntary chains. A wholesaler voluntary chain is one where a wholesaler promotes a contractual relationship with independent retailers, whereby the latter agree to co-ordinated purchasing, inventory and merchandising programmes. The co-ordination enables some of the benefits of bulk buying and group promotion to be realised by smaller operators. Mace and the Independent Grocers' Alliance are UK examples.

Franchise systems. Franchising is fast becoming a major model of contractual arrangement across Europe. Franchising is an ongoing contractual relationship between a franchisor who owns the product concept and a franchisee who is allowed to operate a business, within an agreed territory, in line with the methods, procedures and overall blueprint provided by the franchisor. Managerial support, training, merchandising and access to finance are effectively exchanged for conformity and a specified fee and/or royalties on sales. Franchising will be considered again in Chapter 22.

Administered vertical marketing systems

Co-ordination and control are achieved in an administered VMS through the power of one of the channel members. It is, in reality, a conventional channel within which a dominant force has emerged. Therefore, although each member is autonomous, there is a willingness to agree to interorganisational management by one of its members. Contracts may or may not be used to govern the parameters of behaviour.

> **Example** Marks & Spencer uses an administered VMS to forge very close links with its suppliers, and to dominate decisions about what is supplied, how it is manufactured, quality levels and pricing. Suppliers accept this dominance because they regard M&S as a prestigious and trustworthy customer, and respect its experience of the market. Similarly, Ahold, the Dutch retailer, offers leadership within its distribution channels in terms of product development, manufacturing and purchasing.

The emergence of these integrated forms of channel system is increasingly questioning the traditional approach to channel management. They also provide a context within which behavioural aspects of channel relationships can be examined.

BEHAVIOURAL ASPECTS OF CHANNELS

Most of this chapter so far has concentrated largely on economic issues involved in channel decisions. However, all channel decisions are ultimately made between people in organisations. There is, therefore, always the potential for disagreement over the many decisions needed to ensure that the system operates effectively. Issues such as expected roles, allocation of effort, reward structures, product and marketing strategies are among those that deserve close attention. A channel is an interorganisational social system comprised of members who are tied together by a belief that by working together (for the time being at least), they can improve the individual benefits gained. The channel also offers the potential for one member to have a significant impact on the position of another member, for example the appointment by a manufacturer of a competing retailer in a town.

It is necessary, therefore, to examine the behavioural processes at work and how they are influenced by, and exert influence on, channel decision making.

Co-operation and partnerships

A climate of co-operation is perhaps the most desirable within a channel system. It does not just happen, but needs to be worked on and cultivated with positive co-operation signs and signals. Co-operation can be defined as:

> '**Similar or complementary co-ordinated action taken by a firm in interdependent relationships to achieve mutual outcomes or singular outcomes with expected reciprocation over time**' (Anderson and Narus, 1990).

In other words, you scratch my back and I'll scratch yours, and we shall both be better off. Boyd and Walker (1990), for example, suggest a variety of ways in which the functional performance of channel members in terms of quantities purchased, selling and promotional effort and after sales service levels can be enhanced by incentives.

Some view conflict and co-operation as being at opposite ends of a continuum, while others view them as distinct concepts. Whatever the view, strong co-operation can lead to a feeling of satisfaction and partnership, one of give and take. Co-operation may lead to strong personal and organisational ties that are difficult for outsiders to break. However, not all co-operation need be voluntary. A weaker channel member

TABLE 12.3
Areas of co-operation

■ Advertising allowance	■ Training staff
■ Payment for retailer displays	■ Support for new store openings
■ Contests/competitions	■ Joint advertising
■ Merchandisers	■ Joint selling
■ Demonstrators	■ Joint mailings
■ Samples/bonus goods	■ Delivery costs
■ Local market research	■ Sales promotions
■ Special packaging/displays	■ Own-label supply
■ Automatic reordering	■ Support with store fixtures
■ Returns allowance	■ Price promotions

may think it best to co-operate and comply with the wishes of a more powerful member, rather than risk retribution.

There are many areas of potential co-operation, and Table 12.3 lists some of them.

It is best to assess co-operation in terms of who does what, an approach that requires a clear view of expected roles and functions. An overall agreed package or programme may guide the way in which channel members work together for their common benefit. This programme should be based on obtaining competitive advantage for the whole system, as well as benefiting particular links. The whole approach embodies the notion of partnership rather than competitive relationships. After all, the system is pointless unless it leads to synergies, that is, unless the members feel that they are gaining more by membership than they could achieve alone or by membership of a different system.

Example The growth of independent pubs and high street superpubs during the 1990s has redefined the nature of the relationship between brewer and publican. No longer just vehicles for selling beer in volume, publicans are demanding new support from the brewers, such as niche beers to suit their local clientele, promotions to help sales, and technical service when needed to maintain product quality. Publicans value training, for example, and have sought more input from brewers in areas such as cellar management, merchandising, drinks service and wine (Mellows, 1998). This is creating the need for longer-term business partnerships between independent operators and the brewers by which both parties can gain (*The Publican*, 1998).

Brewers need to develop close co-operation with publicans to ensure service consistency in the bar.

Source: Whitbread Inns.

Conflict

Conflict is a natural part of any social system. A definition of conflict is:

> **'Tensions between two or more social entities (individuals, groups or larger organisations) which arise from incompatibility of actual or desired responses'** (Raven and Kruglanski, 1970).

Conflict may exist where, for example, one channel member feels that another member is not dealing fairly with it, or that the system is not working sufficiently in its favour. The key to dealing with conflict is not to allow it to continue until it reduces channel efficiency or effectiveness, or even results in legal problems. Channel conflict may be issue specific, such as discontent related to changes in margins, or may involve general confrontation on a range of issues. Clark's shoes, for instance, needs to be aware of the potential for conflict as it operates a parallel distribution system. It distributes partly through its own shops, and partly through other shoe retailers. It must support both channels equally.

There are two different types of conflict, each capable of generating varying degrees of intensity in dysfunctional behaviour:

1 *Manifest conflict*, which is overt between channel members and may block goal achievement.
2 *Underlying conflict*, which, although not overt, is capable of developing into manifest conflict, but can still shape willingness to co-operate.

There are numerous possible causes of conflict, some arising from poor understanding, others from a fundamental difference of opinion that goes to the heart of the relationship. The kinds of operational problems either caused by conflict or triggering conflict are shown in Table 12.4. These problems may, however, be symptomatic of deeper pressures, which can be broadly categorised into five areas, described below.

Incompatible goals

Different channel members want different things. One, for example, may be seeking growth, while another is looking towards consolidation and stability. Their goals are incompatible.

Role conflict

Where there is disagreement about who should do what, role conflict may arise. A manufacturer, for example, may feel that a wholesaler is not putting enough promotional effort into reselling a particular product, while the wholesaler may feel that it is the manufacturer's responsibility to promote the product overtly to the retail trade.

Decision domain conflict

This is disagreement about who is in the best position to make marketing decisions. Retailers may feel that because they are closer to the end consumer than the manufacturer, they are better positioned to know what kind of point-of-sale material would perform well, whereas manufacturers, closer to the product, may feel that they should dictate what should be done.

Perceptions of reality

Different channel members may interpret the same phenomena in different ways and may have different perceptions of reality. The Costco example (p. 481 *et seq.*), for instance, shows how the brand manufacturers saw Costco as a beneficial influence in expanding their intensive distribution and better serving the consumer, while the retailers saw it as a threat to their margins and well-being. This certainly caused channel conflict.

TABLE 12.4
Areas of conflict

■ Manufacturer/retailer brands	■ Delivery arrangements/schedules
■ Prices/margins/discounts	■ Product exclusivity
■ Quality	■ Contract flexibility
■ Special services	■ Display/promotion prominence
■ Territory exclusivity	■ General compliance
■ Market information	■ Listing money
■ Direct sales	

Expectations

Different channel members may have different expectations about what should happen in the future. Such conflict may include definition of the best outcomes from a situation, how to overcome resource scarcity, how to allocate resources better, or how profit margins should change in the light of a changing business environment.

> **Example** The danger of conflict in a channel is ever present. Sometimes disputes can become public and embarrassing to both sides. Landmark, a leading buying group in the UK, criticised drinks suppliers for not being supportive during a benzene contamination scare. Many of the suppliers, it was argued, were not prepared to cope with product recalls and gave poor and ineffective advice. With potentially 52 million cans to be removed from the shelves, it was a major headache for retailers to identify which products could have been affected (Dearden, 1998). Also in the grocery trade, cash and carry operator Bestway claimed that some suppliers were giving better terms and conditions to multiples and delivered wholesalers rather than cash and carry operators. It considered such prices to be discriminatory and alleged that this made it more difficult to give its own retailers the best prices. The suppliers rejected this accusation and stated that it was caused by a confusion between normal and promotional prices (*The Grocer*, 1998a).

The response to conflict can even worsen the situation. The exercise of power can be a great source of conflict (Stern and Gorman, 1969), for instance where the strongest member of the channel seeks to impose a solution against the wishes of the others. In contrast, unexercised power could be seen as benev-olent restraint and a sign of willingness to co-operate (Frazier, 1983), thus reducing the tensions.

Conflicts can vary in frequency, intensity, duration, content and impact (Magrath and Hardy, 1988). Some conflict can be a powerful reforming pressure, resulting in a stronger, more efficient channel, but too much becomes dysfunctional. This may involve a refusal to co-operate.

Conflict needs to be spotted early and dealt with before it becomes too overt. This can be helped by regular meetings, frequent communication, and ensuring that all parties emerge satisfied from negotiations. It is critical that each channel member should fully understand their role and what is expected of them, and that this is agreed in advance. If conflict does become overt, communication, formation of channel committees, a fast arbitration service and top management commitment to resolution are all essential to prevent an irrevocable breakdown of the channel.

In any channel, there are likely to be periods of manifest conflict and periods of calm and co-operation. Similarly, there may be conflict in one area, for example profit-margin split, but co-operation in others, for example promotion.

Power—dependency

Power has received considerable attention in the behavioural science literature as a basis for explaining the interaction between two individuals or organisations. It was defined by El-Ansary and Stern (1972) as follows:

> 'The power of a buyer or seller is his ability to control the decision variables in the marketing or purchasing strategy of another member in the supply chain. For this control to qualify as power, it should be different from the influenced member's original level of control over his marketing or purchasing strategy.'

This means that one channel member might wield considerable power over other members, and might clearly be able to exercise that power to the cost of the others, yet can choose not to use that power. Power can be possessed to influence events without it actually being used (Bacharach and Lawler, 1980). Marks & Spencer possesses a great deal of power over its suppliers, but although pursuing rigorous standards and tough bargaining, it values the building of longer-term relationships that do not depend on aggressive or hostile acts.

In a distribution channel, any member might seek to use power-based strategies to influence the others. Power can derive from many sources, real or perceived. A very popular classification comes from French and Raven (1959).

Reward power

Reward power is based on B's perception that A has the ability to provide rewards for B. Such rewards might include volume of business, higher margins or sales and promotional support. As mentioned earlier, a small supplier might feel that a large retailer such as Marks & Spencer has reward power. If the supplier complies exactly with the M&S way of doing things, then that will bring it increased or at least repeat M&S business next season.

Coercive power

Coercive power is based on B's perception that A has the ability to mediate punishments for B. The withdrawal of many of the above mentioned rewards by A could constitute the use of coercive power, for instance the threat of delisting a particular product line. The Costco example given earlier might again be relevant here. The retailers' threats to boycott the brands of certain manufacturers who were also supplying Costco could be interpreted as an attempted exercise of coercive power.

Legitimate power

Legitimate power is based on B's perception that A has the legitimate right to prescribe behaviour for B. This legitimacy could arise from the existence of clauses in formal contracts, or less clearly through the norms or expectations of either party. A contractual VMS, or franchise, often gives one member legitimate power. A franchisee expects the franchisor to specify how the business should be set up and run, since that is part of what the franchisee is investing in.

Referent power

Referent power is based on B's identification with A. In other words, B respects A and might wish to be associated with A to reap reputational and other spin-off effects. A's power might also arise from B's acceptance that both parties are inextricably linked, so that they must succeed or fail together. This kind of power calls for a high degree of empathy and shared communication.

Expert power

Expert power is based on B's perception that A has some special knowledge or expertise, perhaps in market insights, product development or promotion, which gives A influence over B's actions. A small manufacturer or a small retailer might regard an experienced wholesaler as having expert power.

In any channel situation, there may be several different power sources operating, and they may not all be in the hands of the same channel member. When combined, they could provide a basis for an administered VMS, as described earlier. In some situations, one source of power could be cancelled out or counterbalanced by another source wielded by a different channel member.

Example A classic example of the exercise of power is the relationship between the large supermarket chains and the major brand manufacturers. Over the years, each side has tried to exploit power over the other, to the point where the balance of power between them is now a delicate see-saw, tipping slightly in favour of one and then the other. The brand manufacturers have, through brand building, made sure that their products are indispensable to the consumer and thus essential to the retailer, while the retailers have tried to exploit their intensive coverage of the market, making them indispensable to the brand manufacturers. In almost every European country, a small number of distributors account for a very large proportion of business, and this concentration is increasing as retailers join forces, entering into international strategic alliances for purchasing and distribution.

Each party has tried to reduce the power of the other at various times. The manufacturers, for example, have tried to limit their dependence on the big supermarkets by co-operating with the emergent discount chains (Costco springs to mind again), while the retailers have tried to wean consumers off the big brands on to good quality own-brand products (*see* pp. 281 *et seq.*). The uneasy balance, however, remains.

This last scenario raises another concept, *dependency*, that is very closely linked to the development and exercise of power. This is where one party becomes highly dependent for its well-being on the actions of the other party. What is actually happening between the manufacturers and the retailers is that in reality neither can manage without the other, and there is a mutual dependency that limits what each dare do.

Dependency might also be derived from the relative importance of the transactions to the parties involved. If a retailer takes a large share of one supplier's output (say 80 per cent), yet that only represents a small proportion of the retailer's overall needs (say 5 per cent), then that supplier is extremely dependent on the retailer, who immediately has the basis for coercive power at least. If the supplier does not comply, the retailer can easily drop the supplier with relatively little inconvenience to themselves, but with devastating consequences for the supplier.

Finally, B might become dependent on A because there is no obvious alternative, or because the costs and time involved in switching would be too great. As A occupies such a specialist niche in its own market, A may well possess expert or referent power, and the dependency might tempt A to try to exercise coercive power over B. If A pushes this too far, however, B might rebel and decide that locating or developing an alternative partner would now be worthwhile.

All of these tensions and influencing strategies tend to encourage the emergence of channel leaders who regulate and control events. Sainsbury, Tesco and Asda all exercise leadership from the retail end, although as discussed earlier, some aspects of this leadership are questionable. Some wholesale systems, such as those matching up small manufacturers and small retailers, develop leadership at that level rather than at the retail level. Car manufacturers still provide leadership within the automotive trade, because exclusive dealerships and selective distribution mean that the dealers have a great deal to lose if a manufacturer decides not to deal with them any more.

Atmosphere

The tendency towards power–dependency relationships, conflict–co-operation and the general level of trust in the relationships within a channel are important variables affecting the overall climate that governs ongoing relationships and decision making. The way in which all these elements come together sets the scene for the channel either to flourish for the benefit of all parties, or to be plagued by internal strife and inefficiency.

The atmosphere reflects the history of the relationship between the channel members. It is the accumulation of all the positive and negative feelings that have developed during the exchange and operation of the contracts. The atmosphere is, therefore, an outcome of a relationship, and plays a part in influencing future events

(Håkansson, 1982). A climate of hard bargaining may well lead to defensive behaviour if one party feels hard done by. In another situation, problems may be solved not so much by confrontation as by discussion and compromise.

At the heart of the relationships between channel members is trust, defined as:

> **'The firm's belief that another company will perform actions that will result in positive outcomes for the firm, as well as not take unexpected actions that would result in negative outcomes for the firm'** (Anderson and Narus, 1986).

The level of trust existing within a channel can vary from a complete absence to very high degree of completeness. It can also be very long-lasting and set the scene for the conduct of the relationship. Trust can lead to co-operation, good communication and an ability to resolve differences speedily and effectively. Trust is, therefore, an essential requirement for the implementation of relationship marketing within a channel, which in turn should lead to better synergy between channel members. There is a need to understand more fully the role of trust and expectations in channel behaviour in order to explain why some relationships are remarkably well adjusted and others are almost a continual battle between buyer and seller.

THE NATURE OF PHYSICAL DISTRIBUTION AND LOGISTICS

Broadly speaking, **physical distribution** is about the handling and movement of outbound goods from an organisation to its customers. Distribution might be direct, using company-owned transport, or indirect, using external agencies and the kinds of channel structures considered at pp. 462 *et seq.* **Logistics** has a wider brief, since it is concerned with inbound raw materials and other supplies and their movement through the plant as well as with the outbound goods. It also concerns itself with strategic issues such as warehouse location, the management of materials and stock levels and information systems.

The next two subsections look in a little more detail at each of the two areas.

Physical distribution management

Physical distribution management (PDM) is concerned with the organisation and management of the storage and movement of goods from the end of the production line (finished goods) to the end customer. The range of functions undertaken includes receiving and processing orders, picking and packing (materials handling), managing the infrastructure such as warehouses, managing stock and the selection of transportation methods, either direct to the end customer or to a point where bulk will be broken prior to shipment to the individual customer.

In supermarkets, distribution costs take up 3 per cent of sales revenues and in convenience stores the figure goes up to 7 per cent (Rowe, 1998). In order to keep these costs to a minimum, it is important that members in the supply chain work with others to share information, develop responsive stock management and control, and run efficient transport systems. Warehousing and transportation are obvious areas of concern where greater efficiencies can be sought. Companies are moving towards a pan-European approach, but often internal distribution systems are replicated in different countries rather than being considered as part of a Europe-wide system.

Taking an overview of PDM as it relates to a particular channel of distribution, it is important to note that the structure of the *physical* distribution channel may not coincide exactly with that presented earlier in this chapter, unless one or more members decides to undertake those roles directly. Figure 12.8 compares the two structures, showing the increased level of detail needed to describe physical distribution from manufacturer to consumer.

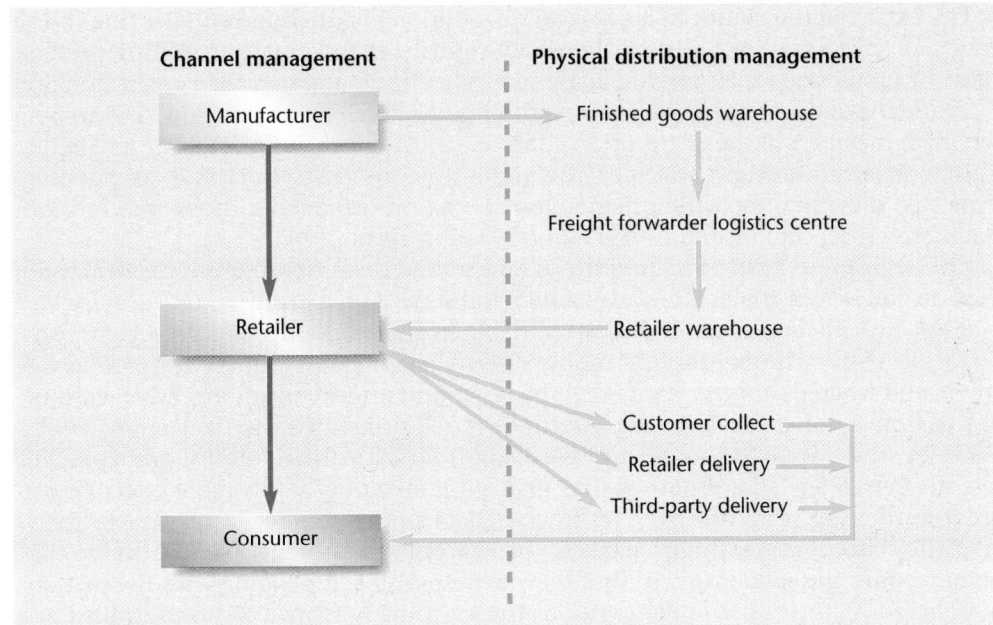

FIGURE 12.8

Channel management and physical distribution management

Example Tibbett & Britten, a British-based international logistics specialist, has over 400 depots in 26 countries, 8000 commercial vehicles and employs over 29 000 people worldwide. Its turnover in 1998 was over £1.1bn. It is market leader in the UK, South Africa and Canada. Tibbett & Britten adds value for its customers by designing distribution systems to customer requirements. This means that a long-term partnership has to be built to justify this specialist investment. In the automotive industry, for example, Tibbett & Britten can undertake pre-delivery inspection, preparation and enhancement as well the normal services of storage, trucking, documentation, import handling and onward delivery. Within the clothing market, it handles hanging garments for multiples and independent retailers.

In 1999, Tibbett & Britten won an order from the Eroski Group in Spain to handle the national warehousing and distribution of non-foods and slow-moving grocery products. As part of the deal, Tibbett & Britten will have to invest in the construction of a 20 000m² dedicated national distribution centre in Spain to supply the retailer's 44 hypermarkets, 86 supermarkets and 663 other stores throughout Spain.

Despite its being a big player in international logistics, you will rarely see a lorry in the Tibbett & Britten livery, as that of the clients is often used (http://www.tbg.co.uk).

Tibbett & Britten adds value to the channel.

Source: Tibbett & Britten Ltd.

The extra intermediaries in a physical distribution channel do not take title to the goods, or take any direct part in their own right in transformation, adding product value or promotion. Such intermediaries are called **facilitators**, as their main function is to undertake the storage and movement of goods to ensure a free flow, and to help the main members of the distribution channel to achieve their objective of having the right goods in the right place at the right time, as cost effectively as possible. Typically, these intermediaries include transportation companies, those who rent out warehouse space and insurance and administration agents.

Although these facilitators might not add product value through transformation, they do add it through creating availability and service.

PDM has emerged as an important variable in the marketing mix in recent years. The links with customer service are obvious. A fast, reliable, timely level of service where and when customers want it can be an important way of adding value, enhancing customer satisfaction and strengthening relationships (Mentzer et al., 1989). However, there are other implications arising from increasingly global and competitive markets. Some stem from retailers managing inventory levels more effectively in order to increase stock turnover. By stocking less and relying on fast, frequent delivery, they have increasingly passed the burden of storage backwards to the manufacturer and wholesaler, so that they are responsible for coping with fluctuations in demand. With the aid of computer technology, many items can be controlled at a level of sophistication not possible a few years ago. Such changes have cost implications that demand careful assessment by the manufacturer or wholesaler.

An additional pressure is that holding stock represents locking up cash, which in turn is likely to increase an organisation's borrowing requirement, leaving it vulnerable to fluctuating interest rates. This is a burden that each channel member would prefer someone else to bear, but the further back up the chain it passes, the fewer options there are for passing it on. The best solution, therefore, is to use management skills and technology to minimise the burden throughout the chain and to evaluate what integration and rationalisation can take place within that chain (Cooper, 1994).

Other areas of PDM have experienced cost pressures. Transportation has been hit by rising fuel costs, the requirement for high levels of safety and pressures to reduce damage to the environment through pollution. Similarly, as organisations internationalise their trading, by definition PDM costs will increase in real terms to cover the additional costs of crossing boundaries. These costs may be direct, for example import duties and extra insurance cover, or indirect, such as time lost through waiting at customs posts (it can take days for commercial vehicles to get across some eastern European borders, for instance).

Given all these pressures, the cost dimension cannot be ignored. The challenge is to find the balance between cost and added value. In some situations there may be little choice. Who wants to be the manufacturer who cannot supply a small replacement part for a capital plant breakdown that is holding up a car assembly line? In other situations, costs will have to be carefully monitored against the achievement of agreed customer service objectives. There is often a trade-off between cost and customer service, offering many possibilities for the marketing manager (Christopher, 1990).

Logistics management

There are limitations to the distribution concept described above, as it fails to reflect the inward flow of materials and parts that also have an impact on the costs and the quality of customer service provided. While it is not argued that marketing should control these inbound logistics, marketers need to be involved in their design and planning to ensure an integrative approach. A definition of *logistics*, amended from Bowersox (1978), is:

> 'The process of strategically managing the movement and storage of materials, parts and finished inventory from suppliers, through the firm and on to customers.'

Logistics, therefore, is an all-embracing concept that focuses on the physical movement and transformation of goods all the way from the source of supply to the point of consumption. Horley (1993) argues that a shift from a PDM to a logistics perspective could lead to significant benefits, including improved customer service, stock minimisation at all levels in the distribution chain, no costly stockouts and, finally, a lower total cost for all members.

Companies are increasingly using logistics to lower costs, yet raise the standards of service to customers. Computers can be customised at the last minute, to match new orders or the market they are supplying, while in book distribution external logistic centres enable rapid selection, packing, transport, invoicing and collection using one provider. In the car industry and for some fmcg products, the results of effective supply chain management are becoming even more important in lowering costs. Some companies are now experimenting with international stock-free delivery chains, the ultimate form of JIT. This means that products from Belgium, for example, are delivered straight on to a production line in Germany with no supporting buffer stock. Similarly, fmcg suppliers may be required to deliver to a distribution warehouse on a cross-docking basis just as a load is being consolidated to send to a particular supermarket. With such pressures to eliminate stockholding costs, suppliers need fault-free supply chains to remain competitive.

The difference between logistics management and PDM can be seen in Fig. 12.9, which shows the all-embracing role of logistics compared with the narrower remit of PDM. Byrne and Markham (1993) highlighted the vital linkage between logistics management and customer service. That linkage is further emphasised through the following scenario. A retailer blames the wholesaler or manufacturer for a delayed part (a physical distribution problem), when it is actually the supplier of the castings to the manufacturer who is the ultimate cause (a logistics problem). Customers may care little; all they know is that they have a service problem, but the marketing manager in the manufacturing organisation needs to look backwards as well as forwards in finding a solution to that problem.

This example shows the integrative nature of logistics and the difficulty of managing it, as it cuts across different functions within a business as well as across different businesses, linking supply sources with demand. It is primarily a framework for guiding forecasting, planning and strategies rather than just another self-contained business function (Smith, 1997). It is therefore important that regular and reliable information is allowed to flow between all the connected parts and that no one part, whether internal or external to the organisation, is allowed to have an undue or negative impact on the others. The supplier who fails on the delivery of castings may subsequently, albeit indirectly, affect the relationship between the manufacturer who uses those castings and its customers, and so on down the line to the end consumer.

The logistics system will, of course, vary from organisation to organisation. In a bank or financial services operation, most of the inward-bound materials are money

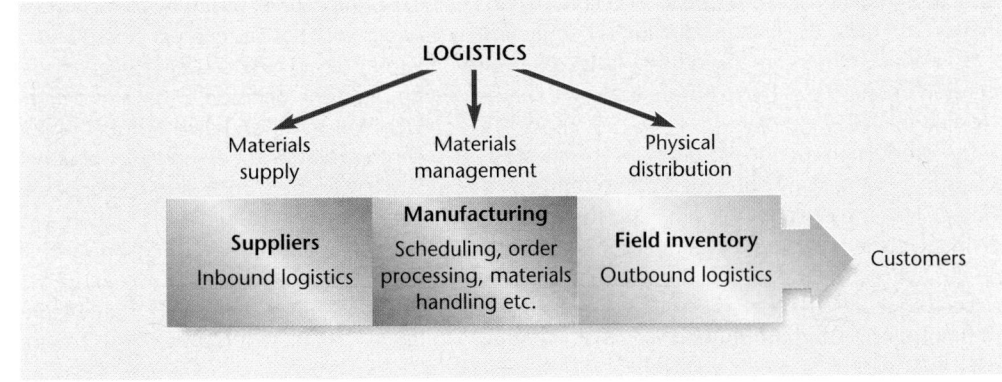

FIGURE 12.9

Physical distribution management and logistics

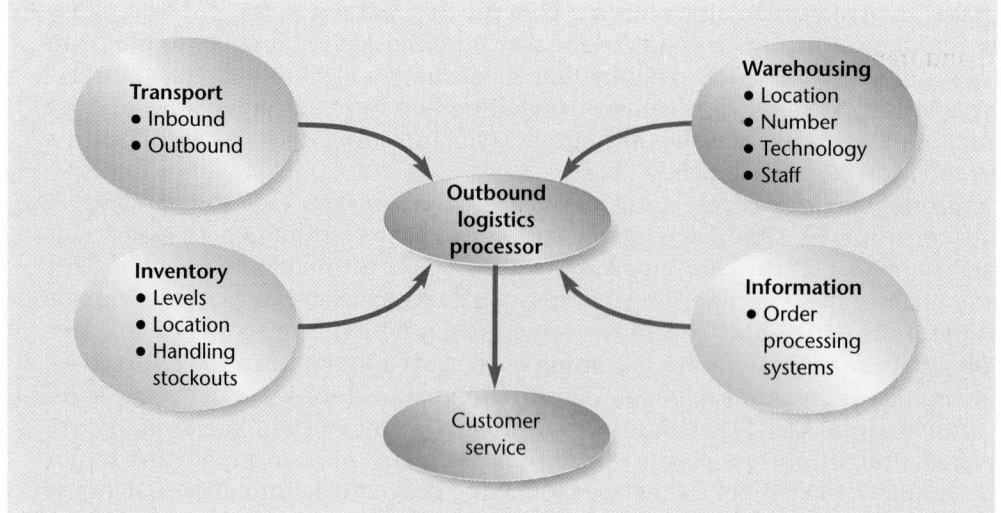

FIGURE 12.10

Influences on the logistics process

and supplies. Logistics, in terms of movement and storage activities, may not be a significant part of the product cost. This contrasts with producers such as Apple, Volvo or BMW, who purchase both raw materials and components from many different sources, and then move finished goods to geographically spread markets and customers. Logistical costs will still vary widely, however, depending on the kind of manufacturer or market concerned. The key variables that will influence the scale and complexity of the logistics process are shown in Fig. 12.10.

MARKETING IN ACTION   **Benetton**

Benetton presents an excellent example of how a global logistics concept can be put into operation in a situation where over 7000 independent stores in more than 120 countries need a regular supply of garments responsive to changing tastes and fashions. At the heart of the operation is an integrated 190 000m² distribution centre and three production facilities at Castrette in Italy. Although garment design is undertaken in-house, manufacturing can also be subcontracted to organisations working to Benetton's tightly specified standards. The facilities at Castrette can manage up to 120m garments per year operating on an IT-controlled production–warehousing–distribution cycle. By using IT, Benetton can delay the final production schedule until the last minute. Orders are taken three times a day and processed during the night to ensure that they can be produced the following day.

After production, the goods enter a sophisticated packaging system. The Robostore 2000 system can divide deliveries by geographic area and then by individual retailer's packaging requirements. Linked with the fully automated distribution centre, garments are received ready for order assembly into vehicles. This highly automated distribution system can handle over 30 000 packages per day but employs just 19 staff. There is also storage space for 250 000 boxes, although the intention is for minimal stocks to be held centrally. The restocking period for European shops is now down to eight days from order and that for the USA to just 12 days. Reductions in re-ordering periods result in lower stock costs for the retailer and less risk of a reduced price rail (http://www.benetton.com).

Shipment is then made direct to the retailers without any use of distributors, wholesalers or regional warehouses. Benetton also went into a joint venture in freight forwarding, as a direct result of the international orientation of its business, to manage and smooth the paperwork flow as carriers cross national boundaries. Various cost trade-offs have been made in this system, not least the decision to have one highly efficient warehouse rather than a number of less automated centres, with a knock-on effect on stockholding. Similarly, order processing costs per garment have been reduced through automation, although transport costs may be somewhat higher. Another main trade-off derives from the decision not to use intermediaries but to supply direct. Effectively, that channel decision influences the rest of the logistics agenda.

Within a channel of distribution, logistical costs will vary from member to member, reflecting the roles undertaken. Whether at this macro level (i.e. the combined logistics of the whole channel of distribution), or at a micro level (i.e. the logistical concerns of one channel member), it is important to focus on the total cost rather than to pursue blinkered strategies that lower costs in one area, only to raise them in another. A decision to close local depots, for example, might increase transportation costs and even inventory costs if the level of goods in transit increases. The effectiveness of this approach, particularly when other organisations are involved, will depend on the nature of the contractual relationships, ranging from informal through to highly prescribed and controlled, and the willingness to work as a system rather than as discrete elements. Many of the issues discussed in Chapter 4 regarding buyer–seller relationships will influence the nature of the supply chain and the sharing of logistical costs. These will be considered further in the next section.

Total logistics cost concept

Implicit within a logistics perspective is the notion that decision making concerning the movement and storage of materials should be done as a whole rather than in discrete parts (Sussams, 1991). There are a number of cost areas that should be considered as part of the logistics and distribution system. These cost areas are often interdependent, because as costs decrease in one area, the costs in another may increase. For example, as the number of stockholding points increases, the cost of holding inventory will also rise, but the cost of transportation may fall as not only are fewer goods moved, but they are moved shorter distances to the end user.

That example may apply at either the macro or the micro level. A channel of distribution consisting of a number of co-operative and integrated members may take an overview of warehousing or distribution depots relevant to the whole channel, and make logistical decisions that may increase the costs of one member, but will decrease the costs and increase the overall efficiency of the entire channel. The member bearing the increased direct costs may be rewarded in other ways, by increased business or increased profit margins to offset the increased operating costs, for example. At the micro level, an organisation may simply look at its own internal cost effectiveness. The trade-off principle can be seen in the hypothetical example shown in Fig. 12.11. The ideal number of distribution outlets is three, when transportation costs are

Set in the heart of the countryside, this Benetton distribution centre uses robotics to proivde an efficient service to its retail outlets.

Source: Benetton UK.

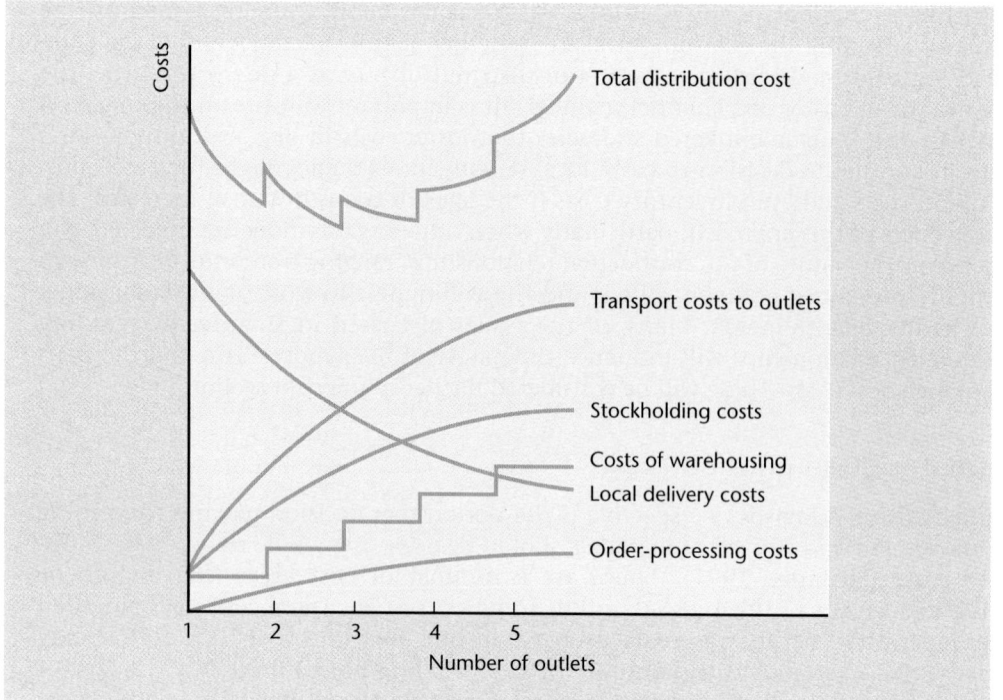

FIGURE 12.11

Total logistics costs: trade-offs
Source: adapted from Christophe (1990)

considered alongside inventory costs. Although neither cost in itself is at a minimum, the total logistics cost is minimised for the system as a whole.

A full understanding of the impact of logistics costs often demands a considerable quantity of accounting data and the use of decision support systems to consider the full range of variables and the effect of 'what if?' scenarios. The use of IT has opened up considerable potential for logistics operations.

However, the principle remains the same: it is the system cost rather than the individual functional cost that is critical. A number of the main cost areas are briefly considered below.

Order processing and administration

Order processing and administration are the areas associated with writing, receiving, acknowledging and processing an order, through to invoicing and confirmation, statements as well as credit checking. They run in parallel with the physical distribution flow but are closely related to it.

These various stages are outlined in Fig. 12.12. In some cases, the whole process may be almost instantaneous. An order placed at Argos, the retail catalogue shopping business, is processed simultaneously with payment as soon as stock availability has been verified. Instructions are issued on-line to the stockroom behind the scenes, and the goods are brought forward for immediate collection by the customer. The whole order processing cycle may take less than five minutes. Large retail chains, their regional distribution depots and their suppliers are increasingly linked, to make the order processing cycle a much faster and more efficient operation. All of this has been made possible by the use of computer-based systems that can handle order processing, transport planning, production planning, inventory levels and account management as part of an integrated system. Such integration is becoming increasingly essential where high-volume transactions are involved.

Inventory

Inventory is often a significant feature of an organisation's assets. Inventory can be in transit or in storage, represented by work-in-progress. Typical costs include financing

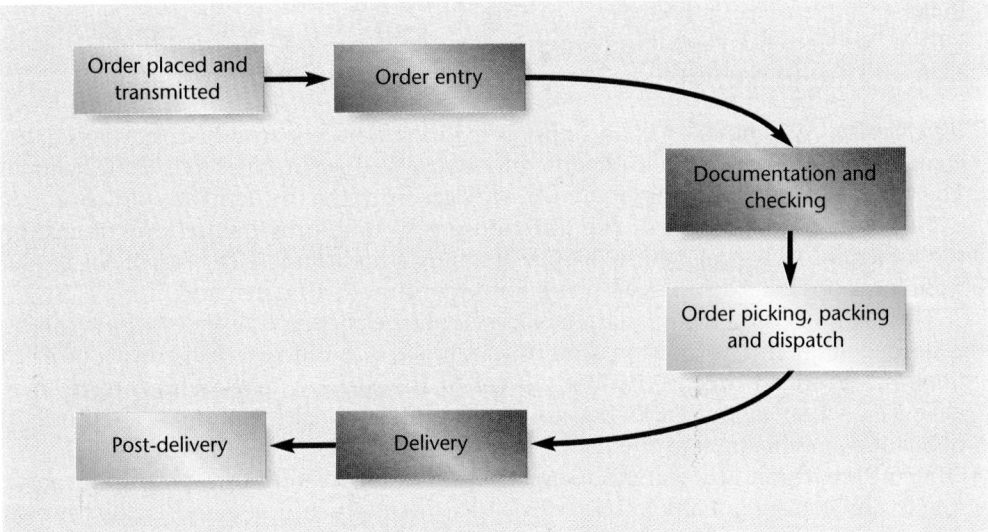

FIGURE 12.12

Stages in order
processing

(the cost of money tied up in stock, storing work-in-progress, insurance etc.), write-offs (depreciation, wastage etc.) and other losses.

Inventory management is central to the problem of how to balance customer service against physical distribution costs. Too much stock, although it will permit a high level of product availability – which may please customers – will result in high carrying and obsolescence costs. Too low a level of stock may result in frustrated customers, brand switching and eventually lost market share. Inventory management can also generate internal conflict between the marketing department, which wishes to maximise choice and availability, the production department, where longer or continuous runs assist lower unit costs but do not necessarily produce the range required in a timely manner, and the finance department, which is seeking to keep costs down through lower inventory levels.

Transport

Transportation is central to any logistics system, moving goods in time and place, thus providing the means to service urgent replacement or maintain inventory levels within a channel system. Across Europe around £75bn is spent on logistics, with £18bn of that spent on logistics that are contracted out to independent service providers (*Supply Management*, 1997).

The selection of alternative modes of transport has different cost and service outcomes that can be used creatively by the marketer. The availability of many perishable foods out of season is a tribute to conscious decisions to use air freight, with the premium price involved. Some market segments are happy to pay premium prices for the benefits of all year round tomatoes or early new potatoes.

There are five main modes of transport that can be considered for product movement. These are rail, road, air, pipeline and water transport. Intermodal transport, where more than one mode of transport is used provides a sixth option. The selection of a mode needs to be made with both company and customer needs in mind. Each mode offers advantages and disadvantages that normally require some trade-off between sometimes conflicting criteria such as speed and cost.

Transport can be either *trunk*, representing bulk movement over a distance between manufacturer and customer or between manufacturer and distribution point, or *local*, representing relatively small shipments to the final user. An example is the postal system. Bulk mailing is undertaken by lorry, rail or air, while delivery to the doorstep is by small van or even on foot.

Outlet

Outlet costs are the capital and operating costs incurred in maintaining facilities to store and handle products.

Warehousing. Warehousing is an important link in the physical distribution chain. It enables goods to be stored and subsequently moved according to customer demand. The type and role of the warehouse will vary according to the demands of the product.

However, the main role of the warehouse is to help provide the level of customer service agreed in the marketing plan by enabling a rapid supply or resupply of products from locations considered appropriate for responding to that demand.

The main decision facing manufacturers and intermediaries is whether a warehouse is needed at all and, if so, what kind of warehouse it should be. The growth of JIT systems has reduced the need for the level of investment in warehousing that was necessary when safety stocks had to be held. In an ideal situation, JIT removes the need for warehousing, but the reality is that even retailers cannot function reliably or efficiently without any warehousing function at all. Warehouses play an important role in smoothing out the imbalances between supply and demand. Take, for example, apples. In the absence of adequate temperature-controlled storage, the market would be awash with local apples in the autumn, yet they would be in scarce supply in the spring unless expensive imported alternatives were introduced. Of course, the storage of goods can be taken to extremes as, for example, where EU intervention has created wine lakes, butter mountains etc. in an effort to regulate the market. However, again, the practice relies on warehouses that can meet preservation needs.

Warehouses may be primarily used to store goods, but they also enable further handling, such as sorting into appropriate storage areas, picking and order assembly, further packing, palletisation or containerisation and, not least, receiving and loading transportation. Increasingly, these tasks are being automated. Sometimes companies have their own warehouses and distribution centres, but an increasing number use the facilities operated by other logistics operators.

The number of warehouses needed is a function of the distribution cost–service trade-off. More warehouses mean higher operating, storage and material handling costs. However, these may be offset against lower long-haul transport costs and improved levels of customer service that may generate more sales. These are finely balanced calculations, especially as customer responsiveness cannot be measured before the event, only estimated. If the decision is taken to operate warehouses, it will be necessary to consider the location of customers and acceptable order cycle times. The location decision will also reflect the accessibility of motorways or other transport modes, such as airports, for both inbound and outbound distribution. For example, the SKF warehouse is on the European motorway network just 15 km from the Dutch border and just 35 km from Germany.

Warehouse costs relate to the purchase and rental of space and the associated infrastructure for picking and packing stock efficiently. The increasing use of computer systems to guide picking has allowed greater use of random storage systems, as companies seek to increase space utilisation. Goods can be stored wherever there is room, and the computer system can quickly identify where they are, thus reducing the need for the more disciplined and orderly storage that a manual system would dictate.

Materials handling. *Materials handling* is essentially an internal operation concerned with moving products into, around and out of the warehouse or manufacturing operation. Materials handling is an integral part of a warehouse operation. The complexity of handling thousands of lines, with increasingly high labour costs, means that mechanisation is playing an ever more significant role. This typically includes automatic picking equipment, mobile platforms, cranes, conveyors and forklift trucks. Some automated warehouses can handle large volumes of goods using robotic equipment and a computerised control centre. In some *retail* warehouses, such as Ikea, some of the picking and handling responsibility for all but the heaviest items has been transferred to the consumer. Given the labour costs inherent in materials handling, the capital infrastructure and the costs of lost or damaged stock, materials handling needs careful planning.

Costs concerned with the materials handling system are concerned with the physical processing of orders into economic shipment sizes in line with customer service expectations and functionally sound protection for movement. This includes palletisation and loading.

CUSTOMER SERVICE CONCEPT

The output of logistics and physical distribution is the level of service that the customer receives (Lambert and Stock, 1997). This can be defined in many ways, according to the specifics of the product-market situation. The challenge is to match the level of **customer service** provided with the need to constrain costs within planned levels. Too high a level of service could lead to excessively high costs that cannot be covered through pricing. Too low a level of service may enable a close control of costs but little positive response from potential customers. The key is to find the balance through careful research, planning and experimentation.

Customer service can be defined as the interaction of all the factors that affect the process of making products and services available to the buyer. These factors, although situation specific, cover such areas as inventory levels, delivery frequency, consistency and reliability of delivery, ease of order administration and the time taken from order placement through to satisfactory installation or consumption. From a study of customer service practices, LaLonde and Zinzer (1976) concluded that customer service variables could be categorised into three areas: pre-transactional, transactional and post-transactional.

Pre-transactional variables

Pre-transactional service activities relate to the corporate policies and procedures that establish the frameworks and administrative systems to achieve the desired levels of customer service. Implicit in this is the setting of customer service standards that can act as a benchmark for measuring achievement. Typical standards cover such areas as reliability, consistency, time, stockouts and accuracy. In practical terms, they might be translated into goals such as:

- 99 per cent of orders fulfilled satisfactorily
- all refunds made within one week of goods receipt
- all orders processed to dispatch within 24 hours
- all orders delivered within 48 hours
- all lunches served within 10 minutes of order.

These standards derive from the competitive position planned and the expectations of the target customers. Different market segments will respond to customer service provision in different ways. Part of the standard setting process, therefore, must be the assessment of the costs of provision and whether the additional costs can be recovered from that market segment. The standards set for customer service thus need to be linked with the strategic marketing plan to provide a cost effective market impact. This will require effective integration of all the activities that are undertaken from order entry through to delivery, to avoid suboptimisation and weak links. It is critical that these standards are clearly communicated to staff to ensure compliance.

Transactional variables

Transactional service activities are the main dimensions of the implementation phase that actually creates customer service. The concern with physical distribution and administration provides performance measures against the predetermined standards.

MARKETING IN ACTION Efficent consumer response

Retailers and manufacturers across Europe are still undecided whether efficient consumer response (ECR) is another fad from the USA or whether it will fundamentally affect the nature of European buyer–seller relationships in the same way that JIT affected organisational markets a few years ago. ECR is about ensuring that the supply chain works in a co-ordinated manner to ensure that the retailer is well served with product without imposing unnecessary strain and inefficiency on the manufacturer. It is concerned with logistics, but also extends to include promotions, assortment and product development. According to Coopers and Lybrand, ECR principles could generate savings of $33bn for European supply chains, the equivalent of 5.7 per cent off consumer prices, 4.8 per cent off operating costs and 0.9 per cent off inventory costs. However, by 1999, despite some retailers claiming to have achieved £50mn in supply chain savings, IGD research suggested that ECR's impact was limited and that it was often treated as a buzzword for logistics rather than a fundamental opportunity to reconsider total supply chain costs and effectiveness in winning new business (Purbrick, 1999). Mitchell (1997), however, argues that ECR can be a major change agent in a supply chain, especially in quality development.

At the heart of ECR is the need for retailers and manufacturers to work more co-operatively than they have done in the past. Adopting a better managed supply chain for branded products could be in the interests of both manufacturers and retailers, not only the discounters, but also reflecting the trend towards home shopping. Often, however, the first step is to co-operate to ensure more efficient replenishment of inventory and greater use of electronic data interchange (EDI).

Tesco has enjoyed benefits from adopting ECR. Its distribution task is challenging, with over 800 stores ranging from the petrol forecourt convenience shop to high street stores and out of town hypermarkets. With the need to lower distribution costs and to reduce the average order time to delivery to within 48 hours, close co-operation with the supply chain has been necessary. Tesco has placed particular emphasis on talking with the chain to agree common standards and operating practices that will lead to customer benefits in price or quality. The Supply Chain Development Director, Graham Booth, described the Tesco approach to ECR as:

'an evolutionary process that requires wide and continuing education to install in today's and tomorrow's managers that underlying philosophy of co-operation between buyer and supplier in order to remove non essential costs from every part of the supply chain' (as quoted by Varley, 1999).

Three aspects of efficient replenishment systems have been piloted in Europe:

1 *Continuous replenishment* means that suppliers generate their orders using inventory data supplied by the retailer in order to provide continuous supply rather than batch delivery. Service levels have improved as a result of the system and inventory and warehouse space costs have lowered.
2 *Cross-docking* is used with fresh produce in particular. At distribution centres, stocks are co-ordinated through the IT system to ensure that the arrival of inbound trucks from suppliers and the departure of retailers' trucks are so close that goods can move from one to the other without going into stock. This means that stock can move easily within the distribution centre. Although trials have shown a loss of transport efficiency, operating costs overall can fall and the shelf life of fresh goods can be increased by up to three days.

Wavin Trepak, a logistics operator from the Netherlands dealing in fresh produce, developed a standardised crate that is fully stackable and can be handled by robots. This system is important for its dealings with Albert Heijn, one of the leading Dutch retailers, as the crates can be rolled straight from the lorry on to the sales floor. This system is also easier for cross-docking.
3 *Roll-cage sequencing* enables products to be stored in the distribution centre by category. This enables easier handling in the distribution centre and results in better packed pallets that are easier for the retail store to deal with. In trials, 200 extra labour hours were incurred in the distribution centre, but this was offset by a saving of 700 hours in stores.

Despite these gains from taking a supply chain perspective, some experts suggest that the traditional leadership of supply chains operated by many UK retailers will restrict the development of ECR in favour of more confrontational and control-orientated methods. Much will depend on how willing the powerful retailers are to give up confidential information and whether their suppliers are sufficiently trusting to reveal insights that could be used to threaten margins (Batchelor, 1998).

Sources: Batchelor (1998); Feary (1999); Mitchell (1997); Murphy (1996); Purbrick (1999); Varley (1999).

The main elements, shown in Fig. 12.13, are discussed below.

Order cycle time

Time is an important measure in physical distribution. The order cycle time relates to the total time between placing an order and satisfactory receipt of the product. The lower the cycle time, the faster stock can be replenished and the lower the inventory levels that need to be held by the customer. Included in order cycle time is the whole process of administration, delivery and installation, where appropriate.

Consistency and reliability of delivery

Delivery must be on time, orders must be filled accurately and goods received in prime condition. In some situations, it is better to have a slightly longer delivery period that is guaranteed, rather than one that may be quicker but could be vulnerable to delays.

Inventory availability

The availability of inventory refers to the range and depth of stock normally held that provides the essential input to delivery. The balance is between stocking in depth on the faster moving, volume products and retaining a sufficient level of stock of, or at least fast access to, slower moving items. Finding parts for obsolete products is always a challenge if their supply is erratic.

Order size constraints

Some companies implement a minimum order policy. This can penalise light users, but reflects the high administrative and delivery costs on small order sizes.

Ordering convenience

Different customers want different convenience standards. These could relate to opening hours, the use of non-cash alternatives or ease of booking.

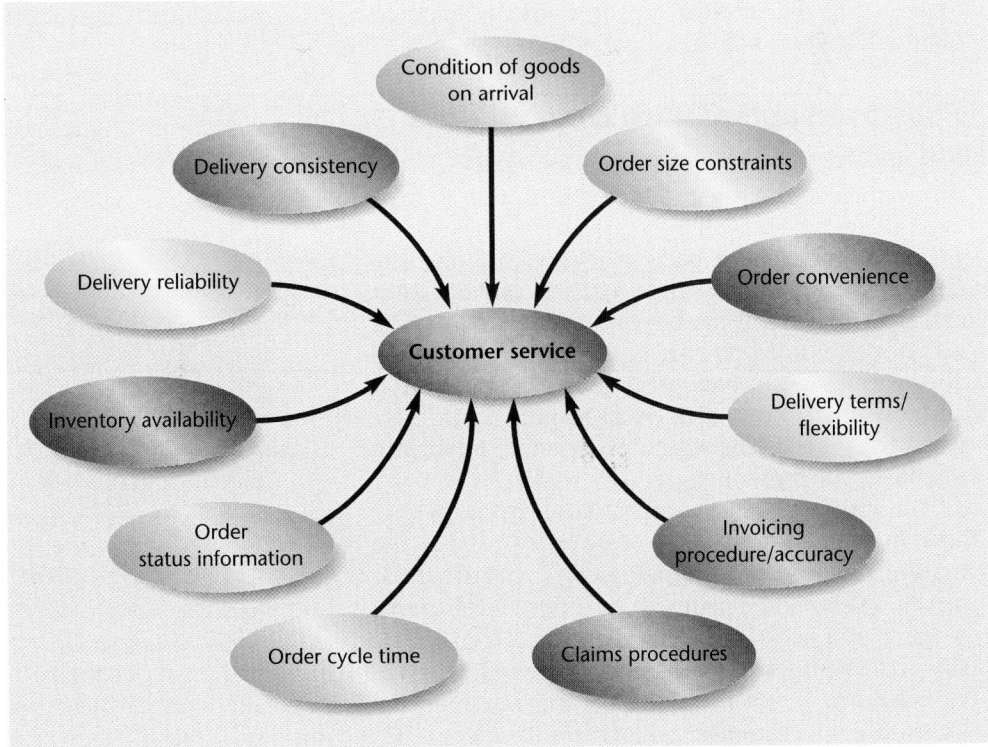

FIGURE 12.13

Consumer service and transactional variables

Delivery times and flexibility

The issues of delivery times and flexibility highlight whether the delivery is on the customer's or the supplier's terms. Customers operating just-in-time (JIT) systems clearly need to be able to specify their delivery requirements. On smaller, less crucial orders, however, it may be necessary for the customer to accept the standard delivery schedule with no guaranteed time of arrival.

Invoicing procedures and accuracy

Customers can be extremely irritated by administrative errors and inaccuracy in such areas as invoicing, as it takes time and effort on their part to point out and help resolve the problem. The kinds of problem that may occur are receiving the same goods twice, inaccurate invoices and poor recording of financial statements.

Claims procedure

A 'no questions asked' approach to alleged shortfalls or damaged stock is critical for customer confidence. In consumer markets, this is an accepted part of customer service for many retailers. Marks & Spencer and W.H. Smith offer full refunds or exchange for goods, whatever the reason for their return. Other retailers are slightly less generous, offering only credit notes for items returned for reasons other than product faults.

FIGURE 12.14

The cost of custom service

Condition of goods on arrival

Quality checking and sensible, functional packaging are vital to service provision. For want of a missing dowel or screw, for example, a customer may need to incur the time and expense of returning to the DIY superstore before they can assemble their flat-pack bookcase.

Order status information

The ease with which shipments may be traced, whether standard or not, and quick identification of where they are delayed or lost, are important means by which to reassure the customer of the management effectiveness of the whole process.

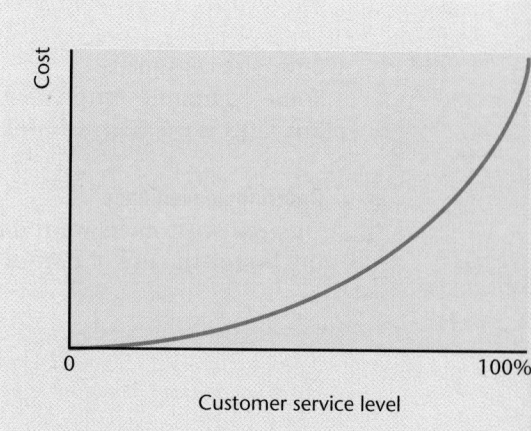

Post-transactional variables

Post-transactional service activities relate to the support given to the product while it is in use. Typical areas include product guarantees, installation support, replacement parts and servicing and the efficient handling of complaints. The sale does not end with delivery. If the buyer cannot use the product properly or if there are delays when something goes wrong, it can be a great source of frustration and dissatisfaction. This is especially important when the purchase represents an essential input into the buyer's own product.

The above elements constitute the cost areas that arise from providing a level of service. Costs, or the margin required, set the parameters within which service levels can be planned. As service levels move towards 100 per cent standards, the costs of provision increase disproportionately, as shown in Fig. 12.14. At very high service levels, the stockholding levels and transport urgency increase dramatically, without necessarily increasing the customer's willingness to respond by paying higher prices. Figure 12.15

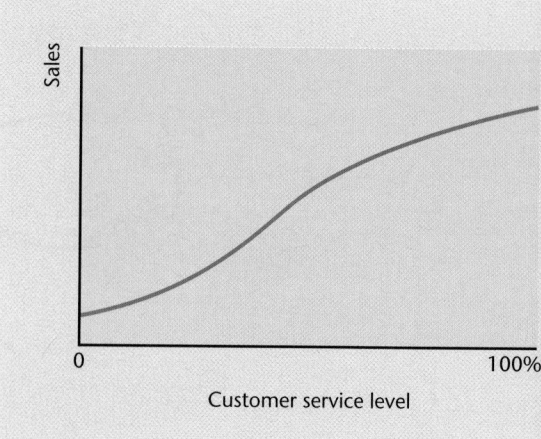

FIGURE 12.15

Customer sensitivi to service

shows that customer sensitivity to high levels of service does not necessarily translate into sales, although it may well enhance loyalty levels. Customers themselves may be prepared to trade service off against cost considerations within agreed parameters.

CHAPTER SUMMARY

The channel of distribution is the means through which products are moved from the manufacturer to the end consumer. The structure of channels can vary considerably depending on the type of market, the needs of the end customer and the type of product. Consumer goods might be supplied direct, but in mass markets for convenience goods, however, this might not be feasible and longer channels might be used.

Organisational markets are far more likely to involve direct supply from manufacturer to organisational buyer. Some organisational purchases, however, particularly routine repurchases of non-critical items such as office stationery, might be distributed in ways that are similar to those used in consumer markets, with various intermediaries involved.

Intermediaries play an important role in increasing efficiency and reducing costs, reduce the manufacturer's risk, gather, store, sort and transport a wide range of goods, and ease cash flow for manufacturers and for customers. These functions are not all necessarily performed by the same member of the distribution channel and the decision as to who does what may be made by consensus or by the use of power in the channel.

Manufacturers are not restricted to using only one channel. Dual or multiple channels can help to reach 'pockets' of a target segment or can help to spread distribution for a mass-market product as widely as possible. There are three broad levels of intensity of distribution, each implying a different set of channels and different types of intermediary: intensive distribution, selective distribution and exclusive distribution.

Channel design will be influenced by a number of factors, including organisational objectives, capabilities and resources. Market size might also constrain the choice of channel, as might the buying complexity associated with the product and the buying behaviour of the target market. The changing environment can also influence the choice of channel, through evolving technology, changing consumer life-styles or changes in regulations.

Selecting specific intermediaries to join a channel can be difficult, especially where selective or exclusive channels are used. This choice can be a critical success factor since, for example, the speed of entry and the degree of penetration into a new market can depend on the right choice of intermediary. Sometimes, however, the intermediary has the power to reject a manufacturer or a specific product.

Vertical marketing systems (VMS) have evolved to create a channel that is more efficient and effective for all parties, ideally working towards the common good in a long-term relationship. The VMS also tries to overcome the threats posed by the various types of channel competition. There are different types of VMS: corporate, contractual and administered.

Clearly, voluntary co-operation is the best way of achieving an effective and efficient channel. However, conflict might arise and, if it is not dealt with promptly and sensitively, channel conflict might lead, sooner or later, to the dissolution of that channel. Behaviour within channels is also influenced by power–dependency relationships.

The interplay of co-operation–conflict and power–dependency creates the climate within which the channel operates. It also determines the level of trust within the channel, which can affect the quality of relationships, the longevity of the channel and its efficiency and effectiveness.

Physical distribution is about the handling, storage and movement of outbound goods, including order processing and transportation. The channels of distribution may include facilitators such as transportation and warehousing specialists. Logistics includes the handling of inbound materials and components, as well as managing outbound inventory, effectively linking supply sources with demand. Logistics can thus provide a framework for guiding planning, forecasting and strategic thinking.

The design of the logistics system will vary depending on the type and size of the organisation, and thus its costs will also vary widely. The main factors affecting the total logistics cost include order processing and administration, stock held or moving through the system, transport and outlet costs relating to warehousing and materials handling.

The overall aim of logistics and PDM is to provide customer service, but this has to be balanced against the cost. The higher the level of service offered, the higher the costs incurred. Thus the organisation or the members of the distribution channel must be careful to match the level of service with actual customer needs, avoiding unnecessary costs.

Key words and phrases

Agents and brokers	**Franchisees**	**Marketing channel**
Bulk breaking	**Intermediary**	**Physical distribution**
Channel strategy	**Inventory management**	**Retailers**
Customer service	**Logistics**	**Vertical marketing systems**
Direct supply	**Market coverage**	**Wholesalers**
Distributors and dealers		

QUESTIONS FOR REVIEW

12.1 What are the different types of *intermediary* that might be found in a distribution channel?

12.2 What is *the short channel of distribution* in consumer markets and what benefits does it offer the manufacturer?

12.3 In what ways can intermediaries make a channel of distribution more *cost efficient*?

12.4 What specific functions can intermediaries undertake that are of benefit to the *manufacturer*?

12.5 What are the five factors influencing *channel strategy*?

12.6 In what ways might *product characteristics* influence channel strategy? Give examples.

12.7 What are the relative advantages and disadvantages of an *administered VMS* compared with the other two types?

12.8 Define the different sources of *power* and explain how each might influence the *atmosphere* within which a channel conducts its business.

12.9 How does logistics differ from PDM?

12.10 What are the three groups into which customer service variables can be categorised and what kinds of sevice does each group cover?

QUESTIONS FOR DISCUSSION

12.1 To what extent and why do you think that the creation of a VMS can improve the performance of a channel and its members?

12.2 What kind of market coverage strategy might be appropriate for:

(a) a bar of chocolate;
(b) a toothbrush;
(c) a home computer;
(d) a marketing textbook;

and why?

12.3 Using Table 12.2 as a starting point, develop lists of criteria that a manufacturer might use in defining:

(a) 'good' retailers; and
(b) 'good' wholesalers to recruit for consumer market channels.

12.4 To what extent and why do you think that warehousing can contribute to effective and efficient PDM?

12.5 Discuss how a power–dependency relationship might work between:

(a) a large brand manufacturer and a large supermarket chain;
(b) a small manufacturer and a large supermarket chain;
(c) a multinational manufacturer of hi-fi equipment and a UK-based high street electrical goods retailer; and
(d) a small manufacturer of high technology, specialised components and an export agent.

CASE STUDY 12.1

Monaghan Mushrooms

Monaghan Mushrooms Ltd is one of the leading mushroom companies in the UK and Ireland. Based in the north-east of Ireland, Monaghan Mushrooms has a turnover of over £20mn, 96 per cent of which is generated from exports. Most of its output goes to the UK and a little goes to continental Europe. Monaghan Mushrooms, despite being an Irish company, does not supply its own domestic market. Its main distribution problem is linking the network of small mushroom producers in Ireland, who operate within a kind of franchised system, with the main grocery buyers in the UK.

Until the 1980s, mushroom producers tended to be large, self-contained organisations that not only grew the mushrooms, but also produced their own high quality compost as a growing medium, and marketed the mushrooms to the trade. As individual organisations, however, they had problems dealing with large, demanding buyers, and they also had problems maintaining consistency and quality at the premium end of the market. There was room in the market, therefore, for a new system of mushroom growing. The Monaghan Mushrooms system enabled a large number of smaller producers to enter the market with minimal capital investment. The system meant that mushrooms were grown in plastic tunnels and growbags as opposed to larger wooden sheds containing locally produced compost, often of variable quality. The key to the Monaghan approach was the production of high quality compost for the small, independent growing units, and the provision of advisory services and centralised marketing. The system enabled the product to have a longer shelf life, an important point considering the distance to the UK market. Also important was the introduction of quality and grading systems that enabled the producers to match their production closely with a buyer's requirements.

The distribution channel linked the producer with the buyer. The product flow moves mushrooms into the grower's cold store, from where they are collected by Monaghan Mushrooms' own specialised transport fleet. They are then taken to five 'added value' plants where further processing operations take place. These are based in Monaghan (supplied by 132 growers), Donegal (29 growers), Cavan (49 growers), Tyrone in Northern Ireland (38 growers) and Fenton Barnes in Scotland (three larger growers). The centralised operations included grading, packaging and canning. The range includes baby button, button, closed-cup, open-cup and flat mushrooms, in white and brown varieties. Packed products include cans and glass jars in a range of sizes for the retail and catering trades, and bulk supplies for other food processors.

A wide range of retail customers are supplied, including the large UK multiple supermarkets such as Sainsbury's, Tesco, Safeway, ASDA and Somerfield, with mushrooms graded and packed to suit requirements. In order to satisfy the demands of these buyers, a rigorous quality control and assurance system is needed to ensure both a quality product to the required freshness, grading and consistency, and high standards of customer service. This includes operating a JIT system to multiple retailers' depots in a temperature-controlled fleet on a daily basis. A split delivery system is used, with 50 per cent company-owned vehicles and 50 per cent contract hauliers.

The UK mushroom market, worth nearly £300mn, is highly competitive. Domestic UK growers produce about 106 000 tonnes, less than 10 per cent of which is exported. Nearly 86 000 tonnes of mushrooms worth £141mn were imported into the UK in 1997. Irish mushrooms accounted for around 30 per cent of those imports. Monaghan is competing with other Irish growers, such as Walsh Mushroom Productions Ltd which represents 110 satellite mushroom growers and exports 10 000 tonnes of mushrooms per year. Some goes into the food manufacturing industry, but like Monaghan, Walsh also sells into the UK grocery multiple retailers. Dutch growers are also strong in the UK market. All growers supplying the retail trade are under pressure. Price wars and the protection of profit margins by the multiples put pressure on suppliers to cut their prices and to become more cost efficient. The multiple supermarkets and chain stores are very important to the growers, however, and thus their demands have to be taken seriously. A Ministry of Agriculture, Fisheries and Food survey of large UK growers showed that they sold nearly 55 000 tonnes through the supermarkets and chain stores in 1998, but only around 15 000 tonnes to wholesalers, the next largest outlet type.

Sources: Adapted from a case prepared by Professor Barra O'Cinneide, University of Limerick; MAFF (1997); http://www.maff.gov.uk; http://www.bordbia.ie.

505

Questions

1 Outline the kind of channel structure appropriate for supplying mushrooms from the producer to:

   (a) an individual consumer; and
   (b) your university or college catering department.

   What kind of market coverage strategies do you think these channels represent?

2 What do you think are the particular problems of producing and distributing a product like mushrooms?

3 What kind of VMS is represented in this case, and what benefits do you think it gives:

   (a) Monaghan Mushrooms; and
   (b) the individual growers?

4 Where do you think the balance of power lies in the relationship between Monaghan Mushrooms and the UK supermarket chains? What could either party do to increase their power?

CASE STUDY 12.2

French hypermarkets and their smaller suppliers

Many French small and medium-sized enterprises (SMEs) which manufacture consumer goods see the hypermarkets as an appropriate and easy way of reaching a mass market. It is not so easy, however, to get a product accepted by the hypermarkets in the first place, nor is it always easy to survive the pressure of dealing with powerful retailers. The hypermarkets put increasing pressure on suppliers to cut prices and to provide more support services, and many smaller companies, especially those which depend too much on a small number of large retailers, cannot survive.

Duarig, for example, was a manufacturer of sports equipment that was forced out of business completely because of the pressure on its profit margins. Over 80 per cent of its output was sold to the hypermarkets. Cipem, a supplier of artificial flowers, realised that it was too small to resist the pressure from the hypermarkets or to negotiate better terms for itself. The hypermarkets demanded more and more services from Cipem, which eventually got to the point where it could no longer deliver. Others found that the only way to survive when dealing with hypermarkets was to make fundamental, and not necessarily welcome, changes in their operations. Lewinger, for example, a manufacturer of knitwear, found that to maintain profit margins, it had to begin to manufacture in low-cost countries such as Poland and Vietnam. Palladium (shoes) tried to maintain control by supplying its goods in limited quantities to the hypermarkets, so that it could get the benefits of mass-market distribution without

the risk of compromising its exclusive image. The hypermarkets responded by producing copies of Palladium's canvas shoes, which meant that Palladium then had to get involved in litigation about the alleged 'counterfeiting'.

Not all SMEs have bad experiences with hypermarkets, however. Those who work closely with retailers can use the relationship as a means of strategic development. Routin, for example, began by supplying own-brand fruit concentrates and juices to Carrefour. As the managing director said, it allowed the company to show what it could do and to demonstrate the quality of its goods. It now also supplies other major hypermarket chains, such as Système U, Auchan and Continent, and had a turnover of FF215mn in 1995. The success of the own-label products gave Routin the experience and the retail contacts to launch a manufacturer brand, Fruiss, a range of fruit syrups. Fruiss was accepted by the hypermarkets for a number of reasons, and not just because it came from a tried and trusted supplier. Fruiss was carefully positioned so that it did not directly compete with any of the own-label products that Routin already supplied. It was thus not seen as a threat. In case there were any residual doubts in the retailers' minds, Routin ensured that the hypermarkets could make a healthy profit margin on the brand. As a final inducement, Routin also developed and installed imaginative point-of-sale display material to reassure the retailers that the product would be noticed by consumers and would be attractive to them.

Acting as an own-label manufacturer, therefore, can be a good way for an SME to develop and grow, and indirectly to become an important force in its product market. Carrefour has signed up a small company with 70 employees to provide all its own-label gherkins! The hypermarkets seem happy enough to deal with small enterprises and to be an influence on their growth. In 1994, Carrefour claimed to have direct relationships with 25 000 SMEs, although in some product areas supply is quite concentrated. Carrefour, for example, sources seven million pairs of socks from eight suppliers, and five million items of underwear from seven other suppliers.

To be successful, any SME has to appreciate how the hypermarkets work in terms of purchasing, and what both the hypermarkets and their customers want. To have a fighting chance of survival, the SME has to try to divert negotiation away from price. Concessions on delivery, quantity, promotion or point-of-sale material, for example, might be easier for the SME to maintain than wafer-thin margins, which can then be put under further pressure later. None of this is easy. A survey of manufacturers, consumers and retailers (*see* Table 12.5) found that each group had different ideas about what factors were most important in the success of a new product.

Metronic, a manufacturer of television aerials, satellite dishes and related products, overcame the focus on price by offering the hypermarkets more in the way of service. To make life easier for the retailer, Metronic offered a complete product-line

TABLE 12.5
Factors in the success of a new product

	Consumers	Retailers	Manufacturers
Attractive price	1	1	6
Quality/performance	2	5	1
Ease of use	3	6	3
Known brand name	4	3	5
Technological innovation	5	4	2
Promotional support	6	2	4

Ranked in order of importance where 1 = most important.

management package, as well as taking responsibility for product display in the stores and giving the retailer regular data on the market and the competition.

Source: Declairieux (1995).

Questions

1 What kind of power do the hypermarkets tend to exert over their small suppliers?

2 What are a small supplier's risks and rewards in dealing with a hypermarket?

3 How can own-label products provide an opportunity for the small manufacturer?

4 Other than going down the own-label route, what can a small supplier do to improve its chances of getting its products listed by the hypermarkets? Are there any potential problems with the strategies that you are suggesting?

References to Chapter 12

A. C. Nielsen (1999), *The Retail Pocket Book 1999*, NTC Publications.

Anderson, J. C. and Narus, J. A. (1986), 'Towards a Better Understanding of Distribution Channel Working Relationships' in K. Backhaus and D. Wilson (eds.), *Industrial Marketing: A German–American Perspective*, Springer-Verlag.

Anderson, J. C. and Narus, J. A. (1990), 'A Model of Distributor Firm and Manufacturer Firm Working Partnerships', *Journal of Marketing*, 54 (Jan.), pp. 42–58.

Bacharach, S. B. and Lawler, E. J. (1980), *Power and Politics in Organisations*, Jossey-Bass Inc.

Batchelor, C. (1998), 'Buzzword or the Way of the Future?', *Financial Times*, 1 December, p. 41.

Bowersox, D. (1978), *Logistics Management*, MacMillan.

Boyd, H. W. and Walker, O. C. (1990), *Marketing Management: A Strategic Approach*, Irwin.

Butaney, G. and Wortzel, L. H. (1988), 'Distribution Power Versus Manufacturer Power: The Customer Role', *Journal of Marketing*, 52 (Jan.), pp. 52–63.

Byrne, P. M. and Markham, N. J. (1993), 'Only 10% of Companies Satisfy Customers', *Transport and Distribution*, December, pp. 41–5.

Christopher, M. (1990), *The Strategy of Distribution Management*, Heinemann.

Clemons, E. (1999), 'When Should You Bypass the Middleman?', *Mastering Information Management, Part 4*, supplement to *Financial Times*, 22 February, pp. 14–15.

Cooper, J. (1994), 'Jeux Sans Frontieres', *Purchasing and Supply Management*, March, p. 4.

Dearden, A. (1998), 'Landmark Hits out at Suppliers', *The Grocer*, 6 June, p. 11.

Declairieux, B. (1995), 'Comment se faire references', *L'Enterprise*, No. 119, Septembre, pp. 26–40.

El-Ansary, A. I. and Stern, L. W. (1972), 'Power Measurement in Distribution Channels', *Journal of Marketing Research*, 9 (Feb.), pp. 47–52.

Feary, H. (1999), 'Fast Fact Takeaway', *The Grocer*, 30 January, pp. 42–3.

Frazier, G. L. (1983), 'On the Measurement of Interfirm Power in Channels of Distribution', *Journal of Marketing Research*, 20 (May), pp. 158–66.

French, J. R. P. and Raven, B. (1959), 'The Bases of Social Power' in D. Cartwright (ed.), *Studies in Social Power*, Ann Arbor, University of Michigan Press.

Gilbert, M. (1995), 'Keeping Them Sweet', *The Grocer*, 28 October, p. 16.

The Grocer, (1998a), 'Pervez Attacks Discriminatory Pricing', *The Grocer*, 1 August, p. 8.

The Grocer, (1998b), 'Mars Stands by Price Marking', *The Grocer*, 7 November, p. 15.

The Grocer, (1998c), 'Mars Blasts High Prices', *The Grocer*, 12 December, p. 12.

The Grocer, (1999a), 'Difficult Future Forecast for Cash and Carry Firms', *The Grocer*, 9 January, p. 12.

The Grocer, (1999b), 'Net Boom – Can Stores Deliver?', *The Grocer*, 16 January, p. 14.

The Grocer, (1999c), *Brokerage Guide*, supplement to *The Grocer*, 10 April, p. 9.

Håkansson, H. (1982), 'An Interaction Approach' in H. Håkansson (ed.), *International Marketing and Purchasing of Industrial Goods: An Interaction Approach*, John Wiley & Sons.

Horley, R. C. (1993), 'Integrated Transport', *Logistics Information Management*, 6(1), pp. 42–5.

Keller, T. (1996), 'A Successful Chain', *European Purchasing and Materials Management*, No. 7, pp. 348–9.

Kumar, N. (1999), 'Internet Distribution Strategies: Dilemmas for the Incumbent', *Mastering Information Management, Part 7*, supplement to *Financial Times*, 15 March, pp. 6–7.

LaLonde, B. J. and Zinzer, P. (1976), *Customer Service: Meaning and Measurement*, National Council of Physical Distribution Management.

Lambert, D. and Stock, J. (1997), *Strategic Logistics Management*, Irwin.

MAFF (1997), *Basic Horticultural Statistics for the United Kingdom: Calendar and Crop Years 1987–1997*, Ministry of Agriculture, Fisheries and Food.

Magrath, A. J. and Hardy, K. G. (1988), 'Ten Ways for Manufacturers to Improve Distribution Management', *Business Horizons*, Nov./Dec., p. 68.

Mellows, P. (1998), 'Beer Necessities of Training Support', *The Publican*, 26 October, p. 24.

Mentzer, J. T. *et al.* (1989), 'Physical Distribution Service A Fundamental Marketing Concept?', *Journal of the Academy of Marketing Science*, 17 (Winter).

Mitchell, A. (1996), 'Two Sides of the Argument', *Marketing Week*, 16 February, pp. 26–7.

Mitchell, A. (1997), *Efficient Consumer Response: a New Paradigm for the European FMCG Sector*, Financial Times Retail and Consumer Publishing.

Murphy, Y. (1996), 'Focus on Warehousing and Distribution', *The Grocer*, 3 February, pp. 53–73.

Nairn, G. (1999), 'A Pioneer in e-procurement', *Mastering Information Management, Part 7*, supplement to *Financial Times*, 15 March, p. 11.

Palamountain, J. C. (1955), *The Politics of Distribution*, Harvard University Press.

The Publican (1998), 'Partnership for Success', *The Publican*, 26 October, p. 19.

Purbrick, L. (1999), 'Enthusiastic Over Creative ECR', *The Grocer*, 13 February, p. 74.

Raven, B. H. and Kruglanski, A. W. (1970), 'Conflict and Power' in P. Swingle (ed.), *The Structure of Conflict*, Academic Press.

Rosenbloom, B. (1987), *Marketing Channels: A Management View*, Dryden.

Rowe, J. (1998), 'Multiples Must Learn to Adjust', *The Grocer*, 1 August, p. 9.

Shapley, D. (1998a), 'French Connection', *The Grocer*, 21 February, pp. 43–4.

Shapley, D. (1998b), 'The Cape Crusaders', *The Grocer*, 20 June, pp. 59-63.

Sharma, A. and Dominguez, L. (1992), 'Channel Evolution: A Framework for Analysis', *Journal of the Academy of Marketing Science*, 20 (Winter), pp. 1–16.

Simkins, J. (1996), 'Borsalino Aims to Recapture Past Glories', *Financial Times*, 19 March, p. 24.

Smith, K. (1997), 'Right to Reply', *Supply Management*, 27 November, pp. 24–9.

Stern, L. W. and Gorman, R. H. (1969), *Marketing Channels* (2nd ed.), Prentice Hall.

Supply Management (1997), 'Life in the Fast Lane', *Supply Management*, 31 July, p. 11.

Sussams, J. E. (1991), 'The Impact of Logistics on Retailing and Physical Distribution', *International Journal of Retail and Distribution Management*, pp. 19(7), 4–9.

Varley, P. (1999), 'Trend Spotter', *Supply Management*, 4 March, pp. 34–6.

Webster, F. E. (1979), *Industrial Marketing Strategy*, John Wiley & Sons.

13 Retailers and Wholesalers

LEARNING OBJECTIVES

This chapter will help you to:

1 understand the role and importance of retailers and wholesalers within the distribution channel;

2 classify retailers according to a number of different organisational and operating dimensions;

3 differentiate between types of retailer, appreciating their individual contribution to the retailing scene and their problems;

4 analyse the particular strategic and operational marketing concerns of retailers; and

5 understand the role played by different types of wholesaler.

INTRODUCTION

Shopaholics of the world unite! Retailing is one of the highest-profile areas of marketing and, like advertising, has had a tremendous impact on society, culture and lifestyles. To some, shopping is an essential social and leisure activity, while to others, it is a chore. It offers some a chance to dream and, for most of us, an opportunity at some time or other to indulge ourselves. We often take for granted the availability of wide ranges of goods and know that if we search hard enough, we will find just what we are looking for. Some people, indeed, find that half the fun is in the searching rather than the ultimate purchase.

Example Dutch retailer Ahold is trying to inject more fun into the grocery shopping experience offered by its Albert Heijn stores. In 1999, it was experimenting with 'circle stores', a radical rethink of the traditional supermarket layout. The store has a market area in the centre with a coffee shop, a bakery, a cooking school and counters with freshly prepared foods. This area has a sophisticated atmosphere and acts as a focal point for socialising and relaxing. A ring of convenience products then lead the shopper from the market to 'themed streets' of other grocery products. The further away from the centre of the store the shopper gets, the lower the prices become. Thus against the walls of the store is an area with a no-frills, warehouse type of atmosphere for all the low-price discount lines. Whether or not the trial of the new format works, it shows that Ahold is trying to innovate, differentiate and develop its mission. According to the project director, 'Besides being a grocery store, Albert Heijn presents itself as a caterer, a meal time consultant, a cooking instructor and a discount outlet' (Hunt, 1998, 1999).

Although to us as consumers retailing means fun, excitement and the opportunity to splash out vast quantities of cash (thanks to plastic cards!), it is a very serious business for the managers and organisations that make it happen. It is often the last stage in the channel of distribution before consumption, which means that there is an important role for the retailer in being so close to the final consumer. Not only do retailers have to buy, sort, store and promote goods, they also have to take the risk of being left with poorly selling and loss-making product lines. To avoid this, retailers have to ensure a close match between their capabilities and the merchandise offered, which in turn arises from a clear understanding of their own market appeal, reflected in such areas as store location, merchandise selection, customer service and general ambience and image. Compare the shopping experience provided by, for example, a large hypermarket and a small clothes boutique. One is large, cheap, cheerful, convenient, busy and impersonal, while the other is small, relatively expensive, cosy and places a distinct emphasis on personal service. These differences are the result of careful retailer strategy decisions focused on developing their individual competitive strengths.

This emphasis on the retailer's strategic thinking in terms of merchandise sourcing reinforces the point made in the previous chapter, that the choice of outlet may not be a completely free decision for the manufacturer. This is because the power balance has progressively swung towards the retailers, given their concentration of purchasing power.

Wholesalers are less evident to the general public, yet they play a vital role in servicing both retail outlets and industrial users, as discussed in Chapter 12. The key to successful wholesaling is to have a clear focus on which target customers are to be served, and then to become highly responsive in terms of stock, service and buying and selling efficiency. For many manufacturers, wholesalers and agents are essential intermediaries, as access to the retail or industrial user could become highly expensive and difficult without their services.

However, the role of retailers and wholesalers is not just restricted to the forward movement and promotion of goods. They also send information back up the distribution channel by providing feedback to the manufacturer about market changes, customer preferences and opportunity areas. Sometimes this feedback can be implicit in a retailer's actions, for instance refusing to re-order, or through established sales patterns. More systematic research and information gathering, however, as described in Chapter 6, may provide especially rich explicit insights sooner and in more depth.

This chapter starts with a review of the importance of retailing and wholesaling in the distribution channel. It then examines in some detail the different forms of retail outlet. Non-store retailing is also considered, as what we are seeing now in this area may lead to significant new developments and fundamental structural change in the retailing world over the next 10 years or so. Finally within the retail sector, current trends and their impact on the main strategy dimensions are considered, with particular regard to such areas as location, merchandising and competitive positioning. The chapter concludes with a more detailed look at wholesaling. Particular attention is paid to the different types of wholesaler and their potential for taking up an effective role within the channel of distribution.

THE NATURE OF RETAILING AND WHOLESALING

Retailing and wholesaling are both about buying and selling for a profit. Of course, that is a gross simplification of the very important roles that both play in bridging the gap between producers and consumers. Both receive goods from a wide range of different sources and then (often) redistribute them to convenient locations along with a marketing package that is valued by their customers or the final consumer. Usually, these locations are shops and warehouses but, increasingly, other forms of non-store retailing are becoming evident, as will be seen later. The main distinction between the wholesaler and retailer is that the wholesaler is primarily focused on other resellers or organisational users, whereas the retailer is focused primarily on the much larger, but highly differentiated, consumer market.

Retailing and wholesaling can best be defined in terms of the main functions that both perform.

Assembling a range of goods

The main function of a retailer is to *assemble a range of products and services* that complement its own strengths and match the needs of the target market. Within a particular product area or market, variety is ensured, as retailers seek to differentiate their offerings from those of their competitors, although increasingly this is becoming more difficult.

Example Think about the variations between music stores in the high street, for instance. Some retailers specialise in a particular style of music, going for depth without breadth, while others go for breadth of coverage without the depth, stocking the bestselling popular items from a variety of music styles, but not much more. Others have heavily diversified into videos and computer games. HMV in the UK, however, has chosen to maintain a tight focus on music, claiming that customers should be able to find any current recording that they want, at least within the larger HMV stores. Its computerised stock-control system means that HMV can assess demand and track the availability of the 270 000 releases current in the UK at any one time.

Through HMV Direct, music lovers can browse through a glossy catalogue at home and then phone through to buy CDs, check availability or get advice from knowledgeable staff. Customers also receive special offers and catalogue updates tailored to their tastes and purchasing habits (*Marketing*, 1997). A further variation on the home shopping theme is HMV's on-line selling operation at http://www.hmv.co.uk, which allows customers to search for an album, see a listing of all the tracks and in some cases to listen to a sample track (Jardine, 1999). Both the catalogue and internet operations emphasise the depth of range offered and enhance HMV's image as a specialist retailer. The product range is also brought to a much wider group of customers, who might only have a small local store with limited stock.

Thus by assembling goods, retailers provide both *place utility* and *time utility*. Place utility means that the goods are at a convenient location that reduces the effort that the customer has to make in finding and purchasing a desired range of goods. It may take place either through providing mail order facilities or home delivery or through providing handy retail premises to receive visiting customers. In the case of home shopping, the catalogue, website or television channel provides the 'showroom' so that customers, from the comfort of their own armchairs, can order by mail, telephone or e-mail for home delivery. This must be the ultimate in place utility. Time utility similarly means reducing the amount of time that the customer has to invest in the purchasing process, and is linked with place utility.

Wholesalers can play a major role in providing the wide assortment of goods required. While some retailers deal directly with manufacturers, others, particularly smaller stores, may prefer the convenience and accessibility of the wholesaler, especially where fast, responsive supply is assured. In the book trade, for example, it is difficult for a retailer to offer anything like the total number of titles available. Instead, the retailer acts as an order conduit, so that either the wholesaler or the publisher can service individual orders that have been consolidated into economic shipment sizes. The wholesaler can maintain a much wider range of products than is possible in all but the largest retail groups, and can provide efficient support activities for rapid stock replenishment.

Providing storage and transportation

The provision of *storage and transportation* has become increasingly important with the widening distance, in terms of both geography and the length of distribution channels, between producer and consumer. Purchasing patterns increasingly include products sourced from wherever the best deal can be offered, whether local or international. As production becomes more concentrated into a relatively small number of larger operations, the need to move products over large distances increases. The distance can be even greater in the foodstuffs area, with the demand for exotic and fresh foods from elsewhere in Europe and well beyond. The availability of Chilean grapes in the UK supermarket in winter, for example, is the end point of a long series of distribution decisions including a number of intermediaries.

Retailers and wholesalers, by allowing larger shipments to be made and then breaking bulk, play an important role in establishing economies of scale in channels of physical distribution. Some wholesalers are themselves heavily involved in performing physical distribution roles such as inventory planning, packing, transportation and order processing in line with customer service objectives. This assists the manufacturer as well as the retailer. Often the wholesaler will incur costs in inward-bound transportation, maintain a safety stock buffer and absorb associated inventory and material handling expenses, all of which represent savings for the manufacturer.

> **Example** Some supermarket chains have to worry about more than just the logistics and transport issues involved in getting goods from manufacturers to supermarket branches. Those offering home delivery have to have a cost effective system to process orders, assemble the required goods and deliver them quickly, accurately and in good condition. This is not necessarily an easy task, considering that a supermarket offers around 20 000 product lines and a superstore nearer 30 000. Home delivery systems also have to work around the normal business of the store (staff assembling home delivery orders should not get in the way of ordinary customers) and deal with the needs of fresh, chilled and frozen goods as well as looking after the more fragile merchandise. The store thus needs staff to process and assemble orders, delivery vans and drivers, and appropriate storage for orders waiting to go out. Brunfaut and Meran (1999) suggest that because 80 per cent of goods ordered by customers for home delivery come from the same 3000 product lines, it could be possible to have a small warehouse facility at the store in which staff can select these goods without going into the main store. Other items can then be selected from the shopfloor with less disturbance to normal shoppers.

Giving advice and information

Both retailers and wholesalers are part of the forward *information flow* that advises customers and persuades them to buy. Although in the supermarket environment the role of personal advice is minimal, many retailers, especially those in product lines such as clothing, hobbies, electrical goods and cars, are expected to assist the consumer directly in making a purchase decision and to advise on subsequent use. These are the kinds of goods that require limited or extended decision-making behaviour, as discussed at p. 104 earlier.

Wholesalers are also important sources of advice for some retailers and users. The more specialised a wholesaler, the greater the opportunity for developing an in-depth market understanding, tracking new or declining products, analysing competitive actions, defining promotions needed and advising on best buys. This role may be especially valuable to the smaller retailer who has less direct access to quality information on broader trends in a specific market. Similarly, an industrial distributor may be expected to advise customers on applications and to assist in low-level technical problem solving.

Example A survey conducted by *Marketing* magazine tested the general standards of service in a range of electrical goods stores selling computers by assessing sales assistants' product knowledge, manner of service and selling ability. One problem that the researcher experienced was having to wait too long to be noticed by an assistant and in some stores even having to go in search of help. Some assistants did not seem to be particularly interested in the customer or closing the sale, while others were too technical or incomplete in their explanations. In general terms, however, product knowledge was pretty good, but the manner of service and selling ability were more of a problem (Murphy, 1999). The best sales assistants notice the customer quickly, take time to find out what the customer wants, talk in terms that the customer can understand, sell the product's benefits, try to sell related products (printers, scanners or Internet access, for example) and coax the customer towards buying without being too pushy.

Quality of service is also important to customers making more routine, low-value purchases. A survey by consultants Nicholson McBride showed that 20 per cent of supermarket shoppers have switched stores because of poor customer service. Much of the poor interaction between staff and customers is simply because staff do not think about the impression they are making. In a self-service store, many staff are not dealing with customers very often and checkout operators are under pressure to keep the conveyor belts moving quickly. All of this is a clear signal that grocery retailers need to invest in staff training and motivation so that staff do make a conscious effort to be more polite, to make more eye contact and to offer a few more smiles and thank-yous (Yeung, 1999).

Transferring title

Both wholesalers and retailers (but not agents) take title to goods and services. Within the context of warranty restrictions, the intermediary accepts legal responsibility for the product, including its storage, security and resale. This has a direct bearing on the pricing, display and control of the products offered, the processing of cash and/or credit transactions, and the implementation of materials handling into and around the showroom and, if necessary, out to the customer. Some of these functions can be passed on to the customer. In IKEA, for instance, the customer can see display products in a showroom and then pick the required products unassisted from warehouse storage racks before going on to the checkout.

When the wholesaler takes title to goods, there are direct financial and other benefits to the producer, for which the wholesaler is rewarded through a profit margin. These benefits include lower distribution and logistics costs, credit and cash flow benefits, reduced selling and administration costs as a result of dealing with a relatively small number of customers, and a valuable information flow back to the manufacturer.

Providing an appropriate environment

Both wholesalers and retailers receive customers in their premises. The wholesaler in the grocery trade will probably operate like an overgrown supermarket, allowing selected and vetted trade customers to choose and even collect goods during their visit. In other situations, such as a builder's merchant, a mixed operation may exist. Some high-value, low-bulk products will be sold by counter service only, rather than on a self-service basis.

In most retail situations, the consumer enters a carefully planned and controlled environment designed to create a retail environment that helps to establish and reinforce the ambience and image desired. In some, this may be a low-cost minimalist approach that reinforces a no-frills, value for money philosophy, with simple picking from racks and pallets or drums. In others, music, decor and display are all subtly developed and designed around themes to create a more upmarket, higher-quality shopping experience. The whole area of retail atmosphere will be readdressed at p. 538 *et seq.*

e-commerce: a new dimension in customer service.

Source: http://www.diy.com, B&Q plc.

The retail environment can also include a range of additional services. Convenient parking is a critical issue where customers are buying in bulk, or want fast take-away services (the 'drive-through' fast food operator has found the logical solution to this one!). Additional services in the form of credit, delivery, returns and purchasing assistance can help to differentiate a retailer.

Example Many retailers are embracing e-commerce as a means of providing additional services to their customers. A website can provide information for customers in their own homes, perhaps on product availability, pricing, special offers or new products. The website can also educate customers, not only by establishing the company's policies on the environment or employee relations issues, for example, but also by giving them ideas about how to use products or about other products in the company's range. On-line ordering then makes it very easy for customers to place an order, which can then be delivered to their homes. In early 1999, DIY chain B&Q was in the process of redesigning its website (http://www.diy.com) to incorporate an on-line ordering service aimed at the amateur DIY enthusiast. B&Q feels that with 289 stores, its on-line service is not so much about extending its geographic reach as adding value for its customers through service and information (Kavanagh, 1999b).

THE STRUCTURE OF THE EUROPEAN RETAIL SECTOR

Retailing across Europe is big business. Table 13.1 shows the value of retail sales across Europe in 1996. In total value terms, Germany, France, Italy and the UK are the leading nations, accounting for 73 per cent of total retail sales between them. On a per capita basis, however, the top five are Belgium, Denmark, France, Germany and Luxembourg.

Table 13.2 shows the top 20 west European retailers, ranked by sales. It is interesting to note that no fewer than 15 of them are grocery retailers, while the remainder consist of two variety stores, one department store and two multisector retailers. In geographic terms, the list is dominated by German, French and UK organisations.

Retailers can be classified on a number of criteria, not all of which are immediately obvious to the average shopper. A later section of this chapter (pp. 521 *et seq.*) will concentrate on store types, but this section discusses other classification criteria, which will also help to shed further light on what retailers actually do and why they are important to both manufacturer and consumer.

Form of ownership

Retailing was for many years the realm of the small-independent business. Some grew by adding more branches and some grew by acquisition, but it is only since the 1950s that the retail structure of the high street has evolved significantly, favouring the larger organisation. Nevertheless, there are still several predominant forms of ownership to be found.

TABLE 13.1
European retail sales, 1996

	Retail sales $bn	Retail sales $ per capita
Austria	38.4	4735.2
Belgium	63.1	6207.7
Denmark	30.4	5795.3
Finland	26.7	5206.7
France	346.2	5934.9
Germany	431.6	5268.7
Greece	29.7	2827.7
Ireland	12.7	3571.4
Italy	290.4	5074.0
Luxembourg	3.9	9513.7
Netherlands	80.9	5194.6
Portugal	15.0	1528.3
Spain	140.9	3551.4
Sweden	37.1	4028.6
UK	234.1	4026.4

Source: Euromonitor (1998), Table 1201, p. 281. Reprinted with kind permission.

TABLE 13.2
Top 20 European retailers by sales, 1997

Rank	Organisation	Country	Core area	Sales, £m
1	Metro	Germany	Multisector	29.9
2	Rewe	Germany	Grocery	18.7
3	Tengelman	Germany	Multisector	17.8
4	Carrefour	France	Grocery	17.7
5	Auchan	France	Grocery	17.0
6	Aldi Group	Germany	Grocery	16.0
7	Intermarché	France	Grocery	14.9
8	Edeka Group	Germany	Grocery	14.8
9	Centres Leclerc	France	Grocery	14.3
10	Tesco plc	UK	Grocery	13.9
11	J Sainsbury	UK	Grocery	13.4
12	Promodès	France	Grocery	11.6
13	Karstadt	Germany	Department store	11.3
14	Lidl & Schwartz	Germany	Grocery	9.5
15	Migros	Switzerland	Grocery	9.1
16	Casino	France	Grocery	8.0
17	Co-operative Society	UK	Variety	7.9
18	Marks & Spencer	UK	Variety	7.8
19	Safeway plc	UK	Grocery	7.1
20	ASDA	UK	Grocery	7.0

Source: A.C. Nielsen (1999), p. 156. The Retail Pocket Book. Published by NTC Publications, Henley-on-Thames. Reprinted with kind permission.

Independent

Still the most common form of ownership in terms of number of retail outlets is independent, with over 62 per cent of UK outlets falling into this category. In sales volume terms, however, this group accounts for less than 30 per cent. Marked variances exist between retail categories, with a significant role for the small independent in the drinks sector and in CTN (confectionery, tobacco and news) retailing. Similar patterns exist across Europe, especially in France, Spain and the Benelux countries, which have above average densities of small retailers. Typically, the **independent retail outlet** is managed by a sole trader or a family business. For the consumer, the main benefits are the personalised attention and flexibility that can be offered. These operations can be highly individualistic in terms of the variety and quality of merchandise stocked, ranging from very upmarket to bargain basement.

Example Independent menswear retailers in London face fierce competition from the multiples for both the best labels and the best sites. A trade journal article, in which a number of independents were interviewed, suggested the following advice:

- offer personal service
- find a niche – the independent retailer Manlee stocks a high proportion of larger sizes, for instance
- invest in attractive design and display
- provide entertainment value within the shopping experience
- think carefully about the product mix – Carlyle and Forge, for instance, sells accessories and furniture as well as clothing, catering for its target customer's total lifestyle
- try to find exclusive labels
- think about own label – for Carlyle and Forge, own label represents 75 per cent of its business
- work hard on getting sourcing right and keeping margins under control.

Source: Rice (1995).

Although it may not be possible for the small independent to compete on price and breadth of range offered, the key is to complement the big multiples rather than to try to compete head on. Howe (1992) is clear about forces that work against the small retailer, such as changing population patterns, the drift towards out of town shopping, supply and resource problems and the sheer scale and professionalism of the large multiple chains. To combat this, the small retailer thus needs to look for niches, specialised merchandise, flexible opening hours and special services and to make more effective use of suppliers. This boils down to sound management and marketing thinking.

Example Many small village grocery shops, faced with losing business to the supermarkets, are trying to maintain their place in the community by expanding the range of services offered. Some, for instance, offer fax and photocopying facilities to their customers, and while these services do not make a profit in their own right, they keep people coming into the store and making other grocery purchases while they are there.

Kishor and Pradeep Patel own a small, independent grocery store in Houghton Regis, on the very outskirts of Luton. Apart from joining the Londis voluntary chain (*see* p. 517), the brothers found other ways of making their store appealing to local residents. Lottery tickets and scratchcards bring in nearly £5000 per week, and commission is also earned from a bank's cash dispenser on the outside wall of the store. The in-store photocopier only makes 1000 copies per week, but it does generate impulse purchases of other products by the users. An arrangement with Video Box Office allows the store to run a video rental section with 330 titles available. The turnover from this is about £750 per week. The average spend per visit to the store is only £3, so it is important for the store to attract as many customers as possible as often as possible. Main selling lines include the sort of goods that a household might run out of between supermarket trips, such as milk, cigarettes, alcohol and confectionery (Hurren, 1999).

Corporate chain

A corporate chain has multiple outlets under common ownership. The operation of the chain will reflect corporate strategy, and many will centralise decisions where economies of scale can be gained. The most obvious activity to be centralised is purchasing, so that volume discounts and greater power over suppliers can be gained. There are, of course, other benefits to be derived from a regional, national or even international presence in terms of image and brand building. Typical examples include Next and C&A. Some chains do allow a degree of discretion at a local level to reflect different operating environments, in terms of opening hours, merchandise or services provided, but the main strength comes from unity rather than diversity.

Contractual system

The linking of members of distribution channels through formal agreements rather than ownership (i.e. a contractual system) was included in the discussion of vertical marketing systems in Chapter 12. For retail or wholesale sponsored co-operatives or franchises, the main benefit is the ability to draw from collective strength, whether in management, marketing or operational procedures. In some cases, the collective

---

MARKETING IN ACTION   ## Voluntary chain, community service

Voluntary chains, or symbol groups, are run by wholesale companies for independent retailers. The retailers join the voluntary chain, which entitles them to trade under the chain's name and fascia (Mace, Spar, Londis, Today's, etc.). Voluntary chains source products for their members. They buy centrally, in bulk to get cost savings, and deal with suppliers on behalf of members. It is sometimes necessary to pressurise suppliers to maintain their service levels. Today's suggested that suppliers were frequently delivering lower than 95 per cent service levels, meaning that its wholesale operation has to keep extra stock in its warehouses to ensure that its members can source the products they want when they want them. It is much easier for a major buyer like Today's to pressurise a supplier than for a small independent retailer with little influence.

Having sourced the products, the voluntary chains redistribute them through their own regional distribution centres to their members, passing on some of the bulk-buying savings. In 1999, Londis was planning to open its third distribution centre, located to serve Scotland and the north of England. This will help it to recruit retailers in those regions. Voluntary chains also develop own-label products and sell them to their members. Londis offers 600 lines, priced at around 10 per cent lower than the leading brands, which account for 20 per cent of its wholesale turnover and 35 per cent of its retailers' sales. Over 40 per cent of wines, spirits, cider and cola sales are own-label products. Not only are the supply prices attractive to member retailers, but the own labels also give the small retailer something unique that the supermarket chains do not sell.

Voluntary chains do provide a service to local communities. Many of their members are small,

neighbourhood retailers trying to compete with the big supermarket chains. The voluntary chains help small retailers to operate more professionally and cost effectively and to stay in business. One of the criticisms levelled at the major UK supermarket chains is that their stores are aimed at car-borne, relatively affluent shoppers and there is little or no provision in the poorer areas of towns and cities for people without a lot of money and without cars. The smaller, local shops that managed to survive in those communities were often expensive and lacking in fresh produce or went out of business, creating 'food deserts'. COR (community-owned retailing) is an organisation committed to changing this situation by bringing manufacturers, wholesalers, community groups, local authorities and government together to provide the means and the support to open, maintain and sustain stores in the deserts with profits going back into the community. Through COR, a pilot store opened in Sheffield under the Mace voluntary chain fascia with an interest-free loan from the Loan Investment Fund, supported by nine well-known manufacturers such as Mars, Birds Eye Walls and Whitbread. Mace has helped by using its geodemographic analysis system to assess spending patterns and the kind of products that should be stocked. The shop expects a turnover of over £50 000 per year and profits of £25 000. It is hoped that not only the products on offer, but also the fact that it is run by the community for the community, will encourage local residents to become loyal to the store. The COR scheme is still in its infancy and the success of its pilot shops will be closely monitored. If they are successful, then the next challenge will be to increase industry support to guarantee a future for the initiative.

Sources: Gannaway (1999a); *The Grocer* (1999b, 1999d, 1998).

strength, as with franchises, can provide a valuable tool for promoting customer aware-ness and familiarity, leading in turn to retail loyalty. The trade-off for the franchisee is some loss of discretion, both operationally and strategically, but this may be countered by the benefits of unity. **Franchising** might also pass on the retailing risk to the fran-chisee. When Benetton's performance was poor in the US market, 300 stores closed, with all the losses borne by the franchisees rather than by Benetton (Davidson, 1993).

If the independent retailer wants to avoid the risks of franchising (*see* Chapter 22 for a more detailed discussion of franchising), yet wants to benefit from collective power, then affiliation to either a buying group or a voluntary chain might be the answer. Buying groups are usually found in food retailing and their purpose is to centralise the purchasing function and to achieve economies of scale on behalf of their members.

Level of service

The range and quality of services offered vary considerably from retailer to retailer. Some, such as department stores, offer gift-wrapping services, and some DIY stores offer home delivery, but in others most of the obligation for picking, assessing and taking the product home rests with the customer.

Three types of service level highlight the main options.

Full service

Stores such as Harrods provide the full range of customer services. This includes close personal attention on the shopfloor, a full range of account and delivery services, and a clear objective to treat each customer as a valued individual. Such high levels of ser-vice are reflected in the premium pricing policy adopted.

Limited service

The number of customers handled and the competitive prices that need to be charged prevent the implementation of the full range of services, but the services that are offered make purchasing easier. Credit, no-quibble returns, telephone orders and home delivery may be offered. This is a question of deciding what the target market 'must have' rather than what it 'would like', or defining what is essential for competi-tive edge. A retailer, such as Next, which claims to sell quality clothing at competitive prices, cannot offer too many extra services because that would increase the retailer's costs. They do, however, have to offer a limited range of services in order to remain competitive with similar retailers.

Self-service

In self-service stores, the customer performs many of the in-store functions, including picking goods, queueing at the checkout, paying by cash or perhaps credit card, and then struggling to the car park with a loaded trolley. Some food and discount stores operate in this mode, but the trend is towards offering more service to ease bottleneck points that are particularly frustrating to the customer. This could include the provi-sion of more staff at the delicatessen counter, more checkouts to guarantee short queues, and assistance with packing.

Merchandise lines

Retailers can be distinguished by the merchandise they carry, assessed in terms of the breadth and depth of range.

Breadth of range

The breadth of range represents the variety of different product lines stocked. A department store (*see* pp. 521 *et seq.* for a fuller discussion) will carry a wide variety of product lines, perhaps including electrical goods, household goods, designer clothing, hairdressing and even holidays.

Depth of range

The depth of range defines the amount of choice or assortment within a product line, on whatever dimensions are relevant to that kind of product. A music store stocking CDs, tapes, minidiscs and vinyl records could be said to have depth in its range. Similarly, a clothing store that stocks cashmere jumpers might be said to have a shallow range if the jumpers are available only in one style, or a deep range if they are available in five different styles. Introducing further assortment criteria, such as size range and colour, creates a very complex definition of depth. A specialty or niche retailer (*see* pp. 526 *et seq.*), such as Tie Rack would be expected to provide depth in its product lines on a number of assortment criteria.

> **Example**   Hennes and Mauritz (H&M) is Sweden's fifth largest company and operates around 500 stores in 12 European countries. It owns over a dozen own labels covering men's, women's and children's clothing, casual and classic wear, and underwear and outerwear. Although it is a speciality retailer in the sense that it specialises in fashion, it provides a broad but shallow range, compared with other fashion retailers who specialise in women's wear only or jeans only (narrow and deep). H&M is happy to offer low prices, reasonable quality and a wide range of fashionable clothing. To keep customers interested in its stores and to broaden the width of range further, new products are introduced every day and no product is kept in the stores for longer than one month (*The Economist*, 1998). This is a departure from the normal practice of fashion retailers, which is to change ranges between two and four times a year.

Figure 13.1 shows the difference between these two terms. It is easy to see, in this figure, how tensions can arise between breadth and depth. Since retailers have limited resources and limited space at their disposal, there is a basic choice to be made between breadth and depth. If they go for breadth, they can provide a wide variety of different kinds of goods, but probably would not be able to stock those products in significant depth. Limits may be placed on the number of different brands, or the range of styles, sizes or colours available within a product area. Sacrificing breadth for depth means that the retailer can satisfy demand for a whole variety of different brands, sizes, colours or styles, but only within a very narrowly defined range of goods.

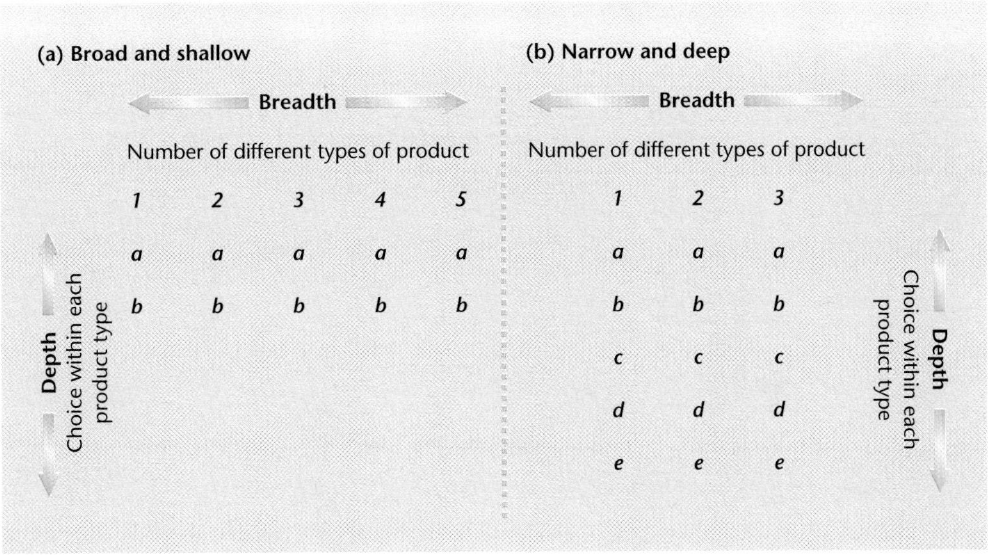

FIGURE 13.1

Breadth vs depth

In many cases, customers are happy to accept a polarised choice, patronising department stores when depth of range does not really matter to them, or where the level of customer service they know they will get from the store matters more. Speciality retailers attract custom from those who do want the depth of choice, perhaps because they are engaged in extended problem solving and want access to as many alternatives as possible, or because they want an unusual combination of size, colour and style, for example, that only a specialist stockist would keep. The speciality retailer might also be seen as more knowledgeable and committed to the product area, and this might reduce the risk inherent in the purchase in the customer's mind.

As Fig 13.2 shows, some retailers do try to compromise by offering a mixed approach. Some products, perhaps popular, fast moving lines, will be stocked in depth.

> **Example** A clothing store might stock a much wider range of colours and sizes for a classic, polo-neck jumper selling at a competitive price than for an extremely fashionable (and therefore short shelf life) velvet jacket selling at a premium price. Breadth and depth might also vary through the year. At Christmas, for instance, most ladies' clothing retailers expand in terms of both breadth and depth for party wear.

The problems caused by the choice of breadth or depth can also be reduced by careful choice of retailing format. A traditional department store has to restrict itself because of the pressures of space and display requirements.

> **Example** A catalogue retail showroom (*see* p. 529), such as Argos, is not expected to display its whole range of stock 'live' and is thus able to provide much greater breadth and depth of range than its department store rivals. It is limited only by its logistical systems and ability to update and replenish its in-store warehouses quickly. Argos has 418 UK stores. Despite the breadth of range it offers, it was felt that Argos was weak in the high-tech product areas and thus a new line of PCs is to be offered. Also, as a means of reducing the complexity of the Argos offering for customers, it has been suggested that a number of specialised Argos catalogues could be produced. A specialised computer catalogue, for instance, could contain everything that the computer user might need and give the impression that Argos is a specialist computer retailer (Edwards, 1999). Similarly, Internet retailing allows organisations to offer a wide range of stock in a space efficient way. Waterstones offers 1.4 million books for sale on its http://www.waterstones.co.uk website and Heffers of Cambridge (http://www.heffers.co.uk) two million, far more than the average bookshop and reaching a much bigger, more geographically dispersed audience (Gilbert, 1998).

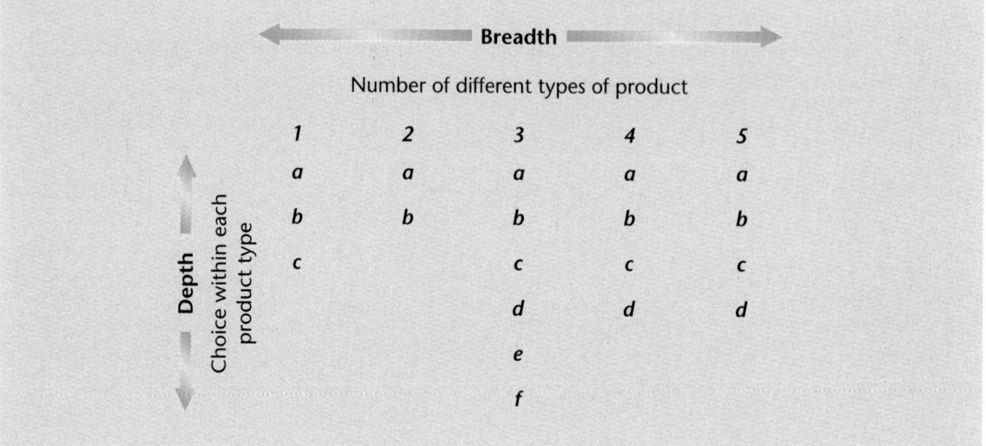

FIGURE 13.2

The mixed approach

Operating methods

The area of operating methods has seen significant change, with the recent growth of alternatives to the traditional approach. Traditional store retailing, which itself includes a wide number of types of retailer, still predominates. These various types are considered in the next section. Non-store retailing, however, where the customer does not physically travel to visit the retailer, has become increasingly popular. This is partly because of changing customer attitudes, partly because of the drive upmarket made by the mail-order companies in particular, and partly because of technological advances in logistics. The whole area of non-store shopping will be further discussed at p. 529 *et seq.*

TYPES OF RETAILER

A walk down any high street or a drive around the outskirts of any large town reveals a wide range of approaches to selling us things. There are retailers of all shapes and sizes, enticing us in with what they hope are clearly differentiated marketing mixes. Taking into account the large number of small independents, there are many thousands of retailers in the UK alone, and yet in the UK, the top three retailers, Tesco, Sainsbury's and ASDA between them hold a 52 per cent share of retail turnover. In Sweden, the top three retailers hold a 95 per cent share between them, but the top three retailers in Greece can only manage a combined 25 per cent share (A.C. Nielsen, 1999).

The following discussion groups retailers according to the type of retail operation that they run. Each type will be defined, and the role it plays within the retail sector will be discussed. This should help to clarify why it is important for the health of the retail sector to support the diversity of shapes and sizes of retailer, and why the small corner shop is just as valuable in its way as the top 10 retailers.

Department stores

Department stores usually occupy a prominent prime position within a town centre or a large out of town shopping mall. Most towns have one and some centres, such as London's Oxford Street, support several.

Examples of department stores are:

- UK: Debenham's, House of Fraser, John Lewis
- France: Printemps, Galeries Lafayette
- Germany: Karstadt
- Netherlands: Vendex
- Switzerland: Manor

Department stores are large and are organised into discrete departments consisting of related product lines, such as sports, ladies' fashions, toys, electrical goods etc. Manor, for example, stocks clothing for all the family, food, cosmetics, entertainment goods, electrical appliances, toys, kitchenware, home furnishing, decorative objects, gifts and accessories, as well as running restaurants in its stores.

To support the concept of providing everything that the customer could possibly want, department stores extend themselves into services as well as physical products, operating hairdressing and beauty parlours, restaurants and travel agencies. In some stores, individual departments are treated as business units in their own right. Taking that concept a little further, it is not surprising that **concessions** or 'stores within a store' have become common. With these, a manufacturer or another retail name purchases space within a department store, paying either a fixed rental per square metre

> **Example** Manchester United Football Club signed a deal with sports retailer Allsports to open 'store within a store' concessions at three Allsports branches. The concessions will sell the full range of 1000 merchandise lines (Buxton, 1999b). This is happening in parallel with the opening of more of Manchester United's own stores and could be seen as allowing retail expansion to happen more quickly at minimum risk. With the concessions, Manchester United will also be getting easy and relatively cheap access to Allsports' prime retail sites. Allsports, of course, gets the benefit of being associated with a big (if not the biggest) sporting name and the concessions are likely to bring many more potential customers into the stores. Liberty, a London-based department store, is also opening concessions, not just in the UK, to sell its women's clothing range (*Marketing Week*, 1999c). Like Manchester United, Liberty is a very well-known name in its market and wants to reach a wider audience quickly and cost effectively.

or a percentage commission on turnover, to set up and operate a distinct trading area of its own. Jaeger, a classic fashion manufacturer and retailer, operates a number of its own stores throughout the UK, but also generates over one-third of its turnover from concessions within department stores such as House of Fraser.

There are sound reasons on both sides for the operation of concessions.

The department store perspective. A concession brings a bit of extra variety and life to a store, and may bring in customers who would not otherwise have patronised that department store. A concession might also trade in a product that the department store owners themselves would not want to take a risk on. Given the uncertainties facing the retail sector, concessions take up what might otherwise be excess floor capacity, and provide a steady income per square metre. Overall, because concessions are clearly distinct from the rest of the store, they are a good way of extending the variety and scope of the store without necessarily compromising its core image.

The manufacturer's perspective. There are two broad reasons that a manufacturer might wish to operate a concession within a department store. The first is a general desire to reduce the influence of the intermediaries and thus have a high street presence, but without going through the lengthy and expensive rigmarole of setting up a retail operation from scratch. One deal, head office to head office, gives the manufacturer a stake in a number of prime sites across the country, as well as giving them access to the department store's facilities and support systems if required. More specifically, the second reason for taking out a concession is that a manufacturer might wish to have tighter control over the way in which its product is displayed and sold. There is always a risk that if your product is only one of many hundreds that a department store sells, it will not get the handling, display or personal selling attention that you think it deserves.

Another retail name's perspective. Why should a department store allow another established high street retailer to have space on its premises? Often, it is because they are both owned by the same parent company. In general terms, there are several possible reasons for this kind of cohabitation:

1 *Encouraging cross-selling*: customers who go into the department store specifically to visit the concession might get drawn into browsing in the wider store (and vice versa).
2 *Lack of suitable sites*: in a particular town, there may not be a suitable property available for opening a new branch. Taking a concession at least establishes a presence in that town until something more appropriate can be found. It also reduces the risk of rushing into a less than desirable property for the sake of it.
3 *Shortage of space*: even if the retailer does have a branch in the town, the shop might not be big enough to display the full range of merchandise. If the original branch

water: 21st century
ling.

z: Photo courtesy of Lend
photographer Adrian Brooks.

cannot be extended, then a concession in the department store in the same town gives some expansion of trading space, although it is a far from optimal solution.

4 *Corporate rationalisation*: high street shops are expensive to operate and maintain. A corporate decision might be made, therefore, to cut back on the number of 'free-standing' branches by closing some down and relocating them in local department stores as concessions. Similarly, if the department store is having a rough time, putting concessions into it might increase its turnover and performance as well as mopping up excess capacity.

The department store is not without problems. In the UK, it is under threat from out of town shopping and the general growth of specialist retailers. There are also difficulties with the high cost of city centre location and operation. The department stores' answer to these threats has been a concerted effort to improve their purchasing policies, to update their image and provide a higher-quality ambience through refurbishment of existing stores, and to locate new stores in out of town retail parks.

Variety stores

Variety stores are smaller than department stores, and they stock a more limited number of ranges in greater depth. C&A, for example, sells only clothing, but provides a great deal of choice within that limited definition, covering ladies' wear, menswear, children's clothing, party wear, sportswear, lingerie etc. Some retailers offer all that in the clothing sector, but add extra ranges too. BhS in the UK, for example, offers housewares and lighting as well as extensive clothing ranges, while Marks & Spencer is respected as much for its groceries as its clothing.

Example Like department stores, the major variety stores such as Monoprix in France and Kaufhalle in Germany operate as national chains, maintaining a consistent image across the country. Some, such as C&A and M&S, also operate internationally. Whatever the geographical coverage of the variety store chain, given the size of the stores, they need volume traffic (i.e. lots of customers) and thus to develop a mass-market appeal, offering quality merchandise at no more than mid-range price points.

Variety stores tend to offer limited additional services, with a tendency towards self-service, and centralised cashier points. In that sense, they are something between a department store and a supermarket.

Supermarkets

Over the last few years, the **supermarket** has been accused of being the main culprit in changing the face of the high street. The first generation of supermarkets, some 30 years ago, were relatively small, town centre operations. As they expanded and cut their costs through self-service, bulk buying and heavy merchandising, they began to replace the small, traditional independent grocer. They expanded on to out of town sites, with easy free parking, and took the customers with them, thus (allegedly) threatening the health of the high street.

The wheel then turned full circle. As planning regulations in the UK tightened, making it more difficult to develop new out of town superstores, retailers began looking at town centre sites again. They developed new formats, such as Tesco Metro and Sainsbury's Local, for small stores carrying ready meals, basic staple grocery goods such as bread and milk, and lunchtime snacks aimed at shoppers and office workers.

Example Generally, supermarkets are large, self-service stores, carrying a comprehensive range of fmcg products, sometimes including in-store bakeries, delicatessens and fish-mongers. A typical supermarket is clearly zoned by product group, but always has central checkout facilities. Branches often also stock some convenience items, such as pharmaceuticals, newspapers, hardware etc. The larger branches of retailers such as Auchan, Carrefour or Tesco may carry clothes, small DIY items, electrical goods etc. Others, such as Sainsbury's, have developed parallel chains (Sainsbury's Homebase) to deal specifically with the less frequently purchased hardware, DIY and gardening goods. Similarly, Auchan has diversified into DIY (Leroy Merlin), sport (Decathlon), electrical goods (Boulanger) and many other areas.

The dominance of supermarkets is hardly surprising, considering that because of their size and operating structures their labour costs are something like 10–20 per cent lower than those of independent grocers, and their buying advantage 15 per cent better. This means that they can offer a significant price advantage. Additionally, they have made efficiency gains and increased their cost effectiveness through their commitment to developing and implementing new technology in the areas of EPOS, shelf allocation models, forecasting and physical distribution management systems.

MARKETING IN ACTION   Discount grocery retailing

Discount grocery retailers are characterised by limited product ranges that generally do not include brand leaders, low-cost 'no-frills' stores and low-priced goods. As they rely on selling high volumes of products to generate profit, they have expanded across Europe in search of greater volumes and economies of scale. Netto started in Denmark, and Aldi and Lidl both originated in Germany, which has a strong discount

Continued

TABLE 13.3

A comparison between discount and mainstream grocery retailers

Discounters	Multiples
Emphasis on low prices	High, medium and low-priced products offered
Small number of product lines (c. 650)	High number of product lines (20 000–30 000)
Focus on fast movng, high-volume products	Focus on providing choice and complete ranges
Unknown brands stocked	Premium brands stocked
Products on sale change as stock is sometimes bought opportunistically on price	Consistant offering from week to week
Price-orientated own-label goods	Both price-orientated and quality-orientated own-label ranges
Mainly operating from small, edge of town sites	Emphasis on out of town superstores/hypermarkets
Minimal services	Extra services developed and emphasised as differentiating features
Minimum staffing	More cashiers, service desk staff, shelf fillers, customers' bag packers
Minimal, low-maintanence, 'no-frills' layout and display	Layout and displays used to entice shoppers, enhance goods and contribute to image and atmosphere
Customer loyalty based on price competitiveness	Customer loyalty based on convenience, service, range, own-brand preference, etc.

retail culture, unlike the UK and other parts of Europe. In Germany the discounters have a 25 per cent market share, while in the UK it is only 2.4 per cent. Hogarth-Scott and Parkinson (1994) researched the effect of a discounter opening a store close to an established supermarket in the UK. They found that although 57 per cent of shoppers had tried the discounter once, only 4 per cent of customers had been lost to the discounter, representing 4.7 per cent of turnover.

Aldi, Lidl and Netto have all found the UK market difficult because the mainstream UK grocery multiples, such as Tesco, ASDA, Sainsbury's and Safeway, have defended their market share vigorously. The UK shopper has been 'trained' not to be price sensitive and to value the service, the ambience, the choice of 30 000 product lines and quality own-label products offered by the multiples (Table 13.3 compares the two types of retailer). While the multiples attract shoppers mainly from the ABC1 social groups who spend over £20 on average per visit, the discounters attract over 70 per cent of their clientele from the C2DE groups and they spend just over £12 per visit. Analysts have predicted that the discounters will start to move more upmarket to try to capture more affluent shoppers and to improve margins. Most of the discounters' stores in the UK, for instance, are relatively small and located on edge-of-town sites to attract non-car-borne shoppers. Netto, however, wants to increase the

number of its stores (it currently has 118) by acquiring premises on out of town sites and retail parks. These sites attract the affluent shoppers and the parking provision means that they can buy more per trip without worrying about how they are going to carry it all home.

The discounters' UK experiences seem to be typical: they have found it hard to generate more than a 5 per cent market share outside their domestic markets. Future expansion also looks difficult. As Aldi and Lidl stand on the brink of entering the Irish market, the messages to them are clear. The trade body representing Irish suppliers feels that Irish shoppers, like the British, do not like price-orientated, no-frills retailing. The trade body is also adamant that both Aldi and Lidl should source 60 per cent of their goods from Irish companies. The problem is that to keep costs low through a streamlined operation, a discounter tends to buy a very limited number of products (Aldi, for example, sells only 650 product lines) at very keen prices in sufficient bulk to serve all its stores across Europe. Thus unless Irish suppliers can give the discounters the kind of very competitive low-priced, mid-quality bargains that they want in bulk volumes, the 60 per cent requirement could have a serious impact on the discounters' cost management, supply chain and margins.

Sources: The Grocer (1999e); Marketing Week (1999a); Robinson (1999).

Hypermarkets

The **hypermarket** is a natural extension of the supermarket. While the average super-market covers up to 2500 m^2, a superstore is between 2500 and 5000 m^2 and a hypermarket is anything over 5000 m^2 (URPI, 1988). It provides even more choice and depth of range, but usually centres mainly around groceries. Examples of hyper-market operators are Intermarché and Carrefour in France, Tengelmann in Germany and ASDA in the UK. Because of their size, hypermarkets tend to occupy new sites on **out of town** retail parks. They need easy access and a large amount of space for park-ing, not only because of the volume of customers they have to attract, but also because their size means that customers will buy a great deal and will therefore need to be able to bring the car close to the store.

The hypermarket format is particularly strong in France, where it accounts for 51 per cent of grocery turnover, the UK (45 per cent), Portugal (41 per cent) and Spain (34 per cent) (A.C. Nielsen, 1999). In Ireland, hypermarkets account for only 11 per cent of grocery turnover. The Irish planning authorities have looked at the effects of hypermarket and superstore developments in other EU countries and concluded that they damage town centres, leading to the closure of small shops, and cause traffic congestion. As a result of this, the Irish government decided to test new planning guidelines designed to prevent further development of superstores and hypermarkets. The new planning guidelines mean that supermarket developments within the Dublin area will be limited to no more than 3500 m^2 and, outside Dublin, no more than 3000 m^2 (*The Grocer*, 1999f).

While the Irish are trying to prevent hypermarkets ever becoming a dominant force, the French authorities are dealing with a very well-developed sector. Planning regulations in France have become very stringent in recent years for any development over 1000 m^2 and this has slowed down the growth in the number of hypermarkets. There are some powerful hypermarket retailers in France and if the planning regula-tions will not allow growth through domestic expansion, then it has to come from international operations or through mergers and acquisitions. Carrefour, for example, operates some of the biggest hypermarkets in France, but it has also been aggressive in its global expansion and by 1998 was generating 30 per cent of its sales outside Europe (Cunningham, 1998). Carrefour also bought Comptoires Modernes and its 800 or so supermarkets (Cook, 1998). Within the French market, Carrefour holds around 18 per cent market share, while Intermarché has 15 per cent. An alliance between Leclerc and Système U gives them over 20 per cent share from the 400 or more hyper-markets that they own between them (*The Grocer*, 1999a).

Out of town speciality stores

An out of town **speciality store** tends to specialise in one broad product group, for example furniture, carpets, DIY or electrical. It tends to operate on an out of town site, which is cheaper than a town-centre site and also offers good parking and general accessibility. It concentrates on discounted prices and promotional lines, thus empha-sising price and value for money. A product sold in an out of town speciality store is likely to be cheaper than the same item sold through a town centre speciality or department store.

The store itself can be single storey, with no windows. Some care is taken, however, over the attractiveness of the in-store displays and the layout. Depending on the kind of product area involved, the store may be self-service, or it may need to provide knowledgeable staff to help customers with choice and ordering processes. Recent years have seen efforts to improve the ambience of such stores and even greater care over their design.

Example IKEA provides an extremely pleasant and user-friendly display area, with mock room settings so that customers can see products in context, free pencils and tape measures for making notes and checking dimensions, and a relaxing restaurant area. This is backed up, however, by an extremely functional and efficient warehouse operation in which customers can self-select the products they want from pallets and then proceed to a checkout, although service is available to help with bulkier items or larger orders.

Toys 'Я' Us in particular has become known as a *category killer* because it offers so much choice and such low prices that other retailers cannot compete. Its large out of town sites mean that it is efficient in terms of its operating costs, and its global bulk buying means that it can source extremely cheaply. Shoppers wanting to buy a particular toy know that Toys 'Я' Us will probably have it in stock, and shoppers who are unsure about what they want have a wonderful browsing opportunity. Additionally, the out of town sites are easily accessible and make transporting bulky items much easier. The small, independent toy retailer, in contrast, cannot match buying power, cost control, accessibility or choice and is likely to be driven out of business.

Toys 'Я' Us is not necessarily having it all its own way, however. In the UK, it is being challenged by Woolworth's plans to open 12 out of town stores (Voyce, 1998). In the USA too, Toys 'Я' Us has lost market share to Wal-Mart (Liebeck, 1998).

Town centre speciality stores

Like out of town speciality stores, town centre speciality stores concentrate on a narrow product group as a means of building a differentiated offering. They are smaller than the out of town speciality stores, averaging about 250 m^2. Within this sector, however, there are retailers such as florists, lingerie retailers, bakeries and confectioners that operate in much smaller premises.

Other examples of products sold through town centre speciality stores are footwear, toys, books and clothing (although often segmented by sex, age, lifestyle or even size). Most are comparison products, for which the fact of being displayed alongside similar items can be an advantage, as the customer wants to be able to examine and deliberate over a wider choice of alternatives before making a purchase decision. Given their central locations, and the need to build consumer traffic with competitive merchandise, the sector has seen the growth of multiple chains, serving clearly

ys 'Я' Us used out town sites to tablish itself as a tegory killer.

Source: Toys 'Я' Us.

defined target market segments with clearly defined product mixes, such as most of the high street fashion stores. To reinforce the concept of specialisation and differentiation, some, especially the clothing multiples, have developed their own-label brands.

Town centre speciality stores are usually a mixture of browsing and self-service, but with personnel available to help if required. The creation of a retail atmosphere or ambience appropriate to the target market is very important, including for instance the use of window display and store layout. This allows the town centre speciality store to feed off consumer traffic generated by larger stores, since passing shoppers are attracted in on impulse by what they see in the window or through the door. The multiples can use uniform formulae to replicate success over a wide area, but because of their buying power and expertise, they have taken a great deal of business away from small independents.

Convenience stores

Despite the decline of the small, independent grocer in the UK, there is still a niche that can be filled by **convenience stores**. Operating mainly in the groceries, drink and CTN sectors, they open long hours, not just 9 a.m. until 6 p.m.

They fill a gap left by the supermarkets, which are fine for the weekly or monthly shopping trip, if the consumer can be bothered to drive out to one. The convenience stores, however, satisfy needs that arise in the meantime. If the consumer has run out of something, forgotten to get something at the supermarket, wants freshness, or finds six unexpected guests on the doorstep who want feeding, the local convenience store is invaluable. If the emergency happens outside normal shopping times, then the advantages of a local, late-night shop become obvious. Such benefits, however, do tend to come at a price premium. To try to become more price competitive, some 'open-all-hours' convenience stores operate as voluntary chains, such as Spar, Londis, Today's and Mace, in which the retailers retain their independence but benefit from bulk purchasing and centralised marketing activities.

The latest development in the convenience sector has been the expansion of the shops operating at petrol stations. Many petrol retailers, such as Jet and Shell, have developed their non-petrol retailing areas into attractive mini-supermarkets that pull in custom in their own right. In some cases, they are even attracting customers who go in to buy milk or bread and end up purchasing petrol as an afterthought.

Discount clubs

Discount clubs are rather like cash and carries for the general public, where they can buy in bulk at extremely competitive prices. Discount clubs do, however, have membership requirements, related to occupation and income.

The discount clubs achieve their low prices and competitive edge through minimal service and the negotiation of keen bulk deals with the major manufacturers, beyond anything offered to the established supermarkets. Added to this, they pare their margins to the bone, relying on volume turnover, and they purchase speculatively. For instance, they may purchase a one-off consignment of a manufacturer's surplus stock at a very low price, or they may buy stock cheaply from a bankrupt company. While this allows them to offer incredible bargains, they cannot guarantee consistency of supply, thus they may have a heap of televisions one week but once these have been sold, that is it, there are no more. The following week the same space in the store may be occupied by hi-fis. At least such a policy keeps customers coming back to see what new bargains there are.

The main problem for consumers is that unless they have large families, or a very spacious garage for storage, the minimum purchase quantities for any single item are intimidating. One solution is to form an informal co-operative with a number of like-minded friends and, acting as a mini-wholesaler, break bulk and resell to them. Most consumers however, would probably not be interested in the management and administration involved, and would prefer to pay the slightly higher prices for the convenience of the local supermarket.

Markets

Most towns have markets, as a last link with an ancient form of retailing. There are now different types of market, not only those selling different kinds of products but street markets, held on certain days only; permanent markets occupying dedicated sites under cover or in the open; and Sunday markets for more specialised products.

Typical market products include fresh food, clothing and housewares. Some goods are downmarket, but others are simply unusual, for example a craftsman or craftswoman selling items that they have made themselves.

Example   The value of the market stall as a first step on the retailing ladder is well understood. The management of the Gateshead Metro Centre, for example, not only rents out permanent retail space, but also hires out a number of mobile barrows, situated throughout the shopping centre, at relatively low rents. This gives a more lively, market type of character to the public areas, but, more importantly, gives an opening for small traders, or individuals with little cash but a lot of entrepreneurial flair, to test a retail concept and to begin developing a business. Many barrow retailers then build up sufficient confidence and resources to take on a permanent shop unit.

Catalogue showrooms

A fairly recent development, **catalogue showrooms** try to combine the benefits of a high-street presence with the best in logistics technology and physical distribution management. The central focus of the showroom is the catalogue, and many copies are displayed around the store as well as being available for the customer to take home for browsing. Some items are on live display, but this is by no means the whole product range. The consumer selects from the catalogue, then goes to a checkout where an assistant inputs the order into the central computer. If the item is immediately available, the cashier takes payment. The consumer then joins a queue at a collection point, while the purchased product is brought round from the warehouse behind the scenes, usually very quickly.

A prime example of this type of operation is Argos, which carries a very wide range of household, electrical and leisure goods. It offers relatively competitive prices through bulk purchasing, and savings on operating costs, damage and pilfering (because of the limited displays).

NON-STORE RETAILING

A growing amount of selling to individual consumers is now taking place outside the traditional retailing structures. Non-store selling may involve personal selling (to be dealt with in Chapter 17), selling to the consumer at home through television, computer or telephone links or, most impersonally, selling through vending machines. Some of these areas clearly have strong roots in direct marketing, which is the subject of Chapter 18, but they will be briefly introduced here.

In-home selling

The longest-established means of selling to the consumer at home is through door-to-door selling, where the representative calls at the house either trying to sell from a suitcase (brushes, for example), or trying to do some preliminary selling to pave the way for a more concerted effort later (with higher-cost items such as double glazing, burglar alarms and other home improvements). Cold calling (i.e. turning up unexpectedly and unannounced) is not a particularly efficient use of the representative's time, nor is it likely to evoke a positive response from the customer. Organisations are more likely now to qualify leads in advance, thus sending representives out to people who have already expressed an interest, for example by returning a 'more information please' coupon from an advertisement, or using the cheaper method of telephone selling to arrange an initial interview.

A more acceptable method of in-home selling that has really taken off is the party plan. Here, the organisation recruits ordinary consumers to act as agents and do the selling for them in a relaxed, sociable atmosphere. The agent, or a willing friend, will host a party at a house and provide light refreshments. Guests are invited to attend and during the course of the evening, when everyone is relaxed, the agent will demonstrate the goods and take orders.

Since the pioneering days of the Tupperware party, many other products have used the same sort of technique. Ann Summers, for instance, is an organisation that sells erotic lingerie and sex aids and toys through parties. The majority of the customers are women who would otherwise never dream of going into 'that kind of shop', let alone buying 'that kind of merchandise'. A party is an ideal way of selling those products to that particular target market, because the atmosphere is relaxed, the customer is among friends, and purchases can be made without embarrassment amidst lots of giggling. One of the best features of party selling is the ability to show and demonstrate the product. This kind of hands-on, interactive approach is a powerful way of involving the potential customer and thus getting them interested and in a mood to buy.

MARKETING AND IT   ## Strolling down the cybermall

One of the pleasures of clothes shopping is wandering around the shops, comparing bargains, seeing what catches your eye, checking fabrics and colours, trying things on to let your friends see what they look like, soaking up the store atmosphere and buying on impulse. It can be very difficult to replicate many of those experiences on the Internet, but retailers and their site designers are trying hard to create 'e-ambience' to make virtual fashion shopping just as rewarding as the real thing. Fashion Trip is a 3-D virtual mall that brings together a number of US retailers such as Levi's, Guess Footwear, Almay and Urban Decay and simulates their stores on screen. Having entered the store, the shopper can look around, pick up clothing and accessories, and then put them on a mannequin to see what they look like. If the shopper likes the garment, it can be ordered on-line directly from the retailer. To simulate the social aspects of shopping, a chat feature allows the shopper to communicate with friends and show them the chosen outfits.

Targeting Europe and the USA, Boo.com (http://www.boo.com) has been launched to sell sports and street wear from a variety of names such as Puma, DKNY, Cosmic Girl and Fubu. An on-line style magazine attracts, advises and involves customers and the virtual 'Ms Boo' acts as a shop assistant. As with Fashion Trip, the graphics are an important part of the retail offering, and at Boo shoppers can zoom in on garments and rotate them to see what they look like from all angles. Shoppers can also choose from a range of European languages and the currency with which they wish to pay.

From the high street, Gap (http://www.gap.com) is about to go on-line in Europe and is offering very wide, deep ranges. In men's jeans, for instance, 3024 size and style options are available. This is far more than a store could offer, but the main benefit that Gap is getting from its European on-line sales is that it allows the company to enter smaller markets in which it would not be cost effective to open real stores.

Sources: Kuchinskas (1998); Rawsthorn (1999); Wills (1998).

The main problem with party selling, however, is that it can be difficult to recruit agents, and their quality and selling abilities will be variable. Supporting and motivating a pyramid of agents and paying their commission can make selling costs very high.

Mail order and teleshopping

Both mail order and teleshopping will be explored further in Chapter 18. This section, therefore, gives a brief introduction in order to acknowledge their place as alternative forms of selling or retailing to consumers. **Mail order** has a long history and traditionally consists of a printed catalogue from which customers select goods that are then delivered to the home, either through the postal service or via couriers. This form of selling has, however, developed and diversified over the years. Offers are now made through magazine or newspaper advertisements, as well as through the traditional catalogue, and database marketing now means that specially tailored offers can be made to individual customers. Orders no longer have to be mailed in by the customer, but can be telephoned, with payment being made immediately by credit card. The strength of mail order varies across Europe, but is generally stronger in northern Europe than in the south. It is strong in Germany through companies such as Otto Versand, Quelle and Nekermann.

> **Example** Otto Versand's main operating areas are Germany, the USA, France and the UK. In the UK catalogue market, it acquired Grattan in 1991 and then proposed to take over Freemans (subject to agreement from the competition authorities) in 1999. This would give Otto Versand a 15 per cent share of the UK market (Darby, 1999). One example of its US operations is its takeover of Crate and Barrel, an American retail and catalogue company in the home-furnishings market. Otto Versand's expertise in mail order helped Crate and Barrel, through advice and training, to think more like a catalogue operator than a retailer. Thus it helped with planning, expanding and managing the product assortment for the mail-order side of the business, co-ordinating products in the catalogue and designing the catalogue as well as advising on targeting the right kind of customer. As a result of this involvement, the response rate from people receiving the catalogues rose, the average order size grew bigger, and sales rose by over 20 per cent. Having got Crate and Barrel better established in its home market, Otto Versand's next step could be to take the catalogue into international markets (Miller, 1999).

Teleshopping represents a much wider range of activities. It includes shopping by telephone in response to television advertisements, whether on cable, satellite or terrestrial channels. Some cable and satellite operators run home-shopping channels, such as QVC, where the primary objective is to sell goods to viewers. Teleshopping also covers interactive shopping by computer, using mechanisms such as the French Minitel system or the Internet. The Internet in particular offers interesting opportunities to a variety of sellers, including established retailers. Many, such as Toys 'Я' Us and Blackwell's Bookshop, have set up 'virtual' stores on Internet sites, so that a potential customer can browse through the merchandise, select items, pay by credit card and then wait for the goods to be delivered.

Through the development of video catalogues and 'specialogues', and through further exploitation of other direct marketing techniques such as telephone ordering and selling via the Internet, mail order and related forms of non-store retailing could have an interesting future, complementing high street retailing in the eyes of the shopper.

Vending

Vending machines account for a very small percentage of retail sales, less than 1 per cent. They are mainly based in work-places and public locations, for example offices, factories, staffrooms, bus and rail stations etc. They are best used for small, standard, low-priced, repeat purchase products, such as hot and cold drinks, cans of drink, chocolate and snacks, bank cash dispensers and postage stamps. They have the advantage of allowing customers to purchase at highly convenient locations, at any time of the day or night. Vending machines can also help to deliver the product in prime condition for consumption, for example the refrigerated machines that deliver a can of ice-cold Coke. A human retailer cannot always maintain those conditions.

In the work-place, vending machines can be a valuable complement to normal catering services. If the machine is situated near to the shopfloor or working area, then employees do not have to waste time trekking across to a remote part of the site to get a drink, for instance. Similarly, the vending machine can help to save time and reduce queues in the canteen by dealing with employees' minor purchases, leaving the canteen staff to handle larger purchases.

Although vending machines take up little space and do not require staff in constant attendance, they do need regular and frequent servicing, whether to replenish stocks or empty the cash box or simply for preventive maintenance to ensure that the service is sustained. Nevertheless, vending machines represent significant business.

> **Example** Consumers are used to vending machines selling snacks, drinks, stamps and parking tickets, but could they get used to buying books in this way? One company, Travelman, is developing the idea of producing short stories on single sheets of paper folded like maps, which would take about 40 minutes to read. This would make them ideal for commuters or travellers, and London Underground would be interested if a suitable vending machine could be developed. Although the distribution method is different, according to the company the idea resurrects the concept of 'the hugely successful . . . short stories that Rudyard Kipling used to sell on the Indian railways' (Alberge, 1998).

RETAILER STRATEGY

This section looks more closely at some of the strategic issues and decisions facing retailers, including location, product mix, competitive positioning, store image and atmosphere, merchandising, the use of technology and, finally, strategic alliances. All these areas could be critical to the marketing success of retailers (Davies, 1992).

Location

Location is a very important area for decision, since if the wrong location is chosen for a store (or, worse, a series of wrong locations for a chain of stores), the retailer can lose a great deal of business by failing to reach or attract the right kind of customer to generate a viable level of trade (Anderson, 1993). In addition to lost business, there is also the waste of the money invested in acquiring the site or premises and building and/or shopfitting. A supermarket chain such as Tesco or Sainsbury's can spend more than £20 million per new store, including site-acquisition costs.

Choice of location is linked to social and demographic changes. For example, increasing rates of car ownership and the rising number of working women with too little time to shop for their families have helped the rise of the out of town superstore site. But there are other, more general factors that also affect the location decision. Some of these are considered in turn.

Catchment

For a given location, the retailer needs to know the size of the population on which the store can draw and, more specifically, what proportion of that population matches the desired market segment profile. Some estimate also needs to be made of the likely average expenditure per customer to see if the store's will generate sufficient turnover, given the likely competitive response to the store's opening. Further work may also be undertaken to assess the market's response to the retailer's presence and promotional activity (Davies and Rogers, 1984; Wrigley, 1988). Catchment is not only about the resident population, but about the location's accessibility and proximity to other attractions, such as railway or bus stations, that will generate passing consumer traffic.

Type of goods

Different locations suit different kinds of goods and shopping needs or habits. Think about the difference between convenience and shopping goods, for instance (defined at pp. 266–7). Convenience goods need to be readily available, geographically close so people can buy almost at whim, whereas shopping goods involve a more deliberate purchasing decision and the consumer is more prepared to travel and invest time and money. Convenience goods, therefore, favour locations with a nearby, dense catchment area or at least a lot of passing, impluse-buying traffic, and shopping goods can be a little more remote, providing that there is the space to present an extensive range of goods for the customer to compare and choose from.

McGoldrick (1990) classifies the factors affecting location decisions as population, accessibility, competition and costs. Figure 13.3 gives examples of some of the factors that might be considered within each category. This figure also outlines the three main stages in an ideal retail-location strategy (Bowlby *et al*, 1984).

Location decision-making process

The location decision-making process consists of three stages.

Search for good locations. At the broadest level, the retailer has to decide which regions, cities or towns to locate in. *Spatial marketing* helps to profile defined geographic areas by socioeconomic categories. It can also establish retail spend potential, thus linking in to minimum threshold requirements, that is, the lowest forecast spend level that makes further investigation worth while.

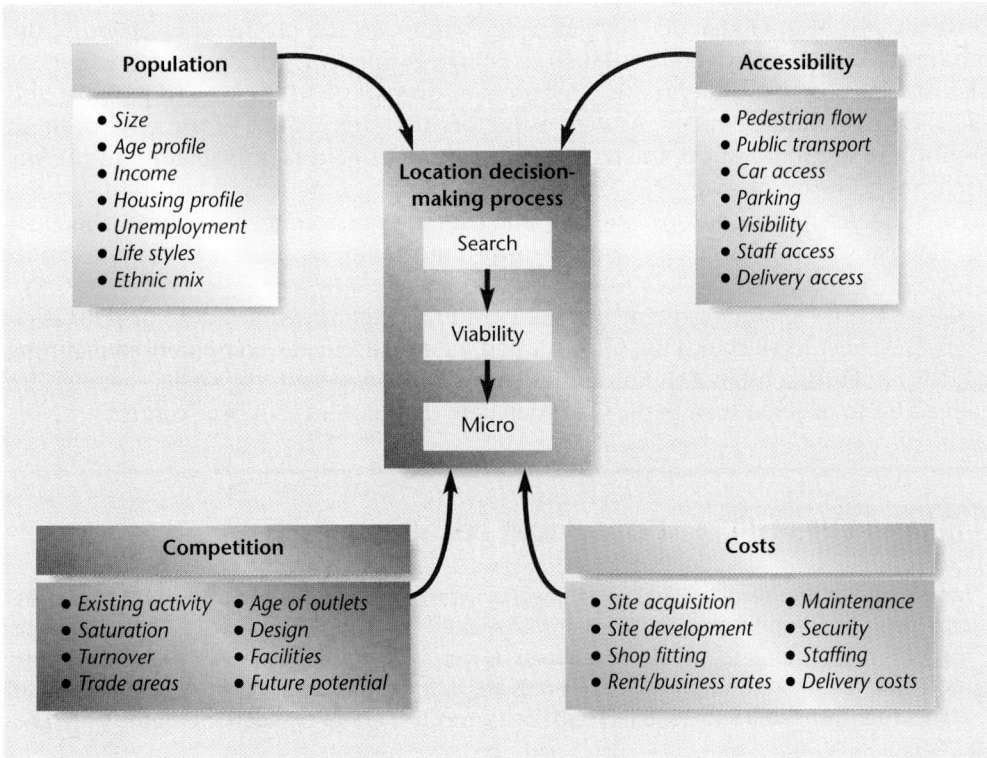

FIGURE 13.3

Factors influencing the location decision-making process

> **Example** Many retailers now use GIS (geographic information systems) to assess potential locations. A GIS includes maps and geodemographic data (*see* pp. 185 *et seq.*) from other commercial databases. The retailer can add any data of its own about its stores, customers and competitors. Companies like Vauxhall Motors can then use it to evaluate catchment areas (for instance the neighbourhood profile of customers, the size of the catchment area to see how dealerships are spread, and to plan new outlets). The GIS can thus profile a geographic area to assess a potential new store location by predicting turnover, profitability and even the amount of store traffic that it would take from existing stores. Supermarket chain Safeway spent around £500 000 developing a GIS that includes loyalty-card data, store data, competitor data and the National Shoppers' Survey data as well as the MOSAIC geodemographic package. This helps Safeway to build up profiles of various customer types and their shopping habits, and to assess the proportion of local grocery spend that a new store would attract, taking into account drive times (i.e. how long shoppers are pre-pared to take travelling to and from supermarkets), its own existing stores and those of its competitors. It also assesses the attractiveness of local stores in terms of the fascia, store format, parking provision, whether there is a petrol station, in-store café or dry cleaner etc. Once a store is up and running, the GIS can help answer questions such as 'What if the competitor builds a new store nearby?' or 'How much more turnover would we generate if we extended our existing store?' (Bowie and Wilcox, 1999).

Assessment of viability. Narrowing down a little, the retailer focuses on the *viability* of a specific site. At this stage, store turnover forecasting using multiple regression techniques may be implemented. This will take into account determinants of sales levels and it is especially important where location is seen as a particularly critical factor. It focuses on the type of customers, public transport and proximity to competitors, among many other things. Being close to competitors may be a good or a bad thing. Generally, for convenience goods it is not good, but with a shopping product, the closeness may encourage consumers to visit both stores and make comparisons and the 'better' retailer will win.

Assessment of micro factors. At the most detailed level, the retailer fine tunes by looking at the impact of micro factors, such as pedestrian flows, the profile of local shops, the proximity of other key retailers (such as Marks & Spencer, which always generates plenty of passing consumer traffic), nearness of car parks and the ease of parking, and the site's overall appearance. As well as factors that are related to the environment around the site in question, the retailer will consider micro factors relating to the site itself, such as ease of access for loading and unloading, the length and terms of the lease or ownership conditions, and any planning permission needed. The challenge is to establish which micro factors are the most important.

Given the level of investment involved, and the high costs of failure or poor decisions, the larger retail chains use sophisticated, often tailormade, computerised planning models rather than rules of thumb or hunches. At the very least, the smaller retailer can gain access to material such as the CACI database that profiles shopping centres.

MARKETING IN ACTION   **Forecourt retailing**

Many petrol stations are located near residential areas or on main roads and this makes them attractive sites for convenience stores to serve local residents as well as motorists. These forecourt convenience stores are bigger (between 1000 and 3000 m²) and have a much wider range of goods on offer than the usual small petrol station shop. Most of the major oil companies are working in conjunction with grocery retailers to develop the convenience store concept. Esso, for instance, has 1980 branded shops, the largest number in UK

Continued

forecourt retailing, and is working with Tesco to open 10 Tesco Express stores at its petrol stations with a view to further expansion later. Total has 568 branded stores, with 188 of them under the Allday's convenience store name. Elf is working with Somerfield, and BP has alliances with Safeway and Budgens. Both Total and Texaco are also developing a much broader approach to retailing on their sites. Texaco, for example, is working with McDonald's, Dunkin' Donuts and Pizza Hut, among others, and Total with Sketchley, Dunkin' Donuts and Blockbuster Video.

Shell has the largest petrol-based convenience chain with 900 Select stores, developed without the involvement of a major retailer. It has one stand-alone Select store (without any petrol retailing attached) in central London and 29 more globally. Of Shell's £350mn planned investment, £140mn is going into Select stores. Shell has a 10 per cent share of the forecourt convenience sector, which is worth over £2.8bn per year (compared with £12.4bn for the whole convenience sector). Convenience stores are important to petrol stations not only because they make more efficient and cost effective use of sites, but also because the profit margins on petrol are so low in the UK. Petrol stations lost money when the supermarket chains started selling cheap petrol and

began something of a price war. Petrol stations are thus having to lure motorists in with cheap petrol and then make higher profit margins on 'top-up' shopping such as milk and bread, as well as impulse purchases of snacks, drinks and confectionery. For some petrol stations, non-petrol purchases account for over 60 per cent of their turnover.

Technological developments could help to keep the motorist out of the forecourt store altogether. Sainsbury's and Tesco have petrol-pump technology that allows the motorist to swipe a credit card through a reader on the pump to pay and get a receipt without having to enter the shop. This speeds up the transaction for the customer, potentially reduces staffing at the cash desk, and keeps the flow of cars past the pumps moving more quickly. It does, however, encourage the motorist just to 'pay and go' without any temptation of an impulse buy. Thus the COPOS (Customer Operated Point of Sale) system has been developed further to allow videos and other displays to appear on a screen at the pump. This could draw customers towards the shop or even allow them to order from the screen, add the cost to the petrol bill, and then wait for a member of staff could bring the goods out to the car.

Sources: Conley (1998a, 1998b); Linnell (1999); Reed (1999).

Classification of locations

In general terms, available locations can be classified into three broad areas.

City centre. In the centre of a town or city, the focus is on offices, shopping and public transport termini. There are usually designated retailing zones within such centres. Famous shopping areas in Europe include Oxford Street in London, the Kurfurstendamm in Berlin and Grafton Street in Dublin. City centres attract the largest stores, and often feature shopping malls and pedestrian precincts, covered or open. The presence of a number of big-name retailers does generate extra consumer traffic, thus they act as magnets for smaller retailers. Such sites are, however, expensive to occupy and maintain, and are dominated by products such as clothing, footwear, jewellery and financial services.

Suburban. In suburban locations, neighbourhood corner shops or small shopping parades are often found at road intersections or on the edges of large housing estates. They largely serve local needs for convenience goods and, to a lesser extent, shopping goods, through shops of about 200 m². Some shopping parades are owned and operated by local authorities which rent the shops to the retailers, others are owned by property companies.

Out of town. First developed in the UK in the 1970s, out of town sites are located at the edges of towns and cities, often next to major roads or at the intersections of major trunk routes. A site can either be dedicated to one massive superstore, such as a supermarket, or be home to a small range of purpose-built stores (say up to 10). The kinds of products sold on out of town sites are typically groceries, furniture, electrical goods and DIY, retailed through well-known supermarkets and discount multiples. The sites are easily accessible and, compared with city centre stores, have lower rents and local authority rates. Most large towns and cities now have them.

The 1980s saw the logical extension of out of town sites into retail parks, with much larger numbers of free-standing stores of 2500 m^2 or more. Under cover, retail parks have developed along the US model into very large complexes indeed. Out of town shopping malls, such as the Metro Centre at Gateshead and Meadowhall, just off the M1 near Sheffield, have taken the traditional mix and range of stores out of the city centre, and reproduced it on a much bigger scale on a purpose-built site with easy access. The Metro Centre, for example, on two storeys, provides nearly 150 000 m^2 of retail space, with the additional bonus of 10 000 car parking spaces (which can all be occupied at peak times near Christmas) and a whole range of leisure activities, such as a multiscreen cinema and a bowling alley (*see also* Case study 13.1 at the end of this chapter).

Product range

Breadth and depth of product range stocked were mentioned earlier (*see* p. 518) as a means of classifying retailers. Speciality stores and niche retailers, such as Tie Rack, concentrate on a few product lines, stocked in considerable depth. Supermarkets and department stores carry a wide product mix. Migros, for example, a Swiss co-operative group, not only retails food but stocks some 22 000 non-food items. Migros is also into travel, printing, publishing, oil, insurance and many other products and services. It is difficult, however, to keep a broad-ranging product mix and substantial product-line depth without investing in large quantities of stock and all the associated costs that go with that.

Product assortment

Most retailers, therefore, will have to compromise, considering product assortment in terms of purpose, status and completeness. *Purpose* means the fit between customer needs and the retailer's revenue requirements. *Status* refers to the relative importance of different products or depths of line. Thus the retailer will define the prime product and then those that are accessories or add-ons to that. The prime product in a petrol station, for example, is obviously petrol, while food and snacks are desirable, but of secondary importance. That last example links into *completeness*, which is the need to meet customer expectations. Thus motorists expect to be able to buy sweets or cigarettes in a petrol station, and feel that they are receiving inferior service if those kinds of goods are not available.

Product type

The type of products stocked is also important. The retailer may wish to fill only a particular quality niche, or may select a range of products covering different quality levels and price points to fulfil the needs of a wider range of customers. Whether to occupy a niche or to develop a wider specialism is an important decision. If the niche is tightly defined with a very deep assortment, then the retailer will have to hold a large quantity of slow moving stock, tying up working capital and storage space. Going for a broader, shallower mix might help things to move a little more quickly. Figure 13.4 summarises various influences on product assortment strategy.

Some retailers do not specialise at all, but take a *scrambled* merchandising approach, by buying in fast moving items that sell in volume but are not necessarily related. This achieves a number of things:

1 *It assists impulse purchases.* As with discount clubs (mentioned at p. 528), consumers come in to see what there is and buy while it is still available.
2 *It can generate more sales and profit.* A careful selection of seasonal items for Christmas that are outside the normal product mix in a convenience store can lead to extra sales.

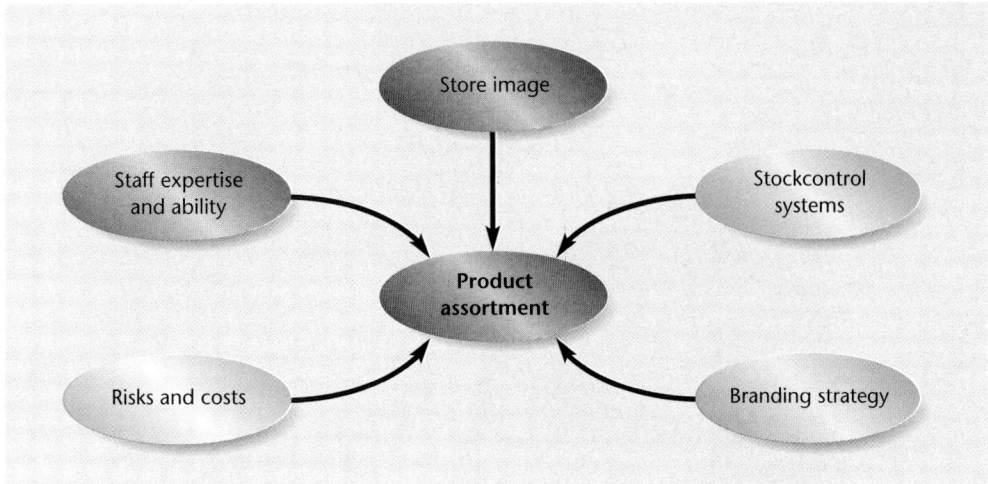

FIGURE 13.4

Factors influencing
product assortment
strategy

3 *It can improve convenience.* The petrol stations, for example, through developing the range of merchandise and services offered in the forecourt shop, have effectively created one-stop shops that can meet most impulse needs of the motorist and those who live close to the garage.

4 *It assists traffic generation.* A wider mix of merchandise attracts a wider mix of customer, certainly for convenience goods.

The retailer does, however, run the risk of losing its distinct image in the mind of the customer. It is also possible to get it wrong, since widening the product mix can project the retailer into unrelated, unknown areas away from its core business, for example a decision to stock CDs in garage forecourt shops, or the newsagent that stocks Christmas trees.

Walters and White (1987) argue that a wide range of issues should be allowed to influence assortment policy. These include careful research, planning and links with corporate strategy. All of this should be focused towards meeting the needs of the target market and is just as important as merchandise style and service.

Retail competitive positioning

Retailers do not operate in a vacuum and they do have to consider how they shape up against their perceived competitors, and how well they differentiate their offering. This clearly means looking at the market, especially at other retailers, in terms of the criteria that distinguish one retailer from another in the customer's mind. This analysis reflects the totality of the offer, in terms of merchandising, brand image, products, pricing, atmosphere and image, and service quality (Davies and Brooks, 1989). An independent clothing retailer specialising in designer labels, for example, will position itself as an exclusive, refined, high-priced outlet, with a high level of personal service. In contrast, a high street multiple targeting the teenage market might position itself as a value for money, lively, vibrant outlet that keeps up with fashion trends. In general, the kind of philosophy applied to product positioning, discussed at pp. 318 *et seq.*, applies equally to retail positioning, although the contributing factors will differ.

Store image and atmosphere

The image and atmosphere of a store are the sum of the physical elements of interior and exterior design, and the layout and displays that create an environment and ambience that consumers find attractive.

Exterior factors that influence perceptions of **store image** include the shop front itself, window displays, the entrance and perhaps even ease of access (traffic congest-

NAUGHTY

NEW LOOK

New Look has created an image
and atmosphere to appeal to the
teenage market.

Source: Advertising Agencies.

ion in the car park, or closeness to car park). The overall impression that these make is
especially important to new customers, who may feel either that the store is exciting
and welcoming and thus worth a visit, or that it is dirty, dingy and worth walking
past. A store may, of course, suffer from influences outside its control, such as the
seediness or cleanliness of the surrounding area and nearby retailers, which all affect a
buyer's mood and perception.

Interior factors contributing to **atmosphere** include lighting, wall and floor cover-
ings and fixtures and fittings, and the effects are very much linked to the senses.

Sight

Sight is stimulated by the use of colour, for example. For a restaurant, red and yellow
attract customers and make them feel hungrier and eat faster. Lighting too affects
mood and perceptions of products and can help to highlight particular items or
ranges or draw customers' attention to the remoter parts of the shop. The general look
of a store as customers walk through the door can either lift their spirits and make
them want to go in and browse, or underwhelm them to the point where they walk
straight out again or only focus functionally on a specific item of interest.

Sound

Total silence is all too rare in retail settings. Most have some sort of music playing,
even if the customer does not consciously notice it. Whether it is pop, middle of the
road, classical or muzak will depend on the retailer's assessment of the preferences of
the target market and the image that is to be projected. Soft music may relax shoppers
and make them stay in the store longer, while loud music can reinforce a stimulating,
vibrant atmosphere that deliberately sets out to excite the customer.

Scent

Smells are very important. Supermarkets make sure that the cooking smells from the in-store bakery are filtered back into the store so that customers can enjoy the smell of fresh bread, start feeling hungry and buy more food. Department stores often site the cosmetics counters near the main entrance so that the customer is hit with an exotic blend of upmarket perfume smells. This can be very pleasant, but they need to be careful that the smell isn't so overpowering that it overloads the senses and makes customers feel nauseous! Some smells communicate cleanliness (pine, for example), some communicate luxury (wood or leather, for example), while others are pleasantly stimulating (coffee and bread, for example). All, however, can be used to create and fix a particular impression in the consumer's mind.

Other sensory experiences

As well as the factors already mentioned, the consumer does have other, largely tactile, experiences in the retail setting. The feeling of walking on carpet rather than lino, the look and feel of natural wood fittings and the texture and feel of fabrics around the store, for example, again enhance or detract from the perceived image of the store. Finally, the retailer must bear in mind the comfort of the customer and how that is affected by the temperature of the store. If it is too hot or too cold, the customer will not feel at ease and will leave the premises more quickly.

It is hard to separate any of these factors, since the consumer tends to experience them as an integrated whole. The consumer will, however, certainly notice if one factor is out of keeping with the rest. The atmosphere thus created can be enhanced by the customer's feeling of the 'user friendliness' of the store. The provision of spacious, cool changing rooms with adequate lighting and mirrors for trying on clothes, easy access for disabled people, enough room to move between the displays without feeling cramped or lost, displays that make it easy to see the goods properly and to their best advantage, and fast, efficient packing and payment handling all help to make the customer feel more relaxed, and thus willing to spend more time, and money, in the store.

Other shoppers

A less controllable factor that can have a profound effect on a customer's behaviour is the degree of crowding in a store. Shoppers walking past an upmarket fashion boutique might be tempted to go in but, if there is no other customer inside, may feel self-conscious, not wanting to be the focus of the sales assistants' attention. Similarly, an empty restaurant might put potential customers off, either because they feel self-conscious about going in, or because they think that the emptiness is a reflection of the quality of the food. The only kind of store that might possibly benefit from lack of crowds is a supermarket, because of its more impersonal atmosphere. There is something inherently satisfying about having a branch of Sainsbury's virtually to yourself and experiencing hassle-free shopping! At the other extreme, overcrowding is no more attractive. Customers cannot move freely or examine the merchandise properly and the queues at the checkouts get longer.

It is not only the number of other shoppers that matters. In some situations, the types of other shoppers affect the consumer. Some people would feel very awkward about going into a fashion store if they felt that they were very different from the shoppers already in there. Similarly, if a shopper was trying to decide whether to buy a particular item of clothing and saw someone old enough to be their grandmother and four sizes bigger choosing the same item, it could make them feel differently about the garment.

As a final thought, remember that store image is not simply a function of the atmosphere factors discussed in this section. It is also affected by additional services offered, merchandise, location, advertising and promotion, brands stocked and pricing. In other words, store atmosphere and store image are simply elements deep inside a detailed marketing mix that must hang together and be linked in with a strategically defined competitive position, as well as meeting the expectations of target customers.

Merchandising strategies

Store image and atmosphere are also affected by the retailer's approach to *layout* and *display*, which can influence both the customer's behaviour within the store and their perception of the retailer's positioning. They affect how people move around the store, which items attract their attention and their propensity to interact with the merchandise. Retailers might, however, be restrained in what they can do with layout and display by the kind of factors shown in Fig. 13.5.

Store layout

McGoldrick (1990) suggests that most store layouts conform to one of three broad types, or combine elements of them. The alternative layouts are shown in Fig. 13.6.

Grid pattern. The grid pattern is the kind of layout adopted by most supermarkets, with systematically arranged aisles. These tend to lead the shopper around the retail space along a largely predictable route that covers most of the store. Supermarkets try to prevent the shopper from taking short cuts by making sure that staple items, such as sugar, bread, milk etc., are placed well apart from each other and scattered around the store. Thus the shopper who only wants a few basic things still has to pass lots of tempting items that might just lead to a few extra, impulse purchases. Routine-response staple items are also piled high to reduce the frequency of shelf refilling, and are placed in narrow aisles to keep shoppers moving, since they do not need to browse around these goods. In contrast, wider aisles are used for the more exotic, less frequently purchased premium goods, such as ready meals, so that shoppers can move more slowly, have their attention captured and browse comfortably.

Grid layouts do make sure that the shopper covers as much of the store as possible, and they are easy and cheap to install and maintain. They can, however, be rather boring and regimental, giving the impression of 'functional' shopping. The shopper

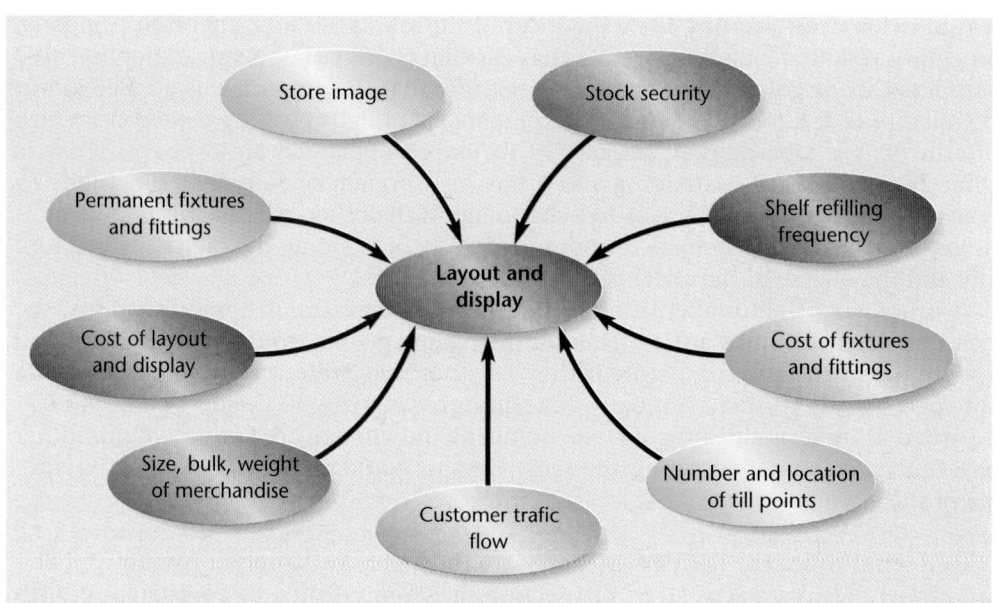

FIGURE 13.5

Factors influencing layout and display

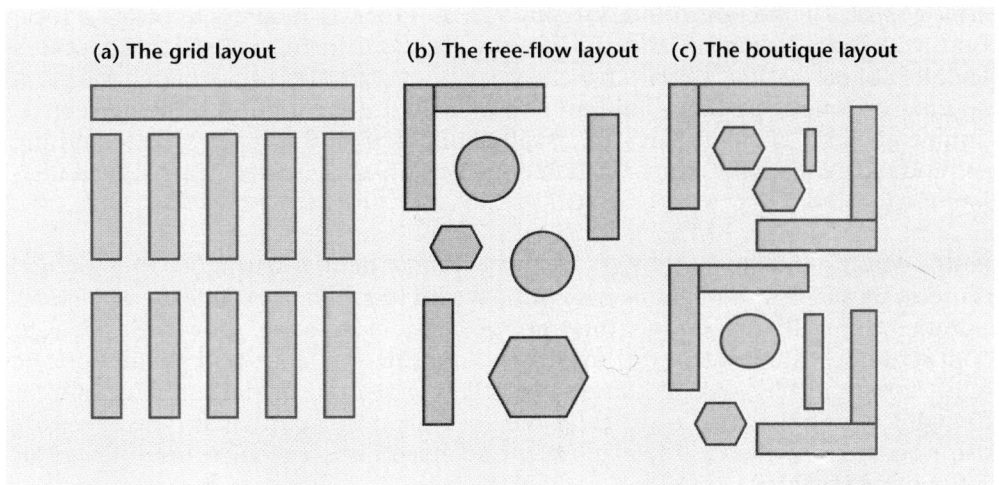

(a) The grid layout   **(b) The free-flow layout**   **(c) The boutique layout**

FIGURE 13.6

Alternative approaches to layout

might also be inclined to associate them with 'pile it high and sell it cheap' discount approaches to retailing, although the fixtures and fittings and the lighting used by some supermarket chains do give a better-quality feel.

Free flow. The free flow pattern is more irregular, involving a variety of different sizes, shapes and heights of fixtures and fittings. Shoppers are free to take any route around the store, and can thus either browse around everything in any order they choose, or cut through directly to one display at the back of the store if they prefer. Fashion retailers and others trying to achieve a strong visual 'look' that stimulates customers but encourages them to take their time browsing use this kind of layout. It can, however, be expensive to set up and maintain, and it does not use the available floor space as efficiently as a grid layout.

Boutique. Whereas in a free flow layout the customer perceives the selling area as essentially a single space, in a boutique layout the perception is of a number of discrete, separate spaces. This might be particularly useful in a large selling space, such as a department store, where very different departments and concessionaires want to create their own unique and more intimate character.

Many stores combine elements of the three types of layout. A superstore might well use a grid layout for its groceries and other fast moving lines, but use a free flow approach for clothing, books or videos, for example. Similarly, a variety store such as Boots will vary its approach. Boots uses a supermarket-style grid layout for fast-moving, staple items such as tights, shampoos, soaps and sticking plasters, but a free flow approach for gift-orientated toiletries, toys and household goods. In some larger stores, the gift department, for example, might even be a boutique layout.

Display

Whatever the type of layout adopted, the retailer also has to think about the way in which merchandise is displayed within it. Rosenbloom (1981) suggests five alternatives.

Open display. Open displays make the merchandise easily accessible to shoppers and encourage them to pick up and examine goods closely. Fashion stores in particular like to encourage such involvement, so that customers can feel the texture and quality of the fabric, can hold a garment up in front of themselves to check its length or whether it suits them, or can be encouraged to try it on.

Theme display. Themes are commonly used in all kinds of retailers to create a focal point to attract a customer's attention. Events such as Christmas, Easter and Mother's Day all provide natural themes for the display of gifts and other merchandise. A supermarket might perhaps build an end-of-aisle display around a theme such as Chinese cookery. These displays are usually temporary and thus provide something new and different for the regular customer to look at, as well as bringing related merchandise together.

Lifestyle display. Lifestyle displays try to create a more natural setting for the product, giving an idea of how it might be used or by whom, through the subtle use of pictures and other props. IKEA and other furniture retailers, for example, show their goods in room settings, with books in the bookcases, lamps on the tables and pictures on the walls. Fashion retailers also use life-style displays, perhaps using large photographs at the point of sale showing a particular type of person in a particular type of setting wearing a particular outfit. The mail-order catalogues have, of course, been doing this sort of thing for years.

Co-ordinated display. A co-ordinated display is similar to lifestyle and themed displays in that it brings together related goods. In a co-ordinated display, goods that are usually sold or used together are displayed together. Thus a women's clothing store might display co-ordinating jackets, skirts and trousers together, or include accessories in a clothing display. Even supermarkets might use co-ordination, for example by displaying marzipan, icing sugar, ready made icing, food colourings and edible cake decorations together near the flour, dried fruit and other home baking goods.

Classification dominance display. The aim of a classification dominance display is to suggest specialisation and expertise within a particular product group through the sheer choice of goods displayed. Thus a branch of W.H. Smith, for instance, might have a display of biros and fountain pens covering a wide range of prices, colours, designs and brands. Displays like this are meant to give the customer the impression that *this* is the only place to shop for these kinds of goods.

Technology

Technological advances have allowed retailers to improve the services that they offer their customers and to increase their productivity for a better competitive edge.

A slice of life, courtesy of IKEA.
Source: IKEA Ltd.

Barcode scanning not only helps to get customers through the checkout more quickly, but also streamlines stock management. Electronic point-of-sale (**EPOS**) systems can monitor exactly what products are being sold and how fast, and can trigger reordering or shelf replenishment through direct links, often to centrally located warehouses.

> **Example** Electrical retailer Curry's delivers small goods to stores in line with EPOS data. Orders for less frequently purchased, larger goods can be sent from the store to a central depot via computer, and then the goods are delivered direct to the customer. Such systems can cost upwards of £50 000, but are essential for giving the customers what they want and expect. Some supermarkets are currently experimenting with self-scanning systems, whereby the customer scans goods as they are put into the trolley. This means that when the customer gets to the checkout, the bill has already been calculated and thus just needs to be paid. This saves on both time and staffing costs.

More strategically, the information gained through EPOS about spending patterns, by brand and by retailer branch, can be used for negotiation with manufacturers or suppliers, or for planning store promotion.

Technology has also fundamentally changed the way in which consumers pay for their purchases. EFTPOS (electronic funds transfer at point of sale) systems have made the use of debit and credit cards very much easier and more acceptable to the retailer and customer alike. Sweeping a card through a reader and letting the till print out the cheque or voucher is much faster and much less prone to error than the old manual systems. For the retailer, it means shorter checkout queues and also faster cash flow, because the day's financial data are downloaded to the bank's computer overnight, instead of the retailer having to pay cheques and credit card slips into the bank manually and then waiting for them to go through the three-day clearing system.

Retailer own brands

There is a fine balance of negotiating power between retailers and suppliers. There are some manufacturer brands that the retailers cannot afford to miss out on, and some retail chains that the manufacturer brands cannot afford to be absent from. One tactic that the retailers have used to tip the balance in their favour a little more is the own brand. Over the last few years, certain supermarkets have been proactive in developing good-quality, value for money, own-brand products across all the main lines

> **Example** Own-label products represent nearly 40 per cent of grocery turnover on average. For some retailers, it is a higher percentage. ASDA, for instance, aims to increase its own-label share of turnover to 50 per cent, whereas other major retailers, such as Sainsbury's, are trying to cut back on own label because they feel that it reduces consumer choice too much. Own-label sales also vary by product. In the confectionery category, for instance, the average own-label share is just under 16 per cent, whereas for delicatessen products it is nearly 86 per cent and for bakery products 64 per cent (A.C. Nielsen, 1998). Fresh bread and bakery products were cited as the most popular own-brand products by 62 per cent of UK shoppers in a MORI poll that looked at consumer purchasing habits and attitudes to own-label products across Europe. Shoppers from the Netherlands buy most own-label products (55 per cent of their purchases), followed closely by the UK (52 per cent), and Italy came bottom of the league (14 per cent). This is not so surprising, given that 57 per cent of UK shoppers think that own labels are as good as the manufacturer brands, compared with only 32 per cent of Italians. The most important criteria for judging own labels were freshness, value for money and quality. Although almost 75 per cent of European shoppers think that own labels represent equal or better value than manufacturer brands, 34 per cent of UK shoppers feel that increased value for money would make own labels more attractive to them (*The Grocer*, 1999g).

they carry. In conjunction with that, they have rationalised the number of brands of any particular product that they stock, deleting the minor ones, so that they now have a major manufacturer brand, their own brand, and perhaps one minor brand of a product. The percentage of shelf space and the proportion of sales accounted for by the own brands have been steadily creeping upwards.

In clothing, most retailers are, and always have been, dominated by own brands, for example M&S, BhS, Principles etc. As discussed at p. 482 *et seq.*, this has also allowed the emergence of the kind of VMS in which the retailer is the dominant force, dictating quality, service levels, packaging and delivery from its suppliers.

Europeanisation and strategic alliances

Many retailers see international activity as an important part of their businesses and for some it represents a significant proportion of their total turnover. IKEA, for instance, generates 88 per cent of its sales outside Sweden, and Delhaize Le Lion, a Belgian food retailer, similarly generates just under 80 per cent of its turnover from international retailing, while for both Tengelmann and Ahold, the figure is between 50 and 60 per cent. The reasons for internationalisation are many and varied. Some are 'push' factors, arising from conditions within the domestic marketing environment that leave the retailer little choice but to internationalise, while others are 'pull' factors, favourable conditions within foreign markets that make them attractive to the retailer. Alexander (1995) neatly summarises the push and pull factors, as shown in Table 13.4.

As mentioned earlier, retailers also form looser international alliances, based on contracts and agreements rather than on degrees of total or co-ownership. These are often geared towards the streamlining of purchasing and logistics rather than direct involvement or interference in each other's retailing operations.

Buckley (1994) raises a few potential problems with alliances that do not involve ownership. While joint buying power may achieve lower prices, that power cannot be used most effectively unless the retailers can threaten the supplier with delisting in *all* the alliance members' stores. Such unanimity might be difficult to achieve. There might also be cultural differences. Products that might be popular and acceptable in one country might not be wanted in another, thus limiting the buying scope of the alliance. Finally, Buckley points out that membership of an alliance might hinder a retailer's ability to expand into its partners' domestic markets, or eventually to take over a partner.

TABLE 13.4

Push and pull factors influencing retail internationalisation

Push factors	Pull factors
Economic instability	Economic stability
Low market growth	High market growth
High operating costs	Underdeveloped retail structure
Poor operating environment	Favourable operating environment
Need for economies of scale	Large market
Hostile competition	Innovative retail culture
Mature domestic market	Investment potential
Small domestic market	Niche opportunities
Format saturation	Company-owned facilities/operations
Restrictive regulatory environment	Relaxed regulatory environment
Consumer credit restrictions	Positive social environment
Political instability	Political stability

Source: Based on Alexander (1995, p. 85).

MARKETING IN ACTION ## Wal-Mart and Wertkauf

Wal-Mart, the US discount retailer, has been very successful in transferring its retail concept and philosophy abroad. It has had to do this because the US discount market is saturated and Wal-Mart has achieved as much growth as it can in its home market, holding a 40 per cent share of the discount market. Wal-Mart has thus expanded into Canada, the Far East and South America very successfully and is the leading retailer in Canada and Mexico. It has around 3000 stores, 20 per cent of which are outside the USA. In 1998, Wal-Mart entered the German market, its first foray into Europe. Although the German grocery market is saturated, with low growth and an environment of restricted shopping hours and strong labour unions, Wal-Mart felt that Germany is at the heart of Europe and would provide a good opportunity to learn about European retailing and find other European targets.

Wal-Mart decided to use acquisition as the means of entering Europe, feeling that because there was already a very strong, competitive retail sector in Europe, starting from scratch would not be viable or even successful. Acquiring an existing company would give Wal-Mart the critical mass that it needed: staff, established stores, a known retail name in the market (the original name to be retained) and customers from day one. Germany provided an ideal takeover target for Wal-Mart in the Wertkauf (literally, 'value buy') chain of 21 stores with 4900 employees. Wertkauf's product range includes food (50–60 per cent of its product offering), consumer durables, clothing and office supplies. Wal-Mart was attracted to Wertkauf because of its large stores, locations, customer base and staff. Germany is not renowned for the quality of customer service offered by retailers, however, so Wal-Mart saw a real opportunity to improve Wertkauf's sales by improving service. This does present a difficult training and cultural task. Wal-Mart sent one US manager to each store to show how Wal-Mart does business and spread the customer service culture. It could also take some time to educate the German consumer about Wal-Mart's low-price, good value, customer service orientated strategy. Wal-Mart then acquired a further 74 stores from Interspar in Germany, which helped its international division to double its profits in 1998 to $551mn. By adding Interspar, Wal-Mart became the fourth largest hypermarket operator in Germany, with a 13 per cent market share and $3.1bn turnover. Wal-Mart was building up to 80 new stores globally in 1999, but noticeably not in Germany. As Troy (1999) points out, this suggests that any further expansion will, by choice, be via acquisition. Then again, it could simply be because the planning regime in Germany is so tight that it is almost impossible to build new hypermarkets.

Analysts do believe that the German market entry is just the start and many European retail chains are nervous in case Wal-Mart is looking at them. The company claims, however, that it is only looking to expand in markets that it is already in, like Germany, rather than looking for wider expansion across Europe. Nevertheless, the rumours have been flying. By May 1999, ASDA and Safeway in the UK, GIB in Belgium, Metro in Germany, Promodès, Carrefour and Casino in France, and even Toys 'Я' Us in Germany had all been discussed in the business press as potential takeover targets. In June 1999, one of the predictions proved correct. Wal-Mart announced its intention to enter the UK market by making a £6.7bn bid for supermarket chain ASDA. ASDA's culture of low prices and frequent price-orientated promotions fits well with that of Wal-Mart, and it will be interesting to see how the takeover works out and whether Wal-Mart's muscle will lead to an all-out grocery price war.

Sources: Buxton (1999c); *The Grocer* (1999c); Lisanti (1999); O'Connor (1998); Tomkins (1997a, 1997b); Troy (1999).

WHOLESALERS AND DISTRIBUTORS

The emphasis of the chapter now shifts up the distribution channel, away from the retailer to the wholesaler. As consumers, we already know a great deal about the structure of retailing and the variety of retailers that exist to serve our needs. We know much less, however, about the organisations that make sure that the retailers have access to the goods we want to buy. Wholesaling is just as complex a world as that of retailing, with as much variety in the sizes, structures and roles undertaken by its organisations. This section, therefore, will define the range of different types of wholesaler.

Full service wholesalers

As the name implies, full service wholesalers offer the fullest range of wholesaling services, from sourcing and bulk breaking to transportation to marketing and management advice. They are of particular value to the smaller manufacturer or retailer that does not have the necessary expertise to do many of these things for itself. Häagen Dazs, for example, used to deliver ice cream direct to independent retailers, but found that the minimum order quantity, or *drop*, required to make this viable was far too high for many small independents. It switched, therefore, to distribution through specialist frozen-food wholesalers so that shopkeepers could buy only one case at a time if they wanted.

Full service wholesale merchants may carry a wide range of product lines, or they might choose to focus on a few lines in depth, or they might be speciality wholesalers, such as the frozen-food specialists mentioned above. All of them, however, sell mainly to retailers. Full service wholesalers that sell to manufacturers or non-retailing organisations are called industrial distributors. Again, they might choose to carry a range of products or to specialise.

Example RS Components is an industrial distributor that relies on high service levels to sell a wide range of electrical components used by small manufacturers, repairers and prototype designers. The typical order size tends to be small, around £100, and a typical outlet could handle over 15 000 orders per day. The focus is on fast service and availability and the higher prices charged reflect the higher added value offered. By having over 50 000 product lines in stock and with a same-day delivery service, its customers do not need to carry extensive stocks themselves. Ordering is now becoming even easier, with the introduction of a CD-ROM as an alternative to the printed catalogue, and the development of on-line ordering facilities. Although 64 per cent of the company's annual sales of £662mn are generated in the UK, the fast service formula has been successful throughout Europe and more recently in Asia and Japan (http://www.RSComponents.com).

Limited service wholesalers

In contrast to the full service operators, limited service wholesalers only undertake clearly defined services, as a means of keeping their costs down. They may, for example, choose not to provide transport services or not to stock large quantities of products.

A typical kind of limited service wholesaler, commonly found across Europe, is the *cash and carry*. These wholesalers serve the needs of the very small retailer, which uses them rather as an individual consumer would use a supermarket. The retailer goes to the cash and carry, browses and selects the required goods, organises payment (either cash or on account), then takes the goods away with whatever transport they have organised for themselves. It is an efficient way for a small retailer to get access to a wide range of branded and other goods at reasonable prices. The cash and carry buys in bulk and then passes on some of the savings to its customers so that they can also make a return or keep their prices lower. Even so, it is still difficult for the small, independent retailer to compete with supermarkets that can sell items to the public at lower prices than the independent can even purchase them at. To try to help with this, many cash-and-carry operators produce own-brand goods, such as Bestway's 'Best-in' range and Nurdin and Peacock's 'Happy Shopper' label, and generic lines, such as Bestway's 'Save-on' products, that allow the small retailer to offer low prices while retaining its margins.

Example Booker is one of the UK's leading food wholesalers, servicing around 450 000 independent grocers, CTNs and multiples. Through a network of 178 branches, it is able to offer both cash-and-carry facilities and a full delivered wholesale service, thus providing the customer with a choice. It is strictly trade only, and even offers business support and advice to its customers. The delivered service is especially important to customers requiring chilled and frozen foods who do not have their own temperature-controlled transport (http://www.booker.com).

CHAPTER SUMMARY

Both retailers and wholesalers bridge the gap between manufacturer and end consumer, but whereas retailers tend to deal directly with end consumers, wholesalers tend to deal with retailers and other organisational buyers. Nevertheless, both can perform broadly similar functions and provide suitable premises for the sale of goods. Suitability can relate to the ambience of the place, services and the facilities provided for customers, as well as the synergy between different manufacturers' products.

Retailers can be classified according to a number of criteria: form of ownership (independents, corporate chains or contractual systems), level of service (full or limited), merchandise lines (breadth and depth) and operating methods (type of store, whether department store, supermarket, variety store or other). Non-store retailing, closely linked with direct marketing, has also become increasingly popular and widespread. It includes in-home selling, parties, mail-order operations, teleshopping and vending machines.

Retailers have particular strategic and operational marketing decisions to make on location, product range, positioning etc. Store image and atmosphere create the character of the store and are important in influencing the customer's perception of it. Both exterior factors (frontage, site, window displays etc.) and interior factors (affecting sight, sound, scent and other tactile experiences) make a contribution. The aim is to stimulate the customer, yet make them relaxed enough to want to stay in the store, browsing and buying. Layout and display can further affect the customer's behaviour. Technology also plays a significant role in the retailer's ability to service customers and to supply them with what they want when they want it. Retailer own brands can help to enhance the image of the store as well as giving the retailer extra bargaining power over suppliers. In addition, some larger retailers have begun to internationalise their operations in various ways. Some have acquired foreign retailers, some have entered into joint ventures and others have entered into looser contractual alliances, usually geared towards pooling purchasing power and offering mutual marketing support.

There are two broad types of wholesaler. Full service wholesalers offer a full range of services, including bulk breaking, transportation, delivery and management advice. Limited service wholesalers keep their costs down by providing only a few, clearly defined services for their customers. They will not usually, for example, undertake deliveries. Cash and carries are the commonest form, serving the needs of small retailers which use the cash and carry just as a consumer uses a supermarket. The wholesaler can buy in bulk and pass on some of the cost savings to the small retailer. Cash and carries also sell own-label goods to give the smaller retailer an opportunity to sell price-competitive goods and to give them a point of differentiation from the large supermarket chains.

Key words and phrases

Atmosphere	Depth of range	Out of town
Breadth of range	Discount clubs	Speciality stores
Catalogue showrooms	EPOS	Store image
Concessions	Franchising	Supermarkets
Convenience stores	Hypermarkets	Teleshopping
Corporate chain	Independent retail outlet	Variety stores
Department stores	Mail order	

QUESTIONS FOR REVIEW

13.1 Summarise the main functions of *wholesalers* and *retailers*.

13.2 Define *place utility* and *time utility*. Why do these concepts matter to customers?

13.3 What factors might be considered in providing an appropriate *selling environment*? How might the importance and the decisions made about these factors differ between retailers and wholesalers?

13.4 What are the predominant forms of *retail ownership*, and what are the main problems facing each of them?

13.5 What are the advantages and disadvantages of allowing *concessions* within a department store?

13.6 What is a *variety store* and what particular advantages does it offer to the shopper?

13.7 What advantages does *out of town retailing* offer to a speciality retailer and its customers?

13.8 Why is choice of *location* so important for a retailer, and what factors are likely to be taken into account when making a location decision?

13.9 What factors influence the *assortment of goods* stocked by a retailer?

13.10 What are the advantages for a retailer or wholesaler of *internationalisation* through strategic alliances? What are the potential drawbacks of such an approach?

QUESTIONS FOR DISCUSSION

13.1 Find examples of:
(a) full service;
(b) limited service; and
(c) self-service stores in the same retail sector.

What contribution does the level of service make to each store's marketing approaches?

13.2 What is a *category killer* and how might its activities affect other retailers? Give examples.

13.3 In what ways and to what extent do you think that *non-store retailing* poses a threat to conventional retailers?

13.4 Choose a retailer and analyse how its store atmosphere is made up.

13.5 Find examples of retailers that use:
(a) grid layout;
(b) free flow layout; and
(c) boutique layout.

Explain how each layout seems to affect shoppers' behaviour within those stores and what contribution it makes to the overall image and atmosphere of the stores.

CASE STUDY 13.1

A large expanse of Bluewater

Bluewater is Europe's largest retail development, covering 50 acres with 1.5 million ft^2 of selling space. It has a strategically chosen location, 40 km from the centre of London, close to the M25 with easy access for major roads in the area, 4 km from the planned Ebbsfleet station on the Channel Tunnel Link railway. Bluewater is valued at £1.2bn and was developed by Lend Lease, an Australian company. It opened in March 1999 with 320 shops, 13 000 parking spaces and a catchment area of nine million consumers spending £5.5bn annually between them. It is expected to attract 80 000 shoppers per day and its aim is to get 30 million visitors per year, with most shoppers coming from within an hour's driving time. To raise awareness of Bluewater's existence and to encourage people to visit it, £2.2mn was initially spent launching the shopping centre in its region with press, television and poster advertising. Its main target is upmarket, ABC1 consumers who are 'shopping centre averse', and thus they are called guests rather than customers and are being offered an 'experience' rather than a 'shopping trip'.

The 'experience' focus is emphasised by the provision of 200 000 ft^2 of leisure and catering as well as 1.5 million ft^2 of retail space. The development has seven lakes, food courts, entertainment areas, a 12-screen cinema and a 200-child crèche. The designers and owners have also tried to build in ways and facilities for making the shopper's visit less stressful. They paid careful attention to the road system and layout, created parking spaces that are 25 per cent bigger than normal, and built welcome lounges at the entrances.

Recruiting retailers begins well before a development like Bluewater is finished. Some 18 months before Bluewater opened, 65 per cent of the retail space had already been let, and seven months before opening it was 95 per cent let. Undoubtedly, the signing up of three key anchor stores – John Lewis, House of Fraser and Marks & Spencer (M&S) – helped to let the rest of the space. The anchor stores were considered important to this development and the developers targeted them first. Lend Lease went to John Lewis and asked the company what it would take to persuade it to open a store at Bluewater. John Lewis came back with a 'shopping list' and Lend Lease made sure that it met all those requirements. John Lewis has a 30 000 ft^2 store. The developers also persuaded M&S and House of Fraser to open 'power branches', i.e. those with a large amount of

investment and innovation. In line with putting the emphasis on 'experience' rather than 'shopping', M&S opened a 146 000 ft^2 store (its largest purpose-built store) with glass elevators and marble floors. A 20 000 ft^2 food hall has 90 employees and 8 ft wide pathways, designer shelving and lighting. The store also has a 140-seater café overlooking the lakes.

The shopping centre is triangular and targets different groups of customers on each side. The anchor stores are situated at the corners of the triangles. One side of the triangle between John Lewis's 330 000 ft^2 store and M&S has mid-range fashion, between M&S and House of Fraser are complementary outlets, and the third side between House of Fraser and John Lewis are designer label stores. Despite the fact that 200 of its 320 stores are flagship stores in their retail chains, Bluewater was not universally welcomed. Some were concerned about its effect on other retail centres such as Gravesend or Dartford. It is noticeable, however, that Bluewater does not have grocery shopping provision (other than the M&S food hall). This will mean, the local council claims, that people will still have to go into other centres for the weekly shop and quick convenience shopping trips.

Bluewater's nearest competitor centre is Lakeside, just 10 miles away and almost as big. By the end of April 1999, it was being reported that retailers that had stores at both shopping centres were doing better at Bluewater than at Lakeside. The Virgin Megastore at Bluewater, for example, was the most successful outlet for Virgin after its London Oxford Street store. All this was making Lakeside think about how it was marketing itself.

Sources: BCSC (1998); Buxton (1999a); Gannaway (1999b); *Marketing Week* (1999d); Parsley (1997, 1998).

Questions

1 What advantages do you think a development such as Bluewater offers (a) the retailers and (b) the consumers?

2 What locational factors will have been taken into account by the developers when choosing a site?

3 If you were the marketing manager at Lakeside, how might you respond to the competition provided by Bluewater?

4 Why do you think some individuals and organisations are concerned about developments such as this? Should these developments be stopped? Could they be stopped?

CASE STUDY 13.2

Amazonian adventures in e-tailing

Amazon, with its motto 'Work Hard, Have Fun and Make History', was set up in 1994 in Seattle as an on-line retailer (or e-tailer) specialising in selling books at up to 40 per cent discount from its http://www.amazon.com site. Since its launch, it has seen its business expand rapidly in line with the general growth in Internet usage and shopping. More than 150 million people around the world have access to the Internet. In the UK, about 20 per cent of the population used the Internet in 1998, and it was predicted that it would be over 30 per cent by the end of 1999. Amazon estimated that in the middle six months of 1998, one million British people made on-line purchases and 30 per cent of those sales were books. Such e-tailing is attractive not just because of the growth potential, but also because the Internet attracts high earning shoppers who can make impulse purchases from their home computers and from the systems at their place of work.

Amazon is in the right sort of market for Internet retailing. According to the Boston Consulting Group, the Internet is best suited for low weight, high value products that can be delivered through the post, such as CDs, videos and books. It is also likely that shoppers know what it is they are buying, whether it is a CD by a favourite artist or a book for mum's birthday, or at least can get a good idea from the website blurb (and many websites operate a generous returns policy, just in case). As Steve Johnson of Andersen Consulting said, 'You've read the review, you want it, you don't need to try it on' (as reported by Kuchinskas, 1998). With over 1.4 million titles on offer, the chances are that Amazon will certainly have anything the customer wants. Amazon argues that the reader reviews, author interviews and browsing system help customers locate what they want, even if they are not sure quite what it is, and more than compensate for the lack of personal selling.

From the start, Amazon has pursued a hybrid strategy, focusing on the one hand on customer service relationship management and on the other hand on the distribution systems and infrastructure. It is clear about the need to have fully integrated and computerised systems. It is linked with its suppliers so that it can deal smoothly and efficiently with its customers' orders. It also has systems designed for dealing

with small, occasional orders from millions of customers. Amazon works with book distributors to dispatch goods quickly without holding large stocks itself. Anything that is not held in stock is delivered to Amazon by the distributor within 24 hours and then repackaged along with the rest of the customer's order and sent out again as soon as possible. Nevertheless, to expand and improve the efficiency of its distribution network in the USA, Amazon was planning to open more distribution centres in 1999 and to increase the amount of stock held. It is not just looking at its distribution efficiency, however. It has introduced an Associates programme, now with 200 000 members, to increase its presence across the entire Web. Associates agree to put Amazon's logo and a link on their own websites and then earn commission on sales from customers 'entering' Amazon through those sites.

Amazon's business is expanding and its customer base now consists of some 6.5 million registered buyers. In April 1998, Amazon bought Bookpages, a UK based on-line bookseller, and used it as the basis for its UK operation, http://www.amazon.co.uk. This makes it quicker and easier for UK customers to order and receive their books. To ensure parity with amazon.com – which UK customers can still access, of course – the idea is that UK book buyers should be paying the same sort of prices as their US counterparts after delivery costs have been accounted for. US customers benefit too. A link between amazon.co.uk and amazon.com means that American customers can access 200 000 UK titles that they could not get in the USA. A similar site has been developed to serve German speaking customers, amazon.de. The UK and German sites between them accounted for 25 per cent of Amazon's $610mn sales in 1998.

Although Amazon has pioneered Internet bookselling, it does face fierce competition from the likes of barnesandnoble.com, borders.com and BOL.com. BOL.com (Books On-Line) admits that Amazon has set high standards in terms of discounts, delivery and choice, and has thus taken a great deal of care in designing systems and its website. To make its presence felt, BOL has entered into agreements with a number of on-line service providers, such as Lycos, EMAP, CompuServe and Freeserve, so that it is the featured bookseller on their sites. It also has an alliance with the Press Association so that people can follow up a news story by buying the relevant books. BOL launched in the UK in March 1999 with an advertising campaign worth over £2mn on print and poster advertising as well as on-line communication. In response to competitive threat, in May 1999, Amazon announced that it was cutting the prices of the bestsellers on the *New York Times* list by 50 per cent for an unspecified period. This is effectively giving cuts on 70 books per week.

Perhaps because of tough competition, Amazon has also started to diversify into different e-tail sectors. As well as selling CDs, gifts and videos, amazon.com is diversifying into Internet auctions. Any of its eight million registered auction customers can buy from and sell to each other. Amazon is acting as an 'infomediary' to link its customers together, effectively creating a horizontal distribution channel. The potential is also there for an infomediary to act as a gatekeeper, representing its customers' interests. If a significant number of its customers wanted to buy a specific product, the infomediary could ask

suppliers to bid for the business or undertake a supplier search, getting a better price through bulk buying. It can also sell access to targeted groups of its customers to interested suppliers. Amazon also bought a large stake in drugstore.com, an on-line retailer of prescription drugs, over the counter medicines and beauty products. This market is thought to be four times more valuable than the book market in the USA.

Sources: Ayres (1998, 1999); Carvajal (1999); Del Franco (1999); *Harvard Business Review* (1999); Kavanagh (1999a); Kavanagh and Dye (1998); Kuchinskas (1998); *Marketing* (1999); *Marketing Week* (1999b); McKenzie (1999); Milliot (1999a, 1999b); Mitchell (1999); http://www.amazon.co.uk; http://www.amazon.com.

Questions

1 What are the differences, from the shopper's point of view, between shopping at Amazon and shopping at a real bookshop?

2 To what extent are image, atmosphere and layout appropriate concepts for an on-line bookshop?

3 Can a high street retailer successfully offer on-line selling in parallel with its more traditional retailing? What factors would have to be considered in setting up the on-line operation?

References to Chapter 13

A.C. Nielsen (1998), *The British Shopper*, NTC Publications.

A.C. Nielsen (1999), *The Retail Pocket Book 1999*, NTC Publications.

Alberge, D. (1998), 'Vending Machines Bring Passengers to Book', *The Times*, 11 July, p. 5.

Alexander, N. (1995), 'Internationalisation: Interpreting the Motives', in P. McGoldrick and G. Davies (eds.), *International Retailing: Trends and Strategies*, Pitman Publishing.

Anderson, C. H. (1993), *Retailing*, West.

Ayres, C. (1998), 'Amazon Looks to Book its Place in the Consciousness of British Readers', *The Times*, 20 October, p. 33.

Ayres, C. (1999), 'Will the Net See the End of the Weekend Shopping Trip?', *The Times*, 2 January, pp. 24–5.

BCSC (1998), 'Bluewater – an Impression', *Beyond the Horizon*, British Council of Shopping Centres, London.

Bowie, S. and Wilcox, I. (1999), 'Location, Location, Location', *Database Marketing*, February, pp. 38–41.

Bowlby, S. *et al.* (1984), 'Store Location: Problems and Methods 1', *Retail and Distribution Management*, 12(5), pp. 31–3.

Brunfaut, O. and Meran, J. (1999), 'Coming Over All Picky', *The Grocer*, 13 February, p. 50.

Buckley, N. (1994), 'Baked Beans Across Europe', *Financial Times*, 14 April, p. 19.

Buxton, P. (1999a), 'Bluewater Experience', *Marketing Week*, 11 February, pp. 34–5.

Buxton, P. (1999b), 'Manchester Utd to Open Retail Outlets', *Marketing Week*, 29 April, p. 7.

Buxton, P. (1999c), 'How the Wal-Mart Deal will boost ASDA', *Marketing Week*, 17 June, p. 19.

Carvajal, D. (1999), 'Three Online Book Retailers Cut Prices on Best Sellers', *New York Times*, 18 May, http://www.nytimes.com.

Conley, C. (1998a), 'BP Taps into Retail Seam to Fuel Profit', *Marketing Week*, 12 February, pp. 20–21.

Conley, C. (1998b), 'Shell UK Launches Standalone Store', *Marketing Week*, 30 April, p. 5.

Cook, R. (1998), 'Carrefour Adds Rival Store to Shopping Basket', *The European*, 7–13 September, p. 21.

Cunningham, S. (1998), 'Shop Till You're Top', *The Times*, 21 November, p. 30.

Darby, I. (1999), 'Otto Versand Builds UK Base in Freemans Deal', *Marketing*, 15 April, p. 15.

Davidson, H. (1993), 'Bubbling Benetton Beats Recession', *Sunday Times*, 4 April, pp. 3–11.

Davies, G. (1992), 'Positioning, Image and the Marketing of Multiple Retailers', *International Review of Retail Distribution and Consumer Research*, 2(1), p. 13.

Davies, R. L. and Rogers, D. S. (1984), *Store Location and Store Assessment Research*, John Wiley.

Del Franco, M. (1999), 'Amazon.com Expansion Continues', *Catalog Age*, April, p. 12.

The Economist (1998), 'Knickers to the Market', *The Economist*, 28 February, pp. 68–9.

Edwards, P. (1999), 'Computer Power Play', *Marketing Week*, 15 April, pp. 37–8.

Euromonitor (1998), *European Marketing Data and Statistics 1998*, Euromonitor, 33rd edn.

Gannaway, B. (1999a), 'Desert Bloom', *The Grocer*, 3 April, pp. 24–6.

Gannaway, B. (1999b), 'Bluewater Horizons', *The Grocer*, 24 April, pp. 40–3.

Gilbert, F. (1998), 'Shift, Command, Read', *The Times*, 12 December, *Metro* Supplement, p. 17.

The Grocer (1998), 'Trading Up – but Watching the Price', *The Grocer*, 25 April, p. 50.

The Grocer (1999a), 'Leclerc and Système U Get Together', *The Grocer*, 30 January, p. 23.

The Grocer (1999b), 'Londis Gearing Up for Expansion into North', *The Grocer*, 13 February, p. 6.

The Grocer (1999c), 'Wal-Mart's New Record', *The Grocer*, 20 February, p. 5.

The Grocer (1999d), 'Poor Service Levels Come under Attack', *The Grocer*, 20 February, p. 8.

The Grocer (1999e), 'Discounters Set to Invade Ireland', *The Grocer*, 20 March, p. 5.

The Grocer (1999f), 'Irish Plan Crackdown on Major Superstores', *The Grocer*, 24 April, p. 11.

The Grocer (1999g), 'The Bigger Picture', *The Grocer*, 24 April, p. 53.

Harvard Business Review (1999), 'Whither Amazon.com?', *Harvard Business Review*, March/April, p. 141.

Hogarth-Scott, S. and Parkinson, S. P. (1994), 'The New Food Discounters: Are They a Threat to the Major Multiples?', *International Journal of Retail and Distribution Management*, 22(1), pp. 20–8.

Howe, W. S. (1992), *Retailing Management*, MacMillan.

Hunt, J. (1998), 'Heijn Works to Fix New Concept', *The Grocer*, 12 September, p. 15.

Hunt, J. (1999), 'Going into Orbit', *The Grocer*, 9 January, p. 32.

Hurren, T. (1999), 'Masters of the Craft', *The Grocer*, 20 March, pp. 44–6.

Jardine, A. (1999), 'HMV Delivers Via Web', *Marketing*, 11 February, p. 16.

Kavanagh, M. (1999a), 'Tangled in the Net', *Marketing Week*, 28 January, pp. 53–5.

Kavanagh, M. (1999b), 'B&Q Plans e-commerce Website', *Marketing Week*, 25 February, p. 40.

Kavanagh, M. and Dye, P. (1998), 'Amazon Launches UK Incarnation', *Marketing Week*, 22 October, p. 42.

Kuchinskas, S. (1998), 'The e-commerce Cometh', *Mediaweek*, 21 September, pp. IQ8–IQ12.

Liebeck, L. (1998), 'A Venerable Concept now Vulnerable', *Discount Store News*, 14 December, pp. 60–4.

Linnell, M. (1999), 'Prime Time at the Pumps', *The Grocer*, 6 February, pp. 34–6.

Lisanti, T. (1999), 'Europe's Abuzz over Wal-Mart', *Discount Store News*, 3 May, p. 11.

Lynn, M. (1995), 'Where Now, Cash Cow?', *Management Today*, March, pp. 46–50.

Marketing (1997), 'New Channel to Market', *Marketing*, 19 June, pp. 10–11.

Marketing (1999), 'BOL Push for e-books', *Marketing*, 11 March, p. 9.

Marketing Week (1999a), 'JWT Wins £2m Netto Supermarket Account', *Marketing Week*, 25 February, p. 12.

Marketing Week (1999b), 'Amazon Lures AA Marketer for Top UK Role', *Marketing Week*, 18 March, p. 6.

Marketing Week (1999c), 'Liberty Targets the High Street with Concessions', *Marketing Week*, 25 March, p. 7.

Marketing Week (1999d), 'Lakeside Axes EURO RSCG to Combat Bluewater Threat', *Marketing Week*, 29 April, p. 13.

McGoldrick, P. (1990), *Retail Marketing*, McGraw-Hill.

McKenzie, A. (1999), 'Aoun Tales the BOL by the Horns', *Marketing Week*, 25 March, p. 38.

Miller, P. (1999), 'Following Otto's Lead', *Catalog Age*, 15 March, p. 10.

Milliot, J. (1999a), 'Amazon.com Eyeing Distribution Improvements', *Publishers Weekly*, March 22, p. 12.

Milliot, J. (1999b), 'Amazon.com's Sales and Losses Soar in 1998', *Publishers Weekly*, 1 February, p. 5.

Mitchell, A. (1999), 'Online Markets Could See Brands Lose Control', *Marketing Week*, 15 April, p. 24.

Murphy, C. (1999), 'Are We Being Served by Electrical Stores?', *Marketing*, 18 March, p. 17.

O'Connor, R. (1998), 'Target Europe: Wal-Mart Sets up a Beachhead in Germany', *Chain Store Age*, March, pp. 55–60.

Parsley, D. (1997), 'At the Heart of a Region's Rebirth', *Financial Times*, 20 November, p. 10.

Parsley, D. (1998), 'Shopping Mall Fund Launched', *Sunday Times*, 6 September, p. 3.3.

Rawsthorn, A. (1999), 'Online Fashion Retailer Sets European Start Up Record', *Financial Times*, 10 May, p. 25.

Reed, D. (1999), 'Fuel Injection', *Marketing Week*, 4 February, pp. 37–42.

Rice, S. (1995), 'The Independents' Lot', *Menswear*, 7 December.

Robinson, P. (1999), 'Economical with the Facts', *The Grocer*, 16 January, pp. 32–4.

Rosenbloom, B. (1981), *Retail Marketing*, Random House.

Tomkins (1997a), 'Wal-Mart Goes Shopping in Europe', *Financial Times*, 20 December, p. 15.

Tomkins, R. (1997b), 'Wal-Mart Eyes Acquisitions in Europe, Japan', *Financial Times*, 23 December, p. 21.

Troy, M. (1999), 'Wal-Mart Germany Beefs up', *Discount Store News*, 4 January, pp. 1, 86.

URPI (1988), *List of UK Hypermarkets and Superstores*, Unit for Retail Planning Information.

Voyce, M. (1998), 'Woollies Plays For Out of Town Sites', *Retail Week*, 18 December, p. 3.

Walters, D. and White, D. (1987), *Retail Marketing Management*, MacMillan.

Wills, K. (1998), 'Look Who's Coming', *Retail Week*, 4 December, p. 8.

Wrigley, N. (1988), *Store Choice, Store Location and Market Analysis*, Routledge.

Yeung, R. (1999), 'Let's Have a Smile', *The Grocer*, 9 January, pp. 34–5.

EXECUTIVE INTERVIEW

Lofthouse of Fleetwood

Interview with
Tony Lofthouse and Duncan Lofthouse, Joint Managing Directors
Rien van Ruremonde, Managing Director, Nedan Zoetwaren BV

As we saw in Case Study 2.2, Lofthouse of Fleetwood manufactures the confectionery/medicinal sweet Fisherman's Friend, but contracts out its marketing to Impex and its distribution to independent distributors. For this interview, we spoke to Tony and Duncan Lofthouse, joint managing directors of Lofthouse of Fleetwood to explore the reasons behind their choice of distributors and then to Rien van Ruremonde, the managing director of Fisherman's Friend's Dutch distributor to discover more about his company's role.

Impex is heavily involved in appointing distributors. It selects and interviews up to six candidate distributor companies, undertaking detailed SWOT analyses on their potential, and it then makes a recommendation to Lofthouse of Fleetwood about which one would be the ideal partner in a particular market. Lofthouse of Fleetwood respects Impex's decision and almost invariably accepts it. The quality of those recommendations is reflected in the fact that over 25 years, only 5 out of 100 distributors have had to be changed. Most of those changes have arisen because the distributor has not agreed with what Lofthouse of Fleetwood wanted it to do in a market, for example not being willing to make an effort to expand the brand's sales significantly.

Among the criteria for selecting a distributor, Lofthouse of Fleetwood includes the following:

- *The products it handles*: a distributor should be selling complementary lines and have experience and suitable contacts in relevant product markets.
- *Its relationship with the competition*: a distributor should not be handling direct competitors' products (and if it was, there would probably be a clause in its contract preventing it from handling Fisherman's Friends); Lofthouse of Fleetwood wants exclusivity.
- *Its structure*: the number of sales representatives and their coverage of the market
- *Its size*: Lofthouse wants a distributor to be small enough for Fisherman's Friend to have an important role and an adequate share of the distributor's management time and attention. The company prefers to be a big fish in a smaller pool. This needs to be balanced, however, against the need to have a distributor big enough to have the right contacts and to achieve the objectives of the product in its market.

- *Its financial status*: the distributor needs to be financially stable and secure and Lofthouse of Fleetwood is looking for a long-term relationship.
- *Its culture*: because Lofthouse of Fleetwood is looking for a long-term relationship, it is important that a distributor has a similar culture and ethos. The company often finds that because it is a family business, it works well with distributors that are also family businesses.

One distributor that has had a long standing and successful relationship with Lofthouse of Fleetwood is its Dutch distributor, Nedan Zoetwaren BV. Its profile certainly fits the criteria above. The company is privately owned and has been in business for over 40 years. It distributes confectionery into the Dutch market and started with Stimorol chewing gum, imported from Denmark. Fisherman's Friend was taken into the portfolio in 1974. The company employs 45 people, 24 of whom are involved on a day to day basis in sales. Four people are involved in account management, and then there are two well established sales forces; 11 people work in the sales force covering impulse outlets (for example petrol stations and convenience stores) and 9 in the sales force covering the grocery trade. The company acts as a distributor representing Wrigley's chewing gum and Cadbury's chocolate as well as Fisherman's Friend, but it also manufactures confectionery products of its own based on liquorice and wine gums, under Nedan's Autodrop brand name.

Nedan estimates that it sold around 750 000 boxes, each with 24 packs of Fisherman's Friend in 1999. That amounts to 18 million packages for a population of 15 million, some 20% above the POPPPPY (packets of product per person per year) target, which puts the Netherlands 5th in the POPPPPY league table, behind Norway, Singapore, Germany and Switzerland. Nedan has only had one year when Fisherman's Friend sales fell, otherwise it has been steady upward progress. The sales force still has to work hard, though, to maintain the success. 42% of Fisherman's friend sales are generated from the impulse sector, tobacconists and petrol stations, and that position has to be defended hard in a very competitive market.

Communication is an important part of the strategy and advertising plays a vital role. Lofthouse of

Fleetwood decided on an umbrella advertising campaign across Europe via satellite television to create a consistent image through one concentrated message. In addition to this, all the regional distributors do their own advertising, within set guidelines, via terrestrial television. A manual, available on CD-Rom, shows distributors how the product and brand should be presented. Nedan's 'Strong Stuff' campaign uses an emotional appeal to communicate the power of Fisherman's Friend both as a taste experience and as a way of making a bad day seem better. The advertising is commissioned and controlled by Nedan in consultation with Lofthouse of Fleetwood and Impex. There is an advertising allowance from the manufacturer, but Nedan spends more than that as a means of developing and defending its own market.

> 'These are our decisions. Although some elements are consistent across the world, such as the packaging and the logo, it would be difficult for Fisherman's Friend to develop a pan-European campaign that is as effective as what we can do for our own market.'

The main medium is television that takes about 85% of the budget and the rest goes mainly on sampling targeting 18 to 24-year-olds. Women aged between 20 and 25 are targeted with the milder variants and men with the original flavour sugar free one. Street sampling works better in the Netherlands than in the UK. In the UK the response is likely to be 'No thanks, I'm not ill' whereas in the Netherlands it would just be 'Thanks'.

In terms of pricing, Lofthouse of Fleetwood cannot dictate resale and retail prices. There is one consistent list price for all distributors, although bulk discounts can be negotiated. Distributors are free, however, to set resale prices according to conditions in their own local markets, although the company will advise a distributor if its prices seem to be too far out of line with those of other distributors. Retail buyers and buying groups, such as Carrefour, Ahold and Tesco, and particularly those operating right across Europe, know very well what prices are like in different European countries and will place their orders in the cheapest market. The advent of the Euro, however, means greater price transparency, although there are still variations in VAT and sales tax rates in different countries which will cloud the issue somewhat. It is true to say, however, that the general increase in and ease of pan-European trade are encouraging more pricing consistency between European distributors which cannot work in total isolation from each other. Although they do have their own defined territories, any decisions distributors make on pricing, for instance, take into account what is happening in neighbouring and other markets. Nedan is confident that its pricing is comparable with that of other European distributors, however, and does not feel that its major customers, such as Ahold, could gain any advantage from shopping around. Pricing in Euros, which is already happening, emphasises the consistency.

As part of their contracts, distributors are expected to carry about one month's stock. In general terms, once a market is established, demand is fairly predictable, unless there is a 'flu epidemic or some other unpredictable effect. Nedan has never had any serious problems in replenishing its stocks from the UK. Nedan, in turn, receives orders electronically from its own customers and undertakes to deliver within 24 hours.

Although the Netherlands – UK ordering routine is very well established, occasional meetings, either in the UK or in the Netherlands, offer an opportunity to discuss any real or potential concerns at a senior level and help to cement the relationship further. Distributors are also encouraged to network with each other and exchange information so that they are more likely to work collaboratively than competitively and Nedan finds this a positive and useful experience. Distributors exchange ideas on how to make cost savings and achieve economies of scale, for example. Lofthouse of Fleetwood facilitates this networking by organising two conferences per year, one in Europe and one in the Far East, so that distributors can meet with each other and with the company to discuss tactics. In 1999, for instance they met in Venice and then in Beijing.

The relationship between Lofthouse of Fleetwood and Nedan is built on mutual trust, co-operation and communication. Nedan feels that Lofthouse of Fleetwood strikes about the right balance between creating and maintaining a consistent brand image across its global markets while allowing local distributors sufficient autonomy to distribute and market the brand appropriately for their own environments. Lofthouse of Fleetwood brings its manufacturing expertise and strategic vision for the brand to the relationship as well as co-ordinating the cohesive network of distributors that allows best practice to be disseminated. The distributors themselves bring their local knowledge and contacts and their operational expertise in marketing and growing the brand to the benefit of all parties.

With grateful thanks to Rien van Ruremonde, Managing Director of Nedan Zoetwaren BV and to Duncan and Tony Lofthouse, Joint Managing Directors of Lofthouse of Fleetwood Ltd.

Part VI

PROMOTION

What is marketing if it isn't communication? The philosophy of marketing (discussed in Chapter 1) as the interface between an organisation and the outside world, particularly its customers, implies that all marketing activities are destined to communicate something to someone, somewhere. This communication may be direct and tangible, an advertisement for example, but it may also be indirect and intangible: think about the ways in which price communicates with a potential buyer, for instance.

There is certainly synergy between direct and indirect communication. Advertising messages centred on product quality can be reinforced by tacit communication though price and packaging, or a sales representative's credibility can be enhanced by what is implicitly communicated by the product's performance. In practice, the direct and indirect elements of communication are inseparable, but in the following six chapters, the emphasis is on the overt means by which organisations communicate.

Chapter 14 introduces the concept of communication and its application in marketing and also looks at some of the factors influencing an organisation's choice of promotional mix elements. Each of these elements is then explored in more detail in Chapters 15 to 17, which look at advertising, sales promotion and personal selling, defining the tools and techniques used within each area, their appropriate use and the problems of implementation. Chapter 18 examines direct marketing, an increasingly important means of injecting a personal touch back into mass markets. It also looks at the role and contribution of on-line marketing. Finally, Chapter 19 explores public relations, sponsorship and exhibitions – all of which are now recognised as valuable marketing communication techniques.

14 Communication and the Promotional Mix

LEARNING OBJECTIVES

This chapter will help you to:

1 understand the importance of planned communication in a marketing context;

2 appreciate the variety and scope of marketing communication objectives;

3 explain the use of promotional tools in the communication process;

4 identify the factors and constraints influencing the mix of communications tools that an organisation uses; and

5 define the main methods by which communications budgets are set.

INTRODUCTION

The promotional mix is the direct way in which an organisation attempts to communicate with various target audiences. It consists of five main elements, as shown in Fig. 14.1. Advertising represents non-personal, mass communication; personal selling is at the other extreme, covering face-to-face, personally tailored messages. Sales promotion involves tactical, short-term incentives that encourage a target audience to behave in a certain way. Public relations is about creating and maintaining good-quality relationships with many interested groups (for example the media, shareholders and trade unions), not just with customers. Finally, direct marketing involves creating one-to-one relationships with individual customers, often in mass markets, and might involve mailings, telephone selling or electronic media. Some might classify direct marketing activities as forms of advertising, sales promotion or even personal selling, but this text treats direct marketing as a separate element of the promotional mix while acknowledging that it 'borrows' from the other elements.

Ideally, the marketer would like to invest extensively in every element of the mix. In a world of finite resources, however, choices have to be made about which activities are going to work together most cost effectively with the maximum synergy to achieve the communications objectives of the organisation within a defined budget. Budgets obviously vary widely between different organisations, and depending on the type of product involved and the communications task in hand.

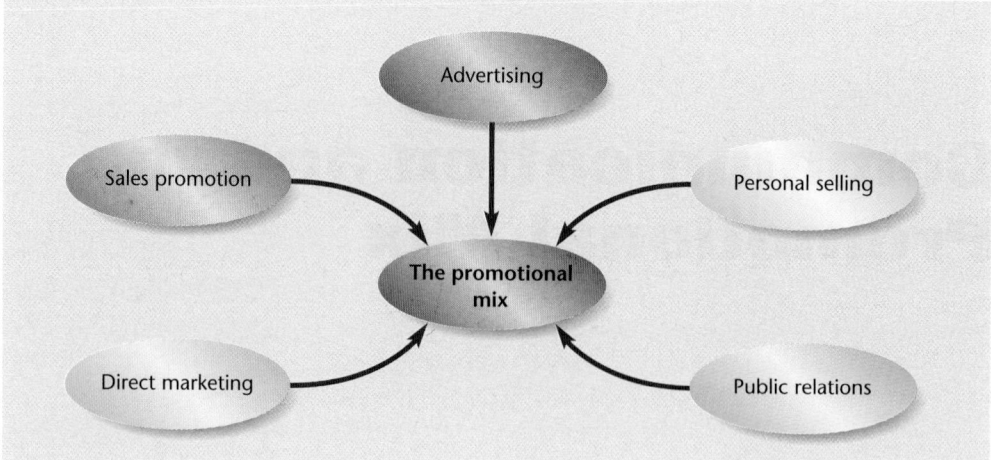

FIGURE 14.1

The elements of the promotional mix

Example St Ivel's Utterly Butterly brand has been skillfully promoted using a number of elements of the promotional mix. The prime objective was to create large-scale awareness and to increase consumer involvement, thus establishing positive attitudes. The £6mn advertising campaign primarily created awareness and concentrated on people's obsession with the spread. The creative focus was on the idea that people recognise obsessive behaviour in others but not in themselves, showing a couple criticising a neighbour for his obsessive car cleaning while going through their own regular breakfast routine with Utterly Butterly. In addition, a major sponsorship deal with Europe's only professional wing-walking team created an opportunity for heightened brand interest. Three bi-planes, Utterly, Butterly and Yum plus a gang of 'Aerobabes' were sponsored by St Ivel to entertain over three million people each year at over 50 airshows. The packaging also featured the Aerobabes. All these activities were supported on the brand's dedicated website (http://www.utterly-butterly.co.uk) where product information and cartoons followed through the slightly wacky theme (*The Grocer*, 1999b; *Campaign*,1999b).

A £6mn advertising campaign and a sponsorship deal ensured a successful launch for Utterly Butterly.

Source: St. Ivel/DmB+B

This chapter, along with the five that follow it, will aim to explain why such choices are made.

Each element of the promotional mix has its own chapter, which discusses in some detail the element's strengths and weaknesses and its appropriate use. This chapter, therefore, provides a more general strategic overview by focusing on the marketing communications planning process. This helps to emphasise some of the influences that shape an appropriate blend within the promotional mix, allowing the marketer to allocate communication resources most effectively.

Communication, even mass market advertising, begins and ends with people, which means that it has plenty of scope for going wrong. The first part of this chapter, therefore, takes a look at communications theory from first principles, building up a simple model of communication. This is then applied in a marketing context to highlight the danger areas where marketing communication efforts can fail. These concepts may appear to be very abstract or theoretical, but they nevertheless form an important foundation for applied decision making and may make the difference between success and failure.

On the basis of these concepts, the main focus of the chapter is on developing a planning framework within which managerial decisions on communication activity can be made. Each of the elements of the simple communication model is incorporated into this framework, whether implicitly or explicitly, with a view to minimising the danger of misunderstanding and failure. Each stage in the planning flow is discussed in turn, with particular emphasis being given to relevant issues and the kind of promotional mix blend that might subsequently be appropriate. It is becoming increasingly important for organisations to design and implement effective marketing communications strategies as they expand their interests beyond their known domestic markets.

COMMUNICATIONS THEORY

Schramm (1955) offers a seminal definition of **communication** that serves as a sound basis for developing a model of communication:

> **'The process of establishing a commonness or oneness of thought between a sender and a receiver.'**

Communication model

Superficially, communication is a very simple process that we all do all the time and take for granted. It would seem from the definition above that all you need is someone to send a message and someone to receive it, as shown in Fig. 14.2.

However, even the three apparently simple elements of Fig. 14.2 raise a number of questions that Fig. 14.2 does not address.

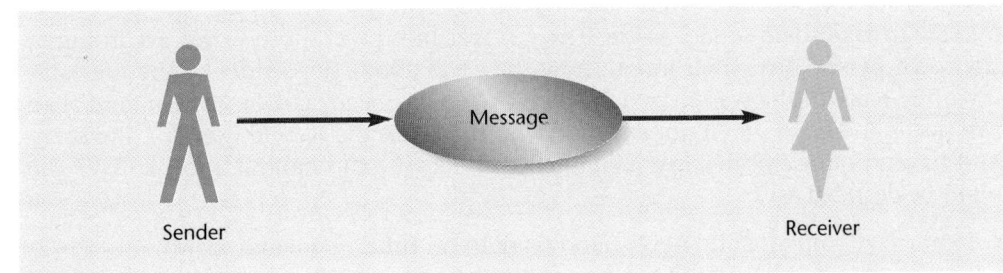

FIGURE 14.2

The basic elements of communication

Encoding the message

Put yourself in the position of having to tell a professor that an assignment will not be handed in on time. The intent of the message is clear enough, but *what* precisely are you going to say and *how* exactly are you going to say it? Here are some alternatives. (This situation is, of course, purely hypothetical. The authors do not hold themselves responsible for the consequences of your using any of these approaches in reality!)

- 'I can't hand in my assignment on time. I'll deliver it on Friday.' (assertive/assumptive)
- 'I'm sorry, but I haven't quite finished my assignment yet. Please can I hand it in on Friday?' (apologetic/appealing)
- 'I've done it, honestly, but the dog ate it, so I need to print it out again – would Friday be all right?' (possibly honest ...)

There are many, many more alternatives. The point is that, as the sender, you would assess each of these alternative approaches in order to predict their likely effect on the receiver of the message. Naturally, you would choose the one most likely to achieve the desired outcome. This relies on your perceptions of the receiver's attitudes, character and state of mind. The third excuse might be appropriate for a professor with a soft-hearted, sympathetic (or gullible) streak, whereas the second excuse would appeal to an honest, straightforward, no-nonsense type. The first excuse guarantees you a 'fail' from any self-respecting academic. In other words, you make a choice as to how you **encode** the message, first so that it will be understood by the receiver and second to increase the chances of achieving the objectives of the communication.

Communication channel

A further complication arises when you consider the means by which the message is relayed to the receiver, that is, the choice of **channel of communication**. Will you deliver the message yourself, verbally, or will you leave a note and run away? The choice of channel might affect the success of the communication. The verbal method allows you to assess the response to your initial message, giving you the flexibility to try again with a different approach, if at first you don't succeed. It also gives you the opportunity to employ non-verbal communication to reinforce the message. The tone of voice used (assumptive, quietly polite or pleading), the look in the eyes (hostile, guilty or pleading) all communicate in their own right, and need to be consistent with the verbal message. The written message, on the other hand, is moderated by its legibility (typewritten or handwritten), and perhaps the physical characteristics of the paper. It does not offer the quick flexibility of message and response of the verbal method.

Decoding

Figure 14.3 extends the initial communication model to include the concepts of 'encoding' and 'channel', and also includes a new element, **decoding**, on the receiver's side of the model. The receiver is not a passive subordinate in the communication process, but is a dynamic influence and partner. It is not enough that you have delivered the message to the receiver's eyes or ears; it has to be understood and interpreted. Your message may well be a sequence of simple words, but the receiver is unlikely to take them at face value. The receiver interprets those words according to their own personality, their mood, how they feel about the sender of the message, how they react to the way in which the message has been sent or worded, and their own needs and wants. So if, for example, you try to use the second excuse – 'I'm sorry, but I haven't quite finished my assignment yet. Please can I hand it in on Friday?' – it might be decoded as:

- 'I am a lazy student and I never hand work in on time – here I go again.'
- 'I am normally a conscientious student, but I genuinely have a problem and I am trying my best to solve it as soon as possible with the least inconvenience to you.'
- 'I'm being honest with you, so do me a favour.'

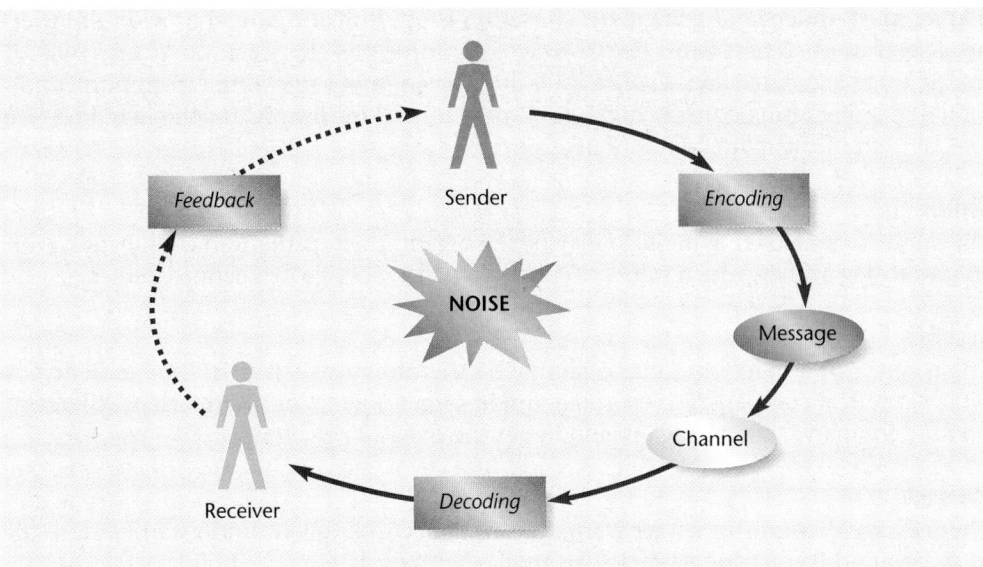

The decoding depends entirely on the receiver's perceptions, and whether the receiver is willing to accept a verbal request or would prefer formal written contact. All this in turn can have a profound effect on the *response* offered. The first decoding option might lead to a flat and unequivocal refusal to comply with the request; the second to a more sympathetic 'Yes, certainly, Friday will do, and do you want to tell me what the problem is?', while the third might elicit a more cynical 'Just this once, but you'd better be on time with the next one'.

Feedback

Whatever the response, it provides **feedback** to the sender on whether the message has been received, understood, interpreted as desired and acted on appropriately. Satisfactory feedback may close this communication episode, whereas unsatisfactory or ambiguous feedback may cause the sender to want to communicate further, going round the model again.

Noise

The final element of the model is **noise**. This consists of all extraneous activity and influences that might interfere and distort information at any point in the communication process. There could literally be physical noise – crackles on a telephone line, other people talking, traffic, background noise etc. – which could blot out or distort part of the intended message. There are, however, other less obvious sources of 'noise' that nevertheless have the same sort of interfering effect, such as the paper running out or crumpling up in a fax machine (thereby distorting or obscuring the message), or perhaps other events distracting the sender's or receiver's attention ('I'll read this message later. I have a train to catch').

Shared meaning

To return to the definition of communication offered at the beginning of this section, the model developed here demonstrates that the process of achieving 'commonness or oneness of thought', or shared meaning between sender and receiver, is not quite as easy and straightforward as it might appear. 'Shared meaning' is more than the successful transmission of words from one party to another, but requires sound mutual understanding of each other, and the active participation of both sender and receiver.

So what has all this to do with marketing? 'Shared meaning' has everything to do with marketing, since an organisation must understand what its market wants, and a market must understand what an organisation is offering and how that will fulfil their needs and wants. There must be two-way communication between buyer and seller if that is to be accomplished. Even a brief attempt to apply the simple communication model in a marketing context highlights some important lessons for the marketer. We look at each of the main components in turn:

Sender

The sender of a marketing message may be the organisation, perhaps in conjunction with an advertising agency, which wants to communicate a message to a defined audience.

Receiver

The receiver of a marketing message may be the individuals within that audience. A pharmaceutical company, for example, might target doctors or pharmacists, whereas a holiday company such as Saga would target the over-50 age group.

Message

The message is what the sender wants the audience to know or understand as a result of receiving the communication. This might be: 'Buy one of our holidays because we understand your needs', or 'This is our new product', or 'Don't drink and drive'.

Encoding

Encoding is where the sender's understanding of the receiver pays dividends. Does the target market only need information? Does it want to be entertained? Persuaded? Threatened? What kind of imagery appeals to this target segment? Artistic? Abstruse? Amusing? What choice of music or voice-over will best enhance the effect of the message in the mind of the target? There are many difficult questions relating to what to say and how to say it that can only be answered through clear knowledge of the target market.

The potential Saga holidaymaker might respond to relaxing scenes, such as almost deserted sunny beaches or gentle activities like rambling, rather than the frenzied disco scene more reminiscent of a Club 18–30 holiday. The core message in each case is actually the same, 'Buy one of our holidays because we understand your needs', but the encoding is appealing to different perceptions of what makes a good holiday.

Channel

The channel is the means by which the encoded message is passed on to the receiver. There are many different choices, for example television, print or personal contact. Again, what is most appropriate can only be established through knowledge of the target market.

Decoding

The decoding phase is a difficult one for the marketer, who can only trust that the right message, encoding and channel decisions have been made in order to increase the chances of the message being interpreted as desired. This becomes particularly problematic where there are mass markets and subtle, sophisticated messages. The more marketers aggregate and generalise behaviour, the less predictable becomes the response of the individual, and the more complex the message, the less likely it is that it will be interpreted by each individual exactly as desired.

As mentioned at pp. 107 *et seq.*, individuals tend to interpret incoming messages very differently, depending on their personalities, experience, interest and knowledge, among other things. Selective perception, for example, means that people will hear what they want to hear, or what is of specific interest at that time, and disregard the rest of the communication. With television advertising in particular, people are exposed to so much of it, so often, that they have learned to screen it out or ignore it. This means that there is greater pressure on the sender to develop messages that are encoded in such a way that they can break through those defences and be interpreted appropriately.

Example Warner Lambert (http://www.warnerlambert.com) wanted to break through the barriers to spread the word that its Listerine mouthwash (http://www.oral-care.com) was clinically proven to kill the bacteria that can develop between teeth and that ordinary brushing could well miss. The objective was to educate consumers on good oral hygiene and to convert non-users to the product. A 30-second television advertising spot was chosen as part of a £4.5mn campaign to show the brand's power by creating a tooth fairy, Keith Allen, introducing his son to the tooth fairy trade in the advertisement. The tooth fairy is bemoaning the stronger, healthier teeth resulting from using Listerine, 'Listerine doesn't just get between the teeth, you know, it gets right up my nose as well' (*Campaign*, 1999a). The humour helped to make the message palatable and attention grabbing and the advertiser hoped that people would recognise the tooth fairy and remember that it is supposed to take away the teeth that have fallen out.

Feedback

Feedback is how the recipient of the message responds to it. This might mean overt action, such as purchasing a product or requesting more information, but it might also be less overt, involving the generation of awareness and the development of attitudes. A great disadvantage of any kind of mass communication, such as television advertising, is that feedback can be slow and painful to collect. This contrasts with face-to-face communication where feedback can be assessed immediately. Even if the intent of the message was to sell the product, sales figures only tell part of the story and more detailed investigation is required to try to establish the role of advertising in those sales and the effectiveness of the message. Meaningful feedback is itself the result of a planned communication effort to collect it on behalf of the organisation.

Since marketing communication is an expensive activity, it is important to monitor the outcomes of what is done and, if necessary, modify or change some aspect(s) of the communication process. Even before mass communication takes place, organisations often test their advertising messages with a limited audience to see whether they achieve what was intended.

Noise

Noise covers any factors that interfere with any aspect of the communication process between sender and receiver. An obvious interference in the receipt of an advertising message, for example, is if the intended receiver is not watching the television when the advertisement is broadcast! Many people regard the commercial breaks as opportunities to make a cup of coffee, or to 'channel hop'. Such behaviour poses a big problem for advertisers. There are no easy answers to this, other than scheduling the advertisement at the beginning or end of a commercial break and starting it with some incredible attention-grabbing device. Other 'noise' includes the clutter of other advertising messages, particularly for competing products, which the receiver is trying to process. The impact of a message may be reduced if it is surrounded by equally stimulating and exciting messages, and there is even the risk of messages becoming confused with each other in the receiver's mind. Noise thus either causes the message to be distorted in the receiver's mind or to fail to reach the receiver's attention at all (Mallen, 1977).

The lessons from this application of the model are fundamental to successful and cost effective marketing communication: know your target market inside out, define exactly what response you would like from the target market and invest in the mechanisms to monitor and evaluate the actual response you receive. This all indicates the need for thorough and logical planning of the organisation's communications activities. The following sections take up this theme, and offer a framework within which marketing communications decisions can be developed and justified.

Example Interactive television can help to reduce the noise surrounding the message. With the average viewer being exposed to 290 commercials per week and a barrage of alternative brands in the stores, interactive television can make the advertiser stand out. The technology means that the product is exposed to the potential customer in real time and a transaction, whether a purchase or a request for more information, can be completed before a competitor gets a chance to present an alternative. That is especially important when over 40 per cent of the advertisements to which we are exposed are forgotten within one week (Turznski, 1999). Dedicated home shopping, banking and holiday channels can be ready for consumer action at the touch of a button. Trials in France indicated that 80 per cent of people pushed the 'yes' button to request a brochure during a car advertisement. Advertisers will have to ensure that they can create attractive advertisements and cope with uncertain response rates. With the growth of digital television, covering 12.5 million homes in the UK and rising, and as targeting becomes ever more sophisticated, interactive television looks set to grow rapidly in popularity.

COMMUNICATIONS PLANNING MODEL

Figure 14.4, adapted from Rothschild's (1987) communications decision sequence framework, includes all the main elements of marketing communications decision making and links closely with the theory of communications discussed above. Given the complexity of communication and the immense possibilities for getting some element of it wrong, a thorough and systematic planning process is crucial for minimising the risks. No organisation can afford either the financial or reputational damage caused by poorly planned or implemented communications campaigns.

Each element and its implications for the balancing of the promotional mix will now be defined and analysed in turn. The first element is the situation analysis, which has been split into three subsections: the target market, the product and the environment. Bear in mind, however, that in reality it is difficult to 'pigeon hole' things quite so neatly as this might imply, and there will, therefore, be a lot of cross-referencing.

Situation analysis (1): The target market

Organisational or consumer market

The *target market* decision most likely to have an impact on the balancing of the overall promotional mix is whether the market is a consumer market or an organisational

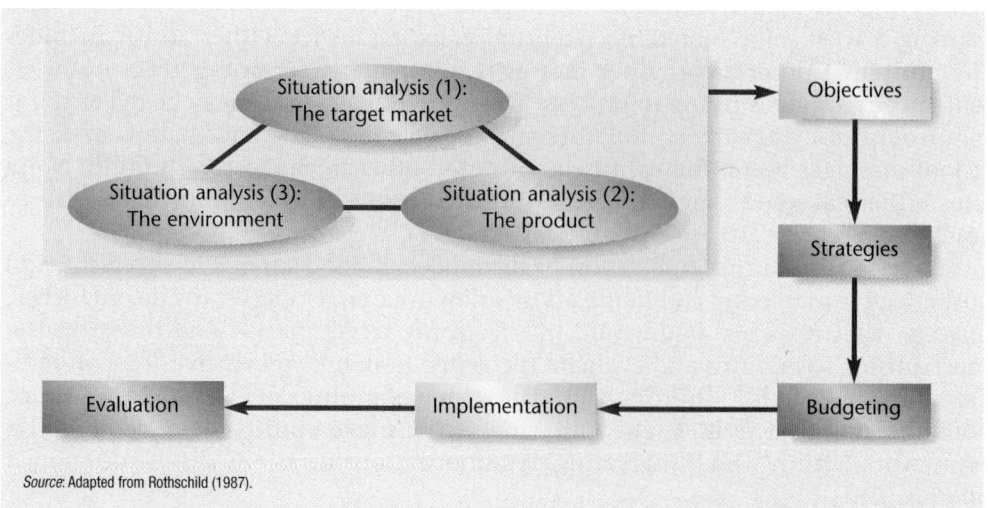

Source: Adapted from Rothschild (1987).

FIGURE 14.4

The communications planning flow

TABLE 14.1

Organisational *vs* consumer market marketing communications: characteristics and implications

Organisational	Consumer
Fewer, often identifiable customers ● *Personal and personalised communication feasible*	Usually mass, aggregated markets ● *Mass communication, e.g. television advertising, most efficient and cost effective*
Complex products, often tailored to individual customer specification ● *Need for lengthy buyer–seller dialogue via personal selling*	Standardised products with little scope for negotiation and customisation ● *Impersonal channels of communication convey standard message*
High value, high-risk, infrequent purchases ● *Need for much information through literature and personal representation, with emphasis on product performance and financial criteria*	Low value, low-risk, frequent purchases ● *Less technical emphasis; status and other intangible benefits often stressed; incentives needed to build or break buying habits*
Rational decision-making process over time, with a buying centre taking responsibility ● *Need to understand who plays what role and try to influence whole buying centre*	Short time scale, often impulse purchasing by an individual or family buying unit ● *Need to understand who plays what role and to try to influence family*

market. Recalling the comparison made in Chapter 4 between consumer and organisational markets, Table 14.1 summarises the impact of the main distinguishing features on the choice of promotional mix. The picture that emerges from this is that organisational markets are very much more dependent on the personal selling element, with advertising and sales promotion playing a strong supporting role.

The converse is generally true in consumer markets. A large number of customers each making relatively low value, frequent purchases can be most efficiently contacted using mass media. Advertising, therefore, comes to the fore, with sales promotion a close second, while personal selling is almost redundant. Figure 14.5 shows this polarisation of organisational and consumer promotional mixes. This does, of course, represent sweeping generalisations about the nature of these markets,

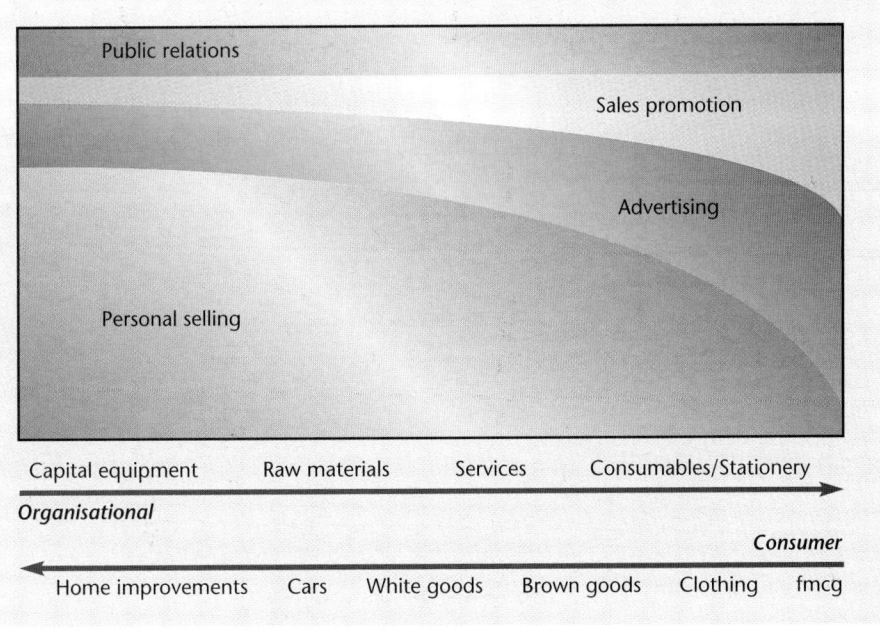

FIGURE 14.5

Organisational *vs* consumer promotional mix

which need to be qualified. The product itself, for instance, will influence the shape of the mix, as will the nature of competitive and other environmental pressures. These will be addressed later (pp. 573 *et seq.* and 576 *et seq.*).

Push or pull strategy

Remember, however, that even consumer goods marketers are likely to have to consider organisational markets in dealing with channels of distribution. Figure 14.6 offers two strategies, push and pull, which emphasise different lines of communication (Olver and Farris, 1989). With a **push strategy**, the manufacturer chooses to concentrate communications activity on the member of the distribution channel immediately below. This means that the wholesaler, in this example, has a warehouse full of product and thus an incentive to use communication to make a special effort to sell it quickly on to the retailer, who in turn promotes it to the end consumer. The product is thereby pushed down the distribution channel, with communication flowing from member to member in parallel with the product. There is little or no communication between manufacturer and consumer in this case.

In contrast, the **pull strategy** requires the manufacturer to create demand for the product through direct communication with the consumer. The retailers will perceive this demand and, in the interests of serving their customers' needs, will demand the product from their wholesaler, who will demand it from the manufacturer. This bottom-up approach pulls the product down the distribution channel, with communication flowing in the opposite direction from the product!

The reality is, of course, that manufacturers take a middle course, with some pull and some push to create more impetus for the product.

> **Example** The Freedown Food Company decided to diversify into exotic meats such as emu, crocodile and kangaroo. The challenge was to gain distribution into a wider market than just speciality butchers and restaurants. As the meats were unusual, the larger retailers had to be sure that there would be sufficient demand to merit their stocking them, while consumers had to be convinced to try the product in the first place. Freedown adopted a push–pull strategy to support the diversification. Information packs were given to butchers and cookery writers, as they were both recognised as credible information sources by the consumer. The butchers were part of the push strategy, in that it was hoped that they

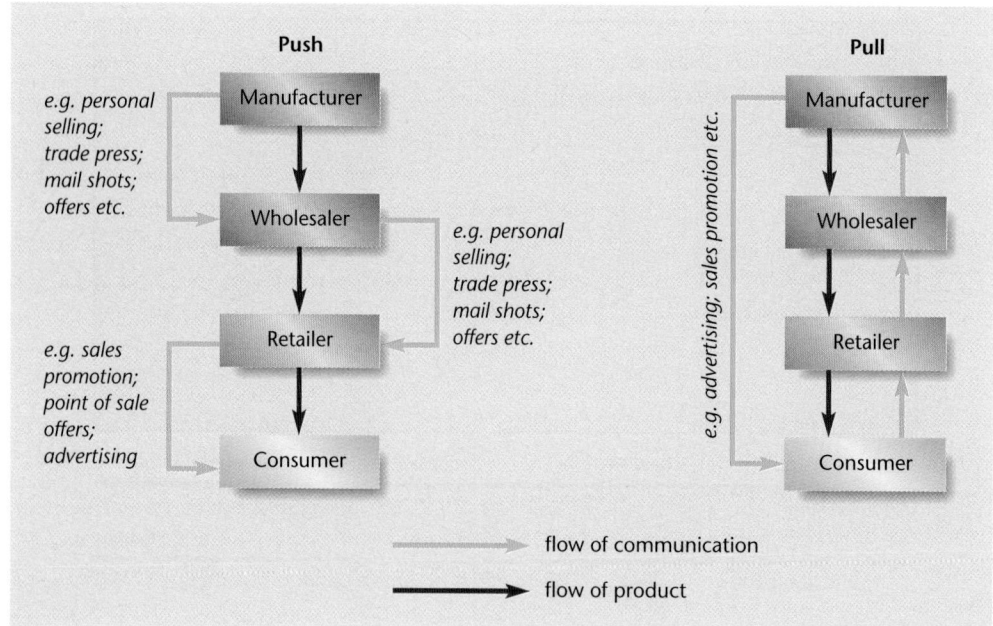

flow of communication

flow of product

FIGURE 14.6

Push–pull strategy

would pass on news of the benefits and effectively sell the meat. The pull strategy involved the writers, who could provide favourable comments and legitimise eating of exotic meat. The restaurants also played an important part in trying to encourage trial. Although Freedown could not afford extensive media advertising, it managed to persuade some large retailers such as Tesco to list the product on a trial basis. This was essential to generate more awareness at the point of sale and to enable sales to be made (Barnard, 1996). Unfortunately, despite this comprehensive communication and distribution strategy, the public did not take to the new meats and the supermarkets soon de-listed them.

Buyer readiness of the target market

In terms of message formulation, a further tempering influence on communication with consumers will be the **buyer readiness** stage of the target market. It is most unlikely that a target market is going to undergo an instant conversion from total ignorance of a product's existence to queueing up at the checkout to buy it. Particularly in consumer markets, it is more likely that people will pass through a number of stages *en route* from initial awareness to desire for the product. A number of models have been proposed – for example Strong's (1925) AIDA model, which put various labels on these stages, as shown in Fig. 14.7 – but broadly speaking, they all amount to the same sequence:

Cognitive. The cognitive stage involves sowing the seeds of a thought, i.e. catching the target market's attention and generating straightforward awareness of the product: 'Yes, I know this product exists.' As part of the 1999 launch of the Rover 75, for example, the company used media advertising, sponsorship and hospitality events to get the brand known and understood as being something different and special.

Affective. The affective stage involves creating or changing an attitude, i.e. giving the consumer sufficient information (whether factual or image based) to pass judgement on the product and to develop positive feelings towards it: 'I understand what this product can do for me, and I like the idea of it.'

> **Example** Some attitudes are extremely hard to change. Croatia faces a difficult task in convincing potential holidaymakers that it is now a safe tourist destination, but nevertheless the tourist board is using advertising to try to overcome preconceptions about the place.

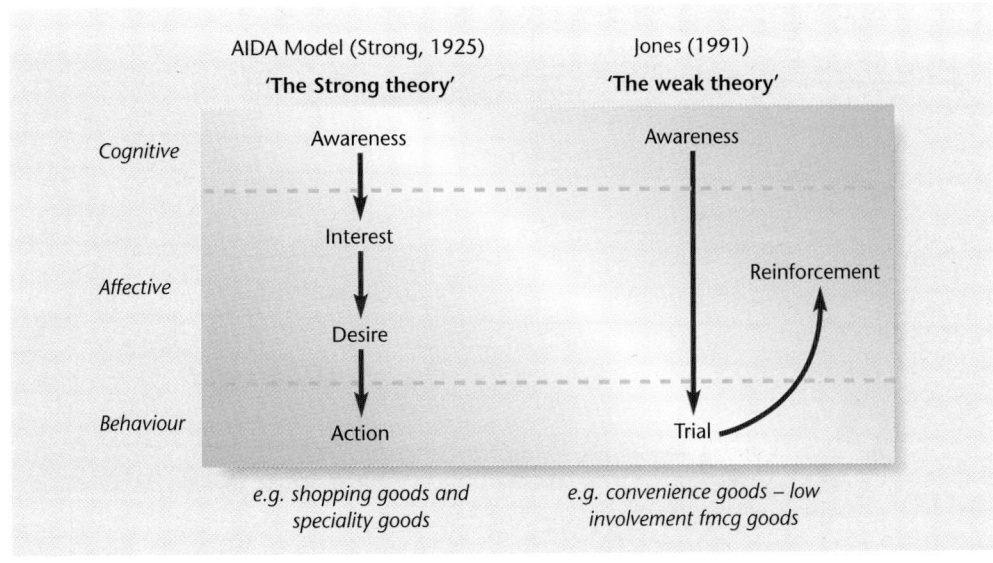

FIGURE 14.7

Response hierarchy models

MARKETING IN ACTION Botton Village

Botton Village, one of eight communities comprising the Camphill Village Trust, is described as a very special place where 160 people with special needs can live in a family community setting that utilises their skills in various craft and agricultural activities. There are five farms and ten workshops on the site selling goods such as hand-crafted toys and environmentally friendly farm produce. Situated in the North Yorkshire Moors national park, the community needs to raise sufficient funds from donors to supplement its income from the state and from its trading activities.

Fundraising is essential for supporting new projects and supplementing income. Open days and fairs are held during the year and a distribution system enables some of the produce, such as honey and toys, to be sold direct at markets or through some retailers. It has a regular net surplus income of around £2.0mn per year raised largely through highly professional and targeted direct marketing. A single mailing can generate between £5 200 and £9 400 per thousand donors mailed in one segment. As a smaller charity, it is not easy for Botton Village to stand out against the better-known charities seeking donations. It has a very small marketing budget, no full- or part-time fund raisers and it needs external professional advice in developing any campaigns.

The main problem facing any charity is the danger of donation fatigue or overload. Sometimes mailing lists are shared and special appeals can divert funds, an important obstacle if the donor has a finite limit to spend with charities. It has been estimated that a charity donor can receive up to 12 appeals during a year. The Botton Village approach to mailing its 73 000 active donors is to maintain communication and nurture the relationship throughout the year, not just during a special appeal. After the first donation, a thank-you letter is sent within 48 hours, regardless of the size of donation. An early response is considered important for building the relationship and has been found to affect future gift giving. Donors also have a wide choice of options, including donation through legacies and covenants, £40 one-off donations and a regular payment plan.

Four mailings per year are sent out, linked with the *Village Life* newsletter. This newsletter focuses on the people helped within the community and outlines key activities and future events. It encourages donors to feel involved and to see tangible effects from their giving. The mailing letters are all personalised and vary in appeal depending on the donor plan adopted. All donations are logged on the database and if no further donations are received during the following year, the

Source: Burnett Associates/The Camphill Village Trust Ltd. Photography by Peter Mernagh.

Continued

donor is sent a reminder. If further contact produces no results, the donor is downgraded to receive only a Christmas card, before finally being dropped after a further two years. Botton is concerned not to be seen as intrusive in its mailings and so donors can opt out of regular communication at any time. Even though some switch to Christmas contact only, donations still run at a high level from this group.

The direct marketing camp been very successful and is now supported by the website. Botton can receive as high as a 50 per cent response rate from some mailings, whereas typical figures are 15 per cent for 'warm' mailings and less than 1 per cent for 'cold' mailings. Even when it shares lists with other charities, it can achieve response rates of around 5 per cent rather than the norm of 1 per cent. The first mailing is crucial and the specially developed pack focuses on the work of the community, its ideals and the lives of those that it is designed to help. By adopting a sensitive and caring approach along with professional marketing, Botton has achieved many of its targets for fundraising.

Sources: *Marketing Week* (1999); http://www.ukonline.co.uk/botton.village.

Behaviour. The behaviour stage involves precipitating action, i.e. where the strength of the positive attitudes generated in the affective stage leads the consumer to desire the product and to do something about acquiring it: 'I want this product and I'm going to go and buy it.' Many press advertisements incorporating a mail order facility are operating at this level.

The speed with which a target market passes through these stages depends on the kind of product, the target market involved and the marketing strategies adopted by the organisation. Nevertheless, each stage becomes increasingly more difficult to implement, since more is being asked of the consumer. Generating awareness, the first stage, is relatively easy as it involves little risk or commitment from the consumer, and may even operate unconsciously. The second stage needs some effort from consumers if it is to be successful, because they are being asked to assimilate information, process it and form an opinion. The third and final stage requires the most involvement – actually getting up and doing something, which is likely to involve paying out money!

The **Strong (1925) theory** proposed these stages as forming a logical flow of events driven by marketing communication. Advertising, for example, creates the initial awareness, stimulates the interest and then the desire for the product, and only then does trial take place. In other words, the attitude and opinion are formed before the consumer ever gets near the product. There is, however, another school of thought that maintains that it does not always happen like that. The **weak theory** (Jones, 1991) accepts that marketing communication can generate the awareness, but then the consumer might well try the product without having formed any particular attitude or opinion of it. Only then, after the purchase and product trial, does the marketing communication begin to contribute to attitude and opinion working alongside consumer experience of the product. This would make sense for low-involvement products, the frequently purchased boring goods about which it is difficult to get emotional, such as washing powder.

Example A consumer might see a television advertisement for a new brand of washing powder and then forget about it until the next trip to the supermarket. The consumer sees that new brand on the shelf and thinks, 'Oh yes, I saw an ad for that – I'll give it a try' and buys a packet. Having tried the product, the consumer might decide that it is quite good and then start to pay more attention to the advertising content as a way of legitimising and reinforcing that opinion.

Whatever the route through the response hierarchy, the unique characteristics of each stage imply that differing promotional mixes may be called for to maximise the creative benefits and cost effectiveness of the different promotional tools. Figure 14.8 suggests that advertising is most appropriate at the earliest stage, given its capacity to reach large numbers of people relatively cheaply and quickly with a simple message. Sales promotions can also bring a product name to the fore and help in the affective stage: using a sample that has been delivered to the door certainly generates awareness and aids judgement and recognition of a product. Adding a coupon to the sample's packaging is also an incentive to move into the behaviour stage, buying a full-sized package.

Notice that in Fig. 14.8 the role of advertising diminishes as the behaviour stage moves closer and personal selling comes to the fore. Advertising can only reiterate and reinforce what consumers already know about the product, and if this wasn't enough to stimulate action the last time they saw/heard it, it may not be so this time either. At this point, potential buyers may just need a last bit of persuasion to tip them over the edge into buying, and that last kick may be best delivered by a sales representative who can reiterate the product benefits, tailoring communication to suit the particular customer's needs and doubts in a two-way dialogue. With many fmcg products sold in supermarkets, however, this is not a feasible option, and the manufacturer relies on the packaging and, to some extent, the sales promotions to do the selling at the point of sale without human intervention. The washing powder brand Radion therefore has bright orange packaging that stands out on the supermarket shelf, commanding attention. This issue will be readdressed at p. 573 *et seq.*

In reality, individuals within the target market may pass through the stages at different times or may take longer to pass from one stage to the next. This means that it may be necessary to develop an integrated promotional mix recognising that the various elements are appealing to sub-segments at different readiness stages, with imagery and content tailored accordingly. The implementation of the various elements may be almost simultaneous, with some fine tuning of the campaign over the longer term.

Knowledge of the target market is an important foundation stone for all of the communication decisions that you are going to make. The more you know about the people you want to talk to, the more likely you are to create successful communication. This does not only mean having a clear demographic profile of the target

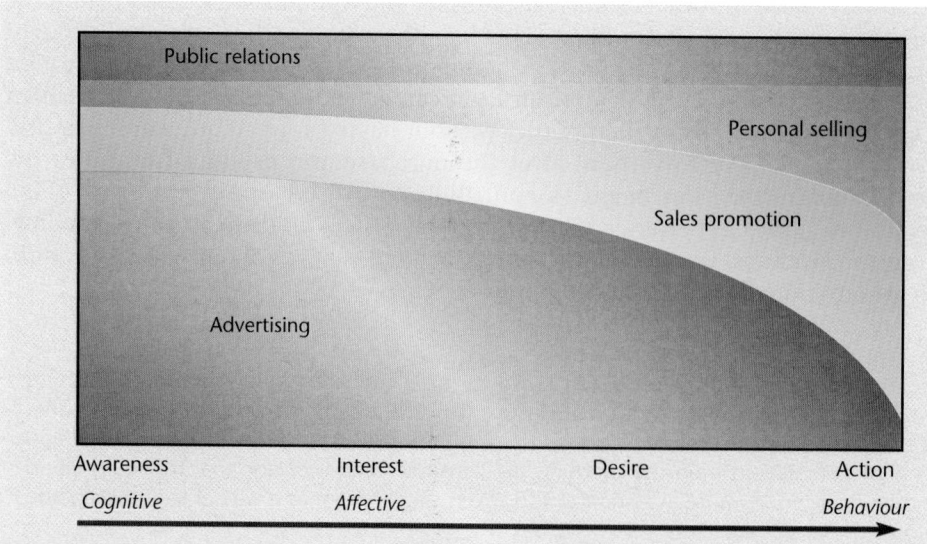

FIGURE 14.8

Buyer readiness stages and the promotional mix.

market, but also having as much detail as possible about their attitudes, beliefs and aspirations, and about their shopping, viewing and reading habits. In addition it is important to understand their relationship with your product and their perceptions of it. This will be explained in relation to communication objectives at pp. 578 *et seq.*

This could be a good time for you to look back at Chapter 5 and revise some of the methods of segmenting markets, whether consumer or organisational, since the criteria by which the target market is defined (including product-orientated criteria) may well have a strong influence not only on the broad issue of balancing the promotional mix, but also on the finer detail of media choice and creative content.

Situation analysis (2): The product

Inextricably linked with consideration of the target market is consideration of the *product* involved. This section will look again at the area of organisational and consumer products in the light of the influence of other product characteristics, and then explore the specific influence of the product life cycle on the promotional mix.

Organisational and consumer products

It is simplistic in the extreme to define a product either as an organisational purchase, personal selling being the best way to sell it, or as a consumer product, which must be advertised. Other product characteristics or the buying habits associated with the product may make such a distinction meaningless.

Example An illustration of this 'grey area' is the sale of double glazing to domestic householders. Strictly speaking, this is a consumer market, in that the product is being purchased by individuals or families for private consumption. There are, however, a number of features suggesting that this particular product has more in common with typical organisational purchases than with other consumer goods. It is an expensive, infrequent purchase with a high level of technical personalisation required to match the product exactly with the customer's needs. It involves a fairly rational decision-making process that takes place over time, and there is a high demand for product information and negotiation before commitment to purchase is made. To the buyer, it is a high-risk purchase that may well involve several members of the family (effectively acting as a buying centre) and will almost certainly involve a great deal of persuasion, reassurance and dialogue from a sales representative.

All these product and customer-orientated characteristics completely override the superficial definition of a consumer product and point to a different kind of promotional mix. Advertising plays a role in generating awareness of a double glazing company's existence and in laying the foundations for corporate and product image building. It also prepares the way for the sales representative, since a potential customer who has seen an advertisement for a sales representative's company will have an impression of what kind of company this is, and will feel less uneasy about the sales representative's credibility and trustworthiness. The personal selling element is, however, the most important and effective element of this mix because of the need for information, product tailoring and negotiation in the affective and behaviour stages. It is also cost effective in relation to the likely value of a single order.

At one end of the consumer product spectrum, a frequently purchased, low-involvement, low unit price bar of chocolate would not, of course, warrant such an investment in personal selling to millions of end consumers, even if such an exercise were logistically possible. The marketing would be more likely to conform to the standard mix, emphasising mass communication through advertising.

Example Another example chosen to illustrate the grey area between consumer and organisational markets is that of day-to-day consumable office supplies, such as pencils, pens and paperclips, for small businesses. This has more in common with the chocolate bar than the double glazing, although technically it is an organisational product, in that it is used to support the production of goods for resale. Compared with most organisational purchases, it is a routine rebuy, a low-priced, low-risk, low involvement purchase, probably delegated to an individual who goes out to the nearest stationer's or office supplies retailer at lunchtime with the contents of the petty cash tin. It is simply not cost effective to use personal selling of such a range of products to that buyer who belongs to a large and ill-defined target market (there are thousands of small businesses, in every kind of activity and market, and geographically widespread) and who makes such small-value purchases. At best, personal selling should be targeted at the stationer's or the office supplies retailer.

These two examples above serve as a warning that some organisational products behave more like consumer products and vice versa.

The product life-cycle stage

One further product characteristic that may affect the approach to communication is the *product life-cycle stage* reached (*see* pp. 303 *et seq.*). Since the overall marketing objectives tend to change as the product moves through each stage, it is likely that the specific communications objectives will also change. Different tasks need to be fulfilled and thus the balance of the promotional mix will alter.

Introduction. With the launch of a new consumer product, it is likely that there will be high initial expenditure on the promotional mix. Advertising will ensure that the product name and benefits become known and spread quickly among the target market, while sales promotions, perhaps based on coupons and sampling, help to generate trial of the product. Sales promotions will also be used in conjunction with intense personal selling effort to gain retailer acceptance of the product.

Example Rivella, a Swiss milk-based soft drink, used *Men Behaving Badly* star Neil Morrisey when it was launched in the UK. The message was designed to focus on the visual contradiction of a product that is milk based but does not look like it, as it is carbonated and amber coloured! Morrisey talked straight into camera claiming that Rivella is made from milk while outlining the sort of lies that women hear from men. The advertisement poses the question: 'Is Rivella made from milk or are all men liars?' This is backed up by the website (http://www.rivella.co.uk), which features questionnaires about men's lying habits and competitions to win cuddly cows. The product is targeted at women aged between 20 and 30 and in Switzerland it is the number two soft drink after Coca-Cola (*Campaign*, 1999c).

Growth. Communications activity is likely to be a little less intense as the product begins to find its own impetus and both retailers and consumers make repeat purchases. There might also be less emphasis on awareness generation and information giving, and more on long-term image and loyalty building. As competitors launch similar products, it is important to ensure that differential advantage is maintained, and that customers know exactly why they should continue to buy the original product rather than switching over to a competitor. This could mean a shift towards advertising as a prime means of image creation that works over a longer period.

Maturity. The maturity stage is likely to be a defensive or holding operation, since competitors with younger products may be threatening to take custom away from the product. Most people know about the product, most people (apart from a few laggards) who are likely to try it already have done so. Thus the role of communication is reminding (about the brand image and values) and reassurance (about having chosen the right product), probably through mass advertising. In organisational markets, this stage is likely to be about further developing and consolidating relationships with customers in preparation for newer products in your portfolio.

Example The relaunch of Tizer, owned by AG Barr Soft Drinks, in the 1990s is a good example of how a mature brand can be revitalised through more aggressive and lively promotion. The brand is targeted at 5 to 15-year-olds and the communications strategy had to reach and convince that audience that the drink was something special. In 1996, the pack was redesigned using a blue can with a red top. The colours carried through to the 'refresh your head' advertising campaign featuring a happy male head with the top sliced off and with Tizer pouring down into it as if into a cup. In 1999, Tizer concluded a sponsorship deal for ITV's Saturday morning pop chart show *CD:UK*, hosted by teen idols Ant and Dec (Barrett, 1999). Tizer is able to run several 45-second indents per show and over the year is expected to reach 91 per cent of kids and 89 per cent of 16–24-year-olds. To support the campaign, there are on-pack promotions and a musical website for 'ice' entertainment (http://www.tizer.co.uk).

Decline. Marketing communication is not going to rescue a product that is clearly on its way out; it can only stave off the inevitable for a while. The majority of consumers and, for that matter, distributors, will have already moved on to other products, leaving only a few laggards. A certain level of reminder advertising and sales promotion might keep them in the market for this product for a while, but eventually even they will drift off. There is little point in diverting resources that could be better used on the next new product.

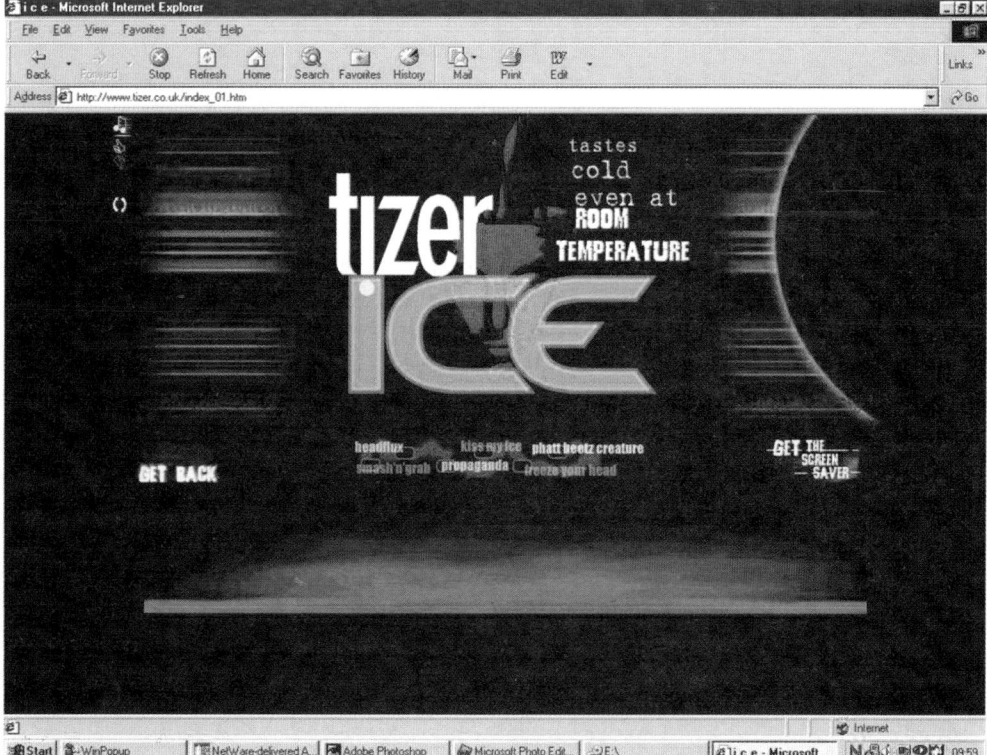

Tizer's campaign is designed to appeal to a younger age group.

Source: A. G. Barr Soft Drinks

The above analysis assumes that a product takes an unexceptional course through the classical stages of the life-cycle. Many consumer goods, however, are revamped at some time during the maturity stage to extend their life-cycle. In such a case, there is every reason to rethink the communications package and treat the process more like a new product launch. There is much to communicate both to the trade and to the consumer about the 'new improved' brand, the increased value for money, the enhanced performance, more stylish looks or whatever aspects are being emphasised. In a sense, this stage is even more difficult than the new product launch, as the marketer has to tread a fine line between overturning old preconceptions about the product, convincing the market that there is something new to consider and confusing and alienating existing users who might think that the familiar, comforting brand values have been thrown out.

The life-cycle concept, as discussed at pp. 303 *et seq*. does have its problems, and in the context of marketing communication, its unthinking, rigid application as a primary basis for communications planning is dangerous. If a product is assumed to be mature/declining, then the application of a communications package appropriate to that stage may well hasten its demise. There are other, more relevant factors, both internal and external, which should have a far greater bearing on the planning process. Some of the external factors will now be discussed.

> **Example** Heinz decided to reposition its tomato ketchup away from its general family appeal to developing a 'laconic, cool, confident brand personality' targeted especially at teenagers. The worldwide revamp cost Heinz $50mn and involved new packaging and design along with a revitalised and changed marketing and advertising strategy. In the UK alone, a media budget of £4mn was allocated to humorous television and poster ads. The messages, showing the bottles about to deliver their sauce, revolved around 'Heinz Tomato Ketchup won't come out until it's ready. No one knows what it does to get ready. It's not like putting on make-up or getting dressed.' Packs were standardised worldwide and the neck collar and fluting were emphasised to highlight the brand heritage and uniqueness. The overall plan was to increase the brand's worldwide share from 28 to 50 per cent (*The Grocer*, 1999a; Hall, 1999).

Situation analysis (3): The environment

Again, some revision of an earlier chapter might stand you in good stead here. Chapter 2 analysed the marketing environment in some detail. This section will, therefore, only look at ways in which environmental elements specifically affect communications.

Social and *cultural* aspects of the environment will mostly have an impact on the message element of communication. What is said about the product and the scenario within which it is depicted in advertisements will reflect what is socially acceptable and culturally familiar to the target market. There must be something that they can recognise, identify with and/or wish to aspire to, if they are going to remember the message, and particularly if they are expected to act on it. This reinforces what was said at p. 566 *et seq*. about the necessity of knowing the target market well.

Organisations are particularly keen to spot changes and shifts in social mores and then to capitalise on them, often creating a bandwagon effect. The 'green' issue is a good example of this. Many companies perceived that there was pressure on them to produce environmentally friendlier products, but rather than lose time in developing really new alternatives (and risk lagging behind their competitors), a few simply created new advertising messages and emphasised green-orientated product claims on their packaging to create the desired image. However, questionable approaches have

Example During the 1990s the safety of silicone breast implants was publicly questioned on several occasions. Activated by anti-implant groups such as Silicone Support and Survivors of Silicone, stories in television documentaries and in the press linked the implants with silicone poisoning and sometimes deformity caused by poor surgery. The Conservatives (twice) and the Labour party both instigated reviews in the UK that could have resulted in the banning or severe restriction of implant use. That would have been bad news for McGhan breast implants from the market leader Inner Medical. A successful PR campaign was mounted by McGhan to remind journalists, politicians and the wider public that breast implants were used not just for cosmetic reasons, but also for reconstruction after a mastectomy.

The most recent governmental review was set up in 1997 and concluded on scientific grounds that silicone was as safe as any other material used in implants, although there were grounds for improving the information available to women so that they could make informed choices. The Independent Review Group consisted of people with no vested interests in the subject, and its report was published by the Chief Medical Officer in May 1998. The sources included implanted women, doctors, lawyers, women's support groups and Members of Parliament capable of studying the scientific evidence from the USA (http://www.silicone-review.gov.uk). Although the industry had a direct opportunity to put its case to the review group, the PR campaign helped to ensure that an alternative view was presented to a public that was starting to believe the negative publicity about implants. However, the controversy continues.

been widely publicised, such as labelling washing-up liquid 'phosphate free', when that kind of product doesn't ever contain phosphate anyway, and emphasising that packaging can be recycled when the recycling facilities do not exist, leading to confusion and suspicion in the consumer's mind about all green claims. Peattie (1992) offers a concise but thorough review of green marketing communication and how it should be done.

A more general criticism of advertisers' influence in the social and cultural area is about their alleged use and reinforcement of stereotypes. The advertisers argue that they simply reflect society as it is, and that it is not their business to change it – they *respond* to the customer's changing attitudes and lifestyle. Should there, however, be concern that if people see stereotypes being constantly presented through advertising as the norm, and even as states to be aspired to, then maybe the impetus to question their validity and to break them will be less urgent? This is a complex 'chicken and egg' debate that you may want to pursue for yourself outside these pages. There are no easy answers.

To be fair to the advertisers, the whole area of stereotypes does perhaps present one of the great insoluble dilemmas of mass communication. In moving away from one stereotype, it is too easy to replace it with another. Because the advertiser is trying to appeal to a relatively large number of individuals (even in a niche market), it is impossible to create an image that reflects every member of the target market in detail. What emerges, therefore, is a superficial sketch of the essential characteristics of that group and its aspirations, i.e. a stereotype! Thus the stereotypical housewife who lives in the kitchen and is fulfilled through the quality of her cooking has been usurped at the opposite extreme by the equally unrealistic power dressing, independent dragon of the board room with the slightest whiff of Chanel and femininity. It seems that the advertisers cannot win.

No communications plan can be shaped without some reference to what *competitors* are doing or are likely to do, given the necessity of emphasising the differential advantage and positioning of the product in relation to theirs. This could affect every stage of the planning, from the definition of objectives, through the creative strategy, to the setting of budgets. These themes will be taken up under the appropriate headings later in this chapter, and will also feature in the chapters on the individual tools of the promotional mix.

Another important factor to take into account is the *legal/regulatory* environment, as discussed in Chapter 2. Some products are restricted as to where they can be advertised. In the UK, for instance, cigarette advertising is not permitted on television. Other products are restricted in when they can be advertised. Restrictions may also exist about what can be said or shown in relation to the product. In the UK, alcohol advertisements cannot show anyone apparently under the age of 21, nor are they allowed to imply that you will not be socially acceptable unless you use this product. Toy advertising similarly cannot imply a social disadvantage through not owning a product, and must also indicate the price of the toy. More generally, advertising aimed at children cannot encourage them to pester their parents to purchase (not that they normally need encouragement). Some regulations are enshrined in law, while others are imposed and applied through monitoring watchdog bodies such as the Advertising Standards Authority. Professional bodies, such as the UK's Institute of Sales Promotion or the Direct Marketing Association, often develop codes of practice to which their members undertake to adhere. As yet, no unified codes have been developed that apply across Europe.

Objectives

Now that the background is in place and there exists a detailed profile of the customer, the product and the environment, it is possible to define detailed objectives for the communications campaign.

Table 14.2, based on the work of DeLozier (1975), summarises and categorises possible communications objectives. The first group relates to awareness, information and attitude generation, while the second group is about affecting behaviour. The final group consists of corporate objectives, a timely reminder that marketing communications planning is not only about achieving the goals of brand managers or marketing managers, but also about the contribution of marketing activity to the wider strategic good of the organisation.

What Table 14.2 does not do is to distinguish between short-, medium- and long-term objectives. Obviously, the short-term activities are the most pressing and are going to demand more detailed planning, but there does still need to be an apprecia-

TABLE 14.2
Possible communications objectives

Area	Objective
Cognitive	Clarify customer needs Increase brand awareness Increase product knowledge
Affective	Improve brand image Improve company image Increase brand preference
Behaviour	Stimulate search behaviour Increase trial purchases Increase repurchase rate Increase word-of-mouth recommendation
Corporate	Improved financial position Increase flexibility of corporate image Increase co-operation from the trade Enhance reputation with key publics Build up management ego

Source: Based on Delozier (1975).

tion of what happens next. The nature and character of medium- and longer-term objectives will inevitably be shaped by short-term activity (and its degree of success), but it is also true that short-term activity can only be fully justified when it is put into the context of the wider picture.

Example Boots the Chemist wanted to increase store loyalty from women in the 25 to 44 age range who were interested in health and beauty issues. It thus launched *Health and Beauty*, a free magazine mailed to 2mn of the 10mn Boots Advantage Card holders. To the reader, the features and columns would appear like any other women's magazine, except that the publication is free and is only issued to a tightly targeted audience. The magazine creates the opportunity to target offers and develop activities to maintain customer loyalty with special events and helplines (Jardine, 1999a). For Vauxhall, however, when launching its new Zafira model the objective was to generate awareness and to stimulate potential customers to take action by enquiring at a dealership or requesting a brochure through the post. The campaign featured comedian Griff Rhys-Jones and used terrestrial and cable TV, radio and press as well as dedicated pages on the main website (http://www.vauxhall.co.uk).

Finally, Table 14.2 also stresses the importance of precision, practicality and measurability in setting objectives. Vague, open objectives such as 'to increase awareness of the product' are insufficient. Who do you want to become aware of the product: the retail trade, the general public, or a specific target segment? How much awareness are you aiming to generate within the defined group and within what time scale? A more useful objective might therefore be 'to generate 75 per cent awareness of the product within three months among A, B and C1 home-owners aged between 25 and 40 with incomes in excess of £25 000 per annum who are interested in opera and the environment'.

Until such precise definitions of objectives have been made, the rest of the planning process cannot really go ahead – how can decisions be made if you don't really know what it is you are aiming for? Precise objectives also provide the foundation for monitoring, feedback and assessment of the success of the communications mix. There is at least something against which to measure actual performance.

Strategies

Having defined objectives, it is now necessary to devise strategies for achieving them. The analysis done so far may already have established the broad balance of the promotional mix, but there is still the task of developing the fine detail of what the actual message is to be, how best to frame it and what medium or media can be used to communicate it most efficiently and effectively.

Example McDonald's ran a very clever campaign to promote the launch of its new 'curry and spice' Indian food range by parodying the 1970s Pearl and Dean cinema commercials. Cinema goers then were often treated to poorly produced, low budget advertisements for the local Indian or Chinese restaurant featuring wooden performances and stunted voiceovers. Despite the dreadful quality of the advertisements, people remember them and nearly 30 years on McDonald's imitated them in its 10- and 30-second commercials using many of the techniques previously employed by Pearl and Dean. Although the commercials would probably not win any awards for technical quality, they were actually well designed and executed and achieved very high recall levels. The humour was not lost, even on a generation that could not remember the 1970s. Such a creative approach to communication has enabled McDonald's to improve its overall market share in the fast food sector (McLuhan, 1999).

Designing the message content, structure and format poses questions for managing any element of the promotional mix. Message content is about what the sender wants to say, while message structure is about how to say it in terms of propositions and arguments. The message format depends on the choice of media used for transmitting or transferring the message. This will determine whether sight, sound, colour or other stimuli can be used effectively. These are important themes, which will be further addressed in the context of each element of the promotional mix in the following five chapters. A money-off sales promotion, for example, is certainly appropriate for stimulating short-term sales of a product, but will it cheapen the product's quality image in the eyes of the target market? Is the target market likely to respond to a cash saving, or would they be more appreciative of a charity tie-in where a donation is made to a specific charity for every unit sold? The latter suggestion has the added benefit of enhancing corporate as well as brand image, and is also less easy for the competition to copy.

Example The Bank of Scotland's credit card tie-in with the National Society for the Prevention of Cruelty to Children (NSPCC) began in 1987 (http://www.nspcc.org.uk). As well as the normal consumer benefit of a credit card, for every £100 spent on the card, 25p is donated to the NSPCC. This is in addition to three bonus donations of £2.50 each, the first when the consumer initially gets the credit card, the second after eight months and the third after twenty months. The credit card holder thus feels that a worthwhile cause is being supported, whatever the indulgence on the card. It has now become one of the leading affinity cards, generating £180 000 for the charity over the 12-year period. The extra benefit is that the card itself, by prominently displaying the logo and imagery associated with the NSPCC, keeps both customers and traders mindful of the charity and its work.

With advertising in particular, the organisation might use a character or a celebrity to communicate a message on its behalf to give it **source credibility**. The audience will see the spokesperson as the source of the message and thus might pay more attention to it or interpret it as having more credibility (Hirschman, 1987).

MARKETING IN ACTION   **Celebrity endorsement**

There are examples of highly successful celebrity endorsements that add to the value of the brand. The use of footballers Michael Owen and Gary Lineker has been a great success for crisp manufacturer Walkers. The re-naming of Salt and Vinegar crisps to Salt 'n' Lineker resulted in increased sales of the brand. Both Michael Owen and Gary Lineker actually appeared in advertisements. Other sports stars lend their support simply by playing. The broadcast vision of Pete Sampras wearing a Nike hat or sports clothes can do no harm at all to the brand while he keeps on winning. It was estimated that during one match in the early rounds at Wimbledon in 1999, Mercedes gained television exposure worth the equivalent of £36 000 in advertising airtime simply by having its logo on Tim Henman's left sleeve.

The use of celebrities can be a high-risk strategy. The allegation that England rugby star Lawrence

Dallaglio had been involved with drugs was not just bad news for him and the team. Nike and Lloyds TSB had sponsorships and Nike had supported Dallaglio with a deal estimated at £30 000 per year for endorsing its kit.

Fortunately for the sponsors, Dallaglio was later reinstated in the team. There has however, been a long line of sports celebrities who have endangered the brands they represent through their alleged misdemeanours on and off the pitch Glen Hoddle and his family had appeared in a wholesome Shredded Wheat advertisement, but they were dropped when it was revealed that he had left his wife for another woman – and all before his final exit from the job as England's soccer manager. Adidas ran an advertisement the morning before the England vs Argentina World Cup game featuring David Beckham and the words: 'After tonight, England v Argentina will be

Continued

remembered for what a player did with his feet.' How prophetic, given Beckham's sending off for kicking out at an Argentinean player. In the arts and pop world, Pepsi dropped Michael Jackson after he became the target of child-abuse allegations. Yardley announced that Helena Bonham-Carter was the new face of its make-up; at the launch press conference, the actress declared that she does not wear make-up!

There are strategies, however, for minimising the risk of sponsorship, ranging from get-out clauses if the star falls from grace through to maintaining a number of celebrities at any one time. In a classic campaign, after Eric Cantona attacked a member of the crowd who had allegedly racially abused him, Nike not only stood by him but developed a campaign showing a repentant Eric condemning racism and violence in football.

Sources: Darby (1999); Jardine (1999b).

Whether the spokesperson, or presenter of the message, is a well-known celebrity or an invented character, it is important to link their characteristics with the communication objectives, as seen in Table 14.3.

TABLE 14.3

The VisCAP model of presenter characteristics and communication objectives

Presenter characteristics	Communication objectives
Visibility ● How well known the presenter is	Brand awareness
Credibility (i) Expertise • Knowledge about the product category (ii) Objectivity • Reputation for honesty and sincerity	Information and attitude building • Both low and high involvement products Information and attitude building • High-involvement products
Attraction (i) Likeability • Attractive appearance and personality (ii) Similarity • To target audience members	Changing attitudes towards the brand • Low involvement products Changing attitudes towards the brand • High involvement products
Power • Authoritative occupation or personality	Create intention to purchase

Source: Based on Rossiter and Percy (1987).

The marketing manager might also have to decide whether or not to use personal or impersonal media. Table 14.4 compares the marketing advantages and disadvantages of a range of media, from informal word-of-mouth contact such as friends recommending products to each other through to a formal professional face-to-face pitch from a sales representative.

Whichever element of the communications mix is being used, the important consideration is to match the message and media with both the target audience and the defined objectives. These issues are covered in further detail for each element of the mix in the following chapters.

TABLE 14.4

Comparison of personal and impersonal media for communications

	Word of mouth	Sales representative	Personalised mail shot	Mass media advertising
Accuracy and consistency of delivery	Questionable	Good	Excellent	Excellent
Likely completeness of message	Questionable	Good	Excellent	Excellent
Controllability of content	None	Good	Excellent	Excellent
Ability to convey complexity	Questionable	Excellent	Good	Relatively poor
Flexibility and tailoring of message	Good	Excellent	Good	None
Ability to target	None	Excellent	Good	Relatively poor
Reach	Patchy	Relatively poor	Excellent	Excellent
Feedback collection	None	Excellent – immediate	Possible – depends on response mechanism	Difficult – costly and time consuming
	Personal			Impersonal

Budgeting

Controlled communication is rarely free. The marketer has to develop campaigns within (often) tight budgets, or fight for a larger share of available resources. It is important, therefore, to develop a budgeting method that produces a realistic figure for the marketer to work with in order to achieve objectives. Even in the same sector, the spend on advertising can vary considerably. In fast food, McDonald's spent £41mn in 1997, an increase of £10 mn from 1994, whereas its nearest rival, Burger King, spent just £9mn, an increase of over 15 per cent from 1994. In music and video stores, however, the spend was more closely matched in 1997, with Blockbuster spending £8.3mn, Our Price £7.7mn and HMV £5.5mn (A.C. Nielsen, 1999).

There are six main methods of budget setting, some of which are better suited to predictable, static markets, rather than dynamic, fast-changing situations.

Judgemental budget setting

The first group of methods of determining budgets are called **judgemental budget** setting because they all involve some degree of guesswork.

Arbitrary budgets. Arbitrary budgets are based on what has always been spent in the past or, for a new product, on what is usually spent on that kind of thing.

Affordable method. The affordable budget, closely linked to the arbitrary budget, is one which, as its name implies, imposes a limit based either on what is left over after other more important expenses have been met or on what the company accountant feels to be the maximum allowable. Hooley and Lynch (1985) suggest that this method is used in product-led rather than in marketing-led organisations because it is not actually linked with what is to be achieved in the market-place.

Percentage of past sales method. The percentage of past sales method is at least better, in that it acknowledges some link between communication and sales, even though the link is illogical. The chief assumptions here are that sales precede communication, and that future activities should be entirely dependent on past performance. Taken to its extreme, it is easy to imagine a situation in which a product has a bad year, therefore its communication budget is cut, causing it to perform even more poorly, continuing in a downward spiral until it dies completely. The judgmental element here is deciding what percentage to apply. There are industry norms for various markets, for example in the pharmaceutical industry, 10 to 20 per cent is a typical advertising/sales ratio, but this drops to less than 1 per cent in clothing and footwear. Double glazing reported 200 per cent in 1996 (A.C. Nielsen, 1999). For industrial equipment the advertising/sales ratio is often lower than 1 per cent although the sales force cost/sales ratio is often considerably higher in such industries. However, this is only part of the picture. The industrial equipment manufacturer might well invest much more in its sales force. Such percentages might simply be the cumulative habits of many organisations and thus might be questionable in their wisdom when considered in the context of the organisation's own position and ambitions within the market.

Percentage of future sales method. None of the budgeting methods so far considered takes any account of the future needs of the product itself. However, the percentage of future sales method is an improvement, in that communication and sales are in the right order, but again there is the question of what percentage to apply. There is also an underlying assumption about there being a direct relationship between next year's expenditure and next year's sales.

Data-based budget setting

None of the methods examined so far has taken account of communications objectives – a reminder/reinforcement operation is much cheaper than a major attitude change exercise – or indeed of the quality or cost effectiveness of the communication activities undertaken. There is a grave risk that the money allocated will be insufficient to achieve any real progress, in which case it will have been wasted. This then paves the way for the second group of techniques, called **data-based budget setting** methods, which eliminate the worst of the judgmental aspects of budgeting.

Competitive parity. The competitive parity method involves discovering what the competition is spending and then matching or exceeding it. It has some logic, in that if you are shouting as loudly as someone else, then you have a better chance of being heard than if you are whispering. In marketing, however, it is not necessarily the volume of noise so much as the quality of noise that determines whether the message gets across and is acted on.

> **Example** Despite the growth in wine sales from £3.8bn to £4.5bn in the UK between 1996 and 1998, the total advertising spend on wine was just £23mn, small by drinks industry standards. However, that might all be about to change as two wine producers have decided to commit significant sums to advertising. Jacob's Creek from Australia and Domaine Boyar have started to test TV advertising. If these tests are successful, it could force other producers to increase their own budgets. Traditionally, wine has been marketed by region rather than through individual brand names and the producers were content to supply in relatively small volumes, both combining to create little need to advertise by brand. If there is a switch to brand advertising in an increasingly global market, it will be a challenge to other producers as well as the supermarkets. The larger retailers have dominated the UK market and have marketed their own brands aggressively alongside selected producer labels. Price segmentation distinguished the brands, so any direct advertising could be regarded as a threat to their structure, especially if non-price variables such as quality and origin are emphasised (Maling, 1999).

If it is to have any credibility at all, then the competitive parity method must take into account competitors' own communications objectives, how they compare with yours and how efficiently and effectively they are spending their money. For all you know, the competitors have set their budgets by looking at how much you spent last year, which takes you all back into a stalemate similar to that of the arbitrary budget method.

Objective and task budgeting. The final method of budgeting, arguably the best, is objective and task budgeting. This is naturally the most difficult to implement successfully. It does, however, solve many of the dilemmas posed so far and makes most commercial sense. It requires the organisation to work backwards. First define the communications objectives, then work out exactly what has to be done to achieve them. This can be costed to provide a budget that is directly linked to the product's needs and is neither more nor less than that required. A new product, for example, will need substantial investment in marketing communication in order to gain acceptance within distribution channels, and then to generate awareness and trial among consumers. A mature product, in contrast, might need only 'maintenance' support, which will clearly cost much less. The only danger with objective and task budgeting, however, is that ambition overtakes common sense, leading to a budget that simply will not be accepted.

The art of making this technique work lies in refining the objectives and the ensuing budget in the light of what the organisation can bear. It may mean taking a little longer than you would like to establish the product, or finding cheaper, more creative ways of achieving objectives, but at least the problems to be faced will be known in advance and can be strategically managed.

> **Example** The European Central Bank is faced with a new challenge in planning a large pan-European campaign to launch the euro hard currency on 1 January 2002. From a spend of around £80mn planned for the countries already in the euro zone, a mix of PR, direct marketing and above the line advertising is required. The objective is to make the bank notes recognisable to all euro-zone citizens and advertising agencies have been asked to outline their ideas as to how that could be achieved within the very broad budgetary parameters (Garrett, 1999).

Mitchell (1993), as reported by Fill (1999), suggested that 40 per cent of companies use the objective and task method, while 27 per cent use a percentage of future sales, 85 per cent use a percentage of past sales, and 19 per cent use their own methods. Overall, across the whole promotional mix, organisations are likely to use some kind of composite method that includes elements of judgmental and data-based techniques (Fill, 1999).

Positioning the budgeting element so late in the planning flow does imply that the objective and task method is the preferred one. To reiterate, there is no point in throwing more money at the communication problem than is strictly necessary or justifiable in terms of future aims, and equally, spending too little to make an impact is equally wasteful.

Implementation and evaluation

The aim of planning is *not* to create an impressive, aesthetically pleasing document that promptly gets locked in a filing cabinet for a year. It is too easy for the planning process to become an isolated activity, undertaken as an end in itself with too little thought about the realities of the world and the practical problems of making things happen as you want them to. Throughout the planning stages, there must be due consideration given to 'what if ...' scenarios and due respect given to what is practicable and manageable. That is not to say that an organisation should be timid in what it aims to achieve, but rather that risks should be well calculated.

Planning also helps to establish priorities, allocate responsibilities and ensure a fully integrated, consistent approach, maximising the benefits gained from all elements of the communications mix. In reality, budgets are never big enough to do everything, and something has to be sacrificed. Inevitably, different activities will be championed by different managers and these tensions have to be resolved within the planning framework. For example, many organisations are reappraising the cost effectiveness of personal selling in the light of developments in the field of direct marketing.

An equally important activity is collecting feedback. You have been communicating with a purpose and you need to know at least whether that purpose is being fulfiled. Monitoring during the campaign helps to assess early on whether or not the objectives are being met as expected. If it is really necessary, corrective action can thus be taken before too much time and money is wasted or, even worse, before too much damage is done to the product's image.

It is not enough, however, to say that the promotional mix was designed to generate sales and we have sold this much product, and therefore it was a success. The analysis needs to be deeper than this – after all, a great deal of time and money has been invested in this communication programme. What aspects of the promotional mix worked best and most cost effectively? Was there sufficient synergy between them? Do we have the right balance within each element of the mix, for example choice of advertising media? Are consumers' attitudes and beliefs about our product the ones we expected and wanted them to develop? Have we generated the required long-term loyalty to the product?

It is only through persistent and painstaking research effort that these sorts of question are going to be answered. Such answers not only help to analyse how perceptive past planning efforts were, but also provide the basis for future planning activity. They begin to shape the nature and objectives of the continued communication task ahead and, through helping managers to learn from successes and mistakes, lead to a more efficient use of skills and resources. The following chapters will discuss some of the techniques and problems of collecting feedback on specific elements of the promotional mix, and Chapter 6 is also relevant in a more general sense.

COMMUNICATIONS PLANNING MODEL: REVIEW

Rothschild's (1987) model of the communications planning process (see Fig. 14.4) is an invaluable framework, as it includes all the main issues to be considered in balancing the promotional mix. In reality, however, the process cannot be as clear cut or neatly divided as the model suggests. Planning has to be an iterative and dynamic process, producing plans that are sufficiently flexible and open to allow adaptation in the light of emerging experience, opportunities and threats.

It is also easy, when presented with a flow-chart type of model like this one, to make assumptions about cause and effect. There is a great deal of logic and sense in the sequencing of decisions indicated by this model – definition of target market defines objectives; objectives determine strategies; strategies determine budgets and so on – but in reality there have to be feedback loops between the later and earlier elements of the model. Budgets, for instance, are likely to become a limiting factor that may cause revision of strategies and/or objectives and/or target market detail. Objective and task is the preferred approach to budget setting, but it still has to be operated within the framework of the resources that the organisation can reasonably and justifiably be expected to marshal, as discussed earlier.

The concluding messages are, therefore, that the planning process:

1 is very important for achieving commercial objectives effectively and efficiently;
2 should not be viewed as a series of discrete steps in a rigid sequence;
3 should not be an end in itself, but should be regarded as only a beginning;

4 should produce plans that are open to review and revision as appropriate;
5 should be undertaken in the light of what is reasonably achievable and practicable for the organisation;
6 should be assessed with the benefit of hindsight and feedback so that next year it will work even better.

Chapter 21 looks at marketing planning more generally, and will further discuss the techniques and problems of implementing plans within the organisational culture.

CHAPTER SUMMARY

Communications theory indicates that a number of dynamic elements are involved in a piece of communication, each of which has the potential to make the process break down. In a marketing context, these risks have to be understood and minimised, given the importance of effective communication to the success of products and given the level of investment often required for marketing communication activity.

As a means of systematically identifying and managing the risks and opportunities inherent in communication, a framework for planning is presented and discussed. The main stages are as follows:

1 *Analyse the situation* in terms of the target market (its characteristics, its buying habits, its state of mind), the product (the type of product, its life-cycle stage) and the external environment (social, regulatory and competitive influences in particular). The outcomes of this analysis may indicate that certain elements of the promotional mix are especially appropriate or cost effective.
2 *Define objectives* for the communication. Again, particular objectives lend themselves to particular techniques, thus shaping the promotional mix. Objectives must, however, be precise, practical and measurable.
3 *Define strategies* for how the objectives are going to be achieved, through what activities, media and messages. These strategies have to be closely matched with situation and objectives.
4 *Set budgets*. Budgets often constrain the activities that can feasibly be undertaken. There are many ways of setting budgets, but the recommended 'objective and task' method closely relates expected expenditure with communication objectives for the budgeting period and thus, if implemented intelligently, will lead to more efficient allocation of resources.
5 *Implementation and evaluation*. This stage involves putting the plan into action, monitoring its progress against what is expected, and assessing performance through information gained from detailed market research. Flexibility in implementation is nevertheless important as problems and opportunities emerge over time.

This framework should not, however, be treated as a rigid series of steps to be gone through once a year. It is an iterative and dynamic continuous process that should aid rather than constrain decision making.

Key words and phrases

Buyer readiness	Encoding	Push strategy
Channel of communication	Feedback	Source credibility
Communication	Judgmental budget setting	Strong theory of communication
Data-based budget setting	Noise	Weak theory of communication
Decoding	Pull strategy	

QUESTIONS FOR REVIEW

14.1 What are the five main elements of the *promotional mix*?

14.2 Define *encoding* and *decoding,* and discuss their role within the communication model.

14.3 How might an understanding of the *theoretical model of communication* help a marketing manager?

14.4 What are the stages in the *marketing communications planning flow*?

14.5 How does a *push* strategy differ from a *pull* strategy, and in what circumstances might each be appropriate?

14.6 What are the three broad stages of *buyer readiness,* and how might the balance of the promotional mix vary between them?

14.7 How and to what extent might the *product life-cycle* concept influence the balance of the promotional mix?

14.8 What are the main categories of *marketing communication objectives*?

14.9 What are the six main methods of *budget setting*?

14.10 Why is the *post-implementation evaluation* of marketing communication plans important? What areas should the evaluation cover?

QUESTIONS FOR DISCUSSION

14.1 Within a marketing communication model, give three specific examples of *noise,* outlining how it might disrupt the communication process.

14.2 How and why might the balance of the promotional mix differ between:

(a) the sale of a car to a private individual; and

(b) the sale of a fleet of cars to an organisation for its sales representatives?

14.3 For each of the STEP factors of the marketing environment, give three examples of influences on the promotional mix.

14.4 What are the main advantages and disadvantages of *objective* and *task* budget setting compared with the other methods?

14.5 To what extent do you think that the advantages of using a systematic planning process for marketing communication outweigh the disadvantages?

CASE STUDY 14.1

Riverdance

The 39th annual Eurovision Song Contest held at the Point Theatre, Ireland, in 1994 saw the birth of a music and dance sequence that has taken the world by storm. Although it was just seven minutes long and was intended only to fill the time until the judges made up their minds about the songs in the contest itself, the *Riverdance* sequence stole the show and had far more impact than any other act featured that night.

The initial briefing to Bill Whelan, the composer of *Riverdance,* was to produce a musical piece that would not only demonstrate Irish culture to an international television audience of 300 million, but also offer high entertainment value. Given Dublin's location by river and sea, an aquatic theme was thought appropriate. The Riverdance sequence involved a troupe of 20 dancers with the lead duo of Jean Butler and Michael Flatley, soon to become household names. Media comments after the show were largely very positive.

Corr (1994), for example, said:

'Combined with Bill Whelan's music, the machine gun feet of Michael Flatley and Jean Butler conjured up visions of a mystic and proud nationality, and reawakened a Celtic revival, providing a fast, sexy link between our dissolving heritage and the genius of a pop moment. So, Riverdance has taken its place in Irish folk history, with a rush of national pride – up there with U2 who conquered the globe in the eighties.'

The combination of ballet, tap, Flamenco and traditional Irish dancing was a big hit. The platform offered by Eurovision, both literally and from a promotional perspective, led to wide public acclaim. A single and a video were produced, and immediately on its release *Riverdance* became the best-selling single in Ireland for 18 weeks.

A Royal Command Performance in the UK and a BBC *Top of the Pops* billing all helped its popularity to grow in the UK. Success followed elsewhere with the release of the *Riverdance* album, which achieved gold status twice in the UK, double platinum in Ireland and Australia and gold in the USA and Canada. Sales were boosted by a series of successful *Riverdance: The Show* tours of America, Australia, Canada, Scotland and Germany, and the show had captured a world-wide following within two years of its introduction. In 1997, *Riverdance* was awarded a Musical Grammy award as the best musical album.

When the show was launched back in Dublin in 1994, there had been no market research to ascertain consumer reaction or pre-testing at a lower-profile event to avoid a potential flop. It was an all or nothing performance. Much depended on the creative genius of Bill Whelan and the quality of the lead dancers. Being performed to such a large captive audience and the 'halo effect' of being associated with the Eurovision Song Contest meant that high consumer awareness and interest were created, but that does not necessarily explain the appeal of the show to large audiences. Snider (1998), along with others, argued that the key was in creating a bridge between culture and entertainment. He said:

> 'The word cultural turns many people off, and that's too bad, because although Riverdance is certainly cultural, it is also a show that can entertain even the most down to earth non-theatre going person.'

Back in Ireland the success was attributed to the presentation and packaging of *Riverdance* into a new and exciting format that awakened 'the plain people of Ireland to the rich heritage of our traditional dance' (Seamus O Se, Vice-President of An Coimisuin le Rinci Gaelecha). The cultural purists remained to be convinced, however, regarding *Riverdance* as 'Broadway with a dash of Irish dancing', a highly professional, clever dance routine designed to have commercial appeal to a wide audience.

Although lead dancers Flatley and Butler had had a powerful impact on the show, when they left in 1995 and 1996 respectively it continued to grow in popularity. There are now three *Riverdance* groups touring the world, the Lee, Liffey and Lagan, all named after Irish rivers, and sell-out audiences are regularly achieved at top-class venues around the world. *Riverdance* merchandise, bags, sweaters, mugs, caps, CDs, cassettes, videos, pens, wallets and books help keep the experience alive or show goers and an official website has been launched (http://www.riverdance.com). To keep up with new technology, in 1999 an interactive digital video disk was launched based on a performance from the Radio City Music Hall in New York. Throughout the five years since *Riverdance*'s

launch, despite new routines and dancers, the basic formula has remained the same with a strong play on Irish cultural roots.

The market has grown with rivals to *Riverdance*. Michael Flatley launched *Lord Of the Dance* in 1996, again initially in Dublin at the Point Theatre, but soon grew the company by creating three troupes, one for Europe and Asia, one in America and Canada and a resident troupe in Las Vegas. Flatley features strongly in the promotions even though he does limit his appearances. Before the French tour he worked on the entertainment press in gaining publicity for the tour. He also supported the summer run of a fourth troupe at the Epcot Centre in Orlando, by undertaking a series of television and press interviews. He has become as closely identified with this show as he was with *Riverdance*. The official website (http://www.lordofthedance.com) has a number of features on Flatley and provides interesting information for hardened fans, such as the fact that he gets through 100 pairs of shoes a year and that his legs are insured for $40mn! This rival to *Riverdance* has also been active in gaining coverage, with over 300 performances in over 100 cities and the biggest-selling performance video of all times in the US, *Feet of Flames*.

Further competition may soon become evident as Jean Butler and Colin Dunne contemplate setting up their own show. All the show formats, however, rely on the same basic concept first experienced in 1994. Despite the sophisticated marketing that has been used to promote the shows since inception, including positioning, personality branding, merchandising and publicity, the question remains as to whether the format can survive in the long term and become classic entertainment or whether saturation and fashion will result in declining appeal. High culture can be very enduring, but popular entertainment tends to have a more limited life-cycle.

Source: Adapted from a case prepared by Professor Barra O'Cinneide, University of Limerick, including Corr (1994); Brophy (1999); Snider (1998); http://www.lordofthedance.com; http://www.riverdance.com.

Questions

1 Is the *Riverdance* phenomenon more of a 'push' or a 'pull' strategy?

2 Outline the promotional mix likely to have been used to sell the video of the show.

3 What are the particular problems of marketing communication for a stage show and what kind of promotional mix is this likely to indicate?

4 What diference do you think the entrance of competition (for example *Lord of The Dance*) would make to the *Riverdance* communications strategy?

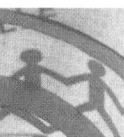

CASE STUDY 14.2

ConvaTec: leader in stoma care

ConvaTec, part of the Bristol Myers Squibb company, is the world leader in a specialised niche of the medical care market, concentrating on colostomy, ileostomy and urostomy bags and associated products. These are used by patients who have undergone major surgery to have parts of their bowel removed, often to prevent the spread of cancer. An artificial opening is created to remove body waste. ConvaTec products mean little to consumers who usually have no awareness and understanding of stoma care, unless they themselves become patients. Then stoma bags become essential for the rest of the patient's life and patients have to learn rapidly about the technology and products used. The number of stoma patients in the UK is around 100 000. Around 350 specialist nurses play a significant role in helping patients to adjust to the use of stoma products, and in advising them what to purchase, how frequently, and how to dispose of the bodily waste. The nurse, therefore, plays a key role in influencing the patient's usage and in directing customer loyalty towards particular brands. The market is a competitive one, with several players competing with ConvaTec for market leadership.

The patient might well be the end user of the product, but actually takes little part in the choice of a stoma case system. Stoma care starts in hospital, and the patient is advised on the best system by the nurse working in conjunction with the surgeon. Initially, this prescription is dispensed by the hospital pharmacy, and once the patient has left hospital, assuming that there are no medical complications, his or her own GP simply gives repeat prescriptions for the same system. The stoma nurses can reinforce product loyalty, because they continue to maintain relationships with patients after they have gone home. The hospital is thus the key for the stoma system marketers. It is not just the surgeon and the nurse who influence the choice, but also the hospital pharmacist and to some extent the accountant. The accountant wants to control the hospital's drugs and appliances budget and the pharmacist wants to streamline the number of different product lines carried and dispensed. The hospitals negotiate prices for the bulk supply of drugs and appliances, and the suppliers often sell to them at a significant discount, effectively as loss leaders, in order to get that initial prescription. Once a

patient on long-term medication has been started on a particular brand, he or she is unlikely to switch, and goods supplied on repeat prescriptions from GPs are charged at the full market price.

ConvaTec and B Braun Biotrol became the main supporters of a BCA project, although they are not allowed to influence the direction of the activities. As part of the project, BCA Direct provides a direct prescription-dispensing company where all funds after costs are donated to the BCA Trust for charity work in the area. The funds released from the trust offer an alternative to the commercial sponsorship approach adopted by many companies. Some nurses felt under pressure working for commercial sponsors, as they were vulnerable to contract re-negotiation and even withdrawal if the funding conditions were not met. One senior nurse is quoted as saying that 'undue influence on dispensing methods is sometimes exerted on sponsored stoma care nurses'. The BCA project allows nurses to be employed by the NHS and recommend the most appropriate treatment for the benefit of the patient, not the sponsor (McCartney, 1997).

ConvaTec has developed a marketing strategy that has achieved a 50 per cent share of a domestic UK market valued at around £35mn. Market research plays a significant role in the formulation of strategy. Some of this research is *ad hoc*, designed to provide information and insights into specific marketing problems, and some is on-going research to track changing patient attitudes and perceptions of the product. ConvaTec recognises that it needs a detailed understanding of two main segments: the patients as the users of the product, and the nurses who play such an important role in shaping patients' usage decisions. A major survey of 5000 patients in 1993 found four main requirements for stoma bags, in descending order:

- security
- comfort
- ease of use
- discretion

These findings reflect patients' concerns over unwanted seepage of fluids or smells that could be embarrassing in social situations. Patients do not usually wish it to be known that they need or use stoma products. Further research into the nurses' views also has an influence on ConvaTec's marketing thinking. Annually, 50 specialist nurses

▶

are interviewed on a semi-structured basis. The findings reinforce the need to be concerned with product quality, innovation and aesthetics. They also confirm the continuing role of nurses in influencing patients' brand choice. Unless significant problems emerge, once a brand has been recommended by the nurse, the GP tends to issue repeat prescriptions without question, and there is little incentive or reason for patients to consider or initiate brand switching. It is, therefore, essential that patients are exposed to ConvaTec products early on to build and retain market share. Other manufacturers are also aware of the importance of that first brand choice and the nurses' influence over it. Around 25 per cent of nurses are sponsored by other manufacturers, which might influence the recommendations they make to patients. This sponsorship also might help the hospital pharmacists and accountants to appreciate the cost effectiveness of stocking certain systems.

ConvaTec has chosen not to pursue the route of building its own nurse base through sponsorship. The marketing approach adopted aims to build a direct relationship with the patient, at the same time as helping the independent nurse to keep up to date with new methods and products in the stoma area. The programme with nurses includes regular symposia where nurses are encouraged to give feedback on their experiences; provision of educational materials, sometimes linked with training, a quarterly journal, *Eurostoma*, to present information on current issues and research, and a resource centre available for stoma nurses to use. This approach is far less direct than that of other manufacturers as the nurses, although clearly being influenced by the various promotional methods, are encouraged to remain independent; and indeed, that is presented as being of benefit to both nurses and patients. Patients are also encouraged to make direct contact with ConvaTec should they be experiencing difficulties or if they have ideas for product improvement. A confidential advisory helpline has been installed and between 2000 to 4000 calls per week are often received. Sometimes, the need is simply to reassure the worried patient. About half the callers are seeking advice on the impact of travel or special diets. Others use the helpline for requesting products or samples, while a small minority use it as a vehicle for making complaints. The important point is that a one-to-one relationship is being forged with the user. This all helps to foster product use satisfaction and to reinforce brand loyalty. All incoming calls are classified according to their content on criteria such as usage, complaints and product ideas. The calls are entered into a database for further analysis and tracking.

A website (http://www.convatec.com) provides on-line brochures and educational services to customers. For example, in the pages on ostomy in teens, considerable effort is taken to convince worried readers that a near-normal life can continue after an ostomy operation, highlighting that around 20 per cent of operations each year are on teenagers. Reassurance is given that modern pouching systems are inconspicuous, lightweight and secure. The site goes on to describe in some detail stoma care with reference to the products supplied by ConvaTec. Practical tips are given on diet, clothing and even how to handle sexual relationships.

Patients and nurses are also used in the new product development process. Patient panels are used to test potential responses at different stages. This is supplemented by encouraging regular patient visits to the factory, where again customer reaction to new ideas and problem areas can be gauged. This is vital in relation to such sensitive products. ConvaTec has taken very seriously indeed the need for direct and meaningful customer relationships, and this has contributed to its marketing success. However, there is still the outstanding issue of whether ConvaTec should build its own nurse base if other manufacturers continue to expand their coverage beyond 25 per cent of the specialist nurse population.

Sources: Management Today (1996); McCartney (1997); http://www.nursing-standard co. uk; http://www.convatec.com; with thanks to Dr Dick Foskett.

Questions

1 Given that the patient has little or no choice in the decision about what stoma care system to use, is marketing communication a total waste of time and money for ConvaTec?

2 What impact do you think ConvaTec's market research and information gathering has on its communications planning?

3 How do you think the communications strategy for stoma products will differ for teenagers and for patients aged over 50?

4 Should ConvaTec change its policy towards sponsoring nurses?

References to Chapter 14

A. C. Nielsen (1999), *The Retail Pocket Book 1999*, NTC Publications Ltd.

Barnard, S. (1996), 'Watching Brief', *The Grocer*, 14 September, p. 15.

Barrett, L. (1999), 'Tizer Links to Pop Show', *Marketing*, 14 January, p. 10.

Brophy, E. (1999), 'The Story of Riverdance', http://riverdance.com.

Campaign (1999a), Listerine's Tooth Fairy to Return in JWT Spot', *Campaign*, 30 April, p. 8.

Campaign (1999b), 'DMB&B Plays Down "Silly" Image in New Utterly Butterly Ads',*Campaign*, 11 June, p. 8.

Campaign (1999c), 'Bates to Use Men Behaving Badly Star to Launch Swiss Soft Drink in UK', *Campaign*, 11 June, p. 8.

Corr, A. (1994), 'Riverdance – The Musical', *RTE Guide*, 30 December, pp. 8–9.

Darby, B. (1999), 'Nike Stands by Scandal Hit Dallaglio', *Marketing*, 27 May, p. 1.

DeLozier, M. W. (1975), *The Marketing Communications Process*, McGraw-Hill.

Dignam, C. (1999), 'Advertisers Tune in to Digital's Interaction', *Marketing*, 20 May, p. 16.

Fill, C. (1999), *Marketing Communications: Contexts, Contents and Strategies*, 2nd edn, Prentice Hall Europe.

Garrett, J. (1999), 'Agencies Contest £80mn "Euro" Brief', *Campaign*, 30 April, p. 1.

The Grocer (1999a), 'Heinz Turns on to Teenager Cool to Win Global Icon Status', *The Grocer*, 12 June, p. 52.

The Grocer (1999b), 'Utterly Butter Wing Girls', *The Grocer*, 22 May, p. 66.

Hall, E. (1999), 'Heinz Ketchup Ads Aim to Unify Image Globally', *Campaign*, 11 June, p. 8.

Hart, N. A. (1993), *Industrial Marketing Communications*, Kogan Page.

Hirschman, E. C. (1987), 'People as Products: Analysis of a Complex Marketing Exchange', *Journal of Marketing*, 51(1), pp. 98–108.

Hooley, G. and Lynch, J. E. (1985), 'How UK Advertisers Set Budgets', *International Journal of Advertising*, 3, pp. 223–31.

Jardine, A. (1999a), 'Boots Puts £3mn into New Loyalty Title', *Marketing*, 27 May, p. 3.

Jardine, A. (1999b), 'Dallaglio Downfall Shows Danger of Endorsements', *Marketing*, 3 June, p. 12.

Jones, J. P. (1991), 'Over Promise and Under Delivery', *Marketing and Research Today*, 19 (Nov.), pp. 195–203.

Maling, N. (1999), 'Wine Makers Press for Brand Emphasis', *Marketing Week*, 19 June, p. 22.

Mallen, B. (1977), *Principles of Marketing Channel Management*, Lexington Books.

Marketing Week (1999), 'IDM Silver Award Winner', *Marketing Week*, 20 May, p. 62.

Management Today (1996), 'Management Today/Unisys Service Exellence Awards'.

McCartney, I. (1997), 'No Strings Attached', *Nursing Standard*, 14 May.

McLuhan, R. (1999), 'McDonald's Curries Favour With 70s Parody for New Line', *Marketing*, 24 June, p. 20.

Mitchell, L. (1993), 'An Examination of Methods of Setting Advertising Budgets: Practice and Literature', *European Journal of Advertising*, 27 (5), pp. 5–21.

Oliver, J. M. and Farris, P. W. (1989), 'Push and Pull: A One-Two Punch for Packaged Products', *Sloan Management Review*, 31(Fall), pp. 53–61.

PR Week (1999), 'Breast Implants', *PR Week*, 4 December, p. 11.

Peattie, K. (1992), *Green Marketing*, Pitman Publishing.

Rossiter, J. R. and Percy, L. (1987), *Advertising and Promotion Management*, McGraw-Hill.

Rothschild, M. L. (1987), *Marketing Communications: From Fundamentals to Strategies*, Heath.

Schramm, W. (1955), *Process Effects of Mass Communication*, University of Illinois Press.

Snider, E. (1998), *The Daily Herald* (Provo, Utah), 26 April.

Strong, E. K. (1925), *The Psychology of Selling*, McGraw-Hill.

Turznski, G. (1999), 'Will Interactive Media Bring Advertisers Relief?, *Marketing Week*, 10 June, p. 16.

15 Advertising

LEARNING OBJECTIVES

This chapter will help you to:

1 define advertising and its role within the promotional mix;

2 appreciate the complexities of formulating advertising messages and how they are presented for both print and broadcast media;

3 differentiate between types of advertising media and understand their relative strengths and weaknesses;

4 appreciate the role played by advertising agencies and the importance of cultivating good agency–client relationships; and

5 understand the stages in the management process of managing advertising activities.

INTRODUCTION

The average European is bombarded daily with an ever increasing number of advertising messages, whether on television, radio, print or posters. Branded goods, machine tools, restaurants, AIDS prevention and thousands of other goods, services and messages are all promoted through advertising. The battle is to attract and hold attention so that the advertising has the opportunity to generate the desired effects. Rarely can this be achieved by one advertisement.

Regardless of the type of organisation, and whatever the mix of media used, any promises made must be consistent between different advertisements and must be delivered when the customer demands them. This implies a high level of integration between advertising decisions and their implementation and the rest of the marketing mix elements.

This chapter examines the role of advertising in the promotional mix and the important aspects of message design and media selection in the development of successful campaigns. The stages in developing an advertising campaign are then presented, along with the main management decisions at each stage. Sometimes these decisions are made in conjunction with the support of an external advertising agency, while in other organisations the campaign process is controlled almost exclusively in-house. The decision to use an agency and the importance of the client–agency relationship are thus also considered within the chapter.

Example Coca-Cola (http://www.thecoca-colacompany.com) is undoubtedly the global brand leader in the cola market, with an image and appeal built up over many years and maintained by significant expenditure on advertising. It would appear that Coke really is 'it'. Pepsi has always struggled, some would say unsuccessfully, to challenge Coke's dominance. 'There are lots of things Coke is concerned about but Pepsi isn't one of them', according to one industry expert. Pepsi's latest challenge consists of a $100mn global campaign of seven advertisements targeting teenagers. One of the advertisements, for instance, features that globally known youth icon, the Manchester United first team. The theme of the advertisements is 'ask for more', which taps into youthful aspirations and philosophies. The campaign is using television and posters to reach the widest possible youth audience in 170 countries, although it will not be used in the USA as Pepsi feels that its home market presents a different communications challenge. An appealing advertising approach is not enough in itself to ensure success, however. Pepsi also needs to make sure that the product is achieving full market coverage in the various international markets and that its pricing strategy is justifiable in relation to Coke's (Tylee, 1999a, 1999b).

THE ROLE OF ADVERTISING IN THE PROMOTIONAL MIX

Advertising can be defined as any paid form of non-personal promotion transmitted through a mass medium. The sponsor should be clearly identified and the advertisement may relate to an organisation, a product or a service. The key difference, therefore, between advertising and other forms of promotion is that it is impersonal and communicates with large numbers of people through paid media channels. Although the term 'mass media' is often used, it has to be interpreted carefully. The proliferation of satellite and cable television channels, along with the increasing number of more tightly targeted special interest magazines and the use of the internet, means that on the one hand advertising audiences are generally smaller, but on the other the audiences are 'better quality'. This implies that they are far more likely to be interested in the subject matter of the advertising carried by their chosen medium. A publication such as *Classic CD*, for example, carries advertising from a wide range of recording companies, both large and small, who see this medium as a cost effective way of reaching a much larger concentrated group from their target market than any other medium, even television, could generate.

Advertising normally conforms to one of two basic types: product orientated or institutional (Berkowitz *et al.*, 1992), as shown in Fig. 15.1. A product-orientated advertisement focuses, as the term suggests, on the product or service being offered, whether for profit or not. Its prime task is to support the product in achieving its marketing goals.

FIGURE 15.1

Types of advertising

Product-orientated advertising can itself take one of three alternative forms, **pioneering**, **competitive**, or **reminder and reinforcement** advertising.

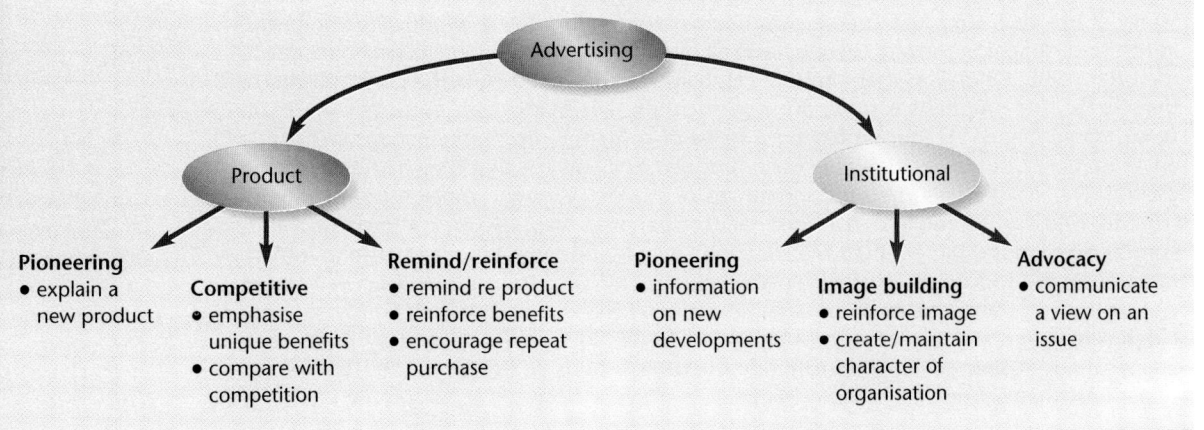

Pioneering advertising

Pioneering advertising is used in the early stages of the life-cycle when it is necessary to explain just what the product will do and the benefits it can offer. The more innovative, technically complex and expensive the product is, the more essential this explanation becomes. Depending on the product's newness, the prime emphasis might well be on stimulating basic generic demand rather than attempting to beat competition.

In these cases, the prime emphasis in the advertising is to provide enough information to allow potential buyers to see how this product might relate to them, and thus to stimulate enough interest to encourage further investigation and possibly trial. Further aspects of this use of promotion were considered in Chapter 8.

> **Example** Gillette (http://www.gillette.com) spent ten years and $750mn developing a three-bladed razor, the Mach 3. To launch the Mach 3 and communicate its 36 new features and its claim to give a closer shave, Gillette spent a further $243mn on a global advertising campaign under the company's corporate slogan, 'The best a man can get'. The pioneering advertising explaining this new concept in shaving is not just benefiting Gillette, however. The American Safety Razor Company has quickly developed a similar product, Tri-Flex, which it is selling to retailers as an own-label product. In the UK, supermarket chain ASDA is selling Tri-Flex at a price 25 per cent cheaper than the Mach 3 (Killgren, 1999). At the point of sale, therefore, Gillette's advertising might well have made the shopper aware of the three-bladed razor and what it can do, and prompted him to think of buying one, but he might well pick up the cheaper own-label product rather than the premium priced Gillette unless he has a very strong sense of brand loyalty. The existence of the own-label competitor makes it harder for Gillette's pioneering advertising to convince the consumer that it is unique and thus to justify a price premium.

Competitive advertising

Competitive advertising is concerned with emphasising the special features of the product or brand as a means of outselling the competition. Usually the seller seeks to communicate the unique benefits, real or imaginary, that distinguish the product and give it its competitive edge. Given that most markets are mature and often crowded, this type of advertising is very common and very important.

> **Example** In the coffee market, each brand is subtly trying to hint that it uses the best quality beans, or that it has the richest or the smoothest taste, or that it represents the best value for money, or that it is the one favoured by the most discerning and sophisticated coffee drinkers. Nescafé, for example, reinforces its advertising with the messages on the jar label: 'best beans, best blend, best taste', 'richer aroma', and 'coffee at its best'. The Nescafé family of brands (http://www.nestle.com/brands) is supported by its worldwide 'Open Up' advertising campaign showing people from all over the world enjoying a cup of Nescafé. In the UK in 1998, £8mn was spent on that campaign (Garrett, 1999). At the premium end of the market, the emphasis is more on sophistication. For many years Nescafé's premium brand, Gold Blend, was supported by a series of romantic, up market, soap opera-style advertisements, but these have now been dropped as it was felt that they had become too clichéd. The idea had also become something of a target. A new campaign from competitor Maxwell House (owned by Kraft Jacob Suchard, http://www.kraftjacobsuchard.com/maxwellhouse) has adopted the soap format but with humourous rather than romantic intent. The spoof Spanish soap opera episodes end with the subtitle 'Maxwell House Gets it Sorted', translated from the Spanish dialogue (Newland, 1999). Seriously sophisticated romance is still in the air, however, with Carte Noire's (also owned by Kraft Jacob Suchard) advertising offering 'Un café nommé désir' alongside imagery more reminiscent of perfume than coffee.

At least with coffee consumers can try the different brands and then decide which one really delivers what they want.

This underlines one of the critical features of good and effective advertising: it must have truth at its core. Advertising simply cannot be used to create a false image, because as soon as consumers try the product or service for themselves, they will compare the reality against the advertising promises and pass judgement.

Comparative advertising

A form of competitive advertising that has grown in significance in recent years is **comparative advertising**. This means making a direct comparison between one product and another, showing the advertiser's product in a much more favourable light, of course (Muehling *et al.*, 1990). Alternatively, the comparison may be more subtle, referring to 'other leading brands' and leaving it up to the target audience to decide which rival product is intended. Initially, it was thought unwise to use a direct comparison approach as it gave a free mention to competitors and was likely to bring about a 'knocking copy' reaction. However, advertisers have now realised that in a competitive world even if they do make a comparison with a market leader with already high awareness levels, the effect need not be negative.

Through careful selection of the benefits and judgement criteria to be emphasised, a comparative advertisement might encourage a perception of relative superiority, despite the selectivity used. The advertiser must be careful with this approach to avoid abusing the competition or presenting false comparisons. Thus any comparative product appeal must be made with care from a legal perspective. Any claims must be clearly sustainable.

A competitor might well see all this as a challenge and run its own comparative advertising to redress the balance. In extreme cases, ill-considered comparative advertising might lead to claims of unfair practice and to legal action.

MARKETING IN ACTION   Comparatively speaking

In 1999, Germany dropped its ban on comparative advertising and a number of companies tried using it for the first time, with mixed success. This prompted Berndt Michael, deputy chairman of agency Grey Europe, to develop guidelines for advertisers thinking of using the technique (Shannon, 1999).

Do not use comparative advertising:

- if your product has no significantly different advantage over the rest that is meaningful to the target market.
- if you are a market leader. Why draw attention to the products that are challenging you? Why tempt competitors to respond by knocking down the claims you have carefully set up or by emphasising your weaknesses?
- if you are trying to build long-term sustainable image. Comparative advertising is a short-term, aggressive tool that risks damaging your image if its seen as 'knocking copy' (i.e. as gratuitous insults to other products). A knocking war between you and your main competitors benefits nobody in the long term

as it simply alienates customers. Similarly, comparative advertising can be good at pointing out provable factual differences between products, but it is harder for it to create an emotional bond with the customer and that too is not helping long-term image.

- unless you are careful about the way in which you communicate direct comparisons. Comparisons can make customers feel uncomfortable, as they are effectively being told that they made the wrong choice when they purchased the competitor's product. To deal with the resulting cognitive dissonance, they are likely to think of reasons for the competitor's product being actually better than yours, despite what your advertising says, and persuade themselves that they did make the right choice.

Thus if it is used sensibly, comparative advertising can play a useful role in informing customers of important differentiating product features and can be a legitimate marketing weapon.

Source: Shannon (1999).

Reminder and reinforcement advertising

Reminder and reinforcement advertising tends to operate after purchase. It reminds customers that the product still exists and that it has certain positive properties and benefits. This increases the chances of repurchase and sometimes might even persuade consumers to buy larger quantities. The main emphasis is not on creating new knowledge or behaviour but on reinforcing previous purchasing behaviour, and reassuring consumers that they made the right choice in the first place.

Such advertising alongside product usage does help the consumer's learning experience. Frequent exposure to advertising that emphasises just how long a bottle of Fairy Liquid lasts makes the washer-up look at the bottle in their own kitchen and think, 'Yes, it has actually been there a while...' Complete victory to the advertiser.

Example Kellogg, the breakfast cereal manufacturer, has a very well-established corporate brand name in the UK market. In the late 1990s, however, it found that it was losing sales to supermarket own-brand products. This was happening because the own-brand ranges have a directly equivalent, but cheaper, product for each of the main Kellogg brands. In Tesco, for instance, Kellogg's Cornflakes are competing against Tesco Cornflakes; Frosties against Frosted Flakes; Rice Krispies against Rice Snaps and Coco Pops against Choco Snaps etc. Kellogg responded to this by targeting lapsed buyers and users of its Cornflakes with a reminder advertising campaign designed subtly to reinforce the brand heritage and quality. Most adults are aware of the existence of Kellogg's Cornflakes and what they are, and so do not need information, just a gentle reminder. The slogan 'Remember How Good They Taste?' takes adults back to the last time they tried Kellogg's Cornflakes, encouraging them to recall their own experience of the brand and how much they liked it. A small price cut, prominently marked on the box, also helped to encourage re-trial.

This kind of advertising clearly relates to established products in the mature stage of the product life-cycle where the emphasis is on maintaining market share at a time of major competition. It is also important if the weak theory of advertising, outlined at p. 571, is accepted. That would mean that post-purchase reminder, image building and reinforcement advertising actually create the attitudes and preferences that lead to further purchases. Consumers might be vaguely aware of a brand name because they have seen advertisements although they do not consciously remember them. This might be enough to make them pick up that product in the supermarket, almost as an impulse purchase, and try it. Then, they begin to take more notice of the advertisements and learn about the product benefits, relating them to their own usage, as in the Fairy Liquid example mentioned above.

Institutional advertising

In contrast, **institutional advertising** is not product specific. It aims to build a sound reputation and image for the whole organisation to achieve a wide range of objectives with different target audiences. These could include the community, financial stakeholders, government and customers, to name but a few. A number of these issues are picked up in Chapter 19 as they form an important part of a public relations campaign.

Institutional advertising may be undertaken for many reasons, as shown in Fig. 15.1, for example pioneering, in the sense of presenting new developments within the organisation, image building, or advocacy in the sense of presenting the organisation's point of view on an issue. Some institutional advertising might be linked with presenting the organisation as a caring, responsible and progressive company. These advertisements are designed to inform or reinforce positive images with target audiences. Others may adopt an *advocacy* perspective, indicating the organisation's view on a particular issue for political, social responsibility or self-interest reasons. There will be more on this in Chapter 19, on PR.

> **Example** Texaco, the petrol company, wanted to raise its profile to compete with Shell, Esso and BP. It decided to do this through promoting the issue of child road safety with the theme 'Children Should Be Seen and Not Hurt'. The television advertisement featured an empty school, representing the 600 children killed or badly injured on Britain's roads every year, and linked into a poster and point-of-sale campaign offering free reflective stickers that could be attached to children's bicycles or clothing. The campaign was reinforced through the availability of car window stickers, catalogues of child road safety products and information leaflets at the point of sale. According to Texaco's advertising agency, DMB&B, the campaign as a whole was appreciated by a wide range of publics, including politicians and schools, and resulted not only in the distribution of 15 million stickers, but also in an increase of 280 per cent in Texaco's rating as 'a company that puts something back into the community' (DMB&B, 1995a).

Advertising within the marketing mix

The above categorisation of product and institutional advertising broadly describes the direct uses of advertising. Within the marketing mix, advertising also plays a less direct but equally important role in supporting other areas of marketing activity. In organisational markets, advertising often directly supports the selling efforts of the sales team by generating leads, providing information on new developments to a wider audience more quickly and creating a generally more receptive climate prior to the sales visit.

Similarly, with sales promotion, a short-term incentive offer may be actively advertised to encourage increased traffic. For example, airlines offering 'two for one' deals or a free ticket competition frequently support their promotions with media advertising. Furniture stores also make frequent use of television and press advertising to inform the public of short-term promotional price cuts or low/no interest financing deals to stimulate interest in furnishing and to draw people into stores that they might not otherwise have thought of visiting at that particular time.

More strategically, advertising may be used to reposition a product for defensive or aggressive reasons in order to improve its competitive position. This may be achieved by demonstrating new uses for the product or to open up new segments, either geographically or benefit based.

In other situations, advertising may support other marketing mix activities to spread demand or to reduce sales fluctuations. The problems of seasonality are well known in the services field, whether in relation to holidays, restaurants or cinemas. Combined with pricing, advertising may seek to spread or even out demand patterns, saving the service provider from having to accept periods of marked under-utilisation of capacity. The various cross-channel ferry companies, for example, advertise low-priced deals and 'booze cruises' to France during the winter to boost passenger numbers.

Overall, advertising's role within an organisation depends on a range of contexts, environments and competitive challenges, and may even change within the same organisation over time. The detailed role of advertising will be specified in the marketing plan, which will clearly specify objectives, resources, activities and results expected. These issues will be revisited at pp. 627 *et seq.*, where the stages in developing an advertising campaign are considered.

Example Although one might expect the British Army to be a defensive advertiser, its 'Be the Best' campaign was definitely on the offensive. The objective was to improve recruitment, not only by raising awareness of army careers, but also by showing that ordinary people can use army training to cope with difficult situations and make life or death decisions. The army was particularly targeting 14–21-year-olds, including graduates. To draw viewers into the television advertisements and get them involved, the advertisements set a problem and invited the audience to solve it. An advertisement at the beginning of a commercial break, for example, showed an army team and its vehicle stuck in heavy snow at night with no cold weather gear and just one blanket between them. 'Who gets the blanket? You have two minutes to decide.' Then, at the end of the commercial break, one wrong answer and a reason for it would be presented and the audience invited to think again. The advertisements were run over the course of two weeks and then towards the end of the run the right answer was given: wrap the blanket around the vehicle's engine or nobody will be going anywhere the next morning. Every advertisement in the series featured a hotline number and this proved to be very successful. The army claims that 1 in 3 callers was converted to an application to join up. This campaign was backed up by radio advertising, which reaches 85 per cent of men aged under 25, and the army's website, which generates about 1000 applications per month (Cozens, 1999a; McLuhan, 1999).

Ten – SHUN! grabbing adverting?

Source: Saatchi & Saatchi/Army Recruiting Group.

FORMULATING THE ADVERTISING MESSAGE

The essence of communication, as outlined in the previous chapter, is to decide what to say, to whom, by what means and with what results. This section centres on the very demanding decision area of designing an appropriate message, with the emphasis on the message content, its tone and how it can then be presented for either print or broadcast communication.

Message

Before producing an advertisement, you need to know who the target audience is and give careful consideration to what you want to say to them. This requires a sound understanding of the targets, their interests, needs, motivations, lifestyles etc. In addition, there needs to be an honest appraisal of the product or service to determine the differential characteristics or benefits that are worth highlighting to achieve the desired results. Table 15.1 shows a range of succinct advertising slogans that convey some complex and sophisticated messages.

Message formulation

Clearly, marketing and promotional objectives are at the heart of message formulation. If the prime objective is to generate awareness, then the message must offer clear information to alert the audience to what is on offer. If the objective is to stimulate enquiries, then the focus would need to be on moving the customer through to action, making sure that the response mechanism is clear and easy to use (more of this in Chapter 18). There also needs to be consistency between the product positioning (*see* pp. 318 *et seq.*) desired and the content and style of the advertisement.

The main aim in message design and execution is to prepare an informative and persuasive message in terms of words, symbols and illustrations that will not only attract attention but retain interest through its presentation so that the target audience responds as desired. Grabbing and holding attention may mean making someone watch an entire 30-second television advertisement, read a long, wordy print advertisement, or simply dwell long enough on a non-verbal graphic image to start thinking about what it means. Whatever the medium or the style of communication, it is therefore essential that the message is understandable and relevant to the audience.

Themes

Sometimes the message may be sent out through both broadcast and print media using the same theme. In other cases, a number of different messages may be communicated in different ways over the length of the campaign.

TABLE 15.1
Advertising slogans

Company or brand	Slogan
Durex	Feeling is everything
Ericsson	Make yourself heard
Nokia	Connecting people
Peugeot	The drive of your life
Rimmel	Make up your own language
Siemens C25	Be inspired
Sloggi Sport	Fit for . . . whatever
Swatch	Time is what you make of it
Toyota	The car in front is a Toyota
Vauxhall	Raising the standard

The formation of the SEM created new opportunities for the adoption of pan-European messages. Some organisations such as Coca-Cola, Martini and Benetton have, for many years, standardised their basic advertising messages throughout Europe. Their view is that their products appeal to market segments, based on factors other than geography, which exist across the whole of Europe. These segments are based on age, lifestyle, beliefs and attitudes. Such transnational life-style segments tend to be the exception rather than the rule, however. It is very difficult in practice to develop pan-European messages that can appeal to the variety of different national cultures and attitudes that still exist across Europe.

Example As Murphy D. (1999) points out, 'Strong advertising may help, drive the product, but the retail environment is where the purchasing decision is actually made'. He argues that it makes sense to extend the themes and images developed in advertising campaigns into other marketing activities such as point-of-purchase (POP) materials. This reminds customers of the advertising messages when and where they are making serious purchasing decisions and provides an opportunity to influence that decision. John Smith's Extra Smooth Bitter, for example, is represented by the six-feet tall cardboard cut-out 'No Nonsense Man', both in pubs and in broadcast advertising. He looks like a typical young casual drinker with a glass of beer in his hand and a tee-shirt saying 'John Smith's doesn't need any nonsense to help sell it (that's why I'm here)'. Supermarket chain Waitrose has also carried its advertising themes through to POP materials. It ran a poster campaign featuring a big yellow sunflower to promote its quality and value. The sunflower also appeared on in-store posters and shopping bags to reinforce the message. Advertising images can make very striking POP displays. Ford dealers use blown-up stills from the Ford Cougar television advertising campaign in the showroom to try to evoke the same emotional response at the point of sale as the original advertisement did.

Message execution

The execution of the message can also be a problem. Research has shown that British advertising shows a sophisticated humour and is high on emotional content. German advertising, in contrast, has much less humour and is more straightforward and informative (Munzinger, 1988). Language barriers can also prevent the effective translation of sophisticated messages from one culture to another. Nevertheless, this can be avoided by largely visual advertising, which completely avoids complicated dialogue. One other solution is to develop fairly bland, inoffensive advertising that can easily be understood and adapted. The same images will be used in different countries, with any verbal elements translated into the local language.

Example Television advertising for Ricola cough sweets from Switzerland, for instance, showed simple, stereotypical images of Switzerland (the Matterhorn, men in ethnic costume blowing long horns, mountain pasture etc.) then cut to an English voice-over describing the product's 13 herbal ingredients. The Ricola advertisement deliberately played on its Swiss heritage and could be used across Europe, because other Europeans could relate in similar ways to the Swiss stereotype shown.

Other organisations go to the opposite extreme and use universal images, familiar in any Western culture, that cannot be associated with any particular country. This brings us back to advertisers such as Benetton and Martini, as well as US companies such as Coca-Cola, IBM and 3M.

The attraction of having a single pan-European approach is the cost savings in development and production of advertising, but this has to be balanced against the potential loss of creativity. It also makes the dangerous assumption that advertising objectives are the same across different countries. Many of these issues are equally applicable to wider international marketing and will thus be discussed further in Chapter 23.

Creative appeals

After the marketing issues of message content have been considered, the creative task can proceed. It is here that agencies can play a particularly major role in the conceptualisation and design of messages that appeal effectively. Two broad dimensions of **creative appeal** guide advertisement production. One dimension is rational or emotive appeals, and the other is whether the advertisement is product or customer focused.

Rational appeals centre on some kind of logical argument persuading the consumer to think or act in a certain way. However, often it is not just a case of *what* is said, but also *how* it is said. The bald logic in itself may not be enough to grab and hold the consumers' attention sufficiently to make the message stick. How it is said can introduce an *emotional appeal* into the advertisement to reinforce the underlying logic of the message. The concern here is not just with facts but also with the customer's feelings and emotions towards what is on offer. It is often the emotional element that gives the advertisement an extra appeal.

> **Example** Many advertisements that feature scientists in white coats have rational appeals at their core. Your toilet is full of germs, but our laboratory tests (enter white-coated bespectacled boffin clutching test tube) have shown that our product kills more germs more quickly with longer-lasting effect than our rival's product (split screen shot: on left sparkling white spotless porcelain, on right dubious-looking murky streaky porcelain), so buy our product (end with reassuring contented smile from boffin clutching pack). Similarly, the dandruff shampoo advertisement that shows over time how washing one side of your head in Head and Shoulders reduces dandruff dramatically when compared with the other side presents unarguable logic to support the product and its claims.

Fear is not, of course, the only kind of emotional appeal. Positive emotions can be equally effective in creating memorable and persuasive messages, which do not necessarily need any solid rational basis in order to be effective. Humour and sex are particularly powerful tools for the advertiser, particularly in appealing to people's needs for escapism and fantasy. A few examples of positive emotional appeals are shown in Table 15.2. Emotional appeals are especially useful when it is difficult to create a meaningful difference and superiority over more rational appeals.

TABLE 15.2
Positive emotional appeals

Company or brand	Slogan
Allure (perfume)	Difficult to define, impossible to resist
Carte Noire	Un café nommé désir
Clinique Happy (perfume)	Wear it and be happy
Hermasetas	Because I'd like to keep the figure I once had
L'Oréal	Because I'm worth it
Nike	Just do it
Regis Hairstylists	Love your hair
Soft and Gentle (body spray)	Create a sensation

Example To capitalise on fear, the toilet cleaner advertisement introduces elements that arouse fear of the health consequences of having a dirty toilet, while the shampoo advertisement subtly hints that having dandruff makes you a social embarrassment. Fear provides an ideal mechanism for advertisements wishing to show a 'problem and solution' or 'before and after' type of scenario. The fear is generated and then dispelled through using the product, and they all live happily ever after.

It may be argued that television is better at creating emotional appeals, as it is more lifelike, with sight, sound and motion to aid the presentation, whereas print is better for more rational, factually based appeals.

Product-orientated appeals

Product-orientated appeals centre on product features or attributes and seek to emphasise their importance to the target audience. The appeals may be based on product specification (air bags or side impact protection bars in cars, for example), price (actual price level, payment terms or extras), service (availability) or any part of the offering that creates a potential competitive edge in the eyes of the target market. Taken to its extreme, this might lead to comparative advertising, as discussed at p. 595–6.

With a product-orientated appeal, there are several options for specific message design strategy. These include:

How to solve a problem. As already discussed, solving a problem can be tied in with an emotional appeal, perhaps with fear of the consequences of not tackling a problem such as body odour or bad breath, for example. The product-orientated element of the advertisement shows how the product provides the solution. In a less emotional way, business to business advertising can also focus very effectively on problem solution.

Example Research company Taylor Nelson offers a service called Nightline, which provides a 500-respondent survey and results by noon the day after it is commissioned. To highlight the speed and to suggest potential reasons for using the service, advertisements for it (for example that appearing in *Marketing Week*, 27 May 1999, p. 54) used a problem-solving approach with a little bit of fear thrown in. The advertisement features a woman screaming under the headline NIGHTMARE. The body text of the advertisement then goes on to outline a marketer's worst fears, for example a product scare or bad press coverage, but then suggests that 'Nightline is the overnight research service you need' to provide the necessary information to start assessing and tackling the problem.

Product comparison. Product comparison forcefully emphasises the product's superiority when compared either directly with a competing brand or generally with other products in the same class. Such an approach was discussed earlier in the Marketing in Action vignette, Comparatively speaking, on page 595–6.

Slice of life. Slice of life advertisements demonstrate how the product fits into a lifestyle that either approximates that of the target market or is one with which they can identify or to which they can aspire.

Example Late in 1998, grocery retailer Sainsbury's (http://www.j-sainsbury.co.uk) developed a television advertising campaign starring John Cleese, based on the 'Value to Shout About' theme. The advertisements were loud and bullying, with Cleese shouting at the customer like a sergeant-major. They were set in an unrealistic store with a rather dim shop assistant acting as a foil for Cleese. The advertisements soon ran into trouble, criticised for being unsubtle, offensive to staff, hauling the brand image downmarket by being too price focused and alienating the target audience. Quite apart from all that, the campaign was not having any impact on sales figures (Jardine, 1999a; Tylee, 1999c). In December 1998, the campaign was voted 'the most irritating ad of the year' (Denny, 1998).

To try to recover lost ground, in April 1999 Sainsbury's announced a £30mn investment package to broaden the appeal of the brand. This investment does not only cover advertising, but also customer service delivery and supplier relationships. Part of the package includes advertising specific offerings. A postcard campaign, for instance, supported the ready meals range. The postcards were distributed through 90 fashionable London venues such as restaurants and on one side ask 'Are you getting enough?', on the other side 'Sainsbury's Ready Meals are now up to 40% bigger' (Jardine, 1999b). The television campaign, replacing the John Cleese advertisements, went back to 'safe' slice of life advertising on the familiar ground of mum shopping with the kids, under the slogan 'Making life taste better'. Sainsbury's marketing director Kevin McCarten was reported as telling staff:

> 'Marketing is not about educating our customers but about understanding their values. If we can appeal to and fulfil their needs, we can make all our lives taste better' (as reported by Jardine, 1999c).

The new advertisement show a harassed mum and a sulky child going through the checkout (with a smiling cashier, of course) and instead of showing the name of each item, the till shows what the item means to the shopper. Thus, for example, a bottle of red wine is scanned as 'memories of France last year £3.99', croissants as 'breakfast in bed 79p', a pizza as 'mum's night off £2.89' and finally a gingerbread man as 'peace offering 39p'. The child is happy again and leaves the store arm in arm with mum, who is safe in the knowledge of shopping well done.

News, facts and testimonials. News, facts and testimonials offer hard information about the product or proof through 'satisfied customers' that the product is all it is claimed to be. Such approaches tend towards the rational, and may be endorsed by a celebrity or by supporting explanation and examples. Magazine advertisements trying to sell goods that the target market might perceive to be more expensive, or goods that sound too good to be true, or goods that a customer would normally want to see or try before purchase, often use testimonials from satisfied customers. These might help to alleviate some of the doubt or risk and encourage the reader to respond to the advertisement.

Example Cafinesse is a concentrated fresh liquid coffee. Sold in chiller cabinets in grocery stores, it is a new concept in 'instant' coffee for British consumers. To establish the concept and generate trial of the product among consumers, an advertising campaign was undertaken. One print advertisement (see, for example, *Sunday Times Magazine*, 13 June 1999, p. 59) shows a porcelain mug tinged with pink and full of steaming coffee. The headline reads, 'Stop, please, you're making me blush'. The source of the mug's embarrassment is the series of quotes from satisfied customers featured in the advertisement. The quotes are carefully chosen to answer some of the doubts that potential customers could have about such a new type of product. The quotes present the product in a favourable light in terms of its:

- taste/flavour
- richness
- smoothness
- ease of use
- flexibility, in that the consumer can make the drink as strong or as weak as desired
- comparison with other instant coffees
- comparison with ground coffee
- value for money.

In a palatable way, the quotes allay fears and reinforce the key benefits of the product, achieving a word-of-mouth kind of effect that will seem more credible and interesting to consumers than an advertisement in which the company brags about its own product. The idea with the quotes is that if Cafinesse is good enough for J. Merry of Surrey, then it is good enough for me. At the end of the advertisement, two additional incentives are offered to encourage the consumer to turn the positive image into purchasing action. The first is a guarantee of 'your money back if you are not satisfied with the product' and the second is news of an on-pack offer to send off for a mug just like the one in the advertisement.

Advertorials. In magazines and trade publications, news and fact-based approaches can also take the form of **advertorials**. These are designed to fit in with the style, tone and presentation of the publication so that the reader tends to think of them as extensions to the magazine rather than advertisements.

Example Advertorials are seen often on US television. Lasting for up to an hour, they demonstrate a product's benefits and uses to a studio audience that becomes increasingly enthusiastic about it. Now, in the UK, Kellogg is planning to move into a similar form of advertiser-supplied programme but with less overt selling, and is currently negotiating the exact format and detail with BSkyB. Initially, it is likely to be a 30-minute life-style programme featuring fashion, health and beauty issues and centred around the Special K brand. This fits well with Special K's positioning and Kellogg's overall marketing strategy of focusing on the health benefits of its products (Crawford, 1999b).

Print media advertorials are also very popular. Between 1993 and 1998, the number of advertorial pages in UK consumer magazines rose by 48 per cent to 238 000 even though they still account for less than 3 per cent of total advertising spend. Research by magazine publisher Emap showed that advertorials work just as well as normal advertising in moving the reader through from awareness to interest, but are a lot better for getting information across and feeling as if they are part of the publication. Because of the association with the editorial style of the publication and the effectiveness of advertorials, media owners tend to charge more for the space, sometimes up to 20 per cent more than if exactly the same space in the same issue was used for ordinary advertising. Research has also shown that readers understand the difference between advertorial and editorial and do not feel 'conned' into reading advertorial. In fact, readers trust advertorials more because of the implied link between them and the publication itself. As long as there is interestingly presented information and no hard sell, readers actually enjoy advertorials (*Marketing*, 1999a).

The overall objective is that the reader's attention should be able to flow naturally from the magazine's normal editorial content into and through the advertorial and out the other side, maintaining interest and retention. This is particularly effective where the advertorial is short.

Customer-orientated appeals

Customer-orientated appeals are focused on what the consumer personally gains through using this product. Such appeals encourage the consumer by association to think about the benefits that may be realisable through the rational or emotional content of the advertisement. Typically, they include the following:

Saving or making money. Bold 2, for example, could sell itself simply on the product-orientated appeal that it incorporates both a washing powder and fabric conditioner in its formulation. In fact, its advertising takes the argument further into a customer-orientated appeal, demonstrating how this two-in-one product is cheaper than buying the two components separately, thus putting money back in the purchaser's pocket.

This is also a strong appeal in cost conscious organisational markets. Lucas Engineering and Systems Ltd offers consultancy to other businesses in the field of purchasing management. Its advertising emphasizes cost saving as the main benefit to be gained from using Lucas, suggesting that a '1 per cent cut in purchase costs can boost profits by as much as 15 per cent'.

MARKETING IN ACTION   Don't drink and drive

Every year around Christmas, the UK government sponsors an advertising campaign to prevent drinking and driving. Over the years, the messages, based around fear of the consequences of drinking and driving, succeeded in raising public awareness generally but were not making the desired impact on the core target audience of 20–35-year-old males. The problem was that the audience felt that for such horrible things to happen, the driver had to be absolutely blind drunk, and since they themselves were never in that state, the message did not apply to them. From 1992 onwards, therefore, the tone of the fear campaign was altered.

The 1994 campaign, for example, pointed out that 'even great blokes can kill', featuring a driver who had only 'had a quick one' and then been responsible for killing the parents of two young children (DMB&B, 1995b). In 1995, the campaign changed direction slightly by showing the damage that 'a quick one' can do to the driver himself. The television advertisement showed a young man, clearly paralysed and brain damaged, being spoon-fed liquidised food by his worn-out mother. With each spoonful, she is encouraging him with 'Come on, Dave, just one more'. In the background as a ghostly echo, pub noises can be heard, specifically a group of lads having a good time and encouraging each other with 'Come on, Dave, just one more'. The message made all the more impact by focusing on what could happen to *me* (i.e. a largely selfish concern) rather than on what I could do to an unknown third party (i.e. appealing to a sense of responsibility or duty).

The 1998 campaign changed direction again. The series of 15 advertisements reconstructed police videos of real fatal accidents with police radio messages talking of dead bodies smelling of alcohol. There was no

GUESS WHAT THOUSANDS OF DRUNK DRIVERS AND BUGS HAVE IN COMMON EACH YEAR?

NO BRAINS.

Source: © Crown copyright (DETR, 1998). Reproduced with permission of the Controller of HMSO.

voice-over, allowing the reality of the video and the messages and conversations between members of the emergency services to speak for themselves. The end shot is of a black screen with the message 'Don't drink and drive' fading to 'Don't drink and die'. Although no bodies are actually seen, some of the advertisements were still graphic enough to have to be shown only after 9 p.m. (*Campaign*, 1998).

Fear avoidance. The use of fear avoidance appeals is a powerful one in message generation and has been extensively used in public, non-profit making promotions, for example AIDS prevention, anti-drinking and driving, anti-smoking and other health-awareness programmes. Getting the right level of fear is a challenge: too high and it will be regarded as too threatening and thus be screened out, too low and it will not be considered compelling enough to act on.

Security enhancement. A wide range of insurance products aimed at the over-50s are advertised not only on the rational basis that they are a sensible financial investment, but also on the emotional basis that they provide peace of mind. This is a customer-orientated appeal in that it works on self-interest and a craving for security. Stairlifts are also sold on the basis of security enhancement, with the implication that they make going up and down stairs easier for the elderly. The advertisements also suggest that with a stairlift, the elderly will be able to retain their independence and remain in their own homes longer, a great concern to many older people.

Self-esteem and image. Sometimes, when it is difficult to differentiate between competing products on a functional basis, consumers may choose the one that they think will best improve their self-esteem or enhance their image among social or peer groups. Advertisers recognise this and can produce advertisements in which the product and its function play a very secondary role to the portrayal of these psychological and social benefits. Perfumes, cosmetics and toiletries clearly exploit this, but even an expensive technical product such as a car can focus on self-esteem and image.

> **Example** Alfa Romeo (http://www.alfaromeo.com) advertises its Alfa 156 model to French executives with macho promises in the headline of 'Power and mastery at your fingertips'. The body copy of the print advertisements starts by emphasising the Formula 1 technology in the car, then goes on to talk about cornering and overtaking abilities and finally implies a certain relaxed superiority, whatever the traffic or road conditions. All of this clearly appeals to a male ego that likes to have its status and dominance reflected in its choice of car and driving style, rather than just being one of the crowd.

Usage benefits – time, effort, accuracy etc. An approach stressing usage benefits is very similar to a rational, product-orientated appeal, but shows how the consumer benefits from saving time, or gains the satisfaction of producing consistently good results through using this product. Such savings or satisfactions are often translated into emotional benefits such as spending more time with the family or winning other people's admiration. They even work in organisational advertising.

> **Example** Toyota sells its cars to organisational fleet managers, not on sexiness or status, but on usage benefits. Its advertisements in trade and business publications (for example that appearing in *Management Today*, June 1999, pp. 6–7) emphasise fuel economy and running and maintenance costs compared with equivalent models from other manufacturers: 'The Avensis 1.8 GS is 1.5p cheaper per mile than the equivalent Mondeo and over 2.5p cheaper than the Vectra or Passat.' Similarly, Siemens advertises its telephone system to French companies on the basis of the product's capabilities and the benefits that it offers to the business user. The advertisement (*L'Entreprise*, May 1999, p. 30) emphasises the telephone directory accessible from all workstations, computer screen display of relevant documents as soon as a caller comes through, voicemail to take messages or the ability to divert calls when someone is out of the office. A website and telephone number are also offered in case the potential buyer wants more information (http://www.siemens.fr/pn).

Execution of consumer-orientated appeals

The execution of consumer-orientated appeals, particularly those with a high emotional content, provides more scope for creative imagination. Approaches may include:

Humour. The series of advertisements centred around the slogan 'I bet he drinks Carling Black Label' showed people (and once a squirrel) performing comically impossible feats to the admiration of a couple of onlookers. Underlying the genuinely funny entertaining structure of the advertisements, however, was the implication that the Carling Black Label drinker is confident, resourceful, witty and admired, which may well appeal to the aspirations of its young male target market.

Sex. Although it is rare these days to see the overtly offensive sexual portrayal of women in advertising, more subtle sexuality is still rife. As long as people are interested in sex, and as long as they feel insecure about their ability to be successful in relationships, then advertisers will find a role for sex in selling products.

Example An advertiser may hint that using a particular brand of deodorant, skin cleanser, aftershave or toothpaste will increase your attractiveness. Alternatively, the effect might be more subtly erotic, such as in the series which ran for many years of Cadbury's Flake advertisements that implied a fantasy-based, self-indulgent pleasure that could be interpreted as bordering on the sexual (it is important to note, however, that this interpretation is strictly in the mind of the beholder and is not explicitly presented on the screen).

As a final point, it is interesting to see that after many years of being criticised for exploiting women, advertisers are redressing the balance and becoming increasingly willing to exploit men.

Example The 'himbo' is almost as common an image as the 'bimbo' used to be. An example of this is the Diet Coke television advertisement, showing female office staff crowding round a window to drool over a rather handsome construction worker having his '11:30 Diet Coke break'.

Animation. Cartoons have an almost universal appeal. As well as using well-known celebrities such as Bugs Bunny or Tom and Jerry to endorse products, advertisers can create exclusive animated characters who can inhabit invented worlds and do impossible things.

Example The adventures of Kellogg's Tony the Tiger, who advertises Frosties, have entertained for over 30 years. Tony also offers the brand a strong, readily identifiable character that can be used both for advertising and as a platform for sales promotion activities. Cartoon characters also have the advantage that while they do not age, they are nevertheless adaptable as the tastes and demands of the target audience mature. Tony's appearance and character are not the same as they originally were.

Music, visual atmosphere. Any emotional effect can be enhanced or reinforced by careful choice of music and/or visual setting. Maxell cassette tapes, for example, used a parody of the song 'The Israelites', entitled 'Me Ears Are Alight', to demonstrate the clarity of the product. The humour and the point of the message, however, depended on the audience's ability to identify the original song. Classical pieces have also been successfully used to create moods in advertisements. British Airways adopted the Flower Duet from *Lakmé* as its theme, while in British minds, Dvorak's *New World Symphony* will forever conjure up images of Hovis bread. Music and strong visual imagery can, of course, serve a useful purpose in international markets by conveying emotion and mood without language problems (Appelbaum and Halliburton, 1993).

Example Using pop tracks in advertisements can benefit both the advertiser and the artist. The choice of track helps to grab attention and to signal to the target audience that this is likely to be their sort of product. It also helps to create emotion and atmosphere in the advertisement itself. Since 1985, Levi Strauss has successfully developed a striking series of jeans advertisements featuring classic pop tracks. Twelve songs used by Levi's, for instance Marvin Gaye's 'Heard it through the grapevine', have subsequently made it into the UK top 10 for a second time. The artist also benefits from what is effectively a mini pop video and many older recordings and artists find a new cult lease of life. An Andy Williams song used in a Fiat Punto advertisement made it to number 1. Similarly, Lenny Kravitz's 'Fly away', used in a Peugeot advertisement, was released as a single afterwards and also made it to the top of the charts (Wilson, 1999).

Once the decisions on message design and execution styles have been made, the framework exists for more detailed consideration of message presentation. We now turn, therefore, to presentation for print media, and then to broadcast media.

Print presentation

The final design of the words, illustrations, symbols and layout completes the message design and execution stage. Whatever the design selected, readers must be attracted to the message and their interest retained for sufficient time to enable them to reach a conclusion. Print is passive, and so it must, by its creativity, create an active and involved reader, whether using a directory, newspaper, magazine or sales literature.

Copywriting

Copywriting is the creative task of putting together the verbal elements of the message. This includes the headlines, any subheadings, body copy and captions. The headline is the main means of attracting attention to the page. Often the first thing read, it will determine whether the reader will be bothered to continue. At its least subtle, the headline aims to communicate a benefit to the reader as an incentive to read on. Where the basic message is very straightforward and rational, the headline might follow suit. 'PC Price Madness' and '50% Off Sale!' are both headlines signalling the type of advertisement that shows lots of different products along with slashed prices, and messages such as 'buy now while stocks last' or 'hurry, sale ends Saturday'.

However, headlines are often a little less direct in their execution, particularly where the appeal is more subtle or emotionally based. If we take a selection of print advertisements for cars – for example 'Safe sex' (Volvo C70 Coupé), 'Without equal, within reach' (Mercedes A-Class), 'How can beautiful be practical?' (Toyota Yaris), 'Stay beautiful' (Renault Mégane) – we see that they either set the mood for the advertisement or seek to raise curiosity, and the incentive to read on emerges from the desire to find out what on earth this is all about. Headlines are not, however, presented in isolation. They can link with an illustration or body copy to stimulate further involvement.

> **Example** The Mitsubishi Shogun's headline 'The kids hate it. They've never had a day off school' means little unless it is read alongside the illustration of the car coping easily with a snowbound country lane. Between them, they manage to give a 'slice of life' feel to the advertisement as well as emphasizing a key benefit of the vehicle.

Following on from headlines, tag lines or sub-headings either offer further explanation, or act as a bridge to the main body copy. The body copy is the main part of the text in the advertisement. It should flow from the headlines and build on the propositions that need to be made. The length will vary and in some cases will be minimal. Assuming that the advertisement has not been deliberately designed to work with just a headline and a strong illustration, the body copy has to retain the interest of the reader through to the conclusion. A large percentage of readers will not get past the headline, but for the small percentage that do, the copy has a persuasive and informative job to do.

> **Example** In the Shogun advertisement, mentioned earlier, the body copy reads as follows:
>
> 'I never quite saw the appeal of an off-roader. That was until I discovered just what the Shogun was like on the road. It's safe and comfortable with masses of room. But best of all, it's fun. For me and the kids. It's got a 3 litre V6 engine which means there is plenty of power whenever you need it. (I chose the automatic version. It's easier in traffic.) It's guaranteed for any amount of miles for

3 years, it has a 6 year anti corrosion perforation warranty and the 3 year pan-European break-down and recovery service that starts at my front door. It's really reliable. And I feel so safe sitting there high up above the traffic. Rupert says it is the only off-roader to have a Super Select transmission system that is able to change between 2 and 4 wheel drive at speeds up to 62 mph. And it's great fun in the mud and snow. But that's Rupert. He's a bit of a kid too. To find out more, including your nearest Shogun Centre, clip the coupon or call free 0800 123 363.'

Guidelines for good copy

There are a number of guidelines in generating good copy which are reflected in the Shogun advertisement.

Sell the benefits. Copy should sell the benefits to the reader, whether product orientated or emotional.

Example The Shogun body copy not only describes the technical features of the vehicle but also converts them into benefits to the owner, even using the magic words 'which means that ...' at one point. 'Safe', 'fun', 'reliable', 'comfortable' are more likely to make an impact on the casual reader than '3 litre V6 engine' and other highly technical descriptions.

Communicate to the individual. The copy should communicate to an individual, not to a mass audience. The message should suggest to readers that the copy has been especially prepared for them. This means using examples and language relevant to the target audience. Remember that they are not obliged to stay with the advertisement all the way to the end. They will stop reading it as soon as they get bored or decide that it's not really talking to them.

Mitsubishi Shogan – understanding the customer.

Source: Butler Lutos Sutton Wilkinson.

THE KIDS HATE IT. THEY'VE NEVER HAD A DAY OFF SCHOOL.

The Shogun advertisement has been written in the first person, almost in the style of neighbours chatting over a cup of coffee. That immediately makes it more personal and welcoming to the target audience of middle-class upmarket housewives. It is also likely that the target audience is conservative, and does not necessarily enjoy driving for its own sake, and may clock up lower than average miles per year. She may view the car simply as a functional means of moving the children around, but because she is rather uneasy about driving in poor weather conditions or in heavy city traffic, she wants a car that will take as much stress as possible out of driving.

The reader of the Shogun advertisement may not necessarily see herself as a Sylvia married to a Rupert (who is probably a merchant banker or a barrister), living in a converted Cotswold farmhouse complete with an Aga, two children (Tristan and Isolde) and a black labrador, but she can enjoy the scenario. She might even go as far as thinking 'If this car is good enough for someone like that, then it's good enough for me'.

Be credible. Copy must be credible, but without using clichés such as 'great prices' and 'best in town'. Credibility is important as it encourages the reader to accept the essence of the sales arguments presented, whether or not they are in the market at that time.

In the Shogun advertisement, the claims made for the vehicle are not unreasonable. The technical specifications and warranties are purely factual, and the benefits to the driver are entirely believable within the context of the character who is supposed to be telling her story.

Keep the message simple, clear and concise. It may not be necessary to cover all the issues in one advertisement. Selectivity and a clearly focused attempt to explain may be sufficient to get the basic message across. This does not mean that the advertising has to be boring. People expect advertising to tell them what they need to know in a digestible, but nevertheless entertaining form. Dull copywriting, however worthy the content, will not retain interest. Imagine how much more boring the Shogun advertisement would have been if it had just been an impersonal list of product features.

The copy must flow from point to point and end in a clear call for action, whether to reflect, enquire or buy. The copy should always end with some request for action. Note that the Shogun advertisement ends with a freephone number and the option of sending off for more information by mail. The specific copy generated will depend also on the overall style. It may be straight copy, but often involves some combination with pictures, artwork and illustrations, and thus the synergy between all the separate elements needs to be carefully thought through, as in the Shogun advertisement.

Finally, the sponsor of the advertisement is usually clearly identified, through the use of words, logos, trade marks or organisation details. Thus the Mitsubishi Motors logo appears at the top left of the Shogun advertisement, with the Shogun logo at the top right.

If the advertisement is designed to generate a direct response from the reader, then the prominence of phone numbers or the design of a reply coupon should be carefully considered. Chapter 18 on direct marketing takes up some of these issues further.

Layout

The **layout** refers not just to the words but also all the artwork, including photography, drawings and logos. The layout shows how the copy and illustration(s) hang together from a rough concept stage through to the final agreed advertisement. This format enables a number of creative ideas to be explored before a final, irrevocable decision is made. The illustrations can sometimes be even more powerful than the headline, particularly as colour reproduction techniques have improved. Often illustrations communicate more symbolism to the reader than words.

Example In *Marketing Week*'s poster watch feature, a sample of 300 adults were shown pictures of ten poster advertisements with the advertiser's name removed. The least cluttered poster scored the highest recall figures, with 59 per cent of adults remembering having seen the poster before. The poster was for Colgate Total toothpaste and had a bright red background with white script, 'Security guard. The only toothpaste proven to work above and below the gumline' and a logo. The Dutch Airline KLM's poster with its fresh, clean image of a swan flying over a reedbed, 'Avoid the rushes', was less well recalled (32 per cent of all adults) but topped the liking scale: 83 per cent of adults liked this poster, compared with 62 per cent who liked the Colgate poster (*Marketing Week*, 1999c). The question is whether it is better to be remembered or to be liked.

Illustrations can be photographs, tables and charts, line drawings and graphs, or indeed any type of non-copy content, including free attachments, such as the scented cards included in perfume advertisements.

Finally, the overall design of the advertisement must be attractive and must encourage the reader to follow through. To achieve this requires, apart from an understanding of what makes the reader tick, a sound understanding of print production processes and the aesthetics of the layout proposed. The aesthetics include the balance between the advertisement elements, the focal point of attention, the eye movement for the reader, the relative proportions of the elements and the unity of style and moods generated.

Broadcast presentation

Broadcast presentation includes television and radio commercials. In contrast to print production, broadcast presentation has no layout, but a script to guide the dialogue, narration, sound effects and music. This ultimately includes the production details to cover camera work etc. where appropriate. The script enables discussion between the creative and marketing staff before the expensive commitment to shooting or recording. Once agreed, the script is developed into a *storyboard*, which has three components: the main scenes and actions, the written description of what occurs and the audio effects. Although at this stage it is still a static format, not using sight, sound or motion, it is a pragmatic response to the problem of incurring production costs at an exploratory stage.

After the initial agreement, the storyboard goes through further stages of refinement prior to final shooting. A number of formats are possible with television commercials. Some advertisements adopt a documentary kind of style, with either an announcer or an expert telling the audience authoritatively about the product on offer. Similarly, demonstrating the product in use gives rational credibility to its claims, especially when its performance is compared with that of rival products. Moving towards a more emotionally based format, some advertisements use a testimonial approach, in which a 'satisfied customer' or a celebrity swears that the product is wonderful. The kind of advertisement that begins with statements like 'I used to have dandruff until I discovered Head and Shoulders' or ends with things like 'So, Mrs Bloggs, you definitely won't swap your one box of new improved Daz for two boxes of your old powder?' falls into this category.

Animation, as discussed at p. 607 above, clearly lends itself to television advertising, and can be used to inform, to entertain, or to create product image, just as using live people can. Much television advertising, though, uses a slice-of-life type of approach to demonstrate the product in context, with strong inputs of emotion and humour to increase the audience's involvement and entertainment impact.

Now you know the secret of her energy.

Source: SmithKline Beecham plc.

Advertising for most branded products is trying to pre-sell the goods, so the advertisement has to be sufficiently impressive for its impact still to be felt some time later when consumers actually get to the supermarket.

> **Example**   A particularly interesting slice of cyberlife showing a product in an appropriate context is Lucozade's (http://www.sb.com) television campaign starring Tomb Raider action heroine Lara Croft. In the advertisement, Lara does her normal job of confronting ravening wolves and generally escaping from tight situations. When she needs an energy boost, she selects the Lucozade glucose drink from her ration pack, then springs back into action again. Lara is such a good choice for the advertisement, partly because she lives an extreme form of the energetic lifestyle in which Lucozade is positioned, and partly because of her appeal and cult status among the under-25 target audience. The campaign cost £25mn and is supported by posters and in-store promotions (Campbell, 1999c; *Marketing Week*, 1999b). The roadside billboards grab attention by showing three of the wolves from the advertisement jumping up to try to reach a 10-feet tall cardboard cut-out Lara trying to climb over the top of the billboard (*Marketing*, 1999e). Unfortunately, two Laras have already been stolen from one site in Bristol. . .

Guidelines for broadcast presentation

There are a number of guidelines to assist in the commercial writing process. Clearly, whatever is shown must attract and hold viewers. It is important that the story is told in an entertaining yet relevant manner. This means using interesting ways of showing people interacting with the product.

In addition, the first few seconds of the commercial need to gain attention, in the same way as the headline in print must. This may be by a direct challenge or an unusual or evocative scene or music. There is, however, sometimes a conflict between aesthetic values and selling in advertising. An advertisement might use stunning special effects, broadcast images that remain in the mind, or create a minor masterpiece of cinematic art, but if viewers cannot understand the commercial message or cannot match the correct product or service with the advertisement, then it has failed.

Advertisers do face problems if they want to avoid clichés or what might be seen as stereotypical advertisements for the sort of product involved. Car advertisements, for example, are typically about speed, performance, status or safety.

Overall, with television the objective is to create 30- or 60-second dramas, vignettes or jokes that are as heavily loaded with emotional connotations as with product benefits.

Example When Peugeot launched its new 406 model, it wanted to get out of that rut. Peugeot felt that consumers, saturated with technical data, saw most competing cars within a particular class as very similar in terms of performance and specification etc. To stand out from the crowd, therefore, the Peugeot 406 advertisement used powerful and emotional imagery in which the car itself played an almost incidental role. The television advertisement was shot in black and white, although some shots featured a little girl in a red coat (a reference to the film *Schindler's List*) and focused on the passing thoughts of the Peugeot driver. The impact came from images such as the girl in the path of a skidding lorry, a man giving a kiss (or possibly the kiss of life – it was deliberately ambiguous) to another man, and a protester in front of a tank. The purpose was to focus on drivers as individuals, making them feel special. This is consistent with Peugeot's slogans, 'The Drive of Your Life' and 'There Is No Such Thing as an Average Person'. To maximise the impact, the initial advertisement was three minutes long and shown simultaneously on every commercial terrestrial and satellite station serving the UK.

The big advantage of television is that it does enable feelings to be attached to the product. The more lively the imagery and believable the advertisement, the greater the effect may be. In a similar way, radio has the benefit of creating lively images in the mind.

ADVERTISING MEDIA

Advertising media are called on to perform the task of delivering the message to the consumer. The advertiser needs, therefore, to select the medium or media most appropriate to the task in hand, given their relative effectiveness and the budget available. Table 15.3 shows the percentage of total advertising spend by medium in different European countries in 1997. It is interesting to note that print takes a higher percentage than television in many countries. This is a stark reminder that most organisations either cannot afford expensive television advertising or find it inappropriate. Print media, such as local and national newspapers, special interest magazines and trade publications, have thus become the primary focus for most organisations' advertising efforts.

This section will look further at each advertising medium's relative merits, strengths and weaknesses, but first defines some of the terms commonly used in connection with advertising media.

Some definitions

Before we proceed to examine the advertising media, several basic terms need to be defined, based on Fill (1999).

Reach

Reach is the percentage of the target market that is exposed to the message at least once during the relevant period. If the advertisement is estimated to reach 65 per cent of the target market, then that would be classified as 65. Note that reach is not concerned with the entire population, but only with a clearly defined target audience. Reach can be measured by newspaper or magazine circulation figures, television viewing statistics or analysis of flows past advertising boarding sites, and is normally measured over a four-week period.

Ratings

Ratings, otherwise known as TVRs, measure the percentage of all households owning a television that are viewing at a particular time. Ratings are a prime determinant of the fees charged for the various advertising slots on television.

TABLE 15.3

Advertising expenditure across Europe: percentage spend by medium, 1997

	Television	Print	Radio	Cinema	Outdoor
Austria	26.9	55.7	10.5	0.5	6.4
Belgium	44.9	52.2	1.3	0.2	1.4
Denmark	18.9	76.4	1.8	0.8	2.1
Finland	14.4	81.0	2.4	0.1	2.1
France	36.0	42.1	9.2	0.7	12.0
Germany	23.5	68.3	3.5	1.1	3.6
Greece	48.5	44.1	5.1		2.3
Ireland	30.7	51.4	9.5	0.9	7.3
Italy	53.4	39.1	4.1	0.3	3.1
Luxembourg					
Netherlands	20.0	71.4	3.0	0.5	5.1
Portugal	48.2	34.1	5.9	0.3	11.4
Spain	32.9	50.1	11.0	1.0	5.0
Sweden	25.3	65.3	3.2	0.6	5.6
UK	33.2	58.5	3.4	0.7	4.3

Source: Euromonitor (1999), Table 1303 p. 314.

Frequency

Frequency is the average number of times that a member of the target audience will have been exposed to a media vehicle during the specified time period.

> **Example** Saturation advertising is a short, sharp burst of advertising for a particular brand that monopolises a medium, television programme or event. The idea is that it cuts through all the normal advertising 'noise' because there is so much of it and thus it is bound to be noticed by the target audience. It hits them hard throughout their involvement in the programme or event. Saturation advertising also tends to generate spin-off PR coverage because of its intensity and often because of its creativity. Carlsberg-Tetley, for example, spent £1mn on nine versions of the same advertisement to be screened around a film on ITV as a means of relaunching the lager brand Castlemaine XXXX. Similarly, £2mn was spent on 90-second advertisements for Blackcurrant Tango to be screened over one weekend. Both Castlemaine XXXX and Tango found a similar effect, however. The saturation advertising certainly helped to generate awareness, but it had a negligible effect on sales, and neither brand has been given saturation advertising campaigns again (Day, 1999). The 'failure' of saturation advertising could be because it misses a proportion of the audience (what if they were out clubbing that night and did not see the film? What if they were away on holiday that weekend?) or it bores the audience because there is so much of it and it is so concentrated. This latter reason might not be so surprising or far off the mark. A survey showed that over 30 per cent of viewers use commercial breaks as an opportunity to go and make a cup of tea, 25 per cent to channel-surf, and 17 per cent to carry on a conversation. Just 16 per cent say that they pay attention to television advertisements (Croft, 1999a).
>
> Perhaps, then, retailer WH Smith and mobile phone operator Orange had the right idea with their joint saturation advertising campaign. They bought the advertising space on all the escalators and four sheet poster sites in London Underground mainline stations for two weeks to advertise their Justtalk pre-pay mobile phone service. This campaign really did have a captive audience, which could only avoid the advertisements by dashing down the escalator a little faster!

Opportunity to see

Opportunity to see (OTS) describes how many times a member of the target audience will have an opportunity to see the advertisement. Thus, for example, a magazine might be said to offer 75 per cent coverage with an average OTS of three. This means that within a given time period, the magazine will reach 75 per cent of the target market, each of whom will have three opportunities to see the advertisement. According to White (1988), it is generally accepted that an OTS of 2.5 to three is average for a television advertising campaign, whereas a press campaign needs five or more. An OTS figure closer to 10 is probably a waste of money, as the extra OTSs are not likely to improve reach by very much and might even risk alienating the audience with overkill!

Ideally, advertisers set targets to be achieved on both **reach** and **frequency**. Sometimes, however, because of financial constraints, they have to compromise. They can either spend on achieving breadth of coverage, that is, have a high reach figure, or go for depth, that is, have a high level of frequency, but they cannot afford both. Whether reach or frequency is better depends entirely on what the advertisement's objectives are. Where awareness generation is the prime objective, then the focus may be on reach, getting a basic message to as many of the target market as possible at least once. If, however, the objective is to communicate complex information or to affect attitudes, then frequency may be more appropriate. An advertiser trying to encourage brand switching, for example, in an fmcg market may find that it takes several exposures to the advertisement before the idea of trying a different brand takes root in the consumer's mind.

Of course, when measuring reach, the wider the range of media used, the greater the chances of overlap. If, for instance, a campaign uses both television and magazine advertising, some members of the target market will see neither, some will see only the television advertisement, some will see only the print advertisement, but some will see both. Although the overall reach is actually likely to be greater than if just one medium was used, the degree of overlap must enter into the calculation, since as a campaign develops the tendency is towards duplicated reach.

Television

Television's impact can be high, as it not only intrudes into the consumer's home but also offers a combination of sound, colour, motion and entertainment that has a strong chance of grabbing attention and getting a message across. Provided that the television is actually switched on, the message in vision or at least sound is being delivered. That does not, however, necessarily mean that anyone is there watching or listening. One of the perennial problems in television advertising is the 'empty arm-chair' syndrome – the tendency of people to go to the bathroom, make a cup of coffee or do a thousand and one other things while the advertisements are on. Even if they stay in the same room, they might be chatting or otherwise making their own entertainment, distracting them from the advertising.

Nevertheless, television advertising does present a tremendous communication opportunity, as indicated by the figures for television ownership across Europe, shown in Table 15.4. Television enables a seller to communicate to a broad range of potentially large audiences. This means that television has a relatively low cost per thousand (the cost of reaching a thousand viewers) and that it has a high reach, but to largely undifferentiated audiences. Some differentiation is possible, depending on the audience profile of the programmes broadcast, and thus an advertiser can select spots to reach specific audiences, for example during sports broadcasts, but the advertising is still far from being narrowly targeted.

The problem, therefore, with television is that its wide coverage means high wastage. The cost per thousand may be low, and the number of thousands reached may be very high, but the relevance and quality of those contacts must be questioned. Television advertising time can be very expensive, especially if the advertisement is networked nationally. Actual costs will vary according to such factors as the time of day, the predicted audience profile and size, the geographic area to be covered, the length of time and number of slots purchased and the timing of negotiation. All of this means that very large bills are soon incurred.

Example   A new product launch in the fmcg sector is almost guaranteed to be an expensive undertaking. When Kellogg launched its cereal bars in the UK, for example, it spent £8.6mn, including £3.3mn on outdoor media and £3.9mn on television advertising. In the mobile phone market, in 1998 One 2 One spent £33mn on its 'Who would you like to have a one to one with?' campaign, of which £23mn was spent on television advertising. The top 10 UK advertisers in 1998 spent £750mn between them and 70 per cent of what went on television campaigns (*Marketing*, 1999b). Companies and brand managers not only have to think of media costs but also of production costs for advertisements. Guinness's 'surfer' ad, featuring surfers riding huge waves with giant white horses leaping out of them, cost £1mn just for production and took a year to make. Although using a celebrity in an advertisement might cause fewer production problems than creating white horse effects, it still costs a lot of money. Murphy C. (1999) estimates that using a recognisable television personality costs around £30 000, whereas a well-known celebrity could cost up to £250 000. Both cost much more if the advertiser wants exclusivity, i.e. the celebrity agrees not to appear in any other company's advertisements over the campaign period.

Quite apart from the cost involved, television is a low involvement medium. This means that although the senders control the message content and broadcasting, they cannot check the receiver's level of attention and understanding, because the receiver is a passive participant in what is essentially one-way communication. There is no guarantee that the receiver is following the message, learning from it and remembering it positively. Retention rates tend to be low, and therefore repetition is needed, which in turn means high costs.

Furthermore, the amount of time allowed for advertising is usually strictly controlled, which tends to force up the rates for prime time advertising and increase the competition for the best slots. The prime slots in the UK and Germany, for example, are often booked over six months ahead, and yet in Spain, advance booking does not extend beyond a few weeks.

The growth of internationally broadcast cable and satellite television channels is changing the shape of television advertising by creating pan-European segment interest groups. MTV, for example, has opened up communication with a huge youth market linked by a common music culture.

Nevertheless, there are still problems with cable and satellite. The levels of penetration differ across Europe. For example cable penetration is high in Belgium, Luxembourg and the Netherlands, as can be seen in Table 15.4, but is still relatively low in Spain, Portugal and the UK. Satellite is also only just taking off and is best established in Austria, Denmark and Germany. Through the advent of digital television and the marketing efforts of its providers, however, it is likely that both cable and satellite will grow significantly by 2005. Also, demand is still weak for true pan-European programmes, and there is not always the flexibility to concentrate on specific geographic markets through these channels. Thus you advertise to the whole of Europe or none of it. Last, but not least, there is the language problem. Whether the channel broadcasts in English, German or French, it is automatically going to exclude a large number of people throughout Europe who do not understand the language, although the capability does exist for broadcasters to feed different things into different regions. Cartoon Network, for example, is available in 40 million homes in 35 countries. It offers tailored packages in different countries, for example broadcasting in Polish in Poland and in Dutch in the Netherlands. On the Netherlands' national Herring Day holiday, Dutch viewers were treated to a feast of Popeye cartoons (Fry, 1999).

TABLE 15.4

Cable and direct-to-home satellite television, 1997

	Television households (TVHH) ('000)	Cable households ('000)	Satellite households (% of TVHH)	Satellite households ('000)	Satellite households (% of TVHH)
Austria	3150	1100	34.9	1570	49.8
Belgium	3860	3800	98.4	110	2.8
Denmark	2370			940	39.7
Finland	2200	863	39.2	270	12.3
France	2210	2232	10.1	2470	11.2
Germany	36877	18880	51.2	11150	30.2
Greece	3346	468	14.0	200	6.0
Ireland	1111	543	48.9	110	9.9
Italy	19121	2868	15.0	760	4.0
Luxembourg	149	122	81.9		
Netherlands	6575	5900	89.7	260	4.0
Portugal	2927	210	7.2	360	12.3
Spain	12020	390	3.2	1130	9.4
Sweden	3855	1962	50.9	720	18.7
UK	24033	2374	9.9	4310	17.9

Source: Euromonitor (1999), Table 1306, p. 317.

Radio

Radio has always provided an important means of broadcast communication for smaller companies operating within a restricted geographic area. It is now, however, beginning to emerge as a valuable national medium in the UK because of the growth in the number of local commercial radio stations and the creation of national commercial stations such as Classic FM and Atlantic 252.

While still not as important as television and print, in general terms radio can play a valuable supportive role in extending reach and increasing frequency. Despite being restricted to sound only, radio still offers wide creative and imaginative advertising possibilities and, like television, can deliver fairly specific target audiences. Narrow segments can be attractive for specialist products or services.

> **Example** Classic FM, with its programming of classical music, has created a new radio-listening segment of older, affluent potential customers who otherwise would be difficult and expensive to contact as a group. Advertisers of financial products, home furnishings and other 'exclusive' products have found a very cost effective medium.

Compared with television, radio normally offers a low cost per time slot. However, as a low involvement medium, it is often not closely attended to, being used just as background rather than for detailed listening. More attention might be paid, however, to the car radio during the morning and evening journey to and from work. Nevertheless, learning often only takes place slowly, again requiring a high level of repetition, carrying with it the danger of counter productive audience irritation at hearing the same advertisements again and again. Radio is, therefore, a high frequency medium. Television for the same budget will provide more reach, but far less frequency. The choice between them depends on objectives, and brings us back to the earlier 'reach vs frequency' discussion. Large advertisers can, however, use the two media in conjunction with each other, with radio as a means of reminding listeners of the television advertisements and reinforcing that message.

Table 15.5 shows the top ten advertisers in the Netherlands in 1993. Although it can be seen that television and the press are the dominant media, radio still has a supporting, albeit small, role to play.

TABLE 15.5

Top 10 advertisers in the Netherlands, 1993

	(mn HFL)	Television	Press	Radio
Procter & Gamble Benelux	156 780	94.0	3.9	1.4
PTT Telecom	77 635	41.7	42.4	8.9
Lever	52 098	84.2	7.5	3.7
Albert Heijn	50 311	22.5	77.4	
Heineken Nederland	46 714	60.3	21.4	8.0
Van den Bergh Foods	43 021	84.3	7.7	4.9
Postbank	36 167	23.1	65.2	7.7
Nestlé Nederland	35 778	80.1	15.3	1.2
Molnlycke Nederland	31 441	88.5	6.1	2.8
Rabobank Nederland	29 818	35.0	53.1	7.5

Source: NTC Publications (1997), p. 212.

One of the main problems with radio is still that there are many commercial stations. Furthermore, the advertising slots tend to be grouped together, creating clutter, and it is difficult to build reach and make an impact. Nevertheless, the costs of production can be low, comprising scriptwriting and delivery. This, combined with the potential of a local orientation, means that radio is still accessible and attractive to the small business advertiser.

Cinema

Cinema is not a major medium, but can be used to reach selected audiences, especially younger and male. In the UK, for example, nearly 80 per cent of cinema goers are in the 15–34 age group. The improvement in the quality of cinema facilities through the development and marketing of multiplexes has led to something of a resurgence in cinema audiences over the last 10 years or so. The popularity of cinema going and the kind of audiences delivered to advertisers are shown in Table 15.6.

Cinema goers are a captive audience, sitting there with the intention of being entertained. Thus the advertiser has an increased chance of gaining the audience's

TABLE 15.6

Cinema screens and attendances, 1997

	Screen (number)	Attendances (millions)
Austria	401	13
Belgium	466	25
Denmark	320	11
Finland	322	6
France	4595	139
Germany	4098	137
Greece	360	15
Ireland	209	13
Italy	3897	92
Luxembourg		
Netherlands	530	17
Portugal	273	8
Spain	2257	101
Sweden	1164	15
UK	2517	124

Source: Euromonitor (1999), adapted from Tables 2407 and 2408, pp. 461–2.

attention. The quality and impact of cinema advertising can be much greater than that of television, because of the size of the screen and the quality of the sound system. Cinema is often used as a secondary medium rather than as a main medium in an advertising campaign. It can also screen advertisements, rated consistently with the film's classification, that would not necessarily be allowed on television.

Magazines

The main advantage of a printed medium is that information can be presented and then examined selectively at the reader's leisure. A copy of a magazine tends to be passed around among a number of people and kept for quite a long time. Add to that the fact that magazines can be very closely targeted to a tightly defined audience, and the attraction of print media starts to become clear. Advertisers also have an enormous range of types and titles to choose from. Table 15.7 shows the numbers of consumer publications in various European countries in 1993/94.

There are several different types of magazine carrying advertising.

General and news-based magazines

With publications such as *Time, The Economist* and *Reader's Digest*, an advertiser needs to ensure that the readership profile matches closely with the target segment, given the general orientation of these magazines. Further selectivity may be possible through regional or country editions.

Special interest magazines

There exists an enormous number of special-interest magazines, each tailored to a specific segment. As well as broad segmentation, by sex (*Freundin* for women in Germany; *Playboy* for men anywhere), age (*Just 17* for teenagers; *The Oldie* for the over-50s in the UK) and geography (*The Dalesman* for Yorkshire and its expatriates), there are many narrower criteria applied. These usually relate to lifestyle, hobbies and leisure pursuits, and enable a specialist advertiser to achieve a very high reach within those segments.

TABLE 15.7

Mainstream consumer publications, 1993/4

	Consumer publications (number)	Combined circulation ('000)	Total audited publications (number)
Austria	33	8 750	42
Belgium	50	6 524	65
Denmark	36	4 128	56
Finland	26	3 739	43
France	120	45 267	149
Germany	87	71 455	160
Greece	28	1 739	50
Ireland	18	817	31
Italy	56	16 647	97
Luxembourg			
Netherlands	56	17 112	75
Portugal	47	3 813	65
Spain	48	10 040	73
Sweden	42	5 988	59
UK	59	24 255	87

NB: Mainstream includes TV guides, business, men's and women's, motoring, home and general interest

Source: Euromonitor (1998), Table 1306, p.311.

Trade and technical journals

Trade and technical journals are targeted at specific occupations, professions or industries. *Industrial Equipment News*, *The Farmer*, *Accountancy Age* and *Chemistry in Britain* each provide a very cost effective means of communication with groups of people who have very little in common other than their jobs.

Whatever the type of publication, the key is its ability to reach the specific target audience. New technology has created this diversity of magazines to suit a very wide range of targets.

Magazines have other benefits. Some may have a long life, especially special-interest magazines that may be collected for many years, although the advertising may lose relevance. Normally, though, an edition usually lasts as long as the timing between issues. The regular publication and the stable readership can allow advertisers to build up a campaign with a series of sequential advertisements over time to reinforce the message. An advertiser may also choose to take the same slot – for example the back page, which is a prime spot – to build familiarity. The advertiser may even buy several pages in the same issue, to gain a short burst of intense frequency to reinforce a message, or to present a more complex, detailed informational campaign that a single- or double-page spread could not achieve.

> **Example** There has been an interesting growth in international rather than purely national magazines. *Vogue*, for instance, is a recognised name across the world, yet produces different editions to suit the different tastes of various geographic regions. Airlines also have to cater for international readerships with their in-flight magazines. BA issues *Business Life* to frequent flyers, *High Life* on certain routes and *Sinbad* for Middle Eastern routes. These magazines carry advertising not only for the airline, but also for hotels, car rentals, computers and business services etc. Long-haul flight magazines also include direct response advertising (*see* Chapter 18), capitalising on the bored captive audience. Although these in-flight magazines conform to high standards in production, their circulation and readership can obviously vary considerably.

Magazines also have one potentially powerful advantage over broadcast media, which is that the mood of the reader is likely to be more receptive. People often save a magazine until they have time to look at it properly, and because they are inherently interested in the magazine's editorial content, they do pay attention and absorb what they read. This has a knock-on effect on the advertising content too. People also tend to keep magazines for reference purposes. Thus the advertising may not prompt immediate action, but if readers suddenly come back into the market, then they know where to look for suppliers.

Improvements in print and paper technology have enabled high quality advertising to be produced, which is especially important if the product is to be shown at its best. Advertisements for food, clothing, holidays or cosmetics, for instance, are all looking to provoke a strong positive emotional desire ('Oooh, that looks nice') through the stimulus provided by the graphic image. Some magazine advertising is almost an art form.

The specific cost of a magazine advertising slot will vary according to a number of factors. These include its circulation and readership profile, the page chosen and the position on the page, the size of the advertisement, the number of agreed insertions, the use of colour and bleed (whether the colour runs to the edge of the page or not), and any other special requirements.

The growth of truly international magazines is partly restricted by language. English language publications are clearly fine for US and UK markets, and to some extent for business segments in Europe, but the proportion speaking English in Europe is widely variable. Figures quoted by de Mooij (1994) suggest that 72 per cent of people in the Netherlands understand English, 44 per cent in Germany and just

12 per cent in Spain. Balkanair, the Bulgarian national airline, compromises by printing all its in-flight magazine articles in both Bulgarian and English on facing pages (presumably either halving the content or doubling the cost in the process).

Newspapers

The main role of newspapers for advertisers is to communicate quickly and flexibly to a large audience. National daily papers, national Sunday papers and local daily or weekly papers between them offer a wide range of advertising opportunities and audiences. Table 15.8 shows the number of newspapers available in each European country in 1997.

Classified advertisements are usually small, factual and often grouped under such headings as furniture, home and garden, lonely hearts etc. This is the kind of advertising used by individuals selling their personal property, or by very small businesses (for example a one-woman home hairdressing service). Such advertisements are a major feature of local and regional newspapers. *Display advertising* has wider variations in size, shape and location within the newspaper, and uses a range of graphics, copy and photography. Display advertisements may be grouped under special features and pages: for instance, if a local newspaper runs a weddings feature it brings together advertisers providing the various goods and services that the bride-to-be would be interested in. Such groupings offer the individual advertisers a degree of synergy. Local newspapers are an important advertising medium, not only for small businesses, but for national chains of retailers supporting local stores and car manufacturers supporting local dealerships. In 1997, regional press had a 20.3 per cent share of advertising revenue, second only to television's 28.3 per cent. National newspapers had a share only of 15 per cent (Croft, 1999b).

TABLE 15.8

Number of newspapers, 1997

	Number
Austria	169
Belgium	31
Denmark	48
Finland	226
France	109
Germany	421
Greece	29
Ireland	10
Italy	686
Luxembourg	6
Netherlands	39
Portugal	28
Spain	140
Sweden	167
UK	120

Source: Euromonitor (1999), Table 1304, p. 315.

During the daily scan for news, readers may notice advertisements and with repetition they may eventually remember them. When a reader is actively seeking information then the newspaper, especially the classified section of a local paper, may be a prime source of products or services.

The main problem with newspaper advertising is related to its cost efficiency – if the advertiser wants to be more selective in targeting. Wastage rates can be high, as newspapers can appeal to very broad segments of the population. Furthermore, compared with magazines, newspapers have a much shorter life span and can have problems with the quality of reproduction possible. Although colour and photographic reproduction quality in newspapers is rapidly improving, it is still inferior to that offered by magazines, and can be inconsistent. The same advertisement, for instance, published in different newspapers or on different days can take on varying colour values and intensities, and be more or less grainy or focused.

Advertising hoardings and outdoor media

The last group of advertising media includes posters and hoardings, as well as transport-orientated advertising media (advertising in and on buses, taxis and trains and in stations). Table 15.9 shows the number of outdoor advertising sites in various European countries in 1993.

Whatever the type of outdoor medium used, the purpose is generally the same: to provide quickly digestible messages to passers-by or to provide something for a bored passenger to look at. As with any medium, the advertising may be a one-off, or it may be part of a multimedia campaign. An advertisement at an airport for a nearby hotel would be a one-off but long-term campaign with a very focused purpose, whereas a hoarding advertising a car would probably be only one element tied into a campaign with a theme extending across television, print and direct marketing as well.

Advertising posters range from small home-made advertisements placed on a noticeboard to those for giant hoardings. This section concentrates on the latter group. Hoarding sites are normally sold by the month. Being in a static location, they may easily be seen 20–40 times in a month by people on their way to and from work or school etc. In the UK, over one-third of poster sites are taken by car or drink advertisers. The reach may be small, but the frequency can be quite intense. They can, however, be affected by some unpredictable elements, out of the control of the advertiser. Bad weather means that people will spend less time out of doors, and are certainly not going to be positively receptive to outdoor advertising. Hoardings and posters are also vulnerable to the attentions of those who think they can improve on the existing message with some graffiti or fly posting.

TABLE 15.9
Number of outdoor advertising sites, 1993

	Number
Austria	123 100
Belgium	56 465
Denmark	15 225
Finland	110 000
France	395 000
Germany	
Greece	12 117
Ireland	5 049
Italy	
Luxembourg	
Netherlands	97 834
Portugal	23 600
Spain	
Sweden	25 446
UK	110 395

Source: Euromonitor (1999), Table 1310, p. 315.

Nevertheless, hoardings offer an exciting medium with great deal of creative scope, capitalising on their size and location. Backlighting, for example, can give a clearer, sharper image, while the potential of video hoardings to create moving, changing messages opens up many possibilities. The latter is especially valuable for attracting passers-by to a restaurant or leisure facility, for example. It pays, however, to be careful in the location of such ultra-creative billboards, since to be the cause of multiple pile-ups by distracting drivers' attention is not desirable PR!

Size is one of the greatest assets of the advertising hoarding, creating impact. Over 80 per cent of hoarding space in the UK is taken by 4-, 6- or 48-sheet sites (a 48-sheet hoarding is 10 feet by 24 feet). Also, sites can be selected, if available, according to the match between traffic flows and target audience. However, in appealing to a mobile

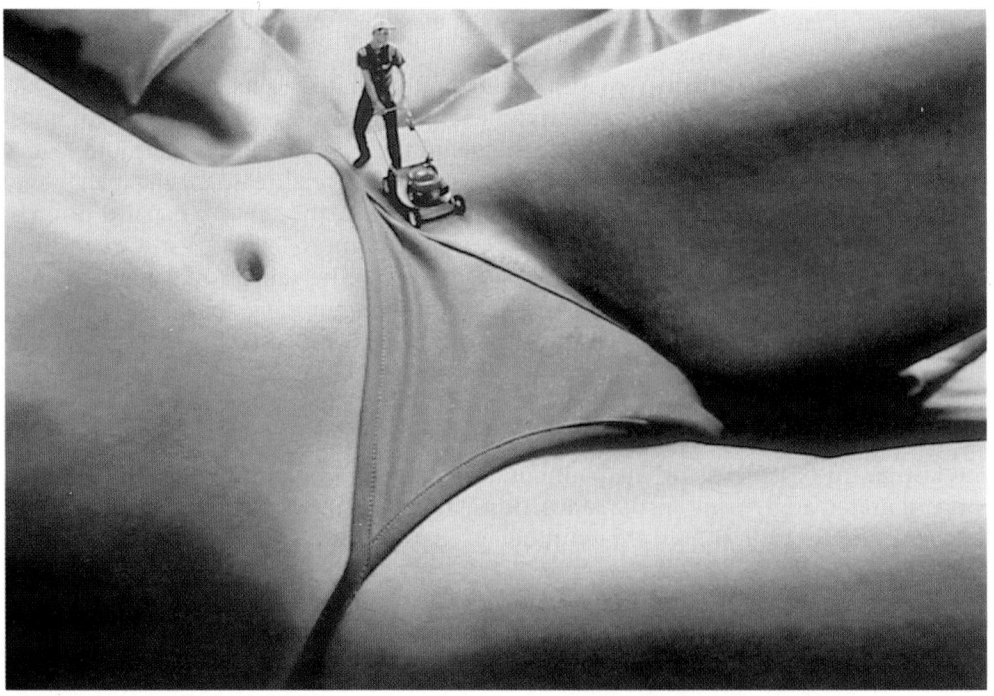

It's a lot more fun than waxing

Source: Kookaï

ARKETING IN ACTION   The Outdoor Life

Almost anything can be used as an advertising medium: bus tickets, tube tickets, hot air balloons, airships, supermarket trolleys, shops' floors, airline meal trays, even cows and toilet walls. Campaigns using these 'ambient media' can be very creative and their value to the advertiser is reflected in the fact that around £64mn is spent every year on this kind of advertising.

Some campaigns are particularly memorable. Cows were recruited to wear coats advertising vegetarian cookery courses, for instance. Toilet walls in pubs and clubs were used by Big City, a dance music radio station, which wanted to generate awareness among young male clubbers. Heat-sensitive stickers were put on the urinal walls and when someone approached, a famous face would appear with a message, for instance David Beckham with the message 'Give David Beckham a warm welcome'.

A more mainstream form of ambient medium is the taxi cab. Taxi Media is a company selling advertising space in and out of 1000 of London's black cabs. Taxis can be branded both inside and out and drivers can participate by handing out freebies or advertising messages. Similarly, Phonesites sells advertising space in telephone boxes. Research suggests that 30 per cent of the UK population uses a payphone every month and that increases to 73 per cent of 16–24-year olds. Phonesites also offers to set up 'hot buttons', automatic direct dialling through to the advertiser.

Research has shown that this generates 40 per cent higher response rates than just printing a full telephone number for the consumer to dial.

Interactive elements can also be built into the most common type of outdoor medium, the advertising hoarding. Volkswagen, for example, ran a poster campaign on bus shelters and garage forecourts consisting of a sheet of real bubblewrap with the VW Polo logo and the heading 'Protective Packaging'. The temptation to go up to the posters and start popping the bubblewrap was surely just too great to resist. Posters can also attract attention through controversy. A poster by French fashion retailer Kookaï showing a tiny man pushing a lawnmower down a woman's bikini line ran on French poster sites and in women's magazines with no problems. Kookaï then wanted to use the same image in a £100 000 campaign in the UK featuring the advertisement on buses in Manchester, London and Leeds. Just before it was due to be launched in London, however, TDI, the agency responsible for selling London Transport bus advertising space, decided to ban the ad as being in poor taste. Kookaï's response was to develop a new advertisement showing a portion of the original advertisement with 'censored' slashed across it. The new caption read, 'They say our ad is too risqué . . . we don't'. The new advertisement duly appeared on the buses.

Sources: Cook (1999b); *Marketing* (1999c); Woolgar (1999).

audience, the message needs to be simple and thus usually links with other elements of a wider campaign, either for generating initial awareness or on a reminder and reinforcement basis.

Finally, there are the *transport-orientated media*. These include advertisements in rail or bus stations, which capture and occupy the attention of waiting passengers who have nothing better to do for a while than read the advertisements. Similarly, advertising inside trains, taxis and buses has a captive audience for as long as the journey takes. Advertising on the outside of vehicles, perhaps even going so as far as to repaint an entire bus with an advertisement, extends the reach of the advertisement to anyone who happens to be around the vehicle's route.

USING ADVERTISING AGENCIES

It is not surprising, given the complexity and expense involved, that many organisations employ an agency to handle the development and implementation of advertising programmes. It is important, however, to select the right kind of agency, not only in terms of its practical ability to do what needs to be done and to solve the problems that need to be solved, but also in terms of their creativity, their culture and their ability to empathise with the product and its target market. In this section, therefore, we will examine briefly the different types of advertising agency, then discuss criteria for selecting an agency, and finally, there will be a few thoughts on client–agency relationships.

Full service agencies

Full service agencies provide a full range of services, including research, creative work, artwork, media buying etc. Larger agencies might also have subsidiaries or sister companies in the sales promotion, PR or direct marketing fields. If a client's account is not large, the agency may bill separately for creative work. With large accounts, some discount can be achieved through the 15 per cent agency commission earned for media buying. Using a full service agency does not mean that the client abdicates all responsibility, but that the advertising is developed jointly. The advantages are that specialist skills can be drawn on as needed; new, different perspectives on the communication problem may be gained; and the client can change agencies if not satisfied. Using a full service agency is also easier to manage and control, and there is less risk of sensitive information leaking out, because everything is self-contained (Smith, 1993). As with any buyer–supplier liaison, however, the quality of the relationship, trust and understanding are all very important.

Limited service agencies

Limited service agencies tend to specialise in one or a small number of parts of the total process. Within advertising, agencies may specialise in creative work, media buying or advertising research, for example. Such agencies may bid on a speculative basis, receiving a fee only for the proposals selected. The advantage of the limited service agency is that it enables the client to select the best talent to suit their various needs. It does, however, mean more work in co-ordinating the effort involved, and there is a risk of information leaks as more different organisations become involved (Smith, 1993).

A few very large organisations might prefer to develop their own expertise in-house with dedicated staff to manage the campaign. The in-house department may provide the full range of services or supplement skills from external sources such as limited service agencies with particular specialisms. At the opposite extreme, there are special difficulties for smaller businesses, as they do not have the expertise or the amount of money to spend to attract significant agency interest. In such a business the owner or the individual responsible for all marketing may handle media and campaign development.

Working in-house gives the advertiser more control and there is no risk of over-dependency on an outside agency. It may even save money, although an in-house department may not have the same media purchasing power as an agency. The organisation will, however, have to be sensitive to potential gaps in its expertise, as well as the risk of becoming too blinkered in its approach to its own advertising. Using outside agencies does at least bring fresh and objective minds to the problem.

Selecting an agency

Clearly, selecting an agency is very important since its work can potentially make or break a product. Different writers suggest different checklists against which to measure the appropriateness of any given agency. The following list has been compiled from the work of Smith (1993), White (1988), and Wilmshurst (1985) and is also shown in Fig. 15.2.

Relative size of agency and client

As already mentioned, it might be useful to try to match the relative sizes of the client and the agency, certainly in terms of the proposed advertising spend. This is to ensure

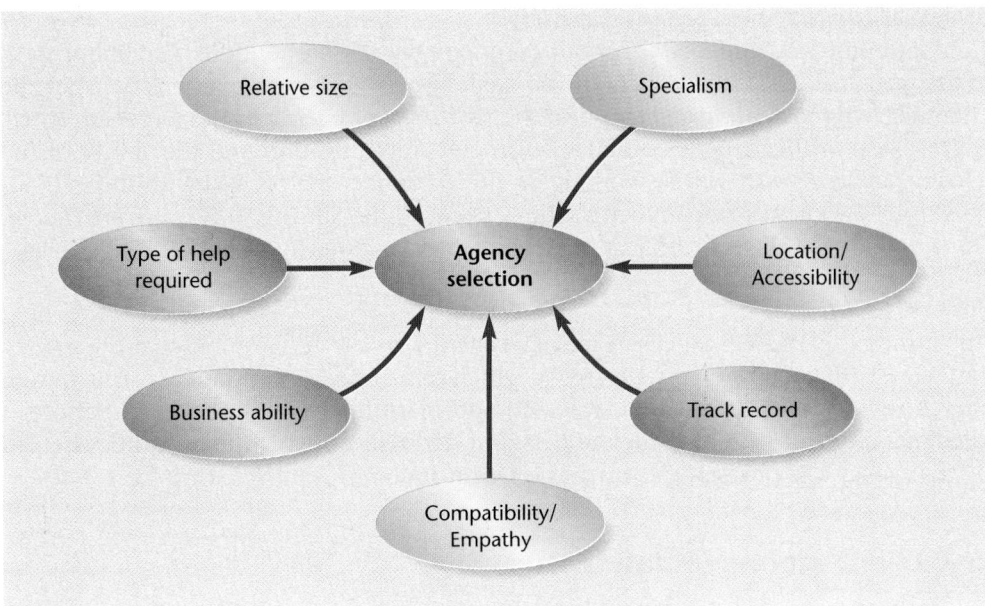

FIGURE 15.2

Criteria for selecting an advertising agency

the right level of mutual respect, attention and importance. The client might also want to think ahead strategically, and choose an agency that will either grow with the client or be able to meet increased future needs. This might mean coping with a bigger account or coping with international advertising.

Location and accessibility

A smaller business with a limited geographic market might prefer to work with a small agency that has deep local knowledge and understanding. A larger business, wishing to keep a close eye on what the agency is doing and thus wanting frequent face-to-face meetings with the account team, might also find it more convenient to use an agency located nearby.

Type of help required

Clearly, a client wants an agency that can supply the kinds of services and expertise required. The client might want a full service agency, or just specialised help in media buying, for example. Any prospective agency thus needs to be measured against its ability to deliver an appropriate package.

Specialism

Some agencies have a reputation for specialising in particular products or services, for example higher education advertising or financial services advertising. Some clients might find this attractive on the basis that they can be sure that the agency has detailed knowledge of the relevant marketing and competitive environments. Others, however, might find it off-putting. They might feel that the agency works for the client's competitors or that they are 'stale' from doing too much work in one field. Nevertheless, a degree of relevant experience in some related area might be a good indicator of an agency's ability to handle this new account.

Track record

Regardless of whether the agency specialises in particular types of advertising or not, a new client is going to be interested in its track record. How has the agency grown? Who is on its client list? How creative is its work? How effective is its work? Does it seem able to retain its clients, generate repeat business from them and build strong relationships?

Compatibility, empathy and personal chemistry

Compatibility and empathy are about corporate culture and outlook and about individual personalities. Clearly, a client wants an agency that is sympathetic to what the client is trying to achieve and can find the right way of talking to the target audience. A great deal of this depends on client–agency communication and the ability of the agency personnel who will be working on the account to get on well with the individuals from the client company with whom they will be liaising. It is quite legitimate, therefore, for the client to ask just who will be working on the account.

Business ability

Advertising is extremely expensive and so a client wants to be reassured that the agency can work within budget, cost effectively, efficiently and within deadlines. This might, therefore, mean looking at their research and planning capabilities. Furthermore, a client should make sure that they understand the basis on which they will be charged by the agency and precisely what is and is not included.

The client–agency relationship

Whatever the type of agency used, a good relationship is essential. With sound briefing, mutual understanding, and an agreed system of remuneration, the agency becomes an extension of the organisation's own marketing team. Co-operation may depend on mutual importance. For instance, a large client working with a large agency is fine, but a small client dealing with a large agency may become lost. There may be other constraints affecting agency choice. If an agency deals with a competitor, for example, then the conflict of interest needs to be avoided.

Research undertaken at the Marketing Forum by Richmond Events Ltd among both agencies and clients looked at the factors most likely to cause a breakdown in client–agency relationships, and those most likely to promote a positive relationship. The top ten factors cited in each category are shown in Table 15.10.

It is clear that the ability to deliver the goods, in terms of timing, creative content and within budget, is crucial to success. Communication and developing deeper mutual understanding and trust are also important if the agency is going to diagnose, understand and solve the client's advertising problem. If these points are taken out of the advertising agency context, they can be seen to be the fundamental criteria for any good buyer–supplier relationship.

TABLE 15.10

Advertising agency–client relationships

Ten factors likely to cause relationship breakdown	Respondents citing factor (%)	Ten factors likely to promote a positive relationship	Respondents citing factor (%)
Lack of personal chemistry	47	Understanding the brand	52
Unreliable delivery	44	Mutual trust	47
Poor creative performance	38	Creative excellence	41
Lack of proactive thinking	30	Long-term partnership	33
Poor communication	23	Proactive thinking	32
Lack of strategic input	22	Planning effectiveness	18
Poor business results	19	Working within budget	14
Inability to learn from experience	18	Continuous improvement	14
Going over budget	17	Respect for deadlines	12
Overpriced production	13	Senior management contact	10

Source: Richmond Events, *The Marketing Forum 1999*. Reprinted with kind permission.

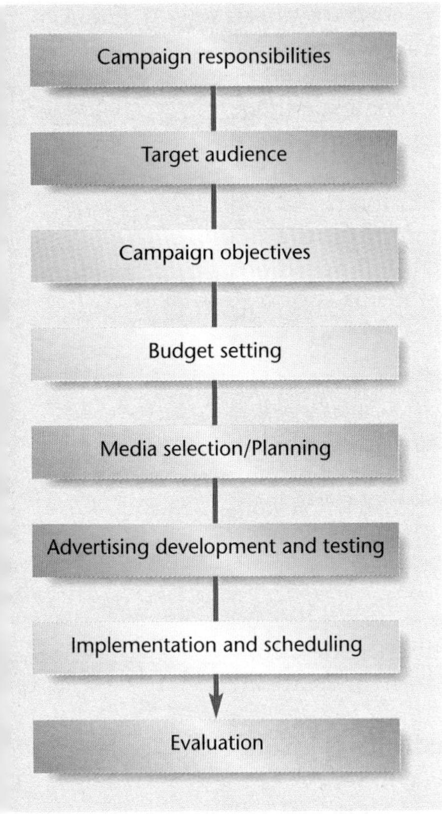

DEVELOPING AN ADVERTISING CAMPAIGN

Campaign responsibilities
Target audience
Campaign objectives
Budget setting
Media selection/Planning
Advertising development and testing
Implementation and scheduling
Evaluation

FIGURE 15.3

Stages in developing an advertising campaign

It is almost impossible that one free-standing advertisement in the press or on television would be sufficient to achieve the results expected, in terms of the impact on the target audience. Normally, advertisers think about a campaign that involves a predetermined theme but is communicated through a series of messages placed in selected media chosen for their expected cumulative impact on the specified target audience. The elements of the campaign are expected to integrate synergistically so that each advertisement placed both supports and is supported by the others. Campaigns can run for varying lengths of time, for a few weeks, for a season, or for many years with little change in formulation. The annual drink–drive campaigns discussed earlier at p. 605, for example, change their approach and message slightly every year, although the broad thrust is always consistent. They also tend to focus mainly on the few weeks around Christmas and New Year.

There are a number of stages in the development of an advertising campaign. Although the emphasis will vary from situation to situation, each stage at least acknowledges a need for careful management assessment and decision making. The stages are shown in Fig. 15.3 and are discussed in turn below.

Deciding on campaign responsibilities

This is an important question of organisational structure and 'ownership' of the campaign. If management is devolved on a product basis, then overall responsibility may rest with the brand or product manager. This certainly helps to ensure that the campaign integrates with sales promotion, selling, production planning etc., since the brand manager is very well versed in all aspects of the product's life. If, however, management is devolved on a functional basis, then the responsibility for an advertising campaign will lie with the advertising and promotion manager. This means that the campaign benefits from depth of advertising expertise, but lacks the involvement with the product that a brand manager would supply. Whatever the arrangement, it is essential to define who is ultimately responsible for what tasks and what elements of the budget.

Example In the motor industry, companies have enormous advertising budgets covering many different car models. Many companies have decided, therefore, to create brand teams, each of which has direct responsibility for one or two models. A typical team might consist of a marketing manager and two brand managers and is responsible for its own advertising and marketing and ultimately for meeting its profit targets. The advantage of this kind of delegation is that the team has a tight focus and thus the interests of the individual car models will be looked after. It is thus also likely that the advertising campaigns will be tightly focused. The disadvantages, however, are that there might be some loss of overall corporate consistency in the different campaigns, and that the advertising agency has to work with five different teams rather than with one.

Selecting the target audience

As discussed at pp. 566 *et seq.*, knowing who you are talking to is the foundation of good communication. Based on segmentation strategy, the target audience represents the group at whom the communication is aimed within the market. In some cases, the segment and the target audience may be one and the same. Sometimes, however, the target audience may be a sub-division of the segment. If, for instance, an organisation served a particular hobby segment, different approaches to advertising would be taken depending on whether they wanted to talk to serious, casual, high spenders, low spenders, general-interest or specific-interest sub-groups. This underlines the need to understand the market and the range of target audiences within it.

A profile of the target audience increases the chances of successful promotion and communication. Any details, such as location, media viewing (or listening or reading) habits, geodemographics, attitudes and values, can be used to shape the propositions contained within the campaign or to direct the creative approach and media choice.

Example An advertising agency thinking about advertising a brand of watches in different European countries found from research that in general, Italians treat watches like fashion accessories and might own several to co-ordinate with different outfits. In contrast, Germans assess watches according to the sophistication of their technology and the number of different functions built in, whereas the British just want a functional and reliable way of telling the time. Clearly, these differences in target market attitudes towards watches will lead to fundamentally different advertising approaches for the brand in those countries.

In organisational markets, the focus is likely to be on understanding the decision-making processes and buying centre membership (*see* Chapter 4), to help create an industry-based segmentation and communication approach.

Whatever the type of product, if the assessment of the target audience is incomplete or woolly, there may be problems in directing campaign efforts later.

Campaign objectives

Communication objectives were considered at pp. 578 *et seq.*, and provide a clear view of what the advertising should accomplish. These objectives need to be specific, measurable and time related. They must also indicate the level of change sought, defining a specific outcome from the advertising task. If there are no measurable objectives, how can achievements be recognised and success or failure judged?

Most advertising is focused on some stage of a response hierarchy model, such as those presented in Fig. 14.7. These models highlight the stages in the process of consumer decision making from initial exposure and awareness through to post-purchase review. Issues such as liking, awareness or knowledge, preference and conviction are important parts of that process, and advertising can aim to influence any one of them. These can thus be translated into advertising objectives with measurable targets for awareness generation, product trial and/or repurchase, attitude creation or shifts, or positioning or preferences in comparison with the competition.

These objectives should be driven by the agreed marketing strategy and plan. Note the difference between marketing and advertising objectives. Sales and market share targets are legitimate marketing objectives as they represent the outcomes of a range of marketing mix decisions. Advertising, however, is just one element contributing to that process, and is designed to achieve specific tasks, but not necessarily exclusively sales.

Campaign budgets

Developing a communication budget was considered at pp. 582 *et seq.* Look back to these pages to refresh your memory on the methods of budget setting. Remember that there is no one right or wrong sum to allocate to a campaign, and often a combination of the methods proposed earlier acts as a guide.

Often the setting of budgets is an iterative process, developing and being modified as the campaign takes shape. There is a direct link between budgets and objectives such that a modification in one area is almost certainly likely to have an impact in the other. Even if the underlying philosophy of the budget is the 'objective and task' approach, practicality still means that most budgets are constrained in some way by the cash available. This forces managers to plan carefully and to consider a range of options in order to be as cost effective as possible in the achievement of the specified objectives.

The first job is to link marketing objectives with the tasks expected of advertising and promotion. Targets may be set, for example, in relation to awareness levels, trial and repeat purchases. Not all these targets would be achieved by advertising alone. Sales promotion, and of course product formulation, may play a big part in repeat purchase behaviour.

Increasingly, computerised models are being introduced to relate objectives and budgets more closely. However, there is still room for managerial judgement and common sense, operating from experience and knowledge of what makes customers and competitors tick. It has been argued that establishing the budget for advertising and marketing is as much a political process as a management task (Piercy, 1987).

Media selection and planning

The various media options were considered individually at pp. 613 *et seq*. The large range of alternative media needs to be reduced down to manageable options and then scheduling (discussed at p. 632) planned to achieve the desired results. The resultant media plan must be detailed and specific. Actual media vehicles must be specified, as well as when, where, how much and how often. This means planning bookings by date, time and space. The plan is the means by which exposure and awareness levels can be achieved. The important aim is to ensure a reasonable fit between the media vehicles considered and the target audience so that sufficient reach and frequency is achieved to allow the real objectives of the advertising a fighting chance of success. This is becoming more difficult as audience profiles and markets change (Mueller-Heumann, 1992).

There are two main approaches to reaching the target audience. The first is a 'shotgun' approach that aims to reach a large number of people across all segments, whether targets or not, accepting that there will be considerable waste. Much television advertising falls into this category. The second approach aims to achieve a close match between the target audience and the advertising media, such as would be the case with a hobby or specific interest group. This approach assumes that the advertiser has a good understanding of the segments and that the media exist for reaching them.

> **Example** Home improvement retail chain B&Q realised that an advertisement placed around ITVs *World's Worst DIY Disasters* could represent an ideal opportunity to reach an interested audience. There was some concern, though, that using the advertising slot would be seen as patronising viewers. To avoid this, a one-off advertisement was produced at short notice to draw attention to the expertise available within B&Q stores and its free 'how to' leaflets. A humorous approach prevented any offence and the theme of doing DIY right and doing it carefully fitted in well with the programming to make the advertisement more memorable (*Campaign*, 1999). VW also took advantage of an interesting media opportunity. It featured its 'wedding' press advertisement for the VW Polo on 52 poster sites in and around Windsor at the time of Prince Edward's marriage to Sophie Rhys-Jones. It was hoped that the posters would not only be seen by the thousands of people lining the procession route, but also that they would be picked up by the television cameras (Barrett, 1999).

The profile of activity is specified in the media plan, which summarises the choices made regarding medium, vehicle and scheduling. The plan has an important role to play in integrating the campaign effort into the rest of the marketing plan and in communicating requirements clearly to any support agencies.

A number of considerations guide the selection of media, as shown in Fig. 15.4. These are discussed briefly below.

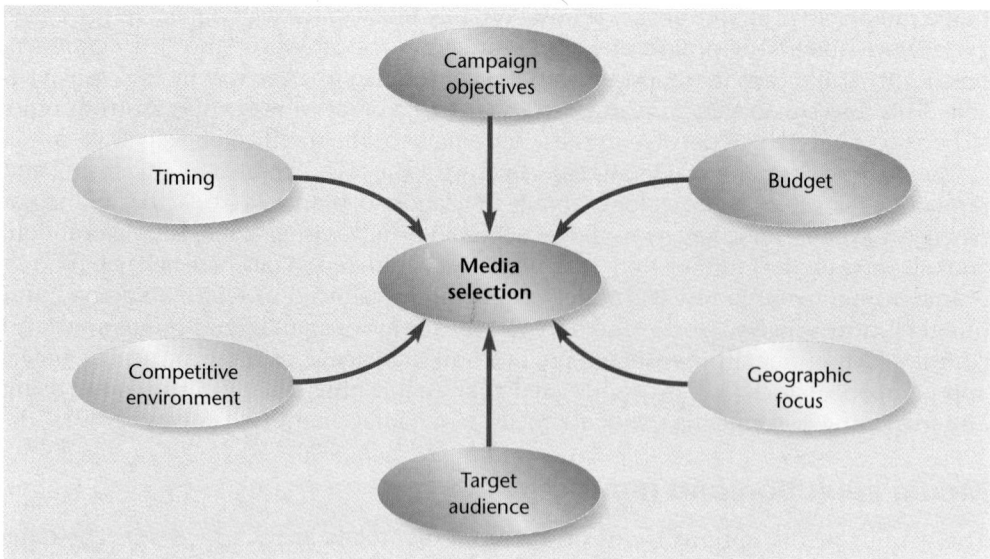

FIGURE 15.4

Factors influencing media selection

Campaign objectives

The media selected must ensure consistency with the overall objectives for the campaign in terms of awareness, reach etc.

Target audience

The target audience is critical to guiding the detailed media selection. As close a fit as possible is required between medium and audience.

MARKETING AND IT   **The man, the ladder and a bucket of paste**

It's a man with a ladder and a bucket of paste. It's the world's oldest advertising medium. It's the poster industry, once derided as the poor relation of newer and more glamorous forms of advertising such as television. But times are changing and the poster business has been cleaning up its act. The reasons for the turnaround in the fortunes of outdoor advertising are varied, but improvements in information technology have been at the heart of some of the changes. Undoubtedly, the biggest change has nothing whatsoever to do with technology – people are spending more and more time travelling and stuck in traffic jams. Outdoor advertising is one of the few markets in which the size of the audience is increasing.

So where does IT come in? For starters, outdoor advertising has become much more targeted. New market research methods have given the industry more information about the profiles of the audiences passing in front of billboards or street furniture panels. In Ireland, Adshel, a bus shelter and outdoor advertising agency, uses geographic information systems (GIS) to manage its poster sites and to allow advertisers to tailor campaigns based on demographic and retail proximity criteria. Food companies, for example, can target sites seen by families with children, while a car manufacturer can target sites near its dealerships.

Advances in display technology are also helping to change the traditional image of the man with the ladder and the bucket of paste. Many posters have moved from paper to vinyl; backlighting is widespread; and more recently, liquid crystal displays (LCD) and light-emitting diode (LED) panels have become very popular for trade shows, conferences and shopping malls. Recent developments have enabled LCD screens to produce a true red, green and blue, which means that they can reproduce colour as faithfully as a television or cinema screen. When 10 000 spectators bid farewell to Hong Kong's Kai Tek airport on 27 July 1998, the evening's events were shown on a massive LCD screen that lit up the stage and allowed every spectator to enjoy the concert in as much detail as if they were standing in the front row. The screen measured 6.4m by 4.8m and featured a definition of 50 lines per metre. As one commentator put it: 'Unlike television, when you book an advertisement on a giant LCD screen, you can be guaranteed that viewers are not watching the other channel when your advertisement is playing.'

Source: O'Connor and Galvin (1999).

Competitive factors

A consideration of the competition includes examining what they have been doing, where they have been doing it, and with what outcomes. A decision may have to be made whether to use the same media as the competition or to innovate.

Geographic focus

The target audience may be international, national or regional, and sometimes a selection of media or vehicles may have to be used to reach dispersed groups within the target audience.

Budget constraints

As discussed at p. 628–9, practicality and affordability usually enter into the planning at some stage. A proposal of 20 prime-time slots on television might well give the chief accountant apoplexy and have to be replaced with a more modest print campaign that makes its impact through stunning creativity.

Timing

The plan needs to take into account any lead-in or build-up time, particularly if the product's sales have a strong element of seasonality. Perfumes and aftershaves, for example, look to Christmas as a strong selling period. Advertisers of these products use glossy magazine advertising all year round, but in the weeks up to Christmas, add intensive and expensive television campaigns (it's a good job we don't have smellyvision yet) to coincide with consumers' decision making for gifts. Similarly, timing is important in launching a new product, to make sure that the right level of awareness, understanding and desire have been generated by the time the product is actually available.

As with any plan, it should provide the reader with a clear justification of the rationale behind the decisions, and should act as a guide as to how it integrates with other marketing activities.

Advertising development and testing

At this stage, the advertisements themselves are designed and made, ready for broadcasting or printing. The creative issues involved have already been covered elsewhere within this chapter. As the advertisement evolves, **pre-testing** is often used to check that the content, message and impact are as expected. This is particularly important with television advertising, which is relatively expensive to produce and broadcast, and also would represent an extremely public embarrassment if it failed.

Tests are, therefore, built in at various stages of the advertisement's development. Initial concepts and storyboards can be discussed with a sample of members of the target audience to see if they can understand the message and relate to the scenario or images in the proposed advertisement. Slightly further on in the process, a rough video of the advertisement (not the full production – just enough to give a flavour of the finished piece) can also be tested. This allows final adjustments to be made before the finished advertisement is produced. Even then, further testing can reassure the agency and the client that the advertisement is absolutely ready for release. Print advertisements can similarly be tested at various stages of their development, using rough sketches, mock-ups and then the finished advertisement.

White (1988) suggests a number of questions that pre-testing advertisements might answer, and these are summarised in Fig. 15.5.

Pre-testing is a valuable exercise, but its outcomes should be approached with some caution. The testing conditions are rather artificial, by necessity, and audiences (assuming even that the testers can assemble a truly representative audience) who react in certain ways to seeing an advertisement in a theatre or church hall might respond very differently if they saw that same advertisement in their own homes under 'normal' viewing conditions.

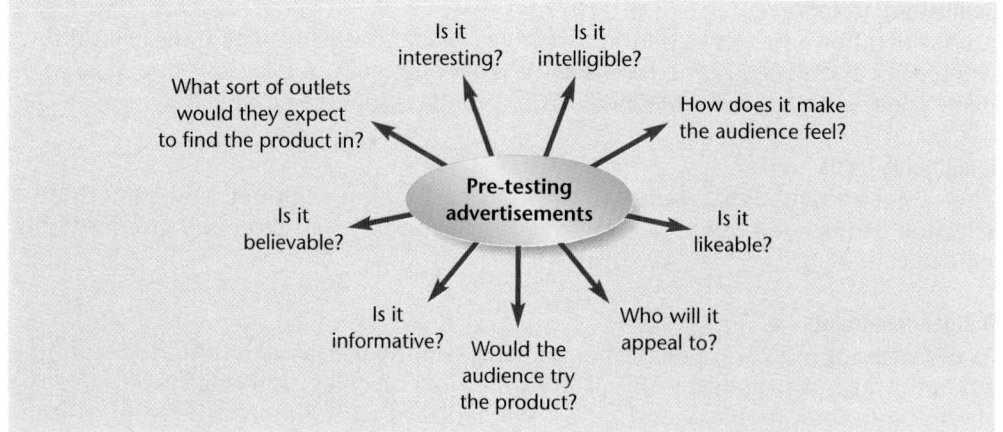

FIGURE 15.5

Information gained
from pre-testing
advertisements

Implementation and scheduling

In the implementation phase, a number of professional experts may be needed to develop and deliver the advertising campaign. These will include graphic designers, photographers, commercial artists, copywriters, research specialists and, not least, media and production companies. The role of the advertising manager is to co-ordinate and select these professionals within a budget to achieve the planned objectives.

A key part of the implementation phase is the scheduling of the campaign. This describes the frequency and intensity of effort and guides all production decisions. There are many different scheduling patterns (Sissors and Bumba, 1989). Sometimes, advertising takes place in *bursts*, as shown in Fig. 15.6. This means short-term, intense advertising activity, such as that often found with new product launches. Most organisations do not have the resources (or the inclination) to keep up such intense advertising activity indefinitely, and thus the bursts are few and far between. The alternative is to spread the advertising budget out more evenly, by advertising in *drips*, also shown in Fig. 15.6. The advertising activity is less intense, but more persistent. Reminder advertising for a frequently purchased mature product might take place in drips rather than bursts.

A number of factors will help to determine the overall schedule, as shown in Fig. 15.7. These are briefly discussed in turn below.

Marketing factors

Marketing factors might influence the speed of the impact required. An organisation launching a new product or responding to a competitor's comparative advertising might want to make a quick impact, for example.

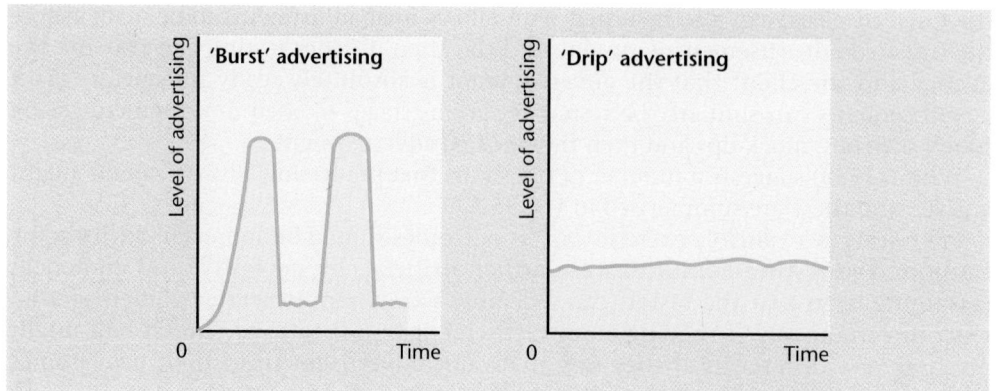

FIGURE 15.6

Advertising
expenditure
strategies; 'bursts'
and 'drips'

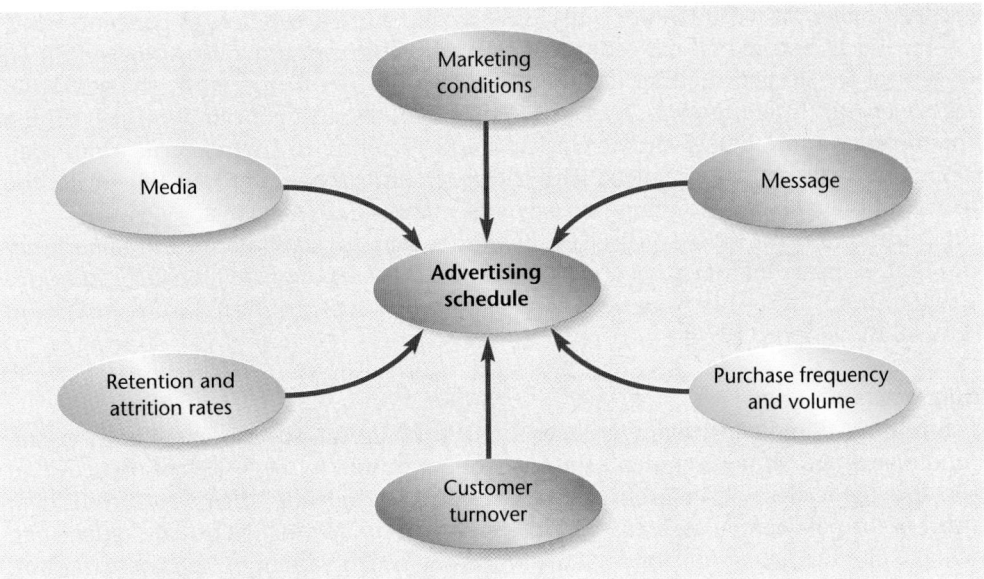

FIGURE 15.7

Factors influencing advertising schedules

The turnover of customers in the market

If turnover of customers is high, then there is a need to advertise more frequently to keep the message available for new entrants into the market.

Purchase frequency and volatility

If demand is highly seasonal or perishable, then the scheduling might provide for a short period of high-frequency advertising. The peak time for advertising perfumes and toys, for example, is in the run-up to Christmas. Similarly, various chocolate products peak at Easter or Mother's day, for example. Alternatively, there may be a link with brand loyalty. Higher loyalty may need less frequency, provided that the product is not under competitive attack. This is, however, a dangerous assumption.

Retention and attrition rates

If the danger of forgetting is high, then the advertiser is likely to need a more active campaign implemented at regular intervals. Different groups learn and forget at different rates. Therefore these retention and attrition rates of the target audience are yet another assessment that needs to be made.

Message factors

A campaign for a new product may need more repetition than one for an established product, because of the newness of the message. More generally, simple messages or those that stand out from the crowd demand less repetition. Similarly, smaller advertisements or those placed in less noticeable spots within a print medium may need more frequency to make sure they are seen.

In broadcast media, however, there is some debate over the relative effectiveness of 10-, 30- and 60-second slots. It seems that longer is not always better. Ten seconds may be sufficient to generate awareness, through a short, sharp impact. Two 30-second slots may be more powerful than one of 60 seconds. However, such a general debate is rather meaningless, since so much depends on the context of the advertising. If there are many other messages (and particularly if they are direct competitors' messages) in the pool, then a much greater impact will have to be made just to create awareness. Finally, impact is not just an issue of how many seconds you buy, it is about what you do with them. A 10-second blast of something stunningly novel and memorable is going to achieve far more than 60 seconds of an advertisement that is a rehash of things that we have all seen before. Research has indeed shown that 10-second advertisements score nearly as highly on recall (34 per cent) as 30-second advertisements (42 per cent) while a 50-second slot scored 58 per cent recall. Nevertheless, the study also showed that 65 per cent of the audience either left the room or did other things while the advertisements were on. Interestingly, it was also found that advertising recall depended on the type of programme being watched, with dramas leading to higher recall than soap operas, and that the more involved with the programme the viewer was, the greater the chances of them actually watching the advertisements (*Marketing Week*, 1999a).

It is important for the advertiser to remember that advertisements and ideas 'wear out', that is, as the audience becomes familiar with them, they are less likely to notice or remember them. This is an effect of selective perception, boredom or irritation (Petty and Cacioppo, 1979).

Media factors

With print media in particular, the better the fit between the advertisement and the surrounding editorial or news content, the fewer opportunities to see (OTS) are needed. This is because the reader is more likely to be interested in the advertisements or to read them as part of the publication, as discussed earlier in connection with advertorials, rather than mentally filtering them out. Similarly, the longer the reader's attention span, whether this stems from interest in the publication, or because the reader is concentrating on the whole content rather than skimming it, the fewer the number of OTSs needed.

The fewer media or advertising vehicles in the plan, the fewer OTSs are likely to be needed. This smaller limit may be important for a smaller business with a limited budget or for a major business seeking to dominate a particular medium by means of monopolising the best slots or positions. Such dominance increases the repetition to those in the target audience. The more congested the medium, the more OTSs there need to be, to cut through the background 'noise'.

Forgetting is part of our daily lives, and so any campaign must seek to minimise forgetting. Time is an important factor, and without reminder advertising or other promotional support, the tendency is to forget. There are exceptions, however. For a consumer durable product, for example, the high involvement necessary may assist in decreasing the rate of forgetting because the purchaser has put a great deal of time and conscious effort into making the decision, as discussed in Chapter 3.

None of this makes one media plan better than another. It depends on objectives and the particular market circumstances prevailing. If the product is new or seasonal, a more intensive effort may be appropriate. The scheduling plan may, of course, evolve over time. During the introduction stage of the product life-cycle an intensive burst of advertising will launch the product, and this may then be followed by a more spread-out campaign as the growth stage finishes. Creating awareness in the first place is expensive, but critical to a product's success.

Campaign evaluation

The evaluation is perhaps the most critical part of the whole campaign process. This stage exists not only to assess the effectiveness of the campaign mounted, but also to provide valuable learning for the future.

There are two stages in evaluation. *Interim evaluation* enables a campaign to be revised and adjusted before completion to improve its effectiveness. It enables a closer match to be achieved between advertising objectives and the emerging campaign results.

Alternatively or additionally, *exit evaluation* is undertaken at the end of the campaign. A number of **post-tests** are possible, and some of them are defined below.

Aided (prompted) recall

In aided (prompted) recall pictures of advertisements are shown to a sample audience. Questions are asked about whether they have noticed these advertisements on television, the radio or in print. The research may go further to investigate level of comprehension.

Unaided (spontaneous) recall

In sponteneous or unaided recall, questions are asked about what advertisements the respondent has noticed recently. No clues are given, so this exercise is much harder for the respondent to do. Sometimes, however, the exercise may be focused on a specific product area, but it is still up to the respondent to remember what advertising they have seen or heard.

Attitude tests

Questions are formulated to measure the respondent's attitude to a product. An attitude test may take place both before and after the advertising campaign so that the level of attitude change effected by the advertising can be measured.

Enquiry tests

The success of the advertising is measured by the number of requests for product information, premiums or sales visits generated. The enquiry test is a simple measure, and is especially useful for small businesses with small budgets, who need to make sure that their advertising works harder. Early in a new campaign, a direct response mechanism (*see* Chapter 18) may be deliberately built in to see what interest is being generated. This gives feedback before the campaign is expanded.

Sales tests

Sales tests are a form of controlled experiment in which an advertising campaign may be run in one area, but not in another. Although it is difficult to keep all other things equal, the running of such a test does give some indication of the impact of the advertising on retail sales etc.

The method of evaluation selected will depend on the original objectives. If these are related to awareness or attitude change, then recognition, recall tests or attitude change tests are appropriate. If the purpose is to influence sales or market share, then the number of enquiries received or sales tests may be used, although neither of these may be a fair assessment, because advertising is only one of many factors contributing to sales. It must be remembered that just because a product's advertisement is recognised or its details are recalled, purchase does not necessarily follow. The consumer might not be able to find anywhere convenient that sells the product, or they might find the price a little too high, or they might be well disposed towards the product, but have even stronger feelings about the competition. These constraints emphasise the need for a fully integrated marketing mix with all its elements working in harmony with each other.

CHAPTER SUMMARY

Advertising is a non-personal form of communication with an identified sponsor, using any form of mass media. It can relate to products, communicating their features, benefits and competitive advantage, or it can relate to organisations, contributing to a strong corporate image or communicating a corporate view on an issue. Advertising can thus help to create awareness, build image and attitudes and then reinforce those attitudes through reminders. It is an invaluable support for other elements of the promotional mix, for example by creating awareness and positive attitudes towards an organisation in preparation for a sales team, or by communicating sales promotions. Advertising also has strategic uses within the wider marketing mix. It can contribute to product positioning, thus supporting a premium price, or it could help to even out seasonal fluctuations in demand.

The advertising message is extremely important. It has to be informative, persuasive and attention grabbing. It has to be appropriate for the target audience and thus speak to them in terms to which they can relate. There are several types of creative appeal that advertisers can use: rational, emotional and product centred. Once the message and its appeal have been decided, the advertisement has to be prepared for print or broadcasting. In either case, the advertisement has to be relevant to the target audience, making a sufficient impact to get the desired message across and to get the audience to act on it.

The advertiser has a wide choice of media. Television has a wide reach across the whole population, but it can be difficult to target a specific market segment precisely. Radio can deliver fairly specific target audiences, and is an attractive medium for smaller companies operating in a defined geographic area covered by a local radio station. Cinema is a relatively minor medium delivering captive, well-profiled audiences. It can make a big impact on the audience because of the quality of the sound and the size of the screen.

Print media broadly consist of magazines and newspapers. Magazines tend to have well-defined readerships who are receptive to the content of advertisements relevant to the magazine's theme. Magazines tend to have a long life span, with each copy being passed around several readers, each of whom is likely to make time to read the publication 'properly'. Newspapers, on the other hand, have a very short life span and are often skimmed rather than read properly. A reader is unlikely to read through the same copy more than once. Outdoor media includes advertising hoardings, posters and transport-related media. They can provide easily digested messages that attract the attention of bored passengers or passers-by. They can generate high frequency as people tend to pass the same sites regularly, but can be spoiled by the weather and the ambience of their location.

Since advertising is so expensive and often requires a lot of creativity if it is to attract attention and communicate a complex message, advertising agencies are often used to provide expertise. Choosing an agency is an important task, and an organisation needs to think carefully about the relevant criteria for choice. Once the client has signed up an agency, it is then important to continue to communicate and to build a strong mutual understanding, with both sides contributing according to expectations.

Managing advertising within an organisation involves a number of stages. First, campaign responsibilities need to be decided so that the process and the budget are kept under proper control. Once the target market and their broad communication needs have been defined, specific campaign objectives can be developed. Next, the budget can be set in the light of the desired objectives. Media choices, based on the habits of the target audience, the requirements of the planned message and the desired reach and frequency, can then be made. Meanwhile, the advertisements themselves are developed. Testing can be built in at various stages of this development to ensure that the right message is getting across in the right kind of way with the right kind of effect. Once the advertising has been fully developed, it can be implemented. Both during and after the campaign, managers will assess the advertising's effectiveness, using aided or unaided recall, enquiry tests or sales tests, depending on the original objectives.

Key words and phrases

Advertising	Frequency	Pre-testing
Advertising media	Full service agencies	Reach
Advertorial	Institutional advertising	Reminder and
Comparative advertising	Layout	reinforcement advertising
Competitive advertising	Limited service agencies	Slice of life
Copywriting	Pioneer advertising	Storyboard
Creative appeal	Post-testing	

QUESTIONS FOR REVIEW

15.1 In what ways can advertising support the other elements of the promotional mix?

15.2 What is *comparative advertising* and what are the risks of using it?

15.3 What are the different ways in which *product-orientated appeals* can be used?

15.4 Define *reach* and *frequency*. Why might there be a conflict between them in practice?

15.5 What can *radio* offer as an advertising medium to a small business?

15.6 What advantages might *cinema advertising* have over *television*?

15.7 In what ways can *magazines* be a better advertising medium than *newspapers*?

15.8 What are the relative advantages and disadvantages of:

(a) full service advertising agencies;

(b) limited service agencies; and

(c) handing advertising in-house?

15.9 Describe the *stages* in developing an advertising campaign.

15.10 What can an advertiser gain from *pre-testing* advertisements?

QUESTIONS FOR DISCUSSION

15.1 Find examples of advertising that uses:

(a) a rational appeal; and

(b) a fear appeal.

Why do you think the advertisers have chosen these approaches?

15.2 What are the guidelines for good copy for a print advertisement? Find a print advertisement and discuss the extent to which it conforms with those guidelines.

15.3 Find a current advertising campaign that uses both television and print media. Why do you think both media are being used? To what extent is each medium contributing something different to the overall message?

15.4 Find out the cost of:

(a) a 30-second advertising slot on your regional commercial television channel at 8 p.m. on a weekday evening;

(b) a 30-second slot at the same time on your local commercial radio station;

(c) a full-page advertisement in your local newspaper; and

(d) a full-page advertisement in a national daily newspaper.

15.5 Develop a checklist of criteria against which a prospective client could assess advertising agencies. Which criterion would you say is the most important, and why?

CASE STUDY 15.1

The spirit is willing. . .

In 1995, the voluntary ban on advertising spirits, whisky, gin, brandy etc. was lifted. Spirits brands turned to television in the hope that it would deliver younger audiences cost effectively. Four years later, however, a senior executive in the spirits industry was complaining that it was simply not working. The task that the spirits industry has set itself to counter an ageing customer base is not an easy one, as wine and to a lesser extent beer are the preferred tipples. It is very important for spirits companies to reach the younger audience, as drinkers tend to develop their preferences in their twenties and stick to them beyond that. Although television advertising spend for spirits had reached £42mn in 1998, over a five-year period, covering brands such as Bell's, Gordon's, Famous Grouse, Bacardi and Smirnoff, sales had, however, fallen £100mn by value. The only product type in the spirits industry that seems to be succeeding with the younger market is vodka: 61 per cent of regular vodka drinkers come from the 18 to 34 age group, whereas 62 per cent of regular whisky drinkers are aged over 50.

Falling sales put the spotlight on television advertising. It was claimed that advertising on ITV, the UKs main terrestrial commercial television channel, had not proved to be effective because while the cost of the medium had risen, the size of the young audience had declined. ITV denied this.

Nevertheless, the spirits manufacturers do believe it and it is driving them to divert a proportion of their advertising budgets into other media, including cheaper television channels, to try to reach more of the target audience than television can deliver. It was also claimed that spirits companies were spreading their resources too thinly over too many brands and media and that supermarket own-label products were also damaging the industry by driving retail prices down.

Some have questioned the creative quality of spirits advertisements on television, pointing out that they do not tend to have the same wit as beer advertisements or direct appeal to the younger market. The advertisements fail to make drinking spirits seem trendy or fun. Some say that this is because the spirits manufacturers do not want to upset the advertising regulatory bodies and are thus playing safe, while others think it is because the advertising agencies involved have not yet mastered the art of developing exciting, creative campaigns for spirits for television audiences. Another criticism is that there are too many shorter advertisements of 10 or 20 seconds being used rather than 30 or 40 seconds. The argument is that if the audience needs persuading about the product benefits, especially an audience that could well be sitting in front of the television nursing a can of lager, it is unlikely to be achieved in a shorter slot that is better for awareness generation. This is seen as a failing of advertising agencies, which have also been blamed for pushing spirits clients into television because agencies are perceived to be obsessed with television and earn good commission on television advertising. It has been calculated that agencies have earned £10mn between them in commission.

The international marketing director for Irish Distillers, which owns Jameson Irish Whiskey, feels that in the UK Irish whiskey has a younger following than Scotch and that television works better because it is not trying to overturn entrenched attitudes. He also points, however, to the US market in which television advertising is not available. His view is that this has made advertisers more creative in other media and that in the UK market, creativity has been lost in the dash to television and advertisers have committed too much to television as a medium and

failed to plan strategically integrated campaigns across different media.

Not all attempts to use television advertising have been a disaster. Baileys successfully repositioned itself from being an old lady's drink into a young woman's drink, both at home and in the pub, and sales doubled. Some companies have withdrawn from television as a medium altogether. Research showed that television failed to deliver either the target audience or the sales for Pernod, and thus the medium was dropped. Others are giving television a further chance and are working on their creativity and message. UDV, the company that owns the Gordon's Gin brand, is spending £12.5mn to try to position the brand in the 25–34-year-old segment without alienating its core 45+ age group. A £1mn television advertisement thus had to make the brand relevant to the younger audience without damaging the image among the older loyal core group. Research showed that the advertisement set in a pool hall, showing a losing player finding his form after a Gordon's and tonic and winning the hall itself from the owner, 'Gordon's as experienced by a hustler', was liked by both audiences. For the older audience, Gordon's continued sponsorship of the Chelsea Flower Show and the National Trust is reassuring and a good fit, partly because gardening is the number one hobby of the 45+ group and partly because Chelsea, the National Trust and Gordon's are all about English tradition and heritage.

Sources: Campbell (1999a, 1999b); Cozens (1999b); Maling (1999); *Marketing* (1999d); http://www.diageo.com.

Questions

1 What are the objectives of advertising in the spirits market? Why do you think that spirits manufacturers were so keen to lift their voluntary ban and move to television advertising as the dominant medium?

2 Why are supermarket own-label spirits a threat in this market, and how might this affect the advertising of the mainstream manufacturer brands?

3 What contribution are the advertising agencies making and how effective do you think they are?

4 When sales are falling, is it fair to blame the advertising?

CASE STUDY 15.2

Business to business advertising and IT

In terms of print media, there are around 4700 magazines and newspapers in the business to business sector or trade press, for example in the computing, financial, medical and even marketing fields. Magazines such as *Nursing Times, Railway Gazette, New Scientist, Utility Week, European Chemical News, Poultry World, Crops, Air Navigation* and *Hairdresser's Journal* all reach highly specialised audiences. The advertising revenue across the sector in 1997 was £1.1bn. NOP research has shown that these magazines and newspapers are seen as authoritative and essential by their readers. Research has also shown that 95 per cent of business/professional people read the trade publications relevant to their area and 68 per cent consider them to be the most important source of information about their industry. A trade magazine like *The Grocer*, for example, is an essential tool in new fmcg product launches and relaunches. It is an important means of communication between manufacturers and smaller retailers in particular and helps to get the product known, stocked and supported in the retail trade. If that did not happen, the product would probably fail.

The trade press is a growing medium with increases in revenues of around 11 per cent per year and an increasing number of titles. Despite this, it is growing no faster than direct marketing and it does appear that some advertisers are using the trade press medium less: 84 per cent of trade press publishers feel that the future will see a shift away from advertising spending with them. According to Donald (1999), this is partly because many business to business advertisers are trying to reach much more diverse audiences than the trade titles deliver, and partly because managers who are busier than ever are harder to reach in the workplace. This has meant that more business to business advertisers are using consumer-orientated national press, on-line and mainstream broadcast media to try to reach decision makers. Techology company NCR, for example, ran a corporate advertising campaign and less than 0.5 per cent of the advertising budget was spent on the trade press. The rest went on national press and television and posters near to target companies' offices. Part of the objective was to reach chief executives and other very senior decision makers. NCR felt that these people would not have much time to focus on the trade press at work and thus that it would be better to try to communicate with them outside the workplace when they were less likely to be busy.

One of the problems with business to business advertising in IT is that IT is relevant to all kinds of businesses, from the public sector through to small businesses and multinationals, in all kinds of industries. Many managers do not read the specialist IT trade publications and it would be unrealistic to expect IT providers to advertise in every other trade publication. Thus many IT providers are turning to the IT supplements developed by the national press to reach the non-specialist business audience. While the IT specialist press is losing advertising revenue, the national newspapers are increasing their IT advertising revenue. There is a general tendency within the IT field for advertisers to use trade press only as part of a bigger package, with an emphasis on television building the corporate image and brand identity and the trade press playing a supporting role in getting across the specific product features and benefits.

Dell Computers uses the personal computer publications, aimed partly at individual consumers and partly at IT professionals, as one of its main media. Thus when potential buyers read a good review of a Dell computer in a magazine, they can find the advertisement in the same issue to get more information or to find a point of contact. Dell does, however, see the trade press as only one element in its communications strategy. National newspapers play an important role in educating people about IT and reaching the smaller business buyer. An on-line advertising presence also plays a role, leading the potential customer towards a purchase and expanding the audience. Couldwell (1999) maintains that growth in the trade press has arisen from advertisers' desire for well-targeted campaigns, but that in the future readers will find it easier to get specialist information over the Internet and thus advertising spend will shift towards the web. In response, some publishers have moved into e-publishing to revitalise their offering to both readers and advertisers. One IT publisher claims that 50 per cent of its website visitors do not read the hard copy of the magazine. According to research carried out across Europe, an IT professional receives an average of 29 magazines per month and, not surprisingly, 61 per cent think that is too many and 89 per cent prefer to get information over the Internet.

Sources: Cook (1999a); Couldwell (1999); Crawford (1999a); Donald (1999); http://www.euro.dell.com; http://www.ncr.com.

▶

Questions

1 What are the advantages and disadvantages of the trade press for the advertiser?

2 To what extent do you think that the views and trends in the IT trade press field might be typical of those found in other professional areas, such as nursing, farming or air navigation?

3 What do you think are the main similarities and differences between advertisements aimed at consumers and those aimed at the business to business market?

4 Is it possible for print and electronic trade magazines to exist side by side?

REFERENCES TO CHAPTER 15

Applebaum, U. and Halliburton, C. (1993), 'How to Develop International Advertising Campaigns that Work: The Example of the European Food and Beverage Sector', *International Journal of Advertising*, 12(3), 223–241.

Barrett, L. (1999), 'VW Links to Royal Wedding with Posters', *Marketing*, 17 June, p. 6.

Berkowitz, E. N. *et al.* (1992), *Marketing*, Irwin.

Campaign (1998), 'AMV Unveils Graphic Anti-drink-drive Xmas Campaign', *Campaign*, 4 December, p. 2.

Campaign (1999), 'Media Choice', *Campaign*, 19 February, p. 20.

Campbell, L. (1999a), 'UDV Chief Slams ITV for Ads Flop', *Marketing*, 4 March, p. 5.

Campbell, L. (1999b), 'Why Spirits Don't Work on TV', *Marketing*, 11 March, p. 19.

Campbell, L. (1999c), 'Lara Croft Signs Up for Lucozade's £25mn Push', *Marketing*, 22 April, p. 4.

Cook, R. (1999a), 'Big Business', *Campaign*, 19 February, pp. 30–1.

Cook, R. (1999b), 'The Business of Ambient', *Campaign*, 14 May, pp. 28–9.

Couldwell, C. (1999), 'IT Overload', *Marketing Week*, 18 March, pp. 49–50.

Cozens, C. (1999a), 'Saatchis Creates New Army Recruiting Drive', *Campaign*, 23 April, p. 7.

Cozens, C. (1999b), 'Gordon's Craves Youth Appeal', *Campaign*, 30 April, p. 14.

Crawford, A-M. (1999a), 'PPA Leads Business Upgrade', *Marketing*, 4 February, p. 8.

Crawford, A-M. (1999b), Kellogg Looks at Branded TV Slot', *Marketing*, 11 February, p. 4.

Croft, M. (1999a), 'Viewers Turned off by TV', *Marketing Week*, 18 February, pp. 36-7.

Croft, M. (1999b), 'Pressing Issues', *Marketing Week*, 22 April, pp. 61–2.

Day, J. (1999), 'The Point of Saturation', *Marketing Week*, 11 March, pp. 40–41.

De Mooij, M. (1994), *Advertising Worldwide: Concepts, Theories and Practice Of International, Multinational and Global Advertising* (2nd edn), Prentice Hall.

Denny, N. (1998), 'Sainsbury's Tops "Irritating" Poll', *Marketing*, 17 December, p. 1.

DMB&B (1995a), *A DMB&B Case Study: Texaco*, DMB&B.

DMB&B (1995b), *A DMB&B Case Study: Drink – Drive*, DMB&B.

Donald, H. (1999), 'Paper Cuts', *Marketing Week*. 17 June, pp. 43–8.

Euromonitor (1998), *European Marketing Data and Statistics 1998*, Euromonitor (33rd edn).

Euromonitor (1999), *European Marketing Data and Statistics 1999*, Euromonitor (34th edn).

Fill, C. (1999) *Marketing Communications: Context, Contents and Strategies*, 2nd edn, Prentice Hall Europe.

Fry, A. (1999), 'Euro TV Builds on Decade's Growth', *Marketing*, 13 May, pp. 43–4.

Garrett, J. (1999), 'Publicis Falls Foul of Nestlé's Global Nescafé Push', *Campaign*, 21 May, p. 12.

Jardine, A. (1999a), 'Sainsbury's Axe Falls on Marketing', *Marketing*, 22 April, p. 1.

Jardine, A. (1999b), 'Sainsbury's Ready Meals in "Suggestive" Campaign', *Marketing*, 20 May, p. 5.

Jardine, A. (1999c), 'Sainsbury's Motivating Staff to Revive Image', *Marketing*, 17 June, p. 3.

Killgren, L. (1999), 'Nicking Gillette', *Marketing Week*, 17 June, pp. 20–2.

Maling, N. (1999), 'TV Money Spirited Down the Pan', *Marketing Week*, 11 March, pp. 26–9.

Marketing (1999a), 'Reading Between the Lines', *Marketing*, 21 January, pp. 21–2.

Marketing (1999b), 'Category King,' *Marketing*, 4 March, pp. 26–7.

Marketing (1999c), 'Hair Today, Gone Tomorrow', *Marketing*, 21 April, p. 80.

Marketing (1999d), 'Gordon's £1mn TV Ad to Pull in More Youthful Gin Fans', *Marketing*, 29 April, p. 8.

Marketing (1999e), 'Lost: Gun-toting Busty Brunette in Tight Shorts', *Marketing*, 3 June, p. 64.

Marketing Week (1999a), 'Commercials Should Break With Tradition', *Marketing Week*, 21 January, p. 12.

Marketing Week (1999b), 'Lara Croft in £25mn Blitz for Lucozade', *Marketing Week*, 22 April, p. 6.

Marketing Week (1999c), 'Poster Watch', *Marketing Week*, 27 May, pp. 38–9.

McLuhan, R. (1999), 'Success for Army's Initiative-testing Recruitment Drive', *Marketing*, 27 May, p. 26.

Muehling, D. D. *et al.* (1990), 'The Impact of Comparative Advertising on Levels of Message Involvement', *Journal of Advertising*, 19(4), pp. 41–50.

Mueller-Heumann, G. (1992), 'Markets and Technology Shifts in the 1990s: Market Fragmentation and Mass Customisation', *Journal of Marketing Management*, 8(4), pp. 303–14.

Munzinger, U. (1988), 'Ad*Vantage/AC-T International Advertising Research Case Studies', *ESOMAR Seminar on International Marketing Research*, 16–18 November.

Murphy, C. (1999), 'Are You paying too Much for Ads?', *Marketing*, 20 May, pp. 24–5.

Murphy, D. (1999), 'Taking Your Ads In-store', *Marketing*, 18 March, pp. 35–6.

Newland, F. (1999), 'O&M Gives Maxwell House Soap Plot', *Campaign*, 4 June, p. 8.

NTC Publications (1997), *European Advertising and Media Yearbook 1997*, NTC Publications.

O'Connor, J. and Galvin, E. (1999), *Marketing and Information Technology*, 2nd edn, Financial Times Pitman Publishing.

Petty, R. E. and Cacioppo, J. T. (1979), 'Effects of Message Repetition and Position on Cognitive Responses, Recall and Persuasion', *Journal of Personality and Social Psychology*, 37(Jan), pp. 97–109.

Piercy, N. (1987), 'The Marketing Budgeting Process: Marketing Management Implications', *Journal of Marketing*, 51(4), pp. 45–59.

Shannon, J. (1999), 'Comparative Ads Call for Prudence', *Marketing Week*, 6 May, p. 32.

Sissors, J. Z. and Bumba, L. (1989), *Advertising Media Planning*, 3rd edn, NTC Business Books.

Smith, P. R. (1993), *Marketing Communications*, Kogan Page.

Tylee, J. (1999a), 'Pepsi to Invest $100m in Global Brand Effort', *Campaign*, 12 February, p. 12.

Tylee, J. (1999b), 'Why Pepsi is Still Desperate to be the Choice of a Generation', *Campaign*, 19 February, p. 16.

Tylee, J. (1999c), 'Sainsbury's to Tone Down Hectoring John Cleese Spots', *Campaign*, 12 February, p. 4.

White, R. (1988), *Advertising: What It Is and How To Do It*, McGraw-Hill.

Wilmshurst, J. (1985), *The Fundamentals of Advertising*, Heinemann Professional Publishing.

Wilson, R. (1999), 'Commercial Sounds', *Marketing Week*, 6 May, pp. 47–52.

Woolgar, T. (1999), 'Outdoor Answers Back', *Campaign*, 16 April, p. 29.

16 Sales Promotion

LEARNING OBJECTIVES

This chapter will help you to:

1 define sales promotion and appreciate its role in the communications mix through the objectives it can achieve;

2 understand the range of available methods of sales promotion in consumer markets and their objectives;

3 understand the range and objectives of sales promotion methods used by manufacturers to stimulate retailers;

4 appreciate the role of sales promotion in other organisational markets and how sales promotion overlaps with other elements of the communications mix; and

5 gain an overview of the issues involved in the sales promotion planning process and their implications for the application and practice of sales promotion methods.

INTRODUCTION

Traditionally the poor cousin of advertising, sales promotion actually covers a fascinating range of short-term tactical tools that can play a vital complementary role in long-term promotional strategy. Its aim is to add extra value to the product or service, over and above the normal product offering, thus creating an extra inducement to buy or try it. Although individual sales promotions are usually regarded as short-term tactical measures, sales promotion generally, as an element of the promotional mix, is increasingly being recognised as a valid strategic tool, working alongside and supporting other promotional elements.

Example   The release of *Star Wars Episode 1: The Phantom Menace* (http://www.starwars.com) in summer 1999 generated a great deal of sales promotion activity from brands anxious to be linked with its predicted box office success. Pepsi (http://www.pepsiworld.com), for instance, developed a £5mn marketing campaign centred around *Star Wars*, including £1mn on television advertising, packaging featuring characters from the film and a number of promotional offers. Consumers who collected five ring pulls from Pepsi cans could send off £2.99 to get an exclusive item of *Star Wars* merchandise (Campbell, 1999b; *Marketing Week*, 1999b) and by offering a range of collectible items, Pepsi is hoping to involve consumers in a collecting habit. Having to collect the ring pulls helps engender loyalty to the brand at least for a short period, while sending money makes the item more valuable to the consumer, helps Pepsi cover its costs, and perhaps keeps the number of respondents down to a manageable level. Even so, Pepsi has done an initial production run of 120 million promotional packs, having learned from its first *Star Wars* promotion in 1997 that generated 250 000 respondents and increased sales over the promotional period by 70 per cent (*The Grocer*, 1999d).

This chapter will define more clearly what sales promotion is and what strategic role it can play within the promotional mix. It considers in detail the various methods associated with consumer, organisational and trade promotions, discussing what each can contribute towards given marketing objectives. If new products are planned, for example, a number of sales promotions may be designed to encourage product trial. If competitive activity is increasing, then sales promotion efforts may be directed at retaining customer loyalty and generating repeat purchases. The chapter will not, however, only look at the implementation issues, but also consider the management concerns that lie behind sales promotion. To be effective, sales promotion programmes must be carefully planned and managed. There are many examples of what can go wrong under poor planning and management, the most spectacular recent example of which was the Hoover free flights sales promotion in the UK (*see* p. 663). The key management issues will be considered from a campaign development perspective.

THE ROLE AND DEFINITION OF SALES PROMOTION

According to the Institute of Sales Promotion, **sales promotion** is:

> '... a range of tactical marketing techniques designed within a strategic marketing framework to add value to a product or service in order to achieve specific sales and marketing objectives.'

The word 'tactical' implies a short, sharp burst of activity that is expected to be effective as soon as it is implemented. The fact that this activity is *designed within a strategic marketing framework* means, however, that it is not a panic measure, not just something to wheel out when you do not know what else to do. On the contrary, sales promotion should be planned into an overall communications mix, to make the most of its ability to complement other areas such as advertising and its unique capacity to achieve certain objectives, mostly tactical, but sometimes strategic (Davies, 1992).

The key element of this definition, however, is that the sales promotion should *add value to a product or service*. This is something over and above the normal product offering that might make buyers stop and think about whether to change their usual buying behaviour, or revise their buying criteria. As the rest of this chapter will show, this takes the form of something tangible that is of value to the buyer, whether it is extra product free, money, a gift or the opportunity to win a prize, that under normal circumstances they would not get.

Perhaps the main problem with the definition is that the area of sales promotion has almost developed beyond it. The idea of the short-term tactical shock to the market is very well established and understood, and will be seen to be at the heart of many of the specific techniques outlined in this chapter. With the development of relationship marketing, that is, the necessity for building long-term buyer–seller relationships, marketers have been looking for ways of developing the scope of traditional sales promotion to encourage long-term customer loyalty and repeat purchasing behaviour. Loyalty schemes, such as frequent flyer programmes or the Shell smart card, are sales promotions in the sense that they offer added value over and above the normal product offering, but they are certainly not short-term tactical measures – quite the opposite. Wilmshurst (1993) clearly states that creatively designed sales promotions can be just as effective as advertising in affecting consumers' attitudes to brands. This means, perhaps, that the definition of sales promotion needs to be revised to account for those strategic, franchise-building promotional techniques:

> '... a range of marketing techniques designed within a strategic marketing framework to add extra value to a product or service over and above the "normal" offering in order to achieve specific sales and marketing objectives. This extra value may be of a short-term tactical nature or it may be part of a longer-term franchise-building programme.'

643

The rest of this section will focus on the objectives that sales promotion can achieve. Sales promotion objectives are best discussed in the context of the relationship within which they are happening, as shown in Fig. 16.1. The techniques linked with these objectives will be discussed in much more detail in later sections of the chapter.

Manufacturer–intermediary (trade promotion)

The intermediary provides a vital service for the manufacturer in displaying goods to their best advantage and making them easily available to the consumer. Any individual intermediary, however, performs this function for a number of manufacturers, and so a manufacturer might wish to use sales promotion techniques to encourage the intermediary to take a particular interest in particular products for various purposes. However, depending on the balance of power between manufacturer and intermediary, the manufacturer might have little choice in the matter. Intermediaries might expect or insist on sales promotions before they will co-operate with what the manufacturer wants.

As shown in Fig. 16.2, and discussed below, trade promotions revolve around gaining more product penetration, more display and more intermediary promotional effort. As Fill (1999) points out, however, this might cause conflict between the manufacturer and the intermediary, since the intermediary's prime objective is to increase store traffic. The level of incentive might thus have to be extremely attractive!

Increase stock levels

The more stock of a particular product that an intermediary holds, the more committed they will be to put effort into selling it quickly. Furthermore, intermediaries have limited stockholding space, so the more space that your product takes up, the less room there is for the competition. Money-based or extra-product based incentives might encourage intermediaries to increase their orders, although the effect might be short lived and in the longer term might even reduce orders as intermediaries work through the extra stock they acquired during the promotion.

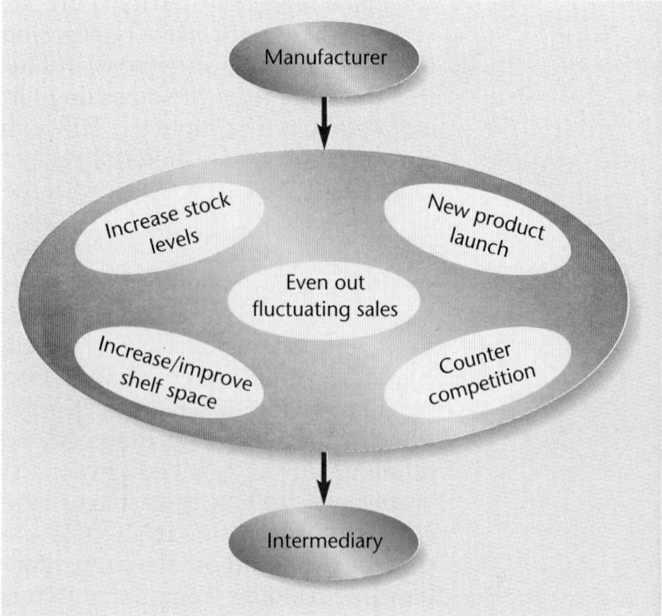

Gain more and better shelf space

There is intense competition between manufacturers to secure shelf space within retail outlets. Demand for shelf space far outstrips supply. Intermediaries are, therefore, willing to accept incentives to help them to allocate this scarce resource to particular products or manufacturers. Again, this may link with money- or product-based trade promotions, but could also be part of a joint promotion agreement or a point-of-sale promotion, for instance. The quality of the shelf space acquired is also important. If a product is to capture the consumer's attention,

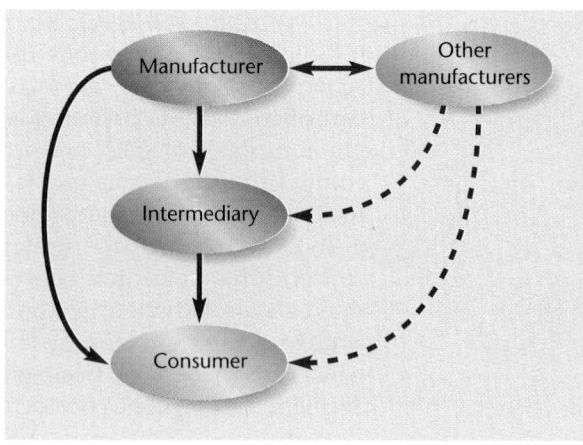

FIGURE 16.1

Communication links through sales promotion

FIGURE 16.2

Manufacturer–intermediary sales promotion objectives

then it needs to be prominent. This means that it must be displayed either at the customer's eye level or at the end of the aisles in a supermarket where the customer is turning the corner and all the trolley traffic jams occur. There is keen competition for these highly desirable display sites, also called *golden zones*, and again, intermediary-orientated sales promotion may help a manufacturer to make its case more strongly.

New product launch

The launch period is a delicate time in any new product's life, and if the distribution aspects of the marketing strategy are weak, then it could be fatal. A new product needs to be accepted by the appropriate intermediaries so that it is available for all those consumers eager to try it. To the trade, however, a new product is a potential risk. What if it doesn't sell? Trade promotions (particularly with a push strategy – *see* pp. 568 *et seq*.) can reduce some of that risk. Money-based promotions reduce the potential financial losses of a product failure, while **'sale or return'** promotions remove the fear of being left with unsaleable stock. Sales force support, meanwhile, can reassure the intermediary that staff are ready, willing and able to sell the product and fully understand its features and benefits. This is particularly appropriate with more complex, infrequently purchased items, such as electrical goods.

Even out fluctuating sales

Some products, such as lawnmowers, ice-cream and holidays, suffer from seasonality. While the design of the product offering or the pricing policies adopted can help to overcome these problems, sales promotion can also play a part. If manufactures are able to encourage intermediaries to take on more stock or to push the product harder during the 'quieter' periods, sales can be spread a little more evenly throughout the year. This process can also be enhanced by a related consumer-orientated promotion, so that the manufacturer is gaining extra synergy through simultaneous push and pull activity.

Counter the competition

It has already been indicated that a manufacturer is competing with every other manufacturer for an intermediary's attention. Sales promotions, therefore, make very useful tactical weapons to spoil or dilute the effects of a competitor's actions. If, for instance, you are aware that the competition is about to launch a new product, you might use a trade sales promotion to load up a key intermediary with your related products, so that at best they will be reluctant to take on the competition's goods, or at worst, they will drive a much harder bargain with the competitor.

Retailer–consumer (retailer promotions)

In the same way that manufacturers compete among themselves for the intermediary's attention, retailers compete for the consumer's patronage. Store-specific sales promotions, whether jointly prepared with a manufacturer or originating solely from the retailer, can help differentiate one store from another, and entice the public in. Retailers also try to use sales promotions in a longer-term strategic way to create store loyalty, for example through card schemes that allow the shopper to collect points over time that can be redeemed for gifts or money-off vouchers. Retailers use sales promotion for many reasons and these are summarised in Fig. 16.3.

Increase store traffic

A prime objective for a retailer is to get the public in through the shop door. Any kind of retailer-specific sales promotion has a chance of doing that. Money-off coupons delivered from door to door or printed in the local newspaper, for example, might bring in people who do not usually shop in a particular store. Such promotions might also encourage retail substitution, giving shoppers an incentive to patronise one retailer rather than another. An electrical retailer might advertise a one-day sale with a few carefully chosen items offered on promotion at rock-bottom prices. This bait brings potential customers to the store, and even if the real bargains have gone early, they will still look at other goods.

Increase frequency and amount of purchases

Even if a customer already shops at one retailer's outlets, the retailer would prefer them to shop there more often and to spend more.

> **Example** Short-term promotions, often price based, are frequently used by retailers to increase store traffic. Sometimes, however, a retailer gets a little more than it bargained for. To celebrate its 25th anniversary of trading in the UK, McDonald's opened 1999 with a 'buy one get one free' offer on Big Macs supported by extensive television and press advertising. The response was overwhelming and brought customers into McDonald's branches in such numbers that some stores had to close because of overcrowding, others had the police in controlling crowds while others simply closed. Many stores ran out of burgers and/or buns and had to withdraw the offer, much to the disgust of their customers. The problem was largely the result of a forecasting error. McDonald's had estimated that stores would see four times as many customers as usual over the promotional weekend, whereas in many stores the actual demand was more like eight times more than normal (Darby, 1999a).

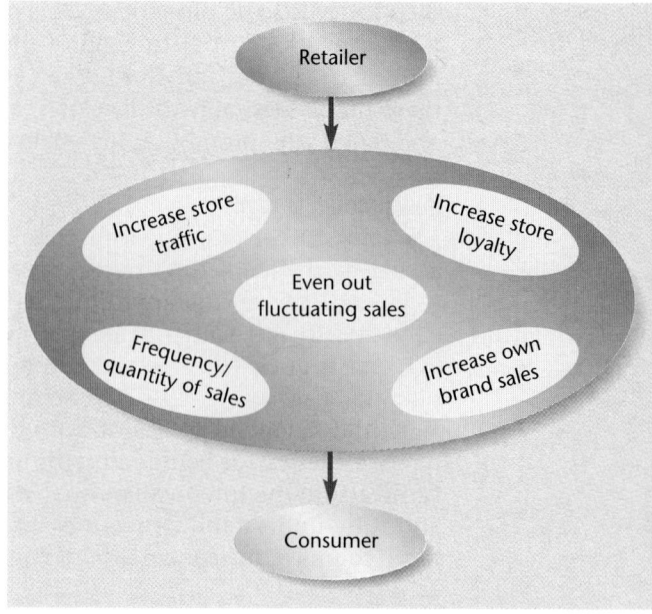

FIGURE 16.3

Retailer–consumer sales promotion objectives

Increase store loyalty

Supermarkets in particular use sales promotion as a means of generating store loyalty. The kinds of activities outlined in relation to increasing the frequency and amount of purchases help towards this, as does a rolling programme of couponing and money-off offers. The problem with this type of promotion, however, is that it risks creating a 'deal-prone' promiscuous customer who will switch to whichever retailer is currently offering the best package of short-term promotions. To counteract this, some retailers have introduced loyalty schemes using swipe cards.

> **Example** In the UK, Tesco was the first with its Clubcard, and Safeway soon followed with its ABC card. Shoppers thus have an incentive to shop regularly at a particular retailer in order to accumulate points. Using the customer database, coupons and money-off vouchers can be regularly issued and delivered to the customer's own home, thus creating a stronger, more personal retailer–customer link (*see also* Case Study 16.2).

Increase own-brand sales

As discussed at pp. 281 *et seq.* and p. 543 *et seq.*, retailers are increasingly investing in their own-brand ranges. These are, therefore, legitimate subjects for a whole range of consumer-orientated promotions. These promotions do not have to be overtly price or product based.

Example In-store free recipe cards can help to promote the store's fresh foods or own-label products by giving the shopper meal ideas and encouraging them to buy the ingredients. This can be linked with other promotions so that, for instance, one of the own-label ingredients could feature a price reduction to encourage purchase further. The magazines sent out with loyalty card statements and vouchers can also promote own-label goods, again through recipes, through editorial copy explaining how products can be used and their benefits, or through the more obvious mechanism of extra money-off vouchers.

Even out busy periods

In the same way that manufacturers face seasonal demand for some products, retailers have to cope with fluctuations between the very busy periods of the week or year, and the very quiet times. Offering sales promotions that apply only on certain days or within certain trading hours might divert some customers away from the busier periods.

Example A one-day sale on a Wednesday or Thursday can be a good way for a retailer to divert shoppers away from the busier weekend, especially if it is well advertised in the local area. One DIY retailer also instituted Wednesday afternoon discounts for senior citizens, presumably because that is an easily defined group who can change their shopping day because they are not likely to be working. Supermarkets in particular find the wide variation in the number of people shopping each day very difficult from the point of view of both making sure that there is adequate staff cover available and keeping the shelves full for shoppers. They are thus considering price-based promotion to reward those who shop at a quieter times and penalise those who are 'cash rich, time poor'.

Manufacturer–consumer (manufacturer promotion)

While it is obviously important for manufacturers to have the distribution channels working in their favour, there is still much work to be done with the consumer to help ensure continued product success. After all, if consumer demand for a product is buoyant, that in itself acts as an incentive to the retail trade to stock it, effectively acting as a pull strategy. There are many reasons for manufacturers to use sales promotions to woo the consumer, and some of these are outlined below and summarised in Fig. 16.4.

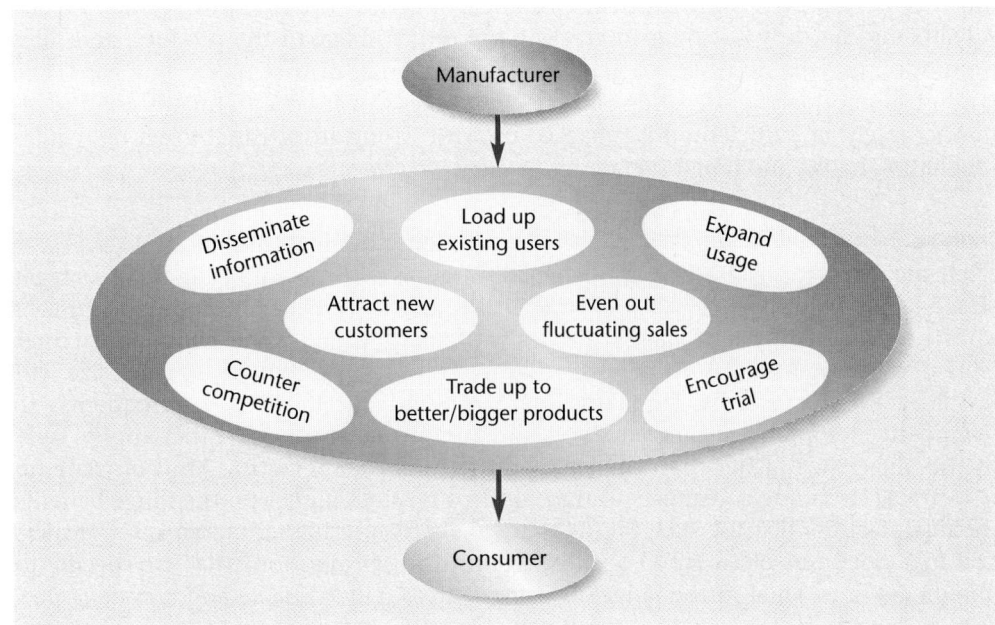

FIGURE 16.4

Manufacturer–consumer sales promotion objectives

Encourage trial

The rationale in encouraging trial is similar to that discussed earlier in relation to the intermediary and new product launches. New products face the problem of being unknown, and therefore consumers may need incentives to encourage trial of the product. Samples help consumers to judge a product for themselves, while coupons, money off and gifts reduce the financial penalty of a 'wrong' purchase. Sales promotions thus play an important role in the early stages of a product's life.

Expand usage

Expanding usage involves using sales promotion to encourage people to find different ways of using more of the product so that, of course, they purchase more.

Example Be-Ro flour produces a low-priced cookery book, available by mail, of reasonably simple but tasty day-to-day recipes, using its products. This encourages a wider range of more frequent home baking, and therefore more consumption of Be-Ro products. Wash & Go shampoo tried to expand usage of its product within households by distributing one-use samples on a door-to-door basis in opaque wrapping with the words 'For Men Only'. Perceived largely as a female-orientated product, this sales promotion was clearly trying to reinforce a wider user base.

Disseminate information

Sales promotions can be used effectively as a means of getting information across to consumers. Even a small sample pack distributed door to door, for example, not only lets the consumer experience the product, but also gives the manufacturer a chance to tell that consumer quite a lot about the product's features and benefits, where to buy it, and related products in the range. While advertising can do the same sort of information dissemination, it is easily ignored. If the consumer is tempted to try the sample, then they may take more notice of the information with it, and only then pay attention to the advertising.

Attracting new customers

An established product may be striving to acquire new customers, either by converting non-users or by turning irregular customers or brand switchers into regular buyers. Advertising can only go so far in creating a positive image of the product, and sales promotion may be necessary to generate that first trial, or that repeat purchase. The kind of promotion that depends on collecting tokens over time to qualify for a mail-in offer might be sufficient, if it is backed up with strong advertising, to set up regular purchasing habits and brand preference.

Trade up

There are two facets to **trading up**. One is getting the consumer to trade up to a bigger size, and the other is to get them to trade up to the more expensive products further up the range. Trading up to bigger sizes is particularly useful where the manufacturer feels that the customer is vulnerable to aggressive competition. The bigger size will last longer and, therefore, that consumer is going to be exposed less frequently to competitive temptation at the point of sale. Any promotional effort that applies only to the bigger size rather than the smaller one might achieve that kind of trade-up objective. Persuading consumers to trade up to a product higher up the range benefits the manufacturer because such products are likely to earn higher margins. Car dealers and manufacturers often try to do this. Again, using promotions that are specific to one model or product in the range, or using increasingly valuable and attractive promotions as the range goes up, can help to focus the customer's mind on higher things. Price-based promotions are probably not a good idea in this case, because of the risk of cheapening the product's image.

Example Protecting the product's image is not just a concern for more upmarket brand owners, however. Even fmcg marketers want to create promotions that will involve the consumer, enhance the product's image, and create something that is difficult for the competition to match. Nestlé achieved all that with its Kit Kat promotion in summer 1999. For a limited period, Kit Kats were made available with special packaging that looked like the usual red sleeve but, when put in the fridge, turned blue with a snowflake pattern. The promotion was emphasised at the point of sale by giving retailers free racks to put in their chiller cabinets so that customers could see the effect and want to try it for themselves. A mail-in promotion also gave consumers an incentive to buy a Kit Kat cool bag for £2.40 and five tokens (*The Grocer*, 1999n; http://www. nestle.com/brands)

Kit Kat is the top selling confectionery brand, biscuit and chocolate biscuit.

Source: Sweet Facts '98, Nestlé UK Ltd.

Load up

Loading up is partly a defensive mechanism to protect your customers from the efforts of the competition. A customer who is collecting tokens or labels towards a mail-in offer with a tight deadline, or who finds a cut price offer particularly seductive, might end up with far greater quantities of the product than can be used immediately. Effectively, that customer is now out of the market until those stocks are used up. This is a two-edged sword: the advantage is that they are less likely to listen to the competition; the disadvantage is that you will not be selling them any more for a while either, as you have effectively brought your sales to that customer forward. Of course, if that customer was originally a brand switcher, or a non-user, then you have gained considerably from loading them up.

Even out fluctuating sales

Evening out fluctuating sales links with the comments made above in relation to manufacturer–intermediary sales promotions. If seasonality is a problem, then sales promotion aimed at the consumer could help to even out the peaks and troughs a little.

Countering the competition

Again, the concept of countering or spoiling competitors' activities was introduced in the discussion of manufacturer–intermediary sales promotions. Diverting the consumer's attention through your own promotion can dampen the effects of the competitors' efforts, particularly if what they are doing is not particularly creative in its own right. Also, as discussed at p. 358, a well-chosen, regionally based sales promotion can seriously distort or introduce an element of doubt into the results of a competitor's test marketing.

Manufacturer–manufacturer (business promotion)

The relationship between manufacturers in the area of business promotion is less clear-cut than any of the other relationships studied so far. When we look at the negotiation of large contracts between organisations, we see that many of the activities that in other circumstances have been classed as sales promotions, such as discounts, added extras and time-limited offers, tend to be included in personal selling as part of the negotiation process leading to the final deal. Manufacturer–manufacturer sales promotions are also tightly linked to trade exhibition attendance, which will be considered in detail in Chapter 19.

Even the freebies, such as calendars, corporate neckwear, and golfing holidays do not class as sales promotions, as they do not link directly with specific products for sale. They are part of the wider area of relationship building between organisational buyers and sellers.

Sales promotion objectives: overview

The previous subsections have looked at sales promotion objectives within specific commercial relationships. They covered a wide variety of objectives, all of which fall into three broad categories as shown in Fig. 16.5: communication, incentive and invitation. These are discussed in turn below.

Communication

Sales promotion has a capacity to communicate with the buyer in ways that advertising would find hard to emulate. Advertising can tell people that a product is 'new, improved', or that it offers certain features and benefits, but this is conceptual information, which people may not fully understand or accept. Sales promotion can, for instance, put product samples into people's hands so that they can judge for themselves whether the claims are true. Learning by one's own experience is so much more powerful and convincing than taking the advertiser's word for it.

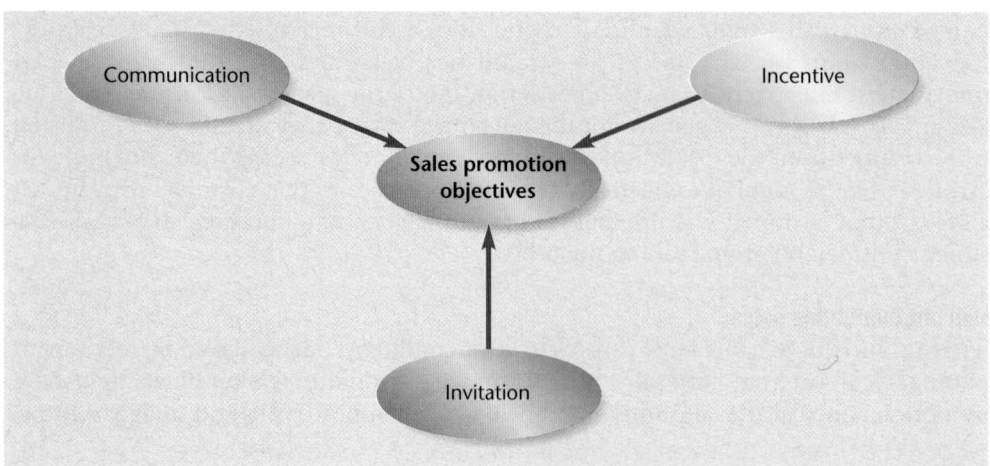

FIGURE 16.5

Sales promotion objectives: overview

As Chapter 14 made clear, grabbing attention is an important starting point for any communication. Thus an on-pack sales promotion, for instance, particularly one that prominently features the word 'FREE', draws the product to the shopper's attention and perhaps makes them receptive to the product's underlying message.

Incentive

The incentive is usually the central pillar of a sales promotion campaign. The potential buyer has to be given encouragement to behave in certain ways, through an agreed bargain between seller and buyer: if you do this, then I will *reward* you with that.

With consumers, the aim may be to encourage brand switching or to fortify wavering existing customers by providing additional rewards and increased value to those who try or repeat buy. If extra benefits are provided, the price conscious or premium conscious customer may be attracted. Similarly, the objective may be to reward those customers who are normally loyal to the brand or producer, but perhaps are the target of competitive action. Occasional rewards for the more frequent purchaser, or those who purchase in larger quantities, can help to maintain their loyalty and goodwill.

> **Example** The EU and the Meat and Livestock Commission (MLC) in the UK are both keen to promote beef sales, especially in the wake of the 'mad cow disease' crisis. Select beef, produced on farms with very high standards in terms of animal welfare, is specially matured and prepared to ensure the best taste and texture and has been the subject of intense promotional activity. The objective of the campaign was not so much to reassure consumers about the meat's safety and quality as to tempt them to try the roasts and steaks cut from Select beef. An on-pack promotion featured a prize draw to win a gourmet weekend of good food and fine wines at the Hotel du Vin in Winchester. The trade marketing director of the MLC said, 'Wine is a natural partner for Select beef and the Hotel du Vin is an aspirational prize which reinforces the quality aspect of the product and adds weight to the temptation strategy' (*The Grocer*, 1999b).

The intermediary also needs incentives as encouragement to stock the product in quantity and to sell it enthusiastically to the end buyer. Like consumers, intermediaries may be price or premium conscious, and incentives help them to swing towards particular brands or manufacturers.

Invitation

The promoted product is saying, 'Buy ME, and buy me NOW'. The promotion is, therefore, an invitation to consider this product, to think about your buying decision, and to do it quickly. The ephemeral nature of most sales promotions reinforces the urgency of taking up the invitation immediately. It prevents the buyer from putting off trial of the product, because the 'extra something' will not be around for long. For the consumer, in particular, the point of sale represents the crucial decision-making time. A product that is jumping up and down, shouting 'Hey, look at me!' through its sales promotion is offering the clearest possible invitation to do business.

Communication, incentive and invitation are all linked together. Elements of all three are present in the objectives of most sales promotions, but their mix and emphasis may change, depending on target audiences and circumstances. Peattie and Peattie (1995) highlighted how sales promotion is not only strong in the fmcg area but can be applied to services marketing, especially through the use of competitions and loyalty schemes.

Within the three main categories of sales promotion discussed earlier in this section (consumer, retail trade and organisation-orientated sales promotions), there are a number of possible techniques for achieving defined objectives. The techniques in each area are not mutually exclusive; ideas can be drawn from any one area and applied in another. The techniques selected will not only depend on the objectives and target audience of the sales promotion campaign, but also be influenced by a range of factors. These typically are market characteristics, competitive levels and activities, promotional objectives and the relevance of each technique to the product and its cost profile.

The following sections outline a number of sales promotion methods, classified by target audience. These methods will be defined and linked with objectives, and then specific examples of applications will be discussed. The list of methods described is not necessarily exhaustive. Sales promotion is an inherently creative area, subject to development as new ideas are introduced. Nevertheless, the following sections do cover the core methods, both established and emerging.

CONSUMER SALES PROMOTION METHODS (1): MONEY-BASED

Money-based sales promotions are a very popular group of techniques used by manufacturers or intermediaries. Sometimes they work on a 'cash-back' basis (*see* p. 655), but more often they are immediate price reductions, implemented in various ways, designed as a short-term measure either to gain competitive advantage or to defend against competitive actions. Such price reductions must be seen to be temporary or else the consumer will not view them as incentives. Furthermore, if money-based methods are used too often, consumers will begin to think of the promotional price as being the real price. They will then think of the product as being cheaper than it really is, and adjust their perceptions of positioning and quality accordingly (Gupta and Cooper, 1992).

Another drawback of this group of sales promotions is that because money-based sales promotions are so common among consumer goods, it is very difficult to raise much enthusiasm about them in the market. The main problem is the lack of creativity that usually accompanies these methods. It is also far too easy for a competitor to copy or match a money-based promotion, and thus any competitive advantage may be short lived.

It is also important to remember that money-based promotion can be an expensive way of putting money back in the pockets of people who would have bought the product anyway. If an organisation offers 10p off a product, then that costs the organisation 10p per unit sold in addition to the overhead costs of implementing the offer. In other words, in most cases money-based sales promotions cost the organisation their full cash value, unlike many of the merchandise offers, yet the long-term effect (especially if the technique is over-used) may be to cheapen the value of the product in the consumer's eyes (Jones, 1990). Effectively, this is a form of indirect price competition, and as discussed in Chapter 11, any price reduction needs to be balanced by volume increases in sales and against the product's reputation. Generally speaking, with money-based sales promotions, the short-term increase in sales needs to offset the extra marketing, distribution and handling costs associated with the promotion, as well as the lost revenue from those who would have purchased anyway (i.e. if you use a 20p coupon against a £1 product that you would have purchased anyway, then for the manufacturer that is 20p lost revenue rather than 80p extra revenue).

In their favour, however, money-based promotions are relatively easy to implement, they can be developed and mobilised quickly, and they are readily understood by the consumer. They appeal to many consumers' basic instincts about saving money, and the value of 10p off a price, or £1 cash back, is easy for the consumer to assess. If the objective of the exercise is to attract price-sensitive brand switchers, or to make a quick and easy response to a competitor's recent or imminent actions, then this group of methods has a part to play. The range of money-based methods is summarised in Fig. 16.6.

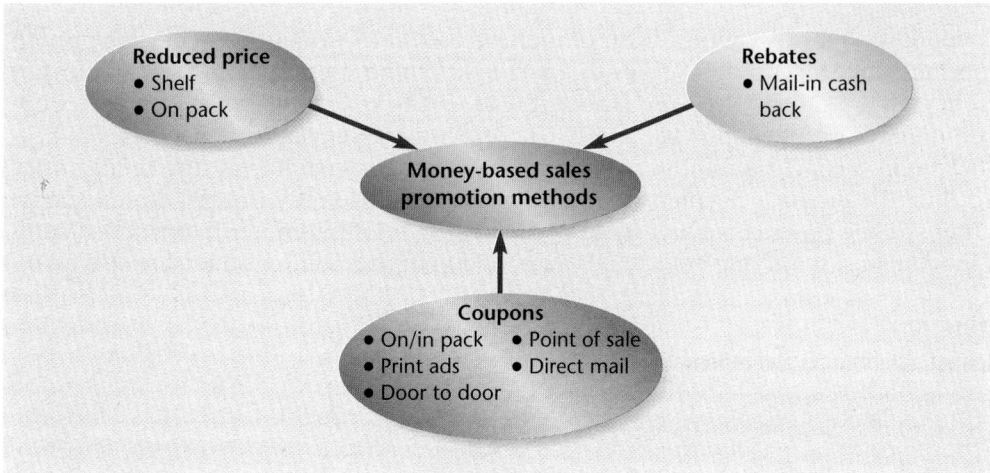

FIGURE 16.6

Money-based sales promotion methods

Reduced price offers (1): Shelf

Retailers frequently implement reduced price offers at the point of sale of the product. Although nothing appears on the product itself, the consumer is drawn to the surrounding notices or leaflets advertising the offer.

Such offers do have a sense of urgency about them, because consumers cannot be sure that the same offer will be available next time they visit that outlet, so they must take advantage of it immediately. They are very simple and quick to implement, costing only what it takes to notify the customers about the offer and the amount given back to the consumer through the reduced price. Local press advertising might be used to communicate a whole range of such offers, available this week only, to help increase store traffic.

Example The major supermarket chains are keen to give the impression that they offer better value for money than their competitors and short-term reduced price promotions are one way of reinforcing this stance. All the major chains have their generic ranges (*see* pp. 285 *et seq.*) at the bottom of the price range and occasionally these are used to make attention grabbing price statements. Thus at various times shoppers have found washing up liquid at 7p per bottle, tins of beans at 3p per can and other products selling at approximately 10 per cent of the price of their premium branded competitors. These are in addition to a day-to-day selection of less drastic short-term price cuts on other own-label and premium brands. The voluntary chains too need to develop their own price cutting strategies in order to compete with the major multiples. Spar, for instance, has its on-going X-tra Value initiative with a series of one-day and seasonal promotions. From time to time there are also two 'Hero' lines with up to 100 per cent extra free to reinforce the value offer (*The Grocer*, 1999a).

Reduced price offers (2): On pack

The second type of reduced price offer features on the product pack itself. The offer is likely to originate from the manufacturer, but sometimes takes the form of a joint promotion between the manufacturer and one particular retailer. Greater expenditure and a longer lead time is required here, as the packaging has to be printed specially for the offer. Again, it is a simple kind of sales promotion, with a sense of urgency, as is a shelf-based offer. Sometimes, reduced price is presented to the customer as a **trial price** when a product is being launched, as discussed at p. 424.

Coupons

Coupons are a more complex form of money-based sales promotion. They are printed vouchers that the consumer takes to a retail outlet and uses to claim a set amount of money off a product. Their use is widespread and flexible, and Table 16.1 shows the extent and value of coupon use in the UK. A manufacturer can issue coupons applicable to one specific product or a range of products, redeemable at any retail outlet stocking the product. Retailers issue coupons redeemable only in their stores against either specific products or any basket of shopping totalling more than a stated sum. Joint coupons, specifying both retail outlet and manufacturer's product, are also used.

TABLE 16.1

Coupon distribution and redemption, 1998

Coupon distribution (billions)	5.1
Coupon redemption (millions)	310.0
Total value of coupons redeemed (£mn)	155.0
Coupons' average face value (pence)	50.0

Source: NCH Marketing Services Ltd.

Coupons are distributed using a variety of means. They are printed within advertisements, on leaflets delivered from door to door, on inserts within magazines and newspapers, through direct mail, at the point of sale and on packs. Table 16.2 shows what proportion of redeemed coupons were distributed through each medium and the average redemption rates for those media. It is interesting to see that of all coupons redeemed, almost 32 per cent were distributed in- or on-pack. On average, nearly one in five in- or on-pack coupons is redeemed. This presumably is because the coupons will be reaching many people who already like and use the product and will therefore be motivated to buy it again, using the coupon. Effectively, this is a reward for current users. In contrast, coupons distributed through mass media perform less well. Fewer than 2 in 100 coupons distributed through newspapers or magazines is redeemed. There is much wastage with these media because many readers will not be even remotely interested in the coupon's product and those who are interested have to remember to keep the magazine, cut the coupon out, take it to the shops and use it.

TABLE 16.2

Coupon distribution and redemption by medium, 1998

	Share of redeemed distribution (%)	Average redemption rates by medium (%)
In/on pack	31.8	19.7
Direct mail	25.6	16.7
Door to door	6.3	6.4
Other	6.0	7.7
In-store	22.6	5.6
Magazines	6.2	1.4
Newspapers	1.5	1.3

Source: NCH Marketing Services Ltd.

The technology is also now available to allow retailers to issue coupons at the checkout, as an integral part of the bill issued to the customer. Checkouts that use laser scanning equipment can analyse the purchasing profile of the current customer, and issue coupons against the next purchase of something that has already been bought, or against a related product, or even against the retailer's own-brand equivalent of a purchased manufacturer's brand.

Manufacturers issue coupons with a number of reasons in mind. They act as a kind of *pull* strategy, creating an upturn in consumer demand for the product, thus encouraging retailers to stock and prominently display the brand. By telling them what is available and by reducing the financial risks of purchase, coupons can help the consumer get round to trying a product, making a subsequent purchase, or trading up, either to larger sizes or to products further up the range. The main problem for manufacturers is misredemption. Some supermarkets, overtly or covertly, will accept any coupon at the checkout, regardless of whether the consumer has actually bought the coupon's product or not. Preventing this from happening is difficult.

Retailer-specific coupons aim to bring consumers into those outlets and to keep them coming back. Like manufacturer coupons, retailer coupons can also have product-based aims. These may include encouraging consumers to try own-brand products, to repurchase or to trade up. As a part of the supermarkets' loyalty schemes, retailer-specific coupons are distributed through direct mail to scheme members. It seems, however, that although the coupons are personalised by having the shopper's name printed on them, a standard set of coupons is issued to all scheme members. This led to Tesco receiving many complaints in the early stages of its Clubcard scheme from vegetarians who had received chicken vouchers!

For whoever issues the coupon, redemption rates are crucial and can vary from just over 1 per cent with coupons in advertisements to nearly 20 per cent with coupons appearing on or in packs. Not surprisingly, it has been found that the higher the coupon value, the greater the interest and redemption. Geographical variations in redemption may also be found. Within the UK, for example, rates tend to be higher in the north than in the south (Wilmshurst, 1993). Overall, the UK is following the lead of the USA where couponing has become one of the main forms of sales promotion because of its flexibility and its direct application to the brand.

Coupons are subtly different from the other money-based promotions already discussed. With shelf and on-pack price cuts, the offer is open to all purchasers, and there is a very direct link between the price cut and the product that may cheapen the brand. A coupon does not look like a price cut, mainly because the price quoted at the shelf or on the product remains intact. The coupon is also a little more selective, in that only those who collect a coupon and remember to redeem it qualify for the discount.

However, to counter that, coupons are very common, and consumers are over-exposed to them. Unless a coupon carries a significant discount on the product, or applies to something intrinsically new and exciting, it is difficult as a consumer to be enthusiastic about them. Increasingly, coupons are being used by people who would have purchased anyway, so the rate of favourable brand switching or recruitment of new users might not be as high as the manufacturers hope. If coupons are being applied to mature products and being redeemed mainly by existing buyers, then all the manufacturer is doing is reducing profits (*see* p. 428).

Rebates

A **cash rebate** or 'cash-back' scheme involves a little more work and loyalty from the consumer. Tokens or labels have to be collected from packaging, involving a number of purchasing episodes, and then mailed in to qualify for either hard cash or a substantial coupon (retailer or product specific). This is similar to gift-based schemes, but involves cash rather than gifts or merchandise. In this case, the 'prize' is widely accepted and valued, and handling costs are considerably reduced.

However if the amounts of money are small, the customer may not develop much interest and may not bother to redeem the offer. It has even been argued (Fill, 1999) that rebates can sometimes be viewed negatively by the customer, who might see them as inconvenient and too much trouble to claim. To some consumers, rebates might even suggest low-quality products that need special help to sell them. For an established product that is well known in terms of image and quality, however, a rebate scheme

> **Example** When Persil did a rebate offer, it not only asked for labels, but also for till receipts showing the product purchases. If consumers responded to this on a large scale, there is potentially a lot of rich information to be had out of this. Most supermarkets now issue itemised till receipts, so the manufacturer can see what other products consumers buy with their Persil, where they purchased (always the same outlet or a variety?), how frequently they purchased, when they purchased (even down to the time of day), the total number of items purchased and the amount spent on each shopping trip. This may not constitute scientifically rigorous market research, but it certainly gives a quick-and-dirty feel for shopping habits, and might indicate directions for future promotional activities with a more specific focus.

might achieve a number of things. It is not seen as a direct price cut to all purchasers, and therefore is less likely to taint the image than other methods so far discussed. The customer is working for the rebate through repeat purchases and the effort of collecting and mailing the tokens, and thus the rebate will be valued when it comes. Depending on the time limit put on the sales promotion and the number of tokens required to qualify for the rebate, it may be possible to increase the number and frequency of purchases, even if it is only existing buyers who take advantage of the offer. Because it is a mail-in offer, the manufacturer gets the added benefit of customer names and addresses, offering future potential of direct marketing (more of this in Chapter 18).

Rebates do not only apply to manufacturer products. Look back to p. 646, where retailer cash rebate schemes aimed at increasing the value and frequency of purchasing were discussed.

CONSUMER SALES PROMOTION METHODS (2): PRODUCT-BASED

One of the risks of money-based promotions that was constantly reiterated in the previous section was the ease with which consumers could relate the promotion to price cutting, and thus the image of the product could, in their eyes, be cheapened. One way of overcoming that problem is to opt for a promotion centred on the product itself. The first method discussed in this section, extra product, demonstrates how this works. The second method, sampling, shows how a product-centred technique can achieve a much greater range of difficult objectives than any money-based activity. Figure 16.7 summarises **product-based sales promotion** methods.

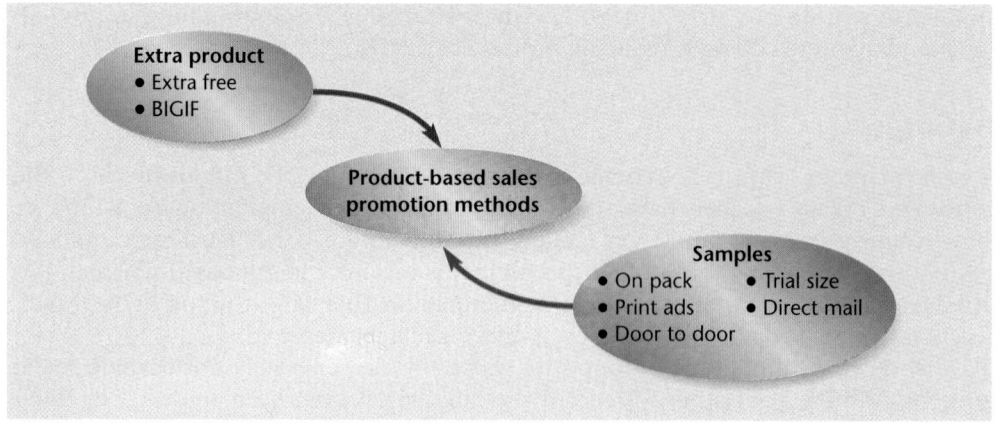

FIGURE 16.7

Product-based sales promotion methods

Extra product

There are two main alternatives for the 'extra product' technique.

Extra free

The 'extra free' technique involves offers such as an own-label can of tomatoes with '20 % extra free'. Just in case the customer has problems understanding what 20 per cent looks like, the can would have a prominent band around the top of the label in a different colour from the usual packaging giving a rough idea of which part of the contents is free. Similarly, a pack of own-label kitchen roll was offering three rolls for the price of two and had a large red flash down the side of the pack proclaiming 'ONE ROLL EXTRA FREE'.

Obviously, such offers require changes in the packaging graphics to communicate the offer, and may even involve major changes in the physical size of the package to accommodate the extra product. If own-label tomatoes are normally sold in 400 gram cans, then producing a 480 gram can will require planned production changes.

A money-based promotion might put 20p back in the consumer's hand; a product-based promotion might give them 20p's worth of extra product free. To the manufacturer, either option rewards the buyer with 20p, but the buyer's perceptions of the two are very different. 20p in the hand is 'giving something back', whereas extra product free is clearly 'giving something in addition' and in the consumer's mind, might be valued at a good deal more than 20p. These product-based promotions, therefore, break the link between promotion and price. This method may be especially attractive as a response to a competitor's price attack, as it can shape the value image of a product without a direct price war.

BIGIF or BOGOFF

In contrast to offering extra free product within a single package, the **BIGIF** (Buy 1 Get 1 Free) or the BOGOFF (Buy One Get One For Free) offers centre on bigger rewards, and are aimed primarily at loading up the customer. Effectively, the offer is saying '100% EXTRA FREE'. As discussed at p. 649, manufacturers may have a particular interest in making sure that the consumer has a kitchen full of their brands, as a means of making them less sensitive to the competition and getting them used to having that product around.

Retailers are increasingly using a variation on this method, based around bulk purchasing, making the offer, 'Buy two and get a third one free' (B2G3F? – it doesn't quite have the same ring as BOGOFF, does it?).

Example Procter and Gamble (http://www.pg.com) launched Ariel Futur Alpine by offering a 1 litre refill free with every 1.5 litre bottle bought. The two packs were presented together in a cardboard box with the word FREE prominently displayed in red on a yellow background. The promotional boxes were also placed in an end of aisle 'golden zone' in Tesco, for example, and extra loyalty card points offered with them. All of this made the new Alpine variant attractive to the consumer, not only to generate awareness and trial, but also to load up customers to protect them from the competition. Supermarkets also regularly offer discounts for bulk purchases with varying conditions, anything from 'buy one get one free' to 'buy six get a seventh free'. Sometimes bulk purchases are encouraged by packaging products together, as in the Ariel example. Tesco offered four cans of its own-label Italian chopped tomatoes banded together with a cardboard sleeve with £1.19 printed prominently on it. This represents a saving on four separate cans and is sometimes made to seem even better value by being reduced on the shelf to £1.09, thus offering a promotion within a promotion.

These offers may need shorter lead times than the 20 per cent extra free type, because they do not involve significant changes to the packaging. Two ordinary packs can be banded together away from the main production line if necessary. In the case of the

MARKETING IN ACTION   Sampling at home and on the move

McVitie's spent £5mn to boost its Go Ahead! brand range and launch two new products within it. £1mn of that was spent on a sampling and couponing campaign to encourage trial and give an incentive to buy. A door to door leaflet campaign reinforces the promotions and brings the brand to consumers' attention in their own homes. Door-to-door sampling like this can be very well targeted thanks to GIS (*see* pp. 185 *et seq.*). These can help the marketer to identify the areas that match the target market profile or some other criterion, for example areas in which the competition has a strong presence. Most marketers will consider an area suitable for a door drop if it has 50 per cent or more households within the target group. Some GIS can profile areas of 450 households (compared with postcode areas of 2500 households), thus offering precise targeting.

Even door to door sampling has to work hard to grab attention and to ensure safe delivery of the sample, however. When Philips wanted to tell consumers about its Softone light bulbs, it dropped a bag through the door with a brochure about the product and a money-off voucher. If the consumer was interested, they left the bag outside the door the next day after ticking a box to say which colour bulb they wanted and the sample was left in the bag for them. This allowed the company to deliver a fragile object safely and allowed consumers to opt out of the

sampling exercise if they wanted to, thus making it more cost effective and better targeted.

Advertising support can enhance the impact of door to door samples. Kellogg, for example, launched its new Honey Rice Krispies with a television advertising campaign and then dropped small 'variety pack' samples through doors. The packaging on the sample was a miniature but otherwise identical version of the full-sized pack so that consumers could recognise it in the stores. The advertising meant that consumers were likely to have heard of the product and would be ready to give it a try. The sample gave them a risk-free and effortless opportunity to sample, thus helping them to make a positive decision to buy the full pack on the next shopping trip.

Home is not the only place where marketers can press samples on to consumers. Railway station concourses can also be good places to carry out a sampling exercise. Concourse Initiatives, a company that markets and manages concourse space, claims that a mainline London station has around 300 000 people passing through every day and that commuters using stations tend to be affluent ABC1s aged under 45, in broad terms an attractive target group for many manufacturers. For one client, a walk-in freezer was built on a concourse and 25 000 ice-cream samples per day handed out. Over three years, Hägen Dazs handed out over 1mn samples in this way. Similarly, samples of draught Guinness have been handed out on a concourse, with a follow-up leaflet giving the consumer money off a Guinness four pack as well as the opportunity to phone in for a free Guinness glass. Interestingly, alcohol sampling is allowed in small measures on concourses but the drink cannot be handed out in bottles or in large quantities. It cannot be given to station staff or consumers aged under 18 and a security guard must be present at all times.

For many manufacturers, the numbers of consumers that concourses deliver is attractive, but there are potential problems. First, size isn't everything. It might be a large audience, but it is a broad one and it is difficult to identify and select a more specific sub-group out of it. Second, consumers on concourses, especially commuters, are often rushing to be somewhere else and, unless they have time to kill waiting for a train, are not likely to be receptive to messages, especially if they are stressed. Nevertheless, leaflets can be handed out quickly for consumers to look at later (on the train?) and incorporating competitions on them is a good way of generating responses and thus leads.

A bright idea for distributing light bulb samples

Source: Circular Distributors Ltd.

Sources: Fletcher (1999); Gray (1999); *The Grocer* (1999j); Miler (1999); http://www. mcvities.com; http://www.guinness.ie.

retailers' B2G3F offers, no banding is needed at all. The offer is made through notices at the shelf, and the computerised checkout is programmed to make the discount automatically when the required number of items have been scanned through.

Samples

Where the main objective is to persuade people to try a product, sampling is often used. People can experience the product for themselves at little or no financial risk and decide on their own evidence whether to adopt the product and buy the full sized pack or not. **Samples** are thus popular and effective. Seventy per cent of households claim to use the free samples that come through the letterbox. The added bonus, particularly with those samples distributed away from the point of sale, is that the sample's packaging can teach the consumer about the product's benefits, and through graphics that relate directly to the full sized pack, aid brand recognition in the store.

The costs of sampling can be very high. The packaging has to be specially designed and produced, and then there are the costs of distribution. The aim is the future generation of sales, and if it takes a sample to convert a 'possibly would buy' into a 'definitely will buy', then it is a justifiable expense.

In the area of traditional sampling, a one-use or one-portion sample is usually sufficient, and there are a number of ways in which it can be distributed. These are discussed below.

Example In 1999, Elida Fabergé launched an extension of its Dove toiletries brand. The new deodorant carries the same branding and 'look' as the other products in the range and like the others contains 25 per cent moisturising cream. The launch was supported by a £10.4mn advertising campaign and 5mn samples were sent out to consumers (*Marketing Week*, 1999a). The samples helped to reinforce the advertising message among the target market and brought the new product directly to their attention, as well as encouraging early trial. A deodorant is not necessarily a frequent purchase, yet the company would not want consumers to wait too long before trying the product. If it is left until the next purchasing occasion, the advertising campaign could have died down by then, the consumer might have forgotten to look for this new product and the routine purchase of the old brand will be made as usual. If the consumer has tried the sample, however, at the point of sale they will remember how nice it was and recognise the packaging and there is a strong chance that the routine purchasing habit can be broken.

ampling was used to elp introduce the atest members of the ove family.

ource: Elida Fabergé Ltd.

On-pack

If a manufacturer is launching a new product in a range, then samples could be given away with existing products. The objective is to inform existing customers of the new product and to allow them to try it. The problem is that this type of promotion is limited to those who buy the existing product. If new customers are required, then usually other mechanisms must be used.

> **Example** William Grant managed to overcome the problem of on-pack sample distribution in launching its new whisky brand Black Barrel. In a pan-European 'Taste the Difference' promotion, anyone who ordered a Scotch or Irish whisky or bourbon was also given a free glass of Black Barrel. Effectively, the new brand was being given away with its competitors' products!

Trial sizes

To recoup some of the costs of producing the samples, they can be sold in retail outlets at a minimal price. Sold as products in their own right, they may attract a wider audience than simply those who already purchase the same manufacturer's existing brands. The small cost is insignificant to the consumer, who still sees it as a relatively risk-free way of trying something different. As with on-pack distributions, it is a good mechanism for introducing new products, or new colours or flavours within an existing product line.

> **Example** New types or variants of detergent are often introduced with a trial size offer priced, for example, between 20p and 50p. When the manufacturers introduced the balls into which the washing powder or liquid had to be poured, the trial-size packs gave consumers a change to see what it was all about and to obtain a ball at low cost. Having used it once with the detergent in the trial pack, it was hoped that consumers would be impressed with the new system and be eager for a repeat purchase of a full sized pack. The trial size also makes it easy and low risk for the consumer to acquire a detergent ball, so that they are not put off from buying a full sized pack just because it needs one.

Print media

Because print media allow the targeting of fairly narrowly profiled audiences, this can be an efficient way of distributing samples to potential buyers. Cosmetics and toiletries, for example, are often sampled through women's magazines. Some samples associated with print media have become very significant in their own right. Computer magazines give away demonstration disks featuring various types of software.

> **Example** In the highly competitive hobby and lifestyle magazine sector, on-magazine gifts are often used to attract and retain readers. *B* magazine in July 1999 carried a free book, *Are you experienced?* by William Sutcliffe, while women's magazines carry free cosmetics samples and gardening magazines packets of seeds from time to time. All of these promotional gifts are relevant to the content of the publication and the target readership.
>
> Some magazines, however, carry free gifts that have become part of their normal offering. *Classic CD*, a monthly magazine specialising in classical music, gives away a full-length (around 70 minutes) CD with every issue, every month, featuring tracks from recent releases. Free CDs regularly feature material from EMI, Phillips, RCA, Deutsche Grammophon, Sony and Hyperion, among others. For the record companies, this is an unbeatable way of whetting the appetite of potential buyers, and for consumers, the CD makes excellent listening, and acts as an audible shop window, reassuring them that they will like particular recordings. This is sampling at a very sophisticated level.

Direct mail

Samples that are small, light and non-perishable can be distributed by direct mail, either to people already on a mailing list, or to those who respond to an offer made in an advertisement.

> **Example** GPs give a book called *Emma's Diary* to pregnant women. The book is produced by the Royal College of General Practitioners but contains advertising from manufacturers and retailers of mother and baby products. Many of these advertisers include forms to fill in and send off to join 'baby clubs' or to receive free samples of products. Retailer Superdrug, for example, asks women to fill in a small questionnaire and then take it to their local store to pick up a 'Mother pack'. This not only builds a database, but also gets women into the stores to spend. Cow and Gate asks women either to mail in a form (again, with a few questions on it) or to telephone to register for 'In Touch' programme. The company then sends regular sample packs, information and advice.
>
> Mailing samples to existing customers means that the samples get into the hands of people who are likely to appreciate them and be converted to the new product. Using direct response advertising allows the organisation to know who has received the samples, and to start building a relationship with them. The companies hope that the women will remain loyal to them throughout the child's infancy and even after subsequent pregnancies.

Door to door

Door to door distribution is a popular but expensive way of distributing samples. Delivering the sample to the house means that you are not dependent on particular existing purchasing patterns (in terms of either store or brand preference), you are not depending on the consumer to notice the sample in-store, nor are you asking them to pay towards the sample. Effectively, you are putting the sample directly into their hands in an environment where it is likely to be remembered and used. Some targeting is possible, using geodemographic segmentation to prioritise distribution areas (*see* pp. 185 *et seq.*), but generally this is mass sample distribution.

Samples might be distributed through the letterbox, or more expensively through a personal call. Personal calls make sure that samples only go to those households that will use them and can also be used for more extensive market research data collection. They also ensure that the sample is put into the hands of a responsible adult rather than being eaten on the doormat by the dog or abducted by the children!

> **Example** When Philips did its door to door sampling exercise with the Softone light bulb (*see* p. 658), a sample bulb was left for the customer on request. The free bulb only had a life span of 10 hours, which was clearly marked on the packaging (Fletcher, 1999). This was long enough to make the consumer think that they were getting good value from the sample and to let them get used to the effect of the Softone bulb, but not so long that they forgot where the bulb came from or what brand it was. Philips would also have been hoping that the consumer would already have used the accompanying money-off voucher and have a replacement bulb handy by the time the sample bulb blew, or that they would still have the voucher and use it on the next shopping trip after the sample was finished with.

CONSUMER SALES PROMOTION METHODS (3):

GIFT, PRIZE OR MERCHANDISE BASED

A wide range of activities depend on the offer of prizes, low-cost goods or free gifts to stimulate the consumer's buying behaviour. Holidays, brand-related cookery books, mugs or clothing featuring product logos and small plastic novelty toys are among the vast range of incentives used to complement the main product sale.

There are many ways in which these incentives can be offered, each with a different impact and its own objectives, as summarised in Fig. 16.8.

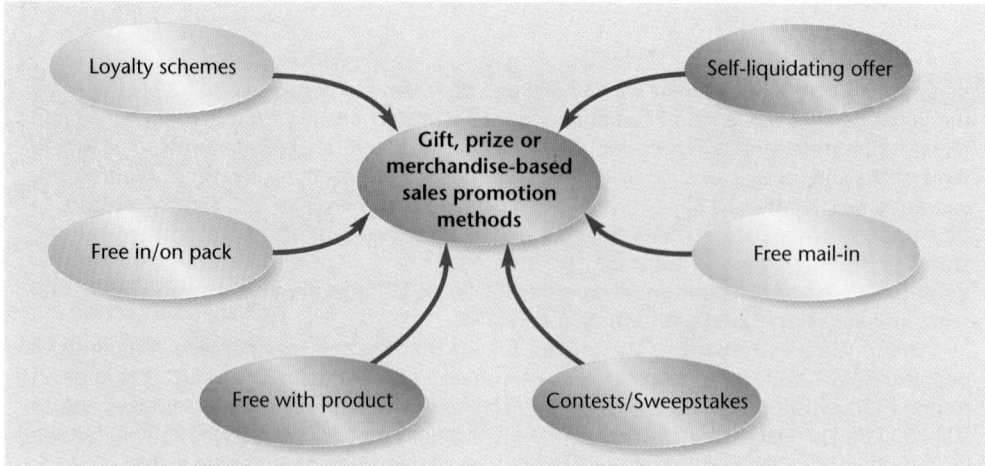

FIGURE 16.8

Gift, prize or mechandise-based sales promotion methods

Example Thomas the Tank Engine has caught the imagination of many young children worldwide. It has also been used by food manufacturers to create permanent consumer loyalty schemes. Seven companies, including MD Foods, Heinz and Pillsbury, joined together to feature on-pack tokens that could be traded in either for free off Thomas the Tank Engine goods or for access to a special catalogue that offered up to 50 per cent off Thomas merchandise. By linking in with around 2000 Thomas the Tank Engine product lines, grossing over £200mn worldwide, the manufacturers hope to improve loyalty by locking parents, pressurised by their children, into their brands in order to 'save' for items from the catalogue (*The Grocer*, 1999m).

Self–liquidating offers

Self-liquidating offers invite the consumer to pay a small amount of money, and usually to submit specified proofs of purchase, in return for goods that are not necessarily directly related to the main product purchase. The money paid is usually just enough to cover the cost price of the goods and a contribution to postage and handling, and thus these promotions become self-financing if the expected number of customers takes them up.

Often, such a promotion is used to reinforce the brand name and identity of the products featuring the scheme.

Example Butcher's dog food followed up its 'Fit as a Butcher's Dog' advertising campaign with a self-liquidating offer. A set of five collectible models, the 'Mischievous Puppy' collection, was designed by Craggley Boggs and made available through the Butcher's Dinner range of dog foods. Three tokens plus £2.60 were required to get one model or five tokens plus £9.99 were required to get the entire set (*The Grocer*, 1999g). The tokens give at least short-term brand loyalty while the money covers the basic costs of the offer to the company. The five tokens plus £9.99 option makes it easier and cheaper for consumers to complete the set within the time limit of the promotion, otherwise the set costs £13 and many tins of dog food. This option is also better for the company as it would involve fewer applications (potentially one per customer rather than five per customer) and be cheaper to administer.

The problem with most self-liquidating promotions is that response levels tend to be low, as consumers have to be prepared to spend money and make an effort to benefit from the offer. Furthermore, the premium itself has to be very interesting and different to get a good response. Plain mugs can easily be purchased cheaply from discount stores, but brand-specific ones that can only be sourced through the promotion have something more attractive about them. They are 'exclusive', and they are only available for a limited time, hence the incentive value.

Free mail-in

In the case of a free mail-in, the consumer can claim a gift, free of charge, in return for proofs of purchase and perhaps the actual cost of postage (but not handling charges or the cost of the gift itself).

> **Example** Kitchen Devils, a kitchen knives brand, offered a free chopping board in return for the barcode from one of its products, a till receipt showing its purchase, and 52p in stamps to contribute to postage. As kitchen knives are by no means frequently purchased, inexpensive fmcg goods, asking for only the one proof of purchase in return for a substantial premium is reasonable. In contrast, fmcg brands such as breakfast cereals are more demanding.

Free mail-ins have increased in popularity in recent years. The free goods attract the consumer and encourage a higher response rate, and the responses potentially provide the organisation with direct marketing opportunities. The main aim, however, in sales promotion terms is to encourage the consumer to make enough additional purchases to collect the necessary proofs of purchase within a carefully assessed time period. The frustration of not quite managing to collect enough to meet an offer deadline, or of feeling coerced into buying unreasonably large quantities of goods in a short space of time, might turn consumers against a brand.

> **Example** A link-up between Coca-Cola and Disney (http://www.disney.go.com) showed good synergy between the partners in the promotion, the premium offered and the target market. A promotion on Coke multipacks gave consumers the opportunity to collect tokens and buy specially commissioned Disney merchandise. Consumers within a 15-mile radius of a Disney store will have to go there to collect their merchandise, otherwise it will be sent by mail. Both companies benefit, as both are targeting young people and families. Coke benefits from the association with the Disney collectibles, a potent brand name in its own right which has a strong appeal to families. Disney benefits from getting consumers into its stores and, again, from the association with a fellow global brand icon. Of course, both companies hope to benefit from increased sales too (Campbell, 1999a).

Of course, the promotion is only free to the consumer. The promoter has to consider carefully the merchandise costs, postage, packing, processing and even VAT. All of this has to be put into the context of the likely response rate, so that the total cost of the promotion can be forecast and an appropriate quantity of merchandise can be ordered and available when the promotion begins.

> **Example** The Hoover free flights deal (two tickets to the US free if you purchase a Hoover product) is a good example of what can happen when the forecasting goes wrong, and there is insufficient 'merchandise' for claimants. This promotion resulted in many dissatisfied customers, litigation, and a great deal of extra expense to Hoover, not to mention damaging PR.

663

Free inside or on pack

Offering free gifts contained inside or banded on to the outside of the pack can make a big impact at the point of sale because the reward is instant, and the purchaser does not have to make any special effort to claim it. One-off gifts are designed to bring the consumer's attention to a product and to encourage them to try it. The offer might shake them out of a routine response purchase and make them think about trying a different brand.

In-pack promotions

In-pack promotions are often used in child-orientated breakfast cereals and, to stimulate repeat purchase, the gifts often form part of a related series.

The costs of in-pack gifts can be high, especially when offered with food products. There may be limitations on size, materials, toxicity, protection and smell in order to conform to hygiene standards. These costs, as well as the direct promotion costs, must be considered.

Example Pepsi is not the only company to have developed promotional activity based on the Star Wars film (*see* p. 642). Kellogg also ran an in-pack promotion featuring statuettes of 10 characters from the film free inside packs of Frosties. The statuettes formed a series to encourage the customer to keep buying in order to get the whole set. As an added incentive, each statuette had a scroll inside it telling the character's history. Cereals targeted at an older audience tend to feature more mail-in offers appropriate to the brand and the target market, such as Kellogg's Healthwise Bran Flakes' offer of a healthy diet 'Breakfast Book' for £3.29 plus two tokens. Similarly, Weetabix's Fruitibix offered a mini folding umbrella for £4.99 and three tokens.

On-pack promotions

Gifts attached to the outside of the pack are less constrained and, again, provide an immediate reward for purchase. They may even be more attractive than in-pack gifts, as the purchaser can actually see and evaluate the gift in advance.

Example PG Tips offered a free tea towel with boxes of tea bags. The consumer's attention was attracted at the point of sale because there was clearly something odd and different about the packs; the tea towel was visible and worth investigating further. Oxo occasionally runs a variant of this technique. Rather than offering a separate free gift, it uses the packaging itself as an incentive. Its stock cubes have been sold (with no increase in price) in attractive tins, plastic money boxes and pencil cases instead of the usual cardboard box. All of these items are kept for a long time and are heavily branded, thus providing the constant reminder. Obviously the costs of such sales promotions are high in terms of product and handling, but the rewards are often very recognisable and tempting to the consumer at the point of sale.

Free with product

'Free with product' is similar to an on-pack offer, except that the gift is not attached to the product but has to be claimed at the checkout. The forerunner of current practice was the plastic daffodil free with soap powder in the 1950s. There are often logistical and practical difficulties for high volume supermarkets in using this method, so its use has declined somewhat. Laser scanning checkouts, however, do allow supermarkets to run their own versions of this kind of offer. The consumer, for example, might be invited at the point of sale to buy a jar of coffee and claim a free packet of biscuits. The computerised checkout can tell whether the conditions of the promotion have been met and automatically deducts the price of the biscuits from the final total.

Customer loyalty schemes

Given the increasingly high cost of creating new customers, organisations have turned their attention to ways of retaining the loyalty of current customers. Major international airlines have their frequent flyer schemes, many different retail and service organisations give away air miles with purchases, and petrol stations and supermarkets issue swipe cards through which customers can accumulate points as mentioned earlier. All of these schemes are designed to encourage repeat buying, especially where switching is easy and generic brand loyalty is low. Brian Woolf, an American database marketing expert, proposes eleven rules for getting the best out of a loyalty scheme. These are outlined in Table 16.3.

TABLE 16.3

The 11 Ps of loyalty marketing

1	Pricing	Be customer specific – reward the best
2	Purchases	Make product-specific offers
3	Point flexibility	Occasionally offer double points, for example
4	Partners	Develop alliances with other retailers
5	Prizes	Weekly prize draw for cardholders, for example
6	Pro-bono	Allow customers to convert points into charity donations
7	Personalisation	Direct mail, specifically targeted at customer
8	Privileges	Invite cardholders to special events, for example
9	Participation	Invite best customers to take part in new variations of scheme
10	Pronto	Generate offers at the point of sale
11	Proactive	Use information to predict/pre-empt customer behaviour

Source: Woolf, as quoted by Mitchell (1995).

Price promotions can be dangerous in that they encourage consumers to become price sensitive, and are easily copied by competitors. Tokens, points and stamps that can be traded in for other goods are all ways of adding value to a product, while avoiding costly price competition. They are thus known as **alternative currencies**.

Trading stamps

Trading stamps are a long-established example of alternative currency. The number of stamps awarded at the point of sale is directly proportional to the value of purchases made. The stamps can be redeemed at the customer's convenience for gifts. Supermarkets and petrol stations widely participated in these schemes until the 1970s. The problem with stamps was that they tended to drive prices upwards at a time when straight price discounting was a more attractive alternative for the consumer.

Points and tokens

In place of trading stamps, new variants have emerged.

Example Walkers developed a promotion offering £200mn of prizes linked with the *Star Wars* film, in which 100mn scratch cards were placed in some crisp packets giving two lucky winners the chance to win £1mn each. There was also £500 000 worth of £5 cash prizes and 100mn Jar Jar Sticky Tongue toys. The promotion was not just communicated on packs and at the point of sale. It was also linked with a £2mn television advertising campaign and £1mn on print advertising in children's and the teenage press (*The Grocer*, 1999l).

One of the problems with loyalty schemes, however, is the sheer number of them. When every airline has a frequent flyer scheme and when every supermarket has a loyalty club, then the competitive edge is lost. Furthermore, there is evidence that the loyalty generated by such schemes is questionable, as will be seen in Case Study 16.2. Nevertheless, loyalty schemes are fast becoming an established part of the marketing scene. The next logical progression is to think about pan-European schemes. There are both cultural and legislative difficulties with this, however. Those in the industry feel that pan-European schemes can at present be built around a broad strategy, but need to incorporate sufficient tailored flexibility to allow for different countries' cultures and legislation covering promotional activities.

Contests and sweepstakes

Gifts given free to all purchasers of a product necessarily are limited to relatively cheap and cheerful items. As Hoover found out, giving away expensive freebies to all purchasers is uneconomic. **Contests and sweepstakes**, therefore, allow organisations to offer very attractive and valuable incentives, such as cars, holidays and large amounts of cash, to very small numbers of purchasers who happen to be lucky enough to win. Such promotions might be seen as rather boring by consumers, unless there is something really special about them.

> **Example** A legal ruling in 1999 cast doubt on whether prize draws and instant-win promotions linked with brands are actually legal. A law was already established requiring draw promoters to state clearly that no purchase is necessary in order to enter, otherwise the draw becomes an illegal lottery. A High Court judgment, however, deemed one such draw illegal because it was too difficult for consumers to participate without making a purchase. In this specific case, a retailer had supplied scratchcards to customers, but the majority of those cards were tied to a purchase (Darby, 1999c). A solicitor suggested that in the light of the ruling, promoters should use advertising and point-of-sale communication to encourage consumers to take the 'free entry' route and that they should ensure that at least 15 per cent of entrants to such a draw come from that route (*Marketing Week*, 1999c). If this ruling is upheld, it could damage a £1bn per year segment of the sales promotion industry.
>
> Daewoo unlikely to face such problems with its prize draw promotion to celebrate the sale of its 100 000th car in the UK. One hundred lucky winners will win the chance to buy a brand new Matiz for £1000. Although existing Daewoo owners have received a mailshot inviting them to enter, press advertising throughout July invited everyone else to participate too (*Marketing*, 1999a). Although non-Daewoo car owners will have to visit a Daewoo outlet in order to pick up an entry form, this is hardly unreasonable and there is a real opportunity for 'free entry'.

Contests

Contests have to involve a demonstration of knowledge, or of analytical or creative skills to produce a winner. Setting a number of multiple choice questions, or requiring the competitor to uncover three matching symbols on a scratch card, or asking them to create a slogan, are all legitimate contest activities.

> **Example** Tesco offered its 9mn Clubcard members the chance to win 2000 holidays in the year 2000 if they were successful in a prize draw. In conjunction with travel agent Going Places, Tesco sent each Clubcard holder a number on a mailed 'passport' and if it matched the one printed on their till receipt, they would win one of the holidays (*The Grocer*, 1999f).

Sweepstakes

Sweepstakes do not involve skill, but offer every entrant an equal chance of winning through the luck of the draw. Additionally, they must ensure that entry is open to anyone, regardless of whether they have purchased a product or not. Thus *Reader's Digest* prize draws have to be equally open to those not taking up the organisation's kind offer of a subscription.

Such activities are popular with both consumers and organisations. The consumer gets the chance to win something really worthwhile, and the organisation can hope to generate many extra sales for a fixed outlay. With price or gift-based promotions, the more you sell, the more successful the promotion, the more it costs you because you have to pay out on every sale. With competitions and sweepstakes, the more successful the activity, the more entries it attracts, yet the prizes remain fixed. The only losers with a popular contest or sweepstake are the consumers, whose chances of winning become slimmer! However, at some stage consumers may become bored with such activities, especially if they do not think they have any reasonable chance of winning. At that point, a more immediate but less valuable incentive might be more appropriate.

All contests and sweepstakes are strictly controlled in the UK under the Lotteries and Amusements Act 1976, and a code of sales promotion practice guides the presentation and administration of such schemes. It is essential for an organisation to seek professional legal and expert advice to avoid any allegation of illegal or questionable practice that could backfire on the promoter. Despite the problems and the need for caution, contests and sweepstakes can, however, provide a lift to flagging product interest and generate additional awareness. Table 16.4 summarises some of the issues on which decisions need to be made before such promotions can be implemented.

TABLE 16.4
Contests and sweepstakes: issues for decision

- Communicating the promotion – on/in pack? leaflet? print media? etc.
- Prize structure and description
- Prize limits
- Entry conditions
- Proof of purchase requirements
- Eligibility and geographic restrictions
- Supplementary rule availability
- Entry method – mail? phone?
- Closing date
- Selection criteria for winner
- Tie breaker
- Notification of results

CONSUMER SALES PROMOTION METHODS (4): STORE BASED

This section looks more generally at what can be done within a retail outlet to stimulate consumer interest in products, leading perhaps to trial or purchase.

Point-of-sale displays

Sales promotion at the point of sale (**POS**) is critical in situations where the customer enters the store undecided or is prepared to switch brands fairly readily. Many different POS materials and methods can be used. These include posters, displays, dispensers, dump bins and other containers to display product. New technology has further changed POS promotion with flashing signs, videos, message screens and other such attention-seeking display material. Interactive POS systems can help customers to select the most appropriate offering for their needs, or can direct them to other promotional offers.

Thomas Cook, the travel agent, for example, uses a system that helps customers to select holidays, while Daewoo uses interactive screens to help consumers 'design' the car they want.

The main objectives of POS promotion are to inform the customer and to persuade them to try or retry the product. In some areas it has been suggested that up to 55 per cent of purchasing decisions are made in-store. This means that the manufacturer has to ensure that the product 'talks from the shelf' to attract attention.

However, as seen in Chapter 13, retailers are increasingly dominating the shelves in their own stores. It is they who decide on the co-ordinated image for the store and strictly control the use of manufacturer-inspired POS material. They want impact, but do not want their stores to look like a loose collection of POS jumble, nor do they want too many flimsy tacky-looking cardboard displays.

MARKETING AND IT

Improving the effectiveness of point of sale displays

Strange as it may seem, more than 70% of all purchase decisions are made at the point of sale. An yet the marketing effort, and marketing research, that goes into this much neglected area is puny. While many of the other elements of the marketing mix have entered the Digital Age, point of purchase languishes in the Dark Ages. Very little effort goes into a serious analysis of its effectiveness. Even if some technology has been incorporated into the point of sale – flashing lights, message boards and videos have all been used to some degree or other – do any of these gimmicks actually help sell more product? Can they be used to predict sales and prevent overstocking or stock shortages? Can displays be improved to increase their effectiveness? Now, there's help at hand to answer exactly these questions. One of the largest market researchers, Research International, has developed a technique for assessing the impact of display stands before they hit the retail floor. Research International had already developed a well-established modelling system, the MicroTest, for pre-testing and analysis in other marketing areas. It has been around for some ten years and has been used extensively by such major manufacturers as Unilever, Kraft and Lyons-Tetley. The MicroTest, according to Maureen Johnson, managing director of RI's retail division, 'was developed to help clients go beyond standard diagnostic information collected in concept or product testing, and actually provides formal sales volume estimates based on the same type of interview. It was intended to provide accurate information as quickly and cost effectively as possible at any stage of the development cycle of a product in order to help clients avoid expensive launches of poorly-manufactured or positioned products.' RI claims a margin of error of plus or minus 20% and says that out of the 150 or so validations it has run (out of a total of 1750 MicroTests), 80% have fallen within this margin. While that may sound like a wide margin, it's an awful lot better than an uninformal guess.

Here's how it works: MicroTest involves a series of intensive interviews with both consumers and shop floor staff. Typically, there are ten to fifteen accompanied shopping interviews per category with each consumer. Each interview lasts about two hours and encompasses visits to three to five different retail outlets. The interviews are designed to allow modelling and analysis of sales volume estimates. The responses are processed and the model is used to fine-tune the stands before they go into action. Point of purchase suppliers seem well-disposed towards this more measurable research technique. Richard Melvern, manager of Kodak's dynamic imaging division, a leading display stand supplier, is enthusiastic. 'This sounds fascinating,' says Melvern, 'and a very valid attempt to be more scientific about point of sale displays. This kind of sales modelling tool will help a lot.'

Source: O'Connor & Galvin (1999).

Demonstrations

In-store demonstrations are a very powerful means of gaining interest and trial. Food product cooking demonstrations and tasters are used by retailer and manufacturer alike, especially if the product is a little unusual and would benefit from exposure (i.e. new cheeses, meats, drinks etc.). Other demonstrations include cosmetic preparation and application, electrical appliances, especially if they are new and unusual, and cars. These demonstrations may take place within the retail environment, but the growth of shopping centre display areas provides a more flexible means for direct selling via a demonstration.

Organisations sometimes use **field marketing agencies** to handle in-store demonstrations and other promotional activities. The agency may well hand out samples and demonstrate products, but they also make sure that products are properly displayed and check where they are positioned on the shelf, particularly in relation to the competition.

> **Example** Linking back to sampling, Birds Eye Wall's believe that providing potential customers with cooked samples of product at the point of sale is extremely effective for stimulating sales. Using a mobile kitchen, 10 000 cooked samples a day can be produced in a supermarket car park.

METHODS OF PROMOTION TO THE RETAIL TRADE

Manufacturers of consumer goods are dependent on the retail trade to sell their product for them. Just as consumers sometimes need that extra incentive to try a product or to become committed to it, retailers too need encouragement to push a particular product into the distribution system and to facilitate its movement to the customer. Of course, many of the consumer-orientated activities considered in previous sections help that process through pull strategies.

> **Example** When Solstis, part of the Lucozade brand family, was launched in the summer of 1999, trade advertising was undertaken to convince grocers that they should stock the product. The advertising highlighted the planned £2mn radio and lifestyle press advertising campaign for the brand, along with a national sampling campaign planned for 250 000 target consumers. The other benefits offered to retailers were associated with profit opportunities and the link with the core Lucozade range (http://www.sb.com).

Some trade promotions are tightly linked with consumer promotions to create a synergy between push and pull strategies.

The main push promotions are variations on price promotions and direct assistance with selling to the final customer. These will now be looked at in turn.

Allowances and discounts

Allowances and discounts aim to maintain or increase the volume of stock moving through the channel of distribution. The first priority is to get the stock into the retailer, and then to influence ordering patterns by the offer of a price advantage. All of the offers discussed here encourage retailers to increase the amount of stock held over a period, and thus might also encourage them to sell the product more aggressively. This may be especially important where there is severe competition between manufacturers' brands.

Individual case bonuses
The most popular form of trade price promotion is the one whereby a retailer or distributor is offered a price reduction on each unit or case purchased (for a limited period only). The advantage of this method is that it is very flexible to introduce and drop, especially with the widespread use of direct ordering systems by phone, fax or computer.

Volume allowances

An allowance or discount could depend on the retailer fulfilling a condition relating to volume purchased. The allowance may take several forms. It could, for instance, be a fixed amount per case provided that an agreed number of cases is purchased. Thus a retailer buying a minimum of 20 cases of a product, for instance, might qualify for a 2 per cent discount on the order total that is not offered to the retailer who only buys 19 cases. Alternatively, the allowance might only apply to those cases purchased over and above the minimum order threshold. Thus the retailer gets no discount on the first 20, but does get a 2 per cent discount on the 21st and subsequent cases. Allowances might also operate on smaller quantities quoted in units.

Discount overriders

Discount overriders are longer-term, retrospective discounts, awarded on a quarterly or annual basis, depending on the achievement of agreed volumes or sales targets. These may be applicable to an industrial distributor selling components as a retail outlet. Although the additional discount may be low, perhaps 0.5 per cent, on a turnover of £500 000 this would still be an attractive £2500.

Count and recount

Count and recount is also a retrospective method in that it offers a rebate for each case (or whatever the stock unit is) sold during a specified period. Thus on the first day of the period, all existing stock is counted and any inward shipments received during the period are added to that total. At the end of the period, all remaining unsold cases are deducted. The difference represents the amount of stock actually shifted, forming the basis on which a rebate is paid. Figure 16.9 shows an example of the calculations involved. This method is not easy to administer and is, of course, potentially time consuming to operate.

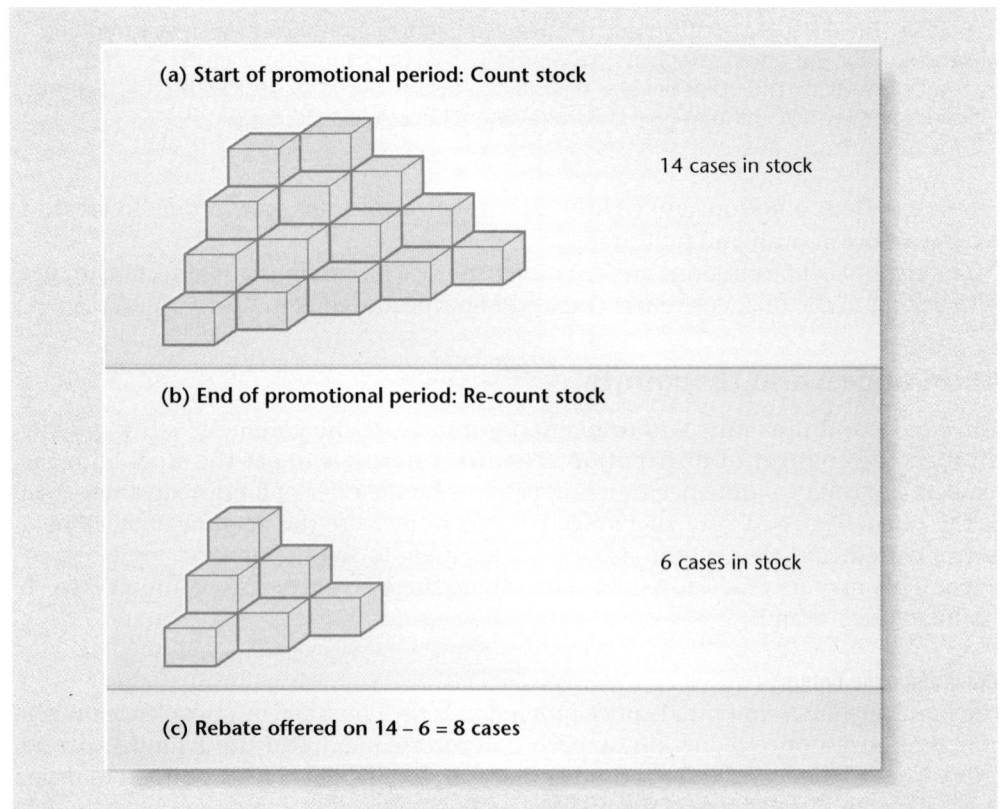

(a) Start of promotional period: Count stock

14 cases in stock

(b) End of promotional period: Re-count stock

6 cases in stock

(c) Rebate offered on 14 – 6 = 8 cases

FIGURE 16.9

Count and recount rebate

Free merchandise

The equivalent of the consumers' BIGIF (*see* p. 657) but on a larger scale, this method involves the offer of free merchandise in return for an agreed level of purchases, for instance buy 10 cases and get another two free. Indirectly, this is a price-based promotion in the retailer's eyes, as it effectively reduces the average cost of all the cases purchased of that brand. The free merchandise need not necessarily be the product itself.

> **Example** SmithKline Beecham ran a six-week promotion on its Lucozade range in 1999 to encourage sales over the summer period: 24 low-calorie 330ml cans could be purchased for the price of 22 and 12 for 10 on Lucozade Sport.

Price-based promotions aimed at the trade are less risky than those aimed at consumers, as the organisational buyer will view them as legitimate competitive tactics rather than using them judgmentally to make emotive evaluations of the product. Price promotions appeal to the trade because they make a direct and measurable impact on the retailer's cost structure, and the retailer has the flexibility to choose

MARKETING IN ACTION Trade promotions

Calypso Cups and Kwenchy Kups are fruit flavoured soft drinks sold in plastic cups with a straw and targeted at children. They are advertised by the manufacturer, Calypso Soft Drinks Ltd, to retailers in the trade magazine *The Grocer*. The advertisement, as well as emphasising the fact that Calypso is 'The UK's number 1 cup drink. Stock up or miss out', offers a summer special promotion of 24 cups per carton for the price of 20. This is to encourage retailers to stock up for the peak season, effectively by offering them more profit per carton through the four free drinks. Free stock does not have to mean giving the retailer more of the same, however. To introduce a new product line, manufacturers can bundle it as free stock with an existing product with which the retailer is already familiar. When Swan launched its extra slim filter tips for smokers, it bundled them with its cigarette papers in cash and carries. Thus when the retailer bought two boxes of packs of cigarette papers, a box of 18 packs of filter tips was also given free. Since each pack retails at 49p, this represents a clear profit to the retailer of £8.82. An offer like this encourages the retailer to consider the new product, stock up with it, and generate awareness and sales with customers, which in turn helps to make the new product a normal part of the retailer's offering.

New product launches are very frequent in the health and beauty sector (see, for instance, Case Study 9.2 on L'Oréal), contributing 10 per cent of market value between 1997 and 1999. This means that retailers are bombarded with new products vying for

the shelf space that is vital to product success. Successful products, those generating at least £1mn annual turnover, tend to be those achieving a high level of retail penetration through trade promotions. Successful products had trade promotions over the first four weeks after launch and over 70 per cent for twelve weeks to ensure retailer commitment. Where the manufacturer is dealing with a large national chain, such as the major supermarket groups, the trade promotions will happen directly between the manufacturer and the retailer. With smaller retailers, as seen in the Swan example above, a promotion can be delivered through a wholesaler or cash and carry using methods very similar to those common in consumer promotions. Sometimes, however, manufacturers prefer to bypass cash and carries and deliver their promotions direct to the smaller retailer. Bulmer, for example, set up a van selling operation to visit 10 000 small retailers to sell its cider brands and to ensure that retailers are displaying them properly. The stock sold like this is taken from local cash and carries and is sold at the cash and carry price to the retailers. The difference, however, is that the van sales team then gives the retailer vouchers off future purchases of those brands to encourage loyalty. The wholesalers and cash and carries are concerned that this might lead to retailers overstocking Bulmer brands, thus neglecting both the other manufacturer brands that the intermediaries offer and the own-label products offered by voluntary chains such as Nisa Today's.

Sources: Calypso (1999); Croft (1999); The Grocer (1999h,1999k).

Who said that trade advertising had to be dull?

Source: Calypso Soft Drinks Ltd.

whether to keep those cost savings or to pass them on to the end consumer. However, in common with price promotions offered to the consumer, trade-orientated price promotions do have the disadvantage of being quickly and easily copied by the competition, leading to the risk of mutually destructive price wars.

Selling and marketing assistance

A number of manufacturer-supported sales and marketing activities assist the reseller by means of promotion at both local and national level.

Co-operative advertising

In co-operative advertising a manufacturer agrees to fund a percentage of a retailer's local advertising, as long as the manufacturer's products are featured in at least part of the advertisement. Normally, the support is limited to media buying rather than creative costs, and is usually set in proportion to the value of product purchased by the retailer from the manufacturer. However, in some cases, standard broadcasting messages or advertising designs, which can be adapted by agreement, are made available to the reseller.

Co-operative advertising support can be very costly, and thus the manufacturer needs to think very carefully before offering it, as it can potentially put far greater pressure on the manufacturer's own promotional budget than some of the methods previously discussed. A further problem arises from the sometimes unco-ordinated advertising programme that may develop. In some regions there may be overlap, but in others the retailer may have little interest in media advertising, resulting in incomplete coverage.

Although in theory manufacturer support may result in better advertising, attempts by resellers to crowd a print advertisement with products, often with price promotions, tend to undermine the position and value of some goods – fmcg brands in particular. Rather than leaving the control of the advertisement in the hands of an individual reseller, therefore, some manufacturers prefer to develop dealer listings. These are advertisements, controlled by the manufacturer, which feature the product and then list those resellers from whom it can be purchased. These are particularly common with cars, higher value household appliances, and top of the range designer clothing, for example.

Merchandising allowances

Using money to provide merchandising allowances rather than for funding advertising may have a more direct benefit to the manufacturer. Payment is made to the retailer for special promotional efforts in terms of displays and in-store promotions such as sampling or demonstrations. This is especially attractive if the product moves quickly and can sustain additional promotional costs.

Sales–force support: consumer markets

A manufacturer may wish to offer training or support for a retailer's sales representatives who deal directly with the public. Such assistance is most likely to be found in connection with higher-priced products of some complexity, for which the purchaser needs considerable assistance at the point of sale. Cars, hi-fi equipment and bigger kitchen appliances are obvious examples of products with substantial technical qualities that need to be explained. With perfumes and fine fragrances, on the other hand, personal service at the point of sale is seen as an important reinforcement of the luxury of the purchase. Manufacturers of such products need retail sales assistants to be well versed in the features and benefits of the products, to be aware of how to match those features and benefits with each customer's needs and, not least, to be enthusiastic about selling the products.

Free training

Free training helps to forge a closer relationship between manufacturer and both retailers and their staff, as well as fulfilling the objective of giving the sales assistants the necessary knowledge base. Even so, such training may not be enough to instil enthusiasm for selling the product and so, to gain an extra selling edge, further incentives aimed at the retailer's sales team might be necessary.

Sales contests

Various prizes, such as cash, goods or holidays, may be used in sales contests to raise the profile of a product and create a short-term incentive. Unfortunately, the prizes often need to be significant and clearly within the reach of all sales assistants if they are to make any real difference to the selling effort. This is especially true when other competitors may adopt similar methods.

Premium money

Other more direct incentives than those already mentioned are also possible. Additional bonuses, i.e. premium money, may be made available to sales assistants who achieve targets. These are useful where personal selling effort may make all the difference to whether or not a sale is made. However, the manufacturer needs to be sure that the cost is outweighed by the additional sales revenues generated.

SALES PROMOTION TO ORGANISATIONAL MARKETS

As the introduction to this chapter made clear, sales promotion in its strictest sense is inappropriate to many organisational markets. The role of discounts and incentives in organisational selling is dealt with in other parts of this book, most notably Chapters 4, 11, and 17. Discounts and incentives are applicable in situations where the buyer and seller are in direct contact and there is room for negotiation of supply conditions. Of course, where organisational marketing starts to resemble consumer marketing, for example in the case of a small business buying a range of standard supplies from a wholesaler, much of what has already been said about manufacturer–consumer or retailer–consumer sales promotions applies with a little adaptation.

The issue of sales force support for retailers selling on to consumers was discussed at p. 673. This same issue will now be looked at from the point of view of an organisational market, as an example of how the same basic techniques and philosophies behind sales promotion can be subtly adapted to a different kind of market.

In industrial distribution situations, it is even more important than in consumer markets for the distributor's sales representatives to have full product knowledge and commitment. As the distributor is likely to carry many product lines, the sales representative is unlikely to be knowledgeable about all products and applications, and thus training through manuals and briefings funded by the manufacturer are likely to assist in selling to the end customer. That takes care of the knowledge base, but even that might not be enough, and the provision of sales aids and a formal sales training programme might need to be introduced for the distributor's sales force. As well as

---

Example JCB decided that it needed to give a boost to its sales of earthmoving and construction machines so it invited a group of 200 or more UK distributors and their top customers to the Torrequebrada Hotel in Malaga. The event was not only a sales conference, but also a forum in which to demonstrate over 30 different machines that were either being introduced for the first time or part of a relaunch. Similar events were held for distributors from France, Italy, Germany and Spain. In total, some 1500 delegates were involved in a series of back to back conferences, the cost of which was claimed to be into six figures.

The sales promotion event was seen as an important part of relationship building with dealers and customers, as well as an opportunity to demonstrate products. Although national events could have been organised, or promotions centred around individual distributorships, an event like this generates a much greater impact, as well as giving JCB a captive audience undistracted by the pressures of day-to-day business. Taking northern Europeans to Spain during a temperate March could also have been an attractive feature of the event!

providing detailed training, the manufacturer's own sales force may undertake joint visits with the distributor's representatives to raise the profile of the product in selected areas. Not only does this directly support the selling effort and provide valuable feedback on customer problems, it also enables informal advice to be given on the best methods of presenting the product and service.

MANAGING SALES PROMOTION

When we look at the range of objectives (*see* pp. 643–652) achievable through sales promotion, we see that the flexibility and directness of many of the methods described are particularly valuable to the marketing manager as part of a co-ordinated promotional programme. Whereas advertising can produce longer-term results, sales promotion can complement that by providing an immediate POS impact that is very important in attracting and keeping loyalty, especially in retail situations.

This statement should not, however, be taken as in any way undermining the strategic role that sales promotion can also play in the promotional mix. In building and maintaining a brand identity, sales promotion (particularly when the techniques used are not price based) can play a role in adding value to the brand, supporting and enhancing its character. Although the specific objectives and themes of sales promotion may alter during the life of the brand, that invaluable support role will not, and thus even if sales promotions only have a short-term impact, they should, in aggregate, contribute towards the long-term objectives of the product.

All of this implies that sales promotions have to be carefully thought through, and properly designed to fit in with wider market efforts, both corporate and brand specific. Sales promotion thus has to be planned and managed, and the various stages in this process are outlined in Fig. 16.10 and discussed below.

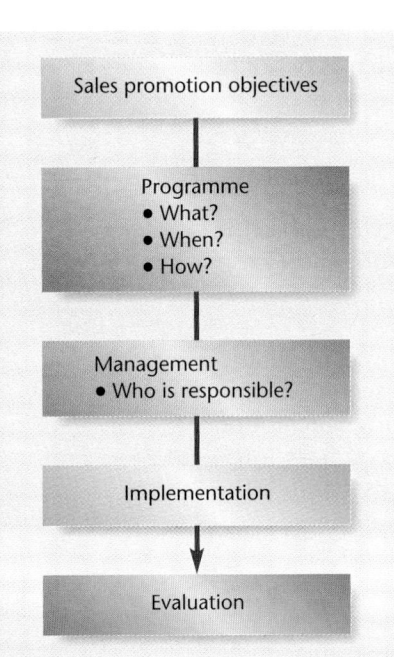

Objectives

As the earlier sections of this chapter have shown, many different sales promotion techniques exist to address a wide range of objectives. The definition of appropriate sales promotion objectives should emerge from a much wider strategic marketing communication plan. Any sales promotion programme undertaken has to fit harmoniously with other activities within the promotional mix, as well as making a positive contribution to achieving the overall objectives of the product's marketing mix.

FIGURE 16.10

The sales promotion
management process

The actual sales promotion techniques employed will themselves depend on the objectives defined and the context within which the sales promotion will take place.

The choice between price and non-price sales promotions may be crucial as the product's life-cycle runs its course. In the early stages, when trial by consumers and retail trade acceptance is vital, the focus may be on samples, coupons and introductory price cuts. Clearly communicating such price cuts as 'trial' or 'introductory' helps to avoid the danger of cheapening the brand's quality.

As the brand develops, so the focus of sales promotion objectives may shift to reminders of the product and retaining loyalty, especially if competing brands are also coming on to the scene. This may be an appropriate point at which to begin to build additional brand value with gifts and competitions. In the mature stage of the life-cycle, price competition may become more intense and so special bonuses and price promotions may predominate.

Programme

In the development of a sales promotion campaign, as with any other promotional activity, there must be a clear link between the activity, its objectives and the target audience.

Target market

The earlier parts of this chapter distinguished between consumer, trade and organisational sales promotions, but even within those broad categories, the specific needs of different *market segments* need to be considered. A number of breakfast cereal sales promotions, for instance, were mentioned earlier in this chapter, some of which are targeted at children (as users and influencers) and some of which are targeted at adults (as purchasers and users). Similarly, consumers vary in their degree of sensitivity to price and coupon offers. Market segmentation, therefore, can help to determine what kind of sales promotion might be most appropriate, and can also be a major guide to the likelihood of a sales promotion's achieving its objectives.

Campaigns and costs

After the definition of the target audience and sales promotion objectives, a shortlist of alternative *campaigns* can be developed according to the budget available. Unlike a media budget, the sales promotion budget can have far-reaching impact across the organisation, which if not carefully assessed can lead to a resource-intensive campaign. This problem is compounded in that the final cost of the campaign may not be known until it is over. Coupon redemption rates, gift take-up and cash-backs, for instance, are difficult to estimate in advance.

There are two main types of cost category in sales promotion.

Communication cost. Communication cost relates to all the costs incurred in bringing the sales promotion to the target groups. These typically include artwork, print costs (including special packaging), media support and distribution.

Fulfilment cost. Fulfilment cost relates to the cost of handling the campaign and financing the programme offers, whether rebates, prizes, merchandise or discounts. As we saw earlier, even free gifts incur postage and packaging costs. Forecasting redemption rates, and therefore fulfilment cost, is notoriously difficult and depends on both internal and external factors, such as trade support, competitive activity and the effectiveness of the rest of the promotional mix. It is often useful to develop a scenario of likely outcomes for budget outline purposes.

Implementation

As with any communication programme, the duration, intensity, coverage and timing of the campaign need to be finalised according to the tasks in hand. Although an individual offer may be short term to gain impact and retain interest, it may itself be a part of a planned series of developing promotional activity, and thus has to be slotted into its appropriate place. Many child-orientated breakfast cereals, for example, permanently feature sales promotions, beginning a new one as soon as the old one ends. These promotions are varied, appealing to different age groups, and utilising different techniques. If the current sales promotion is a free in-pack gift, the next is more likely to be a longer-term mail-in offer. These cereal brands have got to the point where the sales promotion is an expected part of the product offering; it is a shock not to find an offer on the back of a cereal pack!

Guidelines

A number of principles need to be followed to ensure good practice, as outlined by the UK Institute of Sales Promotion and shown in Table 16.5.

TABLE 16.5

Guidelines for good sales promotion practice

Legality	Check any statutory controls/restrictions, e.g. on contests/sweepstakes
Code of practice	What you do should reflect the spirit as well as the letter of the law
Consumer's interests	Deal fairly with the consumer and do not exploit them
Consumer satisfaction	Do not disappoint consumers by raising unrealistic expectations
Fairness	Treat all individuals and participating groups equally
Truthfulness	Do not mislead or deliberately confuse the consumer
Limitations	Exclusions and limitations should be clearly communicated
Suitability	Ensure that the promotion is inaccessible to inappropriate groups where necessary, e.g. children
Administration	Handle consumer queries and responses quickly and efficiently
Responsibility	Prime responsibility lies with the promoter!

Source: Institute of Sales Promotion.

Pan-European guidelines on ethical practice and harmonisation of laws and regulations have not yet been achieved. This means that different countries allow different types of promotion or restrict activities in different ways.

Example It does not appear that the EU sees harmonisation of sales promotion rules across Europe as a priority. Instead, its proposal is that promotional activities will be legal across Europe as long as they are legal in their country of origin. Thus a UK company can undertake any sales promotion in any other EU country as long as it is a legal promotion under British law. This would make things a lot easier for UK companies operating in markets such as Germany, as the UK has fairly liberal promotion regulations and Germany's are very restrictive. The new EU proposal could help to resolve Polygram's long-running dispute with the German government. Polygram wanted to launch a CD club in Germany with introductory discounts (the five CDs for only 50p each type of offer), but German law forbids introductory offers like this. Polygram claims that this is protectionism, because without the offer there is little chance of attracting people away from existing clubs (Murphy, 1999).

Management

The responsibility for sales promotion will depend partly on the company's policies on the use of external agencies, and partly on the use and demands of sales promotion campaigns.

Using an outside agency brings greater flexibility and fresh ideas into sales promotion campaigns. For the smaller organisation, there may be little choice but to use outside help as an extension of the in-house marketing expertise. However, the agency will need to be clearly briefed and at times managed to ensure that an appropriate type and standard of service are achieved. This is especially true if on-going assistance is needed to decide on campaign modifications and review. These will often be costed on a time basis.

In-house provision will depend on the structure of the organisation's marketing department. Responsibility may rest with the product manager, marketing services manager, marketing manager or promotions manager. The important points are that there should be direct accountability for sales promotion decisions, and that they are properly integrated and managed within the context of the marketing plan. Clearly, creating in-house sales promotion facilities enables the acquisition and development of skills that can reinforce subsequent campaigns.

Evaluation

Given the range of sales promotion methods available and the increasing spend on such techniques, it is important to assess thoroughly the effectiveness of the programmes developed. This assessment should cover whether the objectives have been met and whether the results were achieved cost effectively. A number of sources can be used:

1 *Sales force feedback*. Being in the front line, the sales force can quickly get a feel for how a programme is being received by the trade.
2 *Sales data*. Although sales data are a crude measure, early indications of increased shipments may show that a sales promotion is beginning to take off.
3 *Retail audits*. Audits such as Nielson will track changes in distribution, stock levels and market share during and immediately after the campaign.
4 *Consumer audits*. These will indicate changes in customer behaviour, especially that concerned with trial and repeat purchase during the promotion period.
5 *Redemptions*. These are a direct measure of the campaign, such as the number of coupons returned, free gifts claimed, numbers entering the contest etc. These should not be viewed in isolation, but within the context of the campaign and its overall objectives.

However, as with any promotional evaluation, the results cannot be looked at in isolation. Other elements of the mix and the relative level of competitor activity will all play a part in shaping overall results. Only by commissioning pre and post-campaign research can the underlying influences be identified, and the impact on users and non-users of the product assessed.

Joint promotions

Sometimes, the risks and costs of sales promotion can be shared with other organisations by entering into **joint promotions**. If the two products or services have synergy, if they appeal to a similar target audience, or if the two organisations operate on a similar philosophy, then a joint promotion can make a big impact, benefiting both organisations and their customers.

> **Example** British Airways (BA) has a long-term relationship with Associated Newspapers and for three years BA has jointly offered half-price flights with the *Daily Mail* and the *Evening Standard*. The partnership brings benefits to both parties. BA has had around £1mn of media exposure in the newspapers as well as making extra sales that help to fill aircraft and acquiring new customers for its database. The newspapers get something of real value to offer their readers and to drive circulation figure upwards. The fact that both parties share the costs also makes the partnership attractive to them (Beenstock, 1999b).

If a joint promotion is to be successful in all respects, then not only must the right partners be working together, but they must also be clear about what each is bringing to the promotion and how the costs are to be allocated. Joint promotions are not an excuse to try to get someone else to pick up the bill. In many cases, each partner might even pay as much as they would have done for a solo campaign in order to achieve the benefits of reaching a larger audience with a better proposition. Cummins (1989) suggests six factors that help to create successful joint promotions, and these are summarised in Table 16.6.

TABLE 16.6
Factors influencing successful joint promotions

Factor	How to implement
Involve everyone	Include senior management from both parties
Make realistic promises	Only promise what you can deliver
Avoid unplanned changes	Make sure you know at the start what you are committed to
Build in good liaison	Maintain communication and develop problem solving processes
Bargain realistically	Maximise **mutual** benefit at **reasonable** and **fairly shared** cost
Be proactive	Do not sit back and expect the other party to do everything!

Source: Adapted from Cummins (1989).

CHAPTER SUMMARY

Sales promotion is part of a planned marketing communications strategy that is mainly used in a short-term tactical sense, but can also contribute something to longer-term strategic and image building objectives. Sales promotions offer something over and above the normal product offering that can act as an incentive to stimulate the target audience into behaving in a certain way. Manufacturers use promotions to stimulate intermediaries and their sales staff, both manufacturers and retailers use them to stimulate individual consumers and manufacturers might use them to stimulate other manufacturers.

The methods of sales promotion are many and varied. In consumer markets they can be classed as either money based (for example, money off), product based (for example, buy one get one free), or gift, prize or merchandise based (for example, a free toy inside a box of cereal). Customer loyalty schemes in particular have become increasingly popular in the retail trade and in service industries. The problem with them is, however, that as they become more common, they lose their competitive edge and consumers become as disloyal as they were ever inclined to be. Given the high costs of setting up and running such schemes, their cost effectiveness might be questionable. Manufacturers stimulate retailers and other intermediaries by offering money back, discounts, free goods and 'sale or return' schemes, among other methods. They also offer sales force incentives to encourage a more committed selling effort from the intermediary's staff.

Any sales promotion programme has to be planned, implemented and managed. The first stage is to be clear on its objectives, and how those fit into the wider marketing strategy. Then, within the design of the actual programme, the manager must be clear about who the target audience is, what the most appropriate methods of sales promotion are for reaching that audience given the stated objectives, and how much all that will cost. The manager also has to determine the operational issues, such as the timing, duration, intensity and coverage of the promotion, as well as defining any qualifying criteria. All this should be done within current laws and guidelines. The organisation has to decide whether to handle the promotion in-house or to use an agency. Either way, there should be a clear definition of who is responsible for what. Once the sales promotion has run its course, its performance should be assessed and analysed in order to learn from its successes and mistakes. A final issue of sales promotion management is whether to enter into joint promotions with other organisations. Where there is natural synergy between the partners, and a clear division of costs and responsibilities, joint promotions can be very successful. Both organisations can reach a wider audience with a far better proposition than they could have afforded working alone.

Key words and phrases

Alternative currencies	Field marketing agencies	Sale or return
BIGIF	Joint promotion	Sales promotion
Cash rebate	Loading up	Samples
Contests and sweepstakes	Money-based sales promotions	Self-liquidating offers
Co-operative advertising	POS	Trading up
Count and recount	Product-based sales promotions	Trial price
Coupons		Trial sizes

QUESTIONS FOR REVIEW

16.1 What is *sales promotion* and in what ways does it differ from advertising?

16.2 What are the main objectives of *manufacturer sales promotions* aimed at consumers?

16.3 Why do manufacturers offer sales promotions to *retailers*?

16.4 How do the objectives of *retailer–consumer* sales promotions differ from those of *manufacturer–consumer* sales promotions?

16.5 What are the main forms of *money-based sales promotions* aimed at consumers and what are their advantages and disadvantages?

16.6 What specific objectives can BIGIF and similar types of sales promotion achieve?

16.7 How do *self-liquidating offers* differ from *free mail-in offers*, and in what circumstances might each be appropriate?

16.8 What is *count and recount*? Why might a retailer prefer it to a *buying allowance*?

16.9 Outline the key stages in the *sales promotion management process*.

16.10 Once the broad form of a sales promotion has been determined, what specific details need to be sorted out before it can be *implemented*?

QUESTIONS FOR DISCUSSION

16.1 Research a recent new product launch by a manufacturer in a consumer market. What role did sales promotions play in that launch?

16.2 Choose an fmcg product area (breakfast cereals or hot chocolate drinks, for example) and analyse the sales promotions currently offered on the range of available brands in terms of the methods used, duration, size of reward etc.

16.3 To what extent are the sales promotion methods used in consumer markets equally applicable in organisational markets?

16.4 What kinds of sales promotion are:

(a) '20% extra free';

(b) 'send in £9.99 plus five proofs of purchase to get a branded sweatshirt'; and

(c) 'when you open the product packaging, look to see if there is a cheque for £5000 inside'?
Why might manufacturers use them?

16.5 Find three examples of joint sales promotions and discuss the benefits for the organisations concerned and their customers.

CASE STUDY 16.1

Student banking

A prime target market for UK bankers is the student segment. When young people go to college or university, they usually gain greater financial independence and have to learn the art of careful cash management. They thus need bank accounts. There is a lot of competition for this segment, despite the fact that it is not particularly profitable for the banks. The real attraction of the student segment for banks is their longer-term above average earning potential. Customer loyalty to banks can often be high, so once a consumer has decided which bank to use, it can be difficult to encourage them to switch allegiance. At the early stage of the bank–customer relationship, therefore, the banks put up with incurring the costs of providing the full range of facilities that students need, without earning much in return through overdraft charges, as student overdrafts are generally charged at lower preferential rates. The banks also feel that they have a social responsibility not to allow young people to get into so much debt that they cannot cope financially.

In the UK, with the ending of student grants and the introduction of the £1000 contribution to tuition fees for all students except those from low income families, the emphasis has switched to student loans and parental support. Although loans are readily available, it does mean that a student will incur debt which must be repaid as soon as subsequent income reaches a threshold level. It is thus perhaps not surprising that an increasing number of students undertake part-time employment while studying and some, especially mature students, decide either to study part time or not to bother at all. In the UK, however, in contrast with the USA, the tradition is to keep any employment to a minimum, reinforced by sometimes rigid course structures, heavy emphasis on independent study and peer and parental expectation that the student should take three or four years to complete a degree. In the USA, many students take far longer to complete their degrees and select a pace to suit their work demands, maximising the use of flexible credit accumulation models. In the USA, courses are timetabled to meet peaks in demand; for example the same course can be offered day-time and evening. Some universities have gone even further, as has Kettering University in Detroit, by offering degrees that are employer sponsored and in which students spend six month blocks alternating between work and study. With the relative inflexibility of the UK system, despite the introduction of modular schemes, student debt is likely to mount from student loans, tuition fees and any overdraft or bank loan facility topping up the shortfall. A typical student could leave university, in the absence of any parental support or employment income, with as much as £20 000 worth of debt.

Barclay's Bank has emerged as a market leader in the student segment, despite a history of problems in the 1960s and 1970s when students were urged to boycott Barclay's in protest against the company's South African interests. In some instances, Barclay's was prevented from coming on to campuses during freshers' weeks and other forums for meeting new students. Since then, Barclay's has successfully used a series of promotional campaigns to attract students. Locating branches or cash dispensers on campuses, offering subsidised banking and making presentations to student groups are all part of its marketing armoury. A timely talk on 'managing your budget' during induction week, for example, can act as a soft sell, even though the bank's products or services are not overtly promoted.

Barclay's has been especially strong in using sales promotion to attract new accounts. This approach was considered important as students often could not differentiate between the core offerings of the major banks. In the late 1980s and early 1990s incentives such as gift vouchers, Filofaxes, clothes and CDs all played a part in building a strong market position. As the 1990s progressed, however, the focus switched to service and the various financial products that students might need during their course of study.

Barclay's, along with many other banks, offers an interest-free credit overdraft of up to £1600. It also provides a number of extra incentives to attract students. Within the overdraft there is a special £100 buffer to cover special short-term circumstances. As an extra incentive, successful applicants for a student account with a Barclaycard are given an *Easylife* mobile phone worth £119.99 as part of a joint arrangement with Cellnet. This includes no connection fee, no line rental and no monthly charges, although students are required to buy with their Barclaycard £20 of call time every 120 days (but with the first purchase there is a

▶

further £20 worth of free calls). Calls are charged at 49p per minute. For those students not wanting the temptation of a mobile, the alternative is a £15 credit to the student's account and a further £15 off the first monthly Barclaycard statement. Unless other arrangements have been made, the Barclaycard offers a fixed credit limit of £350. Additionally, Barclay's provides free student access to on-line banking as well as free Internet access. Waterstone's bookshop vouchers worth £20 are given as soon as the main student funding cheque hits the account and for those studying subjects in the medical, science and veterinary fields, the figure rises to £40. For the more frivolous student, the vouchers can also be spent in HMV shops! Other discount vouchers are made available during the year, designed to build loyalty and goodwill between the bank and student.

Even the National Union of Students (NUS) has an interest in the success of student banking. It endorses Barclaycard to highlight to the student the importance of managing money. In return for cash sponsorship, NUS university branches often allow Barclaycard to run special promotions on student union premises. Of course, Barclay's, along with the other banks in this segment, has to balance social responsibility against competitiveness. Special student business officers aim to build a trusting relationship with the student in order to identify problems early. Unfortunately, despite all these careful measures, most universities are full of horror stories of how some individuals become seriously burdened with debt due to overspending and abuse of the credit facilities offered.

In general, though, most students manage their finances sensibly and the banks are eager to get their business. Most promotions are heavily displayed at the point of sale, especially in branches close to campuses. The literature provides application details or serves as a guide to further discussion. There is, however, still further scope for imaginative incentive campaigns. One year, Barclay's offered a 'Rent Free' promotion as an incentive for students to visit their local branch and to open an account. The scratchcard based promotion enabled a student to win £2500, at that time a year's rent. The promotion, supported by media advertising, was successful in generating branch traffic. There were seven winners nationwide. With a share of just below 30 per cent in the student segment, it is essential for Barclay's to maintain its innovative promotional edge.

Sources: Croft (1996); Barclay's promotional literature; course handbook, Kettering University; http://www.personal.barclays.co.uk.

Questions

1 What kinds of sales promotions do the banks use in the student segment and what are they trying to achieve?

2 Why do you think the banks have tended to move away from gift-based promotions to money-based offers?

3 What are the problems of using sales promotions in such a highly competitive, concentrated market?

4 How might the use of sales promotion methods differ for a financial services product compared with an fmcg product?

CASE STUDY 16.2

Supermarket loyalty cards

The major UK supermarket multiples have long competed with each other using sales promotion techniques, such as price offers, BIGIFs and free recipe cards available in-store. One or two also used promotions designed to encourage longer-term loyalty and regular shopping habits. These tended to take the form of issuing cards that were stamped at the checkout every time the customer spent more than a certain amount. When the card was full, the customer qualified for a discount. These 'mini-loyalty schemes' were only used infrequently and did not

allow the retailer to track individual shoppers or to analyse their buying patterns and preferences.

Permanent loyalty schemes that allow the retailer to capture and analyse customer data on an on-going basis began to emerge in the UK supermarket sector in 1995. The technology to handle the massive amounts of data about customers and the minutiae of their daily shopping habits existed, and Tesco, the first of the major multiples to develop such a scheme, decided that the time was right to do it.

To participate, customers have to register, filling in a short form giving details about themselves and their domestic situation. They then receive a Clubcard that is swiped through the checkout every time they shop so that points are accumulated electronically, depending on the amount spent. Every quarter, the customer receives a statement showing how many points have been collected, and turning them into money-off vouchers. Tesco makes around 36 million Clubcard related mailings every year. It started with one mailshot to fit all customers, but now has 80 000 variants to target each customer with more relevant offers.

In June 1996, Tesco launched the next phase of its Clubcard: Clubcard Plus. This is a kind of credit card, in that holders pay a fixed sum every month into their Clubcard Plus account and then can use the card to do their shopping and even to withdraw cash at the checkout. A credit facility, up to the same sum as the usual monthly payment, is also available on the card. Whenever the customer's Clubcard Plus account is in credit, however, interest is paid on the balance.

Two weeks after Tesco launched Clubcard Plus, Sainsbury's finally launched a full national loyalty card of its own, called Reward. It cost £15 million to launch, including £5 million on press and television advertising. To offset these costs, Sainsbury's hoped that Reward would lead to an increase of 3 per cent in sales and that it would take customers away from Tesco.

Safeway followed Tesco by launching its own ABC scheme in 1995, while Sainsbury's Reward scheme was launched in 1996. By 1999, Tesco had around 14 million cards in circulation, Sainsbury's 13 million and Safeway 10 million. All three schemes offer 1 penny per £1 spent in the store. In Tesco, customers can only swap points for money-off vouchers, although there are plenty of special offers around the stores giving extra points for buying certain brands or for bulk purchasing. Sainsbury's also gives money-off vouchers, although the customer can opt to swap their points for Air Miles, 'spend' them in Arcadia group clothing stores, or redeem them against specific products in the store with a Reward points value on them (for example, 300 points for a bottle of Bailey's). Safeway also allows shoppers to spend their points in the store.

Not all retailers are convinced about the value of a loyalty card scheme. ASDA, for instance, has never launched one. Its chairman said that he felt that only Tesco's scheme had actually paid for itself, being the most sophisticated scheme on

offer, and that Safeway and Sainsbury's were just wasting money. He said that ASDA had considered such a scheme but so far had rejected it because its philosophy was about permanently low prices in-store, i.e. discounts now rather than points now and money-off vouchers later. Now that ASDA has been taken over by Wal-Mart, it will be interesting to see whether this view of loyalty schemes and pricing will be reinforced in the future. Waitrose, the upmarket supermarket chain owned by the John Lewis Partnership, has also rejected loyalty card schemes as being 'intrusive and hugely expensive'. Waitrose's marketing director claimed that loyalty card points were covered by higher mark-ups on products in the first place and that the supermarkets were making money out of selling the data to other companies. He also claimed that Waitrose was less expensive than the three major chains with schemes, even taking into account the loyalty card discounts. Both Sainsbury's and Tesco disputed that claim, however, on the basis that like-for-like price comparisons had not been made.

It is also true that questions have been raised about the ability of such schemes to influence loyalty. Research has shown that only 22 per cent of consumers are influenced by the loyalty card in choosing where to shop. There is also a problem with promiscuity as consumers hold more than one card, although 58 per cent consumers have at least one card that they do not use. The cards are popular: 90 per cent of customers are aware of the schemes and 64 per cent participate in them. It has also been found that the cards do not do much for loyalty, but are a good way of 'targeting discounts at the people who buy most from you', according to market research company Verdict. Research has shown that cards do encourage customers to spend more. The spending differences between card holders and non-card holders are significant. On average, a card holder spends £33.85 per visit whereas a non-card holder only spends £13.93.

The supermarkets' commitment to their schemes means that they are constantly trying to update them and find better ways of using the data. In spring 1999, it was announced that Tesco would be re-launching its Clubcard by categorising its customers as gold, silver or bronze card holders, depending on their expenditure. It is thought that the top group, the gold card holders, probably the top 20 per cent of customers, will get more benefits in the form of more points or incentives with other retailers linked with the scheme. There are several reasons for doing this. First, it represents good use of the database. By identifying the highest spending, most profitable customers, Tesco can make the effort to nurture them and protect them from the competition, and perhaps even increase their value. Research has shown that on average, the top 5 per cent of a supermarket's customers account for 20 per cent of sales and 30 per cent of profits as they tend to buy the premium, high margin products. Second, Tesco wants to reinvigorate the Clubcard scheme to keep customers interested and using their cards, thus expanding the database. Similarly, after a 14-month trial in 15 stores, Sainsbury's decided to put Reward card kiosks into all its stores. The kiosks have a terminal linking the customer with the loyalty card database to get tailored offers for their shopping that day. The customer swipes their Reward card through the terminal and then uses touch-screen technology to select which offers they are interested in. The machine then prints out vouchers that can be redeemed at the checkout.

None of the supermarkets can risk having its loyalty scheme fade away through customers getting bored and slack about using their cards, because the investment has been too great. It has been estimated that running a loyalty scheme can cost anything from 5–10 per cent of profit in a year and so the scheme has to pay for itself through increased sales or increased customer value. Nevertheless, most managers in the retail trade and industry analysts agree that loyalty does not come from cards. If the scheme is not backed up with the right products, the right stores and the right service, then it is bound to be an expensive failure.

Sources: Beenstock (1999a); Darby (1999b); *The Grocer* (1999c, 1999e); *Marketing* (1999b); Robinson (1999).

Note: All information was correct at time of writing

Questions

1 What factors have led the supermarkets towards these kinds of loyalty scheme and what do they hope to achieve from them?

2 What are the practical problems of setting up, managing and maintaining a promotion like this?

3 What are the potential problems and opportunities arising from Tesco's proposed gold, silver and bronze Clubcard scheme and Sainsbury's kiosks?

4 To what extent and how do you think that retailers and consumers might benefit or suffer from the long-term continuation of these schemes, once the novelty has worn off?

REFERENCES TO CHAPTER 16

Beenstock, S. (1999a), 'Supermarkets Entice the "Ultra" Customer', *Marketing*, 15 April, p. 20.

Beenstock, S. (1999b), 'Why Marketing Partnerships Must not Alienate Their Target Audience', *Marketing*, 29 April, p. 15.

Calypso (1999), advertising in *The Grocer*, 10 April, p 62.

Campbell, L. (1999a), 'Coca-Cola and Disney Link in Dual Promotion', *Marketing*, 22 April, p. 5.

Campbell, L. (1999b), 'Pepsi Backs Star Wars Film with £5mn UK Puch', *Marketing*, 27 May, p. 5.

Croft, M. (1996), 'Student Banking Grows Up', *Marketing Week*, 10 May, pp. 87–90.

Croft, M. (1999), 'It's Looking Good for Beauty', *Marketing Week*, 18 March, pp. 38–9.

Cummins, J. (1989), *Sales Promotion: How to Create and Implement Campaigns That Really Work*, Kogan Page.

Darby, I. (1999a), 'Big Mac Blunder Hits McDonald's', *Marketing*, 7 January, p. 1.

Darby, I. (1999b), 'Asda Chief Lashes out at Rivals' Loyalty Offers', *Marketing*, 27 May, p. 11.

Darby, I. (1999c), 'Court Verdict Threatens Scratchcard Promotion', *Marketing*, 1 July, p. 8.

Davies, M. (1992), 'Sales Promotion as a Competitive Strategy', *Management Decision*, 30(7), pp. 5–10.

Fill, C. (1999), *Marketing Communications: Contexts, Contents and strategies*, 2nd edn, Prentice Hall Europe.

Fletcher, K. (1999), 'Getting the Most out of Mailshots', *Marketing*, 13 May, pp. 38–9.

Gray, R. (1999), 'Targeting Results', *Marketing*, 13 May, p. 37.

The Grocer (1999a), 'Spar Lines up Heroes for its X Files', *The Grocer*, 1 May, p. 5.

The Grocer (1999b), 'Promotional Activity Boosts Select Beef's Sales', in *British Meat Marketing* supplement to *The Grocer*, 1 May, p. iv.

The Grocer (1999c), 'Stores Confused over Building Rapport', *The Grocer*, 8 May, p. 5.

The Grocer (1999d), 'Britvic's Phantom Menace Unleashed in Cola Wars', *The Grocer*, 29 May, p. 47.

The Grocer (1999e), 'Chain Derides Loyalty Card Benefits', *The Grocer*, 5 June, p. 5.

The Grocer (1999f), 'Sun, Sea and Shopping', *The Grocer*, 5 June, p. 8.

The Grocer (1999g), 'Collar this Cute Offer', *The Grocer*, 5 June, p. 54.

The Grocer (1999h), 'Cider Vans Hit the Road', *The Grocer*, 12 June, p. 4.

The Grocer (1999j), 'Biscuit Boost for Go Ahead! Range', *The Grocer*, 12 June, p. 54.

The Grocer (1999k), 'New Lines and Free Stock', *The Grocer*, 19 June, p. 33.

The Grocer (1999l), 'Jar Jar's Sticky Business', *The Grocer*, 19 June, p. 65.

The Grocer (1999m), 'Suppliers Get all Tanked up', *The Grocer*, 19 June, p. 69.

The Grocer (1999n), 'Kit Kat Is Blue for You', *The Grocer*, 26 June, p. 50.

Gupta, S. and Cooper, L. G. (1992), 'The Discounting of Discount and Promotion Brands', *Journal of Consumer Research*, 19 (Dec.), pp. 401–11.

Jones, P. J. (1990), 'The Double Jeopardy of Sales Promotions', *Harvard Business Review*, September/October, pp. 141–52.

Marketing (1999a), 'Daewoo Attracts Visitors in £1,000 Matiz Promotion', *Marketing*, 1 July, p. 4.

Marketing (1999b), 'Sainsbury's Puts Reward Kiosks in all Supermarkets', *Marketing*, 1 July, p. 4.

Marketing Week (1999a), 'Fabergé Extends Dove in £10mn Deodorant Push', *Marketing Week*, 18 February, p. 10.

Marketing Week (1999b), 'On-pack Promotion Launches £5mn Pepsi Star Wars Tie-up', *Marketing Week*, 27 May, p. 8.

Marketing Week (1999c), '"Illegal" Threat to Prize Draws', *Marketing Week*, 1 July, p. 9.

Miller, R. (1999), 'Making the Most of the Concourse', *Marketing*, 6 May, pp. 23–4.

Mitchell, A. (1995), 'Preaching the Loyalty Message', *Marketing Week*, 1 December, pp. 26–7.

Murphy, D. (1999), 'Cross-border Conflicts', *Marketing*, 11 February, pp. 30–1.

Peattie, K. and Peattie, S. (1995), 'Sales Promotion – A Missed Opportunity For Services Marketers?', *International Journal of Service Industry Management*, 6(1), pp. 22–39.

Robinson, P. (1999), 'Played Out?', *The Grocer*, 10 April, pp. 44–6.

Wilmshurst, J. (1993), *Below The Line Promotion*, Butterworth-Heinemann.

17

Personal Selling and Sales Management

LEARNING OBJECTIVES

This chapter will help you to:

1 appreciate the role that personal selling plays in the overall marketing effort of the organisation;

2 define the tasks undertaken by sales representatives;

3 differentiate between types of sales representative;

4 analyse the stages involved in the personal selling process and understand how each one contributes towards creating sales and developing long-term customer relationships;

5 appreciate the issues, responsibilities and problems involved in sales management.

INTRODUCTION

Many organisations employ sales forces to help in the promotional process. Whether that sales force takes a primary role in creating customers and then servicing their needs, or whether it simply receives orders at the point of sale, will vary according to the type of product, the type of customer and the type of organisation. As Chapter 1 suggested, personal selling will probably play a much bigger role in the promotional mix of a high-priced, infrequently purchased industrial good, for example, than in that of a routinely purchased consumer product.

Nevertheless, personal selling is important in some consumer markets. Car manufacturers spend many millions on advertising, but the purchase decision is made and the final deal negotiated at the showroom. The sales assistants thus play a very important role, particularly in guiding, persuading and converting the wavering customer without being too pushy. To do this, the sales assistant not only needs to know the product well, but also needs to be trained to judge the state of mind and the motivations of the potential customer so that a sale is made rather than lost. In the car industry, failure at this stage lets the whole glossy marketing process down. The sales representative selling assembly robots to a car manufacturer faces a slightly different situation. The task is still to try to encourage the buyer to make a decision to buy and then a decision to buy from you. In this case, however, the selling process will involve extensive discussion with operational and financial staff, and might include co-ordination between the seller's own staff and the buyer's decision-making unit, in such areas as technical specification, trials and installation. This is a high level, demanding job, but still needs sound product and sales training and an understanding of customer psychology. Many of these issues were discussed in Chapter 4. In some situations, product differences might be very small and the fit between the buyer's needs and the seller's offering be very close for several competing packages. The sales representative may then make the difference through the way in which the process is handled and the degree of trust and respect generated.

Regardless of whether the sales force is selling capital machinery into manufacturing businesses, fmcg products into the retail trade or financial services to individual consumers, the principles behind personal selling remain largely the same. This chapter will address those principles and show how they apply in different types of selling situation.

> **Example** Reebok, the sports shoe manufacturer, organises its UK selling effort by region. An account manager, effectively acting as a sales representative, covers the entire product range when calling on retailers and wholesalers in a region and thus needs a good understanding of existing lines and how a retailer can also sell them once in stock. The account manager is responsible for negotiating with new and existing customers and, in order to achieve a range of company targets linked with brands, works closely with the display merchandising team. There is little point in the account manager selling into the store if the products do not then sell on to the customer. The link with in-store point-of-sale promotions can be an important part of the overall selling process for both Reebok and its retailers.

As a foundation for discussing the deeper issues concerning personal selling, it is important first of all to establish a definition of what personal selling is, and to look at the different roles it can play and the objectives it can achieve. This can then be put into the context of the wider promotional mix to show how personal selling differentiates itself from the other elements and how it complements them. From this, the chapter moves on to look at some of the skills and techniques involved in selling, using a framework that traces the selling process through from identifying likely prospects to making the sales and following it up. Having looked at selling from such a practical point of view, it is important to round off the picture by considering some of the managerial issues surrounding personal selling. These include the problems of selecting sales representatives, their training, deployment, compensation and evaluation.

THE DEFINITION AND ROLE OF PERSONAL SELLING

According to Fill (1999, p. 7), **personal selling** can be defined as:

> 'An interpersonal communication tool which involves face to face activities undertaken by individuals, often representing an organisation, in order to inform, persuade or remind an individual or group to take appropriate action, as required by the sponsor's representative.'

As a basic definition, this does capture the essence of personal selling. *Interpersonal communication* implies a live, two-way, interactive dialogue between buyer and seller (which none of the other promotional mix elements can achieve); *with an individual or group* implies a small, select audience (again, more targeted than with the other elements); *to inform, persuade or remind ... to take appropriate action* implies a planned activity with a specific purpose.

Note that the definition does not imply that personal selling is only about making sales. It may well ultimately be about making a sale, but that is not its only function. It can contribute considerably to the organisation both before and, indeed, after a sale has been made. As a means of making sales, personal selling is about finding, informing, persuading and at times servicing customers through the personal, two-way communication that is its strength. It means helping customers to articulate their needs, tailoring persuasive selling messages to answer those needs, and then handling customers' responses or concerns in order to arrive at a mutually valued exchange. As a background to that, personal selling is also a crucial element in ensuring customers' post-purchase satisfaction, and in building profitable long-term buyer–seller relationships built on trust and understanding (Miller and Heinman, 1991).

One final thought on the definition: personal selling need not be a face to face activity. Think of it more as a voice to ear activity! Recent years have seen big growth in telephone selling techniques and teleconferencing as cost-effective alternatives (Smith, 1993). Remember too that although personal selling depends primarily on the spoken word, audio-visual aids and demonstrations are often used to enhance that, providing a much more stimulating experience for the potential buyer.

Having thus defined the broad essence of personal selling, it is now appropriate to discuss where and how it fits in to the overall promotional mix.

Chapter 14 has already offered some insights into where personal selling fits best into the promotional mix. We discussed how personal selling is more appropriate in organisational than consumer markets at p. 567, while p. 573 *et seq.* looked at its advantages in promoting and selling high-cost, complex products. The discussion at p. 572 also notes that personal selling operates most effectively when customers are on the verge of making a final decision and committing themselves, but still need that last little bit of tailored persuasion.

All of that discussion in Chapter 14 is relevant here for putting personal selling into context, but there is more to be said. By looking at the main characteristics of personal selling, it is possible to compare it in more detail with the other elements of the promotional mix, highlighting its complementary strengths and weaknesses. The characteristics to be examined are impact, precision, cultivation and cost.

Impact

If you do not like the look of a TV advertisement, you can turn it off, or ignore it. If a glance at a print advertisement fails to capture your further attention, you can turn the page. If an envelope on the doormat looks like a mail shot, you can put it in the bin unopened. If a sales representative appears on your doorstep or in your office, it is a little more difficult to switch off. A person has to be dealt with in some way, and since most of us subscribe to the common rules of politeness, we will at least listen to what the person wants before shepherding them out of the door. The sales representative, therefore, has a much greater chance of engaging your initial attention than an advertisement does.

It is also true, of course, that an advertisement has no means of knowing or caring that you have ignored it. Sales representatives, on the other hand, have the ability to respond to the situations in which they find themselves, and can take steps to prevent themselves from being shut off completely. This could be, for instance, by pressing for another appointment at a more convenient time, or by at least leaving sales literature for the potential customer to read and think about at their leisure. Overall, you are far more likely to remember a person you have met or spoken to (and to respond to what they said) than you are to remember an advertisement. In that respect, personal selling is very powerful indeed, particularly if it capitalises on the elements of precision and cultivation (*see* below) as well.

Precision

Precision represents one of the great advantages of personal selling over any of the other promotional mix elements, and explains why it is so effective at the customer's point of decision making. There are two facets of precision that should be acknowledged: targeting precision and message precision.

Targeting precision

Targeting precision arises from the fact that personal selling is not a mass medium. Advertising can be targeted within broad parameters, but even so, there will still be many wasted contacts (people who are not even in the target market; people who are not currently interested in the product; people who have recently purchased already; people who cannot currently afford to purchase etc.). Advertising hits those contacts anyway with its full message, and each of those wasted contacts costs money. Personal selling can weed out the inappropriate contacts early on, and concentrate its efforts on those who offer a real prospect of making a sale.

Take a simple organisational situation, for instance. A brochure sent to a potential industrial buyer through the post may be addressed to an inappropriate person in the organisation and be put in the bin, the purchasing director's secretary may open the mail and decide not to pass it on, or it may be addressed to someone who is no longer employed within that organisation. In contrast, personal contact with the organisation can establish the identity of the best person to talk to and whether the organisation is even remotely interested in doing business. Both of those issues can be followed through with persistence until satisfactory answers are received. Thus the personal selling effort can then begin properly with a fighting chance of achieving something.

Message precision

Message precision arises from the interactive two-way dialogue that personal selling encourages. An advertisement cannot tell what impact it is having on you. It cannot discern whether you are paying attention to it, whether you understand it or whether you think it is relevant to you. Furthermore, once the advertisement has been presented to you, that is it. It is a fixed, inflexible message, and if you did not understand it, or if you felt that it did not tell you what you wanted to know, then you have no opportunity to do anything about it other than wait for another advertisement to come along that might clarify these things. Because personal selling involves live interaction, however, these problems should not occur. The sales representative can tell, for example, that your attention is wandering, and therefore can change track, exploring other avenues until something seems to capture you again. The representative can also make sure that you understand what you are being told and go over it again from a different angle if you are having difficulty with the first approach. Similarly, the representative can see if something has particularly caught your imagination and tailor the message to emphasise that feature or benefit. Thus, by listening and watching, the sales representative should be able to create a unique approach that exactly matches the mood and the needs of each prospective customer. This too is a very potent capability.

Cultivation

As Chapter 4 implied, the creation of long-term, mutually beneficial buyer–seller relationships is now recognised as extremely important to the health and profitability of organisations in many industries. The sales force has a crucial role to play in both creating and maintaining such relationships. Sales representatives are often the public face of an organisation, and their ability to carry the organisation's message professionally and confidently can affect judgement of that organisation and what it stands for. Sales representatives can also do something that advertising cannot: they can develop personal relationships with people in client organisations. Turnbull (1990) highlighted the information exchange capability and the technical and commercial roles played by sales representatives. These help to reduce the social and cultural distance between buyer and seller. Such relationships can smooth the way to easier inter-organisational negotiation, and they can also make information gathering much easier. A sales representative can potentially find out a great deal more about an organisation's purchasing philosophy by having a friendly chat over a drink with his friend, the purchasing manager from XYZ & Co., than any formal inquiry or survey. Accepting the contention (*see* pp. 165 *et seq.*) that organisational decision making can be affected by less rational human motivations means that the interpersonal bonds between organisations must be fully encouraged and exploited (Cunningham and Homse, 1986).

Cost

All the advantages and benefits discussed above come at a very high cost, as personal selling is extremely labour intensive. In addition, costs of travel (and time spent travelling), accommodation and other expenses have to be accounted for. It can thus cost anything from £50 000 upwards to keep a sales representative on the road for a year. The actual time spent actually selling to the customer, however, has been estimated at just 6 per cent of total time, with 50 per cent spent travelling, 20 per cent on administration and 24 per cent making the call (McDonald, 1984). Although there are likely to be wide variations between organisations, these figures suggest that organisations have to be sure about what their sales force is for, and what it is actually doing that could not be achieved equally well by other means. Only then can the high investment in personal selling be justified as a cost effective use of resources.

Many organisations spend more on this element of the promotional mix than on any other, particularly in organisational markets. Estimates vary, but it is suggested that the number of sales representatives employed in various capacities is very large indeed. In the USA, for example, it has been estimated that around 10 per cent of the work force is employed in positions that involve some kind of personal selling (Zikmund and d'Amico, 1993).

TASKS OF THE SALES REPRESENTATIVE

There is a tendency to think of the sales representative in a one-off selling situation. What the discussion in the previous sections has shown is that in reality, the representative is likely to be handling a relationship with any specific customer over a long period of time. The representative will be looking to build up close personal ties because much depends on repeat sales. In some cases, the representative might even be involved in helping to negotiate and handle joint product development. All of this suggests a range of tasks beyond the straight selling situation.

Clearly, the nature of the selling task and the range of activities with which the sales representative becomes involved will vary according to many factors. The more complex, technical or expensive the product, the more time the representative will have to spend in clarifying what is required, working with the customer to select the right product offering for the situation and ensuring satisfactory post-purchase performance. With routine, low priced, frequent purchases, the sales representative's role becomes much more administrative, just filling in the order forms. In a dynamic, fast-changing market, the representative may be briefed to take on an information-gathering role, finding out through personal contacts who is saying what to whom, and what moves are likely to be planned.

Figure 17.1 summarises the range of typical tasks of the sales representative, each of which is defined below.

Prospecting

Prospecting is finding new potential customers who have the willingness and ability to purchase. For Rentokil Tropical Plants, for example, the role of the sales representative is to contact a range of potential clients including offices, hotels, shopping

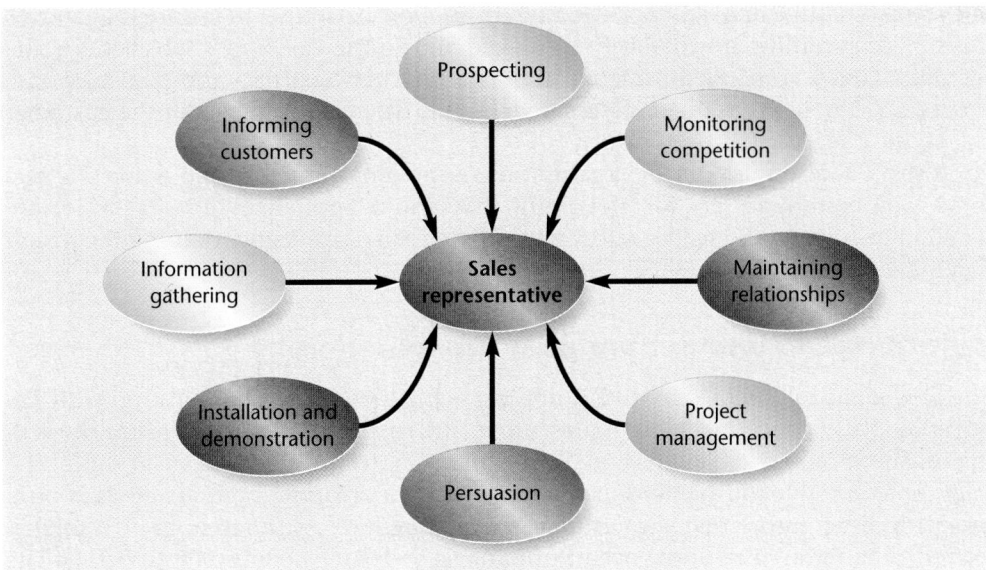

FIGURE 17.1

FIGURE 17.1

Typical tasks of the sales representative

centres and restaurants to design and recommend individual displays of tropical plants on a supply and maintenance basis. Prospecting is an important task, particularly for organisations entering a new market segment or for those offering a new product line with no established customer base.

> **Example** When Pennine Telecom was appointed as a major Dolphin Telecommunications service provider, it had to employ a sales team to launch a new communications technology for businesses. The new communication system offered two-way radio, cellular phone, paging and large volume data transfer within one system. Most of the early work of the sales team was to find potential customers through cold calling and by appointment and then to convince them of the usage benefits of the system compared with its existing one.

Informing

Informing is giving prospective customers adequate, detailed and relevant information about products and services on offer. In organisational markets, once contact has been made with prospects, the sales representative needs to stimulate sufficient information exchange to ensure a technical and commercial match that is better than the competition.

Persuading

Persuading is helping the prospective customer to analyse the information provided, in the light of their needs, in order to come to the conclusion that the product being offered is the best solution to their problem. Sometimes, presenting the main product benefits is sufficient to convince the buyer of the wisdom of selecting that supplier. On other occasions, especially with purchases that are technically or commercially more complex, the persuasion might have to be very subtle and varied, according to the concerns of the different members of the buying team.

Installing and demonstrating

Particularly with technical, organisational purchases, the buyer may need considerable support and help to get the equipment installed and to train staff in its use. The sales representative may join a wider team of support personnel to ensure that all this takes place according to whatever was agreed and to the customer's satisfaction. The representative's continued presence acts as a link between pre- and post-purchase events, and implies that the representative has not stopped caring about the customer just because the sale has been made.

This role is also relevant for organisations supplying the retail and wholesale sectors. Area merchandisers for DeLonghi household appliances, for example, are required to support the selling effort with in-store merchandising, training retail staff and making product presentations in store.

Co-ordinating within their own organisation

The role of the sales representative is not just about forward communication with the buyer. It is also concerned with 'representing' the customer's interests within the selling organisation. Whether concerned with financial, technical or logistical issues, the sales representative must co-ordinate and sometimes organise internal activities on a project basis to ensure that the customer's needs are met. At Duracell, the UK market leader in batteries, a national account manager is responsible for all aspects of the relationship with the large grocery chains. This includes external roles of display, distribution and promotional planning as well as internal co-ordination of logistics and product category management. Similarly in SKF, an account manager for high volume users would be expected to co-ordinate technical problem solving, supply schedules, logistics and contractual matters.

Maintaining relationships

Once an initial sale has been made, it might be the start of an on-going relationship. In many cases, a single sale is just one of a stream of transactions and thus cannot be considered in isolation from the total relationship. An important role for the sales representative is to manage the relationship rather than just the specifics of a particular sale. This means that in many organisations, more substantial and critical relationships have a 'relationship manager' to handle the various facets of the

With complex civil engineering projects such as the second Severn Crossing, building and maintaining relationships with key specifiers and influencers is a major selling task.

Source: Laing-GTM.

buyer–seller evolution (Turnbull and Cunningham, 1981). In some cases, the sales representative might have only one relationship to manage, but in others, the representative might have to manage a network based in a particular sector.

> **Example** The prime responsibility of an account manager at Colgate-Palmolive is to maintain and develop business relationships with major multiple retailer accounts. These relationships in some cases go back over many years. In order to achieve this, the emphasis is on co-operation and customer development through working together in such areas as category management, logistics and merchandising. There is a need to ensure a close fit between retail requirements and Colgate-Palmolive's brand strategies. This means that the account manager must be able to analyse brand and category information in order to develop plans that will help sales of Colgate's personal and household care products. Any account manager who sought short-term sales gains at the expense of customer trust and goodwill would not benefit Colgate-Palmolive's long-term plans for the account.

Information and feedback gathering

The gathering of information and the provision of feedback emphasises the need for representatives to keep their eyes and ears open, and to indulge in two-way communication with the customers they deal with. 'Grapevine' gossip about what is happening in the industry might, for example, give valuable early warning about big planned purchases in the future, or about potential customers who are dissatisfied with their current supplier. Both of these situations would offer opportunities to the organisation that heard about them early enough to make strategic plans about how to capitalise on them. In terms of relationships with existing customers, sales representatives are more likely than anyone to hear about the things that the customer is unhappy about. The representative is in an ideal position, therefore, to make sure something is done to reassure the customer or to put the defect right before the customer's dissatisfaction gets out of hand. It is well worthwhile for the representative to report back even minor problems to give central management as detailed a picture as possible about reaction to products and offerings.

This feedback role is even more important when developing business in export markets, where the base of accumulated knowledge might not be very strong. Personal contacts can help to add to that knowledge over time (Johanson and Vahlne, 1977).

Monitoring competitor action

The representative works out in the field, meeting customers and, in all probability, competitors. As well as picking up snippets about what competitors are planning and who they are doing business with, the representative can provide valuable information about how his or her organisation's products compare with those of the competition in the eyes of the purchasers. During the course of sales presentations, prospective customers can be subtly probed to find out what they think are the relative strengths and weaknesses of competing products, what they consider to be the important features and benefits in that kind of product, and how the available offerings score relative to each other (Lambert *et al.*, 1990).

Thus while selling remains the central activity for a sales representative, the roles of prospecting for new customers, maintaining communication links with customers, servicing customers' needs before and after sale and information gathering are no less important in enhancing the selling process and maximising the investment in such a labour-intensive promotional element.

FORMS OF PERSONAL SELLING

It has already been suggested that different market situations and different product and customer types will vary the demands made on a sales force. These variations relate to the amount of selling effort that needs to be done and the degree of selling skill required to identify and satisfy customer needs. It is important to identify the level of selling required, because the more an organisation demands of its sales force in terms of expertise or skill in handling important long-term customer relationships, the more it has to pay them. There is simply no point in employing a high quality group of professional sales people who can undertake all the roles defined in the previous section if all you want them to do is sit by the phone and fill in order forms. That is an inefficient waste of resources.

Accepting, then, that not all sales representatives will be required to fulfil all those roles, it is possible to define three broad categories of sales representative: the **order taker**, the **order maker** and **sales support** (Moncrief, 1988).

Order takers

As the title implies, order takers tend to have a somewhat administrative role. They either have a regular set pattern of customer contact, or wait for customers to contact them or to come to them. Generally, they are only concerned with routine or low involvement purchasing. This category can be further divided into two subgroups.

External order takers

External order takers are mainly concerned with processing orders where initial contracts have been agreed. The buyer–supplier relationship already exists, and most of the concern is with re-ordering and stocking up. In such cases, the important details of the transaction are already known (pricing, discounts, product offering) and so the representative's role is simply to note details of quantity required and make sure the order is duly processed. In selling to major retailers it is usual for the initial contact to be handled by other, more senior sales people.

The external order taker is typical in selling to retailers, and may have perhaps one or two added functions. A junior sales representative with a confectionery manufacturer, for example, might be given responsibility for visiting garage forecourt shops not only to replenish stock, but also to check displays to make sure that the organisation's products are being given adequate space relative to the competition. The job involves a minimal amount of new selling. The external order taker may also be involved in arranging in-store displays, or in helping the customer to implement special promotions.

Where a steady routine of order taking has been established, the customer may become dependent on the predictability of the representative's visit to keep their own shelves stocked and thus their own business running smoothly. The importance of the external order taker, therefore, as representing the familiar, friendly and reliable face of the supplier should not be underestimated.

Example Aico Ltd manufactures smoke, heat and carbon monoxide alarms. The company mainly deals through the electrical wholesale trade, so the role of the sales representative is to call frequently on existing accounts within a defined geographic area. The sales representative would not only be expected to take orders, but would also ensure that merchandising, stocking and promotions are being used to the full as a means of selling goods on to retailers and the electrical trade. Also in the electrical trade, Pact (http://www.pact-int.co.uk) employs merchandising representatives to manage in-store displays and to take repeat orders from established customers. This is achieved in part by examining stock and sales patterns in a customer's account to ensure that adequate stock levels are being held.

Inside order takers

Inside order takers remain within the confines of the employing organisation and wait for customers to come to them. Again, they can commonly be found in retailing and distribution. A retailer might telephone a manufacturer requesting an urgent delivery of stock. The inside order taker will receive and process that request. A sales assistant working within a retail store waiting for a customer to come through the door is also an inside order taker.

The role of inside order takers may vary. Some will need to be able to answer simple questions, take orders, check delivery and complete transactions. At the other extreme, all that is needed is a telephone sales clerk to handle all incoming calls and to take orders with the minimum of customer contact. An inside order taker of the latter type is likely to be employed either with well-understood products in a straight rebuy situation, or where the buying situation is not at all complex. For example, mail order catalogue companies now use inside order takers to handle telephone sales. The consumer phones up, gives their personal details and the product order to the telephonist, who inputs the data into a computer and can thus immediately tell the customer whether the goods are still available and confirm the order.

Although order taking may seem to be a low level activity, it is nevertheless an important sales function. It is true that order takers do rely on other sales staff or the general marketing effort for contacts, but they represent an efficient means of processing and servicing large numbers of customers properly.

The essence of order taking is not to get involved in detailed explanation, negotiation or new selling. Where the sales representative's role does extend to include those things, or incorporates product demonstration, such as trying to sell a car to a consumer, then the sales representative moves into the next category, order makers.

Order makers

The order maker is what most people understand by the term 'sales representative'. The order maker has to find prospective customers, identify customer-specific problems and needs, sell the appropriate product, then assist with installation and training. In other words, the order maker has to take on most of the roles outlined at Fig. 17.1 above.

The order maker therefore needs a good understanding of each prospective customer's situation and how the product or service being sold can match with that. Order making demands a high level of creativity, the ability to explain and persuade, and the ability and willingness to build relationships with customers. These requirements clearly have implications for the kinds of skills needed and training needed to develop a truly professional approach to the job.

There are two broad facets of order making. One is the generation of new business, requiring an ability to identify and make initial contact. The second is a focus on enhancing the long-term relationship with an existing customer, not just by keeping them topped up with supplies of the current product they already purchase, but by extending the range of products they buy. If they buy more of the same, that is order taking; if they buy products that they have never bought before, that is order making. This means a very close relationship with customers and an in-depth appreciation of their situation and problems.

Attracting new customers can be very demanding. Potential buyers are approached by sales representatives from many organisations, so why should they listen to you or treat you any more kindly than any of the others? Furthermore, when economic times are hard, there is much buyer inertia, meaning that they will put off buying for as long as possible, and then only buy what they really need. The representative has to find a way of cutting through this inertia. Even if the buyer does listen and is will-

Example Microgen is a leading company in the storage, retrieval and processing of information services for business. The sales representative in the company must always be seeking new business solutions to improve customer operational efficiency. This is often taking place with new clients and so high level relationship building skills are required. The salesperson has to take the client from first meeting through to a decision to ordering, and often beyond. Although the challenges are great, so too are the rewards, with on target earnings of up to £100 000 per annum (http://www.microgen.co.uk).

ing in principle to purchase, the time taken between the initial contact and the first significant order places great strain on the sales representative, especially in a market where there may be many alternative products.

Maintaining existing customers can also be very demanding. The representative must not only protect those customers from the competition, but also ensure that the on-going purchase pattern is maintained and even improved with new applications and technology. The representative has also to be alert to opportunities arising from existing customers – don't forget that customers can be a great source of new ideas.

Although order making can be very effective in creating the new customers that keep an organisation moving forward and growing, it is nevertheless a costly part of promotion. The organisation needs to reserve the order making effort for worthwhile prospects and high profile customers, and not waste it on routine follow-up work.

There are risks in classifying selling roles into the three broad groups mentioned above, as it may be a poor guide to selecting the most appropriate selling skills and characteristics. The 1990s have seen the emergence of two powerful forces that have had a major impact on selling. First, relationship management and maintaining the long-term trust and confidence of customers has shifted the emphasis to high level selling activities. Second, order taking is progressively being replaced by telemarketing and field merchandising, both of which will be discussed in Chapter 18. To Sujan *et al.* (1994) it is the difference between effort quality (i.e. working to improve the conversion rate) and effort quantity (i.e. order taking). Darmone (1998) also highlighted the problems of adopting the three categories in dynamic sales environments and proposed that the focus should shift to the amount and processing complexity of information, along with the demands of time management and allocating priorities across a set of customers. The more demanding each becomes, the higher the level of selling skills required.

Sales support

Sales support is a broad term encompassing a variety of staff whose role is to augment the efforts of the mainstream sales force. Sales support staff could, for example, take on the burden of locating and initially screening potential new customers, passing that information on to the sales force so that the real selling process can begin. They may also provide sales training, provide technical support or take care of after sales service.

There are two interesting categories of support staff worth mentioning.

Missionary sales representatives

Missionary sales representatives focus on a particular market segment or product to give enquiries and sales an initial lift. They do not generally work with the selling organisation's customers, but with the customer's own customers. Pharmaceutical companies, for instance, use missionaries to persuade general practitioners to prescribe new drugs for their patients. The actual sales of the drugs, however, are made by the conventional sales force to pharmacists or wholesalers. The missionary is effectively implementing a *pull strategy* (as defined in p. 568 *et seq.*), by communicating with groups a couple of

MARKETING IN ACTION   Is the sales rep an endangered species?

A sales representative is an expensive asset for an organisation to maintain. Representatives need cars, computers, mobile phones, samples, presentation equipment and administrative support. They also run up bills for hotel accommodation and entertaining clients. When economic times are hard, therefore, many organisations cut their sales forces or rationalise them to save on costs. Other factors have also led to a reduction in the number of sales representatives. In consumer goods markets, for instance, there has been a reduction in the number of small independent retailers and a corresponding increase in the share of business taken by the big multiples. The bigger retailers tend to have computerised stock control systems with on-line ordering, so that there is no need for a representative to visit individual branches so often (if at all). HP Foods, for example, had between 70 and 100 sales representatives in the 1970s. In the 1990s, the number has been slimmed down to 12 business development executives who each manage a portfolio of national and regional accounts. The largest proportion of HP's orders, however, comes in via computers or the telephone.

There is, of course, still a role for the representative in consumer goods markets in visiting smaller retailers, both to take orders and to help with promotional events or point-of-sale displays. Many organisations, however, find it cheaper and more efficient to use contract sales staff from field marketing agencies for such tasks. When Mars launched Celebrations, for example (*see* Chapter 7), a field marketing agency was used rather than Mars' own sales force to work with cash and carry and other wholesalers to provide free samples, provide product information and to negotiate special point-of-sale displays. The benefit of contract staff is that the organisation only has to pay for them when they want them, and can have as large or small a 'sales force' as a particular task or project requires. Contract sales staff tend to work in small territories and thus have established close relationships with the retailers and other customers that they regularly visit.

Unilever, Procter and Gamble, Mars and Kraft Jacob Suchard all make extensive use of field marketing agencies, leaving their own sales teams to concentrate on more complex considerations such as category management and logistics with their major accounts. With multinationals being such important field marketing users, a number of agencies are offering pan-European field marketing campaigns.

Some organisations might worry, however, that because contract sales staff are not employed by them full time, there might be questions about their loyalty and motivation. Agencies are well aware of this and try to overcome it by setting up quality control systems to monitor the performance of their staff in the field, and ensuring that staff are fully and properly briefed at the start of an assignment. To try to engender 'loyalty' to the task in hand, the agency will also ensure that a member of staff is only working for one client in a particular product market at a time. Because of the amount of time contract staff spend in the field and because of the wide range of customers and product types they deal with, these agencies can amass a wealth of data about what is going on in the market that a company's own sales force would not have either the time or the resources to collect. Agencies can thus feed information back to clients, providing an additional benefit to their service.

As field marketing has grown in popularity, so its role has expanded from just being point-of-sale merchandising. The contract sellers' sales forces are becoming better trained, more IT literate and skilled in providing useful market information back to the contracting company. There are two broad areas in which contract sales staff are currently used: in fmcg, dealing with retailers, and in door to door selling, covering a wide range of products and services including cable television, utilities and financial services. High pressure selling and mis-selling were exposed in the utilities sector, where untrained and unscrupulous sales people made a wide range of promises that could not be honoured to encourage consumers to change energy suppliers. Most reputable field marketing agencies seek to avoid such problems through careful recruitment, appropriate training and local control. For example, it has been suggested that the ratio of sales representatives to managers should be 10:1 in fmcg and 6:1 in door to door selling.

So, the sales representative might not be about to become extinct. What is certain is that organisations are rethinking how they manage and organise their sales forces and their selling processes. Thus the role and the tasks of representatives will change, and how they are employed might change, but they will always be needed in some capacity.

Sources: Gofton (1998); *Marketing* (1998,1999); Miles (1998); Rines (1995).

stages further down the distribution chain than their own organisation or its direct customers. Figure 17.2 summarises how the missionary approach works.

Sales engineers

Sales engineers, on the other hand, are directly concerned with the organisation's customers and the end users of its products. Their concern is with the technical or application problems of the product. They could be called in at any stage of the sales process. Particularly with a complex organisational product, in the early stages of the selling process they may have to advise on systems design. Later in the process, they might help with installation, training or even maintenance.

Often, these support staff can pick up early warning of problems and emerging opportunities, so they need to have good links with the main sales force, and the organisation needs to have mechanisms in place to make sure that the knowledge they pick up in the field is shared and used.

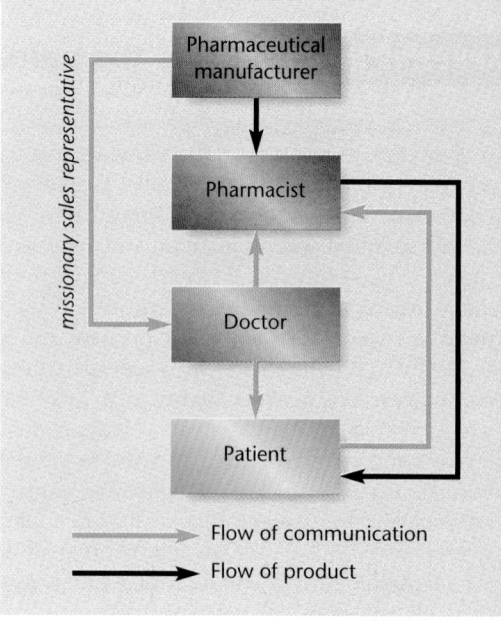

FIGURE 17.2

The role of the missionary

THE PERSONAL SELLING PROCESS

Many textbooks, videos and gurus claim to offer the secret to successful sales presentations. In reality, there is no one approach that is right for all situations, nor is there any one approach that is right for all types of sales representative. This is hardly surprising, because the essential strength of personal selling is the human contact, and the infinite flexibility of the sales representative to create a unique and tailored approach for each prospective customer. At the heart of the sales process is the sales representative's ability to build a relationship with the buyer that is sufficiently strong to achieve a deal that benefits both parties. As shown in Chapter 4, organisations need to buy if they are to achieve their objectives. In many situations the main decision relates to *supplier choice* rather than whether or not to buy. The sales representative's role is to highlight the attractions of the specification, support, service and commercial package on offer. Differences between products, markets, organisational philosophies and even individuals will all have a bearing on the style and effectiveness of the selling activity.

Although it has just been suggested that personal selling does not lend itself to a prescribed formula, it is possible to define a number of broad stages through which most selling episodes will pass (Russell *et al.*, 1977). Depending on the product, the market, the organisations and individuals involved, the length of time spent in any one of the stages will vary, as will the way in which each stage is implemented (Pedersen *et al.*, 1986). Nevertheless, the generalised analysis offered here provides a useful basis for beginning to understand what contributes to successful personal selling.

Figure 17.3 shows the flow of stages through a personal selling process. It does not begin with meeting the customer; that itself is the outcome of an earlier pre-contact stage in which the prospective customer has to be identified. The actual selling stages themselves end with closing the sale, but the model also proposes the extra, necessary stage of following up to ensure a satisfied customer in the post-purchase period. Clearly, at any stage of such a complex human activity things can, and often do, go wrong. Although **conversion rates** between enquiries and real orders vary considerably, it is always useful, if the process ends in failure to make a sale, to look at each stage of the process to establish just where things went wrong. The various stages in the personal selling process are discussed in full below.

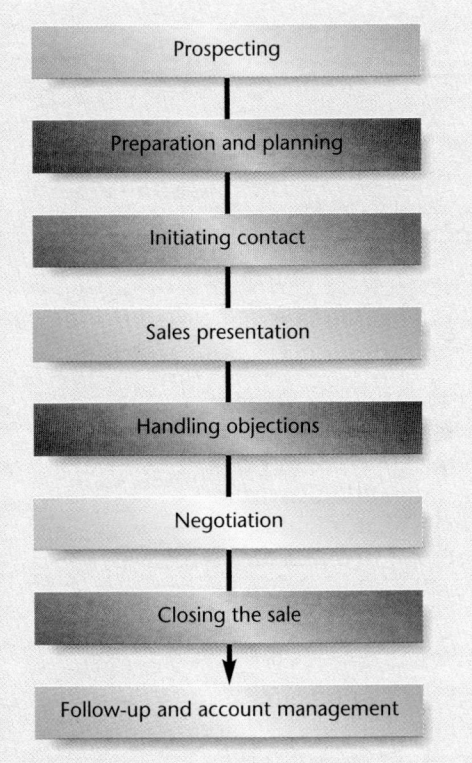

FIGURE 17.3

The personal selling process

Prospecting

Before sales representatives can get down to the real job of selling something, they have to have someone to sell to. This means that there has to be some sort of mechanism for identifying and locating prospects, matching up the prospects' likely needs with what the selling organisation has to offer. In some organisations, perhaps those selling an industrial product with a specific application to a relatively small number of easily defined organisational customers, this will be a highly structured activity, involving sales representatives and support staff, and will lead to the representative going out on a call knowing that the prospect is potentially fruitful. In contrast, double glazing companies often employ canvassers to walk the streets knocking on doors to see if householders are likely prospects. This is not a particularly efficient use of the representatives' time, as most people will say that they are not interested, but in promoting an infrequently purchased, high priced product, yet in a mass market, it is difficult to see what else in the way of prospecting they can do. Consumers seeing advertising for double glazing might get as far as thinking, 'I must get round to doing something about that bathroom window', but because of the expense and the mess involved, it is too easy to put it off and not respond. More direct stimulation, such as that provided by personal selling, is needed to turn that lethargy into 'I will do something'.

The latter example also shows that prospecting is especially difficult with one-time purchases where there is a constant need to replenish contacts. Once a household has bought double glazing, it is not going to repeat the purchase for many years, and so the organisation is constantly starting from scratch, putting considerable resources and efforts into prospecting. In a market where there is the potential for large repeat sales, prospecting may be a smaller part of the selling role, confined to replacing declining or lost customers.

In an organisational rather than a consumer market, the sales representative needs a prospect bank, a pool of potential customers to be drawn on as appropriate. This bank is often a combination of company-inspired and self-researched names and details of prospects. Table 17.1 identifies the wide range of sources of prospects.

Company-inspired prospects are taken from a wide range of sources that can be categorised into three types. First, there are potential customers who have made enquiries or responded to advertising, but not been followed up already. Second, there are those who have already been approached in an exploratory way, for example through telemarketing, and look promising enough to deserve further encouragement. Third, and most problematic, are the lists of names. These lists might be purchased from a list broker or be compiled from a trade directory or a list of organisations attending a particular trade exhibition. While these lists will conform to broad criteria relating to the types of organisations or people on them, so that they are generally relevant to the seller, they are still 'colder' than the first two categories outlined above. This is because there is no means of telling whether those on the list are even in the market for your sort of product, never mind whether they are ready, willing and able to do business with you. Telemarketing support staff may be able to work through such a list and convert some of the names on it into the second category to save the sales representative from much pointless **cold calling**.

TABLE 17.1
Sources of prospects

Company inspired	Sales representative inspired
■ Sales records	■ Scanning directories
■ Invoices	■ Referrals – direct or via sales support staff
■ Advertising responses	■ Observation of new developments
■ Exhibitions and trade show lists	■ Watching the media
■ General enquiries	■ Cold calling
■ Lists from telemarketing campaigns	
■ Purchased lists	

Sales representatives may have to develop their own prospect banks. Their activity falls into two broad classes. First, there may be referrals, either from word of mouth from contacts outside the organisation, or from the telemarketing support staff discussed above. These are 'warm' contacts. Second, they can also compile lists from directories, or from scanning the media for relevant company news that might open up an opportunity. As with the telemarketers above, this might lead to a session of preliminary cold calling (by phone or in person) to establish whether this person or organisation really is a viable prospect.

In summary, there are three stages in prospecting:

1 Generating lists of **leads**, i.e. those individuals or organisations who could be prospective customers.
2 An initial assessment of whether each lead can be developed into a **prospect**, i.e. somebody who is likely to want and can afford to buy the product. This screening is often done prior to a visit.
3 This third stage often only comes after initial contact has confirmed that there is a need (whether the prospect realises that there is a need or not) and that the prospect has the ability, if so motivated, to purchase. This is a **qualified prospect**.

The outcome of this stage of the selling process is a qualified prospect list from which more targeted selling effort can proceed.

Preparation and planning

Identifying a qualified prospect is only the beginning of the process. Before the real selling begins, it is very important to obtain further information on the prospect in order to prepare the best and most relevant sales approach and to plan tactics.

In selling to an organisational customer, this may mean scanning a number of company reports, assessing the norms for that industry in relation to likely buying criteria and needs. Analysing the prospect's company report might promise indications of the strategic direction in which it is moving, as well as revealing its financial situation. It is also necessary to think about the kind of purchasing structures that the representative is going to have to work through, identifying the most likely influencers and decision makers. In industrial situations, for example, a key question may be whether to target the engineering staff early on to get their technical support for the product, encouraging them to re-specify their needs in your favour, or whether to try to motivate the formal buyers to consider alternative sources (i.e. you). Look back at p. 161 *et seq.* to remind yourself about the structure and importance of the buying centre in organisational purchasing behaviour. In addition to finding out who to concentrate on, it is also useful to find out as much as possible about the application of the product and the features and benefits required. This allows the representative to construct a **sales presentation** that will be relevant to the buyer and thus will have more chance of engaging their attention and being persuasive.

Sales representatives in organisational markets are fortunate that sufficient information exists about their buyers to allow them to prepare so well in advance. In consumer markets, it is more likely that representatives have to think on their feet, analysing customers while they are face to face with them. If a couple walk into a car showroom, the sales representative has to work out how serious they are about buying, what alternatives they are considering, what their decision-making criteria are, how price sensitive they are, who the main user will be, and who has the ultimate decision-making responsibility. As if that wasn't enough, there is also the problem of working out the best product offering and deal to match those needs and that profile. If, in the course of a 10- or 20-minute encounter, the sales representative makes any misjudgement about that couple and their needs, then in all likelihood the sale is lost.

Where it is possible, therefore, doing the homework is essential, and it often needs to be very thorough, especially in situations involving large, complex projects with stiff competition. Also, if the competition is already well entrenched in doing business with a prospect, it is even more important to find out as much as possible in advance, since getting that customer to switch supplier will probably be an uphill task unless you can find the right approach with the right people.

Initiating contact

Making the first contact with the prospect is a delicate operation. There are two ways of approaching this stage. First, the initial telephone call that qualifies the prospect may be used to solicit an appointment. Failure to achieve that means that the selling process cannot begin. The phone call should not, however, be allowed to draw the sales representative into detailed discussion, as it is unlikely that serious and fruitful dialogue can take place without the use of sales aids and direct contact. Before the telephone call, an introductory letter may be sent to introduce the sales representative and the organisation so that the phone call does not come as a total surprise, but there still remains the important objective of making an appointment.

The second approach is to use cold calling. This means turning up on the doorstep in the hope that someone will see you, as the double glazing sales representative does. This can be very wasteful in terms of time and travel. There is no guarantee that the representative will get access to the key people, who probably would not in any case be able to spare time without a prior appointment. Even if the representative does get access, it is unlikely that a properly tailored sales presentation will have been prepared if there has not been preliminary contact with the prospect. Cold callers are often seen as time wasters, and do not do themselves or their organisations any favours in the eyes of the prospects.

Once an approach has been made and an appointment secured, the next stage is the initial call. This helps the representative to discover whether the initial assessment of the customer's likely need is borne out in practice. In these early meetings, it is important to build up rapport, mutual respect and trust between buyer and seller before the more serious business discussion gets underway. The time spent in establishing this relationship is well spent. It helps to build a solid foundation for the later stages of discussion.

The challenge at this point is to demonstrate to the prospect that it is worthwhile to talk about their needs, and to entertain the idea of revising their product purchasing specifications or their current practices. The danger here is of allowing the meeting to develop into a detailed product discussion before the prospect's real needs have been fully explored. In some cases, establishing these needs may mean undertaking a more detailed survey of current usage or application before a more formal sales presentation takes place. Remember that customers do not buy products, they buy solutions to problems. The product should be presented to the prospect within the context of how that product is a solution to an agreed problem, not as the sole and abstract object of the discussion.

Again, it must be stressed that it is not easy to generalise. Different products, applications, competitive states, organisational and even individual characteristics are all likely to have an impact on the length and depth of the exploration of customer needs.

The sales presentation

At last, the representative has enough insight and information to allow the preparation of the sales presentation itself that lies at the heart of the selling process. The ease of its preparation and its effectiveness in practice owe a great deal to the thoroughness and quality of the work done in the earlier stages. The objective of the sales presentation is to show how the product offering and the customer's needs match. The presentation must not be product oriented, but be concerned with what the product can do for that particular customer. In other words, do not sell the features, sell the benefits.

Three approaches are possible, although there is a tendency to rely mainly on the third one.

Stimulus–response

The stimulus–response approach works on the simple assumption that given the right stimulus, the customer will respond in the right way. It is most appropriate in consumer markets where people are buying low-risk, low involvement products. In McDonald's, for example, the sales staff will always suggest a drink or french fries if you only ask for a burger. The stimulus is the suggestion of a drink, and that is meant to prompt you into making an instant decision and saying yes to something that otherwise you might not have asked for. Similarly, although buying a pair of shoes can be more of a limited decision-making process (in that they cost a bit more than a burger, and are purchased less frequently), the stimulus–response technique is also used to prompt the purchase of the less expensive extras such as laces and polish.

Formula selling

Formula selling involves training representatives in a standard approach so that they can follow a rigid set of rules as the 'ideal method' to cover the relevant (and irrelevant!) points and achieve results. Formula selling is becoming increasingly less common. One reason for its decline is that customers are wise to it. Another is that it is relatively ineffective and inefficient as it does not feed off an essential strength of personal selling, namely tailoring the message to the customer.

This approach, therefore, usually means that the representative imparts a standard bundle of information to a set pattern, regardless of circumstances and needs. Its last bastions are in door to door selling and telemarketing. Its biggest problem is that it does not allow spontaneity and feedback from the customer, nor does it encourage interaction between buyer and seller. The customer feels that the representative has a set speech to get through, come what may, and begins to resent that they are not being consulted, yet are expected to provide a passive audience to listen to material of doubtful relevance.

Need satisfaction

The most widely used approach, and probably the most effective, is need satisfaction, even though it is more difficult to implement. It involves listening to the customer, asking questions to identify needs, assessing their reactions and tailoring the presentation to suit the circumstance. It is a problem solving approach.

In organisational markets, the need satisfaction technique should be well under way by the selling stage if the preparation has been done properly. The customer's reaction to the sales presentation should concern matters of fine detail, to be explored and resolved. It should not throw up surprises about needs and wants for the representative to have to deal with. In contrast, in a consumer market, selling cars for example, the representative is on more of a knife edge, and the listening and questioning at this stage are incredibly important to establish the customer profile and needs. Clearly, such an approach would not be appropriate in a McDonald's retailing situation where a large number of customers choosing from a very limited range of low-risk product options need to be handled quickly.

In some organisational selling situations, it could even be suggested that the sales representative is acting in a consultative role, using a wider knowledge of the customer's industry to propose informed solutions to the customer's problems. Some advertising agencies, such as Barker's, specialise in advertising for the higher education sector. By building up sound experience of the advertising needs of universities and colleges, especially when recruiting students, they are able to demonstrate a wide and detailed appreciation of the market. Of course, the limiting factor is that some universities would prefer not to use the same agency as their primary competitors (*see* p. 625).

Whatever the broad approach taken, there may be some practicalities to be handled as part of the presentation. The representative may have to demonstrate the product, for example. The product or sample used must look right, and will need to be explained, not in technical terms, necessarily, but in terms of how it offers particular benefits and solutions. A demonstration is a powerful element of a sales presentation, because it gets the prospect involved and encourages conversation and questions. It provides a focus that can dispel any lingering awkwardness between buyer and seller. Also, in getting their hands on the product itself, or a sample, the prospect is brought very close to the reality of the product and can begin to see for themselves what it can do for them. Even in a consumer market, this is important. The car dealer takes prospective buyers out for a test drive so that they can experience the 'feel' of the car, and better imagine themselves owning it. The buyers feel that they are judging the car for themselves, and not just taking the sales representative's word for it. The test drive tells most prospective car buyers much more about the character of the vehicle than half an hour of peering under the bonnet listening to detailed technical specifications from the dealer.

Even where it may be difficult to demonstrate the product, other involvement devices may be used. In organisational markets particularly, it may be possible to visit existing customers who have purchased similar products or systems. This gives the opportunity to see the product in application, and to talk to someone who is reasonably unbiased not only about the product, but also about their experience of the seller's after sales service and ability to honour their promises.

If none of that is possible, then at least the presentation should incorporate plenty of audio-visual aids to keep the attention of the prospect and to prevent any danger of monotony creeping in. Involving members of the sales support team may also help to provide a more detailed and interesting picture for the prospect, and help to answer any of the wider questions or needs that might arise.

Handling objections

It is indeed a rare and skilful sales representative who can complete an entire sales presentation without the prospect coming out with words to the effect of 'that's all very well, but ...'. At any stage in the selling process that involves the customer, objections can and probably will be made. These may arise for various reasons: lack of understanding; lack of interest; misinformation; a need for reassurance; or genuine concern. The sales representative must be prepared to overcome objections where possible, as otherwise the sale is likely to be lost completely. If the customer is concerned enough to raise an objection, then the representative must have the courtesy to answer it in some way. Homespun wisdom among seasoned sales representatives argues that the real selling does not begin until the customer raises an objection.

Table 17.2 summarises typical objections that occur time after time, regardless of the specific selling situation. Some objections are so predictable that it should be pos-

sible to anticipate them and answer them even before the customer gets around to raising them! It is important to develop
counter-arguments. For example, many customers in many different types of market will raise an objection to the effect that the
whole thing is too expensive for them. Whether this is a real concern or a last-ditch attempt to provoke the representative into
price concessions is irrelevant. The representative must have an
answer to it, perhaps using it as an opening to discuss credit or
leasing terms, or to reiterate the savings made by switching to
this product or investing in it.

Organisations that do not subscribe to the formula approach
to selling often do train their sales staff to handle specific objections that commonly arise in their field in a set way. The
following are a selection of objection handling techniques commonly used in personal selling. Each is appropriate for a different kind of objection.

TABLE 17.2
Typical objections

- Your company
- Your product
- Your service
- Your pricing
- You
- You are not competitive enough
- Delivery delay
- I can't afford it
- I don't need it

Ask the objection back

If the prospect comes out with something vague, then it is appropriate for the representative to ask for further elaboration, either to define the objection better, or to find
out whether the objection is real or a stalling excuse. Exploring the objection also
allows the representative and the customer to define whether the objection is fundamental or peripheral.

If a buyer says 'I think your product is not as good as product x', the sales representative should explore what is meant by the use of the word 'good'. This could cover a
whole range of different areas in the competitive offering. The representative's
response may therefore be designed to explore in more detail the underlying problem
by asking 'In what way is it not as good?'

Agree and counter

Agreeing with the objection and countering it is often called the 'yes, but' technique.
Where the objection is founded in fact, all the representative can legitimately do is
agree with the substance of it, then find a compensating factor to outweigh it. Thus if
the prospect argues that the product being sold is more expensive than the competition's, the representative can reply with 'Yes, I agree that value for money is
important. Although our product is more expensive initially, you will find that the
day-to-day running costs and the annual maintenance add up to a lot less ...'. Such a
technique avoids creating excessive tension and argument, because the customer feels
that their objection has been acknowledged and satisfactorily answered.

Boomerang

A variation on the previous technique involves turning the objection into a reason for
buying. Thus if the prospect says something like 'This model's getting a bit old; I
think I'd be better going for the new generation', then the sales representative might
reply with 'This model's technology has been around for a number of years, and that's
the very reason why you should buy it. It's tried and trusted – our customers have five
million of these components in service and the failure rate is less than 0.5 per cent.
The new generation model is twice the price and yet to be proved in practice.'

Feel, felt, found

The previous techniques have all answered rational objections, based on some aspect
of the product or the deal. If the prospect retreats from rationality, and appears to be
making fairly inarticulate, emotional objections, perhaps demonstrating a lack of confidence in their decision-making ability, then this is the appropriate technique to use.
Thus the prospect says, 'Well, I accept what you say, but I just don't feel certain about
this.' To this the representative replies, 'I understand how you feel. Many other people

have felt like that, but they've found that buying this product was actually the best decision.' In other words, the representative is offering the empathy, sympathy and reassurance that will bolster the prospect's confidence in the purchasing decision.

Denial

Denial is a dangerous technique to use unless you are very sure of your ground and your prospect. All the previous techniques have been careful not to contradict the prospect, but all have demonstrated diplomacy and sympathy with the prospect's point of view. Denial, on the other hand, involves telling the prospect that they are wrong. To reduce the risk of antagonising the prospect, any denial must be accompanied by proof of why the objection is wrong or misinformed. Even with proof, the prospect might still be offended that the representative has dared to contradict them, or might feel that somehow they have been made to look foolish, and they therefore decide to take their business elsewhere.

An indirect denial might take some of the edge off the situation. If, for example, the prospect says 'I've heard that you failed to fulfil your delivery promises to Bloggs & Co.,' the representative, rather than using the direct denial of 'No, that's not true', which is defensive and potentially antagonistic, might initially ask the objection back with a reply such as 'Where have you heard that, then?' The dialogue that follows this might allow the representative to discredit the source of the rumour or to set the facts straight without overtly telling the prospect that they are wrong. If the situation is handled well, the prospect may conclude that they were wrong, and the representative is saved from awkwardness.

All in all, handling objections requires a very careful response from representatives. They must not see objections as a call for them to say just anything to clinch the sale, since doing so will only lead to legal or relationship problems later. The representative must assess the situation, the type of objection and the mood of the customer and then choose the most appropriate style of response, without overstepping any ethical boundaries in terms of content. It is critical that winning the argument used to overcome the objection does not lead to a lost sale. Objections may interrupt the flow of the sales process either temporarily or permanently, and unless they are overcome, the final stages of the selling process cannot be achieved.

Negotiation

Some aspects of negotiation have already been covered at pp. 443 *et seq.*, since the trade-off between price and the package offered does tend to be the main subject of most negotiation. To put negotiation in its proper context within the selling process, this subsection broadens the view of negotiation, emphasising the effect of the relative balance of power between the two parties on their negotiating positions.

Once the main body of the sales presentation is drawing to a close, with all the prospect's questions and objections answered for the time being, the selling process may move into a negotiation phase. Negotiation is a 'give and take' activity in which both parties try to shape a deal that satisfies both of them. Negotiation assumes a basic willingness to trade, but does not necessarily lead to a final deal. The danger for the sales representative, of course, is that a deadlocked or delayed negotiation phase may allow a competitor to enter the fray.

There are two types of negotiation:

1 *The co-operative or win–win negotiation.* This assumes that by trading concessions, a better deal can result for both parties. Concessions need not centre on price alone. They can take in issues like delivery schedules, delivery or insurance costs, product specifications, trade-ins or credit terms. For example, the buyer may agree to pay the delivery charges, in return for the seller's agreement to offer an extended war-

ranty. The technique is to trade something that is relatively cheap for you, but is valuable to the other party. Thus an extended warranty costs little to the seller in reality, but means peace of mind and potential repair cost savings to the buyer.

This type of negotiation is especially prevalent when longer-term relationships are being built up. The seller might consider it worth giving away major concessions on a first deal in order to ensure future business from that buyer. There is little point, as a seller, in driving a hard bargain for short-term gain if the long-term relationship flounders as a result.

2 *The competitive negotiation.* The hard bargain focused on short-term gain is appropriate and typical in one-off situations. Rather than seeking a better deal for both parties, the emphasis is on gaining as much advantage as possible over the other party. It still may mean some trading of concessions, especially those that cost you little but are of value to the other party.

Despite the fact that deals are becoming more complex, sales staff are still expected to be able to negotiate. If they are going to be given the power to negotiate on behalf of the organisation, then they need clear guidelines on how far they are permitted to go in terms of concessions, and what the implications of those concessions would be. An extra month's credit, for example, could be quite expensive, particularly for an organisation with short-term cash flow problems, unless it is traded for another prized concession. This effectively means that the sales representative needs financial as well as behavioural training in order to handle complex and sometimes lengthy negotiations.

There are some matters that the representative can consider that might help to establish a successful negotiating position.

The obvious judgement to make concerns the *relative power balance* between buyer and seller. If the buyer has many alternative options, and does not appear to be particularly eager to have that representative's product specifically, then that representative might have to be prepared to give away a considerable amount of ground in order to make a sale. The activities of the competition might also affect what goes on between this buyer and this seller. If the competition have been very aggressive and have already made attractive offers to the buyer, then this seller might feel obliged to make a better offer, depending on how badly the sale is wanted. The only means of saving this situation is if the seller is astute enough not to get locked into purely price-based comparisons with the competition. The representative should, if possible, define the 'better offer' in terms of features, benefits and peripherals other than price, in order to create an offering that is less easy for the competition to copy or undercut, and to blur the distinction between competing products somewhat.

It is, of course, possible that the balance of power lies in the hands of the selling organisation, if it has a unique product, service or expertise to offer that would be difficult to source elsewhere. If that is the case, the seller can afford to be a little less accommodating in terms of concessions.

Another important consideration is the sales representative's assessment of the *limits* within which each party is negotiating. Both parties will enter the negotiation with some idea of their minimum and maximum boundaries in terms of what they want to get and what they are prepared to give way on. The buyer, for example, has minimum performance criteria to which the product must conform, and a maximum price that the organisation is prepared to pay for it. At the same time, the buyer will also have an upper price limit in mind, along with an idea of the extras desired, whether these relate to the product specifications or to peripheral service offerings, the provision of which would justify moving up closer to that limit. The selling organisation too will have defined minimum requirements, in terms of the rock-bottom price they are prepared to go down to, and the maximum they are prepared to give away in concessions. It is a delicate judgement, but if the seller can work out when the buyer is close to their absolute limit, it can make all the difference between a sale and a lost sale. Attempting to push the buyer beyond their threshold means that there is a real risk that they will withdraw from the process.

As a final point, it must be said that negotiation need not be a separate and discrete stage of the selling process. Negotiation may emerge implicitly during the process of handling objections, or may be an integral part of the next stage to be discussed, closing the sale.

Closing the sale

The closing stage of the personal selling process is concerned with reaching the point where the customer agrees to purchase. In most cases, it is the sales representative's responsibility to **close the sale**, to ask for the order. If the sales presentation has been well prepared, if the customer's questions and objections have been satisfactorily handled and if the negotiation issues have been largely resolved, then closure should flow quite naturally with no problems.

Where the representative is less sure of the prospect's state of mind, or where the prospect still seems to have doubts, the timing of the closure and the way in which it is done could affect whether a sale is made. Try to close the sale too soon, and the buyer might be frightened off; leave it too long, and the buyer might become irritated by the prolonged process and all the good work done earlier in the sales presentation will start to dissipate.

Watching the buyer's behaviour and listening to what they are saying might indicate that closure is near. The buyer's questions, for example, may become very trivial or the objections might dry up. The buyer might go quiet and start examining the product intently, waiting for the representative to make a move. The buyer's comments or questions might begin to relate to the post-purchase period, with a strong assumption that the deal has already been done.

A representative who thinks that the time to close is near, but is uncertain, might have to test the buyer's readiness to commit to a purchase. Also, if the prospect seems to be teetering on the edge of making a decision, then the representative might have to use a mechanism to give the buyer a gentle nudge in the direction of closure.

There are many ways of closing the sale (Jacoby and Craig, 1984), and a number are considered below.

Alternative close

The representative may offer the buyer a number of alternatives, each of which implies an agreement to purchase. The buyer's response gives an insight into how ready they are to commit themselves. Thus if the representative says, 'Would you like delivery to each of your stores or to the central distribution point?', there are two ways in which the buyer might respond. One way would be to choose one of the alternatives offered, in which case the sale must be very close, since the buyer is willing to get down to such fine detail. The other response would be something like, 'Wait a minute, before we get down to that, what about ...', showing that the buyer has not yet heard enough and may still have objections to be answered.

Assumptive close

In the assumptive close the sales representative assumes that the customer will buy and carries on into the details of the transaction. The representative will say, 'I'll arrange for delivery within two weeks then', to which the buyer can agree without argument; agree, but argue for one-week delivery time; or disagree and pull the dialogue back into the negotiation or objection handling stages.

Time pressure close

A buyer who is clearly on the edge of a decision may be triggered into action by being offered a limited response time. Thus a suggestion that this is the last item in stock and that if the buyer does not agree to purchase it now, the seller might not be able to source another, could be a powerful incentive to act. Threats of imminent price rises, stockouts, or of the type 'sale ends Saturday' can all increase the sense of urgency, but do run the risk of being challenged by the buyer. The representative needs to be sure that the time pressure can be justified.

The ease of bringing the sale to a close, and the type of closing problems that might arise, will depend on the commercial complexity of the transaction. Sometimes, negotiating a trial order or agreeing to 'sale or return' on goods may reduce the risks of purchase sufficiently to bring the sale to some kind of close. In some situations, the initial commitment to purchase may itself trigger a range of complex negotiations to finalise the deal.

Follow-up and account management

The sales representative's responsibility does not end once a sale has been agreed. As implied earlier at pp. 692 *et seq.*, the sales representative, as the customer's key contact point with the selling organisation, needs to ensure that the product is delivered on time and in good condition, that any installation or training promises are fulfilled and that the customer is absolutely satisfied with the purchase and is getting the best out of it.

MARKETING AND IT   **Three generations of sales force automation (SFA)**

Because the cost of maintaining a direct sales force is high, sales force productivity is an important issue for sales and marketing managers. In many industrial organisations, sales force costs are the largest single marketing expense item. A typical field representative will have a car, mobile phone, expense account and bonus scheme, but there are limits to the number of customers that can be met in any particular day. Many organisations complain that:

- sales force effectiveness is difficult to measure;
- potential business leads slip through the net;
- vital customer information remains hidden on scraps of paper or in the sales representative's head;
- if a sales representative leaves the company, important customer information also leaves;
- sales representatives are always busy but the sales results are often mediocre;
- bonus schemes fail to encourage sales teams to greater efforts.

In response, companies have looked at various methods of automating the sales force to improve productivity and increase sales. The technologies and tools that companies use to automate their sales forces vary significantly. The Yankee Group, a consultancy company, has identified three separate generations of SFA tools:

- *Generation 1: personal information and contact management*. The first generation of SFA tools, products such as ACT!, Goldmine and Maximizer, was designed to help sales representatives to manage contacts and time and increase their selling

effectiveness. Such powerful time- and contact-management tools had not existed previously and were accepted quickly and enthusiastically.
- *Generation 2: networked contact management*. The second generation of tools was essentially networked versions of the first, connecting the contact-tracking database and personal productivity tools of the sales force with the corporate network, contact and prospect database. Sales representatives were equipped with laptop computers that they synchronised or 'replicated' with the corporate network each day.
- *Generation 3: technology-enabled selling*. The third generation of SFA has its primary focus on making the sales force effective where it matters most: in front of the customer. The new generation of tools allows sales representatives to configure products, prepare proposals, give illustrations and quotes, and track orders, using their laptops.

The benefits of SFA can be significant. HP Foods, for example, which sells a variety of food products through shops and supermarkets, replaced its traditional sales force of 100 representatives with 12 business development executives equipped with mobile phones and computers, thus making significant cost savings without compromising service quality. The business case for automating the sales force does not have to stop with the sales representative. If it is extended further into the organisation, the benefits are far more wide reaching. Campbell's Soup, for example, invested $30mn in SFA for some 1000 sales representatives, sales administration, marketing, operations and IT employees in the USA and Canada. The New Jersey-based company, with customers including supermarket chains, other grocery retailers and food service vendors such as KFC and McDonald's, targeted savings of more than £18mn annually through shorter order-cycle times, more accurate invoicing and better control of funds used for product promotions. Campbell's efforts cut across a wide range of functions; distribution, pricing, invoicing, settlement and accounting.

Source: O'Connor and Galvin (1999).

Smile as you dial.
Source: Photodisc

At a more general level, the relationship with the customer still needs to be cultivated and managed. In an organisational market, contacts made with the range of staff involved in the buyer's decision-making unit need to be nurtured. Where the sale has resulted in an on-going supply situation, this may mean ensuring continued satisfaction with quality and service levels. Even with infrequently purchased items, on-going positive contact helps to ensure that when new business develops, that supplier will be well placed. In the case of the consumer buying a car, the sales representative will make sure in the early stages that the customer is happy with the car, and work to resolve any problems quickly and efficiently. In the longer term, direct responsibility usually passes from the representative to a customer care manager who will ensure that the buyer is regularly sent product information and things like invitations to new product launches in the showrooms.

In the organisational market, an important role for the sales representative is to manage the customer's account internally within the selling organisation, ensuring that appropriate support is available as needed. Thus the representative is continuing to liaise between the customer and the accounts department, engineering, R&D, service and anyone else with whom the customer needs to deal.

Turnbull (1990) highlighted six important ways in which personal contact can help to maintain effective relationships with customers. These are shown in Fig. 17.4 and discussed briefly in turn below. At various times in the selling process the buyer and seller may perform different activities in support of each of the following aspects of personal contact.

Example Incyte is at the cutting edge of bio-informatics, trading in genomic information-based tools that help with an understanding of the molecular basis of disease. The key account managers control a small number of accounts in the pharmaceutical and biotechnology industries across Europe and each one can generate many millions of pounds of sales. They work closely with each customer throughout the buying process and beyond and in some cases several projects can be running in parallel. It is often difficult to know where one project ends and a new one begins. Most of the key account managers have PhDs in life sciences and are at least bilingual. In contrast, a national account manager for Jeyes is primarily concerned with wholesale and cash and carry customers. ECR (*see* p. 500) and category management principles along with a good understanding of branding and own-label are considered vital for developing business. This enables account managers to build the confidence of their customers and to implement an agreed plan.

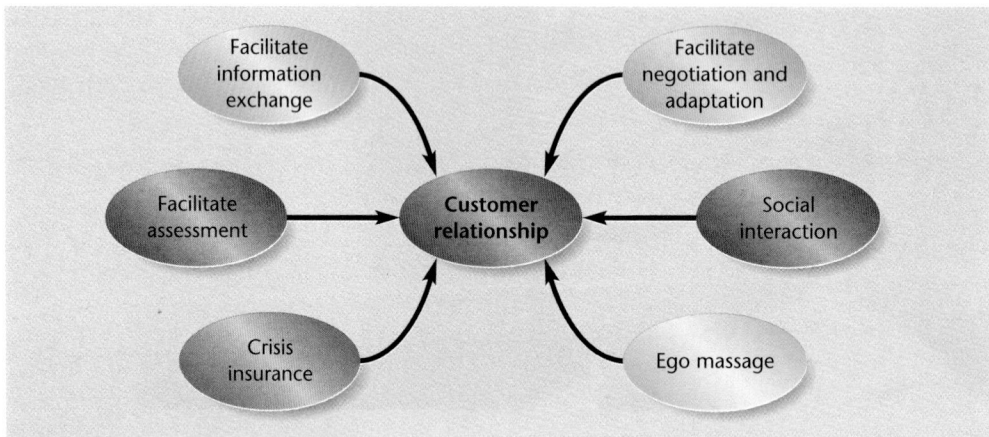

FIGURE 17.4

The role of personal contact in maintaining good customer relationships

Facilitating information exchange

Facilitating information exchange goes beyond hard data concerning the product, and relates to relatively confidential information that can lead to a deeper assessment. Such sensitive information will only be exchanged, however, where experience, trust and respect have been built up through a history of personal contact.

Facilitating assessment

Personal contact, coupled with the free exchange of information, enables the buyer to assess the product and commercial offering in order to make a decision on selecting a supplier.

Facilitating negotiation and adaptation

Facilitating negotiation and adaptation will vary from relatively simple commercial negotiation through to complex technical and commercial discussion to find a fit between the buyer's and seller's respective needs. These discussions could include ways of adapting a product, manufacturing processes and delivery systems.

Crisis insurance

Some personal contacts might only be activated at a time of difficulty and thus could be said to amount to crisis insurance. A supplier to a large buyer, for example, might only plan to meet with the buyer's managing director once a year, out of courtesy. However, if difficulties do arise in the meantime, that contact may be activated as a form of security or insurance, with a direct appeal to intervene.

Non-commercial social interaction

Although most buyer–seller interpersonal interaction takes place within an organisational context, there might also be some private social interaction that will affect the commercial relationship. This might include membership of other social groups, such as a church or sports clubs.

Massaging the ego

An extension of the social and crisis insurance contacts is 'massaging the ego', whereby higher level contact is sought or offered from time to time to enhance one party's feelings of self-importance. Some buyers might, therefore, appreciate a visit once a year from the seller's sales director as a demonstration of the value of their account.

SALES MANAGEMENT

The previous section concentrated on the mechanics of selling something to a prospective buyer. That is important, certainly, because if the selling process does not work well, then there will be no sales and no revenue. Somebody has to show the customer the benefits of dealing with that particular seller. No matter how good the product or the other promotional elements are, they have to be sold.

Equally important, however, is the management of the sales force. Whether in a multinational organisation or a small company, the selling effort needs to be planned and managed. In a very small business, the owner, perhaps with some assistance, may undertake most of the selling and manage it by default. In a larger organisation, a sales manager will be assigned the tasks of achieving sales results through formal management of a sales force. Whatever the size or the character of a business, sales management provides an essential link between the organisation's strategic marketing plans and the achievement of sales objectives by the representatives in the field. Sales management ensures that the selling effort fits with the overall tasks specified in the marketing plan and strategy.

Again, it is difficult to generalise about the specific tasks of sales management, as they will obviously vary between different organisations and different markets. A number of areas commonly found are, however, examined in this section. These include establishing a sales plan and strategy; specifying and recruiting sales representatives; training and developing staff; motivation and compensation policies; and, finally, controlling and evaluating the selling effort.

> **Example** British Midland Airways, the UK's second-largest airline, organises its sales force around a general sales manager. The sales manager is responsible for the control, direction and motivation of a team of national account managers who deal with corporate clients and a team of regional managers who are responsible for developing the retail travel sector across Europe.

Sales planning and strategy

The sales plan outlines the objectives for the selling effort and the details of how the plan should be implemented. This plan itself arises from, and must fit closely with, the marketing objectives set for products and market share etc. In designing and implementing the sales plan, there are three interrelated decisions to be made.

Specifying the sales objectives

There are two types of sales objective to be specified. The first is the general sales targets to be achieved by the sales force as a whole. The second is the definition of sales targets specific to individuals or groups within the sales force.

Setting sales objectives provides an essential yardstick against which to measure progress and to motivate and influence the selling effort. Normally, quantitative measures are used to specify exactly what is required. At the level of the total sales force, the targets will be in terms of sales value and/or volume. Setting objectives in sales and profit terms is often necessary either to avoid the dangers of chasing low profit sales or to lessen the temptation to reduce margins to generate more sales volume but less gross profit (see also Chapters 10 and 11).

Using market share as a basis for sales targets, rather than sales value or volume, carries its own risks. The reasons are similar to those outlined at p. 628 in the discussion of advertising objectives. Although the sales force's efforts are very important for achieving sales, the effectiveness of that selling effort is also affected by other factors. These include such matters as price levels, company image, product specification and the support of other promotional techniques. While measures of product sales compared with the nearest competitor and year on year market share changes are useful indicators of selling performance, they must not be seen in isolation.

For the individual sales representative, many of the same measures still apply. Often, at this level, the sales objectives are called **sales quotas**, and again they are defined in sales value or volume terms. However, it is often useful to clarify these objectives further, perhaps by breaking them down into a number of targets relating to specific product ranges. Where a wide variety of products is offered, there may be weaker ones that need to be highlighted in the setting of objectives, either to boost their sales by setting ambitious targets, or to direct the sales force's attention away from them by setting low targets.

Targets for individual sales representatives need not only relate to selling quantities of products. Performance targets might be agreed in terms of the number of sales calls, the number of new accounts recruited, the call frequency, call conversion rates (i.e. turning prospects into buyers) or selling expenses.

Detailing the sales organisation

Decisions have to be made about organising the sales force. Flexibility in this area depends on whether the organisation already has a sales force or whether one has to be created.

A newly appointed sales manager would normally inherit an existing sales force. One priority for the new manager would be to review the current structure and establish whether it could be modified. Obviously, in a new organisation there are more options available, as the manager does not have to think about the costs of dismantling any existing structure.

For a new organisation, a more fundamental question may be raised about whether a direct sales force is required at all. An organisation may decide to sell through an independent agent (see p. 462) to increase coverage, for example. To do this the organisation must be sure that the agent has the necessary expertise and selling effort. There is little point in losing one's own sales force or opting out of ever setting one up, if the only gain is poorer performance, whatever the savings in salaries and expenses.

Assuming that the selling effort is to be managed internally, the sales manager has four broad choices for organising the sales force: geography, product, customer type, customer importance. Each of these will now be discussed in turn.

Geographic structure. In a European context, a geographic structure normally means dividing Europe up into its individual nations, then subdividing each nation by region, then, if necessary, further dividing each region into sales territories. Thus France, for example, would be a national sales area, Alsace would be a regional division within it, and Strasbourg would be a final subdivision with its own sales representative. Sales representatives are assigned to each geographic territory according to a formula described later (see Fig. 17.5), and represent all or a specified number of company products within that territory.

> **Example** Reebok employs sales people on a geographic basis, so the sales representative in Scotland, for example, would cover all products for his/her customers and have sole responsibility for sales within that territory.

The focus on one area has the advantage of minimising travel costs and avoids the danger of call duplication that exists in the other methods discussed later. In addition, having representatives familiar with the local economy encourages a more knowledgeable approach for identifying and exploiting new opportunities. This could be an advantage in situations where the product or service is sold to a wide range of different customers who are geographically scattered, for example financial services. However, if the organisation operates in a specialised, geographically concentrated industry, or if detailed technical product knowledge is needed, then the geographic option has more limited appeal.

Product-based structure. As an alternative to the geographic approach, a product-based structure means that individual sales representatives specialise in selling only a limited number of products from the organisation's total range. This kind of structure allows the organisation to develop experts in particular product technologies who can act as consultants or problem solvers as well as sales representatives. A product-based structure may also be appropriate where the organisation offers a wide range of very diverse products in its portfolio.

> **Example** Philips (http://www.philips.com) has structured its selling effort around the main divisions of the company. Therefore the consumer electronics division sales force is responsible for sales of such products as DVD players, digital televisions and CD players to retailers. In contrast, the business electronics division would handle such items as digital transmission systems and sell direct to business users. Similar sales teams have been organised around other divisions such as lighting and medical. However, although the company is organised around distinct product types, geographic territories are still used to allocate the defined areas to sales staff.

This approach enables the organisation to recruit more selectively and to develop expertise within its sales force that could give a competitive edge. The disadvantages mirror the advantages of the geographic option. Travel costs increase, as a single representative may have to service customers across Europe. This also has implications for travelling time (and the more time spent travelling, the less time spent selling). Furthermore, the representative may have to acquire a much wider range of knowledge about local conditions and culture relating to the various customers visited. Finally, duplication of calls may increase, because if one customer wants to purchase a wide range of the seller's products, two or three different representatives with different product responsibilities may have to call.

Customer-based structure. A customer-based structure, in contrast, is designed to reflect the needs of different types of customers, rather than being product centred. This might mean dividing customers by industry, so that one representative deals with the automotive trade, while another deals with aerospace. This has an attractive logic, as organisations within a particular industry may well have similar needs, similar applications and similar problems. The representative can develop detailed industry knowledge and form long-term personal relationships with customers. Another way of classifying customers is by the nature of their business, that is, whether they are manufacturers or resellers. Each category would require a very different selling approach, because there are fundamental differences in their buying motives.

Whatever the classification system used, the customer-based approach does ensure a better match between the support and expertise needed by the customer and the skills of the sales representative. However, although call duplication may be low, the potential for geographically spread customers means higher travelling and customer servicing costs.

Customer importance. Finally, a variant of the customer-based approach is a structure based on the size or importance of the customer. The Pareto effect (discussed at p. 192) will identify the important strategic role played by a small number of important customers. If 20 per cent of our customers account for 80 per cent of our business, then that 20 per cent deserves the best care and attention we can offer them. If the major accounts are selected for special attention, the better sales representatives can focus on improving buyer–seller relationships, selling in depth, and co-ordinating the efforts of all the selling organisation's personnel to achieve a high service level for those customers. Those representatives become advanced forms of customer specialists and, where there are very large accounts, may represent only one account.

Research by Pardo (1997) that examined major accounts from the customers' perspectives found that as long as the seller's focused attention gave real added value, not just more frequent, high powered selling visits, there was much to gain for the customer's organisation. It especially enabled problem solving tasks to be handed over to an external organisation that was trusted and competent to advise, thus emphasising the consultancy role and strategic thinking role, as found by Holley (1999) in the computer industry.

> **Example** BASF employs a national account manager to deal with audio, video and camcorder tapes with the regional multiples. It also has sales executives who deal with independent trade customers and retailers through a network of sales territories.

Even in a small business, the owner may choose to retain and maintain a personal relationship with the more important customers, delegating the other accounts to the sales representative(s).

There is clearly no one universally applicable and appropriate organisational structure. Sometimes a mixed structure may be best, combining geographic and major customer specialisation. Johnson & Johnson, for example, employs regionally based territory sales managers for its UK consumer products, but with specific responsibility for certain types of customer, such as independent pharmacies and wholesale cash and carries. This allows the organisation to benefit from the advantages of both types of allocation, while reducing the effect of their disadvantages. The chosen structure will be the right one as long as it reflects the objectives and marketing strategy of the firm. Increasingly, the internationalisation of organisations is causing a reconsideration of the way in which sales are structured across national and EU borders (Hill and Still, 1990). The important point is not to see the sales structure as fixed, but regularly to assess its relevance and its ability to achieve its objectives. If the structure appears to be failing in any way, then questions must be asked and answered, and management may have to be prepared to modify its approach.

Establishing sales coverage and deployment

A further decision has to be made on the ideal size of the sales force. A number of factors need to be considered, such as the calling frequency required for each customer, the number of calls possible each day, and the relative division of the representative's time between administration, selling and repeat calls (Cravens and LaForge, 1983). All these matters will have an impact on the ability of the sales force to achieve the

The inputs

C = Number of customers
F = Average call frequency per customer per year
L = Average number of calls per representative per day
N = Average number of selling days per representative per year

The calculations

Stage 1 T = C × F = Total number of calls per year
Stage 2 D = T/L   = Total number of selling days required per year
Stage 3 S = D/N = Number of sales representatives required

Example

If: C = 300 (number of customers)
    F =   4 (average call frequency per customer per year)
    L =   3 (average number of calls per representative per day)
    N = 133 (average number of selling days per representative per year)

Then: T = 300 × 4 = 1200 = Calls per year
      D = 1200/3 = 400   = Selling days required and
      S = 400/133 = 3.01

Thus 3 sales representatives are needed

FIGURE 17.5

Calculating the size of a sales force

expected sales results from the number of accounts served. For a smaller business, the issue may be further constrained by just how many representatives can be afforded!

Figure 17.5 shows a formula commonly used to assess the size of a sales force. Within the formula, there are several underlying deployment and coverage issues. For example, call frequency will vary according to the size of the decision-making unit within the buying organisation and the frequency of purchase. It may be possible to vary the call frequency depending on the customer's potential and careful use of non-personal communication, such as mail shots etc.

Closely linked with the issue of sales force size is the problem of dividing the whole sales area into individual territories. The size, shape and sales potential may well vary between territories, and these need to be considered when setting sales targets and coverage policies.

The size and deployment of the sales force are not fixed, but must be varied according to emerging opportunities and analysis of resource efficiency. The growth of telemarketing along with the increasingly high cost per personal sales call have made some organisations think much more carefully about where, when and how to employ the sales team.

Recruitment and selection

As with any recruitment exercise, it is important to begin by developing a profile of who the organisation is looking for. A detailed analysis of the selling tasks should lead to a list of the ideal skills and characteristics of the representative to be recruited. As mentioned at pp. 694–696, there are significant differences between order takers and order makers, so the recruiter must at least know where the recruit is to fit in and what tasks they will be undertaking.

Many researchers have attempted to identify the ideal mix of traits that go to make up the super sales representative (Mayer and Greenberg, 1964; Lockman and Hallaq, 1982). The lists of traits rarely agree, contain a huge range of characteristics, and furthermore centre on matters that are difficult to discern and measure in an individual. The challenge for the sales manager is to relate those lists to the specific needs of the

MARKETING IN ACTION 'The Man from the Pru'

'The Man from the Pru' is an advertising slogan that the Prudential, a UK financial services company, has long been trying to put behind it. This has not been an easy task. The man from the Pru is a warm, cosy image, evoking the days when the insurance man (or woman) used to call on customers at their homes every week to collect premiums and update their payment books. Just because the company is trying to shed this image does not mean that it is any less dependent on personal selling, however. Although many financial service companies, including the Pru, have moved towards telephone-based sales and account management, there is still a role for sales forces.

The extra cost of having a sales force has to be justified by generating additional benefits in profitable sales, but this has been increasingly questioned by the Prudential. It estimates that the acquisition cost of a new policy is 119 per cent of the annual premiums for sales through independent advisers and 107 per cent for direct sales. It can take up to seven years to earn any return on a policy and any early cancellation results in an unprofitable sale.

In order to increase the level of sales activity, a detailed examination was undertaken of workloads, motivation and growth opportunities. In 1995, a typical sales representative managed 12 calls per week,

three of which led to fact finding to assess policy needs and 2.5 of which resulted in a proposal. The sales per representative were typically £60 000 per year. The challenge for the Pru was to increase sales to £110 000 to £200 000 per year per representative. It soon became apparent that call rates and proposal conversion rates were difficult to increase and the compensation scheme offered little scope to incentivise the sales force further. Therefore a two-pronged strategy was adopted. First, an integrated sales policy was developed that used a combination of direct sales, telephone sales for routine contact, mail shots and Internet transactions. The development of Internet selling is a longer-term strategy as currently, even in the USA, only 5 per cent of policies are sold over the net. With a customer base of over 6mn in the UK, sales efficiency was a high priority. With non-productive selling time reduced, the second part of the strategy could come into play: attacking the corporate market. By directing sales teams to pursue the corporate sector, especially schools, universities and other organisations employing many professionals, selling in bulk became possible, rather than just one-off policy sales. Sales increased by £50mn per year as a result of the change of strategy.

Sources: Computer World (1999); Howard (1998).

recruiting organisation. This means understanding the market, understanding what customers want from representatives, defining selling requirements, and analysing why certain existing representatives appear to be more successful than others. Table 17.3 lists the attributes of sales representatives typically appreciated by buyers.

TABLE 17.3

Sales representative attributes typically appreciated by buyers

- Thoroughness and follow-up
- Knowledge of seller's products
- Representing the buyer's interests within the selling organisation
- Market knowledge
- Understanding the buyer's problems
- Knowledge of the buyer's product and markets
- Diplomacy and tact
- Good preparation before sales calls
- Regular sales calls
- Technical education

A common dilemma is whether previous experience is an essential requirement. Some organisations prefer to take on recruits new to selling, then train them in their own methods rather than recruit experienced representatives who come with bad habits and other organisations' weaknesses. Others, especially smaller organisations, may deliberately seek experienced staff, wishing to benefit from training programmes that they themselves could not afford to provide. The eventual choice will depend on the organisation's decision on what it requires in terms of such factors as age, background, experience, qualifications etc. A supplier of greeting cards, personalised stationery and postcards considered the most important factors to be experience in sales, a background in retail greeting cards and direct experience of selling into similar outlets. A large car dealer when seeking a new car sales representative demanded two years' new car sales experience as a minimum, although a parallel trainee position highlighted the need for someone who was articulate, with an outgoing personality.

Example Pearl Assurance has over 3.5mn customers who are serviced through a network of area managers and agents. For both types of selling roles, no previous experience in the financial services sector is needed. For the agents there is not even a requirement for sales experience, although some exposure to a customer service background is favoured. Their main role is to follow up domestic and small business sales leads and to deal with basic policies in motor and household insurance. Candidates for the area manager positions are judged more on their stability and interpersonal skills than knowledge of the financial services sector. This fits with the need for sales staff that can be trusted by the prospective customer before they are prepared to commit to a more complex personal pension or life assurance policy.

The actual selection process needs to be designed to draw out evidence of the ability of each candidate to perform the specified tasks, so that an informed choice can be made. The cost of a poor selection can be very high, not just in terms of recruitment costs and salary, but also, and perhaps more seriously, in terms of lost sales opportunities or damage to the organisation's reputation. In view of the importance of making the right choice, in addition to normal interview and reference procedures, a number of firms employ psychological tests to assess personality and some will not confirm the appointment until the successful completion of the initial training period.

Today's sales representative has to be IT literate.

Source: Photodisc.

Training

The recruitment process generally only provides the raw material. Although the new recruit might already have appropriate skills and a good attitudinal profile, training will help to sharpen both areas so that better performance within the sales philosophy of the employing organisation can be developed. Sales force training applies not just to new recruits, however. Both new and existing staff, even well-established staff, may need skills refinement and upgrading.

Training may be formal or informal. Some organisations invest in and develop their own high quality training facilities and run a regular series of introductory and refresher courses in-house. This has the advantage of ensuring that the training is relevant to the organisation and its business, as well as signifying an on-going commitment to staff development.

Other organisations adopt a more *ad hoc* approach, using outside specialists as required. This means that the organisation only pays for what it uses, but the approach carries two serious risks. The first problem is that the training may be too generalised and thus insufficiently tailored to the organisation's needs. The second problem is that it is too easy for the organisation to put off training or, even worse, to delete it altogether in times of financial stringency.

Finally, a third group uses informal or semi-formal 'sitting with Nelly', on the job coaching. This involves the trainee observing other representatives in the field, and then being observed themselves by experienced sales representatives and/or the sales manager. There is nothing quite like seeing the job being done, but with this approach the organisation needs to take great care to deal with a number of points. One concern is to ensure that such training is comprehensive, covering all aspects of the job. Another is to ensure that bad habits or questionable techniques are not passed on. The main problem with this kind of on the job training is that the training is not usually done by professional trainers. Therefore the quality can be variable, and there is no opportunity for fresh ideas to be introduced to the sales force.

There are a number of dimensions that can be covered by training programmes, depending on the training needs identified by the organisation. Programmes may need to cover the organisation's products (and those of the competition), company information (relating to their own organisation, its competitors and their key customers), applications, market information and, not least, developing greater competency in selling and negotiation skills and techniques. It is the job of the sales manager to determine the relative emphasis in the training, its location, who participates, the length of a programme and the overall fit between the training budget, training outcomes and sales objectives.

Whereas larger organisations such as IBM and Xerox will have comprehensive training programmes, smaller organisations and resellers might have only limited facilities and rely on recruiting experienced staff. With resellers, for example, there is a need not only for product knowledge but also for sales skills, yet it could be too expensive to provide sales training for a small number of staff. Thus it could be necessary to group a number of smaller dealers together for sales training to make it worthwhile. Rasmusson (1999) highlighted the potential for industry-related seminars in computing and found that training directly helped encourage incremental sales and customer retention.

Motivation and compensation

Any sales effort needs well-motivated sales people. Apart from the fact that enthusiastic and motivated representatives will sell better, effective sales people are often in high demand by other employers.

An organisation will not only want to motivate new recruits to join its sales force, but also have an interest in making sure that they are sufficiently well rewarded for their achievements that they will not easily be poached by the competition (Cron *et al.*, 1988). There are many ways in which the sales team can be motivated to achieve outstanding results and rewarded, but they are not all financially based.

> **Example** Thomson Directories, advertising to attract sales staff to sell Internet and classified advertising, offered a basic salary just over £18 000, but with commission from on-target earnings (OTE) this could rise to around £30 000. The company also claimed that its top earners made over £50 000 per year. Other benefits were also offered, however, including a car, a mobile phone allowance, contributory pension and a private health scheme. In addition, induction and on-going training along with career development under the Investors in People quality mark were also highlighted.

Even a sense of belonging to a team can be important. Selling can be a lonely activity. Imagine spending your working life out on the road, with mostly only telephone contact with the sales manager, enhanced by the occasional meeting. It is not easy to maintain enthusiasm for the job, or to feel that your work is valued under such conditions. Bringing representatives back to HQ regularly for team meetings, seminars and briefings may help to foster team spirit. It provides an opportunity for the team to share views and experiences, and allows clear two-way communication regarding achievements and expectations. Training programmes can also play a part in reassuring employees that they are valued, and in bringing teams back together again.

By involving the representatives in managerial activities such as developing their own territory sales plan, the organisation gains in two ways. First, it can plan with the benefit of the representative's knowledge and experience of the territory, and second, it gives employees a greater sense of control over their own working as well as a feeling that there is open and co-operative management. Providing representatives with mechanisms for regularly feeding back updated intelligence into the organisation, through a direct data link, makes them feel that they are offering more than just selling expertise and can thus assist in developing positive motivation.

Sometimes, sales managers can create an element of healthy rivalry among sales representatives through sales contests. If the rewards are seen as valuable and achievable, contests can renew a representative's interest in doing a good job. Household goods, holidays or cash bonuses, for example, are tangible and attractive motivators. These contests do not necessarily have to be focused on sales figures. They can be targeted at one or more of a range of important activities, such as creating new accounts, quota achievement by area or product, and increased penetration of existing accounts. These incentives can easily be self-financing if they are taken seriously by the sales force.

The activities outlined so far have consisted of positive reinforcements, but unfortunately, some organisations choose to use penalties and the fear of their implementation to motivate. Demotion and dismissal are extreme responses to poor performance, occurring where an organisation is happy to adopt a hire and fire philosophy rather than investing in staff through careful selection and comprehensive, on-going training. Some organisations in the financial services sector have a reputation for employing sales people in order to benefit from their network of personal contacts and then, when these are exhausted, they are more than happy to terminate sales people's employment if their performance starts to drop.

Pay still remains a vital ingredient in attracting and retaining a committed sales force. The purpose of an effective sales force compensation scheme is to provide the sales manager with the flexibility to focus the efforts of the sales force on the achievement of the sales goals.

Three main methods of compensation exist: straight salary, straight **commission**, and a combination of salary and commission. Each method implies a number of advantages and disadvantages, listed in Table 17.4. The straight salary compensation plan is where a fixed amount is paid on a salary basis. This is most appropriate when

TABLE 17.4
Comparison of compensation plans

	Commission only	Salary only	Part salary/part commission
Motivation for rep. to generate sales	High	Low	Medium
Motivation for rep. to build customer relationship	Low	High	Medium
Motivation for rep. to participate in training	Low	High	Medium
Cost effectiveness for organisation	High	Potentially low	Medium
Predictability of cost to organisation	Low	High	Medium
Predictability of income for rep.	Low	High	Medium
Ease of administration for organisation	Low	High	Low
Organisation's control over rep.	Low	High	Medium
Organisation's flexibility to push sales of particular products	High	Low	High
Overall, best where …	■ Aggressive selling is needed ■ There are few non-selling tasks	■ Training new reps ■ Difficult sales territories exist ■ Developing new territories ■ There are many non-selling tasks	■ Organisation wants both incentive and control ■ Sales territories all have similar profiles

the organisation wants to encourage representatives to spend time developing quality relationships with customers, or where the product sold is technically demanding. The straight commission compensation plan means that earnings are directly related to the sales and profit generated. This encourages a 'sell it quick and move on' attitude, appropriate to low-involvement, uncomplicated products. Finally, the most popular method is the combination plan, involving part salary and part commission. The selection of the most appropriate method will partly be determined by the nature of the selling tasks, and the degree of staff turnover that can be tolerated given the training and recruiting costs. With the trend towards major and key account management, commission on sales volume is becoming less important than achieving a range of relationship-wide objectives covering branding, logistics and merchandising (Holley, 1999).

The overall challenge for the sales manager in this area is to find an appropriate balance between income and incentives, taking into account the pressures of the selling task. This requires knowledge of the market and the sales staff. Although not all effective sales representatives make the transition to become effective sales managers, it is normal for the sales manager to have had direct experience in selling.

Performance evaluation

Given that many sales representatives work away from an office base, the monitoring and control of individual selling activity are vital functions in the sales management role. No valid evaluation can be made without information about performance and the selling effort. Call reports, as part of a systematic means of gathering account information (*see* Chapter 6), form the basis for weekly monitoring of an individual sales representative. They are also valuable, from a strategic point of view, in assessing the general impact of marketing policies at account level. Call reports usually specify who was contacted on the visit, the topics of discussion, particular problems arising, competitive activity and general progress towards the account objectives. Sometimes, these reports are linked to a call plan so that the sales manager can compare planned coverage with actual coverage, and can even assist in advance.

The sales representative's performance can be measured in both quantitative and qualitative terms. Quantitative assessments can be related to either input or output measures, usually with reference to targets and benchmarks (Good and Stone, 1991). Input measures assess activities such as the number of calls and account coverage. Output measures focus on the end rather than the means, and include measurement of sales volume, sales development, number of new accounts and specific product sales.

To create a rounded picture of the sales representative's performance, qualitative measures that tend to be informal and subjective are also used. These could include attitude, product knowledge, appearance and communication skills. Using them in conjunction with quantitative measures, the sales manager may be able to find explanations for any particularly good or bad performance underlying the quantitative evidence of the formal results achieved (McAdams, 1987).

Either way, the assessment can form the basis of a deeper analysis to encourage a proactive rather than reactive approach to sales management. Table 17.5 outlines a number of simple formulae that can be used to assess performance with a view to designing corrective plans or staff development programmes. The analysis might indicate that action needs to be taken on call policy, training or motivation, or even that problems may lie not with the sales force, but with the product or its marketing strategies.

TABLE 17.5
Calculating sales performance

Quantitative measure	Means of measuring
Productivity	
Calls per day	Number of calls/number of days worked
Calls per account	Number of calls/number of accounts
Orders per call	Number of orders/total number of calls
Account development and servicing	
Account penetration	Accounts sold to/total number of accounts available
Sales per account	Total sales value/total number of accounts
Average order size	Total sales value/total number of orders
Expenses	
Sales expenses	Expenses/sales made
Cost per call	Total costs/total number of calls made

Developments in IT are making the task of communicating with and receiving information from the field sales force more effective. This means that trends can be identified sooner, and corrective action planned and implemented more quickly and with more authority.

CHAPTER SUMMARY

Personal selling concerns interpersonal contact between buyer and seller with the aim of encouraging the buyer to behave or think in a certain way. Although it can be an expensive and labour-intensive marketing communication activity, it has a number of advantages over other forms of communication. It makes an *impact*, because it involves face-to-face contact and is less likely to be ignored; it can deliver a *precise and tailored* message to a target customer who has already been checked out to ensure that they fit the right profile; it helps in the *cultivation* of long-term buyer–seller relationships.

The roles undertaken by sales representatives are many and varied. They *prospect* for new customers; they provide customers with relevant and detailed *information*; they *persuade* customers to buy; they help to *demonstrate and install* products; they *represent the customer's interests* within the selling organisation; they help to *maintain good buyer–seller relationships* over time; they *collect information and feedback* from the field, and they *monitor* what the competition are doing in the field and how customers feel about the competition. Clearly, these roles will vary depending on the size of organisation, the type of market and the nature of the sales representative. Some will be order takers, some order makers and some will act in a support role.

The personal selling process can be a long and complicated marketing activity to implement. The process starts with the identification of prospective customers, and then the representative has to do as much background work on the prospect as possible in order to prepare an initial approach and a relevant sales presentation. Initial contact breaks the ice between buyer and seller, allowing an appointment to be made for the real selling to begin. The sales presentation will give the representative the opportunity to present the product in the best possible light, using a variety of samples and audio-visual aids, while allowing the customer to ask questions and to raise any objections they may have. Negotiating the fine details of the deal may lead naturally to closing the sale, and then all that remains is for the representative to ensure the customer's post-purchase satisfaction and work towards building a long-term relationship leading to repeat business and further purchases.

Sales management is an important area of marketing, and involves a number of issues. *Sales planning and strategy* means making decisions about sales objectives, both for the organisation as a whole and for individual sales representatives or teams. *Recruitment* and training are also both important aspects of sales management, and *training* too concerns the sales manager. Apart from benefiting from training programmes, sales representatives have to be properly *motivated and compensated* for their efforts. This means not only designing an appropriate and attractive package of pay and other benefits, but also making sure that representatives are fully involved in the life of the organisation generally and, more specifically, in any decisions involving themselves. A natural part of all this is *performance evaluation*. Sales managers need to ensure that representatives are achieving their targets and, if not, why not.

Key words and phrases

Closing the sale	Order maker	Qualified prospects
Cold calling	Order taker	Sales presentation
Commission	Personal selling	Sales quotas
Conversion rates	Prospecting	Sales support
Leads	Prospects	

QUESTIONS FOR REVIEW

17.1 What is *personal selling* and how does it differ from other elements of the promotional mix?

17.2 What are the major *advantages* of personal selling and what can they contribute to the marketing effort?

17.3 What are the typical tasks of a *sales representative*?

17.4 How might the implementation and importance of each of those tasks vary between *organisational* and *consumer* markets?

17.5 Why might a sales representative's role include co-ordination within the selling organisation?

17.6 What is the difference between an *order taker* and an *order maker*?

17.7 What are the stages in the personal selling process?

17.8 Why is preparation and planning such important parts of the personal selling process?

17.9 How might the sales representative tell whether or not a prospect is ready to *close a sale*?

17.10 What are the main issues that the sales manager must consider as far as sales *planning* and *strategy* are concerned?

QUESTIONS FOR DISCUSSION

17.1 Give examples of three different kinds of sales support staff and analyse their contribution to the personal selling effort.

17.2 In what ways do you think a sales representative could make the sales presentation more relevant and interesting for the prospective customer?

17.3 What techniques might a sales representative use to counter the following objections:

(a) 'Your competitor's product is a lot cheaper ...'

(b) 'I don't think my wife would like it if I bought this ...'

(c) 'I've heard that your service engineers are very inefficient.'

17.4 Summarise the relative advantages of allocating sales responsibilities on the basis of:

(a)   geographic regions,

(b)   product-based criteria; and

(c)   customer-based criteria.

17.5 Find 20 job advertisements for sales representatives and summarise the range of characteristics and skills sought. Which are the most commonly required and to what extent do you think that they are essential for a successful sales representative?

CASE STUDY 17.1

Colomer: Spanish leather

The Colomer Group, based in Vic, Spain, produces high quality leather products for clothing, footwear and gloves. Clothing products represent 85 per cent of sales. It is a world leader in lamb skin, goat skin and pigskin tanning and finishing. Its customers include many of the top design and manufacturing names in Europe.

Raw skins are a by-product of meat production, so the supply of raw material is in no way related to the demand for leather goods. Prices can, however, fluctuate considerably, depending on the availability and quality of skins. Although leather goods are still regarded by many as high priced luxuries, there are marked differences between the average price levels for leather from some of the developing countries and those from producers such as Colomer. Typical price levels per square foot vary from 150 to 800 pesetas. Colomer tends to sell in the 600 pesetas or more price range. Linked with price variations, quality can also vary depending on the consistency and purity of the raw skin. Colomer, for example, only uses skin from the best small sheep such as entrefino, merino and lambs. Careful skin inspection and buying is essential for retaining a premium position. Although the leather industry has been around for many years, in order to retain a competitive edge Colomer has invested heavily in product development, innovation and the use of new technology to enable better, high quality finishes to be achieved. It is in the fashion business and must identify trends and new opportunities

early enough to be prepared for a season up to two years ahead.

Colomer has around 800 customers worldwide, but 600 of them are based in Europe. The company mainly deals with either independent designers or, more normally, designers contracted to clothing manufacturers. Many of the customers are thus small, requiring a sales visit only once or twice a year. The larger manufacturers demand closer attention. The Italian market is of major importance because of the presence of many top designer labels, and currently around 35 per cent of European sales go to this market.

In Europe, Colomer operates through a combination of direct sales and sales agents. Most of the sales staff have had many years in the leather industry and understand the product from a technical perspective. Such knowledge is considered important as the sales people need to help the designers and buyers develop the most appropriate specification for the finished leather. Factors such as regularity, durability and comfort, waterproofing, washability, dry-cleaning capability and perspiration fastness may all have to be considered as part of the sales process. Other issues include whether nappas, sueded leather or shearling finishings are to be selected and the range of colours available. Increasingly, ecological considerations must be taken into account, both in production processes and in the materials used.

The commercial aspects also have to be negotiated. Because volumes tend to be large,

Colomer supplies the leather for chic designer goods

Source: Colomer

margins tend to be small, with limited scope for giving discounts. Although Colomer is the market leader in a range of leathers, there are more specialised niche producers that provide tough competition, even though the range of finishings they offer is limited. The leather manufacturers from developing countries tend to sell on price, but delivery can be erratic, their quality variable and their product ranges narrower. Some markets, such as in the UK, tend to offer more fertile ground for these producers, but premium branded clothing manufacturers across Europe tend to deal only with top quality leather that will be delivered to agreed schedules. Given the fashion seasons, any delay could result in lost sales opportunities, as over 60 per cent of sales are made over the summer period when the trade stocks up for the main winter season. The collection for a season is often developed two years ahead of delivery.

The 15-strong world-wide sales force is organised by product and on geographical lines. In clothing leather, there are three sales staff across Europe while footwear and gloves have one representative each for Europe. The sales director is based in Vic. The role of the sales representatives is to work through designated national agents and to deal directly with some of the larger accounts as well as supporting the agents with technical and sales advice. Because there is a fair amount of travel involved, the company feels that men are better able to be away from home for frequent periods without problems arising from family commitments. Female staff have been employed in

sales roles but in the company's view it was not a great success.

Most members of the sales team have been with the company for many years and few have any formal academic qualifications. Although they understand the leather industry well, there is still an annual sales meeting where new designs and materials are introduced, as well as classes run in sales techniques, delivered by university staff from Barcelona. Around 20 days per year are dedicated to all aspects of training. Most of the sales team are Spanish nationals but they are also proficient in English. Further support in language training is given by the local university. Some of the team can speak Italian and French.

The sales agents comprise an important part of the promotional activity. Normally one agent is selected for each country and is given the responsibility for acting as the day-to-day interface with the customer as the Colomer sales representative is likely to be elsewhere in Europe. Italy is an exception, given the importance of the market. There is a full-time sales representative based there as well as three agents with defined territories. Physical shipments go direct to the customer and the agent is notified of dispatch. In the UK, the agent is based in London, close to the main UK customers, many of who are small Asian-owned businesses. The UK is regarded as a very price sensitive market and the dominance of the large retail chains has restricted the potential for premium leather products. A high proportion of the leather for the multiple retailers comes from cheaper sources in India and the Far East.

The agents tend to be experts in the country market with good trade contacts, but they are not usually technical experts. As part of the induction process, however, the agents spend frequent periods at the manufacturing plant and also receive close support from the sales representatives. Agents are not allowed to sell competitors' lines, but the selling of non-competing lines is allowed, such as car leather. Colomer prefers an exclusive agency agreement to ensure that it receives the dedication and commitment necessary. Most agents are appointed on a one-year trial basis after which a longer-term contract may be negotiated. Colomer is confident that it can assess the value and capability of an agent within one year. The agency commission rates are around 3 per cent of sales, reflecting the low margins earned within the sector. Colomer considers that this rate is high for the sector and encourages more dedicated effort to their products. However, some are considered to be less efficient as repeat sales can be relatively straightforward and co-ordination can be difficult when the direct sales teams are also involved.

Most members of the sales force are on a high basic salary with a low commission. Given the agency support and problem solving role, a high basic salary was considered appropriate as too much reliance on commission could result in shorter-term sales thinking rather than building longer-term relationships based on quality and trust. Commission is linked to achievement of overall sales targets not the profitability of individual orders. With profit margins of only around 10 per cent and the tendency to sell from published list prices, the sales representatives have the discretion only to give up to 5 per cent discount, and even then it has to be an exceptionally large order.

Source: With grateful thanks to Joan Capdevila, Colomer.

Questions

1 What do you think are the ideal characteristics for a successful sales representative working for a company like Colomer in the leather trade? How might these characteristics differ for a representative working for one of the competitors selling mainly on price?

2 What are the advantages and disadvantages to Colomer of giving a high basic salary to the sales representatives?

3 What problems might arise from a mixed selling approach which uses both sales representatives and agents?

4 Can an operation using both geographic and product based sales organisation work? Why does Colomer do it this way rather than using other customer based methods of sales organisation?

CASE STUDY 17.2

Irish Fire Products

Irish Fire Products (IFP), based in the west of Ireland, is a distributor for a range of fire extinguishers, fire blankets, sprinkler systems and other fire-prevention accessories such as alarms, signage and doors. Most of the products sold are of relatively low value compared with an integrated fire-prevention system designed to a customer's specific requirements for protecting commercial premises. Despite the low technology used, IFP, a small business, has prospered for over 20 years, competing with other distributors across Ireland as well as with the direct sales forces of companies such as Nu-Swift and Chubb. The market is mature, with most growth coming from the demands of new legislation. More recently, some customers have been increasingly looking for more sophisticated systems that IFP does not provide.

The company employs around 25 staff. Half are based in the headquarters and warehouse in administrative and logistics functions, and the rest are sales staff and support engineers. A wide range of stock is carried, including many different brands of extinguisher designed to combat different types of chemical and material fires. Goods are normally despatched within a few days of the receipt of an order, and often the sales representative will undertake delivery and installation. Overall, customer service and prices are considered comparable with what competitors are doing, although IFP is concerned about some new entrants to the market who do not give good advice to customers and often sell on price. IFP's owner, Mike Dalton, considers these 'cowboys' to be a threat because they have low overheads that he cannot match. The costs of entering the market are low, and sometimes former salespeople start their own businesses with minimal stock and sales support. In replacement situations, he has found that an increasing number of customers are prepared to buy on price rather than on the pre- and post-sales service offered. Although sales are just about holding up, margins are increasingly being pressurised.

Most organisations need some form of fire-prevention and fire-control systems. Legislation and safety regulations determine the exact specification demanded. The selling process itself differs, depending on whether it is repeat or new business. Regular customers tend to repeat buy with minimal shopping around, unless the value of the item is high. In some cases the sales representative makes additional sales by comparing current equipment against changing fire regulations and changes in material risks. Recommendations are then made to the customer. Customers can vary from a small restaurant or shop to industrial premises, universities and large organisations. Many purchasing decisions cannot be deferred for long because of the insurance and legal implications of being caught out by fire inspectors.

Even where IFP had not supplied a particular prospect before, if a gap in provision was identified, there was a good chance of converting the sale. This also works in reverse from time to time, when other sellers gain sales on the basis of price, once the need has been established. If the sale cannot be closed quickly, there is always the risk of a customer going elsewhere. In new business situations, especially with building extensions and new premises, the demands on the sales representative are sometimes greater because of having to sell through architects and technical experts, as well as having to quote against competition and negotiate the final deal. These customers are often as much concerned with specification match, overall fire system effectiveness and after sales service as they are with taking the lowest price.

Mike Dalton decided early on that the key to his business was an aggressive and motivated sales force. There is a range of brochures, often supplied by the manufacturer, and directories are used, but otherwise, little advertising and few other promotional methods are employed. By 1995, IFP had 10 sales representatives, a national sales manager, a field sales manager based in Dublin, and two sales support engineers who could be used for diagnosis or installation. The national and field sales managers are also expected to handle the major accounts, along with Mike Dalton, leaving the rest of the 10 000 or so potential accounts to the sales team.

For the first three months after appointment, each sales representative is paid a low salary plus commission, but after that it is commission only, although an average sales representative can gross over IR£1700 per month plus personal use of company van or car. Mike Dalton feels that the system employed is right because it keeps the sales team on their toes. With up to 1000 potential accounts per territory and many more unknown prospects, the financial motivation to encourage more cold calling is thought to be essential. Most of the sales team are happy with the arrangement and, even if a bad patch is hit after the trial period, the owner will often provide short-term advances on commission. It is never a long-term problem, as poor performance is normally dealt with by the termination of the representative's contract. The sales managers are paid by part commission and part salary and they are responsible for mentoring the sales team and dealing with any problems.

Although most of the sales team had some previous sales experience, most needed product training in fire prevention and control equipment before starting to sell. This training is normally done by the owner or the sales manager on the premises for two weeks before the representative takes over a territory. No formal sales training system is in place, although from time to time one- or two-day courses are run by staff from the local university. These courses cover general sales topics and tend to be seen as part of the annual sales meeting rather than part of a comprehensive skills development programme. Overall, most of the sales team tend to adjust to the uncertainty of commission only sales and some have been in their jobs for several years. The sales managers have both worked their way through the ranks as super salespeople and so are well versed in giving advice to less experienced colleagues in the job. The managers are particularly concerned with keeping call rates up – at least 10 per day is a minimum expectation – as well as encouraging high standards of product presentation. Over a two-year period, the turnover of sales staff has been around 25 per cent, a figure with which the owner is comfortable.

It is against this background that Mike Dalton contemplated the most appropriate actions for maintaining market position and countering the growing competitive threat.

Questions

1 What kind of remuneration package is used with the sales representatives? What are the problems with it?

2 IFP wants to encourage sales representatives to do more cold calling. Is the company going the right way about achieving this? What else can be done?

3 Is the training programme adequate? What should go into a formal sales training programme?

4 How can Mike Dalton fight the pressure from the more sophisticated integrated systems at one end of the market and the cowboys at the other? What are the implications for the sales force?

REFERENCES TO CHAPTER 17

Computer World (1999), 'Insurers Push Quotes but not Sales On-line', *Computer World*, 26 April, p. 49.

Cravens, D. W. and LaForge, R. W. (1983), 'Salesforce Deployment Analysis', *Industrial Marketing Management*, July, pp. 179–92.

Cron, W. L. *et al.* (1988), 'The Influence of Career Stages on Components of Salesperson Motivation', *Journal of Marketing*, 52 (July), pp. 179–92.

Cunningham, M. T. and Homse, E. (1986), 'Controlling the Marketing – Purchasing Interface: Resource Development and Organisational Implications', *Industrial Marketing and Purchasing*, 1(2), pp. 3–27.

Darmone, R. (1998), 'A Conceptual Scheme and Procedure for Classifying Sales Positions', *Journal of Personal Selling and Sales Management*, 18 (3), pp. 31–46.

Fill, C. (1999), *Marketing Communications: Contexts, Contents and Strategies*, 2nd edn, Prentice Hall Europe.

Gofton, K. (1998), 'Eyes on the Continent', *Marketing*, 15 October, p. 23.

Good, D. J. and Stone, R. W. (1991), 'How Sales Quotas are Developed', *Industrial Marketing Management*, 20(1), pp. 51–6.

Hill, J. S. and Still, R. R. (1990), 'Organising the Overseas Salesforce: How Multinationals Do It', *Journal of Personal Selling and Sales Management*, 10 (Spring), pp. 57–66.

Holley, R. (1999), 'Major Account Management: Not Just Another Job', *Computer Reseller News*, 3 May, p. 125.

Howard, L. (1998), 'UK Direct Sales Force Held to be "Uneconomic"', *National Underwriter*, 15 June, pp. 23–8.

Jacoby, J. and Craig, S. C. (1984), *Personal Selling*, Heath.

Johanson, J. and Vahlne, J. E. (1977), 'The Internationalisation Process of the Firm: A Model of Knowledge Development and Increasing Foreign Market Commitment', *Journal of International Business Studies*, 8(1), pp. 23–32.

Lambert, D. M. *et al.* (1990), 'Industrial Salespeople as a Source of Market Information', *Industrial Marketing Management*, 19, pp. 141–5.

Lockman, B. D. and Hallaq, (1982), 'Who Are Your Successful Salespeople?', *Journal of the Academy of Marketing Science*, 10 (Fall).

Marketing (1998), 'On the Shelf', *Marketing*, 15 October, p. 17.

Marketing (1999), 'Field Marketing, Now a Job That's Going Places', *Marketing*, 7 January, p. 55.

Mayer, M. and Greenberg, H. M. (1964), 'What Makes a Good Salesman', *Harvard Business Review*, 42 (July/Aug), pp. 119–25.

McAdams, J. (1987), 'Rewarding Sales and Marketing Performance', *Management Review*, April, pp. 33–8.

McDonald, M. H. B. (1984), *Marketing Plans*, Butterworth-Heinemann.

Miles, L. (1998), 'Discipline on the Doorstep', *Marketing*, 19 November, pp. 37–40.

Miller, R. B. and Heinman, S. E. (1991), *Successful Large Account Management*, Holt.

Moncrief, W. C. (1988), 'Five Types of Industrial Sales Jobs', *Industrial Marketing Management*, 17, pp. 161–7.

O'Connor, J. and Galvin, E. (1999), *Marketing & Information Technology*, 2nd edn, Financial Times Pitman Publishing.

Pardo, C (1997), 'Key Account Management in the Business to Business Field: the Key Account's Point of View', *Journal of Personal Selling and Sales Management*, 17 (4), pp. 17–26.

Pedersen, C. A. *et al.* (1986), *Selling: Principles and Methods*, Irwin.

Rasmusson, E. (1999), 'Training Resellers to Sell', *Sales and Marketing Management*, May, p. 65.

Rines, S. (1995), 'Forcing Change', *Marketing Week*, 1 March.

Russell, F. A. *et al.* (1977), *Textbook of Salesmanship*, 10th edn, McGraw-Hill.

Smith, P. R. (1993), *Marketing Communications*, Kogan Page.

Sujan, H. *et al.* (1994), 'Effort Quantity and Effort Quality: Learning Orientations, Working Smart and Effective Selling', *Journal of Marketing*, 58 (July), pp. 39–52.

Turnbull, P. W. (1990), 'Roles of Personal Contacts in Industrial Export Marketing' in D. Ford (ed.), *Understanding Business Markets: Interaction, Relationships and Networks*, Academic Press.

Turnbull, P. W. and Cunningham, M. T. (1981), *International Marketing and Purchasing: A Survey Among Marketing and Purchasing Executives in Five European Countries*, MacMillan.

Zikmund, W. G. and d'Amico, M. (1993), *Marketing*, 4th edn, West.

18

Direct and On-line Marketing

LEARNING OBJECTIVES

This chapter will help you to:

1 understand what direct marketing is and why it has risen in importance in recent years;

2 review the various methods used in direct marketing, appreciating their relative strengths and problems in implementation;

3 understand the importance of the Internet as an emerging marketing tool;

4 analyse direct marketing's contribution to achieving marketing communication objectives, and how direct marketing can integrate with other elements of the promotional mix;

5 appreciate the broad issues involved in managing a direct marketing campaign; and

6 appreciate the importance of creating and maintaining a database of customers and understand the importance of using the database as a direct marketing tool.

INTRODUCTION

Over the past decade, direct marketing has grown to become a significant element of the communications mix, emerging from relatively specialised beginnings in traditional mail order and what is derisively labelled 'junk mail'. It can now play an important supporting role, adding an extra dimension to the other elements of the promotional mix. Look at the increasing number of television and print advertisements, for example, which offer some kind of direct response mechanism (phone or mail) to encourage direct dialogue between supplier and customer, over and above the 'normal' objectives of the advertisement. Direct marketing can also be used as a central strategy in its own right as a means of attracting and retaining customers.

As the Harley-Davidson example implies, direct marketing is more than just 'junk mail'. It encompasses a wide range of commonly used techniques, not only direct mail but also telemarketing, direct response mechanisms, mail order and Internet marketing. The latter part of this chapter will look at each of those areas, as well as the use of new interactive communication and computing technology. The main aspects of managing direct marketing campaigns will be explored, starting with the need for careful targeting and working through the construction and maintenance of customer databases. Finally, a number of legislative issues will be discussed, as European governments and the EU seek to regulate the excesses of direct marketing.

Example   For many, a Harley-Davidson (http://www.harleydavidson.com) is *the* motorcycle. It has wide appeal, from those seeking the Rolls-Royce of motorbikes to those seeking to relive their lost youth on two wheels. The focus is on status and Harley's marketing data suggests that the average age of an owner is 44 and the median income is $73 000 in the USA. The Harley-Davidson has an almost cult following and owners congregate each year for rallies held around the country, such as Sturgis, South Dakota. Building on its success in the USA, Harley-Davidson wanted to develop the UK market. Direct mail was used, partly to encourage existing customers to upgrade and partly to tempt potential customers to seek a demonstration. Mailings went to 16 000 targeted individuals and included a teaser video claiming to offer a test drive from the 'comfort of your armchair', only to reveal when opened that nothing can create the Harley experience short of the open road. The £500 000 campaign was integrated with the opportunity to visit a dealer in order to enter a competition to win a dream Harley holiday and a direct response advertising campaign in consumer magazines (Rogers, 1999).

Relive your lost youth with the dream machine.

Source: Harley-Davidson United Kingdom. 1999 models CD. © 1998 Harley-Davidson Motor Company.

First, however, the chapter will begin by defining exactly what direct marketing is, and then examine its role in the marketing plan.

THE DEFINITION OF DIRECT MARKETING

The US Direct Marketing Association has defined **direct marketing** as:

> An interactive system of marketing which uses one or more advertising media to effect a measurable response at any location.

This is quite a broad definition which does, however, capture some basic characteristics of direct marketing. **Interactive** implies two-way communication between buyer and seller, while *effect a measurable response* implies quantifiable objectives for the exercise. *At any location* implies the flexibility and pervasiveness of direct marketing, in that it is not inextricably linked with any one medium of communication, but can utilise any-thing (mail, phone, broadcast or print media) to reach anyone anywhere. What this definition does not do, however, is to emphasise the potential of direct marketing as a primary means of building and sustaining long-term buyer–seller relationships.

It is, therefore, proposed to extend this definition to form the basis of the content of the rest of the chapter:

> **An interactive system of marketing which uses one or more advertising media to effect a measurable response at any location, forming a basis for creating and further developing an on-going direct relationship between an organisation and its customers.**

The key added value of this definition is the phrase *on-going direct relationship*, which implies continuity and seems to contradict the impersonal approach traditionally offered by mass media advertising. Is it really possible to use mass media in a mass market to create a relationship with a single customer? Is it really possible to capitalise on the advantages of personal selling that arise from one-to-one dialogue to build and sustain that relationship without the need for face-to-face contact?

If the answer to those two questions is to be 'yes', then the problem becomes one of information gathering and management. To create and sustain *quality* relationships with hundreds, thousands or even millions of individual customers, an organisation needs to know as much as possible about each one, and needs to be able to access, manipulate and analyse that information. The database, therefore, is crucial to the process of building the relationship. We will look in some detail at the issues of creat-ing, maintaining and exploiting the database at pp. 771 *et seq.*

The definition given above and the comments made about it apply as much to Internet marketing as to the more traditional forms of direct marketing. Indeed, it could be argued that Internet marketing is the ultimate in interactive media. Wherever the customer is in the world, the same messages can be accessed, perhaps even in different languages, thus giving them an enviable consistency and locational flexibility. Measurability and the ability to begin and maintain relationships with enquirers and customers are easily built into website design. Linking data captured from a website with a centralised database is a natural step for an organisation looking to improve its customer knowledge and customer service provision cost effectively. We thus look in detail at this emerging, powerful marketing tool at page 757 *et seq.*, particularly at its capacity to play a role in marketing research and planning, distribu-tion and selling and, of course, communication.

Direct marketing is being used increasingly across a wide range of both consumer and organisational markets. In particular, in consumer markets, it has always been a central feature of the marketing strategies of book clubs, which have seen phenom-enal growth over the past few years and are now expanding into CDs, videos and computer software. Even in the relatively conservative financial services industry, there has been a marked increase in the direct selling and direct marketing of a wide range of banking facilities and insurance. The next section of this chapter looks more closely at the characteristics and conditions that have led to both the enthusiastic adoption of direct marketing by organisations and its acceptance by their customers.

THE RISE OF DIRECT MARKETING

There are a number of reasons for the rapid growth of direct marketing, connected with the changing nature of the customer, the marketing environment and, in partic-ular, technological development.

Changing demographics and lifestyles

In practical terms, many more women are now working, and therefore have less time for shopping, preferring to use what little spare time they have for other leisure activities. Direct marketing, therefore, offers the convenience of shopping by phone, mail or Internet with a minimum of effort, particularly if it is possible to use a credit card for easy payment.

An additional feature of direct marketing that makes it increasingly accepted by consumers is its ability to bring specialist goods within reach. Someone with a particular interest in railways, for example, might find that their local bookshop has a very limited range of titles, and that it takes time (and money) to travel to a place with an appropriate bookshop. Joining a railway, industrial history or general history book club solves many of those problems by bringing the specialist range into the customer's own home.

Increased customer confidence

The big benefit of using direct marketing to build an on-going relationship with an individual customer is that as time goes on, the customer's trust and confidence in the organisation build up. The hardest job is to get the initial purchase, but once customers have had one successful and satisfactory experience, they will be much more receptive and willing to try again. A shrewd direct marketer can capitalise on this by analysing a customer's purchasing habits in order to tailor future offerings to fit that customer's profile, and by gently nudging the customer upmarket into more expensive purchases.

A further aspect to consider is the customer's self-confidence. Some customers prefer to have a discreet direct relationship with organisations, and to make their purchases by mail order. Adult incontinence products, for example, are widely available through pharmacists, yet many customers purchase by mail to avoid what they see as the embarrassment of having to ask for the products or being seen to purchase them.

Increasing competition

Direct marketing offers organisations the opportunity to create loyal customers. If customers have entered into dialogue with an organisation, and have had their needs and wants met through a series of tailored offerings, then it is going to be quite difficult for the competition to poach those customers. Furthermore, using techniques such as direct mail, an organisation can communicate at length and in depth with its customers personally and relatively privately. In contrast, a television or print advertisement is limited in its scope, has to appeal to a much broader segment, and is seen by the competition (who can then work to counter its effects immediately) as soon as it is screened or published.

Media fragmentation

The increasing number of advertising media available, particularly for organisations looking towards pan-European markets, presents both problems and opportunities. It is a problem because the reduced reach per medium makes advertising less attractive for general mass communication. It is an opportunity for direct marketing because audiences are fragmenting into better-profiled groups. The growth of specialist magazines and reading patterns, along with more specialist satellite TV channels, such as MTV, and the Internet, make it easier to locate a defined segment. It also makes it more cost effective to build in direct response mechanisms, because a higher proportion of the audience reached will be interested, and thus a relatively high response rate might be expected.

Increasing media and sales costs

Communication is becoming very expensive. Personal selling is too slow and involves a high cost per call, and is inappropriate for most consumer markets. With traditional advertising, it can be difficult to make the kind of impact that actually leads to action, and thus the outcomes and cost effectiveness of an advertising campaign can be difficult to define. Direct response advertising, followed up by direct mail activity, prompts the customer into action, providing measurable results that allow the cost effectiveness of targeting predetermined receptive audiences to be properly judged.

New distribution channels

Many of the types of direct marketing that have been mentioned not only affect approaches to communication, but also have an impact on the use of distribution channels. Until recently, one of the big drawbacks of mail order was the length of time that a customer had to wait for the delivery of goods. Improvements in the management of logistics (*see* Chapter 12) and increasing competition among carriers means that delivery times have been cut from the old-style 'allow 28 days' to 48 (or even 24) hours, with increased reliability and reduced costs. Combining all that with the convenience factor, cutting out the time and hassle of crowded shopping centres, and the potential of increased merchandise selection, we can begin to see why direct distribution is increasingly becoming acceptable.

> **Example** The growth of telephone call centres, considered later in this chapter, is creating a new channel of distribution between organisations and customers. The UK has the largest call centre market in Europe, followed by Germany with 20 per cent share and France with 15 per cent. Even Air France has centralised its European call centres in London. These centres could, in time, replace the traditional travel agent for air travel reservations. Datamonitor has estimated that there are around 12 000 call centres in the UK and the number will rise to 19 000 by 2003 (Flack, 1999).
>
> The growth of Internet use will further change the shape of distribution channels, as, for example, the growth of Amazon has done in book retailing (*see* Case Study 13.2), encouraging others, such as WH Smith, to go online. Any change of distribution system needs to be handled with care, however, as Packard Bell NEC found with its commercial PC operation in the USA. When NEC started to sell direct as well as through resellers, it ran into a campaign of major resistance that resulted in lost sales. With over 80 per cent of sales going through resellers, NEC could not afford the internal strife, so it changed its policy back to reseller sales only (Woods, 1998).

Increasing computer power and lower data processing costs

It is now realistic for even the smallest company to develop and manage some kind of customer database relatively cheaply. The costs (and size) of the hardware have reduced dramatically, while the power and quality of both hardware and software have increased. Thus it is now possible to hold a vast amount of detail on each individual customer, and it is relatively quick and simple to update and analyse the data held to create better marketing strategies for both existing and future customers.

Impact of new communications technology

There is little point in making any effort to elicit a direct response unless the capability exists to handle the volume of responses generated. With telephone response, for example, it is now possible using automated systems to handle many hundreds of calls simultaneously, reducing the risk of losing potential respondents through the frustration of failing to get through quickly. It is also necessary to keep the costs of response as low as possible for both the organisation and its customers. Freephone numbers and freepost addresses represent the most attractive option for the customer. Both BT and the Post Office are aware of the opportunities that direct marketing offers them as 'middlemen' (or facilitators), and will work with organisations to agree a package that represents the most efficient and cost effective use of their services.

Example Orange (http://www.orange.co.uk) uses call centres to deal with its customers. For account enquiries and other non-revenue earning transactions, Orange offers a 24-hour, self-service facility that uses interactive voice response (IVR). In other cases live operators are equipped to greet the caller by name and the customer's spending patterns are displayed to them. Using sophisticated IT systems, the top customers are identified and not kept waiting. They are routed on a priority basis to the most experienced agents (Clegg, 1999a).

Tektronix's colour printing and imaging division sells networked colour printers. It has established a call centre in Milton Keynes that handles 15 000 calls each month from across Europe, the Middle East and Africa. The average time taken to answer a call was 21 seconds in 1998 and the call can be automatically routed to an operator who speaks the local language. From the caller's perspective, the centre could be in Milan or Cairo (Telemarketing Awards, 1999b).

A final, but extremely important, development in communications technology, which has yet to achieve its full potential in most of Europe, is the use of interactive computers in home shopping. This exciting development is discussed further at p. 762 *et seq.*

Many of the issues mentioned in this section are interrelated. Consumer attitudes to direct marketing have, for example, mellowed as technology has allowed organisations to target personalised mailshots more appropriately, so that what is received through the letter box is less likely to be dismissed outright as 'junk'. The pioneering work of organisations such as the *Next Directory* in developing upmarket, high-quality merchandise, and successfully developing the logistics to fulfil a promise of 48-hour delivery, have also revolutionised UK attitudes to mail order. This has in itself provided the impetus for greater commitment and investment in direct marketing by a wide range of organisations.

The discussion so far has talked generally about the concept of direct marketing, with passing reference to specific areas such as direct mail and direct response, among others. The next section looks more closely at each of these areas and their individual characteristics. Figure 18.1 gives an overview of the range of direct marketing areas.

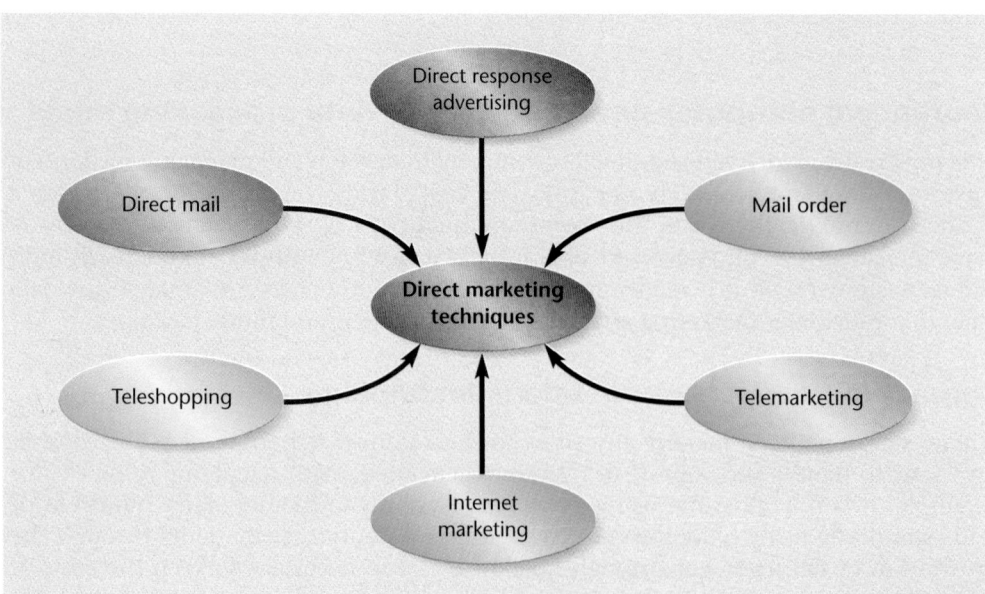

FIGURE 18.1

The range of direct marketing techniques

TECHNIQUES OF DIRECT MARKETING

The scope of direct marketing is very wide. It utilises what might be called the more traditional means of marketing communication, such as print and broadcast advertising media, but it has also developed its own media, through mail, telecommunications and modem. Each of the main techniques in direct marketing will now be considered in turn.

Direct mail

Direct mail is material distributed through the postal service to the recipients' home or business address to promote a product or service. What is mailed can vary from a simple letter introducing a company or product through to a comprehensive catalogue or sample. Many mailshots incorporate involvement devices to increase the chances of their being opened and read, through stimulating curiosity.

Example The wildlife charity WWF UK (http://www.wwf-uk.org) wanted to raise at least £400 000 as the UK's contribution to an international effort to save the threatened Chinese tiger. In the year of the tiger, WWF thought it appropriate to draw people's attention to the threat of extinction caused by loss of the tiger's natural habitat, the use of tiger body parts in Chinese medicine, and illegal trade in tiger skins. WWF worldwide has 4.7 million supporters scattered across 100 countries. From its extensive database it is able to segment donors by country and then into existing and dormant donors and can thus target different messages for each group. In the UK, a special letter was sent to 600 of the most generous supporters; 164 of them responded with cheques averaging over £1000 each. This group received a highly informative and well-produced information pack to reflect the donor's importance. An intermediate pack was sent to potential donors in the £250 and £500 donation category, while the rest of the donors received a basic pack. The campaign successfully raised £540 000 (Gofton, 1999).

Most direct mail is unsolicited. Organisations compile or buy lists of names and addresses, and then send out the mailshot. The **mailing list** used may be cold, that is, where there has been no previous contact between the organisation and the addressee, or may reflect various selection criteria based on data held about previous or existing customers.

Example *The Express* newspaper developed a mailing list of readers who had shown an interest in gardening. Just before the Chelsea Flower Show in 1999, the gardeners received a mailshot offering them the chance to win a trip to see Monet's garden in Giverny, France. They could also dial the newspaper's call centre to win tickets to the Chelsea Flower Show as guests of *The Express*. Enclosed in the mailings were discount vouchers for *The Express* and *Sunday Express* to reinforce loyalty further (*Marketing Week*, 1999b).

Direct mail is widely used in both consumer and organisational markets, as can be seen in Table 18.1. The financial services sector, for example, sends out mailshots to encourage people to apply for credit cards, mortgages, loans and insurance quotes. The pharmaceutical and medical supplies companies send out mailshots to doctors, pharmacists and dentists, partly to make them aware of what is available, and partly to pave the way for a later call from the sales representative. Consultants, contractors and suppliers similarly target organisational buyers and decision makers. Sometimes, different members of the distribution channel can work together.

TABLE 18.1
The UK's biggest mailers by sector

Company	Sector	Estimated number of mailings (Feb–Dec 1998)
MNBA International	Finance	46,848,000
The Associates	Finance	43,778,000
Cornhill Direct	Finance	30,117,000
Barclaycard	Finance	26,839,000
TSB	Finance	24,963,000
Britannia Music Company	Retail	15,883,000
DFS	Retail	14,803,000
Worldbooks	Retail	12,863,000
Littlewoods	Retail	9,577,000
Reader's Digest Associates	Retail	8,833,000
Saga Holidays	Travel	2,062,000
Butlins	Travel	1,415,000
Barclaycard Travel Services	Travel	930,000
Thomson Cruises	Travel	837,000
British Airways	Travel	757,000

Source: DART/ Thomson Intermedia.

Direct mail has the problem that it has suffered from bad PR. All of us as consumers can probably think of a couple of examples of direct mail we have received that have been completely inappropriate, and misconceptions about direct mail's effectiveness are often based on such personal experiences of receiving 'junk'. Historically, this has arisen partly from the lack of flexibility and detail within databases, and partly from poor marketing thinking. In the earlier days of direct mail, marketers were obsessed with the power of databases to generate vast numbers of contacts and to process personalised mailshots at high speed. This created a false bonus in going for volume rather than concentrating on more carefully targeted use, since it was as easy to send 100 000 mail shots as 10 000. If the organisation was looking for a predetermined response rate, then there was an advantage in mailing larger numbers of mailshots, even though the majority were wasted. This then led to resentment among those receiving vast quantities of inappropriate material, and the labelling of direct mail as ineffective junk. Increasingly, though, marketers are using the information at their disposal more intelligently, and mailing smaller groups of well-defined prospective customers, using better-designed creative material. They are also keeping their databases more current, and so a household should not receive direct mail addressed to people who moved away or died over a year ago. In theory, then, an individual should be receiving less direct mail, but what they do receive should be of prime relevance and interest. This should then prompt a 'quality' response (Wilmshurst, 1993).

There is evidence to suggest that direct mail is more effective than its reputation gives it credit for. In 1988, £930mn was spent on direct mail in terms of postage and production. By 1998, the figure had risen to £1665mn (http://www.royalmail.co.uk) and the number of mailshots had increased by 126 per cent over the same period. A survey by the Direct Mail Information Service (DMIS) in 1997 found that in general direct mail scored a 4.4 per cent response rate (over 5 per cent in business to business markets). Underlying that figure, however, 77 per cent of direct mail is opened, 59 per cent opened and read, and 27 per cent kept or passed on. In business to business markets, 84 per cent of direct mail is opened, 12 per cent redirected and 17 per cent filed or answered, and 55 per cent looked at and thrown away. In the DMIS 1999 survey, it was found that the overall response rate had risen to over 11 per cent. This is heartening, but it may not be enough. Think about the hierarchy of effects models shown in Fig. 14.7, and how direct mail fits into those. Using the AIDA model as an example, opening the envelope begins the *awareness* stage, reading the content generates *interest* and *desire* and, finally, the mailshot clearly defines what subsequent *action* is expected. The main objective is to move the recipient quickly through all the stages from awareness to action. The key is not simply the opening of the envelope, but whether the content can pull the reader right through to the completion of action. As a consolation prize, if the recipient reads the content but chooses not to respond, there may still be an awareness or interest effect that may 'soften up' the customer for subsequent mailings or, in organisational markets, a sales visit.

Advantages of using direct mail

Direct mail accounts for 11.6 per cent of promotional expenditure (non-sales force spend) and its biggest users are mail order retailers, financial services companies, retailers and charities (http://www.royalmail.co.uk). There are a number of advantages of using direct mail.

Targeting. Using the post code system, targeted campaigns can be developed based on geodemographic criteria. Combine that with the depth of knowledge held about existing customers, and even more detailed targeting can be achieved. Similarly, with organisational lists, targeted efforts at specific, named individuals within organisations is possible. Even purchased lists can be used for clearly targeted campaigns. The London Herb and Spice Company wanted to create awareness of its fruit teas and so used a mailshot aimed at 90 000 users of competitive products.

When operating on a European basis, however, it must be remembered that regulations on list broking vary from country to country. Laws are more lenient in the Netherlands and France than in the UK and Germany. In the UK list broking is allowed, subject to notifying the subject ('Please let us know if you do not wish to receive offers from other carefully selected companies'), while in Germany heavy regulation reduces the number of lists available.

Example When Scoot, a business directory company (http://www.scoot.co.uk), wanted to warm up potential clients before the sales team called, it turned to direct mail. With a database approaching two million names, the challenge was to pick categories for targeted communication and a follow-up with a sales call. Six broad categories were chosen: food, communications, trade, motor, health and beauty, and retail. A highly creative approach was taken to the insert, with the mailshot shaped like a pair of manicured hands for the health and beauty group and something resembling a sandwich for the food category. The copy content emphasised the number of enquiries that Scoot receives for food establishments. The unusual insert gave the sales person a useful way to generate interest in Scoot's service. The campaign cost £200 000 and is claimed to have grossed £2mn in increased directory listings (Dwek, 1999).

Personalisation. With new technology in ink-jet imaging, laser printing and electronic processing, large numbers of personalised mailings can be undertaken regularly. Although the novelty of receiving mailshots that begin 'Dear Mrs Shufflebottom, You will be the envy of Railway Terrace, Heckmondwyke, if you take advantage of our wonderful offer . . .' has worn off, there is still an undeniable intimacy about personalisation that other advertising media cannot achieve.

Using the correct name and address is not an option, it is essential for direct marketing. MBNA International Bank aggressively markets its credit cards and financial services using regular mailshots. Each letter is personalised and emphasises the speed and ease of application. The freephone 0800 number is mentioned eight times in a typical letter and accompanying reply form. In order to make it even easier for customers, their name and address is already printed on the reply form along with a personal reference number for internal tracking and mailing list management. MBNA is aware that if it does not gain attention quickly or if it gets customer details wrong, the chances are that a response will not be made (Lawson, 1999a).

Response rates. Depending on the quality of the database and the selection criteria underpinning the mailing list, the response rate for direct mailing can be high. This has already been seen in the examples mentioned earlier. All of this is a product of the personal, confidential, selective and flexible nature of direct mail.

Flexibility. The creative scope of what can be included in a mailshot is very flexible, allowing varied and interesting campaigns, which can even be phased if required. This flexibility extends to frequency, size, colour, length, copy, layout and quality, as well as the inclusion of videos, CDs, gifts or samples.

Attention seeking. Even if only for a brief moment, the mailing holds the attention of the reader far more exclusively than advertising. An involvement device that requires the recipient to do something (a competition scratch card; something that needs careful unfolding; a video to play) reduces the chances of the mailing being discarded unread.

Example Advertising agency Saatchi and Saatchi (http://www.saatchi-saatchi.com) decided that it wanted fewer, but higher calibre, applicants for its graduate recruitment programme. In response to enquiries, students were asked to fill an empty envelope with four of their own ideas. These were 'your idea of you' through a visual simile and description of how the student could contribute to Saatchi, 'ideas on a postcard' describing the most important journey in the student's life, 'your best ever idea' and how it became a reality, and finally 'exploiting ideas', developing one of Saatchi's advertisements. Each response was restricted to a maximum of 100 words. These, along with the student's CV and covering letter, gave Saatchi a rich insight into the creative mind of the student without the need to spend too much time on marginal candidates (*Campaign* Direct Awards, 1999b).

Developing a direct mail campaign

It must, however, be stressed that a mailshot is only as good as the data underpinning it. If, for example the mailing list contains many small firms that frequently change their address, or an area of high turnover in residential property, then its quality and its ability to deliver a satisfactory response rate are questionable.

The mailing list is the first of a number of specific areas in developing a direct mail campaign that need to be examined.

Mailing list management. A list is a collection of names and addresses of individuals or companies grouped together on predetermined criteria. Getting the list right (i.e. fit for its purpose) is a major challenge. Direct mail must have accurate targeting, drawing on the same concepts as market segmentation, discussed in Chapter 5.

Lists are either internal or purchased. Internal lists can be compiled from a variety of sources, including past and present customers, enquirers, prospects or compilations from published sources, for example through a systematic scan of trade directories, telephone

WHAT COMES OUT OF THE
WORLD'S MOST FAMOUS AGENCY DEPENDS
ON WHAT YOU PUT IN.

Saatchi & Saatchi is famous for extraordinary ideas.

But to create extraordinary ideas you need to have extraordinary people looking for extraordinary careers.

This is exactly what we have. This is also where you come in. Or rather, this is where you 'put' in.

Because we want to get an idea of what you could put into the agency. So we would like to hear about some of your ideas. But this doesn't mean we want you to send us a load of essays. (You've probably done enough of those already.) We want you to bring your ideas alive. In any way you like. Ready?

1. Your idea of you. Send us a 'visual' simile of yourself and explain how this demonstrates what you will contribute to us.

2. Ideas on a postcard please. What's the most important journey you've made in your life? Send us a postcard.

3. Your best ever idea. What was it and how did you make it become a reality?

4. Exploiting ideas. Take one of our ads and show us how you would exploit it further.

Four ideas. Each accompanied by 100 words.

Finally, put everything, together with your CV, a covering letter saying why you want to work for us and a passport photo, into this envelope. Remove the sticky address label, affix the appropriate postage and send it back to us before the 11th December 1998.

Who knows what might come out of it?

SAATCHI & SAATCHI

Ideas on a postcard, please.

Source: Saatchi & Saatchi.

books etc. Great Ormond Street Children's Hospital (http://www.gt-ormond-st-hospital.
org.uk) is concerned with fundraising to support its development priorities in research,
equipment and treatment. With over 22 000 in-patients and 78 000 outpatients each year,
half of whom are under the age of two, there is always a need for more cash. Although
there is a comprehensive programme of fundraising activities form active donors, including sponsored websites, corporate sponsorship and employee giving, the hospital is also
concerned not to lose lapsed donors. It can target its database of lapsed donors with

special mail campaigns to attract them back. In one campaign, it achieved 6000 responses from the 22 000 lapsed donors at that time. Lists can also be purchased from other organisations who maintain customer databases and wish to trade information.

> **Example** The Boots Advantage loyalty card scheme, launched in September 1997, provided valuable new insights into customer behaviour and the effects of marketing activities and promotional offers. For example, Boots has been able to link the sales of films and photo frames with new baby products. Over time, it will be able to build up a rich profile of the purchasing behaviour of its card holders, which can then be used to send the right promotion to the right person at the right time. Boots is looking at customers in terms of their current and future value to identify the potentially higher spending groups with a view to increasing their value, rather than endlessly attracting potentially low spending customers (Clegg, 1999b; Wilson, 1999).

Lists purchased from external sources need to be carefully checked to make sure that they are relevant and up to date. Next time you fill in a reply coupon, look to see if it has small print at the bottom to the effect that: 'We may wish to pass your details on to other carefully selected companies'. Unless you tick the box stating that you would rather deny the company this privilege, your details are liable to be sold on to another company. Organisations also exist specialising in consumer research and list compilation.

MARKETING IN ACTION   I've got a little list . . .

There is a large number of list providers and the marketer must ensure that the list matches with the required target audience. HLB Ltd provides a list of 20 000 active subscribers to *Feng Shui for Modern Living*. The list comprises ABC1 females, aged between 25 and 45, and 61 per cent of them have incomes in excess of £25 000 per year and are home owners. As professionals in architecture, interior design and landscape gardening, they are targets for upmarket mail order, interior design products, charity and financial services offers. Similarly, Swetenhams offers a list of 100 000 buyers from the Science Museum catalogue, a group who could well be good prospects for offers designed for an educated and affluent audience.

At the other extreme, Dun & Bradstreet offers 48 list options:

■ over 1mn UK decision makers;

■ 1.7mn actively trading UK businesses;
■ 3.5mn European businesses in 18 countries;
■ 2mn directors at home.

Wyvern Direct Response offer lists according to occupational groups such as:

■ 86 000 accountancy professionals;
■ 60 000 investors from R J Temple;
■ 350 000 subscribers to *The Economist*;
■ 45 000 doctors in medical practice;
■ 90 000 hospital contacts.

Some companies offer support services. Wise and Lovey, for example, provides the UK's first fully automated mailing list site at http://www.mailing-labels.com, lists from which are available for purchase. Other directory publishers will need to follow with on-line versions in this fast-moving sector (Witthaus, 1999).

In the UK, the Royal Mail offers a postcode address file (PAF) containing 1.6mn postcodes and 25mn delivery possibilities. This file can be matched with existing or purchased data using specialised software that can run on a PC. These data must be checked and cleaned at regular intervals to ensure that names and addresses are correct. Often this work is handled by a specialist external agency, but there is a threshold of 10 000 records beyond which it becomes more economical to develop in-house capability, especially if the data are complex in their construction and are for specialist mailings and use. No system is 100 per cent accurate and often even the larger companies send their data out for extensive checking and cleansing (Lawson, 1999a).

Once established, the PAF can be used with a mainframe to enable easy selection of geographically based mailing lists, although additional information would be necessary to introduce lifestyle or purchasing behaviour variables.

There is a note of caution, however. Statistics released by the Direct Marketing Association have suggested that of the 3.7bn pieces of mail sent out in 1997, 100mn were marked 'return to sender' and 80mn were so badly addressed as to be undeliverable. The total cost to the industry of inaccuracies is estimated at £100mn per year (Murphy, 1999).

Creative implementation. Designing the content of a mailshot is the realm of a well-briefed copywriter. It is certainly not simply an extension of letter writing. The prime objective of most mailshots is to generate a response, which really means that the recipient's attention and interest have to be engaged quickly, if a rapport is to be established. Even if the recipient starts to read, there is still the danger of distraction and rejection. Personalisation, involvement devices, benefit orientation and flow are therefore critical to holding the reader.

Example In a business to business campaign, Orange Spider, a media production company positioning itself as 'a different animal capable of unconventional work', sent out a black envelope two feet long. Inside was a shining red fish, with the name Orange Spider down its length. For those who did not respond to it, a scaled-down version was sent two weeks later saying 'Gutted! I really thought you would have taken the bait by now', linking with the first mailing. A follow-up telephone call enquiring whether the fish had been received led to an attempt to fix a meeting (Elster, 1999). The question is, was it all just a red herring?

Being too creative, however, can be risky, as computer games manufacturer Eidos (http://www.eidos.com) found when it was the subject of complaints to the Advertising Standards Authority (ASA). At the peak of the NATO Kosovo campaign, Eidos sent out a mailshot designed to look like military call-up papers as part of the launch of a new game, *Commando*. The mock call-up papers were dated April 1940 and were only sent to previous buyers, so most customers should have realised that it was a spoof. Although no complaint was upheld by the ASA, Eidos still withdrew the campaign (*Marketing Week*, 1999a).

The envelope or packaging can also be part of the creative appeal. Placing a message on the outside of the envelope might increase the chances of its being opened, as well as building some sense of anticipation. Teaser messages, coloured envelopes, windows to show a glimpse of an incentive, whether it is a gift or a prize draw, all assist in this process. Thus one of the Great Ormond Street Hospital's lapsed donor mailshot campaigns had the words 'Link up with them this Christmas' on the outside of the envelope, with the 'Link up' presented as a logo written in paper chains.

It should be noted, however, that some organisations take an opposite view. Some consumers will dump an envelope, unopened, straight into the bin, if it is obviously a piece of direct mail. The strategy, therefore, is to make the envelope as innocuous and unobtrusive as possible, so that the recipient has to open it to make sure that it isn't something important. Once the envelope is opened, there is a greater chance that the content will be read. One Amex mailshot was sent in a plain white envelope with just the Amex logo on it. The existing card holders at whom the mailshot was targeted would have assumed that it was something to do with their account.

The response mechanism is also important, especially for business to business direct mail where the main objective is often to generate leads rather than sales *per se*. Response cards not only assist the ease of reply, but also the initial qualification of leads. They can be used to gain additional information on the buyer prior to contact, to assess whether the contact is worth following up, and what kind of follow-up is most appropriate. Reply paid cards should not be an add-on, but a well thought out means of improving the quality of leads generated.

Table 18.2 shows the amount of direct mail received per head of population across Europe. It is interesting to note that the more developed markets have a higher number of mailings than the countries of southern Europe where the infrastructure for communication is less well advanced. Interestingly, in eastern Europe direct mail is in its infancy, but can still attract high levels of readership, as long as a practical, offer-specific orientation is taken.

Direct response advertising

Direct response advertising appears in the standard broadcast and print media. It differs from 'normal' advertising because it is designed to generate a direct response, whether an order, an enquiry for further information or a personal visit. The response mechanism may be a coupon to cut out in a print advertisement, or a phone number in any type of advertisement. This area has grown in popularity in recent years as advertisers seek to get their increasingly expensive advertising to work harder for them.

TABLE 18.2

Number of items of addressed direct mail received per head of population in the EU 1996

	Items per capita (number)
Austria	
Belgium	85
Denmark	46
Finland	52
France	64
Germany	81
Greece	
Ireland	23
Italy	
Luxembourg	
Netherlands	81
Portugal	14
Spain	30
Sweden	67
UK	55

Source: Euromonitor (1998) adapted from Table 1311, p. 316.

Example Slendertone UK (http://www.slendertone.ie) has become the market leader in the body-toning market within three years of its launch and much of this has been attributed to its successful use of direct response media. Market share has grown from 6 to 49 per cent. While sales have gone up sixteenfold, the cost per sale has reduced by 40 per cent in just two years. After building a profile of target customers, the company was able to match it with the reader and viewer profiles of different media. The full range of direct response media was used, including television, press and radio as well as direct mail, catalogues and point-of-sale materials in selected retail outlets. Over 40 titles are used and each is tracked for the number and nature of responses. The UK experience has been replicated by Slendertone subsidiaries in France, Germany and the Netherlands (*Marketing Week*, 1999d).

By using advertising media, direct response advertising's initial targeting, unlike that of some of the other forms of direct marketing, relies much more on an assessment of the medium's reader or viewer profile than on a pre-prepared mailing list. Responses to such advertising, however, can then be used as a database for other forms of direct marketing in the future.

Example Increasingly the telephone is the preferred source of response communication (Reed, D. 1998), although this in turn could eventually be replaced by the Internet. To handle direct responses, it is important to ensure that the call centre is geared up to handle large volumes of calls. Cable and Wireless Communications has set a target of answering 90 per cent of calls within four rings. Caller profiling systems are increasingly being used so that the messages can be tailored to the individual on the line, distinguishing perhaps between time wasters and hot prospects. In a direct response television (DRTV) campaign by Mitsubishi Motors, hot prospect leads were automatically passed on to the local dealer for direct follow-up. This shows DRTV at its best, generating a large volume of responses that are prioritised according to urgency and type of sales approach and then all followed up by either literature mailing and/or a telephone call to encourage, in the case of Mitsubishi, a demonstration or quotation.

Types of direct response advertising

There is a range of types of direct response mechanisms that can be used in advertising. Advertisers can provide an address to write to, a coupon to fill in and send off for more information, telephone numbers or website addresses. Either the advertiser or the customer can pay for any postal or telephone charges. Throughout the rest of this discussion, the costs are considered from the consumer's perspective, i.e. 'freepost' means postal response that is free to the respondent and 'pay post' means that the respondent has to pay normal postage rates.

Freepost (coupon) and freephone

Scottish Widows (http://www.scottishwidows.co.uk) supported its television advertising campaign for ISAs with press advertising that involved freepost, freephone and Internet options for obtaining further information. The coupon was primarily concerned with collecting the enquirer's name and address, but the date of birth and postcode were included to reveal useful background information. A request for daytime and evening telephone details left the enquirer in no doubt what the follow-up approach was going to be!

Franklin Mint, a company specialising in moderately expensive collectibles, regularly advertises to sell straight off the page. An American bald eagle pocket watch was offered for £59 payable by monthly instalments and with a full 30-day money-back guarantee. The advertisement claimed that the watch incorporated the 'original art of the world-renowned wildlife artist [Ted Blaylock] into the design of a precision timepiece'. Although no money had to be sent with the order, an invoice of £29.50 plus £2.95 would be issued on delivery and a further invoice for the final payment the following month. Response could either be by coupon or freephone.

Pay post (coupon) and pay phone

Neville Johnson designs and manufactures exclusive fitted furniture for the home. It uses the Sunday colour supplement magazines to generate enquiries from advertisements showing how loft and sloping roof space can be used as an office with fitted furniture. The coupon asks the customer to provide basic information and a contact telephone number. Interested consumers can either mail the coupon at their expense or can use the telephone, again at their own expense.

Pay post (no coupon) and pay phone

Farmplan Computer Systems offers IT solutions to farmers to cover their financial, accounting and management information needs. The company needs sales leads to enable demonstrations of the software to take place, and so it advertises in the specialist farming press such as *Farmers Weekly*. No coupon is provided and although an e-mail address is provided, any contact as to be at the potential customer's expense.

Freepost and pay phone

Bonusprint, a photo developing company, glued a freepost envelope to its full-page advertisement to make it as easy as possible for readers to order photographic prints at special reduced prices, and claim their free photo album. The loosely attached envelope attracts attention to the advertisement, because it changes the weight and the feel of the page, thus making it difficult to ignore, while the free album offer further encourages response. The envelope has all the necessary information about prices etc. on it so that if it became detached from the advertisement, it could still be used. Given the nature of the response sought in this case, getting people to put their films in the envelope and post them, the lack of a freephone response mechanism is entirely understandable.

Pay post (coupon) and freephone

In contrast to Neville Johnson above, Conquest Fitted Furniture uses direct response advertising in quality magazines to promote interest in its fitted office furniture. It uses a freephone 0800 number, provides a fax number and a coupon to send off to receive a brochure or arrange for a designer to call. It requests no more than the customer's name, address and telephone number for subsequent follow-up.

Freephone only

Although many companies are linking freephone numbers and websites, Volkswagen ran a campaign for its retailer-approved used car programme carrying just a freephone number. Similarly, the Adecco employment agency advertised its new Max and Xpert systems in the trade press, featuring only an 0800 number as the response mechanism.

Internet

With the growth of Internet use, other response mechanisms are also evolving. Screentrade (http://www.screentrade.co.uk) advertises its direct insurance services on the basis of 24-hour access and reduced premiums. Its direct response advertising uses only a website address, with no attempt to provide either a freephone or freepost service. It is one of the first companies in the UK to handle all home, motor and travel insurance through direct Internet sales. Similarly, when Palm Computing advertised its Palm V model in France, it provided just an 0800 number and the website details (http://www.palm-europe.com), a pattern repeated by Siemens Computer Systems (http://www.sni.fr).

Approaches to direct response advertising

As all these examples show, some organisations approach direct response much more seriously than others. The ones who expect the consumer to pay for a phone call or postage, or who expect the consumer to compose a letter rather than filling in a coupon, are immediately putting up barriers to response. Why should consumers make any undue effort, or even pay directly, to give an organisation the privilege of trying to sell them something? In the light of that view, organisations either need to have incredibly compelling direct response advertising that makes any effort or cost worthwhile or, more realistically, they need to minimise the effort and cost to the potential customer. Schofield (1994) confirms that certainly in organisational markets, response should be as easy as possible. The easier the response, the greater the number of enquiries and the greater the conversion rate and revenue per enquiry.

Direct response advertising on television

The use of direct response advertising on television (DRTV) is beginning to grow. Some products are marketed on satellite channels across Europe using toll-free telephone support. CDs and tapes, for example, are actively promoted on the music channel. Holiday companies use a toll-free line to receive requests for brochures, while the insurance industry is starting to appreciate the value of direct response television advertising to generate requests for quotes. If the advertisement is being used to sell off the screen (as opposed to simply generating enquiries) and hard cash is wanted, the risk limit is around £10–£15 and the product must be easily demonstrated and explained.

> **Example** National tourist agencies use DRTV not only to sell their destinations, but also to build databases for future promotions. The Australian Tourist Commission will be spending £57mn globally up to 2001 on a DRTV campaign. The Canadian Tourist Commission has already run three DRTV campaigns in the UK and Ireland and has generated a database of 230 000 enquirers. In the first year of the campaign, simply by putting a telephone response number in the advertisement, 72 000 enquiries were received of which 78 per cent were serious prospects. Now that a database has been established, more attention can be given to regular mailings promoting Canada as a tourist destination (Exon, 1999).

Different media and more creative approaches encourage direct response. Book Club Associates (http://www.bca.co.uk) relies primarily on inserts in magazines relevant to specialist areas such as ancient and mediaeval history, the arts, fantasy and sci-fi and railways to sell membership to its range of clubs. Normally, very low priced introductory offers are designed to stimulate trial, as discussed in the example on page 677. It has also used door drops and television advertising to generate further enquiries.

Example Even the phone number used can help generate responses, especially with radio advertising where the listener might have to remember a number after only hearing it rather than seeing it. Forte hotels, for example, uses the number 40 40 40, of course, while the insurance company Guardian Direct, reminding people of the owl in its logo, uses 28 28 20 (too-whit, too-whit, too-woo). Similarly, BUPA's Dental Cover service has the number 230 230 (tooth hurty, tooth hurty).

Since Forte introduced the 40 40 40 line as part of a programme to centralise its telephone reservation system, it claims to have improved its conversion of enquiries into sales from 25 per cent to 40 per cent. Some numbers are memorable in their own right, without strong links to the company or brand. Disney has 000000, for example, Friends Provident 0800 000080, BT freefone 0800 800 800, and the insurance company Scottish Widows has 678910.

Direct response has only been possible because of allied developments in the widespread use of credit cards that make remote ordering easier, the use of freephone numbers, and improvements in response handling techniques and technology. However, the principles of advertising described in Chapter 15 still have to be applied when the specific elements of direct response messages and media are considered. There is a feeling, however, that the UK market is not properly exploiting direct response, especially through television. Fry (1995) reports the opinion of the head of a direct marketing consultancy who cited the following seven reasons for television-based direct response being less effective than it should be:

- poor forecasting of response
- lack of co-ordination
- ill-considered calls to action
- over-optimistic promises to respondents
- failure to carry the creative message through from the advertisement to the handling of the respondent
- inappropriate evaluation of effect
- inadequate follow-up.

Telemarketing

While direct response advertising and direct mail both imply the use of an impersonal initial approach through some kind of written or visual material, **telemarketing** makes a direct personal, verbal approach to the potential customer. However, although this brings benefits from direct and interactive communication, it is seen by some as extremely intrusive. If the telephone rings, people feel obliged to answer it there and then, and tend to feel annoyed and disappointed if it turns out to be a sales pitch rather than a friend wanting a good gossip. It can be very difficult to curtail a telemarketing call without resorting to rudeness, and many people feel awkward about doing that. At least a piece of direct mail can be dismissed and put in the bin quickly and without leaving a feeling that someone has been offended in some way. Surprisingly, however, research from Datamonitor (*European Business Teleculture 98*) found that many people do accept these calls and in some cases actually enjoy them (Bird, 1998).

Telemarketing, therefore, can be defined as any planned and controlled activity that creates and exploits a direct relationship between customer and seller, using the telephone.

> **Example** Capital Bank (http://www.capitalbank.co.uk), part of the Bank of Scotland group, offers car hire-purchase finance through car dealerships. It uses telemarketing first to welcome new customers and then to introduce the bank's other financial services. Once the customer has taken out a finance package, there is a 'welcome call' to say 'thank you' for the business and to make sure the customer is satisfied with the service received. This is followed up by regular mailings and telephone calls to ascertain whether there are any other financial needs. If the consumer mentions that either they or a family member are interested in buying another car, then the details are transferred to the *Dealer Alert* programme. The focus then is on encouraging the customer to visit the dealer and the bank follows up each *Dealer Alert* with a further phone call to the dealer to check progress. It has been found that qualified leads went up by 52 per cent in one year and the value of loans by a similar amount (Telemarketing Awards, 1999c).

The Capital Bank campaign is an example of **outbound telemarketing**, where the organisation contacts the potential customer. **Inbound telemarketing**, where the potential customer is encouraged to contact the organisation, is also popular. This is used not only in direct response advertising, but also for customer care lines, competitions and other sales promotions.

> **Example** Beiersdorf, maker of Nivea skin cream, wanted to improve the level of customer advice on skincare, give product usage guidance and improve loyalty to its brands. It chose inbound telemarketing to achieve these objectives, setting up a freephone advice line to demonstrate caring concern for customers. In a normal week it receives between 100 and 200 calls, but during an advertising campaign the figure can rise to 20 000 in one week. At the outset of the service, a call was followed by a mailout providing a brochure on the Nivea range, as well as providing usage advice. However, Beiersdorf found that such a passive approach did not enable cross-selling to take place, so the telephone staff now spend much longer with enquirers, examining the various product options and agreeing a usage plan with interested callers (Telemarketing Awards, 1999a).

Scope for telemarketing

Telephone rental or ownership is high across Europe, averaging over 80 per cent of households, and thus if an appropriate role can be defined for telemarketing within the planned promotional mix, it represents a powerful communication tool. As with personal selling (*see* p. 687 *et seq.*), there is direct contact and so dialogue problems can be addressed. Similarly, the customer's state of readiness to commit themselves to a course of action can be assessed and improved through personal persuasion, and efforts made to move towards a positive outcome. Telemarketing can also be used to support customer service initiatives. As the Nivea example indicated, a carefully designed and managed inbound telemarketing operation can provide an important, sometimes 24-hour, point of contact for customers. This is an important part of maintaining an on-going relationship with the customer.

> **Example** Abbey National Direct has a system that recognises the telephone number from which an inbound call originates and can route the call to the staff member who dealt with that customer last time they called. This clearly allows the customer to develop a more personal relationship with the organisation as well as providing consistency. As the one-to-one relationship develops, it also becomes easier for the staff member to try to sell other financial services products to that customer.

Nevertheless, outbound telemarketing in particular is still not widely accepted by consumers and is often seen as intrusive. Where customers have an existing relationship with an organisation, however, and where the purpose of the call is not hard selling, they are less suspicious. Research by Datamonitor, reported by Bird (1998), found that 75 per cent of respondents like receiving calls that check their satisfaction with the product or service or that simply thank them for their custom. The figure drops to less than half if the call is linked to information gathering and a sales pitch. If the outbound calls are badly handled, research by Outbound Teleculture has indicated that 70 per cent of customers become annoyed and in some cases this damages the reputation and prospects for future business for that company.

Marketing tasks. It would be misleading, however, to imply that telemarketing is only about high pressure selling. As a form of personal selling, it certainly lends itself to that kind of application, but there is a whole range of marketing tasks that can be performed using telemarketing methods. As Table 18.3 shows, telemarketing has a clear role at an operational level, not only making sales, but also improving distribution, customer service, technical support, information gathering and credit control. A particular challenge is to integrate it creatively into the rest of the promotional mix.

TABLE 18.3

Applications of telemarketing

- Generate leads
- Screen leads before follow-up
- Arrange appointments for representatives
- Direct sales
- Encourage cross/up selling
- Dealer support
- Account servicing
- Market research
- Test marketing

> **Example** easyJet (http://easyJet.www.com) uses both the Internet and telemarketing to sell its airline seats direct. Although telephone booking is still more popular, the rate of growth in Internet booking could mean that 30 per cent of its business will be conducted through the Internet by 2000. Early in 1999, 87 per cent of bookings were made by phone. easyJet found that in peak periods customers can obtain much quicker service through the Internet and that the company can handle six or seven e-mail bookings per second (Booth, 1999). When Egg launched its new insurance plan, it also geared up for inbound calls, with nearly 95 per cent of all sales coming from direct response advertising and telephone contact. In the first month of the campaign, it received 335 000 enquiries via the telephone and the Internet and soon found its planned response resources stretched (Gofton, 1998).

In a survey of 300 leading organisations carried out by InTelMark for *Marketing* magazine, the total spend on telemarketing as a percentage of the overall marketing budget represented over 10 per cent for 58 per cent of respondents and for 20 per cent of respondents, over 30 per cent of the total buget. Although there was some evidence of the dramatic rise in telemarketing spend levelling off, 42 per cent of respondents reported a relatively larger spend within their budgets over the previous three years (Cobb, 1998). The use of the telemarketing varied widely, as can be seen in Table 18.4.

TABLE 18.4

The use of telemarketing

New business lead generation	28%
Customer care	26%
Customer service	26%
Brand loyalty	14%
Crisis management	6%

Source: Cobb (1998).

Inbound marketing

Customer service and care lines are an important growth area within inbound telemarketing. Ideally these are set up to allow customers to make direct contact with an organisation to ask questions or to pass comment on products and their use. Some centres can also take direct orders. Many companies use external call centres, for example Sitel (http://www.sitel.com) in London has as its clients Norwich Union, Go, Scottish Amicable and Calortex (Curtis, 1998). For Go, BA's discount airline, there are 40 operators handling calls from Germany, Italy, Denmark and Portugal, all in the enquirer's language. Go also has its own centre at Stansted to handle UK calls. The operators in London are even briefed on the weather in the various callers' countries to help give the impression that the call is being taken locally. The Go operation at Sitel handles 2000 calls per day and the operators are trained to check flight availability, take credit card details and assign passengers a reference number. Sitel also works in the business-to-business arena, for example offering technical support and customer help desks, warranty support and account management programmes for computer hardware and software suppliers.

Care line numbers are sometimes included in advertisements and on packaging to assist consumer response. Kellogg provides an 0800 number for comments and enquiries through a customer care line open from 8am to 6pm Monday to Friday.

Example PPP Healthcare uses inbound telemarketing to improve standards of customer care. Initially the concept started as a customer helpline that was staffed by qualified professionals such as pharmacists, midwives and nurses who could dispense advice to the worried caller. The service was not just for those wishing to make a claim, but could handle even routine calls from policy holders such as how to treat an upset stomach or sunburn. The PPP bureau Access 24 has now grown to include healthcare advice on behalf of clients such as Bayer, Boots and Durex, all of which use the centre to increase their own service levels. Pharmaceutical companies have an interest in ensuring compliance with the instructions on medicines to effect a cure and to reinforce brand loyalty as well as avoiding litigation. By printing helpline numbers on bottles or packs, the customer is free to call in and sort out usage problems such as side effects and drug combinations (*Marketing*, 1999b).

There is an added advantage in operating a customer care and service line as it enables the organisation to build a database of enquirers, their concerns and profiles and even buying patterns as in the case of Go. When Boots set up a care line for hayfever sufferers it received over 100 000 calls, an ideal database for building a subsequent promotional campaign offering remedies.

Outbound telemarketing

Outbound telemarketing has also grown in recent years, reflecting the increasing cost of a salesperson's time and a greater acceptance of the telephone, especially in repeat business situations. Productivity can be high from these centres and the calls can be carefully targeted to reach the right audience. The latter is especially true as databases become more sophisticated and various loyalty schemes make a more receptive audience. There is a world of difference between receiving a sales call for double glazing two years after having it installed by a competitor and a call from an insurance company advising you to enhance your cover and take advantage of a special offer. Business to business outbound has been in use for some time, and is regarded as an important means of making appointments or taking repeat business, although the latter is now being strongly challenged by direct IT links. The growth area in this sector is in low value orders for small businesses that may not merit frequent direct calling. Some companies are still reluctant, however, to use outbound telemarketing in consumer markets because of its perceived intrusiveness.

Many of the techniques used in selling, considered in the previous chapter, can be applied to outbound telephone calls. Building trust, conversational styles, empathising with the customer and understanding and being able to communicate with confidence the product benefits relevant to the listener are all crucial. This can

Example American Express calls customers whose credit card spending has dropped below their normal level. It wants to identify whether a competitor's card is being used or if there is some other problem. This enables it to take corrective action to keep the card holder loyal (Bird, 1998). Specialist call centres can handle outbound telemarketing. ADS Telemarketing provides a range of services including data enhancement, mailing follow-up, customer reactivation, lead generation, appointment setting, market research and brand development. Virgin Direct, however, has a policy of not chasing customers and only contacts those who have contacted it first and who have agreed that a return call is in order.

be a challenge if the call centre staff are not well trained or if there is a high turnover of staff so that relationship building becomes more difficult. Perhaps even more important is that the marketer should understand when outbound telemarketing has a role to play, and when it is best to focus on generating enquiries to follow up with a personal visit.

Limitations of telemarketing

In addition, and again in common with personal selling, there are limitations on the practical application of telemarketing, and a number of operational and regulatory issues have to be considered.

Operational issues. For inbound calls in particular, the organisation has to ensure that the system is designed to cope with the expected volume of calls and can handle them speedily and efficiently. Potential customers who cannot get through at all, or who are kept waiting, are likely to give up trying. The problem is made worse by the fact that 80 per cent of responses to a direct response television advertisement, for example, will be made within 10 minutes of the advertisement being screened. After 12 minutes, the response rate is likely to be negligible. Although large volumes of calls are not common within such timescales, a call centre needs flexibility as many organisations set call response time standards, such as '85 per cent of calls to be answered within 20 seconds', and in some cases the target may be as low as 10 seconds. That can be a challenge, such as when the unexpectedly early announcement of the Norwich Union demutualisation generated 9000 calls in 30 minutes (Curtis, 1998)!

Another issue, partly operational and partly strategic, concerns the kind of line to use. Providers such as BT offer a number of options to the marketer, some of which are free or cheap to the caller, others of which carry a premium rate charge.

Clearly, freephone numbers are most attractive to the customer, but do incur costs for the organisation providing the service. These costs have to be balanced against the enhanced service level effectiveness provided by freephone numbers. In 1998, BT reported a 140 per cent increase in customer use of 0345 numbers and a doubling in use of 0800 numbers to 2.7mn minutes. Most customers recognise 0800 as being freephone, but the understanding of the other numbers drops to around 57 per cent for 0345 and just 23 per cent for 0990 numbers. Organisations now use 0800 numbers as an integral part of their promotional strategy, such as Scoot, 0800 192 192, and Guardian Direct, 0800 28 28 20 (Barry, 1998). Marketers need to find the code and tariff system that works best for their business and then ensure that the supporting infrastructure and service are in place to handle customer expectations.

MARKETING AND IT   **Call centre technologies**

Modern telephone call centres are constructed using a variety of telephone and computer technologies from a range of suppliers. The three main technology components in a call centre are:

- **Automatic Call Distribution (ACD) Systems.** The key technology component in the call centre is the ACD. These are the modern version of the old telephone exchanges and have a far greater range of features. They are designed to receive large volumes of incoming calls, answer the calls automatically, place them in a waiting queue and connect them to the next call centre agent who becomes available. While callers wait, ACDs can play recorded announcements to encourage callers not to hang up. As well as managing call routing, ACDs provides status information, such as average wait time, so that managers can make decisions about call handling. Information from the ACD is also very useful for tracking promotions, providing information on where calls are originating from, and other marketing purposes.

- **Voice Response Systems.** One of the major decisions when designing a call centre operation is whether customers are initially routed to a human operator, or to a voice response system. Many companies adopt the latter route in order to keep costs down and in the US, this is the preferred method with most calls never reaching a human operator. In Europe, attitudes are different and some industries such as financial services prefer to maintain human contact

and give callers the choice of speaking to a customer service representative or having their query dealt with by voice response. Voice response systems are referred to as *interactive voice response (IVR) and voice response unit (VRU)* and although both terms are used interchangeably, there is a subtle distinction between the two. VRUs provide a simple recorded message such as the reply that customers typically get when they dial a speaking clock or the local rail timetable. IVRs are interactive, using pre-recorded messages and then accepting responses from touch tone phones to answer queries from callers. IVRs are used to automate certain customer service tasks. Customers interact with IVRs using the keypad on a tough-tone phone, or in some cases, through voice recognition software. The ACD often routes calls first to the IVR, which then handles the call or passes it on to a human operator as needed.

- **Computer Telephony Integration (CTI).** The convergence of telephone and computer technology is known as computer telephony integration. CTI provides the ability to retrieve customer data and deliver it to the customer service representative, or agent, together with the incoming phone call. Automatic retrieval of customer data, based on information given to the IVR, reduces both the amount of time an agent has to spend before addressing the customer's needs and the amount of information the customer has to repeat.

Source: O'Connor & Galvin (1999).

Example   Scoot offers an 0800 freephone line and then directs customers to the nearest store supplying whatever it is they want to buy. This also enables Scoot to track responses from different areas for particular advertisements and to capture data for future selling efforts. Scoot Connect gives the caller details of three local suppliers and information to help them make a decision (Witthaus, 1999).

The Welsh Tourist Board (http://www.tourism.wales.gov.uk) is responsible for marketing Wales as a tourist destination. It uses direct marketing to stimulate enquiries for brochures; campaigns in 1996/97 generated 315 000 request. The board also undertakes image building promotion through television and quality press advertising. The bulk of the image building uses traditional creative execution by showing mountains, castles and beaches, but in 1998 a different element was added to the campaign. A dirty van toured London and Birmingham, looking especially for slow-moving traffic. On the back of the van was the hand-scribbled message, 'Clean air is just two hours away. Wales – two hours and a million miles away'. To support the innovative approach, a freephone number was also given so that interested consumers could obtain more information (Campaign Direct Awards, 1999a).

Outbound telemarketing has its own set of problems. As already mentioned, cold calling for sales purposes is not popular with the public, and has increasingly become the subject of regulation and restriction. In Germany most cold calling is banned

Dusty, but effective direct response advertising.

Source: Welsh Tourist Board.

whereas in the UK it is permitted, although organisations are not allowed to use automatic dialling systems that play prerecorded sales messages. Outbound customer service calls are useful, however. These might be used as an after-sales follow-up to check that customers are satisfied with their purchases. They might also be integrated into a longer-term relationship marketing strategy.

Example Next Directory, for example, tried an experiment with 'welcome calls', made to new customers just after receipt of their first order. After six months, it was found that 92 per cent of those customers who had been 'welcomed' were still active, against only 86 per cent of those who had not received a welcome call. Furthermore, the welcomed customers were spending about 30 per cent more.

Whatever the purpose of outbound telemarketing, it is important to ensure that the operators making the calls are well trained, knowledgeable and courteous. Well-targeted and carefully prepared lists of numbers to call can help to reduce the irritation factor to those called, although pre-screening can be difficult. It can be especially annoying or upsetting to get calls for people who have died or who have moved away. Technology can help to deal with the volume and efficiency of outgoing calls. A central computer dials a number and routes the call to an operator when a reply is detected. If the number called is engaged, or if an answering machine is reached, the computer terminates the call and puts that number to the back of the queue to try again later. The increasing use

MARKETING AND IT Ireland's call centre phenomenon

With more than 100 Irish-based call centres serving the pan-European market, Ireland has claimed more than its share of major international call operations. Although other countries such as Scotland are able to boast a greater number of call centres, Ireland has the distinction that the majority of its call centres are providing multi-lingual, pan-European services rather than national services. In addition to US multinationals like PC manufacturers Dell Computers and Gateway 2000 which support their European operations from Ireland and software company Oracle which does direct marketing across Europe from its Dublin centre, a number of specialist call centre companies have chosen Ireland as their base for their third party operations. One is the Merchants Group which opened its call centre in Cork City in March 1998. The Merchants Group provides third party services for IT, financial services, pharmaceutical, healthcare and utility companies. It investigated sites in Scotland, England and Wales before choosing Cork. Scotland has an attractive grants regime, like Ireland, and the largest concentration of call centres in Europe but Andrew Whiteman, a director of the Merchants Group says 'we decided not to go there because of the competition for staff. We train people to a very high standard and we don't want them going down the road for seven and sixpence more.' The Cork centre, which opened with 60 staff, will eventually employ 600, and represents an investment of several million pounds. The customers

are in 40 different countries, requiring staff with skills in 16 different languages.

The Netherlands and the other Benelux countries are good locations for multilingual call centres because citizens typically have one language. Some companies are also setting up call centres in Finland to serve the Russian market because they prefer the investment climate there.

Major International call centres in Ireland (1999)

Call centre	Year established	Number of agents
Gateway 2000	1994	850
IBM	1996	800
Dell	1993	720
AQL/Bertelsmann	1995	650
Hertz	1996	500
Cutibank	1997	450
UPS	1995	300
Xerox	1998	300
Lufthansa	1998	270
Oracle	1996	250
Compaq	1996	200
Merchants Group	1998	145

Source: Moran (1998); O'Connor & Galvin (1999); Price (1999); Shillingford (1999); http://www.ida.ie

of technology will help to expand and improve the operational capability of call centres. In most cases customers will think that they are talking direct to the company, so if it goes wrong it is the company, not the call centre, that is blamed and risks damaging its image.

Regulatory issues. Pan-European telemarketing is not easy, partly because of language and cultural differences, and partly because of the variation in what is and what is not allowed in different countries. The EU has developed the Distance Selling Directive, an attempt to harmonise regulations to make cross-border direct marketing easier. The original proposals would have meant a complete ban on cold calling by telephone and on unsolicited e-mail. Lobbying by the direct marketing industry, however, managed to get these bans dropped from the proposals. Instead, e-mail can still be used in unsolicited approaches, but prior consent is needed for telephone cold calling. In practice, this actually means that the caller has to identify themselves and the purpose of the call at the beginning, then presumably the recipient has the opportunity to give consent to the continuation of the call.

Another mechanism to protect the consumer from unwanted communication is the use of **telephone preference services**. In the UK, for example, consumers can register with a central agency if they do not wish to receive cold calls. The problem is, however, that currently not all organisations are members of the voluntary scheme, and thus consumers will continue to get calls from non-subscribing businesses. The scheme also excludes calls to business numbers, market research calls and customer service calls. Similar schemes exist in parts of Europe, for instance in the Netherlands, and the EU is looking to impose preference schemes on all member states eventually.

Mail order

Mail order, as the name suggests, involves the purchase of products featured in advertising or selected from a catalogue. The goods are not examined before ordering, and thus the advertisement or the catalogue has to do a good sales job. Mail order companies promote themselves through any media, and receive orders through the mail, by telephone or via an agent. Direct selling through one-off, product-specific advertisements (such as the Franklin Mint operation) has largely been covered at pp. 742 *et seq.* under direct response advertising. This section will therefore concentrate on the mail order catalogue sector.

In the 1960s, the mail order catalogue in the UK was a very heavy and comprehensive document, selling absolutely everything a household could possibly need from clothes, through to toys and power tools, on extended credit. Catalogues were mainly aimed at the poorer sections of society who could not afford to buy things for cash when they wanted them. Mail order catalogues ran on an agency system in which the agent sold to friends and earned commission on sales. The agent was responsible for collecting the owed money weekly. The main strengths of the traditional catalogue were as shown in Fig. 18.2.

Weaknesses of traditional catalogues
Traditional catalogues did, however, have their weaknesses, and these are discussed below.

Lack of speed. Catalogues asked customers to allow 28 days for delivery, and it often did take as long as that for orders to be processed and deliveries made. That lead time was in addition to the time taken for an order to pass through the postal system and be delivered to the organisation. It also took a long time before customers would be informed that an item was out of stock, and then they would have to go through the whole ordering process again.

Downmarket image. The range and quality of merchandise, the emphasis on credit and the presentation of the catalogues meant that mail order was seen very much as a preserve of the C2, D and E socioeconomic groupings.

Lack of targeting. Although the general image was downmarket, there was historically little effort to target catalogue offers closely to customer needs. Catalogues were generalists, so each customer was offered everything. This meant that a great deal of what was offered, including mid-season promotions, was irrelevant to many customers.

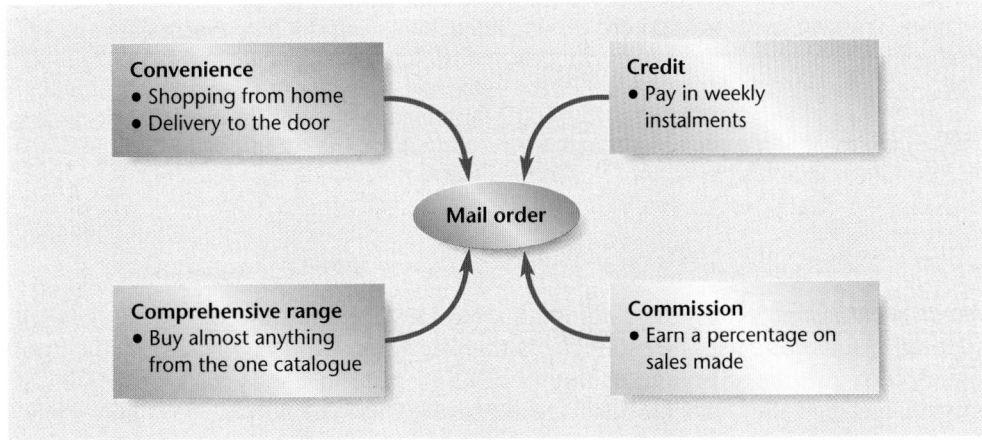

IGURE 18.2

**he traditional
trengths of mail
rder**

The agency system. Many customers just did not want the bother of running an agency. The paperwork and the debt collection involved made it unattractive, even when commission was being earned. Customers wanted to be able to purchase for themselves and their immediate families, with as little administrative responsibility as possible.

Modern mail order catalogues

Figure 18.3 shows how modern catalogues, particularly the new generation pioneered by the likes of the *Next Directory*, have largely dealt with the weaknesses of their predecessors.

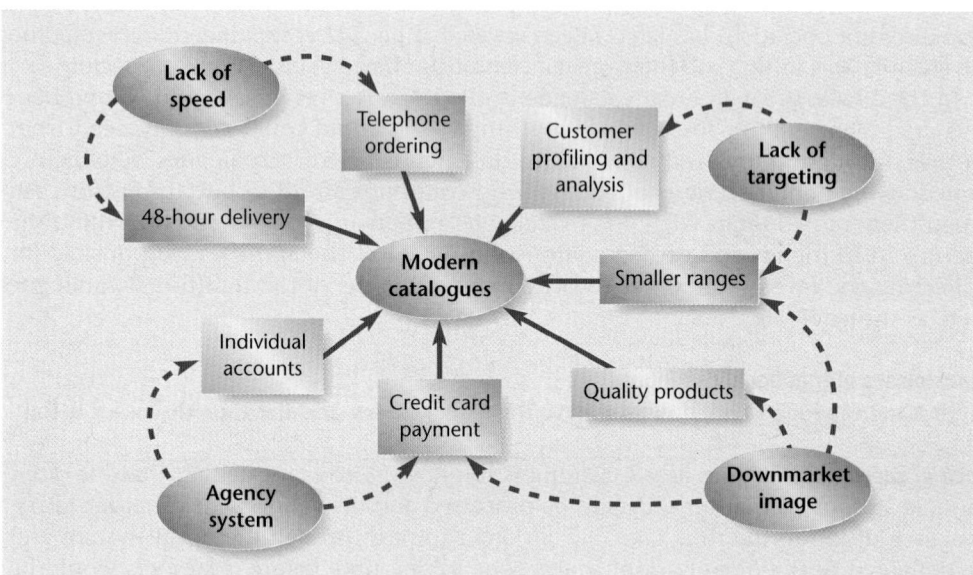

FIGURE 18.3

How modern catalogues overcame mail order's weaknesses

> **Example** The *Next Directory* pioneered the renaissance of the mail order catalogue in the UK, first by trading on its well-established, respected and upmarket high street name. It also speeded up the ordering process and the delivery logistics, through improved technology and distribution systems, to allow telephone ordering and guaranteeing 48-hour delivery. This was the first really high quality catalogue in terms of graphics, photography and the inclusion of fabric swatches. Most importantly, Next Directory targeted the young, trendy end of the market with high disposable income; 40 per cent of its customers were in the A and B socioeconomic groups.
>
> The *Next Directory* broke the mould in terms of attitudes towards mail order, and opened the way for others to move upmarket. The traditional generalist catalogues still exist, albeit much slimmer than in the past, but there is now a wide range of specialist mail order publications, covering goods from garden plants to toys, books and clothing. Even the generalist catalogues now have the technology to analyse their customers' profiles and buying habits and can, therefore, make tailored, relevant individual offers. Payment systems are much more flexible, allowing cash payment, credit if customers want it, or the use of credit cards if they prefer, while the agency system has been pushed into the background.

There are now two main types of catalogue.

Non-store catalogues. Non-store catalogues are catalogues that do not have links with high-street retail outlets. The catalogue is the sole 'shop window'. Traditionally, catalogues carrying the full range of household and fashion goods have been seen as downmarket, and they have found it difficult to move upmarket in the consumer's eyes.

Following Next's example, a number of new smaller catalogues of specialist clothing, such as Lands' End and Racing Green, aimed at a more upmarket audience, have emerged. Other catalogues in DIY, business to business goods, computers and many other sectors also now exist, and there is greater acceptance among more affluent segments of buying from smaller, more targeted catalogues rather than the larger, more traditional blockbusters.

This kind of catalogue is really a form of distribution channel, in that the operator performs the tasks of merchandise assembly, marketing and customer service. The important thing is to find the selection of merchandise appropriate to the market niche served, and to design an appealing kind of service package (in terms of ordering mechanisms, delivery, returns etc.).

Example A number of niche companies use mail order to expand their customer base. James Meade (timeless classic clothes), Robert Humm (old and out of print transport books) and Orvis (fishing merchandise, http://www.orvis.co.uk) have been successful in developing and identifying mail order databases that can be used to target their specialist merchandise. Most specialist mail order companies have expanded their activities by taking out websites for on-line ordering and home shopping. The lists from such mail-order companies can be rented for £120 per thousand, so that cross-selling and complementary sales can be encouraged (Reed, D. 1999).

Store catalogues. As a response to the increasing interest in the non-store sector, some retailers are producing their own catalogues clearly linked with their high street operations. Such catalogues support retail sales by extending the shop window into the customer's home. They also expand coverage, reaching people who might otherwise find it difficult to get to a store, and trade on the retailer's reputation, building on its buying expertise. Companies such as Laura Ashley and Habitat, for instance, operate catalogues.

Example Some retailers, such as Argos in the UK and IKEA, have gone as far as designing their entire retail concept around a catalogue. The shopper can browse through the catalogue at home, select goods and then go into a high street 'showroom' to examine and purchase goods on the spot. This seems to combine the best elements of both the catalogue and the retail outlet. Neither IKEA nor Argos operates a mail order service, however.

TABLE 18.5
Typical advantages of mail order over retail outlets

Advantages of shops over mail order	Advantages of mail order over shops
Can see/touch goods	Delay payment
Can try on/test goods	Choose at leisure
No delay in acquiring purchases	Choose at convenience
Easy to return goods	Easy to return goods
Easy to compare prices	Saves time
Cheaper	No pestering
Shopping is enjoyable	Shopping is not enjoyable
Advice/service available	Home delivery of purchases

Advantages and disadvantages of mail order

Regardless of the type of operation, the basis of the mail order business is the catalogue. As a major selling tool, a great deal of thought and effort is required to get it right and tailor it to the target market. The main advantages of mail order to the consumer are convenience and efficiency and, for some, easy credit. This is especially valuable in areas remote from larger city centres where regular shopping trips are difficult. For the organisation, by avoiding expensive high street locations and the associated display and personal selling costs, the opportunity is provided for a wider variety of lower cost offerings. However, unless catalogues are updated regularly, and unless shoppers are happy not to experience the 'fun' of trial and shopping around for speciality items, the catalogue range may still not suit the more discerning shopper. Table 18.5 shows the perceived advantages and disadvantages of mail order over retailing from the consumer's perspective.

Mail order across Europe

Table 18.6 shows the level of mail order sales in various EU countries and the share of the retail market that mail order takes. While Italy seems to have the weakest mail-order sector, Germany certainly seems to have the strongest. Much of this is due to Otto Versand, the biggest mail order conglomerate in the world. Its catalogue is some-thing of an institution in Germany, and has maintained its edge by pioneering high quality service levels and developing targeted speciality catalogues. Otto Versand generates almost half of its sales outside Germany, however. As already mentioned, it owns Grattan in the UK, as well as 3 Suisse in France, Postalmarket and Eu ronova in Italy, and Spiegel, Eddie Bauer, Crate and Barrel and West Hampton in the USA. It also has inter-ests in Hungary and Japan, and is developing other eastern European and Far Eastern markets.

Although there are over 2000 mail order operators across Europe, most of them specialise in narrow ranges of high quality products. In terms of sales, however, the sector is dominated by the wide-rang-ing generalists. Like Otto Versand, most of them have expanded internationally, largely through acquisition and joint ventures rather than simply by distributing their catalogues across borders. La Redoute is the exception, in having set up operations from scratch in Portugal, Belgium, Spain and Norway, for instance, although goods are supplied from a central depot in France. Cross-border opera-tions and ordering for mail order companies are not easy because of legal, banking and taxation differences, as well as language, taste, pricing and currency problems.

Nevertheless, some mail order companies do try to develop a pan-European identity. Lands' End capitalised on its American origins to present a consistent image in a number of different European markets with catalogues targeting the well-educated, affluent, over-35-year-old audience. Different catalogues are produced for each country to over-come some of the problems outlined above, such as language and pricing, but the print advertisements that invite potential customers to send off for a catalogue are basically the same, with small variations for cultural differences. Lands' End operates in the UK, Germany, France, the Netherlands, Japan and Australia and has a worldwide turnover of nearly $1.4bn (http://www.landsend.co.uk).

TABLE 18.6

Mail order sales and retail market shares in selected EU countries 1994

	Sales through mail order groups ($bn)	Share of total retail sales (%)
Belgium	1	1.3
France	4.4	2.9
Germany	23.1	5.7
Italy	1.1	0.3
Netherlands	1.1	2.1
UK	7.5	2.1

Source: Euromonitor (1998) adapted from Tables 1214 and 1215, pp. 296–7.

Teleshopping

Developments in communications technology in telephone, cable and satellite televi-sion are enabling significant growth in home-based shopping or **teleshopping** (see p. 531 et seq.), even before the impact of the Internet is considered. Direct marketing through these media can vary from fairly standard one-off advertisements screened during a normal commercial break, to slots featured in dedicated home shopping programmes or channels, usually involving product demonstration, often to a live audience. The main problem with developments in this area is not the capability of the technology, but the willingness of consumers to participate. Much depends, of course, on the number of homes connected to either satellite or cable systems, and there are variances across Europe, as we saw in Table 15.4 earlier.

INTERNET MARKETING

The potential audience for Internet usage is very large, as more and more homes and businesses either get connected or develop their own websites. The Internet is a series of connected computers that can be accessed by other parties, rather like a telephone system. Through these connections and the development of the World Wide Web (www or web), hyperlinks and graphical browsers, the potential of the Internet has been expanded rapidly and access to it opened for individuals and businesses alike. The standardisation created by the web has enabled computers to access other computers through embedded links that appear as a screen display of text. The familiar click on part of the text enables the other computer to be found through embedded instructions. The ability to navigate in hyperspace means that the user can access, store and use information contained on every networked computer and made available through websites.

Text-based websites are of limited appeal to the reader unless specific research or information gathering is being pursued. Graphical interfaces have made websites more user friendly. Graphic browsers, such as Netscape Navigator and Microsoft Internet Explorer, enable the viewer to click on images as well as text and also to experience sound and even video. The potential for the Internet as a marketing tool thus emerged in a significant and dynamic way in the 1990s and is still developing further. Even so, the Internet marketing has already had a dramatic effect on marketing and promotional programmes. Mitchell (1999a) argues that the Internet has revolutionised the way in which transactions are done and can reduce interaction costs, both of which are critical aspects of exchange, whether for profit or some other benefit. If sales, marketing and distribution account for around 30 per cent of the cost of a product, then the Internet could reduce them to 20 per cent, with some of those savings passed on to the customer through lower prices. Kavanagh (1999a) goes further by suggesting that the Internet will transform communication in business and that those organisations not appreciating the impact of digitalisation will be dead in 10 years. This section brings together the many aspects of the Internet's impact considered in this book to highlight how direct transactions and interactions between customers and organisations are changing at a very rapid rate. The revolution is far from over yet.

Example Bluewave is a company that designs websites (http://www.bluewave.com). It produced a multilingual pan-European website for Reebok International (http://www.europe.reebok.com). The brief was to show the Reebok 1998/99 collection in a lively and interesting way. The specification included stylish backgrounds, the use of animation and zooming. In the design process, the account manager co-ordinated the work of a variety of experts including the web analyst, web designer, programmer, creative director and a technical manager who ensures that there is functionality between the various screens on the site. An external company was commissioned to handle the advanced interactive technology required. The detailed scheduling and key staff involvement can be found in Figure 18.4.

Most of the web sites connected through the World Wide Web (www), whether individual or organisational, can be accessed for commercial and non-commercial purposes. Throughout this book, various website addresses have been cited to help you to access more information on the organisation highlighted. Some are looking for direct sales, others regard their websites as a means of advertising, generating leads and delivering customer service. The role of websites in public relations and cause-related marketing is also increasing. Annual and financial reports, press releases and general information for the community, investors, job hunters and education can all be found on many of the more sophisticated organisational websites. Other sites are concerned with promoting a particular political, social or environmental viewpoint, which may

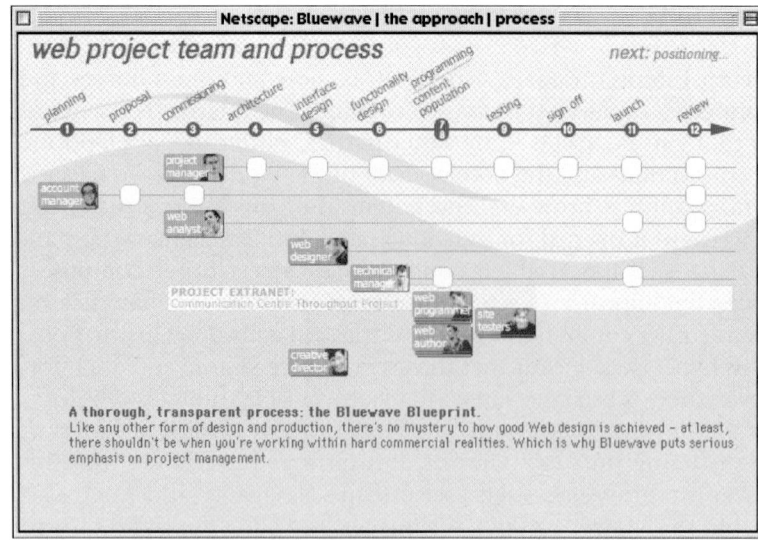

FIGURE 18.4

Bluewave's approach to project management.

Source: http://www.bluewave.com

have to be countered by any organisations targeted (*see* p. 786 *et seq.*, for example). Table 18.7 shows the advantages and disadvantages of developing a website (Fill, 1999).

On most websites, the provider plays a relatively minor role in the viewer's usage. The user is free to search and explore the various pages and links within and between sites. On the McDonald's site, for example (http://www.mcdonalds.com), not only can information relevant to the US market be accessed, but links are also provided to McDonald's operations in many other countries. The messages displayed on a site tend to be fixed in the short term, however, depending on how frequently the site is updated and changed. In fast-moving on-line situations where prices and stock may be changing fairly frequently, for instance, a website needs constant attention.

Increasingly, organisations are introducing an element of fun into their websites to grab and retain attention. Interactive games, web-cam and video feeds, cartoons and relaxed informality have all been introduced to keep viewer's attention and to make company and product information more palatable – there are a lot of choices on the web! The quality of website that we experience is a reflection of the level of investment in the site. Kavanagh (1999e) estimates that a typical e-commerce website project can cost £4.5mn for business to business sites and £8mn for consumer-orientated sites. The

TABLE 18.7

The advantages and disadvantages of website ownership

Advantages	Disadvantages
Relatively inexpensive to create	Varying difficulties in access
Equal access opportunities	Slow access and downloading time
Quick and easy to refresh and update	Possible security difficulties with financial transactions
Open all hours with no constant staff support required	Lack of regulation re content and distribution of material
Can provide cost efficiencies (e.g. collecting information via the web releases staff for other activities)	Corporate rivalry re the development of technology and standards
Global reach	

Source: adapted from Fill (1999) p. 489.

current average is just £1.2mn. Many smaller businesses are spending much less as they try to exploit the technology on very low budgets. However much is spent, a multi-purpose website should provide a powerful supplementary marketing tool. It should have all the creative flair of an advertisement, the style and information of a company brochure, the personal touch and tailored presentation of face-to-face interaction and, not least, always leave the viewer clear as to what action should be taken next.

> **Example** Air Miles (littp://www.airmiles.co.uk), a leading loyalty scheme operator in the UK, introduced a website to increase the proportion of its customers using the Internet and to improve the range and timeliness of its offers and special deals. Rather than constraining customer contact to quarterly mailings, the website could be frequently updated with offers targeted at web users, thus communicating more frequently and more relevantly and yet cost effectively. However, a mixed approach will be needed for a while as only 1.5 million of Air Miles' 3.5 million customers have direct access to the Internet (*Marketing Week*, 1999c).

Despite the significant impact of the Internet, the difficulty for marketers is the technology driving website use. Speeds can still be relatively slow when traffic levels are high. As the number of people logging on to the Internet increases, the problem will become more severe unless bandwidth and capacity problems are resolved. Once on-line, the quality of viewing can be reduced and the irritation level increased if the various graphics take a long time to load and in some cases crash the computer if they overload it. Better video plug-ins and ever more sophisticated browsers will enhance quality and reduce loading times, but as yet for the average Internet user the experience can be frustrating.

Another significant difficulty for the less experienced Internet user is locating material in the first place. The amount of information available at a click is staggering. Although the various search engines such as Yahoo and Excite help our navigation, some familiarity with advanced searches is essential. For example, if you want to find out about the Kronenberg 1664 lager brand, the parent company's website (http://www.danone.com) must be contacted, assuming that you can find out in the first place who owns the brand.

Website usage

The use of websites is still evolving. Household penetration in the UK rose from 5 per cent in June 1997 to 11 per cent by December 1998. The user profile, however, did not change a great deal during that period, still being typically male, from the South of England, younger and from the AB socioeconomic groups (http://www.durlacher.com). Despite the rapidly increasing level of penetration, spurred on by free Internet access providers such as Freeserve and X-Stream, the gap between the numbers willing to purchase goods on-line and those actually doing so is still significant. This has more to do with a lack of consumer confidence in what is being offered through the Internet and concern for transaction security than with people wanting more personal interaction and the opportunity to inspect products. Only 30 per cent of Internet users have actually made a purchase on-line, usually products such as tickets for events and shows, holiday and travel services and low value products such as compact discs and tapes. Less frequently does purchasing extend into clothing, health and beauty products, financial services and motor vehicles (http://www.durlacher.com). Interestingly, pornographic sites (no, you are not getting any addresses for further research!) remain the biggest earners from on-line paid content in the USA and western Europe, generating 70 per cent of the estimated $1.4bn total revenue from on-line payments (*Marketing Week*, 1999e).

In business to business marketing, on-line purchasing has so far fared little better. Although over 80 per cent of businesses believe that e-commerce will eventually underpin their supply chain, only around 20 per cent actually have e-commerce strategies in place to take advantage of the opportunities created. The advantages of moving to e-commerce solutions are clear, such as convenience, cost saving (up to 22 per cent in some supply chains), customer and competitor pressure as well as generating new revenue opportunities (http://www.durlacher.com). A study of larger companies found that 94 per cent of them have corporate websites but only 20 per cent of staff had direct access at work to the Internet (http://www.durlacher.com). Clearly, the revolution is well underway, but the full benefits of Internet use have not yet been realised.

Forrester Research reports predict that e-commerce will grow to between $1.8tn and $3.2tn globally by 2003, depending on the speed of corporate and government take-up of e-commerce (Kavanagh, 1999e). Much will also depend on the uptake in the home. The Henley Centre, as part of its *Annual Futures* study, identified five groups of the UK population with regard to their likely uptake of the Internet. The '@home group' are the current heavy users who are on-line from home and to some extent are influencing the rate and nature of development of Internet marketing. It is predicted that they will remain as the main group for the immediate future. The '@ll group', comprising 14 per cent of the population, are Internet users outside the home and are likely to be the best prospects for the next phase of home use. The 'ne@rly group', 30 per cent of the population, are likely to be a target for Internet use conversion. They tend to be younger with families and finding time pressure a barrier to serious comparative shopping. A family-based appeal would be attractive to this group. The remaining groups, the 'm@ybe group' and the 'not@lls group', together comprising 49 per cent of the population, are not considered as serious prospects at least from now until 2003/4 for Internet use (Rosier, 1999a).

Despite well-argued predictions by industry experts, it is difficult to be sure about actual uptake in the future because of the fast-changing environment within which Internet use exists. This involves any technological advances, the introduction and proliferation of free Internet service providers (ISPs) and efforts to lower call charges. Free ISPs hit the UK scene in 1998 when Freeserve introduced free access and, in the following nine months up to July 1999, the number of free providers grew to around 100 (Curtis, 1999). The key driver for this was the recognition of the benefits to any customer relationship marketing programme of providing free Internet access. This meant that advertisements could be targeted, especially with the company's own products such as on the Toys 'Я' Us, Arsenal FC, Watermans, WH Smith On-line, TescoNet and Virgin Net free access providers. Every time the user switches on, they will be reminded of the ISP provider. There are other benefits in generating a user base. Selling marketing information, storing transaction data, generating advertising revenue and entering into partnerships for co-branding are all possible spin-offs that make offering a free service an attractive proposition (Sumner-Smith and Sumner, 1999).

Example Virgin Net initially started as an ISP offering paid-for access, but it shifted to free access to generate more users. Virgin Atlantic (http://www.virgin-atlantic.com) gave free access to anyone booking Virgin flights through Virgin Net (http://www.virgin.net) and in return established a new means of promoting offers to actual customers as well as keeping its name in front of future travellers. The net access page provides a hyperlink into the main Virgin website, thus enabling ticket ordering, pre-ordering of duty free and even to information about the movies that will be shown on any given flight. The customer support service line is also free, other than local telephone call charges. The initial target set for Virgin Net was one million customers and 200 000 had signed on by May 1999, with 60 000 of them added in the three months after conversion to free access (Kavanagh, 1999d). In 1998 Virgin Net generated £2mn in advertising revenue, but that figure is expected to grow significantly as the number of users also grows.

The next stage in the revolution in the UK could be unmetered calls to the selected ISP's server. This removes another barrier to use, customers being concerned about running up high telephone bills. More and more homes have free Internet access, but that does not mean that they will use it as frequently or for the purposes that the marketers intend. If the user's local telephone charges are waived in order to stimulate their usage, the ISPs might then have to introduce a fixed monthly fee to contribute to the line charges that they incur on the user's behalf. To make up any shortfall, they would also have to generate more advertising revenue and show that they have the sort of customers who will make on-line purchases, or offer linked packages in conjunction with the telephone companies, that combine Internet access with attractive 'normal' telephone tariffs.

Making access cheaper overall to the consumer would generate increased traffic from existing users as well as encouraging new users to go on-line (Curtis, 1999). Research by AOL in the USA found that when a low flat monthly fee was charged, customers spent an average of one hour a day on-line. In the UK with its relatively high local call charges, the average is just 17 minutes per day. Around 41 per cent of UK households have indicated that they would go on-line if telephone charges were dropped and a staggering 95 per cent would spend more time on-line if the charges were lower. X-stream is already leading the way for change. On selected weekends, it buys 0800 line space and offers free calls, aiming to make up the cost from increased banner advertising and generating more e-commerce links. Much will depend on the impact of digital TV and the attitude of BT, which still sets local telephone charges. The latter is difficult for BT, because if it introduced free local calls it could be construed as an unfair competitive advantage as it would encourage users to switch away from other telephone operators. Digital television, however, could change everything, because when the web can be accessed through the television, the local telephone charges become irrelevant as the Internet user is accessing the web via cable. CWC and BskyB are expected to become ISPs via the cable network by 2000.

The marketing uses of a website

There are many reasons for an organisation considering using the Internet, but they tend to group into three broad categories: as a research and planning tool; as a distribution channel; and for communication and promotion, as seen in Table 18.8.

Research and planning tool

The Internet provides direct access to a considerable amount of secondary marketing information. Some sources are free, but many can only be accessed through subscription. Increasingly, the need to visit the library or purchase bulky directories and reports is decreasing as the power, convenience and flexibility of on-line searching become better known. Most organisations offering subscription services will update their sites frequently by adding new and updated information and reports. Many of the secondary data sources considered in Chapter 6 can be accessed on-line.

TABLE 18.8

Marketing uses of the Internet

Research and planning tool
- Obtain market information
- Conduct primary research
- Analyse customer feedback and response

Distribution and customer service
- Take orders
- Update product offerings frequently
- Help the customer buy on-line
- Process payments securely
- Raise customer service levels
- Reduce marketing and distribution costs
- Distribute digital products

Communication and promotion
- Generate enquiries
- Enable low cost direct communication
- Reinforce corporate identity
- Produce and display product catalogues
- Entertain, amuse and build goodwill
- Inform investors
- Detail current and old press releases
- Provide basic product and location information
- Present company in a favourable light – history, mission, achievements, views etc.
- Educate customers on the products, processes etc.
- Inform suppliers of developments
- Communicate with employees
- Attract new job recruits
- Answer questions about the company and its products

As Internet usage increases, the possibilities for primary research are also growing. Through on-line visitor books, feedback using structured questionnaires or via e-mail, web discussion groups and analysing visitor and on-line ordering traffic, useful information can be gathered for marketing planning purposes.

Distribution channel

Many examples have been given throughout this book of the impact of the Internet on distribution channels. Chapter 13 specifically examined on-line retailing and the growth of Amazon shows just how the power of the web can have an impact on a conventional distribution channel. The impact will grow in the future as consumers gain more confidence in on-line purchasing. There are several advantages of on-line distribution that conventional mail order cannot achieve:

- The viewer is actively searching for products and services, and so every site hit could gain a potential customer if interest can be maintained. Regular and loyal customers can take short cuts and skip all the general background information. 'Shopping baskets' help the customer to keep track of what they have bought on this visit and help give the impression of a store just like any other. Four main sectors are considered to be at the forefront of on-line, direct distribution: travel, books, music and software. Revenue in Germany, France and the UK from these areas between 1997 and 2002 is expected to grow from $68mn to $3.3bn (Reed, M. 1999a). CDs, for example, can be ordered on-line from specialist on-line retailers, traditional store-based record companies, music magazine publishers and even direct from fan clubs and the artist's site. Some also offer audioclips as samplers that can be downloaded, although currently the quality can be variable.
- Print and mailing costs are eliminated because no catalogue has to be produced and distributed each season. Although costs will be incurred in developing and maintaining an interesting website, they still represent a saving, especially because a website increases the seller's flexibility as it can be changed far more easily than the printed page with instant updates on prices, product availability and special offers. Amazon (http://www.amazon.com) has over eight million users, yet the cost of communicating with them is a fraction of the cost that would have been incurred through direct mail or media advertising (*The Grocer*, 1999).
- Order processing and handling costs are reduced with on-line ordering as everything is already in electronic form and the customer is handling all the order entry without assistance. McNutt (1998), however, has argued that it is important for organisations to realise that opening the front door to customers with a website providing ordering capability means that they have to ensure that all the 'behind the scenes' logistics operations can cope with changes in ordering patterns. Linking back into the organisational systems for stock control and order fulfilment is essential if customer service levels are to be maintained. The IT systems have to be able to offer real time information flows between the customer, customer support, distribution and the supply chain. Only then can realistic claims be made for cost efficient and effective customer service, whether a small parcel is delivered to Milan or Middlesbrough. Federal Express made a virtue of its integrated system by allowing customers to track the exact whereabouts of a particular parcel on the Internet as a means of reassurance. It also turned this service into an effective selling tool to differentiate itself from competitors.
- Digital products, in the form of magazines, music and video, are capable of being distributed via the Internet, without the need even to send a parcel through the post. The distribution of music products that can be downloaded on to a computer is causing concern to CD manufacturers for copyright and piracy reasons.
- Better after sales service can be provided on-line, not only because of cheaper and easier communication, but also through feedback links, usage information, news flashes on any product changes and mechanisms for fault reporting.

■ In time, however, the growth of powerful ISPs and the emergence of customers in full control of what they will and will not search for and purchase could mean that the most powerful intermediaries in the twenty-first century will be the ISPs and search engine providers who build a wealth of information on individual customer preferences and requirements (Mitchell, 1999b).

Communication and promotion

The Internet is now as good as any other tool for communicating with customers and target audiences. Many of the principles discussed in Chapters 14 and 15 apply equally to the Internet. As well as operating a dedicated website, companies are also taking advertising space on other companies' websites as joint or paid promotions. As can be seen from Table 18.8, extensive use is made of the Internet for communications purposes. Many of the entries are self-explanatory. The main uses are:

As an advertising medium. Advertising on the Internet is similar to advertising through any other medium. The message should be communicated simply, clearly and by creating interest that will move the viewer through to further action, whether that is an enquiry, an order or just getting better informed about what is available. Many of the free Internet access providers exploit this area to the full with comprehensive and sometimes intrusive display and banner advertising messages. Most of these messages are linked to the advertiser's website for further information and action. As the quality of information on web users improves, many of the ISPs have started to target advertising to their users, so for example a user with an interest in sport may receive banner advertisements on sports events and equipment. Amazon has gone further by creating a link with some search facilities, so if you want to know more about an organisation or market, you will be invited to allow Amazon to search for titles on that theme.

Banner advertising is still the main form of Internet advertising, accounting for around 53 per cent of total spend. Banner advertisements normally appear either on a ISP's pages while the customer is logging on to the Internet, alongside a search engine, or as part of a joint promotion on another organisation's website. Overall, Internet advertising was worth just £15mn in 1998, but is expected to grow to £268mn by 2001. Between 1998 and 1999 an additional 500 on-line advertisers began advertising in the UK. When Gillette launched the Mach 3 razor in 1998 (*see* p. 339), it used Internet banner advertisements before the main television and press campaign. Gillette believed that there is a close fit between the typical Internet user and the potential customer for a Mach 3 (Reed, M. 1999b).

Most banner and other display advertisements enable the viewer to access the main information or booking page for the product or company with one click. Despite their power and convenience, there is some evidence from the USA that banner advertisements are being ignored by viewers as wallpaper or background clutter, so their effect is wearing off, despite their intrusive capability. New formats and creative approaches are needed, including high grade graphics, audio and interactive approaches to attract and keep viewer attention. Douwe Egbert coffee (http://www.jamba.co.uk), advertising on the Carlton website, featured a pop-up game similar to Countdown, where viewers could beat the clock to win prizes. The game attracted between 50 000 and 60 000 visitors in the first month.

Table 18.9 gives the top ten on-line advertisers for March 1999, showing that Amazon is at the top of the league with computing and service providers domi-

TABLE 18.9

Top ten on-line advertisers, March 1999

Rank	Advertiser	Spend (£'000)
1	Amazon	72
2	BT	70
3	IBM	64
4	Intel Corporation	61
5	HM Government (UK)	58
6	Last Minute Network	54
7	Guardian Media Group	54
8	United News and Media	53
9	British Airways	53
10	Bertelsmann	51

Source: Fletcher Research (http://www.fletch.co.uk).

nating the rest of the table. The total spend in March was £2.8mn and the estimate for the whole of 1999 was £30mn (MacMillan, 1999).

> **Example** Golfweb Europe (http://www.golfweb.co.uk) is an ideal site for golfers. It provides updated news on golf tournaments, golf courses and all the news that would interest a targeted audience. Websites that are aimed at special interest and lifestyle groups are ideal for marketers and are welcomed by advertisers. On Golfweb's home page alone there are over 10 links to other golf products and services. With one click you could be buying a new set of clubs, taking advantage of a special offer or arranging a tailor-made golfing holiday package.

Loyalty reinforcement. The organisational website itself is also a powerful tool for increasing the level of interaction between the customer and the brand to reinforce loyalty. If the viewer can be entertained and informed, and enjoys coming back to the site, the brand values and image are enhanced.

> **Example** The Carlsberg UK website (http://www.carlsberg.co.uk) aims to appeal to younger lager drinkers. The cost of developing the site was around £650 000 and it offers a news service, screen savers featuring England, Hibernian and Liverpool football clubs (Carlsberg sponsors the latter two clubs), video clips and advice on improving soccer skills along with an on-line competition to win a signed England shirt. There is also a list of the top 40 singles and album charts and a link to the HMV site. Of course, with another click from the home page, the viewer can access information on all the Carlsberg brands (Rosier, 1999b).

Corporate Communications. As will be discussed in the next chapter, the Internet has been widely used by organisations to create goodwill, better understanding and provide important information to shareholders and the community alike. Many organisations detail their financial reports on the web and often provide considerable coverage of their community relations programmes.

Often press releases are automatically placed on the web and so regular updating is necessary. Not only does this service help the media, but it also enables the organisation to get its message across to a wider audience in a more direct manner. Often press release archives can be accessed, going back several years. Even when full text is not available, contact details are provided to the press office for further enquiry.

> **Example** KLM (http://www.klm.com) offers a chronological list of press headlines on its web page along with a search engine to trace any particular topic of interest. The file goes back to 1998 and allows the full text to be read. Through the search facility, it is possible to track significant new events concerning KLM.

Some web pages are designed to counter negative stories and views expressed by unofficial or even anti-lobbying group sites. Shell had to contend with a host of highly critical sites over its environmental record and involvement in Nigeria. It uses both special web-based discussion lines and campaigns, along with a free flow of information, to counter some of the wilder allegations that are not actionable (*see* p. 782).

British Nuclear Fuels (http://www.bnfl.co.uk) offers a web page as part of its site, on its Safety and Environmental Centre. This page, with further links, provides details of the technology used, data on radioactive discharges, and examples of the extensive testing undertaken on marine life around the plants. On request, the viewer can obtain a copy of the annual report on 'Safety, Health and Environment'. This is all part of a campaign to raise public confidence and counter the accusations of 'green' pressure groups and various sites suggesting that the environmental impact from discharges will have a significant long-term effect (*see* for example http://www.necnp.org/sellamox and http://www. equinox.shaysnet.com).

Sales promotion. Because of the relative ease of updating a web page and the flexibility it provides, it is possible to target offers on various products or over a defined period. Offers can be changed by the hour and the response of customers assessed (Wilson, 1999). Using price promotions, gifts and bonuses can all help increase short-term sales.

Ex-Spice Girl Geri Halliwell sent the UK's first digital audio postcard to visitors to http://www.dotmusic.com as part of the promotion of her first single. This is expected to be the forerunner of many more digital audio postcards sent as samples to alert fans to forthcoming releases (Kavanagh, 1999b). Hula Hoops (http://www.hulahoops.co.uk), a crisp snack from KP Foods, ran an interactive on-line knock-out competition for high-tech prizes. This enabled the company to generate more interest in the site and to encourage word of mouth recommendation to visit the site (Kavanagh, 1999f).

Personal selling. By its very nature, the web is impersonal and the Internet is designed more for sales support and generating enquiries rather than for making direct sales. The cost per potential customer hit can be very low, and because people who do visit a site are likely to be interested in what it has to offer, the potential for increasing the level of enquiries is very great as net usage expands. Even in highly routine order-taking roles (*see* Chapter 17), the Internet can be made more interactive if the customer database is able to personalise communication and relate it to offers that could appeal, based on a customer's previous enquiries and sales history.

Overall, the organisation should plan its use of the Internet carefully and be sure that it is integrated into the rest of the marketing mix. Sumner (1999) argues that as much consideration should be given to the off-line use of the website as to its on-line use. By featuring a web address in other advertising and promotional media, the overall site visibility is increased and additional site traffic could be generated. A glance at much poster, print and television advertising will often show a mention of an Internet address for contact. It is important that all of the Internet budget should not be spent on highly interactive, fun websites at the expense of the more mundane, but critical, job of responding to web and e-mail enquiries. A survey by Jupiter Communications, reported by Sumner (1999), found that 42 per cent of top-ranked sites took longer than five days to respond to e-mails and even on retail sites only just over half responded within 24 hours.

THE ROLE OF DIRECT MARKETING IN THE PROMOTIONAL MIX

The previous sections have defined the nature of direct marketing, and some of the tools and techniques involved. This section draws all that together to look at how direct marketing fits in with the other elements of the promotional mix. Although, as previous sections have shown, direct marketing can overlap with advertising, the key distinction between direct marketing and the other elements of the promotional mix is the personalised direct approach that relies on another communication channel, such as a telephone, mail or computer link. At the centre of the activity is a direct response from the customer. For example, a successful mail campaign depends on accurate personalised targeting and a response mechanism that can prompt further contact. It requires action by the customer to generate a measurable response to the promotional effort.

Objectives of direct marketing

There are a number of tasks that direct marketing can perform, depending on whether it is used for direct selling or supporting product promotion. The tasks may be related to on-going transactions and relationships with customers. At its most basic, therefore, direct marketing can fulfil the following objectives.

Direct ordering

Direct marketing aims to enable direct ordering, whether by telephone, mail or, increasingly, by direct computer linkage. The use of credit cards, passwords and specific account numbers makes this possible. All kinds of direct marketing techniques can be used to achieve this, but the example of on-line ordering of CDs, mentioned earlier, is particularly interesting because sellers can both take the order and deliver the product immediately.

Under the EU's Distance Selling Directive, however, customers will have the right to change their minds within seven working days and withdraw from the contract. It will be the supplier's responsibility to make sure that customers have details of how to annul the transaction and to make any refund within 30 days.

Information giving

Direct marketing aims to open a channel of communication to enable potential customers to ask for further information. Information may be given verbally by a sales person, or through printed literature. Again, many techniques can achieve this objective, including customer care lines, as seen on the examples of PPP, Nivea and Boots.

Visit generation

Direct marketing aims to invite a potential customer to call in and visit a store, show or event with or without prior notification. Nissan, for example, used direct mailshots targeted at fleet buyers to encourage them to visit the Nissan stand at the UK Motor Show.

Trial generation

Direct marketing aims to enable a potential customer to request a demonstration or product trial in the home, office or factory.

Achieving the objectives of direct marketing

These objectives can be achieved through a variety of means. They can be regarded as stages in the selling process from making the initial contact to creating a loyal customer. In some cases, the selling company may directly seek business, perhaps by using the telephone to contact lost or former customers, or by introducing a direct on-line ordering system for regular volume customers, such as dealers and distributors. In other cases, the response may come from the customer as a result of other promotional efforts, such as advertising or sales promotion campaigns.

How and when to use direct marketing

Initiation

An important decision in direct marketing is how best to use it at various stages of the relationship with the customer. The earliest stage, *initiation*, can be very difficult, as it involves creating the initial contact and making the first sale. A combination of appealing advertising and sales promotion techniques may be used, for example, to overcome the potential customer's initial apprehension and risk aversion. Thus in its introductory offer, a book club may reduce the customer's perceived risk through drastic price reductions on the first order (any four books for 99p each), and further specifying a period within which the books may be returned and membership cancelled without obligation. Alternatively, a sale on credit or even a free trial may ease the customer's initial fears, despite the high administration costs. Any of these methods makes it easier for customers to part with their cash on the first order, thus opening the opportunity for a longer-term relationship.

Relationship building

Most direct marketing is in fact aimed at the *relationship stage* customer. This is when the seller has started to build a buying profile, supported by more widely available non-purchase specific data. This enables a steady flow of offers to be made, whether by telephone, mailshot or catalogue update. Customers are also likely to be more responsive at this stage, as they have established confidence in product quality and service performance.

Combination selling

Finally, combination selling results from using contacts gained from one medium, such as a trade exhibition, for regular contact by direct marketing means. This could be the mailing of special offers, price lists, catalogues or telephone calls to gain a face-to-face meeting etc. The direct marketing activity is therefore used in combination

---

MARKETING IN ACTION   ## Bibendum: wine goes direct

Bibendum is one of the largest independent wine merchants in the UK, despite having been founded only in the early 1980s. It offers a unique and varied range of wines from around the world along with a fast, efficient and personalised service. Although located in the fashionable Primrose Hill district of London, close to Hampstead and St Johns Wood, Bibendum has established a nationwide customer base from its wholesale and mail order operations. The sales operation is split into catering, the off-trade and supermarket sector, private customers, and a fine wine desk offering exclusive choices.

Although Bibendum has always had a healthy telephone, mail and fax order business, the 2500 ft^2 retail store also generated passing sales, given the attractive catchment area. However in the 1990s, it became increasingly clear that it was the 'backroom operations' that were generating a significant share of the £20mn business. Research indicated that around 90 per cent of sales were handled through the direct marketing operation and the remainder over the counter. Given the floor space that has to be allocated to a retail operation, the management and staffing resources required and the costs of display and presentation, Bibendum took the bold decision to close the retail operation. This enabled it to free valuable space and resources to concentrate on the direct marketing side.

Even the direct marketing mix is changing as customers are substituting on-line ordering for telephone, mail and fax. The website has been extensively overhauled (http://www.bibendum-wine.co.uk) and the expectation is that the Internet will replace the less efficient direct ordering methods. The website has a pull-down menu to let the customer view wines in selected categories and under each category the wine and year are described along with the cases and bottles in stock. Prices vary considerably. A 1997 Cheval Blanc was priced at £750 per case, a 1993 Yquem at £1100 per case and a 1998 Beusejour Becot at just £250 per case.

The next stage is a fully integrated e-commerce system that can link on-line orders with stock control, dispatch and invoicing systems. This is expected to improve customer service and reduce transaction costs. Further research in 1997 indicated that over 60 per cent of Bibendum customers had Internet access or e-mail and this figure was steadily growing. Although telephone and mail ordering will still be possible, this is expected to become a smaller part of the direct operation.

Direct contact with customers will still be maintained, however. The space released from the retail operation will be used to support the tasting programme. Although private tastings are held, normally every month, reservations can be made by Bibendum customers to attend special tasting events, such as the Chateau Pichon Lalande vertical tasting hosted by wine experts costing £90 per person. These events are considered important for retaining customer loyalty and involving customers who are making what to them is a very significant and involved purchase.

Sources: Kavanagh (1999c); http://bibendum-wine.co.uk.

with other methods. As mentioned earlier, Boots used the contacts generated by its pollen count care line to provide a mailing list for material on hayfever remedies and other related products.

MANAGING A DIRECT MARKETING CAMPAIGN

If direct marketing is going to create, build and maintain relationships with new and existing customers, then it needs to be carefully targeted and managed. A failure in any one of the main areas may result in inappropriate messages directed at the wrong targets. The main stages in the development of a direct marketing campaign are outlined in Fig. 18.5 and considered in turn below.

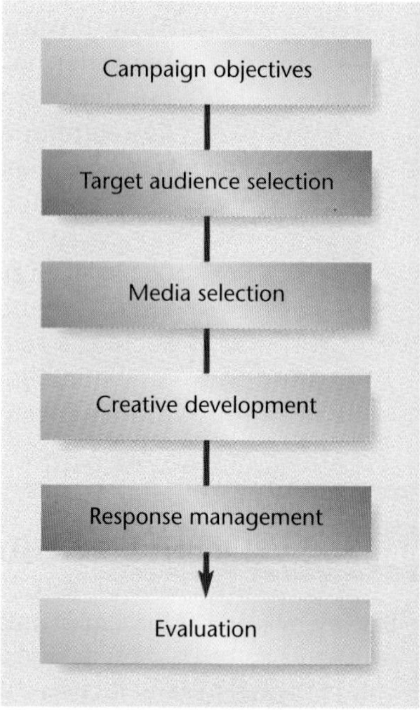

Campaign objectives

As with all marketing activities, the definition of objectives provides an important foundation, guiding subsequent management decisions. Direct marketing objectives must be linked with wider marketing and promotional objectives, and their definition must relate to target audiences and measurable results. Desired outcomes may be expressed in terms of market awareness, number of responses sought or conversion of enquiries into sales.

Prospects and target selection

Prospects can be in a number of states:

1 *possible prospects*: a broad pool of potential customers about whom little is known;
2 *probable prospects*: a list selected through qualification on some predetermined criterion;
3 *unconverted enquiries*: those who have had previous contact with the organisation, showing an interest in its products, but who have not yet committed themselves;
4 *former or lost customers*: those who have purchased in the past, but not recently;
5 *existing customers*: those with an established pattern of custom who are still actively purchasing.

Generally, the nearer the top of that list a prospect falls, the higher the cost per sale. Existing customers will need much less persuasion and incentive to buy than a completely unknown, 'cold' prospect. Note too that information held on present customers can always assist in the targeting of new customers. By identifying the key characteristics of the most valued existing customers, such as demographic, geodemographic and psychographic details (look back to Chapter 5 to brush up on the definitions of these terms), media preferences, products purchased and response profiles, qualification criteria can be defined for screening out the best new prospects, along with an offer that is most likely to appeal to them.

As p. 738 *et seq.* indicated, commercial market research data agencies can provide lists of qualified prospects. The European Direct Marketing Association, for example, provides an international list search service and can also provide details of European list brokers. The sheer volume of information held is surprising and also gives some cause for concern in terms of privacy. CCN database, for example, holds information on 43 million consumers that can be analysed by lifestyle, age, gender, creditworthiness, postcode, purchasing habits or any combination of these. All of this information assists in profiling and helps not only to understand behaviour, but also to predict it. Information systems are slowly, but inexorably, moving from geodemographic level data down to the individual household level.

FIGURE 18.5

Managing a direct marketing campaign

Campaign objectives

Target audience selection

Media selection

Creative development

Response management

Evaluation

Accessing even geodemographic data is, however, less easy in some European countries. Census data (the foundation of most commercial databases) and standards vary in format and timing, and postcode systems may not be so flexible. For example, Germany does not have such a closely pinpointed postcode system as the UK. In Germany, whole cities are often treated as homogeneous for postcode purposes, therefore undermining one of the main methods for direct targeting. Variations in systems mean that we are still some way from having a pan-European database, but international lists are becoming available through conference attendance, car rental, freight companies, hotels and publishers. In practical terms, there are some difficulties in designing pan-European software for database management. Issues of salutation differences, gender, titles, use of first names and different address structures need to be covered. Locally produced software may not easily adapt.

Media selection

After the initial selection of the target customer group, the most appropriate media need to be selected to generate the planned response. The full range of media discussed in Chapters 14 and 15 are available, but their use will be influenced by the size and profile of audience reached, availability, the predicted cost per sale, and their general cost effectiveness for implementing a multimedia or single-medium campaign. In terms of cost, for example, Fill (1999) estimates that to reach a decision maker in an organisation, telephone selling would cost about £10, direct mail about £1.50 and a personal sales call about £175. Although these figures are very generalised, they do underline the importance of cost effectiveness and the need to justify media choices in terms of objectives and expected benefits.

The choice of medium will also depend on what stage in the buying process the prospective customers have reached. Three main stages can be identified.

1 *Response initiation*: The initial contact, generating an expression of interest, can be achieved through almost any medium, for example broadcast and print advertising, magazine inserts, mailshots, or door-to-door leaflet drops. We have already looked at the various response mechanisms (freephone, freepost etc.), and discussed their role in generating the desired outcome (*see* pp. 742 *et seq.*).

2 *Information and action*: Responding to the customer's request for more information and, where necessary, fulfilling the order and delivery process involves more direct contact from seller to buyer. Appropriate media include direct mail, telephone, point-of-sale information and the sales force (particularly in organisational markets).

3 *After-sales*: Once customers have been created, it is important to keep in touch with them and promote new offers from time to time. Again, the seller needs to be proactive through media such as direct mail, telemarketing and the sales force.

Experience with direct marketing suggests the importance of an integrated multimedia campaign. This means ensuring that the best combination of techniques is used to move the potential customer through to a sale.

Example Toyota uses a combination of direct marketing techniques to keep its existing customers and to attract new ones. It has established a central database of new and existing customers and has targeted direct mail campaigns to promote product sales, including the Starlet, Celica and Corolla models. Alongside advertising, it also runs DRTV, national press inserts and general direct mail campaigns as part of a shift from media advertising to direct promotion. Existing customers also receive a quarterly magazine, again driven from the database (*Marketing*, 1999c).

Creative development

Depending on the nature of the direct marketing campaign, a brief may be developed for either internal specialists or external consultants. This brief is similar to that used in advertising and sales promotion, and relates the target customers' needs with marketing objectives and product benefits on offer. There are a number of areas that need to be addressed, as shown in Fig. 18.6. These are discussed in somewhat more detail below.

1 *Objectives*: these indicate what the campaign is expected to achieve and defines the required response targets;
2 *Product benefits*: these describe the key features and relate them to the potential benefits that can be promoted;
3 *Target audience*: this profiles the audience to provide a sound 'feel' for the typical customer;
4 *Offer promise*: this encompasses the key benefits to offer and how they can be supported;
5 *Tone of communication*: the tone will be influenced by the media selected. The formality and communication style need to be specified;
6 *Layout, graphics, scripts*: the physical look of the offer is important for attracting and retaining attention, especially if the campaign is likely to be given only a short period to make an impact. The offer must end by encouraging action relating to the campaign objectives. At a very practical level, it must also be remembered that advertisements used in a campaign may require more space in different countries because of language differences. Compared with English, languages such as Italian and Spanish require 20–25 per cent more space, and German and Scandinavian need 25–30 per cent more. This is quite apart from the normal concerns about translating words and phrases literally from one language to another;
7 *Positioning*: this concerns relating the offer to the many other competitor efforts in the customer's mind;
8 *Restrictions*: any legal and corporate restrictions need to be identified and complied with;
9 *Action*: as the key to direct marketing is action, the mechanism and ease of responding need to be carefully considered.

Response management

One of the main advantages of direct marketing is that the response is direct and usually happens within a limited time span.

> **Example** Digital sent out a mailshot to 60 000 potential customers in France, Germany, Italy, Spain and the UK, to promote its software tools. It estimates that sales worth £2.3 million were generated as a result within a short period.

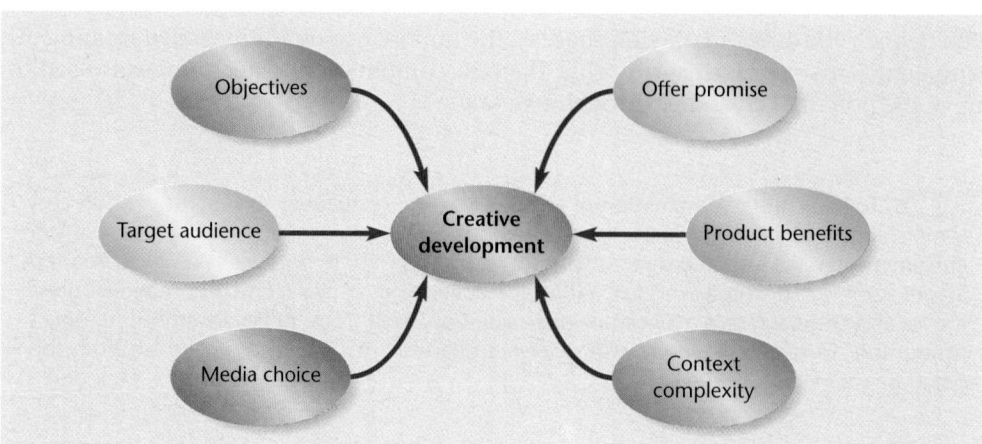

FIGURE 18.6

Issues influencing creative development

A number of ratios can be developed to analyse responses to help increase effectiveness. These ratios include:

- cost per enquiry
- cost per order
- response rate
- conversion rate from enquiry to order
- average order value
- renewal or repeat order rate.

With direct marketing campaigns a unique code can be given to distinguish specific advertisements or promotions. This enables patterns and trends to be identified and these can be used to predict further responses based on customer profiles.

DATABASE CREATION AND MANAGEMENT

Any organisation with a serious intention of utilising direct marketing needs to think very carefully about how best to store, analyse and use the data captured about its customers. This means developing a **database** with as detailed a profile as possible about each customer in terms of geodemographics, lifestyle, purchase frequency and spend patterns. In organisational markets, information might also be held about decision makers and buying centres. Whatever the kind of market, the deeper the understanding of the customer, the easier it is to create effective messages and products. However, if database usage goes wrong, it can cause some unfortunate errors, for example offering maternity wear or prams to pensioners. When the database works well, it can help to offer products that will appeal to the target audience and generate a response, enabling relationships to build and prosper.

This section looks at some of the issues connected with database creation and management, as summarised in Fig. 18.7. Note that the end of the first cycle, customer recruitment and retention, is the start of a stronger second cycle, based on better, recorded information and subsequent targeting.

Customer information

Although internally developed databases are nearly always more appropriate than those available externally, they do take time to develop and maintain. External lists can

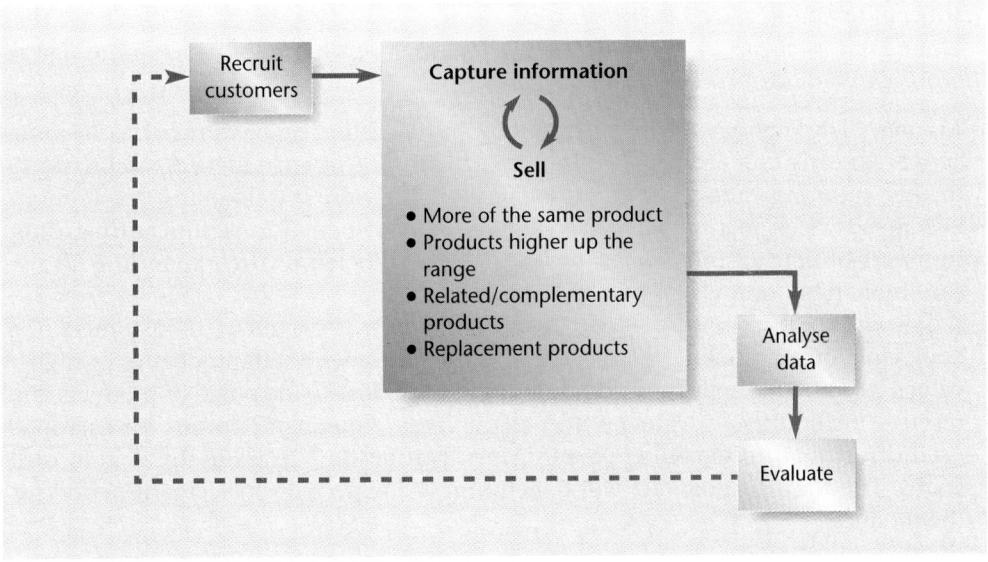

FIGURE 18.7

Database creation and management

be purchased, with over 4000 being available in the UK and some 20 000 in Europe. The selection of the most appropriate list depends on purpose and selection criteria. Geodemographic profiles, such as ACORN and Mosaic, highlight the areas offering the highest probability for identifying the best targets, based on a combination of neighbourhood and demographic detail such as family, education, occupation etc.

The customer and sales database is a most valuable source of information for relationship management and campaign planning. Having the software to edit, sort, filter and retrieve data is essential (Lewis, 1999). Typical information contained in a database describes customer profiles. Through analysis and model building, its predictive potential can be exploited. The first part of Table 18.10 summarises the kind of information that helps to create a rich profile of existing customers, and the second part tracks the developing buyer–seller relationship.

TABLE 18.10

Customer information for database building

- Contact name
- Company name (if applicable)
- Type of company (if applicable)
- Address
- Geodemographic profile
- Psychographic profile

- Previous contacts
- Previous responses
- Purchases actually made
- Frequency of purchases
- Value of purchases
- Types of purchase
- Media responsiveness
- Promotional responsiveness

Keeping customers and reselling to them

As with any marketing effort, the continuation of exchanges will depend on how well needs have been satisfied, service provided and value offered. However, the real challenge for direct marketing is to continue to communicate actively with the customer and win further orders after the initial contact has been made. This can be achieved by keeping in regular contact and developing a range of initiatives to encourage further orders. These could be further sales of the same product, sales of new offers, or cross-selling into related product areas to maximise the returns from established contacts.

Classifying the customer list to reflect loyalty, purchase activity, susceptibility to future offers and age of listing can help to determine the best way of approaching future communication and offers. For example, individual car owners tend to change cars every two or three years, and therefore it might be appropriate to identify customers who are coming to the end of their second year and implement an intensive campaign of sending them financing and product information with a view to getting them into the showroom.

It is always more cost effective to retain customers than to win new ones, so careful use of direct marketing can assist the overall promotional programme. The maintenance and updating of the database provide good means of tracking customer needs, wants and satisfaction, helping to make marketing decisions that maximise the chances of retaining a loyal customer base.

There are five stages in a retention and customer development programme. These are considered in turn.

1 *Welcome*: The obvious first stage applies shortly after the customer has become active. An early contact can be reassuring, and assists in engendering receptivity to further communication. The example of *Next Directory's* 'welcoming' experiment has already been mentioned (*see* p. 751). That scheme led to significantly greater numbers of new customers being retained and also led to their spending 30 per cent more than 'non-welcomed' customers.
2 *Selling up*: Apart from normal repeat business, such as occurs with customers of a book club, organisations should encourage the customer to adopt a better or higher valued model. This approach would be appropriate for a wide range of products and services including cars, cameras and credit cards. American Express, for example, used direct mail to encourage green Amex cardholders to trade up to gold card status. The timing of contact will depend on the expected replacement period for the product.

3 *Selling across*: The selling across or cross-selling stage is where an organisation tries to sell a wider range of products than those in the area originally selected. A customer who purchases car insurance from a particular company might subsequently receive mailings about house insurance or private health cover, for example.

4 *Renewal*: With products that involve annual or regular renewal, such as motor insurance, the timing of appropriate and personalised communication around the renewal date can reinforce repeat purchases.

5 *Lapsed customers*: Customers may be temporarily dormant or permanently lost. A continuation of communication may be appropriate for a period of time so as not to lose contact, especially if reorder frequencies are high.

Review and recycle

As implied above, once a database is up and running it should be monitored, reviewed and evaluated periodically to make sure that it is working well and achieving its full potential. This is not just about 'cleaning' the database (i.e. making sure that it is up to date and that any individuals who have disappeared without trace are deleted from it), but also about data analysis. As part of the strategic planning process, the organisation can look for opportunities to cross-sell to existing customers or to get them to trade up, for instance. Managers can also review whether the nature and frequency of contact are sufficient to achieve full customer potential. Perhaps more importantly, they can assess whether they have recruited the kind of customer expected and whether targets have been met.

All of this analysis can be used to plan the continuation of database building. Although the organisation will be trying primarily to hold on to the customers it already has, there will inevitably be some wastage as customers lose interest, or as their tastes and aspirations change, or as they move house without telling anybody. That wastage, as well as the organisation's own growth aspirations, mean that new customers will have to be sought. Learning from the first implementation of the cycle, managers can assess whether the 'right' kind of media were used to attract the 'right' kind of desired customer. They can refine their profiling and targeting in order to improve response rates and perhaps attract even more lucrative customers. They can review which promotional offers or which kinds of approach were most successful and repeat those with new customers, or try similar activities again.

Ideally, as the organisation builds its relationship with customers over time, and as it repeats the cycle of recruitment and retention with increasing numbers of customers, it should learn and become better at serving its customers' needs. This can only happen, however, within a framework of tight planning, management, analysis and control.

CHAPTER SUMMARY

Direct marketing has made considerable progress in recent years in overcoming its poor image as being just 'junk mail'. It now includes a wide range of tools and techniques, all designed to create one-to-one relationships between organisations and their customers, and to allow organisations to tailor increasingly more relevant offers to individual customers. Direct marketing has become more important in recent years for several reasons, including changing consumer lifestyles, competitive pressure, technological advances and the general move towards relationship marketing.

There are several approaches to direct marketing that an organisation might consider. Direct mail can be very effective in stimulating responses from tightly defined target audiences made up either of existing customers or of new ones. Direct response advertising uses broadcast and print media with the aim of stimulating some kind of response from the target audience. Such advertising can thus be used to create a new database of interested customers who can then be targeted by other direct marketing methods in the future. Telemarketing specifically covers the use of the telephone as a means of creating a direct link between organisation and customer. Outbound telemarketing is generated by the organisation, whereas inbound telemarketing is where the organisation encourages individuals to contact them. The telephone provides a quick, easy and cost effective response mechanism, and can be used both to increase the impact and creativity of advertising and sales promotion, and to provide a human character for the organisation.

Mail order catalogues now target their customers with 'specialogues', providing narrow selections of better quality goods that suit the customer's profile. Some catalogues are solely mail order operations, while others are developed by retailers as a means of extending their established high street business. The most recent development is the catalogue showroom, such as Argos. Within the mail order sector, some organisations expand their operations internationally, usually through the acquisition or partial acquisition of a foreign company.

Part of mail order's appeal is its use of the telephone to speed up transactions. The caller can find out if a particular item is in stock and, if required, make payment immediately by credit card. This principle has been further developed to open up the teleshopping industry. Satellite channels sell the same goods across Europe in this way, and there are whole channels on cable and satellite devoted to home shopping.

Internet marketing is an emerging form of direct marketing that can generate enquiries and sales and can be used to maintain relationships with customers very cost effectively and efficiently.

The internet can be used as a distribution channel, taking orders and delivering digital products. It is a medium for communication and promotion of goods and services as well as for disseminating PR, and a research and planning tool for gathering both primary and secondary data.

Direct marketing thus takes a variety of forms and can achieve a wide range of objectives. As well as direct ordering of goods, it can support the sales effort with information campaigns and after sales customer care initiatives. It can also pave the way towards sales by inviting potential customers to try out products or to make appointments to see sales representatives.

To achieve all this, however, the direct marketing campaign should be well planned, designed and executed. The campaign objectives should be clearly laid out and measurable. The target audience should also be clearly defined. This in turn leads to the selection of the most appropriate media and message. Media choice is also influenced by the campaign's objectives. Once the advertisement or other material has been developed, the organisation has to ensure that all the likely responses can be handled quickly and efficiently. The planning process should also allow for the response to the campaign to be measured and evaluated so that lessons can be learned for the future. Organisations reap the best benefits from direct marketing when they use responses to build databases so that any one campaign or offer becomes just one of a series of relationship building dialogues. It is important, however, to create and maintain a database that can cope with a detailed profile of each customer and their purchasing habits and history.

Key words and phrases

Database	Inbound telemarketing	Outbound telemarketing
Direct mail	Internet marketing	Telemarketing
Direct marketing	Mailing list	Telephone preference services
Direct response advertising	Mail order	Teleshopping

QUESTIONS FOR REVIEW

18.1 What is *direct marketing*?

18.2 What general issues have led to the rise in popularity of direct marketing?

18.3 Summarise what you consider to be the key success factors for a *direct mail campaign*.

18.4 What is *direct response advertising* and what are the relative advantages and disadvantages of using:

(a) television;
(b) radio; and
(c) print media

for it?

18.5 In what ways can *telemarketing* support and enhance the other elements of the promotional mix?

18.6 How do 'modern' *mail order* operations differ from the 'traditional' approach?

18.7 Why might high street retailers want to run mail-order operations in parallel with, and under the same trading name as, their stores?

18.8 What is *teleshopping* and through what media can it be offered to customers?

18.9 Explain the role that direct marketing can play in both creating and retaining customers.

18.10 Define the main stages in managing a direct marketing campaign.

QUESTIONS FOR DISCUSSION

18.1 Collect three pieces of direct mail and for each one assess:

(a) what you think it is trying to achieve;
(b) how that message has been communicated;
(c) what involvement devices have been used to encourage the recipient to read the mailshot; and
(d) how easy it is for the recipient to respond in the required way.

18.2 Carry out your own analysis of the advertising in a magazine. Discuss examples of good and bad direct response advertising from that magazine. What overall conclusions can you draw?

18.3 To what extent, and why, do you think that outbound telemarketing should be controlled by legislation or codes of practice?

18.4 For each of the techniques of direct marketing outlined in Fig. 18.1, assess their relevance to:

(a) consumer markets; and
(b) organisational markets.

18.5 Imagine that you are a customer of a mail order CD club. Specify what information about yourself the club's database should ideally hold. Which parts of that information would be of greatest use to the organisation in designing an appropriate offer for you?

CASE STUDY 18.1

Camp followers

Eurocamp, part of the Holiday Break organisation, is a market leader in European camping and mobile home holidays. It is particularly attractive to families with children looking for relatively inexpensive beach and lakeside holiday locations. Eurocamp has 200 sites in 11 countries and attracts holidaymakers from across Europe. Group sales from Eurocamp and sister companies, Keycamps and Sunsites, are around £75mn per year. The challenge facing Eurocamp, as well as many other holiday operators, is how to extend the season beyond the traditional peaks in July and August. Occupancy during the 'shoulder months' of May, June, September and, in warmer southern climates, October, outside the school holiday period, can

make all the difference to overall profitability. These are important months in which to undertake promotional efforts to extend the season and for that Eurocamp uses direct marketing.

Research has indicated to Eurocamp that its customers do not buy on price and that there is a high degree of satisfaction among past holidaymakers. Eurocamp, like many other holiday operators, has the advantage of being able to build a detailed customer database from enquiries and actual bookings. Family size, car type, postcode information, frequency of booking, site facility information, preferred destinations and even attitudinal data are all available for analysis from routine operations. Generally, the previous year's customers are the best prospects and they normally form the prime target for communication.

Advertising in a range of magazines and newspapers helps to generate enquiries, using freephone or coupon response. This triggers the sending of a brochure as the main selling tool. A multimedia CD-ROM has also been developed to provide a more novel way for consumers to assess a particular holiday camp destination. The website provides extensive information on the various locations, describes packages and special offers and provides a mechanism for customer feedback and brochure requests. The overall key to the promotional campaign, however, is the building of an effective database. Initially, Eurocamp analysed RFV data (recency, frequency and value) relating to the previous five years' bookings. RFV analysis traces the relationship with individual customers over time, how it is changing and provides guidelines for direct promotional activity. From the analysis of such data a three-dimensional model, as shown in Fig. 18.8, can be constructed. For Eurocamp, the RFV data were also considered in terms of family life-cycle and income level information, which could be obtained from the booking forms.

As Eurocamp was able to sell its peak season holidays many times over, it concentrated on the shoulder month customer profiles. Using standard SPSS software, it undertook data cross-tabulation to highlight the loyal and high value customers contained in the data. Customers were grouped into 15 categories ranging from low value spenders

who last visited five years ago to those taking a holiday twice a year with Eurocamp and spending an above-average amount. This enabled the priority value customers to be identified. The relationship with RFV and family life-cycle also proved interesting. Families travelling in June were found to be completely different from those taking a holiday in the peak season. They sought quieter campsites, less busy roads, yet still wanted good weather for the outdoor life associated with camping. All of this analysis resulted in a reshaped database that could be used by the marketing department for special direct promotions.

The refined database was then used to identify those customers more likely to participate in a shoulder month holiday. In particular, families with pre-school children and retired, empty nest couples were identified and the mailshots reflect the needs of these different groups. The pre-school families receive literature showing many happy children eqjoying an almost adult-free zone, except for, of course, the relaxed mum and dad. Mention is made of on-site sports and games, children's couriers and children's discos. The empty nesters would find it hard to see a child in the literature they receive. The focus for them is on healthy walking, bicycling, companionship and a generally peaceful environment. In both cases, the accompanying, personalised letter reminds the reader of last year's holiday in the hope of rekindling happy memories.

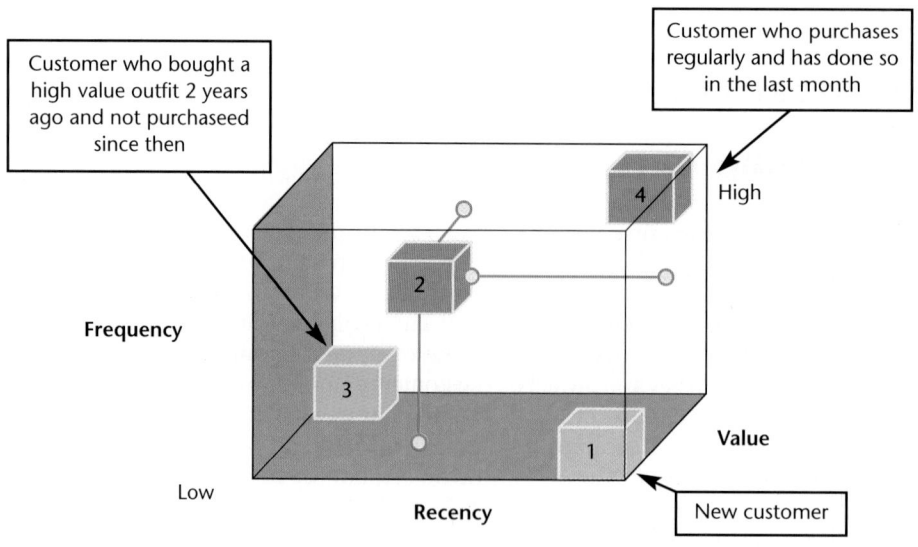

FIGURE 18.8

Recency, frequency and value model

Source: http://www.talkingnumbers.com

Further work is being undertaken to match the main target customers for the shoulder months with the magazines and papers that are used for advertising. Research has already revealed that broadsheet readers (i.e. *The Times, The Independent*) tend to spend more on each holiday but travel less frequently, while tabloid readers spend less but travel more frequently. Responses by postcode are also being examined to establish whether some neighbourhood areas have a greater propensity to take holidays during the shoulder season. This helps guide decisions on the need for targeted mailings. Mailshots are now sent to the priority and targeted customers three or four times a year. Eurocamp's approach to relationship marketing is based on its success in database establishment and subsequent data mining to profile customers to guide marketing decision making.

Sources: Lawson (1999b); http://www.talkingnumbers.com; http://eurocamp.com.

Questions

1 Why do you think Eurocamp is putting such an emphasis on direct marketing?

2 What kind of data could a company like Eurocamp capture about its visitors and how might this be of use to its marketers?

3 Eurocamp has identified groups of higher spending and lower spending visitors. How might the direct marketing approach differ between these two groups?

4 Eurocamp seems to be focusing exclusively on its existing and past customers. How do you think the company could use direct marketing to approach potential customers who have never experienced Eurocamp or perhaps have never even heard of it?

CASE STUDY 18.2

Four websites and a funeral

Buying clothing is for some a very personal affair. The consumer often appreciates the opportunity to inspect and compare styles and designs before purchase. This could involve visiting any number of retail outlets and trying on a wide range of garments. Sometimes friends and other family members can be persuaded to join the 'searcher', so the whole experience takes on a recreational and social dimension (*see* p. 189). Although it is impossible to generalise about consumers' shopping behaviours, most consumers tend to buy through retail stores and spend a variable amount of time searching, depending on the significance and urgency of the purchase. Clearly, shopping for a wedding dress will take a lot more effort than shopping for a pair of socks! So what chance does on-line clothing retailing have to break with conventional shopping patterns? Can it improve on what mail-order and catalogue shopping has done?

As we saw in Chapter 13, Internet distribution is beginning to revolutionise how we learn about products and how we shop, but so far its impact has mainly been in books, music, travel and software. Following on from the vignette on page 530, this case considers the websites of four clothing-related products as a potential mould-breaking approach to clothing purchases. The

target markets vary from minority interest groups through to mainstream clothing buyers.

Virgin Clothing (http://www.virgin-clothing.co.uk) offers a wide range of men's and women's clothing for on-line ordering. Although the merchandise is also available through selected retail outlets and Freeman's mail order catalogue, the prime intention of the site is to encourage direct sales. The clothing selections are presented visually on a rack, to mimic a retail store, and a click enables the garments to be inspected in more detail. The supporting information available includes additional comments on the products, size options, colour choices and, of course, the price range. A typical collection for the women's range includes dresses, skirts, T-shirts, jackets and swimwear. It can be changed on a seasonal basis or whenever the company needs. Underwear is not currently offered. An interesting feature of the site is a mannequin that can model the item under consideration with just one additional click. It is also possible to send a copy of the dressed mannequin to a friend over the Internet for comment.

For shoppers who are undecided about what they want, there is a support facility available in the form of a 'virtual shop assistant'. After some preliminary questions, the main focus is on the reasons for purchase as a guide for making on-line recommendations, i.e. whether the required garment is for work, party, evening wear or casual etc. The assistant can also be asked to tell the viewer more about the particular item of clothing under consideration, to provide that extra reassurance. Other services available include a Customer Service Centre, open daily from Monday to Friday from 9am to 5pm, and a comprehensive clothing care section covering washing, cleaning and other tips to maintain the garments in top condition.

In order to maximise the potential per visit, a link is provided to the locations of all retail stockists of Virgin's clothing ranges and a postcard facility featuring chosen models wearing Virgin clothes that can be sent to friends through the Internet.

Kitbag (http://www. kitbag.com) is an on-line trading company that specialises in football merchandise, including videos, souvenirs and sports clothing, especially soccer shirts. The company, based in Nottingham, provides a detailed step-by-step ordering guide for the selected merchandise and it is hoped to introduce a five-language option in the near future to promote sales from across Europe.

The shirts range covers all the UK's Premiership teams, a wide selection of international teams and a special section on golden oldies, including the 1966 World Cup winning England shirts. The home and away strips are featured, usually with some price discount. The Italian national team shirt was on offer for £44.99 in the summer of 1999. Other items can also be purchased and a small insert screen keeps a running 'shopping basket' total for the shopper buying more than one item.

As an extra feature, a free penalty competition can be played with the viewer taking on an *alter ego* in the form of players including Batty, Southgate, Pearce and Waddle. With on-screen soccer studs for controls, in the unlikely event that the viewer scores a goal a free T-shirt can be claimed. Such interactive fun is clearly designed to attract repeat viewing, as only one shot is allowed per site visit. Instead of a customer service centre, comments are welcome to the virtual soccer manager about the site and any problems. As with the Virgin site, secure credit card ordering services are offered.

Bras Direct (UK) (http://www.brasdirect.com), also based in Nottinghamshire, offers an on-line selection and ordering service for bras and underwear. The problem with bra and underwear purchasing is that the shopper has to be confident that the purchase will not only be a perfect fit but

also match style and colour requirements. As with the Virgin clothing example, the reason for purchase can vary from functional to seductive.

The virtual shop assistant is featured prominently on the site as being 'your personal store assistant' to help the shopper choose the article that's just right for her. A series of qualifying questions are used to narrow down the options before final selection. Initially the 'occasion' selector offers a choice from sporting, special occasion, special gift and normal wear. Then a 'size wizard' requests the size preferred, and for those in any doubt, a measuring guide is also provided to help in self-measurement of bra size and cup size. The size and occasion selectors trigger access to a range of branded choices including Wonderbra, Berlei, Playtex and Gossard. Before final choices are offered, additional questions are asked on preferred style, fabrics, strap requirements, maternity wear, colour etc. This all results in specific brand recommendations to fit the criteria along with details of the price, usually including 25 per cent discount. A collection of items can easily be assembled, using the 'add to basket' option, and a secure credit card transaction service is available to complete the purchase. There is a standard £3.50 delivery charge and the promise of 14-day delivery is normally offered.

The site does not end with the selection of individual brands. Extra features are being added, including a 360-degree view of models wearing the merchandise, a picture gallery of the models that can be downloaded and zoomed into, and two screensavers that can also be downloaded. A screensaver quickly passes through a different selection of models each time it is activated along with a calendar and the Bras Direct logo. Games and other features are also being offered. A multi-lingual customer service team is available for those customers wanting personal queries answered by telephone rather than e-mail.

Tidalwave from Scotland (http://www.erotic-lingerie.co.uk) specialises in a different type of underwear, ranging from the slightly erotic to the pretty way out. It claims to offer 'UK made lingerie for all tastes' and a secure and confidential ordering and delivery service with any products purchased delivered in plain wrappings. Sensitivity about billing has also been considered and discreet entries are made on credit card statements that do not identify the kind of merchandise ordered.

The on-line catalogue is divided into five broad headings under an umbrella brand, Dominion: Ultimate Erotica, Cuddly, Cocktail, Illusions and

Revelation. Typical products include variations of bras, pants, suspenders, bedboots, playsuits, chain bodices and sexy stockings. Most products are not branded, sizes and colours are restricted but each product is normally modelled with a zoom capability. A 'place in the basket option' is available for multiple purchases. As a special incentive, there is a £100 voucher for the user with the sexiest user name. Satisfied customers can make an entry into a guestbook, detailing how delighted they were with their purchases and the service levels received. There is also a link to a range of other erotic sites not owned by Tidalwave.

And the funeral? Well, even that can be arranged over the Internet. Try http://www.funerals.net.uk, a service that includes free consultation, home service arrangements and advice on 'do it yourself' funerals. There is also a useful question and answer page detailing information on cremation.

Questions

1 Outline the main differences between an on-line catalogue, such as those described here, and a more traditional mail order catalogue.

2 What are the main problems that on-line clothing retailers face and how can they overcome them? Are the problems the same for both the underwear and outerwear markets or for women's wear and men's wear?

3 To what extent is the marketing and selling of funeral-related services on-line or through direct mall, direct response advertising or telemarketing really feasible? List the advantages, disadvantages and what you consider to be the best use of each technique in relation to funeral-related services.

4 What are the stages in database creation and management? Explain how each stage would work in an on-line situation.

References to Chapter 18

Barry, K. (1998), 'Cracking the Codes', *Marketing*, 3 December, pp. 36–9.

Bird, J. (1998), 'Dial 0 for Opportunity', *Marketing*, 29 October, pp. 31–3.

Booth, E. (1999), 'Will the Web Replace the Phones?', *Marketing*, 4 February, pp. 25–6.

Campaign Direct Awards (1999a), supplement to *Campaign*, 12 April, p. 5.

Campaign Direct Awards (1999b), supplement to *Campaign*, 12 April, p. 15.

Clegg, A. (1999a), 'Down the Line', *Marketing Week*, 11 February, pp. 41–2.

Clegg, A. (1999b), 'Personal Touch', *Marketing Week*, 10 June, pp. 45–6.

Cobb, R. (1998), 'Talking Business', *Marketing*, 19 November, pp. 31–2.

Curtis, J. (1998), 'Life on the Floor', *Marketing*, 3 December, p. 35.

Curtis, J. (1999), 'Cutting the Cost of Internet Calls', *Marketing*, 8 July, pp. 25–6.

Dwek, R. (1999), 'Business Directions', *Campaign*, 19 February, p. 34.

Elster, L. (1999), 'Client's Choice', Special Report supplement to *Campaign*, 30 April, p. 14.

Euromonitor (1998), *European Marketing Data and Statistics 1998*, 33rd edn.

Exon, M. (1999), 'Databases: No Tourist Trap', *Precision Marketing*, 18 January, p. 12.

Fill, C. (1999), *Marketing Communications: Frameworks, Theories and Applications*, 2nd edn, Prentice-Hall.

Flack, J. (1999), 'Talking Heads', *Marketing Week*, 1 July, pp. 41–2.

Fry, A. (1995), 'Channels of Communication', *Marketing*, 5 October, p. III.

Gofton, K. (1998), 'Campaign Direct', *Campaign*, 20 November, pp. 23–4.

Gofton, K. (1999), 'The Client Culture', Special Report supplement to *Campaign*, 30 April, p. 3.

The Grocer (1999), 'Amazon', *The Grocer*, 22 May, p. 16.

Kavanagh, M. (1999a), 'Tangled in the Net', *Marketing Week*, 28 January, pp. 53–5.

Kavanagh, M. (1999b), 'Ex Spice Girl', *Marketing Week*, 22 April, p. 43.

Kavanagh, M. (1999c), 'Bibendum Shuts Shop to Launch "Virtual" Retailing', *Marketing Week*, 22 April, p. 43.

Kavanagh, M. (1999d), 'Virgin Net', *Marketing Week*, 6 May, p. 45.

Kavanagh, M. (1999e), 'E-volution', *Marketing Week*, 20 May, pp. 45–6.

Kavanagh, M. (1999f), 'Hula Hoops', *Marketing Week*, 8 July, p. 33.

Lawson, J. (1999a), 'Cleaning Up', *Database Marketing*, February, pp. 18–22.

Lawson, J. (1999b), 'Happy Campers', *Database Marketing*, March, pp. 36–8.

Lewis, M. (1999), 'Counting On It', *Database Marketing*, May, pp. 34–7.

MacMillan, G. (1999), 'Online Adspend for March was up £1mn on February', *Campaign*, 25 June, p. 31.

Marketing (1999a), 'The Client Perspective', *Marketing*, 11 March, p. 54.

Marketing (1999b), 'Inbound Swayed by Live Call Trend', *Marketing*, 15 April, pp. 46–7.

Marketing (1999c), 'WWAV Wins Large Slice of Toyota's Direct Business', *Marketing*, 3 June, p. 3.

Marketing Week (1999a), 'Games Firm under Fire over Military Style Mail', *Marketing Week*, 15 April, p. 11.

Marketing Week (1999b), 'Express Mailing Blitz to Target Gardeners', *Marketing Week*, 20 May, p. 12.

Marketing Week (1999c), 'Air Miles Revamps Website to Offer Customised Benefits', *Marketing Week*, 20 May, p. 43.

Marketing Week (1999d), 'Slendertone UK', *Marketing Week*, 20 May, p. 63.

Marketing Week (1999e), 'Porn "Will Continue to Dominate Web Revenue"', *Marketing Week*, 27 May, p. 43.

McNutt, B. (1998), 'A Matter of Priority', *Precision Marketing*, 21 December, p. 16.

Mitchell, A. (1999a), 'Marketers Must Grasp the Net or Face Oblivion', *Marketing Week*, 18 February, pp. 30–1.

Mitchell, A. (1999b), 'Online Markets Could See Brands Lose Control', *Marketing Week*, 15 April, pp. 24–5.

Murphy, C. (1999), 'Addressing the Data Issue', *Marketing*, 28 January, p. 31.

Reed, D. (1998), 'Calls for Concern', *Marketing Week*, 12 February, pp. 45–53.

Reed, D. (1999), 'Purchase History', *Database Marketing*, May, pp. 23–6.

Reed, M. (1999a), 'On-line Sales Go Uptempo', *Marketing*, 7 January, pp. 23–4.

Reed, M. (1999b), 'Going Beyond the Banner Ad', *Marketing*, 28 April, pp. 25–6.

Rogers, D. (1999), 'Harley Chooses Agency for UK Direct Mail Debut', *Marketing*, 24 June, p. 10.

Rosier, B. (1999a), 'New Adopters Will Be Key to Web Future', *Marketing*, 13 May, p. 13.

Rosier, B. (1999b), 'New Carlsberg Site to Target Drinkers', *Marketing*, 20 May, p. 12.

Schofield, A. (1994), 'Alternative Reply Vehicles in Direct Response Advertising', *Journal of Advertising Research*, 34(5), pp. 28–34.

Sumner, I. (1999), 'Web Site Novelties Can Bring PR Opportunities', *Marketing*, 17 June, p. 31.

Sumner-Smith, D. and Sumner, I. (1999), 'The Free Access Revolution', *Marketing*, 4 March, pp. 29–30.

Telemarketing Awards (1999a), supplement to *Marketing*, 17 June, p. 16.

Telemarketing Awards (1999b), supplement to *Marketing*, 17 June, p. 28.

Telemarketing Awards (1999c), supplement to *Marketing*, 17 June, p. 30.

Wilmshurst, J. (1993), *Below The Line Promotion*, Butterworth-Heinemann.

Wilson, R. (1999), 'Discerning Habits', *Marketing Week*, 1 July, pp. 45–7.

Witthaus, M. (1999), 'The Missing Link', *Marketing Week*, 1 July, pp. 51–6.

Woods, A. (1998), 'Packard Bell NEC Back to Resellers', *Precision Marketing*, 21 December, p. 8.

19 Public Relations, Sponsorship and Exhibitions

LEARNING OBJECTIVES

This chapter will help you to:

1 define PR and the areas of marketing activities it covers;

2 understand its role in supporting the organisation's activities and in reaching various groups, or publics, with differing interests and information needs;

3 outline the techniques of PR, their appropriateness for different kinds of public, and how they might be evaluated;

4 appreciate the importance of corporate identity, why organisations might wish to change identity, and the processes involved in change;

5 understand the role of sponsorship in the marketing communications mix and the benefits and problems of different types of sponsorship;

6 appreciate the contribution that exhibitions can make to achieving marketing objectives and how to exploit them to the full.

INTRODUCTION

Looking back to Chapter 2 and the discussion there on the marketing environment, it is clear that organisations need to be concerned about much more than just their trading relationships with their target markets. Customers are important, but a business as a whole cannot function effectively without the support and co-operation of its financial backers, its employees and trades unions, its suppliers, the legal and regulatory bodies to which it is answerable, interested pressure groups, the media, and many more groups or 'publics' which have the ability to affect the way in which the organisation does business. There is no direct trading relationship between the organisation and many of the publics listed above, which means that the objectives of whatever communication takes place are centred more on explaining what the organisation stands for, and creating a strong, positive corporate image than on a hard sell. Public relations (PR) is the area of marketing communications that specifically deals with the quality and nature of the relationship between an organisation and its publics. Its prime concern is to generate a sound, effective and understandable flow of communication between the organisation and these groups so that shared understanding is possible.

Example Shell International decided in 1999 to spend £15mn in an effort to restore its battered corporate image (Jardine, 1999a). The 1990s had seen a series of PR disasters, the most damaging of which concerned the run-in with Greenpeace over the disposal of the Brent Spar oil platform and the execution of Ken Saro-Wiwa in Nigeria, both in 1995 (Denny, 1995). Some consumers boycotted Shell products and even in 1998, MORI found that 10 per cent of people were still highly critical of the company's reputation and operations (Jardine, 1999b). Websites such as http://www.oilcompanies.org.shell run a range of 'facts' and 'stories' severely criticising the company.

Shell's campaign outlined the actions that had already been taken on environmental and human rights issues and sought to encourage wider debate and feedback on these issues. The PR-led campaign included corporate advertising, direct marketing and on-line debate over the Internet building around the theme 'Profits and Principles: Is there a choice?' (http://www. shell. com). Issues such as saving endangered species, protecting the community and environment and sustainable development featured highly. However some critics, such as Greenpeace, believed that more attention should be placed on changing the substance of Shell's operations rather than developing public relations campaigns that they considered were unlikely to change public opinion. The PR battle continues.

As the range of publics implies, PR has a broad brief and a difficult objective to achieve. While publicity or press relations can make a significant contribution, PR utilises a much wider range of activities, which this chapter will cover. First, however, it is important to discuss in more detail exactly what PR is, why it is so important, and what is involved in its management. Then the chapter will go on to look in more detail at some specialist areas of PR, including corporate identity, sponsorship and trade exhibitions. Through this, the chapter will show how PR interacts with other areas of the promotional mix to create synergy, and how it can sometimes draw on techniques such as advertising in achieving its objectives.

THE DEFINITION OF PUBLIC RELATIONS

First, we discuss some formal definitions of PR and the activities covered by it, and then we proceed to a more focused overview of the various publics that might be of interest to an organisation.

Public relations defined

Stanley (1982, p. 40) defined **public relations** as:

> **A management function that determines the attitudes and opinions of the organisation's publics, identifies its policies with the interests of its publics, and formulates and executes a programme of action to earn the understanding and goodwill of its publics.**

The Institute of Public Relations (IPR) is rather more succinct in its definition:

> **The deliberate, planned and sustained effort to institute and maintain mutual understanding between an organisation and its publics.**

The latter is, nevertheless, a more useful definition that gets close to the core concern of PR, which is *mutual understanding*. The implication is that the organisation needs to understand how it is perceived in the wider world, and then work hard to make sure, through PR, that those perceptions match its desired image. Two-way communication is essential to this process. Another interesting element of this definition is the specific use of the word *publics*. Advertising, in its commonest usage, is usually about talking to customers or potential customers. Public relations defines a much broader range of target audiences, some of whom have no direct trading relationship with the organisation, and thus PR encompasses a wide variety of communication needs and objectives not necessarily geared towards an eventual sale. Advertising can certainly be used as a tool of PR, but as this chapter will show, it is not the best communication method for many publics or objectives. Finally, the definition emphasizes that PR is *deliberate, planned and sustained*. This is important for two reasons. First, it implies that PR is just as much of a strategically thought out, long-term commitment as any other marketing activity, and second, it counters any preconceptions about PR simply being the *ad hoc* seizing of any free publicity opportunity that happens to come along.

The essence of PR, as stated in the introduction, is to look after the nature and quality of the relationships between the organisation and its various publics. This means that PR covers the management of a range of activities that create and maintain the character and status of the organisation in the eyes of those who matter. It includes, therefore, activities such as:

- the creation and maintenance of corporate identity and image
- the enhancement of the organisation's standing as a corporate citizen, through activities such as arts and sports sponsorship, charitable involvement and community initiatives
- the communication of the organisation's philosophy and purpose, through activities such as open days, visitor centres and corporate advertising
- media relations, both for the dissemination of good news stories and for crisis management, including damage limitation
- attendance at trade exhibitions, which helps to forge stronger relationships with key suppliers and customers as well as enhancing the organisation's presence and reputation within the market.

All of these activities will be discussed in this chapter, but before we do that, it is important the look in more detail at just *who* the various publics are.

Publics defined

A **public** is any group, with some common characteristic, with which an organisation needs to communicate. Each public poses a different communication problem, as each has different information needs and a different kind of relationship with the organisation, and may start with different perceptions of what the organisation stands for (Marston, 1979).

Example A university has to develop relationships with a wide range of publics. Obviously, there are the students and potential students and the schools and colleges that provide them, both nationally and internationally. The university also has to consider, however, its staff and the wider academic community. Then there are the sources of funding, such as local authorities, the government, the EU and research bodies. Industry might also be a potential source of research funds, as well as commissioning training courses and providing jobs for graduates. It is also important for a university to foster good press relations. Local media help to establish the university as a part of its immediate community, national media help to publicise its wider status, while specialist publications such as the *Times Higher Education Supplement* reach those with a specific interest and perhaps even the decision makers within the sector.

A number of different publics, which relate generally to any kind of organisation, are shown in Fig. 19.1 and discussed below. It is, however, important to remember that any individual may be a member of more than one public. This means that although the slant and emphasis of messages may differ from public to public, the essential content and philosophy should be consistent. Appropriate techniques within PR for communicating with a range of different publics will be looked at later (see pp. 789 *et seq.*).

Commercial

The commercial group includes anyone who has some kind of trading relationship with the organisation, or those who trade in competition with them. It obviously includes, therefore, customers, suppliers and competitors. The main role of PR in relation to this group is to act in synergy with other sales-orientated marketing communication, such as advertising and personal selling. Public relations can be used to convey product information, through editorial coverage in trade magazines, for example, to reinforce attitudes and opinions, or to offer reassurance about product choice, as well as providing a wider umbrella of positive corporate image.

Internal

The internal group consists of those who work within the organisation, and support organisations represented within the workplace. It therefore covers management, administrative staff, production operatives and trade unions. Internal PR is important for keeping employees informed about what the organisation is doing, for boosting morale, engendering a sense of belonging, and helping to reinforce the desired corporate culture.

Financial

Members of this group have some kind of financial interest in the organisation. The group therefore consists of shareholders, potential investors, bankers and the wider financial community. Public relations contributes towards instilling confidence in the organisation, which means that current investors are less likely to pull out, potential investors are more likely to invest and bankers will be more flexible. It goes without saying, however, that PR cannot be used to disguise a basically unsound business, but it might help to buy a little tolerance or flexibility from creditors or backers. Public relations also comes into its own during takeover battles and when mergers are proposed. The planned merger between Rhône-Poulenc and Hoescht was extensively supported by direct communication to shareholders and regular press briefings to ensure that the financial press and community were made aware of the advantages of

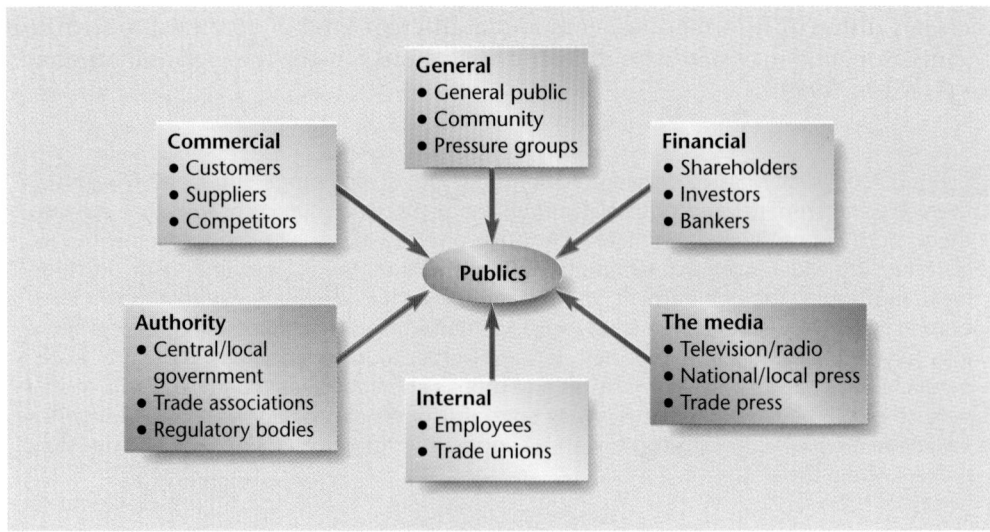

FIGURE 19.1

Publics

the merger. Even a section of the Rhône-Poulenc website was dedicated to the merger (http://www.rp-rorer.com).

Authority

'Authority' is a loose label that covers those who have the power, whether statutory or voluntarily given, to influence the way in which an organisation conducts itself. Central and local government, trade associations and regulatory bodies are all included. Maintaining good relationships with these groups might give the organisation a louder voice in consultation on drafting proposed rules or legislation, or at least give sufficient advance warning of what is in the pipeline to allow them to prepare fully for its implementation or to lobby against it.

Example Dundee City Council wanted to be regarded as a centre for the biotechnology industry in order to attract inward investment. In conjunction with local universities, businesses and research organisations, the BioDundee PR campaign was developed to target international research institutes, venture capitalists, charities and trust funds. The campaign featured the human interest approach, focusing on the leading scientists in the city and their research achievements. A range of media were used, including seminars, events, publications, direct mail, a dedicated website and closer relationships with both specialist and general media. Although the campaign is long term, the messages being sent out clearly position Dundee as a centre of excellence within a rapidly growing industry (Tyrell, 1998; http://dundeecity.gov.uk).

The media

The media are an important group because most members of the other publics listed here will take notice of what they are saying. The media, including television, radio, national and local press and trade and professional press, constitute both a public in their own right and a tool of PR. Good media relationships are essential, whether the organisation wants to feed 'good news' stories to other publics or to minimise the risk of very hostile media reaction in a crisis.

Customers or potential customers are influenced by the non-advertising messages they see or hear in the media, whether on the news, in consumer programmes or as features, and may well change their attitudes and purchasing habits as a result. Celebrity chiefs, it would appear, set an example to us all. Whether it is Delia Smith, Gary Rhodes or Ainsley Harriott, on the television and in the press they extol the virtues of fresh, hygienically prepared, scrumptious home-cooked meals. The reality

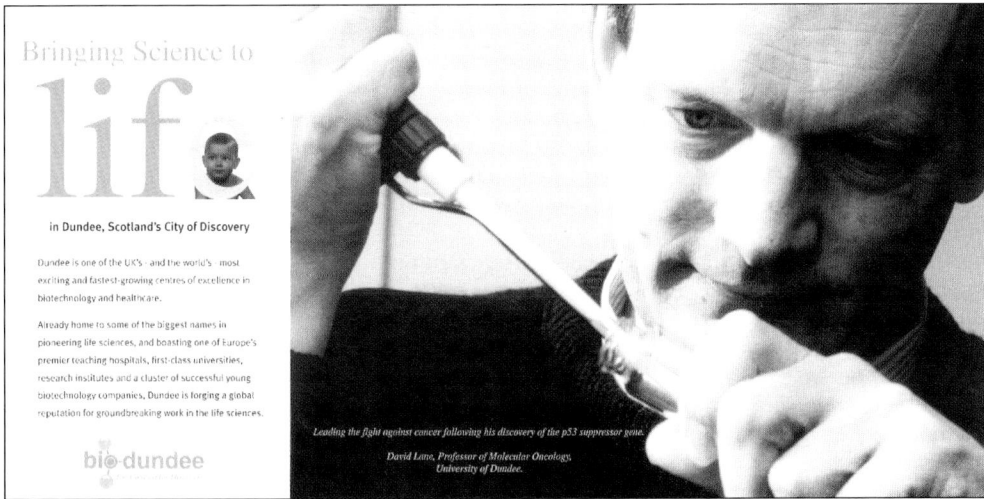

Bringing Dundee's biotechnology expertise to a wide range of international publics.

Source: Dundee City Council.

for an increasing number of people, however, is that they struggle to cook even the most basic food properly and often prefer to patronise the local takeaway or reach for convenience food, and this is especially true for those with busy lifestyles and households in which both partners are working. To allow these consumers to fulfil the expectations that the celebrity chefs raise, therefore, the convenience food manufacturers have expanded their ranges to include interesting and healthy meals and exotic sauces and toppings. At least this creates the illusion of an exotic, well-prepared culinary experience, keeping the consumer interested through variety and quality (Davies and Phillips, 1999).

Sometimes negative events are linked with particular organisations. Product tampering scares (such as glass in baby food), product faults (such as washing powder damaging clothes) or what are perceived to be unethical practices are seen as newsworthy items that could seriously damage an organisation's standing if the coverage were allowed to run on unchecked. The organisation needs to have a mechanism for putting its own side of the story and limiting the damage. Similarly, on the positive side, an organisation with good news to tell, such as job creation, winning a large contract or the launch of an innovative new product, will crave media attention to spread the story far more widely than an advertising budget could, and to give it more credibility.

General

The final group covers the general public at large. This includes the local community, special interest groups and in particular, opinion formers and leaders. It is now accepted that organisations need to be seen as good corporate citizens and have to play a part in the communities in which they are based. Public relations can help this process by, for example, making sure that a company's sponsorship of a local young athlete, environmental project or community group is adequately and positively publicised. It is also clear that organisational activities are under increased public scrutiny from pressure groups who are prepared to publicise and lobby against what they see as unacceptable practices. The nuclear power industry, for instance, is constantly having to use PR to defend itself against a barrage of vocal anti-nuclear pressure groups, while the chemical industry has to deal with environmental groups. Opinion leaders and pressure groups alike have the power to influence public opinion which, in turn, can seriously affect sales or lead to pressure on 'authority' to regulate, legislate or restrict operations.

Example Both the Belgian poultry industry and supermarket chains were hit by a food scare that resulted in chicken and eggs being removed from shop shelves. High levels of cancer-causing dioxins were found in Belgian poultry as a result of contaminated feed from a single producer and there were fears, following on from the 'mad cow' disease scare, that these could be passed on to humans through the food chain. The contamination resulted in a PR crisis both for suppliers in the food chain and for those who regulate it. The Belgian agricultural and health ministers resigned amid accusations from the European Commission that the Belgian government had failed to act quickly enough to protect the consumer's interests. Even retailers in the UK had to take defensive action to reassure customers even though there was no evidence of contamination in the Belgian products they were selling (Smith *et al.*, 1999).

By accepting the resignations, the Belgian government felt better able to regain public confidence that the problem was under control. For the supplier that caused the problem, there may be a more difficult challenge to rebuild its reputation. Perrier never quite recovered lost ground after a product contamination scare. Corporate reputation rebuilding is, however, possible. After the sinking of the car ferry *Herald of Free Enterprise* in 1987, Townsend Thoreson may have disappeared as a brand name, but P&O Stena, through rebranding, advertising and a host of overt safety measures, was able to regain the trust of the public and remain a cross-channel carrier.

Not all publics will be regarded by an organisation as having equal importance. Some will be seen as critical, and be given priority in targeting PR activities, while others will just be left ticking over for the time being. As the organisation's situation changes, the priority given to each of the publics will have to be reassessed (Wilmshurst, 1993).

Even in the quietest and most stable of industries, the membership of each public will change over time, and their needs and priorities will also evolve. This process of change emphasises the need to monitor attitudes and opinions constantly, and thus to identify current and future pressure points early enough to be able to defuse or control them.

THE ROLE OF PUBLIC RELATIONS

As with any marketing activity, managers must be sure that PR integrates with the rest of the organisation's promotional efforts, and that it is clearly related to wider company objectives. Cutlip *et al.* (1985) distinguish between **marketing PR** and **corporate PR**. Although the two are not mutually exclusive, there may be differences in their scope and objectives.

Marketing PR

Marketing PR may be used for long-term strategic image building, developing credibility and raising the organisation's profile, to enhance other marketing activities. When used in this way, it becomes a planned element of the wider promotional mix, working in synergy with the others. A new product launch, or the introduction of a big new innovative advertising campaign, for instance, might benefit from planned PR aimed at specific audiences through specific media to generate interest and awareness.

> **Example** A classic example of the link between advertising and publicity is the launch of the Wonderbra. Playtex spent £300 000 on advertising for this product. The advertisements, featuring headlines such as 'Hello Boys', and 'Or Are You Just Pleased to See Me?' were sexy, funny and somewhat more upfront than traditional lingerie advertisements. Because of this, and because of a deliberate strategy of attracting media attention, Playtex was able to generate publicity equivalent to an estimated £18 million advertising spend.

Corporate PR

It is possible to use corporate PR as part of a long-term relationship building strategy with various publics or as a short-term tactical response to an unforeseen crisis. By definition, short-term circumstances are somewhat unpredictable, and therefore any organisation needs to have contingency plans ready so that a well-rehearsed crisis management team can swing into action as soon as disaster strikes. This means, for example, that everyone should know who will be responsible for collating information and feeding it to the media, and that senior management will be properly briefed and trained to face media interrogation. Such measures result in the organisation being seen to handle the crisis capably and efficiently, and also reduce the chances of different spokespersons innocently contradicting each other, or of the media being kept short of information because everyone thinks that someone else is dealing with that aspect. Although the duration of the crisis may be short, and thus the actual implementation of PR activities is technically a short-term tactic to tide the organisation over the emergency, the contingency planning behind it involves long-term management thinking.

Example Advertising and PR disasters, according to Pitcher (1999), although related, are not the same thing. Typical advertising disasters are like the McDonald's 25th anniversary offer of two burgers for the price of one, which resulted in so many customers that the buns ran out (Rawstorne, 1999), and the launch of Prudential's Egg savings account that completely underestimated demand so that the company could not process all account applications quickly enough. Sales might have been affected in the short term, but the company reputation remained intact. However, PR disasters such as the Brent Spar incident between Greenpeace and Shell or *The Sun*'s decision to publish a topless photograph of Sophie Rhys-Jones just before her wedding to Prince Edward could damage the reputation of the organisations concerned, but sales are not necessarily significantly affected. In all these cases, corporate PR played a role in attempting to preserve the organisation's overall reputation or to minimise the potential damage.

MARKETING IN ACTION ## When the going gets tough. . .

When an organisation gets something wrong, how it handles its public relations can be critical in preserving its reputation. The Bank of Scotland decided to enter into direct banking and needed additional financial backing. It agreed to form a joint venture with US-based Christian Coalition, which was led by US evangelist Pat Robertson. Mr Robertson, known for his outspoken and controversial stand on lifestyle and moral issues, passed a comment on Scotland during an interview on his *700 Club* television programme. He said, 'In Europe, the big word is tolerance . . . and in Scotland you can't believe how strong the homosexuals are. It's just simply unbelievable . . . it [Scotland] could go right back to the darkness very easily.' Understandably, the Scots were outraged and the Bank of Scotland faced a serious PR dilemma.

As a result of the mere association with Mr Robertson, up to 500 accounts had already been closed prior to the live outburst, including those of the Trade Union Congress and a number of charities. The subsequent remarks by Robertson made matters worse. Shares lost 4 per cent of their value on one day and the West Lothian Council threatened to close its £250mn account. The choice facing the Bank of Scotland was whether to convince its customers, shareholders and even employees that the joint venture should still go ahead, despite the affront to Scotland, or to pull out of the deal altogether. Mr Robertson expressed concern at the growing criticism of him in the Scottish press and could not see why the deal should be jeopardised.

The Bank of Scotland chose to pull out of the deal by buying back Robertson's share of the venture, rather than risking further public criticism and censure. Buxton (1999b) claimed that although the Bank of Scotland would have honoured the deal despite the pressure from the church, trade unions and homosexuals, the criticism of Scotland itself was the final straw. The bank proceeded to search for new partners rather than miss out on the business opportunity. However, the board was still severely criticised by shareholders for its lack of judgement in associating with Mr Robertson in the first place.

McDonald's also ran into trouble, this time with year 4 at Filton Hill County Primary School, South Goucestershire. The children complained of poor service, toyless Happy Meals, overcharging and wrong orders at their local McDonald's restaurant. McDonald's responded promptly not just by accepting full responsibility and apologising, but also by providing the missing toys from the Happy Meals, £200 of books for the school and arranging a visit from a representative to explain to the children the complaints handling process. Far from alienating customers, it managed to turn the situation round through good PR.

Coca-Cola, despite its reputation, is not exempt from PR problems. A drinks health scare hit it, causing the withdrawal of its products from four European countries. The problem was traced back to two separate chemical problems at bottling plants in Europe where substandard carbon dioxide had infiltrated a small percentage of bottled Coca-Cola. In Belgium, up to 100 people were affected by stomach upsets, nausea and headaches. Despite the problem, Coca-Cola sought to minimise the damage to its reputation and consumer confidence. By withdrawing the stocks quickly and keeping the media informed of the actions being taken to identify why its high quality standards were breached, more balanced press coverage was generated. The company also detailed the corrective actions planned, in order to minimise the subsequent damage to the brand, unlike in the Perrier case ten years earlier that is believed to have cost Perrier £125mn and a damaged reputation over many years.

Sources: Buckley and Liu (1999); Buxton (1999a, 1999b); Griegson (1999); Grimston and Murden (1999); Nelson and Merrell (1999).

As the above examples show, given PR's wide range of uses and applications, it might be very easy to drift into activities without a clear sense of purpose. It is, therefore, particularly important to define clear objectives as a rationale for action and as a yardstick against which outcomes and achievements can be measured (Stone, 1991).

TECHNIQUES IN PUBLIC RELATIONS

The PR manager has a range of techniques and activities to draw on, limited only by imagination. The first area to look at is that of **publicity** and **press relations**, a major concern within the PR remit. Other external communications and internal PR will then be discussed. While considering techniques, it is important to relate them to the target publics and the PR objectives for which each is appropriate. The range of techniques is summarised in Fig. 19.2.

Publicity and press relations

Public relations and 'publicity' are often mistakenly used as interchangeable terms. Publicity is, however, simply one of the tools available for achieving the overall PR objective of creating and maintaining good relationships with various publics. Publicity is thus a subset of PR, focused on generating media coverage at minimal cost to the organisation. In other words, publicity happens when the media voluntarily decide to talk about the organisation and its commercial activities.

All areas of the mass media can be used for publicity purposes. Within the broadcast media, apart from news and current affairs programmes, a great deal of publicity is disseminated through chat shows (authors plugging their latest books, for instance), consumer shows (featuring dangerous products or publicising companies' questionable personal selling practices, for instance) and special interest programmes (motoring, books, clothing etc.). Print media also offer wide scope for publicity. National and local newspapers cover general interest stories, but there are many special interest, trade and professional publications that give extensive coverage to stories of specific interest to particular publics. It must also be remembered that sections of the media feed each other. National newspapers and television stations may pick up stories from local media or the specialist media and present them to a much greater mass audience.

Generating good publicity

Publicity may be unsought, as when the media get the smell of scandal or malpractice and decide to publicise matters which perhaps the organisation would rather not

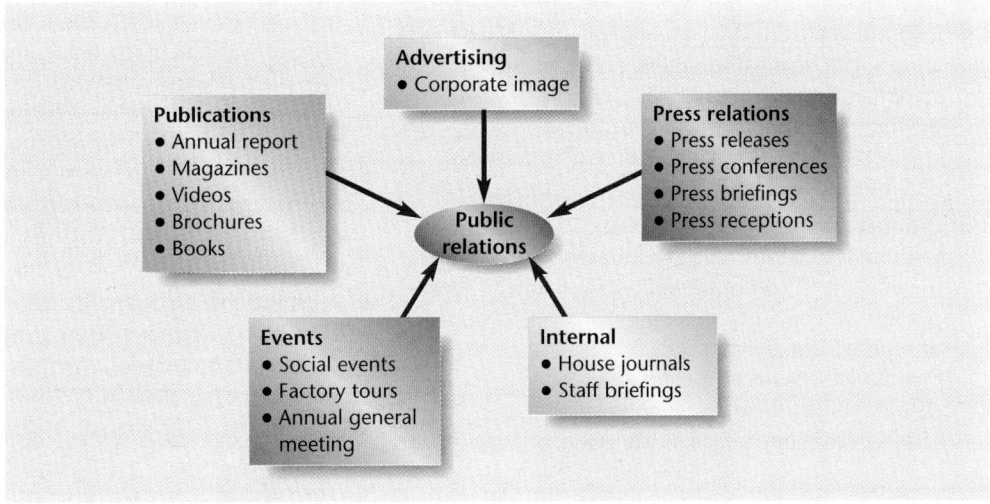

have publicised. To reduce the risk of bad publicity, however, most organisations cultivate good press relations, and try to feed the media's voracious appetite with 'good news' stories that will benefit the organisation. This can be done through a number of mechanisms.

Press releases. Traditionally, press releases consist of a one-page, brief outline of the essential facts behind a story, with a contact name and number being provided for those who wish to obtain more information. It is also common practice to back up a press release with photographic and video material to encourage the media to take up a story.

Many organisations have created snippets of video material that are made available to television news agencies, for example. These snippets feature fairly bland shots, such as the production line or exteriors of the factory or head office, appropriate for backing a wide range of stories about the organisation. Thus a news story about Vauxhall Opel's latest wage agreement will be backed by footage, provided by the company, of diligent workers on the assembly line. The availability of such material means that the organisation's story is more attractive to the news agency and it may give it more air time because it has the pictures to fill out the news item without having to go to a lot of trouble. The news agency can either use the material as it is or edit their own interviews or other coverage into this footage.

Unfortunately, the majority of press releases end up in the news editor's bin. This is partly because organisations produce far too many of them, often covering pretty mundane events, and partly because they are often produced with little imagination. The news editor needs an 'angle' that captures the imagination and might provide the focus for an interesting story.

Press conferences. One of the problems with press releases is that they are used so frequently and it is difficult to make yours stand out from all the others that land on an editor's desk every day. This might make organisations look for more personal contact with the media to make a bigger impression.

MARKETING AND IT   Public relations on the Internet

The Internet is being used more and more for a variety of marketing and corporate public relations activities. Typical public relations activities that are conducted using the Internet include:

■ **Investor relations.** Many companies will place their annual, half-yearly or quarterly accounts or financial statements on the Internet for investors to view or download. Almost all major investors will use corporate websites as a key source of information and intelligence about target companies.

■ **Product and service information.** The Internet has become a key distribution channel for marketing PR material. Most corporate websites will devote most of their web pages to descriptions of their products or services. The general 'look and feel' of a corporate website can significantly enhance (or detract from) the organisation's overall public image. Newspapers such as the *Financial Times* have been known to be scathing in their views about certain corporate websites.

■ **Press releases.** Most companies who distribute press releases on the web will archive these releases so that users can access them easily again. Hewlett-Packard was one of the first companies to launch its own press releases and news information onto a news bulletin board that was shared with several hundred publications worldwide. Most corporate websites will have one or more pages devoted to recent press releases. Marketing departments will now e-mail statements to newspapers for immediate release, as opposed to using fax, courier or mail.

■ **Recruitment.** A company's website can be an invaluable source of reference material for prospective employees. Many companies now solicit and receive job applications over the Internet.

Source: O'Connor & Galvin (1999).

A *news conference* could be used where there is a major story to announce or where a crisis has erupted and there is a need to update the media from the organisation's point of view. Journalists gather to receive information and to ask questions so that they can then go away and write up the material quickly.

Example The NATO conflict in Kosovo was fought from a military and PR perspective. NATO had to be able to cope with the needs of 24-hour news services, over 100 journalists, 600 reporters and camera operators at the headquarters in Brussels alone. The challenge was to manage the news agenda to provide clear and concise information, at the same time ensuring that the public in the various member nations remained fully behind the NATO effort, despite serious setbacks such as the mistaken bombing of the Chinese embassy. Over 40 press officers were assigned for liaison with national governments, monitoring of national press stories and preparing for questions and answers during the daily press conferences. The greatest challenge for the team was to ensure appropriate and consistent news messages without creating television entertainment of live bombing runs. Much also depended on how the chief spokesperson, Jamie Shea, handled the various questions and whether a positive or defensive stance was taken on some issues (Garside, 1999).

A *press briefing* has slightly less urgency about it, and will be used to clarify or explain details about a story. Government departments often use daily press briefings to talk about the background to policy and about on-going activities. This material will then be sourced as contextual material when something really newsworthy happens.

A *press reception* is even more relaxed. This is part of maintaining good press relations and involves inviting chosen members of the press, whether national or trade media, to some kind of party to mingle with executives from the organisation and to chat informally. An organisation might hold a press reception, for instance, as part of a wider PR campaign to allow the media to meet a newly appointed managing director.

Involving the media. Press releases and the other methods of feeding information to the press do work well, but sometimes more can be gained by going a little further and getting the media more involved in what is happening.

Example When P. J. Holloway became the sole UK distributor for fans made by the German firm Rosenberg Ventilation, if it had simply issued a press release, it might have gained limited coverage in the trade press. Instead, it invited key journalists to visit Rosenberg's manufacturing facility in Germany. As a result of this extra investment in press relations, it found that its coverage was considerable and much more complimentary comments than they could otherwise have expected were made about the product benefits.

Advantages of publicity over advertising

The media are obviously very powerful, not only as a public in their own right, but also as a third-party channel of communication with other publics. It may be argued that advertising can do just as good a communication job, in spreading good news to mass audiences, but publicity has a few advantages.

Credibility. Advertising is paid for, and therefore publics have a certain cynicism about the bias within the message. Publicity, on the other hand, is seen as free, coming from a neutral third party, and therefore has more credibility. An advertisement can tell you that a particular make of car has especially good roadholding capacity and you may or may not choose to believe it, but if a newspaper's motoring correspondent or the BBC's *Top Gear* programme concludes that the car demonstrates good roadholding, then that constitutes neutral expert opinion and thus carries more weight.

Reach. To make sure that the widest possible audience is reached with advertising would involve a multimedia strategy that would be extremely expensive to implement. A good PR story that captures the imagination so that it gets wide coverage across both print and broadcast media can achieve an incredible level of reach (*see* p. 613) at a fraction of the cost, and might even make an impact on sections of the audience who wouldn't normally see or absorb advertising.

Excitement. Publicity, by definition, is about news. Whatever is being publicised is of current and topical concern and therefore generates its own excitement. Once a story starts rolling, it can gather its own momentum as the media start vying with each other to generate the most coverage or to find a new angle on the story. Extensive media coverage of the concern over so-called alcopops (alcoholic lemonades and colas) is one such example.

Disadvantage of publicity over advertising

These advantages do, however, need to be balanced against the big disadvantage, *uncontrollability*. Whereas advertising gives the advertiser complete control over what is said, when it is said, how it is said and where it is said, the control of publicity is in the hands of the media. The organisation can feed material to the media, but cannot guarantee that the media will adopt the story or influence how they will present it (Fill, 1999). The outcome of this might be, at worst, no coverage at all, or patchy coverage that might not reach the desired target publics. Another potential risk is distortion of the story.

Example   When BA unveiled its new colour scheme and tail designs for its aircraft in 1997, it was praised for its innovative, ethnic designs, reflecting the various nations that BA serves. Others, however, were less kind, including a very public admonishment when Baroness Thatcher covered up a model with a handkerchief in full view of the national media. Despite the fact that the new designs had cost £60mn, the decision was made in 1999 to return to the British flag for all new planes and to repaint at least half the fleet. This followed a market research report suggesting that in BA's core market, the UK, the ethnic tail fins were extremely unpopular with some customers, who even switched to other airlines in protest (Parsley, 1999).

It is not true to say that there is no such thing as bad publicity. The risks of negative coverage can, however, be minimised by the maintenance of on-going, good press relations, and by setting up a crisis management plan so that if disaster strikes, the damage from bad publicity can be limited and even turned to advantage.

Other external communication

Other forms of external communication are also used for PR.

Advertising

Advertising can be used as a tool of PR, although it is something of a grey area. The kind of advertising to which we are referring here is not the selling or promoting of a specific product or range of products, but the type that concentrates on the organisation's name and characteristics. As previously suggested, although this sort of advertising lacks the impartiality of publicity, it makes up for it in terms of controllability. As a means of helping to establish and reinforce corporate image, it is certainly effective, and as a mass medium will reach members of most publics.

Philips, for example, felt that it needed to refresh its corporate image because its brand was seen as 'too technical'. Mass media advertising, therefore, was used to reach opinion leaders in consumer markets to generate a more user-friendly image.

Events

An organisation can host or participate in various events for PR purposes. As well as press conferences, mentioned above, the organisation may host other social events. If it has just opened a new factory, for instance, it may hold a party on the premises for key shareholders, employees, customers and suppliers. Such one-off events will also, of course, create media interest.

An important public is the one with a financial interest in the organisation. The organisation's annual general meeting is an important forum for both shareholders and the financial media. Efficient administration and confident presentation can help to increase credibility (although none of that can disguise a poor financial position).

Some organisations open their doors to the general public quite regularly, allowing factory tours, and some have even gone as far as building dedicated visitor centres on site, for example Cadbury's Chocolate World, the Sellafield nuclear plant visitors' centre, and Tetley's Brewery Wharf. Such facilities help to involve the public in the work of the organisation, so that they may understand it better, and thus to forge a stronger, more human relationship between organisation and public. Lego has taken this concept a step further by diversifying into Legoland theme parks that are 'products' in their own right, not just PR generators.

Publications

An organisation can commission a wide range of print and video material to support its PR efforts. Videos can be used, as already mentioned, to support press coverage, or can be sent to potential customers or clients to give them a flavour of how the organisation operates. Most universities, for example, will have a recruitment video to send out to schools and colleges to give a more three-dimensional feel for the place than the prospectus alone can manage. At the other end of the university education process, university careers offices stock corporate videos and brochures of organisations looking to recruit graduates.

Annual reports. An important publication is the organisation's annual report, distributed primarily to shareholders and the financial media, but often sent out to anyone who expresses an interest in the organisation. Like the annual general meeting, it is an opportunity to present the organisation in the best possible positive light and to make public statements about the organisation's achievements and its future directions.

Company histories. As a one-off exercise, organisations may even decide to publish their 'autobiographies'.

Pencorp Books specialises in writing corporate histories to contract. The book on Slough Estates, one of the pioneering industrial park property companies in the UK, was distributed to 6000 employees, major shareholders and company contacts. The book also went on sale locally, parts of it were featured in subsequent histories, and a leather bound version was made available for VIP visitors to the company. The original purpose of the book was to raise the profile of the company, especially with existing and potential investors, however it was used much more widely as part of the corporate communications effort (Cassell, 1991).

Lobbying

Lobbying is a very specialised area, designed to develop and influence relationships with 'authority', particularly national and EU governmental bodies. Lobbying is a way of getting an organisation's views known to the decision makers, and trying to influence the development and implementation of policy.

MARKETING IN ACTION **Passports for pets**

The UK animal quarantine laws were introduced at a time when exclusion was effectively the only way to prevent the spread of rabies and other animal diseases from continental Europe. The law, introduced in 1901, required all pets to spend six months away from their owners in detention to ensure that they were disease free and fit to re-enter pet society. The scheme was obviously unpopular with pet owners, not only because of being parted from a pet for six months, but also because of the high accommodation charges. The fines for those smuggling their pets into the country, however, were often also very high. Nevertheless, the general public generally believed that the laws kept the UK a rabies-free zone and changing the rules was not high on the politicians' agenda.

Pressure to change the law by introducing a passport scheme, showing that pets had had relevant vaccinations, started in 1994. The idea was initially rejected by the then Conservative government, so the lobby group, Passport for Pets, expanded its support by persuading other like-minded groups to create a louder voice to argue for change. Animal welfare groups were contacted and veterinary experts were brought in to present scientific evidence that vaccination and microchip implants in pets provided a safe alternative to quarantine. In 1996, the highly respected RSPCA came out in support of changing the quarantine laws and a jointly produced brochure was

mailed to all interested parties, including MPs, to highlight the need for reform. Thus three groups, Passport for Pets, Vets in Support of Change and the RSPCA, formed a powerful alliance under the banner of the Quarantine Reform Campaign.

Successful media campaigns and direct lobbying followed, presenting the rationale for change and the safe alternatives. Eventually, the government commissioned a Special Report through an advisory group on quarantine, which came out in favour of change. The government also consulted interested parties, such as the British Ports Association and the Guide Dogs for the Blind Association. There was 91 per cent support for a passport scheme. Despite the growing evidence supporting passports and successful lobbying, the government has still not openly declared its intention to change the law. Only then would a victory be won. The campaign continues with a new focus on the need for prompt action sooner rather than later in a busy government legislative agenda. This requires further lobbying of MPs and ministers, albeit with a different message from when the campaign started in 1994. The government now plans to introduce a 12-month phase-in campaign for pet passports and perhaps only after that has proved successful can the lobbyists start to relax a little.

Sources: France and Hickmet (1999); http://www. RSPCA. co. uk.

Internal communication

Although employees and other internal publics are exposed to much of the PR that is directed to the external world, they do need their own dedicated communication so that they know what is going on in more detail, and they know it before it hits the wider media (Bailey, 1991). This emphasis on keeping people informed rather than in the dark reflects quite a major change in employers' attitudes towards their employees. It is important for motivation, as well as being a means of preparing people for change and strengthening corporate culture. Two main areas of communication are considered below.

House journals and newsletters

Presented in the style of newspapers or magazines, these are a vital form of communication. Not only can they cover the important trivia of workplace gossip (Maureen from purchasing is getting married on Saturday; marketing beat accounts at five-a-side soccer last weekend; Albert from maintenance will be retiring next month after

50 years' service) which keeps the place vibrant and alive, but they can also be used for crucial managerial communication. Few people would want to read a long working paper written by the managing director on quality management or production targets, but most would at least glance at a well-illustrated, short, clearly written summary of the important points presented in journalistic style. The **house journal** can help to draw disparate parts of an organisation together, renewing a sense of belonging, as well as providing information. This can be particularly important in large organisations, such as retailers and large multinationals, whose staff work in geographically dispersed branches. Shell UK, for example, runs a quarterly in-house magazine called *Shell Focus* covering many topical issues concerning the organisation, including a company-oriented update on the various public debates over Shell's environmental record and its activities in Nigeria.

Briefings

Briefings provide a good mechanism for face-to-face contact between management and staff, and for increasing staff involvement and empowerment. Frequent, regular departmental or section meetings can be used to thrash out operational problems and to pass communication downwards through the organisation. Less frequently, once a year perhaps, more senior management can address staff, presenting results and strategic plans, and directly answering questions. Internal staff briefings are also likely to feature in a crisis management plan. If staff are hearing disaster and scare stories in the media, then they need to be reassured and given full and accurate information about what is being done. After all, their jobs may be at stake.

EVALUATION

Any PR programme should have begun with specific objectives relating to specific publics and, in order to learn from the experience, needs to end with an evaluation of success or failure (Palin, 1982). Haywood (1984) suggests seven commonly used measures of results, some of them qualitative, others less so. They are summarised in Fig. 19.3, and discussed below.

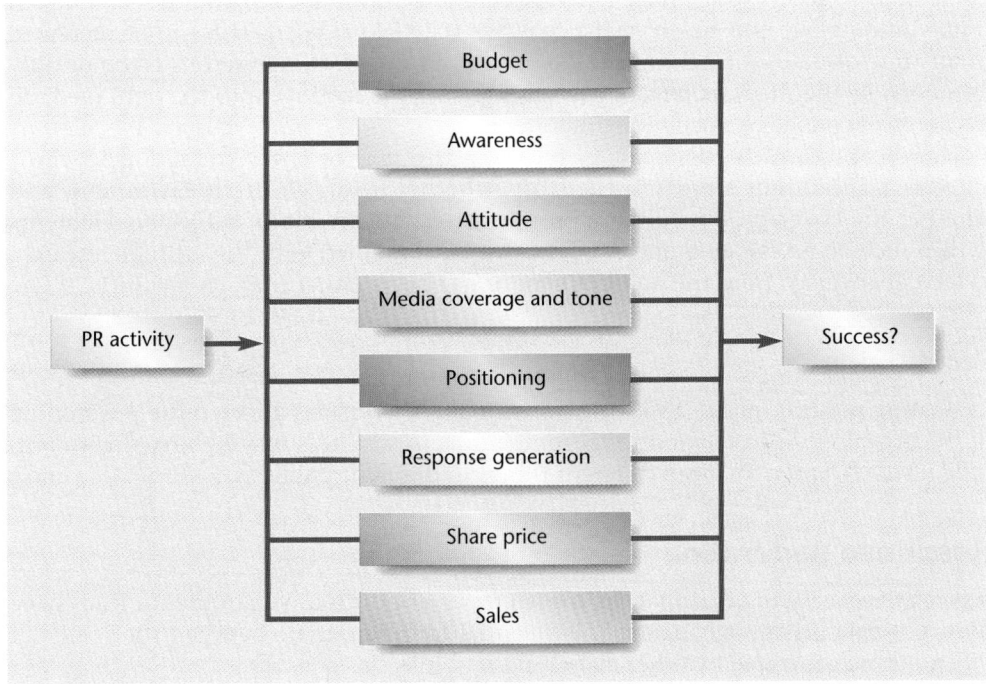

FIGURE 19.3

Evaluating public relations

Not all of these measures will be appropriate for all PR campaigns. The choice of method depends on the defined objective of the PR programme and the target publics involved. In all PR campaigns, however, it is important to define objectives at the start and to define the means by which outcomes will be measured. It is also important to ensure that those measures adequately identify the contribution of PR against the competing background of other marketing techniques.

Budget

This is a straightforward assessment of whether the planned activity has been completed within the given budget and time-scale. This seems fine as a measure of management planning and control, but it does not say much about the quality of the activity or whether it actually made any appreciable difference to anything. Thus it provides no measure of the activity's cost effectiveness.

Awareness

Using standard market research techniques (*see* Chapter 6), an organisation can try to establish whether there has been any increase in awareness of the organisation among the target publics. Care must be taken, however, to try to differentiate between the effects of PR and those of other marketing activities, and also to establish where the synergies between them lie.

Attitude

Building on the identification of changes in awareness, research can establish not only the levels of awareness and knowledge, but also how target publics now feel about the organisation, and to what extent the PR has affected this. Ideally, this post-PR research should be compared with the pre-PR position to give a clearer picture of how far and how deeply the PR has penetrated attitudes.

Media coverage and tone

There are two facets to media evaluation in relation to a PR programme. The first is simply finding out how much media coverage the PR generated. This can be measured in air time or column inches, for instance. It is, however, dangerous to be unduly impressed by the sheer *quantity* of coverage; getting the message into the right medium for the target public is much more important.

The second, and harder part, is assessing the *tone* of the coverage, whether it emphasised the right aspects of the story, whether it was generally favourable, and whether the coverage was suitably prominent. There are many subjective elements within such an assessment, and it might best be combined with the attitude research, to look at coverage from the point of view of its effects rather than its quantity.

Positioning

Evaluating position means assessing how the PR activity has affected the positioning of the organisation in relation to its competitors. Again, this may be linked with attitude research, and may mean different things to different publics.

Response generation

It is relatively easy to quantify response, in terms of how many enquiries or leads have been generated, although, again, it is essential to differentiate between the results of PR and those generated by other marketing activities.

Share price

Some PR activities aimed at the financial public may well have an effect on the organisation's share price. Where an organisation is under threat of a hostile take-over bid, the level of dealing in shares will certainly be a measure of how well the organisation has used PR to persuade its shareholders not to sell out.

Sales

The ultimate measure in evaluating PR is the effect on sales. The problem with measuring this, however, is that most PR is not normally orientated towards affecting sales. As so many other matters have a much greater influence on sales, it might be impossible to state with any certainty what the contribution of PR has been. In an unusual situation, however, such as a product tampering scare, when the story hits the media there will inevitably be a sharp drop in sales, and any slowing or reversal of that decline is likely to be an outcome of the quality of the PR response to the crisis. In such a case, direct attribution is possible with some confidence.

CORPORATE IDENTITY

Corporate identity refers to the way in which an organisation chooses to present itself to the world. It reflects the character and philosophy of the organisation, emphasising those characteristics that it would most like to be associated with (Abratt and Shee, 1988). Although an organisation's logo is the most visible face of its identity, this is only the tip of the iceberg, since the logo should emerge from a deeply ingrained culture. Changing a logo without changing the culture correspondingly is a cosmetic waste of time, and publics will soon recognise that under the fresh veneer lie the same old attitudes.

The creation of new companies as a result of privatisation is a clear opportunity for revising both culture and identity. The 'new' company wants to signal to its external publics that it is a competitive entrepreneurial business and to its internal publics that a fresh start with new attitudes is being made. The privatisation of the British Airports Authority, for example, completely changed its operating structure and its mission. A new identity as BAA linked all its diverse areas of business, presenting a coherent, fresh face to its investors, customers, suppliers, employees and other publics.

Reasons for changing identity

The 1980s saw a boom in the corporate identity business, as organisations both large and small became aware of the importance of presenting a sharp image to their various publics. They realised that they needed to manage and plan their identities rather than letting an image evolve by accident (Bernstein, 1984). There are many reasons that organisations eventually decide to develop or change their corporate image, as shown in Fig. 19.4 and discussed below.

Datedness
An existing identity may come to look old fashioned and it may be considered to be having an adverse effect on publics who see it as a sign of an organisation that is being left behind.

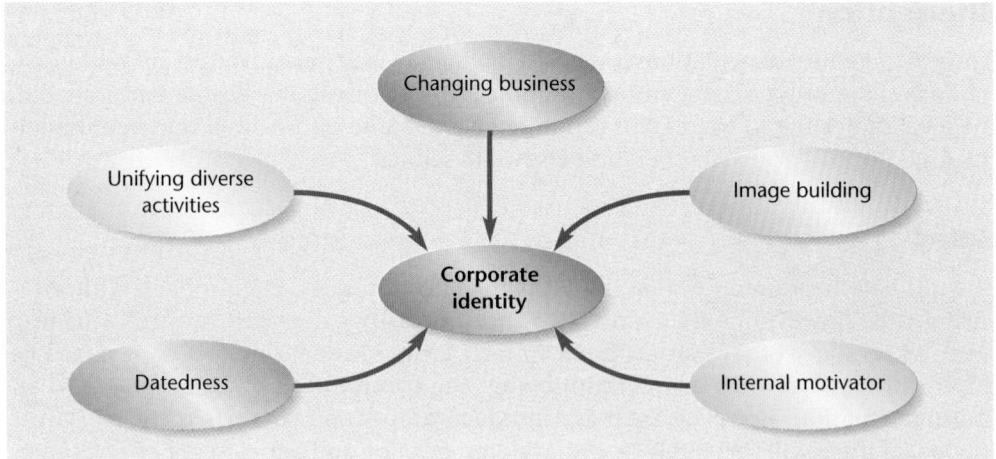

FIGURE 19.4

Reasons for changing
corporate identity

Example Whitbread found that the image of its 200+ budget hotels in the Travel Inn chain had become somewhat dated and so decided on a revamp. Part of this was updating the logo, a rather tired-looking logo with white lettering on a blue background with a small green bed sign, to a new identity featuring a half moon with a human face at rest, in modern colours (see illustration below). This was part of a £300mn investment up to 2004 to upgrade and add bed capacity along with a revitalised advertising campaign. The change in identity was regarded as an important signal to the market of something different (Rogers, 1999).

Before and after: giving
a more human face to
Travel Inn.
Source: Whitbread Plc.

Changing or developing business

Some organisations find that their existing identities are no longer appropriate because of the way their business has evolved.

Example Linked with the points above, an important part of supermarket chain Sainsbury's decision to create cultural change and to signal clearly that it was attempting to reverse market share losses was the re-design of its corporate identity and logo. It had been losing market share to Tesco and other rivals, not because of any decline in service or quality standards, but because others had improved theirs significantly. The new strategy included expanded product ranges, refurbished stores, better customer service and more non-food products. The new identity is being designed to signify these more fundamental changes (Hollinger, 1999a, 1999b).

As mentioned earlier, privatisation creates a strong motivation for rethinking corporate identity. Privatised companies in industries such as water and electricity took the opportunity for radical corporate redesign to emphasise their new found status and to disassociate themselves from any lingering poor reputation of the state owned industries. Mergers or acquisitions might also trigger an identity change. A merger between Smit, a Dutch offshore contractor, and Brown and Root, an American underwater engineering company, created an entirely different kind of organisation from either of its parents. This was reflected in its new identity and logo as Rockwater.

Differentiation

Linked with the previous point is the fact that, as markets become more competitive, organisations strive to differentiate themselves from the competition. While this is obviously done at product and promotional levels, it is also done through corporate identity.

Unifying diverse activities

Large organisations engaged in a wide variety of activities have a particularly fine balancing act to achieve. On the one hand, they want each operating division or subsidiary company to have a certain degree of autonomy and to be seen as a specialist in its own field, yet on the other hand, they still want the divisions or subsidiaries to be seen to have the backing of the wider organisation and to benefit from its standing and reputation. An umbrella style of corporate identity can allow the divisions or subsidiaries to retain their own names and character, but visibly draws them all together under a unified house style that marks them as being related to each other.

> **Example** When organisations formally merge there is a pressing need to develop a new, unified identity that makes a statement to the financial community, shareholders, customers and employees alike about the equality within the merger and the character of the new organisation. When Price Waterhouse merged with Coopers and Lybrand in 1998, the new name became PricewaterhouseCoopers (http://www.pwcglobal.com.). Although Lybrand was dropped, the new organisation had a clear link with the values and strength of the past. Even the name itself was displayed with a bolder C to highlight the link between the two originally separate names. Despite the merger, a clear identity was retained that would still be familiar to the customer. When Guinness and Grand Met merged, however, they chose a new name, Diageo, to signify that there was going to be change and that the post-merger organisation had something new to offer (Gander, 1999; http://www.diageo.com).

Image building

Clearly, a prime motivation for working on corporate image is to communicate the desired image. Careful thought about the elements of the image and the impression they convey can lead to an effective change in attitudes. This can be reinforced by using effective PR and advertising to explain the meaning of the new identity when it is launched.

Internal motivator

Finally, a corporate identity exercise, if managed properly, can be a useful means of effecting internal changes in attitudes. The process of thinking about identity, as discussed below, makes the organisation as a whole look at where it is and where it is going, and what it means to work for that organisation. Launching a new identity can represent a fresh start, or a renewed sense of purpose and direction.

The change process

There are many good reasons for going ahead with a change in corporate identity, but the exercise is only as good as its implementation. It is a sufficiently specialised area to warrant the involvement of professional corporate identity consultants who will oversee the whole process. This subsection deals with the change process.

Figure 19.5 outlines the broad stages involved in the change process, each of which is discussed below.

Research

Before the identity change process can begin, it is essential to carry out research both internally and externally, with a variety of important publics, to establish exactly how the organisation is currently viewed, and what kind of organisation those publics would ideally like to see. Until this is done, the extent and direction of change required will be uncertain.

Setting objectives and criteria for the new identity

A formal statement sets out what the identity is to achieve and what characteristics it is to reflect. This will be based on the research undertaken, and will balance the needs of the various external publics consulted with the organisation's internal mission statement and future direction.

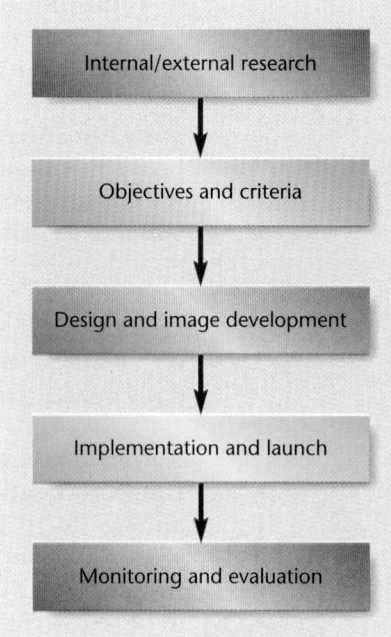

FIGURE 19.5

Stages in the corporate identity change process

Design and development of the new image

It is in the design and development stage that the words and concepts are translated into a visual image. The design team may come up with a number of alternative design solutions, which may have to be tested with focus groups to see whether they evoke the right responses and which one is liked most. In practical terms too the identity has to be sufficiently flexible to be used in a variety of contexts, such as on stationery, vehicles, uniforms and products, for example. It also has to work in a range of media, in both colour and monochrome, and the logo itself has to work in a variety of sizes. This stage may take some time and involve a lot of reiteration, but it is worth it to get the design elements right. An organisation expects to have to live with a new identity for a long time. BAA, for example, had to apply its new image to the exterior of airport buildings, interior signs, stationery, corporate and sales literature, souvenir merchandise, vehicles, luggage trolleys, uniforms and much more.

Implementation and launch

Much work is involved at the implementation and launch stage – in making sure that the new identity is properly installed and utilised throughout the organisation and that it is recognised and understood by internal and external publics. Staff briefing sessions are needed in order to explain the new identity and how it is to be applied and used, and then there are the practical problems of, to name but a few, replacing all the organisation's stationery stocks, repainting the fleet of delivery vans and informing all the interested publics about the new identity. The sheer scale of this task may mean that it is impossible to unveil the new identity overnight and thus a gradual roll-out during a transition period may have to be adopted.

Even if there has been a gradual roll-out, there is still likely to be an official launch date when the new identity is properly recognised and takes over from the old one. This is a good excuse for extensive advertising and a whole range of PR activities to inform publics and to reassure them that the good things they valued about the organisation have not been lost.

Monitoring and evaluation

Finally, it is important to monitor the implementation and evaluate the effects of the new identity as it settles down. This means ensuring that everyone in the organisation is applying the identity correctly and consistently, and that they are adhering to the guidelines laid down for its use (part of the design process will be the production of a manual showing exactly how the identity should be applied on different items and in different contexts). It also means carrying out research to assess how well recognised and accepted the identity has become among various publics, and what connotations are attached to it. The outcomes of this may mean going back to the design team for some fine tuning.

Problems with the change process

Even the brief description of the change process presented here shows that it is a long and potentially difficult task to redesign a corporate identity. There are several pitfalls that can make that task even more difficult, if not downright impossible, and these are summarised in Fig. 19.6. It is essential, for example, for the whole process to have the full commitment of top management. If they are not prepared to drive and legitimise the exercise then there is no reason to expect anyone else in the organisation to take it seriously, or for it to take on anything other than the character of a cosmetic exercise.

It is not enough, however, just to have the commitment of top management. Staff at all levels of the organisation need to know what is going on and where possible to participate in the process, even if only at the research stage. Creating a shared interest and ownership of the new identity is essential for its eventual acceptance. If a new identity is not accepted, then it has to be the fault of some element of the management process. Perhaps the preparatory research was badly carried out (or not carried out at all) or misinterpreted. The design stage may have been skimped so that an identity was hurriedly chosen and implemented without enough thought or staff involvement. Another danger area is implementation and launch. Perhaps staff were not given adequate briefing about the new identity or perhaps PR and other communication aimed at external publics was inadequate.

To be successful, corporate identity change needs to have, as well as top management commitment to the philosophy of change, the right person managing it on a day-to-day basis. This is an important project and should not be given to a junior trainee as something to do between making cups of tea for the office manager. The person in charge needs to have sufficient authority and managerial skills to make it all happen and to win over the doubters. Entrusting the project to a suitably experienced manager reduces the risk of the exercise falling apart because of inadequate research, poor planning, poor control or a lack of attention to detail.

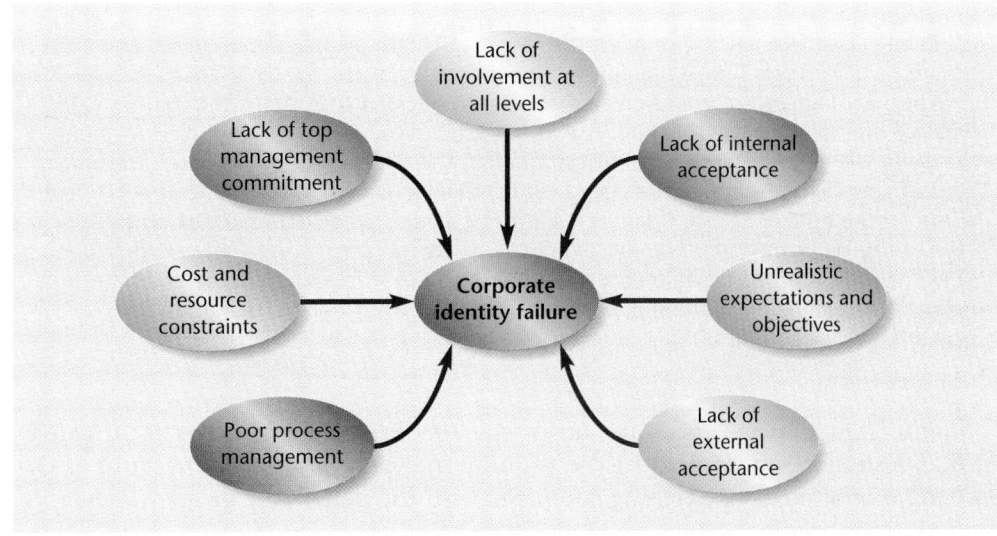

FIGURE 19.6

Reasons for the failure of an identity change

Given the ideals of commitment, thoroughness and participation already suggested, it is clear that this kind of exercise cannot be done cheaply. It is an expensive investment in the organisation's future and well-being. If management starts putting unrealistic cost constraints on the work, then it is likely that corners will be cut and the outcomes will be poor and disappointing. There is a danger that management will view an identity change as a cheap way of avoiding facing up to more fundamental organisational problems. It cannot be emphasised enough, however, that corporate identity should not be used as a cosmetic means of papering over cracks. Changing identity does not compensate for bad management, inadequate or inappropriate products or a poor attitude to customer service. If an organisation has problems of this type, then it needs to do something rather more radical than simply changing the name and/or the logo. If the organisation is unrealistic about what corporate identity can do for it, then the exercise will be a failure.

SPONSORSHIP

Sponsorship is defined by Wilmshurst (1993, p. 367) as:

> **. . . the provision of financial or material support by a company for some independent activity . . . not usually directly linked to the company's normal business, but support from which the sponsoring company would hope to benefit.**

While some sponsorship certainly does have altruistic motives behind it, its main purpose is to generate positive attitudes through associating the corporate name with sport, the arts, charitable enterprise or some other activity. That is why so many companies use sponsorship, including familiar names such as Coca-Cola, JVC, McEwan's lager, Carlsberg, Opel, Lloyds TSB and the Nationwide building society. The arts, sport and broadcast sponsorship are the three main areas creating an industry that is worth an estimated £640mn in the UK, and worldwide in excess of $19.2bn was predicted for 1999 (http://www.sponsorship.com; Tyler, 1999).

Example The Millennium Dome, love it or hate it, has had remarkable success in attracting sponsors. The sponsors include BT, Tesco, BA, BSkyB and McDonald's (http://www.millennium.greenwich2000.com). These organisations hope that they will benefit by being associated with such a high-profile spectacle, although others have suggested that they are partly politically motivated by a desire to be seen as a good corporate citizen by a government that has publicly committed itself to the project (Benady, 1999). The return benefit could be in goodwill when it comes to merger discussions, planning applications and other business activities that have a high public profile.

When Ford agreed to a £12mn sponsorship, it decided to support the Journey Zone, which is intended to show the impact that futuristic travel will have on our lives. Although the Zone will feature all modes of transportation, the opportunity will be used to present Ford as a modern and future-orientated car company (Darby, 1999). Wall's agreed to pay £3mn for the right to sell ice cream at the event, which is predicted to attract up to 25 per cent of the UK population. The success of the event will therefore be measured in direct sales for some sponsors, while others will be looking for less tangible benefits through goodwill and name exposure and whatever links they can generate back into their normal promotional programmes.

Sponsorship grew in popularity during the 1980s, partly because of its attractiveness as a supporting element in the promotional mix, and partly because of the growing cost of media advertising compared with the potentially greater coverage of various sports and arts activities (Meenaghan, 1991). Its growth was also helped by the tobacco companies using it as a means of achieving exposure in spite of the ban on television advertising.

There is a clear distinction between sponsorship and charitable donations (Fill, 1999). Patronage is the giving of gifts in whatever form, with no intention of influencing the commercial success of the company. Examples might include supporting a local hospital, or allowing company sports facilities to be used by outside groups. Sponsorship does seek a return, however indirect it may be, on the investment, although it is mainly about image building rather than selling the product as such. Despite this business orientation, sponsorship may involve only indirect influence on the target audience. The name of the sponsor may only be incidental to the proceedings, for instance the Orange–British Academy Film awards (http://www.bafta.org.com) or Le Crédit Agricole's FF30mn sponsorship of the Tour de France, and there may be no mention at all of products or services. This creates a challenge for the marketing manager, as the effects of sponsorship tend to be long term and, although sponsorship may reinforce a company name, it need not support any understanding of the product ranges on offer. The effect on sales, therefore, is often unclear unless the sponsorship is supported by a promotional campaign or a series of events is planned during a concentrated period.

Types of sponsorship

Four main areas of sponsorship have attracted most interest: sport, broadcast sponsorship, the arts and cause related marketing.

Sport

With the widespread appeal of sport across all ages, areas and life-styles, it is perhaps not surprising that sports sponsorship has grown in popularity. This is especially true when it is linked to the televising of the events. The mass audiences possible through television, even for some minority sports, enable the widespread showing of the sponsor's name.

> **Example** Flora's sponsorship of the London marathon in 1998 demonstrated a clear link between brand values and the nature of the event. The BBC TV viewing figures exceeded 6mn and spontaneous awareness of Flora's sponsorship rose to above 50 per cent, demonstrating the value to Flora of sponsorship (*Marketing Week*, 1999b).

Many sports attract heavy television coverage and so although the typical sponsoring costs may be high, in comparison with the cost of direct television advertising, such sponsorship can actually be very cost effective.

> **Example** In soccer, Carling and the Nationwide building society sponsor the English Premier League and First Division respectively because of the widespread media coverage, especially on television, that is generated. Whether on live transmissions by Sky or on recorded highlights and commentary on various sports programmes, the company names are clearly linked with the leagues and the advertising benefit gained from such a large audience would be beyond most marketing budgets. Littlewoods Pools, however, decided to end its sponsorship of the FA Cup when its three-year £14mn deal expired in 1998. It decided that the £25mn then demanded for a further three years was too high, especially as Littlewoods is more focused on retailing than the pools. AXA, the French insurance company, took over the sponsorship in an attempt to get its name better known in the UK market (Nissé, 1998b).

Sponsorship of sport has the added benefit that although people may ignore commercial breaks, they do pay attention when a 'real' programme is on, and therefore may be more likely to absorb the sponsor's name.

In 1996, UK companies spent over £300mn on sports sponsorship within a sector that worldwide is growing at 10 per cent per year (Mintel, 1996). In 1980 just £30mn was spent on sports sponsorship. One of the problems, however, is that as events become bigger and more international in their coverage, sponsorship becomes more expensive. There is thus a danger that as events such as the Olympic games and the World Cup take on more official sponsors in order to cover their costs, the impact for any one of those sponsors becomes less (Patten, 1998). In France '98 there were 12 official FIFA sponsors paying as much as £250mn each to the world football's governing body. In a survey after the event (Baird, 1998), it was shown that the highest unprompted awareness linking the sponsor with the event was McDonald's with 25 per cent then Coca-Cola (21 per cent) and many sponsors were in single figures, including Philips at 1 per cent. The spontaneous awareness generated by any sponsor was just 55 per cent and 67 per cent of the sample named companies not even associated with the event as sponsors. Interestingly, 75 per cent of respondents considered that too many manufacturers were now associated with the World Cup.

Example One of the objectives of sponsorship is to promote sales, directly or indirectly. Pepsi's FF1.5mn gave it the right to use the French rugby union team in its promotional efforts. The company offered the big retailers an opportunity to give shoppers a chance to win signed rugby balls or seats for matches in the Five Nations tournament. The pay-off was that Pepsi's products should be displayed in 'golden zones', i.e. the prominent and best-selling display areas within a store, for ten days, the duration of the Five Nations tournament. Conscious that the French rugby team interests the whole world, the retailers were very willing to participate. More than 400 hypermarkets, out of 1000, joined the scheme. All Auchan's stores offered two seats for the France–Wales or France–Scotland matches. In Cora, shoppers could win balls or jerseys signed by the players. Everywhere Pepsi gave the same promotional support to emphasise its sponsorship: an offer of seven bottles of Pepsi for the price of six and a poster featuring the team to advertise the promotion. The general impact was that being positioned in the golden zones increased sales 2.5 times (Guerin and Mahout, 1999).

Sponsorship is not just for the big national teams, the global brand names and the big retailers, however. A small menswear retailer, Rodier, struck a deal to dress the players and management of the Perpignan rugby club in its merchandise The deal cost FF100,000, a large sum for a company with a turnover of only FF1.8mn. It did pay off, however. One Saturday, a signing session was organised in the local store featuring Raphaël Ibanez, a Perpignan player who is also in the French national side. The store saw three times as many customers as usual that day and increased its sales by 30 per cent (Guerin and Mahout, 1999). It is also possible for less well-known teams to attract big sponsors. The arch-rival of the Halifax bank, the Nationwide building society, seized the opportunity to sponsor Halifax Town when it gained promotion back to the Football League. Local spectators in the home town of the Halifax would be treated to shirts and advertising boards displaying the Nationwide name. The Nationwide commented, 'We were somewhat surprised to find the club could not find a corporate sponsor locally' (Cole, 1998).

If the sponsorship of tournaments does not appeal, then there is always the option of sponsoring individual athletes or players, or of sponsoring teams or leagues.

Example CGU opted to provide £6mn over four years in sponsoring the National Cricket League (NCL) which replaced the old Sunday League (Baird, 1999a). It joins other sponsors, such as NatWest, in supporting a sport with a declining audience, an ageing customer base and which has just experienced a major change with Channel 4 replacing the BBC for test and county cricket coverage. Even the World Cup hosted in the UK in 1999 struggled to find sponsors, although Pepsi, Vodafone, NatWest and the airline Emirates eventually played a big part. Some critics argue that the problem with cricket sponsorship is that it lacks lively, fmcg brand players such as soft drink or beer manufacturers (Baird, 1999b).

The bails may be flying but CGU scores a six with its sponsorship.

Source: CGU Life Services Limited

On a more limited basis, companies can sponsor match programmes, balls or even the corner flags. Smaller or non-league clubs are appealing for local businesses who want to reinforce their role in the community, and even large organisations can value this.

Example Bedford Town plays in the UK's Ryman League. During any season it plays around 65 games at its home ground. A would-be sponsor has a range of options from £175 per match, £40 to sponsor a player for a season, £50 for a match ball and, for the more adventurous, over £1500 for a special one-off celebrity game, for example against Aston Villa Ex-stars. The low level of sponsorship rates can be attractive to a smaller business with a localised audience (Yarnall, 1999).

All of this works well as long as the sport and the individual clubs continue to maintain a 'clean' image. A riot in the stands or a punch-up on the pitch generate the kind of publicity and media coverage of the type 'What kind of depths has the game sunk to?' that sponsors will not want to be associated with. The fracas between Eric Cantona and a member of the crowd in January 1995, for example, hit the headlines across the world for all the wrong reasons. This, however, is one of the risks of any kind of celebrity endorsement.

The main advantage of sports sponsorship remains the ability to reach large audiences, and sometimes to communicate with audiences that normal advertising scheduling would find difficult.

Example The A and B socioeconomic groups can often be reached through sports sponsorship in tennis, golf, yachting and rugby. Lloyds TSB's sponsorship of the Rugby World Cup qualifiers resulted in awareness of the new, merged company which rose from 4 to 15 per cent in the latter half of 1998. Meanwhile, the Royal Sun Alliance sponsored the all-female international yachting crew of Tracey Edwards and generated an estimated £12mn of media coverage. Unprompted awareness of the sponsorship rose from 10 to 25 per cent (*Marketing Week*, 1999a).

Despite the rising costs, organisations can still gain a lot of value for money, quite apart from the media coverage.

Example There are risks in sponsorship, such as a player, club or indeed tournament running into negative publicity. The Olympic movement is meant to represent all the values of team spirit, individual achievement and the pursuit of excellence that organisations are proud to be associated with. The 'gift' scandal that rocked the International Olympics Federation over the selection of Sydney for the 2000 Games caused concern not just among the public but also among some of the 12 commercial partners who sponsor the event for £30mn each. The sponsors are Coca-Cola, IBM, John Hancock, Kodak, McDonald's, Panasonic, Samsung, *Sports Illustrated*, *Time*, UPS, Visa and Xerox.

McDonald's was concerned, although it agreed to continue its sponsorship, but Johnson & Johnson has actually withdrawn from the 2002 Winter Olympics and US-based John Hancock Mutual Life Assurance has taken the Olympic rings from its advertising and literature while it considers its options. However, despite the negative coverage, the benefits of being a main sponsor of the Games are considerable. Sponsors have exclusive rights in their sector, reach worldwide audiences, have hospitality opportunities at the Games, advertising access and of course the goodwill and reputation gained through being associated with such a high-profile event. The last thing they want is to see a negative association with excessive commercialism and corruption within the Olympic movement that could damage their own and their products' reputations (Lee, 1999).

Broadcast sponsorship

Broadcast sponsorship, sponsoring programmes or series on television or the radio, is a relatively new area in the UK. In 1996 it was worth around £60mn, over 50 per cent growth since 1993. Television sponsorship formed the largest part of broadcast sponsorship, but it still comprises a minor proportion of a channel's commercial income compared with advertising revenue.

Example Domino's Pizza uses broadcast sponsorship as it wants us to watch more television. Research indicated that we are more likely to order a home-delivered pizza if we are glued to our favourite programme. Domino's sponsored *The Simpsons* on BSkyB, believing that the programme's viewers reflected its target customers, as well as, of course, its sponsorship being entirely appropriate given Homer Simpson's special relationship with pizza (Mmmm, pizza). Through television credits, special promotions and hyperlinks from the Sky and Simpson's webpages to the Domino's site, brand share has risen from 15 to 19 per cent and sales of Domino's Pizza increased by 29 per cent in 1998 (*Marketing Week*, 1999c).

In other parts of Europe, the level of sponsorship is much higher than in the UK. Some in the industry claim that the restrictions imposed by the Independent Television Commission (ITC) are too tight. The ITC rules say, for example, that an organisation cannot sponsor programmes directly relating to its products (but a 'good match' is acceptable).

Thus, Lego's sponsorship of *Tots TV* was acceptable, but PPP (a private medical insurance company) was asked to terminate its sponsorship of *Peak Practice*, a medical drama, because of a potential conflict of interest.

Furthermore, a sponsor's products cannot feature in the show, nor can sponsors have any editorial control over the programme's content. Satellite has a little more flexibility and is allowed to incorporate the sponsor's name into the programme title and to have up to two minutes of sponsor's credits. The ITC rules are taken from an EU Directive and are thus the same as those imposed in other parts of Europe, although they may be enforced more rigorously in the UK.

Even within the current regulatory framework, broadcast sponsorship still has much to offer. As with advertising, of course, it is reaching potentially large audiences and creating product awareness. Further than that, however, it also has the potential to help to enhance the product's image and message by association. *London's Burning*, a drama series about fire fighters, for example, was sponsored by Commercial Union, an insurance company. To get the best out of broadcast sponsorship, however, it should be integrated into a wider package of marketing and promotional activities. This might mean using characters or themes from the programme in promotional materials.

Cadbury's decision to sponsor the popular television soap *Coronation Street* with £10mn allowed it to access the characters from the programme in other marketing activities. In addition, of course, the company is able to reach a large audience of over 15 millon households four times a week with an opportunity to stand out in the crowded confectionery market. The sponsorship does not just cover the Cadbury's brand name, but also features individual brands such as Creme Eggs, Roses, Time Out, Crunchie, Wispa and others from time to time. According to Granada it is claimed that 'there is a perfect match between the integrity of the programme and

Cadbury's products are obviously popular on Coronation Street.

Source: Cadbury's Plc.

the commercial expectations of the advertisers' (http://www.cadbury.co.uk). The association has become so successful that the chocolate animations topping and tailing the show are now regarded by many viewers as an integral part of it and Cadbury's has run a number of well-subscribed sales promotions integrated with the *Coronation Street* credits.

The opportunity to reach such a large audience with such frequency and positive association reveals the power of broadcast sponsorship compared with straightforward television advertising. Some broadcasters, however, fear that advertising revenues could fall if broadcast sponsorship grows significantly in popularity.

One of the fears that broadcasters have, particularly when thinking of large deals such as Cadbury's and *Coronation Street*, is that advertising revenues will fall. If Cadbury's spends £10 million on sponsorship, will it then spend £10 million less on standard advertising? Perhaps one of the potential advantages for broadcasters is that sponsorship allows them to build better relationships with advertisers, and thus they might be able to negotiate sponsorship packages that guarantee a certain level of advertising spend too.

The arts

Arts sponsorship is a growing area, second only to sport in terms of its value in the UK. In 1997, arts sponsorship in the UK was worth around £86mn, more than a 75 per cent increase since 1994. Over half of the money, however, went on projects in London. The art forms covered range widely from music, including rock, classical and opera, to festivals, theatre, film and literature. Table 19.1 shows the kinds of activities covered by arts sponsorships and their value.

Oris (http://www/oris.ch), a Swiss watch manufacturer, sponsored the London Jazz festival in 1998 and similar events under the Spirit of Jazz series in 1999 in New York. Oris had its brand logo on all the London festival's print and advertising and claimed a 60 per cent increase in sales as a result. Other large arts sponsors are British Telecommunications, Marks & Spencer, Sun Microsystems with its £500 000 sponsorship for the Institute of Contemporary Art, and Allied Domecq sponsoring the Royal Shakespeare Company, also for £500 000 (Nissé, 1998a).

Example Shell (http://www.shell.co.uk) has been one of the main sponsors of the London Symphony Orchestra for over 20 years. The company provides £120 000 for a scholarship scheme to attract young musicians and a further £200 000 to support the costs of the LSO touring around the UK. Shell gains by being associated with a high quality product that adds directly to the cultural quality of the nation's life. It has also provided corporate entertainment spin-offs for employees, influencers and customers. Meanwhile, the LSO gains by being able to cover the majority of the costs associated with holding its five regional events during the year.

As part of the sponsorship, a number of special programmes such as the Shell–LSO Music Scholarship also operate. This competition is for the UK's talented woodwind, string, brass and percussion players aged between 17 and 20 who can perform in concertos with the LSO. The 1999 National Final for the brass competition was worth a £6000 scholarship, a gold medal and the opportunity to perform with the LSO at the Barbican Centre in London. Tickets were free (Franks, 1997).

Arts sponsorship is not just about music or 'safe options', however. Häagen Dazs sponsored an *avant garde* contemporary art exhibition at the Tate Gallery, while Denton Hall, the international law firm, sponsored Terence Donovan's photographic show *The Eye that Never Sleeps*. The Museum of London venue was considered highly appropriate for business people and the company organised a number of private viewing events for graduate recruits, the business and legal media, and employees, as well as existing or future clients (Goddard, L., 1999). Barclays Bank (http://www.community.barclays.com) also sponsors regional theatre productions of high quality drama, plays by contemporary authors, new stagings of works by Shakespeare and original productions for children. In total, 24 productions have appeared at 90 venues to an audience of over 0.5 million. The overall support for the scheme by Barclays is £2.5mn over three years.

TABLE 19.1

UK arts sponsorship by art form 1994 and 1997

	1994 £mn	%	1997 £mn	%	Percentage change 1994–7
Theatre	5.03	10	16.55	19	+229
Museums	5.78	12	12.78	15	+121
Music	9.65	20	11.09	13	+15
Opera	6.22	13	9.71	11	+56
Festivals	5.19	11	8.12	9	+56
Visual arts	2.19	4	5.06	6	+131
Film	2.64	5	3.85	4	+46
Awards/competitions	3.44	7	3.50	4	+2
Dance	2.37	5	3.01	3	+27
Heritage	0.64	1	2.23	3	+248
Arts centres	1.48	3	1.30	2	–12
Community arts	0.75	2	0.97	1	+29
Literature	0.38	*	0.42	*	n/a
Services	0.10	*	0.36	*	n/a
Photography	0.30	*	0.01	*	n/a
Crafts	0.10	*	–		n/a
Other	3.34	7	7.16	8	+144
Total	**48.77**	**100**	**86.12**	**100**	**+77**

* less than 1%

Data may not equal due to rounding

Source: ABSA/Mintel.

What all of these companies have in common is that they are trying to reach the young intelligentsia, potentially a lucrative market for them, as well as trying to enhance their own images as sophisticated, forward-looking organisations. A wider, if perhaps somewhat less discerning, youth audience can be reached through rock music. Youth audiences are notoriously difficult to reach and to communicate with because of their cynicism about advertising. Various companies have become involved with sponsoring rock and pop events. Lloyds TSB is supporting the TSB Live Tour and pop band The Corrs, while Carling supports the Reading and Leeds Festivals which in 1999 featured such bands as Blur, Red Hot Chili Peppers and The Charlatans. When major pop stars tour a sponsorship deal is often negotiated, such as Avon with Celine Dion and World Online with Cher for their 1999 UK tours.

Ericsson decided to support Homelands, a dance musical event staged in Hampshire and Scotland in 1999. Ericsson featured alongside Bacardi and Bud Ice in sponsoring the event because the company wanted to reach young people to tell them about its new mobile phones that can also operate e-mail. There was space at the festival for Ericsson to demonstrate its phones and so the events were, in Ericsson's opinion, helpful in making the brand credible through association (*Marketing*, 1999).

The important consideration for marketers in deciding whether to sponsor these events is understanding the link between the product and the music. To gain maximum value, it is necessary to ensure that the event features in all aspects of the communications mix, including packaging, advertising and sales promotion. This means exploiting the association before, during and after the music event.

Sponsoring festivals can be particularly useful in boosting unprompted awareness among the target group. The benefit of association between the brand and the event is often enough to justify involvement, but where that can be extended it can add further value to the sponsorship. Sometimes, this can be achieved by a spin-off recording that is released soon after the event.

With arts sponsorship there are a number of opportunities to present the sponsoring organisation, including on stage, in programmes, through associated merchandise including videos and CDs, around venues, and even on tickets. There are also advantages in hosting key customers and suppliers at high profile events, by offering the best seats and perhaps hosting a reception during the interval or after the show.

The popularity of the arts has grown in recent years. While the attractiveness of highbrow cultural activities to A, B and C socioeconomic groups is evident, their ever-widening appeal has created new opportunities to reach different target groups in a quality way. Despite this, however, the arts cannot be complacent about their importance to corporate sponsors. During difficult trading times, organisations have been known to cut their arts budgets substantially. There has also been a change in corporate thinking, with a shift in emphasis towards supporting charities and 'good causes' with more immediate public appeal rather than the arts, which might be perceived as élitist. There are also difficulties in assessing the marketing benefits of arts sponsorship, and the fact that it is easier and cheaper to purchase tailormade corporate hospitality packages than to sponsor one's own event. Nevertheless, there are some positive signs. Sponsorship from large, London-based organisations may be falling, but there is growth in the sponsorship of regional and local arts groups from smaller, provincial based organisations.

Cause related marketing

Linkages between organisations and charities benefit both parties. If, for example, a company runs a sales promotion along the lines of 'We'll donate 10p to this charity for every token you send in', the charity gains from the cash raised and from an increased public profile. Consumers feel that their purchase has greater significance than simple self-gratification and feel good about having 'given', while the company benefits from the increased sales generated by the promotion and from the extra goodwill created from associating its brands with a good cause. Murphy (1999) argues that companies are taking a longer-term view of cause related marketing because of the positive image associated with a good and caring cause.

Example J&B Rare Scotch Whisky associated itself with raising money to help endangered species such as the black rhino by making a donation for each promotional bottle sold. The impact of such activities is greater if there is a clear synergy between the brand and the charity, or at least if the charity has a particular appeal to the same target audience as the brand. A scheme to save rare plant and animal species through sponsorship support was not well subscribed. Tesco did support the skylark with £100 000 and the water vole raised £150 000 from Norsk Hydro, a Norwegian chemical and oil company. Even the dung beetle raised a few thousand pounds and Glaxo Wellcome decided to back a medicinal leech with £18 000. However, around 100 species that still need saving have no backers, including the red squirrel. The issue for a potential sponsor is that there is little direct link between the brands and the animals and the audiences are very specialised, so the only real benefit is a feeling of good citizenship (Nuttall, 1998).

Not all **cause related marketing** is linked with sales promotions, however. Many large organisations set up charitable foundations or donate cash directly to community or charitable causes. Others might pay for advertising space for charities, whether on television, radio, press or posters. This is important at a time when consumers are becoming more conscious of the ethical and 'corporate citizenship' records of the companies they patronise.

Example The Lloyds TSB foundation (http://www.lloydstsbfoundations.org.uk) provides a wide range of support to good causes at a community level. It concentrates on disadvantaged and disabled people of all ages and two-thirds of its budget goes to regionally based charities. Examples include the Radford Care Group in Nottingham, which received £2100 for tables and chairs as part of a care centre for the old and frail, and the National Association of Toys and Leisure Libraries, which advises and lends toys to parents in need. A scheme in Dorset attracted £2700 to extend the service to that area.

Organisations clearly do not just take an altruistic view of their charity involvement. As with any other marketing activity, it should be planned with clear objectives and expected outcomes. Kodak-Eastman (http://www.kodak.com) has clear policies for selecting which causes and events it will sponsor on a worldwide basis. Criteria such as the scale of the impact, the opportunity for spin-off on-site sales, the fit with the core business, target customers and values and the link with the wider media are used. It is also one of a growing number of organisations using the Internet to describe its sponsorship portfolio and to assist potential recipients in approaching the organisation through a structured checklist, although it is mainly orientated towards the USA. The application process also asks the proposer not only to describe the proposed sponsorship but also to indicate the benefits to Kodak on the criteria listed above.

The Woodsy Owl scheme in the USA, linked with the Forestry Service, aims to promote environmental awareness in young children. As part of the scheme, Kodak participates in numerous events held around the USA. The company organises workshops at these events covering picture taking techniques, displays etc. On an international scale, for the Cannes International Film Festival Kodak organises or hosts a series of high-profile events such as being the joint sponsor of the Camera D'Or award, hosting the Women in Film Association and organising the book signing by Henri Alekan on his latest work on cinematographic history. In the Kodak pavilion, the company hosts many opportunities for guests to meet those in the film industry and runs special events for guests from particular countries, such as South Africa in 1999. This clearly shows the close link between event sponsorship and corporate hospitality and relationship building.

The role of sponsorship

Despite the connotations of charity, community support, entertainment and fun, sponsorship is still a serious commercial tool for the marketing manager. As with any other promotional activity, it is important to specify clearly the objectives of pursuing a sponsorship campaign and to plan the activities carefully to ensure that they are relevant and that they are achieved. Evaluation, however, can be a problem with sponsorship, as it is often used in support of other promotional activities, and thus isolating the sponsorship effect may be difficult.

Sponsorship offers the potential to support the broader PR strategy, both directly and indirectly. Directly, it can provide a venue for meeting key customers or suppliers in an informal setting, or more generally improve awareness and attitudes towards the sponsoring company or individual brands (Meenaghan, 1998). Indirectly, it can support employee, government and community relations through emphasising the sponsor's enlightened sense of social responsibility and good corporate citizenship. Furthermore, it can support wider marketing objectives through increasing product awareness and even enhancing product and corporate image. Lee (1998) considers that some companies are turning to sponsorship as it helps them to move into a more glamorous world that can send associated messages to consumers and other publics. BTR, an industrial conglomerate, gains considerable benefit from its sponsorship of the Thrust rocket cars' world land-speed record in achieving recognition among investors and the City.

MARKETING IN ACTION   Computers for schools

When supermarket chain Tesco decided to undertake a cause related community sponsorship programme, it wanted an idea that would give it a high profile and uniqueness that were not readily available from many traditional community-based sponsorship activities. The outcome, the Tesco Computers for Schools annual event, has now been running very successfully since 1992 and has even attracted its own sponsors, such as Nestlé Ice Cream, Coca-Cola and Pringles with the brands linked to the promotion. By 1999, 34 000 computers and 200 000 items of computer equipment worth £44mn had been claimed.

The scheme allows shoppers to collect vouchers, normally over a 10-week period, with one voucher given for every £10 spent in a Tesco store. Programme sponsors, such as Coca-Cola, might fund an extra voucher for the purchase of their brands. The local schools collect the vouchers from willing donor shoppers to cash them in for computer equipment and software from a special 50-page catalogue. The initiative is especially valuable to schools as it provides much needed access to equipment that may not otherwise be available from their hard-pressed budgets. Over 50 per cent of UK schools now take part in the scheme.

Tesco has worked hard to ensure that it receives considerable public relations benefit from the scheme. Not only does it generate increased store traffic, it also enhances Tesco's reputation as a good corporate citizen that is responsible and caring in its community. The chief executive of Tesco stated, 'Education remains a high priority at Tesco. Tesco believes that one of the most important contributions it can make to the community is to help equip schools with resources that will give children the skills they need for the future.' In order to emphasise the community orientation, regionally based launches, alongside the national launch each year, provide an excellent media opportunity. The local launches often feature schoolchildren, Tesco staff and local celebrities and dignitaries. In 1999, 34 000 balloons were launched at 29 Tesco stores to add extra spice and photo opportunities to the launch occasion. The awards events are also well publicised; in 1998 there were 127 equipment presentations involving 133 MPs including Gordon Brown, William Hague and Paddy Ashdown.

Tesco has now become the leading schools-based promotion organisation. The co-ordinated approach between stores, schools and the media has been highly effective. In order to maintain its position, Tesco has extended its involvement in education. It is the Official Education Sponsor for the Millennium, providing £12mn to support the Learning Zone within the Millennium Dome. SchoolNet 2000 offers schools free resources including 340 Internet Centres in Tesco stores and support for 40 advisory teachers to encourage Internet access for children.

Although other companies have also become involved with school-based promotions, the Tesco scheme remains the one to emulate. Walkers crisps and News International's joint promotion for free books to schools, for example, follow many of the principles established by Tesco. As part of the National Year of Reading, 33 000 schools were invited to collect tokens from crisp and snack packets or from within News International publications including *The Times*. The vouchers could then be exchanged for a range of books. The scheme was launched by the minister responsible for education, and the president of Walkers Snack Foods stated how proud the company was to be involved in a scheme to raise the nation's literacy standards. The challenge, however, is to attract the local publicity and high levels of community interest without the local store base that Tesco is able to exploit. There is also a risk that schools and shoppers could see such schemes as naked commercialism, designed to sell more products rather than support those in need.

Sources: Tesco *Computers for Schools* press information, kindly provided by Bell-Pottinger; Wilkinson (1998).

A number of factors need to be considered before a sponsorship decision is made, as summarised in Fig. 19.7.

The first consideration is *relevance*, which is perhaps the most important factor. There needs to be a match between the chosen sponsorship and the target audience that the organisation is seeking to influence.

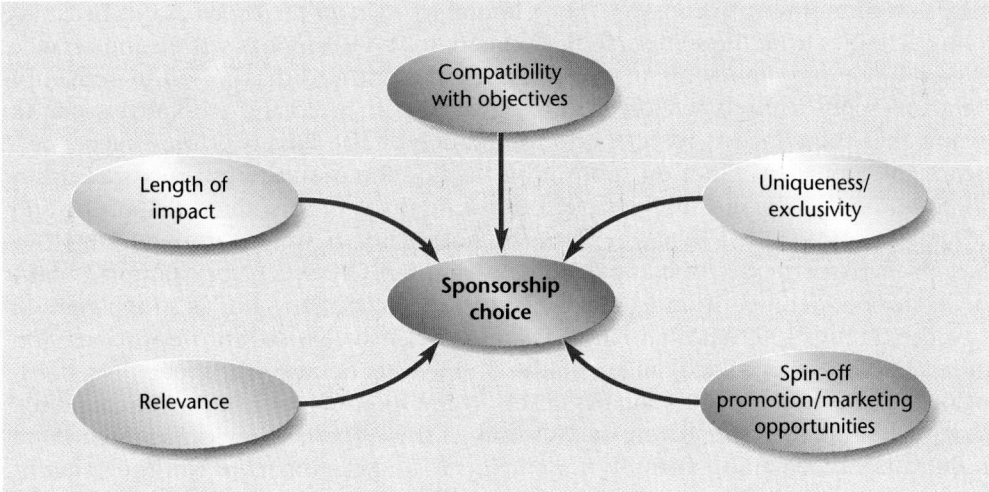

Example *Eurotrash* on Channel 4 is sponsored by Orangina, the popular non-cola French drink brand from Coca-Cola. With the French presenter Antoine de Caunes and the nature of the programme, the partnership was considered ideal since both were trying to shock British viewers in their twenties and thirties with a slightly outrageous and humorous appeal (McLuhan, 1999). Although very popular in France, Orangina had made less progress in the UK and Coca-Cola, after purchasing the brand in 1997, was keen to develop European sales (http://www.cnnfn.com). Occasionally, however, relevance can be a burden. In the mid-1990s, the ruling body controlling women's tennis turned down a three-year, $10 million offer of sponsorship from Tampax for fear of losing other sponsors of individual tournaments within the tour. This appears to have been an incredible decision, coming from a sport that was quite happy to accept cigarette sponsorship (from Philip Morris' Virginia Slims brand) for many years.

The *length of impact* made may also be a consideration. One-off events, unless they are very high profile such as Virgin Cola's and Budweiser's sponsorship of the V99 music festival or the France '98 soccer World Cup, tend not to have the capacity to build the continuity or establish the name familiarity that sponsoring a sports league or series of events would bring. However, there are situations in which a limited length of impact can still be useful if it is part of an integrated campaign. Rover, as part of its launch strategy for the Rover 75, linked up with Classic FM to present two summer concerts featuring Lesley Garrett and the Mediæval Bæbes respectively. The aim was to help generate awareness of the new model with what Rover hoped would be a sympathetic target audience (http://www.classicfm.com).

Uniqueness might be desirable, but as already mentioned, it is not always possible to be a sole sponsor, especially for large international events or where the costs are very high. There is an expectation, for example, that the sponsorship of grand prix racing and its teams will be shared by a range of companies, both within and outside the motor industry. It is difficult, therefore, for any one sponsor to establish a higher profile than the rest unless a particular driver keeps winning. Sponsoring a league or a major event can, however, provide uniqueness. Allied Dunbar's decision to sponsor Rugby's Premiership League was due to the perceived fit between its target market and the sport, largely males aged over 25 in a secure income bracket but with family commitments. Allied Dunbar managed to raise its awareness profile, not just by sponsoring the league but also through the associated television coverage and live debate (Tyler, 1999).

It is also important to consider the potential for *spin-off promotion* and other marketing activities from the sponsorship. Goddard, L. (1999) emphasised the importance of spending more money on advertising and promotion to maximise the impact of the actual sponsorship. Therefore Rover supported both radio and press advertising to ensure that the concerts to celebrate the launch of the Rover 75 were successful. Although Flora spent £1mn on sponsoring the London Marathon, it spent a further £10.5 mn on extra brand support, often featuring the sponsorship deal. Sporting and cultural events provide a focus for corporate hospitality, as well as an opportunity for sales promotion themes. A company sponsoring the Olympics, for example, might run an on-pack competition to win a trip to the games. Thus Kodak's involvement with the Cannes International Film Festival is extensively used for networking and meeting events with a wide range of either influencers or customer groups. Similarly, major sports events provide valuable tickets to the sponsors for relationship building. Charity sponsorship supporting such causes as the Imperial Cancer Research Fund (ICRF) can provide an opportunity for employees and customers to work together in hosting an event, such as a fun run, to raise donations. CGU employees are fund-raising internally for cancer relief and they also feature on the ICRF website (http://www.icnet.uk). As part of the scheme, CGU provides the opportunity for a 10 per cent donation, shared between ICRF and the Macmillan Cancer Relief fund, for any home insurance policy sold through a special hotline.

Finally, it is always important to ensure that the activity is *compatible* with the sponsor's overall promotional objectives. It is easy to get involved with sponsorship because the MD loves soccer or fancies a guaranteed box at the opera for the season. This will cloud judgement over the real fit with the commercial objectives, and call the cost effectiveness of the sponsorship into question. In this sense, sponsorship decisions should be as calculated and unemotional as any other advertising decision.

EVALUATING SPONSORSHIP

Whatever type or method of sponsorship is used, however, it is important to establish the most appropriate means of evaluating results. A number of methods are possible.

1 *Media exposure measurement.* Establishing how much air time on television or radio, or how many column inches in the print media, were given to the event is one measure. The problem is, however, that this measurement takes place after the event, and at best can help to decide whether to continue with future involvement.

2 *Assessing communication results.* Pre- and post-tests on awareness, image etc. can be undertaken to assess whether the sponsorship was noticed and what improvement is made to awareness levels, attitudes and opinions about the sponsor.

3 *Measuring sales results.* Given the indirect nature of sponsorship amid the more powerful impact of other marketing activities, it is unlikely that measuring sales results would yield significant findings proving a causal link between sponsorship and sales.

4 *Feedback from participating groups.* Measurement by obtaining feedback is perhaps easiest to implement where the sponsorship is targeting a small well-defined audience, for example those invited to attend a sponsored concert and its associated hospitality.

EXHIBITIONS AND TRADE SHOWS

Both organisational and consumer sellers may introduce **exhibitions and trade shows** into their promotional mixes. Such events range from small-scale local involvement, for example a specialist bookseller taking a stall at a model railway exhibition, to an annual national trade show serving a specific industry, such as the DIY and Home Improvement Show, or Pakex for the packaging industry. In either case, the exhibition may become an important element of the year's marketing activities, as this section will show. Even those who specialise in organising and supporting exhibitions have their own exhibitions!

> **Example** Allison Transmissions, a subsidiary of General Motors, has successfully used exhibitions to re-establish itself in the European market. As a supplier of automatic transmissions for commercial vehicles, it was having difficulty in getting specified by the vehicle manufacturers. To do so meant a two-pronged approach, influencing users as well as the manufacturers. Unlike in the USA, automatic transmission is not widely used across Europe so part of the job was to convince users that it could be better than manual transmission.
>
> Exhibitions were used to present a unified corporate image and message across Europe. Through product demonstrations, including 'ride and drive', it was possible to show potential customers the benefits of specifying automatic when renewing the vehicle fleet. The company particularly targeted uses where the vehicle is constantly stopping and starting, such as refuse vehicles, buses and fire engines. The national truck and bus exhibitions were targeted, such as the IAA (Hanover) in Germany. Despite having relatively few customers, the power of the exhibition is in the face-to-face contact and high visual impact. Allison now spends 30 per cent of its marketing budget on exhibitions, more than on any other element in the promotional mix (Rines, 1999).

Benefits of attending and participating in exhibitions

Benefits for the small business

Exhibitions and shows can be of particular importance to the smaller business that may not have the resources to fund an expensive marketing communications programme. The exhibition can be used as a cost effective means of building more 'presence' and reputation with the trade, and to generate potential sales leads. Small businesses in the UK, however, seem less inclined to use exhibitions than those from other European countries. According to Hall (1995), in 1994 UK small businesses spent about 10 per cent of their marketing budgets on exhibiting, whereas the French spent 20 per cent and the Italians 30 per cent.

Benefits of international exhibitions

International exhibitions can be particularly valuable because they bring together participants from all over the world who might otherwise never meet, and can thus lead to export deals.

> **Example** The UK's bi-annual International Food and Drink Exhibition (IFE) is attended by over 40 000 visitors and has more than 1000 companies exhibiting. Visitor research indicated that 59 per cent of the audience was looking for new ideas and 38 per cent was actually using the occasion to source new suppliers. There are normally around 30 international pavilions at the event to maximise exposure to new foods from such far-away places as Argentina and Thailand. Although not as large as Anuga in Köln and SIAL in

Paris, the IFE is attractive to international buyers and sellers. While the emphasis is on products and brands, parallel sessions for demonstrations and debates are a popular additional feature. So whether it is treats for children featuring pirate-shaped, cola-flavoured water ice with a lemon centre or the chance to meet over 12 small Irish firms represented by the Bord Bia that the food buyer is looking for, the IFE is a major event in the calendar (*The Grocer*, 1999).

However, as exhibitions have grown in popularity, it has become harder to make an impact in a crowded hall. Between 1992 and 1997, spend on exhibitions in the UK increased from £704mn to £848mn, and thus obtaining the right position and linking the exhibition with invited customers, media activity and seminars can all be important for success (Chetwynd, 1999).

Trade exhibitions and shows

Although some exhibitions, such as the Motor Show, the Ideal Home Exhibition and Clothes Show Live, are open to the general public for part or all of their duration, the serious business of exhibiting takes place in organisational markets. The National Menswear Exhibition may be less well known to the consumer than Clothes Show Live, but it is of far greater importance to manufacturers and retailers in making sure that the right goods reach the right shops at the right time.

The Nürnberg International Toy Fair has been running for 50 years. It represents an opportunity for the trade to present new products to retail buyers from across Europe. New product launches are often planned to coincide with the fair to maximise both the impact to visitors and the subsequent coverage in the trade and hobby press. The main European model railway magazines such as *Continental Modeller* and *Eisenbahn Journal* carry extensive reports on new releases from such manufacturers as Fleischmann, Marklin and Rivarossi.

For the manufacturer, attending exhibitions provides a formal opportunity to display the product range and to discuss applications and needs with prospective customers in a neutral environment. Depending on the type of show and the care that an organisation puts into planning its presence there, an exhibition provides a powerful and cost effective way of getting the message across and making new contacts that may subsequently turn into sales.

Comparison of the benefits of exhibitions and personal selling

Despite the increasing cost of attending shows, a number of benefits can be gained from attendance, which will be compared with what can be achieved through personal selling, the main alternative in organisational marketing.

Product launch and demonstration

An exhibition, as well as providing an organisation with an opportunity to launch or test market new products, enables it to set up working demonstrations of products. This gives potential customers the chance to have hands-on experience of the product and can act as a focal point for discussing applications with individuals or small groups. With a product that is bulky or difficult to set up, a sales representative cannot always provide such demonstrations when visiting potential customers.

Learning experience

The event allows the exhibitor to be present alongside major competitors, learning of new developments and trends and even making comparisons. Taking time to visit other exhibitors' stands can provide a wealth of information that sales representatives would not necessarily pick up in their day-to-day operations.

Lead generation

A valuable aspect of an exhibition is that it concentrates many potential new customers in one place over a short period. A small company with a limited sales force simply does not have the time or resources to generate and follow up large numbers of geographically dispersed leads from scratch. At an exhibition, potential buyers come to you because they are interested, and an initial face-to-face meeting can take place. Even if that meeting does not directly generate a sale, the ice has been broken, the lead has been qualified, and the relationship can be further developed by the sales force after the exhibition. The advantage of an exhibition as a lead generator becomes even more obvious with international events. For a UK company, the cost of attending an exhibition in Frankfurt might be higher than that of one held in London, but the time and effort saved, not to mention the uncertainty involved in trying to locate and follow up foreign leads, should more than compensate. Attendance at a foreign exhibition can be an excellent way for an inexperienced organisation to find its first export customers.

> **Example** The Vitafoods exhibition, held in Geneva in 1999, is an ideal exhibition event for a specialist sector associated with vitality foods and natural medicines. Over 150 000 tickets are distributed free of charge through mailshots and trade journals and the event allows specialist buyers and sellers to meet at one venue. It is especially useful for smaller niche producers who want to meet retail and wholesale buyers (http://www.vitafoods.co.uk).

Relationship building

Even with existing customers, goodwill and relationship building can be furthered if customers are invited to the exhibition stand. Hospitality is an equally important element of the exhibition, and many organisations host parties or receptions for key customers, suppliers or the trade press to foster good relationships. There are also informal, personal networks to develop, renew and refresh. As discussed in Chapter 4, personal relationships between people who work for different organisations within an industry can help to spread information around as well as improving the commercial relationship between their firms.

Visitors' sense of purpose and absorption in the atmosphere

An exhibition takes place in a neutral location over a clearly defined period of time. It is important enough to draw in decision makers and people within an industry who might otherwise be difficult to see. People are there because they want to be, and for the purposes of gathering information and making contacts. The atmosphere can be vibrant, busy and fun, heightening the excitement and stimulation. All of this adds to the visitor's sense of enjoyment and fulfilment. The sales representative, on the other hand, could be calling on someone, in their own workplace, who is extremely busy and reluctant to be seen. The representative might have problems attracting and retaining attention and interest, because the phone never stops ringing, or the manager has made it clear that time is precious and there is a problem on the production line that really must be sorted out immediately.

Brand building

An exhibition can be used to make brand statements very powerfully to customers. This leads to brand-led stand design, which conveys clear messages about the company and what it stands for (Goddard, C., 1999). These should be in line with the desired brand positioning. Through a combination of colour, giant product replicas, furnishings and other imagery, the customer is provided with an insight into what the company is about. For those selling intangible products such as telecommunications, the stand is actually as close as the customer is likely to get to the technology that provides the service.

Market presence

A reasonable objective, particularly for a small company or a new entrant into an industry, is to build awareness, both of the organisation and of the products offered. The larger multi-product company commonly finds that, although the company and its main products are known, there may be several 'blind spots' in the range and thus the exhibition can be used to display them. By comparison, there is a limit to what the sales representative can achieve in this respect. The representative can certainly try to display the full product range to a customer or potential customer, but in terms of raising the organisation's profile within the industry, it would take a long-term determined effort by the entire sales force to achieve as much as a single three-day exhibition could.

PR spin-offs

As the high point in an industry's year, the major national or international exhibition will receive a great deal of publicity within the trade press at least. An organisation with a particularly creative stand or with something exciting to unveil at the show should be able to generate substantial coverage. Some shows generate much more widespread publicity. The Motor Show in the UK, for example, usually has a whole BBC programme devoted to it on a Sunday afternoon when the exhibition is on. This gives valuable airtime to a wide variety of exhibitors, presenting their stands and products to a mass audience.

The hospitality aspects discussed earlier are also a part of the PR effort, whether they centre around customers and suppliers, or cultivating trade press relations.

Corporate boost

Although working at an exhibition can be exhausting, it is different from the day-to-day jobs that most people do. Even for sales representatives, it provides an opportunity to work with colleagues rather than alone, and to meet customers without the slog of travelling. Participating in an exciting event, benefiting from the hospitality, and getting together with old acquaintances all help to boost morale, especially if the exhibition has been a commercial success too.

Importance of exhibitions to organisations

Given these potential benefits it is perhaps surprising that exhibitions do not take a more prominent role in organisations' marketing plans. The overall figures for UK business generally are no more impressive than those for small businesses (quoted earlier). Exhibitions only take up about 8 per cent of the marketing budget of UK organisations, whereas the figures for other countries are: France, 17 per cent, Germany, 21 per cent, Japan, 25 per cent and the USA, 26 per cent (John, 1996). Nevertheless, the exhibition sector in the UK is quite healthy, as shown in Table 19.2, which demonstrates how the number of exhibitions and visitors in the UK evolved between 1991 and 1998.

In a comparison of international exhibition venues, the UK's main sites, the NEC in Birmingham and Earls Court in London, compare very favourably with the other 12

TABLE 19.2

The number of UK exhibitions and visitors, 1991–98

	1991	1992	1993	1994	1995	1996	1997	1998
Exhibitions	660	672	671	691	733	710	841	843
Visitors	9.4	9.1	9.5	10.3	9.7	10.4	10.7	11.0

Source: Exhibition Venues Association, reprinted with kind permission.

The NEC in Birmingham is one of Europe's premier exhibition venues.

Source: The National Exhibition Centre.

members of the European Major Exhibition Centres Association, as can be seen in Table 19.3 in which each is rated on various criteria.

According to the Exhibition Venues Association (EVA) the total number of exhibitions in the UK over 2000 m^2 in 1998 was 843, similar to the previous year. Nearly 60 per cent of these were held either in London or the West Midlands. The EVA also estimated that of the 4200 visitors per exhibition in 1998, on average some 25 per cent were key buyers. Most trade sectors have at least one exhibition per year.

TABLE 19.3
International exhibition venues

	Number of exhibitions	Number of exhibitors	Number of visitors	Exhibition area rented
Barcelona	6	16	5	12
Basel	12	14	14	17
Birmingham	1	2	3	4
Bologna	16	8	6	7
Brussels	=7	17	9	13
Düsseldorf	11	6	11	6
Frankfurt	10	1	7	3
Leipzig	=17	13	17	16
London	2	4	4	8
Lyon	13	12	13	14
Madrid	9	11	8	10
Milan	4	5	2	1
Nürnberg	=7	10	16	9
Paris	3	3	1	2
Paris-Nord	14	7	12	5
Utrecht	5	9	10	11
Valencia	15	18	15	15
Verona	=17	15	18	18

Source: European Major Exhibition Centres Association, reprinted by kind permission.

TABLE 19.4

Exhbition statistics by sector

	Engineering	Computing	Food
Cost per contact (£)	41	35	62
Cost per sale (£)	215	161	182
Average annual budget (£'000)	25.0	44.8	20.3
Spend per exhibition (£'000)	7.4	n/a	3.0
How worthwhile (%)			
Exceptionally	2	3	7
Very	33	35	48
Fairly	40	38	31
Marginally	19	17	14
Not	2	4	0
Under review	3	3	2

Source: Exhibition Venues Association, reprinted with kind permission.

Although international visitors were only a small percentage of total visitors to UK exhibitions, the importance of over 280 000 international buyers for generating leads and sales is well recognised by export-led companies. Table 19.4 looks more closely at the results of a survey undertaken by the EVA, showing outcomes and attitudes to exhibitions by sector.

Reasons for attending exhibitions

The EVA also looked at the reasons for organisations attending exhibitions. These are shown in Table 19.5 alongside the remarkably similar results of a US survey reported by Hart (1993). There has to be more of a reason to attend the show than 'our competitors do' or 'we always go'. Nevertheless, the cost of exhibiting needs to be considered in comparison with alternative ways, if indeed there are any, of achieving the same objectives.

There are many factors to consider before deciding to attend an exhibition. Some of the more important criteria are (Wilmshurst, 1993):

- type of visitors and previous attendance patterns
- participation by main competitors
- advice from agents, trade and local representatives
- exhibition organiser's and independent assessment of previous events
- the promotion and organisation of the event
- the expected costs to be incurred and the objectives to be realised from the event.

TABLE 19.5

Why organisations use exhibitions

UK survey	Per cent	US survey	Per cent
Sales leads	83	Gain qualified leads	71
Presence in the market	70	Maintain image	63
Launch new products	35	Intensify awareness	60
Direct selling	25	Presence in the market	56
		Launch new products	31
		Direct selling	25

Source: UK survey: Exhibition Venues Association; US survey: Hart (1993).

Importance of planning for exhibitors

These reasons for attendance are put into sharp perspective by an examination of the reasons for poor exhibition performance (Dudley, 1990), as shown in Table 19.6. These areas of potential disappointment clearly demonstrate that central to any exhibition decision is the willingness to plan fully, well in advance of the event, including making sure that all participating personnel are comprehensively briefed to handle the event for its duration. Inadequate preparation, even down to poor stand lighting and decor or a shortage of support material, is going to detract from the performance and pull at the event. If added to that there is a parsimonious approach that tries to cut costs through poor-quality space, displays and too few staff, it is easy to see how disappointment might arise.

TABLE 19.6
Reasons for poor exhibition performance

- Inadequate statement of objectives
- Poor-quality visitors
- Bad location of the stand
- Ineffective stand quality/design
- Poor personnel performance
- Lack of follow-up of leads/enquiries
- Ignoring the competition: they get the visitors
- Poor recognition of company by buyers
- Poor corporate identity leading to low recall
- Poor organisation/control of exhibition logistics
- Inadequate staffing arrangements
- Inadequate budget/cost controls

Source: Dudley (1990).

Preparation might also mean co-ordinating the exhibition with the selling effort, making sure that sales representatives invite customers to visit the stand, for example, or with advertising, by featuring participation in the exhibition in advertisements. In all cases, accurate records need to be kept of the visitors to the stand so that the sales force can follow up leads within a short period to take full advantage of the contacts. An exhibition should not be seen as an opportunity for the sales force to get away and have a good time, although enjoyment is not precluded! A sobering thought for those inclined to treat exhibition attendance as a holiday is that the average company spend on exhibiting was £10 500 in 1997. Nevertheless, the EVA has estimated that a sales representative on the road only spends about 180 hours a year on face-to-face selling. How many customers does that represent? At an exhibition, in contrast, a sales team can be contacting up to 50 prospects per hour, a much more efficient use of their time.

Finally, more flexible mobile exhibitions, whether taking the form of a specially fitted caravan or a shopping centre display or a display set up in a hotel room, provide many of the advantages of meeting potential customers without the costs associated with high profile, national exhibitions.

CHAPTER SUMMARY

Public relations is about the quality and nature of an organisation's relationships with various interested publics. These might well include customers and suppliers, but also include shareholders, trade unions, the media, government and other regulatory bodies and pressure groups, among many others. Public relations performs an important supporting role, providing a platform of goodwill and credibility from which other marketing activities can develop and be enhanced. Public relations becomes particularly important in limiting the damage and repairing credibility when a crisis strikes an organisation.

Publicity and press relations are important areas of PR. The media can be valuable in communicating messages to all kinds of publics and even in influencing opinion. Publicity, 'free' media coverage, has the added bonus of being seen as objective and therefore more credible. Organisations are therefore anxious to foster good press relations so that they might be treated less critically should they suffer a 'bad news' crisis. Press releases and press conferences are commonly used ways of getting information to the media, as well as means of fostering personal relationships with key journalists. There are, however, more controllable methods of PR. Advertising can be used to build corporate image and attitudes, and special events and publications can also target key publics. Given the variety of PR methods available, however, it can be very difficult to evaluate PR's success.

Corporate identity is an important consideration for any organisation. Its identity communicates its values and its character, and thus should be strong, clear and distinctive. A desire to change an identity may arise for a number of reasons, but it is not just a cosmetic issue of designing a pretty new logo. It needs extensive research to find out why the old identity was not working and to establish the criteria for the new one. The development of the new image ideally needs to be done in consultation with employees at all levels and, where appropriate, in all divisions of the organisation to make sure that it will be suitable and acceptable from all perspectives. The implementation and launch also need meticulous planning to ensure that all the practical and perhaps even emotional problems of the change are avoided. Finally, the new image should be monitored and evaluated once it has been launched to ensure that it is recognised, properly understood and accepted. Where the change process is not properly planned and managed, problems can occur. Identity change thus needs top management commitment and support and cannot be hurried.

Sponsorship is used by many organisations as a means of generating PR and enhancing both their image and their other marketing communications activities. Sponsorship might mean involvement with sport, the arts, broadcast media or charities or other good causes. Both parties should gain. The sponsor benefits from the PR spin-offs from the activities and the public profile of the organisations and/or events it supports, while those receiving the sponsorship benefit from cash or benefits in kind. Sponsorship might be corporate or brand specific, and the sponsor's involvement might be plainly obvious or quite discreet. Evaluating sponsorship is not easy, but there are a few guidelines for avoiding disappointment. These include the match between the parties concerned, the expected outcomes, potential spin-offs and compatibility with the sponsor's wider marketing objectives.

Exhibitions and trade shows vary from small local events to major national or international shows. They bring together a wide range of key personnel in one place at one time, and can thus generate a great many potential sales leads cost effectively. Sometimes it can be important to be seen at certain high profile exhibitions, among the major competitors, in order to make a statement about one's presence in the market. From the exhibitors' point of view, the main reasons for being there are to generate qualified sales leads and to reinforce the organisation's presence and image in the market. For exhibition attendance to be successful, however, the organisation should ensure that it is a planned element of the overall marketing mix and that it has clear objectives and purposes. It is important to invest adequate funds to make a suitable impact on the show's visitors and to prepare staff carefully so that they make the most of the opportunities offered at the exhibition. After the exhibition, it is crucial that any leads generated are followed up quickly, before the visitors have the chance to forget the good impressions made by the organisation.

Key words and phrases

Cause related marketing	Marketing PR	Public relations
Corporate identity	Press relations	Sponsorship
Corporate PR	Public	Trade shows and exhibitions
House journal	Publicity	

QUESTIONS FOR REVIEW

19.1 What is *PR* and in what ways does it differ from other elements of the promotional mix?

19.2 Differentiate between *marketing PR* and *corporate PR*. To what extent do you think this is a useful distinction?

19.3 List the advantages and disadvantages of *publicity*.

19.4 In what ways can organisations feed material to the media, and in what kind of circumstances might each be appropriate?

19.5 Outline the potential benefits of developing a *house journal*, such as those discussed at p. 794–5.

19.6 Why might an organisation want to change its *corporate identity*?

19.7 Briefly describe the stages an organisation should go through in changing corporate identity, explaining why each is important.

19.8 Why might the lack of top management commitment to a *corporate identity* change mean the failure of the whole exercise?

19.9 What can *sponsorship* offer that media advertising cannot?

19.10 What factors might contribute to successful *exhibition attendance*?

QUESTIONS FOR DISCUSSION

19.1 At p. 783 a range of different publics are mentioned with which a university might have to create and maintain relationships. Draw up a similar list for your own university or college and:

(a) briefly outline what aspects of the institution's activities might be of particular interest to each of those publics; and

(b) suggest appropriate PR methods for each of them.

19.2 Find a corporate story that has made the news recently. It might be a 'crisis', a take-over battle, job losses or creation, new products or big contracts, for instance. Collect reports and press cuttings from a range of media on this story and compare the content. To what extent do you think that:

(a) the media have used material provided by the organisation itself?; and

(b) the story has developed beyond the control of the organisation?

(c) Imagine yourself to be the organisation's PR manager. Write a brief report to the managing director outlining what you feel to be the benefits and disadvantages of the coverage your organisation has received, and what you think should be done next regarding this story.

19.3 Find out as much as you can about a specific trade exhibition in terms of its location, size, range of exhibitors etc. What role do you think the exhibition plays in the exhibitor's marketing strategy and what benefits do you think they derive from attendance?

19.4 What are the dangers of sponsorship from the recipient's perspective?

19.5 Draw up a table outlining alternative methods for evaluating PR, sponsorship and exhibitions, and the potential pitfalls of those methods.

CASE STUDY 19.1

"The sands will rise. The heavens will part. The Power will be unleashed"

The Mummy (http://www.themummy.com), a film released by Universal Pictures and distributed by United International Pictures (UIP), made extensive use of public relations and other elements in the promotional mix to promote and sustain interest in the 're-imagining' of a 1932 film of the same name. Set in the Sahara desert in 1925, it is an 'Indiana Jones' type of adventure that makes excellent use of special effects to frighten and entertain audiences as a 3000-year-old legacy of terror is released on archæologists and treasure hunters when they disturb an ancient Egyptian tomb. As well as being part of the fun and glamour of the movies, *The Mummy* is also a serious new product that had to be launched successfully to cover production costs and to achieve the business objectives set.

Its US launch in May 1999 was very rewarding for Universal and UIP, with $43mn being raised over one three-day weekend alone. This put the film into the top ten list of highest launch receipts. To achieve a Universal top ten all-time position, an important benchmark in the movie industry, the film will have to generate receipts of $130mn. By July 1999, still in the first year after launch, over $117mn had been achieved. Universal had another objective for *The Mummy*, to compete head on with its rival studios to achieve top billings in 1999. The launch was precisely timed to open the film 12 days before the latest *Star Wars* film was released and UIP aimed to follow it shortly afterwards with the appearance of another expected box office smash, *Notting Hill*. *The Mummy*'s UK launch date was set for 25 June 1999, following a similar timing to that used in the US market.

Films are targeted to customers just like any other brand. The prime target for *The Mummy* is the 12–24-year-old, male or female. All other adults could also be regarded as targets, especially those appreciating the fantasy, adventure, high-action romance offerings typified by the *Indiana Jones* series. UIP, therefore, had to prepare for the 25 June launch using a range of promotional techniques designed to make potential customers aware of the launch and familiar with the expected content. Press relations were an important part of the process. Start too early and the impetus may be lost,

especially with the kind of hype surrounding *Star Wars: Phantom Menace* distracting the consumer's attention, but start too late and there would be insufficient time to make any impact at all. A high profile media launch on April 1999 signalled the start of the campaign in the UK. It was attended by some of the stars and the producer, and selected national and regional media were invited to learn more about the film, its content and success. This generated awareness and familiarity among the media and enabled them to prepare their own programmes and features around the proposed June launch date. The film was shown in Reading on 6 June followed by a press conference with one of the stars. Film critics were the main guests.

Support material was also available for the media. In addition to the story-line teasers and general background to the film, the media were given embargoed packs that could not be used until the week commencing 21 June. A standard 'question and answer' print interview with the key stars and producer was made available for regional media. This included colour photography for use with any stories published. For radio a pack of clips with soundtracks, interviews and soundbites was provided just before the launch. A live press conferences with one of the stars of the film was also planned, although specific details were not released until just before the launch.

Closer to the launch date in June, the national and media teaser campaign began. Posters were used to leave the viewer in no doubt as to the nature of the film, which was linked with editorial and media coverage to raise customer anticipation. The title of this case study derives directly from the teaser line on the poster. In London Underground stations, the poster carried an additional quote from *The Express*, 'guaranteed to make you jump, laugh, scream and cover your eyes'. This again shows the advantage of involving the national press and media long before the launch date.

UIP found that 80 per cent of all UK adults visit a Post Office once per month and that a typical main Post Office attracts six million visitors per week. It reached an agreement with the Post Office to insert a trailer for the film before and just after launch on the in-store videos designed to entertain queuing customers. At all 450 Post Offices in June and July *The Mummy* trailer managed 210 showings per week, repeated every 15 minutes, hopefully to new people in the queue. Numerous other joint promotions were launched, for example *The Express* ran a token collecting campaign entitling 10 000 winners to a special pre-launch screening in 30 cities. The paper featured the promotion in its own television advertising, which also benefited the film.

Special events and activities were organised around the launch. *The Mummy* nights were run in resorts, clubs and at 50 end of term student nights. Full information packs were provided to the event organisers along with guidance as to how to theme the event. These included posters, free publicity sheets and material stipulating that the event had to be held in June. Prizes were awarded for the best-dressed mummy or Egyptian fancy dress and the winners won a trip for two to Egypt. *The Mummy* merchandise was available for the runners-up. Bookshops were also targeted for special promotions. Two tie-in books were launched, *Resurrecting the Mummy* on the making of the movie and *The Mummy*. The books were used in a joint promotion organised in bookshops on a National Mummy Day on 12 June. The day featured in the press and awards were available for the best window and store displays, using the support materials provided, such as mini pyramid stands, gold paint, wall friezes and posters, along with plenty of sand. Store customers were also invited through leaflets to enter a *Mummy* competition to win a trip to Marrakech. Over 250 stores were involved in the promotion.

Although the bulk of the promotion was handled by UIP, local cinemas were also encouraged to organise their own publicity and events. The list of activities undertaken by the Warner Village Cinema in Preston is indicative:

- Cinema foyer decorated as a tomb or Egyptian theme.
- Local sand dancers for the launch.
- A competition in the local newspaper to win a free restaurant meal offering a special mummy cocktail that was 'guaranteed to bring you back from the dead'.
- Local newspaper interviews with the make-up artists.
- Use of standard *Mummy* day kit for launch, comprising:
  - 4 tubes of gold paint;
  - 100 armband tattoos;
  - 5 T-shirts;
  - 50 face masks;
  - friezes and posters.

All these activities were in addition to the standard information and press release packs that could be used at a local level.

Other special programmes, events and promotions were linked in to prizes and 'intertextuality', the management of the spin-off products from the film. These included the re-release of the original Boris Karloff 1932 version, television programmes on the Pharaohs, music from the film on radio and CD, press and magazine articles usually offering some prize, such as 'Take a Break' offering a trip to Universal Studios in Florida. *The Mummy* merchandise featured strongly, both as freebies and as licensed merchandising.

There was even a dedicated website through Film Education (http://www.filmeducation.org). This, alongside the main Universal site, was specifically designed to act as a resource to teachers wanting to use the film for historical or more modern media, creativity and marketing education purposes. Some 16 000 study guides for GSCE, NVQ and A level students were supported by dedicated programmes on the BBC Learning Zone. As part of the school-based promotion, a 'Mummy Merchandise Challenge' was issued to 11- to 18-year-olds who were invited to design a piece of original mummy merchandise. The winner not only received a mummy goody bag but their work featured on the website around the same time as the launch.

On the launch weekend all the hard work paid off. In 441 UK cinemas the film grossed nearly £4mn, the 12th biggest opening gross receipts of all time. PR had played its full part.

Sources: http://www.filmeducation.org; http://www.themummy.com.

Questions

1 Which publics were targeted by United Pictures and UIP in launching this film?

2 What PR techniques were used in this case and how effective do you think they were? How were they working with other elements of the promotional mix?

3 What were the advantages and disadvantages of launching *The Mummy* at around the same time as *Star Wars: Phantom Menace*? Do you think on balance that it was a good strategy?

4 What do you think are the differences between using PR for a film and using it for any other consumer product?

CASE STUDY 19.2

Hetty gets her revenge

Compassion in World Farming (CIWF) celebrated victory after a hard-fought battle when on 15 June 1999 the EU Council of Agriculture Ministers voted effectively to put an end to battery hen farming from 2012. The EU Directive stated that from 2003 conventional cages must accommodate a maximum of four hens per cage and from 2007 all perchery systems must move from the current 25 birds per m² to 9 per m². The combination of changes proposed in the Directive will strongly tip the balance towards controlled free-range and barn egg production. This is the culmination of 30 years of campaigning to end a practice that CIWF argued was cruel and detrimental to the health of the hens. Right up to the day of the decision, CIWF fought a campaign using advertising, fund-raising events, video, demonstrations and lobbying to secure change. Even though it knew it had a great chance of being successful, it was still setting up information stands and demonstrating on the need for change right to the last.

CIWF was up against stiff competition from intensive farming groups, some of which are well represented by those in influential positions. It had to use a variety of promotional methods to secure change and the lobbying of influencers and decision makers was particularly critical. Although UK based, CIWF has branches in France and Ireland and offices in Italy and the Netherlands, and all of them approached their local MEPs to present the case for change. Any change had to be Europe wide. Face-to-face meetings, the production of scientific research refuting claims that the economic cost of banning battery farming would be prohibitive and videos were all used to get the message across. Official bodies condemned the practice, including the European Commission's Scientific Veterinary Committee (1992 and 1996) and the House of Commons Agricultural Committee (1981), but despite these endorsements for change, battery farming persisted.

CIWF, therefore, also had to convince the general public in order to put further pressure on decision makers. As early as 1991, it was found that an overwhelming percentage of the British public thought that battery hen farming caused suffering. An NOP poll in 1997 found that 89 per cent of respondents thought it cruel to keep hens in battery cages. Hetty the Hen was a stroke of genius, as she made the issue tangible for many people. She was a 6ft tall, bald, debeaked hen that

made guest appearances at events to create photo opportunities to draw public attention to the campaign. In order to overcome any concern that free-range alternatives would be at a prohibitive price, an argument propagated by its opponents, CIWF was able to present evidence to the public that free-range egg production would only add 1.5p per egg to the price. With increasing public support, its campaign, supported by other animal welfare charities such as the RSPCA, started to have a more significant impact on politicians.

Even after MEPs had accepted the need for change, CIWF found that it was important to keep getting the message across to gain further conviction for action sooner rather than later. The objective was a complete Europe-wide ban on battery hen farming. When the MEPs on the agricultural committee met to consider the proposal for change, CIWF went to Strasbourg and set up an exhibition in the main parliamentary building to show the cruelty of intensive methods and the benefits of free-range farming. The incessant pressure, typified on the CIWF website, meant that when the bill to ban factory farm systems was presented to the full parliament in

Politicians shouldn't mess with *this* chick!
Source: CWIF

January 1999, the MEPs voted for a full ban from 2009, clearing the way for the Council of Ministers' decision in June. However, recommendations and good intentions do not always lead to legislation and further action to reinforce the importance of change and to secure a final ban meant that the campaign continued.

In the six months between January and June 1999, CIWF continued to lobby the agriculture ministers to ensure that the Directive was finally ratified. Further large demonstrations were held for the benefit of ministers in Brussels and Paris. Numerous local events and trade fair demonstrations were organised. In the UK, indoor public events were held, usually screening previously unseen video footage of battery hens suffering, followed by an outdoor demonstration the same or the next day at the regional Ministry of Agriculture offices. A giant 750 000-signature petition was submitted to the UK Minister in March and campaigners came along to give vocal support. The banners proclaimed, 'Minister, we are banking on you to ban battery cages'.

CIWF also commissioned NOP to survey over 1000 people on their attitudes to battery farming in the UK and in May 1999 found that 86 per cent were in favour of a complete ban and that 96 per cent would pay a few more pence to have free-range eggs. Hetty turned up at numerous events, such as the National Pig and Poultry Fair in Warwickshire, along with her retinue of campaigners. Another survey was released in May reporting the findings from nine major supermarket chains. This challenged the myth put out, it was claimed, by opponents, that only 14 per cent of retail eggs sold were from free-range systems. The report found that the average was 30 per cent and in Safeway and Waitrose it was 52 and 65 per cent respectively. Marks & Spencer had gone even further by stocking only free-range eggs. All these findings were sent to the UK's Ministry of Agriculture in good time for the final EU decision. The Campaign Director for CIWF stated, 'The British public were clearly using the power of their purse to show their disgust at the cruel battery cage. Yet still the vast majority of British hens are crammed into these cages so small that they cannot even stretch their wings' (http://www. CIWF.co.uk).

Sources: PR Week (1999); http://www.ciwf.co.uk.

Questions

1 Define the various publics targeted by CIWF.

2 To what extent do you think that Hetty has been useful in CIWF's campaign?

3 Why is PR so important and so prominent in a campaign like this?

4 What PR lessons do you think other campaigners for reform could learn from CIWF's experience?

References to Chapter 19

Abratt, R. and Shee, P. S. B. (1988), 'A New Approach to the Corporate Image Management Process', *Journal of Marketing Management*, 5(1), pp. 63–76.

Bailey, J. N. (1991), 'Employee Publications' in P. Lesly (ed.), *The Handbook of Public Relations and Communication*, (4th edn.), McGraw-Hill.

Baird, R. (1998), 'World Cup Losers', *Marketing Week*, 9 July, pp. 16–18.

Baird, R. (1999a), 'CGU Pours £8mn into Cricket Deal', *Marketing Week*, 18 February, p. 7.

Baird, R. (1999b), 'Sticky Wicket', *Marketing Week*, 25 February, pp. 29–31.

Benady, D. (1999), 'Dome of Contention', *Marketing Week*, 4 February, pp. 26–9.

Bernstein, D. (1984), *Company Image and Reality: A Critique of Corporate Communications*, HRW.

Buckley, N. and Liu, B. (1999), 'Coca Cola Hit by Drinks Health Scare in Europe', *Financial Times*, 16 June, p. 1.

Buxton, J. (1999a), 'Scottish Bank May Be Set to Abandon Evangelist', *Financial Times*, 3 June, p. 1.

Buxton, J. (1999b), 'Bank of Scotland Set on US Direct Venture', *Financial Times*, 7 June, p. 26.

Cassell, M. (1991), *Long Lease*, Pencorp.

Chetwynd, C. (1999), 'The Exhibitionists', *Marketing Week*, 7 January, pp. 33–7.

Cole, R. (1998), 'Team Gets a Little Extra Help from Nationwide', *The Times*, 28 April, p. 1.

Cutlip, S. *et al.* (1985), *Effective Public Relations*: Prentice Hall.

Darby, I. (1999), 'Ford Signs up to £ 12mn Dome Deal', *Marketing*, 11 March, p. 9.

Davies, K. and Phillips, R. (1999), 'Farewell Mrs Beeton', *The Grocer*, 29 May, pp. 34–6.

Denny, N. (1995), 'Oil on Troubled Waters', *Marketing*, 29 June, p. 13.

Dudley, J. (1990), *Successful Exhibiting*, Kogan Page.

Fill, C. (1999), *Marketing Communications: Contexts, Contents and Strategies*, 2nd edn, Prentice Hall Europe.

Fletcher, K. (1995b), 'Good Cause and Effect', *Marketing*, 20 July, p. 31.

France, S. and Hickmet. S. (1999), 'Cracking a Code for Lobbying Probity', *PR Week*, 12 February, pp. 11–12.

Franks, A. (1997), 'Making Much of Music', *Shell Focus*, Summer 1997.

Fry, A. (1995), 'Spreading Across the Small Screen', *Marketing*, 18 May, pp. VIII–X.

Gander, P. (1999), 'Moniker Mayhem', *Marketing Week*, 25 March, pp. 41–3.

Garside, J. (1999), 'NATO Advisers Fight a Comms Battle at Horne', *PR Week*, 30 April, p. 7.

Goddard, C. (1999), 'Brands Make a Stand', *Marketing*, 14 January, pp. 25–6.

Goddard, L. (1999), 'Making the Most out of Being a Sponsor', *PR Week*, 30 April, pp. 15–16.

The Grocer (1999), 'The Business Goes on Show', IFE supplement to *The Grocer*, 30 January, pp. 4–5.

Griegson. J. (1999), 'The Big Mac Kids Get Their Just Deserts', *The Express*, 5 June, p. 35.

Grimston, J. and Murden, T. (1999), 'Bank Pays Preacher £10mn for Lost Deal', *The Sunday Times*, 6 June, p. 11.

Guerin, J-Y. and Mahout, C. (1999), 'Les Bons (et Mauvais) Coups du Sponsoring', *L'essentiel du Management*, 52, June, pp. 6–8.

Hall, C. (1995), 'Get a Fair Share Abroad', *Daily Express*, 26 June, p. 39.

Hart, N. A. (1993), *Industrial Marketing Communications*, Kogan Page.

Haywood, R. (1984), *All About PR*, McGraw-Hill.

Hollinger, P. (1999a), 'Sainsbury Admits Mistakes and Cuts Further 1,100 Jobs', *Financial Times*, 3 June, p. 1.

Hollinger, P. (1999b), 'Sainsbury Recognises the Need for Change', *Financial Times*, 3 June, p. 21.

Jardine, A. (1999a), '£20mn Drive to Fix Shell Image', *Marketing*, 11 March, p. 1.

Jardine, A. (1999b), 'Shell Stresses Ethical Action to Salvage Brand Reputation', *Marketing*, 18 March, p. 9.

John, R. (1996), 'How To Steal the Show', *Marketing*, 4 January, pp. 19–23.

Lee, J. (1998), 'Clamour for the Glamour of Sponsorship', *The Times*, 13 January, p. 31.

Lee, J. (1999), 'Are the Olympics beyond Repair?', *Marketing*, 13 May, pp. 28–9.

Marketing (1999), 'Ericsson Tops Homelands Sponsors', *Marketing*, 15 April, p. 9.

Marketing Week (1999a), 'Corporate Sponsorship', *Marketing Week*, 15 April, p. 57.

Marketing Week (1999b), 'Sports Sponsorship', *Marketing Week*, 15 April, p. 66.

Marketing Week (1999c), 'Brand Sponsorship', *Marketing Week*, 15 April, p. 57.

Marston, J. E. (1979), *Modern Public Relations*, McGraw-Hill.

McLuhan, R. (1999), 'Hitting the Target at Lifestyle Events', *Marketing*, 20 May, pp. 27–8.

Meenaghan, T. (1991), 'The Role of Sponsorship in the Marketing Communications Mix', *International Journal of Advertising*, 10, pp. 35–47.

Meenaghan, T. (1998), 'Current Developments and Future Directions in Sponsorship', *International Journal of Advertising*, 17 (1), pp. 3–28.

Mintel (1996), 'Sport', *Market Intelligence*.

Moran, N. (1998), 'Turning their XXXXX', *Financial Times* survey of Ireland, 22 September.

Murphy, C. (1999), 'Brand Values Can Build on Charity Ties', *Marketing*, 25 March, p. 41.

Nelson, F. and Merrell, C. (1999), 'Robertson May Cost Bank of Scotland £250m Account', *The Times*, 2 June, p. 23.

Nissé, J. (1998a), 'Business Increases Arts Sponsorship', *The Times*, 14 January, p. 25.

Nissé, J. (1998b), 'Littlewoods to End "Too Costly" FA Cup Sponsorship', *The Times*, 16 May, p. 27.

Nuttall, N. (1998), 'Big Business Shuns Call of Wild in Animal Rescue Flop', *The Times*, 6 January, p. 5.

PR Week (1999), 'Bald Bird Beats Battery Barons', *PR Week*, 12 February, p. 8.

Palin, R. (1982), 'Operational PR', in W. Howard (ed.), *The Practice of Public Relations*, Butterworth-Heinemann.

Parsley, D. (1999), 'BA to Fly the Flag Again and Ditch Ethnic Tailfins', *The Sunday Times*, 6 June, p. 1.28.

Patten, M. (1998), 'World Cup Shows More Is Less in Sponsorship', *Marketing Week*, 16 July, p. 14.

Pitcher, G. (1999), 'God Help Those who Confuse Advertising and PR Disasters', *Marketing Week*, 14 January, p. 33.

Price, C. (1999), 'Suppliers Woo the Next Generation of PC Users', *Financial Times*, 3 February.

Rawstorne, T. (1999), 'Big Mac Meltdown', *The Express*, 4 January, p. 3.

Rines, S. (1999), 'Point of Contact', *Marketing Week*, 25 February, pp. 63–4.

Rogers, D. (1999), 'Travel Inn Updates Corporate Image', *Marketing*, 29 April, p. 4.

Shillingford, J. (1999), 'It's not just a Question of Knowing the Language', *Financial Times*, 3 February.

Smith, M. *et al.* (1999), 'Belgian Ministers Quit over Egg Cancer Scandal', *Financial Times*, 2 June, p. 1.

Stanley, R. E. (1982), *Promotion: Advertising, Publicity, Personal Selling, Sales Promotion*, Prentice Hall.

Stone, N. (1991), *How to Manage Public Relations*, McGraw-Hill.

Tyler, D. (1999), 'Sponsorship: Why Bother?', *Management Accounting*, May, pp. 20–1.

Tyrell, N. (1998), 'Dundee Builds on Technology', *PR Week*, 4 December, p. 8.

Wilkinson, A. (1998), 'Schools Sponsorship', *Marketing Week*, 3 December, p. 20.

Wilmshurst, J. (1993), *Below-the-Line Promotion*, Butterworth-Heinemann.

Yarnall, G. (1999), 'A Piece of the Action', *The Grocer*, 15 May, p. 48.

EXECUTIVE INTERVIEW

Alliance & Leicester

Interview with
Tim Pile, Sales and Marketing Director

The Alliance & Leicester is a leading financial services organisation in the UK with an operating income in 1998 of £1,189mn. An interview with Tim Pile, Sales and Marketing Director examined the role of marketing communications within the company. He is responsible for three main parts of organisation: the retail network of 320 branches, business process re-engineering for the whole company and, as Marketing Director, leadership of the marketing strategy including the 4Ps, plus what Tim calls the fifth P – profit. He manages around 2500 staff and a significant marketing budget of millions. The product range includes personal loans, insurances, mortgages, current and savings accounts and credit cards all of which are transacted through the retail branches, ATMs, call centres and Internet banking.

Within Alliance & Leicester, the Sales and Marketing Director has control of all aspects of marketing strategy, including product development, pricing, branch offices and branding, and not just the advertising and promotion mix. An important role for Tim, therefore, is to integrate all marketing activities in the context of the overall strategic plan and direction. Four main benefits are claimed for the Alliance & Leicester approach, most of which have a direct impact upon the marketing communications strategy:

1 *Stronger Branding*: Alliance & Leicester is able to build stronger products within an overall corporate brand. It has a large number of different products and the effort over the past few years has been to ensure that they work together as part of the corporate brand. 'What I seek to do is to ensure that all the marketing programmes take something from the corporate brand but also give something back.'
2 *Cost effectiveness*: it costs more to have separate marketing departments supporting each product rather than having one central team responsible for all products. The diversified model creates a lot of separate cultures and can result in different practices that do not fit well together and/or a duplication of marketing effort. 'We estimate that we can save 30% on costs since by bringing all the marketing departments together. Additionally, we have been able to maximise the scarce expertise of our most effective marketers for the benefit of all Alliance & Leicester's products.'
3 *Strategic clarity*: Through centralised marketing, Tim can ensure that the product range is managed as a portfolio rather than as separate brands and thus can invest more freely in growth areas or focus on areas in decline. For example, Alliance & Leicester has invested heavily in telephone banking and call centre facilities to support all those products that would benefit from direct marketing. It will also be at the cutting edge of Internet banking when it launches its new service for its 1.2 million current account banking customers in January 2000.

4 *Innovativeness*: Centralisation also helps reduce internal politics and brings products to the market much more quickly. Alliance & Leicester's *Moneyback* credit card was conceived, assessed, designed and ready for launch in a few months as significant organisational resources could be devoted to its development without internal barriers having to be negotiated.

It is important to appreciate that Tim does not think of marketing communications as comprising different elements that work in isolation. The key is the integration of the various tools and methods to achieve the desired objectives. The overall marketing communication objectives link right back into the marketing plan, being concerned with delivering transaction volumes and margins through increased customer attention, attraction, retention and satisfaction. Targets are set in each of these areas. To achieve that with multiple products selling into different market segments, Alliance & Leicester focuses on the 'interconnectedness of all communication activities' to create the necessary impact in the competitive markets in which it operates. In financial services, you cannot talk about the brand as a product in isolation as it is an integral part of the service level and customer's service experience.

At a marketing communications strategy level, the aim is to sell products while building the corporate brand. The two must be consistent and interconnected. For that reason, the company has adopted a strong corporate branding framework for its media advertising and product literature. 'All our product literature is consistent in terms of its imagery, style, use of colour, use of logo and the type of language. Only the text varies according to the product claims and benefits. This took some time to achieve as product managers had to sacrifice their promotional and presentational individuality for a standard approach, but they now realise the benefits from working as a part of a corporate brand image and reputation rather than in isolation.'

Tim believes that in financial services the distribution channel is an integral part of the marketing communications strategy as it helps shape how the customer is spoken to and the nature of that contact. For example, one of its competitors MBNA has a direct marketing operation with no branches. He stated that 'it thinks nothing of a mail drop of 15 million to promote a product such as credit cards, whereas the Nat West has an extensive branch network and tends to rely more on direct mailings to support local sales staff with leads for new business. So to us, marketing communications can be a means of distribution for financial services products and this is why we have all been so active in moving to direct marketing approaches'.

Understanding the involvement and interaction between the customer and the product is also important. For example Alliance & Leicester finds that 90% of personal loans can be handled by post or telephone, but that most saving

EXECUTIVE INTERVIEW continued

investment decisions usually involve a visit to the branch. People want the reassurance of a personal contact and to ensure that their trust is well placed. The branch sales staff are trained to handle these situations otherwise it would undermine the achievements of other promotional activities in generating enquiries and interest.

Commenting upon the changes in the promotional mix during the 1990s, Tim highlighted a radical shift from mass marketing to mass customisation. 'Direct marketing has enabled one to one communication, mass customisation if you like, rather than mass marketing which implied large scale media advertising. This means that we can treat each customer as unique and target different financial products at them at different times depending upon our assessment of their needs. Although nationally television advertising revenues have held up over the past five years, that is misleading as it fails to reveal the changes in the typical television advertisers. The emphasis has moved away from a number of the larger fmcg companies and indeed financial service operators to new industries such as computing and telecommunications. Of course we still use television from time to time, but at nowhere near the level of a few years ago. The trend will continue as the media fragments into smaller and smaller audiences.'

Alliance & Leicester has developed a highly sophisticated direct marketing organisation to service its existing 5.7 million customers and also to attract new customers based on the customer profile most likely to respond to a particular mailing. Its data warehouse enables it to prepare response propensity models so that it has a good idea what financial products customers are likely to be interested in at different times. It tracks response rates by each customer cell, products, month, location, customer type, campaign etc. It also tracks the 'cost to acquire' a customer and constantly experiments with different mixes to lower cost and improve effectiveness. Although it has its own in-house database management, it still uses external agencies for the creative themes.

Of course, there is no point in developing a highly professional and sophisticated direct marketing system if the customer contact lets the organisation down. It now has an advanced customer call centres that can handle up to 250 000 calls per month for fulfilment and 2 million customer service calls. It uses different freefone contact numbers to route calls to specialists as it offers such a wide range of financial products. Operators have to be able to offer advice and screen customers to direct them to the most suitable products. All its customer contact staff are trained to high standards in customer handling as well as in the products.

However Tim is less sure about the future impact of the Internet, taking what he describes as a 'heretical view', questioning some of the claims about the future impact on consumers. 'Never has so much hype been given to a new medium and too few people are taking a critical view of its impact. Of course, the Internet has changed and will continue to change financial services marketing and we have invested heavily in our award winning site (http://www.alliance-leicester.com). Currently, we have 65 000 website visitors generating 2500 on-line applications each month. On our website we display brochures, provide application facilities and have hyperlinks to other related pages within the product range. We also intend to be at the forefront of Internet banking but unlike many "experts", I do not think that over the next five years it will replace the branch offices. There will

still be an important role for other communication tools in general and our branch offices in particular. For example the branches will support the Internet to become like a convenience store where products and services can be assessed, discussed and purchased. They will become advice centres and points where personal interaction is possible. In short they will work alongside the Internet, not be replaced by it. For example in the USA the giant internet broker Schwab has recently been opening retail branches to support its internet marketing efforts.'

'In my view, as Internet usage increases, it will be direct mail usage that will decline. The power to link the profile of the Internet user to target advertising messages precisely would benefit financial products. However, the profile of Internet users is not developing as fast as some would like. Interestingly, it is the older market that is becoming the heavier users as they have the time to learn and surf the web. The young professional, an important segment for us, is often too busy to spend hours surfing. I suspect much will also depend upon how quickly legislation catches up with direct marketing. There are already moves to restrict the use of the electoral registers and given the power of the web, inevitably controls will be introduced.'

Tim then discussed the context for his marketing communications strategy and how different elements of the mix support either corporate branding or product promotion. Because of Alliance & Leicester's umbrella approach to product development and management, the challenge is to ensure that the one brand, Alliance & Leicester, is able to meet a plethora of customer needs through the various products within the portfolio. Most of its direct marketing and media advertising is aimed at promoting products, whereas the umbrella brand must be established to make the reception for those products more favourable. However every product promoted must pay a kind of 'brand tithe' to benefit other products in the range. PR and to a lesser extent sponsorship are the main tools for directly building the corporate umbrella brand. The PR team and agency work closely with the marketing staff to develop stories and messages that build the image and reputation of the brand. They are closely involved in the marketing planning process. The reluctance to use sponsorship, however, reflects the difficulty in being able to justify the expenditure when evaluation is so difficult.

There is one final dimension to the umbrella brand: staff. The service they provide, the quality of the interaction with the customer is considered crucial for reinforcing the umbrella brand image and reputation and extends far wider than perhaps the product being discussed. "Total brand communication" is what we are about and that requires an integrated marketing communications strategy, blending the different elements of the promotional mix together to create an impact and then ensuring that staff can live up to the expectations and claims for the brand. We always launch our new products to staff first and we always train, incentivise, communicate and reward staff at the branches due to the critical role they play in supporting the Alliance & Leicester brand. It would all come to nothing if our branch sales staff were not performing in converting product interest into sales and in retaining our customer loyalty. I cannot see Internet marketing changing that. Supporting it, yes, but not changing it.'

With grateful thanks to Tim Pile, Sales and Marketing Director, Alliance & Leicester.

Part VII

MARKETING MANAGEMENT

In offering you a detailed and comprehensive introduction to the important elements of marketing, this book has had to take a 'pigeon hole' approach, treating each element as a separate entity. Throughout the text, however, it has been made clear that all these elements are interdependent and must be integrated into a consistent and coherent overall strategy.

This section, therefore, serves two purposes. First, in Chapter 20, issues of strategic marketing and competitive strategy are addressed. Increasingly, marketing managers are expected to play an additional role in supporting the corporate planning process by focusing on the important areas of product market strategy and marketing resource allocation as well as the more traditional mix management perspectives. Chapter 20, therefore, also outlines the interface between corporate and marketing planning frameworks, and how each influences and is influenced by the other. Second, Chapter 21 examines the marketing planning process, and the role it plays in providing a structured framework within which marketing actions can be undertaken. Finally, Chapter 21 looks at the importance of planning in smaller businesses and how its role changes as the business evolves. The importance of planning, based on sound assessment of the organisation's present position, both internal and external, as stressed in Chapter 14 on marketing communication, cannot be understated.

Chapters 22 and 23 have been included because it is recognised that a broad introduction to a subject such as marketing has to generalise. In some respects this is a strength – it is hoped that the variety of industries, products and experience illustrating this text has been both entertaining and informative for you. This breadth and variety do, however, make it more difficult to envisage how all the elements of the marketing mix mesh together in specific practical applications. Chapters 20 and 21 begin the integration process, but the last two chapters takes it further, in looking at specific situations and types of organisation.

As many of the examples cited in the text so far have related to physical products, Chapter 22 centres on services marketing, such as banking, travel and tourism, and personal services. Marketing tends to be thought of as belonging in large, profit-making businesses. To redress this, Chapter 22 also looks at the non-profit sector, where organisations such as charities, the police, medical and other public services are increasingly adopting a marketing orientation and marketing strategies. Chapter 23 looks at the problems, pitfalls and rewards of international marketing, both within Europe and further afield. The chapter examines the reasons that organisations internationalise and the impact of the international marketing environment on their decisions. Different ways of entering foreign markets are discussed, along with the debate on whether organisations should standardise or adapt their products and marketing offerings in international markets.

Strategic Marketing

LEARNING OBJECTIVES

This chapter will help you to:

1 define marketing strategy and the internal and external influences affecting it;

2 understand the various types of portfolio model used to develop a strategic view of the organisation and the competitive context within which it operates;

3 outline different strategies for achieving growth and their appropriate use;

4 differentiate between types of competitors, appreciate the perspectives from which they can be analysed, and start to define appropriate strategies for dealing with them; and

5 understand the concept of competitive positioning and the range of strategies and tactical actions broadly appropriate for achieving and maintaining a position.

INTRODUCTION

So far, this book has looked at the practical aspects of marketing, from identifying consumer needs and wants through to designing and delivering a product package that aims to meet those needs and wants, and maintains customer loyalty despite the efforts of the competition. The tools that make up the marketing mix are, of course, critical for implementing the marketing concept. Each one adds value to the overall offering, contributing towards a competitive edge that will attract the target market. What exactly constitutes the best mix to adopt varies from situation to situation and must be the subject of research, experimentation and management judgement. So far, the focus on the marketing mix elements has largely been operational and orientated to the short term. Managers must, however, think of their operational marketing mixes in the context of wider, more strategic questions, such as:

■ Which markets should we be in?
■ What does our organisation have that will give it a competitive edge? (This need not necessarily come directly from marketing.)
■ Do we have the resources, skills and assets within the organisation to enable planned objectives to be achieved?
■ Where do we want to be in five or even 25 years' time?
■ What will our competitors be doing in three or five years' time?
■ Can we assume that our current *modus operandi* will be good enough for the future?

These concerns are strategic, not operational, in that they affect the whole organisation and provide a framework for subsequent operational decisions. The focus is on the future, aligning the whole organisation to new opportunities and challenges within the changing marketing environment, as discussed in Chapter 2. The questions suggested above seem deceptively simple, but finding answers to them is, in fact, a highly skilled and demanding task. The future welfare of the whole organisation depends on finding the 'right' answers. As Chapter 2 showed, trends within the marketing environment can be difficult to spot, and even if the organisation does see them, their implications can still be unclear and contradictory. This is particularly true where competitors are concerned. Even the best-laid plans can be severely disrupted by competitive action, especially when the competition refuses to act predictably or to play by 'the rules' as you define them. Thus there is a constant need for information gathering, updating and analysis as a fundamental part of strategic planning in the first place, and then as a part of monitoring and controlling the implementation of those plans.

Gaining an understanding of the external environment is not enough in itself. The organisation also has to take a long hard look at its internal resources, assets and skills to assess whether the organisation is sufficiently well equipped to meet the challenges of the external environment. Strategic marketing planning thus might have long-term implications for the direction and shape of the whole organisation rather than just affecting the operational management of the marketing mix elements themselves. The strategic marketer is, therefore, a catalyst for change through highlighting the need to create a better fit between the market's needs and the capabilities and resources of the organisation. The stakes are high, for the organisation that gets it wrong can face very serious consequences, particularly if long-term investments in plant, machinery or product development have been made on the basis of a particular interpretation of the marketing environment.

Example Tetley Tea (http://www.teafolk.com) undertook a major strategic rethink as the 1990s drew to a close. Although it was the leading manufacturer brand of tea in the UK, with 20.3 per cent market share by volume, compared with PG Tips' 19.5 per cent, Typhoo's 9.8 per cent and retailer own brands' 34 per cent, the market for tea drinking was in decline. The 'share of throat' for tea had declined from 60 per cent in 1995 to 56 per cent in 1999, with younger people in particular switching to fizzy drinks and coffee. The challenge for Tetley was to manage the decline at home while finding new areas for expansion to maintain overall sales. In part, this was to be achieved through product development. New packaging and products such as green tea and fruit and herbal teas are planned, and the idea of launching an iced tea is being given serious consideration. All these developments are designed to capitalise on the strong positive image of the Tetley brand name.

The adverse change in tea demand, coupled with a strong pound in North America and Australia, higher raw tea prices and the economic difficulties in Russia and south east Asia, have all contributed to a 40 per cent decline in operating profits on reduced sales in 1998. Plans to expand into new geographic markets away from the core areas of the UK, Canada, France, the USA and Poland were scaled back in an effort to concentrate on those markets where profits could be realised without significant further investment in marketing or production activity (Pretzlik, 1999a). However more radical plans were also being considered for a chain of 'tea bars' based on a pilot shop called Gaffer's in Manchester. Gaffer is one of the Tetley Tea folk characters that have been featured in Tetley advertising since 1973. It was hoped that a joint venture could be formed to open a Gaffer's chain of tea bars building on the strong Tetley name, emulating the rapid growth in coffee shops (such as Starbucks) and sandwich bars (Pretzlik, 1999b). Tetley will not be alone in this sector if it does decide to enter, however, as Unilever, owner of Brooke Bond and PG Tips, has also been testing the concept with a Ch'a pilot shop in Brighton. Tetley is faced with difficult market choices that will determine its profitability and competitiveness over the next few years.

This chapter first introduces strategic marketing issues by defining some of the commonly used terms and showing how they fit together. Some, however, will not be considered in depth until the next chapter. A number of techniques have been developed for analysing strategic marketing problems, especially those concerned with the interface between the products offered and the dynamics and structure of the related markets. Product portfolio and market attractiveness models are therefore considered at pp. 842 *et seq.* There then follows a review of a variety of strategic options that are closely related to marketing issues. These include growth directions, developing and maintaining a competitive position and deciding on how to compete, ranging from direct attacks to almost independent decision making regardless of competition. Competitive strategies and their impact on marketing are then explored. This area has grown in importance in recent years, reflecting the increased level of competition in many markets, often on an international scale. Chapter 21 will then build further on this chapter by examining the implementation of strategic and operational marketing through the planning process.

DEFINITIONS AND PERSPECTIVES

Marketing strategy cannot be formulated in isolation. It has to reflect the objectives of the organisation and be compatible with the strategies pursued elsewhere in the organisation. This means that marketers must refer back to corporate goals and objectives before formulating their own strategy, to ensure consistency, coherence and relevance.

It would be inappropriate to imply, however, that marketing strategy is always subservient to corporate strategy. Many aspects of marketing actually influence corporate strategy. In a marketing-orientated organisation, the needs of customers and the maintenance of competitive edge are important ingredients in formulating corporate strategic direction and priorities. Furthermore, the product is at the heart of the business and thus marketers' product decisions, for instance deletion, modification or range extension, are likely to have a major impact on the organisation as a whole. In this context, the strategic aspects of marketing are likely to have a major (but not exclusive) impact on the formulation of corporate strategy, as seen in the Tetley Tea example earlier and the Linn vignette on page 836. The two-way process between marketing and corporate strategy is shown in Fig. 20.1.

To help to clarify the two-way interaction, the rest of this section is divided into two. First, we provide an overview of some of the different, and often overlapping, internal strategic perspectives, both corporate and marketing specific, that marketers have to consider in their strategic thinking. We then examine some of the broader factors that affect the formulation of marketing strategy in practice.

FIGURE 20.1

The two-way interaction between marketing and corporate strategy

Strategic marketing frameworks

This subsection outlines some of the strategic perspectives of the organisation, starting with the broad picture required by corporate strategy, then gradually focusing down towards the very specific detail of marketing programmes.

Corporate strategy

Corporate strategy concerns the allocation of resources within the organisation to achieve the business direction and scope specified within corporate objectives. Although the marketing department is primarily responsible for responding to perceived marketing opportunities and favourable competitive environments, it cannot act without the involvement of all other areas of the organisation too. Corporate strategy, therefore, helps to control and co-ordinate the different areas of the organisation, finance, marketing, production, R&D etc., to ensure that they are all working towards the same objectives, and that those objectives are consistent with the desired direction of the business as a whole.

MARKETING IN ACTION   **A sound strategy**

Linn products is a Scottish manufacturer of high quality hi-fi equipment that targets the high-performance, top end of the European market. It made its mark with its first product in 1972, the Linn Sondek LP12, a transcription turntable that became the benchmark against which all the others are judged. The company applied the same standards and positioning to Linn speakers and the first solid state pitch accurate amplifiers. Linn now has over 50 products including CD players, tuners, amplifiers, and speakers that it sells in 30 countries. In just under 30 years, Linn has become a world leader in sound technology, innovative design and precision engineering.

More recently, Linn diversified into the home theatre market, a growing sector at the top end of the hi-fi market. In 1994 the Knekt system was launched, an advanced multi-room sound distribution and control system. It is powerful stuff. A 16-source system, for example, could distribute to 128 rooms. This was followed in 1995 by entry into the digital multi-channel sound market with the Linn AV51, a new home cinema and multi-media high-fidelity sound system. This means that buyers can have a designed-in system in a number of rooms and, because it is multi-channel, they can both watch a movie and listen to audio in the same room from the same entertainment system. People are now taking for granted that they can access all their entertainment needs throughout the home and the Knekt system allows this kind of multi-use.

Linn's mission is 'to thrill customers who want the most out of life from music, information and entertainment systems that benefit from quality sound by working together to supply them what they want when they want it'. Each product has the signature of the product builder. One product builder is responsible for the assembly, testing and packaging of an item. An old fashioned attention to detail does not mean old fashioned inefficient production processes, however. Linn claims to have one of the smallest plants in the world with automated materials handling right up to the assembly point. Within that, 'real-time' manufacturing is practiced, meaning that each day's production is made to order for specific customers. The product designers too are close to the customer and are committed to continuous improvement.

Linn's customer care philosophy extends from the manufacturing process through to the distribution channel. The company is selective about appointing dealers because it sees the key to selling its products as the expertise and product demonstration offered by the retailer. Linn is looking for those retailers that are the best in their area and have a quality reputation that fits with Linn's own. It wants retailers that want to sell quality products and are prepared to spend time with customers demonstrating and installing them. Retailers should be able to:

- work with customers to discover what kind of musical expectations and sound needs they have
- appreciate the cost–value relationship inherent in Linn systems, if necessary comparing them with the competition
- show customers how best to use and accommodate equipment
- help customers consider system expandability.

Linn is very reluctant to supply retailers that are not trained or are unable or unwilling to stock the range for demonstration purposes.

Source: http://www.linn.co.uk.

Linn has diversified into the digital multi-channel sound market.

Source: Linn Products Ltd.

Although the techniques for corporate planning may vary between different sizes and types of organisation, the objective is always the same: to match targeted opportunities with resources, focused activity and strategies. Typical issues of concern to corporate planners might thus be market expansion, product development priorities, acquisition, divestment, diversification and maintaining a competitive edge. In a smaller firm the planning process could be fairly straightforward, but for a larger firm with distinct business areas this planning might mean making tough decisions about resource allocation and strategic priorities, which might create a degree of internal conflict.

To help to make the corporate planning process more manageable, larger organisations often divide their activities into **strategic business units** (SBUs). An SBU is a part of the organisation that has become sufficiently significant to allow it to develop its own strategies and plans, although still within the context of the overall corporate picture. SBUs can be based on products, markets or operating divisions that are profit centres in their own right. Each SBU might face very different marketing environments, achievement targets, strategies and competitors. Given that SBUs might have different growth and financial profiles, it is important at corporate level to assess both the current performance and future potential of each SBU and then decide overall priorities and resource allocation.

Competitive strategy

Competitive strategy determines how an organisation chooses to compete within a market, with particular regard to the relative positioning of competitors. Unless an organisation can create and maintain a competitive advantage, it is unlikely to achieve a strong market position. In any market, there tend to be those who dominate or lead, followed by a number of progressively smaller players, some of whom might be close enough to mount a serious challenge. Others, however, are content to follow or niche themselves (i.e. dominate a small, specialist corner of the market). As we show later (see p. 858), there are many ways of competing, and the choice of competitive strategy guides subsequent detailed corporate and marketing strategy decisions.

Marketing strategy

The marketing strategy defines target markets, what direction needs to be taken and what needs to be done in broad terms to create a defensible competitive position compatible with overall corporate strategy within those markets. It is, therefore, concerned with many of the aspects considered in buyer behaviour (Chapter 3 and 4), as well as the decision to target particular market segments (Chapter 5). Marketing mix programmes can then be designed to best match organisational capabilities with target market opportunities. Many of the cases and examples highlighted in Chapters 7–19 showed how various marketing mix strategies were used to achieve marketing objectives. Chosen strategies will vary, depending on the context (compare, for example, two case studies, Celebrations (Case study 7.1) and Riverdance (Case study 14.1)) but they all share the same marketing-orientated philosophy.

Marketing plan

It is in the marketing plan that the operational detail, turning strategies into implementable actions, is developed. The **marketing plan** is a detailed, written statement specifying target markets, marketing programmes, responsibilities, time-scales and resources to be used, within defined budgets. Most marketing plans are annual, but their number and focus will vary with the type of organisation. The plan might be geographically based, product based, business unit based, or orientated towards specific segments. An overall corporate marketing plan in a large organisation might, therefore, bring together and integrate a number of plans specific to individual SBUs. Planning at SBU level and then consolidating all the plans ensures that the corporate picture has enough detail, and allows overall implementation and control to be managed.

Marketing programmes

Marketing programmes are actions, often of a tactical nature, involving the use of the marketing mix variables to gain an advantage within the target market. These programmes are normally detailed in the annual marketing plan, and are the means of implementing the chosen marketing strategy. Linn hi-fi systems, mentioned earlier in this chapter, found that an advertising campaign of £250 000 using quality journals, a direct mail programme, an annual brochure and a bi-annual magazine was appropriate for stimulating trial and maintaining customer relationships. Programmes provide clear guidelines, schedules and budgets for the range of actions proposed for achieving the overall objectives. These are determined within the framework of the overall marketing plan to ensure that activities are properly integrated and that appropriate resources are allocated to them.

Influences on marketing strategy

Figure 20.2 outlines the various influences on an organisation's marketing strategy, each of which is then discussed in turn.

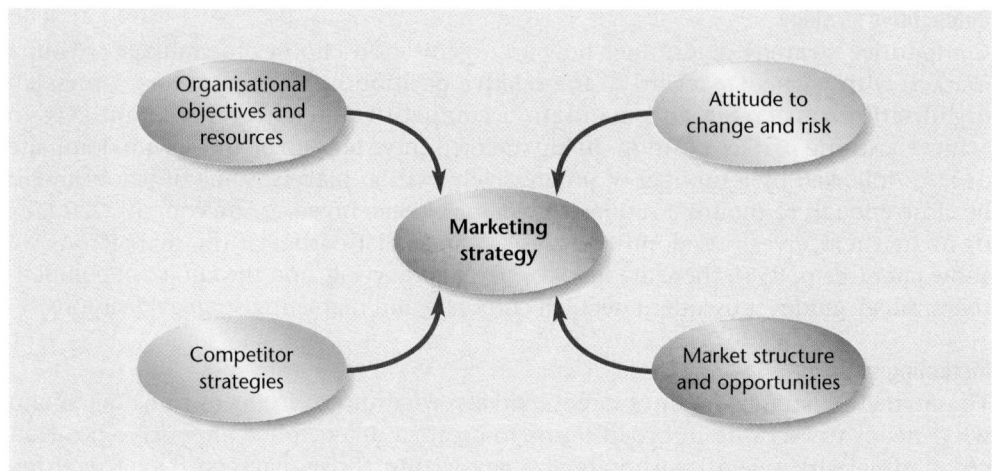

FIGURE 20.2

Influences on marketing strategy

Organisational objectives and resources

Marketing strategists need to be guided by what the organisation as a whole is striving for – what its objectives are and what resources it has to implement them. Some organisations might have very ambitious growth plans, while others might be content with fairly steady growth or even no growth at all, that is, consolidation. Clearly, each of these alternatives implies different approaches to marketing.

Example Aston Martin Lagonda (http://www.astonmartin.com) is one of the world's most prestigious car manufacturers, reflecting many of the traditional values of craftsmanship, attention to detail and exclusivity. Its advertising material promises owners an 'exclusive, exhilarating adventure in an individually produced, true British sports car'. With maximum speeds of up to 200mph and a desirable marque, the famous wings, it represents the aspirations of many, but only a few can afford the price tag of around £85 000 to join the most exclusive owner's club. The Aston Martin DB7 Volante was voted the year's ultimate Christmas present in the USA in 1998, despite the catalogue price of $150 000. In little more than 86 years, only 15 000 cars have been produced and it is claimed that around 13 000 of them are still in use.

The organisational objective for Aston Martin is primarily to maintain the exclusivity tag. Over 70 per cent of cars are exported, especially to the USA and Canada, followed by Germany, Japan, Italy and Switzerland. Although there is certainly sufficient demand to expand production from the 700 or so cars built each year, that might mean not only a reduction in exclusivity but also a departure from the traditional production methods based on individuality and craft. Customers can watch their cars being produced and talk to the craftsmen involved. The specifications are chosen not for speed of assembly but the quality of the finish, with each car produced individually to the exact customer requirements. Materials include Connolly leather, Wilton carpet and Burr walnut veneer and every engine has the signature of the craftsman who produced it.

Despite restricted production volumes and resistance to mass production methods, considerable investment is made in both product and process development. For example, the V12 engine was the result of collaborative research with the Ford Research and Technology Group and Cosworth, and significant investment has also been made in the paint factory and final assembly plant at Bloxham, near Banbury. Careful attention is given to dealer support, special pick-up and assistance services, advanced driving tuition and a fast turnaround on parts orders.

Resources are not only financial. They also include skills and expertise, in other words any area of the organisation that can help to add value and give a competitive edge. The exploitation, through marketing, of things that the organisation does well, such as manufacturing, technical innovation, product development or customer service, might help to create non-financial assets such as reputation and image, which are difficult for competitors to copy.

Example Swiss Company Holderbank SA (http://www.holderbank.com) is one of the world's largest suppliers of cement, aggregates and concrete with sales of CHF11 268mn in 1998. For any company of this nature to survive, there have to be economies of scale in production, consistent supplies of raw material and low transport costs. Holderbank has established three fundamental strategic principles to guide its competitive position: cost leadership in its many overseas markets, market leadership to achieve volume sales, and strong vision and firm control over central strategy yet still allowing local autonomy.

To achieve cost leadership, Holderbank invests heavily in technology to reduce unit costs and often locates plants either near to raw materials or near to customers. Through a process of acquisition and new plant openings, it now has over 40 cement plants in Europe alone, 108 aggregate and 307 ready-mix concrete plants. On a worldwide scale, there are over 630 ready-mix concrete plants. Wherever Holderbank decides to expand, largely driven by construction opportunities because of demographic development or infrastructure renewal, the formula is the same: large volumes, efficient operations and local service. The strategic risk is spread by involvement in over 60 countries, both developing and developed, and thus little thought has been given to diversifying away from the core cement business. Indeed, the most recent strategy suggests divesting any activity outside the core as a means of maintaining world leadership.

As the cases of Aston Martin and Holderbank show, marketing strategies do need to be compatible with corporate objectives and to capitalise on available resources.

Attitude to change and risk

The corporate view on change and risk often depends on the approach of top management. Risk tolerance varies widely from individual to individual, and from management team to management team. Managers will also, of course, be guided by the nature of the organisation and their interpretation of its business environment. The managing director of a small business may not want to take on high risk projects, feeling that the firm's size makes it more vulnerable to failure through its lack of resources. A larger firm might be able to absorb any losses, and therefore feel that the risk is worth taking.

Example The reverse is true in some new industrial sectors such as the biotech industry. Smaller biotech companies have been found to be more inventive and efficient than the larger pharmaceutical companies in which the enterprise spirit can sometimes be lost (Piling, 1999). This can be an issue if the smaller company is acquired by the larger organisation and if any subsequent integration and even cost cutting lead to a stifling of ideas. However, when pharmaceutical giant American Home Products (http://www.ahp.com) took a 54 per cent stake in the Seattle-based company Immunex (http://www.immunex. com), which specialises in cancer treatment and immunity systems, it ensured that a considerable degree of managerial and R&D freedom was retained in the absorbed organisation. Roche, from Switzerland, went further when it took a share in Genentech from San Franciso (http://www.gene.com), ensuring that its shareholding was not so large that it dominated and controlled local management.

The Performance Group (1999) in its studies of corporate innovation has found that enterprise depends on a willingness to accept mistakes rather than punish them, and that this stance, along with a tolerance of risk and innovation, is essential for a culture that welcomes change and significant development. Archie Norman, the chairman of ASDA, is quoted as saying:

> A failing organisation is almost invariably an organisation that ceases to innovate and to experiment because innovation and experimentation are risky.
>
> (as quoted by Burt, 1999)

The organisation that can encourage change, ideas and innovation may be better able to exploit emergent product and market opportunities as they arise.

Market structure and opportunities

Markets vary considerably in their structure and dynamics. Some are fairly stable and not a great deal happens in them unless one of the major players decides to become aggressive and seeks to improve its competitive position. Some markets are simply too complacent. A good example would be the Dutch agriculture sector, which has been criticised for failing to keep up with market changes and increased levels of European competitiveness. Although competitiveness has been maintained in cut flowers and seeds, ground has been lost in the dairy, vegetable and pork sectors. The real problem has arisen from changes in the marketing environment, as consumers have sought a wider variety of products and higher product specifications, and European supermarket buyers have sought greater efficiency.

> **Example** Mothercare (http://www.mothercare.co.uk) is a retailer of specialist accessories and clothing for babies and children up to eight years old. In the UK, it is claimed that over 90 per cent of pregnant women visit one of its 340 stores before giving birth, generating a turnover of over £300mn. From its launch in 1961, Mothercare worked hard to establish a reputation for quality, own-label brands, an attractive retail environment and a comprehensive range including maternity wear. Since 1984, export sales have been developed through direct retail outlets and franchises, resulting in operations in over 30 countries.
>
> In more recent years, however, Mothercare's performance has been questioned after a string of poor sales results and a loss of UK market share (*Marketing*, 1999). The focus was particularly on loss of market share in the four- to eight-year-old sector, which had become much more fashion conscious. This led to a review of Mothercare's product range and even discussion about stocking other brand names. Mothercare managed to retain its market leadership position, although advertising expenditure was reduced to just £1mn in 1997 and market share was lost to ASDA, which built up a comprehensive children's wear range at lower prices. Mothercare also suffered from changing retail patterns and had to close 68 of its smaller high street stores as part of a shift to out of town shopping and the more popular Mothercare World hypermarket format.

The impact of the increasing internationalisation of organisations is that previously dormant markets can be suddenly transformed into dynamic competitive arenas by the entry of a new, foreign competitor. This can be seen in the UK construction industry. Companies suffered badly in the 1990s, partly because of the depressed state of the construction market generally, but also because of increasing difficulties in competing with European, Japanese and American rivals entering the UK market. For many years, contracting was often a national and sometimes even a regional business with a large number of smaller firms. With the arrival of international competitors, most of whom are much larger, smaller firms were finding it harder to win contracts and to do battle in European markets.

Often, such turbulence only happens over a limited period until a new *status quo* is reached through a new market structure that redefines relative market shares. In the case of construction, that could mean considerable rationalisation within the UK industry. Sometimes, the turbulence is created by innovation and new product technology that again has the potential to redefine how players actually compete. In some growth markets, turbulence can be high until the market stabilises and competitors become more entrenched, leaving fewer opportunities for new entrants.

> **Example** The household paper products market in the UK is split into three main sectors: toilet tissue, kitchen towels and facial tissues. Although the kitchen towel sector was at one time regarded as a commodity in a stable market, new product development caused the market to grow again ahead of inflation. Fort St James claimed that its Kittensoft Thirst Pocket kitchen towels, offering air drying, 'air pocket' technology, grew by 113 per cent in one year. Similarly, Procter & Gamble innovated with rinsed and reusable kitchen towels along with microwavable paper in its Bounty range and also experienced growth. Increased interest in home decoration has led to a wider variety of colours and designs beyond the former white standard kitchen roll. Although the retailer own brands still dominate the market, the increased versatility and performance of new products is helping to create turbulence in a mature market (Carmichael, 1999).

Competitor strategies

The competitive structure in different product markets will vary to create conditions of strong or weak competition. In markets such as computer chips, the dominant competitor has a major influence over the level and nature of competition. Challenges can still arise, but nevertheless, within constraints set by governmental competition policy and public pressure, a dominant competitor is effectively able to decide when and how to compete. The dominant competitor is likely to be confident that it has sufficient strength through its market position, volume sales, and thus perhaps through its cost base to fight any serious challenger successfully.

> **Example** Computer chip manufacturer Intel dominates its markets through size and speed. It dominates world manufacturing capacity and has geared up its R&D to shorten the development time for new generations of chips. Through its dominant strength, Intel has developed a strong capacity in motherboards and chip sets for PCs, regardless of the individual brand name of the final computer sold. This has created a situation that competitors find increasingly difficult to overcome.

Achieving such dominance provides a strong basis for competitive advantage as it makes building, sustaining and defending a market position relatively easier. The strategies that lead to this will be explored in the next section.

STRATEGIC MARKETING ANALYSIS

Strategic marketing planning makes use of a number of analytical models that help to develop a strategic view of the business, and thus can be used as decision-making aids. The various models outlined below can be applied either to SBUs or to individual products, and thus the use of the word 'product' throughout the discussion should be taken to mean either. The fundamental concept of many of these models is that although products may be managed as individual entities on an operational basis, strategically they should be viewed as a **product portfolio**, that is, a set of products, each of which makes a unique contribution to the corporate picture. The strategist needs to look at that corporate picture and decide whether, for example, there are enough strong products to support the weak ones, whether the weak ones have development potential or whether there are appropriate new products in development to take over from declining ones. The product portfolio at corporate and product range level can be clearly identified in the Nestlé vignette (at page 843).

Managing SBUs or a product portfolio means that management has to consider products *relative* to each other and ensure that each is fulfilling its allotted strategic role and that the overall balance is right. Management might decide, for example, that the strategic role of a mature product is to generate revenues to provide the stability and investment needed for a risky new product. The new product's role, on the other hand, might be to become sufficiently well established within the next three years to take over from the mature product as it declines.

Product portfolio analysis: the Boston Box

Sometimes referred to as the **Boston Box**, or the BCG matrix, the Boston Consulting Group (BCG) market growth–relative market share model, shown in Fig. 20.3, assesses products on two dimensions. The first dimension looks at the general level of growth in the product's market, while the second measures the product's market share relative to the largest competitor in the industry. This type of analysis provides a useful insight into the likely opportunities and problems associated with a particular product.

Feeding the world

Nestlé is the world's largest food company, with 522 factories, 230 000 employees and sales in excess of CHF71 000mn. The company plans globally by product groups, within each of which is a portfolio of brands. Nestlé's challenge is to manage the portfolio of activity at product group level while allowing individual regions or countries to operate at a devolved divisional level. There are specific brands dedicated to national or regional markets, although this is tending to consolidate towards fewer, more global brands (Rosier, 1999). It is still largely a food and drink company with plans to dominate globally in such sectors such as coffee, water, pet foods and ice cream. This priority influences many aspects of strategic marketing planning between the headquarters in Switzerland and the respective divisions around the world.

Nestlé does not just focus on growth for existing brands and product groups. It is very active in acquiring and divesting brands to ensure a close and sensible fit within the overall brand portfolio. The strategy is to build strength in long-term priority areas and to divest in areas with limited potential and strategic fit. In 1998, a number of key product categories benefited from acquisition. Nestlé acquired the San Pellegrino brand, to fit with its other international mineral water brands, Klim milk powder, which is especially strong in Colombia and Taiwan, and Cremora, a coffee whitener popular in Africa and the Middle East. Whole companies are also acquired. Again in 1998, the purchase of Spillers enabled Nestlé to become the number two producer in the European pet food market and enabled a good fit with the existing Friskies brands, in terms of distribution coverage and product range. In earlier times, the acquisitions of Maggi, Carnation and Perrier had a major effect on the portfolio balance.

Despite the acquisitions, a number of marginal brands were also sold, including the canned tomato brand Contadina, Libby's Meats and Locatelli cheeses in Italy. The overall net expenditure on acquisitions and divestments was CHF4047mn in 1998. The frozen food business with the Findus brand is also to be sold off so that Nestlé can concentrate on high value added products such as pizzas and prepared dishes that are in a rapidly growing market. The portfolio has to be managed closely to achieve a target real internal growth of 4 per cent, compared with the 3.2 per cent achieved in 1997 and 3.3 per cent in 1998.

Two of these product groups will now be briefly considered in turn to demonstrate the issues of portfolio management at both company and brand levels.

Beverages

This division contains the world's leading coffee brand, Nescafé, which generates significant cash for the business. Launched in 1938, the brand has grown to market leadership and claims that over 3000 cups are drunk per second. Nestlé also has world leadership in chocolate and malt-based drinks such as Nesquik, Milo and Nescau. Other products in the group include roasted coffee, teas, fruit juices and cereal drinks.

In order to retain the lead position for Nescafé, Nestlé still supports the brand with marketing and new product variants. In 1998, the priority was to innovate with new speciality tastes and to improve the distribution channels for corporate sales. In this group, the strategic attention tends to be on global development rather than focusing on individual countries. Within the product portfolio new products are also introduced or new markets attacked on a rolling launch basis to safeguard the longer-term viability of the portfolio. in 1998, ready-to-drink Nescafé in a can was launched in Thailand and liquid concentrate for iced coffee was introduced to Japan.

The mineral water division is a significant growth market for Nestlé. Formed by the acquisition of Perrier in 1992, it now has the strong brands of Perrier, Vittel and Contrex to enable a strong competitive position to be realised. Investment is still taking place in this product group. San Pellegrino, the leading Italian water brand, was purchased in 1998 and marketing efforts are being intensified in the emerging markets in China, parts of south-east Asia, Pakistan, Brazil and Mexico. Investment is also needed to support the growth markets and to improve efficiency in European markets, such as with the Perrier plant in France.

Within this product group, sales in 1998 amounted to CHF19.8mn with trading profit at 16 per cent.

Chocolate and confectionery

Nestlé is also a world leader in chocolate and confectionery, with such international brands as Kit-Kat, Smarties, Lion and After Eight. Other brands such as Femina and Babe Ruth are specific to certain geographic regions. Acquisition has been used in the past, most notably in the UK with the purchase of Rowntree. Both sales and profit have been under pressure in this group. New product development has been active, however, with the launch of a white chocolate After Eight in Germany and new Smarties concepts such as Smarties eggs and mini Smarties. Sales were especially badly hit in eastern Europe, but that did not stop Nestlé acquiring Perm and Barnaul.

Within this product group, sales in 1998 amounted to CHF10.5mn with trading profit at 9.3 per cent.

Continued

Other product groups include ice cream and dairy products, prepared foods and cooking aids, and pharmaceuticals. With all these distinct product areas, Nestlé must plan its portfolio. The organisational structure is still primarily national rather than regional and this has had an effect on the slower development of worldwide marketing, in advertising and brand development. In the UK market it has been suggested that its image is poorer than many other areas and consumers are not aware of the extent of Nestlé brand ownership (Tungate, 1999). However, with such a large portfolio covering over 70 countries, it is a challenge to achieve any type of focused image. The recent wave of acquisitions and divestments is not only being resourced by the more successful brands in each product area, but also by targeted investment across the portfolio to enable more resource intensive options to be pursued. This may in time result in less discretion for national divisions in strategic marketing decision making.

Source: Rosier (1999); Tungate (1999); http://www.nestle.com.

Market growth reflects opportunities and buoyancy in different markets. It also indicates the likely competitive atmosphere, because in high growth markets there is plenty of room for expansion and all players can make gains, while in low growth markets competition will be more intense, since growth can only be achieved by taking share away from the competition. The model assumes a range of between zero (or decline) and 25 per cent growth (or more, if relevant to a particular industry). Some fine tuning is possible to reflect market circumstances.

Market share position is measured on a logarithmic scale against the product's largest competitor. Thus a relative share figure of 0.2 means that the product only achieves 20 per cent of the market leader's sales volume, a potentially weak competitive position. Similarly, a share figure of 2 would mean that the product has twice the market share of its nearest rival. A share figure of 1 means roughly equal shares, and therefore joint leadership.

Figure 20.3(a) gives an example of the resultant matrix after all the products of an organisation have been thus analysed. The next stage is to plot the products within a simpler four-cell matrix that reflects the differing competitive positions, as shown in Fig. 20.3(b). Each cell offers different types of business opportunities and imposes different resource demands. The general labelling of the cells as 'high' and 'low' gives an instant and sufficient feel for each product's situation, and the circle that represents each SBU's contribution to the organisation's total sales volume provides a further indication of the relative importance of different products. In Fig. 20.3(b), for example, Product 2 can be seen to be the biggest contributor to overall sales volume, whereas Product 1 contributes very little.

FIGURE 20.3

BCG matrix

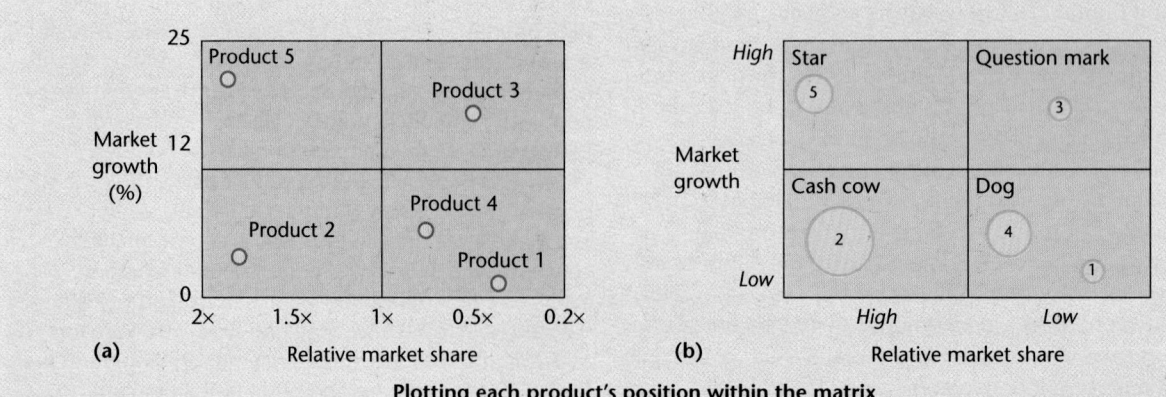

(a)

(b)

Plotting each product's position within the matrix

This model provides a guide to the most appropriate corporate investment and divestment options. The 'ideal' model is one where the portfolio is reasonably balanced between existing strength and emerging opportunity. The great advantage of the model is that it forces managers to reflect on current and projected performance, and to ask important questions about the continued viability of products, their strategic role and the potential for performance improvement.

We now look in turn at each cell of the matrix.

Dog (low share, low growth)

A dog holds a weak market share in a low growth market, and is likely to be making a loss, or a low profit at best. It is unlikely that its share can be increased at a reasonable cost, because of the low market growth. A dog can be a drain on management time and resources.

> **Example** Liptonice, a cold, fizzy, canned lemon tea, and other products like it had proved to be successful in continental Europe and its owners were confident that it could succeed in the UK market too. What they had not taken into account, however, was the nature of the British consumer's love affair with tea and the perception of it among younger consumers. In the British mind, tea should be drunk hot and milky – even drinking it hot and black with lemon is considered a bit risqué. The ritual of making tea 'properly' is also deeply culturally ingrained. Add to that the young person's view that tea is for grannies, and the prospects for canned, cold, fizzy lemon tea start to look less promising. A £6mn product launch and later a £4mn relaunch failed between them to achieve the product's target of £20mn sales per year and the product quietly disappeared from UK stores. Do you think this a dog that was shot?

The question, therefore, is whether or not to shoot the dog, that is, withdraw the product. Much depends on the strategic role that the dog is fulfilling and its future prospects. It may, for example, be blocking a competitor (a guard dog?), or it may be complementing the company's own activities, for example creating customers at the bottom of the range who will then trade up to one of the organisation's better products (a guide dog, or a sheep dog?). Otherwise, a dog may be worth retaining if management feels that there will be an upturn in the market soon. It may also be possible to retain the product with less marketing support (which might improve the profits, but is unlikely to help its market share), or to reposition it into a narrower segment where it is more highly valued.

> **Example** After a rapid rise in the UK associated with the success of the National Lottery launch, the market for lottery tickets and scratchcards has become more mature, making some 'products' vulnerable. Pools operator Vernons decided to terminate its 'Easy Play' National Lottery-based football game within a year of its launch, despite an alliance with Camelot, the company holding the National Lottery franchise. Launched in August 1998 to coincide with the new soccer season, Easy Play's weekly revenue quickly dropped from £1.5mn to just £250 000. Vernons committed £12mn to the promotion of Easy Play with a door-to-door mailing drop and a television and press advertising campaign. The idea of the game was that each player was allocated a random selection of 11 matches from 49 and prizes were offered for any player achieving more than 5 'score draws' in their 11 matches. Unlike the football pools format, however, more drawn matches meant more winners and thus smaller prizes. The failure of the game was attributed to poor coverage of winning numbers in the press; existing pools players failed to be inspired by a game requiring no skill; and unlike the National Lottery, Easy Play failed to attract a significant number of women (Bell, 1999b).

Question mark (low share, high growth)

The high market growth of a question mark is good news, but the low share is worrying. Why is relative market share so low? What is the organisation doing wrong, or what is the competition doing right? It may simply be that the question mark (also sometimes called a problem child or a wild cat) is a relatively new product that is still in the process of establishing its position in the market. If it is not a new product, then it might just need far more investment in plant, equipment and marketing to keep up with the market growth rate. There is also a risk, however, that a question mark with problems might absorb a great deal of cash just to retain its position.

> **Example** The challenge for Sega (http;//www.sega.com) in the launch of its Dreamcast computer games console is to move the new product quickly from question mark status to being a star product in the portfolio. It is fails, some pundits believe it will mean the end of Sega's presence in the console market. The console itself offers unique features compared with the market leader, Sony (http://www.sony.com), and follower, Nintendo (http://www.nintendo.com). These include a built-in modem to enable free Internet access, e-mail and on-line gaming across Europe, along with 128 bit capacity. However, it could be a tough challenge to capture the planned 50 per cent share of the global console market, given Sony's domination with nearly 70 per cent share in 1998 and Nintendo's 27 per cent. Success in this market is not just about up-to-date hardware, but also hinges on the range of associated software. If software developers do not support the product platform with new and exciting games, the console could be in difficulties as early as its launch. The Dreamcast product is being offered at around £200 compared with around £100 for Sony and Nintendo consoles. With that kind of price premium, even a £60mn pan-European marketing drive and a launch into a growth market that nearly quadrupled between 1996 and 1999 may not be sufficient to guarantee success (Campbell, 1999b; Littlewood, 1999).

Some of the alternatives for question marks, such as dropping or repositioning, are the same as for the dogs, but there are some more creative options. If the product is felt to have potential, then management might commit significant investment towards building market share, as mentioned above. Alternatively, if the organisation is cash rich, it might seek to take over competitors to strengthen its market position, effectively buying market share.

Star (high share, high growth)

A star product is a market leader in a growth market. It needs a great deal of cash to retain its position, to support further growth and to maintain its lead. It does, however, also generate cash, because of its strength, and so it is likely to be self-sufficient. Stars could be the cash cows of the future.

> **Example** Following on from the previous example, the market leader in consoles, Sony, is in a very strong position despite the challengers. In 1998, it sold 50 million PlayStations worldwide and can offer a comprehensive range of software. Its success was due to technological innovation, strong marketing and clever market development in moving the console from being a bedroom toy for kids to being a mainstream home entertainment system. Whereas the average age for use was 12 in the early 1990s, it is now around 17 years old. Sony still invests heavily in the product. In 1998, it spent over £3.7mn on advertising computer entertainment compared with Nintendo's £1.7mn and Sega's spend of just £60 000. New product development has also been a high priority and a new model is planned for 2000 that is compatible with existing software, can take DVD, and is claimed to be faster than Dreamcast (Littlewood, 1999).

Cash cow (high share, low growth)

As market growth starts to tail off, stars can become cash cows. These products no longer need the same level of support as before since there are no new customers to be had, and there is less competitive pressure. Cash cows enjoy a dominant position generated from economies of scale, given their relative market share.

Example It could be argued that Heinz baked beans is a cash cow product. Certainly, without the baked beans sector it is the clear market leader and, although threatened to a certain extent by supermarket own brands, it retains cow status and it could be argued that the market is low growth as it is mature and fairly stable. This analysis does depend, however, on a narrow definition of 'the market'. If the market was defined as 'canned foods', then perhaps Heinz would be defining its SBUs differently, possibly looking at the whole beans-based range (including beans with sausages etc.) rather than just the plain baked bean product. Would the beans SBU still be a cash cow?

The management focus here is on retention and maintenance, rather than on seeking growth. Management might be looking to keep price leadership, and any investment will be geared towards lowering costs rather than increasing volumes. Any excess cash can be diverted to new areas needing support, perhaps helping to develop dogs and question marks into stars.

Two further categories were proposed by Barksdale and Harris (1982):

War horses (high share, negative growth)

War horses are market leaders, but their cash generating position is under threat because of negative market growth. Management options depend on whether the decline is terminal or temporary. If it is terminal, then the strategy should be to harvest for as long as possible, offering minimal marketing support, as most volume comes from repeat sales based on loyalty. Any investment, whether in promotion or plant, should look for a swift payback. If the decline is temporary, it is probably worth riding the storm, maintaining support to enable cash generation to continue.

Dodos (low share, negative growth)

As the name implies, the dodo product is almost certain to become extinct, as low share of a declining market means that sales volumes are dwindling away. Management needs to undertake regular reviews of returns generated, adopting a contribution-based approach to such a product. As soon as the product's contribution becomes negative, it is a candidate for early termination.

Once the BCG matrix has been developed for an organisation, it can be used to assess the strength of the company and its product portfolio. Ideally, a strong mix of cash cows and stars is desirable, although there may be embryonic stars among the dogs and question marks. The situation and the portfolio become unbalanced where there are too many dogs and question marks and not enough cash cows to fund new developments to allow them to break out of those cells. There is also a risk dimension to all this. The organisation as a whole is vulnerable if there are too many products with an uncertain future (question marks).

Four main assumptions underpin the BCG model:

1 gains in market share are made by investing in a competitive package, especially through marketing investment;
2 market share gains have the potential to generate cash surpluses as a result of economies of scale and the learning curve;
3 cash surpluses are more likely to be generated when products are in the maturity stage of the life-cycle;
4 the best opportunities to build a strong position occur during a market's growth period.

MARKETING IN ACTION   Philips manages its portfolio

Philips operates in a number of markets that require considerable R&D if the company is going to remain competitive. In 1998, Philips' R&D spend was 6.7 per cent of sales and over 1300 patents were registered. It is active in 80 businesses and claims world leadership in digital technologies for television and displays, wireless communication, lighting, speech recognition, storage and optical products. The scale of activity is impressive. It produces 2.4 billion incandescent lamps every year and 30 million picture tubes. One in seven of the world's televisions contain a Philips picture tube and 60 per cent of all telephones have Philips components. In lighting, 30 per cent of all offices around the world are lit by Philips, as are 55 per cent of all soccer stadia.

Such volumes make Philips a world leader in a number of sectors. In lighting, shavers (Philishave), colour picture tubes, one-chip TV circuits and PC video cameras it is number one. In Europe it is number two for steam irons, medical diagnostic imaging equipment and consumer electronics such as video and audio equipment. All this requires Philips to manage its product portfolio at divisional level to maximise the cash available to support investment as well as achieving growth targets. Since 1994, overall growth has been in excess of 10 per cent per annum, but this has varied markedly between divisions. The overriding strategy has been to build a high volume electronics business, but to retain or build market share only in selective consumer and business markets. Philips is not a niche operator and has to think about its portfolio in global terms to achieve the necessary volumes.

Philips has eight divisions:

- Domestic appliances and personal care
- Components
- Medical systems
- Consumer electronics
- Semiconductors
- Lighting
- Business electronics
- Origins (IT).

The Lighting division is critical to the portfolio as it generates the cash needed by other areas. Growth was only around 2 per cent in 1999, in line with the market, but over 24 per cent return on net assets was achieved. Even in a relatively mature market, Philips cannot afford to be complacent. Recent innovations have included Halogena, a light with a two-year guarantee with a whiter light than standard incandescent lamps and that lasts three times longer, while Ecotone Ambience is the first energy-saving lamp for Europe that offers a soft light and the shape of a normal light bulb. Improving margins through operational efficiency is a priority in this area.

The consumer electronics division is cash hungry to support new technological formats and products. With the convergence of audio, video, communication and IT technologies (see, for example, the Linn vignette on p. 836, digital networks producing and recording images and the growth in video conferencing, Philips has to invest in R&D to achieve its 6 per cent growth in sales. It is at the forefront with Star products in a 4.5in deep 42in flat television screen, a recordable CD, DVD players and mobile computing. Not all of these products will offer formats that will become the industry norm, so Philips has to plan for some failure within the new technologies. Price competition can be intense if no product distinctiveness is offered and margins have been depressed in the division.

The semiconductor division is a tough area for Philips. It is only eighth in the world and specialises mainly in customers in the audio, video and communication systems businesses. Some areas do return a high market share, such as specialist chips for one-chip TV integrated circuits, but overall, the economic downturn in the Far East in the late 1990s created over-capacity and heavy price discounting. Even in this division there is a need to invest in new products to exploit opportunities in chips for videophones, interactive digital television and multimedia computers. In 1999 sales dropped by 6 per cent in this division and profits continued to fall.

The medical division also needs investment to keep abreast and ahead of technological change, so the cash generated particularly from lighting has to service many other divisional developments when cash is scarce. Focus on areas of strength and compatibility is essential and thus Philips has also been divesting areas in which it cannot find the investment needed to grow. In 1998, the Polygram music business was sold along with Philips Car systems and over 20 other businesses.

Source: Millar (1999); http://www.philips.com.

Abell and Hammond (1979), however, identified a number of weaknesses in the BCG model and its assumptions, for instance that cash flow and cash richness are influenced by far more than market share and industry growth, and that return on investment (ROI) is a more widely used yardstick of investment attractiveness than cash flow.

Although it is conceptually neat, the BCG matrix does not adequately assess alternative investment opportunities when there is competition for funds, as for example when it is necessary to decide whether it is better to support a star or a question mark.

Market attractiveness model: the GE matrix

Developed first by General Electric (GE), the market attractiveness–business position portfolio assessment model was designed to overcome some of the problems of models such as the BCG matrix.

The **GE matrix** adds more variables to aid investment decision appraisal. It uses two principal dimensions, as seen in Fig. 20.4: *industry attractiveness* (the vertical axis) and *business strengths* (the horizontal axis). Within the matrix, the circle size represents the size of the market and the shaded part the share of the market held by the SBU.

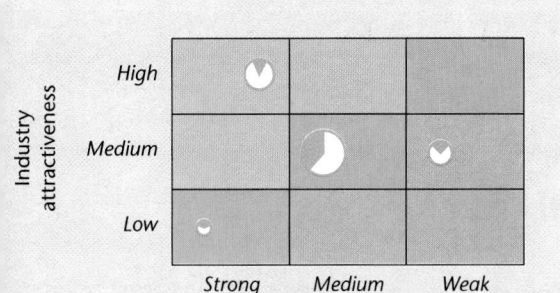

The first dimension, industry attractiveness, is a composite index determined by market size, rate of growth, degree of competition, pace of technological change, new legislation and profit margins achieved, among others. The second dimension, business position, is another composite index, comprising a range of factors that help to build stronger relative market share, such as relative product quality and performance, brand image, distribution strength, price competition, loyalty, production efficiency etc. Both dimensions need to work positively together, since there is little point in having a strong position in an unattractive market, or a weak position in strong market.

Within the matrix, there are three zones, each implying a different marketing and management strategy:

1 *zone 1 (high attractiveness, strong position)*. The strategy here should be investment for further growth;
2 *zone 2 (medium attractiveness)*. Because there is a weakness on one dimension, the strategy here should be one of selective investment, without over-committing; and
3 *zone 3 (least attractive)*. Either make short-term gains or proceed to pull out.

The main areas of concern with this model are linked to methodology and the lack of clear guidelines for implementing strategies.

> **Example** ECCI, English China Clay International (http://www.ecci.co.uk), was purchased by Imetal (http://www.imetal.fr) in 1999, bringing to an end a period of reformulation and restructuring to establish a strong position in attractive and core markets. Imetal, with its headquarters in France, is a world leader in minerals and metal processing and ECCI represented an ideal acquisition for a company looking to grow the mineral side of its operations as part of its strategy.
>
> ECCI, from its origins in the nineteenth century, became a major international player in industrial minerals and white pigments, especially kaolin and calcium carbonates along with speciality chemicals. These are widely used in the paper, board, plastics and paints industries. ECCI is the world leader in speciality minerals, supplying 7 million tonnes across five continents. Sales immediately before the takeover were $1.2bn. The success of the company was achieved by a programme of divestment and investment during the 1990s. Early in the 1990s, ECCI found that funds were too limited to build world-class businesses in areas of strength, so those activities offering relatively poor potential or which did not fit well with the core business were divested. The building materials division, for example, worth about £350mn and the second largest operation in the group, was sold (Lorenz, 1995). The funds

released enabled ECCI to build in the more attractive areas of industrial and speciality chemicals, which were considered to be higher value added but required considerable R&D to keep pace with user industry needs. Investment was also needed to fund expansion in the competitive US market.

The process of divestment is still not complete as Imetal now considers rationalising the portfolio further. In 1999 after the takeover, it sold off the speciality chemicals division for $425mn, despite its having been purchased by ECCI as recently as 1993. This was part of a further phase of realignment to build strength in the more attractive speciality minerals sector.

English China Clays sets sail towards the next century with a streamlined portfolio of SBUs.

Source: English China Clay International.

Example In 1998, Philips (http://www.philips.com) decided to sell Polygram to Seagram's music label. After a strategic review, Philips decided that Polygram did not fit strategically with the rest of its portfolio (see the Marketing in Action vignette on p. 848), despite its being a successful part of the company. The music industry has characteristics that are very different from Philips' main electrical operations area, so there was little scope for synergy in marketing or product development etc. To Seagram, however, a leading operator in the music business, the acquisition for $10.4bn was considered a bargain because of its compatibility with existing distribution channels and the value chain. In the first year, Seagram had to restructure at a cost of $405mn, causing first-quarter losses, but it was expected that the situation would be reversed as the restructuring benefits were realised. Philips, meanwhile, was then free to focus on areas in which competencies were strong and could build or maintain leadership (Rubythorn, 1999).

Shell's directional policy matrix

Shown in Fig. 20.5, the **Shell directional policy matrix** has two dimensions, competitive capabilities and prospects for sector profitability. The nine cells of the matrix offer different opportunities and challenges, so that placing each product in an appropriate cell provides a guide to its strategic development.

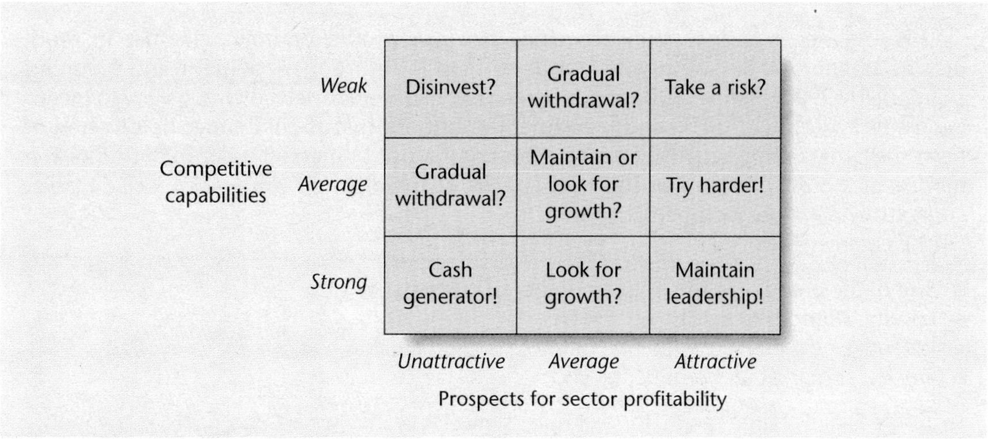

	Weak	Disinvest?	Gradual withdrawal?	Take a risk?
Competitive capabilities	Average	Gradual withdrawal?	Maintain or look for growth?	Try harder!
	Strong	Cash generator!	Look for growth?	Maintain leadership!
		Unattractive	Average	Attractive

Prospects for sector profitability

FIGURE 20.5

Shell matrix

Review of models

Portfolio models have been criticised, but they have, nevertheless, been useful in forcing managers, especially in large complex organisations, to think more strategically. They can certainly be used as diagnostic tools to give an overview of the current position and to stimulate debate on what could happen if direction is not changed. These models do not, however, give solutions about what strategies should be adopted, and they need to be supported by clear action plans. The main problem with them is the rather simplistic use of variables that contributes to the axes and the decision rules sought from the models. The preoccupation with market share is of particular concern, since it might be just as valid to consolidate and perform better as to pursue high growth, high share business. The models also fail to consider the synergies between businesses, where one may support another.

In some situations, it might be more appropriate to focus on a small number of areas and perform really well in these than to over-extend in the pursuit of market share or market growth. In many markets, a set of businesses survive with little reference to market share as niche operators. They might, therefore, develop attractive returns without necessarily seeking market share for its own sake or incurring the costs and risks associated with the pursuit of relative sales volume. This is also true in situations where technological change and obsolescence can quickly erode any significant advantage gained.

Some methodological weaknesses emerge when the models are implemented in practice:

1 how to weight the variables for a composite index such as that which the GE model uses. Different managers could have different opinions about how to weight variables, leading to very different-looking matrices for the same organisation;
2 the guidelines used to distinguish zones or cells are open to some debate. Different rules may apply in different situations;
3 the measures used on each matrix also need careful examination. Often, the preoccupation with market share, SBUs and production suggests a bias away from the smaller business and the service business. In a small business, share may be of minimal importance compared with dependable niches. The service business has very different operational concerns from a manufacturing organisation, given the focus on service performers and facilities rather than production lines.

Although these models are commonly described in textbooks, they are not so widely used in practice. They are conceptually easy to design, but very difficult to implement effectively. They require considerable management skill and judgement, because of their focus on the identification of variables, weighting decisions and future changes, rather than just on present, tangible, measurable factors.

Unilever (http://www.unilever.com), in a review of its portfolio, classified its products as category A or category B brands to help in future management and planning (Campbell, 1999c). Some 1800 brands in the portfolio were reviewed with a view to identifying those worthy of marketing investment and those that should either be divested or have their marketing activity reduced. The criteria used reflected a combination of the models previously discussed in this chapter, but adapted to suit Unilever's specific market contexts with a more judgmental approach.

The criteria were:

- Size of the brand: volume, value, number of customers
- Loyalty: strength of loyalty
- Potential: new market segments, brand extension etc.
- Trends: at market and product levels.

From the Elida Fabergé range, for example, typical A brands were Dove, Lynx and Impulse, while brands in the B category included Pears Shampoo, Timotei and Brut. For the B brands in any organisation, the main difficulty is likely to be gaining management support for the divestment of products that may have a long history or affectionate following within the company.

Overall then, although portfolio models can be useful planning tools, company-specific and pragmatic approaches used by organisations such as Unilever could be more appropriate. Where they are used at all, there is often a tendency to use them as diagnostic tools rather than as predictive tools. Their real advantage is their focus on corporate objectives, and the contribution that marketing decision making makes to that process. Above all, however, it must be remembered that they are tools to assist decision making, not a series of rules that lead to inevitable conclusions and decisions.

GROWTH STRATEGIES FOR MARKETING

The previous section looked at the corporate perspective on strategic planning, presenting a number of models that can guide marketing strategy development. This section examines a number of different strategies that organisations might adopt if their priority is *growth*. It is important to remember, however, that growth is not always a priority. In many small firms, for example, survival or sustaining the *status quo* might be the main objective. In other situations, standing still might be the right strategy if the market is starting to tighten up. The preoccupation with growth, therefore, should not be assumed to be relevant to all organisations all the time.

Managing growth is not without problems, because of the demands it imposes on management time and resources, and not least because of the additional risks created. For those who are facing growth opportunities, and who have the capabilities to exploit them, a number of options are available. The product–market matrix proposed by Ansoff (1957) provides a useful framework for considering the relationship between strategic direction and marketing strategy. The four cell matrix shown in Fig. 20.6 considers various combinations of product–market options. Each cell in the **Ansoff matrix** presents distinct opportunities, threats, resource requirements, returns and risks, and will be discussed in the next two subsections.

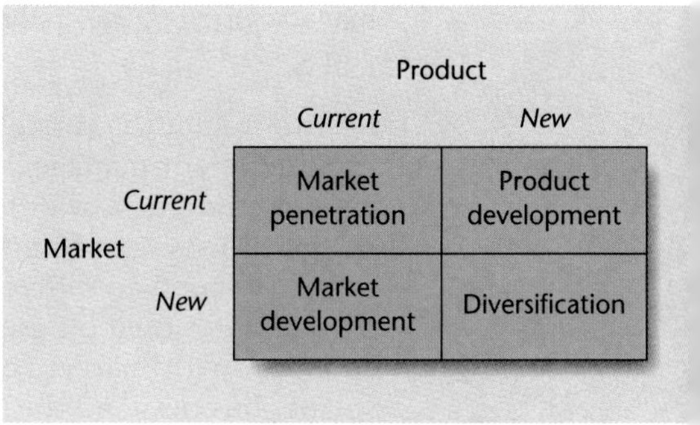

FIGURE 20.6

Ansoff's growth matrix

Source: Ansoff (1957).

Intensive growth

Three cells of the Ansoff matrix offer opportunity for sustained growth, although each one has different potential according to the market situation.

Market penetration

The aim of **market penetration** is to increase sales volume in current markets, usually by more aggressive marketing. This means using the full range of the marketing mix to achieve greater leverage.

Example Ericsson (http://www.ericsson.com) wanted to increase its share of the rapidly growing mobile phone market in the UK and thus decided to strengthen its relationship with independent retailers. The new deal developed meant that the retailers would use the Ericsson illuminated shop-front signs alongside their own identification. In addition, a branded zone was set up within stores to display Ericsson products, although retailers were also free to stock competing brands such as Nokia and Motorola. Other retailer support strategies had already been introduced as part of the deal, including shop assistant/dealer training programmes and a dealer loyalty programme, Partner Net. The overall market in the UK is very competitive, with Ericsson in third place with a 25 per cent share behind Nokia and Motorola, so this initiative is just one of Ericsson's activities, including price promotions, user package bundling, media advertising and product development, to gain and retain share (Campbell, 1999a).

Market development

Market development means selling more of the existing product to new markets, which could be based on new geographic segments or could be created by opening up other new segments (based, for example, on age, product usage, lifestyle or any other segmentation variable). Danish firms control nearly half of the world's market for wind turbine machines. Companies such as Vestas Wind Systems and Nordtank Energy Systems depend heavily on achieving growth by developing new markets.

Example The prime objective of these companies is to grow by opening up new markets around the world. Vestas Wind Systems (http://www.vestas.com) is the world's leading manufacturer of wind turbines. The world market for wind turbine systems is expected to continue growing over the next ten years due to greater energy consumption, more environmental awareness and greater efficiency as technology continues to lower unit costs. From its origins in Scandinavia, Vestas now has a 23 per cent share of the world market, with just 19 per cent of its installed megawatts (MWs) in Scandinavia. Europe has been opened up, with especially strong sales in Germany (17.6 per cent) and Spain with 30 per cent of total sales. Further markets are also being developed, including the USA and China, both of which may offer excellent long-term potential for wind turbines.

Part of the market development strategy is to establish local production facilities through acquisition or direct investment. In addition to Denmark, factories exist in Germany, Spain and India and sales offices are also being opened to support the development of a market, as it may take some time to achieve regulatory approval and to negotiate with power providers. Despite the international coverage, the success of Vestas has been built on the platform of product development, occupying 9 per cent of the workforce, quality, pre- and post-sales service, efficient production and competitive pricing. Although still primarily a wind turbine producer, Vestas' sales had grown from DK1510mn to DK2830mn by 1998 and the order book stood at a record eight months.

Wind power at work.
Source: John Beaumont-Kerridge

Product development

Product development, as covered in Chapter 9, means selling completely new or improved products into existing markets.

Example   St Ivel (http://www.st-ivel.co.uk), capitalising on the success of its Utterly Butterly Brand (see page 560), launched Utterly Cheddarly spreadable cheeses combining English cheddar, sour cream and butter in a crumbly or smooth variant. These new products, although with their own small marketing budget, could also benefit from the £6mn spend and favourable consumer reaction to the original Utterly Butterly range. However, with the cheese spread market in decline, to be successful the high quality spread will have to reverse a trend (*The Grocer*, 1999c).

At the other extreme, British Aerospace Regional Aircraft (BARA) has been working on a RJX series of regional aircraft building on its success with the BAe 146 and RJ series. Although the growing market makes it highly competitive, it is essential for manufacturers such as BARA to develop new planes even to keep up with the competition, let alone beat them. Bombardier of Canada, Embraer of Brazil, Fairchild-Dornier and Boeing are all also planning planes around the 100-seat class (Donne, 1999).

Diversified and integrative growth

Growth through **diversification** takes place outside the value chain, for example developing new products and new markets, whereas growth through integration takes place within the chain, for example making components yourself rather than buying them in.

Example   Specialist Computer Holdings (SCH) achieved very rapid growth in its computer sales and service group by moving into mail order computer sales and through the Byte chain of computer stores. This integrative growth was partly organic and partly through acquisition. By developing in unfamiliar but related technology areas (diversification growth), it was able to increase its turnover rapidly.

Both diversification and integration might involve radical new departures into unknown technical, managerial or marketing areas.

The BAe 146: flying high across Europe.

Source: British Aerospace.

Growth through diversification

Diversification, the final cell in the Ansoff Matrix, happens when an organisation decides to move beyond its current boundaries to exploit new opportunities. It means entering unfamiliar territory in both product and market terms. One of the main attractions of this option is that it spreads risk, moving the organisation away from being too reliant on one product or one market. It also allows expertise and resources to be allocated synergistically, for example theme parks diversifying into hotel accommodation, or airlines diversifying into tour packages. Calori and Harvatopoulos (1988), in a study of diversification in France, found both offensive and defensive reasons for diversification, with outcomes such as a stronger financial position or greater synergy with existing operations. The danger is, of course, that the organisation spreads its effort too widely into areas of low expertise, and tries to position itself against more specialist providers.

There are two main types of growth through diversification:

Concentric diversification. Concentric diversification happens where there is a link, either technological or commercial, between the old and the new sets of activities. The benefit is, therefore, gained from a synergy with current activities. An organisation could, for example, add new, unrelated product lines to its portfolio, but still use the same sales and distribution network.

Example Mars (http://www.mars.com) decided to move into the UK processed organic market as one of the first major food manufacturers to venture into this new and growing sector. Although the market had been considered by other food manufacturers, there was some uncertainty as to how consumers and retailers would react to a sector that still could not boast large volumes and is certainly small by global food standards. In 1997, the sector was estimated to be worth just £260mn, but was thought to have the potential to reach £1bn by 2001 (The Soil Association). Heinz, Nestlé and Procter & Gamble, although involved in the sector, are not planning immediate activity in the UK, leaving Mars with an opportunity to exploit existing marketing and distribution strengths. The Seeds of Change range from Mars initially covered pasta sauces and dried pasta, but in the USA the range also includes soups, salsa and salad dressings and these are expected to be added to the UK range. The advertising campaign spend was planned at £1.5mn and the company was confident that by entering into the market early, with its existing strengths in retail distribution, the launch would be a success (*Marketing Week*, 1999; Wilkinson, 1999).

Conglomerate diversification. The conglomerate diversification route is taken when an organisation undertakes new activities in markets that are also new. This involves risks in both the product development area and gaining acceptance in the market place.

Example American Express decided to become a multi-product business, building on its image and experience with certain lifestyle segments gained through its credit cards. Not only was direct banking piloted in Germany, but consideration was also given to mobile phone services, travel products and private health care. The common thread for the diversification was the use of the Amex name.

Growth through integration

Meanwhile, integrative growth means staying within the same value chain but entering new roles or processes, either to ensure greater control of the overall process or to gain expansion. There are a number of options.

Backward integration. The focus in backward integration is on guaranteeing the quantity and quality of supply within acceptable cost guidelines. This could mean looking closely at raw materials, semi-processed materials, components or services supplied. A large manufacturer of vehicle refrigeration units in Ireland, for example, acquired the capacity to produce one of the components. This meant that these components were now made in-house, thus effectively terminating supply arrangements with some local small suppliers. Marks and Spencer, in contrast, does not seek formal ownership of its suppliers, but firmly controls their operations through tight specifications, prices, quantities and exclusivity agreements.

Backward integration might not be undertaken by choice. Suppliers may not be able to meet the buyer's specifications, or the buyers might want access to the supplier's technology to allow them to redesign and control the specification, for example.

Forward integration. Forward integration occurs where the organisation sets up or acquires dealers, distributors, wholesalers or retailers in order to control the distribution process in terms of physical supply, inventory, selling effort etc. This could also include controlling the major customers for your product.

> **Example** Cockerill Sambre (http://www.cockerillsambregroup.com), the major Belgium-based steel producer, has set up companies further down the distribution channel, primarily through acquisition, to process its products to meet specific applications, such as coatings and galvanising. In addition, it has established a dense network of steel service centres to cover a number of European markets. For example, Disteel in Belgium, Dikema & Chabot in the Netherlands and Scandinavia, the PMU Group, France's leading steel distributor, and in the UK ASK McGowan all provide the local technical expertise and ready machined stock close to users. These centres sell 4.5mn tonnes of steel per annum, of which 50 per cent comes from Cockerill's steel division, thus helping to retain overall competitive strength in main markets such as the automotive, packaging, agricultural and construction industries.

Horizontal integration. The objective of horizontal integration is to absorb competitors, to strengthen either market coverage or market position. This route might result in cost savings if, for example, product distribution overlap can be eliminated and a common distribution network used. Within the greeting card industry, for example, larger producers tend to acquire the more successful smaller operators who find it difficult to break out of confined niches as they lack the distribution and merchandising strengths to deal with the larger retailers. In other horizontal acquisitions, the partners may be complementary rather than direct competition.

> **Example** The merger of UBS and the Swiss Bank Corporation in 1998 created Europe's largest banker. By eliminating a major competitor, UBS thought it would be better placed to pursue a worldwide dominance in global asset management and investment banking. Although the merger did enable UBS to become the world's biggest bank for wealthy private customers, who generate half its profits, some analysts question whether size is important for growth in private banking. This contrasts with the investment banking sector in which there is evidence, especially from the USA, that larger firms are better able to increase margins and profits (Hall, 1999).

Each of the alternative growth strategies is summarised in Table 20.1. As has been seen in the Philips and Nestlé vignettes (p. 848 and 843), acquisition is still used as a growth strategy, but increasingly organisations are finding at a wide, diversified port-

TABLE 20.1
Alternative growth strategies

Intensive growth

- Market penetration
- Market development
- Product development

Diversified growth

- Concentric diversification
- Conglomerate diversification

Integrative growth

- Backward integration
- Forward integration
- Horizontal integration

folio might well spread risk, but does little to help achieve a dominant position in the market. Nestlé tended to acquire companies only in areas that were compatible with its aim of leadership in certain food and beverage sectors and divested where the fit was poor, such as the plans for the sale of Findus. Philips also divested where there was little synergy, such as with the Polygram music label.

United Biscuits (UB; http://www.ubs.com) and its McVitie's biscuits have been going through a similar process. After a period in the 1980s when diversification, both geographic and product based, was actively pursued, the focus is now on the core business, biscuit making. It found that moving into unrelated areas achieved only limited success, whereas its real strength lay in its familiarity with marketing and operations in biscuits and snacks. In order to remain competitive, and to regain the market share lost in its core business, UB decided to dispose of its frozen goods business. The cash released is being used to invest in new flavours and types of biscuits, such as low-fat, caramel-covered Homewheats and Jaffa Cakes in a tube (Urry, 1999).

Other 'no growth' options

Not all strategies have to be growth orientated. *Harvesting* is a deliberate strategy of not seeking growth, but looking for the best returns from the product, even if the action taken may actually speed up any decline or reinforce the no growth situation. The objective is, however, to make short-term profit while it is possible. Typically, products subjected to harvesting are likely to be cash cows in the mature stage of their life-cycles (*see* pp. 303 *et seq.*), in a market that is stable or declining, as considered at pp. 842 *et seq.* Harvesting strategies could involve minimal promotional expenditure, premium pricing strategies where possible, reducing product variability and controlling costs rigidly. Implementing such strategies helps to ensure that maximum returns are made over a short period, despite the potential loss of longer-term future sales. Effectively, the company is relying on the short-term loyalty of customers to cushion the effect of declining sales.

In more extreme cases, where prospects really are poor or bleak, *entrenchment* or *withdrawal* might be the only option. A timetable for withdrawal or closure would be developed and every effort made to maximise returns on the remaining output, in the full knowledge that harm will be done to sales volume in the short term. Some care should, however, be exercised when considering withdrawal, as highlighted in our discussion of dogs (*see* p. 845). Although the profit potential may be poor and the costs of turnaround prohibitive, the loss of a product in a range may affect other parts of the range adversely. Thus entrenchment, protecting the product's position as best you can without wasting too many resources on it, might be the most appropriate course of action.

Example In the example of managing Unilever's product portfolio (*see* p. 852), the category B brands were identified for early withdrawal or harvesting in order to free resources and shelf space to support the A brands with growth potential. Unilever did, however, exercise some caution in its approach to pruning. Care was taken not to sell off brands that could be used by an aggressive competitor to damage other Unilever brands. Pears, for example, had a 200-year heritage in the soap market, yet offered little potential to Unilever, but could offer an opportunity to another company prepared to invest in the brand heritage. EMVI successfully turned around a former Unilever product when it purchased the Harmony hair care range in 1998, capitalising on high brand awareness and an opportunity to modernise and internationalise the image. In short, one company's divestment may be another's opportunity for growth with creative marketing support (Campbell, 1999c).

Sometimes brands might be allowed to die slowly rather than be subjected to a firm decision to terminate.

MARKETING AND COMPETITIVE STRATEGY

No organisation operates in isolation. The organisation is not free to develop a business and marketing strategy without reference to the competitive environment. In recent years, the analysis and development of competitive strategy has become a major area of concern in many markets, reflecting the changing economic environment, and especially the internationalisation of trade. Competitors are an important factor that will influence the eventual success or failure of a business in any market. Ignore competition, and the likelihood of being taken by surprise or of being caught out by a strong new product or a major attack on a loyal customer base is very great and can create severe problems. That is why it is important to consider systematically a number of aspects of competitive behaviour.

Competitor analysis

Competitor analysis is a systematic attempt to identify and understand the key elements of a competitor's strategy, in terms of objectives, strategies, resource allocation and implementation through the marketing mix. A sound understanding of these areas enables stronger defences to be built and sustainable competitive advantage to be created and, not least, provides a foundation for outmanoeuvring the competition to gain share or market position.

At the macro level, Porter (1979) in his Five Forces Model defined the competitive forces that operate in an industry. They are:

- the bargaining power of suppliers
- the bargaining power of customers
- the threat of new entrants
- the threat of substitute products and services
- the rivalry among current competitors.

Porter's five forces form a useful starting point for undertaking a competitive analysis, in particular because they encourage a very wide definition of competition. Competition is not just about established, direct competitors at end-product level, but also about indirect and future competitors and about competition for suppliers. Before the development of the Channel Tunnel, the cross-channel ferry companies felt little need to compete aggressively with each other. Once the concept of the tunnel became a reality, however, they were shaken into action because of the perceived competitive threat.

The Porter model gives a sound foundation, but there are still several areas that should be analysed, if there is to be a full appreciation of competitors.

Competitor identification

As the Porter model implies, the identification of competitors is often broader than it first appears. The exercise should look at potential competitors, focus on the extent to which market needs are being satisfied and look at the needs that are emerging, as well as evaluating the activities and capabilities of the obvious competition. Latent or new competitors can take a market by surprise.

There are several types of competitors:

- *Similar specific* – same product, technology, and target market, for example Sega *vs* Nintendo
- *similar general* – same product area, but serving different segments, for example Häagen Dazs *vs* Wall's ice cream

■ *different specific* – same need satisfied by very different means, for example Eurostar *vs* British Airways between London and Paris

■ *different general* – competing for discretionary spend, for example a holiday *vs* a new car.

An organisation needs to decide with whom it is really competing, and from which category of competition the main threats are emerging. A market leader might base its marketing strategy on the overall stimulation of demand (i.e. tackle the *different general* competitors, on the basis that it will pick up the largest share of any new business created), while a minor player might be more concerned with taking share from *similar specific* competition.

Any organisation should take a wide view of who it is competing with. Small local shops discovered the hard way that they were competing with the supermarket multiples. The process can, however, work the other way round: it is possible for what appears to be a small niche operator to shake up a market. Häagen Dazs, for example, entered the UK by opening up a whole new 'adult indulgence' segment in the ice-cream market which grew so fast that it caused existing players to rethink their marketing strategies.

Competitive clusters

Once competitors are identified, it might be possible to group them into clusters, depending on their focus and strategy. Figure 20.7 shows how advertising agencies can be clustered.

The vertical axis in Fig. 20.7 covers a geographic spectrum. At one end are the purely local, typically small operators, perhaps based in a town or city. Then come regional agencies, for example based in Lyon or Leeds, that may have some national accounts. These are followed by national agencies that operate throughout the country, and are often based in the capital. European agencies handle European accounts, working through a network of offices in other capitals, while at the far end of the spectrum are the international agencies, operating from major world capitals. The horizontal axis covers the range of services, beginning with the specialists (handling for example only one task, such as media buying or one type of advertising, such as direct response). Limited service agencies handle mostly advertising work, but not research or wider aspects of marketing, while full range agencies offer most services

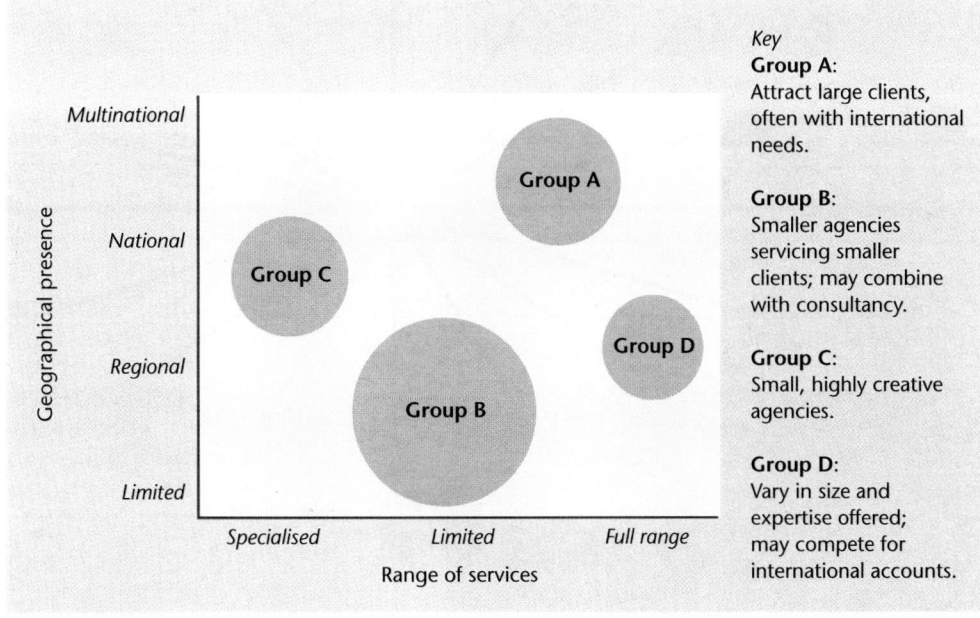

FIGURE 20.7

Strategic groupings: advertising agencies

directly or by affiliation. Finally, diversified agencies offer all marketing services on a 'one-stop shop' basis.

Once the clusters have been identified, the strong and weak competitors in each group can then be considered, and strategic opportunities defined. It is clearly easier to enter the market as a local, specialised or limited service agency than as a major international player, but subsequent evolution may be possible. It is important to remember, however, that there might still be competition between different clusters. A local agency could bid for a national contract, for example, but might find it difficult to convince a potential customer that they have the expertise, resources and track record.

There are a number of different characteristics that can be used for identifying strategic clusters, as shown in Fig. 20.8. This can provide a useful framework for identifying opportunities, but remember that in order to implement the technique, the organisation needs detailed competitor information, not just on financial performance but also on segments served and marketing strategies etc.

Competitive strengths and weaknesses

Examining a competitor's strengths and weaknesses provides a valuable insight into their strategic thinking and actions. A full range of areas should be examined, for example manufacturing, technical and financial strengths, relationships with suppliers and customers and markets and segments served, as well as the usual gamut of marketing activity. It is particularly worth undertaking a detailed review of the product range, identifying where volume, profits and cash come from, where the competitor is the market leader, where it is weak and where it seems to be heading.

Of course, the required information may not all be readily available. Shared customers or suppliers can be a useful source of information, but the organisation might also have to make use of secondary data, especially sales reports, exhibitions and press cuttings etc. The analysis of this information should be considered in the context of *critical success factors*. These are the factors or attributes that are essential if an organisation is to have any chance of success in a particular industry. Often, they evolve around technology, image, finance, service, quality, distribution, management

FIGURE 20.8

Characteristics that define strategic groups

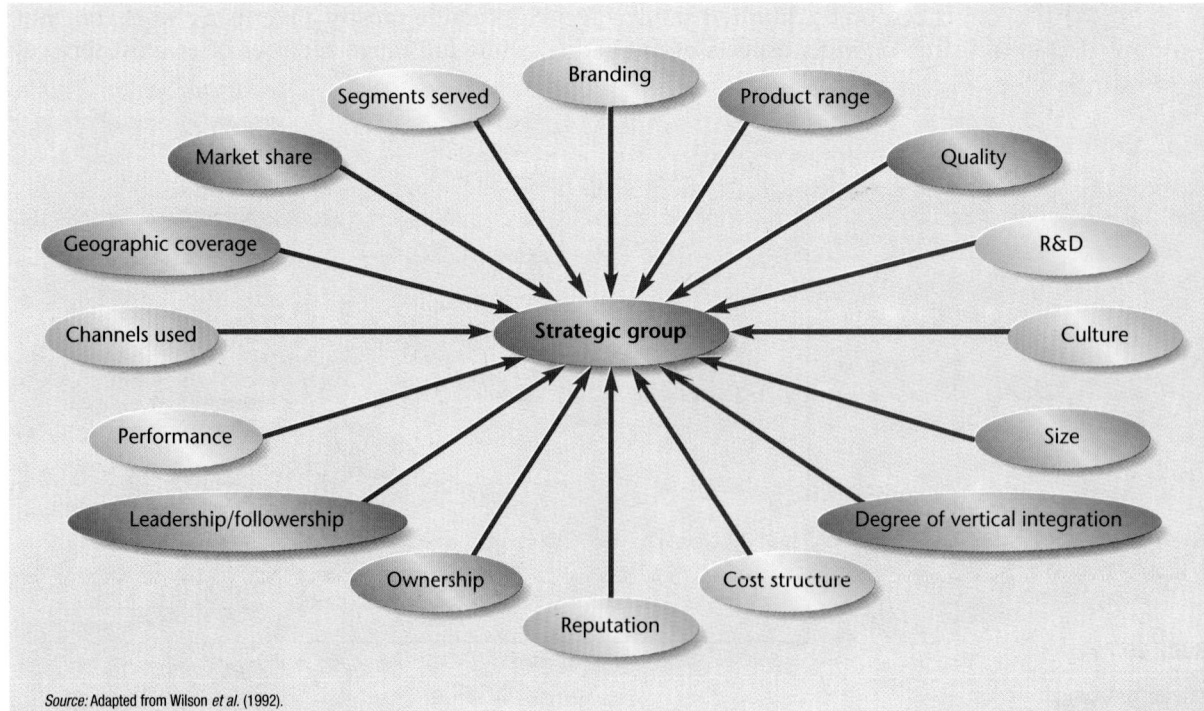

Source: Adapted from Wilson *et al.* (1992).

or the skills of the work-force. Each competitor can be rated on each factor to assess their strong and vulnerable points. This information can be used later to plan and launch an attack.

Example When the Central European countries emerged from their managed market regimes, a number of companies had to re-appraise their relative competitive strengths and weaknesses quickly in order to survive. Alpina (http://www.alpinasports.com), in Zirl, Slovenia, had built up an internationally known brand name with cross-country skiers and had already established an 25 per cent share of cross-country ski boots, making it number two in the world against Adidas-Salomon. The USA and Norway were the prime markets. However, it had also diversified into hiking boots and roller skates in the sports segment as well as exporting fashion shoes to the former Soviet Union. Half of the demand for sports and fashion shoes came from the former USSR, and much of this was lost after the political changes, making an assessment of alternative options a necessity.

The strategic re-appraisal indicated to Alpina that it needed to rationalise its product range, invest in technology and brand its shoes more heavily if it was to compete in new global markets. With a European market worth 1.3bn pairs of shoes annually, the 1.2 million pairs from Alpina may be insignificant. In the short term, Alpina went into low margin sub-contract work for other Western European producers. This provided cash flow and exposed it to alternative quality systems. It also realised, however, that this sector could not be the basis of long-term survival, with even lower labour costs being offered in Bosnia and the Italians starting to use very low-cost Albanian producers. It therefore sought out new fashion niches under the Simona brand name and found success in the German market where its below-average prices were attractive. Retail and production facilities also had to be upgraded before it felt confident that any competitive strength could be sustained (March, V., 1999).

Competitors' objectives and strategies

It is important to understand what drives competitors, what makes them act as they do. Most firms have multiple objectives beyond the simple notion of profit. Objectives could relate to cash generation, market share, technological leadership, quality recognition or a host of other things. Sometimes developing an understanding of a competitor's product portfolio provides a valuable insight into likely competitive objectives. Once you understand their objectives, you have strong clues about how their strategy is likely to unfold in terms of their positioning, marketing mix and vulnerable points for attack, or your best means of defence. Furthermore, if you can assess the relative importance of their objectives, you can go further in assessing their likely future plans and their reaction to market or competitive events. Competitive retaliation, for example, is likely to be more intense if the competitor has a strong vested interest in the market, such as profit contribution, growth, opportunities etc.

Example For the launch of Persil's innovative detergent tablets in 1998, it was essential for Lever to understand and be prepared to combat any retaliation from its main competitors, especially Procter & Gamble's (P&G) Ariel, Bold and Daz. It had been a failure to under-stand competitor thinking and reaction in 1994 that had resulted in a serious decline of Persil as a laundry products brand. Then the new version of Persil, Persil Power, contained a manganese accelerator to make a cleaner wash. The problem was that according to tests undertaken by P&G on the new product, some clothes were shredded by the brand's manganese module, so P&G insisted that the product be withdrawn or it would go to the press. Since Lever refused to back down, the subsequent negative publicity damaged Persil and the whole laundry detergent market as consumers switched away from concentrates, having been made aware of the risks and complexity. The withdrawal of Persil Power was followed by a price and advertising war as the market contracted and Persil's overall sales dropped by 20 per cent. Lever had perhaps underestimated the strength of reaction to what P&G considered a direct attack on its market position (Benady and Mitchell, 1998).

Competitive reaction

It is very important to be able to assess competitors' responses to general changes in the marketing environment and to moves in major battles within the market. These responses could range from matching a price cut or an increase in promotional spend, through to ignoring events or shifting the ground completely. An organisation can learn from experience how competitors are likely to behave. Some will always react swiftly and decisively to what is seen as a threat, others may be more selective depending on the perceived magnitude of the threat.

Example Following from the previous example, Lever had to plan its marketing strategy very carefully again when it launched the detergent tablet. P&G would be likely to retaliate if the tablets were successful and most manufacturers had the ability to produce their own version, so any lead could have been short lived. Doubts were expressed by some that the tablets would dissolve in the wash, while others regarded them as a gimmick that could make dosage decisions easier but added little to wash performance. However, the tablets proved to be a great success and helped restore Persil as the number one brand, with 23 per cent share compared with 21.5 per cent for P&G's Ariel brand. P&G was left with no alternative but to launch its own version in 1999 under the Ariel name, but chose to use different pack sizes to avoid direct comparison, although the price per tablet was considerably less than Persil's (Bell, 1999a).

It is not always easy to predict competitive reaction, as it is likely to be influenced by a range of factors, including cost structures, relative market positions and the stage reached in the industry or product life-cycle.

Competitive information system

The above discussion of competitor analysis demonstrates the need for a well-organised and comprehensive competitor information system. This would be part of the MIS discussed in Chapter 6. Often, data need to be deliberately sourced on an ongoing basis, collated, analysed, disseminated and discussed. Then, management at all levels can learn what is happening. They may dispute the findings or the data may provide a basis for seeking further insights. It is impossible to provide a complete checklist of areas that need to be considered, but Wilson *et al.* (1992) provide useful guidelines, as shown in Table 20.2.

Clearly, information is the key to outmanoeuvring and limiting the threats of competition, and should be gathered and analysed on both an individual competitor and competitive cluster basis.

TABLE 20.2
Useful information about competitors

- Sales
- Customers
- Products
- Advertising and promotion
- Distribution and sales force
- Pricing
- Finance
- Management
- Anything else ...

Source: Wilson *et al.* (1992).

Alternative competitive strategies

It has been argued that organisations should select a generic strategy that provides the direction for subsequent operational decisions, including marketing (Porter, 1980). Three **generic strategies** are proposed, as shown in Fig. 20.9. Each one imposes different pressures on the organisation to ensure that resources and capabilities are consistent with the requirements of the strategic alternative selected. The expectation is, however, that the vigorous pursuit of the chosen strategy will create a *sustainable competitive advantage*. The three alternatives are cost leadership, differentiation and focus. Each one is now considered in turn.

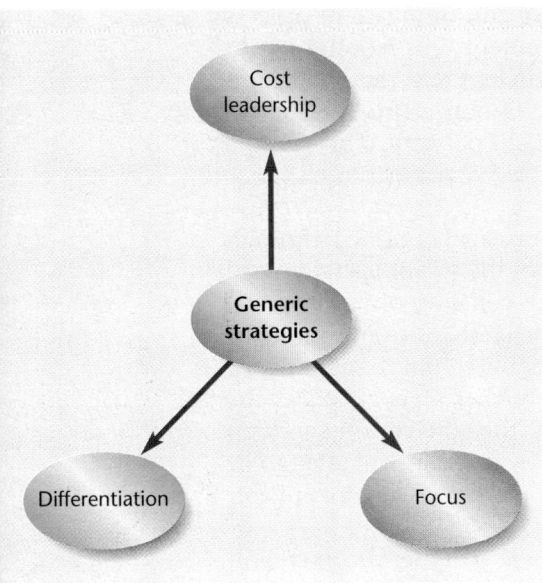

FIGURE 20.9

Generic strategies

Cost leadership

Through the strategy of cost leadership, the organisation seeks a cost advantage over its competitors. This might involve efficiency drives, tight cost controls or a preoccupation with low-cost production. It almost certainly means a ruthless attack on waste, in the drive to gain cost advantage. It might mean investment in production to achieve productivity gains, or it might mean investment in marketing to ensure that adequate sales volumes are achieved.

Example In the earlier example of Holderbank SA (*see* p. 839), the main element of its competitive strategy was to ensure consistent and appropriate quality and the lowest unit of cost. To achieve a cost leadership position there had to be careful plant location decisions and investment in production technology to ensure that it always kept one step ahead of the competition. Large volumes also required large orders, so contracts were pursued aggressively using a direct sales force.

In the above example, the low-cost position was designed not so much to cut prices as a market leader, but to maintain and build its market dominance. The problem with cost leadership is, however, that it tends to put undue emphasis on price. A cost leader can entertain a price war and, with a more efficient cost base, can contemplate winning. Cost leadership can also give a defensive cushion. A competitive supply market might, for example, encourage a powerful buyer to demand yet lower prices. The cost leader can deliver on those prices and perhaps still retain a small advantage. Such a focus on costs and price can also have the advantage of making it less attractive for new entrants to come into the market.

In short, the firm with cost leadership will feel the pinch last. There are two main sources of cost leadership, productivity and linkage effectiveness.

Productivity. There are a number of ways within a manufacturing environment to reduce and maintain low or lower average unit costs compared with the competition. *Economies of scale* suggest that as production volume increases, unit costs decrease. Plant and equipment might be more efficient or be able to cope with additional volume without a proportional increase in overheads and support services. A 20 per cent increase in production volume does not mean a 20 per cent increase in staffing, R&D or supplies management costs. The increased production gives more volume over which to spread fixed costs, thus lowering the average unit cost.

Such economies of scale may be linked with higher overall annual volumes, or an ability to better utilise capacity to the full over the course of the year if the overall capacity is fixed. Many service providers, including airlines and hotels, face problems in how to fill off-peak capacity. Often it is the ability to solve this problem that will determine overall success.

The *experience curve* is another means of building a low cost base. This concept suggests that as cumulative volume increases, so does experience in manufacture, which might mean less wastage or higher productivity, and thus have a beneficial influence on cost. In other words, the more you do something, the more proficient you become at it. That benefit will only be achieved, however, if management responds to the opportunity for cost reduction created. Thus as electronics companies become more experienced in the mass production of DVD players, their manufacturing efficiency should rise and costs decrease accordingly.

This means that through learning to produce, specialise and innovate in process design, improving the performance of production equipment and redesigning or standardising production, the operation becomes more efficient and the opportunities for cost reduction increase. The Boston Consulting Group estimated that as cumulative output doubles, average cost is reduced by 15–20 per cent. This favours those firms aggressively seeking market share gains, as they can further enhance their competitive position.

Of course, there are limits to how far cost efficiencies can be gained through economies of scale and learning. Economies of scale arise from the size of operation and volume produced compared with competitors. There may come a point where the economies of scale turn to diseconomies, as a result of unmanageable size and complexity. Learning curve effects arise from cumulative effects over time, regardless of operational scale. The benefits of learning might lead to further scale effects as the market position of the cost leader increases. In many ways, the efficient organisation will be chasing ever smaller gains in average unit costs. The biggest gains are often to be had during the launch and early stages of a new product, not during the maturity phase.

Linkage effectiveness. Not all gains come from production itself, whether the operation is a factory or a hotel. Some can derive from linkages with other areas of the organisation, the supply network and customer and channel interfaces. Large production volumes need successful marketing and logistics to ensure their efficient throughput to customers. In particular, pricing and distribution strategies and promotional approaches need to generate a sufficient flow of trade. Mass production requires mass distribution to keep goods flowing. One of the reasons that Wal-Mart's prices are something like 17 per cent lower than those of its US competitors is that despite the volumes of goods handled, it has a very efficient logistics systems that minimises the amount of stock held while ensuring availability on the shelves.

Working closely with suppliers to ensure timely and competitive component and materials supply can be a source of cost saving. The need to reduce inventories both before and after the production line emphasises the role of 'just in time' systems, supplier partnerships, efficient physical distribution and the right dealer network or channel. All of these are essential if the cost advantages created in production are actually to reach the market place. Some organisations go further and integrate supply lines either horizontally (thus sharing costs in some areas, for instance physical distribution) or vertically, by controlling suppliers and the distribution network. Not all control and gains from integration have to be based on legal ownership. Managed supply chains based on supplier dependency, such as those created by large retail multiples, can achieve many of the same results without the problems of ownership.

Problems of cost leadership. There are, however, several problems with a cost leadership position:

1 The focus is on cost as a competitive weapon rather than on the range of other factors that customers might find important. Some customers will be prepared to pay more for added value or a stronger brand image.
2 The focus is purely on product cost, not the total cost of purchase to the customer, including after sales costs, change costs and usage costs.
3 As we saw in Chapters 10 and 11, price is the easiest of the marketing mix variables to replicate in the short term, and price wars are rarely beneficial to all suppliers in the long run.
4 The cost leader may become more resistant to change, becoming locked into obsolete or less relevant production technology. New technology can erode both the scale effect and the benefits of learning. The benefits of the technological efficiency gained might thus become the cause of inertia and eventual demise.

Differentiation

The second generic strategy is differentiation. In order to succeed, an organisation must offer something to the buyer that the buyer values, and that is different from the rest. This differentiation is usually defined in terms of better performance, better design or a better fit with the customer's needs. The tradition within Germany's long-established piano manufacturers is to seek high quality and excellent design in the face of stiff competition from the Far East. Manufacturers such as Bechstein in Berlin, Steinway in Hamburg and Bluthner in Leipzig have all resisted the temptation to go downmarket, and although the market is relatively small the industry has survived. The value added must be sufficient to command a price premium, but that in no way means that the organisation can forget about costs. The offering still needs to be competitive, and the organisation must justify the price–value relationship.

The aim is to create an edge over rivals and to have a differentiation package that is sustainable over time. In marketing, this can be 'real' (e.g. a product design feature) or 'imaginary' (a strong brand image or advertising campaign). People really do have to believe that there is a difference. Remember, though, that this approach might not achieve market leadership, even if the product is regarded as superior. Buyers might still be prepared to accept second best at a lower price.

Example Teuscher (http://www.teuscher.com) truffle shops claim to offer a fairytale experience to all their visitors. Through its 25 shops worldwide, top quality chocolate surrounded by elaborate store design helps Teuscher stand out from the crowd. The designs are deliberately themed and changed simultaneously in all shops four or five times per year. Examples have included autumn pheasants, pink flamingos and bears, to name but a few, all set amid plants and flowers. Attention to detail also extends to the products themselves. The raw material is carefully selected couverture that has been specially tempered and has a high cocoa content and low melting point. Such delights as champagne truffles, a favourite with the UK's Queen Mother, chewy florentines, candied orange slices, hearts and fish shapes, golf balls, trains and pianos are all offered – in chocolate, of course. This attention to detail, a high level of creativity and an emphasis on premier class make Teuscher shops very special places (Style, 1999).

The main advantage of a differentiation strategy is that it takes the focus away from price, and therefore might lead to the possibility of charging a price premium. It might also generate buyer loyalty, reducing their tendencies towards substitution or switching. The organisation does, however, have to think through the marketing activity that supports this strategy very carefully, and must plough back any price premium into sustaining its position. In the case of Aston Martin, mentioned earlier (p. 839) and Ferrari, with prices around £100 000 it is essential that the design, image, performance and service package justify the asking price.

The sources of differentiation can emerge from any area of the market offering:

- *product*: branding; innovation; quality; specification; design; image; patents
- *price*: price positions; price–value combinations
- *place*: intensive distribution, exclusive distribution; back-up, service support
- *promotion*: creativity; spend
- *service*: strong trusting relationships with customers; adaptation; transaction-specific investments.

The difficulties with this approach stem from environmental changes. More experienced consumers may see through 'imaginary' differences, and even question the value offered for the price premium. As the market matures, imitators might reduce margins, and it becomes more difficult to retain the level of marketing investment required. New types of competitors might also disturb the *status quo*, for example telephone banking or chains of opticians offering 'your glasses in one hour or less'.

Focus

An organisation adopting a focus strategy is deliberately selective, focusing on a narrow group of customers, rather than on the whole market. There are many ways of selecting appropriate segments, but the organisation building a long-term strategy needs to ensure that they are durable. The philosophy here is to do a little thing thoroughly and well by meeting the needs of a clearly defined group far better than anyone else. Focus in itself might not be enough, however, and the organisation might have to combine it with cost leadership or differentiation to build advantage.

Example   Wolfking (http://www.wolfking.com) is a Danish manufacturer of specialist machinery for the food processing industry. The company has always focused its operations on narrow areas and then sought to be the best in those areas. From its early origins in mink farming equipment, then in stainless steel meat processing machines in the 1970s, it has expanded into computer control systems and pet foods, but has always been associated with meat processing. With an overall objective to be a leading global manufacturer and supplier of machinery and advanced processing lines for minced meat and raw materials, Wolfking has established a market leadership position through direct operations and acquisition. For example, when it wanted to get into the allied processing of cured and marinated meat sector it purchased Belam BV in the Netherlands in 1992 and Scanio in Denmark in 1998.

To help achieve the focused strategy there has had to be heavy investment in new technology, product development and new systems that can offer tailor-made complete solutions, if necessary, to the meat trade, retail and processors. The other critical element of the strategy is expanded market coverage. It sells through distributors and sales offices in most major markets and operates sales and service companies in China, the USA, the UK, Germany and Brazil.

If a focus strategy is to succeed, the organisation must understand segments thoroughly, how their needs are changing and what range to offer. If you are not serving a segment more effectively than your competitors, then you are in a poor position. To some extent, the scope for focus strategies has been opened up by the advent of the SEM. It is easier now for organisations to adopt a European market segmentation approach. Similar segments may exist in different countries, and thus although the segment may be small in each country, aggregated across Europe, it becomes an attractive option. Imagine, for example, the pan-European segments for premium brands of designer clothes, sports cars, fragrances and jewellery. An organisation operating in one of these segments might adjust its offering slightly to reflect local differences, but the key is the focus on a pan-European segment. It could be possible to define subsegments, perhaps based on natural clusters, for example Nordic, German or Iberian markets, but the danger here is that the segmentation becomes purely geographic rather than behavioural.

The risk with this segmentation approach is that the segments identified might not be sustainable long term, or might be undermined locally by competition. Although there is pressure on larger organisations to take a fairly standardised approach across Europe, with minor implementation variances, there is still room for the smaller business to compete. Many small organisations, perhaps with a local or regional orientation, survive alongside larger suppliers because of their local presence, local service and responsiveness and differentiation to reflect specific local characteristics, for example food taste or the need for personalised attention.

Choice of generic strategy

The actual choice of generic strategy depends on three criteria:

- the fit between the demands of the strategy and the organisation's capabilities and resources
- the main competitors' abilities on similar criteria

■ the key criteria for success in the market and their match with the organisation's capabilities.

Once these criteria have been assessed, the organisation can select the best strategy to build a strong position. In some cases an organisation might not have a free hand, since the nature of the marketing environment and the competitive stances already taken by other firms might force a particular strategic direction.

Assuming, however, that an organisation does have a free choice, it should take into account its potential sources of advantage and how they might best be used to exploit each alternative strategy. These sources of advantage might be:

1 *skills*: The question of skills concerns the hiring, training and development of key staff, who could be in R&D, selling, quality assurance or any area that could help to implement a particular strategy;
2 *resources*: The issue of resources refers both to the level and deployment of resources, for example promotional spend, R&D investment, financial reserves, production facilities and market coverage, and to brand strength;
3 *relationships*: The quality and long-term stability of supplier–customer relationships provides an asset that is durable in the face of many of the short-term pressures that are created by new entrants and competitors. Such relationships might tend to favour a focus strategy, for example.

Whichever strategy an organisation chooses, there must be ruthless commitment to it. Half-hearted implementation will mean that the strategy is ineffective and the organisation will be vulnerable to attack. Trying to implement parts of all three strategies in some kind of hybrid is equally dangerous. The organisation might then have to deal with the worst of all worlds: having no cost advantage, poor differentiation and an inappropriate or fuzzy focus. Nevertheless, there is some interrelationship between the three strategies. Although differentiation is the opposite of a cost leadership strategy, because differentiation incurs costs, a dominant position achieved through differentiation may itself help to achieve volume economies in manufacturing and distribution.

Furthermore, even if the commitment to the chosen strategy is strong in theory, it can still be difficult to stick to it in practice. If cost leadership is the chosen strategy, then beware of the customer requesting special modifications. Although flexible manufacturing methods are enabling more scope for variation during the assembly process, such customising needs to be within defined cost parameters. Despite the fact that Cummins produces a specified range of diesel engines, for example, it is also able, through flexible manufacturing, to accommodate some variability for customer specification, including colour, features and even packaging. However, Cummins would not be in the business, within a mass production system, of building prototypes and limited batch produced lines. Similarly, if differentiation is the chosen strategy, there are risks in the pursuit of the low price option. If the focus strategy is to be implemented on a pan-European basis, then decisions have to be taken on how much adaptation can be allowed for local needs in different countries.

COMPETITIVE POSITIONS AND POSTURES

A final stage in the determination of a competitive strategy is to decide how to compete, given the market realities, and how to either defend or disturb that position. This means that the organisation has to consider its own behaviour in the context of how competitors are behaving, and select the most appropriate strategy that will enable overall objectives to be achieved. Two aspects need to be considered, competitive position and competitive posture. **Competitive position** refers to the impact of the organisation's market position on marketing strategies, whereas **competitive postures** are the strategies implemented by organisations in different positions who want to disturb the *status quo*.

867

Competitive positions

An organisation's competitive position usually falls into one of four categories, according to its relative market share. The four categories, and the kinds of marketing strategies that go with them, are shown in Fig. 20.10 and are now considered in turn.

Market leader

In many industries, one organisation is recognised as being ahead of the rest in terms of market share. Its share might only be 20–25 per cent, but that could still give it a dominant position. The market leader tends to determine the pace and ways of competing in the market. It sets the price standard, the promotional intensity, the rate of product change and the quality and quantity of the distribution effort. Effectively, the market leader provides a benchmark for others to follow or emulate.

> **Example** In an industry dominated by the 'Mrs Mop' image, a strong emphasis on price, labour casualisation and sometimes unskilled staff working in small transient firms, ISS has become the world's largest cleaning company. That is no mean achievement, given that in the EU alone 2.4 million people are employed in around 54 000 cleaning companies. The ISS approach is to focus on maintaining high service standards from its well-paid, well-presented, well-trained 195 000 staff who are all aware of the quality standards that have to be achieved. It has also developed a reputation in special application areas, such as hospitals, food hygiene and high-technology environments. The leadership position in Europe and Asia has been achieved largely through acquisition and a commitment to internationalisation. It was clear early that the home base, Denmark could not offer sufficient growth potential. ISS now has 70 companies in 32 countries and in 1999 it added to the list with the purchase of Abilis in the Netherlands, Europe's second largest provider of cleaning and specialised services. So the next time you check your computer keyboard, if there are crumbs in it, ISS cannot be the cleaning contractor (MacCarthy, 1999).

Market leadership can be at company, product group or brand level. Hellmans claims over 50 per cent of the UK mayonnaise market, just ahead of a series of own-brand products. Chivers Hartley is the market leader in jams and marmalades, and Otto Versand is Germany's market leader in mail order. In each case there are a

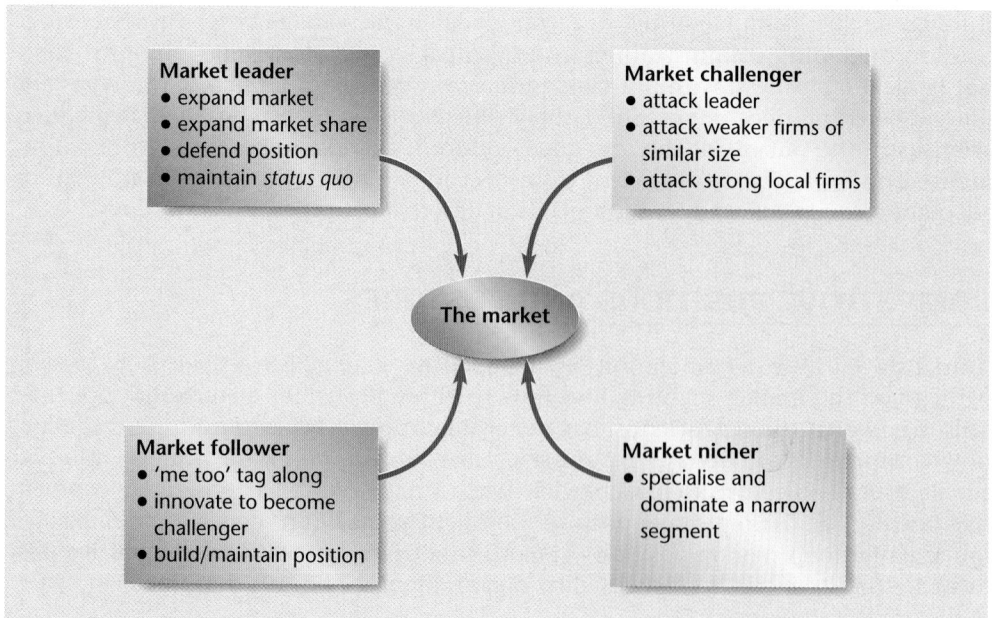

FIGURE 20.10

Competitive position and strategy

number of rivals, so the power associated with being a leader might not necessarily be very great, especially if markets are defined from a European rather than a domestic perspective.

Market leadership lends itself to a number of strategic alternatives, none of which is mutually exclusive:

- *expand total market* by creating new uses, new users, or more intense use
- *expand market share* via the marketing mix. This assumes that share and profit are related
- *defend position* against challengers, through continuous innovation, or through expanding the range to get more shelf space. This strategy has been seen in many high-profile marketing battles between leaders and challengers, such as Coca-Cola *vs* Pepsi, Avis *vs* Hertz, Unilever *vs* Procter & Gamble.
- *seek stability* and retention of customer base, as have organisations such as Kodak, Benetton, Nestlé and L'Oréal.

MARKETING AND IT | **e-Commerce and the importance of first mover advance**

In the digital age, huge advantages can accrue to those who are first movers. For example:

- **Amazon.com versus 'The Rest'.** In 1995, Barnes and Noble was one of the premier book retailers in the US and Amazon.com had just been established by Jeff Bezos, a former investment banker with an idea that there was a market for books to be sold over the Internet. Amazon gave its customers access to far more books than a physical bookstore could carry, and often at a lower cost. However, Amazon's real advantage was not just access to countless books, but access to countless book reviews, discussion forums, Eyes (the e-mail service that automatically notifies customers of books that might be of interest to them), etc. Two years later, Amazon had made sufficient inroads into the book retailing market that Barnes and Noble launched its own on-line service. In early 1998, the European publishing giant Bertelsmann announced that it was planning to launch its own global electronic bookstore called Books Online in the US later that year. By October, it became clear to both Bertelsmann and Barnes and Noble that neither of their ventures was likely to be as successful as Amazon, which had quickly established itself as the market leader. Bertelsmann and Barnes and Noble decided to merge in order to compete against the upstart. By early 1999, Amazon had solidified its position as market leader and had moved into several new business areas including CDs, on-line auctions as well as purchasing a 40 per cent share in Drugstore.com, an online pharmacy.
- **Sky versus BSB.** Rupert Murdoch's Sky Corporation launched a satellite pay-TV service in the UK on

5th February 1989, a full 14 months ahead of its main rival BSB, which had missed its original target launch date by nine months. The lost time was critical. Despite having deeper pockets that Sky, BSB failed to build a customer base quickly enough to overtake Sky. By late summer 1990, Sky had 750 000 satellite subscribers against 110 000 for BSB. By November that year, financial problems and mounting losses forced both companies to merge, but it was the management of Sky that survived in the newly-merged entity called British Sky Broadcasting – virtually all of BSB's 580 employees were fired or left of their own accord. By 1992, BSkyB was generating its first profits and when the company was floated two years later, it had a valuation of £4.4 billion.

First mover status has been very important to Internet-based companies, in particular. While many virtual companies generate no profits, they have managed to attract extremely high market capitalisations. When iVillage.com was floated in early 1999, its share price rose to over $100 per share, valuing the company at more than $300 million, despite the fact that it generated losses of more than $40 million the previous year. Amazon.com's market value at the same point in time was in the billions of dollars, also despite the fact that it had never generated a single cent in profits. However, the market expectations are that these Internet-based companies will be bought out, at high prices, by larger organisations intent on buying their way into cyberspace. Hence the large market valuations. Being second or third into the market often confers the status of also-rans.

Source: O'Connor & Galvin (1999).

Market challengers

Market challengers are organisations with a smaller market share, but who are close enough to pose a serious threat to the leader. However, an aggressive strategy can be costly, if the challenger is thinking of attacking where there is uncertainty over winning. Before making a concerted effort to steal share, therefore, the challenger needs to ask itself whether market share really matters so much, or whether there would be greater benefit from working on getting a good ROI from existing share. Dolan (1981) found that rivalry is greater where there is stagnant demand (i.e. growth can only come through stealing share from competitors), and where fixed costs or investment in inventory are high (i.e. economies of scale can bring benefits, but you need to have a higher market share to achieve them).

> **Example**   Toyota's plans for its prestige car brand, Lexus, are taking it head first into a challenge to the leadership of BMW and Mercedes. The Lexus IS200, a compact executive car, is designed to compete with the BMW 3 series and the Audi A4 in a sub-market consisting of around 50 per cent of the premium-price car market. Central to this strategy is the creation of a separate network of 300 Lexus-only European dealerships by 2005. These will be able to reinforce the luxury image and position it away from the mass market Toyota appeal. The price point will be 2 to 5 per cent lower than that of the established competitors and an aggressive promotional programme will support the attack. Although it is unlikely that BMW will respond with price discounting, it is also very unlikely that it will fail to respond in other ways to what is a serious challenge (Maling, 1999).

Assuming that the decision is made to attack, there are two key questions: where to attack, and what the likely reaction will be. There are several options:

- attack the market leader
- attack weaker firms of a similar size
- attack firms who are strong but very local.

It is never easy to attack leaders, who tend to retaliate through cutting prices or by investing in heavy promotion etc. It is, therefore, a high-risk but high return route. The challenger needs a clear competitive advantage to exploit to be able to neutralise the leader. When Quaker Petfoods challenged Pedigree Petfood's Whiskas' dominance of the catfood market, for instance, it did it by product improvement to create a high-quality brand with premium packaging, supported by appealing press and television advertising. Despite Whiskas' £10mn spend (compared with Felix's £3mn), its market share fell within three years from 50 to 35 per cent. The challenger might also have to be prepared to absorb short-term losses as a result of defending against the leader's retaliation. Again, Felix had to increase its advertising spend considerably to attack the leader. The moral of this story is not to enter the fight unless you are really convinced that you can win and are prepared to invest in the battle. The difficulty in some markets is spotting the market challengers of tomorrow. Whereas BMW can track the progress of Lexus, a new competitor that could radically change the shape of marketing must also be considered.

> **Example**   Fogdog (http://www.fogdog.com) may not be a name that readily springs to mind in the sporting goods market, but it may be an organisation that will challenge traditional sports retailers in the same way that Amazon did in bookselling. Fogdog established its reputation in the USA as a single source for any sports or outdoor equipment purchased over the Internet. With over 250 brand names including Nike and Reebok represented by 15 000 products and over 60 000 stocking units, a vast choice is offered. The site has around 200 000 hits per month and the US product range would fit into four shops the size

of Harrods! Even without trying, Fogdog makes 15 per cent of its sales in Europe and thus is planning a major push into this prime market. The website blends a wide range of merchandise with the benefits of on-line shopping. With a sports market estimated to be worth £3bn and a 12 per cent mail order market share, Fogdog could be a market challenger for tomorrow (Rigby, 1999).

Market followers

Given the resources needed, the threat of retaliation and the uncertainty of winning, many organisations favour a far less aggressive stance, acting as market followers. There are two types of follower. First, there are those who lack the resources to mount a serious challenge and prefer to remain innovative and forward thinking, without disturbing the overall competitive structure in the market by encouraging open warfare. Often, any lead from the market leader is willingly followed. This might mean adopting a 'me too' strategy, thus avoiding direct confrontation and competition.

> **Example** The Holiday Autos car rental company competes with the 'giants' of Hertz and Avis by offering lower and inclusive prices. Car rental customers are often concerned that low basic rental prices are then supplemented with many additional costs. The Holiday Autos system for the leisure market aimed to remove many of those difficulties through inclusive pricing. Despite being a late entrant, launching in 1987, it now operates in 50 countries and 4000 locations. From a UK base, by 1998 international turnover exceeded that of its UK business (*Marketing*, 1998).

The second type of follower is the organisation that is simply not capable of challenging and is content just to survive, offering little competitive advantage. Often, smaller car rental firms operate in this category by being prepared to offer a lower price, but not offering the same standard of rental vehicle or even peace of mind should things go wrong. A recession can easily eliminate the weaker members of this category.

Hammermesch *et al.* (1978) and Saunders (1987) found that some market followers seek deliberately to build and maintain that position through a range of strategies, which include careful and narrow segmentation, highly selective R&D and a focus on quality, differentiation and profitability rather than on cost and share gains.

Market nichers

Some organisations, often small, specialise in areas of the market that are too small, too costly or too vulnerable for the larger organisation to contemplate. Niching is not exclusively a small organisation strategy, as some larger firms may have divisions that specialise. The key to niching is the close matching between the needs of the market and the capabilities and strengths of the company. The specialisation offered can relate to product type, customer group, geographic area or any aspect of product/ service differentiation.

> **Example** Although in the context of the sports goods market La Boule Obut is an almost insignificant player, it has captured 70 per cent of the market for the manufacture of steel petanque balls, the essential accessory for a favourite French pastime, boules. Although over 30 countries play boules, there are only 600 000 licensed players worldwide, two-thirds of whom are in France. Prices range from FF75 to FF400 per boule and of the 7000 customers, 60 per cent buy through large distributors. This small market niche is of little interest to larger sports or steel manufacturers. The niche, however, has enabled La Boule Obut to thrive since 1955, a one-product company that has even turned its back on the expansion possibilities through the wooden jacks that are needed for boules (Owen, 1999).

Success in a niche market.

Source: Obut.

The main problem for market nichers is the challenges created if the niche starts to disppear due to innovation and change. One of the problems faced by Sock Shop, the niche hosiery retailer, for example, was that larger retailers such as Marks & Spencer encroached on its niche by providing equally wide and deep hosiery assortments at competitive prices, thus eroding the differential advantage of the niche operator.

Competitive postures

The previous section considered the underlying rationale for defending, attacking or ignoring what is going on in the market from the point of view of an organisation's relative market position. This section examines *how to attack* or *how to defend* a position. A number of analogies from texts on warfare have been used (*see* e.g. Kotler and Singh, 1981) to describe the various options and the difficulties associated with them. Four broad postures are considered here, although the final two owe their roots to diplomacy rather than warfare.

Aggressive strategies

Aggressive strategies are implemented when one or more players in a market decide to challenge the *status quo*. Again, the question of who to attack, when to attack and where to attack all need to be answered carefully in the context of the resources needed, the competitive reaction and the returns to be gained at what cost. Even in warfare, head-on assaults can be costly and do not always succeed. Five broad aggressive strategies can be contemplated, as shown in Fig. 20.11.

Frontal attacks. A challenger contemplating a head-on attack in marketing terms needs to be very well resourced relative to the market leader. A full-scale attack means matching and winning on all the competitive variables such as price, mass distribution, product features and the rest. A more limited frontal attack may pick off some customer groups who could be more vulnerable to a new offering, for example those who are more service conscious.

Flank attack. Many successful attacks occur because the enemy has been outflanked and its strategy has been disrupted. By attacking particular segments, product weakness areas or poor distribution facilities, progress can be made despite the overall strength of the competition. Such tactics are called technological flanking and segmental flanking.

Flank attacks can lead to encirclement if the poorly defended segment is used by the challenger to build an image and reputation in the market in preparation for a further attack in an area of direct concern to the leader.

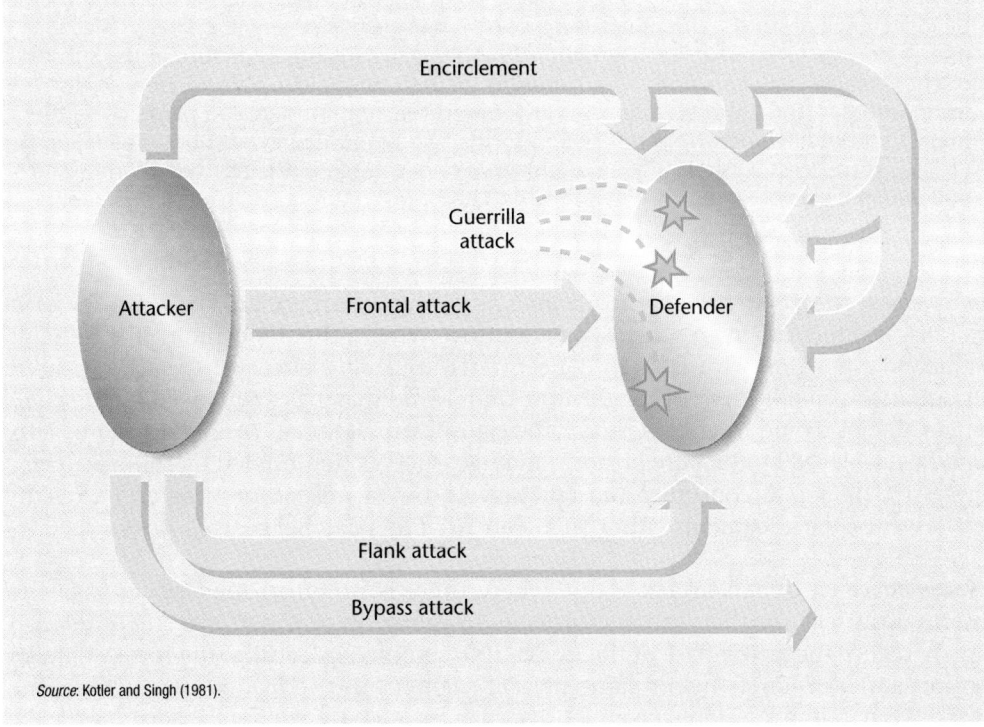

FIGURE 20.11

Attack strategies

Source: Kotler and Singh (1981).

Example The wet shaving market has seen many upheavals since Bic (http://www.bic.fr) took the market by storm in the 1960s with the disposable razor. The Bic attack was full frontal, offering convenience, low prices and ease of repurchase supported by heavy advertising and mass distribution. Gillette and Wilkinson Sword retaliated within three years with their own versions, but a third of the market had already been lost. Since then there have been many other shaver wars as one party seeks to gain a product or market advantage over the other. In the early 1990s, for example, innovation took place in the premium wet shaving sector with the launch of the Sensor and Protector close shave systems. In 1999, the battle continued as Wilkinson Sword launched a high-tech response, the FX Diamond, to the Gillette Mach 3 (*see* p. 339) triple-blade razor. The Wilkinson FX Diamond is a flexible twin-bladed razor that is considered to stay sharper for longer as it is four times harder than the Mach 3. It has also been ergonomically designed and comes with a stand for storage and travelling. The investment required exceeded £30mn and a £13mn advertising launch was planned to support the launch. Gillette claims to have invested £600mn in the Mach 3.

However, the big three manufacturers have not been left to fight it out among themselves. ASDA launched a cheap alternative to the Mach 3, manufactured by the American Safety Razor Company. It was even claimed that the Tri-Flex blades could be used with Gillette handles, an issue that caused legal action between the parties (*The Grocer*, 1999a, 1999b).

Example When the Prudential (http://www.prudential.co.uk) wanted to enter the Internet and telephone banking service, it had to compete with established banking methods in general and with the successful new telephone banking offerings from such companies as Virgin, Tesco and Marks & Spencer. As had Virgin before it, the Prudential also used technological flanking to attack the main high street banks, but also had to try to outflank the other new entrants by segmental outflanking. It has been argued that established financial service brands have difficulty in being stretched into new market segments, making them fair game for a new entrant (Bell, 1998). The Prudential sought to outflank through extensive research to identify the real needs and concerns of potential customers when buying service products (McLuhan,1999). One major point identified was that people wanted to be treated as individuals rather than as a part of a mass market segment, perhaps reflecting one of the perceived benefits of traditional high street banking. Therefore in the subsequent promotional campaign the advertising focused on individuals and individualism, using Zoë Ball and Linford Christie. It also found that the Prudential's name had little impact and positive benefit in this sector, so the Egg brand name was born. The launch was a great success. Over 150 000 customers were generated in the first two months and 500 000 in the first six months. The outflanking had worked through careful positioning.

Encirclement attack. Encirclement means launching an attack on many fronts with rapidity and force so as to spread panic and overwhelm the opposition. It is difficult to defend a position with enough concentrated force and effect when faced with an all-out attack on all sides. Although short-term losses may be experienced by the challenger, the outcome might eventually be significant advances in market share. This could be achieved by the pure breadth of range, such as that offered by Seiko watches, aggressive pricing at consumer and retail levels, heavy pull promotion, and a relentless drive to attack segments either on a sequential or a parallel basis.

Bypass attack. A bypass attack is one where there is no effort made to engage the enemy in direct conflict, but the tactic is to move on and perhaps surround and slowly reduce the power base of the leader. In a commercial setting, the focus could be on unrelated products in the same market segment as the leader, new geographic markets, and always seeking a competitive edge through technological advances.

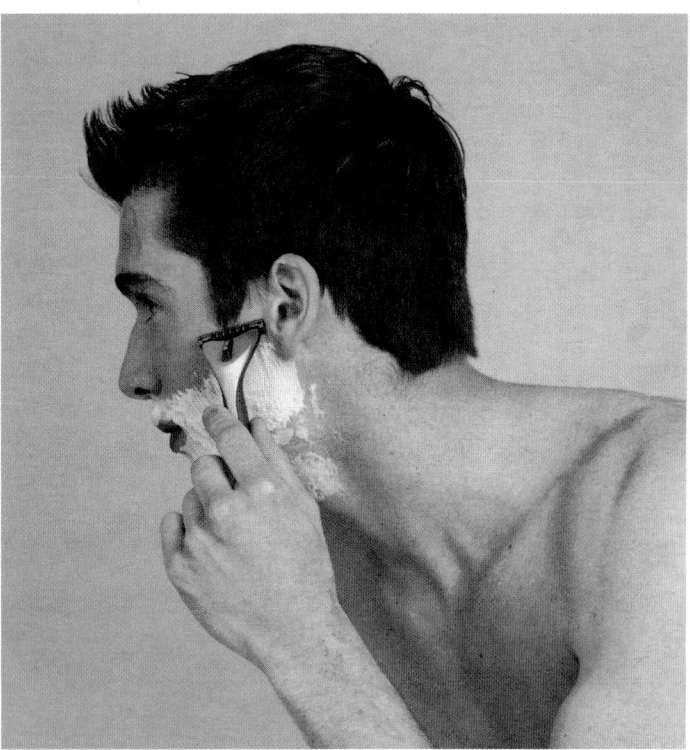

Wilkinson Sword: competing at
the cutting edge.

Source: Wilkinson Sword Limited

Guerilla attack. Guerrilla action is a well-known strategy for a small group operating against a much more powerful force that it dare not meet head on. In business, the purpose of such a strategy is to make short-term marginal gains that can still be important for the smaller organisation, although not very significant to the larger operator. It could mean bursts of activity, perhaps in price promotions, dealer loadings or geographically concentrated campaigns, or even in recruiting some of the market leader's key staff. It is about hitting poorly defended targets hard, and then quickly retreating.

Defensive strategies

Defensive strategies might be adopted by a market leader under attack, or by a market follower or nicher put under pressure by competitive activity. Even a challenger needs to reflect on likely competitive retaliation before committing itself to aggressive acts. Figure 20.12 shows a range of possible defences.

Fixed position defence. One option is to sit tight and defend the current position. This can be risky, in that such defences might then be bypassed rather than attacked directly. In commercial terms, the organisation that seeks to hold position without adopting fresh ideas can run into trouble. Travel agents have been accused of being too complacent about the threat of direct links between supplier and customer that are made possible by the Internet (Daneshkhu, 1999). Although the power of the Internet is recognised, travel agents tend to believe that it is an alternative distribution channel, not a force that could radically reshape the industry. A number of the main UK travel agents do not offer on-line booking facilities, allowing specialist providers such as http://www.bargainhols.com to build a niche in offering package holidays and general travel, http://www.travelocity.com and http://www.expedia.com to sell flights, hotel rooms and car hire. A survey by MORI for the Association of British Travel Agents concluded that 45 per cent of holiday makers would buy holidays over the Internet, but only 1 per cent currently do so. However, travel agents also argue that given the significance and amount of a family holiday and the complexity

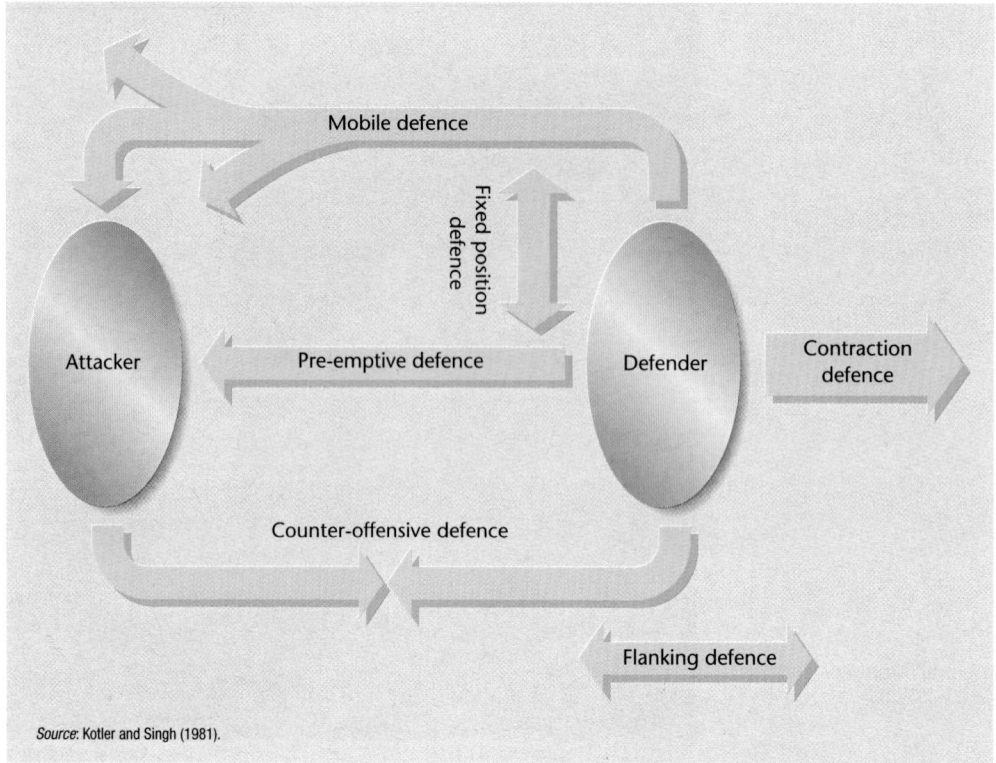

Source: Kotler and Singh (1981).

FIGURE 20.12

Defence strategies

of finding and sorting out a package holiday, on-line holiday bookings will pose little threat as customers prefer direct contact with expert sales staff in a travel agent.

Mobile defence. Rather than defending existing products, the focus in mobile defence turns to broadening the market appeal and even diversifying away from that market, as the cigarette companies have done. This means, however, that an organisation must be prepared to redefine its priorities and the type of business it is in, and keep an open mind. It does not mean a retreat, but it does reduce vulnerability and opens up new segments, for example developing bicycles into an item for the health and leisure segments.

Flanking defence. In military situations, the rear or flank is often seen as a weak area. If it is attacked, this can turn the course of a battle.

> **Example** Sotheby's (http://www.sothebys.com) and Christie's (http://www. christies.com) have been competing head on for many years to take the title of the world's leading auction house. However, the traditional auction room atmosphere, the auctioneer and the hammer may soon be a thing of the past if on-line auction companies have their way. Although both Sotheby's and Christie's are moving to establish website auctions, they believe that this will only divide the market between live and Internet business rather than completely replacing the traditional format. They are worried about integrity, honesty and warranties offered with on-line auctions and believe they will only be popular for lower-priced items. Some 80 per cent of auction sales are for less than £8000 (Gwyther, 1999). Despite its concerns, Christie's has already created a separate on-line business and Sotheby's chose a sale of baseball memorabilia to launch its own Internet operations (Labate, 1999).
>
> The main advantage of Internet auctions is convenience, instantaneous participation and perhaps entertainment, but that must be tempered with initial legal teething difficulties

associated with fraud, taxes and the sale of regulated goods (Price, 1999). In the USA, an increasing number of Internet auction sites are being launched; eBay claims to add 250 000 new items each day with 1.4 million items sold and 800 000 bids providing on-line auctions between sellers and buyers (Kehoe, 1999). On its website, it has recreated a market atmosphere with colourful characters behind stalls along with crowds of shoppers. The range of items is extensive, from stamps, books, figurines and toys to many other areas. The buyer bids and specifies how much they are prepared to pay. Even antiques dealers use the service as an alternative to maintaining expensive premises. Sotheby's and Christie's cannot afford to be left out of the on-line auction growth, but still wish to keep their options open.

A flanking defence therefore means paying attention to the market to ensure that any weak spots are identified and defended before a competitor becomes too powerful. The marketing history books are full of examples of poor flank defending. Smiths Crisps, for example, used to dominate the potato crisp market until Golden Wonder entered the fray. Smiths was considered to be an adult snack, with one flavour option only, and to be purchased in pubs. The Golden Wonder market entry was based on a children's snack, sold through shops and supermarkets. The rest is history. The flank was not defended by Smiths and it lost its market dominance position.

Contraction defence. In contraction defence, rather than risk the threat of being overwhelmed in one major defensive position, an organisation undertakes a selective withdrawal, to delay or even offset the attacking force. In commercial terms, that could mean withdrawing from marginal segments and areas where the presence is small and cannot be defended. This might mean that in areas where strengths do exist a better, more concentrated fight can take place. When under threat, the core business must be defended at all costs.

Pre-emptive defence. The phrase 'the best form of defence is to attack' is now a recognised business strategy. If an organisation feels that it might soon be under attack, rather than wait for that to happen it takes deliberate aggressive actions. This might mean a particular marketing mix emphasis, for example advertising, dealer loaders or new products. Alternatively, signals can be sent that any attack would be vigorously defended.

Counter-offensive defence. Once hostilities have begun, a number of counter-offensive measures can be taken in defence. Many of these actions are aggressive, but retaliatory. Three responses are possible. First, *head to head confrontation* means matching action with action. This, incidentally, is how price wars start. It does not just centre on price moves, however: it might also mean investing as much in advertising as the competition or launching a similar new product. It shows that no competitive advantage can be gained. The second possible response is to *outflank and attack*, which means finding the competitor's weak spots, in terms of product areas, market segments, marketing methods, for example, and ruthlessly attacking them so that it hurts deeply and quickly. The final response is to *hit where it hurts most*, which means attacking the cash

Example Price wars are common in the package holiday market and so Thomson Holidays decided to outflank and attack its competitors by launching a new credit card that also serves as a loyalty card. In conjunction with Mastercard, Air Miles Holiday Points were given for every £10 spent on the credit card and these could be redeemed against a holiday booking with Thomson. This is designed to create more loyalty and provide an incentive to stick with Thomson rather than buying solely on price (Rogers, 1999).

cow or resource base of the attacker. The attacker will make efforts to defend the cash cow, and in this way the attentions of the attacker can be deflected.

Co-operative and independent

It would be incorrect to assume that all competitive behaviour is challenging and confrontational. Many situations are characterised by peaceful co-existence and at times by co-operative alliances between competitors. In independent situations, a firm may neither know nor care about competition. That does not mean to say that competition does not exist. Competitive threats could be overlooked. You might, for example, own the only bee farm in an area, but you will still be competing for the time, attention and interest of the day tripper with many other local attractions, albeit very different from your own. Alternatively, an organisation may see others as operating in ill-defined but parallel segments. One fencing contractor might specialise in farming/industrial jobs and another in consumer markets. They might advertise accordingly, and while not turning any work away, peacefully work alongside each other. In these cases, aggressive marketing behaviour is unlikely to be provoked unless a major new competitor disturbs the *status quo*.

Ignoring the competition can be folly if a significant, unseen threat is developing, but many of the actions undertaken by organisations that do this are implemented on the assumption that there will be no special competitive turbulence in the market.

Strategic alliances were briefly covered in Chapter 13 (p. 544 *et seq.*) in the context of retailing. Strategic alliances occur when organisations seek to work together on projects, pooling expertise and resources. This could include R&D, joint ventures or licensing arrangements, sometimes on a worldwide scale. Many large construction projects demand that different firms work together to provide a turnkey package. The alliance can be general, on many fronts or specific to a certain project.

Not all joint ventures work out as expected, however. After ten years of participating in a joint venture in the construction and earthmoving sector, Volvo decided to buy out its partner Clark Equipment to form the Volvo Construction Equipment Corporation from the formerly jointly owned VME Group. The purchase added to the financial strength of Volvo as the operating margins from VME exceeded those earned from both Volvo trucks and the automotive division. Another advantage of the purchase was the ability to co-operate more closely in engine development. It was also felt that the Volvo name would be a marketing advantage in a highly competitive market dominated by Caterpillar with a worldwide share of 34 per cent compared with VME's 5 per cent (Baxter and Carnegy, 1995).

Example Carlsberg (http://www.carlsberg.com) and the Coca-Cola Company formed a joint venture in 1997 to form Coca-Cola Company Nordic Beverages (CCCNB). This joint venture became the 'anchor bottler' in the Nordic region, handling all production, sales and distribution of Coca-Cola products in the area. With a still growing market worth 2.8 billion litres, Carlsberg took a 51 per cent shareholding to capitalise on its own expertise in manufacturing and regional distribution. In each country existing bottlers would be part of the CCCNB agreement, so in Sweden, for example, Coca-Cola Dryker Sverige near Stockholm services 12 000 trade customers across the country. From Coca-Cola's perspective, the joint venture enabled much-needed capital investment to be created in new production facilities in alliance with a company that understands the bottling and distribution business.

There are many forms of alliance that can be created for mutual benefit. A number of non-competing organisations in the consumer goods area are forming marketing alliances to reduce costs and improve market impact. P&G, with its Pampers nappy brand, and toy company Fisher-Price formed an alliance to share customer information, perform joint direct marketing and sampling programmes and co-operate on in-store activities. Although no joint branding on products was considered, the two companies plan to spend £2mn establishing 13 playgrounds across Europe as part of a joint advertising theme, 'Let's Play Together', that both parties can use for promotional purposes. Possibilities also exist for a joint babycare section within large supermarkets to strengthen the category. The link has positive attractions to both sides. Fisher-Price is an expert on child development and has a strong brand image, whereas P&G has considerable strength in marketing and distribution. It is expected that more alliances of this nature will be formed in complementary market sectors as companies seek to maximise impact and exploit category management principles to the full (Marsh, H., 1999).

Joint ventures and alliances are also widely used in international marketing as a means of market entry and development. These will be considered on p. 1025 *et seq.* when international marketing strategies are discussed.

Finally, *collusion* is where firms come to an 'understanding' about how to compete in the market. Legislation prevents this from extending to deliberate price fixing, as seen in the investigations into price fixing in the UK electrical goods market (*see* p. 400). Neither retailers nor manufacturers can openly collude to set retail or supply prices between them, although they can, of course, watch each others' pricing policies carefully and choose to match them if they wish.

CHAPTER SUMMARY

This chapter has been concerned with marketing strategies, the longer-term consideration of where the organisation wants to be and how it can get there using its products and its marketing mixes. The implication of this is that marketing strategy is intertwined with the wider issue of corporate strategy. Marketing strategies will not only be influenced by corporate goals, but also by competitive strategy. The organisation has to decide how it wants to position itself relative to the competition, whether it wants to be perceived as a leader, a follower or a niche operator, and how it wants to deal with competition. Marketing strategy thus creates, maintains and reinforces corporate positioning and how it is perceived, by using the elements of the marketing mix to capitalise on strengths, overcome weaknesses, defend against threats and exploit opportunities within the business environment. Outcomes of this analysis are the marketing plan that specifies the overall direction of the organisation and marketing programmes that spell out the operational tasks to be undertaken in order to implement the plan.

Central to this is as deep an understanding of competitors as possible, since only then can competitive advantage be deliberately created and maintained, and defences put in place to protect it. Models such as Porter's five forces can help to analyse competitive structures systematically and provide a starting point for building strategies. In designing marketing strategies, it is also important to understand how competitors are likely to react and the implications of that reaction for the successful implementation of the strategies. The depth of information thus required underlines the need for a comprehensive and well-maintained information system.

In terms of the strategies themselves, there are broadly three generic options. The first is cost leadership, seeking to gain a cost advantage over the competition. An alternative is to seek differentiation, offering something different, better or more valued by the customer than that offered by the competition. The third generic strategy, a focus strategy, means concentrating on one specific segment of the market and serving it thoroughly. The actual choice of generic strategy depends on the organisation's capabilities and resources, the nature of the competition faced and the key factors for success in that market. In practice, it might be difficult to stick rigidly to one of these strategies alone and there might have to be some flexibility.

Strategic marketing planning often revolves around analysis of the organisation's product portfolio. The Boston Box provides a diagnostic tool that can act as a basic foundation for strategic decisions. The Boston Box does, however, have its critics because of its emphasis on the desirability of market growth and high market share. Other portfolio models, such as the GE matrix and the Shell directional policy matrix, have therefore been developed to try to overcome some of the Boston Box's weaknesses by redefining the axes in more detail, increasing the number of cells, and thus trying to be more specific about associated courses of action.

Where growth opportunities are identified, there are a number of alternative strategies available, as defined, for example, by the Ansoff matrix. Not all strategies revolve around the concept of growth. Harvesting, associated with cash cows, means reaping the benefits of a product without actively seeking growth for it. Entrenchment, protecting a current position, might be appropriate for a dog deemed essential to the overall portfolio, while withdrawal might be considered for a completely useless dog.

An organisation also needs to consider competitive position and competitive posture. Competitive position defines an organisation as a market leader, a market challenger, a market follower or a market nicher. Competitive posture is about how to attack or defend a position. This covers aggressive strategies for attacking competitors in different ways, and defensive strategies to be used when the competition attacks.

Competition need not always involve confrontation, however. It is possible to work co-operatively with competitors or other organisations. Strategic alliances or joint ventures have become increasingly appreciated as ways of exploiting synergies between organisations and opening up new opportunities that neither party would have the resources to pursue alone.

Key words and phrases

Ansoff matrix	Generic strategies	Product development
Boston Box	Market development	Product portfolio
Competitive position	Market penetration	Shell directional policy matrix
Competitive posture	Marketing plan	Strategic business units
Competitive strategy	Marketing programmes	
Diversification	Marketing strategy	
GE matrix	Porter's five forces	

QUESTIONS FOR REVIEW

20.1 Define the main factors influencing organisations' *marketing strategy*.

20.2 What is a *product portfolio* and what is the point of *portfolio analysis*?

20.3 Define the four cells of the *Boston Box*.

20.4 How does the GE matrix define *industry attractiveness* and *business position*?

20.5 What are the problems of implementing portfolio models in practice?

20.6 Which three cells of the Ansoff matrix offer *growth opportunities*?

20.7 Differentiate between three different types of *integrative growth*.

20.8 What issues might an organisation take into account when undertaking *competitive analysis*?

20.9 What are the three *generic strategies* and how might each be implemented?

20.10 Define the four different types of *competitive position*.

QUESTIONS FOR DISCUSSION

20.1 To what extent do the cells of the Boston Box reflect the stages of the product life-cycle (PLC)? What does the Boston Box offer as an analytical tool that the PLC does not?

20.2 For each cell of the Ansoff matrix, find and discuss an example of an organisation that seems to have implemented that particular growth strategy.

20.3 Choose an organisation and apply Porter's five forces to its industry or market. What are the implications of your findings for your chosen organisation's strategic development?

20.4 To what extent do you think that market leadership is the best competitive position to aspire to?

20.5 Discuss the relative merits and appropriate use of each of the competitive postures described in this chapter.

CASE STUDY 20.1

easyJet, easyRide? (B)

As discussed in Case Study 1.1, the deregulation of the European airline routes helped to open up a new market for low-cost, low priced budget airlines such as easyJet, operating from secondary airports on a limited number of carefully selected routes. They offer minimum service, minimum flexibility once the passenger has purchased a ticket, and ticket sales are made directly between the airline and the passenger by telephone or the Internet, rather than through travel agents. For easyJet, for instance, the Internet accounts for 15 per cent of its ticket sales. Even business travellers are turning to the low-cost airlines. A Barclaycard survey showed that 25 per cent of respondents had travelled with one of these airlines and 96 per cent of them intended to do so again, and easyJet appeared in the top ten list of airlines most frequently used by business travellers.

Up until 1998, the main budget operators in the UK market were easyJet, Ryanair and Debonair, all independently owned airlines set up specifically to serve the budget market. Late in 1997 it was announced that British Airways (BA) wanted to enter this market too. This was not an overnight decision by BA, however. The company spent six months researching the market, assessing its potential longer-term profitability and its likely future before making a decision. When BA first announced its intentions, the response from existing airlines was perhaps predictable. The chairman of Debonair said:

I believe very strongly in competition, but if BA is going to use the brute force of their financial system to eliminate small competitors, then they should be stopped. . . . Deregulation was created to give the consumer a choice – not for people already in a position of strength to take advantage of every single

scrap, like a vulture in the desert. (as quoted by Ashworth, 1997)

The chief executive of Ryanair said:

If British Airways think they can set up a discount airline, they must be smoking too much dope. (as quoted by Parsley, 1997)

and easyJet saw Go as 'the biggest challenge to our survival so far'.

Analysts supporting BA's move saw it as a bold, pre-emptive idea to get BA early into what was predicted to be a fast growing market. Looking at the US experience, it was apparent that at the time of deregulation in 1978, the major airlines had underestimated the potential of the budget market and allowed operators such as Southwest Airlines to take domestic market share from under their very noses. Nevertheless, it had also been the experience in the USA that although many budget operators sprang up following deregulation in 1978, over 80 per cent of them eventually went out of business. Those that are left now account for something like 30 per cent of the domestic air travel market between them. Industry insiders and analysts who were against BA's move perhaps thought that BA was seeking to hasten this 'shakeout' in the market place and prevent the budget operators from getting too well established and from building too high a market share in the first place. Long before BA decided to enter the market, the Civil Aviation Authority had feared that it was possible that aggressive price competition between carriers on the same route could lead to one or more of them going out of business. Nevertheless, the established budget operators have tried to block Go. In 1999, for instance, British Midland took legal action against Go, objecting to its application to fly to Prague with fares half the price of those of the other three operators on that route.

It is alleged that BA invested an initial £25mn in Go and offered it favourable aircraft maintenance rates and other benefits to get it off the ground. It is perhaps not surprising, then, that one of the competitors' big fears was that BA could and might easily cross-subsidise its new subsidiary, although BA denied that this would happen and insisted that Go would have a separate brand, separate management and a totally independent financial set-up. Some analysts said, however, that by doing this, BA was handicapping Go by denying it the use of BA's biggest asset: its brand name. BA was adamant about Go's independence and simply saw its creation as a logical move, responding to a significant change in the marketplace. Go's offices were set up at Stansted airport rather than within BA's own territory near Heathrow. To emphasise Go's separateness even further, although its chief executive came from BA, few other staff did because it was claimed that Go needed to have a different kind of culture. In operational terms this seems to make sense. A budget airline is a long way from the service-orientated internationally established brand name that BA is, with all the implications that has for profit margins, strategic alliances, distribution through a network of travel agents across the world and service levels delivered. Go was entering a market in which the existing budget operators had already established pricing norms of one-way fares on most routes of

less than £100 and Go would have to work within revenues generated from that kind of pricing and from a limited number of leased planes flying a limited number of routes.

At the end of its first year of trading, Go was flying to 15 destinations and, although it was making losses, expected to break even within the next two years. Meanwhile, the European Commission is watching carefully to see whether there is any evidence that BA is using its resources or influence in an anti-competitive way.

Sources: Ashworth (1997); *Credit Management* (1999); Davidson (1999); Gresser (1997); Leathley and Keenan (1997); Lennane (1999); Lennon (1999); Lynn (1997); Oliver (1998); Parsley (1997).

Questions

1 What is the role of a low-cost subsidiary in the portfolio of a major international airline like BA? What relevance does portfolio analysis have for a smaller company like easyJet?

2 Which growth strategy was BA using when it developed Go and why? Apply the Ansoff matrix in general terms to a major international airline, discussing the advantages and disadvantages of each cell.

3 How would you classify and assess BA's initial competitive position and posture in this market? What effect do you think that BA's entry into the market might have had on an existing operator's (such as easyJet) strategic postures?

CASE STUDY 20.2

Is the market wearing out?

The life-cycle of the denim jeans market shows a series of peaks and troughs as jeans go in and out of fashion. In 1999 the market was definitely in a trough, with sales volumes falling at about 11 per cent per year, for a number of reasons. As denim moves through the fashion cycle and becomes 'uncool' again, other products take over. This time it was combat pants and sportswear. Combat, cargo and carpenter pants became popular because opinion formers such as the band All Saints and clubbers wore them, and this style filtered through to the youth market generally. They also appealed because the youth market was bored with denims and the obvious marketing efforts that went with

them. Combats were practical and, initially at least, unbranded and unmarketed. Some companies spotted the trend early and responded accordingly. Both The Gap and Wrangler, for instance, introduced combat ranges relatively early on, before companies like Levi's had probably even noticed that there was a trend to spot! Some analysts were suggesting that because of innovative use of fabrics and design these products could stay around and challenge denim in the longer term. Nevertheless, as with any fashion product, combats could suffer from the 'trickle-up' effect, i.e. as the combat look moves upwards from the streets into mainstream fashion and then into designer labels, its 'cool factor' will decrease accordingly. Once the marketers start branding and advertising combats and distributing them through high street stores such as Marks & Spencer for an older audience, the youth market is surely going to move on.

Certain brands in the jeans market were not just losing out to the combat cult, however Middle-of-the-road jeans, such as Levi's 501s, found themselves stranded between the designer brands at the top end of the market and retailer own brands, such as The Gap, at the mass market end, both taking sales away from them. Demographic factors have also made life a lot tougher. The core market, 18- to 25-year-olds, is declining in numbers in Europe as well as turning away from jeans as 'something dad wears'. In the UK, jeans sales overall fell by 14.3 per cent in 1998.

In such a difficult environment, companies have to be alert to changes in the market and have strategies in place for dealing with them and even for survival. Part of Levi's problem was that it was not responsive enough. It was rather internally focused on 'doing very well what has always been done' (Heller, 1999). The US company, for instance, spent two years and $850mn reducing the time it took to get new products to the market from 15 months to 3 months and retail stock replenishment time down from three weeks to a target level of three days. The problem was that not only had nobody thought through the cost implications of offering that kind of service, but more fundamentally, while this systems development was going on, the company failed to pay due attention to the marketplace and sales just evaporated.

In the UK and Europe Levi's suffered particularly badly, being so dependent on one brand, the 501s. Through the late 1980s and early 1990s, the 501s brand had shown rapid and satisfying growth and, unlike its competitors, Levi's had seen no reason to innovate or to spread its risk. It was so sure of its customers that it forgot to check how their needs and wants were changing as the market matured and to see how the competition was better meeting those needs and wants. Effectively, Levi's was a one-product company offering no new or different 'looks' to its customers. In the UK market, Levi's further alienated some customers by refusing to supply 'non-approved' retailers such as supermarket chain Tesco with jeans. When Tesco started selling Levi's sourced on the grey market (*see* Case Study 11.1) at reduced prices, this focused the consumer's attention on price and value for money. It is thus perhaps not so surprising that when Levi's increased the wholesale price of its jeans by £1, lending to an increase in the retail

price of £3, sales began to fall. With similar problems in its other geographic markets, Levi's sales fell to the point where plans to shut 29 factories in the USA and Europe with the loss of over 16 000 jobs were announced over a two-year period. In 1998 alone, Levi's lost £1bn of sales.

Once Levi's had identified its problems, it began at act, first with a restructuring. The post of UK marketing director was abolished and replaced with a regional marketing and development director for Northern Europe (including the UK, Benelux countries, Norway and Sweden). In the UK, market research showed that lack of innovation was the key issue among the core 18- to 25-year-old market and furthermore that new products would bring back young customers. Levi's therefore defined three main segments to be targeted and gave each segment its own marketing team and new product development priorities. The three segments are:

■ urban opinion formers
■ extreme sports
■ regular girls and guys.

The idea is that each segment will have its own targeted range of styles and new products and that the pricing bands within which Levi's works will be stretched to cover a wider range. Levi's does not, however, want to lose its main focus or compromise its brand image. Whether it is doing enough remains to be seen. Can it develop the products and implement the marketing communications strategies to put the cool back into jeans and attract customers back? Is it doing too little too late, given the competitive threats posed by The Gap, Diesel and Pepe, for all of which innovation is an everyday part of commercial life?

Sources: Barrett (1998); Heller (1999); Jardine (1999); Lee (1999); Munk (1999).

Questions

1 Into which cells of the Shell directional policy matrix would you place (a) Levi's 501s and (b) The Gap's combat pants? Justify your answer, stating clearly any assumptions that you are making.

2 What kind of defensive strategy do you think that Levi's chose to use in the short term against the combat pants threat? Is this the most appropriate strategy? Why?

3 What are the advantages and potential problems of replacing the UK marketing director with a regional marketing brand development director for Northern Europe?

4 What can Levi's learn from the combat pants experience and what impact might those lessons have on its future marketing strategies?

References for Chapter 20

Abell, D. E. and Hammond, J. S. (1979), *Strategic Market Planning*, Prentice Hall.

Ansoff, H. I. (1957), 'Strategies for Diversification', *Harvard Business Review*, 25(5), pp. 113–25.

Ashworth, J. (1997), 'BA Goes in Search of Blue Skies with No-frills Travel Operation', *The Times*, 18 November, p. 33.

Barksdale, H. C. and Harris, C. E. (1982), 'Portfolio Analysis and the PLC', *Long Range Planning*, 15(6), pp. 74–83.

Barrett, L. (1998), 'Hard-hit Levi's Cuts Top UK Role', *Marketing*, 22 October, p. 1.

Baxter, A. and Carnegy, H. (1995), 'Gaining Ground in the Earthmover Industry', *Financial Times*, 13 March, p. 19.

Bell, S. (1998), 'Financial Players Catch Segmentation Bug', *Marketing*, 6 May, p. 13.

Bell, S. (1999a), 'P&G Ariel Tablet Set for UK Push', *Marketing*, 28 January, p. 5.

Bell, S. (1999b), 'Vernons Pulls Plug on Failed Easy Play Game', *Marketing*, 22 April, p. 9.

Benady, D. and Mitchell, A. (1998), 'Persil's Gamble', *Marketing Week*, 12 February, pp. 29–31.

Burt, T. (1999), 'All Change for Profits', *Financial Times*, 29 June, p. 15.

Calori, R. and Harvatopoulos, Y. (1988), 'Diversification: Les règales de conduite', *Harvard – L'Expansion*, 48 (Spring), pp. 48–59.

Campbell, L. (1999a), 'Ericsson Links up with Small Retailers', *Marketing*, 15 April, p. 4.

Campbell, L. (1999b), 'Nintendo and Sega to Upgrade in Sony Fight', *Marketing*, 20 May, p. 4.

Campbell, L. (1999c), 'Why Unilever B Brands Must be Cast Aside', *Marketing*, 10 June, p. 13.

Carmichael, M. (1999), 'Anything but Bog Standard', *The Grocer*, 10 July, pp. 35–7.

Credit Management (1999), 'Low Cost Airlines Take Off', *Credit Management*, April, p. 14.

Daneshkhu, S. (1999), 'Travel Agents on Stand by as Internet Take off is Delayed', *Financial Times*, 15 July, p. 7.

Davidson, A. (1999), 'The Andrew Davidson Interview: Barbara Cassani', *Management Today*, August, p. 66.

Dolan, R. J. (1981), 'Models of Competition: A Review of Theory and Empirical Evidence', in B. M. Enis and K. Roering (eds.), *Review of Marketing*, American Marketing Association.

Donne, M. (1999), 'Smaller Airliners will Create Much Interest', *Aerospace* supplement to *Financial Times*, 14 June, p. XII.

Gresser, C. (1997), 'Blue Sky: Rival Airlines Fear Destruction', *Financial Times*, 19 November.

The Grocer (1999a), 'Diamonds Are for Shaving', *The Grocer*, 10 July, p. 47.

The Grocer (1999b), 'Razor Wars Break out as Asda Goes to Court', *The Grocer*, 17 July, p. 8.

The Grocer (1999c), 'Spreadable Turns Utterly Appealing to Adult Eaters', *The Grocer*, 17 July, p. 43.

Gwyther, M. (1999), 'Sold to the Man on the Internet', *Management Today*, June, pp. 78–85.

Hall, W. (1999), 'Change of Fortune as UBS Struggles to Meet Targets', *Financial Times*, 2 July, p. 24.

Hammermesch, R. G. *et al.* (1978), 'Strategies for Low Market Share Business', *Harvard Business Review*, 56 (May–June), pp. 95–102.

Heller, R. (1999), 'When Goliaths Start Wobbling', *Management Today*, June, p. 34.

Jardine, A. (1999), 'Life for Denim in Combat Era', *Marketing*, 4 March, p. 19.

Kehoe, L. (1999), 'On-line Mecca for Avid Collectors', *Electronic Business* supplement to *Financial Times*, 24 March, p. III.

Kotler, P. and Singh, R. (1981), 'Marketing Warfare in the 1980s', *Journal of Business Strategy*, 2 (Winter), pp. 30–41.

Labate, J. (1999), 'Christie's Creates Internet Post', *Financial Times*, 13 May, p. 28.

Leathley, A. and Keenan, S. (1997), 'BA Flies into Europe with No-frills Service', *The Times*, 18 November, p. 6.

Lee, J. (1999), 'Can Levi's ever Be Cool Again?', *Marketing*, 15 April, pp. 28–9.

Lennane, A. (1999), 'Still the World's Favourite Airline?', *Airfinance Journal*, June, pp. 30–34.

Lennon, D. (1999), 'Travelling Cheap', *Europe*, April, pp. 20–21.

Littlewood, F. (1999), 'Sega Gearing up for the Final Fight', *Marketing*, 27 May, pp. 28–9.

Lorenz, A. (1995), 'English China Clays' New Chemistry', *Management Today*, October, pp. 48–52.

Lynn, M. (1997), 'BA's Iron Lady Gets her Wings', *Sunday Times*, 23 November, p. 3.5.

Maling, N. (1999), 'Lexus Euro Drive Shifts up a Gear', *Marketing Week*, 7 January, p. 17.

Marketing (1998), 'Holiday Autos in Global Refocus', *Marketing*, 15 October, p. 4.

Marketing (1999), 'Mothercare Web Strategy Aims to Halt Retail Losses', *Marketing*, 27 May, p. 4.

Marketing Week (1999), 'Mars Creates New Organic Food Range', *Marketing Week*, 22 April, p. 7.

Marsh, H. (1999), 'P&G Enters the Age of Alliances', *Marketing*, 11 Febrary, p. 18.

Marsh, V. (1999), 'A World Leader in Ski Boot Production', *Slovenia* supplement to *Financial Times*, 7 June, p. 13.

MacCarthy, C. (1999), 'A Sweeping Success at Cleaning Up', *Financial Times*, 8 June, p. 15.

McLuhan, R. (1999), 'Careful Research Continues to Pay', *Marketing*, 15 April, pp. 31–2.

Millar, S. (1999), 'CBS Market Watch: Philips Electronic Quarter Profits Falls', http://cbs.marketwatch.com, 22 July.

Munk, N. (1999), 'How Levi's Trashed a Great American Brand', *Fortune*, 12 April, pp. 82–90.

O'Connor, J. and Galvin, E. (1999), *Marketing and Information Technology*, 2nd edn, Financial Times Pitman Publishing.

Oliver, J. (1998), 'BA's Cut-price War Cleared for Take-off, *The Express*, 14 May, p. 59.

Owen, D. (1999), 'Boules Capital of the World', *Rhônes Alpes* supplement to *Financial Times*, 28 June, p. 18.

Parsley, D. (1997), 'BA Ruffles Rivals with Discount Airline Plan', *Sunday Times*, 2 November, p. 3.3.

Performance Group (1999), *Breakthough Performance through People*, The Performance Group, Oslo, Norway.

Pilling, D. (1999), 'Big Boys Eye Bit-sized Bios', *Financial Times*, 15 July, p. 22.

Porter, M. E. (1979), 'How Competitive Forces Shape Strategy', *Harvard Business Review*, 57(2), pp. 137–45.

Porter, M. E. (1980), *Competitive Strategy*, Free Press.

Pretzlik, C. (1999a), 'Gaffer, Young Sidney and Co Lament Losing "Share of Throat"', *Financial Times*, 26 July, p. 18.

Pretzlik, C. (1999b), 'Tetley Seeks Partner to Open Tea Bar Chain', *Financial Times*, 26 July, p. 18.

Price, C. (1999), 'Rush to Bid in Cyberspace', *Electronic Business* supplement to *Financial Times*, 24 March, p. III.

Rigby, R. (1999), 'How Valley Culture Provided a Sporting Chance', *Management Today*, July, pp. 87–9.

Rogers, D. (1999), 'Thomson Loyalty Card Braves the Annual Price War', *Marketing*, 6 May, p. 1.

Rosier, B. (1999), 'Nestlé to Unify Brands with Net's Global Reach', *Marketing*, 27 May, p. 3.

Rubythorn, T. (1999), 'Never Complain, Never Explain', *EuroBusiness*, 1(2), pp. 42–5.

Saunders, J. (1987), 'Marketing and Competitive Success', in M. J. Baker (ed.), *The Marketing Book*, Macmillan.

Style, S. (1999), 'Step Right in here for the Chocoholic's Dream Shop', *Greater Zurich* supplement to *Financial Times*, 29 June, p. IV.

Tungate, M. (1999), 'Nestlé Makes Moves to Befriend the British', *Marketing*, 20 May, p. 15.

Urry, M. (1999), 'When it Comes to the Crunch McVitie's Take the Biscuit', *Financial Times*, 16 August, p. 10.

Wilkinson, A. (1999), 'Mars Tries to Exploit Organic Foods Boom', *Marketing Week*, 29 April, p. 24.

Wilson, R. M. S. *et al.* (1992), *Strategic Marketing Management*, Butterworth-Heinemann.

Marketing Planning, Management and Control

LEARNING OBJECTIVES

This chapter will help you to:

1 understand the different types of plan found within organisations and the importance of formal planning processes;

2 define the stages in the marketing planning process and their contribution to sound, integrated plans;

3 appreciate the various methods of estimating or forecasting both market and sales potential;

4 outline alternative ways of structuring a marketing department and their advantages and disadvantages;

5 understand the need for evaluation and control of marketing plans and their implementation, and the ways in which this can be achieved;

6 understand the special characteristics of a small business and how marketing helps small businesses from their start-up to maturity.

INTRODUCTION

Much of this text so far has been concerned with the development of competitiv advantage through the careful design and implementation of an appropriate and inte grated marketing mix. After selecting the most appropriate target markets, th organisation can create an offering that is of value to the chosen market segment(s through a tailored package of pre-sale, consumption and post-sale benefits. This is dynamic process because the marketing environment changes, competitive action change and, not least, customer needs and preferences are also liable to change. Thi process of matching between the organisation and all aspects of the environmen cannot be left to chance since it requires careful planning and management. Marketing at both strategic and operational levels, plays an important part in that process.

The previous chapter looked at marketing planning's contribution to the process o matching organisational capability strategically to the environment. The product offered, the markets targeted and the basis of competitive advantage all have a signifi cant impact on company success and the operational plans of the various function within the organisation. Marketing planning, alongside other areas such as financia and production planning, are part of the functional planning that takes place at divi sional, business unit or individual company level. Its aim is to ensure that marketing activities are appropriate to the achievement of corporate objectives, can be implemented within resource limits and are capable of creating and sustaining a competitive position.

> **Example** Marketing planning is important to companies operating in the chilled snacks market because of the fast-changing consumer environment that is encouraging innovation and new product opportunities. Lunch on the move is now a common phenomenon in offices which, along with longer working hours, allows opportunities for greater snacking between meals. A company like Ginsters which sees innovation as an important means of meeting and keeping up with changing consumer eating habits and preferences needs to plan its new product introductions carefully. This is especially true as Ginsters has a policy of introducing two new limited edition sandwich flavours each month. These new flavours have to be researched and developed, demand for them forecast and then sold through to the trade to hit the shelves at the right time. One of the products for August 1999, for instance, was an Eclipse sandwich to celebrate the UK's first total eclipse for over 70 years. If that product had been delayed until September, after the eclipse hype had died down, the impetus and the sales would have been lost. It is a similar story for Ginsters' less transitory product lines. Ginsters came to the conclusion that its pasty and savoury pastry brands were in a market that was 'perceived as deeply traditional and out of touch' (Hardcastle, 1999). This might well have been identified as a result of the monitoring and control mechanisms built into marketing plans. Whatever triggered the discussion, it led to a complete rethink of the product ranges in the context of current consumer demands. This in turn led to the introduction of a six-pack of miniature Cornish Pasties called Pocket Pasties, ideal for those eating on the move or from lunchboxes. The success of this product will no doubt be measured in terms of its planned performance and sales targets.

The first part of this chapter examines some of the issues associated with designing a planning system for marketing and how it fits into the organisational planning process. Then, the various stages of the marketing planning process are discussed in detail. Although the implementation of the planning process may vary from situation to situation, the outline given here at least demonstrates the interrelated nature of many planning decisions. Attention then turns to the important role of forecasting, which is sometimes neglected, but is nevertheless a fundamental part of the planning process. Poor forecasting increases the likelihood of formulating inappropriate plans, whether at a strategic or operational level.

The chapter then moves on to examine other managerial issues associated with managing marketing. Making sure that the organisational structure of the marketing function is appropriate, for example, is essential to the achievement of the tasks specified in the plans. Within any kind of structure, the degree of specialisation, motivation, responsiveness and expertise of staff will be a major factor in determining how well and how successfully those tasks are performed and completed. Issues of marketing control and analysis are considered because without adequate and timely control systems, even the best-laid plans may be blown off course without managers realising the seriousness of the situation until it is too late to do anything about it. Finally, the chapter looks at the particular problems of managing marketing and planning for smaller businesses.

STRATEGIC MARKETING PLANS AND PLANNING

Planning can be defined as a systematic process of forecasting the future business environment, and then deciding on the most appropriate goals, objectives and positions for best exploiting that environment. Organisational and functional strategies and plans provide the means by which the organisation can set out to achieve all that. All organisations need to plan, otherwise both strategic and operational activities would at best be unco-ordinated, badly focused and poorly executed. At worst, the organisation would muddle through from crisis to crisis with little sense of purpose, until eventually competition would gain such an advantage and demand reach such a low level that continuation would just not be viable.

Planning is therefore an activity, a process in business that provides a systematic structure and framework for considering the future, appraising options and opportunities, and then selecting and implementing the necessary activities for achieving the stated objectives efficiently and effectively. The marketing plan provides a clear and unambiguous statement concerning what strategies and actions will be implemented, by whom, when and with what outcomes.

It is important to distinguish between *plans*, the outcomes of the planning process, and *planning*, the process from which plans are derived. While the process of planning is fairly standard and can be transferred across functions and organisations, there are often wide variations in the actual use of plans to guide strategy and operations. This is partly because there are several different types of plan that can emerge from a planning process. The next subsection looks in detail at some of them.

Types of plan

Plans can be developed to cover many different aspects of an organisation. In some cases, they may be designed and developed as part of an integrated corporate system of long-term planning, encompassing the whole organisation, while in others, they may be used to address specific short-term issues of concern. Plans may be differentiated in terms of a number of features. These are as follows.

Organisational level

Managers are involved with planning at all levels of an organisation. The concerns of managers, however, change at higher levels of the organisation, and the complexities affecting planning also change. The more senior the manager, the more long term and strategic becomes the focus. At the highest level, the concern is for the whole organisation and how to allocate resources across its various functions or units. At lower levels, the focus is on implementation within a shorter-term horizon, and on operating within clearly specified parameters. The marketing director may thus have a particular concern with developing new innovative products and opening new segments, while the sales representative may have to focus on sales territory planning to achieve predetermined sales and call objectives.

MARKETING IN ACTION   **Strategies for sporting success**

In 1998, Adidas was delighted to overtake Nike as the best-perceived sports brand in the UK, and certainly in Europe as a whole Adidas has a slightly larger turnover (at about £1.4bn) than Nike's £1.3bn. These achievements led to a review of the structure of the marketing function and marketing strategies. As the UK and Ireland managing director put it:

We have to think as a number one brand; up until now we've been thinking as number two. I wouldn't say we followed but we were watching. (as quoted by Darby, 1999a)

One of the first actions was to review the marketing team of 75 people and to recruit more managers with successful track records in major consumer brands. One of the reasons identified for Nike's decline was that it had focused too much on fashion and not enough on its 'credibility' and 'authenticity' in the sporting sense. Adidas is thus looking to strengthen its positioning by using its sponsored sports people, such as boxer Prince Naseem, footballer David Beckham and tennis player Anna Kournakova, more strongly in its marketing communications strategy. Serious sports credibility and a focus on products rather than

Continued

fashionability, built through sponsorships, advertising and direct marketing, is seen as important as Adidas diversifies into less mainstream sports such as snowboarding in which credibility means a lot more than celebrity.

This is remarkable, considering that in the early 1990s Adidas, a German-based company, nearly went out of business altogether. It was operating under a wide variety of brand names in a wide variety of markets, not just sporting goods, and had clearly lost any sense of focus. It was losing market share and making financial losses because of relatively low quality goods manufactured in its own high-cost European factories, rather than outsourcing production to cheap but high quality contractors as Nike and Reebok were doing. The turnaround under new chairman Robert Louis-Dreyfus involved rationalisation, streamlining and better planning and control of both production and products, better defining its strategic business units, to make the company more focused and competitive. Louis-Dreyfus also overhauled the organisational culture, clearing out the 'old' management and empowering more marketing-orientated managers, many brought in from outside.

The turnaround at Adidas was not accomplished by 'management'; it was begun by a bunch of guys who believed in the brand, believed in the company and who cared. (Tom Harrington, Adidas's director of communications, as quoted by Puris, 1999)

It must be said, however, that belief and creativity alone were not enough to get Adidas out of danger. These qualities had to be tempered by strong leadership and visionary planning to strengthen the company as a whole. Even now, while the UK operation is making important long- and short-term strategic plans for the positioning and day-to-day marketing of Adidas products in its own market, it is still dependent on the central organisation under Louis-Dreyfus for the overall longer-term mission, culture, corporate objectives and organisational focus to be followed. It is also dependent on the central organisation to ensure consistency between the different divisions around the world, while protecting their autonomy to make strategic and tactical plans appropriate to their own markets.

In 1999, however, Adidas's commitment to 'serious sportswear' was questioned when it was announced that the company would probably be launching a fashion label with the working title Attribute in 2001. The target market would be 20- to 35-year-old urban males with high incomes. While the new label would allow Adidas to benefit from an involvement in street fashion without being overtly connected with the core Adidas brand, some analysts worry that entry into a highly competitive market like this would divert resources and focus away from Adidas's core business (Day, 1999).

Time scale

Plans may be short-, medium- or long-term in focus. '*Short-term*' normally means the shortest period of time appropriate to the operations of the organisation. Normally this is one year, or in some industries, such as fashion, one season. Such plans are usually about implementation, the achievement of specified objectives and allocating clearly defined responsibilities. *Medium-term plans* are more likely to cover a one to three year period. The focus is not so much on day-to-day operations and detailed tactical achievement as on renewal. This involves the redesign and redefinition of activities to create, maintain and exploit competitive advantage. This could include the opening up of a new market, a new product innovation, or a strategic alliance to improve market position, for example. *Long-term* plans can be anything from three to 20 years, with the time scale often dictated by capital investment periods. If it takes 10 years to commission, build and earn a payback on a major capital project, such as a new manufacturing plant or new machinery, then the planning horizon will have to be extended to take into account the various influences that could affect the feasibility of the project. Long-term plans are nearly always strategic in focus and concerned with resource allocation and return.

> **Example** Carphone Warehouse is the UK's largest independent mobile communications retailer with 180 stores. It also has a division dealing with direct sales. In the short term, it was also planning an on-line store. Like any organisation, however, it has to balance long-term strategy with short-term tactics and responsiveness to changes in the marketing environment. In October 1998, for instance, the company was facing up to a potential threat in the Christmas market. All the major supermarket chains were planning to start selling pre-pay mobile phone packages, competing purely on price. Carphone Warehouse was realistic enough to realise that it was unlikely to be able to compete with the likes of Tesco on price, even if it wanted to, and instead decided to reinforce its positioning on good service and independent expert advice. The website would also provide some of the convenience shopping features offered by supermarkets. In the longer term, the company will be concerned about the saturation of the retail market with not only the supermarkets but also other independent chains, such as The Link, planning to open more stores. To consolidate and improve its long-term competitive position, Carphone Warehouse is not only planning to open more stores of its own, but also strengthening its links with manufacturers and service providers; developing new products, such as text input to mobiles and mobile e-mail; and looking at new tariffs, networks and pre-pay arrangements. It is also providing an information service to give impartial advice, particularly to reassure consumers and refute the health scares connected with mobiles such as brain tumours and the impact of low frequency radio emissions on blood pressure (Benady, 1998; http://www.carphonewarehouse.com).

Regularity

Most longer-term plans have annual reviews to monitor progress. Shorter-term plans are often part of a hierarchy linking strategy with operations. Some plans, however, are not produced regularly as part of an annual cycle, but are campaign, project or situation specific. A *campaign plan*, for example, might have a limited duration to achieve defined objectives. As seen in Chapter 15, advertising is normally linked to a theme built into an integrated campaign covering perhaps media advertising, sales promotion, selling, distribution and pricing. *Project plans* are specific to particular activities, perhaps a new product launch, a change in distribution channels, or a new packaging innovation. These activities are of fixed duration and are not necessarily repeated.

Contingency plans are efforts to cater for the 'what if?' questions that emerge in more turbulent environments. Planned responses to any possible scenarios that might occur are prepared. A major new competitor entering the market, a supply shortage or a radical product innovation from a competitor could all affect the best-laid plans. By thinking through the implications and alternatives before the crisis arises, a number of options can be identified to support management if the scenario really materialises.

Focus

Plans will vary in their focus across the organisation. *Corporate plans* refer to the longer-term plans of the organisation, specifying the type of business scope desired and the strategies for achieving it across all areas of the business. The focus is on the technology, products, markets and resources that define the framework within which the individual parts of the organisation can develop more detailed strategies and plans. *Functional or operational plans* are, therefore, developed within the context of the organisational corporate plan but focus on the implementation of day-to-day or annual activities within the various parts of the organisation.

Organisational focus

Plans will vary according to the nature of the organisation itself. A number of alternative ways of organising marketing are considered later (*see* pp. 915 *et seq.*). If the organisational focus is on products, then plans will also take that focus, while if markets or functional areas are emphasised, plans will reflect that structure. For example, a functional organisational marketing plan will have distinct elements of pricing, advertising, distribution etc. If SBUs are formed, then there is immediately a requirement for a two-tier planning structure: (a) considering the portfolio of SBUs at a corporate level, and (b) for each SBU, looking at the more detailed organisational design. Similarly divisional, regional, branch or company plans may all be used in different circumstances.

MARKETING IN ACTION   ## Starbucks comes home

Starbucks, after a highly successful launch in the USA, is now planning the expansion of its European operations. It has the objective of being the most recognised coffee brand in the world. It buys and roasts whole-bean coffees and sells them through a range of distribution channels alongside rich-brewed, Italian-style espresso, pastries and confectionery. Before Starbucks, coffee was almost a commodity sold by the 'giants' of P&G, General Foods and Nestlé. Starbucks sold a retailing concept around the coffee bar, the emotional experience of good conversation and relaxation along with quality coffee made from quality beans. Despite the premium price, Starbucks became a way of life (Kim and Mauborgne, 1999).

Effective positioning and the integration of strategic and operational marketing have been central to the on-going success of Starbucks as the concept is replicated in new retail outlets. To have become the leading retailer and roaster of specialist coffee in the world, enterprise, flair and a strong commitment to marketing planning have been critical. Regardless of location, the product ranges are similar and the overall store and marketing formulae well defined and centrally directed.

Based on an idea of a coffee bar culture experienced during a visit to Milan with its many espresso bars, an opportunity for a new concept in coffee retailing was introduced to the USA in Seattle, Washington in 1983. From a pilot launch, the directly owned coffee shop network had grown to 84 locations by 1990 and 2400 locations by 1999. These shops are in addition to a speciality sales division, a direct response business, supermarket sales and, most recently, an on-line ordering service. Combined with an active programme of product development, the US market has been taken by storm and Starbucks is regarded as a category killer (*see* p. 527 *et seq.*) in what was once a mature, sleepy sector.

In 1996, international stores were opened in Tokyo and Singapore and in 1998 the first European outlet was opened following the acquisition of the Seattle Coffee Company in London. Through acquisition, Starbucks will have 82 stores in the UK by the end of 1999, 18 new and 15 converted from the Seattle Coffee Company. The remainder await a name change by end of 1999 when the integration is complete. In addition, a recent joint venture with Sainsbury's in the UK will lead to six in-store coffee shops being opened. Starbucks is well on the way to becoming the leading brand of speciality coffee in the UK in the same way that it has in the USA, and the next step will be a dramatic impact on the European mainland. Then Starbucks really will be coming home.

Sources: The Grocer (1999); Kim and Mauborgne (1999); http://www.starbucks.com.

Café society.

Source: Starbucks Coffee Company.

Planning: benefits and problems

There are several benefits to be gained from taking a more organised approach to planning marketing activity. In summary, the benefits can be classified as relating to the development, co-ordination or control of marketing activity, as shown in Fig. 21.1.

Despite the obvious benefits, we cannot assume that all organisations practise planning, and even those that do might not achieve all the results they expect. Planning in itself does not guarantee success. Much depends on the quality of the planning, its acceptance as a fundamental driving force within the organisation, and the perceived relevance of the resulting plans. There are thus many ways in which the process can go wrong.

One major pitfall is a tendency to become technique orientated, losing sight of what planning is actually for. The production of big, complex, multicoloured BCG or GE matrices becomes an end in itself, and too little time and attention is devoted to working out what they mean and their implications for strategic decision making and planning. There is also a risk that because techniques produce clear, pretty pictures, with things neatly pigeonholed, managers take them too literally and look for formulaic solutions. 'This product is a dog, therefore *we must* do THIS or THIS.' Such attitudes stifle creativity and ignore the true complexity of the world. Techniques such as the BCG matrix were never meant to be used in this way; they act as guides, they stimulate debate, but they do not offer pat solutions.

Finally, managers can become very fond of certain techniques. This is dangerous because any one technique only gives a partial insight, and occasionally looking at things from a new perspective can add new dimensions. That is not to suggest, of course, that the organisation should go to the opposite extreme of concentrating too much on the planning process itself. Too many techniques may just confuse the real issues, creating a fog around the whole process. A complementary portfolio of carefully chosen techniques needs to be defined, and regularly reviewed for appropriateness.

Another potential problem arises perhaps from embracing planning rather too eagerly. The urge to set up dedicated planning departments can divorce the professional planner from the managers who have to live with the resulting plans and implement them. Differentiating so clearly between the planner and the manager is

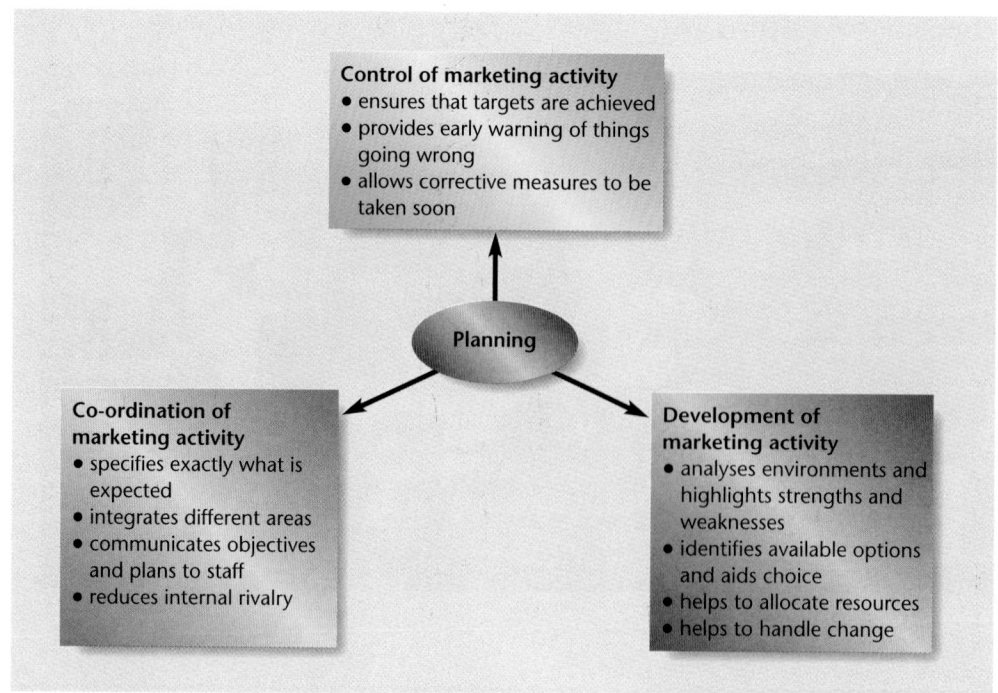

FIGURE 21.1

Benefits of planning

> **Example** In Chapter 20, Nestlé's long-term strategies to build market dominance in selected product sectors were discussed. This involved a regular re-appraisal of the contribution of different product areas and the portfolios contained within them. The longer-term strategic marketing plans would, therefore, have defined the desired position and outlined the strategies to achieve it, such as innovation, joint ventures and acquisition/divestment. The operational marketing plans would, however, be more focused, concentrating on particular products and indicating actions and responsibilities. The launch of the new Junior range in the UK nutritional market, for example, targeted at one- to three-year-olds, is consistent with Nestlé's strategic development plans for the nutritional sector, but will require detailed actions for advertising, packaging, distribution etc. (Darby, 1999b).

far more likely to lead to plans that are not valued and end up locked in a filing cabinet, unused. The way to reduce this risk and to overcome such problems is to make sure that managers are still wholly involved in the process so that they feel some ownership of the plans. Clear and regular communication is absolutely crucial.

In practical terms, marketing planning can fall down simply because of unreliable marketing information. As Chapter 6 made clear, accurate and timely information is essential if the planning process is going to mean anything at all. Good information is only part of the story, however. Planning is about using that information to forecast trends in the market and its environment, then to develop strategies and budgets in response to it, in an iterative and integrated way. Some organisations are good at the forecasting part, while some are good at the budgeting part, but too many fail to bring all this together in an analytical planning process, centred on strategic thinking.

In summary, there is a need for full integration between the **planning process** and the resulting plans. There is no room for a weak link in the chain, since the plans are only as good as the process that generated them, and the process is pointless if it does not result in acceptable, implementable plans.

THE MARKETING PLANNING PROCESS

The process of marketing planning in an organisation will vary, depending on whether a strategic or operational perspective is adopted. The **strategic marketing plan** differs from an **operational marketing plan** on two key dimensions, according to Abell (1982). First, the strategic marketing plan deals with the total strategy in a market linking customers, competitors and organisational capability. Operational marketing plans, on the other hand, normally deal with the marketing mix strategy that will be used to gain leverage in a market. The strategic marketing plan, therefore, guides all planning and activities at a functional level, not just in marketing but across the whole organisation. Second, strategic marketing plans tend to be prepared at an SBU or company level, while the operational marketing plan is more often concerned with products and market segments.

> **Example** Pilkington Glass developed long-term corporate strategies aiming to make it the number one or number two supplier in selected geographic markets. Essential to achieving this was a detailed review and restructuring of its marketing positioning and activities (Lorenz, 1996a). The longer-term strategic marketing plans would, therefore, have defined the desired position and outlined the strategies for getting there (e.g. improving margins, increasing control over distribution channels and increasing the added value of the products), whereas the operational marketing plans would have told managers precisely how to put that into practice.

The previous chapter dealt with many of the issues associated with the strategic marketing plan and its contribution to the overall strategic management process in an organisation. In the corporate planning process, marketing acts as a critical link between customers, competitors and the strategic direction and objectives of the organisation. Thus appraising opportunities, market attractiveness, competitive positioning and portfolio management are important tools in the corporate planning process. The marketing plan, however, although well subsumed in the strategic planning process, still operates as a means of integrating activities, scheduling resources, specifying responsibilities and providing benchmarks for measuring progress.

The purpose of marketing planning has been defined as:

> **to find a systematic way of identifying a range of options, to choose one or more of them, then to schedule and cost out what has to be done to achieve the objectives.**
> (McDonald, 1989, p. 13)

If this definition is to work in practice, an organisational structure is needed to ensure that the process is properly managed. Without such a structure, there is a danger that key stages may be omitted, or given insufficient attention. Although the structure will vary according to the complexity and variability of the organisation, and the emphasis may vary according to the turbulence in the environment and the resultant challenges facing the organisation, a number of broad phases in the planning process are likely to operate in any case. The main stages in the planning process are shown in Fig. 21.2 and each stage is considered in turn. The early stages of this planning process form part of strategic marketing planning.

Corporate objectives and values

Corporate objectives are at the heart of the planning process, since they describe the direction, priorities and relative position of the organisation in its market(s). These objectives help to create guidelines for marketing plans, since the output of the corporate planning process acts as an input into the marketing planning process.

Objectives are normally presented in terms of different kinds of targets.

Quantitative financial targets
Quantitative financial targets are items such as market share (by value), sales, profit and ROI, over a set time period. These could be broken down into specific targets for each of the various organisational units. Therefore within a university, the student number targets (the equivalent of sales targets) could be allocated across different faculties, and these will in turn determine the financial allocations.

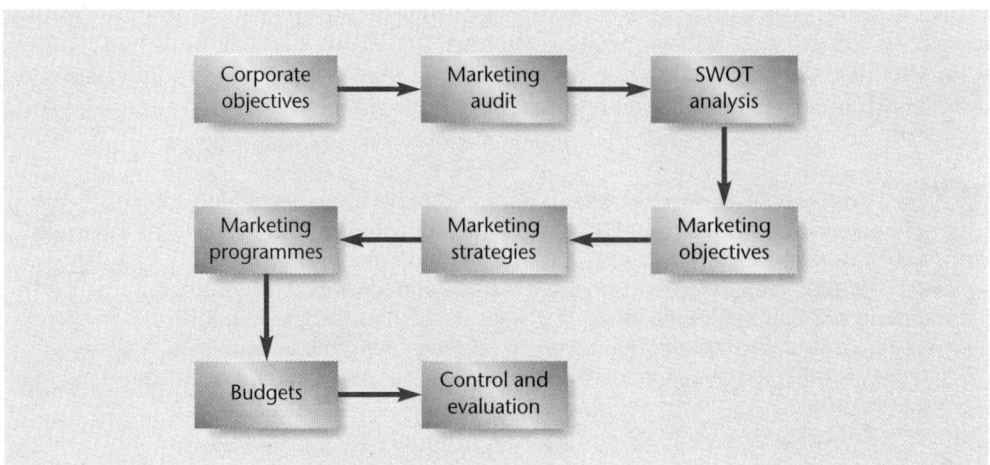

FIGURE 21.2

Stages in the planning process

Philosophical targets

Philosophical targets are likely to be contained within a mission statement. A mission statement represents a vision of where the organisation is today and where it wants to be in the future. It expresses the core values of the organisation and is intended to guide functional and business unit areas in their strategic development. It should encompass segments served, the needs to be fulfilled in the market, and the technological or service character of the organisation (Abell, 1982). It should encapsulate the distinctive and principal values of the organisation, but from a market rather than a product orientation.

Day (1990) identified four characteristics of a well-thought-through mission statement:

- *Future orientated*: linking the future with its impact on the business
- *Reflecting the values and orientation of the leader*: providing support and clear guidelines to staff
- *Stating strategic purpose*: indicating the direction and strategy to be followed, the targets and competitors to beat
- *Enabling*: providing clear guidelines to managers lower down the organisation in their preparation of SBU or functional plans.

To Wensley (1987), mission statements should be 'short on numbers and long on rhetoric but remaining succinct'. The mission statement provides the essential guidelines for managers in making their day-to-day decisions and when preparing operational plans. Nevertheless, the corporate mission statement needs to be supported by quantitative and qualitative targets that reflect this mission.

ARKETING IN ACTION   Companies with a mission

Mission statements vary in length, complexity, detail and philosophy. Gillette (http://www.gillette.com) has adopted a 'Mission and Values' approach. The mission is described as 'to achieve or enhance clear leadership worldwide in the existing and new core consumer products in which we choose to compete'. The core areas include male and female grooming, alkaline batteries, the oral care markets and writing instruments. Supporting the mission are three value statements summarising the company's philosophy about people, customer focus and good citizenship.

Dell (http://www.dell.com) the computer systems company, specifies in more detail the parameters that directly support the more generalised mission statement. It aims to be 'the most successful computer company in the world at delivering the best customer experience in the markets we serve'. In doing so, Dell will meet customer expectations in terms of:

- highest quality
- leading technology
- competitive pricing
- individual and company accountability
- best in class service and support
- flexible customisation capability
- superior corporate citizenship
- financial stability.

Boeing (http://www.boeing.com), meanwhile, specifies its mission statement through a vision and core competencies approach. The vision is for 'people working together as one global company for aerospace leadership'. Three core competencies relate to internal and external focus around closeness and understanding of customer needs, large scale systems integration and efficient, cost effective design and production. These statements are then followed by an extensive list of values.

Subway (http://www.subway.com), a sandwich retail chain, has adopted a core values and philosophies approach to describe its philosophical targets. They are:

- commitment to customer satisfaction through high-quality food with exceptional service and good value
- taking pride in serving customers and community
- valuing a sense of urgency, to emphasise innovative and entrepreneurial behaviour
- to ensure fairness, mutual respect and teamwork.

Finally, Avis (http://www.avis.com) aims to provide 'a stress free rental experience by providing safe, dependable vehicles and special services to win the customer's loyalty'. The vision is to become the world's leading car rental company.

The above examples demonstrate the range of approaches used by organisations to capture their values and purpose. Although most do tend to be very generalised, they provide a sense of direction to guide more detailed planning and strategy formulation.

Qualitative targets

Qualitative targets include items such as service levels, innovation and scope. These rarely have just one objective, but are often found in a mixture with defined priorities. Drucker (1955) highlighted eight areas, as shown in Fig. 21.3.

Whatever the type of objective, they all must be realistic, achievable within a specific time-scale, and cited in order of priority. This will lead to a hierarchy of interlinking objectives. In any case, objectives should reflect the competitive and market positions considered in Chapter 20. In practice, however, defining objectives is often a case of managing trade-offs, such as those suggested by Weinberg (1969) in Table 21.1.

The outcome of this stage should be a clear statement of what is expected of the functional units within the organisation and their plans.

TABLE 21.1
Trade-offs in setting objectives

- Short-term profit *vs* long-term growth
- Profit margin *vs* market positioning
- Direct sales effort *vs* market development
- Penetrating existing markets *vs* developing new ones
- Profit *vs* non-profit goals
- Growth *vs* stability
- Change *vs* stability
- Low-risk *vs* high-risk environments

Source: Weinberg (1969).

The marketing audit

Audit is a term more commonly used in financial management to describe the process of taking stock of an organisation's financial strengths, weaknesses and health, through checking and analysing changes in its assets and transactions over a given period. The philosophy of the **marketing audit** is very similar, in that it systematically takes stock of an organisation's marketing health, as the formal definition implies:

> [The audit] is the means by which a company can understand how it relates to the environment in which it operates. It is the means by which a company can identify its own strengths and weaknesses as they relate to external opportunities and threats. It is thus a way of helping management to select a position in that environment based on known factors.
>
> (McDonald, 1989, p. 21)

The marketing audit is really the launching pad for the marketing plan, as it encourages management to reflect systematically on the environment and the organisation's ability to respond, given its actual and planned capabilities. The marketing audit, just

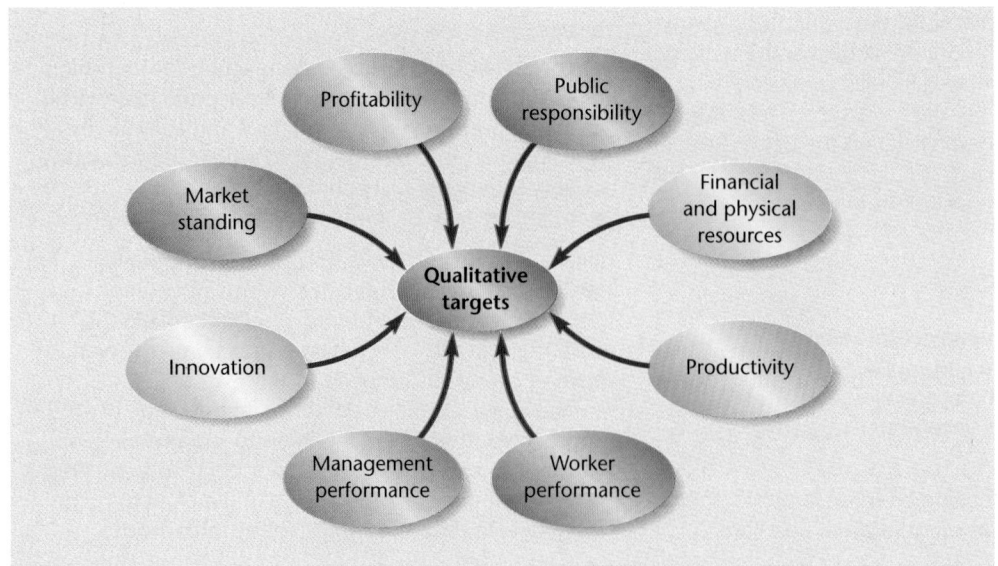

FIGURE 21.3

Qualitative targets

like its financial counterpart, is first and foremost about developing a shared, agreed and objective understanding of the organisation. It thus concerns such questions as:

1 What is happening in the environment? Does it pose threats or opportunities?
2 What are our relative strengths and weaknesses for handling and exploiting the environment?
3 How effective are we in implementing marketing activity?

In order to answer such questions, managers have to look at both environmental variables (i.e. an external audit) and operational variables (i.e. an internal audit).

The **external audit** systematically looks at the kinds of issues covered extensively in Chapter 2 as the STEP factors. Sociocultural changes, such as in the demographic make-up of a market or in public concerns or attitudes, may well influence the future strategic direction of an organisation. The early identification of technological change might also change strategic direction, as the organisation plans ways of exploiting it to make cheaper, better or different products ahead of the competition. Economic and competitive factors are both, of course, very important. Low disposable incomes among target customers may force the organisation towards more rigorous cost control or into changing its product mix, while high interest rates on organisational borrowing might delay diversification or other expansion plans. Competition also has to be analysed very carefully on all aspects of its marketing activities, including its response to STEP factors and its choice of target markets. Finally, the external audit should note what is happening in terms of the legal and regulatory frameworks, whether national or European, that bind the organisation.

Example National Car Parks (NCP) is the UK's biggest car park operator, with around 500 car parks, including 10 at UK airports. If it were to undertake an external audit, it might raise the following issues, among others:

1 *Competition*: a number of rivals from mainland Europe and the USA have entered the UK market.
2 *Negotiating for sites*: increased competition means that acquiring new sites or even renewing the leases on existing ones is more difficult. On the other hand, competitors who are struggling provide an opportunity for NCP to pick up sites and contracts.
3 *Management contracts*: many site owners (local authorities, airports, hotels, shopping centres etc.) now prefer to award management contracts to car park operators, rather than giving them complete autonomy over the car park operation. NCP's traditional approach has been one of autonomy, and its competitors have been faster to accept management contracts.
4 *Service*: direct parking is now available from operators such as Interlink (http://www.webworld.co.uk/mall/inter-link). These competitors offer lower prices and collect customers from their hotels.
5 *Government policy for transport*: the government's drive to get cars off the road could have an adverse effect on demand for parking. On the other hand, city centre traffic restrictions and proposed tolls to get into centres could lead to an increase in demand for 'park and ride' schemes and thus edge of town parking.
6 *Security*: both the general public and the police are pressurising car park operators to install increasingly sophisticated security systems.
7 *Shopping habits*: the rise of out of town shopping with ample free parking not only pulls shoppers away from town centres, NCP's traditional territory, but also highlights the high cost of town centre parking. 'Park and ride' schemes operated from edge of town sites into the centres might provide an opportunity for NCP in co-operation with local authorities.

Sources: Foster (1996); http://www.ncp.co.uk

The **internal audit** focuses on many of the decision areas discussed in Chapters 3–19 and their effectiveness in achieving their specified objectives. It is not just, however, a *post mortem* on the 4Ps. Auditors will also be interested in how smoothly and synergistically the 4Ps fit together, and whether the marketing actions, organisation and allocated resources are appropriate to the environmental opportunities and constraints.

Table 21.2 summarises the issues that a marketing audit should consider.

TABLE 21.2
Marketing audit issues

- Macro environment: STEP factors (*see* Chapter 2)
- Task environment: *competition, channels, customers* (*see* Chapters 3–5)
- Markets (*see* Chapter 20)
- Strategic issues: *segmentation, positioning, competitive advantage* (*see* Chapters 5 and 20)
- Marketing mix (*see* Chapters 7–19)
- Marketing organisational structure and organisation (*see* Chapter 21)

The audit should be undertaken as part of the planning cycle, usually on an annual basis, rather than as a desperate response to a problem. The audit is a systematic attempt to assess the performance of the marketing effort, looking from the present backwards, although when it is done thoroughly it can be a time-consuming activity. To help the audit process, it is critical to have a sound marketing information system covering the marketing environment, customers, competitors etc., as well as detail on all areas of the organisational marketing effort, as outlined in Chapter 20.

The main risk in undertaking the marketing audit is a lack of objectivity. This may arise from being too close to the situation to see it clearly, or from a fear that if the audit is too objective, a manager's past decision making might be criticised. The use of external consultants could overcome these problems, but nevertheless, going through the process itself internally can be a valuable experience for managers.

Marketing analysis

The marketing audit is a major exercise which ranges widely over all the internal and external factors influencing an organisation's marketing activity. It generates, therefore, a huge amount of material that has to be analysed and summarised to sift out the critical issues that will drive the marketing plan forward.

SWOT analysis

The commonest mechanism for structuring audit information to provide a critical analysis is the **SWOT analysis** (strengths, weaknesses, opportunities, threats).

Strengths and weaknesses. Strengths and weaknesses tend to focus on the present and past, and on internally controlled factors, such as the 4Ps and the overall marketing package (including customer service) offered to the target market. The external environment is not totally ignored, however, and many strengths and weaknesses can only be defined as such in a competitive context. Thus, for example, our low prices may be seen as a strength if we are pricing well below our nearest competitor in a price sensitive market. Low prices may, however, be a weakness if we have been forced into them by a price war and cannot really sustain them, or if the market is less price sensitive and our price is associated with inferior quality when compared with higher-priced competitors in the minds of the target market.

Opportunities and threats. Opportunities and threats tend to focus on the present and the future, taking a more outward-looking, strategic view of likely developments and options. Thus the organisation that is the price leader in a price sensitive market might see the opportunity to get its costs down even further as a means of maintaining its position and pressurising any challengers. The challenger's SWOT analysis would define that same scenario as a threat, but might see an opportunity in opening up a new, non-price-sensitive segment. Many opportunities and threats emerge from the marketing environment, when shifts in demographic and cultural factors are taken into account; when developments in emerging markets, such as eastern Europe, are analysed; when, in fact, the implications of anything included in Chapter 2's STEP factors is considered.

> **Example** If UK book and stationery retailer WH Smith were doing a SWOT analysis, it might identify the rise in on-line bookselling as both a threat and an opportunity. It is a threat in the sense that it has generated new competitors such as http://www.amazon.co.uk focusing on the UK as well as making it relatively easy for UK consumers to buy from the USA or anywhere else. The threat is intensified with the evidence that there is a significant shift towards on-line book buying. Related opportunities for a high street retailer could be that the on-line market is young enough to support more providers and a retailer could open a parallel distribution channel to sell on-line to compete directly with the likes of Amazon. In the light of WH Smith's strengths as an established retail name and as a distributor, this could be feasible and successful. WH Smith has also identified a trend in consumer preferences, accelerated by the on-line revolution and the associated fragmentation of mass markets, towards more focused retailers rather than generalists. One way that WH Smith has tried to capitalise on this is by acquiring Hodder Headline, which is involved in children's and educational publishing. This backward integration could improve WH Smith's expertise and focus in those areas as well as strengthening any on-line offer (Hollinger and Rawsthorn, 1999).

Understanding the SWOT analysis

The SWOT analysis, therefore, helps to sort information systematically and to classify it, but still needs further creative analysis to make sense of it. The magnitude of opportunities and threats, and the feasibility of the potential courses of action implied by them, can only really be understood in terms of the organisation's strengths and weaknesses. If strengths and weaknesses represent 'where we are now' and opportunities and threats represent 'where we want (or don't want) to be' or 'where we could be', then the gap, representing 'what we have to do to get there', has to be filled by managerial imagination, as justified and formalised in the body of the marketing plan.

> **Example** West Coast Fish Products is a small fish processing company in Ireland, which smokes salmon, trout and mackerel, using a special blend of woods, herbs and spices to achieve a distinctive flavour. Although its main market is in Ireland, it is looking towards European markets, especially Germany and Switzerland. Even though it is a small company, it uses a formal approach to marketing planning, identifying priorities for marketing strategy development. Its SWOT analysis revealed the following issues:
>
> **1** *Strengths*
>
> (a) reputation for quality in raw materials and processes;
> (b) value added products using herbs;
> (c) knowledge of the market and contacts in Germany, France and Switzerland;
> (d) good location for accessing raw materials.

2 *Weaknesses*

    (a) no formal organisation for marketing;

    (b) emphasis on quality and production rather than on systematic market development;

    (c) buyers tend to initiate contact – company not sufficiently proactive;

    (d) limited resources for intensive market development;

    (e) most competitors have larger market share;

    (f) remote European location means higher transport costs and reduces shelf life of products by up to seven days;

    (g) retail and catering trade dominated by a few large customers.

3 *Opportunities*

    (a) increasing European consumption of smoked salmon;

    (b) fish seen as a healthy product, low in fat and cholesterol;

    (c) contract catering sector relatively underdeveloped;

    (d) the rural, green image of Ireland reflects positively on Irish food products;

    (e) government aid programmes for small businesses in exporting, marketing etc.;

    (f) new potential in US and Japanese markets.

4 *Threats*

    (a) seasonal demand, peaking at Christmas;

    (b) domestic Irish market relatively small;

    (c) smoked salmon regarded in Ireland as luxury speciality food;

    (d) pressure on prices in domestic market from retail and catering buyers;

    (e) low levels of supplier loyalty;

    (f) highly competitive European market (80 competitors in Ireland alone) with strong competition from Norway and Denmark in particular;

    (g) market pressure to raise quality standards, especially with smoked salmon;

    (h) business vulnerable to impact of disease and pollution in fish stocks;

    (i) tougher European legislation affecting processing, additives, handling, marketing etc.;

    (j) variety of tastes and demands (colour, saltiness, dryness etc.) across different European markets.

From this profile, marketing objectives could then begin to be formulated.

Marketing objectives

As the previous subsection implied, the desire to exploit strengths and opportunities, and to overcome weaknesses and threats, gives a foundation for the definition of marketing objectives. Objectives are essential for clearly defining what must be achieved through the marketing strategies implemented, and also provide a benchmark against which to measure the extent of their success. **Marketing objectives** do, however, have to be wide ranging as well as precise, as they have to link closely with corporate objectives on a higher level but also descend to the fine detail of products, segments etc. They must, therefore, be *consistent*, with each other and with corporate goals, *attainable*, in that they can be achieved in practice and their progress can be measured, and *compatible* with both the internal and external environments in which they are to be implemented. These criteria are generally applicable, despite the fact that marketing objectives can vary over time and between organisations.

    Guiltinan and Paul (1988) identified four fundamental areas within which marketing objectives may be defined:

1 achieving market share growth or maintenance;
2 the maintenance or improvement of profitability;
3 establishing an opening marketing position;
4 maximising cash flow, harvesting.

Example BUPA is Britain's largest private healthcare company, with a 41 per cent share of all private health insurance policies, a market worth about £2bn. At the end of 1998, however, it decided to review its marketing structures and strategies because it felt that the market as a whole was not growing and yet competition was increasing. Its biggest competitor, PPP, is increasing its market share, which currently stands at 30 per cent

The first thing senior management did to bring better focus was to create five divisions: healthcare, nursing homes, hospitals, Sanitas (the Spanish subsidiary) and new businesses (for example dental services and travel insurance), each with a team of experienced consumer goods marketers. Overall, there is a perceived need to strengthen the BUPA brand name generally and to ensure that the brand image adequately reflects the whole range of the company's activities. The company will also clearly want to stem any fall in market share and strengthen its competitive position against the equally well-known mainstream insurance companies that are entering its markets. Improving service levels is also seen as a means of not only strengthening the brand image but also improving the retention rate. Some 20 per cent of customers fail to renew their policies when they expire (Murphy, 1998b).

BUPA's advertising aims to win new customers and clean up in the marketplace.

Source: BUPA.

Whatever the basis of the objectives, they cannot be left at such a descriptive level. It is not enough to say that our objective is to increase our market share. That leaves too many questions unanswered, such as:

■ Volume (i.e. focus on quantity) or value (i.e. focus on revenue) share?
■ How much more share?
■ For which products?
■ In which segment(s)?
■ At which competitor's expense?

It is essential to quantify and make explicit precisely what is intended. Even when those questions have been answered, the objective is still quite general, and a number of detailed subobjectives, which will perhaps relate to constraints or parameters within which the main objective is to be achieved, should be also defined. The main objective of increasing market share, for example, may have subobjectives relating to pricing. Thus the marketing manager might have to find a way of increasing market share without compromising the organisation's premium price position.

For West Coast Fish Products, introduced earlier, the primary broad marketing objective might be to improve its profitability in the domestic Irish market through more effective and efficient marketing. It might also strive to improve its marketing position in selected European markets. With limited resources, however, this can only be done if there is a disciplined approach to developing one or two markets in depth rather than seeking orders from a wide geographic area. Detailed marketing objectives would then have to be defined that outline quantified targets relating specific products to specific markets.

Marketing strategies

A marketing strategy is the means by which an organisation sets out to achieve its marketing objectives. The main areas of focus are the definition of the target market and the marketing mix employed. They are not only described in qualitative terms, but are also specified in terms of the resources required and the structure and allocation of responsibility for implementation.

In terms of the target market, the planner needs to ensure that the right group has been selected, matching with the conclusions drawn from the SWOT analysis. The organisation should, of course, be able to make an attractive offering to that segment, and have the expertise to create and sustain differential advantage, whether it is looking for defendable niches or to compete head-on in a crowded mass market segment. Chapter 5 looked more closely at segmentation bases and target market selection. The choice of target segment will be influenced by the competitive structure of the market, and thus by the organisation's choice of competitor against whom it wants to compete, and how. This in turn links with generic competitive strategies and the concept of competitive positioning, as outlined in Chapter 20 (pp. 862 *et seq.*).

In reality, an organisation will be presented with a range of strategic options, relating to its defined objectives. Some will be related to increasing volume (as in Ansoff's product and market matrix presented in Fig. 20.6), while others relate to improving profitability and holding on to what the organisation already has (reducing costs, increasing prices, changing the product mix, streamlining operations etc.).

Within each area examples of actions might be to:

1 *Improve product packaging*: Supermarket chain Sainsbury's developed a range of 12 meals called Fresh Creations in conjunction with Hazlewood Foods. All the ingredients required to make a high quality meal are contained within the one pack, thus there will be meat, fish or a vegetarian focal point, accompanied by fresh vegetables, potatoes or rice, and a sauce. Each item is in its own transparent inner pack and they are put together within outer packaging that is also transparent so that customers can see what they are getting. This gives the customer the pleasure of cooking from fresh foods but without the chore of finding recipes or choosing all the ingredients. Packaging like this can also command a premium price (Hunt, 1999).

2 *Alter prices*: Kellogg decided to use price cuts on its leading brands in an attempt to kick start the UK cereal market. For many years it had resisted serious price cutting, preferring to build a strong brand image associated with quality and healthy eating. Retailer own brands tended to compete on price, but stagnation in the market combined with an increasing share going to own brands meant that Kellogg decided to lower prices, which had been as much as 33 per cent higher than own-brand products. Advertising was also used to inform consumers of the lower prices (Rogers, 1998).

3 *Improve productivity*: in the late 1980s when Ford took over Aston Martin, one of the first objectives was to increase productivity as a means of improving both the cost profile of the organisation and sales volumes.

4 *Standardise*: the Boss Group is a leading manufacturer of lift trucks (for example fork-lift trucks and other loading and unloading machinery). It uses a common chassis for a range of different lift trucks. By standardising the component, the

A combination of productivity, style and design

Source: Aston Martin Lagonda Limited

organisation can achieve cost efficiency in both logistics and manufacturing, yet can still offer a wide range of trucks to meet different customer needs.

5 *Change sales or customer mix*: Sellotape still derives over half its sales from its original product launched in the 1930s, but it has gradually developed a more segmented approach, to change both the product and customer mix. There are products for DIY, children, gift wrapping and general home stationery, as well as a brand aimed at the small office.

> **Example** For West Coast Fish Products, the strategy might be to occupy a narrow niche with high quality, clearly differentiated, unique products. Within the domestic Irish market, this would mean increasing the promotional effort targeted at top class restaurants and hotels, and opening up a new segment of high-class catering services. This is not just a question of promotional activity, of course, but also needs to be carried through to product appearance, packaging, delivery and order processing etc. Prices, however, are under pressure from competitive forces, so it might be difficult to accompany any push upmarket with a corresponding price increase. In the international market, the priority is to fine tune the marketing mix strategy to meet the needs of selected European wholesale and retail markets.

Marketing programmes

Whereas the previous stage was about designing marketing strategies, this one is about their detailed implementation. The marketing programme will precisely specify actions, responsibilities and time scales. It is the detailed statement that managers have to follow if strategies are to be put into operation, as it outlines required actions by market segment, product and functional area. Within the marketing programme, each mix element is considered individually, covering all the decision areas outlined in Chapters 7 to 19. This is in contrast to the marketing strategy itself, which stresses the interdependency between elements of the mix for achieving the best synergy between them. Now, the individual strands that make up that strategy can be picked out, and for each functional area, such as pricing, managers can go through planning processes, audits, objectives, strategies, programmes and controls.

On the basis of the overall marketing strategy, managers can emphasise those areas of comparative strength where a competitive edge can be gained, strengthen those areas where the organisation is comparable with its competition, and work to develop further or overcome those where the organisation is more vulnerable. The key challenge at the end of it all, however, is to ensure that the marketing mix is affordable, implementable and appropriate for the target segment. With that in mind, and given the dynamic nature of most markets, managers will also have to review the mix on a regular basis to make sure that it is still fresh and still serving the purposes intended.

Example West Coast Fish Products drew up a series of planned actions for the main segments served. In the domestic Irish market, for example, the programme aimed at the trade segment might entail:

- sales visits to the top 25 hotels and restaurants
- sales visits to 30 large catering companies
- attendance at relevant trade shows and fairs
- improving design, labelling and durability of packaging
- improving logistics to reduce order processing and delivery times
- launching a new line of fresh eels
- encouraging bigger average order size to improve sales volume and efficiency.

In each case, responsibility will have to be allocated, resources specified, schedules drawn up and activities described in much more detail. For this company, it might well mean that the directors have to spend time meeting customers and developing new business rather than concentrating on the manufacturing processes.

Marketing budgets

The marketing plan must specify and schedule all financial and other resource requirements, otherwise managers might not be able to accomplish the tasks set. This is partly about costs, such as those of the sales force which include their associated expenditures, advertising campaigns, dealer support, market research etc., and partly about forecasting expected revenues from products and markets. In determining budgets, managers need to balance precision against flexibility. A budget should be precise and detailed enough to justify the resources requested and to permit detailed control and evaluation of the cost effectiveness of various marketing activities, yet it also needs the flexibility to cope with changing circumstances.

We discussed budget setting, and some of the issues surrounding it, in Chapter 14 in a marketing communications context (*see* pp. 582 *et seq.*). Many of the points

Example When Cadbury Schweppes introduced its Managing For Value (MFV) programmes (*see* p. 303), it had far-reaching effects on marketing planning and budgeting. The underlying concept of MFV is that all existing and proposed products have to be profitable to survive. This means assessing a brand's impact, not just in terms of marketing returns, but also in terms of the total capital investment, such as in production machinery and logistics. To assess the return, marketing managers were expected to consider a variety of cost equations and schedules on different marketing and production options. The MFV also focused more attention on the effectiveness of the marketing budget and its contribution to market share, volume and earnings growth. The sponsorship of *Coronation Street* (*see* p. 807) was an outcome of the MFV drive, as it enabled a stonger focus on the master brand. It also allowed advertising expenditure on some individual brands to be reduced or redirected away from media advertising, although this was subsequently modified to allow individual brands also to be featured in the sponsorship. With a £22mn spend on advertising alone, of which £10mn goes on *Coronation Street*, Cadbury's has to manage budgets very carefully to realise the benefits of the MFV programmes.

Source: Murphy (1999).

Bringing chocolate to life takes nearly half of Cadbury's advertising budget.

Source: Cadbury's Plc.

made there are more widely applicable, particularly the relative strengths and weaknesses of objective and task budgeting compared with methods based on historical performance (for example basing this year's budget on last year's with an arbitrary 5 per cent added on).

Marketing controls and evaluation

Control and evaluation are both essential if managers are to ensure that the plans are being implemented properly and that the outcomes are those expected. As part of the planning process, therefore, managers will have to specify what will be measured, when, how and by whom. Although the defined marketing objectives provide the ultimate goals against which performance and success can be measured, waiting until the end of the planning period to assess whether they have been achieved is risky. Instead, managers should evaluate progress regularly throughout the period against a series of benchmarks reflecting expected performance to date. If, for example, the overall objective is a 20 per cent increase in volume sales over 12 months, managers might expect after three months to see at least a 5 per cent improvement on the equivalent figure for the previous year, as strategies begin to take effect and gather momentum. At that three-month staging post, managers can then decide whether their strategies appear to be well on target for achieving objectives as planned or whether the deviation from expected performance is so great that alternative actions are called for.

Control and evaluation can take either a short- or a longer-term perspective. In the short term, control can be monitored on a daily basis through reviewing orders received, sales, stockturn or cash flow, for example. Longer-term strategic control focuses on monitoring wider issues, such as the emergence of trends and ambiguities in the marketing environment. This has strong links with the marketing audit, assessing the extent to which the organisation has matched its capabilities with the environment and indeed the extent to which it has correctly 'read' the environment.

This whole area of control and evaluation will be considered in greater detail at pp. 919 *et seq.*

MARKET POTENTIAL AND SALES FORECASTING

The extent to which plans can be successfully implemented depends not only on managers' abilities in setting and implementing strategies, but more fundamentally on their ability to predict the market accurately. This means two things: first, assessing the market potential, that is, working out how big the total cake is, and second, forecasting sales, that is, calculating how big a slice of that cake our organisation can get for itself. The following subsections will look at both of these areas, especially the factors influencing their calculation and the methods used.

Market and sales potential

The concept of **market potential** is very simple, but in practice it is very difficult to estimate. Market potential is the maximum level of demand available within the total market over a given period, assuming a certain level of competitive marketing activity and certain conditions and trends in the marketing environment. This definition immediately raises problems in calculating a figure for market potential, as it involves many assumptions about competitors and the environment, needs a precise definition of 'the market' and requires methods of quantifying the variables concerned.

Market potential

We now look more closely at some of the difficulties in estimating market potential.

Maximum level of demand. The calculation of maximum level of demand should be product or service specific, and means calculating the demand if all possible buyers were to purchase to their fullest realistic extent in terms of volume and frequency. It is an idealised concept that is difficult to measure, for many reasons. For example, any individual's decision about whether to purchase, how much and how often is, in practice, influenced by many factors. One factor is marketing activity, such as campaigns encouraging product substitution or increased consumption. If market potential is partially dependent on marketing effort, then a range of alternative 'maximum levels of demand' become immediately possible.

Total market. The potential total market is really a question of boundaries. In the same way that calculation of profit can vary according to the way in which an accountant interprets the rules, total market size can vary according to the definitions used to mark market boundaries.

Level of competitive activity and trends in the marketing environment. As we showed in Chapter 2, the marketing environment is a very dynamic and complex phenomenon that has a fundamental impact on the organisation. A change in any aspect of the marketing environment can, therefore, have a corresponding effect on market potential. Competitors can also implement strategies that change the nature of the market as a whole, either by opening up new segments, increasing demand through marketing communication efforts, or by launching new products that effectively create a new market.

> **Example** Eidos has been successful in establishing a share of the computer games market with titles such as *Tomb Raider* and *Championship Manager*. However, that market can also be defined in terms of the games format, i.e. PC, Nintendo etc.; as 'action games', including games like *Tomb Raider*; or even as part of a wider entertainment sector. Depending on the definition used, market size and therefore potential could vary significantly, and thus the prospects of Eidos could be redefined. For example, a wider market definition could be important to Eidos, as it develops an Internet games portal and after the sale of film rights to Paramount to continue the adventures of Laura Croft (Price, 1999).

Over time, market potential will change, depending on the forces at work. All of these forces are beyond the organisation's control, yet the organisation has to try to predict them. It is also important when looking at the environment to be clear about the time period being considered, the stage of growth reached by the market, and the rate of change, especially in technology that is likely to affect the environment. Clearly, the further ahead the organisation is looking, the greater the uncertainty in predictions.

Sales potential

Even after the potential has been estimated for the market as a whole, an organisation will then need to determine its own **sales potential**, that is, the share of the market that it could reasonably expect to capture. Obviously, sales potential is partly a result of the organisation's marketing effort and its success in attracting and holding customers. Although the level of total market potential will create a ceiling for an organisation's individual sales potential, in reality sales potential should be based on a clear understanding of the relative success of individual organisations' marketing efforts. The decision to launch a new range or to increase promotional expenditure could help to raise the level of sales potential. As already mentioned, in some situations the actions of an individual organisation can increase the potential for all competitors by expanding the market potential as a whole. Thus if a major player in the market or a number of competitors increase their promotional spends, that might stimulate the market for all competitors, not just those undertaking the marketing effort.

Having a clear idea of market and sales potential provides a useful input to the marketing planning process. It is especially important for planning selling efforts and allocating resources. The allocation of sales force effort, and the establishment of distribution points and service support centres, for example, can reflect sales potential rather than actual sales, thus allowing scope for expansion. Similarly, sales potential can also be used to plan sales territories, quotas, sales force compensation and targets for prospecting.

Estimating market and sales potential

The methods used for estimating sales and market potential will vary, depending on just how new or innovative the product or service is, and how mature the market is. The two main groups of methods discussed here are *breakdown*, that is, working from the aggregate level of the whole market down to the segment of interest, and *build-up*, that is, starting with individual customers then aggregating up to industry or market totals.

Breakdown methods

Breakdown methods fall into two main groups: those based on total market measurement and those based on statistical series analysis.

Total market measurement. The total market measurement method begins with any total industry or market data that may be available from secondary research, and then breaks that information down to market segment level and thence to the organisation's own sales potential. This method relies heavily on the availability of a long series of data on industry sales volume and consumption by segments within that market, but rarely are such complete and detailed data available. Potential is thus often estimated from what data are available and then adjusted to take account of the current marketing environment. Once market and segment potentials have been established, sales potential can be derived by estimating competitors' relative market shares and then calculating how those might change as a result of expected actions, for example a new product launch.

Statistical series analysis. Statistical series analysis is a means of calculating potential for market segments. It is based on developing a statistical relationship, correlating sales and key factors influencing them. The success of this method depends on identifying the right factor or combination of factors (i.e. statistical series) to use in the analysis. Cox (1979), for example, quotes the case of a company trying to establish potential for production machinery. The analysis was based on a single factor, the number of production employees within each industry using that kind of equipment. Several other statistical series, such as expenditure on new equipment and value of products shipped, had been tested but discarded. In some industries, the appropriate factor to use is fairly obvious. The potential for building material sales in a region, for example, is closely related, as one might expect, to the number of building contracts and the size of their floor area. The calculation might be further influenced by weightings reflecting managerial judgements on the relative importance of segments and the likely effect of other environmental factors on the future development of those segments. Thus knowledge that the authorities in a certain region are about to invest in an extensive campaign to attract new industry into its neighbourhood might make the building materials company weight that region more highly than a similar region with lower future growth prospects.

Build up methods

There are three main methods for aggregating data to produce reliable market and sales potential figures: census, survey and secondary data.

Census. The census method is based on a detailed consideration of every buyer and potential buyer in a market. This may be difficult, if not impossible, in mass consumer markets, but is more feasible in industrial situations, where demand might be concentrated and orders infrequent but of high value. With large capital plant, such as turbine generators or aircraft engines, for instance, a census could provide a good indication of market and sales potential as the customer base is very small. The market potential is effectively the sum of all the potentials estimated for individual purchasers.

Survey. The survey method is more widely used in consumer markets where a representative sample (look back at Chapter 6) of consumers are asked about their purchase intentions. This information can then be used as a basis for calculating total market or sales potential. The main problem, however, is that respondents might lie about their intentions, or fail to follow them through in the future. Consumers might well be genuine in saying that yes, they do intend to replace their car within the next 12 months, but an unexpected redundancy, repairs to the roof of the house, or the allure of an exotic holiday might cause them to revise their intentions. Even more problematic is establishing intent to purchase a particular brand. A consumer might genuinely intend to replace their car with a Ford, but if at the time of the actual purchase Renault or Volvo are running a particularly attractive promotion, then ... who knows?

Secondary data. Finally, secondary data can be used to establish sales and market potential. Internal sales records can be used to predict individual customers' purchasing on the basis of past behaviour. In this approach, the sales potentials are produced first and the market potential is then derived from those figures.

Market and sales forecasting

Marketing often plays a central role in preparing and disseminating **forecasts**. This is perhaps one of its most important functions, as the sales and market forecasts provided are the basis of all subsequent planning and decision making within most areas of the organisation. Whether the organisation is a car manufacturer forecasting the demand for each model, a tour operator forecasting demand for specific destinations, or a university forecasting numbers of full-time, part-time and overseas students by programme area, the forecast is the starting point for all subsequent decisions. Get it wrong and the whole organisation can be caught out by major capacity or cash flow problems. In fashion markets, for example, it can be very difficult to forecast what styles are going to sell in what quantities, hence the popularity of 'end of season' sales as retailers try to sell off surplus stock. Holiday companies also find forecasting difficult, and again find themselves selling off surplus holidays at a discount right up to departure dates.

Example Both Boeing and Airbus forecast a decline of between 30 and 40 per cent in demand for civil aircraft in 1999 and no recovery until 2001, based on the impact of a slowdown in economic activity and the aftershocks of the Asian financial crisis. Although the age of passenger fleets is well known, replacement dates can be deferred and so market forecasting can still be challenging. In addition, the type of aircraft required has to be assessed. Although there has been consideration of 'super jumbos' seating 550, Boeing is wary of over-committing to a project, as it forecasts that the real demand in the future will be for direct flights with smaller planes rather than trunk/hub type flights involving a change (Skapinker, 1999).

Forecasting and planning are, however, different functions. Forecasting attempts to indicate what will happen in a given environmental situation if a specific set of decisions and actions is implemented with no subsequent changes. Planning assumes that the environmental situation, especially that relating to the competitive arena, can be influenced, or at least better dealt with, by changing management decisions and actions. The focus of planning is, therefore, on alternatives and outcomes. Of course, there needs to be interaction between planning and forecasting, so that forecasts can be revised to take account of the new conditions likely to be created by the implementation of proposed plans.

Example Bridon (http://www.bridon.com), part of the FKI Group, is one of Europe's largest wire producing companies and its production is mainly concentrated in Doncaster. Its customers come from various industrial sectors, buying wire for cranes, oilfields and mining, mooring systems and structural systems. It has even supplied wire for the Millennium Dome project.

In looking to the future, a company like Bridon has to try to forecast the future needs of current customers and any likely changes or developments, but also sources of new business, perhaps in emerging growth industries or from new products. This forecasting has to be done early so that Bridon can make any necessary capital investment to ensure that it is ready when the demand is there, although it also needs an in-depth understanding of the probabilities of winning tenders. In the early 1990s, Bridon had recognised that it was taking too long to get new products on the market and by cutting the time taken down from five years to eight months on specific projects, any forecasting effort is looking less far into the future. Forecasting was also helped by improvements in customer service. A new ordering and scheduling system alongside simpler administration brought more information about individual customers together, perhaps making it easier to identify ordering patterns and trends and to spot future opportunities. Product sector forecasts and plans can also be assisted by a combination of industry trend analysis and the 'expert' opinion of the sales force and management.

There is no such thing as a rigid or absolute forecast. Different forecasters using different forecasting methods are almost certain to come up with different results. Forecasts should, however, share some common characteristics, as suggested by Wheelwright and Makridakis (1977). They should:

- be based on historical information from which a projection can be made
- look forward over a specific, clearly defined time period
- make clearly specified assumptions, since uncertainty characterises the future.

Forecasts often evolve from the general to the specific through a process of information assessment, sharing and iteration between senior staff, professional planners and line managers. This evolution allows managers to arrive eventually at a forecast based on an agreed set of assumptions regarding the industry and market environment, and compatible with planned effort at a corporate level. The process of reconciliation between the 'specialists' and line managers in sales and marketing is important for generating commitment and a sense of responsibility for the forecasts agreed.

If forecasts are to be operationally relevant, they should progress through four levels of detail, so that formulating assumptions, identifying key trends, and operational planning and decision making can all be included. These four stages, proposed by Wolfe (1966), are shown in Fig. 21.4.

Each stage clearly builds on the previous one, and thus the impact of changes can be traced throughout the process. A range of methods can be used for forecasting,

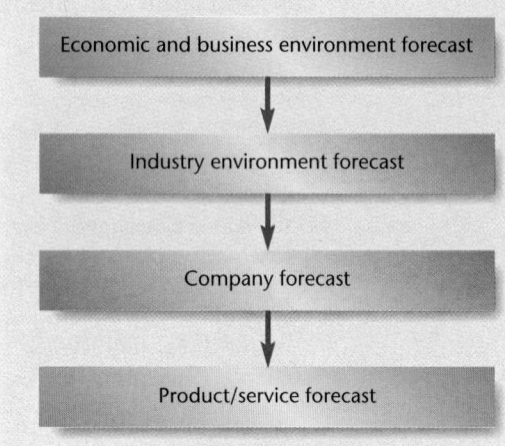

FIGURE 21.4

Four-stage approach to forecasting

Improve sales forecasts, slash costs

The effect of accurate sales forecasts can be profound. Raw materials and component parts can be purchased much more cost effectively when last minute, spot market purchases can be avoided. Such expenses can be eliminated by accurately forecasting production needs. Perhaps most important, accurate forecasting can have a profound impact on a company's inventory levels. In many firms, inventory exists to provide a buffer for inaccurate forecasts. Thus, the more accurate the forecasts, the less inventory that has to be carried (Moon *et al.*, 1998). And sales forecasts are rarely near the mark. In a 1997 survey by the magazine *Purchasing*, nearly 60 per cent of the purchasing outfits surveyed said that the sales forecast information they received was only somewhat accurate. Another quarter said that the information was not accurate (Genna, 1997). Another study of 208 companies found that many system disconnections still exist between the forecasting function, the information needed to produce accurate forecasts, and the forecast users (Mentzer *et al.*, 1999).

So how can sales forecasting be improved? The answer is not simply to use technology. Another survey of 478 US companies revealed that an average of 1.82 sales forecasting computer systems were used by those companies (Kahn and Mentzer, 1997). Yet most of the companies surveyed used only personal computers and had very little access to mainframe systems where the *real* information to support accurate sales forecasting is often held. The answer is to create an integrated forecasting function, allowing both your customers and your suppliers into the process. The technology comes in through:

- EDI linkages to allow everybody access to what inventory is where in the supply chain
- electronic point-of-sale systems (EPoS) to provide instant feedback on how well different products and product lines are selling.

The ultimate effects of sales forecasting excellence can be dramatic. Brake Parts, Inc., a manufacturer of automotive after-market parts, improved its bottom line by $6 million per month after launching a company-wide effort to improve sales forecasting effectiveness.

Source: O'Connor and Galvin (1999).

depending on the stage being undertaken. Each method differs in its cost profile, complexity in preparation, rigour and ability to generate the range of projections needed to plan the next stage. The following subsection looks at a number of forecasting methods.

Forecasting methods

Forecasting methods fall into two main groups. *Qualitative techniques* are often used in the earlier stages of forecasting to describe the likely changes and to help define more precisely the assumptions used. *Quantitative techniques* tend to be used in the later stages, when production schedules and financial planning require hard numbers on which to make plans. All these techniques are shown in Fig. 21.5.

Qualitative methods

Qualitative methods do not rely on hard, statistical data, but centre on 'soft' data based on expertise, knowledge and judgement. There are several methods of qualitative forecasting.

Management judgement. Management judgement is perhaps the riskiest source, as it relies on the people at the top or on experts within the organisation to predict what will happen. While the people involved may have a wealth of expertise and knowledge between them, there is a risk that they are too close to the organisation, its way of doing things and its markets to be truly objective. Their assumptions and prejudices may lead to an incomplete or inaccurate picture. Although management judgement does not lead to rigorous forecasts, it does at least encourage the systematic analysis and justification of available data and management attitudes.

Example Despite Sony's leadership of the games console market (*see* p. 846), the company has forecast that its sales will fall in 1999–2000 from 21.6 million units to 17 million units as a result of increased competition. Although it will be responding to the launch of Sega's Dreamcast, until the PlayStation 2 is available Sony must manage the difficult transition without undermining current sales by encouraging customers to wait for the new product. Management judgement is often needed to assess the impact of a competitor's launch and the impact of any short-term marketing strategies designed to stop customers shifting to competitors before the new product launch (Abrahams, 1999).

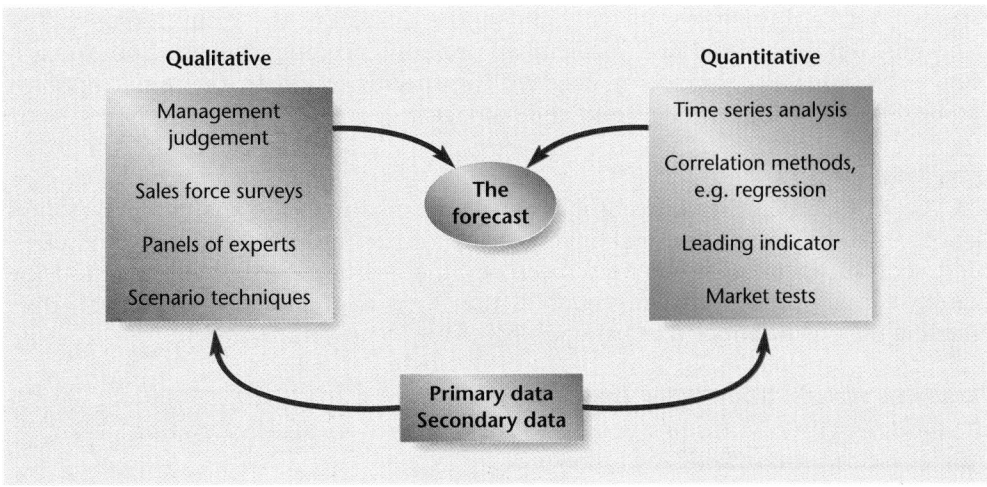

FIGURE 21.5

Forecasting methods

Sales force surveys. Sales force surveys can provide a wealth of information. Such surveys involve asking sales representatives to provide forecasts on customers, dealers, accounts etc. The sales force is a valuable source of expert opinion, since representatives are very close to customers on a daily basis, and will learn of likely changes in purchasing intentions early. As with a primary research survey, however, any forecast derived from this method should be treated with caution. In addition to any bias introduced by the customer, the representatives might also influence the forecast, either through naivety or through consideration of their own agendas. A naive representative, for example, underestimating barriers and constraints, might assume that when our new product is launched, sales to certain customers will boom. More insecure representatives might prefer to underestimate future demand and overestimate the barriers so that their own performance will look better. The cynical representative, on the other hand, might underestimate future demand because sales targets and bonus arrangements depend on it. Thus the more pessimistic the forecast, the lower the sales target and the sooner the bonuses start to accrue.

Representatives might thus be over-optimistic or pessimistic, or protective of their own position and interests, but rarely realistic. Management do, of course, recognise these biases, and try to make allowances for representatives' involvement, motivation and realism. Nevertheless, the sales force survey is still an attractive technique, as it slots into the existing structure of the organisation and can easily provide forecasts for individual customer groups, sales territories, areas, operating divisions or products.

Panels of experts. Panels of experts consisting of specially chosen eminent industrialists, economists, management consultants or academics, for example, may be asked for their opinions. These individuals are chosen for their sound knowledge and opinions of a market or its environment, and the membership of the panel will be balanced to represent a range of areas of expertise. The panel will be presented with forecasts and views of the future, and then asked to comment. The quality of the results will depend on the quality and commitment of the experts used, but even the best experts get it wrong sometimes.

Scenario techniques. Scenario techniques aim to provide a complete picture of trends and events to create a more integrated and complete view of alternative situations. Although a panel of experts can be used for such a purpose, the main method used tends to be the Delphi technique. The *Delphi method* pools expert opinion, on the assumption that group opinion is better than that of an individual. It is especially useful for very long-range forecasting and technological forecasting. The experts used are not brought together, and they do not know who else is involved. Each one is questioned on issues and trends, then the collective responses are distributed to all members of the team with a further, more detailed questionnaire. This process is repeated until a rounded profile is obtained, the median of the group response. The main problem is potential bias, as members are influenced by feedback from the collective responses. For short-term, organisation-specific forecasts, the same approach can be used involving the sales team and managers.

Quantitative methods

The majority of quantitative techniques are concerned with the analysis of historical data to establish trends and make projections for the future based on a time series. More sophisticated models have also been developed, however, that aim to reflect the complex interactions between variables that help explain cause and effect, thus enabling the organisation to be better prepared for an uncertain future.

Time series analysis. Time series analysis is a means of using historical data to predict the future. Analysis of historic data can reveal patterns in the organisation's sales figures. These patterns include the following.

1 *Trends*: extrapolation of data on a straight or curved line basis can give a broad view of the general direction in which sales are moving.

2 *Cycles*: these reflect periodic changes in patterns over a period of time. It is important to analyse the reasons for cycles. Some may be caused by external factors, such as fluctuations in the economy leading to upturns and downturns in business, while other short-term fluctuations could reflect the outcomes of successful marketing activities. Cycles may last years or months, and tend to recur. The UK's construction industry is used to 'boom and bust' cycles linked with the state of the UK economy. When the economy is depressed, nobody wants to build new offices, factories, supermarkets or other retail space. Furthermore, a long-term depression in the housing market means that there is little building work in that sector either. Normally, when the economy recovers, the construction industry follows close behind.

3 *Seasonality*: this covers shorter-term fluctuations around an overall trend, and may even be observed on a daily or weekly basis, if the organisation wants to get down to that level. Obviously, some markets are naturally highly seasonal, such as summer holidays, toys as Christmas gifts and gardening products, and any forecasting is going to produce pronounced seasonal effects.

4 *Random factors*: these are very difficult to predict, but nevertheless, any forecast is going to have to make allowances for the effects of strikes, riots, civil commotion and acts of God, as the insurance industry would put it.

At the end of this detailed analysis of trends and patterns, managers are better able to estimate the sales forecast for the coming period, perhaps giving pessimistic, optimistic and expected figures. Time series analysis builds on long-term trends and short-term fluctuations, and can be smoothed exponentially, placing more emphasis on recent data. The problem with time series analysis, as with any technique based on historical data, is that it assumes that things will carry on steadily into the future without any major deviation. This might be a reasonable assumption if the market concerned is stable and predictable, but a highly dangerous assumption in unstable, fluctuating markets.

Correlation method. If time series analysis is felt to be inappropriate, the forecaster might prefer to use a correlation method (or statistical demand analysis). Techniques such as multiple regression are, like time series analysis, based on historical data but instead of assuming that sales are simply a function of time, they try to identify other factors that influence sales. Thus, for example, sales of domestic conservatories might be expressed as a function of a number of other variables:

$$Q = f(x_1, x_2, x_3),$$

where Q is the quantity of conservatories demanded,
  x_1 is disposable income,
  x_2 is the cost of borrowing and
  x_3 is the number of households with gardens, but without conservatories.

By analysing statistically a series of historic data relating to Q and x_1 to x_3, an equation can be developed which gives the best explanation of the quantitative relationship between sales and the other variables involved. Thus analysis might reveal that

$$\text{Sales} = c + 3(x_1) + 50(x_2) - 0.05(x_3).$$

It would then be possible to forecast future sales by inserting estimated future values of x_1 to x_3 into this equation, or to forecast sales in a different region, for example by inserting known values of x_1 to x_3 from that region.

This type of method can be difficult to implement, since it needs an extensive historic data bank to work with if the best possible equation is to be devised.

Managers still need to exercise a certain degree of caution when using such equations. The forecast is never going to be 100 per cent accurate, and there is still the underlying assumption that the relationship between all the variables is going to continue into the future in the same way as it has in the past. The main problem with using an equation like this for forecasting, however, is the estimation of future values of x_1 to x_3. Any unforeseen swings in their behaviour might render the whole forecast meaningless.

Leading indicators. Leading indicators are useful for shorter-term forecasting. These indicators give advance warning of trends and changes in the marketing environment so that the organisation can adjust or plan accordingly. The definition of the key indicators will vary from industry to industry. A carpet manufacturer, for example, might look at the rate of new business start-ups or the amount of new office space being developed (on the basis that new businesses might want to carpet their new offices). In consumer markets, the leading indicators might be house sales, the rate of new house building, or even trends in average disposable income or unemployment levels. These all affect consumers' willingness and ability to buy new carpets, and will have an impact on the type, quality and price of carpets that the manufacturer produces.

Market tests. Market tests, as discussed at pp. 356 *et seq.* give an insight into real behaviour rather than focusing on intentions. They are very useful as a part of new product development and launch programmes, and can help to forecast likely future performance. Managers need to be sure, however, that the structure of the test and the area in which it takes place are as truly representative of the target market and the planned marketing mix as possible.

Overall, the more cross-checking of forecasts that takes place using different techniques, the more tailor-made the techniques to suit the industry, the organisation's product and its target market's purchasing characteristics, the better and more reliable the forecast will be.

Primary research. Primary research looks outside the organisation by surveying customers. In an organisational market, key customers could be asked their opinions of trends and how their own consumption patterns are likely to change. In consumer markets, a sample of consumers within a segment could similarly be surveyed, although this is more likely to be part of a bigger quantitative survey. In either case, it is essential that the research is sufficiently deep to allow the assumptions underlying the respondent's opinion to be thoroughly understood. Respondents are not always willing, however, to give information or may simply not know much about the issues raised. There is also a risk that organisational customers may feel that they are being asked to reveal commercially sensitive information that might be used against them in future negotiations. This may lead to non-response or to lies! Respondents may even be over-optimistic about their own intentions so that when customer intentions to purchase are aggregated, the resulting forecast is far too high.

Secondary data. Some secondary data can also be used to help create a general picture. Organisations can make use of published research data (*see* pp. 226 *et seq.*), such as those published by Euromonitor, to validate their own understanding of the way the market is moving, to raise new issues, and to act as a basis for further detailed investigation. Similarly, publications by various banks and government bodies provide the kind of background information on economic and industrial trends, demographics and social trends that can lead to a deeper understanding of the marketing environment.

ORGANISING MARKETING ACTIVITIES

Effective marketing management does not happen by itself. It has to have the right kind of infrastructure and place within the organisation in order to develop and work efficiently and effectively. First, therefore, we discuss the role and place of the marketing department within the organisation as a whole. That is followed by an overview of different ways of structuring a marketing department, and finally we consider issues surrounding the implementation of marketing plans.

Organisational location of marketing

Central to the marketing philosophy is a focus on customer needs. As discussed in the early chapters of this book, marketers act as an interface between customers and other functions within the organisation. By understanding markets, customers' needs and wants and the ways in which they are changing and why, the marketer is providing essential information for planning corporate direction and the activities of other functions within the organisation. The production department, for example, needs to know what products will be demanded, with what variations, to what specifications, in what quantities and when, so that they can plan to produce them. Most, if not all, of these decisions will be marketing driven.

So that marketing can fulfil its role effectively, therefore, and be taken seriously, marketing managers should be equal in status to senior managers from other functional areas. They also need to work closely with other managers, not just for information exchange but also on joint projects, for example new product planning and development, inventory management, physical distribution or logistics management.

It is important, however, to distinguish between a functional marketing department and marketing orientation as a management philosophy. A small organisation might not have a marketing department as such, but it can still practise a marketing orientation very effectively through the closeness of its relationships with its customers and its responsiveness to their needs. In contrast, any organisation can have a marketing department, yet not be truly marketing orientated. If that marketing department is isolated from other functional areas, if it is just there to 'do advertising', then its potential is wasted. Marketing orientation permeates the whole organisation and *requires* marketing's involvement in all areas of the organisation.

Whether or not there is a marketing department, and how it is structured, depends on a number of factors. These might include the size of the organisation, the size and complexity of the markets served, the product and process technology and the rate of change in the marketing environment. There are several ways of incorporating and structuring marketing within the organisation, and these are discussed below.

Organisational alternatives

In thinking about how marketing might be organised, it is important to be clear about the tasks involved in marketing. Marketers have to research and analyse markets and customers. They have to forecast sales and then plan, develop, implement and manage elements of the marketing mix. They also have a wider corporate role in supporting the organisation's strategic development, interfacing with other functions. The marketer's focus is not just on today, but on the future as well. These tasks open up a number of choices for organising staff, delegating authority and responsibility and specifying line management relationships. The purpose is to clarify who makes what decisions and who is responsible for their implementation, and to ensure that all this is done at an appropriately senior level with proper monitoring and control.

There are four main choices for structuring marketing management within a department, focusing on function, products, regions or segments. The marketing

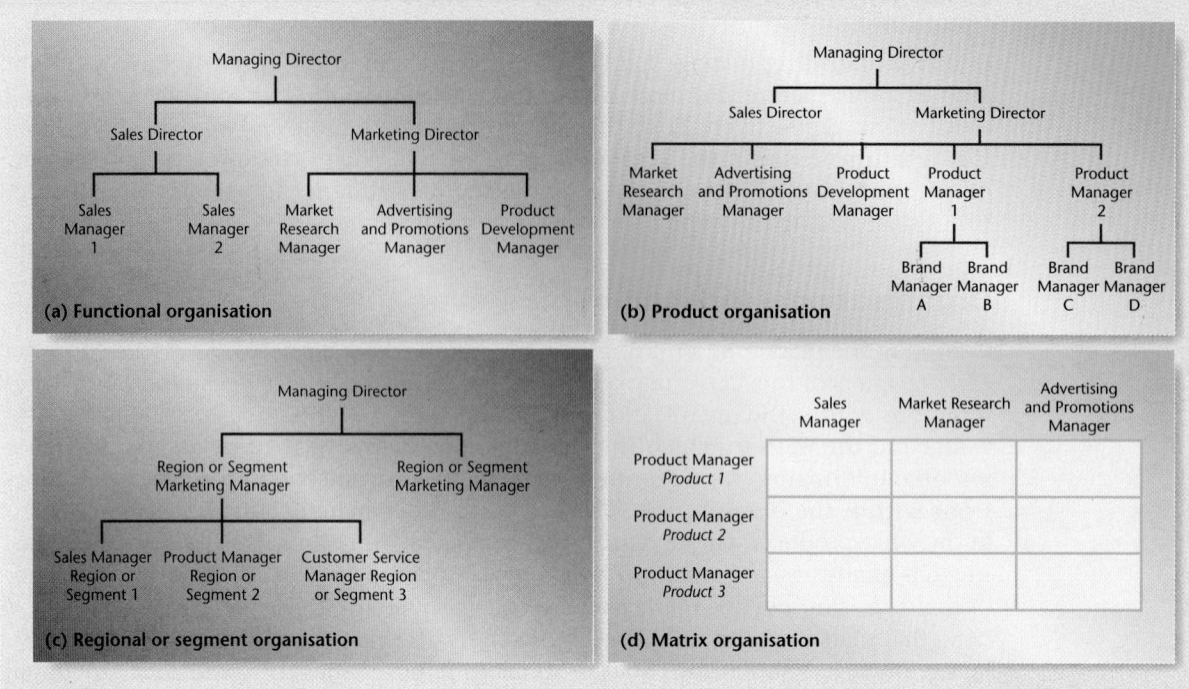

(a) Functional organisation

(b) Product organisation

(c) Regional or segment organisation

(d) Matrix organisation

FIGURE 21.6

Forms of marketing organisation

department might also choose to develop a matrix structure, allowing an equal focus on both function and products, for example. These are all shown in Fig. 21.6. The organisation might, of course, choose not to have a formal marketing department at all. Each of these choices is discussed below.

Functional organisation

A functional department is structured along the lines of specific marketing activities. This means there are very specialised roles and responsibilities, and that individual managers have to build expertise. Such a department might have, for example, a market research manager, an advertising and promotions manager and a new product development manager, each of whom will report to the organisation's marketing director.

This system works well in organisations where the various business functions are centralised, but problems can arise where they are decentralised. Then, functional marketing tasks have to be co-ordinated across diverse areas, with greater or lesser degrees of co-operation and acceptance.

> **Example** Many university marketing departments are organised on functional lines. A number of specialised roles concerned with public relations, print and prospectuses, advertising, schools liaison and market research can often be found reporting to a marketing manager. Product development issues and fees tend to be the domain of the faculties and departments rather than the marketing department due to the significance of academic quality control, curriculum design and delivery, often within a regulated setting.

Product organisation

Giving managers responsibility for specific products, brands or categories of product might suit a larger company with major brands or with diverse and very different product interests. The manager, reporting to a product group manager or a marketing director, builds expertise around the product, and is responsible for all aspects of its development, its strategic and marketing mix planning and its day-to-day welfare. Other specialist staff, such as market researchers, might be involved as necessary to help the product manager.

Example Forte, the hotel division of Granada, restructured its marketing department so that its four individual brands could be marketed separately. Therefore Posthouse, Heritage, Le Meridien and London Signature each had a managing director reporting to the chief executive. This structure was considered more appropriate for the development of each brand, despite the potential for some duplication of marketing effort (Barrett, 1999).

The product, brand or category management approach is very popular in fmcg markets. It gives clear lines of management responsibility, but there is still a need for a central function to co-ordinate the overall portfolio. As mentioned at pp. 329–300, there are potential problems with internal rivalry as managers seek to champion their own brands. A little healthy rivalry is not necessarily a bad thing, but it must not be allowed to get out of hand or to cloud management judgement.

The typical tasks of a product or brand manager include:

- the development of competitive strategies and plans consistent with corporate objectives
- the production of annual marketing plans, forecasts and budgets
- the design and development of support strategies for the sales and distribution team
- the gathering or commissioning of primary and secondary data on the product, market, competitors etc.
- management of the product in terms of innovation, modification and deletion.

The main problem with product organisation is working with other functions, such as production, finance etc. to get the resources, attention and effort that the product needs. There is also the risk that too many management layers will be introduced, hence the move towards category management (i.e. responsibility for a group of brands) rather than individual brand management.

Regional organisation

An organisation with its activities spread over a wide geographic area, or one operating in markets with distinct regional differences, might find regionally based marketing responsibility attractive. The regional marketing manager, along with a support team, will make all marketing decisions relevant to planning and operations in that territory. There will then be some mechanism for co-ordinating regional efforts at a national or international level to ensure consistency and strategic fit. As larger organisations become more international, this approach is becoming more common. The main benefit is that local managers develop the knowledge and expertise to know what is best for their region. They can then develop the most appropriate, fully integrated marketing mix package, as well as contributing intelligently to the organisation's overall strategic planning for that region.

Example Procter & Gamble decided to centralise its strategic marketing activities in Europe by moving the senior marketers from four regional units into seven business units in a new European HQ in Geneva. The business units are fabric and homecare, food and beverages, feminine hygiene, beauty care, tissues and towels, baby care and health care. However, the R&D and product design specialists would remain close to production and operational marketing decision making. Eight market development organisations have the job of tailoring global programmes to local markets and designing local marketing plans based on local consumer knowledge. Although national marketing staff are to be retained alongside the sales force to tailor products and programmes, the move to centralisation is thought likely to assist in more pan-European development and to increase the speed of decision making to get new products to market more quickly. Thus a new product launched in Germany might quickly be rolled out across Europe, as marketing staff in other locations will be aware of its potential because they are part of the same division (Bell, 1999a, 1999b).

Regionally based marketing departments are particularly attractive to organisations with a great emphasis on selling in the field, where close co-ordination and control are necessary. It is also appropriate for service industries, such as hospitality, where local conditions may differ and where, again, close control and co-ordination of service delivery are required.

Segmental organisation

An organisation that serves diverse groups of customers with very different needs might choose to develop marketing teams dedicated to each of those groups. This is because the marketing decision making and the marketing mixes have to be tailored to the individual needs of segments in which the competitive threats may be very different.

A brewery, for example, will market to the licensed trade (for instance pubs and clubs) and the retail trade (for instance supermarkets and off licences) very differently; a manufacturer of wound dressings will market differently to the hospital sector and to the pharmacist; a car dealer will market differently to the family motorist and to a fleet buyer. The volume purchased by individual customers within the same segment might create differences that are reflected in the marketing effort. An fmcg manufacturer will create a different kind of marketing mix and customer relationship with the top six multiple supermarket chains than with the many thousands of small independent grocers.

The marketing manager for a particular segment or customer group will have a range of specialist support staff and will report to a senior marketing manager or director with overall responsibility for all segments.

Matrix organisation

A matrix approach allows the marketing department to get the best of more than one of the previous methods of organisation. It can be particularly useful in large diverse organisations or where specialists and project teams have to work on major cross-functional activities, for example PR, new product development or marketing research programmes.

Example The Cendant (http://www.cedant.com) leisure and direct marketing holding company manages through a matrix structure, with each business unit supported by marketing specialists working across the company. This enables a wider cross-fertilisation of ideas into divisions, for example the direct marketing company can be used to promote discount travel services and hotel reservations.

No department

Of course, another option is not to have a department at all. Small organisations might not be able to afford specialist marketing staff and thus perhaps the owner finds himself or herself performing a multi-functional role as sales representative, promotional decision maker and strategist rolled into one. If a small organisation does decide to invest in marketing staff, the recruit might be put into an office-based administrative support role or into a sales role.

Sales-driven organisations

Some organisations are still driven by sales. They might have a few very large customers and be selling a complex technology. In such a case, the role of marketing is relegated to a support role that is largely concerned with PR and low-key promotional activity. Other organisations, particularly those currently or previously in the public sector, are still in the process of developing marketing departments. Universities, for example, are re-appraising the role of marketing. Although they might have marketing departments, many of the key variables are beyond the control of their marketing managers. For example, academics, with or without the benefit of market research, develop and vali-date new courses; in another area, domestic full-time student fees and student numbers are agreed with the government. Often, universities see the marketing department's role as purely functional, handling student recruitment fairs, prospectuses, schools liaison and advertising. In short, there is no guarantee that having a department means that there will be a marketing orientation in the organisation.

CONTROLLING MARKETING ACTIVITIES

Control is a vital aspect of implementing marketing plans, whether strategic or opera-tional. It helps to ensure that activities happen as planned, with proper management. It also provides important feedback that enables managers to determine whether or not their decisions, actions and strategies are working appropriately in practice.

Strategic control takes a wide, long-term view, considering whether the overall mar-keting strategy is actually driving the organisation in the desired direction. This is normally assessed through the marketing audit process outlined at pp. 896 *et seq.* and is often conducted on an annual basis, either as a special *ad hoc* process or as part of the marketing planning cycle. *Operational control* takes a shorter-term view, checking whether detailed, functional marketing programmes are actually working in practice. These checks can take place on a daily basis if necessary, and certainly happen fre-quently enough to determine whether problem areas are developing. Operational control needs to pick up problems early, before too much damage is done, so that cor-rective action can be taken more easily. Designing an effective control system to suit the needs and characteristics of the organisation is a critical part of managing marketing effort.

FIGURE 21.7

Marketing control

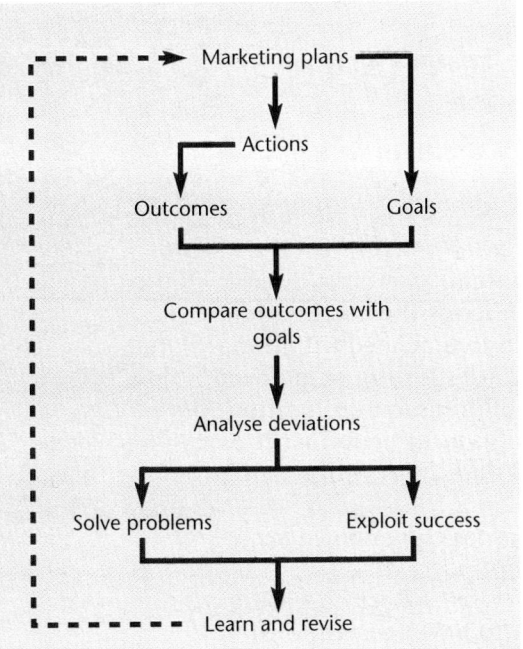

The marketing control process

The marketing control phase, shown in Fig. 21.7, is not an afterthought to be bolted on to the end of the plan-ning process, but should be designed as an important part of that process. In setting marketing objectives, it is important to define them in terms of detailed time-spe-cific goals against which performance can be measured. This makes the task of control more manageable, since those areas where serious deviation is occurring can then be easily diagnosed. Management effort can thus be focused on areas of greatest need rather than being spread too thinly.

When setting performance targets for marketing activities, however, it is important to ensure that they are realistic, that they can be measured and that the measurement criteria used are meaningful and relevant. This is especially important where managers' perfor-mance is partly judged by their achievement of the agreed targets. Typical measures might be sales volume or value, the number of new customers created, the number of enquiries generated, stock turnover, satisfaction surveys or relative market share. The MIS system considered in Chapter 6 should provide the essential flow of information that enables performance to be measured as well as highlighting emerging problem areas. This flow of data must, therefore, be timely and sufficiently detailed to allow deeper analysis.

As soon as the control mechanism shows that a gap is opening between proposed targets and actual achievement, managers can start to look for reasons for this happening. Sometimes the reasons might be obvious, for example a stockout in a particular region or the loss of a major customer. In other situations, however, further research might have to be commissioned to support deeper analysis of the underlying causes. If, for example, a brand's market share continues to decline despite increased marketing effort, managers might start asking serious questions about customer responsiveness and the brand's competitive positioning.

Unless managers can be sure about why performance is off target, they cannot reliably define the right corrective actions. In some cases they might decide that no corrective action needs to be taken, in others they might devise a programme of major or minor changes to bring the marketing strategy back on track. Where a regional stockout occurs, the solution may be obvious, if brand share is declining unexpectedly, a fairly radical revision of the brand's marketing strategy might be called for. Failure to achieve targets does not, however, mean automatic condemnation of the marketing plan and its manager. It could be that targets were hopelessly optimistic, in the light of the emerging market conditions. Alternatively, other departments within the organisation, for example production or logistics, may have failed to achieve their targets.

Managers should, however, be wary of overreaction. A certain amount of deviation is to be expected since no forward plan can be absolutely right. Part of the planning process is to agree what the threshold is between tolerable and intolerable deviation. Real customers buying real products in a real competitive market do not necessarily behave to order, and therefore some flexibility and patience should be exercised. There is also sometimes a lag effect between implementing marketing action and seeing the results of that action. Declaring a crisis and taking corrective action too soon might well be counterproductive. If, however, a major event happens that represents discontinuous change, corrective action might have to be taken long before its effects start to show in the computer printouts.

Methods of evaluating operational performance

There are several ways of evaluating marketing performance, two of which, sales analysis and costs and profitability analysis, are discussed here.

Sales analysis

Sales analysis is at the heart of any performance control system, as it most directly relates to the product and is likely to be widely understood across the organisation. Through the ordering and invoicing system, sales data can be accumulated within the MIS. These data include future order files, current sales, and sales history by product and perhaps even by individual customer, giving detailed information on location, price, quantity etc. Sales analysis can thus provide a ready measure of performance to date, and through analysis of the variances between expected and actual performance, it can form a basis for planning remedial actions.

Sales analysis can be broken down into various subdivisions for more refined analysis, as shown in Fig. 21.8.

Sales analysis can also be linked with market share analysis, reflecting general trends within the industry. It is possible for an organisation to have increasing sales,

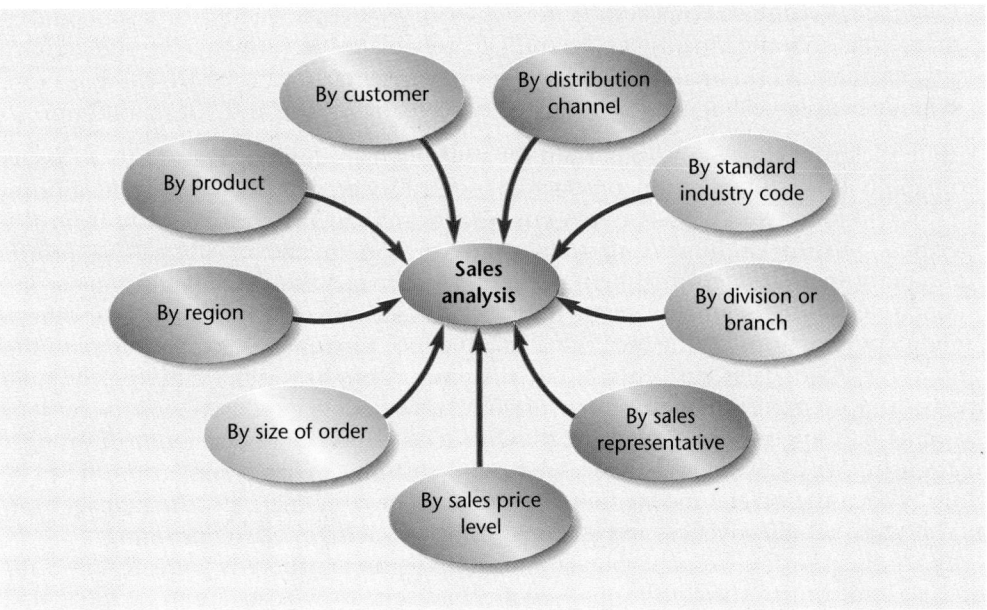

FIGURE 21.8

Bases for sales analysis

but to be losing market share (because competitors' sales are growing faster). Equally, it is possible to see a decline in sales at the same time as market share is rising (because competitors' sales are declining faster). In some situations, for example during harvesting and strategic withdrawal, an organisation might be happy to see both sales and share declining, as long as short-term profits are maintained or improved. Linking sales analysis with market share analysis is useful for putting the organisation's performance in its proper competitive context. It could give indications of how well a marketing mix has been formulated, as well as raising debate about the controllable and uncontrollable factors at work in the market.

Marketing costs and profitability analysis

Figure 21.9 shows the three controllable elements of marketing that contribute towards profit and those that create costs (Wilson *et al.*, 1992). Thus marketing profitability is created by what is sold, in what quantity and at what price, but reduced by the costs associated with achieving those results.

Although the categories of costs seem to be reasonably straightforward, it can be difficult in practice to identify and control some aspects of marketing costs. Wilson *et al.* (1992) suggest a number of characteristics of marketing costs that make them difficult to estimate, allocate or evaluate, a few of which are discussed below:

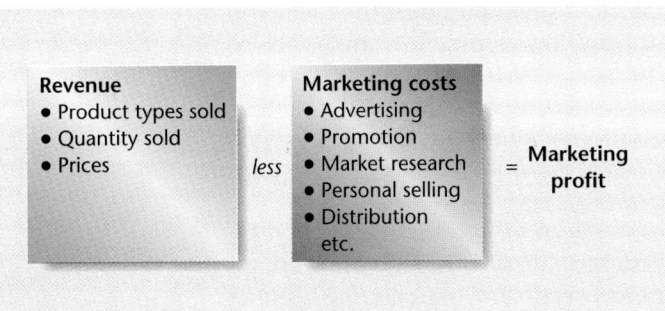

FIGURE 21.9

Marketing costs and profit

1 *Long-term or lagged effects*: an advertising campaign running now might only start to generate sales next year and the effects of that advertising might last much longer than the campaign itself. How should this be reflected in terms of profitability analysis?

2 *Joint costs*: some costs, for example corporate advertising or trade exhibition attendance, will be spread across different products, sales territories or segments etc. Then there are the indirect central costs, such as general administration, some of which will be apportioned to the marketing department. What is the fairest way of allocating all these shared costs?

3 *Isolating effects:* marketing results are achieved as a consequence of an integrated marketing mix and thus it can be difficult to isolate the influence of one activity and evaluate its financial efficiency. This is particularly true where there is close synergy between elements, for instance between advertising and sales promotion.

Despite such difficulties, it is important for strategic planning purposes to try to assess profitability by customer group, product, sales territory etc., rather than just measuring sales. Conducting such assessments encourages managers to move away from the relentless pursuit of increasing sales volume as a means of increasing profit. Profitability analysis might highlight, for example, the fact that certain customer types, products, territories, segments, marketing activities etc. are more lucrative than others. Certain combinations might be more attractive too. Customer A might purchase the same value of goods as customer B, but customer A might purchase more profitable goods from the range, demand fewer discounts, or be less expensive to service than customer B. It might, therefore, be worthwhile to invest more in developing a stronger relationship with customer A, or seeking more customers with a similar profile to A. Thus by focusing on the more profitable elements or combinations, the manager can increase the cost effectiveness and efficiency of the cash invested in marketing.

As an organisation becomes bigger and more complex, there is a greater need for analysis and control through formalised mechanisms. How costs are to be calculated and allocated should be clearly defined and the limitations of financial analysis in a marketing context should be understood. It is also important that there is close liaison between marketing and the accounts department to ensure that timely and appropriate information is gathered and disseminated.

MARKETING PLANNING FOR THE SMALLER BUSINESS

Although marketing principles, both strategic and operational, apply equally across all organisations regardless of their size, the application of marketing often varies greatly. A large business with a well-defined management structure and a strong resource base applies marketing principles very differently from a small firm with limited resources and managerial skills trying to establish itself or grow in the marketplace. This is often reflected in the marketing planning process and the final marketing plans adopted.

This section examines the marketing planning issues facing the small business. After brief consideration of the definitions and nature of small business, the focus will shift to marketing in the various stages of a small firm's development from launch to maturity. Although there is some dispute over the actual stages of development and the criteria that should be used to describe them, small business marketing strategy will nevertheless be shown to evolve as the organisation changes and grows.

Characteristics of small business

According to Burns (1989), **small businesses** are easier to describe than define. Perhaps that is not surprising, given that the small businesses sector includes a large number of organisations at different stages in their development, displaying different strengths and weaknesses and operating in different markets. Often small businesses have a number of characteristics that identify them from their larger counterparts.

Small share of the market. A small share of the market means that a small business cannot influence either supply or prices in the same way as a market leader could. As previous chapters have suggested, however, a lot depends on how the market is defined. An organisation with a small share of a generally defined national or international market might nevertheless hold a dominant position in a specifically defined segment or niche.

Personal ownership. Many small businesses are characterised by the fact that it is not uncommon to find the owner at the heart of all the strategic decisions and in many operational issues. If the owner is not careful, however, this can lead to too much time spent on operational fire fighting, and not enough priority given to strategic marketing and external activities (Pettitt and Kirkwood, 1986). The reality for many owners is that they are market analysts, strategists, sales representatives and service deliverers all rolled into one. Only as the business grows and a more formal organisational structure starts to form can the owner manager start to delegate and use specialists where appropriate.

Independence. This means that there is no external interference. A wholly owned subsidiary, for example, might have its decisions influenced by a remote management board. It might make its own promotional decisions, but have product range and pricing decisions imposed by the parent organisation. The small business thus has much more autonomy in its decision making, but of course cannot benefit from the resources and expertise of a parent company.

Other differentiating factors. There are other approaches to describing the difference between large and small firms. Wynarczyk *et al.* (1993), for example, suggest that the level of uncertainty, the approach to innovation and organisational evolution are important factors that help to distinguish between large and small businesses. The degree of *external uncertainty* facing the small firm is thought to be greater than that facing the larger organisation. Without a diversified base of activity, any organisation can be vulnerable to sudden and unexpected changes in the business environment. There are also issues associated with *internal uncertainty*. In a smaller firm, the motivation and aspirations of the owner are key influences on the organisation's strategy and performance.

It has traditionally been thought that small firms are at the cutting edge of *innovation*. A greater degree of flexibility, a higher tolerance of risk and a willingness to enter non-standard niches are all held to be supportive of small firms' innovative approaches. By providing specialisation in product or service terms the smaller firm can exist alongside the larger operator. The smaller firm might be highly successful in bringing non-standard technology to a market, but unless the venture is carefully planned and resourced, it might lack the resources to exploit the opportunity effectively. The truly innovative small firm is the exception rather than the rule, however. Finally, a small firm can be distinguished from a large one by its tendency to evolve more quickly and change, often with step-like growth as particular projects achieve success. Each might require fundamental change within the business if it is to exploit the opportunity.

From a quantitative perspective a consensus is emerging across the EU for defining different types of enterprise, based on the number of employees (Storey, 1994):

- micro enterprises: 0–9 employees
- small enterprises: 10–99 employees
- medium enterprises: 100–499 employees
- large enterprises: over 500 employees

These definitions are not sector specific, where wide variations are likely and the 99 employees top limit means that the definition of small business encompasses both very small new starters and more established enterprises. For comparative purposes, this EU definition is probably the best available at a general level. Small firms, however they are defined, are a dominant force across Europe and comprise 95% of all enterprises. Italy, Greece, Portugal and Spain have a higher percentage of their workforces employed in small business, with a correspondingly larger number of enterprises per 1000 inhabitants than the rest of the EU.

Despite this level of economic and political significance, many of the special marketing problems faced by the small firm as it starts and grows are often ignored, compared with those of the larger organisation. The next section, therefore, turns to marketing planning during an enterprise's evolution.

Example According to Bradley (1999), Internet marketing has the potential to be a great leveller between small and large businesses in many retail and distribution areas. By giving an opportunity to new and small businesses to reach mass markets very cost effectively, products and services can be sold without the need for expensive marketing and distribution infrastructures. Investment in premises, stock, and sales staff can make a more traditional business much less flexible than an on-line business. Furthermore, the lower level of investment required by an on-line business means that the cost of market entry can also be much lower. In the US, however, Bradley believes that it is often new entrants rather than existing small businesses using the Internet to expand that are better exploiting the opportunities.

IDC in a study of small/medium/large business users of the Internet in the US in 1997 found that small business users made up just 17% of 'total net use' despite being the largest group in terms of the number of businesses. While most of the Fortune 500 companies now have websites, the same cannot be said for smaller businesses. In another study by Cyber Dialogue, of 1000 businesses with fewer than 100 employees only 37% were on-line and even then a large majority were mainly using it for e-mail rather than for direct marketing and advertising. Whether a business is a real estate operator displaying houses, a manufacturing company displaying on-line brochures for spares and machinery or a restaurant highlighting a new menu, the Internet can enhance the information available to potential customers.

Marketing planning during small business development

The business launch and development process can be generalised as a model, as shown in Fig 21.10. This model reflects the same basic concept as the product life-cycle (plc) model considered in Chapter 8. As with the plc, different businesses might exhibit very different profiles. Some might not even get as far as the start-up stage, if the initial business assessment appears to be too problematic. Others might never get beyond the survival stage as a result of a combination of marketing, financial or operational problems. Eventually, the owners might decide that the returns are not sufficient to justify all the risks and hours expended. The lucky and well-managed businesses, however, might continue to grow into ever larger organisations, becoming significant players in their industries. The rate of development of a small business might also vary depending on the nature of the industry, its stage of maturity and the degree of innovativeness of the new product or service idea. In the high-tech and innovative service sectors, growth can be very rapid indeed because of the faster rates of product adoption and acceptance. However, given that most businesses in Europe are small rather than large, the achievement of growth and significant size is the exception rather than the rule. The majority of micro enterprises start small and stay small throughout their existence. They either do not want to grow or lack the marketing and management impact to manage the transition (Gallagher and Miller, 1991).

Each of the five stages in the development will now be considered in turn.

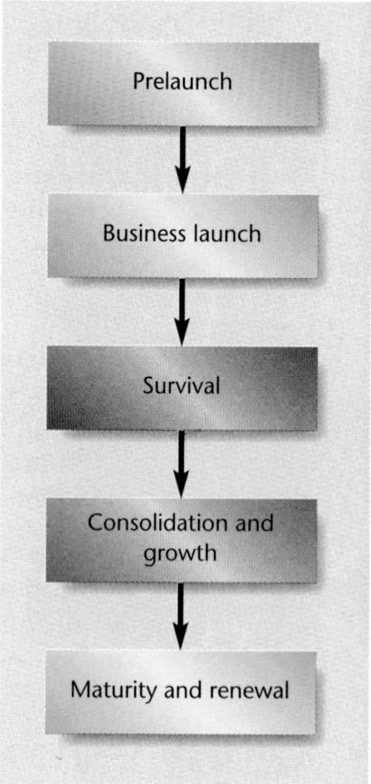

FIGURE 21.10

Business launch and development stages

Marketing and planning in the prelaunch stage

The prelaunch stage covers the period up to the start of trading. There might be a few months or several years between a person first having the idea for a business venture and the launch of the business itself. People start their own businesses for many different reasons. Some are driven by a desire to succeed, and to experience independence and wealth through self-enterprise (McClelland, 1961). For others, however, it is not 'pull' factors but 'push' created by unemployment, frustration from being in a dead-end job, or other unexpected shocks to career or life development patterns (Birley, 1989). This latter group is less likely to be opportunity or wealth driven and more intent on making a living and surviving. Consequently, they might be far less market orientated. Many even lack any idea about which might be the best product or market area to enter. To this group, the idea of the entrepreneur as an innovator is rather a remote concept. Others may have acquired sector experience while in employment so may bring some market understanding and even contacts to a new start situation.

For example in the USA, 1 in 12 adults is trying to start a business compared with 1 in 67 in Finland (Campbell, 1999). In joint research undertaken by London Business School, Babson College and the Kauffman Centre for Entrepreneurship (http://www.entreworld.org), the conclusion was drawn that there is a link between economic growth rates and the number of start-ups, although it is of course more problematic to assess whether those start-ups are a cause or an effect of growth. Factors such as perception of opportunity, demographic profile, culture, education and the small business support infrastructure were all found to play a role in encouraging more start-ups.

Once the decision to start in business has been made, it is important to find an idea and then assess the chances of success carefully. This concerns far more than marketing issues and includes, for instance, staffing, finance, operations, premises etc. Sometimes, these things are formally described in a business plan, but unfortunately many new businesses fail to give them serious consideration, and many assumptions and poorly researched decisions are used as a substitute. It is, however, often the marketing decisions that will determine the success of the business launch. The battle in any start-up situation is to generate sufficient revenue from customers before the initial reserves are exhausted.

> **Example** A budding entrepreneur had the idea to produce a boot warmer for those cold winter mornings. Switching on the warmer a few minutes before the boots were required meant that the feet would not be exposed to a nasty cold shock. Unfortunately, a preliminary assessment of the market revealed a low level of customer interest and questionable business viability given the low market price that could be realised. There was also general indifference from the retail and wholesale trade and direct marketing was not considered an option for a one-person business.

The nature of the initial business plan will be determined, in part, by the innovativeness of the product or service idea. If the idea is genuinely innovative in the planned market (even if it has been transferred from other geographic markets), the main focus should be on developing or transferring the concept and on developing the most appropriate marketing mix for local conditions. This might mean a detailed examination of current demand for whatever alternatives are currently available in that market, and their usage (*see* Chapter 5). The broad parameters of the marketing mix might then become evident from this comparative research, but what is actually the issue is whether that marketing mix is sufficiently targeted and resourced in the most effective manner. It must be compatible with the skills and resources of the prospective entrepreneur.

Particularly in situations where there is potentially a lot of competition, there has to be a clear understanding of why the launch will be successful. Market assessment and research should provide some insights into competitor vulnerability and weaknesses, and the sensitivity of potential customers to alternative marketing mix offerings. The entrepreneur should understand whether the focus should be on niching, service differentiation, pricing, branding, heavy promotional spending or whatever. For the inexperienced marketer, none of these decision areas is easy (*see* Chapter 20).

An important part of this process is the testing of the product or service idea. With a tangible product, it might be possible to undertake trials to iron out any problems before the full launch. In some cases, these might take the form of bench tests to minimise the risks of outright failure on specification – performance grounds. This might be followed or replaced by trials involving a sample of customers. The main risk, however, is of another organisation stealing the idea, if it is truly innovative. Many new starters do not have the resources to defend against such acts from larger, better-resourced competitors. Testing the product on real customers at the launch can prove to be even more costly and risky for the entrepreneur.

Marketing an planning for survival

After the initial launch, the emphasis in the new business is on ensuring survival. This means creating the niche in the market and using marketing tools to become competitive. The speed with which a market can be penetrated can often be over-estimated, however. Customer loyalty to existing suppliers or even risk aversion to changing suppliers can slow down the rate at which new products or suppliers will be tried. The time taken to locate potential customers, agree specifications, negotiate contracts, manufacture and deliver the goods, and of course to be paid can put a lot of pressure on cash flow. This is particularly acute for a manufacturing business where lead times can be prolonged. Service and retail businesses can generate positive cash flows relatively quickly, as long as sufficient attention is paid to creating customer awareness and willingness to try. It took nine months for an Irish manufacturer of diamond cutting heads to receive its first significant revenue from a customer. In contrast, a small bakery or takeaway business could generate customer revenue on day one. A number of factors will influence the ability to achieve a successful launch:

Example Ocean Home Shopping was launched in 1995 by Aamir Ahmad as a mail order company specialising in up market home and office accessories. Within three years, sales had grown to £1.6mn from over 20 000 customers. The marketing and business plan has had to evolve during this time around the critical success factors for any small mail order business: buying attractive stock and building and retaining a customer base. The difference between a retail store and a mail order catalogue business is that in a retail store if an item does not sell, the price can quickly be lowered, but with a catalogue, the price is fixed for six or twelve months. There is also a problem with items that sell better than expected, as suppliers have to be flexible enough to increase output at short notice. Supplier management has been a major learning area for the new entrepreneur and Ocean has restricted its product range to 800 items in order to have large volumes and more effective product management. Selling out has also been a challenge. An internal call centre operation was introduced to handle customer orders and queries effectively and pressure started early on to build a customer database that could be used for marketing as well as distribution. By early 1999 no website had been established, but consideration was being given to relationship marketing techniques that could consolidate and grow the business (Gracie, 1999).

Perceived, valued product differences. It is relatively easy for the entrepreneur to think that what is being offered is clearly differentiated from the competition and will be of value to the customer, but often the difference is either not perceived by the customer, or does not matter to them. Even where there is a technological lead, it may still take time for the product to be tested and evaluated.

Size of market niche. Even when some customers do find the product of interest, the size of the niche may be too small to generate a sufficient volume of initial or repeat business. Sometimes, the opposite might be true, and the market potential can prove to be too large. Full exploitation of the opportunity is beyond the resources of the individual operator. Better-capitalised and more experienced operators might quickly move in and start to dominate the market.

Market entry strategy. A well-thought-out entry plan in which all aspects of the mix are co-ordinated increases the chances of success. Areas of particular focus should include ensuring that product quality is maintained on a consistent basis and that there is a match between the product positioning and its price. Too low a price might mean that the business is not generating enough revenue to support marketing effort, and too high a price might not attract enough customers. Rarely, however, do the owners of small firms have a sufficient grasp of all the marketing tools and how they interact.

Ability to attract key customers. In manufacturing situations, the business launch is often based on promises of orders from one or two key customers. Attracting firm orders from these key customers could be crucial to the successful launch of the business. If the entrepreneur is completely unknown, it could take some time for potential customers to overcome the risks of dealing with an unproven supplier. The key requirements for winning orders are likely to be a combination of the product package offered and the way it is presented to the potential customer. Often, this latter point is overlooked.

Competitive reaction. It is surprising how often a small business start-up plan fails to take into account the likely reaction of competitors to a new entrant. Although clear market leaders might not be that bothered, other recent entrants and smaller operators might well increase their own marketing effort to combat the new threat. This could mean pressure on margins from price competition and the need for increased promotional effort from the new business. These two forces might not be compatible for the vulnerable and stretched new business, and result in stunted growth.

Distribution coverage. The best-laid launch plans can be thrown off course if the entrepreneur cannot gain distribution coverage. If the range is new, unproven and not supported with advertising and sales promotion, there might be little chance of getting shelf space in retail or wholesale outlets. Even if intermediaries choose to stock the product, they might not actively promote it. Direct distribution options are often not viable because of the cost efficiency reasons discussed in Chapter 12. However, the growth of Internet usage is making on-line ordering an attractive option for some new-start businesses.

Awareness and interest generation. This is often a major challenge for the new business, as with a limited communications budget it could be very difficult to make any impact in the market. In organisational markets, the priority is likely to be to develop a campaign of personal sales visits, with sales letters and publicity material supporting direct sales. In consumer markets, the priority is often to create a basic level of awareness. Local media are often used, with the business graduating from the classified small advertisements to the display columns as resources grow.

Flexibility and responsiveness. During the start-up period, the entrepreneur has to learn very quickly from experience and try new ways of doing things. The business plan should have provided a general match between customer needs and the small business offering, but the start-up period enables the fine tuning to take place. Sometimes the changes can be very radical indeed as new opportunities are perceived. Those entrepreneurs who cannot learn face failure.

Example It is alleged that an Irish entrepreneur got the idea for a ready to eat breakfast cereal when his girlfriend spotted someone eating a bowl of cereal in a car! With support from a 50 per cent development agency feasibility grant, Ennis Foods was born. Careful

▶

market research into the breakfast cereal market was followed by investment to establish how to bring wet milk to a dry cereal conveniently outside the normal domestic setting. This involved compartmentalising the wet and dry areas in a unique, patented single pack that also doubled as a cereal bowl.

The project could not be entered half-heartedly. Around £4mn of investment was needed to go into production under the brand name Rumblers. This was raised from a selection of shareholders, including a cereal producer and a milk supplier. The owner had to accept just a 20 per cent share to get the business off the ground. The market research paid off, as sales started to build through three distinct sectors: vending (10 per cent), airlines (15 per cent) and retail (75 per cent). The uniqueness and convenience of the product were well received and many retailers were prepared to give the product a trial. Sales have now reached half of the modern plant's capacity and output is soon expected to exceed 1mn cartons per month. Already the likes of Nestlé and Kellogg are keeping track of the company, and the next significant stage could be international commercialisation, albeit with new owners and an expanded bank balance for the successful entrepreneur (Rubythorn, 1999).

Marketing factors are, of course, not the only consideration during this stage of development. All the business functions have to be well managed and mistakes can easily be made. Those businesses that cannot overcome the barriers might survive a year or two and then perhaps give up the struggle, if cash reserves do not build because of either poor inflows or poor expenditure management. Others move into the consolidation and growth stage.

Marketing and planning for consolidation and growth

The next stage occurs after the small business starter has survived the first year or so and has reached a position of having built a customer base and adjusted to the unexpected aspects of the launch. The character of the business might have already changed by this stage as a result of either new market opportunities, redefinition of target segments, or changes in the product or service concept emerging from practical experience. The first priority after survival is to consolidate any progress made. This might mean encouraging repeat purchases and expanding the customer base sufficiently to provide some security. Unfortunately, it is very easy for a smaller business at this stage to drift into a significant trading relationship with a major customer, as a result of which dependency starts to develop. The attractions of regular cash flow from a major customer are very tempting, but if the customer base is not diversified, the small business is extremely vulnerable to sudden changes in policy and buying patterns.

Example Barefoot Books (http://www.barefoot-books.com) has successfully developed a niche in the children's publishing market. Its books are targeted at children up to 12 years old and are well produced to reflect themes such as folk tales and legends from across the world, all with lots of illustrations. The two female owners started with very little, other than a talent for spotting a good story when they started in 1993. Gaining a market proved challenging at a time when education authorities were cutting back on book expenditure and large publishers were often reluctant to experiment with untried new books. Perseverance paid, however. Barefoot went for direct sales to book distributors and larger retail stores and the business now employs five staff and 15 commissioned sales staff for the UK and continental Europe. The owners work closely with teachers, librarians and children's theatre directors when formulating new series and themes and they are not averse to testing some ideas on their own children. Titles can all be purchased on-line through the website. The US market is now being developed, again on a direct distribution basis, and this is expected to help achieve the objective of improving turnover tenfold by 2003 to £10mn (Hobson, 1998).

Consolidation assumes some kind of on-going balance between cash inflows and outflows. Many small business owners are happy to stay at that level because they do not want to have to tackle the problems of growth or they feel that they do not have the capability to manage growth. The price for not moving far beyond survival might, however, be fairly low personal returns and a degree of vulnerability to external forces.

Only a small percentage of small businesses plan and achieve rapid growth. Storey (1994) argues that there are three key influences on the growth rate of a small firm. The first is the entrepreneur's background and access to resources. Factors such as previously acquired skills, education and experience might all play a part, but the central factor is often the motivation of the entrepreneur. Those who were 'pushed' into self-employment through redundancy tend to be less growth orientated than those starting a small business for the attractions of independence and wealth (Kinsella *et al.*, 1993). The size of the company could also be a factor, as evidence suggests that the smallest firms are least likely to grow compared with larger businesses of between 25 and 49 employees (Hakim, 1989).

The quality of the strategic decisions taken once the business has been launched and has survived the difficult early period are of particular importance. The marketing areas that can be significant to the growth business include product and range development and refinement to better meet changing customer needs, regulations and competitive offerings; market development, perhaps reconsidering whether the original market niche pursued is still large enough to sustain the growth; professionalising the approach to marketing, perhaps taking the first steps towards developing a marketing plan to support planned expansion and to sustain business growth; and the strength of positioning because, as the business starts to grow, serious competitor reaction could emerge.

> **Example** Delahaye (http://www.delmovblue.com) has become a small pan-European business employing a staff of just 20. Based in London and Paris, it specialises in packing and moving at the premium end of the market, with most of the clients being corporate. By concentrating at the premium end of the removal market, a 40 per cent margin can often be generated, but this reflects the service levels demanded and the quality that is essential for moving valuable items. The company, according to Lloyd's of London, has the lowest record of damage in the industry. The staff employed tend to be inexperienced in removals so they can be trained to high standards, rather than focusing on curing bad habits. Most of the marketing is through word-of-mouth recommendations and through high level social networking handled by the owner, Elizabeth Delahaye. The niche developed has become a source of profit per annum over £500 000 (Chapple, 1999).

If there are real product or service advantages, a close match between customer specifications and the product offering, or a clear added value position, it can be harder for competitors to retaliate and the entrepreneur could have a slightly easier context in which to create and sustain planned growth. In order to do this, the entrepreneur will also have to learn how to use the marketing mix to good effect. If the organisation operates in a consumer market, very careful scheduling of media is required. Mass media are usually well beyond the limited resources available. Instead, targeted media such as specialist magazines can provide more effective communication, and direct marketing might also offer attractive and cost effective options. In organisational markets with clearly defined customers, there will be a need to ensure that regular contact is maintained and that suitable promotional material and exhibitions are used to support the selling effort. Where intermediaries are used, gaining their support will be crucial at this stage. This might mean gaining distribution or encouraging intermediaries to promote the product more heavily. Only by developing trade promotion policies can growth be maintained.

All these factors interact to encourage or restrict the development of the small firm. To cope with these forces, the entrepreneur must change and respond to emerging opportunities. The whole process will be highly demanding in terms of time and expertise. There are likely to be considerable demands on working capital for the growth business as the pursuit and achievement of new business drives up marketing and operational costs. This can lead to under-capitalisation that could restrict the pace of growth. Some businesses become high growth companies, star performers, that may become attractive to larger firms, as for example in the biotechnology and pharmaceutical sectors where innovative solutions have been found. Others may plateau and move into a steady state stage. Those who are better able to adapt and manage the market threats and opportunities will be better able to continue with high growth, reinvesting capital into further innovation.

Marketing and planning for maturity and renewal

This marks the end of the transition from start-up to established enterprise. The size and profile of the micro enterprise may have evolved to a small business or even to a medium enterprise with a management structure. At this stage, many of the marketing principles described in this book can become practical possibilities. As the organisation grows, specialist staff in sales and marketing might be recruited, although the entrepreneur might still keep a close watch on key customers. The critical decision at this stage is whether to move forward with growth or whether to consolidate and primarily seek to retain market share. However, even then, no growth does not mean that there can be no change in the marketing and operation of the business (Gibb and Scott, 1985).

> **Example** A packaging company specialising in shoe boxes decided not to seek further growth but to maintain sales to its established customer base. This was possible for a number of years because there was no significant market change. But there are risks in this approach. The company dealt with customers primarily by telephone and only visited them once every 18 months or two years. The company had little information about new opportunities or specification changes even within its core market, let alone the threat of new competition.

Even to stand still, because of turbulence and market forces, the entrepreneur might have to respond to new competitive threats, customer need changes and market dynamics. This could mean new products, product development and finding new customers to compensate for any losses. If there is no change and stagnation sets in, a decline may soon follow.

> **Example** Express Group, a 26-year-old medium sized enterprise based in Gateshead, has changed its business in the 1990s from primarily being an engineering jobbing shop with little distinctiveness to a 'design-intensive supplier of engineering solutions' in the supply chain that ends with products for larger companies such as Nissan, Electrolux and Gillette. The key to the approach was to ensure that the sales and design staff were involved with the buying organisation before rather than after the specification was finalised. Product design contracts now comprise 25 per cent of revenues with conventional subcontracting making up the rest for the UK and overseas market. By seeking to become closer to customers in a problem solving, customer focused manner, the group now expects to grow further in a competitive market (Marsh, 1999a).

It is not always the lack of desire to grow that affects the smaller business. Italy, for example, has the world's highest concentrations of small engineering companies, but many lack the capital to expand even if opportunities do become available. Some, however, do find strategic routes to avoid stagnation. HTP, near Milan, has built the business to offer a variety of specialist machines for the textile industry in printing and preparing fabric. It has been successful in growing through acquisition, product specialisation, yet offering a range of integrated solutions, retaining resource flexibility and pooling marketing and research across the various facets of the business. Innovation has been a high priority and around 20 of the 120 employees are involved with product development. It has also sought a diversified market base, with over 75 per cent of production exported, especially to South-east Asia (Marsh, 1999b). In the UK, also in the textile machinery sector, James Holdsworth, a family-run business since 1790, innovated with a 'card clothing clip'. Fitted to knitting machines, it enables the use of high-pile furry fabrics for soft toys such as teddy bears. The new clip is expected to help increase overall company sales from £5mn by 50 per cent in the first three years of launch to 1999. In an industry that has suffered considerable rationalisation, innovation, niching and close customer relations have enabled Holdsworth to survive and perhaps even grow (Jones, 1999).

The stages presented in this section are by no means universal. High growth companies can move very quickly through the stages, often by large incremental steps as new projects are introduced. Others might stabilise very early and change very little, in line with the owner's wishes. This could mean that marketing is always treated as *ad hoc*, is poorly informed and is not integrated into the organisation. The attitudes, expertise and objectives of the owner or ownership team will be paramount.

Many small businesses have to run very hard just to survive. Many do not make it. As a generalisation, younger rather than older businesses are more likely to fail, very small micro enterprises are more vulnerable than larger ones and, most interestingly, those that grow soon after starting have a better chance of survival. It is interesting to consider some of the managerial deficiencies that can cause failure. The small business might fail (adapted from Burns, 1989) if:

■ it cannot identify the target market or target customers
■ it cannot delineate its trading area
■ it cannot delegate
■ it considers advertising as an expense not an investment
■ it has poor knowledge of pricing and strategy
■ it has an immature understanding of distribution channels
■ it does not plan.

Marketing is indeed at the heart of small business development.

CHAPTER SUMMARY

Marketing planning is about developing the objectives, strategies and marketing mixes that best exploit the opportunities available to the organisation. Planning should itself be a planned and managed process. This process helps organisations to analyse themselves and their marketing environments more systematically and honestly. It also helps organisations to co-ordinate and control their marketing activities more effectively. There are, however, risks in allowing planning to become an end in itself, as its managers might then become too technique orientated or too formulaic in their approach. It might also encourage the rise of the 'professional planner'. Planning should, therefore, be a flexible, dynamic activity that is fed with accurate, reliable and timely information, and is not divorced from the managers who have the day-to-day responsibility for implementing the plans.

Marketing plans can be strategic or operational. The plans help to integrate activities, schedule resources, specify responsibilities and provide benchmarks for measuring progress. There are eight main stages in the planning process: corporate objectives, the marketing audit, marketing analysis, setting marketing objectives, marketing strategies, marketing programmes, controls and evaluation and budgeting.

In order to construct realistic plans, managers need to estimate what total market demand could be, and what their own organisation's sales potential within that market might be. The whole area of forecasting is an important one for marketers. The more accurate the view of the future, the more appropriate the plans are likely to be. Forecasts can be general or specific, qualitative or quantitative. There are a number of forecasting techniques. The qualitative group includes management judgement, sales force surveys, expert opinion and scenario techniques. Quantitative techniques include time series analysis, multiple regression, leading indicators and market tests.

In order to fulfil its function properly, the marketing department should have a central role within the organisation, with senior management of equal status to those in other functional areas. It is also important, however, that the marketing philosophy pervades the whole enterprise, regardless of the size or formality of the marketing department. There are several approaches to structuring the marketing department itself. These are the functional, product based, regional, segmental or matrix approaches.

As marketing plans are being implemented, they have to be monitored and controlled. Strategic control concerns the longer-term direction of marketing strategy, whereas operational control assesses the day-to-day success of marketing activities. Using information gathered in the monitoring process, the actual achievements of marketing strategies can be compared with planned or expected outcomes. Managers can then analyse gaps and decide whether they are significant enough to warrant corrective action. Although this can be a quantitative analysis, it should still be looked at in the context of more qualitative issues concerning customer needs and synergies between customers, markets or products.

Small businesses are difficult to define, but do tend to have certain characteristics in common. They have relatively small market shares, their owners tend to be closely involved in all aspects of both strategic and operational management, and they are often fully independent. Small businesses also face a high degree of uncertainty in their environment and can find innovation difficult because of shortage of resources. The four-stage model of small business development suggests that marketing plays an important part in the process of starting and developing a business. In the prelaunch stage, the entrepreneur must assess the feasibility and viability of the business idea. During the launch period, it is a fight for survival, ensuring that sufficient sales volume is generated to sustain the business. Many small businesses do not grow, but start small and stay small either because they do not want to grow or because there is no growth in the market. A small percentage of small firms do grow, some very rapidly indeed. This requires a more professional strategic marketing approach to maintain differentiation. The final stage, maturity and renewal, determines whether the business will grow even further to become a medium or large enterprise or stabilise. Stability does not, however, mean that strategic marketing can be neglected. Innovation in products and marketing might still be necessary to maintain the status quo. At any one of these four stages, failure can occur. Many of the factors contributing to failure are based on poor marketing.

Key words and phrases

Control and evaluation	Market potential	Sales potential
Corporate objectives	Marketing audit	Small businesses
External audit	Marketing objectives	Strategic marketing plan
Forecasts	Operational marketing plan	SWOT analysis
Internal audit	Planning process	

QUESTIONS FOR REVIEW

21.1 Why do organisations need *marketing planning*?

21.2 Define the stages in the *marketing planning process*.

21.3 What is a *SWOT analysis*?

21.4 To what general criteria should 'good' marketing objectives conform?

21.5 What is the difference between *marketing strategies* and *marketing programmes*?

21.6 Define *market potential*.

21.7 What is the difference between *breakdown* and *build-up* methods of assessing market potential?

21.8 What are the:

(a) *qualitative*; and
(b) *quantitative* techniques

of forecasting?

21.9 What are the four main choices for structuring the marketing department?

21.10 How can *operational performance* be evaluated?

QUESTIONS FOR DISCUSSION

21.1 What is the mission statement of the university or college at which you are studying? From your general knowledge of the organisation and your experience as a customer, discuss the extent to which you feel it is fulfilling its mission.

21.2 Using whatever information you can find, develop a SWOT analysis for the organisation of your choice. What are the implications of your analysis for the organisation's short- and long-term priorities?

21.3 Discuss the importance of market and sales forecasting in the marketing planning process and outline the relative advantages and disadvantages of three different forecasting methods.

21.4 What kind of marketing organisational structure would be appropriate for each of the following situations and why?

(a) a small single product engineering company;
(b) a large fmcg manufacturer selling a wide range of products into several different European markets;
(c) a pharmaceutical company manufacturing both prescription and 'over the counter' medicines.

21.5 Discuss the role played by control and evaluation in both the planning and implementation of marketing strategies and programmes.

CASE STUDY 21.1

Sparks fly at Marks & Spencer

By the end of 1998, it was clear that the UK's hitherto star retailer Marks & Spencer (M&S) was in crisis. The media and customers all joined in to help the senior management undertake an internal audit to identify the problems and develop solutions. These are a few of the issues identified:

■ M&S thought that customers understood what it stood for without marketing. In a sense it was product orientated, concentrating on the quality of stock and assuming that it would communicate everything the customer needed to know. It was spending very little on marketing communication, around £4mn, compared with other big retail names spending anything from £20mn to £50mn.

■ M&S was complacent about its customer service standards. These used to be exceptional in the UK retail trade, but even the supermarkets have

not only caught up with M&S but also surpassed its service levels, thus negating one of the prime advantages that M&S had.

■ It did not (and at the time of writing still does not) accept major credit cards, which is at least an irritation to many customers and again a small sign that customer service is not quite what it should be.

■ Its recent clothing ranges have been described as 'uninspired' and 'dreary' and the fact that in 1998/99 profits fell by nearly half, around £600mn, perhaps indicated that customers were not impressed with the ranges or value for money offer in the stores. For the autumn 1998 season, M&S had bought £2.5bn of clothing and at the end of the season 10 per cent of it remained unsold. The discounting had started only weeks after the ranges had gone into the stores and by Christmas a major sale was underway. Overall, sales were well down despite a large increase in selling space through expansion.

- Some had also questioned whether the clothing quality was as good as it used to be, especially when viewed from a value for money perspective. This issue descended almost to farce, much to the glee of the media, when at the Annual General Meeting in July 1999, a shareholder took the podium and waved her knickers at the startled audience to make a point about slipping standards of quality and design.

- Even food sales, a traditional area of great strength for M&S accounting for 40 per cent of revenue, were under threat. The mainstream supermarket chains, such as Tesco with its Finest range, had developed top-quality premium products, for instance chilled ready meals, to rival M&S's offerings. M&S also lost impetus with its store locations. With its town centre sites, it had been ideally placed to sell its foods to those either shopping or working in town who wanted to make a convenient short food shopping trip. Recently, however, the mainstream supermarkets have been opening or refurbishing their town centre sites and are competing effectively for those same customers (Murphy, 1998a).

- It had very ambitious expansion plans, looking to invest over £200bn over three years to expand selling space by 25 per cent, as well as investing to refurbish existing stores. Clearly, to fund and support such plans, strong trading is required from the existing retail space and this was not happening.

- It had also had poor results from its overseas stores, in North America, Asia and continental Europe, yet still had ambitious and expensive expansion plans. This was seen as important, however, to try to reduce dependency on the UK domestic market, which still accounts for 85 per cent of sales and over 90 per cent of profits.

Some blame an arrogant, inward-looking complacency for the problems. M&S had been the most popular, most profitable, number one UK retailer for so long that it forgot to monitor competitive threats. Whatever the reasons for the problems, the crisis caused a shake-up at the top of the organisation and Peter Salsbury took over as chief executive (Gwyther, 1999). He himself said, 'We lost touch with our customers and forgot about the competition.' One of his first acts was to sack nearly one-quarter of the company's top executives to slim down the senior management team and the lines of communication. In January 1999, M&S created its first ever marketing department and started to look at its communications strategy in response to its crisis. A spokesman said:

'it will enable us to present to our customers our full range of products in a co-ordinated way. It will also allow us to understand the aspirations of individual customers in much greater depth.' (as quoted by Jardine, 1999)

More dialogue, and perhaps tension, was encouraged between buyers and store managers and buying decisions were pushed further down the hierarchy to involve more marketing and selling staff in those decisions. A tendency for store managers just to stock what buyers, who were sometimes out of touch with the customers, gave them had been partly responsible for poor sales figures. Senior managers were also reviewing relationships with suppliers, looking to them to cut their costs and prices and perhaps to outsource production to cheaper countries. The initial target was to cut the number of UK suppliers from 65 per cent of the total to 50 per cent. It was also decided to reduce the 100 per cent dependency on the St Michael own label by introducing more sub-brands to give better targeting and perhaps even introducing designer names into the stores.

By July 1999, the signs were better, certainly on the product front. The fashion writers felt that the autumn/winter range for 1999/2000 was sharper, more attractive and stylish (Finn and Robinson, 1999). Also, the international expansion programme was cut back to reduce costs and the increase in domestic selling space slowed down to allow the company to concentrate more on improving the returns from existing space. Store refurbishment was seen as a priority, and 100 stores were picked for major refurbishment to signal visibly that M&S was changing and to freshen up the image to go with the autumn/winter collection. Also, £20mn is to be spent on the 19 largest stores installing new display equipment and catwalks for mannequins.

All of this is just the start, however. Changes to corporate culture could take a little longer.

Sources. Bellamy (1999); The Economist (1999); Finn and Robinson (1999); Flynn (1998); Gwyther (1999); Jardine (1999); Marketing Week (1999); Murphy (1998a); Robinson (1999); The Times (1999).

Questions

1 How do you think M&S survived for so long without a marketing department?

2 You have been asked to make a presentation to the board of M&S about the benefits of introducing a structured marketing department and the strategic role of marketing planning. Summarise the key points of your presentation.

3 Using the information in the case, outline a rough SWOT analysis for M&S. Has M&S identified the right immediate marketing priorities? Assess its immediate actions.

CASE STUDY 21.2

Chuft Toys and Gifts

Chuft Toys and Gifts, launched in 1992, is a small business manufacturing a range of specialist wooden toys. After graduating, both partners in the business became quickly disillusioned with working in large companies and met each other by chance while backpacking in Australia. Although their degrees were in production engineering and product design technology, their first business venture was developing a backpacker's travel guide based on their first-hand experiences. This guide still survives today. However Chuft, the young entrepreneurs' second venture, was the real basis for developing a full-time business. Sales grew from £150 000 in the first year to £500 000 by year four.

The initial product was a wooden steam train whistle, which they designed. The prototype and first production run were produced in a draughty garage at the home of one of the partners. They both enjoyed the fun of designing and establishing the most appropriate way of manufacturing the early batches. They approached the heritage line, the North Yorkshire Moors Railway, which agreed to place a pilot order in its station shops to see how well the whistles sold. To everyone's surprise, 30 whistles were sold in one weekend. Chuft thus made the transition from being a possible enterprise to being a trading concern. The partners managed to raise capital for production machinery and found premises in an Enterprise Centre. Although resources were tight, they had just sufficient to build a basic business infrastructure.

The company now sees itself as primarily being in the gift market. The steam train whistle, with a few variants, is still the company's core line, although other products have also been developed, including low-priced wooden novelties and puzzles and 'equilibria', balancing wooden clowns. Another range is 'Toys With Noise', a tractor, a traction engine, a steam engine, a fire engine and a police car, each of which makes a suitably characteristic noise when pushed or blown. Chuft also markets a whistling train, comprising a wooden locomotive, caboose and carriage as a boxed set. The locomotive whistles when you blow into the cab.

A common characteristic of all the toys and gifts is the high quality of the materials and finish, and the attention paid to packaging, which follows a strong, unified and coherent design and image. Considerable thought has gone into the colours, materials, information provided and not least the shape of the packaging, so that it stands out in display areas and communicates the product's quality. Wooden toys and gifts tend to be bought on impulse rather than as planned purchases. Although cheaper alternatives are available, the quality positioning commands an above average price and this is supported by a selective distribution strategy.

Finding the best price and trade margin took some time, a few mistakes, and considerable trial and error. Initially, the toys were exhibited at national and regional toy and trade fairs. The partners decided to expand further, however, by carefully selecting outlets that valued premium quality rather than cheap products. These included preserved railways, Harrods, Jenners (Edinburgh), the National Trust and other heritage sites. One of the partners was responsible for selling while the other managed production. They did not meet very much sales resistance, as they allowed retailers to try small pilot orders to assess whether larger-volume sales could be realised.

While they expanded steadily in the home market, the first export enquiries were received. This was a source of surprise to the partners. Attendance at exhibitions generated the enquiries that soon led to further trial orders. There was no plan to move into exports or to modify their activities to suit export markets. Orders from these buyers were taken on a reactive basis, with the view 'Why refuse an order?' This exposed the partners to some of the problems of exporting, including documentation and procedures. From these initial export orders, a number of buyers suggested that they themselves should become agents for Chuft in their own markets. Chuft did not feel that it had the resources to become directly involved in developing new markets, so any arrangement with foreign intermediaries was considered appropriate.

Although no major changes in the marketing mix took place for export customers, a number of new decisions had to be made. First, changes were made to the product packaging to emphasise 'Heritage' and 'Britishness' as the selling points, thus taking into account comments from the foreign buyers. New languages such as French, Japanese and German were introduced to the packaging. Price setting was never very sophisticated, but the partners decided to apply a standard discount, with little variation for the volume of orders. Agents were selected mainly on the strength of trust and a feeling that they were reliable, rather than on any kind of objective criteria. Regardless of trust, however, Chuft always insisted on cash in advance for export orders.

Exports have grown to 30 per cent of output, although profit margins are tighter than in the domestic market. This volume is considered useful for spreading the load of the factory and in reducing the effects of concentrating on just one market. The main markets are Japan, America and Germany, although other European markets also provide some sales. The partners do not want to sell to developing countries and are determined not to be swamped by US demand.

The future challenge for the business is in keeping the product range fresh. Life-cycles are

tending to become shorter as the range increasingly moves into novelty products. Despite the success, there are still many other problems to overcome. Deciding on whether to manufacture or subcontract, obtaining suitable premises as production expands, achieving production efficiency and assembling the resources to hit a market harder than has been possible in the past have all become priorities. Although the business now employs 20 people, sales are still handled by the partners. There appear to be many opportunities for further expansion, but the need to develop a sound strategy to enable further growth to be properly managed is starting to occupy the partners' minds. They think that they have reached a crossroads. Should they continue to expand, should they consolidate, or should they seek radically new options?

The increased contact in mainland Europe led to a French distributor approaching Chuft in 1997 with the prospect of a significant order, provided it could deliver in time for the Christmas season. This would require an immediate start in production and raw material planning so that the first deliveries could begin soon after the initial contract was placed. The partners were delighted at the prospect of an order that could provide the funds for further expansion, but were nervous over the scale of the order as it would require both additional machinery and staff. They were not yet strong enough financially to absorb the risk or loss if the sales volume did not materialise, yet they knew risks would have to be taken if they were to grow. The distributor was, however, confident of success and had already given a verbal go ahead to start production.

Note: Some case details have been modified to protect the partners' interests.

Source: Adapted from a case prepared by Gerry Kirkwood.

Chuft Toys and Gifts expanded and diversified its product range as the business grew.

Source: Chuft.

Questions

1 What do you think are the problems facing two young graduates wanting to start a new business?

2 To what would you attribute Chuft's initial success?

3 Where does Chuft go from here? What do you think might be the main dangers facing this firm?

4 Should Chuft accept the big French order?

Reference for Chapter 21

Abell, D. F. (1982), 'Metamorphosis in Market Planning,' in K. K. Cox and V. J. McGinnis (eds.), *Strategic Market Decisions*, Prentice Hall.

Abrahams, P. (1999), 'Sony Forecasts Fall in PlayStation Sales', *Financial Times*, 28 April.

Barrett, L. (1999), 'Forte Axes Role in Brand Review', *Marketing*, 4 February, p. 2.

Bell, S. (1999a), 'P&G Restructures Global Operations', *Marketing*, 10 June, p. 1.

Bell, S. (1999b), 'P&G Forced by Rivals to Change Old Habits', *Marketing*, 17 June, p. 15.

Bellamy, E. (1999), 'Buyers Take Blame for M&S Losses', *Supply Management*, 27 May, p. 10.

Benady, A. (1998), 'Carphone Fights off Retail Giants', *Marketing*, 15 October, p. 23.

Birley, S. (1989), 'The Start Up', in P. Burns and J. Dewhurst (eds.), *Small Business and Entrepreneurship*, Macmillan.

Bradley, D. (1999), private correspondence between Professor Bradley of the University of Central Arkansas and the authors.

Burns, P. (1989), 'Introduction', in P. Burns and J. Dewhurst (eds.), *Small Business and Entrepreneurship*, Macmillan.

Campbell, K. (1999), 'Varying Stakes of Start Up', *Financial Times*, 22 June, p. 16.

Chapple, B. (1999), 'Kitchen Sink to a Renoir', *EuroBusiness*, 1(3), pp. 109–10.

Cox, W. E. (1979), *Industrial Market Research*, Wiley.

Darby, I. (1999a), 'Can Adidas Go the Distance?', *Marketing*, 28 January, p. 18.

Darby, I. (1999b), 'Nestlé to Launch Kids' Food Range', *Marketing*, 13 May, p. 2.

Day, G. S. (1990), *Market Driven Strategy*, Free Press.

Day, J. (1999), 'Fashion Kits', *Marketing Week*, 12 August, pp. 28–9.

Drucker, P. F. (1955), *The Practice of Management*, Heinemann.

The Economist (1999), 'Food for Thought', *The Economist*, 10 July, p. 56.

Finn, H. and Robinson, E. (1999), 'M&S Collection Signals Fashion Comeback', *Financial Times*, 7 July, p. 26.

Flynn, J. (1998), 'Marks and Sparks Isn't Throwing off any', *Business Week*, November 16, p. 64.

Foster, M. (1996), 'NCP Fights for its Space', *Management Today*, February, pp. 54–8.

Gallagher, C. and Miller, P. (1991), 'New Fast Growing Companies Create Jobs', *Long Range Planning*, 24(1), 96–101.

Genna, G. (1997), 'What's Wrong with Sales Forecasts?', *Purchasing*, 5 June.

Gibb, A. and Scott, M. (1985), 'Strategic Awareness, Personal Commitment and the Process of Planning in the Small Business', *Journal of Management Studies*, 22 (6), 596–631.

Gracie, S. (1999), 'Help Suppliers Catch the Growth Wave', *Sunday Times*, 14 February, p. 3.2.

The Grocer (1999), 'Starbucks Set for Six Sainsbury Stores', *The Grocer*, 14 August, p. 11.

Guiltinan, J. P. and Paul, G. W. (1988), *Marketing Management: Strategies and Programs*, McGraw-Hill.

Gwyther, M. (1999), 'King Richard: a Tragedy in Three Acts', *Management Today*, April 1999, pp. 78–85.

Hakim, C. (1989), 'Identifying Fast Growth Firms', *Employment Gazette*, January, pp. 29–41.

Hardcastle, S. (1999), 'Cone-venience', *The Grocer*, 17 July, pp. 37–40.

Hobson, R. (1998), 'A £1mn Homespun Story of Publishing Success', *The Times*, 13 January, p. 23.

Hollinger, P. and Rawsthorn, A. (1999), 'WH Smith Books a Place in New Retailing Era', *Financial Times*, 25 May, p. 21.

Hunt, G. (1999), 'Shapely Partners', *The Grocer*, 27 March, pp. 39–40.

Jardine, A. (1999), 'Time for M&S to Follow Tesco', *Marketing*, 28 January, p. 17.

Jones, S. (1999), 'Combing the Market Brings Success to Textile Company', *Financial Times*, 14 May, p. 8.

Kahn, K. and Mentzer, J. (1997), 'State of Sales Forecasting Systems in Corporate America', *Journal of Business Forecasting*, Spring.

Kim, C. and Mauborgne, R. (1999), 'Coffee Blended with Emotion', *Financial Times*, 20 May, p. 18.

Kinsella, R. *et al.* (1993), *Fast Growth Firms and Selectivity*, Irish Management Institute.

Lambin, J. J. (1993), *Strategic Marketing*, McGraw-Hill.

Lorenz, A. (1996a), 'Pilkington Picks Up the Pieces', *Management Today*, March, pp. 37–41.

Marketing Week (1999), 'M&S Unveils Fresh £20m Revamp', *Marketing Week*, 22 July, p. 6.

Marsh, P. (1999a), 'Teams Glued to Engineering Solutions', *Financial Times*, 13 May, p. 17.

Marsh, P. (1999b), 'Pattern for Survival in the Textile Business', *Financial Times*, 27 May, p. 14.

McClelland, D. (1961), *The Achieving Society*, Van Nostrand.

McDonald, M. H. B. (1989), *Marketing Plans*, Butterworth-Heinemann.

Mentzer, J. *et al.* (1999), 'Benchmarking Sales Forecasting Management, *Business Horizons*, May–June.

Moon, M. *et al.* (1998), 'Seven Keys to Better Forecasting', *Business Horizons*, September–October.

Murphy, C. (1998a), 'How Can Marks & Spencer Prevent the Sales Slump?', *Marketing,* 29 October, p. 19.

Murphy, C. (1998b), 'BUPA Looks for Better Health', *Marketing*, 3 December, p. 21.

Murphy, C. (1999), 'Cadbury's Quiet Revolution', *Marketing*, 11 February, pp. 24–5.

O'Connor, J. and Galvin, E. (1999), *Marketing and Information Technology* (2nd edn), Financial Times Pitman Publishing.

Pettitt, S. and Kirkwood, G. (1986), 'Developing Marketing within the Owner Managed Firm', paper presented to 31st Annual World Conference, ICSB, Denver.

Price, C. (1999), 'Games Popularity Buoys Eidos', *Financial Times*, 28 May, p. 24.

Puris, M. (1999), 'The Big Turnaround', *EuroBusiness*, June, pp. 74–8.

Robinson, E. (1999), 'Change of Tone in M&S Makeover', *Financial Times*, 15 July, p. 20.

Rogers, D. (1998), 'Kellogg Blitz to Push Price Cuts', *Marketing*, 17 December, p. 1.

Rubythorn, T. (1999), 'The Spirit of New Ireland', *EuroBusiness*, July, pp. 55–6.

Skapinker, M. (1999), 'Airbus and Boeing See Decline in Aircraft Demand', *Financial Times*, 14 June, p. 27.

Storey, D. (1994), *Understanding the Small Business Sector*, Routledge.

The Times (1999), 'M&S Adds to Sub-brands', *The Times*, 25 August, p. 26.

Weinberg, R. (1969), 'Developing Marketing Strategies for Short Term Profits and Long Term Growth', paper presented at Advanced Management Research Inc. Seminar, New York.

Wensley, J. R. C. (1987), 'Marketing Strategy', in M. J. Baker (ed.), *The Marketing Book*, Heinemann.

Wheelwright, S. C. and Makridakis, S. (1977), *Forecasting Methods for Management* (2nd edn), Wiley.

Wilson, R. M. S. *et al.* (1992), *Strategic Marketing Management*, Butterworth-Heinemann.

Wolfe, H. D. (1966), *Business Forecasting Methods*, Holt, Rinehart and Winston.

Wynarczyk, P. *et al.* (1993), *The Managerial Labour Market in Small and Medium Sized Enterprises*, Routledge.

Services and Non-profit Marketing

This chapter will help you to:

1 define the characteristics that differentiate services from other products and outline their impact on marketing;

2 develop an extended marketing mix of 7Ps that takes the characteristics of services into account and allows comprehensive marketing strategies to be developed for services;

3 understand the importance of interactive and internal marketing for service products and their impact on issues of quality and productivity;

4 appreciate the impact of franchising and its role in service markets;

5 understand the special characteristics of non-profit organisations within the service sector, and the implications for their marketing activities.

INTRODUCTION

The focus of this chapter is on the marketing of services, whether sold for profit or not. Service products cover a wide range of applications. In the profit making sector, services marketing includes travel and tourism, banking and insurance, and personal and professional services ranging from accountancy, legal services and business consultancy through to hairdressing and garden planning and design. In the non-profit-making sector, services marketing applications include education, medicine and charities through to various aspects of government activity that need to be 'sold' to the public.

Marketing these kinds of services is somewhat different from marketing physical products. The major marketing principles discussed in this book, segmenting the market, the need for research, sensible design of the marketing mix and the need for creativity, strategic thinking and innovation, are, of course, universally applicable, regardless of the type of product involved. Where the difference arises is in the detailed design and implementation of the marketing mix. There are several special factors that provide additional challenges for the services marketer.

> **Example** Hoteliers want every visitor to thoroughly enjoy an overnight stay with them. If there is a mismatch between customers' expectations and their experiences, if they are unhappy with the room, service or choice in the hotel, they may not make a return visit. As discussed throughout this book, most businesses rely on repeat business. This requires a considerable attention to detail on the part of the hotelier, for example communicating the location of the hotel, providing car park security, levels of service in the front office, and not least creating the ambience and ensuring the functionality of the room itself. Although there is a trade-off between price and the value offered, the experience must be up to scratch. With the impact of IT and its ability to create and update a guest database, the accommodation experience will soon become far more personalised. Your preferred room temperature, a television that lists your favourite programmes and videos, a menu displayed on the television tailored to your tastes, a mini bar with your choice of drinks, a room with your preferred style and location (type of bed, floor covering, smoking etc.) are just some of the variables that a database could flag up to make your experience that bit more special. Oh yes, and all this would be in your native language (Warren, 1999)!

This chapter will, therefore, examine in detail the special aspects of services that differentiate them from physical products. It will then look at the issues involved in designing the services marketing mix and the marketing management challenges arising from its implementation. The chapter also provides a detailed consideration of franchising. For many franchisees the franchise route is an attractive way of getting into business, and for franchisors it is an attractive way of expanding an easily replicated service idea. The decision to enter such a relationship, however, has major implications for the marketing strategies of both parties. Finally, the whole area of marketing services in the non-profit sector will be considered.

PERSPECTIVES ON SERVICE MARKETS

Services are not a homogeneous group of products. There is wide variety within the services category, in terms of both the degree of service involved and the type of service product offered. Nevertheless, there are some general characteristics, common to many service products, that differentiate them as a genre from physical goods. It is often especially important, for example, to adopt an integrative approach to linking customers, employees and operations within service situations (Looy *et al.*, 1998). This section, therefore, explores the criteria by which service products can be classified, and then goes on to look at the special characteristics of services and their implications for marketing.

Classifying services

There are few pure services. In reality, many product 'packages' involve a greater or lesser level of service. Products can be placed along a spectrum, with virtually pure personal service involving few, if any, props at one end, and pure product that involves little or no service at the other. Most products do have some combination of physical good and service, as shown in Fig. 22.1. The purchase of a chocolate bar, for example, involves little or no service other than the involvement of a checkout or till operator. The purchase of a gas appliance will involve professional fitting, and thus is a combination of physical and service product. A new office computer system could similarly involve installation and initial training. A visit to a theme park or theatre could involve some limited support products, such as guides and gifts, while the main product purchased is the experience itself. Finally, a visit to a psychiatrist or a hairdresser may involve a couch, a chair and some minor allied

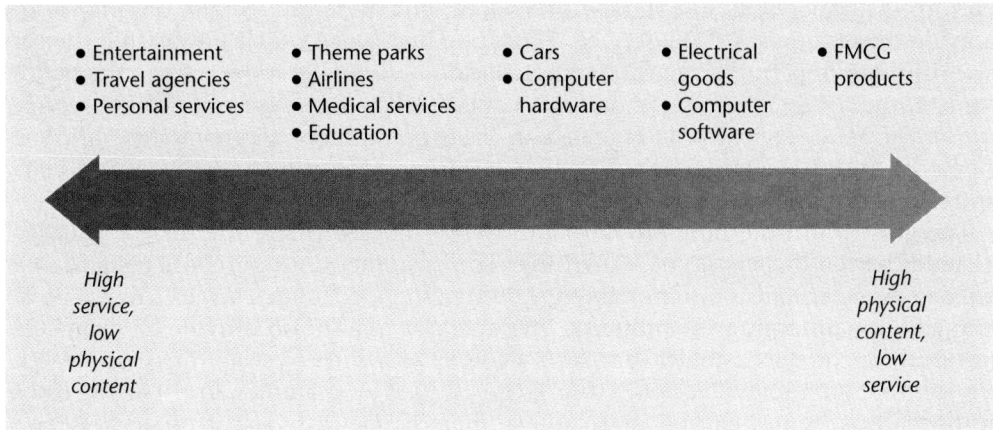

props such as an interview checklist or a hair-dryer. The real product purchased here, however, is the personal service manufactured by the service deliverer, the psychiatrist or the hairdresser.

Tangibility is not the only way of classifying service products. Lovelock (1996) suggests several other ways of grouping services along dimensions that might have implications for the marketing mix employed in designing and delivering the service. These include how the service is delivered, the extent to which supply is constrained or demand fluctuates, the degree of involvement of people and facilities in the service, the level of customisation, the relationship between the service organisation and its customers, the duration of the benefits of the service and the duration of the service delivery.

Special characteristics of service markets

Five main characteristics, as shown in Fig. 22.2, have been identified as being unique to service markets (*see*, e.g., Sasser *et al.*, 1978; Cowell, 1984).

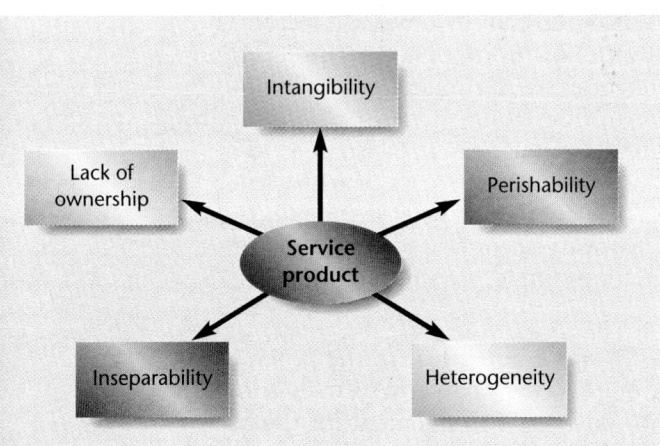

Lack of ownership

Perhaps the most obvious aspect of a service product is that no goods change hands, as such, and therefore there is no transfer of ownership of anything. A legal transaction does still take place; an insurance company agrees to provide certain benefits as long as the premiums are paid and the terms and conditions of the policy are met. A car rental company allows the customer full use of a vehicle for an agreed length of time, subject to some restraints on named drivers and type of usage, but the ownership of the vehicle remains with the rental company. A train seat can be reserved for a journey, but it is not owned. A subscription to the National Trust provides rights of access free of charge but no actual share in the ownership of its properties. The access, use or experience of the service is, therefore, often time specific, usage specific and subject to contractual terms and conditions.

The lack of ownership raises the issue of the transient nature of the purchase. Most service products involve some kind of 'experience' for the customer. This might be surrounded by props, for example a stage, lighting and sound systems, a lecture theatre, an insurance policy, a vehicle or a room, but these only serve to enhance or degrade the experience of the service. The faulty fuel gauge which means that the car hirer runs out of petrol in the most remote location, the hotel room next to the building site, the ineffective microphone at a concert all spoil the memory of the service consumed. Most service products are about the expectation of 'temporary use' and the memories arising therefrom, for example the stories of the annual holiday in Marbella or trekking through the Himalayas.

The growth of timeshare provides an interesting case where the service package includes partial ownership of something. The customer does purchase a share in a holiday property, but is also purchasing the timeshare operator's services in administering and maintaining the property. The operator might also provide an exchange service, whereby the customer can join a network of owners to swap timeshares. With services that do not involve ownership, frequent flyer programmes, membership clubs and loyalty schemes can encourage customers to feel a sense of ownership and belonging to the service product.

Intangibility

A visit to a retail store reveals an inviting display of products to purchase. These products can be examined, touched, tried on, sampled, smelt or listened to. All this can help the customer to examine what is on offer and to make choices between competing brands. The consumer regularly uses the whole range of senses to assist decision making (*see* Chapter 3). Touch, sight, sound, smell and taste are powerful influences on consumer purchasing, enabling them to assess what is being offered, to weigh up value, and to develop the confidence to act. This is especially important before the purchase is made, but even after the sale the product can be assessed in terms of its use, its durability and whether it lives up to general expectations. If there is a fault with a physical product, it can be returned or exchanged.

With service products, it is far more difficult to use the senses in the same way as a means of making a purchase decision because the actual service experience can only take place after that decision has been made. The heart of a service is the experience created for the customer, whether individually as with a personal service such as dentistry or hairdressing, or as a group experience, such as a lecture, a show or a flight. In many cases, once the purchase decision has been made, all the customer will receive is a ticket, a confirmation of booking or some promise of future benefit. The service experience itself is intangible, and is only delivered after the customer is committed to the purchase.

Despite the problem of **intangibility**, the potential customer can make some kind of prior assessment of the service product. Using available tangible cues, the customer can assess whether a particular service provider is likely to deliver what is wanted. The actual cues used and the priority given to them will vary according to the customer's particular needs at the time. In choosing a hotel, for example, a customer might look at the following:

1 *Location*: if the customer is on holiday, then perhaps a hotel near to the beach or other tourist attraction would be preferred, or one in a very peaceful scenic setting. A business traveller, in contrast, might look for one that is convenient for the airport or close to the client being visited.

2 *Appearance*: a customer's expectations about a hotel are likely to be affected by its appearance. Does it look shabby or well kept? Is it too big or too small? Does it look welcoming? What is the decor like, both internally and externally? Do the rooms seem spacious enough and well appointed? Those who are familiar with the Parador hotel chain in Spain will realise what an impact can be made by building a hotel around the conversion of historic buildings such as castles and stately homes.

3 *Additional services*: the customer might be concerned about the peripheral aspects of the service on offer. The tourist who will be spending two weeks in a hotel might

be interested in the variety of bars and restaurants provided; hairdressing, laundry or creche facilities; shopping and postal services; or the nightlife. The business traveller might be more concerned about car parking, shuttle buses to the airport, or fax and telephone provision.

4 *Customer handling*: if the potential customer contacts the hotel for further information or to make a reservation, the quality of the handling they receive might affect the purchase decision. Courtesy and friendliness will make a good impression, as will a prompt and accurate response to the query. This kind of efficiency implies a commitment to staff training and good operating systems to assist easy access to relevant information and the speedy processing of bookings.

Example A visit to the cinema has been revolutionised over recent years, and further changes are still expected as efforts continue to be made to upgrade the customer experience. It is not very long ago that going to the cinema meant a choice of one main feature and a 'B' film and that was all. Stern-faced usherettes guided you with their torches towards a seat (usually the one you did not want), then they doubled up as ice-cream sellers during the interval (until they ran out of stock). Parking was usually non-existent, as cinemas were located in town centres, and queueing was the norm for more popular shows as no advance booking was possible. The seating was not particularly comfortable, and the whole episode was not very customer friendly. It is perhaps not surprising that cinema audiences declined over many years as people switched to new leisure pursuits.

All that has now changed in many cinemas, as marketing strategies have become far more orientated towards the needs of the consumer. This is very evident from a visit to a multiplex cinema, a format which has been a major influence in the rise in cinema attendances in the UK. A multiplex is a large building containing a number of small, individual cinemas around a central circulation area. A multiplex can thus show 12 or more different films at any one time and can seat up to 3500 customers in total. The size of the individual cinemas varies, so that, for example, blockbusting new releases can be put into bigger ones or even be shown in two cinemas at once, reflecting the expected popularity of the film. The seating in all the cinemas is invariably of a high standard.

Pre-booking is possible, at least to guarantee entry although not necessarily to have a specific seat allocation, and there is plenty of opportunity to purchase a wide range of snacks in the central circulation area while you wait to be admitted to the cinema itself. Parking is rarely a problem, as most multiplexes are on large, out of town sites. Whereas town centre sites tend to attract primarily a local audience, multiplexes tend to pull audiences from greater distances. Careful marketing, through advertising and brochures, for example, ensures that people know what range of films is on offer at any one time. Once customers are in the cinema, trailers for forthcoming features also help to encourage 'repeat purchases', keeping more regular cinema goers aware of new releases.

Efforts to upgrade the customer experience are not over yet. Bars and catering are expected to be upgraded further, even though on many sites a number of fast food franchises have been licensed. Improved booking systems are likely to be introduced to speed up pre-booking (with seat allocations) and payment, in some cases using the Internet. Although the supply of quality cinema viewing is increasing, the service enhancement is still essential as part of the package to encourage cinema goers to visit more often by making it easier and more pleasant for them.

Sources: Daneshkhu (1996); Murphy (1996); Rawsthorn (1996).

In a wider sense, marketing and brand building are also important, of course. These help to raise awareness of a hotel chain's existence and positioning, and differentiate it from the competition. These communicate the key benefits on offer and thus help the customer to decide whether this is the kind of hotel they are looking for, developing their expectations. Advertising, glossy brochures and other marketing communications techniques can help to create and reinforce the potential customer's perception of location, appearance, additional services and customer handling, as well as the brand imagery. Strong marketing and branding also help to link a chain of hotels that might be spread worldwide, giving the customer some reassurance of consistency and familiarity. A business traveller in a strange city can seek out a known hotel name, such as Novotel, Holiday Inn, Sheraton, Campanile or Formula 1, and be fairly certain about what they are purchasing.

The more intangible the product, the greater the pressure on marketers to create what tangibility they can. This makes it easier for the consumer to do some pre-purchase evaluation and gives them the confidence to buy. The secret of franchising's success is to make a service offering tangible so that the customers know what to expect before purchase, regardless of the geographic location of the outlet.

> **Example** Pizza Hut's menu, decor, servers, order processing, equipment, cooking procedures etc. are all standardised (or allow minor variations and adaptations for local conditions), creating a consistent and familiar experience for the customer all over the world. Customers thus have a strong tangible impression of the character of Pizza Hut, what to expect of it, and what it delivers.

One of the greatest problems of intangibility is that it is difficult to assess quality both during and after the service has been experienced. Customers will use a combination of criteria, both objective and subjective, to judge their level of satisfaction, although it is often based on impressions, memories and expectations. Different customers attach significance to different things. The frequent business traveller might be extremely annoyed by check-in delays or the noise from the Friday night jazz cabaret, while the holidaymaker might grumble about the beach being 20 minutes' walk away rather then the 5 minutes promised in the brochure. Memories fade over time, but some bad ones, such as a major service breakdown or a confrontation with service staff, will remain. In a restaurant, assessing the quality of the food or the cleanliness of the cutlery might well be straightforward and consistent between different customers, but atmosphere, music and interaction with the serving staff are much more individual and subjective.

Perishability

Services are manufactured at the same time as they are consumed. A lecturer paces the lecture theatre creating a service experience that is immediately either consumed or slept through by the students. Manchester United, Ajax or AC Milan manufacture sporting entertainment that either thrills, bores or frustrates their fans as they watch the match live. Similarly, audiences at Covent Garden or La Scala absorb live opera as it unfolds before them. With both sport and entertainment, it is likely that the customer's enjoyment of the 'product' is heightened by the unpredictability of live performance and the audience's own emotional involvement in what is going on. This highlights another peculiarity of service products: customers are often directly involved in the production process and the synergy between them and the service provider affects the quality of the experience. A friend might tell you, 'Yes, it was a brilliant concert. The band were on top form and the atmosphere was great!' To create such a complete experience, the band and their equipment do have to perform to the expected standard, the lighting and sound crews have to get it right on the night, and the venue has to have adequate facilities and efficient customer handling processes. The atmosphere, however, is created by the interaction between performer and audience and can inspire the performer to deliver a better experience. The customer therefore has to be prepared to give as well as take, and make their own contribution to the quality of the service product.

Perishability thus means that a service cannot be manufactured and stored either before or after the experience. Manufacture and consumption are simultaneous. A hotel is, of course, a permanent structure with full-time staff, and exists regardless of whether it has customers or not on a particular night. The hotel's service product, however, is only being delivered when there is a customer present to purchase and receive it. The product is perishable in the sense that if a room is not taken on a particular night, then it is a completely lost opportunity. Room 101 for the night of Wednesday, 3 September 2003 is a unique, time-dependent service product. The same is true of most service products, such as airline seats, theatre tickets, management consultancy or dental appointments. If a dentist cannot fill the appointment book for a particular day, then that revenue-earning opportunity is lost for ever. In situations where demand is reasonably steady, it is relatively easy to plan capacity and adapt the organisation to meet the expected demand pattern.

Example Some airlines are considering whether to address the issue of special services for business travellers head on. Rather than concentrating on fast-track security and passport checks, special airport lounges, extra leg room and special menus, the idea of 'business travellers only' flights is being considered. Both Boeing and Airbus Industrie are examining the option of producing a number of jets designed only to take business-class passengers. For example the A319, which normally carries 124 passengers, could be reconfigured to take just 50 business travellers. That would also mean that on normal services, the first-class and business-class areas could be reduced or eliminated to allow for more economy-class passengers. The main stumbling block is ensuring that the business-travellers only flights run on routes that will guarantee an economic loading and that the extra seats created in economy class on the other flights can be sold. Select the wrong routes or suffer from an economic downturn and the changes could have a disastrous effect on already tight margins in the airline industry (Bray, 1999).

Even where demand does fluctuate, as long as it is fairly predictable managers can plan to raise or reduce service capacity accordingly. A larger plane or an additional performance might be provided to cater for short-term demand increases. It can be more difficult, however, if there are very marked fluctuations in demand that might result in facilities lying idle for a long time or in severe overcapacity. The profitability of companies servicing peak-hour transport demands can be severely affected because vehicles and rolling stock are unused for the rest of the day. Airlines too face seasonal fluctuations in demand.

Example Balkanair mothballs a number of its holiday jets over the winter, as the Black Sea resorts in Bulgaria virtually close down and there is little demand from foreign tourists. Sports and entertainment can be hit by unpredictable demand fluctuations. A football team that hits a run of bad luck can see its crowd fall to 5000 but still have to maintain a 50 000-seater stadium. More drastically, a West End show that gets universally bad reviews might have to end its run early because it cannot fill the theatre on a regular enough basis.

Sometimes, of course, changes in demand or events within the marketing environment mean a flood of extra customers. This can put severe strain on the service delivery system and on capacity, if the service provider cannot respond in sufficient time.

In summer 1998, both Air Canada and North West Airlines pilots went on strike over pay and employment conditions and many European travellers where caught in the aftermath. Although the run-in to both strikes was long and very public, the airlines would generally not change reservations on standard economy tickets until the strikes were formally announced. Many thousands of domestic and international passengers were faced with disrupted plans, delays or even no alternative travel arrangements at all along with a frustrating time in trying to make alternative arrangements. Given the volume of inbound telephone calls when the Air Canada strike was announced, there was little chance of getting any help over the telephone. At many of the airports, the queues meant a wait of several hours without any refreshments and an uncertain outcome. Although Air Canada did manage to find alternative carriers for many passengers, goodwill and the reputation of the airline suffered badly.

In happier circumstances, success might lead to increased demand. A non-league football team experiencing a good cup run might 'borrow' a bigger and better-equipped ground for a fixture against a high-profile opponent, or a show that gets good reviews and good word-of-mouth recommendations might extend its run or insert extra performances.

The concept of perishability means that a range of marketing strategies is needed to try to even out demand and bring capacity handling into line with it. These strategies might include pricing or product development to increase demand during quieter periods or to divert it from busier ones, or better scheduling and forecasting through the booking and reservation system.

Example Since the return of Hong Kong to Chinese control, some hotels have found that the number of foreign tourists prepared to pay premium prices has fallen considerably. The Peninsula Hotel has seen its occupancy levels fall to around 50 per cent despite a drop in the average room rate from HK$2905 to HK$2790. The more downmarket Kowloon Hotel has maintained its occupancy rates, but has seen average room rates drop from HK$559 to HK$464 in one year. The financial problems in Asia have not helped the local hotels, but in the short term, other than changing prices and increasing promotional activities, the options are limited (Jacob, 1999).

Similarly, the capacity and service delivery system can be adapted to meet peaks or troughs in demand through such strategies as part-time workers, increased mechanisation or co-operation with other service providers. These will be considered in more detail later (*see* pp. 962 *et seq.*).

Inseparability

Many physical products are produced well in advance of purchase and consumption, and production staff rarely come into direct contact with the customer. Often, production and consumption are distanced in both space and time, connected only by the physical distribution system considered in Chapter 13. Sales forecasts based on reasonable expectations of changes in demand provide important guidelines for production schedules. If demand rises unexpectedly, opportunities might well exist to increase production or to reduce stockholding to meet customer needs.

As has already been said, with service products, however, the involvement of the customer in the service experience means that there can be no prior production, no storage and that consumption takes place simultaneously with production. The service delivery, therefore, cannot be separated from the service providers and thus the fourth characteristic of service products is **inseparability**. The terminology used to order a service product might vary: booking, making an appointment, reserving a seat or prepaying an entrance fee. All of these terms, however, imply that the customer is being granted legitimate access to consume a service experience at an agreed time and place in the future, with the co-operation and participation of the provider.

Inseparability means that the customer often comes into direct contact with the service provider(s), either individually, as with a doctor, or as part of a team of providers, as with air travel. The team includes reservations clerks, check-in staff, aircrew and perhaps transfer staff. In an airline, the staff team has a dual purpose. Clearly, they have to deliver their aspect of the service efficiently, but they also have to interact with the customer in the delivery of the service. An unco-operative check-in clerk might not provide the customer's desired seat, but in contrast, a friendly and empathic air hostess can alleviate the fear of a first-time flyer. The service provider can thus affect the quality of the service delivered and the manner in which it is delivered.

Example British Airways (BA) is training all of its 14 000 cabin staff to be more aware of other cultures. The airline carries people from many different nationalities (over 60 per cent of its passengers are not from the UK) and it feels that it is important for cabin crew to think about different cultures and how they might behave when on board. Handling sensitive issues around food and drink can be especially important for cabin crew, for instance. How different cultures handle conflict situations with other passengers or crew can also vary. In addition to training, BA is looking to employ more staff from ethnic minority backgrounds. The recruitment drive improved numbers by 14 per cent from an average of just 85 UK-based flight attendants and 3000 extra staff world-wide from a diverse range of ethnic backgrounds (Skapinker, 1999).

While the delivery of a personal service can be controlled, since there are fewer opportunities for outside interference, the situation becomes more complex when other customers are experiencing service at the same time. The 'mass service experience' means that other customers can potentially affect the perceived quality of that experience, positively or negatively. As mentioned earlier, the enjoyment of the atmosphere at a sporting event or a concert, for example, depends on the emotional charge generated by a large number of like-minded individuals. In other situations, however, the presence of many other customers can negatively affect aspects of the service experience. If the facility or the staff do not have the capacity or the ability to handle larger numbers than forecast, queues, overcrowding and dissatisfaction can soon result. Although reservation or prebooking can reduce the risk, service providers can still be caught out. Airlines routinely overbook flights deliberately, on the basis that not all booked passengers will actually turn up. Sometimes, however, they miscalculate and end up with more passengers than the flight can actually accommodate and have to offer free air miles, cash or other benefits to encourage some passengers to switch to a later flight. At theme parks, much more time can be spent waiting to get on to a ride than on the ride itself during times of peak demand. Although attempts are made to manage that situation by providing information about waiting times, planning the queueing procedure to give the impression of constant forward movement, and providing entertainment while people wait, customers would still prefer shorter queues and less competition for the park's facilities.

What the other customers are like also affects the quality of the experience. This reflects the segmentation policy of the service provider. If a relatively undifferentiated approach is offered, there are all sorts of potential conflicts (or benefits) from mixing customers who are perhaps looking for different benefits. A hotel, for example, might have problems if families with young children are mixed with guests on an over-50s holiday. Where possible, therefore, the marketer should carefully target segments to match the service product being offered. By attracting like-minded individuals, not only will the service experience be enhanced for all customers, but there will also be less opportunity for those seeking a peaceful retreat at a hotel being disturbed by a Club 18–30 all-night rave!

> **Example** On a more positive note, soccer and rugby clubs in the UK have been following the North American experience by trying to appeal to the family rather than just to sports-orientated men. Although the sports event itself is still at the heart of the attraction, the total experience has been modified by creating family enclosures, improved catering and toilet facilities, pre-match entertainment, and encouraging a club interest and following. At Saracens and the Bradford Bulls rugby clubs, pop music, competitions and dancing girls have all helped to enhance the experience. Players at these clubs are also expected to participate in the community. By creating a sense of belonging and fun, the wider appeal appears to have been working in raising gate receipts in some spectator sports (Richards, 1999).

Finally, the behaviour of other customers can be positive, leading to new friends, comradeship and enjoyable social interaction, or it can be negative if it is rowdy, disruptive or even threatening. Marketers prefer, of course, to try to develop the positive aspects. Social evenings for new package holiday arrivals, name badges on coach tours, and warm-up acts to build atmosphere at live shows all help to break the ice. To prevent disruptive behaviour, the service package might have to include security measures and clearly defined and enforced 'house rules' such as those found at soccer matches. Of course, there can be real problems for marketers in keeping some segments apart, for example in soccer grounds.

The implications of inseparability for marketing strategy will be considered at pp. 959 *et seq.*

Heterogeneity

With simultaneous production and consumption and the involvement of service staff and other customers, it can be difficult to standardise the service experience as planned. **Heterogeneity** means that each service experience is likely to be different, depending on the interaction between the customer and other customers, service staff, and other factors such as time, location and the operating procedures. The problems of standardising the desired service experience are greater when there is finite capacity and the service provided is especially labour intensive. The maxim 'when the heat is on the service is gone' reflects the risk of service breakdown when demand puts the system under pressure, especially if it is unexpected. This might mean no seats available on the train, delays in serving meals on a short-haul flight, or a queue in the bank on a Friday afternoon.

Katz *et al.* (1996) found that people significantly overestimate the amount of time they spend in queues and quickly become very impatient, especially when their time is unoccupied. For that reason, clever service operators make sure that there is some entertainment while customers are waiting and plan the queuing area layout to encourage a number of short, moving lines, rather than the appearance of one long line stretching all the way to eternity!

> **Example** Virgin Trains has been struggling to make a success of its rail service. It is a tough challenge, with one in five trains running late or cancelled, and yet 75 per cent of the problems are out of Virgin's control, resting with the railway infrastructure. If the track or signalling is not up to scratch, or the non-Virgin locomotive in front breaks down, then it is difficult to offer a reliable service. With 28 million passenger journeys a year, there is plenty of scope for the complaining passenger and ironically, although many other train operators are also failing in service reliability, the high profile of Virgin often means that it is subject to more complaints. The company is so used to dealing with complaints that when one passenger wrote to compliment Virgin on its service, Virgin wrote back and apologised to him, promising to look into the matter! Providing a consistent and reliable service in such an environment may need a lot more than the promised high-speed trains (Killgren, 1999).

Sometimes the differences are more subtle, but they can still affect the perception of service performance. On one day a lecturer might deliver an entertaining and informative lecture, but on the next day, perhaps suffering from the effects of a late night, the performance might be well below average. Following an inconsistent soccer team can be a rollercoaster; a great match and a convincing win one week, but an eminently forgettable performance the next. A multi-location service provider might regularly provide excellent service in one branch, but very poor service in another. There can also, of course, be inconsistencies between different service providers. Within a single branch of a bank, some clerks can be bright, friendly and helpful, while others will be surly and offer service grudgingly. Some travellers assess the check-in staff at an airport to decide which one looks more likely to turn a blind eye to excess luggage or to allocate the best seats!

Some of the heterogeneity in the service cannot be planned for or avoided, but quality assurance procedures can minimise the worst excesses of service breakdown. This can be done by designing in 'failsafes', creating mechanisms to spot problems quickly and to resolve them early before they cause a major service breakdown. Universities, for example, have numerous quality assurance procedures to cover academic programmes, staffing and support procedures that involve self-assessment, student evaluation and external subject and quality assessment.

Not all service breakdowns are caused by the service provider, but, whatever their cause, they can still fundamentally affect the quality of the service experience. Technical problems with a plane are the responsibility of an airline, but not the fog, air traffic delays or problems with the baggage handlers. A state agency might have responsibility for promoting regional tourism, but is dependent on the hotels, guest houses, tourist attractions, taxi drivers and other service providers to deliver the required service to a proper standard for the region's tourism to develop.

Example A *Which? Hotel Guide*, published by the Consumers' Association, raised serious questions about the quality of British hotels at the lower end of the market and suggested that they had fallen behind many other European destinations. Even the unified grading system introduced to rate English hotels does not really help at the bottom end of the market, as many hoteliers will not even enter the system. Instead these hoteliers rely on the unwary tourist on the basis that they do not want repeat business. Faulty plumbing, poor bed comfort, ill-equipped rooms, noise, poor hygiene and low service levels can all be found in various combinations and there is little that the tourist agencies can do about it. For many of these hotels, it is a vicious circle: poor, ungraded amenities may lead to low occupancy, which means that there is little potential for investment to break out of the cycle. Of course there are noticeable exceptions, but the risks to the holiday experience in the great British tourist resorts is clear (Young, 1998).

Management therefore has to develop ways of reducing the impact of heterogeneity. To help in that process, they need to focus on operating systems, procedures and staff training in order to ensure consistency. New lecturers, for example, might be required to undertake a special induction programme to help them learn teaching skills, preparing materials and handling some of the difficulties associated with disruptive students. Managers have to indicate clearly what they expect of staff in terms of the desired level of service. This must cover not only compliance with procedures in accordance with training, but also staff attitudes and the manner in which they deal with customers. Many franchising chains have successfully managed growth, yet maintained service consistency and control through the careful design of the operating manual, extensive staff training, and regular monitoring and feedback.

Example The Welsh Tourist Board (http://www.visitwales.com) operates a quality assurance scheme that establishes the minimum standards that a tourist might expect when visiting or holidaying in Wales. Inspectors examine all aspects of the accommodation before awarding a star category. These range from five stars for exceptional quality and exemplary service to one star for a fair to good standard of furnishings and adequate service and guest care. The scheme extends to activity holidays and self-catering accommodation, and is designed to provide some standardisation in an inherently non-standard holiday experience for tourists.

A short break in Wales promises an escape from the rat race.

Source: Welsh Tourist Board.

Lovelock (1996), however, feels that these characteristics are somewhat over-generalised and are not necessarily applicable to all service products. An alternative list of eight generic differences between physical products and services, summarised in Table 22.1, is therefore suggested as a more practical approach. This list does, nevertheless, include many of the concepts discussed above, albeit under different labels.

The characteristics of service products, regardless of how they are defined, create problems for marketers. They have to build and maintain competitive advantage through service design, delivery, differentiation and efficiency, while regularly providing consistent service. The next section, therefore, looks in more detail at the impact of the particular characteristics of service products on the design and implementation of the marketing programme.

TABLE 22.1

Generic differences between services and physical goods

1 The nature of the product
2 Customers' involvement in the production process
3 People as part of the product
4 Greater problems in maintaining quality
5 Harder for customers to evaluate
6 Absence of inventories
7 Relative importance of time factors
8 Structure and nature of distribution channels

Source: Lovelock (1996).

SERVICES MARKETING MANAGEMENT

So far, this chapter has looked at the characteristics of service products in a very general way. This section looks further at the implications of those characteristics for marketers in terms of formulating strategy, developing and measuring quality in the service product and issues of training and productivity.

Services marketing strategy

The traditional marketing mix, consisting of the 4Ps, forms the basis of the structure of this book. For service products, however, additional elements of the marketing mix are necessary to reflect the special characteristics of services marketing. Shown in Fig. 22.3, these are:

- *people*: whether service providers or customers who participate in the production and delivery of the service experience
- *physical evidence*: the tangible cues that support the main service product. These will include facilities, the infrastructure and the products used to deliver the service
- *processes*: the operating processes that take the customer through from ordering to the manufacture and delivery of the service.

Any of these extra marketing mix elements can enhance or detract from the customer's overall experience when consuming the service. However, despite the special considerations, the purpose of designing an effective marketing mix remains the same

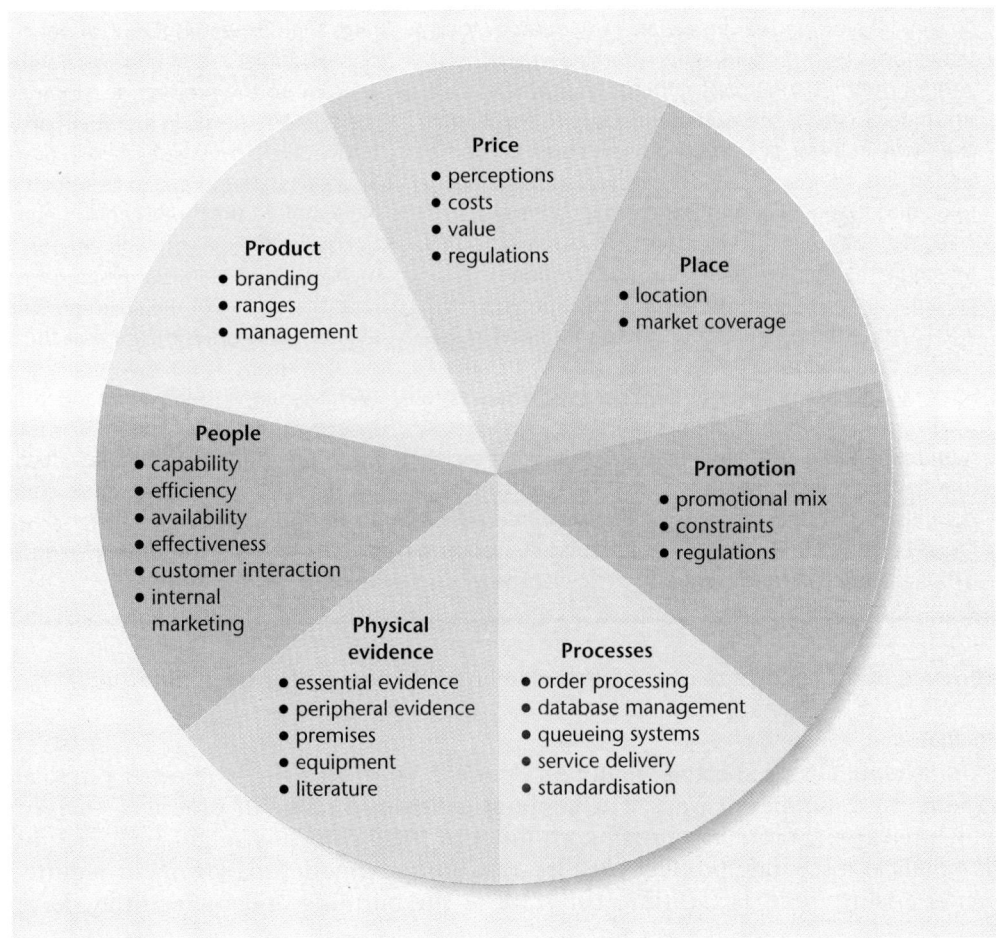

FIGURE 22.3

The services marketing mix

whether for services or physical products. The marketer is still trying to create a differentiated, attractive proposition for customers, ensuring that whatever is offered meets their needs and expectations.

MARKETING IN ACTION **The less than magic kingdom?**

The Disneyworld and Disneyland theme parks in the USA have long proved to be popular attractions for US, European and global tourists. It seemed to make good business sense, then, to extend the concept and bring it closer to non-American visitors by building Disney theme parks in other parts of the world. EuroDisney was opened in 1992 in France to give Disney a focal point within Europe. Disney had assumed that because European tourists enjoyed going to Florida to experience the all-American Disney culture, it could replicate that experience almost exactly on the outskirts of Paris.

Although it is the biggest attraction of its kind in Europe, the 'Magic Kingdom' did not quite live up to the expectations of America's biggest theme park export, nor did those early visitors seem to feel that the experience was quite right. Some things were out of Disney's control. With the best will in the world, Paris does not have Florida's climate and any outdoor tourist attraction is going to look different if it is experienced in grey, overcast conditions rather than in wall-to-wall sunshine. Some visitors also found a trip to EuroDisney expensive in terms of travel and hotel costs. For some UK families, for instance, it actually worked out cheaper to go and spend a week in Florida than in Paris!

Disney thus reviewed all aspects of its marketing mix to enable the theme park to reach its maximum potential. Very large numbers of visitors are required, and to make the park a success the hotels need to sell rooms, the restaurants food and the stores gifts and merchandise. Many changes from the highly successful US formula were thus implemented. An insufficient number of guests used the hotels in a European society that has less discretionary spend and perhaps greater budget consciousness than its American counterpart. From a planned occupancy rate of around 80 per cent, the actual levels were closer to 60 per cent. The entrance fee to the park and the prices of hotel rooms, meals and merchandise all had to be reduced to stimulate more demand. Even the food products had to be revised. It had been assumed that the French would want to eat a light breakfast of coffee and croissants, but they actually wanted full sit-down service, resulting in queues in hotels with not enough breakfast places. Also, the 37-year-old Disney rule of no alcohol in the theme park appeared to put off many Europeans who wanted a beer or wine with a meal. When alcohol was eventually served, after much soul searching, it was realised that when they were in the park, Europeans acted more like the Americans in wanting fast food on the run!

Even the distribution channels proved problematic. In the USA, direct ordering is normal for booking hotels etc.; in Europe the tradition was not so strong and the growth of inclusive packages meant higher commission rates than expected. Only 25 per cent of Europeans booked direct. All of these mix adjustments were in addition to the product development that is considered normal in a theme park. To generate repeat business and renewed interest, new attractions such as Space Mountain have to be added at regular intervals. New minor attractions can sometimes help solve queuing problems at peak periods. The role of the 'cast members', i.e. staff, remained the same, however – to raise the quality of the customer experience – although financial difficulties meant that the park had to make do with nearly 1000 fewer staff than planned. Finally, even the name itself was changed from EuroDisney to Disneyland Paris, with some consumers regarding the Euro connotations as negative. It all goes to show the dangers of transferring service marketing mix assumptions across international borders when it is difficult to test market before launch.

Source: Eisner (1999).

All seven of the services marketing mix elements will now be considered in turn.

Product

From a supplier's perspective, many services can be treated like any other physical product in a number of ways. The supplier develops a range of products, each of which represents profit earning opportunities. A hotel company might treat each of its hotels as a separate product with its own unique product management requirements arising from its location, the state of the building and its facilities, local competition, and its strengths and weaknesses compared with others in the area. These products might, of course, be grouped into product lines and SBUs based on similarities and differences between them, just as physical products can be.

Similarly, an insurance company might have many different policies on offer, including pension plans, endowments, life insurance, house buildings and contents insurance, and motor or holiday insurance. Each one again might be considered as a product or as part of a range.

Many of the product concepts and the decisions concerning them that were discussed in Chapters 7 to 9 apply equally to services and physical products. Positioning, branding, developing a mix, designing new services and managing the product life-cycle are all relevant.

> **Example** British Airways seeks to brand itself as a friendly, reliable and professional airline; Formula 1 positions itself as a no-frills, low-cost motel chain; BSkyB offers a range of satellite channels to cover sport, news, movies and other entertainment. Services can be repositioned too. Spain, for example, is trying to reposition itself and change its appeal because of too many new competitors in the sea, sun, sand and cheap alcohol segment of the market. It now wants to be regarded as a destination that still offers good value, but a wider range of tourist attractions and cultural activities. Parques Reunidos, for example, is a leading operator of amusement parks, zoos and water parks in Spain. It has six venues that attract 3.6 million visitors per year, with 1.9 million visiting the Parque de Atraccionnes in Madrid alone. The success of that park since 1994 has been largely due to an on-going programme of enhancing the facilities, developing merchandising and catering, as well as raising the entrance fee. Such facilities along with cultural and heritage sites all help attract a wider range of tourism segments (Burns, 1999).

Product development Product development in some service situations can be complex as it involves 'packaging' otherwise separate elements into a service product. Therefore a holiday company may need to work with airlines, hotels and local tour companies to blend a package for the target segment. From a consumer perspective, any failure in any part of the system will be regarded as a criticism of the holiday company, even though air traffic delays or faulty plumbing may not be directly under the company's control. At a regional and national level, government and private companies may work together to develop new attractions and infrastructure for tourists.

> **Example** In China, tourism outside the main centres of attraction is still in its infancy and requires product development and packaging. In Heilongjiang Province in the northern region, tourism is regarded as a significant growth product by the provincial government. The province has opened up 1397 scenic spots in snowfields, forests, wetlands and by rivers to make the destination more attractive. In the winter, ice and snow package tours are being developed including dog sleigh rides and ice skating. The targets are not only international tourists, but also those from China seeking the wilderness areas in the north of the country (Bin, 1999). In Israel, at town level, a biblical theme park is planned for Nazareth, portraying life as it was around 2000 years ago. Over $60mn is required, but if it is completed it could provide a much-needed boost to tourism in an essentially Muslim city (Dunn, 1998).

Price

Because services are intangible, their pricing can be very difficult to set and to justify. The customer is not receiving anything that can be touched or otherwise physically experienced, so it can be hard for them to appreciate the benefits they have gained in return for their expenditure.

> **Example** A solicitor's bill or the labour charges added to a repair bill can seem to be incredibly high to customers, because they do not stop to think about the training that has gone into developing professional skills nor of the peace of mind gained by having the job done 'properly'. As with any product, therefore, the customer's perception is central to assessing value for money.

The prices of some services are controlled by bodies other than the service provider. The amount that dentists charge for work under the National Health Service or that pharmacists charge to dispense a prescription is imposed by central government. Similarly, the BBC is funded by licence fees determined by government and charged to television owners. Other services price on a commission basis. An estate agent, for example, might charge the vendor a fee of 2 per cent of the selling price of the house, plus any expenses such as advertising. Some solicitors in the UK who specialise in pursuing compensation claims would like to be able to charge their clients a fee based on a percentage of the compensation achieved, but currently that is not allowed by their regulatory body, the Law Society.

Other service providers are completely free to decide their own prices, with due respect to competition and the needs, wants and perceptions of customers. In setting prices, however, service providers can find it very difficult to determine the true cost of provision, perhaps because of the difficulty of costing professional or specialist skills, or because the time and effort required to deliver a service vary widely between different customers, yet a standard price is needed. Perishability might also affect the pricing of professional services. A training provider, for example, who has little work on at the moment might agree to charge less than the normal daily rate, just to generate some income rather than none.

In service situations, price can play an important role in managing demand. By varying the price, depending on the time at which the service is delivered, service providers can try to discourage customers from purchasing at the busiest periods. Customers can also use price as a weapon. Passengers purchasing airline tickets shortly before the flight or visitors looking for a hotel room for the night might be able to negotiate a much lower price than that advertised. This is a result of the perishability of services: the airline would rather have a seat occupied and get something for it than let the flight take off with an empty one and, similarly, the hotel would rather have a room occupied than not.

> **Example** The rail pricing system has changed considerably in the UK in recent years. Traditionally, the passenger bought a ticket, walked on to the train and found a seat. Few bothered to pay the additional charge for a seat reservation. The emphasis is now on encouraging advance booking so that capacity can be better planned. The price mechanism is used to achieve a spread of customers. Suitably indexed to give equivalents in today's prices, an 'ordinary return' from London to Manchester was £51 in 1949. In 1969, period returns, usually for return travel within a month, could bring the price down to £41. By 1989, 'savers' again gave a price of £41, and a low of £32 could be found in 1994 with advance booking. Virgin Rail has three price bands: Virgin Value 7, with seven days' advance booking at £20; Virgin Value 1, available the day before; and walk-on tickets costing around £41. The customer now needs to be highly aware of the different pricing schemes yet, contrary to popular opinion, rail travel really can be as cheap as it was 50 years ago (Doe, 1999).

Place

According to Cowell (1984), services are often supplied direct from the provider to the customer because production and consumption are simultaneous. Direct supply allows the provider to control what is going on; to differentiate through personal service; and to get direct feedback and interaction with the customer. Direct supply can take place from business premises, such as a hairdresser's salon, a solicitor's office or a university campus. Some services can also be supplied by telephone, such as insurance and banking services. Others are supplied by the service provider visiting the customer's home or premises, such as cleaning, repair of large appliances, equipment installation and servicing, or home hairdressing services.

Whatever the mode of direct supply, it can cause problems for the service provider. It limits the number of customers that can be dealt with and the geographic coverage of the service. For sole traders or small businesses who particularly value the rapport and personal relationships built up with regular clients, this might be perfectly acceptable. Businesses that want to expand might find that direct supply involving the original proprietor of the business is no longer feasible. Professional service businesses, such as accountants or solicitors, might employ additional qualified staff to expand the customer base or to expand geographic coverage.

> **Example** The health and fitness industry experienced high growth in the 1990s and, with an estimated 5 per cent of 18- to 65-year-olds joining clubs, there was a significant increase in the number of new independent entrants to the business. It is highly fragmented, with the top 11 operators taking just 7 per cent of the market. The larger operators such as Cannons Group (21 clubs), First Leisure (18 clubs) and Fitness First (24 clubs) have to manage each club location to an agreed blueprint if they are to replicate the standard of experience needed (Daneshkhu, 1999). This is achieved by specifying the location, size, layout, equipment and level of staff expertise needed to operate a successful club. Each club location must develop close personal relationships with members if it is to compete with the individuality offered by the independents. The next stage in development for the clubs could be European expansion. The Netherlands, Germany and France are considered relatively under-developed and a number of UK operators are thinking of established clubs. Fitness First already has 14 in Germany through buying a share in a German fitness club (Robinson, 1999).

Other service businesses such as fast food outlets, domestic cleaners or debt collection agencies might opt to expand by franchising, an area which will be later in this chapter. Some services will decide to move towards indirect supply through intermediaries paid on a commission basis. Thus the local pharmacist might act as an agent for a company that develops photographic film; a village shop might collect dry cleaning; insurance brokers distribute policies; travel agencies distribute holidays and business travel; and tourist information offices deal with hotel and guest house bookings. In some of these cases, the main benefit of using an intermediary is convenience for the customer and spreading the coverage of the service. In others, such as the travel agency and the insurance broker, the service provider gains the added benefit of having its product sold by a specialist alongside the competition.

Place is not just important for delivering the service; it also covers access to reservation and information systems. Travel agents, for example, have direct computer links with tour operators and other central reservation systems that are not available to the consumer. The tour operator benefits from being able to distribute information cost effectively and having its holidays sold by trained agents. The growth of Teletext, interactive shopping and the Internet might revolutionise this aspect of the services marketing mix still further.

Promotion

Marketing communication objectives, implementation and management for services are largely the same as for any other product. There are a few specific issues to point out, however. As with pricing, some professional services are ethically constrained in what marketing communication they are allowed to do. Solicitors in the UK, for example, are allowed to use print advertising, but only if it is restrained and factual. An advertisement can tell the reader what areas of the law the practice specialises in, but it cannot make emotive promises about winning vast amounts of compensation for you, for example.

Service products face a particularly difficult communications task because of the intangibility of the product. They cannot show you pretty pack shots, they cannot whet your appetite with promises of strawberry and chocolate-flavoured variants, they cannot show you how much of this amazing product you are getting for your money. They can, however, show the physical evidence, they can show people like you apparently enjoying the service, they can emphasise the benefits of purchasing this service. Testimonials from satisfied customers can be an extremely effective tool, because they reassure the potential customer that the service works and that the outcomes will be positive. Linked with this, word-of-mouth communication is incredibly important, especially for the smaller business working in a limited geographic area. Overall, if the service provider can use communication to build a reputation for quality, reliability and trustworthiness, then it is well on the way to overcoming potential customers' doubts and overcoming intangibility.

> **Example** Jarvis Hotels (http://www.jarvis.co.uk) uses direct marketing to promote conference business in its 62 hotels in the UK. The information pack, which is targeted at potential business customers, includes a complete directory of locations, room configurations and prices along with a lot of visual imagery to show the standard of meeting rooms, food service and the range of staff who are employed to make the conference or meeting a success. The messages throughout stress quality and reliability.

Finally, it must be remembered that many service providers are small businesses, who could not afford to invest in glossy advertising campaigns even if they could see the point of it. Many can generate enough work to keep them going through word-of-mouth recommendation, websites and advertisements in the *Yellow Pages*. Much depends on the level of competition and demand in the local market for the kind of service being offered. If the town's high street supports four different restaurants, then perhaps a more concerted effort might be justified, including, for example, advertising in local newspapers, door-to-door leaflet drops and price promotions. Local service outlets that are franchises are likely to benefit from large scale national corporate promotion, designed to create a consistent image for all branches. Nevertheless, franchisees might also have some discretion and flexibility to do their own communication tailored specifically to local conditions.

It is important to remember, however, that customers are likely to use marketing communication messages to build their expectations of what the service is likely to deliver. This is true of any product but, as will be discussed at pp. 959 *et seq.*, because of intangibility, the judgement of service quality is much more subjective. It is based on a comparison of prior expectations with actual perceived outcomes. The wilder or more unrealistic the communication claims, therefore, the greater the chances of a mismatch that will lead to a dissatisfied customer in the end. The service provider does, of course, need to create a sufficiently alluring image to entice the customer, but not to the point where the customer undergoing the service experience begins to wonder if this is actually the same establishment as that advertised.

Example The Australian Tourist Commission also makes heavy use of imagery to portray the natural and cultural delights of Australia to European audiences. Whether it is kangaroos, Ayers Rock, the Great Barrier Reef or Sydney Opera House, the visual message is the same: vibrant, exciting and surprising. The media advertisements and PR usually reinforce these themes, making full use of holiday programmes and travel shows as well as supporting Australia-themed national supplements in some of the daily newspapers. Although Australia retains an exotic image, campaigns are also highlighting new messages of 'affordable, achievable and accessible' to attract a wider pool of potential visitors (Gray, 1998).

The Australian Tourist Commission used pan-European advertising to improve its sales potential.

Source: DMB&B.

People

Services depend on people and interaction between people, including the service provider's staff, the customer and other customers. As the customer is often a participant in the creation and delivery of the service product, there are implications for service product quality, productivity and staff training. The ability of staff to cope with customers, to deliver the service reliably to the required standard and to present an image consistent with what the organisation would want are vital concerns to the service provider. This is known as *internal marketing*, and will be discussed later at pp. 962 *et seq.* The role of the customer in the service is known as *interactive marketing*, and will be discussed at pp. 959 *et seq.*

Physical evidence

Physical evidence comprises the tangible elements that support the service delivery, and offer clues about the positioning of the service product or give the customer something solid to take away with them to symbolise the intangible benefits they have received. Shostack (1977) differentiates between *essential evidence* and *peripheral evidence*. Essential evidence is central to the service and is an important contributor to the customer's purchase decision. Examples of this might be the type and newness of aircraft operated by an airline or of the car fleet belonging to a car hire firm, the layout and facilities offered by a supermarket (*see* pp. 532 *et seq.* for more on this), or a university's lecture theatres and their equipment as well as IT and library provision. Peripheral evidence is less central to the service delivery and is likely to consist of items that the customer can have to keep or use.

Example   Aillwee Cave is situated in the remote Burren region of Ireland, famous for its limestone scenery, cultural heritage and spring flowers. Although lacking the size of the cave
systems in the Dordogne in France or the accessibility of Cheddar caves in the UK, it has
nevertheless become a major day visitor attraction. The cave owners have worked hard at
creating an atmosphere for its visitors. The cave experience itself is similar to many others,
with effective use of lighting on natural rock formations and fascinating tales of bears and
mysteries. The staff are, however, well trained and are called 'actors', reflecting the role
they are meant to play in raising the excitement during the visit. The guiding principle is an
impeccable tour experience every time. However, surrounding the cave a number of other
facilities have been opened, making full use of the local limestone and sympathetically
designed to blend with the natural environment. Therefore, although cheese making and
craft shops may not fit exactly with a cave experience, they do enhance the overall day-
visitor attraction and, of course, generate further on-site expenditure. The longer the
visitors stay, the more they tend to spend.

Processes

Because the creation and consumption of a service are usually simultaneous, the production of the service is an important part of its marketing as the customer either
witnesses it or is directly involved in it. The service provider needs smooth, efficient
customer-friendly procedures. Some processes work behind the scenes, for example
administrative and data processing systems, processing paperwork and information
relating to the service delivery and keeping track of customers.

Example   The Royal Mail in the UK works largely out of the public view. The scale of operation is enormous: 76 million letters per day, and 210 000 collection points feeding into 26
million delivery points in the UK alone. The logistics chain offers plenty of scope for things
to go wrong. The stages are collection, concentration, outward processing at one of 74
mail centres, network distribution using 55 trains, 37 aircraft and 7500 long distance lor-
ries, inward processing at mail centres, local distribution and eventually delivery to your
door. Despite all that, the customer expects the service to operate smoothly and efficiently
and will soon complain if mail is late or damaged (Brewer, 1999).

Systems that allow the service provider to send a postcard to remind customers that
the next dental check-up or car service is due certainly help to generate repeat business, but also help in a small way to strengthen the relationship with the customer.
Other processes are also 'invisible' to the customer, but form an essential part of the
service package. The organisation of the kitchens in a fast food outlet, for example,
ensures a steady supply of freshly cooked burgers available for counter staff to draw
on as customers order. Well-designed processes are also needed as the service is delivered to ensure that the customer gets through with minimum fuss and delay and that
all elements of the service are properly delivered. This might involve, for example, the
design of forms and the information requested, payment procedures, queueing systems or even task allocation. At a hairdressing salon, for instance, a junior might wash
your hair while the stylist finishes off the previous customer, and the receptionist will
handle the payment at the end.

Banks have thought seriously about ways of making their services more accessible
to their customers. Telephone banking, for example, with processes designed to protect customer security and to provide 24-hour coverage, allows customers easy access
to their accounts from their own homes whenever they want it. In addition to this,
there is an expectation that full use of on-line banking with the major banks is not far
away. Already in Scandinavia, electronic banking services have made a big impact.
The regional banks are encouraging customers to use on-line services for retail transactions as well as share trading and foreign currency transactions. Loans usually still

require face-to-face meetings. SEB now has 260 000 customers using on-line banking, 20 per cent of its retail base. Svenska Handelsbanken has 140 000 Internet customers, including 15 000 small businesses in which the service flexibility has been especially well received. The banks are offering incentives for customers to use the Internet, including lower commission charges, and they believe that the next phase of competition between banks will be on customer service rather than price (Burt, 1999). If Internet banking takes off across Europe, it could revolutionise the whole banking scene and remove many of the barriers associated with geography. The bank processing system could as easily be in Amsterdam or Bilbao as in Tokyo or New York. This could lead to new forms of alliances and mergers between the major banks (Graham, 1999).

Interactive marketing: service quality

Central to the delivery of any service product is the *service encounter* between the provider and the customer. This is also known as **interactive marketing**. This aspect of services is an important determinant of quality because it brings together all the elements of the services marketing mix and is the point at which the product itself is created and delivered. The challenge for the service marketer is to bring quality, customer service and marketing together to build and maintain customer satisfaction (Christopher *et al.*, 1994). Quality issues are just as important for service products as they are for a physical product, but service quality is much more difficult to define and to control. These difficulties arise from the essential intangibility of the service,

---

MARKETING AND IT   ## I'd like to talk to the person who made my laptop, please

Call centres are expected to deliver top quality customer service. Sometimes they do. And sometimes it is just too difficult to please everybody, all of the time. The problem is that service quality depends on the call centre equipment being linked to a variety of customer and other company databases. Indeed, one of the biggest obstacles that call centres face is the lack of integration with other company systems. However, as the two examples below demonstrate, if integration can be achieved, the customer service benefits can be significant.

Dell Computers

With the recent announcement of 3000 new jobs, in addition to the 1400 already employed at its manufacturing plant in Limerick, and Dell Direct Call Centre in Bray, County Dublin, Dell computers will soon be one of the largest private-sector employers in Ireland. Every Dell PC shipped in Europe, the Middle East and Africa is custom built in Limerick and sent directly to the customer. It takes four working days from order to delivery. Dell maintains a database of every machine it ships, giving full details of the configuration and service history. This provides customer support staff with a very precise history of the PC, which they can access as soon as they receive a call. It also allows support staff to talk directly to the person who made the machine, if necessary. All this happens because Dell uses CTI technology to link its call centre staff to the database.

Shimano

The Japanese company Shimano, a manufacturer of bicycle components and fishing gear, also uses CTI technology to improve customer service. Shimano wanted a CTI system that could help it manage a wide variety of customer calls and enable it to capture customer information from those customers that could be fed back to its headquarters to help in product development and improving products. The CTI system, from Siemens Rolm, had to be integrated with the computer system that manages its customer database records. The Shimano account manager now receives the following information automatically from the CTI system:

- who is calling
- customer data from the customer database
- a history of previous calls made by the customer
- past queries and requirements of the customer
- how these queries were handled
- products bought by the customer
- the degree of customer satisfaction.

Source: O'Connor & Galvin (1999).

the fact that it is produced 'live' and the involvement of the customer in the production process. Because there is no physical product to look at and measure, service quality assessment is largely dependent on the customers' perceptions of what they have received and the extent to which that has fulfilled or exceeded their expectations. Authors such as Devlin and Dong (1994) and Zeithaml *et al.* (1990), for example, stress the importance of customer perceptions and use them as the basis for frameworks for measuring service quality.

> **Example** Home delivery of pizzas is usually associated with supplier guarantees of free pizzas if delivered outside a certain period. This helps emphasise the speed of delivery and reinforces the convenience of home ordering services. Pizza Hut could be going a step further in the UK by introducing on-line ordering. By being able to access the local store, plan choices and with on-line ordering and credit card transaction, the speed and convenience aspect of service quality will be reinforced (Rosier, 1999).

Measuring service quality

Some aspects of the service product can, of course, be measured more objectively than others. Where tangible elements are involved, such as physical evidence and processes, quality can be defined and assessed more easily. In a fast food restaurant, for example, the cleanliness of the premises, the length of the queues, the consistency of the size of portions and their cooking, and the implementation and effectiveness of stock control systems can all be 'seen' and measured. Whether the customer actually *enjoyed* the burger, whether they *felt* that they had had to wait too long, or whether they *felt* that the premises were too busy, crowded or noisy are much more personal matters and thus far more difficult for managers to assess.

A particular group of researchers, Berry, Parasuraman and Zeithaml, have developed criteria for assessing service quality and a survey mechanism called SERVQUAL for collecting data relating to customer perceptions (*see*, e.g., Parasuraman *et al.*, 1985; Zeithaml *et al.*, 1988; Zeithaml *et al.*, 1990). They cite 10 main criteria that between them cover the whole service experience from the customer's point of view:

1 *Access*: how easy is it for the customer to gain access to the service? Is there an outlet for the service close to the customer? Is there 24-hour access by telephone to a helpline?

2 *Reliability*: are all the elements of the service performed and are they delivered to the expected standard? Does the repair engineer clean up after himself after mending the washing machine and does the machine then work properly? Does the supermarket that promises to open another checkout when the queues get too long actually do so?

3 *Credibility*: is the service provider trustworthy and believable? Is the service provider a member of a reputable trade association? Does it give guarantees with its work? Does it seem to treat the customer fairly?

4 *Security*: is the customer protected from risk or doubt? Is the customer safe while visiting and using a theme park? Does an insurance policy cover all eventualities? Will the bank respect the customer's confidentiality? Can the cellular telephone network provider prevent hackers from hijacking a customer's mobile phone number?

5 *Understanding the customer*: does the service provider make an effort to understand and adapt to the customer's needs and wants? Will a repair engineer give a definite time of arrival? Will a financial adviser take the time to understand the customer's financial situation and needs and then plan a complete package? Do front-line service staff develop good relationships with regular customers?

Those first five criteria influence the quality of the *outcome* of the service experience. The next five influence the quality of the *inputs* to the process to provide a solid foundation for the outputs.

6 *Responsiveness*: is the service provider quick to respond to the customer and willing to help? Can a repair engineer visit within 24 hours? Will a bank manager explain in detail what the small print in a loan agreement means? Are customer problems dealt with quickly and efficiently?

7 *Courtesy*: are service staff polite, friendly and considerate? Do they smile and greet customers? Are they pleasant? Do they show good manners? Do service staff who have to visit a customer's home treat it with proper respect and minimise the sense of intrusion?

8 *Competence*: are service staff suitably trained and able to deliver the service properly? Does a financial adviser have extensive knowledge of available financial products and their appropriateness for the customer? Does a librarian know how to access and use information databases? Do theme park staff know where the nearest toilets are, what to do in a medical emergency or what to do about a lost child?

9 *Communication*: do service staff listen to customers and take time to explain things to them understandably? Do staff seem sympathetic to customer problems and try to suggest appropriate solutions? Do medical, legal, financial or other professional staff explain things in plain language?

10 *Tangibles*: are the tangible and visible aspects of the service suitably impressive or otherwise appropriate to the situation? Does the appearance of staff inspire confidence in the customer? Are hotel rooms clean, tidy and well appointed? Do lecture theatres have good acoustics and lighting, a full range of audiovisual equipment and good visibility from every seat? Does the repair engineer have all the appropriate equipment available to do the job quickly and properly? Are contracts and invoices easy to read and understand?

It is easy to appreciate just how difficult it is to create and maintain quality in all 10 of these areas, integrating them into a coherent service package. Parasuraman *et al.* (1985) suggest that there are four barriers to service quality, all of which are the fault of the service provider, and all of which will affect the customer's perception of the service experience. These barriers thus mean that there is a mismatch between what customers expected and what they perceived to be actually delivered.

1 *Misconceptions*: management misunderstands what the customer wants and thus delivers an inappropriate or incomplete service product.

2 *Inadequate resources*: if a service provider is trying to cut costs, for example, the customer might suffer. There could be long queues because there are too few staff available, premises might be ill-equipped or shabby, or administrative support systems might start to break down. Students are often all too familiar with the effect of large classes and increasing staff–student ratios in many universities.

3 *Inadequate delivery*: lack of training or poor recruitment might lead to staff with poor knowledge or with no real interest in the customer. This might mean that elements of the service package are not delivered at all or delivered in a very cursory and inadequate way.

4 *Exaggerated promises*: a service provider desperate to gain customers in a highly competitive environment might be tempted to be somewhat economical with the truth. In some cases, when choosing a hotel in a foreign holiday resort from a brochure, for example, customers can only really test the validity of the promises made after they have committed themselves to the purchase. The true picture emerges as the service is being consumed. Thus a hotel brochure might boast that it is within five minutes' walk of the beach and that all rooms have a sea view. Unless customers have been to the resort before, or can get word-of-mouth verification from friends, relatives or travel agents who have stayed there, the fact that they

would have to be Olympic sprinters to get to the beach in five minutes and that they would need to stand on a chair with binoculars to see the sea might emerge too late. In this case, expectations are being raised that simply cannot be fulfilled. The customer's perception of service quality is therefore bound to suffer.

MARKETING IN ACTION ## Smartcards keep queues moving smartish

Reducing queues is a means of improving the service experience that is of concern to many service providers. Airports in particular have a lot of potential for involving passengers in slow-moving queues at check-in desks, security scanners, passport control and departure gates. Checking in for a flight, for instance, can be a very tedious, long-drawn-out affair that dampens the spirits of even the most enthusiastic traveller. Swissair is thus experimenting with a check-in system based on a smartcard that passengers 'show' to a card reader machine as they go through passport control. The scanner checks the passenger's identity and the reservations database and then prints the ticket. The scheme is being piloted with a selected number of members of Swissair's frequent flyer programme travelling with hand baggage only from Zurich airport. Eventually, it is hoped that the scheme will be extended to more airports and be developed further to issue boarding cards as well as tickets. Airports themselves are constantly trying to address the queuing problem. Heathrow, for example, has developed the world's biggest off-airport check-in facility at Paddington station for those travelling to the airport by train.

Railway stations themselves are not strangers to queues, however. London Transport has awarded a £1.2bn contract to a consortium to develop, supply and maintain an integrated ticketing and revenue collecting system for London Transport trains and buses for 17 years. The passenger buying a card for the first time pays an amount of money that is programmed on to the card and then as each journey is made, its price is deducted from the card's value. The passenger can 'top up' the card as necessary. The cards are also very flexible in that they are not bounded by travel zones or time restrictions as are normal season tickets or travel cards. The card reader at the station will take account of the time of day and the distance travelled when calculating the fare to be deducted from the card. Discounts for frequent travellers, promotions or other concessions can also be implemented easily. It is likely that the mainline train operators running services into London will also adopt the same technology to be integrated seamlessly with the Underground system, and it could even be of interest to taxi operators or to the government for road toll schemes.

The good news is that smartcards can help to speed passenger flows and reduce the frustration factor. Operationally, they also mean that there is less cash handling to be done at stations because most passengers will pay for and top up their smartcards using credit cards. The cards also should reduce fraud, in that the card reader can check that the right fare is paid for any specific journey. From a strategic planning perspective, the new system will also collect accurate information about who is travelling, between what destinations and when, as well as helping to monitor the effects of promotions, discounts and differential pricing initiatives. The only potential disadvantage, however, is that smartcards do also reduce contact with staff and some of the personal touch of services marketing.

Sources: Cohen (1999); Glover (1999).

In summary, Fig. 22.4 shows the service experience and the factors that affect consumers' expectations of what they will receive. The criteria that influence their perception of what they actually did receive are also shown, as well as the reasons that there might be a mismatch between expectations and perceptions.

Internal marketing: training and productivity

Because of the interaction between customers and staff in the creation and delivery of a service, it is particularly important to focus on developing staff to deliver high levels of functional and service quality. This does not mean a take-over of personnel and operational management functions by marketing, but marketers must work closely with these line managers to ensure that the right staff are recruited, inducted and trained and that they then perform to the service standards set. The pay and rewards

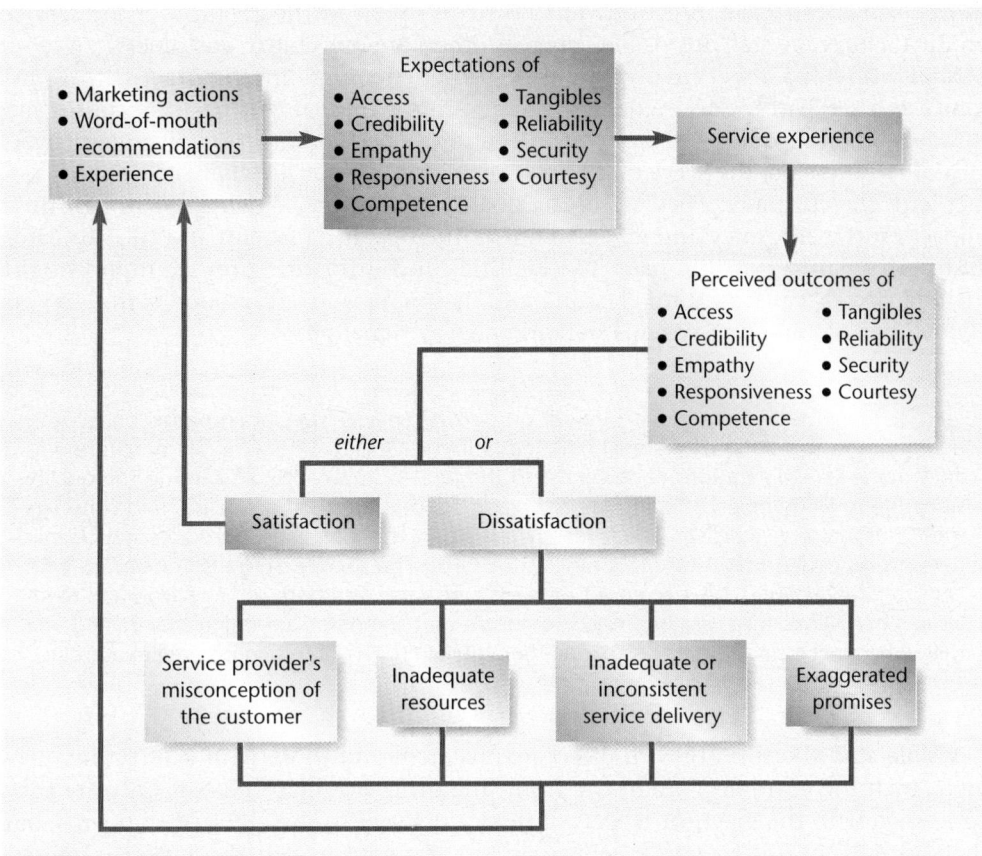

FIGURE 22.4

Service quality: expectations, perceptions and gaps

system employed can also help to boost staff morale and encourage them to take a positive approach to service delivery. Heskett *et al.* (1997) highlighted the connection between employee and customer satisfaction within services. The 'satisfaction mirror' can actually enhance the customer's experience if the service personnel are approaching service delivery in a positive way. They suggested that employees feeling enthusiastic about their job communicate this to customers botil verbally and non-verbally and are also more eager to serve the customer. Similarly, employees who remain in the job longer reach higher capability levels and often a better understanding of customers, which again can enhance customers' feelings of satisfaction. Defining the ideal profile and right remuneration package for staff is not easy.

> **Example** Recent research from MORI suggested that staff attitude was more important than quality or price in influencing consumer choice when buying a service. It would appear that the young (aged between 15 and 34) and the more affluent are especially sensitive. Whether it is poor advice, indifferent attitudes, a failure to keep promises or just poor attention to detail, the message is clear to service providers. Many readers will almost certainly recall situations where poor staff attitude has had a bearing on the quality of the experience. B&Q has been especially sensitive to ensuring that its staff project the right attitude and it operates a policy of hiring mature staff over 50 to offer advice and ensures that all staff are trained to deal effectively with customers (Gofton, 1999).

Staff training

Many service failures actually do stem from staffing problems. To minimise the risk of failure, therefore, it is important to identify all functions that involve customer contact and to train and remunerate staff for these functions accordingly. As Table 22.2

shows, some staff have direct or indirect involvement in the creation of the service product, and some staff are visible, whereas others are invisible to customers.

Staff who have direct involvement are those who come into contact with a customer as a key part of service delivery. In an airline, these might be air hostesses and stewards, check-in staff, and those at the enquiries desk. Indirect involvement covers all staff who enable the service to be delivered, but do not normally come into contact with the customer. They affect the quality of the service delivery through their impact on the efficiency and effectiveness of the operating system and the standards and performance possible from the facilities and infrastructure. Examples might include aircraft catering staff, cleaning and maintenance staff, ground staff at sports venues, banks' computer systems staff and railway signalmen.

Example Jarvis Hotels (mentioned earlier on p. 956), places special emphasis on its staff training in its promotional material. Entitled 'Summit Quality Signature', its brochure outlines the various dimensions of training and the phased approach to awarding the quality signature to all members of staff. The first stage concentrates on core values and considers such issues as service delivery, clear merchandising, first impressions, introductions, cleanliness, freshness and how to encourage extra sales. The second stage is concerned with consistency. Quality standards are set for each core value and both self-checking and regular external 'flight tests' are organised to ensure that standards are being maintained and that, where necessary, corrective action is being taken (Jarvis Hotels corporate literature).

Visible staff (both those with direct involvement and those with indirect involvement with the customer) are in the front line of service delivery. Not only are they concerned with the practical aspects of service delivery to the required standards, but their appearance, interpersonal behaviour and mannerisms will also make an impression on the customer. Airlines, for example, will pay particular attention to a cabin attendant's personal grooming and dress standardisation to ensure a consistent visual impact. Dress is often used to help the customer identify visible staff, both those directly involved in the service, such as aircraft cabin crew, and those who are indirectly involved, such as stewards at soccer matches or security staff.

Indirect visible staff also include people such as the cleaners at McDonald's, chamber maids in hotels, or staff supporting the cashiers in banks. Invisible staff might or might not have direct contact with customers. Staff who take telephone bookings or those who deal with customer queries on the telephone are heard, but not seen. In some cases, these staff might be the only major point of contact for the customer, and thus although their visibility is limited, their ability to interact well with customers is still extremely important.

TABLE 22.2
Staff in the service function

	Visible to the customer	Invisible to the customer
Direct involvement	■ Airline cabin crew ■ Cashiers ■ Sales assistants ■ Medical staff ■ Receptionists	■ Telephone based services – order takers – customer helplines – telephone banking
Indirect involvement	■ Hotel chamber maids ■ Supermarket shelf fillers	■ Office cleaners ■ Airline caterers ■ Administrative staff

The organisation's strategy for **internal marketing** will vary, depending on the different categories of staff employed. Staff who are in the front line of service delivery, with a high level of customer contact, will have to be trained to deliver the standards expected. Staff who do not have direct contact still have to be motivated to perform their tasks effectively and efficiently. They have to understand that what they do affects the quality of the service delivered and the ability of the front-line staff to perform to expected standards. All of this strongly implies, however, that the different groups of staff have to work closely and efficiently together, and deliver a quality service to each other, which in turn will affect the quality of service delivered to the end customer (Mathews and Clark, 1996).

Lee (1997) argues that although internal marketing will not reverse a company's fortunes, it could strengthen the overall marketing effort if staff are committed to the company, brand(s) and mission. This is especially true in service situations where the employee often comes into direct contact with customers and may be part of the service delivery process. This means listening to staff and their ideas as well as involving them in shaping strategy and plans. An Institute of Employment Studies survey of staff and customer attitudes in a major retailer found a direct and strong link between employee commitment and customer satisfaction. The importance of creating a positive organisational culture and good-quality line management all contribute to enhancing the service experience (Bevan and Barber, 1999).

Staff productivity

Staff productivity within services is also a difficult issue for managers. According to Cowell (1984), there are several reasons for **service productivity** being difficult to measure. The main reason is that services are 'performed' not 'produced' and there are too many external factors influencing this live creation of a product. The service production process simply cannot be controlled and replicated as reliably and consistently as a mechanised factory line. Service productivity particularly suffers from the involvement of the customer. If customers do not fill forms in properly, if they are not familiar with procedures or they do not really know what they want, if they turn up late for appointments, if they want to spend time in idle chatter rather than getting on with the business in hand, then it will take service staff much longer to deliver the product. Where productivity is measured in terms of the number of transactions handled, the amount of revenue generated, or the number of customers processed, such delays essentially caused by the customer can reflect unfairly on service staff. This raises the whole question, however, of what constitutes appropriate and fair measures of service productivity. A customer who is given a great deal of individual help or who feels that service staff have taken time for a friendly chat with them might well feel that they have received a much better-quality service and appreciate not being treated with cold, bureaucratic efficiency. It might be worth tolerating a slightly longer queue if you feel that you will be treated with care, respect and humanity when you get to the front of it. Definitions and measures of productivity therefore need to be flexible and sympathetic, striking a fine balance between the customer's needs and the business's need to work efficiently.

None of this absolves managers from looking at ways in which service productivity can be improved. There are several possibilities for delivering services more efficiently without necessarily detracting too much from their quality.

Staff. Through improved recruitment and training, staff can be given better skills and knowledge for dealing with customers. A clerk in a travel agency, for example, can develop a better knowledge of which tour operators offer which resorts so that the key brochures can be immediately pulled out in response to a customer query. Library staff can be fully trained in the use and potential of databases and on-line search mechanisms so that customers can have their problems solved immediately without having to wait for a 'specialist' to return from a lunch break. Improving the staff profile might also allow more delegation or empowerment of front-line service staff. A customer does not want to be told 'I can't do that without checking with my supervisor' and then have to wait while this happens. Staff should be given the responsibility and flexibility to deal with the real needs of customers as they arise.

Systems and technology. The design of the service process and the introduction of more advanced technology can both help to improve service productivity.

> **Example** Onboard catering on trains has always posed an operational nightmare for operators, yet in airlines the problem has been largely solved through a combination of systems and technology. Whereas most airline food is standardised, precooked, paid for in advance and delivered to a programmed schedule to passengers in predetermined seats, on some rail services it was not unusual to find a cook frying eggs or cooking vegetables at 80mph in a confined space and waiters taking orders from an albeit limited menu. Meals were not part of the ticket price, so likely demand per journey had to be forecast. On some occasions, the restaurant on wheels would even break down or supplies would not be forthcoming. Train catering became the butt of many jokes, even though the quality of food, when available, probably exceeded airline levels.
>
> Some of the problem rested in the ambience of on-train facilities. For many years the layout was fixed: a 20-seat dining area, a kitchen in the middle and a take-away bar at the other end of the carriage. There was little space for passengers to mingle and socialise and the counters were far too small so that produce could not be displayed, an essential part of any food operation. Queues became excessive and often extended back into the adjacent carriage. Eating was functional and rarely pleasurable.
>
> The new generation of operators are trying to change things. In France on the Atlantique TGV, a whole coach is allocated to catering with a small bar at one end and a large social area for eating and drinking at the other, all separate from the restaurant facilities. On German trains (DBAG), a bistro facility has been incorporated to offer light meals, snacks and drinks, again in a social environment. The focus has been on enhancing the experience for the traveller. On some of the UK trains, the focus appears to be on adding systems and controlling the customer. Virgin West Coast now restricts the full restaurant service to first-class passengers only and meals are included in the ticket price. Other passengers are not allowed to use the facilities, even if there are empty seats. Many trains have been divided into three seat zones in which different standards and styles of catering are provided, ranging from full service to trolley service. Virgin is finding it difficult to please all groups of passengers. Some are complaining that breakfast should not be included in the ticket price. Standard-class passengers resent being refused entry to restaurant car facilities. At times service has been inconsistent, with no trolley at all appearing. The quality of food offered is good; it is the service delivery problem that is the cause of concern. Even if the coach layouts are changed to allow more customer flexibility, it would take two or three years to complete the programme. To some train operators, catering remains a cost and a necessary evil (and perhaps to some customers too!), rather than a means of adding value. The trouble is that customers themselves do not want to be treated the same as on a plane (Perren, 1999a, 1999b).

Technology combined with well-designed systems can be very powerful. Libraries, for example, have used technology to improve their productivity. Laser scanning barcodes in books make it far quicker to issue or receive returned items than with the old manual ticketing systems. This has also allowed them to improve the quality of their service. The librarian can immediately tell you, for instance, which books you have on loan, whether or not another reader has reserved a book you have, and which other reader has borrowed the book you want. Some technology means that the service provider need not provide human interaction at all. In the financial sector, 'hole in the wall' cash machines, for instance, give customers 24-hour, 7-day-a-week access to their bank accounts, usually without long queues, and because of the way these machines are networked they provide hundreds of convenient access points.

Within service premises, post offices, banks and supermarkets all use express tills or checkouts, for instance, to process customers with small or straightforward transactions faster. Supermarkets also use laser scanning of barcodes not only to help in stock control but also to move goods through the checkout more quickly. The problem with this, however, is that the customer still intrudes. Customers pack their shopping bags at their own pace, and then have to fumble in purses or wallets for enough cash or for a credit card to pay for it all.

MARKETING AND IT   ## Service through the ATM

The ATM is ubiquitous. There are nearly 150 000 machines already installed across Europe – one for every 3000 people. On average, more than 3000 withdrawals are made from each machine every month. However, ATMs are more than simply a means of withdrawing cash or making routine transactions. Many banks have added new marketing functions to their ATM networks. More interestingly, many of them are now becoming web-enabled as well, providing the promise of bringing e-commerce directly to your local cash machine. For example, the latest ATMs, located away from banks, enable customers to withdraw cash, buy cinema tickets, which the machine prints itself, and make hotel reservations. The technology company Moneybox announced that it would install 1000 ATMs in convenience stores and petrol stations in the UK, later spreading to nightclubs and betting shops. As well as dispensing cash, they will sell cards for pre-paid mobile phones and run promotional advertising. At present, Moneybox's ATMs will not be linked to the Internet. But later, says Moneybox's managing director Paul Stanley, they will be, enabling customers to purchase goods and bring e-commerce to the cash machine.

Sources: Buxton (1999), *Electronic Payments International* (1996); O'Connor and Galvin (1999).

Reduce service levels. Reducing service levels to increase productivity can be dangerous if it leads to a perception of reduced quality in the customer's mind, especially if customers have become used to high levels of service. Reducing the number of staff available to deliver the service might lead to longer queues or undue pressure on the customer to move through the system more quickly.

Example If a busy doctor's surgery introduces a system that schedules appointments at five-minute intervals, one of two things might happen. A doctor who wants to maintain the schedule might hurry patients through consultations without listening to them properly or allowing them time to relax enough to be able to say what is really worrying them. Patients might then feel that they have not got what they came for and that the doctor does not actually care about them. Alternatively, the doctor may put the patient first, and regardless of the five minute rule take as long as is needed to sort out the individual patient. The patient emerges satisfied, but those still in the waiting room whose appointments are up to half an hour late might not feel quite so happy.

Reducing service levels also opens up opportunities for competitors to create a new differential advantage. As discussed in Chapter 13, discount supermarkets such as Aldi, Netto and Lidl keep their prices low partly through minimising service. Thus there are few checkout operators, no enquiries desk, and nobody to help customers pack their bags. The more mainstream supermarkets have been able to use this as a way of emphasising the quality of their service, and have deliberately invested in higher levels of service to differentiate themselves further. Thus Tesco, for example, promised its customers that if there were more than three people in a checkout queue, another checkout would be opened if possible. Tesco also announced that it was taking on extra staff in most of its branches, simply to help customers. These staff might help to unload your trolley on to the conveyor belt or pack your bags, or if you get to the checkout and realise that you have forgotten the milk, they will go and get it for you.

Customer interaction. Productivity might be improved by changing the way the customer interacts with the service provider and its staff. It might also mean developing or changing the role of the customer in the service delivery itself. The role of technology in assisting self-service through cash machines has already been mentioned. The whole philosophy of the supermarket is based on the idea of increasing the customer's involvement in the shopping process through self-service.

Customers might also have to get used to dealing with a range of different staff members, depending on their needs or the pressures on the service provider. Medical practices now commonly operate on a group basis, for example, and a patient might be asked to see any one of three or four doctors. If the patient only wants a repeat prescription then the receptionist might be able to handle it, or if a routine procedure is necessary, such as a blood test or a cervical smear, then the practice nurse might do it. The role of students in the delivery of educational services has also evolved, partly as a means of improving academic staff productivity. Student-centred learning, for example, means that students are encouraged to take more responsibility for their own education, with academic staff providing the broad structure, on-going guidance and assessment rather than handing out the whole learning experience to a passive audience on a plate. This has led to a greater degree of partnership between staff and students, and in many ways has actually improved the quality of the service delivered.

If any measures are taken that relate to the nature of customer involvement and interaction, the service provider might have a problem convincing customers that these are for their benefit and that they should co-operate. Careful use of marketing communications is needed, through both personal and non-personal media, to inform customers of the benefits, to persuade them of the value of what is being done and to reassure them that their co-operation will not make too many heavy demands on them.

Reduce mismatch between supply and demand. Sometimes demand exceeds supply. Productivity might well then be high, but it could be higher still if the excess demand could be accommodated. Some customers will not want to wait and might decide either to take their business to an alternative service provider or not to purchase at all. At other times, supply will exceed demand and productivity will be low because resources are lying idle. If the service provider can even out some of these fluctuations, then perhaps overall productivity can be improved.

The service provider might be able to control aspects of supply and demand through fairly simple measures. Pricing, for example, might help to divert demand away from busy periods or to create extra demand at quiet times. Off-peak or off-season tariffs, prices or fares or time-specific promotions ('10 per cent off the price of a haircut on Wednesday afternoons between now and Christmas', for example) might help to achieve this. An appointment booking system might also help to ensure a steady trickle of customers at intervals that suit the service provider. The danger is, though, that if the customer cannot get the appointment slot that they want, they might not bother at all. Finding alternative uses for staff and facilities during quiet times can also create more demand and increase productivity. Universities, for instance, have long had the problem of facilities lying idle at weekends and during vacations. They have solved this by turning halls of residence into conference accommodation or cheap and cheerful holiday lets in the vacations, or hiring out their more attractive and historic buildings for weddings and other functions at weekends, with catering provided.

If the service provider cannot or does not wish to divert demand away from busy times, then the ability to supply the service to the maximum number of customers will have to be examined. If the peaks in demand are fairly predictable, then many service providers will bring in part-time staff to increase available supply. There might be limits to their ability to do so, however, which are imposed by constraints of physical space and facilities. A supermarket has only so many checkouts, a bank has only so many tills, a barber's shop has only so many chairs, a restaurant has only so many tables. Nevertheless, part-time staff can still be useful behind the scenes, easing the burden on front-line staff and speeding up the throughput of customers.

In other situations, physical constraints are less important.

Example A business school operating a modular scheme might find that there are substantial numbers of students wanting to take marketing options. This might not put too much pressure on the weekly lecture programme, since as long as a large enough lecture theatre is available, a lecturer can talk to 200 students as easily as to 50. The problems arise with the number of seminar groups to be serviced and part-time staff might be brought in to take some of the burden off full-time staff. Physical facilities are not likely to pose too many problems in this case, especially if staff and students are prepared to tolerate less popular timetable slots such as 4 p.m. on a Friday!

Internal marketing is an extremely important element of service creation and delivery. As Heskett *et al.* (1994) suggest, there is a direct link between employee satisfaction and productivity, customer satisfaction and loyalty, and profit. If service creation and consumption are inseparable, then it is logical to assume that staff attitudes, efficiency and competence are also inseparable from the customer's judgement of quality, and thus satisfaction.

FRANCHISING

As mentioned in Chapter 12, a **franchise** is a kind of vertical marketing system with a contractual relationship between the **franchisor** and the **franchisee**. Generally, it means that the owner of a product, trade mark, process or service licenses another person or organisation to use, buy, sell or operate it in exchange for some form of payment. This might be in the form of a royalty, a licence fee or a commitment to purchase products at supplier-dominated prices. Franchising is therefore both a distribution method through which market coverage can be extended and a business system through which enterprises can launch or grow. Table 22.3 highlights a number of the better-known international franchises.

Example Marco Leer from Rotterdam in the Netherlands specialises in leather upholstery refinishing. After several years of R&D, the owner found an innovative way of mixing and applying paint to leather upholstery. This significantly reduced labour costs and created an opportunity to standardise prices. Soon after the launch in the Netherlands, the owner decided that franchising was the best method of expansion. He first appointed franchisees in other parts of the Netherlands, then in Europe, where there soon were 20 franchises across Belgium, Germany, the UK and Switzerland. The key ingredients of the package for franchisees are detailed business and technical training, field support and advice over finding a suitable business location. Location is important for the collection and delivery of furniture and premises adjacent to highways are preferred. It is the product concept, however, that lies at the heart of a franchise system that has led to business success. The ability

▶

to refurbish leather products to high standards, to train franchisees to achieve that standard, and the creation of a business system that can be replicated are central to growth. Although the sector is not as glamorous and as high profile as fast food or retailing, the franchising method has enabled an otherwise limited site operation to expand on a European scale (http://www.marcoleer.nl).

TABLE 22.3

International franchisors in fast food

Franchise name	Outlets (no.)	Co-owned outlets (%)[b]	US outlets (no.)	Countries covered (no.)	Total sales ($bn)	International sales (%)
Burger King	10 526	7.10	8 020	54	10.3	n/a
KFC	10 423	26.40	5 132	76	8.2	52
McDonald's	25 341	22.60	c. 12 700	116	35.9	60
Pizza Hut	12 285	32.30	8 471	86	7.4[a]	c. 36
Subway	13 937	n/a	11 817	70	3.5	11

Notes:
All figures are approximate based on 1998/99 data available from published sources except:
(a) 1996 data from published sources
(b) excludes joint ventures.

Although franchising is primarily a method of marketing goods and services, it can also offer a small business a route for achieving more rapid growth, as seen in the Marco Leer case. From a slightly different perspective, it can also provide a prospective entrepreneur with a *quasi*-independent entry into a market with a tried-and-tested concept. Such an entrepreneur might be new to franchising or even new to business, but can nevertheless bring a bundle of skills and competencies acquired in a previous career.

There are five different types of franchise relationship, covering distributorships, licences to manufacture, celebrity endorsements, trade marks and the most popular form in recent years, business format franchising. The latter has emerged as the most potent and dynamic growth area in the retail and service sector throughout the developed world and will now be discussed in detail.

Business format franchise

A business format franchise provides opportunities for small, independent entrepreneurs, without a novel idea, to enter business and is an attractive route for existing business with a proven concept to expand.

The **business format franchise** implies access not only to a product concept, but also to a comprehensive package that enables the product or service to be delivered in a standardised way, regardless of location. The package or format might include a wide range of different requirements and supports.

The business format therefore includes such issues as intellectual property rights relating to trade marks, trade names, shop signs, designs, copyrights, know-how or patents. All of these can be used to market more effectively, thus facilitating the resale of goods or the provision of services to end users.

Example McDonald's (http://www.mcdonalds.com) is probably the most famous franchisor in the world. With over 24 500 outlets in 116 countries, the influence of the golden arches continues to spread at a rapid rate. Around 80 per cent of all outlets are franchised. The typical cost to the franchisor is a start-up investment of between $363 000 and $600 000, a franchise fee payable to McDonald's of $45 000, and an on-going royalty on sales of 12.5 per cent. The benefits in return can be very significant: access to one of the biggest global brands, a highly experienced and professional support team, proven procedures in food quality preparation, exceptional brand consistency, support with site development and launch, and on-going national advertising and sales promotion to retain an interest in the brand. In the UK alone, the 870 restaurants are visited by more than 2.5 million customers every day, over 2800 in each store. Worldwide, it is over 38 million per day. The menu may change a little depending on where you are in the world, but the basic propositions and the burger are ever present. Staff training is central to the franchise. Regardless of who they are and what experience they have had, the franchisee must attend a five-day restaurant assignment as a crew member, with no special treatment, and undergo any subsequent training as suggested by McDonald's.

Despite such an impressive operation, there can be no room for complacency. Increased competition from other franchise systems such as Burger King, especially in the US market, and possible cannibalisation of sales as new franchisees are taken on have caused difficulties for some franchisees (Richards, 1998). The market leadership position in the US (c. 40 per cent of the burger market) and UK (c. 78 per cent share) is being challenged and McDonald's is experimenting with new product lines to fight back (Murphy, 1999).

Types of business format franchise. There are four main types of business format franchise:

1 *Executive*: this involves white collar orientated businesses, such as consultancy, estate agencies and personnel recruitment, where the franchisee usually visits the client to perform the service.
2 *Retail*: the franchisee operates from premises either in prime locations or from carefully selected sites. Examples of this type of franchise are fast food, picture framing and wine stores. Many of the issues considered in Chapter 13 apply to this group. Investment can be high, but so too can the returns.
3 *Distribution*: these franchisees often operate from vans delivering to retailers or direct to the public. Products include greeting cards, tools and pet accessories. The sales territory is normally firmly specified.
4 *Job*: these tend to be service franchises where the franchisee performs a service on the customer's premises. They often operate from a home base with a van. Cleaning, repairs and security services are all good examples.

The business format contract. A number of elements are incorporated into the business format franchise, providing the basis for the content of the contractual agreement and the mutual responsibilities created (Mendelsohn, 1992):

1 The contract should specify the nature and terms of the relationship. This should cover its duration, the geographic extent of any exclusive sales territory and the franchisee's and franchisor's mutual expectations and responsibilities.
2 The franchisor must have developed a successful, proven business format system with an identified brand name before offering it to franchisees. This is normally a requirement of the various national bodies that register and regulate bona fide franchises. It protects potential franchisees from the small minority of unethical franchisors who would take money from franchisees and leave them with an unproven concept that will quickly fail.
3 The franchisor should train the franchisee in the system before opening and fully assist in the planning and implementation of the opening.

4 The franchisor should maintain a business relationship with the franchisee through on-going support in marketing and management. Such a relationship is important in the early stages of the franchise when the franchisee is still learning the business.

5 The franchisee is permitted, under the control of the franchisor, to use the brand name and to operate the business system in a defined geographic area. The franchisee is allowed to benefit from the goodwill created.

6 The franchisee should make a capital investment to launch the business.

7 The franchisee should legally own the business. This means that the consequences of business failure will fall primarily on the franchisee rather than on the franchisor.

8 The franchisee must pay the franchisor for the rights acquired and the on-going services provided. This is normally by a combination of licence fee, royalty or mark-up on supplies purchased.

MARKETING IN ACTION **La Compagnie des Petits**

The first shop belonging to La Compagnie des Petits opened in March 1992. Founded by three partners who all had experience in the textile industry, the purpose of the store was to offer children's clothing that was of good quality, well designed and fashionable, but not too expensive. The owners selected the franchise route as a means of expansion. By 1999, the network had grown to include 64 units, mainly in France, with 44 operated on a franchise basis and the rest run by the owners. The results have been sufficiently promising to raise sales to FF129mn, 54 per cent of which was generated from the franchised units.

In its advertisement, the company offers potential franchisees premises, fixtures and fittings, as well as professional advice and support. It also claims to offer attractive gross margins on goods sold. Because it manufactures its goods in countries with low labour costs, and supplies its franchisees at cost price, gross margins of around 52 per cent are possible. The company's research suggests that the average spend in one of its stores is FF350, on goods priced between FF30 and FF350.

As one might expect, the company, as a franchisor, says that it is looking for motivated people who want to take the welfare of an enterprise into their own hands. The franchisor claims too that because of their stake in the business, franchised stores in the chain perform a lot better than the wholly owned branches. The company thus wants to establish a real partnership with its franchisees, developing an extensive network without losing sight of the interests of the individual franchisee.

Franchisees, however, have to be able to raise sufficient finance to set themselves up in business. The franchisor will find and equip the premises to ensure that the right locations are selected. The 'entry fee' to buy into a franchise is FF70 000 and an investment in opening stock means that the franchisee should have around FF500 000 to put into the business with at least 60 per cent of it from personal quity. There is also an annual royalty of 4.1 per cent of sales and an advertising contribution of 1.2 per cent to cover the on-going involvement of the franchisor in the franchisee's business and the costs of developing the brand image and awareness of the franchise system as a whole.

Source: http://www.franchiseguide.de

Business format franchising can help the aspiring entrepreneur to start a new business in a new area. By providing the innovative idea and a potentially successful formula, franchisors are active in encouraging this route into self-employment. Typical advantages for the franchisee are the independence of ownership, control over one's own working environment and the freedom to guide one's own destiny. In the view of Felstead (1991), however, the degree of independence is highly variable depending on the design of the system, varying from high to low discretion franchising, as shown in Table 22.4.

TABLE 22.4

Variations in franchise independence

	High discretion/ 'Soft' franchising	Low discretion/ 'Hard' franchising
Controls on and nature of the productive process	High service content/low product content	Low service content/ high product content
	High level of expertise at the point of consumption	Low level of expertise at the point of consumption
	Exclusive territory served by mobile operation	Single fixed store location
	High levels of local advertising/low levels of national advertising	Low levels of local advertising/high levels of national advertising
Revenue payments	Low royalties	High royalties
Ownership of the means of production	Absence of trade secret/special equipment/special products	Trade secret/special equipment/special products
	Weak 'ties' on physical means of production	Strong 'ties' on physical means of production

Source: Felstead (1991).

The scope and growth of franchising

Although franchising is often regarded as a relatively recent phenomenon, its origins can actually be traced back to the tied house system in British brewing in the eighteenth century. Although such arrangements did not demonstrate the characteristics of a business format system, their roots lay in exclusive purchasing arrangements. The modern genesis of franchising, especially of the business format type, can be traced back to the USA with the Howard Johnson restaurant chain in the 1930s, which was followed by many other well-known franchises. Some of the early franchises centred on product and trade names in such areas as petrol retailing and soft drinks bottling. Most of the major growth in the USA, however, has been through business format franchising. It has been estimated that in the USA there are something like 800 000 franchisees and over 3000 franchisors. Not all these franchisors offer international systems, but even this grew at a fast rate in the 1990s.

Europe has also experienced the franchise revolution. Many of the trends that fuelled growth in the USA have also been seen in Europe. Growing disposable incomes, urbanisation and home-centred families have all played their part in creating more service-orientated operations. Franchising is particularly well suited to services and people-intensive activities, especially where geographic proximity is needed. In Europe, it has been estimated that there are over 170 000 franchised outlets belonging to around 4000 franchise systems, with a total turnover of around £70bn, employing 1.5 million people.

The impact of franchising in Europe has been greatest in France, Netherlands and the UK, although Germany and Spain are also experiencing a growth in new systems. In the UK, around 20 per cent of retail sales are generated in franchised situations, deriving from 29 100 franchised outlets and 568 franchisors. The combined turnover is £7bn and the industry employs 275 000 people. Interestingly, over 92 per cent of franchisees are thought to be operating at a profit, indicating the strength of proven franchised systems compared with new independent business start-ups in which failure rates can be high.

The franchisor's perspective

Benefits

Both small and large companies can expand through franchising. The two main benefits are financial and managerial. From a financial point of view, rapid growth in market coverage and penetration can be achieved using the resources provided by the franchisees. To open a new directly owned outlet would involve an investment both in capital assets (shop fittings, equipment, property etc.) and in working capital for stock and other operating costs. There would also be the risk of failing to achieve sales targets and financial projections. Many of these risks are effectively borne and financed by the franchisees through their start-up capital investment, licence fees and any other royalty payments.

> **Example** The Perfect Pizza (http://www.perfectpizza.co.uk) franchise chain has taken a steady approach to growth and has focused on the UK and Ireland. It has established 200 stores in the UK, with a further 80 planned by 2004, enabling it to claim the number one spot in pizza home delivery in the UK with a 15 per cent share of the market estimated at £360mn. Management at Perfect Pizza is primarily concerned with keeping the system working effectively through franchisee support and group marketing and new product development. Over 90 per cent of stores are franchised and as part of the start-up package, full training is given to ensure that the operation soon moves to the norm of between 300 and 600 orders per week with an average value of £8 to £12. The system employs 2500 people, either directly or through the franchise arrangements.

A franchise offers a recognisable corporate image and a proven business and operating system to the franchisee.

Source: Perfect Pizza.

The franchisee also represents a committed management resource. The franchisee becomes the legal owner of the business and will therefore suffer from failure or benefit from success. By applying entrepreneurial skills within the framework of the franchise agreement, the franchisee will have to manage the local operation, promote sales and control resources. It would be very hard for the franchisor to motivate salaried staff to make the same effort, because they would not be running the same personal risks as a franchisee (Barrow, 1989).

There are other benefits from franchising. Of particular importance is the ability to develop economies of scale in purchasing, marketing and corporate image and branding without having a large organisation. Indeed, a small enterprise seeking to expand quickly can gain these benefits on the basis of the franchisees' capital. The important benefit of a business format franchise system, however, is that it can divorce service design and planning from service delivery and operations. The skill for a successful franchisor might therefore lie in opportunity assessment, system design and franchisee recruitment rather than in the technical area of production.

Example The Subway restaurant chain provides an excellent example of the pace of network development possible through a franchised system. The chain was started in 1965 in the USA by a 17-year-old high school graduate wanting to pay his way through college. The franchise concept is simple: the provision of high-quality hot and cold sandwiches, deli style, with salad and hot and cold drinks, offering value and speed of service. The average store is between 50 and 150 m², with a take away and small eating-in area. Since starting to use franchising in the 1970s, the chain has opened over 12 600 units in 70 countries. The number of outlets doubled between 1994 and 1999. Sales are in excess of $3.5bn and although Subway is still primarily a North American operation, there are 129 outlets in Japan, 210 in Australia and 31 in the UK. European penetration has not been so strong to date, perhaps reflecting the alternative traditions in sandwich making. There are two stores in Germany and none in France, although these areas may be targeted over the next few years (http://www.subway.com).

Disadvantages

There are, nevertheless, also problems associated with franchising a business. Some of them relate to handling difficult, ineffective or remote franchisees, especially as they become highly experienced in trading in the system area. This could lead to some questioning of the franchise relationship, if poor or ineffective support is being provided by the franchisor (Pettitt, 1988). Furthermore, if the franchisor is felt to be abusing its power, franchisees might start to group together to negotiate on more equal terms with the franchisor. Reputable and better-established franchisors often welcome the formation of formal franchisee groups, as a means of generating feedback and working together to develop a more effective franchise system.

The franchisee's perspective

In some respects, for the franchisee, the decision to start a franchised business is similar to the decision to start a fully independent one. The main difference is the need to select the most appropriate business sector from the franchise opportunities available. Some of the benefits of entering a franchise agreement are generic, in that they are related to the growth prospects in that particular product or service sector. Other benefits might only be realised if a 'good' franchisor is selected, one that offers a first-class support package and meets their commitments over time.

Ultimately, the decision is based on the individual's preparedness to accept a lower return for a lower risk. As indicated in the previous section, many new small businesses fail. This often reflects a lack of preparedness, experience or real and reasonably permanent market potential. Through careful site selection, concept packaging and training, the franchisee entrepreneur does not have to go through the same learning experience and trial-and-error process. While the returns may be lower, given the need for royalties and other means of remunerating the franchisor, because the concept is entirely proven, the risk in the launch phase might be much lower. The failure rate for franchised systems is often between one-eighth and one-tenth of failure rates of independent ventures.

Advantages of franchising

The main advantages in adopting a franchise are:

1 Participation in a system with an established image, name and reputation, often on a regional or national scale. As shown in Chapter 14, it can take a considerable time to get a company or brand name established in the consumer's mind. The franchisee can cut out much of this building process and, where a reputation already exists, it can be traded on.

> **Example** Domino's Pizza (http://www.dominos.com) has a well-respected reputation in fast food franchising. With over 6000 stores generating $3.1bn of sales and operations in 64 countries, including 318 in Europe, Domino's needs a flow of new franchisees to continue its expansion programme. It offers a comprehensive initial and on-going training and support programme for its franchisees. Before starting the franchise outlet, the franchisees participate in a franchise development programme focusing on operations, production, planning, food presentation, local marketing and business development. A preference is given to franchisees who have worked in a pizza retail environment, as this is found to speed up the induction process.

2 In well-organised systems, the franchisee receives a number of services as part of the start-up package. With the Prontoprint system these include site selection, planning and launch assistance, training for the franchisee and key staff in all aspects of the business, support in raising finance and, where necessary, the best combination of opening stock or supplies, marketing information and launch publicity. Often franchisors can provide special finance facilities for new franchisees.

3 National or regional advertising in addition to any undertaken by the franchisee can play an important role in building a stronger system (brand) identity. Prontaprint (http://www.prontaprint.com) can claim sales of $57mn through 220 business communication centres in the UK and Ireland. It operates a central support function for marketing, advertising campaigns and PR and at a local level it will assist with launch events, organise sales promotion and local point-of-sale materials. However, it does expect the franchisee and local teams to be very active in direct customer contact, from prospecting to over-the-counter service and repeat business calling. Sales and telesales training is provided and in the franchisee selection process selling skills are considered to be crucial.

4 Where supplies or equipment have to be purchased, the franchisee will at least receive considerable guidance to avoid shortages or surpluses. At best, preferential terms might be passed on.

5 On-going advice and support might be available for management problem solving, whether in marketing, finance or any other aspect of business development. Amtrack Express Parcels goes further by covering all invoicing, cash flow and debt collection services for its franchisees.

6 New product development can also be important if a stream of product or service improvements would help the franchisee to keep the product portfolio fresh. From its origins in the full print design and copy service for smaller business, Prontaprint has had to reinvent the business with the changing impact of technology.

Although it retains the core service of designing and printing letterheads and forms etc., new business areas have also been launched such as the web design service that enables franchisees to design sites, advise on on-line ordering and analyse visitor traffic. This has meant new manuals and training for all Prontaprint staff.

7 Some territorial protection will be offered if franchisees are given defined licence areas in which to trade. Of course, that is no protection from competitors operating within other franchise systems or independent operators. A Domino's Pizza franchise does not mean protection from Pizza Hut, Pizza Express or indeed non-pizza fast food outlets.

Problems in franchising

Despite the advantages of franchising that might contribute to an increased likelihood of success, there are potential problems that also need to be considered by the prospective entrepreneur before signing the franchise agreement. Perhaps the greatest problem arises from the contract itself.

1 The contract has to ensure systems compliance. This means rigorous control over the product range offered, its quality and specification, its delivery and the way in which it is marketed. Much of the freedom to experiment and adjust to the local environment might well be denied to a franchisee. In more mature franchise chains, such as Prontaprint, some local flexibility might be allowed, but in most franchise chains close control is exercised.

2 The option always exists for the independent operator to expand, sell out or cease trading according to personal objectives. Most franchisors, however, require that any franchise transfer can only be made with their approval, and that they must approve any new franchisee. Similarly, restrictions on market development might limit growth. Although EU competition law prohibits franchisors from delineating where franchisees can draw customers from, it does not affect their ability to restrict the number of new licences or to define broad sales territories.

3 A fundamental tension can creep into the franchise relationship. The franchisor might seek to increase volume in the system to achieve greater market presence and to raise royalties based on turnover. The franchisee might be more interested in return on investment than in chasing extra turnover for lower margins.

4 Any loss of reputation or poor decision making by the franchisor might have negative effects on the franchisee. Some franchisors have been criticised for failing to fully develop their national promotional campaign in support of franchisees. Some franchise systems have failed.

Example Franchise systems can fail, even though the majority succeed. Notable failures include Athena poster shops, the Pierre Victoire restaurant chain, and The Tanning Shop, which went into receivership owing £6mn (Gwyther, 1998). The failure of the franchisor leaves many angry franchisees who have often invested personal savings and perhaps have built an effective local business.

When The Tanning Shop chain folded, franchisees lost between £7000 and £50 000 each. They claimed that the locations selected were poor and that the financial forecasts used to encourage them to sign up were over-inflated, as were the prices of the supplies they were required to purchase from the franchisor. The network for the vertical tanning booth outlets grew quickly from one store in London in 1992 to 150 stores by 1996. However, the sales and thus the cash flow forecasts were not realistic. Regardless of location, the sales and business plans were based on inner London performance, levels that could not be sustained in market towns and small cities. Many of the prospective franchisees were not business wise and did not challenge the figures before joining. It really was a case of franchisee beware (Murray, 1998).

On balance, the advantages and disadvantages of the franchised route are a trade-off between the benefits of being associated with a franchised chain and the costs associated with the loss of complete independence and the on-going franchisor involvement. Given the worldwide growth of franchising and the fact that many franchisees do renew their agreements when the original contract period expires, it would appear that many entrepreneurs are prepared to sacrifice their independence for lower start-up risk and that they do feel that operating a franchise is worthwhile.

Franchise blueprints and contracts

The keys to success in any franchise system are the development and testing of an unusual or attractive market concept, patented equipment and/or a readily identifiable trade mark and image. In the view of Mendelsohn (1992), any business that is capable of being run under remote management is also capable of being franchised. Table 22.5 indicates the wide range of areas that are currently being franchised across Europe. From a marketing perspective, there is really no difference between developing a successful independent business and developing a successful franchise system. The product or service must be valued, differentiated from its competitors by real or imaginary criteria and sustainable over time. There are, however, some other considerations that are relevant when an entrepreneur is deciding on the appropriateness of the franchising route. The system must be capable of replication according to the franchisor's design. This could include product, service and marketing effectiveness. It must also be capable of generating margins that can sustain the continued interest of both franchisor and franchisee.

TABLE 22.5
Business areas franchised in Europe

Business area	Specific products/services franchised
Food and drink	sandwiches; pizzas; burgers; petfood; Chinese take-aways; Mexican restaurants; off-licences; sweet shops
Clothing and consumer goods	leisure wear; children's wear; bridal/formal wear; accessories; sports goods and clothing; greeting cards; toiletries
Domestic services	home cleaning; double glazing repair/maintenance; upholstery/carpet cleaning; interior decoration; drain clearance
Car services	windscreen replacement; scratch/dent repairs; car cleaning/valeting; servicing
Personal services	dating agencies; hairdressing; sunbeds; nursing care; party planning
Legal/business services	courier services; stock auditing; utility auditing; office training; computer training; workwear; office cleaning; printing; will writing; property sales.

The decision to build a franchise chain can stem from an existing business seeking to expand or from a new business start-up, where the investment may be large, as is typically found in the fast food business, or quite small, as in such areas as domestic services.

> **Example** The cost of entering a franchise can vary significantly. It can be over $1mn for a KFC franchise, £35 000 for Prontaprint plus a £12 500 franchise fee, and at Flower Forever the fee is just £4250, although a further £9000 is needed for start-up. Subway has a $10 000 initial fee but a further $100 000–$200 000 is required to get started with stock, premises, equipment charges etc. Although Subway can arrange for preferential finance terms, at least 50 per cent of the investment must be in cash. This investment must be recouped from profits after all royalties have been paid, although in the case of Subway a 20-year renewable contract is offered. Most franchisors claim that the invest can be recouped within three years.

In the case of a new start rather than an outgrowth such as the Marco Leer example (*see* p. 969 above), it is normally expected that the franchise package will have been piloted before being offered to potential franchisees. This enables the concept to be fully tried and tested in field conditions.

Launching a new franchising system

There are seven stages in launching a new franchised system, as shown in Fig. 22.5.

Developing the franchised business system concept. As indicated above, a franchised business system should offer many of the characteristics of any successful business plus the ability to replicate without the direct intervention of the concept owner. The more complex and technically orientated the business, the greater the difficulty of franchising, because of problems in replicating. The impact of franchising in industrial markets is, therefore, marginal, being reserved mainly for industrial services rather than manufacturing. In contrast, a fast food system can be standardised through the use of similar equipment, kitchen design, premises, raw materials, cooking instructions, food presentation, menu, seating configuration etc.

As with any business launch, it is very important to have a clear idea of the target market and to assess the potential business likely to be generated across a geographic area. In some cases, the availability of suitable premises might be an important consideration. Often a franchisor agrees a town or city and even a site before advertising for franchisees. This might be especially crucial where impulse or passing trade is required.

Undertaking a pilot operation. Before the franchise is offered to a wider audience, it should be piloted in at least one location for at least one year. This enables a full market test to take place and the package to be fully developed and refined. If the franchisor is new to the trading concept, the experience gained will be invaluable later when advising others on managerial and operational problems. Many national franchise associations insist on a pilot period as a precondition of membership. Without such a

FIGURE 22.5
Stages in launching a new franchised business system

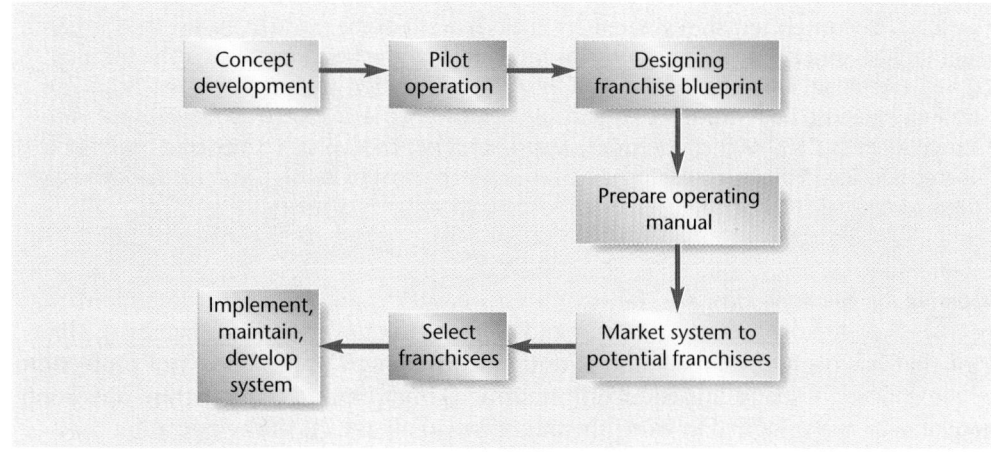

pilot the franchisees, if they are prepared to take a chance, are effectively working on a trial-and-error basis and might not receive the same benefits as they would if they were entering a proven system.

Designing the franchise blueprint. The proven franchise package should be the output of the pilot period. The package represents the **franchise blueprint** for a successful operation, the key factors that are likely to maximise the chances of success. Obviously, these factors will vary from one system to another, depending on innovativeness, positioning and competitiveness.

As mentioned above, an important part of the blueprint will be the site selection, both specifically and in a general trading area. The way in which the area and site decisions are made will be similar to that of any other retail location decision, as discussed at pp. 532 *et seq.* Issues of market potential, customers' preparedness to travel and competition might all play a part in the decision to locate in a particular area. Proximity to other attractions might be important, for example siting a multiplex cinema in an edge of town retail park close to a Burger King and a Pizza Hut. The selection of specific sites might also consider such factors as traffic flow analysis, space requirements, access, parking and, of course, rental or freehold costs. Perfect Pizza, for example, advertises for franchisees both for new territories yet to be developed and to take over existing stores.

Other areas for consideration in the blueprint will be the equipment, layout, service specification, interior design, product range etc. These issues should all be detailed in the development of the operating manual. Similarly, work systems, material requirements, staffing, marketing literature and management systems such as stock control and accounting will have to be tested and included in a refined state in the package. A final part will be the development of a finance package that can help potential franchisees to raise capital. This must allow franchisees to generate a start-up proposal that will survive the close scrutiny of financiers and analysts. A franchisee might have a better chance of obtaining start-up capital from banks and leasing companies with the franchisor's support than if it was a completely independent business.

Some operators decide to adopt a mixed system in which some outlets are franchised and others are company owned. This enables the franchisor to maintain control and contact with the market, and allows for continuing updating of the concept and blueprint.

Example It was a long way for John Dys to go to escape from serving in the Dutch army, but a move to Canada with the concept of the popular *pannekoek* house eventually gave rise to the De Dutch (http://www.dutchpannkoekhouse.com) franchise chain. The attraction is that the restaurants, in addition to being themed around Holland with menu items such as De Snack and Eggs Hollandict, also only serve breakfast and lunch, and allow both a lifestyle change for franchisees and a specialisation not possible in full-range restaurants. The choice of menu has been extensively tested to position the chain apart from the many other fast food restaurant facilities and considerable effort goes into selecting the best ingredients. The blueprint covers the menu, ideal site location and the food preparation and operating methods. The equipment and fittings are specified and are included in the c. C$250 000 investment. The franchise fee is C$37 000 and a royalty charge of 5 per cent, plus a 3 per cent advertising charge is levied. Although the franchise chain is still regional to British Columbia and Alberta, perhaps one day the first outlet will be exported back to the Netherlands.

Preparing the operating manual. The operating manual is an important document that specifies exactly how the franchisee should conduct the business. It formalises the blueprint that has been developed, and is usually copyrighted to provide extra protection for the concept. Usually, any induction training is built around the **franchise operating manual**, which is designed to guide the franchisee in all aspects of the operation.

The manual will vary according to the type of franchise. Operating instructions can be quite specific, down to such details as opening hours, staff schedules, pricing policies, staff duties, service standards, accounting procedures and point-of-sale promotion. Any standard forms that have to be regularly submitted to the franchisor are provided, along with associated instructions. In situations where the service is more technical and requires careful delivery, a technical supplement might explain in some detail the equipment used and how it must be maintained to ensure high standards.

Manuals not only serve as a practical guide to operations and as a constant source of reference, they can also be used to ascertain the maturity of the franchisor for a would-be franchisee. However, the more detailed the manual, the more control the franchisor has over the franchisee in terms of inspecting premises and assessing local systems, creating additional pressure to comply with quality standards (Chaplin, 1999).

All franchisees receive the manual and are expected to inform their staff of the relevant parts. In a restaurant franchise, for instance, the level of detail can even include how the food should be arranged on the plate!

Marketing to franchisees. Once the system has been designed and the necessary support made available, the franchisor needs to find and select suitable franchisees. There is little point in recruiting 'unsuitable' candidates, as they are more likely to fail or to demand excessive franchisor time. Poor franchisees might also reflect badly on the reputation of the franchisor. Often the expansion of the network proceeds slowly in the first year or two in order to fine tune the system and franchisee recruitment.

> **Example** Elite Introductions (http://www.eliteintroductions.com) has the clear mission of bringing people together. It achieves that by matching potential partners on its register in a tasteful and confidential manner. From a one-office beginning in 1994, it has grown to 40 outlets and each franchisee needs £25 000 to start an office in an otherwise highly people-orientated business. Often working from home, the attraction to potential franchisees is the relatively low cost of entry and no need for extensive working capital, as stock and rent are not required in what is an essentially cash-based business. It advertises for new franchisees using franchise magazines and through its own website.

Franchisors use a variety of methods to reach prospective franchisees. Magazines such as the *Franchise Magazine* are an obvious source, as are franchise exhibitions such as the European Franchise Exhibition, and advertising in general media. Once potential franchisees have made an initial approach, there should be a preliminary screening before a detailed analysis of the suitability of a potential candidate.

Selecting franchisees. The level of detail and formality in the selection phase will often depend on the care taken by the franchisor, the range of alternatives, and the scale of the investment required. In reality, this phase is actually about mutual selection, since the franchisee must also be convinced that the relationship is worth the investment and commitment.

A number of issues might be explored by the franchisor, including the candidate's motivation, commitment, transferable skills, financial resources, career history and ability to adopt a multi-functional entrepreneurial role. Many franchisors develop a franchisee profile to guide their selection. Over time, this can reflect the franchisor's actual experiences of franchisees rather than an idealised profile. Certain skills might emerge ahead of others. Sometimes, these skills are marketing and sales related, reflecting an ability to adopt a planned, proactive approach to market development.

> **Example** Domino's Pizza's main priority in franchise selection is finding good people who are committed to building the franchise outlet. Staff training and the operating manual provide guidelines for inexperienced franchisees, but one of the most important factors in selecting applicants is their knowledge of their local environment and a willingness to become involved in the community through clubs, schools and churches etc. There is also a preference for franchisees who are prepared to take their turn in all aspects of the operation, including delivery, to keep them in touch with customers and being better able to understand service levels.

The franchisor does have a responsibility to avoid selecting unsuitable applicants, despite the temptation of more licence fees. Often, a potential franchisee is investing a significant sum of money, perhaps from savings or redundancy. The loss of this through business failure could be devastating. Ultimately, any franchise system will only sustain itself if all its parts are strong. Rumours of high failure rates among franchisees will soon spread and deter potential candidates.

From the franchisee's perspective, the decision to take out a franchise should be treated just like any other investment decision. The franchisee should thoroughly investigate the character and track record of the franchisor, as well as thinking through the feasibility of the franchise itself under different market conditions. The franchisee should be particularly concerned about the level of initial and on-going support offered by the franchisor in site selection, opening, training and marketing. Often the best source of information is existing franchisees. Any franchisor who is reluctant to provide such contacts might be regarded as dubious. If the system appears to be working well, the real question is whether it will transfer to the area being considered and whether the applicant has the necessary skills and interest to make it work.

The franchise contract specifies, usually very precisely, the obligations of both parties and the basis on which the agreement may be terminated. It is a legal document, is rarely negotiable and always needs careful scrutiny before signing. Once the agreement is signed it is legally binding for the contract period. The agreement normally specifies (based on Barrow and Golzen, 1990):

- the nature and name of the activity being franchised
- the franchise territory
- the terms of the franchise
- the franchise fee and royalty
- franchisor responsibilities
- franchisee obligations
- the conditions under which the franchisee may sell or assign the business
- the conditions under which the franchisee may terminate the franchise
- the terms and obligations of the franchisor in similar circumstances.

It is often considered that once the contract has to be quoted, normal working relationships have either become very strained or broken down. Most franchise systems have less confrontational ways of resolving difficulties as they emerge. These include regular meetings and associations of franchisees to represent the collective interest.

Maintaining and developing the franchised system. After the contract has been signed, an initial franchise fee will be payable. This normally reflects a payment for the initial service in establishing a new unit, including site selection and acquisition, training and an element of goodwill in entering an established network. To the franchisor much of this payment represents a direct contribution. Other capital for specified equipment, leases etc. will have to be paid directly or to specified suppliers. In some cases, a turnkey package might be offered in which the whole operation, including equipment, is prepared by the franchisor, leaving the new franchisee to concentrate on staffing, learning new systems and launch marketing. To the franchisor, especially in the early stages, this return for the systems investment can be an important source of income.

Example Worldsites (http://www.worldsites.net) offers a comprehensive training programme to cover induction and advanced training. Specialising in consultancy for and the development of websites, it aims to bring Internet technology close to the smaller business customer. It has 35 franchises in 20 countries, with the UK divided into five master franchise areas to allow for the development of franchises within areas. The induction training concentrates on team leadership, prospecting and maintaining customer relations. Initially, the local franchisees can ask Worldsites to undertake website development, but after a five-day technical course, the franchisees are better equipped to handle website design software and site upgrades along with making full use of e-commerce systems. Support is provided to franchisees for the launch and for any technical problems, as well as with business development. In return, a royalty has to be paid.

Continuing fees are also normally paid in order to cover the provision of on-going services, especially in advertising, product development and management advice. This is based on a direct fee for management services, a royalty on sales, or a mark-up on goods that have to be purchased from the franchisor.

Example KFC (Kentucky Fried Chicken) operates a royalty scheme of 4 per cent on sales with no additional royalty payment for advertising. That royalty contributes to KFC's overall 'interest' in maintaining the franchisee and the system, as well as allowing for system-wide branding and promotion. KFC has to compete in a global market for consumers' discretionary spend on fast food, and any one of the 400 franchisees in the UK and Ireland plays only a small part in the process. Corporate marketing, using the Colonel's face as a familiar advertising icon, is designed to give reassurance of the chicken quality, consistency and the expertise needed in its preparation to make it stand out from the rest (McLuhan, 1999).

In some cases, a special levy may also be imposed solely for advertising, on the basis that national advertising and promotion benefits all members of the system. Central co-ordination also enables the franchisor to control the form and content of the advertisements for the whole system.

As with any business, the inflow of fees from the franchisees must not only meet the franchisor's profit requirements, but also be able to support the renewal of the franchise system. This can be achieved by new product lines, fresh advertising campaigns, more effective training or any other means of maintaining competitive edge. As it becomes harder to find really innovative service ideas, competition between similar franchise systems and fully independent operators is increasing.

NON-PROFIT MARKETING

The marketing concerns of **non-profit organisations**, including those in the public sector, became increasingly important over the 1980s and 1990s for a number of reasons. In the UK, the government pursued a deliberate policy of exposing public sector services to commercial market forces and of increasing their autonomy and accountability. The main focus of this section, however, is the charities aspect of non-profit marketing, reflecting the growth of cause related marketing (CRM) and the radical changes in the ways in which charities generate revenue, their attitudes to their 'businesses' and their increasingly professional approaches to marketing.

Example The National Missing Persons Helpline (NMPH) was registered as a charity in the UK in 1993. It was set up because at any one time there are up to 250 000 people 'missing' in the UK, yet there was no central body to offer advice and support to missing persons' families, to co-ordinate information on missing people, or for missing people to contact for help. Although many people do 'go missing' on purpose and do not wish to be found, others disappear because they are distressed, ill or confused and need help and reassurance to solve their problems. A few are the victims of abduction.

The NMPH therefore offers a number of services, including:

- a national 24-hour telephone helpline for families of missing people
- a confidential 'Free Call Message Home' 24-hour telephone helpline so that missing people who do not want to be 'found' can at least leave a message to reassure their families that they are all right
- a national computerised database of missing people
- searching for missing people, using contacts among the homeless population, and advertising and publicity
- An image-enhancing 'age progression' computer that can create a photograph of what someone who has been missing for several years might look like now.

The charity's 'customers' are not just missing people and their families. The police find the NMPH and its database invaluable in assisting with identifying corpses and helping with missing persons cases generally.

In marketing terms, the NMPH's main problem is generating a steady and reliable flow of income. NMPH does not charge commercial rates for its services, even to the police. It hopes, of course, that those who have benefited from the service will make a donation, but this is unlikely to cover the full cost. It thus relies heavily on cash donations, corporate donations of goods and services, fundraising and promotional events. It is particularly dependent on some of the 'donations in kind', for example television airtime or print advertising space, in order to carry on its work effectively.

Sources: NMPH literature; briefing given by Elaine Quigley at Buckinghamshire Chilterns University College.

Like many other organisations, they have found that the environment within which they operate has changed. There are many more charities competing for attention and donations, and the attitudes of both individual and corporate donors has changed. The case of the corporate donor was discussed earlier at pp. 810 *et seq*. Thus all sorts of organisations that have not traditionally seen themselves as 'being in business' have had to become more businesslike, fighting for and justifying resources and funding.

This section, therefore, discusses the characteristics that differentiate non-profit from profit-making organisations. Then, the implications for marketing will be explored.

Classifying non-profit organisations

As suggested above, non-profit organisations can exist in either the public or private sectors, although the distinction between them is rather blurred in some cases. A hospital that treats both National Health patients and private patients, for example, is involved in both sectors. Table 22.6 gives examples of organisations in both sectors.

Characteristics of non-profit organisations

Clearly, all non-profit organisations operate in different types of market and face different challenges, but they do have a number of characteristics in common that differentiate them from ordinary commercial businesses (Lovelock and Weinberg, 1984; Kotler, 1982). These are as follows.

TABLE 22.6
Non-profit organisations

Public sector	Private sector
Public hospital	Private hospital
University	Private school
Public library	Charity
State railway	

Multiple publics. Most profit-making organisations focus their attention on their target market. Although they do depend on shareholders to provide capital, most day-to-day cash flow is generated from sales revenue. Effectively, therefore, the recipient of the product or service and the source of income are one and the same. Non-profit organisations, however, have to divide their attention much more equally between two important groups, as shown in Fig. 22.6. First, there are the customers or clients who receive the product or service. They do not necessarily pay the full cost of it. A charity, for example, might offer advice or help free to those in need, whereas a museum might charge a nominal entry fee that is heavily subsidised from other sources. Thus clients or customers concern the non-profit organisation largely from a *resource allocation* point of view. The second important group is the funders, those who provide the income to allow the organisation to do its work. A charity, for example, might depend mainly on individuals making donations and corporate sponsors, a medical practice on government funding and a museum on government grants, lottery cash, individual donations and corporate sponsorship as well as entrance fees. Thus funders concern the organisation from a *resource attraction* point of view.

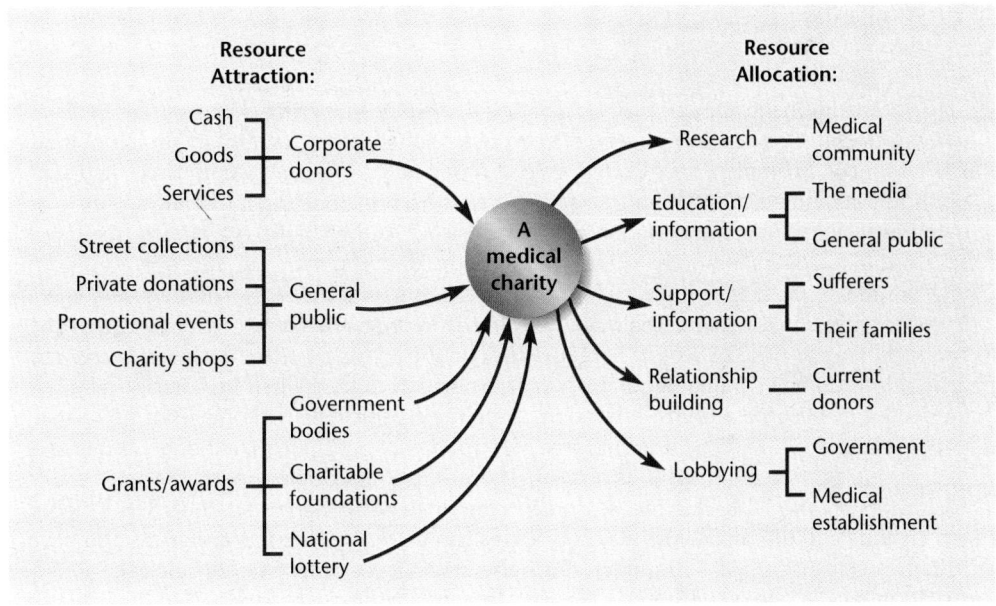

FIGURE 22.6

Non-profit organisations: Multiple publics

Example Great Ormond Street Children's Hospital (http://www.gosh.org.uk) offers the widest range of paediatric care in the UK, with over 22 000 inpatients and 78 000 outpatients, 50 per cent whom are aged under two years. In order to provide care, to maintain its position at the frontier of medical research and to enhance its reputation for pioneering surgery, it needs to supplement the income it gets from the government via the National Health Service. Each year, it aims to raise £10mn from donations and sponsorship to provide the opportunity to purchase new equipment and to extend its range of facilities.

The hospital must therefore interact with a number of publics if it is to achieve its targets. Its core activities mean that it is working with patients, parents, local hospital consultants and doctors. Each has an interest in the paediatric care work of the hospital. The government and the National Health Service also have an interest in the hospital, given its role, profile and of course its prime funding source. However, the donor publics are critical to the future of GOSH and thus the hospital has an active fundraising programme. Schemes include sponsorship, advertisements on the website, private donations, payroll covenants and legacies, company giving and joint sales promotions such as one undertaken with Baby Bio, which raised £20 000. Employee fundraising through adopting GOSH for a month, a year or for a special event provides a further source of funds as well as raising the profile. Even credit card holders can contribute, with a charity Mastercard scheme offered through the Bank of Scotland whereby a small donation is automatically transferred to GOSH for each transaction made on the card. Furthermore, individuals can run the London marathon to sponsor GOSH. All this means that GOSH has to plan its activities carefully to maintain good relations with individuals and organisations to attract resources and in return to ensure that the gratitude and goodwill from the well-being of its patients is fed back to the supporters.

Multiple objectives. One definition of marketing offered earlier in this book is to create and hold a customer at a profit. As we have seen, there are many different ways of achieving this and many possible subobjectives on the way, but in the end for most organisations it is all about profit. As a result, success criteria can be fairly easily defined and measured. In the non-profit sector, however, there might be multiple objectives, some of which could be difficult to define and quantify. They might concern fundraising, publicity generation, contacting customers or clients (or getting them to visit you), dispensing advice, increasing geographic coverage or giving grants to needy clients.

Example The Swanage Railway is a heritage line owned by its members in southern England and concentrates on running preserved locomotives, often steam, on a short stretch of track from Swanage to Norden, near Corfe Castle. It is primarily a line run by enthusiasts and supported by volunteers all intent on recreating scenes from bygone days. Members donate as much as they can afford and life membership costs £250, which allows as much free travel as is wanted. General fundraising and special appeals to members are also operated from time to time, such as the appeal to find the £122 000 to help towards extending the line a few extra miles to Wareham. The main objective is to finish the complete reopening of the line and to run as wide a range of heritage stock on the line as possible. However, in order to achieve this objective a number of other objectives have to be realised first. Realistically, the line needs to become a tourist attraction, bringing in customers who may not be railway enthusiasts as such. This could mean some compromise of purist ideals, although in this case this has not yet extended as far as running Thomas the Tank Engine specials. The line runs 19 services per day in the summer season and the more passengers are on board, the higher the revenue and the sooner the main objectives can be realised. Grants and loans also have to be won, such as £500 000 funding from the Rural Development Commission for a 130-space car park at one of the stations. Similarly, the local authority has supported the line as it regards it as a valuable tourist feature. Therefore fundraising, membership and revenue earning operations have to be undertaken successfully, even though they may conflict at times, if the core enthusiasts want to catch a whiff of steam and nostalgia (Jones, 1999).

Service rather than physical goods orientation. Most non-profit organisations are delivering a service product of some sort rather than manufacturing and selling a physical product. Many of the services marketing concepts already covered in this chapter therefore apply to them. In some non-profit bodies, the emphasis is on generating awareness about a cause, perhaps to generate funds, and giving information to allow people to help themselves solve a problem. Particularly where charities are concerned in generating funds, donors as a target audience are not directly benefiting from their participation in the production of this service, other than from the warm glow of satisfying their social conscience. This contrasts with the more commercial sector, where the customer who pays gets a specific service performed for their benefit (a haircut, a washing machine repaired, a bank account managed for them etc.).

Example Oxfam International (http://www.oxfam.org) is not only delivering a service product, but one that is often directed at beneficiaries many thousands of kilometres away. Its many programmes vary from very high profile activities such as dealing with the humanitarian disaster in Kosovo or helping in the aftermath of hurricanes, or participation in longer-term projects lasting many years. The Great Lakes project in East Africa, for example, is planned to last for 30 years and is concerned with human rights, humanitarianism and reconstruction in water, sanitation and farming.

Oxfam needs high profile media coverage to make the suffering of people and the effective impact even of small donations more tangible. With natural disasters, much of the media coverage is done for Oxfam and the focus is on directing goodwill and sympathy to make donating easy. In other cases, more subtle lobbying and influence are required to achieve the mission of 'saving lives and restoring hope'. Reports highlighting, for example, that in the world there are 870 million illiterate people, that 70 per cent of them are women, that 125 million children do not start school and that another 150 million drop out after four years are designed to stimulate debate. Reports and briefing papers are published and sent to politicians alongside lobbying for change. One campaign has focused on debt relief for developing countries and this has been actively pursued with G8 members, while another campaign has called for fairer trade by allowing tariff-free imports from developing countries to the EU. The greater the publicity, the more tangible the problems and the more powerful the call for help.

Public scrutiny and accountability. Where public money is concerned or where organisations rely on donations, there is greater public interest in the activities and efficiency of the organisation. To maintain the flow of donations, a charity has to be seen to be transparently honest, trustworthy and to be producing 'results'. The public wants to know how much money is going into administrative costs and how much into furthering the real work of the charity.

Example Greenpeace (http://www.greenpeace.org) relies exclusively on support from individuals and foundations. It makes a deliberate point in its publicity of stating that it does not seek funds from governments, corporations or political parties and will not take individual donations if they compromise its independence of action. It is proud to state that it has no permanent allies or enemies. Such a principled stand means that Greenpeace must be entirely transparent if it is to avoid criticism from parties who have suffered from its direct action, or even the wider publics that support its cause.

To achieve a policy of openness, Greenpeace must make public its campaigns, its governance arrangements and its financial affairs. The annual reports reveal detailed information in all areas. The campaigns in climate, toxins, nuclear, oceans, forests, ocean dumping and genetic engineering are all specified and details provided of the main achievements in each area. For example, the 1998–99 report highlights Greenpeace's role in the EU ban on drift net fishing, the decision by a number of DIY stores to ban timber from native forests in British Columbia, and the delisting of genetically modified foods by an Austrian supermarket. The financial breakdown of income and expenditure reveals a net income of $101mn and the surplus being used to modernise the fleet and infrastructure. Of expenditure, c. 34 per cent went on direct campaigns, 24 per cent on campaign support and 14 per cent on administration. This indicates that over half of any donation is ploughed back into the campaigning for which it was intended. Finally, details of the 40 offices and the various boards of trustees are presented along with the respective roles of Greenpeace International in the Netherlands, the overall strategy group, and each local board is specified. With many powerful detractors and 2.4 million supporters on a global scale, Greenpeace must show the results and the methods used to reach them.

Marketing implications

In general terms, the same principles of marketing apply equally to non-profit organisation as to any purely commercial concern. There are, however, a few specific points to note. A non-profit organisation might have quite a wide-ranging **product portfolio**, if the needs of both funders and customers or clients are taken into account. Their products might, for instance, vary from information, reassurance and advice to medical research and other practical help such as cash grants or equipment. Donors might be 'purchasing' association with a high profile good cause or the knowledge that they have done a good deed by giving. Because the products vary so much, from the extremely intangible to the extremely tangible, and because there are so many different publics to serve, a strong corporate image and good marketing communication are particularly important to pull the whole organisation together.

> **Example**   The National Meningitis Trust (http://www.meningitis-trust.org.uk) has a specialised, highly focused portfolio concerned with meningitis. It aims to create awareness of the disease, to fund research and provide support to patients via grants and on-line support. A particular success was in its participation in the campaign to get students better informed of the dangers of meningitis within university halls of residence.
>
> Compare this with the National Trust (http://www.nationaltrust.org.uk), which has a large portfolio of activity and interests. It owns 240 000 hectares of countryside, 575 miles of coastline and 200 buildings and gardens, including 19 castles and 49 churches and chapels. It operates nearly 2800 listed buildings of which 263 are open at a charge. The National Trust must manage its portfolio to generate sufficient revenue to support the acquisition, maintenance and development of its property and land. The portfolio includes entrance fees, memberships, individual and corporate donations, fundraising, including special appeals, renting out 200 holiday cottages, and the sale of branded merchandise such as gifts, china, glass and over 60 book titles. It must manage its resources from 35 000 volunteers, 2.5mn members and 12mn visitors annually. Although the objectives are not commercial, a businesslike approach is needed to portfolio management to ensure adequate returns on activities and that any cross-subsidisation is appropriate.

If dispensing information and advice or increasing the profile of a cause are central objectives of the non-profit organisation, then **marketing communication** is an essential tool. This might mean using conventional advertising media, although that can be expensive for organisations such as smaller charities unless advertising agencies and media owners can be persuaded to offer their services cheap or free as a donation in kind.

Publicity can also be an invaluable tool for the non-profit organisation, not only because of its cost effectiveness, but also because of its ability to reach a wide range of

> **Example**   The Royal Academy has used marketing communication effectively to manage the flow of viewers to its galleries. With the 'Monet in the Twentieth Century' exhibition run in 1999, a marketing support budget of £500 000 was allocated. The exhibition itself was planned to net revenues of between £15mn and £20mn through tickets, sponsorship and merchandising. Normally, most of the marketing costs are covered by sponsorship and in return corporate entertaining opportunities are opened up, for example Ernst & Young used the gallery for five or six events per week in return for sponsorship during the 12-week opening (Marsh, 1999). Press and magazine advertising and direct marketing were all designed to raise awareness, Merchandise such as Monet seeds and Monet ceramics were designed to increase the visitor spend. At a time of declining grants from the government, arts organisations need both 'blockbuster' art exhibitions and regular patronage and fundraising to supplement their income to enable them to invest in new projects. Galleries and museums are increasingly becoming brands in their own right.

audiences. Publicity might encourage fundraising, help to educate people or generate clients or customers. Association with high-profile commercial sponsors can similarly help to spread the message, through publicity, sponsored fundraising events or joint or sponsored promotions.

Example As seen in the Monet example above, the arts attract a great deal of interest from corporate sponsors. The opening of the Tate Gallery of Modern Art (http://www.tate.org.uk) in London is planned for spring 2000. Although a £50mn grant was given by the Millennium Commission, further funds were also needed. It sought corporate sponsors in an effort to raise the additional £14mn needed to open the Bankside site. The sales approach adopted with companies was not the 'begging bowl', but highlighted the commercial, cultural and environmental benefits that sponsors will enjoy when the Tate on Bankside is opened. A world-class museum attracts additional tourists, creates jobs and becomes a venue for corporate hospitality. Twenty-four Founding Corporate partners were sought, each contributing £250 000 for five years. Pearson (the group which includes the publisher of this book), Railtrack and CGU were early members. The partners will be able to use the gallery for evening or breakfast entertaining and employees will have privileged access (Thorncroft, 1999).

In sectors where a non-profit organisation offers a more clearly defined product to a specific target segment within a competitive market, then a more standard approach to marketing communication might be used. A university, for example, is offering degree courses to potential students. As discussed elsewhere in this book, it might use advertising media to tell potential students why this is the best place to study; printed material such as the prospectus, brochures and leaflets to give more detail about the institution, its location and the courses on offer; visits to schools and education fairs to meet potential recruits face to face, and publicity to increase awareness and improve its corporate image.

Pricing is applied somewhat differently in the non-profit sector than in the commercial world. As mentioned earlier, those providing income might be totally different from those receiving the product. It is accepted in most areas of the non-profit sector that the recipient might not have to bear the full cost of the service or product provided. In other words, the recipient's need comes first rather than the ability to pay. In the profit-making sector it is more likely to be the other way around: if you can pay for it, you can have it. Non-profit pricing, therefore, might be very flexible and varied. Some customers will not be asked to pay at all, others will be asked to make whatever donation they can afford for the service they have received, others will be charged a full market price.

Example The National Trust, mentioned earlier, has to apply many pricing principles to generate sufficient revenue to meet the preservation objectives. In addition to pricing merchandise and in some cases charging entrance fees, a comprehensive range of membership options are available. For example, individual members pay £29 per year, families £56 and a child £14.50. Life membership options are also available starting at £700, but with lower prices for pensioners. Educational group memberships allow benefits to groups of up to 60 students and pupils. The 2.5mn members in return are granted free access to sites, can participate in local clubs and associations, and receive newsletters and magazines. The management of the Trust do not seek to charge premium pricing for sometimes exclusive and unique sites; instead a more moderate approach is adopted that rewards loyalty and frequent users, but still generates enough revenue from all sources to meet the planned development needs.

Issues of distribution, process and physical evidence, where applicable, are similar for non-profit organisations to those of other types of organisation. The organisation has to ensure that the product or service is available when and where the customer or client can conveniently access it. This might or might not involve physical premises. Clearly, non-profit institutions such as universities, hospitals, museums and the like do operate from premises. They face the same issues as any other service provider of making sure that those premises are sufficiently well equipped to allow a service to be delivered and to deal with likely demand. They also have to realise that the premises are part of the marketing effort and contribute to the customer's or client's perception of quality. Prospective students visiting a university on an open day might not be able to judge the quality of the courses very well, but they can certainly tell whether the campus would be a good place for them to live and work, whether the teaching rooms are pleasant and well equipped, and how well resourced the library and IT facilities seem to be.

Some non-profit organisations that focus mainly on giving information and advice by mail or by telephone do not, of course, need to invest in smart premises. Their priority is to ensure that customers or clients are aware of how to access the service and that enquiries are dealt with quickly, sympathetically and effectively.

Example The Samaritans (http://www.samaritans.org.uk) exists to provide a confidential counselling service to those in a desperate emotional state who are contemplating suicide. The service is offered 24 hours a day from 200 branches staffed by volunteers. There is no move towards developing a central call centre as it would undermine the whole structure of the service. Volunteers are carefully selected and trained locally, and give of their time for no charge. In 1999, there were 19 600 volunteers on various shifts, normally giving no more than 180 hours per year each. Although the caller may not care where the Samaritan is located, the organisation insists that its volunteers should not have to travel more than 60 miles to an office. There were 4.5 million calls in 1998 and the operation had to be able to cope with that demand, especially during the recognised peaks between 10 p.m. and 2 a.m. Each volunteer takes over 250 calls per year, and some calls can last for a long time, depending on the needs of the caller. Each branch runs as an autonomous operation, generating its own funds to cover the c. £17 000 cost per phone line and office expenses.

Marketing in non-profit-making areas is rapidly evolving and the techniques used in commercial situations are being transferred, tested and evolved to cope better with the complexity of causes, ideas and attitude change in a wide range of situations. Marketing thinking is being applied to encouraging more 'users' and 'customers' to come forward to benefit from supportive contact for people or children at risk, such as that provided by the Samaritans and the NSPCC. It is also being applied backwards to attract resources into charitable organisations that often rely on voluntary staff and generous donations from individuals and corporations.

CHAPTER SUMMARY

Many goods include some element of service as part of their product package, but those for which service is a major element of what the customer is buying are known specifically as *service products*. Although the variety of service products is very wide, everything from air travel to accountancy, fast food to pharmacies and doctors to degrees, all of them share some common characteristics that differentiate them from other types of product. With service products, for instance, there is often no transfer of ownership of anything, because a service is intangible. Services are also perishable, because they are generally performed at a particular time and are consumed as they are produced. This means that they cannot be stored in advance of demand, nor can they be kept in stock until a customer comes along. The customer is often directly involved in the production of the service product and thus the manufacture and delivery of the product cannot be separated. It also means that there is extensive interaction between the customer and the service provider's staff. Finally, because of the 'live' nature of the service experience and the central role of human interaction, it is very difficult to standardise the service experience.

These peculiar characteristics of services have implications for marketing strategies and management. The normal model of a marketing mix consisting of the 4Ps is useful, as far as it goes, and many of the principles associated with the 4Ps and physical products are also appropriate to services. Overall, however, the 4Ps are insufficient, and an additional 3Ps, people, processes and physical evidence, have been added to deal with the extra dimensions peculiar to services. *People* takes account of the human interactions involved in the service product; *physical evidence* looks at the tangible elements that contribute either directly or indirectly to the creation, delivery, quality or positioning of the service; and *processes* defines the systems that allow the service to be created and delivered efficiently, reliably and cost effectively.

Service quality is an important but difficult issue for managers, because it is hard to define and measure. Judgement of quality arises largely from customers' comparisons of what they expected from various facets of the service with what they think they actually received. Management can ensure that the service product is designed with the customer's real needs and wants in mind; they can make sure that it is adequately resourced; they can make sure that it is delivered properly; and they can try not to raise unrealistic expectations in the mind of the customer. In the end, quality is a subjective issue. Different customers will pick up on different aspects as being of prime importance, and the same customer might even react differently to the same service on different occasions.

Staff are an important element of service and its delivery. The service provider has to ensure that staff are fully qualified and trained to deal with customers and their needs, and to deliver the service reliably and consistently. The emphasis that is put on this will vary depending on whether staff have direct or indirect involvement with customers, and whether they are visible to customers or not. Like quality, productivity is a difficult management issue because of the live nature of services and the involvement of the customer in the process. Managers have to think and plan carefully in terms of staff recruitment and training, systems and technology, the service levels offered and the way in which customers interact with the service, to try to maintain control and efficiency in the service delivery system. Trying to manage supply and demand can also help to streamline productivity.

Franchising represents a way for established businesses with a good idea to grow rapidly and achieve wider geographic coverage, and also a way for individuals to get into business with a relatively low risk. Most franchised systems are governed by a contract that formally lays out both parties' obligations and rights. There is also likely to be a blueprint or manual that can specify a wide range of operating procedures and systems that allow each individual franchise to be operated effectively and to the same standards as others. Failure in franchise situations is lower than for independent small businesses. Although the franchisee must sacrifice a certain amount of independence, the risks are greatly reduced and the franchisee can benefit from the franchisor's experience and managerial support.

Non-profit organisations, which might be in the public or private sector, form a specialist area of services marketing. They differ because they are likely to serve multiple publics; they have multiple objectives that can often be difficult to quantify; they offer services, but the funder of the service is likely to be different from the recipient of it; and finally, they are subject to closer scrutiny and tighter accountability than many other organisations. It is also possible that where non-profit organisations are in receipt of government funding or where their existence or operation is subject to regulation, there will be limits placed on their freedom to use the marketing mix as they wish. Pricing or promotion, for example, might be prescribed or set within narrow constraints.

Key words and phrases

Business format franchise	Inseparability	Perishability
Franchise	Intangibility	Service productivity
Franchisee	Interactive marketing	Services
Franchisor	Internal marketing	Visible staff
Heterogeneity	Non-profit organisations	

QUESTIONS FOR REVIEW

22.1 What are the main characteristics that distinguish *services* from physical products?

22.2 How can *tangibility* be introduced into service products?

22.3 Define *inseparability* and its implications for the service product.

22.4 What are the 7Ps of the services marketing mix?

22.5 What are the 10 criteria that affect customers' perceptions of service quality?

22.6 Define the barriers to service quality.

22.7 What is *internal marketing* and why is it important in service products?

22.8 In what ways can service *productivity* be improved?

22.9 In what ways do *non-profit organisations* differ from other types of business?

22.10 What benefits does *franchising* offer

(a) the franchisor and
(b) the franchisee?

QUESTIONS FOR DISCUSSION

22.1 Discuss the impact of perishability on the management and marketing of a service business.

22.2 Choose a service business and analyse its marketing offering in terms of the 7Ps.

22.3 Design a short questionnaire for assessing the quality of service offered by a local dental practice.

22.4 In what ways might the following service organisations define and improve their productivity:

(a) a theme park;
(b) a university;
(c) a fast food outlet?

22.5 What do you think might be the main sources of revenue for the following types of non-profit organisation and what revenue generation problems do you think each faces:

(a) a small local charity;
(b) a National Health Service hospital;
(c) a public museum?

22.6 Find out about a potential franchise opportunity. How much is the licence fee and what does it include? What benefits would the franchisee derive and what risks would they run if they decided to take up this opportunity?

CASE STUDY 22.1

Developing a new franchise proposal: budget-priced hostels

(The name of the company featured in this case has been changed.)

Western Hostels were based in a picturesque part of Ireland, overlooking the Atlantic Ocean. The area was popular with tourists, although the

season tended to be short. The business idea for a budget tourist hostel developed from the owners' experience in running a small hotel. They saw two backpackers having breakfast by the side of the road early one morning and after some investigation they realised that there was a gap in the market for accommodation located somewhere between a tent and a bed-and-breakfast guesthouse on the luxury scale. This gap was not just based on price but also on the customer's preferred accommodation experience. Independent backpackers are not just young people, but come from all age ranges. What they have in common is the desire for a different type of more informal holiday experience.

The entrepreneurs, having done some careful analysis, developed a business plan and opened a hostel for all age ranges. They were surprised with the scale of the response. It was especially attractive to the French and Germans who were visiting Ireland on walking or cycling holidays. In the main season, the hostel was often fully booked and was turning customers away. Demand was even steady in the shoulder months of March–April and October–November at the beginning and end of the main season. There was little demand in the winter months, so they decided to close for refurbishment and a rest. The owners did not live on the premises, but they did live nearby so that they could keep a watch on the hostel. The cost of the hostel was around IR£100 000, which had been covered by a secured business loan.

The hostel concept was simple: communal, single-sex sleeping, a community kitchen and lounge, all of which allowed plenty of opportunity for guests to mingle and share experiences. The range of facilities was basic, but of high quality, and prices were a little lower than typical bed-and-breakfast rates. No food was served, although guests could cook their own. Most of the marketing that was undertaken was through travel guides and some specialist hiking magazines. Organised groups such as walking clubs, universities, schools and churches were direct mailed. A few add-on services were offered, for example a rent-a-bike scheme, a *bureau de change*, a limited selection of groceries, stationery etc., along with musical instruments that could be hired for the evening.

After two seasons the owners contemplated the next stage in development. They became interested in the franchise option after attending a business seminar. Although there were other hostels in Ireland, they were independent and of variable standard. By franchising the product concept to a specified standard and then developing and implementing a brand identity and group marketing, the basis of a successful franchise system seemed possible. The direct experience they had gained would enable them to produce an operating manual, especially covering start-up, maintenance, pricing, promotion and service standards. If a number of franchisees could be found, an advertising royalty could be used to develop a centralised reservation system and to produce a central brochure for key markets. The initial capital would be around IR£50 000 to cover equipping premises with 30 or more beds, and a levy on sales would also be made. In addition, the property could be acquired by the franchisee on a mortgage basis, so the capital and interest charges could be extended over a longer period.

They thought they knew the main ingredients for a franchise package, but they were still not entirely convinced that it was the best way to expand. Their plan would be for five franchises in Ireland and at least 10 in the UK within five years. Each franchisee could expect to generate around £3000 per week in the high season, based on a price of £12 to £15 per person per night and at least 30 beds. Ancillary sales would add to those revenues. After an advertisement in a franchise magazine, the owners have arranged to meet with three serious franchisee enquiries. They started to prepare for the meeting.

Questions

1 Is franchising the best way forward for this business? What are its alternatives?

2 Is the product concept, as outlined in this case, a good candidate for franchising?

3 If you were one of the potential franchisees at the meeting, what questions would you be asking?

4 What are the next stages the owners will have to go through to create and implement a franchised system?

CASE STUDY 22.2

'Stop it, Daddy'

The NSPCC (http://www.nspcc.org) has one simple aim: to ensure that cruelty to children stops. However, it has to decide between many different, and sometimes conflicting, objectives to achieve its aim. The challenge is to ensure that the public is aware of the extent of the problem, when sometimes it is uncomfortable to think that such cruelty goes on in a modern society. The message has to be got across that, for example, in the UK one child per week dies of abuse and neglect, 26 per cent of all rape victims are children and 35 000 children are on child protection registers.

The main objective of the charity is to make its *raison d'être* superfluous, but unfortunately it is a long way from that goal. It runs a series of programmes and campaigns to attack child abuse in the home, at work, at school and in society and the community. The immediate objective is to raise sufficient funds to help 100 000 children per year, five times more than at present. That would mean being able to handle more calls on its National Child Protection Helpline, expanding its schools service, producing parenting packs and working directly with over 6000 children. To achieve its main objective, it must raise donations directly from individuals, through corporate contributions and through fundraising. These sources provide 86 per cent of its income. It needs volunteers to raise funds and to help with some of the core services. All of these contributors must believe they are doing a worthwhile thing in supporting the NSPCC rather than another charity. The NSPCC is therefore a prime lobbying and pressure group on child welfare issues. Campaigns have been run to influence government to raise such issues on the political agenda, government spending priorities and in law and policy making.

The society needs to publicise its campaign and achievements to retain support. It is lobbying for change in, for example, indeterminate prison sentences for sex offenders and the keeping of proper criminal records for those working with children, as well as promoting more generally the non-violent discipline of children. Even local authority play areas are not left unnoticed, given that 81 per cent of them are unsupervised. To achieve all this, public support and donations must be activated through working with the media in PR and advertising terms. The latest campaign, 'Full Stop', is both very powerful and very controversial, as it addresses issues of which many of the public do not want to be reminded.

The NSPCC actually ran into trouble for being too hard hitting with some advertisements as part of the Full Stop campaign. Overall, the campaign aimed to shake the reader out of complacency and to change public attitudes to enlist more support. The campaign's first stage was targeted at raising awareness of the brutality and types of child abuse that go on through a series of advertisements following a high-profile launch supported by Ewan McGregor and Madonna. The advertisements' imagery was very powerful and disturbing: 'Stop it, Daddy, stop it'. It featured well-known personalities such as pop group the Spice Girls, cartoon character Rupert Bear and footballer Alan Shearer covering their eyes as background voices focused on adults either physically abusing or just about to molest a child. Such an approach was considered necessary to shock readers and to bring home the reality of what sadly does go on for a small percentage of children.

The NSPCC also entered into a marketing partnership with South Wales Electricity and Gas company (SWALEC). For every customer that switched to SWALEC, the NSPCC would be given £15, minus an administration charge. Potential customers were also sent a sales promotion offering a £60 discount on fuel bills. When the offer, using the 'Stop it, Daddy' theme, started dropping through potential customers' doors, complaints were made. Some recipients were shocked, others regarded it as intrusive, and some thought it simply tasteless exploitation of a charity by SWALEC (Beenstock, 1999). Consumers complained to the ASA and the drop of 7mn leaflets was aborted, pending further research. Meanwhile, the ITC received over 150 complaints about the television campaign, including some from people previously abused as children, but none of the complaints was upheld, on the grounds that a strong approach was justified for this kind of subject matter, even if it made some viewers uncomfortable (Dignam, 1999).

As NSPCC relies on donations for 86 per cent of its income, it is essential that it gets its message across. It seeks direct donation pledges, volunteer support for fundraising and corporate sponsorship such as the SWALEC example. With a plan to raise £250mn over five years in support of its revitalised action programmes, the NSPCC believes that it must use sometimes shocking promotional techniques to stir people out of complacency. Funds are also needed for the distribution of 900 000 publications, to maintain the child protection helpline. The latter has received 72 000 calls about children at risk, of which 7 per cent are from children themselves. Faced with the reality, it is perhaps not surprising that it is prepared to push the frontiers of shock campaigning.

The challenge for many cause related non-profit organisations is that there are many needy and worthwhile causes, all competing for limited discretionary funds. Even just looking at the small number of examples highlighted in this text, all are seeking funds for very worthwhile causes and, if there is to be a response, the advertising and promotion must make an impact through linking a donation with a real tangible benefit to the child, environment or society. The range of choices is very large, from the genuine and highly valued causes at an international level to localised good causes in supporting a community group or town hospice. Similarly, the causes themselves can range

from the mainstream to downright dubious and even obscene. The larger cause related organisations need to ensure that their positioning is clearly identified and the brand name has a real impact with donors and supporters.

Sources: Beenstock (1999); Dignam (1999); Jardine (1999), http://www.nspcc.org.

Questions

1 In what ways do the special characteristics of services and the 7Ps of the services marketing mix apply to a charity?

2 List the multiple publics for both resource attraction and resource allocation that an organisation like the NSPCC might be targeting. What kind of problems do you think might arise from having such diverse target audiences?

3 What benefits does a charity get from a promotional tie-in, such as the one between the NSPCC and SWALEC??

4 To what extent can 'shock' campaigns such as NSPCC's Full Stop be justified? What are the potential advantages and disadvantages of such a campaign?

A disturbing image to shock all of us out of complacency.

Source: NSPCC.

References for Chapter 22

Barrow, C. (1989), 'Franchising', in P. Burns and J. Dewhurst (eds.), *Small Business and Entrepreneurship*, Macmillan.

Barrow, C. and Golzen, G. (1990), *Taking Up a Franchise*, Kogan Page.

Beenstock, S. (1999), 'Why Marketing Partnerships Must not alienate their Target Audience', *Marketing*, 29 April, p. 15.

Bevan, S. and Barber, L. (1999), 'The Benefits of Service with a Smile', *Financial Times*, 24 June, p. 15.

Bin, J. (1999), 'Northeast Province to Develop Ecotourism', *China Daily Business Weekly*, 11–17 April, p. 7.

Booms, B. H. and Bitner, M. J. (1981), 'Marketing Strategies and Organisation Structures for Service Firms', in J. Donnelly and W. R. George (eds.), *Marketing of Services*, American Marketing Association.

Bray, R. (1999), 'In a Class on their Own', *Finanacial Times*, 12 July, p. 13.

Brewer, N. (1999), 'Royal Mail's Needs as a Rail Customer', *Modern Railways*, August, pp. 577–81.

Burns, T. (1999), 'Parques IPO Aims to Lift Spain Tourism', *Financial Times*, 19 May, p. 29.

Burt, T. (1999), 'The Northern Lights of Electronic Banking', *Financial Times*, 19 July, p. 17.

Buxton, J. (1999), 'Cashing in on the Hole-in-the-Wall', *Financial Times*, 21 July.

Chaplin, D. (1999), 'Do You Know What You Want to Know?', *Franchise International*, March/April, pp. 124–7.

Christopher, M. *et al.* (1994), *Relationship Marketing: Bringing Quality, Customer Service and Marketing Together* (2nd edn), Butterworth-Heinemann.

Cohen, A. (1999), 'A Departure in Efficiency', *Financial Times*, 16 August, p. 10.

Cowell, D. (1984), *The Marketing of Services*, Butterworth-Heinemann.

Daneshkhu, S. (1996), 'Leisure Parks Fund Launched', *Financial Times*, 10 February, p. 9.

Daneshku, S. (1999), 'Professional Push Pumps Iron into Growth Market', *Financial Times*, 20 May, p. 30.

Devlin, S. J. and Dong, H. K. (1994), 'Service Quality From the Customers' Perspective', *Marketing Research*, 6(1), pp. 5–13.

Dignam, C. (1999), 'ITC Clears Hard Hitting Abuse Ads from NSPCC', *Marketing*, 15 July, p. 3.

Doe, B. (1999), 'Service Please', *Modern Railways*, August, p. 597.

Dunn, R. (1998), 'Nazareth to Become Site of Biblical "Theme Park"', *The Times*, 27 November, p. 18.

Eisner, M. (1999), 'The Miracle that Turned Sour', *EuroBusiness*, June, pp. 64–9.

Electronic Payments International (1996), 'Sweden Heads ATM League Table', *Electronic Payments International*, April.

Felstead, A. (1991), 'Facing up to the Fragility of "Minding Your Own Business" as a Franchise', in J. Curran and R. A. Blackburn (eds.), *Paths of Enterprise: the Future of the Small Business*, Routledge.

Glover, J. (1999), 'London Joins the Smartcard Set', *Modern Railways*, August, p. 585.

Gofton, K. (1999), 'Staff Attitude Key to Winning Sales', *Marketing*, 3 June, p. 2.

Graham, G. (1999), 'Alternatives to Mergers', *Financial Times*, 19 July, p. 17.

Gray, R. (1998), 'Australia as a Brand', *Marketing*, 26 November, p. 30.

Gwyther, M. (1998) 'Franchise Nation', *Management Today*, December, pp. 40–46.

Heskett, J. L. *et al.* (1994), 'Putting the Service–Profit Chain to Work', *Harvard Business Review*, March/April, pp. 164–74.

Heskett, J. *et al.* (1997), *The Service Profit Chain*, Free Press.

Jacob, R. (1999), 'Hotel Group Profit Drops 90%', *Financial Times*, 23 July, p. 27.

Jardine, A. (1999), 'SWALEC's Child Cruelty Ad Pulled after Outcry', *Marketing*, 22 April, p. 3.

Jones, R. (1999), 'From Southern to Swanage Railway: Spot the Seam', *Heritage Railway*, August, pp. 26–31.

Katz, K. *et al.* (1996), 'Managing Perceptions of Waiting Times and Service Queues', *International Journal of Service Industry Management*, 7(5), pp. 44–61.

Killgren, L. (1999), 'Off the Rails', *Marketing Week*, 18 February, pp. 26–9.

Kotler, P. (1982), *Marketing for Non-Profit Organisations* (2nd edn), Prentice Hall.

Lee, J. (1997), 'Customising Staff to Win Hearts and Minds', *The Times*, 9 December, p. 31.

Looy, B. *et al.* (1998), *Services Management: an Integrated Approach*, Financial Times Pitman Publishing.

Lovelock, C. H. (1996), *Services Marketing* (3rd edn), Prentice Hall.

Lovelock, C. H. and Weinberg, C. B. (1984), *Marketing for Public and Non-Profit Managers*, John Wiley and Sons.

Marsh, H. (1999), 'Making Money from Monet', *Marketing*, 4 February, p. 12.

Mathews, B. P. and Clark, M. C. (1996), 'Comparability of Quality Determinants in Internal and External Service Encounters', in *Proceedings: Workshop on Quality Management in Services VI*, Universidad Carlos III de Madrid: 15–16 April.

McLuhan, R. (1999), 'The Colonel Steps in to Revitalise KFC's Brand Identity', *Marketing*, 6 May, p. 18.

Mendelsohn, M. (1992), *Guide to Franchising*, Cassell.

Murphy, C. (1996), 'Front Seat for Cinema Brands', *Marketing*, 28 March, p. 15.

Murphy, C. (1999), 'How McDonald's Conquered the UK', *Marketing*, 18 February, pp. 30–31.

Murray, I. (1998), 'Franchisees Furious over Tanning Loss', *The Express*, 12 January, pp. 31–2.

O'Connor, J. and Galvin, E. (1999), *Marketing and Information Technology* (2nd edn), Financial Times Pitman Publishing.

Parasuraman, A. *et al.* (1985), 'A Conceptual Model of Service Quality and Its Implications For Future Research', *Journal of Marketing*, 49(Fall), pp. 41–50.

Perren, B. (1999a), 'Service on Board', *Modern Railways*, May, p. 352.

Perren, B. (1999b), 'Service on Board', *Modern Railways*, August, p. 595.

Pettitt, S. (1988), 'Marketing Decision Making within Franchised Systems', *Proceedings of the Society of Franchising*, San Francisco, USA.

Rawsthorn, A. (1996), 'UCI Set to Open Six More Cinema Complexes', *Financial Times*, 30 January, p. 18.

Richards, A. (1998), 'Falling Arches', *The Express*, 13 September, p. 56.

Richards, H. (1999), 'Crowd-puller Returns to Run with the Pack', *Financial Times*, 5 March, p. 11.

Robinson, E. (1999), 'Fitness First Pushes for Europe', *Financial Times*, 5 February, p. 22.

Rosier, B. (1999), 'Pizza Hut Debut Site to Extend Home Delivery', *Marketing*, 29 April, p. 13.

Sasser, W. E. *et al.* (1978), *Management of Service Operations: Text, Cases and Readings*, Allyn & Bacon.

Shostack, L. G. (1977), 'Breaking Free From Product Marketing', *Journal of Marketing*, 41(April), pp. 73–80.

Skapinker, M. (1999) 'Variety Taken on Board', *Financial Times*, 2 June, p. 14.

Thorncroft, A. (1999), 'Tate Puts City in the Frame', Weekend supplement to *Financial Times*, 3–4 April, p. X.

Warren, P. (1999), 'Welcome to the Hotel Room that Knows You Better than Your Mother', *The Express*, 17 January, p. 24.

Young, R. (1998), '"Seaside Hotels" are what Drives us to the Costas', *The Times*, 30 September, p. 10.

Zeithaml, V. *et al.* (1988). 'SERVQUAL: A Multiple Item Scale for Measuring Consumer Perceptions of Service Quality', *Journal of Retailing*, 64(1), pp. 13–37.

Zeithaml, V. *et al.* (1990), *Delivering Quality Service: Balancing Customer Perceptions and Expectations*, The Free Press.

International Marketing

This chapter will help you to:

1 understand what international marketing is, and why it is so important to many organisations;

2 appreciate the problems of analysing international marketing environments and selecting markets to enter;

3 define the various available methods of international market entry, outlining their advantages and disadvantages within the context of the broad factors influencing the choice of market entry method;

4 develop an overview of the factors that encourage organisations to adapt their marketing offerings to suit specific international markets, and those that push them towards standardisation; and

5 appreciate the reasons that individual elements of the marketing mix might have to be treated differently in different international markets.

INTRODUCTION

Although international trade has been a feature of civilisation for thousands of years, this century has seen an enormous growth in the scale and complexity of trade across national frontiers. Now, most large organisations and many smaller ones assume that they will have to trade across national boundaries, and indeed for many such organisations, international trade is essential for their survival. For some organisations, an international orientation is so deeply ingrained into their strategy and operations that the domestic market in which the corporate headquarters are located is regarded as a relatively minor part of the total trading picture. Others, however, take a much more *ad hoc* approach, simply responding to any export enquiries that might drift in but with no special commitment to developing new markets. In between are those who proactively want to develop an international strand to their businesses. Many smaller firms in Europe have learned and benefited from the potential offered by the SEM and are now actively pursuing marketing opportunities wherever they occur in the world.

Organisations that are looking to expand their customer base internationally, however, face challenges that might be very different from those encountered in domestic markets. Decisions have to be made about the most attractive markets to pursue and develop, the best methods of entering new markets, and how much adaptation of the marketing package is necessary to achieve the desired positioning in the context of

Example Cansum Guralp is a highly specialist manufacturer of seismic detectors that monitor undersea and land earthquakes. Although only having 31 employees and sales of just over £2mn, it depends on exports for virtually all of its business. The US takes 44 per cent of sales, Japan 20 per cent and Europe 16 per cent. Its customers, mainly government institutions and universities, only have two other choices worldwide, Swiss and American companies. The need being satisfied is universal, the provision of high-quality information, and Cansum needs to meet that need on a global scale given that the home market has little to offer. From the outset, the company treated international markets as the only market to penetrate if it were to be successful (Pretzlik, 1999).

local needs and buyer expectations. These decisions are not, of course, too different from those required for domestic markets, and many of the key concepts presented in this book are just as applicable when dealing with Americans, Japanese or Danes. What are different, however, are the practice and implementation of marketing in order to take into account local customs, trading contexts, competition and other special factors that might inhibit or encourage free trade. Some organisations, such as McDonald's and Coca-Cola, choose to ignore any differences and market in the same way internationally, but the majority have to modify their marketing carefully to suit local conditions.

Example To Barlows (http://www.barlows.com), a South African multinational, internationalisation is a fundamental part of its growth strategy. Although now diversified, it has especially strong interests in marketing the brands of other manufacturers in the capital equipment, earthmoving and materials handling markets as well as manufacturing its own paints, speciality chemicals and cement products. Its managed brands include Hyster trucks in the south-east USA and Europe, and Caterpillar in Siberia. It has manufacturing plants in several countries concentrating on its own brands such as Plascon and Melles Groit and two of its eight divisions are based outside South Africa, reflecting the international nature of the company: materials handling in North Carolina and the scientific division in Staffordshire.

The strategy has been to build world-class brands in selected niches that can compete with other global players. There is a high degree of standardisation in many of its products, although some customisation is possible. In the UK lift truck market, for example, Barlows was able to change the rules of the market by shifting buyers to rental rather than purchase options, in line with its international policy. In order to achieve global capability, Barlows places considerable emphasis on organisational learning and sharing. Interdivisional task forces in such areas as IT, logistics and industrial relations enable ideas to be identified and implemented in all its global operations. All this means that its international interests have grown from 22 per cent of its annual operating profits in 1994 to 57 per cent in 1998 (*Business Report*, 1999).

This chapter starts with an examination of the rationale for international marketing and the philosophy behind it in different types of organisation. This will help to explain better the motivation and direction that organisations take as they plan their marketing strategies. The next part of the chapter, building on the concepts introduced in Chapter 2, will consider the special environmental forces that affect international markets. Sometimes these forces can be so great that it becomes undesirable, difficult or extremely risky to enter a market. The analysis of environmental forces can help to identify which countries (for example Peru, Ukraine or Vietnam) or regions (for example South America, eastern Europe or South-East Asia) should be given priority in the organisation's international development plans. Having decided on which market(s) to target, the organisation then has to decide on a market entry method. Each method carries its own risks and benefits and is appropriate for different kinds of organisations and situations. We look at this decision area later in this chapter (*see* pp. 1016 *et seq.*). Finally, the more practical issues of designing the international marketing mix are introduced, applying the concepts outlined elsewhere in this book. In this section, the most important issue is balancing the pressure to adapt and modify the marketing mix to suit local needs against the benefits of adopting a standardised approach across a whole range of different international markets to achieve economies of scale and a greater sense of consistency.

THE MEANING OF INTERNATIONAL MARKETING

International marketing is, of course, concerned with marketing across national boundaries. At its simplest, the small business that receives an order to supply its product to a buyer in another country is involved in international marketing. Even in such a simple situation, however, practical problems will have to be solved. Decisions will have to be made, for example, about what currency the price is quoted in and whether it has to cover shipping costs, import duties or other taxes. Special documentation will probably be necessary to enable the product to be shipped and transferred across national boundaries, and then the specific transportation and insurance arrangements will have to be made. The mechanism through which payment for the goods is to be transferred from country to country will have to be agreed between the buyer and the seller and might have to involve their bankers. In some cases, the seller might also have to consider installation and after-sales service arrangements. All these activities differ from normal domestic arrangements in complexity and design.

As soon as the organisation decides to seek markets proactively beyond its own national boundaries, the complexity increases still further. Promotional material and methods will have to be fine tuned to suit the local market environment in terms of language, culture, business practice etc. Successful trading on a longer-term basis might require a physical presence in the market through a sales office or distribution point from which customers can be serviced. Regardless of how committed or long term the presence, however, the principle of simple international marketing still holds: the organisation operates from its home base and supplies customers in a country other than its own. This is *exporting*.

> **Example**   Often, it is progress in export markets that has a big impact on the performance of a company. This can be seen by looking at EU companies exporting industrial machinery. North America is a major market for EU companies and between 1997 and 1998, export sales of such items as aerospace equipment and rolling stock increased by one-third. Vehicles and machine sales account for 47 per cent of all merchandise exports from the EU to the USA. Any trade dispute between the USA and the EU, for example the banana wars or the hormone-treated beef row (*see* page 1042), could have a damaging impact on exporters in these unrelated areas. However, the economic difficulties in Asia resulted in a decline in EU exports to that region by 20 per cent, wiping out most of the gain for exporters from growth in US trade. This demonstrates the need to spread risk when exporting to unpredictable export markets (Marsh, 1999f).

The difficulty with such a simple principle of international marketing, however, is that it can become less applicable as the organisation intensifies its international activity. An organisation might, for example, acquire or set up a manufacturing company to serve the market in a foreign country. That company is part of an international group, but at a local level it does not market across national boundaries but concentrates on its own domestic market. The parent organisation might get involved to a greater or lesser extent in critical issues such as strategic direction, resource allocation or product strategies, but otherwise the manufacturer is largely autonomous. Truly global organisations such as Shell, Rank Xerox and McDonald's, therefore, are likely to have production, distribution and/or marketing organisations to serve different nations or regions. International marketing is, therefore, far more complex and less easy to define than the simple principle suggests. Its complexity arises not only from operational considerations, but also from the attitude of organisations towards it. International marketing could be an integral part of the corporate culture or it could be viewed as an add-on extra of less importance than domestic marketing.

Lynch (1994) proposed five broad categories of European organisation that will differ in their attitude and approach towards international marketing:

1 *Local scale organisations* operate within national or even local boundaries and have little opportunity or desire to trade internationally. This group might include the local garage, a television repair shop or a small metal fabricator, for example. There might be little competitive advantage to be gained in transferring existing skills and experience to new markets. In some cases, 'exporting' could mean trading in another part of the same country rather than going abroad.

2 *National scale organisations* focus mainly on their own domestic market, but might find a number of changes affecting them as a result of the SEM. In the retail sector, for example, such organisations as Leclerc and Karstadt are still primarily national operators in terms of their origins and main markets. Although Karstadt generates around 90 per cent of its sales from its domestic market, it is pursuing opportunities for international expansion based on its existing expertise.

3 *Regional scale organisations* might experience some growth with the economic changes in Europe. Rather than operating throughout Europe, their first stage of development may be to operate on a regional scale, for example in Scandinavia or Benelux/Northern Germany. Irish companies have a long tradition of exporting to the UK as a first experience of operating beyond national boundaries. UK companies often used to focus on Commonwealth countries as export markets, although there is now more emphasis on Europe.

> **Example** Gerbit has been a maker of high-quality sanitary systems for 125 years. The Swiss company has concentrated on the premium sector and is not interested in low-margin sanitary ware such as ceramic basins and bath tubs, where there is over-capacity in Europe. Instead, it focuses on higher margin internal water supply, drainage and lavatory flushing systems along with low noise and touch-free electronic systems. It has developed this niche on a selective regional scale within Europe, deliberately not attacking the UK and Scandinavia. The focus instead has been on Germany, Italy, Austria, the Netherlands, France and Belgium which, along with the Swiss domestic market, has enabled a 30 per cent sales growth rate over five years in what is otherwise a stagnant market. By selecting markets in which a strong presence can be established and in which there is less sensitivity to premium prices, Gerbit has become a leading regional scale organisation in its sector (Hall, 1999).

By operating on a regional scale, a firm gains early experience of operating beyond the domestic market, and is exposed to such issues as cultural differences, administration and logistics within a less hostile setting. Often organisations in this category are in transition as they seek similar niches beyond their domestic markets.

4 *European scale organisations.* It is perhaps in this area that there will be considerable growth over the next 10 years as organisations with a strong national presence expand to take advantage of the single market. Hennes & Mauritz from Sweden is moving from being a regional scale to being a European scale organisation with parallel moves into the North American market. Siemens AG (with 61 per cent of its sales in Europe, Promodès (with virtually all of its sales in Europe) and Marks & Spencer (with over 90 per cent of its sales in the UK and Europe) are already at various stages of transition from Europe to world scale companies. Others are now seeking to strengthen their European presence from a traditionally strong domestic base.

Example Alliance Unichem (http://unichem.co.uk), a wholesale drugs company, is seeking to manage its transition into the dominant European player in its market. It is already number two in Europe after its merger with Alliance Santé in 1997 giving it a 16 per cent share after Gehe in Germany. Its shares in specific EU countries vary from around 30 per cent in France and the UK and 25 per cent in Italy to much smaller shares in Germany, southern Europe, Scandinavia and the Netherlands. The strategy is to improve overall market share in Europe by acquiring smaller rivals in low-share markets and being more aggressive in its marketing in high-share markets. This dual approach is considered essential in a market where pharmaceutical manufacturers will favour pan-European wholesalers that can be effective in all their markets (Bilefsky, 1999a).

Hennes & Mauritz (http://www.hm.com), the leading Swedish clothing retailer and Sweden's third biggest company, is now looking to become a world-scale organisation. Expansion has already been successful in Europe, with 156 of its 576 stores located in Germany and a presence in many other EU countries. Even though it has a small percentage of the German market, at 1.7 per cent, for its low-priced, well designed, value for money fashion lines designed for younger age groups, Germany generated 32 per cent of its European sales in 1998 compared with 18 per cent from the Swedish market. Some experts have, however, questioned H&M's decision to open a New York store as part of a strategy to move to world scale retailing. Concerns were expressed that even in Europe, when it came up against tough competition, such as in the UK, it has not made such a big impact as in Germany and the Netherlands. In the UK its share is just 0.3 per cent, so any US move will pitch it up against well-established and highly efficient competitors who could make H&M's aspirations difficult to realise (George, 1999).

5 *World scale organisations* have a strong European base, but now operate in a range of different world markets on a direct investment, joint venture or exporting basis. Companies such as Shell, Unilever, Pilkington and Glaxo-Wellcome derive a significant proportion of their sales from outside Europe. Often Europe is seen as one geographic market containing segments that transcend national boundaries, and the priority is to compete against powerful international competitors, especially from the Far East and the USA. A successful European base provides a good foundation from which to compete internationally.

Example As we saw at p. 843, Nestlé is a major global organisation. It operates in more than 100 countries and has nearly 500 factories around the world. It does, however, use a wide variety of methods to grow internationally. Acquisitions, for instance, have provided a fast route into some markets, strengthening its international market presence and its product portfolio. In some markets, joint ventures with the likes of Coca-Cola and General Mills were felt to be more appropriate, while in others it has set up its own directly owned marketing and production facilities.

Despite being a prominent international player in the food industry, Nestlé still faces major international competition. When it plans its marketing, although it must take national markets into account, the regional and global competitive scenes are important aspects of strategy formulation. Thus while broad strategies are determined at an international level, they are fine tuned and implemented at a local level to ensure that cats eat Gourmet and humans eat Lion bars in sufficient numbers to achieve the objectives set.

The distinction drawn between different types of organisations is important, as it highlights a Europe in transition. It could be argued that within the SEM there is no such thing as exporting, but just one large domestic market. Some organisations might adopt a European niching strategy as a matter of course, and see that as their 'home' market. For others with a national or local bias, moves to expand within Europe would be regarded as significant strategic developments that require major learning and adjustment. To these organisations, the decision to trade elsewhere within Europe differs little from a decision to trade in the USA, which is seen as just as risky and diffi-cult. Although some of the risks and barriers to trade have been eliminated within Europe, others such as language or different distribution and communication channels require a different marketing approach.

Thus international marketing means different things to different organisations. To small organisations and companies still primarily operating from one main man-ufacturing base, most marketing involves product movement across national boundaries and the design of a marketing mix for each market. For other organ-isations, the scale of international operation has become so great that product movement across national boundaries is minimal or part of a carefully planned strategy. To such multinational or transnational organisations, the distinction between international and domestic marketing becomes very artificial from a strate-gic marketing perspective.

Example   Some organisations manufacture around the world and, like General Motors (GM) and SKF, might concentrate on particular products in different nations as part of their inter-national product strategies. Thus GM's Astra model could be manufactured in Germany and sold into the home market, but it will also be shipped across international boundaries. Similarly, SKF (http://www.skf.com) might produce spherical roller bearings in Sweden, sell-ing some in the domestic market and exporting the rest. When volumes and profitability drop in a market, the future potential must be re-appraised. SKF found that it had a small share of the US automotive market for taper roller bearings and thus decided to close the plant in Glasgow, Kentucky, then ship the products in from another plant overseas. Taper roller bearings are no longer produced by SKF in the USA. However, it still maintains 80 fac-tories in 23 countries around the world.

SKF developed from its Swedish beginnings to become a world-scale organisation.

Source: SKF.

The rationale for international marketing

Nations encourage their businesses to export their goods and services as a means of earning the foreign currency to pay for necessary imports, whether oil or oranges. The smaller and less well-endowed a nation, the greater the need for foreign trade. But even the more powerful economies in the world still need exports and positively encourage their business communities to generate them. A number of small firms in the USA, for example, have been accused of not giving exporting sufficient priority because of the size and potential of the domestic market.

Apart from the warm glow arising from the sense of having done one's duty as a good corporate citizen in contributing towards the nation's balance of payments, there are other reasons, both positive and negative, that organisations consider international development as an option. For many, there is in fact no choice, unless the objective is to remain a local or national operator. This might be possible where careful positioning or regulation provides a shelter from which the organisation can ignore most of what is happening in the international market place. In reality, however, few businesses are immune from the impact of international trade. As trade become more liberalised and domestic markets consequently become less well protected, tough and sometimes powerful competitors can enter the market with a sufficiently attractive product and the resources to make a significant impact.

Example The UK wine market has enjoyed so much growth since the 1980s that it has been suggested that it is now a mass market and no longer enjoys the élitism and luxury image of the past. If demand levels off, as has been suggested, then there could be over-supply. If a gap then emerges between production and consumption, there is likely to be fierce competition between the traditional and more recent wine producers. France still dominates the market with over 30 per cent share, but 'New World' competitors as a group claim that they have a larger share than the French, although not on an individual nation basis. The success of Chilean wine is indicative of the impact of New World producers.

In the 1980s, Chile sought to develop its international sales of wine but made little impact because of quality and marketing problems. In the 1990s, however, it increased its efforts in European and North American markets with an offering based on quality, consistency and price competitiveness. By 1998, Chile had carved out a 3.5 per cent share of the market by value, and a higher percentage by volume. Through its careful strategy, it had become the third largest New World producer after Australia and South Africa and experienced double-digit growth through such brands as Terra Andina and Campero. Argentina could be the next significant entrant and it has started to concentrate on quality wines, rather than its previous focus on unbranded wines. Sales into the UK grew by over 20 per cent in 1998 but still represent less than 1 per cent share. With these aggressive new entrants, sales from Bulgaria, Portugal and Hungary have suffered (*The Grocer*, 1999e, 1999f; Palmer, 1999).

Whole industries have been effectively wiped out by the inability of domestic producers to withstand the impact of international competition.

Example More recently, many traditional industries in Central Europe have found it difficult to withstand the onslaught of aggressive international competitors. The Hungarian glass industry suffered very badly from exposure to European competition. In 1997, Hungary abolished the import duty on bottles, making imports 13 per cent cheaper, and within two years around 30 per cent import penetration for bottles had been achieved compared with just 5 per cent before. That was bad news for Owens-Illinois, a US glass bottle maker, which decided to introduce much needed investment by buying some Hungarian manufacturers in 1995. The changes in market conditions and the effect of many years of neglect forced it to close down all but one plant. It lost over 50 per cent of sales from one plant when exports to Russia and the Ukraine ceased in 1997. However, some companies are able to refocus their strategy to survive. Guardian Glass, in contrast, established a joint venture in 1998 with the then state-owned company and through investment in quality and productivity, along with product specialisation, managed to resist the changes and grow profitably (Wright, 1999).

To ignore or underestimate international competitors and to position poorly against them can have serious consequences. Waiting until the competitor has entered and gained a foothold in the market could be too late.

Defending the organisation against the worst effects of foreign competition might involve rather more that just creating a strong positioning strategy for products, however.

> **Example** In the 1970s and 1980s, many companies found themselves trying to withstand competitive pressure from a resurgent Japan, seeking world domination in various sectors. Some companies, for example those manufacturing cameras, photocopiers or motorcycles, succumbed, but other European and American producers survived. Ford, for example, wanted to restructure and integrate its worldwide operations to enable it to become more competitive. Similarly, SKF undertook major rationalisation and manufacturing concentration to ensure that its cost base was low enough to compete, whereas Bosch relied on technical superiority and close customer relations, even developing plants near its main automotive customers as a means of defence. The threats have not receded but these organisations are better able to survive and to compete on equal terms in the international arena.

There are also positive reasons for organisations actively pursuing international opportunities. Each of these, shown in Fig. 23.1, is considered in turn.

Small or saturated domestic markets

If the domestic market is limited in size or has become saturated (in that there are too many suppliers chasing too few customers), the organisation might look towards international markets sooner rather than later. An Irish producer of specialist furniture, for example, might soon find that with a domestic population of around 3.5 million there are too few potential customers to maintain a viable level of business activity. In this case, the feasibility of exporting and willingness to try it might have been an important part of the business start-up process, as considered in Chapter 21. A similar manufacturer in Germany or Italy might, however, have a much larger domestic market to target before reasonable opportunities are exhausted.

The more an organisation decides to niche, the smaller the segment and the greater the chance of reaching saturation.

> **Example** Bruno Magli (http://www.magli.it) designer shoes now have worldwide appeal, with the home market, Italy, taking just 20 per cent of production. North America and Japan account for over 40 per cent of sales. The home market could not support the business objectives of the company even though it only sells around 800 000 pair of shoes per year, so developing export markets became essential. The fashionable designer footwear has a premium position and is sold mainly through franchised retail stores in many leading cities around the world. The segment served is treated as universal and the positioning is the same all over the world (Monk, 1999).

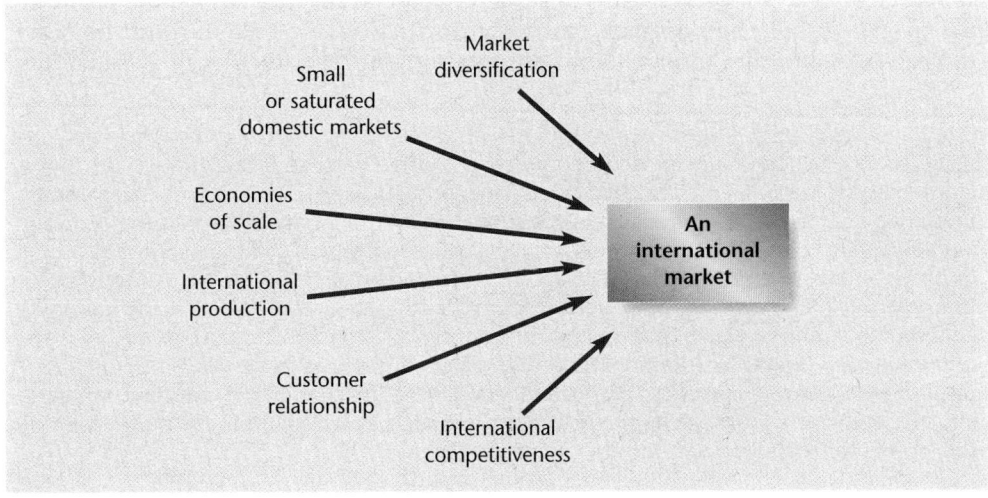

FIGURE 23.1

Reasons for internationalisation

Ultimately, the judgement as to whether a market is too small or too saturated lies with the organisation. What might be a comfortable niche for a small business might appear to be not worth the effort for a large organisation. In a mainstream market, if two or three very large organisations hold most of the market share between them, other companies might decide that there is no room for them to develop as they would wish, and thus they might look to foreign markets for opportunities. The significant development of Japanese companies in world markets was partially stimulated by the limited growth potential in the domestic market, where domination had already been achieved.

Example The elevator and escalator market is dominated by large players such as Schindler of Switzerland, Otis of the USA and Thyssen Krupps Industries of Germany (TKI). As the number three manufacturer, TKI (http://www.thyssen-elevator.com) must compete on a global scale if it is to achieve low unit costs. Half its sales are generated in Germany, 25 per cent in the rest of Europe and 20 per cent in the USA, giving it a 13 per cent world share. International marketing is not an optional luxury, it is a necessity. In order to bring it closer to the market leaders and to improve its competitive position and presence, particularly in the US market, TKI recently purchased Dover, a US lift company. Not only did this move expand the product range, but it also enabled TKI to benefit from Dover's strong regional presence with branch offices and established contacts (Marsh, 1999e).

Economies of scale

The TKI example above also demonstrates the importance of developing internationally to achieve economies of scale. Serving a large market with high volumes from one plant enables cost competitiveness to be maintained. Ford believes that there will only be six major car makers within a decade. This is inevitable when operating margins are very tight, heavy R&D costs have to be recouped, and marketing becomes more global. To achieve low unit costs in production and to spread marketing costs, Ford has to ensure a high degree of standardisation in critical parts such as the chassis and engines, allowing more superficial styling changes for local markets, for example air conditioning. To achieve such economics of scale a consolidation of factories is likely to be inevitable and some smaller manufacturers, such as Volvo, have already been acquired. In the latter case, although the marque will be maintained for its market appeal, opportunities are also created for savings in adopting common components in some areas (Pitcher, 1999a).

While the prospect of economies of scale is not necessarily enough in itself to push an organisation into international markets and does not guarantee success, it can provide a flexible foundation for developing the international marketing package.

International production

Differential labour costs around the world have been an incentive for some organisations to shift production abroad. Not only do they save on labour and possibly operating costs, but they also save on transport and import costs as well as benefiting

Example VW established a manufacturing presence in the Czech Republic through the purchase of Skoda in 1991. It provided much needed capital investment and design and marketing skills to the ailing company. One of the main attractions for VW was the operating and labour costs, which are just one-tenth of those in Germany. With new models built on VW platforms, Skoda is now seeking to export to western Europe as well as continuing to expand its manufacturing operations in central and eastern Europe. It already has low volume car assembly plants in Bosnia and Poland and is considering adding Russia as a means of overcoming high import tariff barriers (Anderson, 1999). VW also operates a plant in Bratislava and intends to produce cars under the VW brand from the plant, including the second line for the Polo, previously concentrated in Wolfsberg in Germany. Again, the incentive is linked to much lower labour costs (Done, 1999).

from government incentives to encourage inward investment. Furthermore, the organisation might want to develop a regional presence for marketing purposes.

Customer relationships

As customers become more international in orientation, suppliers have to follow suit. Those supplying components to the automotive industry might have to be able to supply standard parts to any one of several manufacturing plants around the world. They might even be expected to expand their own manufacturing operations so that they themselves have plants close to the car manufacturer's locations.

> **Example** Siemens (http://www.siemens.com), a German electronics group, decided to expand its business in the French railway equipment market. The national market is dominated by Alstom, a UK-French consortium, but Siemens was planning to use its purchase of the transport arm of French company Matra as a base to expand its share of the market. Although it had contacts with most of the main buyers for trams, signalling and electronics, it found that French buyers often bought from French companies, despite a so-called free market. By leaving 5 per cent of shares in the new Matra Transport International in French hands, Siemens hoped to appease buyer sensitivities and capitalise on pre-existing customer relationships. The acquisition also benefited Siemens in the German market through Matra's expertise in driverless trains and Matra benefited from access to Siemens' worldwide contacts and distribution network, especially in the growing markets of the USA and Far East (Batchelor, 1999).

In service industries in particular, it might be necessary to locate closer to customers, wherever they might be. Engineering consulting and testing service providers or advertising agencies, for example, might also feel that they can develop better customer relationships and better service by having branch offices or subsidiaries in a number of foreign markets where potential customers are concentrated.

Market diversification

The broader the range of markets served, the less likely it is that failure in any one market will cause terminal corporate decline. As discussed in Chapter 20, different markets are at different stages of development and competitive intensity, and make different resource demands. If, therefore, the organisation has a well-spread portfolio, resources can be shifted for further development, for combating short-term difficulties, or even to allow withdrawal. Central and eastern Europe and the Far East are currently regarded as markets that need investment if a long-term presence is to be built, whereas many western European markets are generally regarded as mature, with any growth arising from aggressive techniques for stealing share from competitors.

> **Example** Netherlands-based United Pan-Europe Communications, Europe's largest private cable television operator, has been building a presence in Hungary, Slovakia and the Czech republic. In Poland, however, there was strong competition between Polish-owned At Entertainment and French pay TV company canal Plus. Experts suggested that the market was not big enough for two, despite its being central Europe's largest for advertising revenue, let alone three operators, so UPC agreed to buy At Entertainment. The additional marketing, financial and technical strength of UPC should enable At Entertainment to expand its share of the market and to launch new services such as Internet via digital television (Bobinski and Cane, 1999).

International competitiveness

Finally, it should not be forgotten that one of the main reasons for international development is the pursuit of market opportunities, with a view to either beating the competition or strengthening one's position against them.

> **Example** Pitcher (1999b) argues that UK retailers have to be proactive in expanding their international operations. Argos, the GUS-owned catalogue retailer (*see* p. 529), for example, has probably reached near saturation in the domestic UK market with a catalogue circulation of 14 million, yet it has only just started to develop internationally with four stores in the Netherlands. This compares with Tesco, which has developed over 100 stores internationally, especially in central Europe, and Dutch retailer Ahold, which owns a number of subsidiaries in South America (a turnover of $4.5bn), Asia ($0.5bn), USA (around $20bn), Europe (not including the Netherlands, a turnover of $2bn) (Pring, 1999).
>
> For French battery company Saft, it is essential that it has an international profile if it wishes to compete. In a market dominated by US and Japanese companies, Saft, part of Alcatel, must 'think global' to sell its rechargeable, high value batteries that are particularly used by industrial customers. Only one-quarter of its staff are in France, the rest are in the Americas and Asia, and it considers itself an international company that just bappens to be based in Paris. International markets are also important for recouping the 6 per cent of revenue spent on R&D, which in the case of a new high energy, lithium-based battery came to $200mn (Marsh, 1999d).

Whatever the motivation for entering and developing international markets, a planned approach considerably increases the chances of success. The main stages in that process include identifying opportunities, assessing markets, planning entry and allocating resources to ensure a match between opportunities, objectives and capabilities.

UNDERSTANDING INTERNATIONAL MARKETS

Once the decision has been made to pursue international development, the organisation has to choose which foreign markets to target. It might already have a shortlist of two or three areas that clearly show potential, but further, more detailed analysis is necessary in order to choose between them or to set priorities. Understanding the marketing environments involved can form the basis of detailed market assessment and selection.

International marketing environment

The STEP factors making up the marketing environment have already been covered in detail in Chapter 2. Much of that discussion is as relevant to international markets as it is to the domestic situation. This section, therefore, will simply highlight briefly a few issues under each factor that might influence international marketing decisions and strategies specifically.

Sociocultural factors

As well as the normal consideration of market structure in terms of demographics, the international marketer needs to pay special attention to sociocultural factors, issues of cultural difference. These could affect not only the way in which a product is marketed to consumers, but also the way in which business negotiations are handled. Cultural differences might be seen in terms of language, social structures and mores (including class structure, gender roles and the effect of religion) and prevalent values and attitudes.

Language. Language is a minefield for the international marketer. Many British exporting companies assume (and indeed expect) all foreigners to speak and to negotiate in English. Unfortunately, this arrogance is often misplaced. In much of continental Europe, small and medium-sized companies cannot operate in English, and others resent being expected to do so. It is not unreasonable to expect a marketing-orientated organisation to make the effort to deal with customers in the customer's own language.

Example There are two broad approaches to the handling of international languages. First, staff can be trained to the required level. When Peebles Transformers from Edinburgh won a contract to supply the Tianhuangping pumped storage site, it used a multimedia training package in Mandarin as well as hiring a local translator for support. In contrast, Simpson Photo Imaging, a small ceramics decorating business, employed a linguist who spoke nine languages for customer contact, especially at exhibitions, although again it also encouraged other staff to learn a second language consistent with its export priorities (Bloom, 1998). DSM, the Netherlands' largest chemical manufacturer based in Limberg, is a European organisation that trades internationally rather than a domestically orientated company that happens to export. It now considers Germany as much of a domestic market as the Netherlands, and German, along with the other main European languages, is widely spoken (Cramb, 1999).

Language can also be a problem within the marketing mix. As seen at p. 286, brand names do not necessarily transfer easily across borders. Not only might the name itself have an unfortunate meaning or be difficult to pronounce in other languages, but the subtle associative elements of some names might be lost in translation or when used by people ignorant of the original language. Sales brochures and literature, manuals and instruction leaflets have to be carefully translated. Most of us have come across instruction books for Japanese electronic goods that have been translated by someone with a less than perfect grasp of English idiom. At best this is amusing, but it can irritate and frustrate the customer, and it does not give the best impression of the organisation that has produced it.

Social structures, customs and mores. Social factors can affect what is or is not acceptable in terms of the product itself, its marketing mix, or the business negotiation process. In any consumer market, the marketer needs to understand as much as possible about the individual and the influences of various groups on them (*see* pp. 107 *et seq.* and 117 *et seq.* to revise these concepts). The role of women in society or the structure and centrality of the family might affect product positioning and what is portrayed in advertising, for example.

Example Any exporter to South Africa has to be aware of the changing social structure in the post-apartheid period. In a society in which 73 per cent of the population is black and the middle-class/middle-income black consumer is a fast growing segment, traditional racial segmentation approaches are no longer appropriate. Marketers have to be aware of changing values and attitudes within a group that has been suppressed for so long, such as its aspirational orientation, symbols of personal achievement and group belonging, which are especially powerful within the emergent black middle class. Race is no longer a sufficient segmentation base and it is even risky to treat the middle-class black group as homogeneous. Instead, lifestyle variables cutting across race and gender are now more appropriate for an international marketer (Ives, 1999).

Business culture also needs to be understood in detail. Negotiating styles and etiquette can differ widely. Figure 23.2, based on Mead (1990), summarises some of the considerations that the international marketer has to take into account.

In international markets, there is a strong chance that ethical problems will have to be faced sooner or later. The ethical standards exhibited in the conduct of business in one environment might not be the same in another. This poses a moral dilemma as to whether to participate in practices that would be considered offensive or illegal in the home environment. If the marketer does not participate, however, it could jeopardise sales and the employment of staff back home. In short, what price morality?

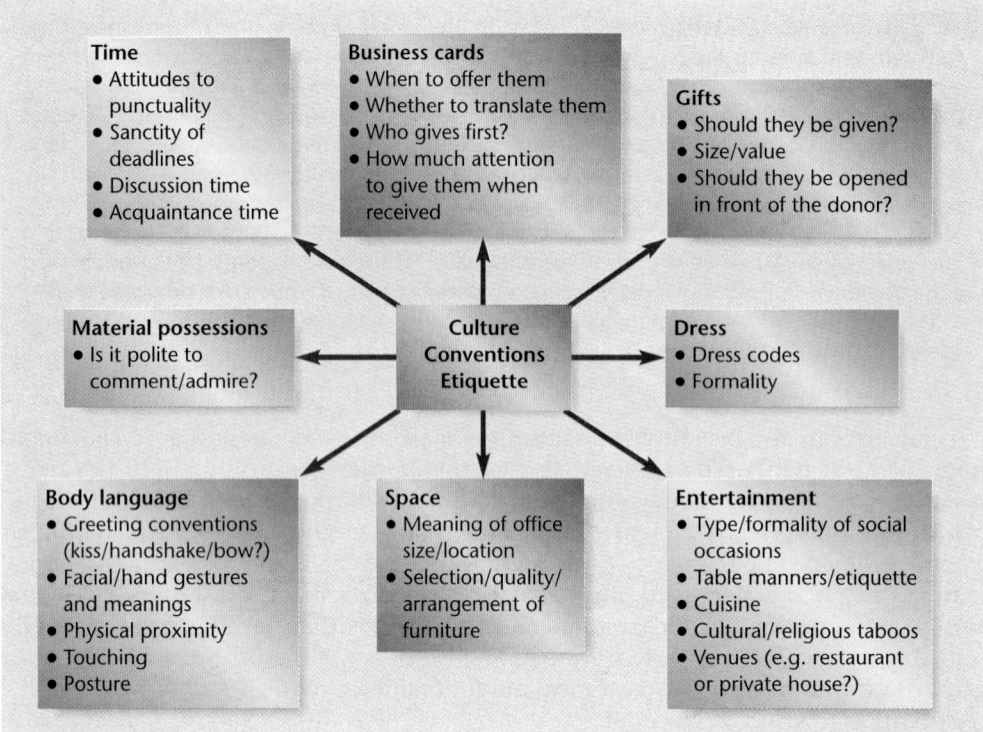

FIGURE 23.2

Behavioural factors influencing business conduct

Source: Adapted from Mead (1990)

Shell had to face such a dilemma through allegations of guilt by association. By opposing the environmental protection views of Ken Saro-Wiwa in Nigeria, the company was seen as being linked with the political regime that eventually ordered his execution as part of the human rights oppression of the Ogoni people. In the West, scandals and corruption have affected organisations, with even the Olympic games bidding process being questioned (*see* p. 806). Some companies have been heavily criticised for buying from firms using child labour in Asia and the Far East. With the growth of the Internet, it is becoming increasingly difficult for organisations to turn a blind eye to questionable practices in far-away places.

The EU has just drawn up a voluntary code of conduct to guide multinationals operating in the developing countries. It covers best practice on the environment, employment issues, corruption and human rights. The OECD anti-bribery convention could end the common practice of treating bribes as deductible operating expenses. The full impact of these measures is yet to be realised, however, as this is a large-scale problem.

ICI believes that compromising core values and common standards, ranging from 'commission', 'expediting payments' to fundamental breaches of human rights, should not be allowed and it makes a point of telling customers of the standards within its ethical code, turning a potential problem into a competitive strength. Perhaps there is some business that is simply not worth the price of winning (Maitland, 1999).

Values and attitudes. Values and attitudes can affect reaction to a product or to its origins. During the days of apartheid, consumer pressure and trade sanctions imposed by governments meant that South African products were not imported, while consumer boycotts affected those European companies that invested in South Africa. Quite apart from such specific political issues, some cultures are more resistant to foreign goods than others. As seen at pp. 189 *et seq.* (Paitra, 1993), even within Europe there are different attitudes to the origin of goods. Germans tend to be traditionalists, orientated more towards long-established home-produced products, whereas France and Italy are much more open to new foreign ideas.

Example Sara Lee and its Kiwi Shoe Polish (http://www.kiwicare.com) brand found interesting differences between the South African and some European markets in terms of attitudes to shoe care. It is important for Kiwi to understand these differences if it is to maintain its 72 per cent share of the South African market after building brand share from 24 per cent in 1984. South Africa is a nation with one of the highest levels of shoe polish penetration. Interestingly, consumers take a keen interest in the preservation and presentation of their shoes, unlike in some other markets where cleaning is often an act of last resort. In part, the consumer involvement is driven by climatic differences given the relatively high dust levels in South Africa, and also reflects a desire to extend the life of a shoe. Sara Lee does not only need to understand differences between nations, it also needs to track whether there are significant differences in attitudes and values within the country (Dorrian, 1998).

Nevertheless, some companies do trade successfully using their country of origin as a major international selling point. IKEA, for example, emphasises its Swedishness because in most countries Scandinavian design is much admired. Both Burberry and Laura Ashley trade on their Englishness, with an image of quality and quaint heritage. Meanwhile, McDonald's and Coca-Cola carry the American dream around the world. This can backfire, of course, if customers in a foreign market do not hold or believe the 'right' stereotypical images of Englishness or Swedishness. National images can also be damaged by international political events. During the Gulf war, for example, associations with the UK or the USA became a distinct disadvantage for products in some international markets.

When candles went out of fashion after the Second World War, the industry virtually died. In the 1980s, however, the atmospheric impact of ambient light led to a resurgence in demand for candles from bars and restaurants and for home use. Candles became a lifestyle product, even offering scents such as lavender and chocolate. For UK producer Colony, around 15 per cent of production is exported, especially to the USA, Japan and mainland Europe, reflecting the style, fragrance and gift potential of candles that are now anything but white. It would appear that the lifestyle appeal transcends national borders in western-dominated value systems (Jones, 1999).

Not surprisingly, many organisations prefer to gain international experience initially by choosing countries that are culturally as similar as possible to their own. Thus smaller Irish companies might begin by exporting to the UK, while Swedish companies might begin by trading in other Scandinavian markets. This reduces the risks and barriers to market entry and allows the organisation to learn a little about what international marketing means before it launches itself into more far-flung territories.

Technological factors

The stage of technological development that a market has reached can have many implications. A manufacturer of 'ready-to-microwave' meals might not have much success selling into markets where the penetration of microwave ovens is very low! Similarly, sophisticated computer peripherals or software need markets with an established IT base. Technology available within a market might also affect goods handling, stock control or the preservation of perishable goods. This raises questions as to whether the exporter can work within the existing technological infrastructure or whether investment will have to be made in developing it or finding alternative solutions.

Example The technological infrastructure also limits the potential for Internet use, with its benefit of on-line trading and building stronger customer relationships regardless of geographic location. Internet use reveals big differences between nations for technological, economic and attitudinal reasons. In terms of the number of Internet users, the US dwarfs its nearest contenders in the UK, Germany and Japan, but as a percentage of the

▶

population the Scandinavian countries have higher Internet penetration. In contrast, China, Spain and even France show low levels of penetration. The implications of these differences concern not just what is possible when developing a foreign market, but also indicate the competitive headstart that many US companies have in developing the use of the Internet (Taylor, 1999).

Economic and competitive factors

As might be expected, the international marketer is interested in the size of the foreign market and its market potential. Basic information about per capita disposable income, consumption patterns and unemployment trends can help to paint a background picture of how that market is developing in the longer term. The international marketer will also be interested in inflation, the stability of exchange rates and any exchange control regulations. An exporter wanting payment in hard currencies such as sterling or dollars rather than in the importer's local currency might face problems if the importer's government tightly controls their access to hard currency. The existence and levels of import tariffs, duties and local taxes can also add to the costs and problems of entering foreign markets. We discussed the impact of VERs on the car market at p. 65 *et seq.* Chapter 2 also discussed the problems of varying VAT rates and excise duties on cross-border trade within the EU.

In terms of competitive analysis, the procedure is the same as for any domestic market, and organisations need to look at the number of competitors, the structure of the market and the sophistication of market positioning and marketing mixes. Of particular interest in foreign markets is the extent to which other exporters have managed to penetrate that market and the problems they have faced in doing so.

Example Although economic considerations predominate in international marketing decisions, it is also important to remember the broader impact, both positive and negative, on the societies with which the organisation is doing business. This is especially true in developing nations. A few facts published by the United Nations Development Programme in its *Human Development Report* make interesting reading (Wolf, 1999b):

- By 1997, 20 per cent of the world's people were producing 82 per cent of the world's exports. The bottom 20 per cent contribute just 1 per cent.
- Ten countries account for 84 per cent of global research and development.
- 20 per cent of nations generate 93 per cent of Internet usage, the bottom 20 per cent just 0.2 per cent.
- The widening gap between rich and poor brings responsibilities to governments and organisations alike. Whereas convergence has taken place in countries like Singapore, South Korea and Hong Kong, and is taking place in China and Brazil, in many developing countries, especially in Africa, it is slipping back. Over 1.3 billion people in the world exist on less than $1 per day and some of these societies are failing due to disease, terrorism, war and migration. Organisational policies that promote local development and enable skills and competencies to be assimilated are making a direct contribution to the economic development potential of that economy. In China, for example, the insistance on joint ventures in many sectors has enabled faster rate of indigenous change through improved know-how.

Clearly, these are political and policy problems. However, they also affect trade. Instability is not good for any business and can restrict and curtail business development. Even in Northern Ireland, it proved difficult to reach the full potential for inward investment due to the troubles. This also affects tariff and other barriers. The EU has argued for the abolition of duty on imports from the poorest countries to aid development and wishes to see the elimination of very high tariffs on industrial products that may benefit developing countries (Williams, 1999a). However, such moves will not extend so easily into agricultural products if they conflict with EU farming interests.

Political and legal factors

Some countries are more politically stable than others. In some a change in government makes little difference to commercial life, but in others the changes can be dramatic. The last thing an organisation needs is to invest in setting up a manufacturing plant in a country with a liberal regime, only to have it 'confiscated' by a subsequent hardline government with a hostile attitude to foreign ownership of assets. This is an extreme case, although it must be said that some governments do restrict foreign ownership. This might mean, for example, that the foreign manufacturer has to enter into a joint venture with a local company, with the local company retaining 51 per cent ownership of the joint enterprise.

Political problems do not always arise from specific conditions in the foreign market itself. Individuals and groups in the domestic market might have strong views about trade with certain countries and regimes, as mentioned earlier in relation to South Africa. Action taken by trading blocs and governments working together also has a profound influence. In spring 1996, for example, there was a worldwide ban on the sale of British beef and beef products in response to the 'mad cow disease' crisis that completely devastated a major UK export industry. Although the ban has been lifted, it cost the UK £1.5bn in lost export sales and there are no guarantees that meat exporters will win back lost markets. Initially the marketing is to be focused on Belgium and the Netherlands, with the emphasis on premium lines such as Aberdeen Angus (Smith, 1999).

Organisations thinking about setting up a manufacturing plant in a foreign country are going to have to look not only at ownership restrictions, but also, for example, at employment law, health and safety regulations, financial law and patent protection relevant to that market. Any organisation wanting to sell or market a product will also need to know about advertising, sales promotion and direct marketing constraints, pricing regulations, contract law and consumer protection legislation.

Example Coca-Cola dominates the European market for carbonated soft drinks. It has become so strong that it considers its greatest competitor to be tap water! This has attracted the interest of the EU regulators concerned over the marketing practices in member states. 'Good marketing' – in terms of bringing the product close to the consumer in chilled cabinets, top positioning in supermarkets and in drinks dispensers, often to the exclusion of competitors – is disliked by the regulators, who see it as abuse of a dominant position. Despite Coca-Cola's assurances that practices such as loyalty bonuses and rebates would be discontinued, Pepsi Co has made allegations that exclusivity clauses are still being used in Italy (Willman and Blitz, 1999).

Market selection

Once the marketing environment is understood, the organisation needs to look at it in their own context. This means matching the opportunities and threats emerging from the marketing environment with the organisation's own strengths, weaknesses, assets, skills and aspirations.

Example When Toad, a car audio and alarm group, decided to develop the continental European market, it had to select a market in which car radio theft was high and in which it could soon gain a foothold. It chose France in general and Paris in particular as a prime market because of the large number of car parks in the city. The greater the number of car parks, the greater the chances of car crime, especially radio theft. Another attraction was Toad's UK alliance with Autoglass that could also transfer to France, given Autoglass's 26 per cent share of the French replacement car window market. These two factors dominated the market selection decision (Malkani, 1999).

Some of the issues associated with market selection that might be considered are shown in Fig. 23.3 and discussed below.

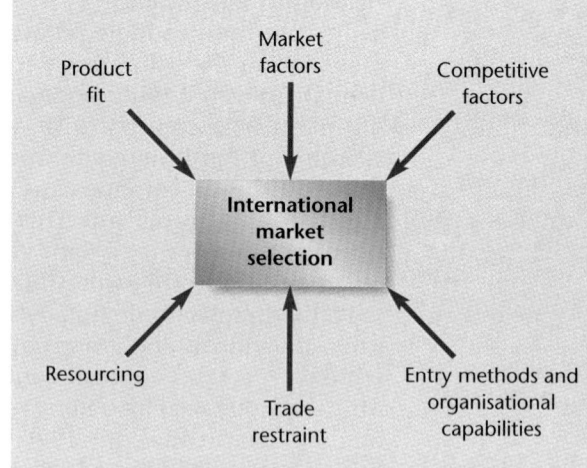

FIGURE 23.3

Factors influencing international market selection

Product fit factors

Is there a gap in the market for our product? Is there demand for our sort of product? Would we have to adapt the product to suit local conditions and, if so, how much?

Market factors

Is it a completely undeveloped market, is it still in its growth stage, or has it reached maturity? Is there sufficient potential future demand to warrant our long-term commitment to this market? Are there established distribution channels we can use or would we have to invest in creating them? How long are the distribution channels and how sophisticated is their infrastructure?

Competitive factors

Who are the existing competitors in this market and how well established are they? How intense and how aggressive is the competition? To what extent have existing competitors obtained control over distribution channels? How likely are competitors to react aggressively to our entry into the market and what barriers to entry can they raise?

Entry factors

What market entry methods are feasible for this market, and how much would each cost us? Do we have any established contacts in this market who could help us? What marketing costs are going to be incurred in getting established in this market and developing a market share? How similar is the culture in this market to our own, and how well do we understand any differences? Is this going to cause us problems in entering the market?

Resourcing factors

What are we going to have to invest in entering this market? Are we going to have to recruit local staff and/or relocate our own staff? Are we going to have to train staff in languages, export procedures, business culture etc.?

Trade restraint factors

What legal and regulatory factors will influence our operation in this market? Do we have to manufacture to different quality or safety standards? Can we use advertising and sales promotion as we would wish? Are there import tariffs or quotas that apply to us? Will we be allowed to repatriate any/all our profits (i.e. take money out of the

> **Example** The US government has threatened, demanded, exhorted and nagged the Japanese over the size of the trade gap between the two nations ($4bn), yet the deficit has continued to climb (Dunne and Nakamoto, 1999). It is a situation that concerns manufacturers in both nations and constrains the potential for a would-be exporter. Bilateral pacts have been developed in such areas as construction, computers and paper products. However, the impact has been negligible. In construction, US firms have won just a 1 per cent share of public contracts; in computing foreign market share has actually fallen, and in paper products the 1 per cent import penetration is the smallest in the industrialised world. The automotive sector has a $33mn deficit in Japan's favour. The problem is not so much the trade regulations as business practices in a highly cartel-based business culture. Often, Japanese distributors and retailers fear selling competitive foreign products as it may affect relationships with their main Japanese suppliers.

MARKETING IN ACTION   China and the WTO

The WTO (World Trade Organisation) is an international body that implements and monitors the trade agreements and conventions negotiated and agreed between its members. China is the largest trading nation still outside the WTO and it has been trying to get in for 13 years. The progress of China's negotiations with the WTO and its members depends, of course, on the wider political climate between them as well as on trade issues. NATO's bombing of the Chinese embassy in Belgrade during the Kosovo conflict, for instance, meant that talks were suspended by the Chinese. In economic terms, however politically desirable it may be to see China join the WTO, its entry cannot be seen to be too easy. Not only would it upset developing countries that are competing with China, it would also send the wrong messages to other countries with weak economies that are knocking on the WTO's door, such as Russia. It thus has to negotiate and meet conditions for entry relating to economic and trade reforms. As Fidler (1998) points out, however, the longer China's entry is delayed, the higher the barriers to entry will get as existing members incorporate new agreements into the WTO system.

To help its application, which it needs to boost falling foreign investment, the WTO is considering further trade liberalisation measures in financial services, retail, telecommunications and agriculture. It also reduced import tariffs on over 1000 products and was considering 300 more. It has promised to reduce average tariffs to about 10 per cent from an average of 17 per cent, although they are much higher on some goods. Cutting tariffs on cars from 80 to 60 per cent would still not be enough for the USA and EU, which want to see average tariffs of about 8 per cent.

Reductions in tariffs would certainly have a direct effect on foreign firms trading with China, but the whole issue of WTO membership is also important as a means of making business with China more secure in the longer term. One of the areas in which a reduction in tariffs is still being considered, for example, is civil aircraft. US aviation company Boeing has been trading with China for nearly 30 years and 68 per cent of the large passenger jets operated by Chinese airlines are Boeing aircraft. The market is far from saturated: it is predicted that a further 1800 jets will be needed within the next 20 years. Politics is important to companies like Boeing that want long-term trade with China. For Boeing in China, this is not only because all the major Chinese airlines are state owned and aircraft orders have to have government approval, but also because it is in Boeing's interests to ensure that investment is made in the long-term development of Chinese aviation. If US government was to favour Sino–US trade by awarding China 'Most Favoured Nation' (MFN) status, it would make it a lot easier to do business, as would China's WTO membership. Boeing is lobbying for both these things.

As China progresses towards WTO membership and continues to reform its economy, becoming less protectionist and more liberal in terms of trade, it will also become a much more attractive market for foreign investors and traders. Trade volumes between China and the USA, for example, have grown rapidly and are now 35 times bigger than in 1980. The USA is China's second biggest trading partner and China is the USA's fourth largest partner. US companies have invested over $45bn in projects in China, while Chinese companies have invested over $700mn in the USA. Nevertheless, there is still plenty more trade potential that WTO membership could help to exploit to the benefit of all parties.

Sources: Fidler (1998); Kynge and de Jonquières (1999); Robinson, G. (1999); Walker and Fidler (1999); Wei (1999); Yu'an (1999).

China believes that it has a lot more to offer than just tourism.

country)? Are there any constraints on foreign companies operating in this market, for example a ban on foreign ownership of companies?

Throughout the whole process, there is a need for sound market intelligence and information. It is very difficult to undertake detailed research on 180 sovereign states, hence the need for a scan to reduce the shortlist to two or three serious contenders. The screening process will become more detailed as options are eliminated. Early screening will soon reveal the options that are unattractive because of clearly unfavourable environmental forces. Desk research alone can show up markets with low potential, leaving a much smaller number for more detailed investigation. In reality, however, market screening can be random, driven as much by enquiries or knowledge gained through media and personal networks as by systematic research. At some point, however, it is likely that a visit will have to be made to a potential market to see at first hand how it operates and to make preliminary contacts.

MARKET ENTRY METHODS

Once an organisation has decided which are the best markets to enter, it must then decide how to enter. The choice of **market entry method** depends on a number of factors. Paliwoda (1993) cites six main factors, as summarised in Fig. 23.4. They are briefly outlined here, but will be further considered as each entry method is discussed later in this section.

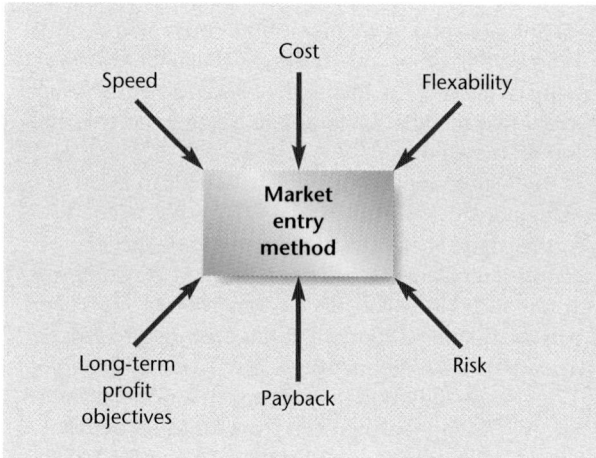

1 *Speed*: how quickly does the organisation want to get into the market? Some market entry methods might take many months or even years to plan and implement, whereas others can be put into action almost immediately.
2 *Costs*: how much is it going to cost to enter the market by each method? Do the benefits derived from using one method rather than another justify its higher cost?
3 *Flexibility*: how much flexibility does the organisation want to retain? Some entry methods allow the organisation to leave the market or expand further relatively easily. Others require long-term contractual agreements or long-term financial commitments that could restrict the organisation's future options.
4 *Risk factors*: these are wide ranging, covering all aspects of the marketing environment, but particularly competitive and political risks. Again, some entry methods can help to reduce certain types of risk. Long-term investment in a manufacturing plant in a foreign country, for example, not only helps to overcome import quotas and duties, but also might be viewed more kindly by the government.
5 *Payback period*: there might be pressure from within the organisation to produce a quick return on any investment in a foreign market. If this is the case, acquiring an established manufacturer might be a more appealing option than building a new factory from nothing, if it means that revenues can be generated within one year rather than five years.
6 *Long-term profit objectives*: the organisation has to look ahead to what it wants to achieve in the future and how it can best exploit the opportunities available in the foreign market. The choice of market entry strategy is just the first stage in a longer-term strategic plan for that market.

FIGURE 23.4

Factors influencing the choice of market entry method

Of course, much also depends on the nature of the product itself and its market. Some services lend themselves naturally to international franchising, while mass production can make it cost effective to manufacture abroad. As discussed in Chapter 2, Japanese car manufacturers have established manufacturing plants within the EU to overcome import quotas and to delete the costs of shipping finished goods half-way across the world.

The range of market entry methods from which the organisation can choose is wide and varied, as can be seen in Fig. 23.5. When looking at this figure, remember that the definition of *customer* needs to be flexible. In some cases, it might mean an individual consumer or end user, in others it might be a wholesaler or retailer within a longer distribution channel, but in others it might be a manufacturer who is buying in components or raw materials.

The classification of market entry methods is not easy, as there are many relevant criteria, such as the level and type of investment involved and whether it is indirect or direct; whether the goods or services are manufactured or produced at home or abroad; whether the exporter deals directly or indirectly with the buyer, or whether the transaction involves exporting goods and services, knowledge and expertise or investment. For further exploration of these issues *see*, for example, Brooke (1992), Young *et al.* (1989), or Paliwoda (1993). The groupings presented in Fig. 23.5 are largely based on Brooke (1992) and will now be discussed in turn.

Trade in goods and services

There are two main methods of trading in goods and services: **direct export** and **indirect export**.

Direct export
Direct exporting means that the organisation produces the product at home and then sells to the foreign customer without the use of an intermediary. The seller thus has to take responsibility for finding customers, negotiating with them, processing their orders and arranging shipment and after sales service.

FIGURE 23.5

Market entry methods

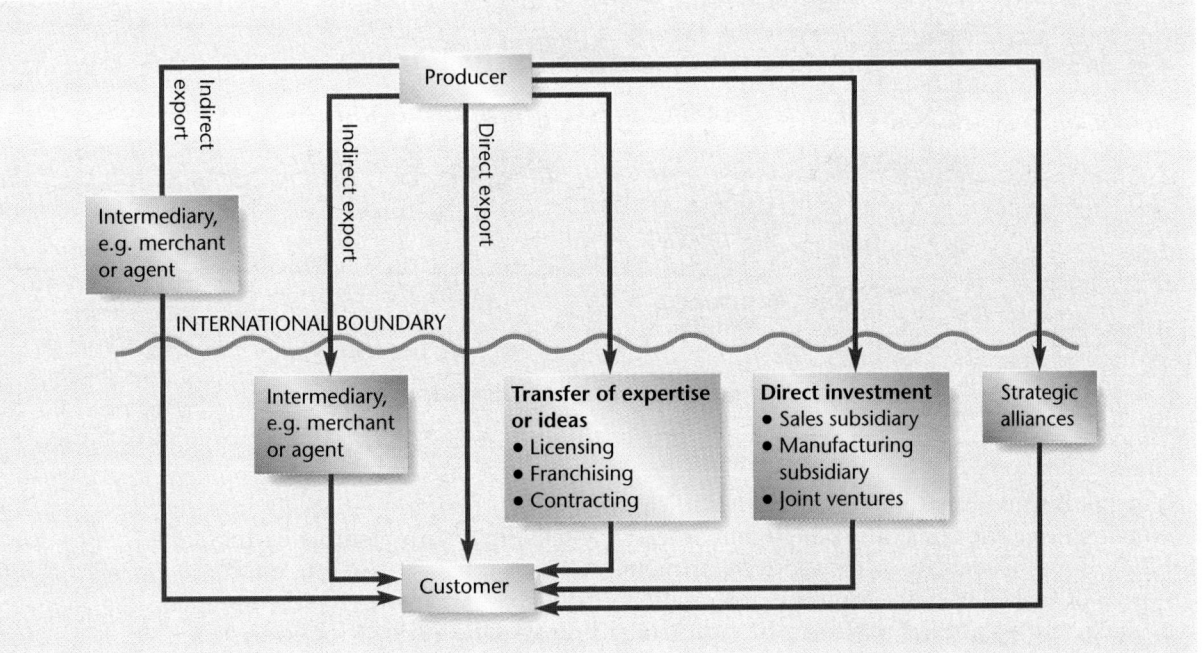

Example Boss, part of the Jungheinrich group, manufactures lift trucks for international markets. In order to benefit from economies of scale in production, it manufactures at a small number of sites and then ships the trucks on an export basis. It has found that with containerisation and improved transport efficiency, typical transport cost as a percentage of sales vary between just 3 and 6 per cent. To support the direct sales, it has established a network of sales and service points to handle negotiations, local spare parts, after sales service, technical advice, training and to build closer relationships with customers.

The Boss Group Limited has used a variety of market entry methods in order to develop its global sales.

Source: Boss Group Limited.

Clearly, this involves some investment and can represent a big step, especially for the smaller firm. The costs can be high, but at least the seller maintains complete control by selling through its own export department and sales force. The selling effort can be co-ordinated and run from the organisation's home base with sales representatives making trips abroad, or it can be run from a branch sales office located in a foreign country. It depends on the organisation's objectives and the volume of business it expects to handle. Ultimately, the organisation might decide to set up a sales subsidiary, which will be considered at p. 1023.

> **Example** It was a matter for celebration when the Eurofighter consortium won its first export order from Greece (*see* p. 140). The order was for 80 Typhoons to the value of £2.8bn to be supplied when the fighter becomes available in 2005, but after consortium members' orders have been filled. Despite competition from the F-16 made by Lockheed Martin, the Mirage, the Sukhoi and a plane from Israel, the Greek government chose the Typhoon, although there was a suggestion that the Greek aerospace company Hellenic Aerospace Industry saw the order as a means of gaining a direct share of the production (Lorenz, 1999). Such complexity is not untypical in the exporting of large-scale industrial products. To win some export orders, it is necessary to offer a consortium approach consisting of partners with different expertise and resources. In order to win a $100mn contract for the development of the port of Abidjan on the Ivory coast, TCI, a small technology group, formed a group containing Standard Bank, Christiani and Nielsen and OT Africa along with a shipping company. The expertise offered by TCI was in specialist telecommunications equipment, while the other partners offered finance and construction capabilities (Cane, 1999).

As well as providing control over the selling process, direct exporting also has the advantage of building a clear presence in the market. It creates contacts and helps to develop stronger buyer–seller relationships, which might be an important factor for buyers looking for committed suppliers.

Indirect export

Indirect exporting takes place where an organisation produces goods at home and then sells them through an intermediary and thus indirectly to the foreign buyer. The intermediary could be based either in the seller's home country or in the foreign market (although technically this is classed as direct exporting) and could be acting on behalf of the seller, on behalf of the buyer or totally independently. An export agent, for example, acts on behalf of the seller, undertaking to sell on a commission basis into a particular market. A confirming house or a buying house, on the other hand, acts on behalf of foreign buyers and earns commission from them. An export merchant is effectively a wholesaler who buys goods outright from a number of manufacturers and then resells them, perhaps to foreign retailers at a profit. Whether the intermediary is a merchant or an agent, the exporting manufacturer benefits from the intermediary's knowledge of the foreign market concerned, their contacts within the distribution channel, and their experience of how business is done in that country. Similarly, the foreign buyer using a buying agent is also benefiting from the intermediary's knowledge and contacts in the export market.

> **Example** Trustin Unimerchants is importing genuine Mexican foods under the brand name La Sierra. It sourced a range of Mexican products from factories in Mexico that were only too pleased to work with an intermediary to open up a new market for them. Such delights as *Salas taquera molcajete*, tender cactus, jalapeño peppers and tortilla soup were identified by Trustin Unimerchants as having potential in the UK by offering ethnic as opposed to TexMex foods. It, in turn, sells on to supermarkets and the grocery trade (*The Grocer*, 1999c).
>
> Brand Marketing International (BMI) is a food broker in the barbecue, ethnic food, savoury snacks and long-life speciality bread categories. Its speciality is the barbecue market, a fast-growing UK sector. It has sourced from a number of overseas suppliers such as Stubbs Legendary Kitchen from Texas, Africa Braai from South Africa and Great Aussie BBQ from Australia. The portfolio developed is enhanced by a partnership with the exporters designed to create and modify brands to find stronger market niches rather than a straight buy-and-sell approach (*Brand Marketing International*, 1999).

Because of the reliance on the expertise of an intermediary, indirect exporting is an ideal starting point for a small business entering the international arena. It also carries little risk and little commitment because there is no investment in market development. It can, therefore, be a useful method if the organisation is dealing in small volumes or is somewhat uncertain, either about its own future or whether the product is appropriate for an international market.

Trade in knowledge and expertise

So far, the methods discussed have involved the transfer of goods or services from a domestic producer to a foreign customer. Here, however, we look at the transfer of ideas, concepts and processes, a transfer that is usually carried out so that goods and services can be produced abroad by foreign producers. This gives the originating organisation the benefit of selling a product with a 'made in ...' label that shows that it was produced in the country in which it is being sold rather than being overtly a 'foreign' product.

The main methods to be covered here are licensing, franchising and contracting.

Licensing

Licensing can be an attractive option for entering international markets. The licensor grants a licensee the right to manufacture a product, use patents, use particular processes or exploit trade marks in a defined market in return for a royalty payment. Franchising applications of licence agreements are considered separately.

In manufacturing, **licensing** is useful for markets that are very remote or not worth the costs of direct involvement. The domestic manufacturer might be producing up to full capacity in its own plants and might not want to invest in new facilities or to divert capacity for a particular foreign market. Licensing helps to overcome high import tariffs, but also avoids the costs and commitment of direct investment. The licensor does, however, need to be sure that the licensee can handle the necessary production and marketing, otherwise a gap might be left for competition.

Licensing can be a particularly effective way of achieving technology transfer, that is, the movement of technological advance to new nations.

> **Example** Love it or hate it, Spam (http://www.spam.com) is big business. Tulip International gained the UK licence for producing Spam, a product that sells £88mn in the USA, £129mn worldwide and £7mn in the UK. The licensor, Hormel Foods in the USA, wanted to work with a licensee that would seek to move the brand away from a speciality, almost nostalgic position, more into the mainstream. Tulip decided to commit £150 000 supporting the brand, showing how versatile the product actually is to a nation reared on Spam fritters rather than Spicy Spam kebabs and stuffed peppers. Changing perceptions will not be easy in a canned meat market that declined by 9 per cent in 1997 (*The Grocer*, 1999m).

Licensing can thus be viewed favourably by foreign governments, as it brings in new technology and helps in the training and skilling of the local work force. Licensing can also be useful in some specific industrial sectors, such as defence, as a means of winning government contracts.

The financial risk of licensing could be relatively low, as the licensee is the one who will be investing in plant, machinery and marketing. There could, however, be risks to the licensor's reputation if the licensee degrades or abuses the licensor's name or intellectual property. There is also a risk that the licensee, having gained experience, might then decide to go it alone at the end of the contract period and turn into a competitor.

A major strength of licensing is that it combines the skills and knowledge of the licensor with the local contacts and experience of the licensee. Its success, however, is very dependent on whether production quality and marketing effectiveness can be created and sustained. Like any distribution decision, the choice of licensing as an entry strategy is based on a trade-off between the increased coverage and lower risk gained, and the potentially reduced financial returns because of the high level of involvement of the licensee.

Franchising

The previous chapter looked at the impact of franchising across Europe and the development of some large international franchisors such as KFC, Subway and Domino's Pizza. Some franchisors, such as McDonald's in the UK, have grown through direct involvement between the franchisor and its franchisees. Sometimes, however, indirect methods are adopted that involve a sharing of know-how, resources and marketing effort. McDonald's, for example, preferred to use a joint venture to enter the Russian market because of the alien and relatively unknown nature of the marketing and operating environment. By far the most popular indirect method, however, is the **master franchising** system.

Master franchising. Master franchising means that an individual or organisation in a country is given an exclusive right to develop the franchising system. The master franchisee can then develop a network of sub-franchises on a regional, multiple or individual unit basis. The master franchisee might receive extensive training from the franchisor, not only in operating a unit, but also in franchisee recruitment, staff training and managing a franchised system. It is then the master franchisee's responsibility to use local knowledge and contacts to develop the network in a manner that is satisfactory to the franchisor. The master franchisee earns a percentage of the fees or royalties paid by individual franchisees.

> **Example** Specialising in improving air quality and water damage restoration, BMS Technologies (http://www.steamatic.com) from the USA uses master franchises in 20 countries to develop its markets. In Portugal, the master franchisee is responsible for developing the national market, appointing individual franchisees or directly owned branches as appropriate. BMS concentrates its expertise in field support, training and continued research and development rather than being concerned with detailed operation (*Franchise Magazine*, 1999).

Area development agreement. The franchisor might not want to appoint a single master franchisee to cover a whole country. After all, this does put a great deal of power into the master franchisee's hands, and if the master franchisee fails to fulfil their part of the agreement or to maintain high standards among the sub-franchisees, the franchisor stands to lose both reputation and the competitive initiative in that country. The franchisor might, therefore, prefer to enter into *area development agreements* in which several master franchisees are appointed, each with responsibility for a clearly defined regional territory. The agreement might also specify that a certain number of outlets are expected to be opened over a defined period of time in return for the exclusive territory. This approach has all the benefits of the master franchisee system, in terms of reducing the network development costs, the time taken to develop a new market and exploiting the local knowledge of the master franchisees, while reducing the potential losses from a poor master franchisee.

> **Example** Subway uses development agents in new countries to open up the market. These agents are contracted to find an agreed number of franchisees, either through master franchise arrangements or direct to individual franchisees. They use their local knowledge to assist with site selection, site negotiation, setting up the operation, training and on-going operations. In return, they receive a percentage of the start-up franchise fee and a percentage of the company royalty from that area.

Contracting

A manufacturing contract means that the manufacturer contracts with a company in the foreign market to produce or assemble the product on their behalf. This saves the time and costs involved in physically transporting the finished product from abroad. This allows a more flexible approach for entering markets where inter-national logistics costs might otherwise reduce effectiveness and margins. Like licensing, **contracting** also avoids the problems of currency fluctuations and import barriers, but potentially creates a new competitor. Nevertheless, contracting can be particularly useful if the volume of business in the foreign market is too much for direct importation of goods, but not sufficient to warrant direct investment in production facilities. As Gilligan and Hird (1986) make clear, contracting also allows the contractor to retain control over marketing and distribution, unlike licensing.

Management contracts are widely used in service markets, such as hotels. An independent enterprise contracts to operate all the management functions in return for a fee, and occasionally for a share in the profits. The company awarded the contract has responsibility for operational matters such as human resource management, financial control, marketing and service delivery, but does not normally get involved in strategic or policy issues, nor does it have any share in the ownership of the business.

Example Hilton Hotels (http://www.hilton.com) operates over 400 hotels worldwide in 50 countries. It has a combination of directly owned, franchised and management contract-run hotels. In the latter case, it has no equity stake, but uses its management expertise and knowledge at a local level. For example, it entered into a contract with London and Regional properties to manage the 163-bed luxury Hilton London Green Park Hotel. The various arrangements enable the Hilton to do what it does best, operating and marketing hotels, without the risks and problems associated with building and capital investment. However, franchise operations are the most popular operating method, with 74 per cent of the sites and over 50 per cent of the rooms operated under franchise agreements.

The careful use of management contracts can help the 'exporter' to increase market coverage and to develop international segments more quickly.

Investment

This group of entry methods involves a major commitment for the organisation because it involves some level of investment in the foreign market. As mentioned earlier, this might mean simply setting up a sales subsidiary to market and distribute goods imported from the home country, or it might mean acquiring a local company or setting up a new manufacturing facility to produce goods closer to the market, thus avoiding international logistics costs and import barriers. Whatever the type of investment, it certainly helps the organisation to create a presence in the market and to build much closer relationships with customers.

Example The UK has been highly successful in attracting inward-bound investment. It has 23 per cent of all inward investment made in the EU, including 40 per cent of Japanese and US investments in the EU (Groom, 1999). This makes the UK the leading investment destination in Europe. In 1997, over half the inward investment projects in the UK were from the USA, with Japan, Germany and France accounting for under one-fifth of the total between them. These figures reflect the ease with which US companies can work in the UK, with fewer language and cultural barriers.

Because investment is such a big decision, there are a number of specific issues to be taken into account. These are summarised in Fig. 23.6, based on Walsh (1993), and cover the whole range of operational and marketing environmental factors.

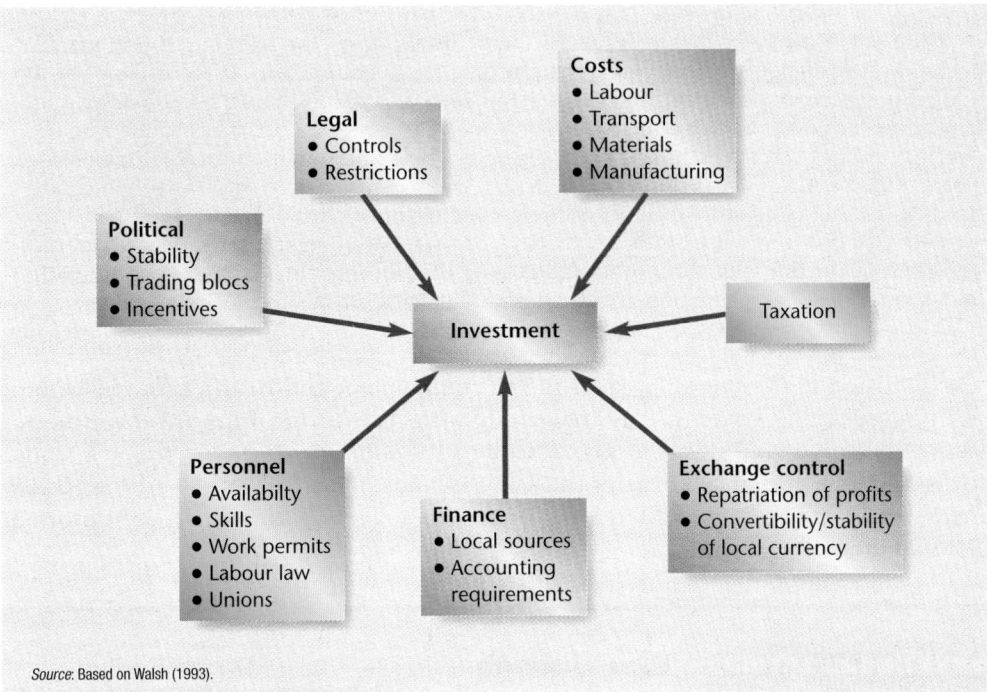

Source: Based on Walsh (1993).

Within this section, three particular forms of investment are considered: **sales sub-sidiaries**, **manufacturing subsidiaries** and **joint ventures**.

Sales subsidiaries

Sales subsidiaries play no part in manufacturing the product, but do take responsibility for marketing, selling and distributing it. They might also get involved in after sales service. Sales subsidiaries can be specially created or they can be developed from an existing acquired company. Staff, therefore, can either be transferred from the parent organisation or recruited locally. With local staff, the organisation acquires local contacts and knowledge, but might have to give product and management training. With transferred staff, the product and management knowledge might well be in place, but local knowledge will have to be developed.

The advantage of selling through sales subsidiaries rather than through the domestic sales force lies in the dedicated local knowledge and expertise that builds up and the closeness to the customer. Also, in the event of failure in that market, any losses can be confined to the subsidiary rather than having an extensive impact on the parent company.

Manufacturing subsidiaries

The establishment of manufacturing subsidiaries involves assembling or manufacturing the product in local markets. Again, such an operation can be set up from scratch or developed from an acquisition. It becomes an integral part of the manufacturing base of the host country, and can thus become a significant contributor to the local economy.

> **Example** JCB, a UK construction equipment company, is at the first stage of direct overseas investment. It derives 70 per cent of its sales from exports, for which the USA is a prime market. In an attempt to compete better with large US competitors such as Caterpillar and Case, it decided to open its first non-UK plant in Savannah, Georgia, that could build machines appropriate for the US market (Marsh, 1999b). This could be a sound move, as the US now accounts for 24 per cent of the company's output, ahead of domestic sales. European sales will, however, still be satisfied on an export basis from the UK (Marsh, 1999c).

The Belgian steel wire maker Bekaert is much further down the road in creating manufacturing subsidiaries, some of which are run on a joint venture basis. It has established a global presence in a series of specialist niches such as making the wire for champagne corks, in which it has 80 per cent of the global market. Other product lines include wire for fencing, bridges and filters. It has been developing the South American market for over 40 years through taking a stake in existing or new steel wire producers in most of the countries. As a result of creating over 20 of these manufacturing subsidiaries, Bekaert has now gained a 40 per cent share of the South American steel wire market. New ideas are transferred from the European and other markets so that local businesses can keep up with industry standards and continue to outperform other local competitors (Marsh, 1999a).

As discussed in Chapter 2, because of the employment and wealth creation potential involved, many governments are keen to attract this sort of inward investment, offering incentives and grants to manufacturers to set up plants in key regions. Many of these manufacturing subsidiaries themselves export their goods to nearby markets. Japanese cars, for example Nissan and Toyota, manufactured in the UK are exported to other European countries.

MARKETING IN ACTION   War games

In early 1999, British Aerospace (BAe, http://www.bae.com) made a £6.9bn bid for the Marconi defence division of GEC. This acquisition was designed to strengthen BAe's portfolio of both civil and defence products and thus increase its importance in international markets. BAe already had substantial interests in both military and civil aircraft through its partnerships in the Eurofighter project (see p. 140) and in Airbus Industrie. Marconi brings international expertise in bulk ammunition and missiles, electronics (radar, infra-red systems, avionics etc.) and military ships and submarine building. Although both Marconi and BAe are UK companies, BAe also has international interests through joint ventures, partnerships and shareholdings, strengthening its presence not only in aircraft, but in satellite technology, electronics missiles and sonar. If the BAe–Marconi deal is approved, it would put BAe third in the world in the defence market in terms of sales behind Lockheed Martin and Boeing. The deal would create Britain's largest manufacturing company.

Source: British Aerospace Photo Library 1999.

In political terms, the acquisition is seen as desirable by industry analysts in the UK. European governments have long been worried about US dominance, especially in such a sensitive area as defence, and wanted a European challenger both to serve European needs better and to compete in world markets. The overall philosophy in the European market has been that consolidation is desirable to compete with the USA. If smaller European companies could merge into a bigger one, it would improve international competitiveness and reduce the risk of their being taken over by US companies. Across Europe, both the industry and governments recognised the logic of this. Other European companies and analysts are less sure about the deal than their UK counterparts, however, because it is a British–British alliance. BAe had been in talks with DASA (DaimlerChrysler Aerospace) in Germany, but the Marconi deal eclipsed this. Politically, the deal is somewhat embarrassing for the UK government, which had supported the concept of European integration but had assumed that the first stage would be a deal with DASA. The 'new' BAe will now be far bigger than any of the other European companies and makes any future mergers less likely to be partnerships of equals. Other major European companies such as DASA, Aérospatiale and Thomson-CSF feel that they have been sidelined because of the deal. Will they wait and see what the outcome of the competition authorities' scrutiny is and then continue to seek consolidation with BAe? Alternatively, will they consolidate between them without BAe or will they start looking for deals with US companies?

Source: Colver (1999); Financial Times (1999a); Nicoll (1999a, 1999b).

Joint ventures

A joint venture is set up when two organisations come together to create a jointly owned third company. The two parents share the ownership, control and profits, as well as the risks. There are many reasons for taking this route. The partners might feel that separately they do not have the necessary resources (whether financial, physical or managerial) to develop or make an impact on a market. This motivation could be especially important if they are up against larger, more powerful competitors. The partners are likely to have complementary assets or skills. One might have cash, the other know-how; one might have technical expertise, the other might be an ailing manufacturing plant at the geographic heart of the market; one might have marketing and distribution skills, the other an unexploited product idea. A joint venture might be the only choice if an organisation wants to enter a country whose government is hostile to foreign companies having 100 per cent ownership of any aspect of production (whether physical assets or know-how).

Example Fiat has taken a more cautious approach in Russia. A planned $840mn investment with the Gaz Auto Company at Nizhny Novgorod has been phased over five years, but if successful will see 150 000 Marea, Siena and Palio 'world cars' produced on a greenfield site next to the Gaz plant, famous for its Volga saloon. Fiat's stake covers know-how, machine tools and equipment. Gaz will be concerned with land, labour and distribution. Fiat aims to have a long-term presence in Russia, but must plan carefully in the short term given the continued economic crises (Robinson, A., 1999).

Joint ventures have been an important force in the privatisation and regeneration of the industries of central and eastern European countries. Western companies have been encouraged to invest cash and managerial skills in joint ventures with local companies that provide production facilities that can be updated, labour that can be retrained and access to the market. The partners work together to develop products and markets and share the benefits. Not all joint ventures run smoothly, however.

Example China has proved to be a tough market for Unilever. It trails not only its US rival Procter & Gamble (P&G), but also a number of local Chinese competitors. Whitecat, a local company, is for example the leading washing powder company and P&G dominates the shampoo market. Unilever's relatively poor showing has been attributed to poor distribution and inefficient joint ventures. Many of the joint venture companies are partly state owned and they also require considerable investment. Often management, marketing and distribution functions overlap, resulting in cost inefficiencies and slow decision making. Because of the difficulty in attracting a significant market share in some sectors, Unilever has mothballed one of its Shanghai companies making detergents and has pulled out of the Omo detergent factory in Zhangjikou near Beijing. As part of a renewal strategy, Unilever plans to replace the joint ventures with a joint stock company embracing the Chinese partners but with Unilever having the dominant share. This will enable more centralisation of marketing and distribution as well as helping to eliminate inefficiencies. The plan will require approval from the Ministry of Foreign Trade and Economic Co-operation in Beijing (Harding, 1999a).

This example shows just how exposed to risk the organisation is when entering a market with such a level of commitment. Political, legal and economic issues all add to the normal commercial and marketing problems of operating in relatively unknown environments. Opportunities that seem attractive on the surface could prove to be far more difficult to exploit in practice. Commitments made by local partners or even governments have to be honoured. Although access to an otherwise difficult or prohibited market may be gained, distribution and competitive structures could mitigate against rapid change. Benefits are rarely realisable in the short term and those organisations looking for quick success are often frustrated and can become disillusioned.

> **Example** In the Ukraine, a link between Daewoo and Avtozaz, the makers of the popular Tavria model, went badly wrong. The venture planned to bring to the Ukraine semi-knocked-down kits for the home market and for export to Russia. Demand in both markets has collapsed. Even with the cheapest Daewoo at $8200, it is too expensive for most Ukrainians. The unfashionable Tavria became increasingly difficult to sell with its 'Lada-like reputation', despite an injection of ideas from Daewoo. Second, the Ukrainian government's promise to ban the import of used cars over five years old and to impose a $5000 customs value on younger imports was not workable in practice. Both factors have now raised considerable doubt as to whether in the short term the venture will return any profit (Sych, 1999).

Nevertheless, joint ventures can be very successful, as long as both partners plan the venture carefully and are clear about their objectives. They also need good communication and mutual understanding of what each party is bringing to the venture, what each one's responsibilities are within it and what each expects to get out of it. Figure 23.7 suggests a number of factors that might contribute towards a more successful joint venture partnership.

Strategic alliances

The term **strategic alliance** is wide ranging, covering any kind of collaborative agreement or activity between two or more organisations. It can include joint ventures, but not all strategic alliances have to be joint ventures. Whereas a joint venture specifically means creating a separate, jointly owned entity, a strategic alliance can be much looser and informal. It could be two companies joining R&D forces to develop a specific product for a specific market, or agreeing to share a distribution channel, or agreeing to sell each other's products. The benefits from a strategic alliance are similar in principle to those derived from a joint venture, in that it brings together complementary assets and skills creating synergy. Strategic alliances do not, however, necessarily carry the same degree of long-term commitment and risk, as there is no equity stake, just commitment to a specific project or activity.

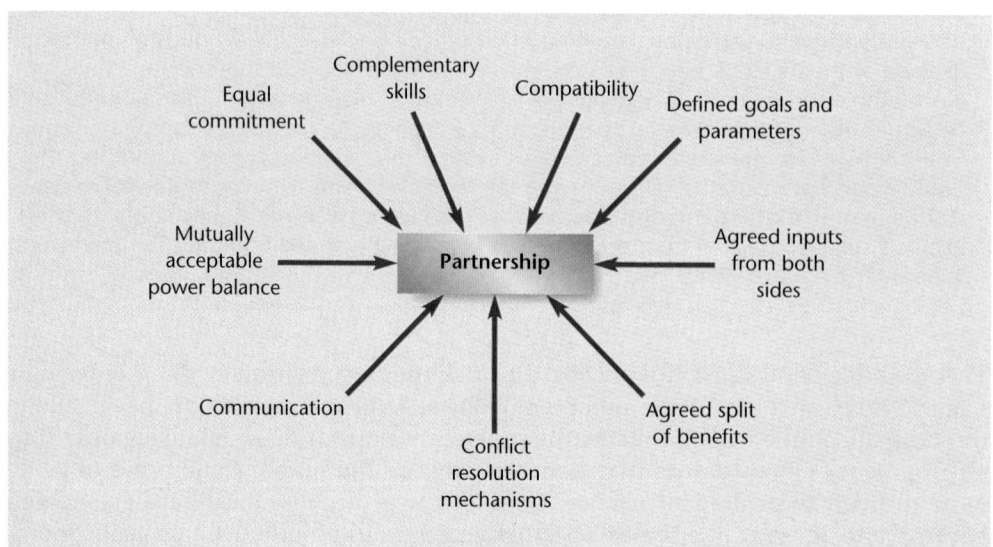

FIGURE 23.7

Factors contributing to a successful joint venture partnership

> **Example** Mattel, a large US-based toy manufacturer whose products include the Barbie doll, and Bandai, the Japanese toy maker of the Tamagotchi virtual pet, formed a global alliance to improve marketing and distribution for both companies. Bandai planned to sell Mattel products including Barbie and Hot Wheels in Japan, a market that often proves tough for foreign competitors. In return, Mattel would promote Power Ranger dolls and other Bandai products in Latin America. An added benefit for Mattel and Bandai would be the access to the growing on-line market in the USA, a trend that Mattel planned to exploit with its own direct ordering website (Nusbaum, 1999).

The number of strategic alliances of all kinds has increased rapidly over the last 10 years or so. As competition has become more aggressive, markets have become more global and technology has increased its rate of change. Alliances are particularly prevalent in fast moving, high technology industries such as defence, communications, pharmaceuticals (all requiring heavy investment in R&D to keep up with the pace of technological change and to deliver necessary innovation) and airlines (under pressure from competition and national protectionism). As Houlder (1995) points out, a strategic alliance can help an organisation to enter new markets, obtain access to expertise and technology and achieve economies of scale much more quickly. She does, however, sound a note of caution, quoting a survey that suggested that only 17 per cent of US managers thought that alliances were effective while 31 per cent thought they were downright dangerous. The risks arise from ill-matched partnerships, poor definition of the alliance's purpose and the mutual responsibilities involved, or poor implementation of the alliance. Figure 23.7 suggests ways of creating more successful joint ventures, but imagine how much damage can be done when one or more of the factors considered there goes wrong, as they often do in practice. Houlder (1995) sums up the real-world problems neatly:

> **There is a dilemma at the heart of alliance-making. Trust, flexibility and commitment are widely seen as the keys to success. But companies dare not blind themselves to the risks involved. Today's ally may be tomorrow's competitor; a joint venture may turn out to be a takeover by the back door. For the growing number of companies engaged in alliances, ambiguity is a fact of life.**

> **Example** Despite the difficulties of establishing strategic alliances, powerful international combinations have the potential to make a significant impact on domestic markets. The alliance between Goodyear and Sumitomo Rubber Industries in Japan is bound to affect EU manufacturers such as Continental in Germany, Pirelli in Italy and Michelin in France. A large, efficient competitor with reduced costs, strong distribution and powerful brands could stimulate further alliances within Europe as a defensive measure. The Goodyear–Sumitomo alliance will establish joint ventures in Europe, Japan and the US, and share global purchasing and tyre technology as part of a rationalisation of operations on a global scale (Griffiths, 1999).

INTERNATIONAL MARKETING STRATEGY

Once an organisation has analysed the characteristics of the target foreign market and has decided how to enter it, the next stage is to design the marketing programme. In principle, this is no different from designing a marketing mix in a domestic market. The organisation has to define and select target segments, position the product and decide whether to modify the marketing mix to suit conditions in the foreign market, whether it is close to home in Europe or elsewhere in the world. Just because a particular marketing mix is successful in the domestic market, however, it cannot necessarily

MARKETING IN ACTION   'No way, BA'

The announcement of a proposed strategic alliance between British Airways (BA) and American Airlines (AA) was a further move in the changing face of competition in the transatlantic passenger market. International alliances are increasingly being used as a means of controlling routes and for developing new business. To competitors, however, the proposed BA–AA alliance was seen as dangerous, as they thought it would create a very powerful airline partnership that could distort fair trade. Ironically, BA had used a similar argument to criticise the Lufthansa–United Airlines alliance that was designed to seek antitrust immunity in the USA.

The BA–AA proposal might, at first glance, appear to be straightforward. All BA and AA flights between the UK and the USA would have co-ordinated schedules that would enable smoother transfers for passengers between the two airlines. By placing joint flight codes on their UK–USA flights, they would also share the revenues generated. It would also mean, however, that around 40 per cent of weekly take-off and landing slots at Heathrow, 60 per cent of the total transatlantic market, and 70 per cent of flights between London and New York would be covered by the agreement. They would also be able to access parts of each other's database for mailing and promotion purposes. This could seriously affect the competitive position of a number of smaller airlines who are excluded from similar deals. Richard Branson, speaking for Virgin Atlantic, claimed that the BA–AA alliance would be bad for the market, because it could lead to reduced competition and higher fares.

Not surprisingly, regulatory bodies on both sides of the Atlantic were very interested in the proposal. What should have been an April 1997 launch for the alliance was postponed as the EU Competition Commissioner deliberated over the implications of the deal and considered what conditions should be imposed if it was to go ahead. BA–AA had always known that they

would be required to give up some slots as part of the deal, but the question was how many. They had offered 196 per week, whereas the EU initially demanded 350. The EU ruling eventually came in July 1998: 267 slots had to be given away free. BA–AA said that this was too many and that they wanted to sell slots for around £2mn each. Some argue that this should be allowed as the slots are a legitimate valuable asset of the airlines, others argue that the slots were given free to the airlines in the first place and if a sale is allowed at all, the proceeds should go to the taxpayer.

The issue has become more complicated because the BA–AA deal has become entangled in the wider debate between the US and UK governments on 'open skies' policies, i.e. allowing each other's airlines to fly freely to each other's airports without restriction. Under the current agreement, only BA and Virgin Atlantic from the UK and AA and United Airlines from the USA are allowed to fly to the USA from Heathrow. US approval for the BA–AA alliance hinges on the governments' resolving the 'open skies' issue, but by July 1999 there was still no agreement about opening Heathrow Airport to more competition. Within the inter-governmental discussions there are still some sticking points, for example whether BA–AA should be allowed to conclude their deal and code share (i.e. transfer passengers between the two airlines freely and jointly set prices) before or after open skies is implemented. There is also some doubt still as to whether the US authorities will give BA–AA antitrust immunity, i.e. allow them to code share without falling foul of antitrust laws. The UK is also demanding more liberalisation within the US domestic market to allow, for instance, UK carriers to operate domestic flights within the USA. As things stand, there is no sign yet that a resolution is in sight either for the open skies agreement or the BA–AA alliance.

Sources: Ashworth (1998); Parsley (1998); Skapinker (1999a, 1999b).

---

be successfully transferred elsewhere. A whole range of factors within the marketing environment, for example culture, customs or competition, might point to the wisdom of adapting some or all of the marketing mix elements.

We now look more closely at the pressures affecting the debate on the merits of the standardisation as compared with adaptation, and later we take a more general view of the implementation of the marketing mix in international contexts.

Standardisation or adaptation

The decision on whether to standardise or to adapt is a major one for any organisation operating in more than one environment. There could be conflicting pressures, some of which push the organisation towards adapting the marketing mix to suit

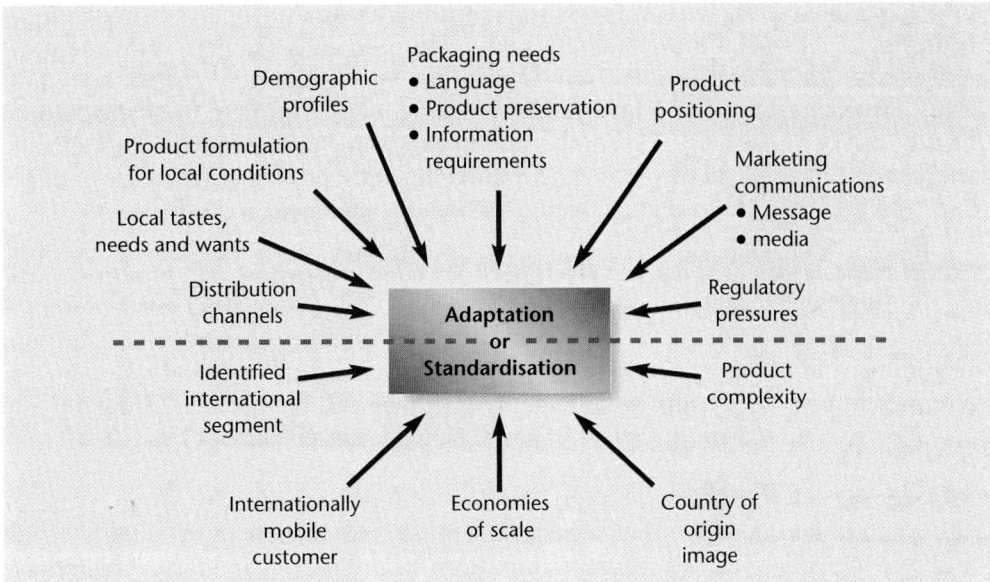

FIGURE 23.8

Factors influencing
the adaptation or
standardisation
decision

local conditions, and some of which push the organisation towards standardisation of the marketing approach, regardless of local market.

There are risks in either approach. If there is too much adaptation, the organisation could fail to exploit the synergies possible from operating in many different markets. Global branding and the transfer of new product ideas across boundaries are all possible with standardisation. In the extreme case of adaptation, each domestic market is treated differently and that can create vulnerability if the product is up against powerful internationally branded competitors (Shay, 1998). If, however, a multinational loses touch with local markets, it can also cause difficulties. Wind (1998) argues that a serious global company should have representatives of different parts of the world in key management positions, be sensitive to different cultures and employ managers that are capable of operating anywhere in the world. We look first at pressures leading towards **adaptation**, which are summarised in Fig. 23.8.

Pressures towards adaptation

Customer needs. Any organisation has to think carefully about customer needs and wants and the extent to which the marketing mix satisfies them. If those needs and wants are different in an international market, then some adaptation might be necessary. A food product, for example, might have to be flavoured differently, be more or less sweet, be more or less salty, be more or less fizzy, contain less fat, have a different smell or be a different colour to meet the preferences and expectations of the local market. Clothing too might have to be adapted for the local market and use different fabrics, different colours, and be produced in different size ranges. In an earlier chapter (*see* p. 183), for example, it was shown how Gossard, the lingerie company, had to vary its product mixes across Europe to cater for different average sizes, different attitudes towards the purpose of lingerie, and different fabric preferences. Benetton produces garments centrally to the same designs for all its worldwide markets in undyed yarns and fabrics. Batches of garments are then dyed on demand to meet the colour requirements of different markets.

Parker (1995) argues that customer needs in markets cannot fully converge because of the physioeconomic framework. Climate, natural resources and other environmental influences all help to shape society and the individual, creating different attitudes and physiological needs. There is an inverse relationship, for example, between the number of calories people eat and the ambient temperature. In colder climates, for example, more alcoholic drink is consumed, which generates a lot of calories to retain body heat (that's our excuse, anyway). These fundamental influences all help to create cultural diversity, but of course may be less important in explaining differences within a climatic zone. Other influences, however, such as natural minerals, proximity to oceans or major rivers, could all then play a part in shaping customer preferences and behaviour.

Practical considerations. It is not just customers' aesthetic preferences that prompt adaptation, but practical considerations as well. The paper used for printing postage stamps has to be adapted depending on the climate of the destination country. This is because the gum used in a temperate climate could not withstand the humidity of some Far Eastern countries. The stamps would simply go gooey and be unusable. Similarly, the paper used to wrap soap in hot climates has to be treated with a mould inhibitor.

Packaging and communication. It might not, of course, be necessary to go as far as redesigning or reformulating the product itself. The focus of adaptation could be brand imagery, packaging or marketing communication, for instance. Brand image might have to be adapted to avoid embarrassing connotations in foreign languages or to create a clearer and stronger positioning statement within the local marketing environment.

Example Cadbury's Yowie is a big hit in Australia. The 52g hollow milk chocolate shapes are based on six Yowie characters and inside there is a toy animal, information on its rarity and a game. When Yowies were launched in the UK, as the toy animals are so central to the product's appeal, consideration was given to replacing the Australian animals with those more relevant to British wildlife. However, consumer research showed that the Australian wildlife had a certain exotic appeal and so they were retained in the collection (Gray, 1999; *The Grocer*, 1999g).

Packaging can also be varied to suit local preferences. SmithKline Beecham was the first company to sell toothpaste without the cardboard carton outer packaging in the German market. This led to an increase in sales and moved the product to a leadership position in the oral healthcare market, especially as it was linked with an environmentally friendly message. In the UK, however, it did not sell so well. Retailers did not like loading the tubes on the shelves and consumer research suggested that the lack of a carton indicated a poorer value perception (Parker, 1996). A similar situation but in reverse has been found in the wine market. Wine cartons are cheaper, lighter, easier to handle and can keep wine more fresh, yet they are not popular in the UK and they are perceived to contain downmarket wine. Tetra Pak has been successful elsewhere in Europe, capturing 7 per cent of the table market wine segment in Germany with its packs and 350 million and 250 million cartons were sold in 1998 in Spain and Italy respectively. In Argentina, 66 per cent of all table wine is sold in cartons, but the British consumer remains unconvinced (*The Grocer*, 1999h).

Packaging design can help to reinforce image, but might also have to be adapted in practical terms for the local language or to give instructions relevant to local usage of the product. Nevertheless, some consumer products do manage to standardise their packaging for a number of international markets, regardless of language. Provided that the same brand name is used, it is possible to print lists of ingredients and basic instructions in several languages.

Marketing communication. All of this is likely to follow through into the adaptation of advertising and other marketing communication activities, again to create something to which the local target audience can better relate, and to differentiate the product more clearly.

> **Example** HSBC Holdings (http://www.hsbc.com) purchased the Midland Bank in the UK in 1992, but retained the familiar high street brand name for a period to reassure customers. Although mention was always made to 'Member of the HSBC Group' and the distinctive HSBC logo was featured, the separate names survived. This applied to other familiar names around the world such as the Hong Kong Bank and Marine Midland Bank. However, HSBC eventually decided to abandon its policy of retaining local names in its global empire, arguing that in a global market with rapid international communication, retaining separate names could reduce the impact of the overall brand. The global campaign to establish HSBC as the umbrella brand was estimated to have cost £30mn, including a £7mn television advertising campaign in the UK. The move from local names to an umbrella brand was considered important to strengthen the competitive position of HSBC and to enable global financial products to be developed (Graham, 1999a).

Marketing communication might also have to be adapted to take account of the different buyer readiness stages of different markets. A product that is mature in the domestic market, and only needs reminder advertising and low key promotional activity, might be unknown in a foreign market and need a promotional mix that is much more geared towards awareness, generating trial and attitude building. Communication might also have to be adapted to the effects of local media availability and consumption habits.

> **Example** When Swedish company Target Games wanted to develop US sales of its refillable candy dispensers, it decided that originality was everything. It developed three brand names with appropriately designed dispensers. The names were Snot!, Fart! and Burpp! and the dispensers were designed with orifices that gave off appropriate sounds (*The Grocer*, 1999b).

Distribution channels. Another practical consideration is the sophistication and structure of distribution channels. An fmcg producer selling into eastern Europe, for example, will not find the same concentration of retailing in hypermarkets and superstores owned by large chains as in western Europe. This means that the producer has to find ways of achieving geographic coverage through thousands of small independent grocers, which could prove to be difficult and expensive, particularly if the wholesale sector is similarly underdeveloped. Logistics might also have to be adapted, if deliveries are being made direct to small stores rather than to a big retailer's regional depots. Also, if it takes longer to get the product into the shops, perhaps because of poor transport infrastructure to outlying areas, then the producer might have to address issues of product freshness. This problem could be compounded if retailers cannot provide appropriate and reliable storage conditions. Shops might not have the capacity to keep food chilled at a safe temperature or might not have sufficient freezer or chiller space to store any significant quantity of goods.

> **Example** In service situations, managers still need to consider how the service will be sold and delivered. Provident Financial, a UK credit company, decided to expand in Poland and the Czech Republic. It replicated its domestic distribution model by using agents, often women, making loans to low-income customers, again mainly women, and then collecting repayments on a weekly basis. The domestic home credit business would be the same in Poznan as in Peterborough, as Provident resisted the temptation to adapt (Graham, 1999b).

Product positioning. Some products might require a high degree of customisation, regardless of where they are sold. In some organisational markets, the supply of engineering components for example, the product and its associated marketing and service mix are designed and tailored for the specific customer. Similarly, large capital projects for bridges, tunnels or major public buildings are unique and have to be designed, managed and implemented according to local conditions and customer requirements. Clearly, in such circumstances, there is little room for standardisation. Linked with the practical need for adaptation, the organisation could develop a deliberate strategy to seek special niches in the market and to position itself as a specialist in tailor-made packages to suit individual customer requirements.

Example When McVitie's acquired French company Biscuiterie Nantaise, it had to decide whether to move any of its brands into other markets. Extensive research was undertaken in the UK to establish whether the children's biscuit brand needed to be adapted to suit local tastes. The large square sandwich biscuit with a smiling face was prominent on the packaging and had a high recall in France, where the brand was very popular. McVitie's concluded that the position of the brand, targeted at children, did not have to be changed and this proposition was far stronger than the issue of a country of origin (Gray, 1999).

Mode of entry to market. It is also possible that the organisation's mode of entry to the market might influence its willingness to adapt. If the product is being manufactured locally, either under licence or through a subsidiary, then it might be easier to design adaptations into the product or the manufacturing process and to allow local marketing managers to adapt the marketing approach to suit local conditions. In an organisation that is more centrally controlled and where more functions, such as R&D and manufacture, are undertaken by the parent organisation, the more likely it is that there would be a standard marketing approach.

Example A Hungarian company has become a success in selling buses to city transport networks across the USA. In order to penetrate the US market, it was necessary to have a manufacturing facility in the USA. The company, North American Bus Industries (NABI), has a plant in Hungary from which bus bodies are shipped to a plant acquired in Anniston, Alabama, for final assembly. By having a US base it is better able to service the market, can become closer to customers and can also overcome some of the regulations and tariff barriers that could otherwise restrict growth (Eddy, 1999).

Regulations. Finally, the organisation might be forced towards adaptation by technical or commercial regulations. Toys imported into the EU, for example, have to conform to certain safety standards. Some Far Eastern manufacturers, therefore, have had to adapt their product designs and improve their quality standards or face exclusion from European markets. Regulations might also cover product labelling (relating to weight, country of origin or declaration of ingredients, for example) and product claims (relating to the extent to which it can be recycled, health warnings, nutritional or other alleged benefits).

Example The world's first cholesterol-cutting food ingredient, Benecol, had to overcome extensive regulatory barriers before it could be sold in the North American market. Raisio (http://www.raisio.com), the Finnish company behind the product, and Johnson & Johnson, which has the international marketing and production rights, were in a race against time to beat an alternative offering from Unilever. Although the USA is considered the prime market for health-conscious low fat margarine and spread buyers, Europe proved an easier bet for regulatory acceptance of the product's health claims. The US Food and Drug Administration disrupted the launch in the USA by classifying Benecol as a food ingredient rather than dietary supplement, which meant a different approach to product positioning and an undermining of the health claims (Burt, 1999a).

As discussed in Chapter 2, other elements of the marketing mix, such as pricing, sales promotion, advertising and direct marketing, are likely to be subject to widely differing regulation in different international markets, and therefore might have to be adapted in order to conform.

Pressures towards standardisation

If an organisation is operating in a market where customer needs and preferences are largely universal, then there might be little enthusiasm for adaptation and **standardisation** might be considered to be preferable. Unfortunately, such markets are not very easy to find. Coca-Cola has virtually created such a market, but even it occasionally adapts the sweetness or fizziness of the product to suit local market preferences.

Identified international segment. What is more likely to happen is that the organisation will define an international lifestyle or usage segment (*see*, for example, the discussion of Euro-segments at pp. 189 *et seq.*) which cuts across geographic borders and allows a standardised marketing mix to be developed.

> **Example** Finding an international segment is not necessarily easy, but is attempted by brands such as Cadbury's, Wash & Go, American Express, Nescafé and Carte Noir. Car manufacturers also try to standardise their marketing approaches as much as possible, across Europe at least. Some retailers, particularly the franchised ones, including companies like Benetton, The Body Shop, Toys 'Я' Us, and IKEA, also aim for standardisation.

As mentioned earlier, some retailers and product manufacturers use their country of origin as a key element of the product's appeal, and that is clearly going to imply a degree of standardisation.

> **Example** Skane, a Swedish dairy company, developed a fruit drink to appeal to those consumers with upset stomachs. The drink, Provita, claims to help restore the balance in the body's gastrointestinal system and even ease disorders such as irritable bowel syndrome and stress-related stomach problems. The health-conscious and non-prescription medicinal segment was thought to be similar across most northern European countries, so the product is being rolled out, unmodified other than the packaging, into the UK and then into five other countries (*The Grocer*, 1999a).

Economies of scale. Such standardisation does not stem just from the existence of international lifestyle or usage segments, but also from a practical desire to achieve economies of scale, where possible. If aspects of the marketing mix can be standardised, then costs will be lower. A standardised product with standardised packaging can be produced in larger, more economic quantities and then distributed to a number of

> **Example** Electrolux (http://www.electrolux.com) is moving towards standardising many of its household appliances around common European platforms. Although knobs and gadgets can be adapted to suit local markets, the basic oven or vacuum cleaner will be built on a common platform. For example, the euro-oven may have a special pizza setting for Italy, or special shellfish compartments in France, but the common platform can be built at all plants and all models designed around that platform. This enables considerable economies of scale to be realised in production and in component costing. It also means that a pan-European approach can be taken towards marketing, rather than relying on national approaches, so logistics and promotional campaigns as well as production will reflect a standardised market (Burt, 1999b).

different markets. If a product is particularly complex to manufacture or involves sophisticated technology, then the pressure towards standardising it in all markets might be considerable. The costs and implications of trying to adapt could be just too high.

Mobile customers. International service industries aim to standardise their offerings as far as possible, as discussed in Chapter 22. A hotel chain serving business travellers, for example, will want to create a strong international brand image so that experiencing a stay at a Sheraton hotel in Sofia is as similar as possible to a stay at a Sheraton hotel in London. In this case, although the hotels are located in different countries, the market segment served is not geographically tied and thus the product has to be standardised for consistent positioning in the customer's mind. Other products, also targeted at internationally customers, implement a deliberate standardisation strategy. Kodak or Fuji films, for example, have to be immediately recognisable by tourists wherever they are.

Degree of adaptation or standardisation

As this discussion has implied, the degree of adaptation can be total or partial, or there can be no adaptation at all. If the marketing environment warrants it, adaptation could mean a complete overhaul of all elements of the marketing mix. At the other extreme, it could just mean a standardised product with slight alteration to the labelling on the package to make it conform to local regulations. Keegan (1969), looking at adaptation in terms of product and promotion in particular, came up with five alternative strategies, reflecting differing levels of adaptation. These are summarised, with examples, in Fig. 23.9. The important point, however, is that any adaptation, however great or small, should be justified by the market or its environment, although its cost effectiveness should also be taken into account. It is equally important that a decision to standardise should be based on an appreciation of different market needs rather than on cultural arrogance. For Wind (1998), there will always be a tension between global strategy and local interest. What is needed is a blend of standardisation and differentiation that can allow local adaptation to suit local market needs, yet still enable cross-country co-ordination, integration and synergy. The challenge, according to him, is to 'think and act globally, regionally and locally'.

International marketing mixes

The principles of designing a marketing mix for international markets are the same as those employed in domestic markets. Sound market analysis and understanding should precede any detailed decision making in the selection and scheduling of the marketing tools. As discussed above, the marketing strategy and programme might have to be tailored to exploit strengths and opportunities and minimise weaknesses and threats in the context of the local marketing environment. This includes the need

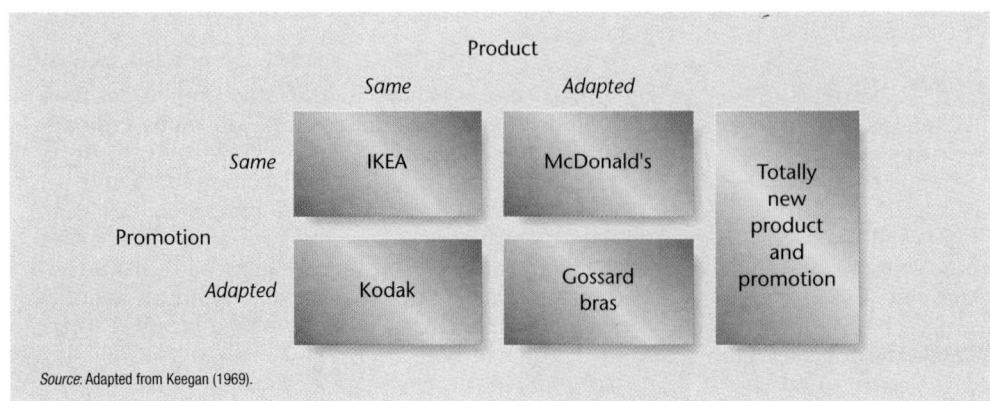

Source: Adapted from Keegan (1969).

FIGURE 23.9

Five product adaptation strategies

to appreciate the social and cultural influences on consumer decision making, the state of technological capability and the sophistication of distribution channels. Also, as considered at p. 1000 *et seq.*, the segmentation and positioning strategy will be an important determinant of the shape of the marketing mix.

As a way of summarising many of the points made throughout this chapter, each element of the marketing mix will now be considered briefly.

Product

The specification of the whole product package must be driven by customer needs and wants rather than pure convenience. It might be possible to define a standard product that can be sold across a number of international markets, for example consumer electronic goods, kitchen appliances or some toiletries. Otherwise, the product might have to be adapted for local needs in major or minor ways. Part of the success of many Australian wines within the traditional markets of the EU has been due to their careful positioning as premium wines, attracting higher price points. This has been supported by technological advances such as pioneering 'bag-in-a-box wines' and using computers for maintaining product quality and consistency (Smith and Robinson, 1999). Packaging and brand imagery are likely to have to be adapted to reflect local culture or to help create a market position that is compatible with the local marketing environment.

> **Example** Some national products are difficult to transfer across boundaries. Kellogg, for example, could have a problem if it tried to move its cereal Hoshi No Yasaibatake (The Vegetable Garden of Star) into European markets. Although popular with Japanese children, a mix of dehydrated carrot, spinach and pumpkin in brown sugar and honey might not be to British or German tastes. However, there may be no reason why the product could not be exported to some other Asian countries where tastes could be similar (*The Grocer*, 1999d).

Packaging might also have to be redesigned to cope with different physical conditions and handling. The climate might be hotter and drier or more humid, or the product might have to be better protected to survive a longer journey time or a longer shelf life, especially if storage conditions within the distribution channel are less than perfect.

Price

In any market, domestic or otherwise, the primary consideration for price is what the market will bear. The organisation has to be aware of the pricing structure within the market, customers' price perceptions and the implications of price for product positioning. A price level that might represent excellent value for money in the home market could seem to be very expensive in a foreign market. The opposite is true in the case of McDonald's pricing, where US menu prices tend to be lower than in many European countries on a straight currency conversion basis. This in part reflects the highly competitive state of the fast food market in the USA, as well as a willingness for European consumers to value the offer regardless of comparison. Clearly, price perceptions and positioning are partly affected by competitors' approaches to pricing. The organisation thus has strategic decisions to make about whether to match the competitors' prices or to price significantly higher or lower.

> **Example** The growth of on-line trading is removing some of the opportunities for companies to offer different prices in different markets. Amazon (http://www.amazon.com) can take orders from the same customer on its European websites and on its US main site (*see* pp. 550 *et seq.*). It is possible, therefore, for the consumer to compare prices allowing for exchange rates and any additonal delivery costs.

The cost structure associated with a product might also change in international markets. If an organisation is exporting goods, it potentially faces higher logistics costs, for example in terms of insurance and transportation, especially if the goods are being sent to quite remote markets. There could also be additional administration and banking costs in arranging shipping and payment. If, for example, a buyer wants to pay for the goods through a letter of credit, then banks have to act as intermediaries, checking documentation and arranging the international transfer of funds. Banks charge for this service, as well as charging for foreign currency exchange. Price might also have to reflect a 'cushion' against fluctuations in exchange rates, to avoid losses.

Selling costs can also be higher, for example if sales representatives are being sent abroad on sales trips or the organisation is attending international trade fairs and exhibitions. In addition to these costs, there is the cost of preparing sales materials, brochures and other sales aids. A great deal of cash might have to be invested in market development before any significant level of orders is generated. This cost will have to be recouped somehow.

Longer-term capital investment in a country can also affect cost structures. Building a manufacturing plant, for example, might lead to a lower unit cost and reduce distribution costs, but nevertheless a return will be expected on the capital. Alternatively, if there is major adaptation and market development activity, there might be pressure to get a faster payback. Where goods are traded between the home organisation and a foreign subsidiary, issues of transfer pricing (as discussed at pp. 448 *et seq.*) arise. If transfer prices are set too low, and cannot be defended in commercial terms, then the organisation might be open to accusations of 'dumping', that is, exporting goods at unfairly low prices in order to get rid of them outside the home market. Different countries regulate transfer pricing to different extents and in different ways, and thus the organisation should investigate carefully how much flexibility there actually is with transfer prices.

Place

The organisation should develop an appreciation of what is 'normal' in the local market for distributing products similar to its own. This includes an understanding of how customers purchase, where they expect to find the goods and what support services they expect from intermediaries. Unless the organisation is prepared to invest heavily, its distribution strategy needs to be built around available intermediaries and their capabilities, including their stock control systems, on-line ordering capacity, goods handling capacity and storage conditions.

> **Example** Unilever in China, mentioned earlier on p. 1025, had to regain distribution control for its Wall's ice-cream brand after trying to get coverage in 80 cities quickly. The problem was that the freezers designed to support the Wall's products often disappeared without trace or were full of products other than Wall's ice cream. After that experience, Unilever decided to establish exclusive distributors and to develop a strong regional network. This has enabled an efficient operation to supply over 500 cities and even to allow penetration into more rural areas (Harding, 1999b).

Delivery size and frequency will have to be tailored to suit the channel. Logistics thus have to be planned around intermediaries' needs and available modes of transport. They also have to be timed to take into account problems such as crossing borders.

Example The safety of Alpine road tunnels following fires in the Mont Blanc and Tauern tunnels is leading to reconsideration of how dangerous some products are when transported through confined spaces. Rail operator DB in Germany started a marketing campaign highlighting that dangerous goods should be moved by rail, and legislation could be stiffened to restrict dangerous and hazardous materials from using the network of tunnels through the Alps (Gough, 1999).

MARKETING AND IT ### Have a cigar (or a Beanie Baby, or some erotica)?

The Internet is making its mark on international pricing. For a start, there are concerns in many quarters that the impact of the Internet will be to force prices down, permanently. More realistically, the Internet will be a force for harmonisation of prices across the globe. Today, it is easy to scour the world for any item, find it, pay for it and have it shipped – and all within minutes. (OK, perhaps a little longer – the Internet is so *slow*, after all, isn't it?) So just how easy is it to find stuff on the Internet? Here's a real-life example.

Cigars are less easy to find on the Internet than Beanie Babies. At least, that's the opinion of Jango, the Internet shopping agent from Excite Shopping. On 5 August 1999, we searched for the best value Arturo Fuente Brevas Royale cigars on the web. Jango could only find two on-line retailers that sold them: Cigar Express and The Cigar Box. Beanie Babies were a different matter altogether. Although we specifically told Jango that it had to find the cheapest Scoop the Pelican Beanie Baby, this was no problem to our digital shopping assistant. Within seconds, Jango returned 353 results from a variety of Internet classified advertising sites and on-line auctions. For $7.00, we could purchase Scoop from one of Yahoo!'s classified advertisements. Alternatively, we could choose from a variety of auctions, including 19

different Yahoo! auctions, all of which were due to start within eight hours. Guide prices ranged from $3.00 up $9.00, the highest prices being reserved for Scoops with free heart-shaped tag protectors or similar value added paraphernalia. If we were in a hurry, the on-line auction house eBay had an auction starting within six minutes and there was a Scoop the Pelican going for $9.99.

To go with the cigar and the Beanie Baby, some soothing music, perhaps? This time, we asked MySimon if he could find Madonna's *Erotica* CD (there's no accounting for taste). MySimon was almost as efficient as Jango, returning quickly with 73 results from 42 different merchants, including Amazon.com, Compact Disc Connection, Borders.com, BestPrices.com and Wal-Mart. BestPrices.com even offered a choice between the clean version and the stickered version of the CD. Unfortunately, it was out of our price range at over $14.99. Eventually, we settled for Amazon's offer of shipping within 24 hours for a mere $12.99.

That's how easy it is to shop on the Internet. And although shipping costs will discourage the purchase of low value, bulky items, many items will soon be priced in the global currency of Internet dollars. Now, where's that cigar?

Source: O'Connor and Galvin (1999).

Promotion

Promotional mixes are highly likely to have to be tailored to suit the local environment. Advertising has to conform to local regulations, in terms of both media choice and content. Furthermore, a campaign has to take into account available media and their costs, as well as the target market's media consumption patterns. Sales promotion, as seen in Chapter 16, is also subject to different degrees of regulation. The choice of sales promotion techniques therefore has to respect local regulations and reflect the target market's preferences. In some markets, for example, coupons distributed through print advertisements might stimulate more response than those printed on packs.

Public relations activities, particularly publicity, might call for the services of a local PR agency that knows the media scene and has established contacts. Public relations can be particularly useful if the organisation wants to be seen to be integrating into the local community. Some kind of sponsorship, for example, gives an opportunity to demonstrate a willingness to give something back to the community, and to participate in its life. Finally, personal selling in a foreign market might mean training sales staff in language and culture, including negotiation styles, business etiquette and social interaction. If the organisation does not have an established name in the international market, the sales force could face a great deal of cold calling and rejection. The sales manager, therefore, should take particular care to ensure that the sales force is properly motivated and supported, and that their morale is kept up, especially if they are working a long way from home.

Example Care must be taken in designing the messages and promotional mix so that they avoid causing offence and alienating consumers through approaches that do not transfer easily across international markets. It has been argued that the US company Monsanto (http://www.monsanto.com) seriously misjudged the European attitude to genetically modified food and as a result faced some difficult PR problems that it did not originally envisage (Tornkins, 1999). In 1998, Monsanto ran a £1mn campaign to prepare the consumer for accepting more genetically modified foods with what was effectively a consumer education campaign that even invited people to consider the alternative views of Greenpeace and Friends of the Earth. The informed debate that Monsanto sought revolved around the promise of biotechnology and the risks associated with it.

The outcome was perhaps predictable; the scientific debate was lost in an aggressive counter-campaign to discredit GM food that was still raging at the time of this book going to press and was certainly well beyond the original campaign period planned by Monsanto.

After the BSE scare, consumers became very cynical about what they are told and sensitive to what they eat. There is a mistrust of government, big business and scientists on GM and other food-related matters and thus the view in many quarters was that GM was being imposed on Europeans by arrogant US companies (Blackledge, 1999). In the USA, hormone-treated beef and other genetically modified products have been widely accepted, although even that is now under threat as questioning campaigns have been stirred up by European concerns. In the UK and the rest of Europe, there are still major concerns in these areas, showing markedly different attitudes from those of the typical US consumer. Inadvertently, Monsanto identified itself as being at the forefront of a debate that it could not realistically win and that had the potential to do its image and reputation harm.

CHAPTER SUMMARY

International marketing is of concern to organisations of all types and sizes, whether they drift into it accidentally through the receipt of unsolicited orders from abroad or whether they treat it as a major planned part of their marketing strategy. International marketing is complex, not only because it potentially involves greater administrative and operational marketing effort, but also because it involves an understanding of marketing environments that might be very different from the domestic market.

There are many reasons that organisations seek international marketing opportunities. The limitations of the domestic market might encourage organisations to look further afield for growth opportunities, or the domestic market could be under threat from foreign competition. International marketing might open up an opportunity to manufacture more cheaply abroad or to develop economies of scale in the home manufacturing operation. Customers who operate internationally might also expect their suppliers to follow and do the same.

Whatever the reason, the choice of foreign market has to be made carefully and a full analysis of the STEP factors should provide a foundation for an informed decision. By comparing a number of possible markets on criteria such as product fit, market factors, competitive factors, market entry issues, resource constraints and trading constraints, an organisation can decide which one presents the best opportunity.

There are many possible market entry methods, and the choice depends on how quickly the organisation wants to get into the market, what it is prepared to invest in terms of time, money and long-term commitment to do so, its willingness to take risks and its financial objectives. Some organisations begin their international careers by direct exporting, selling to a foreign customer or through a foreign-based intermediary, or by indirect exporting, selling through an intermediary based in the domestic market. If an organisation is selling expertise or knowledge rather than goods and services, then available options include licensing, franchising and contracting. Where an organisation wishes to make a long-term commitment to a market or region, then investment might be appropriate, acquiring or setting up manufacturing or sales subsidiaries, or entering into joint ventures or strategic alliances. By having such a strong local presence in the market, an organisation might be able to overcome any political hostility to importers and might gain a better understanding of how best to adapt the product and its marketing package to suit local needs.

A major concern for any organisation is whether to standardise or adapt its marketing offering for an international market. If it decides to adapt, it needs to think about which elements of the marketing mix should be adapted and to what extent. Standardisation is attractive, in that it can lead to economies of scale and easier marketing administration, but it can be dangerous unless there are clear indications that it is appropriate within the international marketing environment.

In any market, even if the product can be standardised, it is likely that the price will have to be adapted. Different markets face different cost structures and are subject to different taxes and import duties. Customers might have different price perceptions and expectations. Advertising and other marketing communication activities will face different regulatory environments and might well have to be adapted to conform, quite apart from any cultural differences.

Key words and phrases

Adaptation	Joint ventures	Master franchising
Contracting	Licensing	Sales subsidiaries
Direct export	Manufacturing subsidiaries	Standardisation
Indirect export	Market entry methods	Strategic alliance
International marketing		

QUESTIONS FOR REVIEW

23.1 Why is marketing in an international context more complex than in the domestic market?

23.2 Define Lynch's five categories of international European organisation.

23.3 Why do organisations internationalise?

23.4 For each STEP element of the marketing environment, outline three factors that might make the international market different from the domestic one.

23.5 What six broad groups of factors should be taken into account when selecting a foreign market?

23.6 What factors influence the choice of *market entry method*?

23.7 Differentiate between *direct* and *indirect exporting*.

23.8 What are the main strengths of *licensing* as a market entry method?

23.9 What are *joint ventures* and what are the risks associated with them?

23.10 Summarise the factors that might create pressure towards *adapting* the marketing mix for a foreign market.

QUESTIONS FOR DISCUSSION

23.1 To what extent do you think that internationalisation is essential for today's organisations?

23.2 Choose an fmcg product from your home market that has not yet become an international product. Decide which foreign market you would like to launch this product in and find out as much relevant information as you can about the marketing environment in that country. What recommendations would you make to the manufacturer of your chosen product about the launch?

23.3 Discuss the problems that small businesses might face in internationalising and the feasibility of the various market entry methods for them.

23.4 Find an example of a successful joint venture in an international market. What benefits have the parties to the venture derived from it?

23.5 Citing examples that you have found, discuss whether standardisation is possible or desirable in international markets.

CASE STUDY 23.1

Wal-Mart comes to town

Wal-Mart is America's biggest retailer and has a successful track record in internationalisation. It opened its first international store in Mexico City in 1991 through a joint venture with Cifra and now has an international division generating sales of $12.2bn and profits of $55lmn. It now operates in nine countries, including China, South Korea and several south and central American countries, as well as the USA. International sales account for only 9 per cent of Wal-Mart's total sales, but the target within five years is 30 per cent.

As we saw on p. 545, its first European venture was the take-over of Wertkauf in Germany. This was followed fairly quickly by entry into the UK market through the take-over of supermarket chain ASDA. In February 1999, Wal-Mart senior managers visited the Prime Minister at Downing Street for a 'social visit'. Some speculated that Wal-Mart wanted reassurance that it would be welcome in the UK and even that it was trying to get agreement that planning regulations would be relaxed to allow it to expand more easily in the UK. The bid for ASDA was then announced in June 1999. Germany and the UK are two of the three most important grocery markets in Europe (France is the third) and UK is the most mature of those markets. At £6.7bn, the ASDA deal is Wal-Mart's biggest yet. Wal-Mart's entry has been taken very seriously by the retail sector as it is a formidable presence in the UK market. Globally, it has well over 3000 stores and sales of £85bn, compared with Tesco's 639 stores and £18.5bn sales. ASDA adds over 200 stores to Wal-Mart's portfolio and £8bn in sales (as things stood at the time of the take-over). The UK market entry fitted with government thinking at the time that the grocery

sector was over-pricing its goods and would benefit from more competition. A survey showed that 80 per cent of UK consumers thought that they paid more for food and groceries than other nationalities did.

ASDA is already very efficient in terms of its cost structures and operates on the same net margins as Wal-Mart. Nevertheless, analysts predict that there will be severe price cutting sooner or later, if not a price war. ASDA's suppliers could be the ones bearing the brunt of this, or alternatively margins could be cut to almost suicidal levels for a year or two to get the discount principle established and to hit the competition hard. In both Germany and Canada, Wal-Mart reduced prices immediately on entering the market. It struggled to make profits in Canada for three years, but Canada eventually became the most profitable market. If the same strategy is used with ASDA, it could lead to consolidation within the European market so that its competitors can combine strength and gain better economies of scale and more buying power. Companies like Carrefour might well be interested in joining forces with other retailers, especially if it considers that Wal-Mart might be looking towards the French market in the future. As far as the UK is concerned, consolidation really has to be pan-European, because UK-only mergers would fall foul of monopoly rules.

Speculation is also rife about which retail sectors in the UK will be hardest hit by Wal-Mart. It could be electrical goods and variety stores such as Argos, Woolworth's and Littlewoods, as Wal-Mart is perceived as being strongest in non-food retailing. Some retailers are less worried than others, however. Matalan, for example, is an out of town, no-frills clothing retailer. It has 90 stores and a database of

3.4mn customers, each of whom has paid a £1 membership fee, and so there is a lot of direct marketing and targeting to build relationships. It has twice as much clothing selling space as ASDA and feels that with its out of town sites it can undercut Wal-Mart by up to 25 per cent on average on clothing prices. An identical blouse is sold at ASDA for £20 and at Matalan for £10. Only time will tell whether Matalan is underestimating Wal-Mart's buying power. In the supermarket sector, the marketing director of Waitrose thinks that shoppers who would want to shop at Wal-Mart already shop at ASDA, Aldi or Netto and so there is little threat to more upmarket retailers. It could be the case that companies like Tesco respond to Wal-Mart in the same way that they responded to the European discounters (*see* p. 545) with limited price cutting and major emphasis on value added through service, quality and choice. Neither Wal-Mart nor ASDA has a loyalty scheme and Wal-Mart has a much smaller range of grocery goods on offer than, for example, Tesco. It offers fewer prepared foods and less own-brand choice (although its own-label Cola is the third biggest in the world behind Coca-Cola and Pepsi).

Wal-Mart might thus have to adapt to the UK market. It is used to significantly bigger outlets (four or five times bigger) than ASDA can offer. Furthermore, Wal-Mart's primary buying strength is in non-foods. So the question is how ASDA can retain food focus yet take advantage of Wal-Mart's non-food strength within limited space. Big extensions and huge new stores are not so easy under planning rules, although some analysts think that planning regulations will be relaxed to help Wal-Mart and it could spark an expansion in the number of hypermarkets operated by Tesco and Sainsbury's *et al.* In the US market, however, Wal-Mart has taken share from traditional food supermarkets, despite its relatively recent commitment to food. Currently, Wal-Mart only generates about 16 per cent of its sales from grocery-type products (food, tobacco and confectionery). Nevertheless, in the USA, a typical basket of groceries costs about 17 per cent less in a Wal-Mart hypermarket than in a more traditional supermarket. Food sales in its hypermarkets were worth about $15bn per year in 1999 and that is expected to more than double by 2003. If ASDA can use Wal-Mart to improve its non-food offering and margins, that would give it leeway to reduce food margins more safely. Initial price attack could be in health and beauty, where margins are biggest and where global buying could reap rewards.

Even before the take-over, ASDA had learned from Wal-Mart how to reduce the time taken to build a new hypermarket from 30 weeks to 15 weeks. Within days of the take-over, the two companies were exchanging staff and ideas to help the integration along. ASDA has a lot to learn about more efficient use of the supply chain and IT. In a typical ASDA store, for example, up to 45 per cent of space is used for storage. At Wal-Mart, it is typically 12 per cent. ASDA will also benefit from Wal-Mart's global sourcing arrangements with big suppliers. Wal-Mart accounts for about 20 per cent of Procter & Gamble's sales volumes, for instance. Where the two companies have suppliers in common there may be synergies that will benefit both. The plan is to retain the ASDA name, however, to reassure loyal customers.

ASDA has a lot to teach Wal-Mart about UK retailing and Wal-Mart, on past experience, is not likely to impose its US methodology in the UK regardless. In Mexico, for instance, Wal-Mart has adapted to run a variety of store formats, from fast-food outlets to department stores to suit local demand, and it does take some ideas home to try out in the USA.

Sources: Bilefsky (1999b); *The Grocer* (1999j, 1999k, 1999l); Hollinger (1999); Jardine (1999a, 1999b); Robinson *et al.* (1999).

Questions

1 When Wal-Mart entered the Mexican market, it entered into a joint venture. In both Germany and the UK it took over existing retailers. Why do you think it used a different strategy?

2 What other market entry strategies could Wal-Mart have used and why do you think they were rejected?

3 What kind of factors do you think led Wal-Mart to internationalise in the first place? What do you think is the appeal of the UK market as a target for market entry?

4 To what extent do you think adaptation is necessary for a retailer entering a foreign market?

Will Wal-Mart revolutionise European retailing?

Source: Wal-Mart.

CASE STUDY 23.2

Banana wars

Governments and other trade bodies can have a serious effect on international business and companies' freedom to import and export what they want. Throughout the 1990s, for instance, there was a long-running dispute between the US government and the EU over bananas. These 'banana wars' erupted because the EU was restricting the volume of American and South American bananas imported into Europe. The EU's position was that it wanted to favour certain Caribbean, African and Pacific producers that were ex-colonies or dependencies, particularly of France and the UK. The WTO (World Trade Organisation) had already ruled that this amounted to unfair protectionism, but the USA and five Latin American co-complainants went back to the WTO in 1999 asking for sanctions after the EU failed to comply with the 1997 WTO ruling against the banana regime.

Thus in April 1999, the WTO officially authorised the USA to impose trade sanctions worth over $191mn on EU goods, although the USA had actually been looking for $520mn in compensation. Nevertheless, the WTO was anxious that the EU should introduce a banana regime consistent with WTO rules and authorised the sanctions to encourage the EU to rethink. The EU maintains, however, that the Caribbean producers do need protection. Their farms are smaller and the land poorer than that found in Latin America. In addition, their shipping costs are a lot higher because they cannot achieve the same economies of scale. Places like the Windward Islands are extremely dependent on the banana as it accounts for 60 per cent of export earnings. The Caribbean as a whole is only the world's tenth largest banana exporter. Ecuador alone exports something like 4.5 million tonnes compared with the Caribbean's 0.3 million tonnes. In Wolf's (1999a) opinion, however, the EU regime is long overdue for revision as it does not in fact protect the livelihoods of small, uncompetitive producers. It has been estimated that the banana regime costs the EU $2bn per year of which only $150mn goes to subsidise the actual growers. Over $1bn goes as 'quota rent' to cover the difference between the market value of the bananas and the cost of acquiring them, which effectively goes to the distributors. The regime does not exclude 'dollar' bananas (i.e. those from the Americas) but there is an upper quota limit and imports into the EU above that limit attract a tariff of 150 per cent.

Initially, the EU said that it could take until January 2000 to sort all this out. By July 1999, it had not yet drafted its revised proposals for the banana regime and so it looked unlikely that anything could be passed through the European Parliament and implemented by January 2000. It appeared, however, that producers on both sides of the dispute were losing patience. In mid-July 1999, it was announced that Caribbean producers would be meeting initially with industry and government representatives from Ecuador to see if they could come to an agreement to resolve the dispute. This signalled a shift in strategy from 'push' to 'pull'. Before, the Caribbean producers had tried to resolve the situation by trying to get the USA and the EU to take action. Now, they were trying to devise a solution at the grower level and then present it to governmental bodies.

When a trade war like this blows up, exporters are left holding their breath to see if their products are on the 'hit list'. In the banana wars, for example, initially British biscuits were on the list to have 100 per cent duty imposed on them. Even though the list was subsequently revised and biscuits deleted from it, it still caused problems. Walkers' Shortbread generates 15 per cent of its business in the USA and its customers were hanging back to see whether biscuits would be included on the list or not. Customers knew that the punitive tariffs would be backdated and held off buying just in case they effectively ended up paying for the goods twice – once to the supplier and then the 100 per cent backdated duty to the US government.

Bananas are not the only food causing tension between the USA and the EU. In July 1999, the USA was again authorised to impose sanctions on EU goods, this time because of the EU's ban on importing US hormone-treated beef. The WTO decided that sanctions worth $116.8mn would adequately represent the trade lost over the 11 years of the beef ban. The sanctions took the form of 100 per cent import duty on certain products, particularly from France, Germany, Italy and Denmark, as these countries were seen as being most influential in the beef ban. The WTO supported the sanctions because it said that there was insufficient scientific proof that the US beef was a health risk. About 95 per cent of US beef is hormone treated and it is exported to nearly 140 countries worldwide. The WTO had asked the EU to lift its ban, but the EU preferred to retain it while scientific research was being conducted.

In the countries targeted by the sanctions, producers were hit hard. Adding 100 per cent duty to the cost of a product is at best going to wipe out profit and at worst price it out of the market altogether. French café owners decided to support producers of Dijon mustard, foie gras and Roquefort cheese, which were among the products hit by the tariffs, by imposing their own trade sanction. Overnight, the price of a bottle of Coca-Cola went up to £50! It was only a small shot in a much bigger war, but it made a point.

Sources: Financial Times (1999b); James (1999); James and Wilson (1999); McCooey (1999); Suzman and de Jonquières (1999); Williams (1999b, 1999c, 1999d); Wolf (1999a).

Questions

1 Summarise the STEP and market selection factors from the point of view of a South American banana producer wanting to do business in the EU.

2 What options does a company such as Walker's have if its product category is targeted by sanctions?

3 How do you think generally that the international marketing of fresh fruit might differ from the international marketing of packaged goods, such as biscuits?

4 To what extent do you think that governments should be allowed to interfere in what is imported into a country or trading bloc?

References for Chapter 23

Anderson, R. (1999), 'Skoda Drives VW's Success Story', *FT Auto* supplement to *Financial Times*, 1 March, p. IV.

Ashworth, J. (1998), 'Brussels Ready to Set Terms for BA's Tie-up', *The Times*, 6 July, p. 48.

Batchelor, C. (1999), 'Siemens Lines up Expansion into French Railway Business', *Financial Times*, 14 May, p. 29.

Blackledge, C. (1999), 'Benefits that Go Against the Grain', *Life Sciences* supplement to *Financial Times*, 15 March, p. IV.

Bilefsky, D. (1999a), 'Alliance Unichem Sets out its Battle Plan to Conquer Europe', *Financial Times*, 28 May, p. 25.

Bilefsky, D. (1999b), 'Matalan Steps out of the Shadows to Take on the US Giant', *Financial Times*, 20 July, p, 22.

Bloom, J. (1998), 'Mind Your Language', *Management Today*, August, pp. 72–3.

Bobinski, C. and Cane, A. (1999), 'UPC to Buy Polish Cable TV Company', *Financial Times*, 3 June, p. 25.

Brand Marketing International (1999), 'Barbecues Burning Bright', *Brokerage Guide* supplement to *The Grocer*, 10 April, p. 5.

Brook, M. Z. (1992), *International Management* (2nd edn), Stanley Thornes (Publishers) Ltd.

Burt, T. (1999a), 'Benecol Launch in Europe Expected', *Financial Times*, 3 February, p. 34.

Burt, T. (1999b), 'Electrolux Plans Global Platforms', *Financial Times*, 17 February, p. 23.

Business Report (1999), 'Barlows Blooms Offshore', *Business Report*, 6 August, p. 11.

Cane, A. (1999), 'British Win West African Port Deal', *Financial Times*, 12 January, p. 6.

Colver, H. (1999), 'We've No Need to Say Sorry', *Sunday Business*, 24 January, p. 18.

Cramb, C. (1999), 'Dutch Group Holds its Own', *Rhine-Maas* supplement to *Financial Times*, 11 May, p. III.

Done, K. (1999), 'VW to Double Capacity in Slovakia', *Financial Times*, 21 January, p. 27.

Dorrian, P. (1998), *Marketing Magic*, Zebra Press, South Africa.

Dunne, N. and Nakamoto, M. (1999), 'US Short of Answers as Japan Trade Gap Swells', *Financial Times*, 23 February, p. 3.

Eddy, K. (1999), 'Bus Group on Road to Success', *Financial Times*, 26 May, p. 28.

Fidler, S. (1998), 'Very Long March to Join the "Club"', *China* supplement to *Financial Times*, 16 November, p. VI.

Financial Times (1999a), 'Europe Stung as BAe Opts for Marconi', *Financial Times*, 20 January, p. 1.

Financial Times (1999b), 'Trade War Escalates as EU Fights US Sanctions Move', *Financial Times*, 5 March, p. 1.

Franchise Magazine (1999), 'BMS Technologies', *Franchise Magazine*, March–April, p. 186.

George, N. (1999), 'Fashioning a Store of Value', *Financial Times*, 18 June, p. 4.

Gilligan, C. and Hird, M. (1986), *International Marketing: Strategy and Management*, Croom Helm.

Gough, J. (1999), 'Alpine Road Tunnel Safety Question', *Modern Railways*, August, p. 592.

Graham, G. (1999a), 'HSBC Is Challenged on Planned Rebranding of Midland', *Financial Times*, 4 February, p. 9.

Graham, G. (1999b), 'Provident Steps Up Expansion in Eastern Europe', *Financial Times*, 26 February, p. 18.

Griffiths, J. (1999), 'Europe Stands by for a Rolling Tide', *Financial Times*, 4 February, p. 34.

Gray, R. (1999), 'Moving Brands across Borders', *Marketing*, 22 July, pp. 25–6.

The Grocer (1999a), 'Serious Swedish Cure for Funny Tummies', *The Grocer*, 9 January, p. 48.

The Grocer (1999b), 'International', *The Grocer*, 16 January, p. 54.

The Grocer (1999c), 'Authentic Mexican Products Cross the UK Border', *The Grocer*, 23 January, p. 49.

The Grocer (1999d), 'International', *The Grocer*, 20 February, p. 52.

The Grocer (1999e), 'Challenge for the New World', *The Grocer*, 27 February, p. 57.

The Grocer (1999f), 'Trouble Ahead for Global Wine Industry', *The Grocer*, 27 February, p. 57.

The Grocer (1999g), 'Yowie Animals Arrive to Take UK by Storm', *The Grocer*, 24 April, p. 59.

The Grocer (1999h), 'Will Wine Cartons Catch on in the UK?', *The Grocer*, 29 May, p. 55.

The Grocer (1999j), 'Wal-Mart out to Kick Ass', *The Grocer*, 19 June, pp. 16–17.

The Grocer (1999k), 'Nobody Does it Better', *The Grocer*, 19 June, pp. 18–19.

The Grocer (1999l), 'Getting IT Right', *The Grocer*, 19 June, p. 20.

The Grocer (1999m), 'The Unbelievable Spam', *The Grocer*, 1 August, p. 45.

Groom, B. (1999), 'Rising Tide of Investment Flows from Overseas', *Financial Times*, 15 July, p. 9.

Hall, W. (1999), 'Swiss Sanitary Group Prepares to Test the Water', *Financial Times*, 22 April, p. 32.

Harding, J. (1999a), 'Unilever Plans Revamp of China Business', *Financial Times*, 17 June, p. 27.

Harding, J. (1999b), 'Unilever Sets out to Scale a Formidable Chinese Wall', *Financial Times*, 17 June, p. 32.

Hollinger, P. (1999), 'When the Price Is Not Right', *Financial Times*, 15 June, p. 22.

Houlder, V. (1995), 'Today's Friend, Tomorrow's Foe', *Financial Times*, 2 October.

Ives, V. (1999), 'Black Magic', *Marketing Mix*, July, pp. 26–32.

James, C. (1999), 'Banana Peace Bid by Rival Growers', *Financial Times*, 15 July, p. 4.

James, C. and Wilson, J. (1999), 'The Big Place of the Banana in a Small Part of the World', *Financial Times*, 19 March, p. 7.

Jardine, A. (1999a), 'Wal-Mart Arrival Shakes up Retail', *Marketing*, 17 June, p. 2.

Jardine, A. (1999b), 'Can UK Retail Repel a US Invader?', *Marketing*, 24 June, p. 15.

Jones, S. (1999), 'Candle Makers Get a Flicker of Hope as US Lifts Threat of Trade Sanctions', *Financial Times*, 17 April, p. 5.

Keegan, W. (1969), 'Multinational Product Planning: Strategic Alternatives', *Journal of Marketing*, 33 (Jan).

Kynge, J. and de Jonquières, G. (1999), 'Beijing Ponders How to Meet Demands to Open Economy', *Financial Times*, 15 February, p. 3.

Lorenz, A. (1999), 'Eurofighter Clinches First Export Order', *Sunday Times*, 14 February, p. 3.

Lynch, R. (1994), *European Business Strategies: The European and Global Strategies of Europe's Top Companies*, Kogan Page.

Maitland, A. (1999), 'A Code to Export Better Practice', *Financial Times*, 26 January, p. 14.

Malkani, G. (1999), 'Toad to Begin European Drive', *Financial Times*, 12 August, p. 19.

Marsh, P. (1999a), 'Bekaert Ties up the Wire Market', *Financial Times*, 10 February, p. 21.

Marsh, P. (1999b), 'JCB Chief Digs in to Keep the Business in the Family', *Financial Times*, 16 March, p. 12.

Marsh, P. (1999c), 'JCB Lifts Exports 6% Despite Strong Pound', *Financial Times*, 24 March, p. 25.

Marsh, P. (1999d), 'French Company Powers Ahead', *Financial Times*, 10 May, p. 18.

Marsh, P. (1999e), 'Diverse Group is a Leader in Lifts and Escalators', *Engineering* supplement to *Financial Times*, 30 June, p. VIII.

Marsh, P. (1999f), 'EU Industrial Exporters Savour Success in North America', *Financial Times*, 18 August, p. 6.

McCooey, C. (1999), 'Banana Splits', *The Grocer*, 24 April, pp. 36–8.

Mead, R. (1990), *Cross-cultural Management Communication*, John Wiley & Sons.

Monk, C. (1999), 'Every Cloud has a Silver Lining', *EuroBusiness*, September, pp. 38–40.

Nicoll, A. (1999a), 'Gunfight at the UK Corral', *Financial Times*, 20 January, p. 19.

Nicoll, A. (1999b), 'When Size Matters, it's Best to Aim for Being Number One', *Financial Times*, 20 January, p. 24.

Nusbaum, A. (1999), 'Mattel and Bandai Plan Global Link', *Financial Times*, 22 July, p. 28.

O'Connor, J. and Galvin, E. (1999), *Marketing and Information Technology* (2nd edn), Financial Times Pitman Publishing.

Paitra, J. (1993), 'The Euro-consumer: Myth or Reality?', in C. Halliburton and R. Hunerberg (eds.), *European Marketing: Readings and Cases*, Addison-Wesley.

Paliwoda, S. (1993), *International Marketing* (2nd edn), Butterworth-Heinemann.

Palmer, T. (1999), 'Broadening Horizons', *Wine Guide* supplement to *The Grocer*, 21 August, p. 3.

Parker, G. (1996), 'Getting the Balance Right', *European Purchasing & Materials Management*, 7, pp. 262–3.

Parker, P (1995), *Climatic Effects on Individual, Social and Economic Behaviour: a Physioeconomic Review of Research across Disciplines*, Greenwood Press.

Parsley, D. (1998), 'BA Fights for Right to Sell Airport Slots', *Sunday Times*, 13 September, p. 3.4.

Pitcher, G. (1999a), 'Ford Takes Pole Position in the Battle for Worldwide Domination', *Marketing Week*, 4 February, p. 25.

Pitcher, G. (1999b), 'Why Overseas Growth is Crucial for the UK Retail Sector's Success', *Marketing Week*, 12 February, p. 25.

Pretzlik, C. (1999), 'Making Waves', *Financial Times*, 21 April, p. 15.

Pring, A. (1999), 'In Pursuit of the Best', *The Grocer*, 9 January, pp. 28–32.

Robinson, A. (1999), 'Fiat Well Placed to Profit from Russian Recovery', *Financial Times*, 21 January, p. 27.

Robinson, E. *et al.* (1999), 'Wal-Mart in £6.7bn Bid for Asda', *Financial Times*, 15 June, p. 1.

Robinson, G. (1999), 'Chinese and US Officials Resume Talks', *Financial Times*, 29 June, p. 5.

Shay, A. (1998), 'Finding the Right International Mix', *Mastering Marketing* supplement to *Financial Times*, 16 November, pp. 2–3.

Skapinker, M. (1999a), 'US and Britain Plan Open Sky Deal this Year', *Financial Times*, 20 May, p. 9.

Skapinker, M. (1999b), 'UK Calls off Open Sky Talks with US', *Financial Times*, 1 July, p. 6.

Smith, M. (1999), 'Brussels Expected to Lift Ban on British Beef', *Financial Times*, 9 July, p. 1.

Smith, M. and Robinson, G. (1999), 'Australia's Confident Winemakers Ready to Pit Themselves against World's Best', *Financial Times*, 18 May, p. 8.

Suzman, M. and de Jonquières, G. (1999), 'UK Escapes 100% Tariffs as US Retaliates over EU's Beef Ban', *Financial Times*, 20 July, p. 20.

Sych, V. (1999), 'Break Down', *Business Central Europe*, February, pp. 24–5.

Taylor, P. (1999), 'Business Urged to "Get a Connection" as Web Turns out to be More than a Fad', *Financial Times*, 6 July, p. 9.

Tomkins, T. (1999), 'Monsanto Scores an Own Goal', *Financial Times*, 23 February, p. 16.

Walker, T. and Fidler, S. (1999), 'US and China Pull out Stops for WTO Deal', *Financial Times*, 15 February, p. 3.

Walsh, L. S. (1993), *International Marketing* (3rd edn), Pitman publishing.

Wei, G. (1999), 'Constructive Partnership Vital', *Sino-US Friendship* supplement to *China Daily*, 8 April, p. S-1.

Williams, F. (1999a), 'EU to Press Case for Poor', *Financial Times*, 26 February, p. 3.

Williams, F. (1999b), 'EU "Needs 8 Months" to End Banana Crisis', *Financial Times*, 20 April, p. 9.

Williams, F. (1999c), 'Reforms to EU Banana Import Regime Delayed', *Financial Times*, 27 July, p. 8.

Williams, F. (1999d), 'US Wins Approval for Beef Sanctions', *Financial Times*, 27 July, p. 8.

Willman, J. and Blitz, J. (1999), 'Coca-Cola's Style Offends European Regulators' Taste', *Financial Times*, 22 July, p. 2.

Wind, J. (1998), 'Strategic Thinking in the Global Era', *Mastering Marketing* supplement to *Financial Times*, 16 November, pp. 8–9.

Wolf, M. (1999a), 'Going Bananas', *Financial Times*, 24 March, p. 18.

Wolf, M. (1 999b), 'A World Divided', *Financial Times*, 14 July, p. 16.

Wright, R. (1999), 'Shattering Blow for Hungary's Glass Industry', *Financial Times*, 14 May, p. 33.

Young, S. *et al.* (1989), *International Market Entry and Development: Strategies and Management*, Harvester Wheatsheaf.

Yu'an, Z. (1999), 'Boeing Offers China Support to Join WTO', *Sino-US Friendship* supplement to *China Daily*, 8 April, p. S-4.

EXECUTIVE INTERVIEW

Jardine Fleming

Interview with
Adam Williams, China Country Head

In recent years, China has rapidly opened up to become an attractive target for Western companies looking for new export markets. As an economy in transition, however, China has a very different and rapidly changing marketing environment, with some elements of a free market and some tight state regulation affecting many potential market entrants. Some companies are looking to enter the Chinese market through joint ventures may often use advisers to help them find their way through the regulations, to locate suitable partners then get the deal set up and working. One such company offering advisory services to multinationals is Jardine Fleming. The company started as a joint venture between Jardine Matheson, the Hong Kong based trading group and Robert Fleming, the UK merchant bank but is now a subsidiary company of Robert Fleming. It is a traditional style merchant bank that provides a wide range of financial services to its corporate customers. Adam Williams is China Country Head of Jardine Fleming, based in Beijing. He outlined some of the services provided by Jardine Fleming, discussed the general business environment in China and then gave some advice for managers and companies trying to get established in this market.

Apart from the fundamental job of a merchant bank of raising and lending money, Jardine Fleming fulfils a number of major roles in the Chinese market. First, it is into corporate finance, assisting Chinese companies to list on the Hong Kong, Shanghai or Shenzhen stock exchanges. It also has a role as a broker, with seats on the Shanghai and Shenzhen stock exchanges, trading in Chinese "B" shares. It undertakes research into China and Chinese companies and has a sales network throughout Asia.

It also undertakes investment fund management. Globally, the Fleming group manages funds worth around $120bn. The company cannot yet be a fund manager in the Chinese market because foreign companies are not allowed to do it, but it is hoped that the rules will change, allowing at least the management of joint venture mutual funds if not full fund management rights. Legislation covering Joint Venture Fund Management companies is presently waiting approval from China's State Council.

Listed companies are generally state owned enterprises. Recently, there has been the first acknowledgement of the contribution of the non-state sector to the economy and this has been seen by many as a tacit acceptance of capitalistic enterprise (albeit with "Chinese characteristics!"). This private enterprise exists within a society in transition. Since China opened up to the West in the 1970s, it has been gradually dismantling the Stalinist structures that have become stagnant. They suffer from bad management and overstaffing. As this happened, village or township enterprises took on some of the characteristics of private companies. There are thousands of these enterprises now ranging from sole traders to large manufacturing concerns creating wealthy owners. The non-state sector is worth more than 50% of GNP and rising.

The government wants inward investment and so there has been lots of reform. The President and the Prime Minister are both reform minded and provide strong leadership with the rest of the government behind them. Like Mrs Thatcher, they will take tough decisions and inflict necessary short-term pain for the longer-term benefit of the country. Tough decisions affect people, however. The government has cut the number of Ministries from 40 to 28, deploying 47% of staff. It is a slow process, and the government is helping people find other jobs. For the first time too, Chinese business is having to face up to the concept of bankruptcy. Privatisation is on the agenda and the market economy is accepted as controlling industry and enterprise. The financial sector is also being reformed and Jardine Fleming has to adapt quickly as there is a lot of reform happening very fast.

'Management' is an important new idea in China as is the concept of a customer focused rather than management focused organisation. In Communist thinking, it is the other way around. Previously, if a factory had the best machine then that was 'better' but in Western markets, it's the competitive advantage delivered by the machine that matters. The government's objective is to create 3000 fine international organisations from the state owned sector, but where are they going to get 3000 fine managers with the necessary skills? In many sectors, joint ventures can help in management skills transfer. There are also more Chinese students now going to business schools and doing MBAs and many managers have now studied in the UK or USA. Thus management quality is improving and more English is spoken. But Chinese managers still need more experience and a different management culture from the old hierarchical organisations in which juniors do not argue or question seniors.

Despite all the changes (and when China joins the World Trade Organisation these will accelerate), China is still a protected, regulated environment. It is a common experience for companies to have to wait a long time for licences and yet even a joint venture cannot do certain things without a licence. Lobbying for licences and de-regulation is thus a big issue for foreign companies, expecially in financial services, telecommunications, sales, distribution and retail. Licences are frequently given, not on objective commercial grounds, but on political criteria. For instance, four insurance licences were given to US companies just before a state visit to the USA. Power matters and the USA has a lot of leverage for getting companies into China and trading. Europe has not quite got the same status yet. A company's chances of getting a licence can be increased by being helpful to regulators. The regulators themselves are struggling to develop legislation or whatever, and companies can often provide information or expertise that the regulators could not access themselves. This is all very well for a company that has an established presence in China, but new entrants clearly needed expert help from experienced advisors like Jardine Fleming!

It can also be very expensive to get into the market and buy goodwill. Some insurance companies, for example, have set up $1bn investment funds in attempts to establish a more prominent place in the queue for licenses. It takes persistence too. It can cost £250 000 a year to run an office and you might not get a contract for four or five years. Thus not many companies actually have offices and it would be very tough for a small or medium sized company to demonstrate the commitment to the market and to relationship building that Chinese partners consider so important.

Some things are changing. In the past, deals relied on mutual understanding but now there is a well developed body of contract laws and international accounting practises are becoming the norm. All the same, a good underpinning relationship is still essential. Surety in China is understanding the mutual self-interest in a deal. Contracts now commonly contain arbitration clauses, either in Singapore or Stockholm usually, but how do you enforce a ruling? Relationships are much more important as is 'saving face' i.e. living up to and delivering on one's promises in what is a shame-based rather than guilt-based culture.

In setting up joint ventures, Jardine Fleming is often the middleman fostering and nurturing mutual understanding, even if the involved parties do not quite realise that this is what is happening. Most Fleming staff are Hong Kong Chinese who understand both Western and Chinese cultures (as well as the geographically diverse cultures within China). The fastest joint venture Jardine Fleming has set up took 13 months but in other cases it has been known for deals to take ten years or more from initial discussions to completion.

It does take time to cultivate business people and regulators and to build relationships. Time is not of the essence and patience is a virtue. Negotiation is trench warfare with argument over the most minute detail. It will change and is changing, mainly through the entrepreneurial sector.

In summary, Adam suggested ten hot tips for managers sent to negotiate in China, although they are necessarily very generalised:

1 Appreciate the culture and read up on the country and the business environment before you go there.
2 Appreciate that while the basic business dynamics are the same, i.e. mutual gain, how you negotiate requires cultural sensitivity. The Chinese are not usually blunt and Westerners can cause a lot of difficulties for themselves by being too blunt. Remember that the back door is more important than the front door i.e. leave sticky points to the end of a formal meeting then give the senior managers time and space to get together to sort them out less formally.
3 Align your self-interest with theirs. Remember that what is logical to you is not necessarily seen the same way by them, so do not make assumptions. What you think they want is not necessarily what they do want.
4 Do not give away anything in hope of a quick fix because you will not get it. Do not give now what you wouldn't have given later in any case.
5 They respect a hard bargain. Anything you do for them needs to be costed in somewhere. Travel is a good thing to build into contracts, for instance. It is valued and if it is costed in as a 'fact finding' or 'training' visit then it is seen as an integral and necessary part of the deal. Offer no charity!
6 Do not believe what people are telling you. Corroborate information from other sources such as market research agencies or Reuters etc. Consult professional advisory companies with a track record of doing business in China.
7 Surprisingly there are no secrets in China. Everyone knows what their rivals are up to. There is a lot of apparent openness – which can confuse the unwary more than closed doors!
8 Expect enormous expense on generating goodwill, but have defined objectives and cost them into a long-term plan. For example, even when a financial services company gets a licence to operate in China, it will take time to generate profit and perhaps it will be ten years before the fund management market becomes lucrative. Know your payback period and have a defined plan, including prioritising who to target in your goodwill exercise.
9 … thus do not go to China looking for short-term profit. In many industries long-term relationship building will be the only way to guarantee repeat business and an expanding customer base.
10 Do not leave your brains at the airport!

With grateful thanks to Adam Williams, China Country Head of Jardine Fleming.

Glossary

(Words which are set in *italics* have their own entries in the glossary, where they are further defined).

4Ps: otherwise known as the *marketing mix*, these are the basic tools of marketing: product, place, price and promotion.

7Ps: an extended *marketing mix* that takes account of the particular characteristics of services markets: product, price, place, promotion, physical evidence, people and processes.

Adaptation: (a) tailoring a product or other aspects of the *marketing mix* to suit the different needs and demands of other markets, usually international; (b) changing production methods or product specifications in an organisational market in order to better meet an individual customer's requirements.

Advertising: a paid form of non-personal communication transmitted through a mass medium.

Advertising media: the means through which advertisements are delivered to the target audience. Media include broadcast media, print media, cinema, hoardings and outdoor media.

Advertorial: a form of print *advertising* that is designed to mimic the editorial content, style and *layout* of the publication in which it appears.

Agents and brokers: *intermediaries* who have legal authority to act on behalf of a seller in negotiating sales, but who do not take title to goods themselves.

Alternative currencies: trading stamps, tokens or loyalty scheme points awarded on the basis of the amount spent by the customer that can be accumulated and then exchanged for gifts or discounts.

Ansoff matrix: a framework for considering the relationship between general strategic direction and *marketing strategies*. The four-cell matrix looks at permutations of new/existing products and new/existing markets.

Atmosphere: (a) the elements that come together to make an impact on retail customers' senses as they enter and browse in a store; (b) creating a feeling appropriate to the character of the store and the desired mood of the customers.

Attitude: the stance that individuals take on a subject that predisposes them to act and react in certain ways.

Augmented product: add-on extras that do not form an integral part of the product but which might be used, particularly by retailers, to increase the product's benefits or attractiveness. Includes guarantees, installation, after sales service etc.

Awareness: the consciousness that a product or organisation exists.

Behaviour segmentation: grouping consumers in terms of their relationship with the product, for instance their usage rate, the purpose of use, their willingness and readiness to buy etc.

BIGIF: a form of *product based sales promotion* – buy one get one free also known as BOGOFF.

Boston Box: (also known as the BCG matrix) a tool for analysing a *product portfolio*, plotting relative market share against market growth rate for each product. The resultant matrix classifies products as cash cows, dogs, question marks and stars.

Brand loyalty: occurs when a consumer consistently buys the same brand over a long period.

Branding: the creation of a three-dimensional character for a product, defined in terms of name, packaging, colours, symbols etc., that helps to differentiate it from its competitors, and helps the customer to develop a relationship with the product.

Breadth of range: the variety of different *product lines* either (a) produced by a manufacturer; or (b) stocked by a retailer.

Breakeven analysis: shows the relationship between total costs and total revenue in order to assess the profitability of different levels of sales volume.

Bulk breaking: buying large quantities of goods and then reselling them in smaller lots, reflecting some of the cost savings made through bulk buying in the resale price. A prime function of *intermediaries*.

Business format franchise: allows a *franchisee* access not only to a product concept, but also to a comprehensive package that allows the product or service to be delivered in a standardised way regardless of the location.

Business to business marketing: see *organisational marketing*.

Buyer readiness stages: categorise consumers in terms of how close they are to making a purchase or a decision. Stages range from initial awareness, through to interest, desire and, finally, action.

Buyer–seller relationship: the nature and quality of the social and economic interaction between two parties.

Buying centre: a group of individuals, potentially from any level within an organisation or from any functional area, either contributing towards or taking direct responsibility for organisational purchasing decisions. The buying centre might be formally constituted, or be a loose informal grouping.

CAPI: computer aided personal interviewing.

Cash rebate: a form of *sales promotion* usually involving the collection of a specified number of proofs of purchase in order to qualify for a cash sum or for a *coupon*.

Catalogue showrooms: a high street store selling goods through catalogues displayed in the outlet, with the customer collecting goods immediately from a pick-up point on the premises.

CATI: computer aided telephone interviewing.

Cause related marketing: linkages between commercial organisations and charities that can be used by both parties to enhance their profiles and to help achieve their marketing objectives.

Channel of distribution: the structure linking a group of organisations or individuals through which a product or service is made available to potential buyers.

Channel strategy: decision taken about the allocation of roles within a *channel of distribution*, and the way in which the channel is formally or informally managed and administered.

Closed questions: market research questions which offer the respondent a limited list of alternative answers to choose from.

Closing the sale: the stage of the *personal selling* process in which the customer agrees to purchase.

Cognitive dissonance: a state of psychological discomfort arising when a consumer tries to reconcile two conflicting states of mind, for example, the positive feeling of having chosen to buy a product and the negative feeling of being disappointed with it afterwards.

Cold calling: unsolicited visits or calls made by sales representatives to potential customers.

Collaborative R&D: pooling resources and expertise with one or more other organisations to undertake a research and development project jointly.

Commission: a percentage of the value of goods sold paid as total or partial remuneration to a sales representative or agent.

Comparative advertising: a type of *advertising* that seeks to make direct comparison between a product and one or more of its competitors on features or benefits that are important to the target market.

Competitive advertising: a commonly used type of *advertising* that communicates the unique benefits of a product, differentiating it from the competition.

Competitive edge: having a clear advantage over the competition in terms of one or more elements of the *marketing mix* that is valued by potential customers.

Competitive position: the organisation's strategic position in a market compared with its competitors: leader, challenger, follower or nicher.

Competitive posture: an organisation's means of dealing with competitors' actions in a market, proactively or reactively. Postures can be aggressive, defensive, co-operative or independent.

Competitive strategy: how an organisation chooses to compete within a market, with particular regard to the relative positioning and strategies of competitors.

Concept testing: the presentation of a new product concept, in terms of its function, benefits, design, branding etc., to a sample of potential customers to assess their reactions, *attitudes* and purchasing intentions towards it.

Concessions: also known as stores within stores; trading areas usually within *department stores*, sold, licensed or rented out to manufacturers or other retail names so that they can create their own distinctive trading image.

Consumer decision making: the process that consumers go through in deciding what to purchase, including *problem recognition*, information searching, evaluation of alternatives, making the decision, and *post-purchase evaluation*.

Consumer goods: goods that are sold to individuals for their own or their families' use.

Contracting: a type of *market entry method* whereby a manufacturer contracts with a company in a foreign market to produce or assemble goods on its behalf.

Contests and sweepstakes: a form of *sales promotion* in which customers are invited to compete for a specified number of prizes. Contests must involve a degree of skill or knowledge, whereas sweepstakes are effectively open lotteries.

Continuous innovation: products are upgraded and updated regularly in relatively small ways that make no great changes to the customer's buying behaviour.

Continuous research: research undertaken, usually by commercial market research organisations, on a long-term, ongoing basis, to track changing patterns in markets.

Control and evaluation: mechanisms for ensuring that *marketing plans* are properly implemented, that their progress is regularly measured and assessed and that any deviations are picked up early enough to allow corrective action to be taken.

Convenience goods: relatively inexpensive frequently purchased consumer goods; related to *routine problem solving* buying behaviour.

Convenience stores: usually small neighbourhood grocery stores that differentiate themselves from the *supermarkets* through longer opening hours and easy accessibility.

Conversion rate: the number of enquiries from potential customers or sales visits made by sales representatives that actually turn into orders or sales.

Co-operative advertising: a form of *sales promotion* targeted at *intermediaries* through which manufacturers agree to fund a percentage of the *intermediary's* local advertising costs as long as the manufacturer's product appears in the *advertising* material.

Copywriting: writing the verbal (written or spoken) elements of an advertisement.

Core product: the prime purpose of a product's existence which might be expressed in terms of functional or psychological benefits.

Corporate chain: multiple retail outlets under common ownership, usually with national coverage.

Corporate identity: the character and image of an organisation, reflecting its culture, that is presented to its various *publics*, including the organisation's name and logo.

Corporate objectives: the overall objectives of the organisation that influence the direction of *marketing strategy*.

Corporate PR: *public relations* activities focused on enhancing or protecting the overall corporate image of an organisation.

Count and recount: a form of *sales promotion* targeted at *intermediaries* through which rebates are given for all stock sold during a specified promotional period.

Coupons: a form of *sales promotion* consisting of printed vouchers, distributed in a variety of ways, that allow a customer to claim a price reduction on a particular product or at a particular retailer's stores.

Creative appeal: the way in which an *advertising* message is formulated in order to provoke the desired response from the target audience. Types of appeal include rational, emotional, product-orientated or consumer-orientated appeal.

Culture: the personality of the society in which an individual lives, manifest in terms of the built environment, literature, the arts, beliefs and value systems.

Data-based budget setting: setting *advertising* or marketing budgets using methods that do not involve guesswork or arbitrary figures. The two main methods are competitive parity and objective and task.

Database marketing: compiling, analysing and using data held about customers in order to create better tailored, better timed offers that will maximise customer value and loyalty.

Decision making unit (DMU): see *buying centre*.

Demographic segmentation: grouping consumers on the basis of one or more *demographic* factors.

Demographics: the measurable aspects of population structure, such as birth rates, age profiles, family structures, education levels, occupation, income and expenditure patterns.

Department stores: large stores, usually located in town centres, which are divided into discrete departments selling a very wide range of diverse goods, from clothing to travel, from cosmetics to washing machines.

Depth of range: the amount of choice or assortment within a *product line*.

Derived demand: where demand for products or components in organisational markets depends on consumer demand further down the chain; for example demand for washing machine motors is derived from consumer demand for washing machines.

Differential advantage: see *competitive edge*.

Diffusion of innovation: a concept suggesting that customers first enter a market at different times, depending on their attitude to innovation and new products, and their willingness to take risks. Customers can thus be classified as innovators, early adopters, early majority, late majority and laggards.

Direct export: selling goods to foreign buyers without the intervention of an *intermediary*.

Direct mail: a *direct marketing* technique involving the delivery of promotional material to named individuals at their homes or organisational premises.

Direct marketing: an interactive system of marketing that uses one or more *advertising media* to effect a measurable response at any location, forming a basis for further developing an on-going relationship between an organisation and its customers.

Direct response advertising: *advertising* through mainstream *advertising media* that encourages direct action from the audience, for example, requests for more information, requests for a sales visit, or orders for goods.

Direct Supply: a distribution channel in which the producer deals directly with the end customer without the involvement of *intermediaries*.

Discontinuous innovation: represents a completely new product concept unlike anything the customer has yet experienced, and thus involves a major learning experience for the customer with much information searching and evaluation.

Discount clubs: similar to *wholesalers*, but reselling in bulk to consumers who are members of the club rather than small retailers.

Distributors and dealers: *intermediaries* who add value through the provision of special services associated with the selling of a product and the after sales care of the customer.

Diversification: developing new products for new markets.

DSS: decision support system; an extension of the *MIS* that allows the marketing decision maker to manipulate data to explore scenarios and 'what if ...' questions as an aid to decision making.

Durable products: products that last for many years and are thus likely to be infrequently purchased, such as electrical goods and capital equipment.

Dynamically continuous innovation: the introduction of new products with an element of significant innovation that could require major reassessment of the product within customers' buying behaviour.

Economic and competitive environment: trends and developments in terms of the economic well-being and condition of individuals, nations or trading blocs, including taxation and interest rates etc.; the structure of markets in terms of the number of competitors and their ability to influence the market.

Environmental scanning: the collection and evaluation of data and information from the marketing environment that can influence the organisation's *marketing strategies*.

EPOS: electronic point of sale systems which streamline stock control and ordering systems through barcode scanning and allow the automatic processing of credit card payments for goods.

Eurobrand: also known as a pan-European brand; a brand which is marketed and sold with a standardised offering across a number of different European countries.

Evoked set: the shortlist of potential products that the consumer has to choose from within the purchasing decision making process.

Exchange process: the interaction between buyer and seller in which each party gives the other something of value. Usually, the seller offers goods and services, and the buyer offers money.

Extended problem solving: a *purchasing situation* usually involving a great deal of time and conscious information searching and analysis, as it involves high-priced goods which are purchased very infrequently; the consequences of making a 'wrong' decision are severe and thus the customer is prepared to invest time and effort in the process.

Extending the product line: adding further *product items* into a *product line* to extend coverage of the market, for instance introducing a bottom of the range cut-price version of a product, or developing a premium quality product to extend the top end of the range.

Family life-cycle: a model representing the way in which a family's structure changes naturally over time.

Field marketing agencies: agencies which undertake in-store *sales promotions*, *sampling*, and/or the setting up and maintenance of POS material.

Filling the product range: adding further *product items* into a *product line* to fill gaps within the range, for instance introducing additional flavours, pack sizes or packaging formats.

Fmcg products: fast moving consumer goods; relatively low-priced, frequently purchased items, such as groceries and toiletries.

Focus group: a small group of people, considered to be representative of the target segment, invited to discuss openly products or issues at their leisure in a relaxed environment.

Forecasts: estimates of future demand, sales or other trends, calculated using quantitative and/or qualitative techniques.

Franchise: a contractual *vertical marketing system* in which a *franchisor* licenses a *franchisee* to produce and market goods or services to criteria laid down by the *franchisor* in return for fees and/or royalties.

Franchisee: an *intermediary* who holds a contract to supply and market a product or service to operating standards and criteria set by the *franchisor*.

Franchisor: the individual or organisation offering *franchise* opportunities.

Frequency: the average number of times that a member of the target audience will have been exposed to an advertisement during a specified period.

Full service agencies: *advertising* agencies that provide a full range of services, including research, planning, creative work, advertising production, media buying etc. Such agencies might also offer other marketing communications services such as *direct mail*, *sales promotion*, and *PR*.

GE matrix: a tool for analysing a *product portfolio*, plotting industry attractiveness against business position for each product, resulting in a nine-cell matrix.

Generic strategies: three broad strategic options that set the direction for more detailed strategic planning: cost leadership, differentiation and focus.

Geodemographics: a combination of *geographic* and *demographic segmentation* that can either give the demographic characteristics of particular regions, neighbourhoods and even streets, or show the geographic spread of any demographic characteristics.

Geographic segmentation: grouping customers in either organisational or consumer markets in terms of their geographic location.

Heterogeneity: a characteristic of *services*, describing how difficult it is to ensure consistency in a service product because of its 'live' production and the interaction between different customers and service providers.

House journal: an internal publication produced by an organisation in order to inform and entertain its employees and to generate better internal communication and relationships.

Hypermarkets: very large self-service *out of town* outlets, 5000 m² or more, stocking not only a wide range of grocery and *fmcg products*, but also other consumer goods such as clothing, electrical goods, home maintenance products etc.

Independent retail outlet: a single retail outlet, or a chain of two or three stores, managed by either a sole trader or a family firm.

Indirect export: selling goods to foreign buyers through *intermediaries* such as export agents, export merchants or buying houses.

Industrial marketing: see *organisational marketing*.

Information overload: having so much information available that the consumer either cannot assimilate it all or feels too overwhelmed to take any of it in.

Inseparability: a characteristic of *services*, describing how service products tend to be produced at the same time as they are consumed.

Institutional advertising: a type of *advertising* that does not focus on a specific product, but on the corporate image of the advertiser.

Intangibility: a characteristic of *services*, describing their non-physical nature.

Interactive marketing: (a) in *services* markets, the encounter and interaction between the service provider and the customer. (b) see *Internet marketing*.

Intermediary: an organisation or individual through whom products pass on their way from the manufacturer to the end buyer.

Internal marketing: the development and training of staff to ensure high levels of quality and consistency in service delivery and support. Internal marketing includes recruitment, training, motivation and productivity.

International marketing: a particular application of *marketing* concerned with developing and managing trade across international boundaries.

Internet marketing: also known as on-line marketing the use of the Internet to disseminate information, communicate with the marketplace, advertise, promote, sell and/or distribute products or services.

Inventory management: controlling stock levels within the *physical distribution* function to balance the need for product availability against the need for minimising stock holding and handling costs.

Joint demand: where demand for one product or component in an organisational market is dependent on the supply or availability of another, for example a computer assembler's demand for casings might depend on the supply or availability of disk drives.

Joint promotion: *sales promotion* activity undertaken by two or more brands or manufacturers jointly, for example collecting tokens from Virgin Cola in order to get two Eurostar tickets for the price of one.

Joint ventures: a jointly owned company set up by two or more other organisations: (a) as a means of *market entry method;* or (b) as a means of pooling complementary resources and exploiting synergy.

Judgemental budget setting: setting advertising or marketing budgets using methods that involve some degree of guesswork or arbitrary figures. Methods include: arbitrary, affordable, percentage of past sales, and percentage of future sales.

Layout: (a) in retailing, the arrangement of fixtures, fittings and goods in the store; (b) in *advertising,* the arrangement of the various elements of a print or poster advertisement.

Leads: names, addresses and/or other details of individuals or organisations which could be potential customers.

Learning: the change in behaviour that results from experience and practice.

Licensing: an arrangement under which an organisation (the licensor) grants another organisation (the licensee) the right to manufacture goods, use patents, use processes, or exploit trade marks within a defined market. Often used as an international *market entry method*.

Lifestyle segmentation: grouping consumers on the basis of *psychographic* characteristics.

Limited problem solving: a *purchasing situation* usually involving some degree of conscious information searching and analysis, as it involves moderately high priced goods which are not purchased too frequently, and thus the customer might be prepared to shop around to a limited extent.

Limited service agencies: advertising agencies that specialise in one or just a few parts of the whole *advertising* process; for example they might specialise in creative work, or media buying or advertising research.

Loading up: an objective of *sales promotion*, encouraging customers to advance their buying cycles, i.e. to buy greater quantities of a product in the short-term than normal.

Logistics: the handling and movement of inbound raw materials and other supplies as well as outbound *physical distribution*.

Macro segments: segments in organisational markets defined in terms of broad organisational characteristics such as size, location and usage rates, or in terms of product applications.

Mail order: a form of non-store retailing usually involving a catalogue from which customers select goods, then mail or telephone their orders to the supplier. Goods are delivered to the customer's home.

Mailing list: a list of names and addresses, which can be compiled from organisational records or purchased, used as the basis for *direct marketing* activities.

Manufacturer brands: *branding* applied to goods that are produced and sold by a manufacturer who owns the rights to the brand.

Manufacturing subsidiary: a subsidiary company set up in a foreign market to manufacture or assemble a product.

Mark-up: the sum added to the trade price paid for a product to cover the *intermediary's* costs and profit. Mark-up can be measured as a percentage of the trade price or as a percentage of the resale price.

Market coverage: ensuring that the product is made available through appropriate *intermediaries* so that: (a) the potential customer can access it as easily as possible; and (b) the product is properly displayed, sold and supported within the *channel of distribution*. Market coverage might involve intensive distribution, selective distribution or exclusive distribution.

Market development: selling existing products into new segments or geographic markets.

Market entry methods: ways of getting into international markets, including *direct exporting, indirect exporting, licensing, franchising, sales* or *manufacturing subsidiaries, joint ventures,* or *strategic alliances.*

Market penetration: increasing sales volume in current markets.

Market potential: the total level of sales achievable in a market assuming that every potential customer in that market is buying, that they are using the product on every possible occasion, and that they are using the full amount of product on each occasion.

Market segmentation: breaking a total market down into groups of customers and/or potential customers who have something significant in common in terms of their needs and wants or characteristics.

Marketing: creating and holding customers by producing goods or services that they need and want, communicating product benefits to customers, ensuring that goods and services are accessible, and that they are available at a price that customers are prepared to pay.

Marketing audit: the systematic collection, analysis and evaluation of information relating to the internal and external environments that answers the question 'Where are we now?' for the organisation.

Marketing concept: a philosophy of business, permeating the whole organisation, that holds that the key to organisational success is meeting customers' needs and wants more effectively and more closely than competitors.

Marketing environment: the external world in which the organisation and its potential customers have to exist, and within the context of which *marketing* decisions have to be made.

Marketing mix: the combination of the *4Ps* that creates an integrated and consistent offering to potential customers that satisfies their needs and wants.

Marketing objectives: what the organisation is trying to achieve through its *marketing* activities during a specified period. Closely linked with *corporate objectives*.

Marketing orientation: an approach to business that centres its activities on satisfying the needs and wants of its customers.

Marketing plan: a detailed written statement specifying target markets, *marketing programmes*, responsibilities, time-scales, controls and resources. Plans may be short term or long term, strategic or operational in focus.

Marketing PR: *public relations* activities focused on particular products or aspects of their marketing campaigns.

Marketing programmes: specific marketing actions, specified within the marketing plan, involving the use of the *marketing mix* elements in order to achieve marketing objectives.

Marketing research: the process of collecting and analysing information in order to solve marketing problems.

Marketing strategy: the broad marketing thinking that will enable an organisation to develop its products and *marketing mixes* in the right direction, consistent with overall *corporate objectives*.

Master franchising: a *franchisor* grants an individual or organisation in a particular country or other trading region the exclusive right to develop a *franchise* network by sub-franchising within that territory.

Micro segments: segments in organisational markets defined in terms of detailed organisational characterics such as management philosophy, decision making structures, *purchasing policies* etc.

MIS: marketing information system; the formalised collection, sorting, analysis, evaluation, storage and distribution of marketing data.

Modified rebuy: goods and services purchased relatively infrequently by organisations which might want to update their information on available products and suppliers before making a repeat purchase decision.

Money-based sales promotions: *sales promotions* that centre around some kind of financial incentive: money-off packs, *cash rebate* offers, or *coupons*.

Motivation: the driving forces that make people act as they do.

Multiple sourcing: the sourcing of a particular *organisational good* or service from more than one supplier simultaneously.

Multivariable segmentation: using a number of different variables to develop a rich profile of a target group of customers.

Negotiation: a give and take process between a buyer and a seller in which precise terms of supply, specification, delivery, price, and after-sales service etc. are agreed.

New product development (NPD): the process of seeking and screening new product ideas, analysing their commercial feasibility, developing and *test marketing* the product and its associated *marketing mix*, launching the product fully, then monitoring and evaluating its initial progress.

New task purchasing: goods and services that are purchased extremely infrequently by organisations, and involve a high level of formalised information collection and analysis before a purchasing decision is made.

Non-durable products: products that can only be used once or a few times before replacement, such as groceries or office stationery.

Non-profit marketing: marketing activities undertaken by organisations which do not have profit generation as a prime corporate objective, such as charities, public sector health care, and educational establishments.

On-line marketing: see *Internet marketing*.

Open-ended questions: market research questions which do not offer a respondent a list of alternative answers. The respondents are encouraged to answer spontaneously and to enter into explanation of their answers.

Order maker: a sales representatives with responsibility for: (a) finding new customers and making sales to them; and (b) actively increasing the volume or variety of sales to existing customers.

Order taker: a sales representative who either has a set pattern of customer contact or waits for customers to contact him/her when they want to buy.

Organisational goods: goods that are sold to organisations for: (a) incorporation into producing other products; or (b) supporting the production of other products directly or indirectly; or (c) resale.

Organisational marketing: (also known as industrial marketing or business to business marketing) activities directed towards the *marketing* of goods and services by one organisation to another.

Out of town: describes large retail sites located away from the town centres so that they are easily accessible to large numbers of car-borne shoppers.

Outsourcing R&D: commissioning other organisations or research bodies to undertake specific research and development projects, rather than handling them in-house.

Own label brands: *branding* applied to goods that are produced by a manufacturer on behalf of a retailer or wholesaler who owns the rights to the brand.

Penetration pricing: setting prices low in order to gain as much market share as possible as quickly as possible.

Perception: the way in which individuals analyse and interpret incoming information and make sense of it.

Perishability: a characteristic of *services*, describing how service products cannot be stored because they are produced and offered at particular moments in time.

Personal selling: interpersonal communication, often face to face, between a sales representative and an individual or group, usually with the objective of making a sale.

Personality: features, traits, behaviours and experiences that make each person a unique individual.

Physical distribution: the handling and movement of outbound goods from an organisation to its customers.

Pioneer advertising: *advertising* used in the early stages of a *product life-cycle* to explain what a product is, what it can do and what benefits it offers.

Political and regulatory environment: the governmental influences, at local, national and European levels, that inhibit or encourage business; the legal and regulatory frameworks within which organisations have to operate, including national and European law, local by-laws, regulations imposed by statutory bodies and voluntary codes of practice.

POS: point of sale; marketing communication activity, for example *sales promotions,* displays, videos, leaflets, posters etc., which appears in retail outlets at the place where the product is displayed and sold.

Post-purchase evaluation: the stage after a product or *service* has been purchased and used in which the consumer reflects on whether the product met expectations, exceeded them or was disappointing.

Post-testing: evaluation undertaken during or after an *advertising* campaign to assess its impact and effects.

Potential product: what the product could and should be in the future to maintain its *differentiation.*

PR: see *Public relations.*

Premium price: a price which is distinctly higher than average to reflect better product quality, exclusivity or status.

Pre-testing: showing an advertisement to a sample of the target audience during its development to check whether it is conveying the desired message in the desired way with the desired effect.

Press relations: cultivating good relationships between an organisation and the media as an aid to *public relations* activities.

Price: a medium of exchange; what is offered in return for something else; usually measured in terms of money.

Price comparison: using price as a means of comparing two or more products in order to judge: (a) their likely quality in the absence of other information; (b) which offers the best value for money.

Price differential: any difference in the prices charged for the same product to different *market segments* or in different geographic regions.

Price elasticity of demand: the responsiveness of demand to changes in prices. Elastic products are very responsive, so that a price increase leads to a fall in demand, while inelastic products are very unresponsive and thus a rise in price leads to little or no change in demand.

Price negotiation: bargaining between a buyer and a seller to agree a mutually acceptable price.

Price objectives: what the organisation is trying to achieve through its pricing, measured in financial or market share terms, and closely linked with overall *corporate* and *marketing objectives.*

Price perception: a customer's judgement of a price in terms of whether it is thought to be too high, about right or extremely good value for money; this judgement might vary with different circumstances and is often formed in the light of what other alternative products are available.

Price sensitivity: the extent to which price is an important criterion in the customer's decision making process; thus a price sensitive customer is likely to notice a price rise and switch to a cheaper brand or supplier.

Pricing method: the means by which prices are calculated. Methods can be cost-orientated, demand orientated, or competition-orientated.

Pricing policies and strategies: the overall strategic guidelines for the pricing decision, specifying pricing's role within an integrated *marketing mix.*

Pricing tactics: short-term manipulation of price to achieve specific goals, as for example in *money-based sales promotions.*

Primary research: *marketing research* specially commissioned and undertaken for a specific purpose.

Problem recognition: the realisation, triggered by either internal or external factors, that the consumer or the organisation has a problem that can be solved through purchasing goods or services.

Product-based sales promotions: *sales promotions* that centre around some kind incentive connected with the product: extra product free, *BIGIF,* or *samples.*

Product development: selling new or improved products into existing markets.

Product items: the individual products or brands that make up a *product line.*

Product life-cycle (PLC): a concept suggesting that a product goes through various stages in the course of its life: introduction, growth, maturity and decline. At each stage, a product's *marketing mix* might change, as will its revenue and profit profile.

Product lines: a group of products, closely related by production or *marketing* considerations, that exists within the overall *product mix.*

Product manager: the individual within an organisation responsible for the day-to-day management and welfare of a product or family of products at all stages of their *product life-cycle,* including their initial development.

Product mix: the total sum of all the *product items* and their variants offered by an organisation.

Product orientation: an approach to business that centres its activities on continually improving and refining its products, assuming that customers simply want the best possible quality for their money.

Product portfolio: the set of different products that an organisation produces, ideally balanced so that some products are mature, some are still in their growth stage while others are waiting to be introduced.

Product positioning: developing a product and associated *marketing mix* that: (a) is 'placed' as close as possible in the minds of target customers to their ideal in terms of important features and attributes; and (b) clearly differentiates it from the competition.

Product repositioning: refining the product and/or its associated *marketing mix* in order to change its *positioning* either: (a) to bring it closer to the customer's ideal; or (b) to move it further away from the competition.

Product specification: the criteria to which an organisational purchase must conform in terms of quality, design, compatibility, performance, price etc.

Production orientation: an approach to business that centres its activities on producing goods more efficiently and cost effectively, assuming that price is the only factor important to customers.

Promotional mix: the elements that combine to make an organisation's marketing communications strategy: *advertising, sales promotion, personal selling, direct marketing* and *public relations*.

Prospecting: in *personal selling*, finding new potential customers who have the ability, authority and willingness to purchase.

Psychographics: (also known as lifestyle segmentation) defining consumers in terms of their *attitudes*, interests and opinions.

Psychological pricing: using price as a means of influencing a consumer's behaviour or perceptions, for example using high prices to reinforce a quality image, or selling at £2.99 instead of £3.00 to make the product appear much cheaper.

Pull strategy: a communications strategy that focuses on the end consumer rather than other members of the *channel of distribution*. Thus a manufacturer might focus on communication to consumers, rather than to wholesalers or retailers, thus helping to pull the product down the channel.

Public relations (PR): a deliberate, planned and sustained effort to institute and maintain mutual understanding between an organisation and its *publics* (Institute of Public Relations definition).

Publicity: a tool of *public relations* focused on generating editorial media coverage for an organisation and/or its products.

Publics: any group, with some common characteristic with which an organisation needs to communicate, including the media, government bodies, financial institutions, pressure groups etc. as well as customers and suppliers.

Purchasing policy: an organisation's preferences, systems and procedures for purchasing including, for example, attitude towards favoured or approved suppliers, *single* or *multiple sourcing*, and rules and guidelines.

Purchasing situation: the context in which a consumer purchasing decision is made, defined by the frequency of purchase, the risks involved, and the level of information searching undertaken: *routine problem solving, limited problem solving,* and *extended problem solving.*

Push strategy: a communications strategy that focuses on the next member of the *channel of distribution* rather than on the end consumer. Thus a manufacturer might focus on communication to wholesalers or retailers rather than to consumers, thus helping to push the product down the channel.

Qualified prospects: potential customers who have been screened to check that they meet relevant criteria as potential purchasers, for example checking their financial status or that they do actually need the product.

Qualitative research: the collection of data that are open to interpretation, for instance on *attitudes* and opinions, and that might not be validated statistically.

Quantitative research: the collection of quantified data, for example sales figures, *demographic* data, purchase frequency etc., that can be subjected to statistical analysis.

Rating scales: a form of multiple choice market research questionnaire question in which respondents are asked to indicate their answer on a scale, for example ranging from 1 to 5 where 5 = 'strongly agree' and 1 = 'strongly disagree' with a given statement.

Reach: the percentage of the target market exposed to an advertisement at least once during a specified period.

Reference groups: groups to which an individual belongs or to which the individual aspires to belong, and which influence the individual's *motivation, attitudes* and behaviour.

Relationship life-cycle: the evolution of *buyer–seller* relationships in organisational markets, through stages including awareness, exploration, expansion, commitment and dissolution.

Relationship marketing: a form of *marketing* that puts particular emphasis on building a longer-term, more intimate bond between an organisation and its individual customers.

Reminder and reinforcement advertising: a type of *advertising*, targeted at consumers who have already tried and used the product before, that reminds consumers of a product's continued existence and of its unique benefits.

Repeat purchase: the purchase and use of a product on more than one occasion by a particular customer.

Retailer: an *intermediary* which buys products either from manufacturers or from *wholesalers* and resells them to consumers.

Rolling launch: the gradual launch of a new product, region by region.

Routine problem solving: a *purchasing situation* usually involving low-risk, low-priced, regularly purchased goods, which does not involve much, if any, information searching or analysis on the part of the buyer.

Routine rebuy: goods and services purchased frequently by organisations from established suppliers, with little, if any, formal decision making involved in the *repeat purchase*.

Sales orientation: an approach to business that centres its activities on selling whatever it can produce, assuming that customers are inherently reluctant to purchase.

Sales potential: the share of a total market that the organisation can reasonably expect to capture.

Sales presentation: the stage of the *personal selling* process in which the sales representative outlines the product's features and benefits.

Sales promotion: usually short-term tactical incentives offering something over and above the normal product offering to encourage customers to act in particular ways.

Sales quotas: the sales targets that a sales representative has to achieve, broken down into individual product areas and specified as sales value or volume.

Sales subsidiaries: a subsidiary company set up in a foreign market to handle marketing, sales, distribution and customer care in that market.

Sampling: (a) a form of *product-based sales promotion* involving the distribution of samples of products in a variety of ways, so that consumers can try them and judge them for themselves; and (b) in market research, the process of setting criteria and then selecting the required number of respondents for a research study.

Sampling process: defining the target population for a market research study; finding a means of access to that population, and selecting the individuals to be surveyed within that population.

Secondary research: data which already exist in some form, having been collected for a different purpose, perhaps even by a different organisation, and which might be useful in solving a current problem.

Self-liquidating offers: a form of merchandise-based *sales promotion* that invites the consumer to send cash, and often proofs of purchase, in return for merchandise. The price charged covers the cost of the merchandise and a contribution to handling and postage.

SEM: single European market; since 1992, completely free trade has been possible between member states of the EU, although the process of harmonising marketing regulations, product standards, tax rates etc. is an ongoing process that has not yet been fully achieved.

Semi-structured interview: a form of market research that involves some *closed questions* for collecting straightforward data and some *open-ended questions* to allow the respondent to explain more complex feelings and *attitudes*, for example.

Services: goods that are largely or mainly non-physical in character, such as personal services, travel and tourism, medical care or management consultancy.

Shell directional policy matrix: a tool for analysing a *product portfolio*, plotting competitive capability against prospects for sector profitability for each product, resulting in a nine-cell matrix.

Shopping goods: consumer goods purchased less frequently than *convenience goods*, and thus requiring some information search and evaluation; related to *limited problem solving* buying behaviour.

SIC code: standard industrial classification; a means of categorising organisations in terms of the nature of their business.

Single sourcing: the sourcing of a particular organisational good or service from only one supplier.

Skimming: setting *prices* high in order to attract the least price-sensitive customers and to generate profit quickly before competitors enter the market and start to force prices down.

Slice of life: a style of *advertising* that shows how the product fits into a lifestyle that is similar to that of the target audience, or represents a lifestyle that they can identify with or aspire to.

Small business: small businesses are usually defined as those with fewer than 100 employees.

Social class: a form of stratification that structures and divides a society, often on the basis of income and occupation, for marketing purposes.

Social marketing: a marketing focus that is concerned with ensuring that organisations handle marketing responsibly, in a way that contributes towards the well-being of society as a whole.

Sociocultural environment: trends and developments within society as a whole, affecting the *demographic* structure of the population, life-styles, *attitudes*, culture, issues of public and private concern, tastes and demands.

Source credibility: the trustworthiness, likeability, respect or expertise of the perceived source of a marketing message in the minds of the target audience. Source credibility might be transferable to the actual subject of the message, or might at least ensure that the message is listened to.

Speciality goods: expensive, infrequently purchased consumer goods; related to *extended problem solving* buying behaviour.

Speciality stores: stores which tend to concentrate on one clearly defined product area, focusing on *depth of range*.

Sponsorship: the provision of financial or material support to individuals, teams, events or organisations, outside the sponsor's normal sphere of operations. This might involve sport, the arts, community or charity work.

Standardisation: a deliberate strategy to maintain the same *product* and *marketing mix* across all international markets without adapting it for local conditions.

STEP factors: the four broad categories of influences that create the *marketing environment*: sociocultural, technological, economic and competitive, and political and regulatory.

Store image: the *positioning* of a store in terms of its *branding*, product selection, interior and exterior design, fixtures and fittings, lighting etc.

Storyboard: part of the process of developing a television or cinema advertisement, a storyboard shows sketches of the main scenes in the advertisement, describes what is happening at that point, and what sound effects should be used.

Strategic alliance: a collaborative agreement entered into by two or more organisations with a specific purpose in mind. It might include *joint ventures* or looser arrangements that do not involve any equity stakes.

Strategic business unit (SBU): a group of products, markets or operating divisions with common strategic characteristics, that is a profit centre in its own right. An individual product, market or operating division could also be defined as an SBU if appropriate.

Strong theory of communication: a theory that assumes that marketing communication takes the potential buyer through the *buyer readiness stages* in sequence, thus forming *attitudes* and opinions before a purchase has taken place.

Supermarkets: self-service stores carrying a wide range of grocery and *fmcg products*, with smaller branches located in town centres and larger stores located on *out of town sites*.

Switchers: consumers who are not loyal to any one brand of a particular product and switch between two or more brands within the category.

SWOT analysis: a technique that takes the findings of the *marketing audit* and categorises key points as strengths, weaknesses, opportunities or threats.

Tangible product: the way in which the concept of the *core product* is turned into something 'real' that the customer can interact with, including design, quality, *branding*, and product features.

Targeting: deciding how many *market segments* to aim for and how to do it. There are three broad targeting strategies: concentrated, differentiated and undifferentiated.

Technological environment: trends and developments in the technological field that might: (a) improve production; (b) create new product opportunities; (c) render existing products obsolete; (d) change the ways in which goods and services are marketed; or (e) change the profile of customers' needs and wants.

Telemarketing: using the telephone: (a) to make sales directly; or (b) to develop customer relationships and customer care programmes further. Calls might be: (a) outbound, instigated by the organisation; or (b) inbound, instigated by the customer.

Teleshopping: a form of non-store retailing including shopping by telephone and shopping via computer networks.

Tendering: where potential suppliers bid competitively for a contract, quoting a price to the buyer.

Test marketing: the stage within the *new product development* process in which a product and its associated *marketing mix* are launched within a confined geographic area to get as realistic a picture as possible of how that product is likely to perform when fully commercialised.

Trade shows and exhibitions: centralised events, large or small, local or international, focused on an industry or a product area, that bring together a wide range of relevant suppliers and interested customers under one roof.

Trading up: an objective of *sales promotion*, encouraging customers either to buy bigger sized packs of products, or to buy the more expensive products in a range.

Transfer pricing: prices charged for the exchange of goods and services between different departments or operating divisions within the same organisation.

Trial: the purchase and use of a product for the first time by a particular customer.

Trial price: a very low or minimal temporary price often used for new products to encourage consumers to try them.

Trial sizes: a form of *product-based sales promotion* involving the sale of products in smaller than normal packs, so that consumers can buy and try them with minimal risk.

Unsought goods: goods that consumers did not even know they needed until either (a) an emergency arose that needed an immediate purchasing decision to help resolve it; or (b) an aggressive sales representative pressurised them into a purchase.

Value: a customer's assessment of the worth of what they are getting in terms of a product's functional or psychological benefits.

Value management: the analysis of products and processes to see where the greatest costs are being incurred and where the greatest value is added. This can lead to cost savings and better value for money to the customer.

Variety stores: smaller than *department stores*, variety stores stock a relatively limited number of different product categories, but in greater depth.

Vertical marketing systems: a *channel of distribution* which is viewed as a co-ordinated whole and is effectively managed or led by one channel member. The leadership might be contractual, or derived from the power or dominance of one member, or arise from the ownership of other channel members by one organisation.

Weak theory of communication: a theory that assumes that marketing communication creates awareness of products, but that *attitudes* and opinions are only created after purchase and *trial*.

Wholesaler: an *intermediary* which buys products in bulk, usually from manufacturers, and resells them to trade customers, usually small retailing.

Index

Index of company names